Texts, Temples, and Traditions

Menahem Haran

Texts, Temples,
and
Traditions

A Tribute to Menahem Haran

Edited by

MICHAEL V. FOX, VICTOR AVIGDOR HUROWITZ,
AVI HURVITZ, MICHAEL L. KLEIN,
BARUCH J. SCHWARTZ, AND NILI SHUPAK

EISENBRAUNS
Winona Lake, Indiana
1996

Acknowledgments

The publication of this book was made possible by the generous financial support of:

The President of the Hebrew University, Jerusalem
The Philip and Florence Dworsky Foundation for Biblical Research
Dr. S. Z. and Mrs. Ayala Sachs Abramov
The Institute for Jewish Research, the Hebrew University, Jerusalem
The University of Haifa
The Moriah Foundation
Professor Sa-Moon Kang

Library of Congress Cataloging-in-Publication Data

Texts, temples, and traditions : a tribute to Menahem Haran / edited by Michael V.
    Fox . . . [et al.].
        p.   cm.
    Chiefly English; some essays in Hebrew.
    Includes bibliographical references and index.
    ISBN 1-57506-003-5 (cloth : alk. paper)
    1. Bible. O.T.—Criticism, interpretation, etc.   2. Priests, Jewish—Biblical
teaching.   3. Hebrew language—etymology.   I. Haran, Menahem.   II. Fox,
Michael V., 1940–
BS1192.T49   1996
296′.09′01—dc20   96-5780
                                                                              CIP

CONTENTS

PART 5
Language and Writing

HEBREW ESSAYS

PREFACE

THIS VOLUME CELEBRATES MENAHEM HARAN'S ILLUSTRIOUS CAREER as scholar and teacher. The appreciation in the following pages surveys his scholarly achievements. This preface will mention some of his personal accomplishments.

Menahem Haran began his Bible studies in secret as a child in Soviet Russia, studying with a tutor hired by his father. He came to Palestine with his family in 1933 and grew up in Tel Aviv. He served in the Israeli army during the War of Independence and subsequently became a major in military intelligence. He received his B.A., M.A., and Ph.D. degrees from the Hebrew University, the institution to which he has devoted his career. He was also active in the spread of academic Bible study throughout Israel and was instrumental in organizing the Bible departments at the Universities of Beer-Sheva, Tel Aviv, and Haifa, and guiding them in their early years. He also served in visiting professorships in Europe and America.

The editors of this volume have had the privilege and pleasure of being counted among Menahem's students and colleagues. Some of us began our Bible studies at the Hebrew University, others arrived on the scene from abroad. We were all taken under Menahem's tutelage and steered by him at critical points in our academic journeys. We share memories, recent as well as distant, of his unfailing helpfulness and warmth. We have all maintained close relations with him and his wife, Raya, over the decades.

Menahem is the descendant of an illustrious rabbinical line, as is Raya, and theirs is a scholarly family. Raya is also famous for Sabbath afternoon *salons*, in which all of us, starting in our student days, have been privileged to meet some of the most prominent scholars of Judaica and other fields over the years.

As students we learned to treasure Menahem's scholarly discipline and intellectual integrity, his insistence on clear writing and uncompromising logic, alongside a firm but courteous, even gracious, mode of criticism. These qualities are exemplified most notably in his own lectures and writing. We came to admire his extensive knowledge of the best of biblical scholarship and his refusal to run after trendy new "methods." His standards became a sort of "conscience," watching over our shoulders as we worked. At the same time, his infectious love for learning conveyed to his students—hundreds of undergraduates as well as doctoral students—a sense of the seriousness and significance of the work in which we are engaged.

Fortunately, Menahem's career is far from over. He has undertaken a major project in an area he himself defined, and he is pursuing it with unabating vigor and creativity. Soon this work will appear and make its mark on international scholarship. We look forward to his contributions to Jewish learning and to his friendship for many years to come.

The Editors

CONTRIBUTORS

Shmuel Aḥituv
Ben Gurion University

Yairah Amit
Tel Aviv University

Gershon Brin
Tel Aviv University

Ronald E. Clements
University of London

Mordechai Cogan
Ben Gurion University

Chaim Cohen
Ben Gurion University

Frank M. Cross
Harvard University

Graham I. Davies
Cambridge University

John A. Emerton
Cambridge University

Michael V. Fox
University of Wisconsin, Madison

Richard E. Friedman
University of California, San Diego

Moshe Greenberg
Hebrew University

Edward L. Greenstein
Jewish Theological Seminary

William W. Hallo
Yale University

Victor Avigdor Hurowitz
Ben Gurion University

Sara Japhet
Hebrew University

Sa-Moon Kang
Korean Presbyterian Seminary

Michael L. Klein
Hebrew Union College, Jerusalem

Israel Knohl
Hebrew University

James Kugel
Harvard University

François Langlamet
École Biblique

William McKane
St. Andrews University

Carol Meyers
Duke University

Bustenai Oded
Haifa University

Shalom M. Paul
Hebrew University

Rolf Rendtorff
Heidelberg University

Henning Graf Reventlow
Ruhr-Universität Bochum

Alexander Rofé
Hebrew University

Magne Sæbø
Free Faculty of Theology, Oslo

Nahum M. Sarna
Brandeis University

Baruch J. Schwartz
Tel Aviv University

Nili Shupak
Haifa University

J. Alberto Soggin
Waldensian Seminary, Rome

Shemaryahu Talmon
Hebrew University

Zipora Talshir
Ben Gurion University

Jeffrey H. Tigay
University of Pennsylvania

Raymond Jacques Tournay
École Biblique

Emanuel Tov
Hebrew University

Meir Weiss
Hebrew University

Hugh G. M. Williamson
Oxford University

Yair Zakovitch
Hebrew University

Ziony Zevit
University of Judaism, Los Angeles

Editorial Assistants: Kathleen Wiskus and Tamara Lanaghan

MENAHEM HARAN'S CONTRIBUTION TO BIBLICAL AND JUDAIC STUDIES

Victor Avigdor Hurowitz

I

PROFESSOR MENAHEM HARAN IS HONORED in this volume by a chorus of colleagues, disciples, and friends from Israel, Europe, North America, and the Far East. Before we present him with the fruits of our labor, it is customary and altogether fitting that we recall a few of the bountiful contributions he has made to the world of biblical and Judaic studies over the past forty years of illustrious and prodigious scholarly creativity.

The jubilarian is an outstanding representative of the first generation of Israeli scholars to have been trained in fully modern, critical approaches to the Hebrew Bible. Although heirs to and informed by the interpretive acumen of the great traditional Jewish exegetes, these scholars have adopted the scientific philological and literary-historical methods of Europe and North America developed over the last two centuries. A student of the renowned Yehezkel Kaufmann, Menahem Haran maintains his mentor's revision of what is considered "classical" biblical scholarship, although for reasons and with results uniquely his own. Kaufmann attacked the philosophical foundations of the so-called Wellhausen school by denying a genetic, developmental relationship between prophecy and the Torah literature. Haran's approach proves to be more that of a historian, particularly a historian of religious phenomena. He rejects Wellhausen's theory of Israelite religion and the growth of Pentateuchal literature, not only because of its alleged preconceived notions of historical dialectic and determinist evolutionary tendencies; his departure from the earlier dominant school is also based on his own attempts to link religious revolutions, particularly the composition of the Priestly (P) and Deuteronomic (D) sources and the promulgation of the Torah, with decisive historical events such as the cultic-religious reforms of Hezekiah and Josiah, the apostasy of Manasseh, and the activity of Ezra (146, 149, 159).[1]

---

1. Numbers in parentheses in this article of appreciation refer the reader to numbered works by Prof. Haran in the bibliography (pp. xxiii–xxxvii).

For Haran, Julius Wellhausen is not someone to be excoriated as a hostile force with whom the Jewish Bible scholar should feel compelled to do battle for nationalistic or religious reasons. Haran praises Wellhausen's accomplishments wholeheartedly and, in a way, regards himself as an intellectual descendant of that great scholar (138). He warns against those who would reject solely for apologetic reasons the firm philological foundations of Gentile biblical scholarship (90, 95).

Haran's debt to classical source criticism is manifold. First of all, he embraces the source-critical literary analysis of the Pentateuch, as well as of the Former Prophets. He utterly rejects the apologetic approaches associated with such scholars as U. Cassuto and M. H. Segal, as well as the more recent harmonizations that go under the name of literary or aesthetic criticism. For him, the four documentary sources, J(ahwistic), E(lohistic), P(riestly), and D(euteronomic) (practically in that order), are the tangible components of the Torah. With all due respect for the "final," received form of the Pentateuch, the steps that led up to it are for Haran just as real, just as tangible, and just as worthy of scholarly investigation. The four documents even extend beyond the book of Deuteronomy and, in fact, encompass the books of Joshua, Judges, Samuel, and Kings (67, 124). Although many scholars, including Kaufmann, refrain from distinguishing between J and E, Haran not only regards the Elohist document as an identifiable stratum but argues that it in particular is the source of many ideas and historical conceptions found in D (102). On the other hand, Haran follows Kaufmann in placing P before D, emphasizing that P was made public only after D. Thus, Haran developed his own argument for preferring the above-mentioned order to that of Wellhausen.

Haran resists attempts to discern substrata within the four major sources. He has a rather limited regard for certain dominant trends in biblical scholarship, such as form criticism and tradition history. Although he has made important contributions to certain literary problems, such as the meaning of the graded number sequence (97, 120) and the prosody of the priestly blessing (188), he has resisted the recent wave of literary-aesthetic criticism. All these approaches essentially neglect the distinct nature of the documents and undermine any attempt to associate the various documents with particular scribal schools. By so doing, they run contrary to Haran's nearly instinctive feel for completeness and plasticity in the literary documents and in their real-life background.

Haran considers the fundamental issues raised by classical biblical scholarship in general, and by Wellhausen in particular, to be perennially relevant and realizes that in many cases the incisive answers given by nineteenth- and early twentieth-century scholars still must be addressed. He has often delighted in drawing our attention to the still-valid insights he has gleaned from little-known Renaissance and Enlightenment scholars, whose writings he has perused during his many visits to the libraries of the old European universities.

An example of the way Haran responds to certain "postclassical," fashionable trends in source criticism is in order. According to a theory expounded by Frank Moore Cross and popularized by several of his students, there were two Deuteronomic redactions of the book of Kings: one at the time of Josiah, and the other after the destruction of the temple. Haran rejects this theory and rarely refers to it, but he is well acquainted with it. In one of his writings (169, p. 351 n. 40) he mentions the theory, briefly adduces a few arguments against it, and refers to scholars who rejected the idea earlier.

Most significantly, Haran points out the all-embracing model by which Wellhausen dealt with Israelite cult. The comprehensive, elementary categories where, what, when, and who, as translated by Wellhausen into "place of worship," "sacrifice," "sacred feasts," and "priests and Levites," are recognized by Haran as the four essential aspects of cult that are to be investigated and as providing the conceptual framework within which one must trace the cult's historical development. Any attempt to modify Wellhausen's approach to ancient Israelite cult must be conducted within this framework of discourse (138).

Haran's numerous scholarly contributions touch on nearly all of the major realms of inquiry investigated by modern biblical scholarship. It is the Bible's own character that mainly shapes the agenda of Haran's scholarly enterprise. The Bible is a collection of writings that evolved over a long period of time and was then transmitted and studied over an even longer chronological span. Accordingly, Haran's various studies probe the way the biblical writings came into existence, their transmission after having reached finalized form, the meaning and literary qualities of the writings themselves, and the historical events and real-life circumstances that both produced and are reflected in the Bible.

II

Menahem Haran is best known as one of the world's most influential scholars of ancient Israelite cult. In scholarly circles one cannot discuss matters of ancient Israelite cult without referring to Haran and coming to terms with his views. The numerous studies that were eventually distilled into his definitive work *Temples and Temple-Service in Ancient Israel* (138) would secure him a permanent place in the annals of both biblical studies and the study of ancient Near Eastern religion.

Fundamental to Haran's understanding of ancient Israelite cult is his categorical distinction between two institutions. On the one hand, the Bible knows of a dozen or so "Houses of Yhwh/God," to which, for the sake of brevity, Haran refers as "temples" (89, 137). The Bible describes in great detail four such temples—the tabernacle, the First Temple in Jerusalem, the Second Temple, and the visionary temple of the future prescribed by Ezekiel—while a fifth temple, the one in Shiloh, is frequently mentioned as a precursor to the one in Jerusalem. Other temples, about a dozen in number, are known to us from sporadic allusions in formulaic language. Haran has examined all of these facilities in detail. The Israelite temple is based on and derives from similar installations in the ancient Near East (13, 188, 189). These "houses of God" were permanent fixtures housing some symbol of divine presence, manned by priestly families, preferably of Levitical descent, and the cult performed within them symbolically represented a daily-life routine for their divine resident and an appeal to his perceptive faculties (29, 32). In distinction to the synagogue, the temples were not essentially places of community worship but were, rather, domains of the priest (143, 145, 162, 172, 183). Laymen could enter temples only as guests and linger in the outer court, with no access to the inner cultic sanctity.

On the other hand, the Bible refers to innumerable open cultic precincts. These sacred *temenoi* were characterized by an altar, or *bāmāh*, and possibly by some symbol of divine presence such as a sacred tree or a pillar. Some of them may even have reached prominence and become subjects of cult legends associating them with national patriarchs or great historical events (128). Nonetheless, they were open-air facilities located outside the cities and lacking permanent priestly officiants and a regular cult.

P's tabernacle, D's laws of sacrifice, and the festival regulations of J and E relate to the first type of cultic installation, while J's and E's sacrificial doctrine and various narratives refer to the latter. Haran on several occasions urges his archaeologist colleagues to adhere to these distinctions when classifying their finds and, in general, to refrain from applying to silent remains of questionable nature specific biblical terms that in the Bible belong to well-defined phenomena (140, 197). Another biblical relic to be distinguished from a "House of God," was the Elohist's "Tent of Meeting." Both P and E refer to an *ʾohel moʿed* in the desert; however, whereas P conceives of this structure as a portable temple and casts it in the image of the Temple of Jerusalem, E, followed by D, regards it as an oracular tent pitched outside the camp (11, 27).

More than any other modern scholar, Haran has been a pioneer in bringing the Priestly system to life and making it comprehensible to contemporary scholars. With a sense for completeness, a feeling for reality, and a thirst for finding the essence of whatever he chose to study, Haran found order and purpose in the endless, confusing details of the Priestly tabernacle and the daily duties of its priestly officiants. Although never using the popular term *sacred space*, Haran describes just this crucial phenomenon in his groundbreaking studies of the tabernacle, as well as his marginal notes about the Solomonic Temple (34, 44). He establishes the related principles of material gradation and graded holiness. Put simply, the closer to the divine presence in the innermost recesses of the temple, the more valuable, the more complex, the more restricted, and the more holy the men and materials involved must be (49, 51). This recognition forms the basis for various observations and studies by other scholars concerning the sacrificial system. The concept of graded holiness and its physical manifestation in material gradation can also help illuminate the decor of Solomon's Temple.

Not only does Haran clarify the general nature and organizing principles of the tabernacle and its ritual, but he also delves into the specific nature of some of its major appurtenances. In particular he studies the ark and cherubs (17, 23, 53), the incense altars and incense pans (15, 28), and the garments of the high priest (8). His studies of these implements take into account the biblical descriptions, as well as comparative material from the ancient Near East. He works his way deftly through a maze of details, traditions, and scholarly opinions about these various items and in the end presents us with a clear picture of their physical nature and symbolic functions within the tabernacle and the daily cult (29, 32).

One of his recent studies, relating to the small altars discovered throughout the land of Israel, especially at Tel-Miqneh (Ekron), emphasizes the essentially aristocratic nature of the incense altars used in biblical temples. He distinguishes the altars intended for incense offerings and located within the temple from those scattered about the country and on which simple grain sacrifices were offered by the common folk (197, 201). He often employs socioeconomic factors in interpreting texts and artifacts, so as to reconstruct ancient realia. For instance, Haran insists that meat was enjoyed by the average Israelite only rarely and on special occasions, and this economic reality is to be seen as enabling the Priestly source to prohibit nonsacrificial slaughter altogether. Even when interpreting the abecedaries found throughout the land of Israel and denying that they indicate the presence of schools and widespread literacy, Haran brings social realities and possibilities to bear on the interpretation of archaeological finds (182).

Although Haran's most prominent contributions have been to our understanding of ancient temples and the ritual performed in their midsts (the "where" and "what" in the above terminology), he has added significantly to the other two categories ("who" and "when") as well. He has studied the history of the Israelite priesthood from earliest times down to the time of the Second Temple Period and shown that the tribe of Levi was never a secular caste of warriors but was always a priestly tribe, even in the narrative documents J and E (130, 138). The Zadokite priesthood recommended by Ezekiel is not a predecessor to P's Aaronide priesthood but a refinement of it. As for the Gibeonites, the slaves of Solomon, and the Second-Temple Nethinim, Haran has shown them to be ethnically distinct, non-Israelite groups who resembled each other legally and functionally; they worked in the temples at Shiloh and Jerusalem in paracultic roles. Ezekiel accuses Israel, perhaps through hyperbolic exaggeration, of having employed them instead of Levites in more prestigious functions and calls for the end of such practices (16, 25, 30).

Haran has also studied the three pilgrimage festivals and in particular the festive occasions of the first month. He has shown that the Paschal sacrifice was known as a temple sacrifice and was associated with the Passover even in the J and E documents (116, 117, 118, 119). Haran also calls attention to previously unnoticed family celebrations alluded to in the Former Prophets and the narrative portions of the book of Job. These were regular occasions, but their fixity was a matter of customary family practice rather than a function of a national calendar (88, 93, 96).

III

Haran has also made significant contributions to our understanding of prophecy and prophetic literature, being especially attracted to the books of Deutero-Isaiah, Jeremiah, Ezekiel, and Amos. Just as he is able to find method in the myriad details of the cult, so in one of his early studies of prophetic literature he was able to find major factors bringing order to the seemingly amorphous mass of prophecies of Deutero-Isaiah (46, 47, 147). He is also capable of pointing out criteria of selection and order in the books of the three major prophets and the twelve minor prophets. The surviving utterances of each prophet are grouped into categories of oracles of doom, oracles of consolation, oracles concerning foreign nations, and stories about the prophet. On the basis of this commonality Haran suggests that all prophetic literature was gathered, redacted, and even canonized, not in a long, drawn-out process, but simultaneously, at a single point (126). Regarding the nature of the written prophecies themselves, Haran defends the position that the oracles preserved in the books of the classical prophets are not some verbatim transcript of the prophets' publicly pronounced message or their *ipsissima verba*, and thus do not accurately reflect the prophets' thoughts at the moment of inspiration. Rather, they are deliberate, literary creations, only distantly echoing the public address or the prophetic experience. A parade example of a prophecy meant to be written down and studied is the law code of Priestly pedigree found in Ezekiel 40–48, a unit to which Haran has dedicated a major study (129, 144; compare 165). His interest in prophecy has drawn him also to investigate several individual pericopes and literary problems in the books of Jeremiah (1, 126, 144) and Amos (55, 86).

Haran has also addressed the question of the differences between preclassical and literary prophecy. Whereas preclassical prophecy was distinguished by group ecstasy and association with permanent institutions such as holy places and temples, classical prophecy was a largely literary phenomenon with low levels of ecstasy and high emphasis on moral values and an ethical message (131, 136). Even though certain prophets such as Jeremiah and Ezekiel were priests, there was no particular association between their prophetic activity and the temple. Although Haran insists on distinguishing categorically between prophet and priest, he does point out that some of the moral concerns commonly associated with classical Israelite prophecy are not foreign to the writings of the Israelite priesthood as embodied in the Pentateuchal Priestly code (143).

His interests span a great variety of additional topics as well. The exceptional scope of his scholarship is evidenced by his contributions to Samaritan studies. His investigation of a medieval liturgical poem enumerating the 613 precepts resulted in the discovery that the poem's total was based on Maimonides' count. The author, Aharon Ben Manir, a resident of Damascus, was shown to have had access to Maimonides' writings (14, 98, 142). He also studied the messianic idea in the Samaritan conception (6). Some recent investigations (for example, 154, 173, 190, 198, 203, and items in progress), as well as one from the beginning of his career (2), have taken him into later fields of Jewish studies.

IV

Haran's penchant for the tangible has led him on occasion into the realm of iconography. In one early study he discusses the bas-reliefs on the sarcophagus of Ahiram, king of Byblos, using the Bible to interpret the mourning rites, as well as to identify the main figure as a god rather than a king (9, 19). In a penetrating review of Othmar Keel's book about the prohibition of seething a kid in its mother's milk, Haran rejects the author's attempt to impose on the biblical injunction an interpretation derived from a questionable artistic analysis of a well-known ancient Near Eastern decorative motif (158, 167; compare 137, 142). A more recent article illuminates the nature of the mask Moses would place over his face when not addressing the people. On the basis of comparative material from ancient Near Eastern texts and art, he suggests that Moses, having encountered God, is himself the bearer of divine radiance. Haran makes the interesting proposal that, when he commissioned Joshua to succeed him as the head of the people, Moses actually transferred some of this radiance to his appointed successor (168, 181).

Haran has always been acutely aware of the importance of comparative material for illuminating the Bible. With all due cognizance of the uniqueness of the Hebrew Bible and the necessity to study the Bible and ancient Israel from within and on their own terms, he emphasizes the fact that Israel of the biblical period did not exist in a vacuum. Relevant material from contiguous cultures, when used properly, can be of utmost importance for properly understanding the culture and writings of ancient Israel. Whenever necessary, Haran incorporates in his own work the insights and results of the best and most authoritative scholarship in the related fields of archaeology, Assyriology, Egyptology, and Northwest Semitics. He often encouraged his students to study these cognate disciplines in order to enable themselves to work independently outside the Bible and to undertake competent comparative research.

A problem that has always been central to Haran's concerns is the later development of the Bible, starting with the time of its canonization. In one of his earliest articles discussing the status of the book of Ben Sira, he demonstrates that there was never an official process of canonizing previously noncanonical books (11). In fact, rabbinic statements supposedly describing a decision-making process actually referred to the confirmation of a situation established generations earlier. As part of his investigation into the early history of the canon, Haran has provided two interesting studies touching upon certain problems in the book of Psalms. He demonstrates that the fivefold division of the Psalter is a relatively late development and that the four doxologies are only signs of the liturgical use of this book after its canonization (186). In a brilliant analysis of Psalm 151 from Qumran, Haran shows that the Hebrew Qumranic version postdates the shorter Hebrew *Vorlage* of the Septuagint version. He also defends the unity of the psalm and confirms the late, postcanonical origin of the psalm in all of its known forms (175, 185, 194).

Over the last decade Haran has undertaken and brought to fruition an innovative project in codicology, extensively studying the development of the physical form of the Bible as it existed from biblical times until the invention of printing (151, 153, 154, 155, 173, 198). He has amassed much material relating to the realia of scribal practices, bookmaking, and the physical forms of books from the biblical period and later, and he attempts to determine how the physical realities of writing books leave their mark on literary creations. During the First Temple Period, papyrus was commonly used for writing, while long, important compositions were inscribed on parchment (151). The Deuteronomic laws would have been written on a single parchment scroll, while P, which is by its literary nature composed of numerous shorter units, would have been composed originally on papyrus. The division of the Torah into five books, and the Former Prophets into four was not merely mechanical, and it was not simply the result of the physical necessity to produce short books. It was, rather, the result of a literary division and was imposed on the compositions by the final redactors. A Priestly editor redacted the Torah, while a Deuteronomic editor redacted the Former Prophets. The divisions into smaller books reflect the redactors' perception of changing times and theological conditions (169, 191). In contrast, it was the practical necessity of limiting book scrolls to a certain size that determined the division of the Chronicler's work into a book of Chronicles and a book of Ezra–Nehemiah (170, 174). Once put in two scrolls, the two parts of what was basically a single literary work were linked by catch lines, a scribal device well known from the writings of other ancient Near Eastern cultures.

Haran has shown with the help of written and pictorial evidence that the large Torah scrolls to which we are accustomed today were actually latecomers to Jewish religious practice, whereas earlier, each book of the Torah was written on a separate scroll (190). He has also suggested that at a certain time all of the books of the Prophets or all of the books of the Writings could have been written on a large scroll, making a *bibliotheca*. Such a practice is the realia behind the rabbinic discussions about the order of biblical books (200, 202).

Professor Haran has now brought to fruition a monumental study of the concept of canon and the process of canonization. He demonstrates that canonization of the Hebrew Bible was not a process of selecting a few remarkable works from a large corpus of available material but was, rather, an ongoing collecting of what remained of ancient Israelite inspired literature. The first of three volumes making up this major work is completed.

V

Menahem Haran's special commitment to biblical studies in the Hebrew language must be noted. His interest in and concern for biblical studies in Modern Hebrew is more than strictly an academic one. He is recognized as a true master of the Hebrew language, and anyone who has ever been moved by the elegance of his writing can confirm this evaluation. Moreover, out of commitment to the language and to the development of critical scholarship within Israel, he has ensured that most of what he writes appears in Hebrew, even though he knows that his widest audience is among the scholars who can only read the English versions of his works. In the same vein, he contributed extensively to *Encyclopaedia Biblica* and served as one of its editors, thereby ensuring that the Hebrew language would be host to one of the world's finest biblical reference works (35–42, 68–83, 118–19, 132, 160). In order to make available the best of biblical scholarship to educated laymen in Israel, Haran has been a regular participant in the Bible study group held in the residences of the President and Prime Minister, and several of his scholarly articles have found more popularized expression in the publications of that group (54, 126, 147, 152, 156, 176, 177, 178, 195, 196).

First as a doctoral candidate at the Hebrew University, and eventually as an incumbent of the Yehezkel Kaufmann Chair of Bible Studies at the Hebrew University, Haran has enjoyed a unique perspective from which to write extensively about the emergence of modern biblical scholarship in Jewish and Israeli circles and in the Hebrew language. In his prolific writings describing biblical studies in Hebrew, he admits that there were sporadic critical statements in the writings of the Talmudic sages, certain Medieval exegetes, several Jewish biblical scholars of the nineteenth-century Enlightenment, and the *Wissenschaft des Judentums* movement. He stresses, nonetheless, that Jewish scholars on the whole have excelled principally at exegesis rather than criticism. Religious sentiment made even the *Wissenschaft* and the *Maskilim* reluctant to subject the Bible to truly critical surgery and analysis. Ahad Ha⁽am himself expressed admiration for Gentile study of the Bible but hindered the publication of biblical criticism in the Hebrew-language journal he edited. Abraham Kahana and Yehezkel Kaufmann belatedly brought fully critical Bible scholarship to the Hebrew language with their respective publications of a commentary to most of the Bible and a major study of Israelite religion. But it was only within the Hebrew University that critical study of the Bible found a place to flourish fully among Jews and in the Hebrew language (5, 57, 90, 91, 92, 95, 98, 123, 178, 179, 180).

Professor Haran, through his own writings, through his many students, and through the leading role he has played in the international academic community, has ensured that Israel and the Hebrew University will remain among the foremost centers of academic Bible studies. He has warned us against surrendering the critical pursuit merely because of the inevitable weaknesses, uncertainties, and vicissitudes (90). Through the example of his own research and teaching, he has shown us how fruitful and rewarding the unflinchingly critical pursuit can be.

The participants in this volume wish our friend and teacher Menahem Haran many more years of good health and happiness, so that he may continue the productive, illuminating study of the Bible, not only in its received form, but also in its original setting and historical development.

בָּרֵךְ ה׳ חֵילוֹ וּפֹעַל יָדָיו תִּרְצֶה

BIBLIOGRAPHY OF THE PUBLISHED WRITINGS OF MENAHEM HARAN

1947

1. שריד ארכאי בספרות הנבואה, ידיעות החברה לחקירת א״י ועתיקותיה, י״ג, תש״ז, עמ׳ 7–15.

2. רמזי בקורת-התורה בספרו של רנ״ק, תרביץ י״ח, תש״ז, עמ׳ 59–61.

1948

3. תולדות האמונה הישראלית (ביקורת), מאזנים, א׳, תש״ח, עמ׳ 186–188.

4. מכבשונה של הספרות הנבואית (ביקורת), בצרון ט׳, תש״ח, עמ׳ 258–265.

1951

5. חקירת המקרא בעברית מראשית התקופה הלאומית עד זמננו (סקירה ביבליוגראפית-היסטורית), בצרון כ״א, תש״י, עמ׳ 100–114, 174–178, 256–262; כ״ב, תש״י, עמ׳ 189–196; כ״ג, תשי״א, עמ׳ 38–41, 115–126, 187–193.

1952

6. מושג ה״תהב״ בדת השומרונית, תרביץ כ״ג, תשי״ב, עמ׳ 96–111.

1954

7. מבוא לספרות המקרא, האוניברסיטה העברית, ירושלים, תשי״ד.

1955

8. צורת האפוד במקורות המקראיים, תרביץ כ״ד, תשט״ו, עמ׳ 380–391.

9. התבליטים שעל דפנות הסרקופגוס של אחירם מלך גבל, ידיעות החברה לחקירת א״י ועתיקותיה י״ט, תשט״ו, עמ׳ 56–65 [נוסח אנגלי להלן, מס׳ 19].

10. פרשת הכיבוש הישראלי הראשון (ביקורת), הארץ, המוסף הספרותי 17.6.55.

1957

11. מהותו של אהל-מועד, תרביץ כ״ה, תשט״ז, עמ׳ 11–20 [נוסח אנגלי להלן, מס׳ 27].

12. מבעיות הקנוניזציה של המקרא, תרביץ כ״ה, תשט״ז, עמ׳ 245–271.

13. מגמות וסגנונים בפולחן המזרחי הקדמון (בעית "הדפוס הפולחני"), בית
מקרא, א', תשט"ז, עמ' 76–85.

14. מניין המצוות להרמב"ם בפיוט שומרוני, ארץ ישראל ד' (ספר יצחק בן-צבי),
תשט"ז, עמ' 160–169.

15. קטורת מחתות וקטורת תמיד, תרביץ כ"ו, תשי"ז, עמ' 115–125 [נוסח
אנגלי להלן, מס' 28].

16. הגבעונים, הנתינים ועבדי שלמה (היסטוריה של קיבוץ כנעני ביהודה),
יהודה וירושלים (קובץ), הוצאת החברה לחקירת א"י ועתיקותיה, ירושלים,
תשי"ז, עמ' 37–45 [נדפס גם בתוך: ארץ בנימין, תל-אביב, תשל"ב, עמ'
151–157; נוסח אנגלי להלן, מס' 30].

1958

17. הארון והכרובים (משמעותם הסמלית, צורתם, בעית המקבילות
הארכיאולוגיות), ארץ ישראל ה' (ספר ב' מזר), תשי"ח, עמ' 83–90 [נוסח
אנגלי להלן, מס' 23].

18. ערי הלויים: אוטופיה ומציאות היסטורית, תרביץ כ"ז, תשי"ח, עמ' 421–439
[נוסח אנגלי להלן, מס' 31].

19. "The Bas-Reliefs of the Sarcophagus of Ahiram King of Byblos."
Israel Exploration Journal 8: 15–25.

1959

20. עתפה, מחמל וקבה (לחקר מוצאם של דפוסי הפולחן המקראי: בעית המקבילות
הערביות), ספר דוד נייגר, ירושלים, תשי"ט, עמ' 215–221.

21. המסורת המקראית על כיבוש חצור (יה' יא, א-טו) לאור החפירות (תקציר),
ידיעות החברה לחקירת א"י ועתיקותיה כ"ג, תשי"ט, עמ' 100–101.

22. ספר במדבר: פרקים נבחרים, לפי הרצאותיו של מ' הרן, בעריכת נחמן סירקין,
אוניברסיטת תל-אביב, סיון תשי"ט.

23. "The Ark and the Cherubim: Their Symbolic Significance in Biblical
Ritual." *Israel Exploration Journal* 9: 30–38, 89–94.

1960

24. המשכן: הדירוג הטכני-החמרי, ספר נ"ה טור-סיני (בעריכת מ' הרן וב"צ
לוריא), ירושלים, תש"ך, עמ' 27–42.

25. הגבעונים: מקומם במערכת כיבוש הארץ ובתולדות ישראל, עיונים בספר
יהושע (דברי חוג העיון בתנ"ך בבית ראש הממשלה), ירושלים, תש"ך,
עמ' 101–126.

26. מבוא למקרא, לפי הרצאותיו של מ' הרן, נרשמו ונערכו על-ידי גדעון בנימיני,
אוניברסיטת תל-אביב.

27. "The Nature of Ohel Mo^ced in the Pentateuchal Sources." *Journal of Semitic Studies* 5: 50–65.

28. "The Uses of Incense in Ancient Israelite Ritual." *Vetus Testamentum* 10: 113–29.

1961

29. המערך הפולחני הפנימי ומשמעותו הסמלית, ספר היובל ליחזקאל קויפמן, ירושלים, תשכ״א, עמ׳ כ–מב [נוסח אנגלי להלן, מס׳ 32].

30. "The Gibeonites, the Nethinim and the Sons of Solomon's Servants." *Vetus Testamentum* 11: 159–69.

31. "Studies in the Account of the Levitical Cities." *Journal of Biblical Literature* 80: 45–54, 156–65.

32. "The Complex of Ritual Acts Performed inside the Tabernacle." Pp. 272–302 in *Studies in the Bible*. Edited by C. Rabin. Scripta Hierosolymitana 8. Jerusalem.

33. סילוק ארון הברית, ידיעות החברה לחקירת א״י ועתיקותיה כ״ה, תשכ״א, עמ׳ 211–223 [נוסח אנגלי להלן, מס׳ 45].

1962

34. שילה וירושלים (יסודה של המסורת הכהנית שבתורה), תרביץ ל״א, תשכ״ב, עמ׳ 317–325 [נוסח אנגלי להלן, מס׳ 44].

42–35. אנציקלופדיה מקראית, כרך ד: כהנה, כהנים (עמ׳ 14–47); לחם הפנים (עמ׳ 493–495); מאכלים ומשקאות (עמ׳ 543–558); מזבח (עמ׳ 763–780); מכס (עמ׳ 964–965); מלאה (עמ׳ 975); מלבושי כהונה (עמ׳ 1045–1049); מלואים, מלואי יד (עמ׳ 1049–1050).

43. האנציקלופדיה העברית, כרך ט״ו: וטה, וילהלם מרטין לברכט דה-, עמ׳ 1003–1004.

44. "Shiloh and Jerusalem: The Origin of the Priestly Tradition in the Pentateuch." *Journal of Biblical Literature* 81: 14–24.

1963

45. "The Disappearance of the Ark." *Israel Exploration Journal* 13: 46–58.

46. "The Literary Structure and Chronological Framework of the Prophecies in Is. XL–XLVIII." Pp. 127–55 in *Congress Volume, Bonn 1962*. Vetus Testamentum Supplements 9. Leiden.

47. בין ראשונות לחדשות, מחקר ספרותי והיסטורי בחטיבת הנבואות שבספר ישעיהו פרקים מ–מח, ירושלים, תשכ״ג.

1964

48. קווים לתיאור אמונתם של האבות, ע״ז לדוד (ספר היובל לדוד בן-גוריון),
ירושלים, תשכ״ד, עמ׳ 40–70.

1965

49. המשכן: טאבו מודרג של קדושה, ספר מ״צ סגל (בעריכת י״מ גרינץ וי׳
ליוור), ירושלים, תשכ״ה, עמ׳ 33–41.

50. "The Religion of the Patriarchs: An Attempt at a Synthesis." *Annual of the Swedish Theological Institute* 4: 30–55.

51. "The Priestly Image of the Tabernacle." *Hebrew Union College Annual* 36: 191–226.

52. "Review of *Christian News from Israel*, Vol. 16, Nos. 1–2, 1965." *Annual of the Swedish Theological Institute* 3: 43–47.

1966

53. "Review of *Das altisraelitische Ladeheiligtum*, by J. Maier." *Journal of Biblical Literature* 85: 248–49.

54. קרבנו של גדעון, עיונים בספר שופטים (דברי חוג העיון בתנ״ך בבית ראש
הממשלה), ירושלים, תשכ״ו, עמ׳ 235–250.

55. מבעיות הרקע ההיסטורי של ״נבואת הגויים״ שבספר עמוס, ידיעות החברה
לחקירת א״י ועתיקותיה ל׳, תשכ״ו, עמ׳ 56–69 [נוסח אנגלי להלן, מס׳ 86].

56. עלייתה וירידתה של ממלכת ירבעם בן יהואש, ציון ל״א, תשכ״ו, עמ׳ 18–38
[נוסח אנגלי להלן, מס׳ 66].

57. בשליחותה של תקופת מעבר: על הפירוש המדעי של אברהם כהנא לתורה,
נביאים וכתובים, מאזנים כ״ג, תשכ״ו, עמ׳ 237–245.

58. *Universal Peace in Isaiah's Prophecy.* Excerpts from the Writings of Yehezkel Kaufmann. Edited and with a Foreword by Menahem Haran. Jerusalem.

59–61. כנ״ל (מס׳ 58), בתרגומים לצרפתית, ספרדית ורוסית.

1967

62. תרבותם הדתית של האבות: האמונה והפולחן, היסטורייה של עם ישראל,
כרך ב׳: האבות והשופטים (בעריכת ב׳ מזר), תל-אביב, תשכ״ז, עמ׳ 111–124
[נוסח אנגלי להלן, מס׳ 100].

63. על גבול האמונה, מאזנים כ״ד, תשכ״ז, עמ׳ 52–55.

64. כיבושה של דרך, הוראת המקרא באוניברסיטה העברית, האוניברסיטה,
כרך 13, חוב׳ ב, תשכ״ז, עמ׳ 12–18.

1970

95. *Biblical Research in Hebrew: A Discussion of Its Character and Trends.*
Lecture Delivered November 5, 1968 at the Inauguration of the Yehezkel
Kaufmann Chair of Bible Studies. Jerusalem.

96. זבח הימים, ספר שמואל ייבין (בעריכת ש׳ אברמסקי, י׳ אהרוני ועוד),
ירושלים, תש״ל, עמ׳ 170–186 [נוסח אנגלי לעיל, מס׳ 88].

97. סוגיות מקרא: דגם המספר המודרג לצורותיו ויחסו אל הדפוסים
הפורמאליים של התקבולת, תרביץ ל״ט, תש״ל, עמ׳ 109–136 [נוסח
אנגלי להלן, מס׳ 120].

98. בין מסורת לבקורת: דרכו של מ״ץ סגל בחקר המקרא, מולד, סדרה חדשה,
כרך ג (כ״ר), תש״ל, עמ׳ 97–106.

1971

99. שירת המצוות לאהרן בן מניר: פיוט שומרוני ליום-הכיפורים על תרי״ג
מצוות על-פי הרמב״ם, דברי האקדמיה הלאומית הישראלית למדעים, כרך ד,
חוב׳ 15, ירושלים, תשל״א, עמ׳ 229–280 [נוסח אנגלי מקוצר: מס׳ 127].

100. "The Religion of the Patriarchs: Beliefs and Practices." Pp. 219–45 in
The World History of the Jewish People, volume 2. Edited by B. Mazar.
Tel Aviv.

101. "The Sacking of Thapsacus by Menahem ben Gadi (2 Kings 15:16) and
Its Historical Background." Pp. 108–9 in *Proceedings of the 27th Inter-*
national Congress of Orientalists. Wiesbaden.

102. דרכיהם של יוצאי מצרים: מסעי ישראל ממצרים לפי מסורות המקרא
והנתונים הטופו-גיאוגראפיים של חצי-האי סיני, תרביץ מ׳, תשל״א, עמ׳
113–143.

103. השגות גיאוגראפיות משתנות ומצע אחד: הערות מיתודולוגיות על תפיסת
מסעם של ישראל ממצרים במקורות התורה, ארץ ישראל י׳ (ספר ז׳ שז״ר),
תשל״א, עמ׳ 138–142 [חלק ממס׳ 102].

104–115. *Encyclopaedia Judaica*: "Amos"; "Holiness Code"; "Menorah";
"Nehushtan"; "Poor, Provision for the"; "Priests and Priesthood";
"Priestly Vestments"; "Proverb"; "Show Bread"; "Vatke, Wilhelm";
"Wette, Wilhelm Martin Leberecht de-" "Winckler, Hugo."

1972

116. קדמותו של זבח הפסח, המקרא ותולדות ישראל—מחקרים לזכרו של יעקב
ליוור (בעריכת ב׳ אופנהיימר), תל-אביב, תשל״ב, עמ׳ 93–103.

117. דין זבח הפסח בספרי הברית (שמ׳ כג, יח; לד ,כה), דברי הקונגרס העולמי
החמישי למדעי היהדות, חטיבה א, ירושלים, (תשל״ב), עמ׳ 68–78.

118–119. אנציקלופדיה מקראית, כרך ו: עמוס (עמ׳ 271–287); ערכים [של הקדשות] (עמ׳ 391–394).

120. "The Graded Numerical Sequence and the Phenomenon of 'Automatism' in Biblical Poetry." Pp. 238–67 in *Congress Volume, Uppsala 1971.* Vetus Testamentum Supplements 22. Leiden.

121. "The Passover Sacrifice." Pp. 76–106 in *Studies in the Religion of Ancient Israel.* Vetus Testamentum Supplements 23. Leiden.

122. "Études bibliques à l'Université de Jérusalem." *Études théologiques et religieuses* 47: 47–49.

123. "La recherche biblique en Hebreu: Son caractère et ses tendances." *Études théologiques et religieuses* 47: 145–59.

1973

124. תקופות ומוסדות במקרא: עיונים היסטוריים, תל-אביב, תשל״ג.

125. סוגיות מקרא: ריכוז הפולחן בתפיסת המקור הכוהני, באר-שבע א, תשל״ג, עמ׳ 114–121.

126. חיבורו של ס׳ ירמיהו וחיבורם של ספרי נביאים אחרונים, עיונים בספר ירמיהו (דברי חוג העיון בתנ״ך בבית נשיא המדינה), חלק ג, גבעתיים, תשל״ג, עמ׳ 105–118.

127. "The Song of the Precepts of Aaron ben Manir: A Samaritan Hymn for the Day of Atonement on the 613 Precepts as Listed by Maimonides." Pp. 174–209 in *Proceedings of the Israel Academy of Sciences and Humanities*, 5/7. Jerusalem.

1975

128. פרקי שכם, ציון ל״ח, תשל״ג [תשל״ה], עמ׳ 1–31.

129. סוגיות מקרא: קובץ החוקים של יחזקאל (מ-מח) ויחסו לאסכולה הכוהנית, תרביץ מ״ד, תשל״ה, עמ׳ 30–53 [נוסח אנגלי להלן, מס׳ 144].

130. "The Historical Beginnings of Priesthood in Ancient Israel." Pp. 17–18 in *Actes du XXIXe Congrès international des Orientalistes.* Études Sémitiques. Paris.

1976

131. בין הנבואה הקדומה לנבואה הקלאסית, הצבי ישראל—אסופת מחקרים במקרא לזכרם של ישראל וצבי ברוידא (בעריכת י׳ ליכט וג׳ ברין), תל-אביב, תשל״ו, עמ׳ 83–91 [נוסח אנגלי להלן, מס׳ 136].

132. אנציקלופדיה מקראית, כרך ז: שבת, ממחרת השבת (עמ׳ 517–521).

133. "Exodus, The." Pp. 304–10 in *The Interpreter's Dictionary of the Bible, Supplementary Volume.* Nashville.

134.   בעקבות הכוהן מדאר, בית מקרא ס״ט, תשל״ז, עמ׳ 177–182.

1977

135.   "A Temple at Dor?" *Israel Exploration Journal* 27: 12–15.

136.   "From Early to Classical Prophecy: Continuity and Change." *Vetus Testamentum* 27: 385–97.

1978

137.   גדי בחלב אמו, ארץ ישראל י״ד (ספר ח״א גינזברג), תשל״ח, עמ׳ 12–18 [נוסח אנגלי להלן, מס׳ 142].

138.   *Temples and Temple-Service in Ancient Israel: An Inquiry into the Character of Cult Phenomena and the Historical Setting of the Priestly School.* Oxford [reprinted with slight changes, Winona Lake, Indiana, 1985, 1995].

1979

139.   המסגרת ההיסטורית של יציאת מצרים: נתונים ופתרונות, מחקרים במקרא ובמזרח הקדמון—ספר היובל לשמואל א׳ ליונשטם (בעריכת י׳ אבישור וי׳ בלאו), ירושלים, תשל״ט, עמ׳ 153–169.

140.   במות ומקדשים: מערד עד דן, בית מקרא ע״ר, תשל״ט, עמ׳ 94–105.

141.   ברוך בן נריה, שיחות במקרא, כרך ב (בעריכת ב׳ צביאלי), ירושלים, תשל״ט, עמ׳ 191–193.

142.   "Seething a Kid in Its Mother's Milk." *Journal of Jewish Studies* 30: 23–35.

143.   הכוהן, המקדש והעבודה, תרביץ מ״ח, תשל״ט, עמ׳ 175–185 [תרגום לשבדית: מס׳ 150; לגרמנית: מס׳ 162; נוסח אנגלי בשינויים: מס׳ 164].

144.   "The Law-Code of Ezekiel XL–XLVIII and its Relation to the Priestly School." *Hebrew Union College Annual* 50: 45–71.

1980

145.   העבודה והתפילה, הגות במקרא—מבחר מתוך עיוני החוג לתנ״ך לזכר ישי רון, כרך שלישי, תל-אביב, תש״ם, עמ׳ 120–125 [נוסח מקוצר של מס׳ 143].

146.   מאחורי הקלעים של ההיסטוריה: לקביעת זמנו של המקור הכוהני, ציון מ״ה, תש״ם, עמ׳ 1–12 [נוסח אנגלי להלן, מס׳ 149].

147.   ישעיהו השני: בשורתו הנבואית וצורתה הספרותית, עיונים בספר ישעיהו (דברי חוג העיון בתנ״ך בבית נשיא המדינה), חלק ב, ירושלים, תש״ם, עמ׳ 1–30.

1981

148. "Temples and Cultic Open Areas as Reflected in the Bible." Pp. 31–37 in *Temples and High Places in Biblical Times: Proceedings of the Colloquium in Honor of the Centennial of Hebrew Union College–Jewish Institute of Religion* (1977). Jerusalem.

149. "Behind the Scenes of History: Determining the Date of the Priestly Source." *Journal of Biblical Literature* 100: 321–33.

150. "Präst, Tempel, Bön." *Svensk exegetisk årsbok* 46: 55–68.

151. מלאכת הסופר בתקופת המקרא: מגילות הספרים ואביזורי הכתיבה, תרביץ נ', תשמ"א, עמ' 65–87.

152. הנבואה המקראית—קווי ייחוד ורקע, עיונים בספר תרי-עשר (דברי חוג העיון בתנ"ך בבית נשיא המדינה), ירושלים, תשמ"א, עמ' 33–54.

1982

153. מגילות הספרים בתחילת ימי בית שני: המעבר מפפירוסים לעורות, ארץ-ישראל ט"ז (ספר מ"צ אורלינסקי), תשמ"ב, עמ' 86–92 [נוסח אנגלי להלן, מס' 163].

154. מגילות הספרים בין קומראן לימי הביניים: עורות יהודיים ונכריים למיניהם ולתקופותיהם, תרביץ נ"א, תשמ"ב, עמ' 347–382 [נוסח אנגלי להלן, מס' 173].

155. אנציקלופדיה עולם התנ"ך, כרך 1—בראשית, ערכים על בר' א, א; פרק ד; מג, יא (דבש).

156. "Book-Scrolls in Israel in Pre-exilic Times." *Journal of Jewish Studies* 33: 161–73.

157. הערות לחוקתו החזונית של יחזקאל, עיונים בספר יחזקאל (דברי חוג העיון בתנ"ך בבית נשיא המדינה), ירושלים, תשמ"ב, עמ' 3–22 [השווה מס' 129].

1983

158. סוגיות מקרא: הגדי בחלב אמו והגדי היונק חלב אמו, תרביץ נ"ב, תשמ"ג, עמ' 371–392 [נוסח גרמני להלן, מס' 171].

159. "The Character of the Priestly Source: Utopian and Exclusive Features." Pp. 131–38 in *Proceedings of the Eighth World Congress of Jewish Studies: Bible Studies and Hebrew Language.* Jerusalem.

160. אנציקלופדיה עולם התנ"ך, כרך 11—ירמיה, ערכים במבוא: "סידורו של ספר ירמיה"; ועל א, יא–טו; פרק ב; ג, א–ד, ד; ד, ה–ו, ל; ז, א–ח, ג; ח, ד–ט, כה; פרק י; י, יא; פרקים יא–יב; פרק יג; יד, א–טו, ד; טו, ה–כא; פרק טז; פרק יז; כא, יא–כג, ח; לב, ג; לז, כא; לח, א–יג; נא, סד; נב, כ; נב, כח–ל.

161.   עוד על מגילות הספרים בתקופת המקרא: הראיה החמישית, תרביץ נ"ב,
תשמ"ג, עמ' 643–644.

162.   "Priestertum, Tempeldienst und Gebet." Pp. 141–53 in *Das Land Israel in biblischer Zeit: Jerusalem-symposium 1981*. Edited by G. Strecker. Göttingen.

163.   "Book-Scrolls at the Beginning of the Second Temple Period: The Transition from Papyrus to Skins." *Hebrew Union College Annual* 54: 111–22.

164.   "Priesthood, Temple, Divine Service: Some Observations on Institutions and Practices of Worship." *Hebrew Annual Review* 7: 121–35.

1984

165.   אנציקלופדיה עולם התנ"ך, כרך 12—יחזקאל, ערכים במבוא ועל-פני כל הספר
(כולל רוב הערכים בפרקים מ–מח, עמ' 200–250).

166.   "More concerning Book-Scrolls in Pre-exilic Times." *Journal of Jewish Studies* 35: 84–85.

167.   "Review of *Das Böcklein in der Milch seiner Mutter und Verwandtes: Im Lichte eines altorientalischen Bildmotivs*, by Othmar Keel." *Journal of Biblical Literature* 103: 97–99.

168.   "The Shining of Moses' Face: A Case Study in Biblical and Ancient Near Eastern Iconography." Pp. 159–73 in *In the Shelter of Elyon: Essays on Ancient Palestinian Life and Literature in Honor of G. W. Ahlström*. Journal for the Study of the Old Testament Supplement Series 28. Sheffield.

169.   גודלם של ספרים במקרא והיקפם של ספרי תורה ונביאים: היבטים
פליאוגראפיים וקומפוזיציוניים בסידור האסופה המקראית, תרביץ נ"ג,
תשמ"ד, עמ' 329–352.

1985

170.   "שורות קישור" בפליאוגראפיה הקדומה ובאסופה המקראית, ארץ-ישראל
י"ח (ספר נ' אביגד), תשמ"ה, עמ' 124–129 [נוסח אנגלי להלן, מס' 174].

171.   "Das Böcklein in der Milch seiner Mutter und das saugende Muttertier." *Theologische Zeitschrift* 41: 135–59.

172.   "Cult and Prayer." Pp. 87–92 in *Biblical and Related Studies Presented to Samuel Iwry*. Edited by A. Kort and S. Morschauser. Winona Lake, Indiana.

173.   "Bible Scrolls in Eastern and Western Jewish Communities from Qumran to the High Middle Ages." *Hebrew Union College Annual* 56: 21–62.

174. "Book-Size and the Device of Catch-Lines in the Biblical Canon." *Journal of Jewish Studies* 36:1–11.

175. שני הנוסחים של מזמור תהלים קנא, תרביץ נ"ד, תשמ"ה, עמ' 319–329 [נוסח אנגלי להלן, מס' 185].

176. מקומו של ספר מלכים בספרי נביאים ראשונים, עיונים בספר מלכים (דברי חוג העיון בתנ"ך בבית ראש הממשלה), חלק א', ירושלים, תשמ"ה, עמ' 390– 418–414 ,399 [השווה מס' 67].

177. עבודת האלהים במלכות ישראל הצפונית, עיונים בספר מלכים (דברי חוג העיון בתנ"ך בבית ראש הממשלה), חלק ב', ירושלים, תשמ"ה, עמ' 157–191.

178. על משנתו של פרופ' יחזקאל קויפמן, עיונים בספר מלכים (דברי חוג העיון בתנ"ך בבית ראש הממשלה), חלק ב', ירושלים, תשמ"ה, עמ' 275–280.

1986

179. פרשנות המדרש והפשט והשיטה החביקורתית בחקר המקרא, מחקרים במדעי היהדות: אסופת ההרצאות והדיונים שנישאו בכנס יובל הששים של המכון למדעי היהדות, ירושלים, תשמ"ו, עמ' 62–88.

180. "Midrashic and Literal Exegesis and the Critical Method in Biblical Research." Pp. 19–48 in *Studies in the Bible*. Edited by S. Japhet. Scripta Hierosolymitana 31. Jerusalem.

1987

181. כי קרן עור פני משה, מחקרים במקרא יוצאים במלאת מאה שנה להולדתו של מ"ד קאסוטו (בעריכת ח' ביינארט וש"א ליונשטם), ירושלים, תשמ"ז, עמ' 127–136 [נוסח אנגלי לעיל, מס' 168].

1988

182. "On the Diffusion of Literacy and Schools in Ancient Israel." Pp. 81–95 in *Congress Volume, Jerusalem 1986*. Edited by John A. Emerton. Vetus Testamentum Supplements 40. Leiden.

183. "Temple and Community in Ancient Israel." Pp. 17–25 in *Temple in Society*. Edited by Michael V. Fox. Winona Lake, Indiana.

184. הקודקס, הפינקס ולוחיות הדיו, תרביץ נ"ז, תשמ"ח, עמ' 151–164.

185. "The Two Text-Forms of Psalm 151." *Journal of Jewish Studies* 39: 171–82.

1989

186. ארבע הברכות וחמשת ה"ספרים" שבספר תהלים, דברי האקדמיה הלאומית הישראלית למדעים, ח, 1, ירושלים, תשמ"ט, עמ' 1–32.

187.   הקדמה לספרו של מאיר פארן: דרכי הסגנון הכוהני בתורה—דגמים, שימושי
לשון, מבנים, ירושלים, תשמ״ט, עמ׳ 1–7.

188.   ברכת כוהנים מכתף הינום—המשמעות המקראית של התגלית, קתדרה, 52,
תשמ״ט, עמ׳ 77–89.

189.   בשולי הקודקס והפינקס, תרביץ נ״ח, תשמ״ט, עמ׳ 523–524.

1990

190.   ספרי תורה וספרי מקרא במאות הראשונות לספירה הנוצרית, שנתון למקרא
ולחקר המזרח הקדום י׳, תש״ן, עמ׳ 93–106.

191.   "Book-Size and the Thematic Cycles in the Pentateuch." Pp. 165–76 in
*Die hebräische Bibel und ihre zweifache Nachgeschichte: Festschrift für
R. Rendtorff.* Edited by E. Blum, C. Macholz, and E. W. Stegemann.
Neukirchen-Vluyn.

1991

192.   יהדות ומקרא בתפיסתו של יחזקאל קויפמן, מדעי היהדות 31, תשנ״א,
עמ׳ 69–80.

193.   ח״א גינזברג—דברים לזכרו, עת לעשות מס׳ 3, תשנ״א, עמ׳ 18–23 [נוסח
מקוצר בתוך: מדעי היהדות מס׳ 31, תשנ״א, עמ׳ 86–88].

1992

194.   המגילה QPs[a]‏11 ובעית חיבורו של ספר תהלים, שערי טלמון: מחקרים
במקרא, קומראן והמזרח הקדמון (בעריכת ע׳ טוב ומ׳ פישביין),
Winona Lake, Ind., עמ׳ *123–128* [נוסח אנגלי להלן, מס׳ 199].

195.   זבחי הימים של אלקנה בשילה, עיונים בספר שמואל (דברי חוג העיון
בתנ״ך בבית ראש הממשלה), חלק א׳, ירושלים, תשנ״ב, עמ׳ 23–44
[רישום סטינוגראפי; השווה מס׳ 96].

196.   הוקעת בני שאול על-ידי הגבעונים, עיונים בספר שמואל (דברי חוג העיון
בתנ״ך בבית ראש הממשלה), חלק א׳, ירושלים, תשנ״ב, עמ׳ 249–279.

197.   "מזבחות הקטורת" בממצא הארכיאולוגי והפולחן של מלכת השמים
במלכות יהודה, תרביץ ס״א, תשנ״ב, עמ׳ 321–332.

198.   "Technological Heritage in the Preparation of Skins for Biblical Texts in
Medieval Oriental Jewry." Pp. 35–43 in *Pergament: Geschichte, Struktur, Restaurierung und Herstellung.* Edited by Peter Rück. Sigmaringen.

1993

199.   "11QPs[a] and the Canonical Book of Psalms." Pp. 193–201 in *Minḥah le-
Naḥum: Biblical and Other Studies Presented to Nahum M. Sarna in
Honour of His 70th Birthday.* Edited by M. Brettler and M. Fishbane.

Journal for the Study of the Old Testament Supplement Series 154. Sheffield.

200. "On Archives, Libraries and the Order of Biblical Books." *Journal of the Ancient Near Eastern Society of Columbia University* 22 (Y. Muffs Festschrift): 51–61.

201. "'Incense Altars': Are They?" Pp. 237–47 in *Biblical Archaeology Today, 1990: Proceedings of the Second International Congress of Biblical Archaeology*. Edited by A. Biran and J. Aviram. Jerusalem.

1994

202. על ארכיונים, ספריות וסדרם של ספרי המקראי, המקרא בראי מפרשיו: ספר זיכרון לשרה קמין (בעריכת שרה יפת), ירושלים, תשנ"ד, עמ' 223–234.

1995

203. "Altar-ed States: Incense Theory Goes Up in Smoke." *Bible Review* 11: 30–37.

In Press

204. ספריות בעת העתיקה וראשיתן אצל יהודים, מכמנים [מוזיאון ראובן ועדית הכט], מס' 9, ירושלים תשנ"ה.

205. האסופה המקראית—מחקר היסטורי ופליאוגראפי על גיבושה ועל צורתה במהלך הדורות עד מוצאי ימי הביניים, חלק א: אקדמות להסברת הקאנוניזציה של המקרא כתהליך היסטורי, ירושלים.

206. "The *běrît* 'Covenant': Its Nature and Ceremonial Background." *M. Greenberg Festschrift*. Edited by M. Cogan et al. Winona Lake, Ind.

ABBREVIATIONS

General

A(m)T	*The Bible: An American Translation* (ed. Smith and Goodspeed; Chicago: University of Chicago Press, 1927)
AT	Ancien Testament
AV	Authorized Version
DSS	Dead Sea Scrolls
DtrH	Deuteronomistic History (Historian)
EB	English Bible
EBH	Early Biblical Hebrew
GNB	Good News Bible
Heb.	Hebrew
JB	Jerusalem Bible
JPSV	Jewish Publication Society Version
KJV	King James Version
LBH	Late Biblical Hebrew
LXX	Septuagint
MT	Masoretic Text
NAB	New American Bible
NASB	New American Standard Bible
NEB	New English Bible
NIV	New International Version
NJPSV	The New Jewish Publication Society Version
NRSV	New Revised Standard Version
P	papyrus
Pesh.	Peshiṭta
PN	Personal name
REB	Revised English Bible
RS	Ras Shamra texts
RSV	Revised Standard Version
RV	Revised Version
Sam. Pent.	Samaritan Pentateuch
Syr.	Syriac version
Tg.	Targum
TM	Texte massorétique
Vg.	Vulgate

Books and Periodicals

AB	Anchor Bible
ABD	*Anchor Bible Dictionary*
ABL	R. F. Harper (ed.), *Assyrian and Babylonian Letters*
AfO	*Archiv für Orientforschung*
AHw	W. von Soden, *Akkadisches Handwörterbuch*
AnBib	Analecta Biblica
ANEP	J. B. Pritchard (ed.), *Ancient Near East in Pictures*
ANET	J. B. Pritchard (ed.), *Ancient Near Eastern Texts Relating to the Old Testament* (3d ed.)
ANETS	Ancient Near Eastern Texts and Studies
AnSt	*Anatolian Studies*
AO	Der Alte Orient
AOAT	Alter Orient und Altes Testament
AOS	American Oriental Series
AP	J. Marouzeau (ed.), *L'anné philologique*
AS	Assyriological Studies
ASOR	American Schools of Oriental Research
ASTI	*Annual of the Swedish Theological Institute*
ATANT	Abhandlungen zur Theologie des Alten und Neuen Testaments
ATD	Das Alte Testament Deutsch
ATK	*Arbeiten zur Theologie und Kirche*
BA	*Biblical Archaeologist*
BAL	R. Borger, *Babylonische Assyrische Lesestücke* (2d ed.; Rome, 1979)
BAR	*Biblical Archaeologist Reader*
BASOR	*Bulletin of the American Schools of Oriental Research*
BASORSS	Bulletin of the American Schools of Oriental Research Supplement Series
BBB	Bonner biblische Beiträge
BDB	F. Brown, S. R. Driver, and C. A. Briggs, *Hebrew and English Lexicon of the Old Testament*
BETL	Bibliotheca ephemeridum theologicarum lovaniensium
BHK	R. Kittel (ed.), *Biblia Hebraica*
BHS	*Biblia Hebraica Stuttgartensia*
Bib	*Biblica*
BiMes	Bibliotheca Mesopotamica
BIN	Babylonian Inscriptions in the Collection of James B. Nies, Yale University
BiOr	*Bibliotheca orientalis*
BIOSCS	*Bulletin of the International Organization for Septuagint and Cognate Studies*

BJRL	*Bulletin of the John Rylands University Library of Manchester*
BK	*Bibel und Kirche*
BKAT	Biblischer Kommentar: Altes Testament
BN	*Biblische Notizen*
BR	*Biblical Research*
BWANT	Beiträge zur Wissenschaft vom Alten und Neuen Testament
BZ	*Biblische Zeitschrift*
BZAW	Beihefte zur ZAW
BZNW	Beihefte zur ZNW
CAD	*The Assyrian Dictionary of the Oriental Institute of the University of Chicago*
CAH	Cambridge Ancient History
CahRB	Cahiers de la Revue biblique
CB	Cambridge Bible for Schools and Colleges
CBC	Cambridge Bible Commentary
CBQ	*Catholic Biblical Quarterly*
COHL	G. Posener, *Catalogue des ostraca hiératiques littéraires de Deir el Médineh*. Vols. 1 (1938), 2 (1951), 3 (1977–80 = FIFAO XX). Cairo
ConBOT	Coniectanea Biblica, Old Testament
CT	Cuneiform Texts from the British Museum
CTA	A. Herdner, *Corpus des tablettes en cunéiformes alphabétiques*
DBAT	*Dielheimer Blätter zum Alten Testament*
DISO	C.-F. Jean and J. Hoftijzer, *Dictionnaire des inscriptions sémitiques de l'ouest* (Leiden, 1965)
DJD	Discoveries in the Judaean Desert
EA	J. A. Knudtzon, *Die El-Amarna Tafeln* (2 vols.; Leipzig, 1915; reissue, Aalen, 1964)
EBib	Études bibliques
EncJud	*Encyclopaedia Judaica*
ErIsr	*Eretz-Israel*
ETh	*Études théologiques*
EvT	*Evangelische Theologie*
ExpB	Expositor's Bible
FIFAO	Fouilles de L'institut Français d'Archéologie Orientale
FOTL	Forms of the Old Testament Literature
FRLANT	Forschungen zur Religion und Literatur des Alten und Neuen Testaments
GB	Wilhelm Gesenius and F. Buhl, *Hebräisches und aramäisches Handwörterbuch über das Alte Testament*
GKC	*Gesenius' Hebrew Grammar*, ed. E. Kautzsch, trans. A. E. Cowley

HALAT	L. Koeher and W. Baumgartner, et al., *Hebräisches und aramäisches Lexikon zum Alten Testament*
HAR	*Hebrew Annual Review*
HAT	Handbuch zum Alten Testament
HBC	*Harper's Bible Commentary*
HKAT	Handkommentar zum Alten Testament
HSM	Harvard Semitic Monographs
HSS	Harvard Semitic Studies
HTR	*Harvard Theological Review*
HUCA	*Hebrew Union College Annual*
ICC	International Critical Commentary
IDB	G. A. Buttrick (ed.), *Interpreter's Dictionary of the Bible*
IDBSup	Supplementary volume to *IDB*
IEJ	*Israel Exploration Journal*
Int	*Interpretation*
JAAR	*Journal of the American Academy of Religion*
JANES(CU)	*Journal of the Ancient Near Eastern Society (of Columbia University)*
JAOS	*Journal of the American Oriental Society*
JbBiblTh	*Jahrbuch für biblische Theologie*
JBL	*Journal of Biblical Literature*
JCS	*Journal of Cuneiform Studies*
JEA	*Journal of Egyptian Archaeology*
JEOL	*Jaarbericht . . . "Ex oriente lux"*
JJS	*Journal of Jewish Studies*
JNES	*Journal of Near Eastern Studies*
JNSL	*Journal of Northwest Semitic Languages*
JPS Torah Commentary	Jewish Publication Society Torah Commentary
JQR	*Jewish Quarterly Review*
JSJ	*Journal for the Study of Judaism*
JSOT	*Journal for the Study of the Old Testament*
JSOTSup	Journal for the Study of the Old Testament Supplement Series
JSPSS	Journal for the Study of the Pseudepigrapha Supplement Series
JSS	Journal of Semitic Studies
JTS	Journal of Theological Studies
KAI	H. Donner and W. Röllig, *Kanaanäische und aramäische Inschriften*
KAR	*Keilschrifttexte aus Assur religiösen Inhalts*
KAT	Kommentar zum Alten Testament
KB	L. Koehler and W. Baumgartner, *Lexicon in Veteris Testamenti libros*

KB³	L. Koehler and W. Baumgartner, *Lexicon in Veteris Testamenti libros* (3d ed.)
KHAT	O. F. Fridelin (ed.), *Kurzgefasstes exegetisches Handbuch zum Alten Testament* (Leipzig, 1812–96)
KTU	M. Dietrich, O. Loretz, and J. Sanmartín, *Die keilalphabetischen Texte aus Ugarit* (AOAT 24; Neukirchen-Vluyn, 1976)
LÄ	*Lexikon der Ägyptologie*
LAPO	Littératures anciennes du Proche-Orient
LKA	E. Ebeling, *Literarische Keilschrifttexte aus Assur*
MARI	*Mari: Annales de recherches interdisciplinaires*
MSL	Materialien zum sumerischen Lexikon
MVAG	*Mitteilungen der vorderasiatisch-ägyptischen Gesellschaft*
MWJ	*Magazin für die Wissenschaft des Judentums*
NCB	New Century Bible
NCBC	New Century Bible Commentary
NICOT	New International Commentary on the Old Testament
NKZ	*Neue kirchliche Zeitschrift*
OBO	Orbis biblicus et orientalis
OBT	Overtures to Biblical Theology
OED	*Oxford English Dictionary*
OLZ	*Orientalische Literaturzeitung*
Or	*Orientalia*
OTL	Old Testament Library
OTS	*Oudtestamentische Studiën*
RA	*Revue d'assyriologie et d'archéologie orientale*
RAcc	F. Thureau-Dangin, *Rituels accadiens*
RB	*Revue biblique*
RdE	*Revue d'Egyptologie*
REJ	*Revue des études juives*
ResQ	*Restoration Quarterly*
RevQ	*Revue de Qumran*
RLA	*Reallexikon der Assyriologie*
RQ	*Römische Quartalschrift für christliche Altertumskunde und Kirchengeschichte*
SAA	State Archives of Assyria
SAAB	*State Archives of Assyria Bulletin*
SAHG	*Sumerische und akkadische Hymnen und Gebete*
SAK	Studien zur altägyptischen Kultur
SAOC	Studies in Ancient Oriental Civilization
SB	Sources bibliques
SBL	Society of Biblical Literature
SBLDS	SBL Dissertation Series

SBLMS	SBL Monograph Series
SBT	Studies in Biblical Theology
ScrHier	Scripta hierosolymitana
Sem	*Semitica*
SOTSMS	Society for Old Testament Study Monograph Series
SS	Studi semitici
STDJ	Studies on the Texts of the Desert of Judah
SthZ	*Schweizerische Theologische Zeitschrift*
TDOT	G. J. Botterweck and H. Ringgren (eds.), *Theological Dictionary of the Old Testament*
THAT	E. Jenni and C. Westermann (eds.), *Theologische Handwörterbuch zum Alten Testament*
ThB	Theologische Bücherei (Zürich)
ThR	Theologische Rundschau
TLZ	*Theologische Literaturzeitung*
TRE	*Theologische Realenzyklopädie*
TWAT	G. J. Botterweck and H. Ringgren (eds.), *Theologisches Wörterbuch zum Alten Testament*
TZ	*Theologische Zeitschrift*
UF	*Ugarit-Forschungen*
UT	C. H. Gordon, *Ugaritic Textbook*
VT	Vetus Testamentum
VTSup	Vetus Testamentum Supplements
WBC	Word Biblical Commentary
WC	Westminster Commentaries
WHJP	World History of the Jewish People
WMANT	Wissenschaftliche Monographien zum Alten und Neuen Testament
WO	*Die Welt des Orients*
WZKM	*Wiener Zeitschrift für die Kunde des Morgenlandes*
ZA	*Zeitschrift für Assyriologie*
ZÄS	*Zeitschrift für ägyptische Sprache und Altertumskunde*
ZAW	*Zeitschrift für die alttestamentliche Wissenschaft*
ZDMG	*Zeitschrift der deutschen morgenländischen Gesellschaft*
ZDPV	*Zeitschrift des deutschen Palästina-Vereins*
ZNW	*Zeitschrift für die neutestamentliche Wissenschaft*
ZTK	*Zeitschrift für Theologie und Kirche*

Part 1

Priests and Their Sphere

THE DISTRIBUTION OF THE PRIESTLY GIFTS
ACCORDING TO A DOCUMENT OF
THE SECOND TEMPLE PERIOD

Sara Japhet

A

THE SUBJECT OF THE *priestly gifts* receives much attention in all the strata of biblical law and arises once and again in the literature of the restoration period, in Nehemiah and Malachi.[1] The *priestly gifts* thus became one of the central issues in the discussion about the dating of the Pentateuch sources, the Priestly source in particular.[2] However, although the subject has been extensively discussed in the scholarly literature, it has been analyzed from too narrow a perspective, generally centering on the relationship of the Pentateuch sources to one another, and their dating.

2 Chr 31:4–19 contains interesting and detailed evidence about the *priestly gifts*, but this has drawn only limited attention, which has centered on one verse alone. This is the reference to *the tithe of cattle and sheep* (2 Chr 31:6), from which Wellhausen deduced that "the tithe of cattle" was first established in the Second Temple Period, and even that this was the source of Lev 27:32–33, which refers to this tithe.[3] Other scholars also discussed the evidence of 2 Chronicles 31 in regard to the *tithe of cattle*.[4] The material in Chronicles seems to have been neglected both by scholars of the Biblical period, who viewed it

---

1. The main sources are: Exod 22:28–29; 23:19; 34:19–20, 26; Leviticus 6–7; 23:15–20; 24:5–9; 27; Num 5:8; 6:19–20; 15:17–21; 18; 31; Deut 14:22–27; 15:19–20; 18:3–4; 26:1–11; Mal 3:8–12; Neh 10:33–40; 12:44–47; 13:10–13, 31. See Y. Kaufmann, *History of the Religion of Israel* (Jerusalem, 1960) 1.143 [Heb.].

2. See the discussions by Wellhausen and Kaufmann, which have become the classic literature on the topic: J. Wellhausen, *Prolegomena to the History of Israel* (Eng. trans.; Edinburgh, 1885) 152–59; Kaufmann, *History of Religion*, 143–59.

3. Wellhausen, *Prolegomena*, 157.

4. See for example: R. de Vaux, *Ancient Israel: Its Life and Institutions* (Eng. trans.; London, 1961) 404–5.

as late and tendentious, and by the scholars of Halakah, who concentrated their attention on the halakic literature itself and not on its biblical precedents.[5]

Only recently, with the accumulation of halakic material from the Dead Sea Scrolls,[6] has there been a certain shift in scholarly interest to the intermediary period, of which Chronicles is a major representative. It is no coincidence that 2 Chronicles 31 drew the attention of Y. Yadin in his discussion of priestly gifts in the *Temple Scroll*,[7] but he too touched only upon the similarities between the two works. Yadin's attention naturally focused on the *Temple Scroll* rather than on 2 Chronicles 31, and he therefore dealt only with isolated details of the chapter. The *Temple Scroll*, and the Qumran Halakah in general, now allow us to view the halakic evidence in the book of Chronicles in a new light.[8] I hope that this article will be a contribution to this effort.

B

2 Chronicles 31 forms part of a larger unit devoted to the reform of Hezekiah (2 Chronicles 29–32). The chapter continues the description that begins with the purification of the temple (2 Chronicles 29) and proceeds with the celebration of Passover in Jerusalem (2 Chronicles 30) and with the purification of the land from all traces of idolatry (2 Chr 31:1). According to the Chronistic account, after these accomplishments, Hezekiah turned to establishing the daily service in the temple; he appointed the priests and Levites "division by division, each according to his service" (31:2), and he took ap-

---

5. See for example the division of topics in the *Encyclopaedia Judaica*. The entry "Tithe" is almost entirely devoted to biblical sources, and Chronicles is mentioned only in passing (*Enc. Jud.* 15.1158–62; the text in Chronicles, p. 1161), while the entry "*Terumot* and *Ma^caserot*" (ibid., 1025–27) deals primarily with Halakah, and mentions only 2 Chr 31:6.

6. See L. Schiffman, *The Halakah at Qumran* (Leiden, 1975); J. Zussman, "The History of *Halakah* and the Dead Sea Scrolls," *Tarbiz* 59 (1990) 11–76 [Heb.]; and Zussman's revision of the same article in *The Scrolls of the Judean Desert: Forty Years of Research* (ed. M. Broshi et al.; Jerusalem, 1992) 99–127 [Heb.].

7. Y. Yadin, *The Temple Scroll* (3 vols; Jerusalem, 1983) 1.141, 154–56, 167–68, 264–66, et al. One of the points upon which Yadin expands is the tithe of honey, which is mentioned in 11QTemple LX 9. In Yadin's view, the author of the scroll prescribed this law on the basis of 2 Chr 31:5: "The deliberate inclusion of the honey in the discussion of the hunt suggests that the author knew he was setting forth a polemical law. He doubtless drew upon the verse: 'as soon as the command was spread abroad . . .' (2 Chr 31:5)" (pp. 167–68). Two observations on this issue are in order: The book of Chronicles does not refer directly to "the tithe of honey." It does mention the "firstfruits of honey" and adds at the end of the verse, "and they brought in abundantly the tithe of everything." While the "tithe of everything" may include tithe of honey, it is not mentioned specifically. The "firstfruits of honey" is alluded to in Lev 2:11–12 as well and is not the innovation of Chronicles. My second observation is that it seems more reasonable that Chronicles and the author of the *Temple Scroll* have a common halakic tradition than that Chronicles is the basis for the *Temple Scroll*'s innovation.

8. For another aspect of this topic, see: S. Japhet, "The Prohibition of the Habitation of Women: The Temple Scroll's Attitude toward Sexual Impurity and Its Biblical Precedents," *JANESCU* 22 (*Comparative Studies in Honor of Yochanan Muffs*; 1993) 69–87.

propriate steps to maintain the temple both by seeing to the provision of sacrifices for the regular offerings and by establishing the system of economic sustenance for the temple personnel. While the provision of sacrifices is described as the responsibility of the king himself (v. 3), he turns to the people for the financial support of the temple personnel: "to give the portion due to the priests and the Levites" (v. 4). The chapter then proceeds to describe in detail how Hezekiah's command was carried out and the administrative steps that were taken (vv. 5–19).

The bulk of 2 Chronicles 31 suits this theme in terms of its literary nature and style. It is a narrative description of the actions and statements of the personalities involved: Hezekiah, the people, the priests, and others.

> And he [the king] commanded the people to give the portion. . . . As soon as the command was spread abroad the people of Israel gave in abundance . . . they brought in abundantly of everything . . . when Hezekiah and the princes came and saw they blessed the Lord. . . . And Hezekiah questioned the priests and the Levites about the heaps. . . . Azariah the chief priest answered him. . . .
>
> (vv. 4ff.)

The narrative part ends with a concluding statement:

> by the appointment of Hezekiah the king and Azariah the chief officer of the house of God. (v. 13)

2 Chr 31:14 introduces a change in both the topic and style. The passage shifts from a narrative description to an administrative document that is built entirely of nominal clauses and that has no narrative or rhetorical elements. There is not one instance of speech, direct or indirect,[9] no narrative time of any kind, and the entire section contains only two declined verbs, both in subordinate clauses, which serve an adjectival function.[10] The topic also changes from collection or storage of the contributions to the apportionment of the contributions to the priests and Levites.[11] The document presents the mechanisms for

---

9. This can be compared to the preceding narrative section, which has four references to indirect speech (v. 4: "and he commanded the people . . . to give the portion due to the priests and the Levites, that they might give themselves to the law of the Lord"; v. 8: "When Hezekiah and the princes came and saw the heaps, they blessed the Lord and his people Israel"; v. 9: "And Hezekiah questioned the priests . . ."; v. 11: "Then Hezekiah commanded them to prepare chambers . . ."; and a long citation of the statement of "Azariah the chief officer of the house of God" (v. 10).

10. In v. 18 in a causative clause: "for they were faithful in *keeping themselves holy* (יתקדשו)," and in v. 19 in a relative clause: "men in the several cities *who were designated* (נקבו) by name."

11. The different topics are expressed terminologically: that which follows the heading "to give the portion due to the priests and the Levites" (v. 4) deals with the 'bringing' of the gifts (vv. 5, 6, 10, 12), while the document deals with their 'apportionment': "to apportion (לתת) the contribution reserved for the Lord and the most holy offerings" (v. 14), "to distribute (לתת) the

the distribution of the priestly gifts and the rules governing the status of the recipients of the gifts and the logistics of distribution; it has its own heading (v. 14), which reveals a certain tension with the facts related by the preceding narrative.[12] Verses 14–19 would, therefore, seem to represent an independent document that dealt generally with the apportionment of priestly gifts and that was integrated into the narrative in order to anchor the enactment of the administrative procedures to Hezekiah's time, endowing them thereby with antiquity and authority.[13]

The document in its present form is undoubtedly from the Second Temple Period,[14] not only in terms of language and style but also in content, for the order of service described is based on the system of priestly courses, which certainly originated in the Second Temple Period.[15] The conjecture can, of course, be made that the chapter reflects a historical memory of the origins of the various procedures relating to the temple and the clergy in the days of Hezekiah.[16] The centralization of the cult in Jerusalem and the abolition of the highplaces certainly entailed the necessity for financing the various groups of the cultic personnel. The laconic remark in 2 Kgs 23:9 provides a hint of reform in this

portions to their brethren" (v. 15), "to distribute (לתת) portions to every male among the priests" (v. 19). The term 'to bring' is not mentioned once in the document.

12. The narrative mentions several types of priestly gifts: firstfruits and tithes in v. 5 ("the firstfruits of grain, wine, oil, honey. . . . they brought in abundantly the tithe of everything"); tithe in v. 6 ("the tithe of cattle and sheep"), the meaning of which is clear; and "the dedicated things that had been consecrated to the Lord," which is not. Some scholars believe that the text is corrupt; see W. Rudolph, *Chronikbücher* (HAT; Tübingen, 1955) 304–5; and BHS. In the following verses, all the gifts are called 'contributions' (תרומה, v. 10) or 'contributions, tithes, and the dedicated things' (תרומה, מעשר, קדשים, v. 12). All these gifts belong to the category called by the sages 'light holy' (קדשים קלים) and tithe, which is the Levite gift (see M. Haran, "Priestly Gifts," *Encyclopedia Biblica* 4.39, 43 [Heb.]). In contrast, the heading in v. 14 has three other terms: 'free-will offerings to God' (נדבות האלהים), 'contribution reserved for the Lord' (תרומת ה'), and the 'most holy offerings' (קדשי הקדשים). Without entering into detail (see below, pp. 15–16), I would mention that 'the most holy offerings', which are an integral part of the document, are gifts of another kind; they were not mentioned in the narrative and have no connection to it.

13. For the concept of the king as the source of cultic authority, see S. Japhet, *The Ideology of the Book of Chronicles and Its Place in Biblical Thought* (Frankfurt, 1989) 234–39, 438–44.

14. See also Licht's statement: "The action attributed to Hezekiah apparently reflects the custom of the Second Temple period" (J. Licht, *A Commentary on the Book of Numbers [XI–XXI]* [Jerusalem, 1991] 129 [Heb.]); this view is accepted by most of the commentators.

15. See: S. Japhet, *I and II Chronicles: A Commentary* (OTL; London, 1993) 423–24. According to Williamson the courses are a later stratum in Chronicles, for they were not established until after the book's composition. However, in his discussion of chap. 31, Williamson's position on this issue is not unequivocal. See H. G. M. Williamson, "The Origins of the Twenty-Four Priestly Courses: A Study of I Chronicles XXIII–XXVII," *Studies in the Historical Books of the Old Testament* (ed. J. A. Emerton; VTSup 30; Leiden, 1979) 251–68; idem, *I and II Chronicles* (NCBC; London, 1982) 373–77.

16. See for example, I. Knohl: "It seems to me that a reliable tradition concerning reforms in the system of collection and distribution of the contributions and tithes carried out in this period lies at the basis [of the chapter]" (*Temple of Silence* [Jerusalem, 1993] 196 n. 41 [Heb.]).

sphere: "Nevertheless the priests of the high places came not up to the altar of
the Lord in Jerusalem, but they did eat unleavened bread among their brethren." However, the questions remain. Can one date the centralization of the
cult—with all its ramifications—as early as Hezekiah's reign? Can one link
this reform to the specific procedures depicted in our document, or even to
their basic principles? In any event, we are concerned here not with the entire
chapter, its contents and presuppositions, but with 2 Chr 31:14–19 alone, the
document that deals with the allocation of the priestly gifts.

C

There are two criteria in 2 Chr 31:14–19 by which the temple clergy who
are eligible for priestly gifts are divided: a distinction is made between priests
and Levites and between those who officiate at the temple and those who live
in the provincial towns. Thus, four groups are created: priests who serve in
the temple, priests who live in the provincial towns, Levites who serve in the
temple, and Levites who live in the provincial towns. The originally clear
structure of the document has been somewhat distorted by a small textual corruption in the Masoretic Text. In the interest of precision, let us first clarify
the text of the document and the difficulties it presents.

The obvious point of departure is 2 Chr 31:19, which refers to all the
members of the tribe of Levi who are in the provincial towns, both priests and
Levites:

> As for the sons of Aaron, the priests, who were in the fields of common land
> belonging to their cities (בשדי מגרש עריהם), . . . to distribute portions to every
> male among the priests and to every one among the Levites who was registered
> by genealogy.

The wording of the opening phrase, "as for the sons of Aaron," indicates
that the verse deals with a different group from the one discussed previously.[17]
The question is, to whom are those "who were in the fields of common land
belonging to their cities" contrasted? Who are the "others" discussed earlier?
Reason would dictate that they are the sons of Levi who are in Jerusalem and
officiate in the temple and that v. 19 indeed points to a differentiation between
these two groups. However, the wording of v. 15, which mentions "the cities of
the priests," militates against this simple answer. The wording of the text as it
now stands thus contrasts the priests in the "priestly cities" (v. 15) and those
"in the fields of common land belonging to the cities" (v. 19). This contrast
presents several difficulties.

17. See, for example, the NEB translation, 'As for the priests of Aaron's line . . .', and similarly
the NJPSV and others.

(a) The terms 'priestly cities' (ערי הכהנים) and 'the fields of common land belonging to the cities' (שדי מגרש עריהם) refer to the same thing with a minor change in terminology, for the book of Chronicles attests to the evolution of the term עיר מגרש ('a city of common land') or even מגרש ('common land') as a term for the Levitical cities.[18] The "fields of common land" is a quotation from Lev 25:34, but the meaning is changed. It does not mean the common land that surrounds the city, as opposed to the built-up area inside it, but means the Levitical city or priestly city itself.[19]

(b) In the extant text, the document seems to deal twice and in two different ways with the priests who live in the provincial towns, while the priests of Jerusalem who officiate in the temple are not classified as a special group. However, it is particularly the priests of Jerusalem who are the primary candidates to receive the priestly gifts, both because they are officiating in the temple and because they are cut off from any other source of income. The "most holy offerings" taken "from the fire" are certainly designated for them alone. The focus of the document, as it stands, on the priests of the provincial towns seems very strange.[20]

(c) 2 Chr 31:16 seems to refer to the temple clergy: "all who entered the house of the Lord as the duty of each day required." However, in its present form, the syntactical context of this phrase is unclear, and it is unconnected to the preceding phrase. Its connection to v. 15 (the priestly cities) on the one hand, and to v.16a ("except those registered by genealogy") on the other, leads to some strange and unacceptable interpretations.

The root of all these problems seems to be a minor corruption in the MT of 2 Chr 31:15 that is not easily detected, since it causes no difficulty when one reads the verse on its own. The difficulties become evident only when the syntax and internal logic of the entire section are examined. The text of the Septuagint preserves the original version and provides the solution. Instead of 'in the cities of the priests' of the MT, the Septuagint reads: διὰ χειρὸς τῶν ἱερέων, in which 'in the cities' (בערי) is presented as 'by the hand of' (על יד). This cannot be an internal Greek corruption, for there is no connection be-

---

18. S. Japhet, "The Supposed Common Authorship of Chronicles and Ezra–Nehemiah Investigated Anew," *VT* 18 (1968) 348–50.

19. Not all the commentators realized the significance of "the fields of common land belonging to the city" as the technical designation for a Levitical city and explained the contrast between v. 19 and v. 15 as being between the priests living in the "fields" around the city and those living in the city itself (see for example, Rudolph, *Chronikbücher*, 309; Williamson, "Origins," 377; and others). This differentiation is not supported by any other source, biblical or later, and seems forced. See also: E. L. Curtis and A. A. Madsen, *The Book of Chronicles* (ICC; Edinburgh, 1910) 484.

20. This is indeed Elmslie's conclusion: "ver. 15 states that the distribution was to be made to priestly and levitical persons resident in the priestly cities but (ver. 16) *not* to those who were for the time being on duty at the Temple, since these no doubt would receive their share at the Temple itself " (W. M. L. Elmslie, *The Book of Chronicles* [CBC; 1916] 315). Regarding his understanding of the entire section, see below, n. 34.

tween the translation of the MT to be expected (ἐν [ταῖς] πόλεσιν τοῦ/τῶν) and the extant version διὰ χειρός.

On the other hand, the similarity between the Hebrew basis of the Septuagint and the Hebrew of the MT is undeniable, making clear the process by which the error crept in.[21] The ל was changed to ר in the original על יד, because of the phonetic similarity of the two consonants[22] and so the meaningless word עריד was created. The final ד was erased in a hyper-correction, and the word ערי remained as a construct form: ערי הכהנים. When we accept the Septuagint version, the text becomes coherent, its internal structure and meaning become perfectly clear, and all the difficulties that were listed above (and others that were not mentioned) disappear.

D

The document (2 Chr 31:14–19) before us is thus composed of two unequal parts: after the heading in v. 14, vv. 15–18 deal with the clergy in Jerusalem, while v. 19 is devoted to the members of the tribe of Levi who live in the provincial towns. Verses 15–18 are also divided into two subunits: one dedicated to the priests, which ends with a summarizing clause, and one dealing with the Levites, which ends with an explanatory clause. In each of the subunits, the expression 'according to their offices by their divisions' is repeated in order to emphasize the fact that the text deals with those who actively officiate in the temple.

The section reads thus:

Part I, vv. 15–18

Ia (15–17a):

ועל ידו עדן ומנימן וישוע ושמעיהו אמריהו ושכניהו על יד הכהנים באמונה,
לתת לאחיהם במחלקות כגדול כקטן (מלבד התיחשם לזכרים מבן שלוש
שנים ולמעלה) לכל הבא לבית ה׳ לדבר יום ביומו לעבודתם במשמרותם
כמחלקותיהם. זאת[24] התיחש הכהנים לבית אבותיהם.[23]

---

21. For the considerations that apply to the preference of one version of a text to another, see E. Tov, *Textual Criticism of the Hebrew Bible* (Minneapolis, 1992) 293–311.

22. See GKC §6 o–p / pp. 34–35.

23. The division of verses in the MT does not fit the syntax of the passage. The conclusion is severed from the passage that it ends and becomes a heading where what follows ("and the Levites from twenty years old . . .") is unconnected to it. This break is further emphasized in some editions (see BHK/BHS) by a closed passage (פרשה סתומה), which creates an even greater separation between the conclusion and what came before. This may be a reflection of redactory activity, which attempts to overcome the problematics in the meaning of the text by changing its structure.

24. The reading of the MT is ואת, but with many other commentators I prefer the version of the Septuagint: זאת (οὗτος). See, for example, BHK, BHS, and others. The formula X זאת serves in the priestly literature both as a heading and as a conclusion. As a heading, see, for example: Exod 12:43; Lev 6:2, 7, 18, and many more. As a conclusion, see: Lev 7:35, 37; 12:7, et al. Generally

And by his side Eden, Miniamin, Jeshua, Shemaiah, Amariah, and Shecaniah alongside the priests in offices of trust, to distribute [the portions] to their brethren, old and young alike, by divisions, (except those registered by genealogy, males from three years old and upwards), to all who entered the house of the Lord as the duty of each day required, for their service according to their offices, by their divisions. This is the registration of the priests according to their fathers' houses.

Ib (17b–18):

ותלוים מבן עשרים שנה ולמעלה במשמרותיהם במחלקותיהם. ולהתיחש
בכל טפם נשיהם ובניהם ובנותיהם לכל קהל, כי באמונתם יתקדשו קדש.

And the Levites from twenty years old and upwards according to their offices, by their divisions. They were registered by genealogy with all their little children, their wives, their sons, and their daughters, the whole multitude, for in their faithfulness they sanctified themselves in holiness.

Part II, v. 19:

ולבני אהרן הכהנים בשדי מגרש עריהם בכל עיר ועיר אנשים אשר נקבו
בשמות,לתת מנות לכל זכר בכהנים ולכל התיחש בלוים.

As for the sons of Aaron, the priests, who were in their cities (which have common land), there were men in the each city who were designated by name to distribute portions to every male among the priests and to every one among the Levites who was registered by genealogy.

2 Chr 31:15–17a defines the priests of Jerusalem who are eligible for the priestly gifts. First are mentioned all those in service ("their brethren, old and young alike, by divisions"), but this is interrupted by a parenthetical sentence that begins with the word 'except': "except those registered by genealogy, males from three years old and upwards" (v. 16a). The description of the priests who perform the temple service is thus: "to distribute the portions to their brethren, old and young alike, by divisions, . . . to all who entered the house of the Lord as the duty of each day required, for their service according to their offices, by their divisions." All the terms used are part of the linguistic corpus connected to the temple service; some appear in Chronicles alone and some in other sources as well.[25] The priests eligible for priestly gifts are therefore com-

---

speaking, the conclusion is longer than the opening and has a celebratory style. See, for example: Lev 7:35–37; 11:46; 13:59, and so on. See also: M. Paran, *Forms of the Priestly Style in the Pentateuch* (Jerusalem, 1989) 152, 156–60, 223–25, 237 [Heb.].

25. 'Their brethren' (אחיהם), as an expression of the relationship between the priests and the Levites, or between one group of the clergy and another, is widespread in Chronicles. See, among others: 1 Chr 6:44 [MT: 6:29]; 9:32; 15:16, 17, 18; 23:32; 24:31; 2 Chr 29:15, 34. The term 'divisions'

posed of two groups that are essentially one: the priests who officiate in the temple and all males above age three, that is to say, all male priests. This definition is summed up in v. 17a: "This (MT: and) is the registration of the priests according to their fathers' houses." It is repeated in v. 19 regarding the provincial towns: "to every male among the priests." The criteria for the priests are thus personal and individual. Each priest is eligible for priestly gifts from age three on, that is from the time he is weaned[26] until his death, his entire life.

2 Chr 31:17b–18 opens with a new heading, "And the Levites," and defines the criteria for their eligibility. Here, too, the reference is to those who officiate "according to their offices, by their divisions," but in contrast to the priests they are not registered from age three but "from twenty years old and upwards." This difference becomes significant in the sequel: "They were registered by genealogy with all their little children, their wives, their sons and their daughters, the whole multitude." That is, in contrast to the priests, the eligibility of the Levites is a function of their household, and every household is defined according to its head, who must be twenty or more.[27] This definition is also repeated very briefly regarding the Levites in the provincial towns: "and to everyone among the Levites who was registered by genealogy" (v. 19).

Although the document focuses on the men officiating in Jerusalem, the basic terms of eligibility seem no different for the priests of Jerusalem and the priests of the provincial towns or for the Levites in Jerusalem and the Levites in the provincial towns. The essential difference (upon which the document centers) concerns the various administrative bodies responsible for distribution of the gifts.[28] The difference in terms of eligibility lies between the priests and

---

(מחלקות) is a common term in Chronicles, see: 1 Chr 23:6, 24:1ff., et al.; and see: Japhet, "Supposed Common Authorship" 344–48; and see n. 15 above. The term 'offices' (משמרות), both in singular and plural, is a standard term in the priestly material in the Pentateuch, in Ezekiel, in Ezra–Nehemiah and in Chronicles, and so is the term 'service' (עבודה). See J. Milgrom, *Studies in Levitical Terminology* (Berkeley, 1970) vol. 1. The following terms should also be included in this category: כגדול כקטן: 1 Chr 25:8, 26:13; דבר יום ביומו: 1 Chr 16:37, 2 Chr 8:14, etc. Concerning the term כל הבא as a *terminus technicus* that indicates membership in a specific group, see: S. Lieberman, "The Discipline in the So-Called Dead Sea Manual of Discipline," *JBL* 71 (1952) 202; idem, *Greek in Jewish Palestine* (New York, 1965) 80. It is possible that it is already *terminus technicus* in our text.

26. Regarding age three as the age of weaning, see H. Z. Hirshberg, "Weaning," *Encyclopaedia Biblica* 2.519–20 [Heb.]. There is no explicit reference in the Pentateuch to the age at which the priests become eligible for the priestly gifts.

27. Twenty is the generally accepted age of full maturity in the Bible. It is the age when the male is included in the census, the age of military service, and so forth. See for example Exod 38:26; Num 1:3ff., 26:2ff., et al. For the age of twenty in the Dead Sea Scrolls, see 1QSa I 9–11. See also L. Schiffman, *Sectarian Law in the Dead Sea Scrolls: Courts, Testimony, and the Penal Code* (Chico, Cal., 1983), 55–65; idem, *The Eschatological Community of the Dead Sea Scrolls* (Atlanta, 1989) 16–20, and the literature mentioned there.

28. A comparison between the detailed language of 2 Chr 31:14–15 and the general description in v. 19 should be made, but this is outside the purview of our article. On the practical level,

the Levites. In this regard, the document agrees with what we know from the Pentateuchal laws. In the Pentateuch as well there are separate categories of gifts, one for the priests and one for the Levites, with different terms of eligibility of each group. However, despite the general similarity, many differences in detail appear between the document and the Pentateuch. In order to clarify these details, their scope and significance, let us first turn to the Pentateuchal sources, the most detailed and orderly presentation of which is found in Numbers 18.[29]

E

According to Numbers 18, the priestly gifts are divided into two categories:[30] 'the most holy offerings' (קדש הקדשים)—"this shall be yours of the most holy things [reserved] from the fire" (v. 9); and 'the gift offering' (תרומת מתנם), called by the sages 'light holy offerings'—"and this is yours, the offering of their gift" (v. 11). The first category is designated only for the males of the priests and it must be eaten in a holy place: "In the most holy place you shall eat it, every male shall eat it" (v. 10). The second category is for all the priestly families, and can be eaten in purity everywhere: "I have given them to you, and to your sons and your daughters with you, . . . everyone that is clean in your house shall eat of it" (v. 11).[31]

According to the guidelines in Numbers 18, enjoyment of the priestly gifts is given to the priests and their families. The most holy offerings are reserved

---

there was probably a difference between the priests of Jerusalem and the priests in the provincial towns: since there was only one central temple, one would assume that the parts of the sacrifices given to the priests—the "most holy offerings" and some of the "light holy offerings"—were not delivered to the provincial towns. This may explain the claims of the priests, testified to in sources of the Second Temple Period, to a portion of the tithe.

29. The common view is that Numbers 18 belongs to source P. See, for example, Licht: "It is generally accepted that chapters 17–18 come from P; this is clear . . ." (*Commentary*, 132). Recently, Knohl has claimed that this chapter belongs to H, which in his opinion is later, and expresses different views from P (*Temple of Silence*, 56–57). Since one may assume that Chronicles already knew the complete Pentateuch, this dispute has no direct bearing on our analysis, but it is of interest regarding Chronicle's position vis-à-vis the various trends in Israel, the laws and ideologies they propound.

30. For further details, see Haran, "Priestly Gifts," 39–44; also Licht, *Commentary*, 121–31.

31. The question of the household slaves is a separate issue. According to Lev 22:10 it is clear that "every stranger" (anyone who does not belong to the family of the priest) is forbidden to eat of the holy offerings. But slaves are not included in this category: "But if the priest buys a slave as his property for money, he may eat of it, and those that are born into his household may eat of his food" (22:11). How then, are we to understand Numbers 18, which does not enter into detail on this issue. Is one to emphasize "to you and to your sons and daughters with you" (Num 18:11), that is only family members, or "everyone that is clean in your house" (18:11), which may include the slaves? It is impossible to decide this issue for lack of detail, but it should be emphasized that the different texts need not be harmonized. They may reflect different legal positions.

for "every male," while the other gifts, which are the majority, (the firstfruits, the firstborn, and so on) are intended for the entire family: "everyone that is clean in your house shall eat of it" (v. 13).

In contrast to the great number of gifts intended for the priests,[32] the Pentateuch designates only one gift for the Levites, the tithe, called by the Rabbis מעשר ראשון ('the first tithe') (Num 18:21ff.).[33] The following Pentateuchal guidelines for the tithe relate to the issue under discussion:

1. The Levites are obligated to deduct from the tithe תרומת מעשר (a tithe contribution), equal to a tenth of the tithe (Num 18:26), intended for the priests.
2. After the תרומה is deducted, the tithe loses its holiness and "shall be reckoned to the Levites as the produce of the threshing floor and as the produce of the winepress" (v. 30).
3. It may be eaten anywhere, and the definition of those who eat it is general: "And you may eat it in any place, you and your households" (v. 31).

Thus, Numbers 18 lists three kinds of priestly gifts, which differ in their origin, the level of their holiness, those allowed to eat them, and the place where they may be eaten:

1. *Most holy offerings*—given to every male priest and eaten in a holy place.
2. *Light holy offerings*—(תרומת מתנם)—given to all the priestly families and eaten in purity everywhere.
3. *The Levite gifts (tithe)*—given to all the Levite families and eaten everywhere.

There is a similarity between the light holy offerings and the Levite gifts, for both are eaten by the entire family and are not limited to the males, but the light holy offerings are holy and must be eaten in purity, while the tithe is not holy.

The exact definition of those who may eat the gifts is another issue. There is a clear reference to familial ties for the priests: "to you, and to your sons and your daughters with you" (v. 11), "you and your sons with you" (v. 19). Regarding the Levites, general terms are used: "you and your households" (v. 31).

---

32. Even in the Pentateuch, where the various sources have different views of what the priestly gifts constitute and at times call the same gift by different names, the number of priestly gifts is quite large. This is certainly the case in rabbinic law, whose enumeration of priestly gifts integrated the details given in all the sources. See Kaufmann, *History of Religion*, 143.

33. Some of the questions regarding the tithe—should it be viewed as an annual obligation or as a voluntary donation? what is the relationship between the different types of tithe? and what is the history of the tithe in the biblical and postbiblical periods?—are not relevant to our analysis and cannot be dealt with here. See the literature referred to above, the commentaries on the relevant texts, and recently: M. Herman, *Tithe as Gift: The Institution in the Pentateuch and in Light of Mauss's Prestation Theory* (Lewiston, N.Y., 1991) and the literature mentioned there.

F

As we have seen above, 2 Chr 31:14–19 does not have three categories of eligibility for priestly gifts, but only two: "every male among the priests" and "every one among the Levites who was registered by genealogy." That is, one category of priests and one of Levites. Moreover, the categories of Numbers 18 and those of 2 Chronicles 31 are not identical, and these differences demand a detailed examination.

2 Chronicles affirms only the first of the Pentateuchal categories, "every male among the priests," and nullifies the second, which relates to the priestly families. Correspondingly, it sustains the category of Levites but offers a definition that differs from that given in Numbers 18. Instead of "you and your households," 2 Chronicles 31 defines the Levites as "everyone among the Levites who was registered by genealogy," that is, everyone who is a Levite according to his genealogy. This category instead matches the category of the priestly families in Numbers 18. 2 Chronicles 31 thus introduces two changes into the definition of those eligible for priestly gifts: the category of the priestly families is abolished, and the degree of sanctity of the Levites is raised by applying to them the guidelines previously used for the priests.

The major difficulty of this new categorization concerns the priests. Does it mean that the priestly families are not allowed to enjoy the priestly gifts? Such an interpretation contradicts the Pentateuchal source to such an extent that the spontaneous reaction of the commentator is to reject it and to search for ways to harmonize the various testimonies. This may be done either by reading the text in 2 Chronicles 31 differently from the way we have read it above or by interpreting it so that the tacit assumptions of Numbers 18 will be implicit in this text as well. I cannot present here all the solutions suggested by the commentators, but will give a few illustrations.

The easiest way to resolve the difficulty is to forego a precise explanation of the document and to make only general statements, claiming that the text is not sufficiently clear, that it has been corrupted, or that it was modified by secondary additions.[34] This method cannot be used by the translators, who must confront the text in its entirety. They therefore attempt to apply 2 Chr 31:18, "They were registered by genealogy with all their little children, their wives, their sons and their daughters," both to the priests and to the Levites[35] or, alternatively, to the priests alone.

There are several variations to this exegetical procedure. Curtis, for instance, proposes that 2 Chr 31:17aβ–b "and the Levites . . . by their divisions,"

---

34. So, for example, Elmslie in 1916: "The exact meaning and sequence of these verses is hard to follow, and probably the obscurity is due to faults in the Hebrew text" (*Book of Chronicles*, 315), and Dillard in 1987: "The flow of thought and the precise significance of some of the details in this section are difficult" (R. B. Dillard, *2 Chronicles* [WBC 15; Waco, Tex., 1987] 251).

35. So in the Septuagint and the Targum, and so in various modern translations, such as the AV, NJPSV, and others. See also Pseudo-Rashi to v. 17.

is a parenthetical sentence and that vv. 17aα and 18 are a continuum, so: "This is the registration of the priests according to their fathers houses (לבית אבותיהם), who were registered by genealogy with all their little children. . . ."[36] The RSV, in contrast, achieves the same goal by changing the text via translation. It concludes the sentence with v. 17, ignores the conjunctive *waw* at the beginning of v. 18 (ולהתיחש), and adds a new heading at the beginning of v. 18: "The priests were enrolled."[37] The difficulties with these interpretations are clear: there is no sign in the text that 2 Chr 31:17aβ–b is a parenthetical sentence; presenting it as such makes it meaningless; the new reading, according to both suggestions, is in total contradiction to the explicit testimony of v. 19 ("every male of the priests" and "every one among the Levites who was registered by genealogy").

Pseudo-Rashi follows a different direction, reading an a fortiori inference into 2 Chr 31:19 that includes the directives of Numbers 18. The commentary on v. 19 reads:

> "To every male among the priests." And also to all their wives, sons and daughters. And what was stated here: "to every male" is meant to add something new, for if they provide even for male minors . . . all the more so they provided for their wives and sons and daughters.[38]

Another means of harmonization is to assume that 2 Chr 31:14–19 does not refer to all the priestly gifts but only to part of them, that is, to the most holy offerings on the one hand (which are eaten by the male priests as per Num 18:9–10) and to the tithe on the other (intended for the Levites, as in Num 18:24ff). The text then would not refer to the light holy offerings, the other priestly gifts.

In order to examine this avenue of interpretation, the document in 2 Chr 31:14–19 should be analyzed within the two contexts in which it appears: the primary context, in which the document is a separate literary unit, whose subject is set by its special heading in v. 14 and the secondary context created by the inclusion of the document in chap. 31.

2 Chr 31:14 designates the priestly gifts by three terms: 'freewill offerings to God' (נדבות האלהים), 'the contribution reserved for the Lord' (תרומת ה), and "the most holy offerings" (קדשי הקדשים). We cannot examine the meaning of the term 'freewill offerings to God' in light of its use in other places, for it is peculiar to this verse, but its literal meaning and its place within the verse may indicate that it is a general term that includes the other two and perhaps more: "And Kore the son of Imnah the Levite . . . was over the freewill offerings to

---

36. Curtis and Madsen, *Book of Chronicles*, 483–84. David Qimḥi, the Medieval commentator, may have interpreted these verses similarly. See the conclusion of his commentary on v. 16.

37. It should be remarked that the translators did not note these changes.

38. See *Miqraot Gedolot*. David Qimḥi has another explanation: "to every male among the priests: Portions suitable to be eaten by the male priests."

God to apportion the contribution reserved for the Lord and the most holy offerings." Freewill offerings to God apparently include all the gifts and holy offerings, while the gifts that are to be apportioned (לתת) are the contribution reserved for the Lord, on the one hand, and the most holy offerings, on the other.

The third term, 'most holy offerings', is a well-defined term, equivalent to the priestly gifts described in Num 18:9: "This shall be yours of the most holy things [reserved] from the fire, every offering of theirs, every cereal offering of theirs, and every sin offering of theirs and every guilt offering of theirs which they render to me shall be most holy to you and to your sons."[39] The term 'the contribution reserved for the Lord' may be interpreted in two ways. In Numbers 18 it is used for the tenth part of the tithe that the Levites reserve for the priests (Num 18:26, 28, 29); if we seek an exact parallel between the texts, 2 Chr 31:14 would also refer to the tenth part of the tithe. However, according to its literal meaning, its use in other sources,[40] and its function in the document before us, 'the contribution reserved for the Lord' seems to serve as a more general term that describes many gifts, among them the priestly gifts detailed in Num 18:11–18 and called there 'their gift contribution' (תרומת מתנם), and the Levite gifts, the tithe, which is also called 'contribution': "For the tithes of the children of Israel, which they offer as a contribution unto the Lord, I have given to the Levites to inherit" (Num 18:24). Indeed, no matter how we interpret the contribution reserved for the Lord, even in its most narrow sense of a tenth part of the tithe, it thereby refers to the light holy offerings, which according to Numbers 18 are intended for the priests. It cannot be interpreted as meaning the tithe alone.

As for the context of 2 Chronicles 31 as a whole, it contains an explicit reference to the tithe (vv. 5–6) and to the firstfruits (v. 5), which is certainly one of the light holy offerings, that according to Numbers 18 are intended for the entire families of priests.

The conclusion to be drawn is that no matter in what context 2 Chr 32:14–19 is read, it does not exclude the light holy offerings from the gifts, and no reasonable harmonization can be made with the positions of Numbers 18. The question whether the priestly families are allowed to enjoy the priestly gifts remains; even though the document mentions the two types of gifts, it limits the recipients to "every male of the priests."

G

2 Chr 31:14–19 also expresses a different view from the Pentateuch regarding the status of the Levites. By describing the eligibility of the Levites as

39. See also Ezek 42:13 (twice), 44:13.
40. In Exod 30:14–15 the term תרומה describes the half-shekel, the census toll. In Exod 35:21, 24 it describes the people's donation to the building of the tabernacle, also called תרומה לה' (v. 5), and in Num 31:29, 41 it refers to the tax on the booty.

being according to their registration by genealogy, the text transfers to the Levites certain concepts that originally belonged to the priests. The use of the term 'holy' in v. 18 may be connected to this trend as well. It is apparently no coincidence that the only time the document uses the term 'holy' is in relation to the Levites, as a justification for their eligibility: "for in their faithfulness they would sanctify themselves in holiness."

As is well known, the Pentateuch does not assign holiness to the Levites. Although the Levites perform their duties in the courtyard of the tabernacle and carry its vessels, what is demanded of them, except for their origin, is purity and not holiness.[41] This is not the case in Chronicles, where the holiness of the Levites is a basic concept that is repeated several times. Not only is holiness demanded of the Levites, but they are even quicker to fulfill this obligation than the priests. See, for example, the following verses: "And the priests and the Levites made themselves holy (or: sanctified themselves) to bring up the ark of the Lord the God of Israel" (1 Chr 15:14); "Hear me, Levites, now make yourselves holy (or: sanctify yourselves) and make the house of the Lord the God of your fathers holy" (2 Chr 29:5); "And the Levites arose . . . and they gathered their brethren and made themselves holy (or: sanctified themselves)" (2 Chr 29:12–15); "their brethren the Levites helped them, . . . for the Levites were more upright in heart to make themselves holy (or: in sanctifying themselves) than the priests" (29:34); and others.

The 'holiness' of the Levites is no doubt linked to the Chronicler's unique position regarding the functions of the Levites and is a necessary consequence of this view. The Levites' involvement in the temple service in Chronicles is much broader than the service designated for them by the Pentateuch: some of the functions that Chronicles assigns to them were originally, or according to other views, the legacy of the priests. 2 Chr 31:14–19 fits in very well with the book in its entirety in the increased functions assigned to the Levites, in their higher status, and in the increased level of their holiness.

Various scholars since the earliest scholarship of Chronicles have noted the unique position of this work vis-à-vis the Levites. Some saw in its pro-Levite tendency one of the cornerstones of its world view, while others viewed it as the major motivation for the composition of the book.[42] However, the discovery of the Dead Sea Scrolls, chief among them the *Temple Scroll*, has

---

41. One may compare the rite of purification of the Levites (Num 8:5–22) with the initiation ceremony of Aaron and his sons (Leviticus 8–9) in order to appreciate the difference. In contrast to the priests, whose holy state obligates them to remove themselves from impurity and imposes on them various matrimonial restrictions (Leviticus 21), no such rules apply to the Levites. See also J. Milgrom in Yadin, *Temple Scroll*, 1.169 n. 1.

42. See, among others: G. von Rad, *Das Geschichtsbild des chronistischen Werkes* (Stuttgart, 1930) 88–119; A. C. Welch, *The Work of the Chronicler* (London, 1939) 55–67; R. H. Pfeiffer, *Introduction to the Old Testament* (New York, 1941) 795–801; O. Eissfeldt, *The Old Testament: An Introduction* (Eng. trans.; Oxford, 1965) 537–38, etc.

changed the perspective from which this position is to be considered. It has become evident that this was not the personal inclination of one author, but a
more widespread view, aspects of which are expressed in the writings of the
Dead Sea sect. As Yadin justly claims, "the tendency of the Scroll . . . [is] to
emphasize the status of the Levites."[43]

The strong similarity between the *Temple Scroll* and Chronicles regarding
the status of the Levites raises another question, that of the claim of the Levites
to a share in the priestly gifts. We have seen above that the heading of the document found in 2 Chr 31:14 lists two types of gifts: most holy offerings and contributions reserved for the Lord. We have also seen that the document mentions
two eligible groups: (1) every male of the priests and (2) every one of the Levites who was registered by genealogy. The obvious question is, should one
press this dichotomy in order to claim that there is complete parity between the
two principles of classification and to conclude that the most holy offerings are
intended for every male of the priests, while contributions reserved for the Lord
are intended for every one of the Levites who is registered by genealogy. Since
we have concluded above that the term 'contribution reserved for the Lord' is
not restricted to tithes, but includes the light holy offerings as well (some or
all), this equation would imply a claim by the Levites for gifts that according to
the Pentateuchal law are intended for the priests.

This conclusion may be formulated in two alternate ways, one more extreme than the other. According to the most extreme interpretation, the claim
made by the Levites would be for all of the contributions reserved for the Lord,
leaving the priests with only the most holy offerings. According to the more
moderate view, the contributions reserved for the Lord would be shared by the
priests and Levites, and the exclusive rights of the priests would be abolished.
In either case, this equation may infer the demand to include the Levites in the
gifts that were originally the legacy of the priests. The elevation of the sanctity
of the Levites would be associated with this demand; it would be a necessary
condition of their eligibility for the priestly gifts.

As Yadin pointed out, there is a clear correlation between 2 Chronicles 31
and the *Temple Scroll* on this issue as well. The *Temple Scroll* testifies explicitly to the Levite demand for part of the peace offerings and designates the
shoulder for the Levites: "And to the Levites one tenth of the grain and the
wine and the oil . . . and the shoulder from those offering a sacrifice"
(11QTemple LX 6–7). In Yadin's view, this prescription is based on biblical
sources, among them 2 Chronicles 31.[44] He relies mainly on the term מנה ('por-

---

43. Yadin, *Temple Scroll*, 1.155.

44. "In my opinion, however, the prescription in the scroll is based, as well, on several passages that, when taken simply, probably hint that the portions from the dedicated things are to
be shared with the Levites" (ibid., 155). Yadin enumerates among these sources: 2 Chr 31:4ff.,
19; Neh 12:44ff.; 13:10. According to Milgrom, this demand is based on Num 18:1–3 (see ibid.,
169–70).

tion'), common to these works and the *Temple Scroll*. However, it should be emphasized that one can find in 2 Chronicles 31 at most hints of the claims of the Levites, rather than explicit statements, so Yadin's view remains a hypothesis for the time being.

H

We have seen that 2 Chr 31:14–19 limits the eligibility of the priests to "every male of the priests," and in light of the distinction made in Num 18:9–10 and 11–18, this seemed to exclude the priestly families. In fact however, this limitation affects only the women,[45] rather than the entire family, for "every male of the priests" includes all males with no age limit, young and old alike. More precisely, the women in the priestly families are divided into two groups according to their genealogy, and this difference can have a direct bearing on their eligibility to enjoy the priestly gifts. The first group includes the wives of the priests. Since a priest is not restricted to marriage with only the daughters of priests,[46] the wife of a priest may be an Israelite, having no priestly genealogy of her own. If individual priestly genealogy is the guiding principle for eligibility to enjoy the priestly gifts, this may explain the exclusion of the wives of priests from those eligible. However, this principle is not applicable to the second category, the daughters of priests who do have priestly origins and to whom the Pentateuch explicitly refers.[47] Both according to halakic reasoning and according to the Pentateuchal sources, there is no reason to deny the rights of the daughter of a priest to eat from the holy gifts.

2 Chr 31:14–19 abolishes the rights of all women to partake of the holy offerings, without reference to their genealogy. This position (which seems most extreme and seems to lack any halakic basis) is connected to another aspect of the ideology of Chronicles and may be explained in that context.

As I have shown elsewhere, and in an entirely different connection, one finds in Chronicles a more extreme position regarding sexual impurity than the position of the Pentateuch. It demands a complete separation between "holiness" and "women." This tendency, which demands that women be kept away from all sacred objects, is found in the writings of the Dead Sea sect as well, and the two sources shed light on one another.[48] This fundamental outlook

45. See also Rudolph, *Chronikbücher*, 309. Rudolph applies this to the Levites as well, and considers the words "their wives, their sons and their daughters" in v. 18 a late addition. I cannot accept this view.

46. Lev 21:7. It is possible that such a restriction applies to the High Priest: "he shall take a virgin of his own people (מעמיו) to wife" (Lev 21:14), if we interpret 'of his own people' (מעמיו) in the narrow sense of 'his family' (as does *HALAT* 3.792). It is certainly not applicable to priests in general. As far as we know, this restriction was never observed in reality (see Exod 6:23).

47. Lev 22:12–13; Num 18:11, 19.

48. See "Prohibition of the Habitation of Women," which deals with 2 Chr 8:11. Rudolph already noted the affinities between 2 Chr 31:16 and 2 Chr 8:11 (*Chronikbücher*, 309).

seems to serve as the basis for 2 Chronicles 31: the extraordinary sanctity of the priestly realm and its inherent relationship to the temple and its service demand the maximum distancing from women. The priestly gifts are holy, and their defilement by women *qua* women should be prevented, including mothers, wives, and daughters.

I

We came across the ideational and halakic similarity between Chronicles and the Dead Sea Scrolls in two different and independent contexts; 2 Chr 8:11, on the one hand, and 2 Chr 31:14–19, on the other. This close affinity sharply delineates the question of the place Chronicles holds within the framework of the different streams of Second Temple Judaism, as well as demanding a new look at these streams themselves. The fact that Chronicles contains laws and positions that deviate from the Pentateuch has been noted in the past, although the general tendency in scholarship has been to emphasize rather the similarities between Chronicles and the biblical literature, particularly its priestly and Deuteronomistic traditions. As long as these issues were examined independently, they were generally interpreted as an expression of the individual, idiosyncratic tendencies of the Chronicler. Now, with the testimony of the Dead Sea Scrolls, the ideational proximity of Chronicles to these writings is beginning to be clear, particularly the issues in which Chronicles deviates from the Pentateuchal tradition. These phenomena delineate new isoglosses that traverse the lines of canonical and noncanonical status and emphatically raise the question of the "sectarian" nature of works, laws, and views.

The affinity between Chronicles and the writings of the sect became clear to me, as stated, with my detailed study of two separate issues. It is of course possible that the correlation is merely coincidental, and it is certainly too early to draw general conclusions, but it seems to me, nonetheless, that this ideational proximity cries out for further investigation. It is to be hoped that new research and additional discoveries will enlighten us concerning these questions; I have intended but to open a small window upon this fascinating world.

THE HOLINESS OF ISRAEL AND THE LAND IN SECOND TEMPLE TIMES

James Kugel

IN HIS LONG AND FRUITFUL CAREER, Menahem Haran has contributed greatly to our knowledge of all things connected to holiness and cultic worship in ancient Israel. In this paper, I should like to explore in his honor the relationship between the idea of sacred place as it is found in various Second Temple texts, and the idea of Israel as a sacred people, a people holy to God. Underlying this choice of topic is the belief that these two notions were indeed closely connected, if not their origins, then at least in later times. It will not, of course, be possible for me to begin to do justice to the complexities of this interrelation in this brief format. Rather, I should like to try merely to suggest some of the more obvious ways in which sacred place and sacred people might have come to overlap in the late and postbiblical periods, as well as to examine in some detail one or two brief passages that may have bearing on this overall theme.

The idea that the people of Israel are both held to be and enjoined to be holy to God is an idea that has been explored at some length by modern biblical scholars.[1] Israel's holiness turns out to be a complex and multifarious notion, so much so that there would be little point here in seeking to list all the different aspects of holiness that scholars have identified in their examination of various biblical texts and social milieux. Let me, however, permit myself one observation with regard to this body of evidence: among the many things that Israel's holiness may have meant in early times, it does *not* seem at first to have implied anything about what might be called the "genetic" purity of this people and the necessity of maintaining such purity through strict endogamy,

1. In addition to Haran's own writings (and see in particular, in connection with our particular subject, his *Temples and Temple Service in Ancient Israel* [Oxford, 1978] 175–88 [repr. Winona Lake, Ind., 1985]), a number of studies have focused specifically on the concept of holiness; for a recent survey of the literature, see J. G. Gammie, *Holiness in Israel* (Minneapolis, 1989). One important new study is that of I. Knohl, *The Sanctuary of Silence* (Jerusalem, 1992), especially 169–75 [Heb.].

21

avoidance of contact with strangers, and so forth. This is hardly a surprising observation, but it perhaps ought to be stated at the outset of our inquiry.

Thus when, for example, God proposes to the people at the time of the Sinai covenant that they be to Him "a kingdom of priests and a holy nation" (Exod 19:6), the latter phrase (as well as the former, in my opinion) is intended to mean a nation whose every citizen is in direct fealty to this Deity, "holy" in the sense of "given over entirely to God." Israel's "holiness" is thus a matter of its special tie to God, an idea given expression in the preceding verse in the phrase *ᶜam sĕgullâ*. Whatever this may imply about the origins of Israel's holiness, one thing seems indisputable: such holiness has no particular implications here for the people's homogeneity or genetic purity.

A somewhat contrasting view of Israel's holiness is found in Jer 2:3, where the prophet speaks of Israel as holy to God but then immediately goes on to define that holiness in terms drawn from the realm of sacral law: "Israel is holy to God, the firstfruits of his harvest: those who consume her will be found guilty." This is to say that they will be guilty of consuming what has been sworn to the Deity, a grave crime: "evil shall fall upon them, says the Lord." Here the prophet appears to draw on the rather separate notion of Israel as God's firstborn (Exod 4:22) in order to suggest that they are, as a people, therefore in the same legal category as another "firstborn," the firstfruits of the harvest, which are also given over to God and so belong wholly to Him. If so, then "consuming" Israel (the verb *ᵓkl* here is intended to suggest the cultic crime of eating produce belonging to God) is a crime against God and one that the Deity himself will therefore severely punish. The notion of Israel's holiness underlying this prophetic oracle is hardly *identical* with that of the previous passage; as noted, this one seems to derive from a cultic analogy predicated on the tradition of Israel as God's firstborn and the ancient and direct attachment of this supreme Deity to one particular people (compare with Deut 32:8–9). Nevertheless, the two are united in seeing Israel's holiness as implying a direct connection to God. Israel is God's own people, to whom He stands in extraordinary relationship. Once again, this notion of Israel's holiness says nothing about the people's internal purity or homogeneity.

Internal purity is also not quite the notion underlying the famous priestly injunction, "You shall be holy, for I, the Lord your God, am holy" (Lev 19:2). The complex of legal prohibitions and exhortations that follows this general summons makes it clear that Israel's "holiness" here refers to their proper *behavior*, their conformity to a host of ethical and cultic concerns that together will vouchsafe their overall purity and make possible God's presence in their midst. In this catalog of the do's and don'ts of holiness, such matters as respect for the sanctuary and proper procedure with regard to sacrificial food are strikingly juxtaposed to love of one's neighbor and the avoidance of concealed hatred and revenge—for neither purely cultic, nor purely ethical matters alone constitute the standard of holiness to which Israel is to be held, but both together.

Now, to be sure, holiness in this behavioral sense is indeed contrasted in direct fashion to the practices of other nations: "You shall not follow the practices of the land of Egypt, in which you have dwelt, nor shall you follow those of the land of Canaan, to which I am bringing you, nor keep their statutes" (Lev 18:3), "You shall not walk in the custom of the nation which I am casting out before you. . . . I am the Lord your God who have separated you from the peoples" (Lev 20:23–24). Yet it is clear that the danger represented by these nations belongs to the sphere of forbidden *actions*; it is not that contact with them ipso facto spells corruption, only that such contact might lead to corrupt actions.[2]

And indeed, any such idea would be quite incompatible with priestly injunctions elsewhere about the merciful treatment of strangers and sojourners "in your midst." In the same vein, there are such varied biblical topoi (spanning the whole range of sources and social milieux represented in preexilic writings) as the ones depicting Israel as being accompanied by a "mixed multitude," a ragtag band of different peoples who went out from Egypt (Exod 12:38, Num 11:4), or the legally prescribed acceptance of Edomites and Egyptians into the "congregation of the Lord" (Deut 23:8), the captive foreign woman of Deut 21:10–14, the Egyptian-Israelite marriage mentioned in Lev 24:10–23, or the foreign brides taken by various distinguished ancient Israelites, including Joseph, Judah, Moses, David, Solomon, and so on and so forth.

One must, of course, qualify this overall observation with the specific tradition regarding the original Canaanite inhabitants of the land. As is well known, a number of narrative texts suggest that intermarrying with Canaanites is a bad thing, and Deut 7:3–6 specifically bans such intermarriage. But it is interesting to observe the stated basis for this ban:

> You shall not make marriages with them [the Canaanite tribes], giving your daughters to their sons or taking their daughters for your sons. For they would turn away your sons from following me, to serve other gods. . . . But thus shall you deal with them: you shall break down their altars and dash into pieces their pillars and hew down their Asherim and burn their graven images with fire. For you are a people holy to the Lord your God; the Lord your God has chosen you to be a people of his own possession, out of all the peoples that are on the face of the earth.

Once again we are in the plane of forbidden actions. Marriage with the Canaanite peoples will lead to idolatry, the great sin of Deuteronomy, and it is for this reason that such marriage has been forbidden.

However, this passage in Deuteronomy certainly stands behind another from a later period, Ezra's famous description of the mixed marriages that he found Jews had entered into in their restored homeland—and here indeed a new note is sounded:

> The people of Israel and the priests and the Levites have not separated themselves from the peoples of the land . . . for they have taken some of their daughters to be

---

2. See Knohl, *Sanctuary of Silence*, 170–71.

wives for themselves and for their sons, and the holy seed has become mingled with
the peoples of the land.   (Ezra 9:1–2)

It has been pointed out that the actual list of foreign peoples that accompanies
this indictment—"the Canaanite, the Hittite, the Perizzite, the Jebusite, the Ammonite, the Moabite, the Egyptian, and the Edomite [emended for "Amorite" on
the basis of 1 Esdras 8:69]"—is a composite. The first four are the names of
long-extinct Canaanite peoples included in the prohibition of Deuteronomy
cited above, whereas the latter four peoples were, in Ezra's time, still quite real,
flesh-and-blood neighbors of restored Israel. Certainly, then, this text's purpose
in evoking the first four is to suggest that the latter four belong in the same category and so imply that Deuteronomy's ban on intermarriage applies as well to
Edomites, Egyptians, and so on (although that is hardly Deuteronomy's view).[3]

Apart from this, however, it is of interest to observe the notion of Israel's
holiness that stands behind the last sentence, "the holy seed has become mingled
with the peoples of the land." The clear implication is that *holy* seed should not
become mingled with anything. Moreover, it seems that this highly unusual
phrase (it occurs only once elsewhere in the Hebrew Bible, Isa 6:13) is being
used here in order to suggest one of the prohibitions of *kil°ayim*, namely, 'sow-
ing with mixed seed' (Lev 19:19, Deut 22:9). For, surely, it is no accident that
this text speaks of holy 'seed' rather than merely "the Israelites," "the people,"
or even "the holy people." If it is the holy *seed* that has become *mingled*, this
very fact acquires the resonance of a violation of cultic law. Here, then, is a
striking extension of the implications of Israel's holiness in postexilic times:
holy now means that Israel is not to be mingled with other peoples; marrying
foreign women is a violation of Israel's sacred status.[4]

The political reality out of which such an idea grew is not hard to pin down.
For, as several scholars have recently stressed, this was a time when matters of
self-definition could no longer simply (but were they ever simple?) be equated
with geography; "Israel" does not necessarily equal the people living in Israel's
territory.[5] The striking difference of views on the matter of self-definition found
in the books of Chronicles on the one hand and those of Ezra and Nehemiah on
the other has already been pointed out.[6] To live as a distinct people in a land
held to belong to that people, yet one also inhabited by others—this was a situation that elicited a whole range of reactions; the view attributed to Ezra that we
have just examined was merely one strategy. But it is of interest to us precisely
because it bears witness to a new wrinkle in the old notion of Israel's holiness.

---

3. See the discussion of this verse in Sara Japhet, "People and Land in the Restoration Period,"
in *Das Land Israel in biblischer Zeit* (ed. G. Strecker; Göttingen, 1983) 114–15.

4. Ezra 9:2 likewise uses another term with cultic resonance, *m°l*, to describe the offense in
question; cf. Ezra 9:4, 10:2, 6, 10; Neh 13:27.

5. See in this connection Japhet, "People and Land," 104–6; also W. D. Davies, *The Territorial
Dimension of Judaism* (Berkeley, 1982) 28–45; Doron Mendels, *The Land of Israel as a Political
Concept in Hasmonean Literature* (Tübingen, 1987) 5–8.

6. S. Japhet, *The Ideology of the Book of Chronicles* (Frankfurt am Main, 1989) 267–351.

As noted, this view was not the only one witnessed in Second Temple times; the same political reality elicited different sorts of reactions in different quarters. But I should like now to turn to an extreme version of this view presented in a text of somewhat later date, the book of *Jubilees*, which is generally held to be a product of the second century B.C.E., although a still earlier date is not to be excluded.[7]

Jubilees' view of Israel's holiness is rather surprising. Israel is "holy" virtually in the sense of angelic, a people whose existence and function on earth is comparable to that of God's own sacred hosts on high. As a result, any mingling—and particularly, any sexual union—between an Israelite and a foreigner is monstrous. *Jubilees* defines such unions as "unclean" and "an abomination," an act of "fornication" that belongs to the same order of sexual sacrileges as incest, bestiality, and the other forbidden unions of the priestly code.

This angelic nature of the people of Israel perhaps deserves some elaboration here. It is first suggested in *Jubilees* by the account of the Creation and God's resting on the seventh day. In retelling those events, the angel who is the speaker of the book of *Jubilees* says to Moses:

> And he gave us [angels] a great sign, the Sabbath day, so that we might work six days and observe a Sabbath from all work on the seventh day. And he told us—all of the angels of the presence and all of the angels of sanctification, those two great [i.e., highest] kinds [of angels]—that we should keep the Sabbath with him in heaven and on earth. Then he said to us: "Behold, I shall separate off for myself a people from among all the nations, and they also will keep the Sabbath. . . ."
> And thus he created a sign by which they might keep the Sabbath *with us* on the seventh day. . . .   (*Jub.* 2:17–18, 21)

Behind this passage stands an old and thorny exegetical problem: If God rested on the seventh day, then what happened to the institution of the Sabbath thereafter? The Bible never again mentions God resting on subsequent seventh days, nor does the Sabbath ever emerge as an organizing principle of the universe (as its role in the Creation account might suggest). Instead, it seems to be put into suspension until it comes to be enjoined upon one people, the Israelites, at the time of the Sinai covenant. But if the Sabbath as a phenomenon was embodied in the very creation of the universe, then why was it not enjoined upon *all* peoples? And what had become of this divine institution between that first cosmic Sabbath and the commandment to observe it given to the Israelites at Sinai?

The answer proposed above by *Jubilees* is characteristically bold. Here, the Sabbath is essentially a *heavenly* institution: God rests, and the two highest classes of angels rest, and so they will continue to rest throughout the ages (God commands them to "keep the Sabbath with him," apparently, henceforth

---

7. See my article, "Levi's Elevation to the Priesthood in Second Temple Times," *HTR* 86 (1993) 52–58; R. Doron, "The Non-dating of Jubilees" *JSJ* 20 (1989) 1–11.

forever). But one earthly people is also to participate in this heavenly institution, the people of Israel—and this, it seems, because of their special status. The fact that they alone are to take part in this heavenly observance is in itself an expression of their utter uniqueness on earth, indeed, their quasi-angelic holiness. As the angel of *Jubilees* goes on to observe:

> On this day [the seventh], we kept the Sabbath in heaven before it was made known to any human to keep the Sabbath thereon on earth. And the creator of all blessed it, but he did not make any people or nations *holy* to keep the Sabbath with the sole exception of Israel. To them alone did he grant it, that they might eat and drink and keep the Sabbath thereon on earth.   (*Jub.* 2:30–31)

The same theme of Israel's connection with angels recurs with regard to circumcision. Israel is commanded to be circumcised

> because the nature of all of the angels of the presence and all of the angels of sanctification [again, the two highest classes of angels] was such [i.e., they were as circumcised] from the day of their creation. And in the presence of the angels of the presence and of the angels of sanctification he made Israel holy, so that they might be with him and with his holy angels.   (*Jub.* 15:27)

One further reflection of Israel's angelic status occurs with regard to the laws of incest. As frequently happens in *Jubilees*, the angel here speaks to Moses about what is written in the "heavenly tablets." The contents of these tablets are never directly defined, but they seem to embody the Pentateuch-to-be as well as certain other bits of divine teaching found elsewhere in the Bible or oral teaching. In this case, the angel, after mentioning that the heavenly tablets contain one stipulation concerning the crime of lying with one's father's wife (presumably the one found in Lev 20:11), speaks of a second reference to this crime:

> And it is written a second time: "Let anyone who lies with his father's wife be cursed, because he has uncovered his father's shame." And all the holy ones of the Lord said, "So be it, so be it."   (*Jub.* 33:12)

Here the allusion is to Deut 27:20—with one difference! In Deuteronomy, the text concludes "And let all the *people* say, 'So be it, so be it.'" Since, however, the "heavenly tablets" are the timeless and supernal Torah, the author of *Jubilees* has substituted for the word "people" (that is, Israel) in this text Israel's heavenly correspondent, that is, "the holy ones of the Lord," the angels.[8]

---

8. This view is reflected (albeit in somewhat narrower terms) in the Qumran *Hôdāyôt*, where it is the members of the sect who are like the angels: "For you have granted your glory to all those of your counsel [i.e., members of the sect] in common with the angels of the presence, and there

In short, Israel's holiness is not, for the author of *Jubilees*, merely an expression of their unmediated dependence on, or special relationship to, God, nor yet of their being held to a special standard of purity and sanctity (though all of these ideas are likewise to be found in this book). For *Jubilees*, Israel's holiness means first and foremost that Israel belongs to an order of being different from the order of being of other humans so that Israel is, in effect, wholly different, the earthly correspondent to God's heavenly hosts. Under such circumstances there is no possibility of Israel's mingling or intermarrying with other peoples. In retelling the story of Dinah, the author of *Jubilees* uses the occasion to address the subject of intermarriage:

> And if there is any man in Israel who wishes to give his daughter or his sister to any man who is from the seed of the Gentiles, he shall surely die; they shall stone him with stones, for he has committed a disgrace in Israel. And also the woman will be burned with fire, because she has defiled the name of her father's house and will be uprooted from Israel. . . . For Israel is holy to the Lord, and any man who causes defilement shall surely die.   (*Jub.* 30:7–8)

Similarly, when in *Jubilees* Rebecca warns her son Jacob not to take a Canaanite wife, the text again specifically connects this interdiction to Israel's holiness:

> And now my son, listen to me and do your mother's bidding, and do not take a wife for yourself from the daughters of this land . . . but take for yourself a wife from the house of my father, and the Most High God will bless you, and your children will be a righteous generation and *a holy seed.*   (*Jub.* 25:3)

Here is Ezra's phrase again, "holy seed," and its appearance can hardly be coincidental. The holy seed cannot be sown among other nations; it is not a question of learning their evil ways, but of mixing unlike substances.

That such a view is found in *Jubilees* may not surprise those acquainted with its general tenor. It is somewhat more surprising to note that its further identification of intermarriage as the crime of "giving one's seed to Molech" is reflected as well in *Tg. Pseudo-Jonathan* to Lev 18:21, as well as in the Mishna (albeit disapprovingly), *m. Meg* 4:9.[9] Still more striking is that a similar attitude toward intermarriage is formulated in Pseudo-Philo's *Book of Biblical Antiquities*, which finds this issue to be the point of several biblical stories even when it is not specifically mentioned. For example, this book asserts that

---

is no intermediary between them and your holy ones" (1QH VI 13). See Jacob Licht, *Megillat ha-Hodayot* (Jerusalem, 1957) 113, also Introduction, p. 49. The phrase "no intermediary" is apparently based on Gen 42:23; the implication is thus that sect members are not only at the same level as the angels of the presence but commune freely with them.

9. See G. Vermes, "Lev. 18:21 in Ancient Jewish Bible Exegesis," *Studies in Aggadah, Targum, and Jewish Prayer in Memory of Joseph Heinemann* (ed. E. Fleischer and J. Petuchowski; Jerusalem, 1981) 108–24.

Tamar, who, in the Bible, tricks her father-in-law into having sexual relations with her (Genesis 38), did so out of the purest motives:

> Her intent was not fornication, but, being unwilling to separate from the sons of Israel, she reflected and said, "It is better for me to die for having intercourse with my father-in-law than to have intercourse with Gentiles." . . . And her intent saved her from all danger.[10]   (*Book of Biblical Antiquities* 9:5)

It was not doubt because of the views embodied in such texts as these that the Jews acquired their reputation for xenophobia attested by many Greek and Roman writers. "To have no communication with foreigners," wrote one (Pompeius Trogus, in the first century B.C.E.), "gradually became a religious institution of the Jews."[11] (This is not a bad description of the evolution that we have been tracing.)

It was suggested above that such views came in response to the problems of self-definition inherent in the geopolitics of postexilic Judea. If the people of Israel were *not* necessarily coterminous with the people living in Israel's territory, then the issue of borders needed to be handled in some nongeographic fashion, and this is precisely what Ezra–Nehemiah, *Jubilees*, and other early texts seek to do. In the extreme, as we have seen, this led to the assertion that the people of Israel were radically discontinuous with the rest of humanity.

But these views of Israel in turn may have inspired some readjustments in the notion of the sanctity of Israel's land. For, if (in the Priestly view) the land belongs to God and is inhabited by Israel only on condition that God's laws of holiness are properly observed, how can this stipulation be reconciled with the presence of non-Israelites in the midst of this sacred space? The fact that Israel was now, at least for some, *by nature* a holy people, separate and, in the extreme, belonging to a different order of being, may in turn have encouraged the very notion of the land's holiness to be reunderstood or reformulated.

I believe this to be the case for example with the *Book of Jubilees*. This book, as we have glimpsed briefly, has a most radical notion of Israel's holiness, a notion that cannot but have helped shape its attitude toward the presence of foreigners in the land. According to *Jubilees,* it is Israel's exclusive covenant with God that will allow this people "not to be uprooted from the Land," the clear implication being that other peoples *will* be uprooted, and the text then adds specifically:

> For the Lord did not draw Ishmael and his sons and brothers, nor Esau, near to himself, and he did not choose them, though they are [also] the sons of Abraham, for

---

10. Incidentally, the *Testament of Judah* (in the *Testaments of the Twelve Patriarchs*) likewise is at pains to exonerate Tamar's union with Judah. The text stresses that her previous marriages to Judah's sons were never consummated, thus lessening or eliminating his guilt (*T. Judah* 10:3–5). On the contrary, Judah's great sin, according to the *Testament of Judah*, was his marriage to Bathshua, *because she was a Canaanite* (*T. Judah* 8:2–3; 11:1–2, 4–5; 17:1–2).

11. M. Stern, *Greek and Latin Authors on Jews and Judaism* (Jerusalem, 1984) 1.338.

he knew them. But he chose Israel that they might be a people for him, and *he made them holy* and gathered them up from all the [other] sons of men.

(Jub. 15:30–31)

Here, then, Israel's radical holiness has radical territorial implications: they are to dwell apart from the other sons of men, even their brethren, the Edomites and Ishmaelites. Elsewhere in *Jubilees*, the same note is sounded: Isaac says to his son Esau (as he does *not* say in the Bible) that Esau's seed "will be rooted out from under heaven" *(Jub.* 26:34), and he had earlier predicted the same fate for the Philistines *(Jub.* 24:29–30), both potential encroachers on the sacred territory of Israel. Most specifically, Abraham elsewhere tells Jacob:

God . . . brought me out from Ur of the Chaldeans so that he might give this land to me to inherit forever and to raise up a *holy seed.* . . .   *(Jub.* 22:27)

Once again, Ezra's phrase "holy seed" is invoked in *Jubilees* and is here connected directly to the very grant of the land to Abraham by God.

This is not to say, however, that the only way in which this new notion of Israel's holiness made itself felt was in the demand that Israel's land be purified of foreigners. It may well be that the feeling of radical discontinuity that sometimes accompanies the concepts of holy land or holy city in some other Second Temple texts was likewise fostered by this same evolutionary reformulation of Israel's holiness as a people that we have been charting.[12]

By "discontinuity" I certainly mean even something as innocent as Pseudo-Philo's stipulation that the "holy land" is watered from its own, special part of heaven:

Then the Lord showed him [Moses] the land and all that is in it and said, "This is the land that I will give to my people." And he showed him the place from which the clouds draw up water to water the whole [rest of the] earth, and the place from which the river takes its water, and the land of Egypt, and the place in the firmament from which *only the holy land drinks.*   *(Book of Biblical Antiquities* 19:10)

Certainly (this author reasons) if Moses could, according to Deut 34:1, see "the whole land . . . as far as Dan" from where he stood, he must have actually been standing inside heaven itself at the time. Such reasoning apparently allowed this author to suppose that Moses had been able to glimpse at this opportunity

12. I should stress here my own reluctance to connect radically discontinuous peoplehood with radically discontinuous territory in any simple cause-and-effect relationship. No doubt a great many factors helped to shape later ideas about the holiness of the land of Israel or the city of Jerusalem in different periods (including, certainly, the raw facts of political independence or domination by an outside power, the physical configurations of geographic Israel at any given time, as well as the particular politics—and, hence, accessibility—of Jerusalem and the temple itself to the totality of Israel or some subset thereof). Yet, without diminishing the importance of any of these (or yet other) factors, it seems nonetheless worthwhile to seek to explain some of the feeling of radical discontinuity that accompanies the concepts of holy land or holy city in some Second Temple writings in terms of the reformulation of Israel's holiness that has been seen above.

that which only a heavenly voyager could glimpse, that the holy land's water supply is (as one might likewise infer from Deut 11:11–12) separate from that of the rest of the world. But if so, then here is a relatively minor instance of what I just mentioned, an understanding of the holy land's being holy in the same, radically discontinuous way that Israel the people is alleged to be holy by the same author.

The holy land as reflected in the *Testament of Job* (dated to the first century B.C.E. or C.E.) is quite other-worldly and in this way discontinuous. Indeed, it is not clear whether *this* holy land is on earth or in heaven:

> The whole world shall pass away and its splendor shall fade. And those who heed it shall share in its overthrow. But my throne is the holy land, and its splendor is in the world of the changeless one. Rivers will dry up, and the arrogance of their waves goes down into the depths of the abyss. But the rivers of my land, where my throne is, do not dry up nor will they disappear, but they will exist forever.
>
> (*T. Job* 33:4–7)

In a well-known passage from the *Testament of Dan* (part of the *Testaments of the Twelve Patriarchs*) evoking the New Jerusalem, it is certainly a happy coincidence to find specific reference to the "holy ones" who will populate it and, as well, evidence of the same radical discontinuity between this New Jerusalem, an Eden free of outside domination, and the old Jerusalem, presumably well-known to the author:

> And he shall turn the hearts of the disobedient ones to the Lord and grant eternal peace to those who call upon Him. And the holy ones shall refresh themselves in Eden, the righteous shall rejoice in the New Jerusalem, which shall be eternally for the glorification of God. And Jerusalem shall no longer undergo desolation, nor shall Israel be led into captivity.
>
> (*T. Dan* 5:11–13)

Here again, sacred place is not sacred merely because of the presence of the Deity—it is a true utopia, "eternally for the glorification of God," and no longer subject to the ups and downs of ordinary existence.

A further illustration of the varied interrelationship of holy people and sacred place is from the *Psalms of Solomon*, dated to the first century B.C.E., and the arrival of Roman political domination in the region. This work refers frequently to God's "holy ones," who in context appear to be synonymous with both the "righteous" in general and the people of Israel in particular. Indeed Israel is, according to the *Psalms of Solomon*, righteous or holy by definition, except for those who have fallen under the influence of foreigners.[13] Foreign-

---

13. The historical and social setting of *PsSol* 17 has been much discussed. See A. Caquot, "Les Hasmonéens, les Romains et Hérode: Observations sur PsSal 17," in A. Caquot (ed.), *Hellenica et Judaica* (Louvain, 1986) 213–18; R. R. Hahn, "The Community of the Pious: The Social Setting of the Psalms of Solomon," in *Studies in Religion/Sciences Réligieuses* 17 (1988) 169–89;

ers are, equally axiomatically, bad; they are destined to be banished from the holy city's precincts.

> The lawless one laid waste our land, so that no one inhabited it; they massacred young and old and children at the same time . . .
>
> Because the enemy was a stranger and his heart alien to our God, he acted arrogantly.
>
> So he did in Jerusalem all the things that Gentiles do for their gods in their cities.
>
> And the children of the covenant among the Gentile rabble adopted these [practices].
>
> No one among them in Jerusalem acted [with] mercy or truth.
>
> Those who loved the assemblies of the devout fled from them as sparrows fled from their nest.
>
> [They became] refugees in the wilderness to save their lives from evil.
>
> The life of even one who was saved from them was precious in the eyes of the exiles.
>
> They were scattered over the whole earth by [these] lawless ones.
>
> (*Pss. Sol.* 17:11–18)

Here the holy people are (in keeping with the views seen earlier) corrupted by mere contact with the "Gentile rabble." Their only chance of escape is to flee the holy city like sparrows fleeing their nest. At least for now, holy people will constitute in and of themselves a new holy place, "scattered over the whole earth," since the old holy place has been corrupted.

And yet there is, once again, a future Jerusalem that will once again become a holy place, but only if it is made radically discontinuous with its present reality—that is, if it is utterly purged of its foreign contaminators:

> See, Lord, and raise up for them their king, the son of David, to rule over your servant Israel, in the time known to you, O God.
>
> Gird him with the strength to destroy the unrighteous rulers, to purge Jerusalem from the Gentiles who trample her to destruction; in wisdom and in righteousness to drive out the sinners from the inheritance [again: inherited land, *naḥalah*]. . . .
>
> He will gather a holy people whom he will lead in righteousness; and he will judge the tribes of the people that have been made holy by the Lord their God.
>
> He will not tolerate unrighteousness even to pause among them, and any person who knows wickedness shall not live with them.
>
> For he shall know them that they are all the children of their God.
>
> He will distribute them upon the land according to their tribes; the alien and the foreigner will no longer live near them.   (*Pss. Sol.* 17:21–28)

However much this author may wish it to appear so, this predicted future is not exactly a return to an old biblical ideal, for, as noted, the foreigner "within your

---

John Collins, *The Scepter and the Star: The Messiah of the Dead Sea Scrolls and Other Ancient Literature* (New York, 1993) 51–53.

midst" or "at your gates," a biblical commonplace, will now not only *not* be in your midst, but not even nearby.[14] Instead, these lines present a strikingly new vision and one that once again suggests a connection between the radically discontinuous understanding of the people's holiness and a similarly discontinuous vision of the holy land and holy city. For while the rhetoric of this passage seems designed to evoke the past, there stands behind it a stark and cold new order. In it, Israel cannot suffer contact with Gentiles without corruption, so "the alien and the foreigner will no longer live near them" (though they may come to pay homage to Israel's God, v. 31). Only those who have fled the Gentiles may hope to emerge as a newly reconstituted "holy people," whose holiness therefore demands a holy place purged of all foreign elements.

We have seen above a number of texts from, roughly, the second century B.C.E. through the first century C.E., all of which seem to share, on the one hand, a view of Israel's holiness that makes of Israel a race apart, and, on the other, a notion of sacred place characterized by its radical discontinuity from present, real places.[15] It is suggested that these two developments are not unrelated. Of course, disjunction is in itself a component inherent in the very idea of the holy, the "completely other," in Rudolf Otto's famous phrase, and it is thus not impossible to find adumbrations of such views in earlier periods of Israel's history. It seems, nonetheless, undeniable that a change in Israel's self-understanding as a holy people did occur along the lines described above, and that this new self-understanding in turn had consequences for the idea of the holiness of the land of Israel and the city of Jerusalem that had come down from an earlier day. At least in some quarters, this holiness would henceforth require that some radical purification or transformation of the holy place occur so that its present corruption, by foreigners or their agents, might be utterly removed. This certainly resonated with the themes of return and purification sounded first during the Babylonian Exile and once again turned the eyes of expectant Israel to a day in the near future when all would be set aright, a day in which, in the view of some, a radically discontinuous Israel would serve God in a radically transformed homeland.

Postscript: Since this article was completed, a number of other articles and books touching on its overall subject have appeared. Particularly relevant is the study by Betsy Halpern-Amaru, *Rewriting the Bible: Land and Covenant in Postbiblical Jewish Literature* (Valley Forge, Penn., 1994). The curious reader will discern certain differences in approach and conclusion that must, however, await another occasion to be addressed.

---

14. Indeed, this redistribution of the land to the old tribes recalls Ezekiel 47 and 48, except that there, aliens are to be *included* in the redistribution, "they are to be to you as the native sons of Israel" (Ezek 47:22).

15. At the end of the period under consideration the work known as *2 Baruch* was composed; see 42:4–6 and 48:22–24 for further echoes of our theme. The phrase "holy seed" occurs repeatedly at Qumran as well, and its use there seems in keeping with the hypothesis offered here. I hope on a later occasion to examine this evidence in detail.

REALMS OF SANCTITY: THE CASE OF THE "MISPLACED" INCENSE ALTAR IN THE TABERNACLE TEXTS OF EXODUS

Carol Meyers

Introduction

THE BASIC STRUCTURE of the tabernacle texts in Exodus involves, first, a detailed set of instructions in chaps. 25–31 for the fabrication and consecration of the tabernacle structure with all its appurtenances and priestly vestments. Then, following the discrete three chapters (32–34) recounting the golden calf incident, a lengthy description in chaps. 35–40 reports the construction and assembly of the sacred complex and all its ritual components. Most of the materials in these two sections of Exodus are identical in their depiction of the tabernacle and its accoutrements, with the specifications in the second, descriptive section clearly related to those in the first, prescriptive section.

Despite the similarities in content of the two sections, there are important divergences in the ordering of the materials. The descriptive section has often been understood[1] as a document that, like 1 Kings 6–7, is apparently related to ancient Near Eastern modes of accounting such as might have been kept in the archival materials of Mesopotamian temples.[2] However, "archival" may not be the most useful way to describe these texts; it does little more than indicate where they may have been stored. As a genre, the term *monumental* may be more appropriate.[3] This designation would apply to the entire tabernacle account of Exodus. Although there may be compelling reasons to treat all the

---

1. See J. Montgomery, "Archival Data in the Book of Kings," *JBL* 53 (1934) 46–52; B. A. Levine, "The Descriptive Tabernacle Texts of the Pentateuch," *JAOS* 85 (1965) 307–18.

2. Cf. O. Eissfeldt, *The Old Testament: An Introduction* (trans. P. R. Ackroyd; New York, 1965) 289.

3. See V. Hurowitz, "The Priestly Account of Building the Tabernacle," *JAOS* 105 (1985) 21–30, esp. 21.

tabernacle sections of the Pentateuch as a literary whole,[4] the fact remains that the descriptive unit of Exodus 35–40 is organized in a different way from the prescriptive section that precedes it. That is, the descriptive text seems to be organized according to architectural conceptions of a building. Thus Exodus 35–39 (40 being an account of the consecration of the structure), like 1 Kings 6–7 in its description of the temple, begins with the structure itself and then proceeds to specify its internal furnishings. This arrangement may reflect royal Mesopotamian building inscriptions,[5] although the biblical accounts in Exodus and 1 Kings contain a wealth of detail not present in those accounts (though perhaps reflecting other kinds of Mesopotamian documents).

Whatever the nature of the descriptive texts, it is clear that the core (chaps. 25–27) of the prescriptive section of the tabernacle texts embodies a somewhat different organizational principle than does its descriptive counterpart. The sequence of materials, despite the similarity of content, bespeaks a priestly conceptual framework rather than an administrative architectural and archival framework. Identifying the priestly conceptualization in its ordering of the prescriptive texts is important in dealing with the item under consideration in this paper, the apparently "misplaced" incense altar of Exod 30:1–10.

The prescriptive section begins with the most sacred contents of the tabernacle, that is, the ark and the associated cherubim and 'cover' (or 'mercy seat'). Next it gives instructions for fashioning the cultic furniture to be placed inside the tabernacle. Then the details involved in making the tent itself are provided. Finally, the text sets forth specifications for the sacred precinct (the courtyard and its altar and vessels) outside the tabernacle. While others have noted that the order of instructions in chaps. 25ff. proceeds from the most holy and most important (the ark) to objects and domains of lesser sanctity,[6] Menahem Haran's scholarship is outstanding in providing a detailed and compelling analysis of such gradations of holiness. He has examined the Pentateuchal texts, especially those of Exodus, that provide information about the tabernacle; and he has recognized the continuum of sanctity, in both its material and cultic components, that is reflected in the materials, workmanship, and rituals associated with this sacred structure. Building on earlier studies and culminating in *Temples and Temple-Service in Ancient Israel*,[7] Haran has brought great clarity and profound insight to scholarship dealing with the Israelite cult in

---

4. Ibid.

5. See V. Hurowitz, *I Have Built You an Exalted House: Temple Building in the Light of Mesopotamian and Northwest Semitic Writings* (JSOTSup 115; Sheffield, 1992) 244–59.

6. See, e.g., U. Cassuto, *A Commentary on the Book of Exodus* (trans. I. Abraham; Jerusalem, 1967) 328; M. Noth, *Exodus* (trans. J. J. Bowden; OTL; Philadelphia, 1962) 202.

7. For his earlier studies, see M. Haran, "The Complex of Ritual Acts inside the Tabernacle," *Studies in the Bible* (ScrHier 8; Jerusalem, 1961) 272–302; idem, "The Priestly Image of the Tabernacle," *HUCA* 30 (1965) 191–226. For the latter, see *Temples and Temple-Service in Ancient Israel* (Oxford, 1978; repr. Winona Lake, Ind., 1985).

general but especially to our understanding of the realms of sanctity of the tabernacle and temple and their sacral activities. His work clearly informs the nature of this essay, which is offered here as an indication of my indebtedness to him in this piece as well as in my other attempts to understand the cult of ancient Israel.

The Problematic Position of the Incense Altar Text

Despite the overall organizational coherence of both sets of tabernacle instructions, there are some features that seem to disrupt the notion of an orderly and intentional arrangement of materials. Prominent among the apparent aberrations are chaps. 30 and 31. Some of the items specified in these chapters seem to be out of place. (Others, such as the Sabbath regulations of Exod 31:12–17, seem to be of no consequence at all for the enterprise of tabernacle construction.) The very first section of chap. 30, setting forth instructions for the golden altar of incense, is a case in point. It will be considered here as a way of examining whether its problematic position is a disruption of the ordering of the prescriptive texts, or whether it in fact helps preserve the gradated coherence of the sanctuary and its rituals that is the conceptual hallmark of those texts.

As noted above, the prescriptive section of Exodus begins (in chap. 25) with instructions for constructing the most important component of the tabernacle, the ark, and then the 'cover' or 'mercy seat' (*kappōret*) with its cherubim. These items are the furnishings of the inner sanctum or 'most holy place' (Exod 26:34). This innermost and holiest space is separated from the outer sanctum or 'holy place' by a veil (*pārōket*). The text then delineates the furnishings of the outer sanctum: the golden table for the bread of the presence, and the golden lampstand or menorah. It continues (chap. 26) with a blueprint for the tabernacle (*miškān*) itself, with all its curtains, clasps, frames, and bars; and it proceeds (chap. 27) to set forth the way in which the altar (of sacrifice) should be built and to specify the construction of the court, outside the tent structure itself, in which the altar is to be situated. Chapter 28 goes on to delineate the priestly vestments, and chap. 29 provides instructions for consecrating the tabernacle and its personnel.

This sequence is indeed orderly, in progressing from the most holy to the least. However, there is a glaring omission in the graduated scheme. Other passages in Exodus (31:8; 37:10–28; 39:36–38; 40:4–5, 22–27) as well as one in Numbers (4:7–11) describe three, not two, items of furniture in the outer sanctum. In fact the central item in that space, the one to be situated directly in front of the veil and flanked by the table and the lampstand, is the golden altar of incense, which is absent from the core chapters (25–27) of the prescriptive section and is specified only in the problematic collection of materials in chaps. 30–31. In these chapters it occupies pride of place, coming first (vv. 1–10 in chap. 30) and perhaps thereby indicating its prominence as a cultic appurtenance. Yet it is conspicuously missing from its seemingly logical place, with the other items of the outer sanctum, in chap. 25.

This apparent displacement of the instructions for making the golden incense altar has long attracted the attention of scholars. Indeed, as early as the Greek translation of the Hebrew text, the absence of the incense altar from the presentation of the holy items to be placed in the 'holy place' inside the tabernacle was deemed problematic. The Septuagint thus omits the incense altar in its translation of Exodus 37, where the MT has a description of it in vv. 25–28, immediately following the account of the fabrication of the golden table and the golden lampstand. By omitting the incense altar from the descriptive section, the Greek probably sought to balance its absence from chap. 25 in the prescriptive section of Exodus.[8]

The approach of modern biblical scholarship to the incense altar dilemma was established by Wellhausen and has held sway in most quarters until the present. Since the verses (Exod 29:43–46) immediately preceding the presentation of the incense altar serve as a general conclusion to the specifications for the tabernacle and its furnishings, the incense altar presented in Exod 30:1–10 must be seen as an appendix or addition to chaps. 25–29[9] and not part of P's conceptualization of the tabernacle. With most of the second half of Exodus assigned to P, Exodus 30–31 as an added "cultic miscellany"[10] must therefore be attributed to the work of a successor to P, designated P[s].[11] Since Wellhausen and his disciples assigned P to the Second Temple Period, with the whole notion of the tabernacle and its service being a fictitious representation of the Second Temple, the putative insertion of the incense altar specifications in chap. 30 would thus have occurred at a time well after the Exile.

Wellhausen's dating of P and the accompanying notion that the concept of the tabernacle was invented by the postexilic priesthood have long been replaced by views of P and the tabernacle that recognize both the authenticity and antiquity of much of P's materials.[12] Still, the idea that the incense altar is either a later addition or is out of place for some polemical reason has continued.[13] The arguments for a greater antiquity for the incense altar than classical source theory allows are thus worth considering.

For one thing, the presence of an incense altar in the First Temple is specified in 1 Kgs 7:48 (compare 1 Kgs 6:20, 22) along with instructions for

8. See J. P. Hyatt, *Exodus* (NCB; London, 1971) 291; D. W. Gooding, *The Account of the Tabernacle* (Cambridge, 1959) 3, 66–69, 76.

9. J. Wellhausen, *Prolegomena to the History of Ancient Israel* (original German ed., 1878; Cleveland, 1957) 63ff.

10. G. H. Davies, *Exodus* (Torch Bible Commentary; London, 1967) 223.

11. B. Baentsch, *Exodus-Leviticus-Numbers* (HKAT 1/2; Göttingen, 1903) 258ff.

12. See most recently, R. E. Friedman, "Tabernacle," *ABD* 6.292–300.

13. E.g., Noth, *Exodus*; R. E. Clements, *Exodus* (CBC; Cambridge, 1972); B. S. Childs, *The Book of Exodus* (OTL; Philadelphia, 1974).

the table and the lampstands. The allusions to an incense altar in Solomon's temple were thought to be secondary interpolations by adherents to source theory, since it was felt that incense was not a legitimate part of the Israelite cult until the seventh century.[14] However, the archaeological discovery of incense altars of the Iron II Period, contemporary with the First Temple, indicates the widespread use of four-horned incense altars similar in size and shape to the one presented in Exodus 30 and 37.[15] Furthermore, several biblical texts outside P seem to indicate the use of incense in both the First Temple and also in a pre-Solomonic shrine.[16]

The existence of extrabiblical and extra-P evidence from the First Temple Period and earlier certainly is consistent with positing the antiquity of P traditions of an incense altar. Indeed, as Cassuto points out, a cultic innovation from "pagan religion" in the Second Temple Period would be far more unlikely than for earlier periods.[17] If the antiquity of the use of these altars in ancient Israel seems assured, then the seemingly incongruous or extraneous position of the prescriptive verses in Exodus 30 must be addressed. In doing so, the assumption that they have been secondarily added there, by P[s] or a similar later hand, must be ruled out. Again, Cassuto's comments are apt; he points out that if someone wanted to add an incense altar not present in the actual core text of Exodus 25–27, that person would more likely have put it where it would seem to belong, in chap. 25, rather than in its present apparently anomalous position.

If archaeological materials and biblical passages external to P indicate that the incense altar would have been part of the tabernacle/temple cult and thus that its appearance in Exodus 30 is out of place, looking at evidence internal to the tabernacle texts also suggests that the Exodus 30 passage is misplaced. Several features of its fabrication, in addition to its appearance together with the table and the lampstand elsewhere in P, link it inextricably to the set of appurtenances in the outer sanctum as set forth in Exodus 25. Its primary physical characteristic is its material; like the table and lampstand, it is made of gold. In addition, it shares with the table (and probably the lampstand)[18] the fact that it has a core of acacia wood and is overlaid with gold. It also features

14. See Hyatt, *Exodus*, 291.

15. See, most recently, S. Gitin, "New Incense Altars from Ekron: Context, Typology, and Function," *ErIsr* 23 (Biran Volume; 1992) 43–49; idem, "Incense Altars from Ekron, Israel and Judah: Context and Typology," *ErIsr* 20 (Yadin Volume; 1989) 52–67. See, for an earlier such study, H. M. Wiener, *The Altars of the Old Testament* (Leipzig, 1927). But also see the view expressed by Haran that these small altars were not intended for incense: *Temples and Temple-Service*; idem, " 'Incense Altars'—Are They?" *Biblical Archaeology Today, 1990: Proceedings of the Second International Congress on Biblical Archaeology, Jerusalem, June–July, 1990* (Jerusalem, 1993) 237–47.

16. See the discussion in K. Nielsen, *Incense in Ancient Israel* (VTSup 38; Leiden, 1986) 71–73, 100–102.

17. Cassuto, *Commentary on the Book of Exodus*, 390.

18. See C. L. Meyers, *The Tabernacle Menorah: A Synthetic Study of a Symbol from the Biblical Cult* (ASOR Dissertation Series 2; Missoula, Mont., 1976) 31–34.

a molding like that of the table (and like the moldings on many archaeologi-
cally retrieved examples and perhaps also like that of the lampstand's complex
decorations),[19] as well as that of the ark in the inner sanctum. Finally, it has
rings and poles for transport, as do the table and the ark. With respect to transport, it should be noted that the instructions in Numbers 4 include the incense
altar in the sequence of directions for packing up the tabernacle's furnishings:
ark, table, lampstand, and incense ("golden") altar.

Such evidence leads to the conclusion that the incense altar was an integral part of the furnishings of the outer sanctum of the tabernacle, just as the
descriptive section stipulates. It is difficult to agree with the suggestion that it
has been omitted from the prescriptive section as a way of dealing with illegitimate use of incense,[20] since the incense altar would then, presumably, have
been deleted from other parts of P. Nor can it be accepted that Exodus 30 contains four *accessories* to worship;[21] the incense altar with its aromatic substance is integral to the constellation of interior cultic acts. If anything, the
altar of incense was more important, not less important,[22] than the other ritual
appurtenances of the outer sanctum, as will become clear below.

The Function of the Incense Altar

The fact that the incense altar was an essential and original part of the interior furnishings of the tabernacle (and temple) seems well established. The
location of the prescriptive text delineating its fabrication apart from the core
texts specifying the other items to be placed in the outer sanctum must therefore be deliberate. Haran, by the way, though quite adamant in demonstrating
the precision and logic of P in many places, falters in considering the incense
altar passage of Exod 30:1–10. He assumes that our expectation that it ought
to be in Exodus 25 is a result of our sense that being there would simply "sat-
isfy the requirements of classical taste."[23] Thus we should not regard its present
position as "slovenliness" but as an imposition of later ideas of organization on
an ancient text. We should "explain the misplacement of the passage in question by assuming that the copyist or editors themselves were not sufficiently
careful about inserting it where it belonged, and that this was the natural result
of an editorial method which gave rise to loose joints and rough edges."[24]

Although it is always possible that retrojecting later standards on an ancient document such as the tabernacle texts leads to faulty judgment about the

19. Ibid., 82.
20. Noth, *Exodus*, 192.
21. J. I. Durham, *Exodus* (WBC; Waco, Tex., 1987) 351.
22. P. P. Jenson, *Graded Holiness: A Key to the Priestly Conception of the World* (JSOTSup
106; Sheffield, 1992) 96.
23. See Haran, *Temples and Temple-Service*, 228.
24. Ibid., 229.

organization of its contents, it is also possible that in certain cases there are other factors at work that override the basic system that governs the arrangement of the prescriptive texts. That is, the absence of the incense altar from what would seem to be its logical place may be a sure sign that another kind of logic is operative for this appurtenance.[25] Indeed, in this instance it may be that the very notion of gradations of sanctity that is reflected in the sequence of specifications in Exodus 25–27, and that Haran has meticulously demonstrated, prevents the inclusion of the incense altar in that section.

The appurtenances and materials present in the core of the prescriptive section are not simply static objects. They are conceived as part of the furnishings of a functional household of the deity. Thus the mode of usage associated with the tabernacle's furnishings is as important as are their physical properties. With this aspect of the Exodus texts in mind, the specific function of the incense altar perhaps holds the key to understanding why this item of the cultic repertoire does not appear in what would otherwise seem to be its logical place. This altar's function, in turn, can be considered by examining the vessels associated with it.

The task of identifying the incense altar's vessels is more difficult than might be expected. The golden plates, spoons, cups, and libation vessels for use with the table in the outer sanctum are enumerated at the end of the depiction of that piece of furniture (Exod 25:29 = 37:16). Similarly, the lampstand's utensils are itemized at the conclusion of the passage setting forth the details of that object's construction (Exod 25:38–39 = 37:23–24). Furthermore, the summation in Exodus 39 (vv. 36, 37, 39) mentions utensils for the table and the menorah, and also for the courtyard altar (for which utensils are similarly itemized in both the prescriptive and descriptive passages.) However, the details of the incense altar's fabrication, in both chaps. 30 and 37, have no mention of vessels or utensils necessary for the use of the incense altar. Likewise, the description in Numbers of packing and transporting the tabernacle omits instructions for incense altar vessels, even while specifying carrying instructions for the table and lampstand (Num 4:9–12). Although the general term "all the service vessels" of v. 12 could conceivably include incense altar vessels,[26] such a possibility is unlikely in light of the omission of incense altar vessels in other texts.

The absence of this information is surprising and can certainly not be taken as an indication that the incense altar had no functional role. The Exod 30:1–10 passage presenting specifications for its fabrication contains, in fact, two details not included in Exodus 25 for either the table or the lampstand; and the second detail, if not also the first, relates to function. First, the spot where this object is to stand in the outer sanctum is specified: "place it in front of the curtain that is over the Ark of the Covenant, in front of the cover

25. J. Milgrom, *Leviticus 1–16* (AB 3; New York, 1991) 236.
26. Cf. J. Milgrom, *Numbers* (JPS Torah Commentary; Philadelphia, 1990) 27.

that is over the Ark of the Covenant" (Exod 30:6). Analogous information about the placement of the lampstand and table does not appear in the prescriptions for these objects in Exodus 25. The inclusion of instructions for positioning the incense altar within the passage specifying its fabrication shows an importance for location not present for the other items of the outer sanctum and surely relates to one of its functions (see below, pp. 44–45). Second, the regular use of the altar is specified: incense is to be offered twice daily at the time the high priest tends the lamps (Exod 30:7–8); and also, once annually, as a purgation rite, the horns of the incense altar are to be daubed with blood (Exod 30:10). Neither of these features is repeated in the descriptive incense altar text in Exodus 37, which thus appears abbreviated but which in fact fits well with the other descriptions of outer sanctum furnishings, which also do not delineate function.

These two features of the incense altar instructions in chap. 30 thus point to a way in which its usage diverges from the use of items flanking it in the inner sanctum: it has a central location, and it has a special usage beyond the daily service of the divine household. This usage will be considered below, but first the apparent absence of vessels must be examined. Were there really no vessels connected with the function of the incense altar? This could hardly be the case, since both the daily use of incense and the annual expiation rite involved the transfer of materials used in those rituals. Although the requisite containers are not specified in the Exodus texts, at least not in association with the incense altar itself, there are other biblical texts that indicate the existence of such items.

The most explicit text to name the kind of vessel associated with the use of the incense altar appears in a prophetic book. At the end of Second Zechariah, in a passage depicting the pervasive holiness of the future age, when all mundane objects will become as sacred as the holiest of cultic objects, the prophet mentions "basins before the altar" (Zech 14:20). In the eschatological future, horses' bells will, "on that day," be inscribed in a way that is suggestive of the inscription on the headpiece of the high priest, part of the most sacred aspect of the priestly vestments.[27] Similarly, the "pots" associated with the courtyard ritual will become as holy as the "basins before the altar."

Can this be a reference to vessels used with the incense altar? The use of the term 'basins' itself is not conclusive. The Hebrew word *mizrāqîm* (or *mizrāqôt*) can denote cultic items of silver, gold, or bronze in various contexts and with different usages in Israelite rituals.[28] In this case (Zech 14:20), their linkage with 'altar' is the only indication of which particular basins are indicated. Yet the term 'altar' itself is not otherwise identified in this passage. In Zech 9:15, where 'basin' and 'altar' appear together, the text refers to the bronze courtyard altar, since only for that altar are its 'corners' specified (as *zāwiyyôt*

---

27. See C. L. Meyers and E. M. Meyers, *Zechariah 9–14* (AB 25C; New York, 1993) ad loc.
28. See note to "basins before the altar" in Zech 9:15 in ibid., 483–86.

in Zech 9:15 and as *pinnôt* in priestly texts [Exod 27:2, 38:2; compare with Ezek 43:20, 45:19]). In denoting the courtyard altar, where basins at its corners would often be 'full',[29] the 'altar' of Zech 9:15 provides the appropriate imagery for the poetic language of Zechariah 9.

Zechariah 14 probably does not refer to that outer, courtyard altar. Contextual considerations support the conclusion that the altar of Zech 14:20 is the incense altar. As noted above, the last few verses of Second Zechariah deal with contrasts between formerly mundane objects and objects of greatest holiness, like the horses' bells, that are to become "holy to Yahweh," a designation linked to priestly garments worn *inside* the sanctuary. The "pots" of this verse are also to become as holy as possible, that is, as holy as vessels designated 'basins' (*mizrāqîm*), serving the interior of the sanctuary, where the incense altar was situated, rather than the courtyard.

Presumably such basins would be made of gold, in keeping with the material principal whereby all ritual items within Israel's temple and tabernacle were made of the metal deemed most precious.[30] This would seem to fit the cursory information provided in 1 Kgs 7:48–50 about the appurtenances, vessels, and structural features of the Jerusalem Temple. Verses 49 and 50 list utensils associated with the interior furnishings, and 'basin' is included in this list of golden objects (compare with 2 Chr 4:21). Similarly, the account of the sacking of the temple in 2 Kings and at the end of Jeremiah lists 'basins'. In Jer 52:19 the basins appear to be gold, with bronze basins being mentioned in 52:18. The text in 1 Kgs 15:15, however, is less clear about whether the basins are bronze or gold. In both places, it is to be noted, the basins are listed with 'firepans', items perhaps used with the incense altar,[31] separate from the bronze vessels of the courtyard altar.

The ambiguity of the Kings passages as well as Jeremiah about the material of the basins is noteworthy; it may indicate a functional merging of altar basins (and firepans?).[32] Although the term 'basins' is not present in the priestly texts presenting the incense altar, it does appear as a designation for a bronze vessel used in association with the courtyard altar. Those vessels were probably fairly large containers, perhaps to be related to the ceramic kraters or drinking bowls recovered in archaeological excavations. Because the krater was among the finest wares produced by Israelite potters,[33] it would be a fitting ceramic prototype for or equivalent to a metallic vessel ("basins") used in a sacred context.

29. See J. Kelso, *The Ceramic Vocabulary of the Old Testament* (BASORSS 5–6; New Haven, 1948) 22–23.

30. Haran, *Temples and Temple-Service*, 158, 164–65.

31. See V. Hurowitz, "Solomon's Golden Vessels (1 Kings 7:48–50) and the Cult of the First Temple," *Pomegranates and Golden Bells: Studies in Biblical, Jewish, and Near Eastern Ritual, Law, and Literature in Honor of Jacob Milgrom* (ed. D. P. Wright, D. N. Freedman, and A. Hurvitz; Winona Lake, Ind.; 1995), 151–64.

32. Cf. C. L. Meyers, "Firepan," *ABD* 2.796.

33. See Kelso, *Ceramic Vocabulary*, 23.

Although some basins were used for tribal grain offerings (of flour plus oil; Num 7:13, 19, etc.), the dominant cultic use of the term 'basin' is for the bronze basins of the courtyard altar.

The function of courtyard altar basins is not directly specified. However, indirect evidence suggests that they may have had something to do with the quantities of blood that were poured out at the base of the sacrificial altar, presumably at its corners, after some of the blood was smeared on the horns at the corners of that altar (for example, in Lev 4:34; cf. Exod 24:6, where Moses puts some blood in vessels and then throws [verb *zrq*] the blood on the altar). The use of basins (*mizrāqôt*) at the corners of the altar of burnt offerings also fits the imagery of Zech 9:15 mentioned above. Basins were meant as receptacles for liquid, presumably blood.

As such, in terms of their size and function, basins are appropriate to the ritual acts of the sacrificial altar and not the incense altar. For the latter, smaller and typologically different vessels would be in order, but only to bring incense to the altar; the burning of incense would have left no residue to be carried away. Such vessels are not specified: perhaps they are subsumed under the incense dishes for the golden table (Exod 25:29 = 37:16; compare with 1 Kgs 7:50, which links basins and incense dishes as part of the table's vessels);[34] or perhaps they are omitted because the basins for the incense altar are omitted. More likely, the vessels for bringing any substances into the sanctuary, whether for the table or lampstand, are not specified. Only the vessels for holding or tending the substances in their ritual usages are mentioned. For the incense altar this means the surface of the altar itself in terms of the daily ritual, unless firepans, if they are truly golden vessels associated with the golden altar of the tabernacle as well as the temple, were somehow used for the burning of incense.

This brings us back, finally, to the absence in the priestly texts of basins used for the incense altar. Clearly they were not part of the daily service, that is, the incense-burning function of the interior altar. Rather, they are functionally linked to the basins of the large outer altar, as receptacles for blood. In that capacity, a basin for the incense altar would have been used regularly only in the annual purgation rite, which involved the transfer of blood from the outer altar into the sanctuary and, only in this instance in all of priestly legislation, into the Holy of Holies (Lev 16:11–19). The exact sequence of this ritual, meant to maintain the sanctity of the sanctuary, is tantalizingly vague, though it can be reconstructed using biblical evidence along with the information in *m. Yoma* 5:3.[35] The incense altar lay directly in the path the priest would have had to take, and the special incense (as described for the incense altar in Exod 30:26) of this altar was used in the priest's ritual acts. Thus it is possible that "the altar before

34. See Hurowitz, "Solomon's Golden Vessels," 158.
35. See B. A. Levine, *Leviticus* (JPS Torah Commentary; Philadelphia, 1989) 103ff.

Yahweh" of Lev 16:12 refers to the incense altar, as it surely does in Lev 16:18, which relates how the combined blood of the sacrificed bull (for the sins of the priesthood) and of the he-goat (for the sins of the people) was to be smeared on the incense altar's horns and then sprinkled on it seven times.

In addition to this annual rite of purgation and purification, which dealt with the defilement that could be introduced to the sanctuary by the priesthood itself and with the impurity of the Israelite community that also could reach the divine dwelling and cause God to withdraw,[36] expiatory sacrifices were prescribed in Leviticus 4 and 5 for inadvertent or unwitting offenses incurred by the priests or the people. The ritual involved the slaughter of an unblemished bull at the courtyard altar and then the carrying of some of its blood into the sanctuary. There the priest was to dip into the blood, sprinkle it seven times in front of the curtain, and smear some of it on the horns of the incense altar (Lev 4:5–7, 16–18).

The rituals described above involve the incense altar, but not in the way this altar might be expected to be used: (1) they do not include its incense-burning function; (2) they are not part of the daily service; and (3) they specify the introduction of matter (blood) produced by a ritual act taking place in a different realm—the courtyard—of the sacred precinct. For these reasons, it is possible to conclude that while certain vessels, that is, basins, were in fact used in association with the incense altar, they originated with the altar of burnt offerings outside the entrance to the outer sanctum and were primarily intended as receptacles for blood spilled at the corners of the courtyard altar in the rituals of animal sacrifice. Thus the basins used for the blood of purgation and purification to be sprinkled in front of the curtain and smeared on the incense altar's horns would have been part of the elaborate set of vessels connected with the use of the sacrificial altar. The basin regularly appears as an item in the repertoire of the bronze altar's utensils; for example, "you shall make pots to receive its ashes, and shovels and basins and forks and firepans; you shall make all its utensils of bronze" (Exod 27:3; compare 38:3). Consequently, the vessels, or 'basins', used with the incense altar were not used exclusively or primarily with it. They were actually part of the regular functioning of the courtyard altar and were only occasionally used with the incense altar. The incense altar thus did not have its own discrete basins. It would not have needed them for the daily ritual, and its need for them for special occasions involved a ritual originating in the court.

Conclusion

The passage in Exod 27:3 cited above stipulates, as would be expected, that the bronze altar of burnt offering was to be served by bronze utensils.

---

36. See ibid., 99; J. Milgrom, "The *ḥaṭṭāʾt*: A Rite of Passage?" *RB* 98 (1991) 120–24.

Consequently, the basins used to carry blood from it into the sanctuary would have been bronze. The fact that a bronze vessel could thus enter a sacred realm otherwise characterized by gold appurtenances and vessels constitutes something of an anomaly. It is unlikely that the basin for this specific purpose was cast of gold. Yet the logic of having such a golden vessel may somehow underlie the ambiguity in the Kings and Jeremiah texts discussed above concerning whether the basins were included among the bronze, silver, or gold elements of the temple.

The fact that the vessels used with the *golden* incense altar are *bronze* basins made for the courtyard altar strongly suggests that the conception of the incense altar is complex in a way that does not obtain for the other two items of golden furniture in the outer sanctum of the tabernacle. It differs from the other appurtenances in critical ways. The following features of the golden incense altar and its use are salient in this regard:

1. It is used in a regular daily ritual related to the service of a divine dwelling. But it also plays a central role in maintaining or reestablishing the purity of the entire sacred precinct.

2. As a golden object, it partakes of the material gradation that sets the items inside the sanctuary apart from the bronze items of the courtyard. Yet it is homologous with respect to one of the latter items, namely the bronze altar, in its morphology, its detail of fabrication, its function, and in its very name. Like the altar of burnt offering, it is square in shape, has horns at its corners, is used for the burning of a substance, and is designated an 'altar' (*mizbēaḥ*). This designation may be derived the fact that it is shaped like the courtyard altar.[37] However, it is just as likely to indicate its inherent role as an internal altar for the use of sacrificial blood obtained from its counterpart outside the sanctuary. That the text of Exodus 30 expressly forbids the use of the incense altar for burnt offerings, among other things (v. 9), indeed suggests that its form is an invitation for sacrifice as much as for incense.

3. The close connection of the incense altar with an item from outside the sanctuary is further indicated by the fact that the incense to be used on the altar is 'most holy' (*qōdeš qodāšîm*), not simply 'holy'. In the account in Exodus of the anointing of the sacred complex, the superlative designation is not used for the tabernacle and its furnishings, which are made 'holy' (*qōdeš*) by the anointing procedure; but the altar of burnt offering and all its implements are thereby made 'most holy' (Exod 40:9–10; compare with 29:37). Thus the blood to be carried from the outer altar and smeared on the horns of the incense altar is also 'most holy' (Exod 30:10).

4. The incense altar and the courtyard altar are both located on the tabernacle's central axis. The latter is to be installed in front of the 'entrance of the tabernacle of the tent of meeting' (Exod 40:6, 29), in front of an elaborate

37. So N. Sarna, *Exodus* (JPS Torah Commentary; Philadelphia, 1991) 194.

'entrance screen' (*māsak happetaḥ*, Exod 35:15); the former is to be placed in front of the entrance to the inner sanctum (Exod 40:5), in front of an elaborate 'curtain for the screen' (*pārōket hammāsāk* Exod 40:21).

The central axis of the sanctuary runs from the inner sanctum or most holy place, with the ark representing God's presence, to the incense altar of the outer sanctum or holy place, to the outer altar of the court. Moreover, both altars are at access points, or entrances, which allow movement to the inner-most realm of holiness of the tabernacle complex from the outermost realm. Such points have an extremely important role in ancient architecture, both secular and sacred. Entryways are points of accessibility and also of vulnerability.[38] They allow essential passage but also risk the admission of unwanted persons or substances. The special vocabulary and ritual associated with both tabernacle altars must be seen as a function of their location on the path between the ultimate sacred space, the inner sanctum as locale of absolute purity and divine imminence, and the outer world with its burden of pollution.[39]

It is no wonder then that the Israelite attempts to secure the purity and holiness of the sacred space embodied in the tabernacle and temple involved special attention to the point of access to the holiest spot within the sacred precincts. Materials that move from an outer zone of sanctity to the inner zone, or that are associated with such movement, thus belong in some ways to both realms. The incense altar, while part of the triad of furnishings in the outer sanctum, was also part of the ritual that attempted to prevent outer pollution caused by priestly or community transgressions from contaminating sacred space and interfering with God's availability to the community. Inner altar and outer altar, therefore, were functionally homologous in certain purgation rituals.

The prescriptive tabernacle texts, in laying out a blueprint governed by zones of sanctity, thus could not include in the instructions for the furnishings of the outer sanctum the specifications for the altar of incense. This item, or at least some of its most critical functions, involved the transgression of boundaries. At one end, at the point of utmost sanctity, it provided smoke that apparently penetrated into the inner sanctum as the cloud of divine presence (Lev 16:12–13).[40] In this regard, it is to be noted that one later tradition has the incense altar actually *within* the Holy of Holies (see Heb 9:4). In the middle, as an item of furniture of the outer sanctum, the small golden altar was used for an incense rite that was an inseparable part of the complex of acts performed in that zone of sanctity.[41] At the other end, with respect to the court as a zone

---

38. See C. L. Meyers, "*sap*," *TWAT* 5.898–902; A. van Gennup, *Rites of Passage* (trans. M. B. Vizedom and G. L. Caffee; Chicago, 1960) 15–25.

39. Cf. J. P. Brereton, "Sacred Space," *Encyclopedia of Religion* 12 (1987) 526–35; J. J. Preston, "Purification," *Encyclopedia of Religion* 12 (1987) 91–100.

40. See discussion in Milgrom, *Leviticus*, 1024–31; B. A. Levine, *Leviticus*, 103–4.

41. Haran, *Temples and Temple-Service*, 241–45.

of lesser holiness and with its own separate complex of ritual acts, it received blood from the outer altar. The blood, some of which was thrown against the screen in front of the ark, was intended to remove impurities introduced to sacred space by human transgressions.

The connection of the golden incense altar with the three realms of sanctity of the tabernacle complex thus sets it apart from the golden appurtenances of the outer sanctum, or the middle zone, that were otherwise similar in conception and material. The text of Exodus 25–27 signifies an ordered sacred reality. As such, the text could not be disrupted by the presence of an object that functionally interrupted this order. The golden altar of incense is hardly misplaced in its present position. It appears outside the carefully gradated sequence of the core of the prescriptive texts precisely because it crosses the realms of sanctity that the texts represent with such exquisite precision.

HEZEKIAH AND THE TEMPLE

H. G. M. Williamson

THE STORIES ABOUT HEZEKIAH in Isaiah 36–39 have been the subject of a number of studies in recent years, most of which have been concerned to point out their suitability within the present form of the book of Isaiah as a whole and to argue that they are by no means the isolated historical appendix to the first half of the book alone that they were once thought to be. Indeed, so strongly has this appreciation impressed itself on some scholars that they have even gone as far as to suggest that the stories were not transferred to their present setting from 2 Kings 18–20, as the consensus has long maintained, but rather that they were first composed for the book of Isaiah and that it is their setting in the Deutero-nomic History that is secondary from a literary point of view.[1]

It is by no means certain, however, that this second conclusion is a necessary consequence of the first. A convenient point at which to test it is Isaiah 38 = 2 Kgs 20:1–11, the account of Hezekiah's illness and recovery, for in this chapter there are rather greater differences between the two forms of the narrative than is generally the case in this set of parallel passages. Needless to say, a full study even of this one passage would far exceed the limits necessarily imposed on the present article, let alone an examination of the parallel material as a whole. There are, for instance, complex textual issues that reflect on the point at hand but that cannot be examined here.[2] Rather, my concern will be to

---

Author's Note: It is a pleasure to be invited to contribute to this volume in honor of Menahem Haran, who amongst his many contributions to Biblical scholarship has shed so much light on the role and rituals of the temple in ancient Israel.

1. See, for example, K. A. D. Smelik, "Distortion of Old Testament Prophecy: The Purpose of Isaiah xxxvi and xxxvii," *OTS* 24 (*Crises and Perspectives: Studies in Ancient Near Eastern Polytheism, Biblical Theology, Palestinian Archaeology and Intertestamental Literature*; Leiden, 1986) 70–93; C. R. Seitz, *Zion's Final Destiny: The Development of the Book of Isaiah—A Reassessment of Isaiah 36–39* (Minneapolis, 1991).

2. See A. H. Konkel, "The Sources of the Story of Hezekiah in the Book of Isaiah," *VT* 43 (1993) 462–82.

suggest that there is a previously unnoticed connection between two important elements in the chapter and that when these elements are taken together they point rather firmly to the usual conclusion that it is the text in Isaiah that is dependent on the one in 2 Kings and not vice versa.

The most obvious difference between the two versions of the story is the inclusion of the Psalm of Hezekiah in Isa 38:9–20. This is almost universally regarded as having been added to the account at a late stage in its development. As far as I am aware, even among those who think that this material has been taken over by Kings from Isaiah, only Seitz has suggested that this passage was already in place and was omitted by the Deuteronomic historian, but even then he expresses uncertainty: "It is impossible to determine whether the psalm of Hezekiah was brought over from Isaiah as part of the original depiction of the DtrH."[3] Moreover, though he suggests that "its omission is certainly consistent with the other modifications that have occurred in the story of Hezekiah's illness," it is clear that he is working on the basis of the conclusion that he has already reached that the Kings version is dependent on the Isaian. He does not appear to advance any independent arguments to support the proposal that the psalm was deliberately suppressed by the historian.

On the usual view, of course, such an addition presents no difficulty. Beyond this, however, Ackroyd has made out a case for regarding the inclusion of this psalm as purposeful within the context of the role these chapters play specifically within the book of Isaiah. "It is not," he writes, "simply an appropriately worded psalm of thanksgiving for deliverance in time of distress, here seen as apposite to the recovery of the king. It is a comment on the larger significance of that recovery in the context of the whole work."[4] He supports this conclusion with the following observations: the psalm uses a series of metaphors that speak of restoration to life from the pit; in Lamentations and parts of Jeremiah these metaphors are used in relation to the experience of exile; and the climax is reached with the individual joining the community in worship at the temple. The inclusion of the psalm thus has the effect of heightening the typological significance of Hezekiah's illness. On the one hand, "the illness of Hezekiah and the death sentence upon him thus become a type of judgment and exile, and in that measure they run parallel to the theme of judgment which is found in the ambassador story which follows."[5] On the other hand, the conclusion of the psalm points forward to the possibility of restoration for the community.

---

3. Seitz, *Zion's Final Destiny*, 187.

4. P. R. Ackroyd, *Studies in the Religious Tradition of the Old Testament* (London, 1987) 165. Ackroyd's proposal has been developed by a detailed analysis of the psalm's various themes by J. H. Coetzee, "The 'Song of Hezekiah' (Isaiah 38:9–20): A Doxology of Judgement from the Exilic Period," *Old Testament Essays* 2/3 (1989) 13–26; see also J. W. Watts, *Psalm and Story: Inset Hymns in Hebrew Narrative* (JSOTSup 139; Sheffield, 1992) 118–31.

5. Ackroyd, *Studies in the Religious Tradition*, 165.

Whereas the Deuteronomic History is reticent about speaking of such restoration, it is entirely suitable within the book of Isaiah.

It is difficult to be sure quite how far we should go in agreeing with all of Ackroyd's observations. The elements to which he draws attention are, of course, paralleled in a number of the psalms,[6] so that we may need to distinguish carefully between their meaning in what could have been an originally independent psalm and their reuse in the present setting of the book of Isaiah, a situation in which it is always a delicate decision to what extent the person including the material was conscious of the full impact of his choice on as sensitive a later reader as Ackroyd shows himself to be. An exception to this reservation should probably be drawn, however, with regard to the conclusion of the psalm, both because of its climactic position and because of its striking shift to first-person plural forms, of which the writer could hardly have been unaware. The psalms inserted at 1 Sam 2:1-10 and Jonah 2:3–10 seem similarly to conclude with consciously climactic statements. There need be no doubt, therefore, that part of the reason for including the psalm of Hezekiah was to associate the deliverance of the king with the cultic well-being of the people as a whole, a theme familiar from many other parts of the Hebrew Bible.

The second major difference between Isaiah 38 and 2 Kgs 20:1–11 relates to the fact that the narrative part of the chapter is considerably shorter in Isaiah than in 2 Kings. Not all the minuses should necessarily be accounted for in the same way. For instance, it is possible to believe that 2 Kgs 20:4a, "And before Isaiah had gone out of the middle court," has been added at a later stage in order to emphasize the speed with which the godly king's prayer was heard;[7] the use of שוב (2 Kgs 20:5) instead of הלוך (Isa 38:5) can then be neatly explained as a necessary change consequent upon the addition. On the other hand, it might be supposed that the description of Hezekiah as נגיד־עמי 'the prince of my people' in 2 Kgs 20:5 has been omitted from Isa 38:5 because it was thought to detract from the strongly positive portrayal of the king that the Isaian context requires. It is less easy to explain as a purposeful addition to Kings. However, such small differences are not of great significance when taken alone, since the possibility of accidental loss in the course of transmission must always be borne in mind.

Greater weight attaches to the reasons that Isa 38:6–7 is so very much shorter than 2 Kgs 20:6b–11a. In the Kings account, as has often been noted, there appear to be two narrative elements that are rather roughly juxtaposed.[8]

6. See especially J. Begrich, *Der Psalm des Hiskia: Ein Beitrag zum Verständnis von Jesaja 38:10–20* (FRLANT 42; Göttingen, 1926); H. Wildberger, *Jesaja, 3. Teilband: Jesaja 28–39* (BKAT 10/3; Neukirchen-Vluyn, 1982) 1454–67.

7. Wildberger, *Jesaja*, 3.1446. For a different interpretation, see M. A. Sweeney, *Isaiah 1–4 and the Post-Exilic Understanding of the Isaianic Tradition* (BZAW 171; Berlin, 1988) 14.

8. F. J. Gonçalves, *L'Expédition de Sennachérib en Palestine dans la littérature hébraïque ancienne* (EBib n.s. 7; Paris, 1986) 333–36, with bibliography.

Verses 1–7 are complete in themselves, because they tell of Hezekiah's illness, his prayer, and his recovery through the intervention of the prophet at God's instruction. This comes to a clear literary conclusion in v. 7: "And Isaiah said, 'Take a cake of figs.' And they took and laid it on the boil, and he recovered" (RV). As most commentators recognize, there is no other legitimate way of translating the MT. A number of the English translations seek to harmonize the account with what follows by rendering the *wāw*-consecutive + imperfect verbs as though they continued the imperative mood of Isaiah's direct speech; see, for example, the RSV: "Bring a cake of figs. And let them take and lay it on the boil, that he may recover." Though this urge to harmonize was perceived as early as the LXX and Peshiṭta, it should be resisted.[9] The climactic "and he recovered" forms an effective contrast to the "you shall not recover" in v. 1, so that vv. 1–7 may be taken as a self-contained narrative unit as they stand (without the revocalization that tacitly lies behind the harmonizing approach). The roughness of the transition to the following paragraph is to be explained as the result of the joining together of two originally independent narrative elements, not explained away as due to an error in the vocalization by the Masoretes. To this first narrative, then, there is added in vv. 8–11 the account of Hezekiah's request for a sign and the favorable response by the prophet. In the present form of the text, the way for this is partly prepared by the words in v. 5: "behold, I will heal you; on the third day you shall go up to the house of the Lord."[10] This only highlights the fact, however, that these two sections were not written originally as a single narrative, for in that case we should logically have expected the request for a sign before the statement of recovery. We may thus safely conclude that 2 Kgs 20:1–11 is a composite narrative, the editor of which[11] has chosen, for whatever reason, to juxtapose the various items at his disposal rather than to integrate them into their expected order.

This expected order is, in fact, what we find in the Isaiah version, where a variant form of 2 Kgs 20:7 has been moved to the end of the account in Isa 38:21.[12] On this basis, Cogan and Tadmor argue that the Isaiah version must be the later of the two: "The rearrangement in Isaiah sought to smooth out the difficulty of 2 Kgs 20:7 noted above, by removing it to the end of the chapter; therefore the text of Kings is earlier."[13]

---

9. Contra, most recently, E. Ruprecht, "Die ursprüngliche Komposition der Hiskia-Jesaja-Erzählungen und ihre Umstrukturierung durch den Verfasser des deuteronomistischen Geschichtwerkes," *ZTK* 87 (1990) 33–66 (39).

10. Cf. v. 8.

11. Identified most recently as the Deuteronomist by S. L. McKenzie, *The Trouble with Kings: The Composition of the Book of Kings in the Deuteronomistic History* (VTSup 42; Leiden, 1991) 106–7.

12. The function of this verse in its new setting has recently been discussed by V. Hoffer, "An Exegesis of Isaiah 38:21," *JSOT* 56 (1992) 69–84. Her conclusions fit well with my understanding of the earlier part of the chapter.

13. M. Cogan and H. Tadmor, *II Kings* (AB 11; Garden City, N.Y., 1988) 257.

Jeremias reaches the same conclusion on different grounds.[14] He observes
that the removal of 2 Kgs 20:7–8 to the end of the chapter has created an un-
evenness in the representation of who is speaking in Isa 38:5–8: God speaks in
the first person through Isaiah in vv. 5b–6; he is referred to in the third person
in v. 7; and the first-person singular in v. 8 is ambiguous, since it could refer
either to God or to the prophet. Since in the Kings version exactly the same material all makes sense because it is distributed through more than one scene,
Jeremias concludes quite reasonably that this is an indication of a previously
unnoticed difficulty consequent upon the abbreviation in Isaiah. It is unfortunate that Seitz appears to have been unaware of Jeremias's article. His analysis
of Isaiah 38 proceeds on the assumption that Isa 38:1–8 + 21–22 is a coherent
narrative that has been confused in Kings.[15] Jeremias has shown, however, that
this is not the case; rather, as we have seen, the apparent confusion in Kings
should be explained as resulting from the juxtaposition of the two narrative
blocks in 2 Kgs 20:1–7 and 8–11. The writer of Isaiah 38 has tried to smooth
this out into a single whole but has thereby unconsciously introduced confusion
of a different, and clearly secondary, sort.

The conclusions of Cogan and Tadmor and of Jeremias seem convincing as
far as they go, but they do not account for the whole of the matter. The Isaiah
version does, after all, retain Isaiah's offer of a sign to Hezekiah, albeit now in
its expected position. In this connection, some other differences between the
two accounts need to be examined, and the explanations for them will be seen
to differ. First, in Isaiah Hezekiah is offered a sign without his first requesting
one (contrast 2 Kgs 20:8). This may be due to two related factors that have been
noted by various scholars on other grounds, namely, the concern in the Isaiah
narratives to portray Hezekiah as a wholly pious king and in particular the desire to contrast him with the portrayal of Ahaz in Isaiah 7.[16] Second, some of
the details of what the sign was intended to confirm are systematically eliminated, namely that Hezekiah will be "healed" and that he will go up to the
house of the Lord on the third day. It is possible that part of the motivation for
this is the account of Hezekiah's visits to the "house of the Lord" in the earlier
narratives (at 2 Kgs 19:1 and 14 = Isa 37:1 and 14), but since the occurrence
of this material in 2 Kgs 20:8 is as part of a longer passage (vv. 6b–8) for the
omission of which we have seen that there were other motives as well, not too

14. C. Jeremias, "Zu Jes. xxxviii 21f." *VT* 21 (1971) 104–11.

15. Seitz, *Zion's Final Destiny*, 149–82; see especially pp. 162–66. Other scholars who regard
the Isaiah version as prior include P. Auvray, *Isaïe 1–39* (SB; Paris, 1972) 315; A. Laato, *Who Is
Immanuel? The Rise and Foundering of Isaiah's Messianic Expectations* (Åbo, 1988) 277.

16. Cf. R. E. Clements, *Isaiah and the Deliverance of Jerusalem* (JSOTSup 13; Sheffield,
1980) 65; idem, *Isaiah 1–39* (NCB; Grand Rapids, 1980) 290; Ackroyd, *Studies in the Religious
Tradition*, 173. Sweeney (*Isaiah 1–4*, 12–16) appeals to the narrative's desire to portray Hezekiah
as a wholly pious king to explain more or less all the differences between 2 Kgs 20:1–11 and Isaiah
38. However, I am arguing for a variety of reasons, of which this is only one. Also cf. E. W. Conrad, *Reading Isaiah* (OBT; Minneapolis, 1991) 44–45.

much should be built on it. Third, however, there is the excision of these same
words from 2 Kgs 20:5, and here none of the considerations just advanced appear to apply. They could have been left there in the Isaiah version without pos-
ing any problem whatever of the sort that we have been examining up until
now. Moreover, there is no evidence for Jeremias's conjecture that 2 Kgs 20:5
and 8 were added only later, and so were no part of the Kings text that was copied in Isaiah. Some other explanation must therefore be sought.

I suggest that the answer lies in the new interpretation put upon this whole
incident by the inclusion of the psalm of Hezekiah. There, it will be recalled,
the climax of the poetic account of the king's restoration comes with the statement that he and his children will give praise to God throughout their lives in
the house of the Lord:

> The living, the living, he thanks thee,
>   as I do this day;
> the father makes known to the children
>   thy faithfulness.
> The Lord will save me,
>   and we will sing to stringed instruments
> all the days of our life,
>   at the house of the Lord.
>
> (Isa 38:19–20)

Whereas in the Kings account the focus of attention is entirely on the individual
Hezekiah, in Isaiah his restoration is seen typologically as adumbrating the restoration of the community, and of the royal line in particular, characterized by
worship in the house of the Lord. In this new context, the reference to a single
visit to the temple by the king alone as a sign of restoration would have been
inappropriate. It was therefore deleted and reinterpreted by the inclusion of the
psalm in the manner indicated.[17]

If this is the case, it follows that the reshaping of the first part of Isaiah 38
and the inclusion of the psalm were part of the same process (thereby confirm-
ing that it is the Isaiah version that must derive from Kings, and not the other
way about), although, as we have seen, other considerations were simultaneously at work. As in not a little of the other postexilic literature (working under the assumption that these chapters were added to the book of Isaiah at that
time), the loss of monarchy could be sustained as long as a temple still stood
as a focus for the community's present cohesion and future hopes, which they
had formerly vested primarily in their kings. But included among these hopes
was, paradoxically, the expectation that one day the temple would again see the
descendants of Hezekiah included in its congregation.

---

17. In this respect, therefore, I should take issue with Watts's conclusion that "Hezekiah's
Psalm has no effect on the prose plot" (Watts, *Psalm and Story*, 125).

THE EARTHEN ALTAR LAWS OF EXODUS 20:24–26 AND RELATED SACRIFICIAL RESTRICTIONS IN THEIR CULTURAL CONTEXT

Ziony Zevit

EXOD 20:24–26 RECORDS what are generally considered to be the basic altar laws of ancient Israel. In defining the requirements for an altar, these laws restricted the range of possible altar types that may have been used or deemed acceptable. The objectives of this study are to describe the physical appearance of such altars, to indicate what the altars meant symbolically in the context of monolatrous or monotheistic Israelite Yahwism, and to analyze how other encumbrances on accepted sacrificial procedures nuanced and diminished the symbolic meaning of these altars.

מִזְבַּח אֲדָמָה תַּעֲשֶׂה־לִּי וְזָבַחְתָּ עָלָיו אֶת־עֹלֹתֶיךָ וְאֶת־שְׁלָמֶיךָ אֶת־צֹאנְךָ וְאֶת־
בְּקָרֶךָ בְּכָל־הַמָּקוֹם אֲשֶׁר אַזְכִּיר אֶת־שְׁמִי אָבוֹא אֵלֶיךָ וּבֵרַכְתִּיךָ. וְאִם־מִזְבַּח
אֲבָנִים תַּעֲשֶׂה־לִּי לֹא־תִבְנֶה אֶתְהֶן גָּזִית כִּי חַרְבְּךָ הֵנַפְתָּ עָלֶיהָ וַתְּחַלְלֶהָ. וְלֹא־
תַעֲלֶה בְמַעֲלֹת עַל־מִזְבְּחִי אֲשֶׁר לֹא־תִגָּלֶה עֶרְוָתְךָ עָלָיו.

24. An altar of earth you will make for me, and you will offer on it your burnt offerings and your well-being (or peace) offerings and your flock animals and your herd animals.[1] In every place where I cause my name to be mentioned I will come to you and I will bless you.

25. And if an altar of stones you will make for me, do not build them

---

1. The phrase "and your flock animals and your herd animals" could have been the original version of this prescription, which was then glossed by "your burnt offerings and your well-being offerings." This second phrase, which could also have arisen as a variational doublet, clarified the specific application of these altars. In the extant context, despite the absence of a prepositional *mēʾēt*, the phrase carries the import of "from your flock animals and your herd animals."

53

hewn[2] because you wielded your tool[3] over it[4] you profane it.[5]
26. Do not ascend my altar by steps so that you do not reveal your nakedness on it.

Slaughtering itself did not (usually) take place on altars, for a range of practical considerations: it would have been physically difficult to get a living animal, whether partially restrained or not, up on an altar; the active, kicking animal, even in its death throes, could damage the altar and harm those who held it down and slaughtered it. Furthermore, disemboweling animals is un-aesthetic, smelly and messy, and skinning animals is done more easily and efficiently when the carcass is suspended than when horizontal in its own gore.[6] For these reasons, the expression *zbḥt ᶜlyw* in Exod 20:24 must be interpreted 'you will offer on it'. In other words, in this context, the meaning/function/intent of the verb *zbḥ* has been influenced secondarily by the meaning and function of the noun *mizbēaḥ* 'installation or artifact on which something is displayed or presented to (or before) a deity' (compare with 2 Chr 33:16). The word itself never refers to the place of slaughter.

2. A literal rendering of *gāzît* is 'hewing', which is to say, do not turn the natural stones into shaped, dressed ashlars. The intent of the prohibition is to ensure that the altar stones are naturally whole. See Deut 27:6 where this rule from Exodus is paraphrased and prescribed for a specific altar. The altar to be constructed there is of unworked *ʾăbānîm šĕlēmôt* 'complete stones'. (Note that Deut 27:5–7 is an inclusio interrupting legislation about the establishment of an inscribed monument, vv. 4 + 8.)

3. Hebrew *ḥereb* could be properly translated 'sword', but here, as Ibn Ezra suggested, *ḥereb* is the name of a tool used in stonecutting; compare with Deut 27:5, ". . . an altar of stones, do not wield *barzel* 'iron' over them." This is repeated in Josh 8:31. The shape of the tool most likely determined its name; compare Isa 2:4 and Mic 4:3, "they will beat their swords (*ḥrbwtm*) into pruning hooks." The *ḥrbwt ṣrym* 'flint swords' of Josh 5:2–3 were not weapons of war but hand implements for circumcision (compare with Exod 4:25). In this case, as in Ezek 26:9, *ḥereb* may refer to a straight stone chisel. See P. McNutt, *The Forging of Israel: Iron Technology, Symbolism, and Tradition in Ancient Israel* (Sheffield, 1990) 217–18. Although the law in Deut 27:5–6 helps illumine the basic altar law of Exodus, the two are not necessarily identical with regard to their restriction. The prohibition in Exodus is against the use of tool-cut stones; that of Deuteronomy against stones cut with iron. Developing an idea of Nachmanides in his comment on Exod 20:23, I suggest that perhaps Deut 27:6 considered stones cut by bronze implements to have been 'complete stones'. This interpretation hinges on the significance of the use of the term *barzel* 'iron' by the legislator.

4. The implicit, logical antecedent of the feminine pronoun is a 'stone of hewing' *ʾeben gāzît*. The sense of the verse is that stones not be turned into cut building blocks. The 'because' clause focuses on a single instance that can desacralize the complete undertaking. The lack of elegance in the English reflects a similar lack in the Hebrew.

5. The last phrase could be rendered 'lest you wield your sword over it and profane it', but this would create an association with a sword as a weapon of war and a false connection between a weapon (that is also a specialized tool) and the profanation of the stones.

6. One important narrative exception is what almost took place in Gen 22:9–10, but the story presupposes that Abraham was following proper procedure. The parallel language in 1 Kgs 18:33 has Elijah placing a dismembered ox on the piled wood. The difference between these two cases can, of course, be explained by noting that the kicking ox, even if trussed, could destroy the altar, whereas Isaac was a compliant victim.

Alternatively, the preposition ‘al, in the collocation, could have the sense of 'by, adjacent to', in which case the phrase could be translated 'and you will slaughter next to it . . .' (compare with Gen 14:6, 16:7, 18:5; Exod 2:15, 14:2; and especially Lev 1:11, where the object of the preposition is a vertical surface). However, accepting this alternative renders the many details of the altar's construction superfluous since its function would be to be the place next to which the offering is slaughtered rather than the focus of the legislator's attention, and its use would never be spelled out. The only contexts in which the expression can be rendered 'you will slaughter on it' involve human victims (see 1 Kgs 13:2, 2 Kgs 23:20), a category of offering that is explicitly ruled out by the stated intent of the law here and will not be considered below.[7]

Altars for the burning of ‘ōlôt and (zebaḥ) šělāmîm sacrifices could be made either of piled-up earth or unhewn stones, depending on what was readily at hand and the preference of the individual (vv. 24–25). These two types of sacrifices were the least cumbersome of the offerings, both with regard to the types of animals and to their attendant rituals. In addition, insofar as they were often optional and not linked with other cultic requirements specifically prescribed in P, they were motivated primarily by the individual's desire to know that he was under divine supervision and in some sort of communion with the divine (Lev 22:17–24, Num 15:1–8).[8] These two sacrifices would have been the most common type made, and concern for their proper execution at a site sanctioned by law, cultic norm, oracle, or tradition would have been significant.

These altars were imagined as being used in such a way that an individual would have to be on top of it either to arrange the sacrifice properly or to perform some ritual. They were also imagined as being of such a height that steps would be convenient, if not necessary, for ascending to the top (v. 26). Since a person whose height was 150–155 cm (= 5 ft. to 5 ft. 2 in.), the average height of adult males in the Iron Age according to skeletal remains,[9] could easily step onto an altar raised 25–30 cm (= 10–12 in.) above the ground, the minimal height of an altar that might demand steps (note the plural in v. 26) is about three times this height, that is, 75–90 cm (= 30–36 in.), hip level or higher. Steps, however, are prohibited, since they might force an individual to raise his

7. Although slaughter on the altar did not occur in prescribed or reported cultic, blood offerings elsewhere in the Bible, the story of the "Binding of Isaac" has Abraham build an altar, stack a pyre, truss Isaac, and deposit him on top of the wood where he intended to slaughter him (Gen 22:9–10). On the strength of the presupposition of this story that such a procedure is normal, we must allow that slaughter on the altar itself was perceived as acceptable with certain types of offerings under certain circumstances.

8. See Baruch Levine, *In the Presence of the Lord* (Leiden, 1974) 22–27; Jacob Milgrom, "A Prolegomenon to Leviticus 17:11," *JBL* 90 (1977) 273–74.

9. Oral communication by J. Zias of the Israel Dept. of Antiquities (January, 1987). This is about the height of contemporary citizens from the more rural sections of lesser developed Mediterranean basin countries and of many Europeans who reached maturity prior to World War I.

knees so high that he might expose himself.[10] The implication of the prohibition is that a graduated ramp was permitted.

Furthermore, since the law assumes that people had to mount the altar in the course of its use, for whatever reasons, it also assumes that whatever had to be done could not be done by someone standing on the ground, either because the altar was too high or because its surface dimensions were so large that its central section could not be reached.

Assuming an altar of a minimal height of 75 cm and an average adult male whose maximum height was 155 cm, a man's reach into the altar would have extended approximately 100 cm (= 40 in.). Round altars must therefore have had minimal diameters of about 200 cm, while square altars had sides of no less than 200 cm. On the basis of these dimensions, it can be determined that such altars had a surface area ranging between 3.1–4.0 square meters. This area would suffice for the burning of the dismembered carcass of a large herd animal and more than suffice for the carcass of a smaller flock animal.

The volume of earth or stones involved in constructing an altar of the minimal dimensions presented above ranges between 2.3 cubic meters for the round one and 3.0 cubic meters for the square. Allowing realistically for sloping sides with an angle of 45 degrees could increase the volume of material by about 30 percent, raising the volume to 3.1 and 3.9 cubic meters respectively. This volume could be carried by a pickup truck, though the weight might strain the springs. Naaman the Aramean estimated that two mules could haul such a load from Israel to Damascus (2 Kgs 5:17). Once the materials were assembled, the time involved in heaping up and arranging the altar would have been minimal, a few hours of work at most. Higher altars or altars with larger surface areas would have required more material and more work.

Although the text lacks specific dimensions, Num 23:1–3, 14, 29–30 presupposes that an individual, Balak, could build seven altars, each sufficient for the offering of a bull and a ram. The nature of the sacrifices indicates that the surface area involved was similar to what we have described above for the field altar, although the height may have been lower. The story indicates that Balak alone did the building since they were intended for his ultimate benefit. He wanted to be able to determine the outcome of future events by having Balaam curse Israel. Balaam, to Balak's consternation, was simply prognosticating a good future for Israel. If we assume, along with most commentators, that each set of altars was constructed in a single day, this story supports our estimation of the time involved in building an altar.

---

10. The implication is that steps functioned like boosts and were widely spaced. Another implication is that the offerer is imagined as wearing either a short kilt that might slide up his thigh or a robe that could flap open. Were he wearing an undergarment, this would not be an issue. Furthermore, the law is not concerned with what might be seen by somebody lying flat on top of the altar or what might be exposed to the altar, since the ramp solution does not remove the problem of nakedness from that perspective.

Even though they did not match Balak's prodigious activity, Abraham is described as constructing an altar large enough to sacrifice Isaac in part of a day (Gen 22:9) and Moses as building an altar and setting up twelve *maṣṣēbôt* 'standing stones' in a single morning (Exod 24:4). The significance of these narratives lies in their apparent verisimilitude to both the author-narrator and to his Iron Age audience.

No shape is specified by the altar law. Nevertheless, the dumping of earth to the minimum implicit height would tend to produce a structure more round and oval than square. Undressed stones, of course, could have been manipulated to produce a squarish structure with rounded corners. Even if constructed primarily of stones, dumped earth would have been used to fill in the spaces, to eliminate the movement of the stones, to bond the structure together, and to provide a flat, working surface on top.

The demands of the law in Exodus, when both its explicit and implicit elements are considered, were that animal offerings be made on an unmistakably artificial surface raised significantly above its natural environs, so much so that one might need two or three steps to ascend its top, and that this platform be made of earth materials. Why?

Insistence that the altar be a platform raised noticeably above the immediately adjacent terrain is to be explained by the fact that YHWH was perceived essentially as a celestial deity overseeing and managing affairs from on high. This hypothesis is consistent with all the imagery and metaphors associated with him. And, what is even more important, no imagery makes him a denizen of subterranean habitations. The hypothesis is supported further by the initial words of the divine speech that introduces the altar laws: "You saw that I spoke with you from the heavens" (Exod 20:22). Offerings on the ground or close to the ground would have been considered dedicated to chthonic deities.

A consideration of classical practice is instructive: (1) animals dedicated to Olympians were slaughtered face up; to chthonic deities, face down; (2) to Olympians on an altar built up of stones; to chthonic deities, on the ground or on a slightly raised mound into which a pit that drained into the ground was excavated; (3) Olympians were worshiped in temples built on high spots or on a three-stepped base; chthonic deities were sometimes worshiped in caves or dark recesses; (4) Olympian sacrifices were made in daylight and the meat to be consumed had to be apportioned before sundown; sacrifices to chthonic deities were made at night, and if meat was consumed, it had to be consumed before sunrise.[11] Sacrifices were offered to chthonic deities in the classical world

---

11. Walter Burkert, *Greek Religion* (Cambridge, 1985) 199–200; S. M. Grintz, " 'Do Not Eat on the Blood': Reconsideration in Setting and Dating of the Priestly Code," *Annual of the Swedish Theological Institute* 8 (1970–71) 88; W. A. Jayne, *The Healing Gods of Ancient Civilizations* (New York, 1962) 215; C. G. Yavis, *Greek Altars: Origins and Typology including the Menoan-Mycenean Offeratory Apparatuses* (St. Louis, 1949) 55.

not so much for worship as for placation, the aversion of evil, and for obtaining dreams or other signs for divinatory purposes.[12]

An instance of such slaughter is described as having taken place after a compulsory fast and a long day's victorious battle in 1 Sam 14:32. The tired warriors took herd and flock animals from the booty, "and they slaughtered on the ground (or in the direction of the ground, *ʾārṣâ*), and the people ate on the blood."[13] This is represented as occurring at night (vv. 24, 34, 36) and being stopped by Saul who himself slaughtered the remaining animals on a large rock (v. 33).[14]

Lev 19:26 prohibits 'eating on the blood', that is, eating meat without draining off the blood, listing it with two forms of prognostication, divination and soothsaying, indicating thereby that it too was a cultic practice associated with future-telling.[15] The preposition *ʿal*, in the expression *lʾ tʾklw ʿl hdm*, means 'along with, in addition to, next to' (compare Exod 12:8, 9 [with the verb √ʾkl 'to eat']; Lev 2:2; 3:4; Num 9:11; Deut 16:3). Since there is no prohibition against eating meat per se in biblical legislation, the disqualifying, operative element in this apodictic law must have been the blood. Accordingly, this verse sheds light on the above-mentioned story.

It is likely that the type of slaughter and ingestion practiced by the Israelites was associated with divination, since Saul, after setting things right, constructed an altar and sought an oracle from a priest concerning a planned military campaign (1 Sam 14:35–37).[16] In other words, the storyteller por-

---

12. Grintz, "Do Not Eat," 88.

13. If the *waw* of *wyʾkl* in v. 32b is a *waw explicativum*, *wyʾkl* could be translated 'that is to say, the people ate on the blood'. In other words, slaughtering on the ground is termed 'eating on the blood'. Although theoretically possible, other biblical data presented below support treating these as two distinct, yet related cultic acts. See the following note.

14. Saul's act is presented as being a reaction to the report that the people were 'eating on the blood'. His response is to have the slaughter take place on the rock, off the ground, indicating that the narrative presupposes that if not slaughtered on the ground itself the consumption of blood had no value, a point with which Lev 19:26 disagrees. There is nothing in this story to suggest that it reflects the solution to slaughtering on the ground proposed in Leviticus 17, on which see below. However, the accusation 'you have committed treason' *bgdtm*, in v. 33, does indicate that from Saul's (and from the narrator's) perspective, an accepted norm was indeed violated.

15. Grintz, "Do Not Eat," 78–80, citing discussions from late antiquity through modern times. The exact nuance of Hebrew √nḥš is unclear. It is best explained as being a byform of the root lḥš 'to whisper incantations', but the actual practice may have involved reading the lees from wine in a cup (compare Gen 44:5, 15); Hebrew √ʿnn may have to do with reading omens from the shape of clouds, *ʿănānîm*.

16. The functional parallel between Saul's altar and those constructed by Balak are obvious and need no elaboration. The ritual parallels between what is described in 1 Samuel 14 and classical chthonic worship are similarly obvious. A connection between them may be proposed, but the direction of borrowing or influence is unclear, since recent research suggests that many elements in Greek religion that emerged in the Late Bronze and Iron Ages were influenced by West Mediterranean practices. One important link may have been the Philistines, whose Aegean origins and cultural affinities are even more obvious now than before, thanks to the excavations at Ashkelon

trayed Saul as obtaining legitimately what the Israelites attempted to achieve illegitimately. This was apparently not an isolated case of such practice, a fact that may be ascertained from a study of other laws in Leviticus.

Lev 17:1–9 prescribes that all animals sacrificed by Israelites and resident aliens be brought and presented first at the YHWH sanctuary and dedicated to YHWH. The core prescription is stated in vv. 3–4 and repeated paraphrastically in vv. 8–9, which function as a resumptive repetition, a *Wiederaufnahme*. The intervening verses are an expansion of the core.

2. Speak to Aaron and to his sons and to all the Israelites and say to them: "This is what the Lord commanded:

3. Any Israelite who slaughters an ox or a sheep or a goat in the camp, or who slaughters outside the camp

4. and does not bring it to the entrance of the Tent of Meeting to present it as an offering to YHWH, before the dwelling of YHWH, bloodguilt will be imputed to that man. He spilled blood; and that man will be cut off from the midst of his people;

5. In order that the Israelites bring their sacrifices, the ones that they sacrifice on the face of the field, that they bring them to YHWH at the entrance of the Tent of Meeting, to the priest; and they will slaughter them as sacrifices of well-being for YHWH.

6. And the priest will dash the blood on the altar of YHWH at the entrance of the Tent of Meeting and turn the fat into smoke, a pleasing odor to YHWH.

7. And they will no longer slaughter their sacrifices to the *śĕ^cîrîm* after whom they go astray.
This shall be an eternal law for them, for their generations."

8. And say to them: "Any Israelite or stranger who lives among them, who offers a burnt offering or sacrifice

9. and does not bring it to the entrance of the Tent of Meeting to make it for YHWH, that person will be cut off from his people." [17]

Although vv. 3–4a appear grudgingly to allow slaughtering in areas outside of the sanctuary, their real intent, as stated explicitly in vv. 4b–5, is to

---

(Lawrence Stager, "When Canaanites and Philistines Ruled Ashkelon," *BAR* 17/2 [1991] 31–42). Their rapid acculturization to Eastern Semitic civilization appears to be well established through finds at Ekron and inscriptions from Philistine and related Sea-People sites along the Phoenician coast, indicating that they spoke a West-Semitic dialect and that they worshiped deities with Canaanite names.

17. P's prohibitions against the consumption of blood are found also in Lev 3:17, 7:26–27, where they are somewhat out of place. There, the situation presupposes the presentation of all sacrifices to priests at shrines, and it is difficult to see what an offerer could have gained by not following the shrine's normal practices. Only Leviticus 17 provides the background against which the origin of these prohibitions may be understood.

restrict all sacrifice to the sanctuary premises by likening improper disposal of the blood and meat to the spilling of blood and by making slaughter away from it inconvenient, if not physically impossible. This was in order to eliminate the *zĕbāḥîm* that Israelites offered "on the face of the field," that is, on the surface of the ground (cf. *ᶜal pĕnê* in Gen 1:2, 6:1).

Distinguishing between the actual prescriptions in this section (vv. 3–4, 6, 7b–9) and the stated reasons motivating their enactment (vv. 5, 7a) reveals a connected series of outlawed cultic practices: Israelites slaughtered "on the face of the field" (v. 5) to unnamed deities other than Y<small>HWH</small>;[18] they did something with the blood, which the legislator insists should be thrown on the altar, and with the burned parts, which should be burned on the altar (v. 6); they dedicated their *zebaḥ*-offerings to what the legislator termed *śĕᶜîrim* (v. 7a), goat deities of the wilderness (compare Isa 13:21, 34:14).[19] This term may have been the way the Yahwistic priest who drafted this legislation referred vaguely to deities whose conventional emblem was a goat but whose reality he could not fathom.

The natural continuation of the core prescription is vv. 10–12, which prohibit the ingestion of blood (v. 10), claiming that the proper use of blood is on the Y<small>HWH</small> altar (v. 11; compare with v. 6) and implying that Israelites were eating the blood to gain what putting the blood on the altar would achieve for them. Lev 19:26, discussed above, clarifies the objective of ingesting blood.[20]

Verses 13–14 deal with the blood of hunted animals, prescribing that their blood be poured on the ground and covered up (v. 13) and demanding, in an expansive paraphrase of v. 10, that their blood also not be consumed (v. 14). The implication of v. 13 is that, while the spilling of a hunted animal's blood directly on the ground is permissible, leaving it uncovered is not. Blotting up the blood in a covering of soil is seen as eliminating any taint of its ritual purpose; conversely, leaving it to drain into the ground slowly is perceived as a sacral act. The two cultic practices outlawed in Lev 17:10–14 then, are consuming blood and letting it pour out onto the ground.[21] Since no other deities are even

18. This last point is implicit but clear. Contrast the emphasis on the divine name in v. 5 ("they will bring them to Y<small>HWH</small>" and "they will offer . . . to Y<small>HWH</small>") and in v. 6 ("altar of Y<small>HWH</small>" and "sweet smell for Y<small>HWH</small>"), with the nonmention of any deity's name in the offerings on the "face of the field" found in v. 7. The legislation here does not perceive of these rituals as being misguided or illegitimate rituals dedicated to Y<small>HWH</small>.

19. For a possible connection between this and the scapegoat ritual of Leviticus 16, as viewed through astute medieval commentators, filtered through anthropological studies and contemporary philological intuition, see Baruch Levine, *Leviticus* (JPS Torah Commentary; Philadelphia, 1989) 114, 250–53.

20. A detailed literary study of this chapter is available in Baruch Schwartz, *Selected Chapters of the Holiness Code: A Literary Study of Leviticus 17–19* (Ph.D. diss., Hebrew University, Jerusalem, 1987). I have not had an opportunity to study this dissertation but thank Avigdor Hurowitz for bringing it to my attention.

21. The net effect of the legislation in Leviticus 17 was that the killing of all consumable animals fell into one of two categories: sacred slaughter or hunted animal. All of the former had to

hinted at here, we cannot assume that these verses reflect the concern of Lev 17:1–9 with the *śĕ^cîrîm*. Only ritual acts that P recognized or intuitively perceived to be symbolically inappropriate for Yhwh were proscribed.

These practices that the legislation of Leviticus 17 declared illegitimate thus correspond, in part, with the objectives and ritual pattern of chthonic worship in classical sources.[22] The story in 1 Samuel 14 presupposes a similar complex of objectives and rituals, although the narrative there does not indicate that they may have been directed to a foreign deity.

It is interesting to note that the first presentation of the core law in Lev 17:3 is stated in terms of the animals to be presented, "ox or lamb or goat," while in the paraphrastic *Wiederaufnahme* of 17:8, the law is stated in terms of the types of sacrifices, the *^cōlâ* and *zebaḥ*. Although the altar law in Exod 20:24 does not use the identical vocabulary, it refers to the same sacrifices and to the same animals.

Read in the context of the complex of ritual acts underlying Leviticus 17 and 1 Samuel 14, the altar laws of Exodus 20 provided a solution to the perceived problem—sacrifice that could appear to be dedicated to a deity other than Yhwh or to Yhwh as a chthonic figure—which was different from the problem proposed in Leviticus. In Exodus, the solution was to have individual Israelites use a type of altar that would clearly mark the celestial nature of the intended recipient, Yhwh; in Leviticus, the solution was to compel individual Israelites to have a sanctioned clergy officiate on their behalf at a sanctioned altar.

If we assume that P accepted the altar legislation of Exodus, then the difference between the two may be explained as follows: for Exodus, a proper altar was a sufficient condition for legitimate sacrifice, whereas for P, it was a necessary, but insufficient one. The mythopoeic thinking underlying the Exodus laws cannot be reconstructed with any certainty, but we can say minimally that it involved the concept of deity. The thinking underlying Leviticus 17 is more patent. For the author of this chapter, what was at stake was more than a concept of deity; it was a theory of sacrifice. Here P asserted a theory in which

---

the animal finally fell. For the Israelite who wished to consume meat without having to make his way to a Yhwh altar where priests could manipulate the blood but who wished to adhere to the regulations of this chapter, one possibility existed. He could kill an animal at home, but the animal would have to be considered a "hunted animal," and its carcass would fall under the category of *nĕbēlâ* 'an animal that fell or died by itself' (v. 15). As a consequence, those who consumed it would need to undergo ritual cleansing prior to entering a sanctuary (v. 16). The legislation of Deut 12:15–16, 20–24 allows nonsacrificial slaughter for consumption without recourse to the possible subterfuge perceived above, warning only that the blood be "poured out on the ground like water" (vv. 16, 24), without a proviso that it be covered over, and that it not be consumed (vv. 16, 23). Possibly, the "pouring out like water," which is to say, scattering it over a distance so that it not puddle and sink down, was intended to achieve the same effect as covering it over, getting rid of the blood in an unmistakably nonsacral way.

22. See Milgrom, "A Prolegomenon to Leviticus 17:11," 154–56.

the objectives of sacrifice were purification, expiation, and communion. These were readily obtainable for Israelites when (the power inherent in) sanctioned blood was presented properly by priests at a legitimate altar. P polemicized against a theory of which one objective was communion with noncelestial beings or with a noncelestial aspect of Yhwh, and another was self-empowerment to divine the future through the ingestion of blood (compare Ps 16:4, Zech 9:7).[23]

23. One of Balaam's oracles in Num 23:24 likens Israel to a lion that eats its prey and drinks its blood. The significance of the metaphor is clear from the preceding v. 23, where Israel is described as lacking divination or augury because "Jacob is told at once / Yea Israel, what God has planned" (njpsv). In other words, divine revelation is akin to eating meat like a lion (on the ground) and 'drinking' *yišteh* blood (which lions do not do).

Part 2

The Torah

THE OTHER EGYPT: A WELCOME ASYLUM

Mordechai Cogan

OPPROBRIUM BEST DESCRIBES THE VIEW of Egypt and the Egyptians presented by most biblical writers. And with good cause. Tradition taught that Israel had been enslaved in Egypt for 430 long years (Exod 12:40) under conditions that threatened its very existence. Though Jacob and his sons were once the welcome guests of the Pharaoh who had appointed Joseph his second-in-command (Gen 47:1–12), their descendants were enslaved by a later ruler and forced to labor on state projects (Exod 1:11–14), a fate similar to the fate of captives brought back from Canaan by victorious Egyptian armies.[1] The memory of life in this "slave house" (Exod 20:2, Deut 5:6; the Hebrew *bêt ʿăvādîm* is usually rendered 'house of bondage') left its indelible mark on all strata of biblical law; the deprivations of Egyptian bondage repeatedly served as the base for enjoining upon the Israelites the humane treatment of the poor and the stranger who might be found among them: "Do not oppress the stranger, for you have experienced the life of a stranger, for you were strangers in the land of Egypt" (Exod 23:9; also see Exod 22:20; Lev 19:33–34; Deut 15:15; 24:18, 22).

Besides being described as an "iron furnace" (Deut 4:20, an allusion to the conditions under which the enslaved were kept: all who entered the blast furnace that was Egypt were broken down; see also 1 Kgs 8:51; Jer 11:4), Egypt was remembered as a country of disease and sickness (compare Deut 7:15, 28:27), a place one would certainly have been glad to forget or, at best, to leave to history. This feeling was so strong that the Law of the Monarchy (Deut 17:14–20) restricted any future Israelite king from developing extensive trade

Author's note: This article is dedicated to Prof. Menahem Haran in appreciation and thanks for his timely and sober advice approximately thirty years ago, which set the course of my scholarly training and vocation.

1. E.g., see the booty list of Thutmose III from Megiddo and northern Canaan, in J. A. Wilson (trans.), "Egyptian Historical Texts," *ANET*, 237; and the text of Seti I referring to prisoners taken in the same general area (ibid., 254).

in horses, "so as not to return the people to Egypt . . . for the Lord enjoined you: 'You shall not return by this way again'" (v. 16).[2] Only under one circumstance would Israel go down to Egypt again and its history, so to speak, be reversed: as punishment for breach of the Lord's covenant the Israelites would be transported to Egypt by ships, there to be put on the block and sold as slaves (Deut 28:68).[3]

It is, then, with some surprise that one reads of the freed Israelites, who, when faced with the hardships of the desert trek through the Sinai to Canaan,[4] longed for Egypt's plenitude: "We remember the fish we ate in Egypt for free, the cucumbers and the melons, and the leeks and the onions and the garlic . . ." (Num 11:5–6; see also Exod 16:3). Indeed, Egypt could be described as a veritable "Garden of the Lord" (Gen 13:10), a "vegetable garden," thanks to the Nile River's dependable flow (as compared to the land of Canaan, which was dependent on the Lord's beneficence from the skies; cf. Deut 11:10–12). And who would have believed that many Israelites, when faced with hard fighting in order to enter Canaan, would cry out: "If we had only died in the land of Egypt, or died in this desert. . . . Our wives and little ones will become prey. Wouldn't it be better for us to return to Egypt?" (Num 14:2–4). The Egyptian enemy who was routed at the Sea of Reeds, whom they were "never to see again" (Exod 14:13), no longer looked threatening!

Such reactions are intelligible, coming as they did from a generation of emancipated slaves, who, at the first signs of adversity were ready to abandon their newly-won freedom. But from a later period, an even more striking *volte-face* in the biblical attitude toward Egypt is found in the law concerning nations who were to be excluded from the Israelite community in Deut 23:4–9:

> An Ammonite or a Moabite shall not be admitted into the congregation of the Lord; even in the tenth generation, he shall not be admitted into the congregation of the Lord, because they did not meet you with bread and water on the way when you left Egypt, and because they hired Balaam son of Beor, from Pethor in Aram-naharaim, to curse you. . . . You shall never concern yourself with their welfare or benefit as long as you live. Do not abhor an Edomite, for he is your brother; do not abhor an Egyptian, for you were a stranger in his land. Children born to them in the third generation may be admitted to the congregation of the Lord.

2. This restriction echoes King Solomon's business dealings with Egypt, in particular his extensive trade in horses and chariots (1 Kgs 10:28–29). In the late eighth century, Egyptian military aid to Judah was still centered around its horse and chariot components (Isa 30:1–5, 31:1).

3. The unusual detail of reaching Egypt by ships is clarified in a reference to the manner in which Ashurbanipal's army reached Egypt; they sailed to the Delta from the Phoenician coast (A. L. Oppenheim [trans.], "Babylonian and Assyrian Historical Texts," *ANET*, 294). Judean soldiers enlisted in this campaign may have "gone down" to Egypt in this manner.

4. The contradictory Pentateuchal traditions on the route through the Sinai Peninsula were unraveled by M. Haran, "From Egypt to Canaan," *Ages and Institutions in the Bible* (Tel Aviv, 1972) 37–76 [Heb.].

An Ammonite or a Moabite was not to be admitted, even after ten generations, into the congregation of the Lord,[5] that is to say, could not participate in the public and cultic life of the Israelite community;[6] an Edomite or an Egyptian could do so after only three generations. These restrictions are grounded in historical terms: Ammon and Moab are shut out forever, because they did not come to Israel's aid as it moved through the desert on the way to the Promised Land;[7] Edom because of its familial ties with Israel, and Egypt because of its hospitality towards Israel, could gain entry in a relatively short time. Of special note is the use of the formulation "for you were a stranger in his land"; in all other contexts the hardships of the Egyptian enslavement are recalled.

Israel's judgment of its neighbors was often read backwards into tales told about the forefathers of the neighbors. For example, the Canaanites were held to be a lewd and shameless folk and always had been so, as attested by the behavior of their eponymous ancestor in the days of Noah (Gen 9:20–25); the Moabites and the Ammonites were an incestuous lot by birthright (Gen 19:30–38). In other cases, events associated with the Egyptian sojourn and the desert wanderings were seen as affecting subsequent relations between peoples. Thus the unprovoked attack by the Amalekites upon Israel's faint and weary as they left Egypt earned them the harshest of sentences: "Wipe out the memory of Amalek from under heaven. Do not forget!" (Deut 25:17–19; cf. Exod 17:8–16, 1 Sam 15:2). And the predominant recollection of Egypt, forged by sad experience, was as an enslaver of the nation—in all references except the one under discussion, Deut 23:8–9, "Do not abhor an Egyptian, for you were a stranger in his land. . . ."[8]

Because it is "common sense" that Israelites "might loathe" the Egyptians (Malbim at Deut 23:8), traditional Jewish commentators felt obliged to explain this veering from the normal path. Rashi proffered: "'Do not abhor an Egyptian' completely, even though they threw their male (children) into the Nile. What is the rationale? They had served as your refuge during the hour of need . . . ," that is, during the seven-year famine that struck Canaan in the days

---

5. On the late term *qāhāl* 'congregation', which replaced the earlier term *ʿēdâ*, see J. Milgrom, "Priestly Terminology and the Political and Social Structure of Pre-monarchic Israel," *JQR* 69 (1978) 65–81.

6. On this sense of *lābōʾ biqĕhal*, see Lam 1:10; and see Z. Falk, "Those Excluded from the Congregation," *Beth Mikra* 62 (1975) 342–51 [Heb.]. On the forced interpretation of the phrase in rabbinic sources as a prohibition of marriage with these groups, see S. J. D. Cohen, "From the Bible to the Talmud: The Prohibition of Intermarriage," *HAR* 7 (1983) 23–39.

7. There is some question about the historical reference made here, for one tradition did tell of the Moabites' selling food to Israel (Deut 2:29) and of Israel's avoiding contact with the Ammonites (2:19; cf. Num 21:24). See the attempt of Nachmanides at Deut 23:5 to reconcile the passages.

8. Later still, Ezra included Egyptians in the list of nations forbidden in marriage to Israel (Ezra 9:1-2); but his rigorous amplification of Deut 7:1–4 was contrary to Deut 23:8–9. See M. Fishbane, *Biblical Interpretation in Ancient Israel* (Oxford, 1985) 114–29, for a discussion of Ezra's exegetical method and motives.

of Joseph. Ibn Ezra pointed out other evidence of Egyptian kindnesses: ". . . the honor they bestowed upon our father (Jacob) and that they installed one of our own (i.e., Joseph) as a captain and governor. . . ." Modern commentators, as well, remark that there is here a noted "preferential treatment of the Edomites and Egyptians," "certainly very old," but are hard put to explain its background.[9] The issue simply stated is this: How did the mistreated stranger come to think kind thoughts about his former master? A look at the political and social relationships between Israelites and Egyptians over the centuries clarifies the point further.

Relations between the two peoples are only randomly reported in the Bible; what emerges is a picture of ups and downs. If, as seems likely, Israelites were to be found in Canaan as early as the end of the thirteenth century B.C.E., there must have been some contact between them and the Egyptians who maintained their hold over the land for the early part of the next century. The oft-cited "Israel Stele" of Pharaoh Merneptah claims an Egyptian victory over a group of Israelites in Canaan.[10] Yet the biblical writers, true to their historiographic point of view, avoid all mention of contact with Egypt or the Egyptians after the encounter at the Sea of Reeds (Exodus 14–15), in fulfillment, it seems, of the Lord's promise that "the Egyptians whom you see today you will never see again" (Exod 14:13)—until the reign of Solomon, that is. Solomon's marriage with a Pharaoh's daughter (1 Kgs 3:1), an unheard-of deed from the Egyptian perspective,[11] together with a dowry of territory in the

9. See, e.g., G. von Rad, *Deuteronomy* (OTL; Philadelphia, 1966) 145–46; also cf. idem, *Studies in Deuteronomy* (SBT 9; London, 1953) 20; a stylistic consideration, that is, a perceived apodictic formulation, seems to be the criterion for his setting an early date for the law. See also K. Galling ("Das Gemeindegesetz in Deuteronomium 23," *Festschrift Alfred Bertholet* [Tübingen, 1950] 176–91), who thinks that the tensions between Egypt and Israel during most of the monarchic period would not have given birth to the pro-Egyptian stance of Deuteronomy 23; this argument supports his taking the "law of entry" to be early. Galling's position is adopted by A. D. H. Mayes, *Deuteronomy* (NCB; Grand Rapids, 1979). The early moderns noted the uniqueness of the attitude toward Egypt in this passage but do not seem to have been greatly bothered by it; see for example, A. Bertholet, *Deuteronomium* (HKAT; Freiburg, 1899) 72. More recently, P. A. H. de Boer ("Egypt in the Old Testament: Some Aspects of an Ambivalent Assessment," *OTS* 27 [*Selected Studies in Old Testament Exegesis*; ed. C. van Duin; 1991] 152–67) suggested an early date for the positive assessment of Egypt in Deuteronomy 23. To do so, he transferred the Exodus credo and its image of Egyptian bondage into a late post-prophetic slot. But the assessment of O. Eissfeldt ("The Exodus and Wanderings," *CAH* 2/2A.321) is to be preferred: "It is quite inconceivable that a people could have obstinately preserved traditions about a dishonourable bondage of its ancestors in a foreign land, and passed them on from generation to generation, unless it had actually passed through such an experience."

10. See J. A. Wilson (trans.), "Egyptian Hymns and Prayers," *ANET*, 378.

11. That Egyptians did not marry their daughters to foreigners is clearly documented for much of the second millennium B.C.E.; see the discussion of A. Malamat, "Aspects of the Foreign Policies of David and Solomon," *JNES* 22 (1963) 1–17. As for the days of Solomon, K. A. Kitchen (*The Third Intermediate Period in Egypt* [*1100–650 B.C.*] [Warminster, 1973] 280–83) has found evidence of some openness. Regarding Gezer, Pharaoh Siamun seems to have been unable

vicinity of Gezer (1 Kgs 9:16), trade with Egyptian merchants (1 Kgs 10:28–29), and even the exchange of wise men between the courts (1 Kgs 5:9–11), made for rich and varied contact between Jerusalem and Tanis. This flowering quickly wilted with the attack of Pharaoh Shishak on Jerusalem, five years after Solomon's death, which cost Judah dearly (1 Kgs 14:25–26).

At this point our sources fall silent and only resume after approximately two centuries, toward the close of the eighth century. For the next one hundred years, Egypt is seen as supporting attempts by the kingdoms of Israel and Judah, and the Philistine cities on the Mediterranean coast, to rebel against Assyria (2 Kgs 17:4, 18:21). Such help was Egypt's way of maintaining a foothold in its onetime province in Canaan and also served to keep the imperial danger at arm's length. For a very brief interval, between the debacle at Megiddo in 609 B.C.E. and the arrival of the Babylonians in 604 (2 Kgs 23:29–35), Egypt was even master over Judah. This short-lived Egyptian domination did not prevent the last generation of Judeans from seeking Egyptian support in their revolt against Nebuchadnezzar (Jer 37:5) or from fleeing to the land of the Nile in advance of Babylonian reprisals against Judah (Jer 42:7–43:7).

Assessing this historical record, it is difficult to single out a particular age that might have provided the *Sitz im Leben* for the softening of Israel's attitude toward its former oppressor, as reflected in Deuteronomy 23. It is noteworthy that the Deuteronomistic editor of Kings seems to have found Solomon's taking an Egyptian princess of more than passing interest. This marriage is referred to no less than five times in the account of Solomon's reign (see 1 Kgs 3:1; 7:8; 9:16, 24; 11:1). But only in 1 Kgs 11:1 is there a hint of any criticism of the king's act. The other passages, likely based on contemporary sources, refer to the marriage with equanimity. In those early times, union with Egyptians was not viewed with disfavor (evidence the accepted tradition that the tribes of Ephraim and Manasseh were of Egyptian descent, through Asenath, the wife of Joseph, daughter of Potiphera, priest of On, Gen 41:50).[12] Thus, it does not seem likely that Deut 23:8–9, which allowed the entry of Egyptians into the Israelite community, albeit only in the third generation, was formulated with Solomon in mind.[13]

---

to hold onto the gains he won in northern Philistia and so compromised with the stronger Solomon by transferring this strategic border town to Judah (A. Malamat, "Aspects of Foreign Policies," 13, 16–17).

12. Refer to the tradition recorded in 1 Chr 4:18 regarding the marriage of an early descendant of Judah with Bithiah, a Pharaoh's daughter. See the discussion on the Chronicler's interest in presenting this and other examples of foreign marriages, by S. Japhet, *The Ideology of the Book of Chronicles and Its Place in Biblical Thought* (Frankfurt am Main, 1989) 346–51.

13. That is, unless one adopts Milgrom's suggestion ("Priestly Terminology," 173–74) to take Deut 23:4-9 as a Northern Israelite polemic against Judah and the Davidides. Even the regulations concerning the Ammonites and Moabites (Deut 23:4–7) seem to be of another age; note, for

But though the historical circumstances that might have motivated the unique approach *vis-à-vis* Egypt expressed in Deut 23:8–9 seem irretrievable, its humanitarian perspective is manifest. And, in point of fact, the change of attitude expressed in the rationale "for you were a stranger in his land" is in harmony with the overall moral and humanistic character of the Deuteronomic law code,[14] which has deep roots in wisdom literature.[15] The sundry rationales for exclusion or admission of nations into Israel's community in Deut 23:4–9 echo wisdom teachings. Thus, the Ammonites and Moabites were to remain outside the community because they treated Israel worse than enemies by not extending them food and drink (cf. Prov 25:21). Not so the Edomites, who as kin to Israel,[16] were worthy of regard, and likewise the Egyptians, who had opened their door to Jacob and his family in their hour of need (cf. Job 31:32).

The slave experience colored and indeed even dominated most biblical perceptions of Egypt; yet, at the same time, other realities apparently required Israel to move beyond stereotypes. In reconciling the two communities, a human face was put on Israel's Egyptian experience: the slave house became a welcome asylum.[17]

---

example, that Rehoboam, who succeeded Solomon to the throne, was the son of Naamah of Ammon (1 Kgs 14:21). The violation by Solomon of Deut 23:8-9 did give cause for some raised eyebrows among the traditional commentators: see, for example, Gershonides at 1 Kgs 3:1. Qimḥi (ad loc.) adopts the stance that the Egyptian princess had converted to Judaism, thus legitimizing the marriage. This was the rabbinic position respecting Deut 23:8-9: male Egyptians were restricted until the third generation; females who converted were accepted immediately; see *m. Yebam.* 8:3; *b. Yebam.* 76a–b. The Greek traditions also reflect an exegetical concern "over whether Solomon actually married Pharaoh's daughter or not, and if he did, exactly when"; see D. W. Gooding, *Relics of Ancient Exegesis* (SOTSMS 4; Cambridge, 1976) 107 and 66–73.

14. This is especially manifest in legislation that has parallels in the other Pentateuchal codes; for example, the Sabbath law in Deut 5:12-15 enjoins rest on the seventh day upon all who live within Israel, even to servants: "Remember that you were a slave in Egypt" (contrast the Creation rationale of the Sabbath in Exod 20:11).

15. This has been convincingly demonstrated by M. Weinfeld, *Deuteronomy and the Deuteronomic School* (Oxford, 1972) 244–81, 282–97; repr. Winona Lake, Ind., 1992.

16. Israel's kinship with Edom is the rationale for the respect shown Edomite territory in Deut 2:2–8. Both Deuteronomic passages are at variance with the dominant hatred expressed toward Edom in other biblical passages; see my comments on this ambivalent attitude towards the Edomites, in *Obadiah* (Mikra LeYisrael; Tel Aviv, 1992) 8–12.

17. The dominant image of Egypt as slave master was kept alive in the yearly re-enactment of the freeing of Israel from Egyptian enslavement in the Passover Seder ritual; but even there, the image was not static. In a particularly unique midrash quoted in the Hagaddah, the cruelty of Pharaoh is mitigated, with the Syrians made out to be more calculating than the Egyptians: "Pharaoh decreed (the destruction of) only the males, while Laban (the Aramean) sought to uproot them all." As understood by L. Finkelstein ("The Oldest Midrash: Pre-rabbinic Ideals and Teachings in the Passover Haggadah," *HTR* 31 [1938] 299-304), the background of this homily may have been the rivalry between political parties in second-century B.C.E. Palestine, torn between loyalties to Ptolemaic Egypt and Seleucid Syria.

THE COMPOSITION OF THE BOOK OF EXODUS:
REFLECTIONS ON THE THESES OF ERHARD BLUM

Graham I. Davies

AFTER NEARLY TWENTY YEARS of debate about the composition of the Pentateuch, in which sometimes the only consensus has seemed to be that the old four-source theory will no longer do, there are signs that substantial agreement has now been reached around the following theses:

1. The earliest major composition extending from the patriarchs to the beginning of the settlement in Canaan (or, more modestly, the earliest one we can now detect) was produced in a Deuteronomistic environment, not earlier than the seventh century B.C.E., and probably not before the sixth century B.C.E.[1]

2. The Priestly (P) material comprises a supplement (or series of supplements) to this composition, not an independent account of Israel's origins that once existed separately from it and was secondarily combined with it by a redactor.

The two books by Erhard Blum,[2] together with several shorter publications by him, represent the most thorough and rigorous presentation of these theses to have appeared. Blum was a pupil of R. Rendtorff, but even in his

Author's note: It is both an honor and a pleasure for me to offer to a scholar and a friend who has opened my eyes to many aspects of the book of Exodus these reflections on a recent book by another scholar whose work promises to make some lasting contributions to our understanding of the heart of the Torah.

1. It does not greatly matter for this purpose whether one uses or rejects the specific title "Deuteronomistic" for this composition; for its rejection see, e.g., J. Van Seters, "The So-Called Deuteronomistic Redaction of the Pentateuch," *Congress Volume, Leuven, 1989* (VTSup 43; Leiden, 1991) 58–77; idem, *Prologue to History: The Yahwist as Historian in Genesis* (Louisville, 1992) 227–45.

2. Erhard Blum, *Die Komposition der Vätergeschichte* (WMANT 57; Neukirchen-Vluyn, 1985); idem, *Studien zur Komposition des Pentateuch* (BZAW 189; Berlin, 1990).

earlier book he went well beyond his teacher in both the depth and the breadth of his investigations. With his treatment of Exodus and the following books in *Studien zur Komposition des Pentateuch* he leads the field, and this volume is an obvious representative to choose for an evaluation of these fresh departures in Pentateuchal study.[3]

Blum's arguments and conclusions about the composition of Exodus may be summarized as follows. He begins by examining the present text of Exodus 1–14(15) for signs of its coherence as a composition. He finds this in several groups of texts, which all turn out to be linked to Exod 3:1–4:18. Thus, as has often been noted, Exod 14:31 echoes 4:31, which is itself the sequel to key sections of chaps. 3 and 4, especially 3:16–17 and 4:1–9. Exod 11:1–3 and 12:25–36 are linked to 3:21–22, and 11:1–3 is also bound to 5:22–6:1, which in turn echoes 3:8, 10, 19b. The "commemoration" passages in 12:21(25)–27 and 13:3–16 pick up 10:2 and beyond it features of chaps. 3 and 4 (cf. 4:29, 31 with 12:21, 27; and 3:8, 17 with 13:5). These texts Blum describes as a "composition-layer" (*Kompositionsschicht*), that integrates the whole narrative into a coherent theological scheme.[4] He then argues that Exod 3:1–4:18, the account of Moses' meeting with Yahweh at the mountain of God, is an insertion into the surrounding context (because of the Reuel/Jethro inconsistency at the beginning and the lack of continuity between 4:18 and 4:19 at the end, whereas 4:19 connects straightforwardly with 2:15–23aα). In this he follows a proposal of B. D. Eerdmans[5] that has generally been rejected because of a preference for a source-critical solution to these difficulties. But according to Blum, there is no need for the traditional source-critical explanations in 3:1–4:18; it is to be seen as a unified composition, except for 4:13–16, a passage that contradicts 3:18 and must have been added later.[6] Similarly he proposes that Exod 11:1–3, which has often been seen as an extract from the E source because it breaks up the connection between 10:29 and 11:5, should be regarded as a fresh composition added to the existing context at this point.[7]

The setting for the addition to the Exodus narrative of the "composition-layer" of which these passages form a part is deduced from the parallel between Exod 14:13, 31 and 1 Sam 12:16–18. Taking the latter as a purely Deuteronomistic composition (with Noth), Blum argues that Exodus 14 must also be Deuteronomistic. He claims further support for such an origin for the layer

3. Although Blum's treatment of the theologies of the Pentateuch and of the political context of the final stages of its formation are not discussed in detail here, they are also of the highest importance; cf. ibid., 188–207, 287–382.

4. Ibid., 17–19.

5. B. D. Eerdmans, *Alttestamentliche Studien, III: Das Buch Exodus* (Giessen, 1910) 18.

6. That 3:1–4:17 (sic) is a literary unity is a conclusion that has been reached independently by G. Fischer, *Jahwe unser Gott: Sprache, Aufbau und Erzähltechnik in der Berufung des Mose (Ex 3–4)* (OBO 91; Freiburg/Göttingen, 1989).

7. E. Blum, *Studien*, 20–30.

as a whole from other studies, including that of H. H. Schmid on Exodus 3–4 and his own earlier work on Genesis.[8] He does not, however, hold that the whole layer was created *de novo* by the Deuteronomistic writer(s); he finds evidence of an earlier basis for it in 5:22–6:1, 12:21–27, parts of chap. 14, and even in 3:1–4:18.[9] It is important to note the implications of this, to which Blum returns at a later point.[10]

Next Blum turns to the Sinai pericope, Exodus 19–24, 32–34.[11] His method is similar: to look first for the coherence of the pre-Priestly composition and then to attempt a diachronic account of its contours. By this means he identifies further parts of the "composition-layer." He begins with chaps. 32–34, where he attributes to this layer 32:7–14 and, rather awkwardly, the whole of chapters 33–34 (apart from 34:11–26, which he has already [pp. 69–70] argued was composed as a secondary expansion of the reference to the "ten words"). The inclusion of most of these two chapters enables him to make further connections with a series of passages outside the Sinai pericope: Numbers 11–12; Deut 31:14–15, 23; 34:10 (–12). From these it is possible to strengthen the links (already given by the narrative correspondence between Exod 24:12ff. and 32:1ff.) with chaps. 19–24, for both Joshua, Moses' *mĕšārēt* (24:13), and the seventy elders (24:9; cf. v. 14) occur outside the Sinai passages. Within chaps. 19–24 themselves, a "string" of related passages is comprised by 19:3b–8, 20:22, and 24:3–8, the last being also part of an older narrative framework of the Book of the Covenant. In its present narrative context, it is bracketed by 24:9–11, whose wider links have already been noted, and the closely related vv. 1–2. Both 19:3b-8 and 20:22 are held to show affinities with the Deuteronomistic History.[12]

In his next section, Blum widens his sights to take in the remainder of this "Deuteronomistic Composition" (KD), adding some further important characteristics (including the connection in Exod 1:6, 8), defining the limits of the work (it begins at Gen 12:1–3), and extending the analysis into the wilderness narratives before and after Sinai. In Exodus 15–18 he finds no trace of KD in 15:22–27 and 16:1–36, agreeing with other scholars that the editing here is post-Priestly. On the other hand, both pericopae in Exodus 17 (1b–7, 8–16) have features reminiscent of KD elsewhere (cf. Num 14:22; Exod 24:13–14). Exodus 18 has often seemed isolated to earlier scholars, and Blum finds no

---

8. H. H. Schmid, *Der sogenannte Jahwist: Beobachtungen und Fragen zur Pentateuchforschung* (Zürich, 1976) 19–43; E. Blum, *Die Komposition,* 255–56; cf. Exod 3:16–17 with Gen 50:24.

9. Blum, *Studien,* 30–42.

10. Ibid., 208–18.

11. Ibid., 45–99. For an earlier treatment of the Sinai pericope, cf. idem, "Israël à la montagne de Dieu: Remarques sur Ex 19–24, 32–34 et sur le contexte littéraire et historique de sa composition," *Le Pentateuque en question* (ed. A. de Pury; Geneva, 1989) 271–95.

12. Blum, *Studien,* 98. In his book, Blum appears to reckon with identifiable pre-Deuteronomistic material in the Sinai pericope to a greater extent than he had earlier done; cf. idem., "Israël à la montagne de Dieu," in *Le Pentateuque en question* (ed. A. de Pury; Geneva, 1989) 298.

place for it in K<small>D</small>. He does, however, note several correspondences to Exodus 3–4 that he attributes to the fact that in each case the underlying narrative derives from one and the same "continuous Moses-tradition" (*zusammenhängende Moseüberlieferung*).[13] The introduction of Exodus 18 into the Exodus narrative belongs, according to him, to a later stage of composition than K<small>D</small>, because of some aspects of the language and concerns of the chapter. Blum concludes his examination of K<small>D</small> by reverting to some more general issues.[14] He dates K<small>D</small> in the Persian Period, seeing it as presupposing the Deuteronomistic History but too distinct from it in style to be part of the same original work.[15] It is by no means a mere prelude to that work, but is rather a "history of origins" that defines Israel's being and constitution. By its extensive development of the promise to the patriarchs and in other ways, it reassures the people that exile is not the end and that both enjoyment of the promised land and a permanent covenant relationship with her God remain Israel's destiny. Prophecy is subordinated to Moses, and the incorporation of the Book of the Covenant further emphasizes the importance of law. Finally Blum considers the relation of K<small>D</small> to earlier traditions.[16] He sees no basis in Exodus–Numbers for tracing earlier shorter works (like the patriarchal cycle already identified by Rendtorff), except for the story of Balaam; the rest of the underlying material seems to him most likely to derive from a continuous earlier narrative that we may call "A", perhaps a *vita Mosis*. This narrative is apparently to be distinguished from another version of the Exodus-Moses tradition (which we may call "B"), which provided K<small>D</small> with some of the material in Exodus 3–4 and a late redactor with the basis of Exodus 18. Such indicators of date as there are suggest to Blum that "A" cannot be earlier than the late monarchy period, after the fall of the Northern Kingdom, though it will itself have been based on still earlier traditions, as the allusions in the book of Hosea show.[17] Elsewhere Blum has allowed that Deuteronomy itself must in some places have known this same underlying tradition.[18]

When he comes to deal with the "Priestly Composition" (K<small>P</small>), Blum finds no need to spend time on the identification of Priestly texts; he can, for the most part, accept what is generally agreed. He does, however, insist that Num 27:12–23 is the end of K<small>P</small>—what follows is a series of later supplements—and he appears to regard the Holiness Code as an integral part of the work.[19] Where he parts company with most earlier critics, though in agreement with several recent ones, is in his denial that P was ever a separate source-document. The

---

13. Blum, *Studien*, 156.
14. Ibid., 164–207.
15. Ibid., 164 n. 276.
16. Ibid., 208–18.
17. Ibid., 218 n. 144.
18. Ibid., 176–88.
19. Cf. ibid., 324–28.

reasons for this are set out in detail.[20] For our present purpose we shall chiefly limit ourselves to the sections that deal with the book of Exodus, though it should be recognized that Blum, like some others, believes that it is particularly in Genesis that the character of P as a 'reworking' (*Bearbeitung*) of older material is evident. Following Cross and Rendtorff, he holds that in Genesis 12–50 the verses ascribed to P are insufficient to form an independent narrative, the genealogies serve to divide up and "frame" the older material, and the longer theological passages both show a knowledge of their older parallels and were evidently designed to stand alongside the latter to correct them.

In Exodus, too, Blum finds that there are verses belonging to P that must be seen as "reworkings" of the older material: 15:19, 20:11, the references to Aaron, Nadab, and Abihu in 24:1 and 9, 31:18, 32:15–16, 34:29–35. Moreover, with Cross, Blum finds it inconceivable that so important a figure in the story as Moses would be brought onto the stage, as it were, in 6:2 without any prior introduction.[21] Later on, further Priestly passages are mentioned as having had no independent existence: 11:9–10; 12:1–20, 28, 37a(?), 40–42, 43–51; 13:1, 20.[22] At the same time Blum is well aware (more so than most recent advocates of this view of P) that there are features of P, particularly in Genesis 1–11, Exodus, and Numbers, which contrast very sharply with the older material. His detailed discussions of some longer passages are designed to show how, even where this is the case, a "supplementary" view of P can be maintained, though only with a much subtler view of P's intentions than is usually presumed. This may be seen in his preference for "compositional" over "redactional" as a description for P's activity, a change that has come in since the publication of his earlier work on the patriarchal narratives.

The first longer passage to be discussed is Exodus 6(–7). Blum acknowledges the tensions that exist between the account here of God's promises to Israel and the older materials in Genesis and in Exodus 3, but he also draws attention to several ways in which Exod 6:2–7:13 is closely related to the surrounding (non-Priestly) context, particularly in Exodus 5. Here he builds on earlier work.[23] This encourages him to investigate the "synchronic-compositional meaning" of the combination of the earlier and later accounts. In relation to the most glaring and most famous of the contradictions between them, the knowledge (or rather, lack of it) of the name Yahweh by the patriarchs, he proposes that Exod 6:3 gives a "binding interpretation" of the older material: the latter was not altered, but the reader or hearer was intended to make the necessary corrections mentally. Blum also endeavors to accommodate the

---

20. Ibid., 229–85.
21. Ibid., 230–31.
22. Ibid., 260 n. 116.
23. See M. Greenberg, "The Thematic Unity of Exodus III–XI," *Proceedings of the Fourth World Congress of Jewish Studies* (2 vols.; Jerusalem 1967) 1.151–54; J. L. Ska, "Les plaies d'Egypte dans le récit sacerdotal (Pg)," *Bib* 60 (1979) 23–35.

observations of the older source-criticism in another way, as can be seen in his explanation of the fact that the Kᴘ sections in Exodus 1–7 (1:1–5, 7; 2:23–25; 6:2–7:13) may be read as a coherent narrative, which suggests at first sight that they may once have existed separately.[24] He presumes that the Priestly tradents had an eye on the continuity of the material that they were composing themselves, as well as on the coherence of the total text that developed from its combination with the older narratives.

Secondly Blum considers the plague-cycle in Exod 7:17–11:10. His analysis of the text is similar to that of Noth: 7:19–22*; 8:1–3, 11–15; 9:8–12, 22–23, 35; 10:12–13a, 21–23, 27; and 11:9–10 belong to Kᴘ; the remainder to the older Kᴅ (Noth's J). A notable feature of this analysis that distinguishes it from many earlier ones is the attribution of the brief, "non-J" portions of the plagues of hail, locusts and darkness (9:22–23, 35; 10:12–13a, 21–23, 27) to P rather than to E. This is important for Blum's argument about the nature of the Priestly material, for (as he observes) the P elements at the beginning of the plague-cycle have several aspects that seem *prima facie* once again to point to an independent P source. They provide a coherent account of the successive plagues, with a recurring motif of the contest with the Egyptian magicians, and in the case of the gnats (כנים) and the boils (שחין), which are entirely from P, we seem to be dealing with parallels to the purely Kᴅ (J) narratives about flies (ערב) and pestilence (דבר). However, against such a view of P, Blum asserts that what he (following Noth) takes to be P sections of the hail and locust plagues "lean on" the older material, that is, they cannot have existed apart from it; by themselves they would give a weak and anticlimactic continuation of the P narrative. Moreover, the Priestly texts refer to the plague of the first-born but do not describe it (Exod 11:4–8 and 12:29–33 are from Kᴅ/J), so here too they presuppose the older narrative; and the "knowledge" theme in 7:5 (P) is not picked up in the P sections of the plague-cycle, but only in Kᴅ passages there (7:17 etc.) and in the P account of the crossing of the sea (14:4, 18). The conclusion is that here too P is not a "source" as traditionally supposed. Yet the evidence noted above from the beginning of the cycle shows that Kᴘ must have worked with an existing tradition that was already partially shaped ("partiell vorgeprägte [priesterliche] Überlieferung"), a view that was anticipated by J. Reindl.[25] Thus, Blum concludes, Kᴘ is neither simply a source nor a purely creative redactional layer:[26] it is a "composition" that from time to time incorporates other pre-existing material as well as Kᴅ. This, we may note, is almost identical to the view of R. E. Friedman.[27]

24. Blum, *Studien*, 240.

25. J. Reindl, "Der Finger Gottes und die Macht der Götter: Ein problem des ägyptischen Diasporajudentums und sein literarischer Niederschlag," *Dienst der Vermittlung* (Erfurter theologische Studien 37; Leipzig, 1977) 49–60.

26. Blum's subtitle for the section beginning on p. 228: "Weder 'Quelle' noch 'Redaktion.'"

27. R. E. Friedman, *The Exile and Biblical Narrative* (HSM 22; Chico, Calif., 1981).

A further indication of Blum's readiness to take seriously earlier critical work and as a result to develop a rather complex picture of KP may be seen in his treatment of the "sea" narrative in Exodus 14. He begins by acknowledging that the now traditional analysis into (at least) two parallel sources is firmly founded, with Exod 14:21 providing an impressive point of departure. The relative completeness of the account preserved in the Priestly sections[28] proves that it once existed independently, and Blum acutely notes that this is confirmed by the fact that in the existing text v. 15a has nothing to refer back to (for example, "Moses cried to the Lord"). There can therefore be no question here of KP mentally conceiving his narrative as a unified whole before inserting it into KD. (A similar concession is subsequently made with regard to Numbers 16.) However, according to Blum, to attribute the independent account to a Priestly source is impossible, because the preceding Priestly sections do not come from such a document.[29] In fact, as he says, much of the so-called P account in Exodus 14 is not distinctively "Priestly," to such an extent that several earlier scholars attributed all or most of it to, for example, E. This suggests that KP derived this account from elsewhere, in the same way as his opening contributions to the plague-cycle (though not necessarily from the same "source"). Be that as it may, Blum notes again how carefully the combination of the two strands of the narrative has been made, so that their distinctive emphases on the deliverance of Israel and the demonstration of divine power against the Egyptians both stand out and indeed find a new integration in the appearance of the divine glory in the cloud (vv. 17–20).

It is perhaps useful to try to locate Blum among the varied voices of recent discussion about the Pentateuch. One reviewer has proposed the epithet "a new Wellhausen."[30] There is some justification for this. Blum, like Wellhausen, has sifted the conclusions of a creative period of Pentateuchal research and produced a synthesis of his own that may prove to be the foundation for a new, more settled period of textual study. Though it lacks the elegance of the *Prolegomena*, Blum's book shows a similar willingness to take into account all of the biblical evidence and put it in its place. Blum may even be described as a moderate, a mediating figure, in the current debate. Yet there are two major ways in which he differs from Wellhausen (apart from the conclusions!). One is (perhaps intentionally) evident in the book's final sentence, where Blum characterizes his study as a "(necessary) prolegomena to an appropriate exposition of the final form (that is, of the text)."[31] This is something very different from Wellhausen's revised title "Prolegomena to the History of Israel." We

28. According to Blum, these are vv. 1–4, 8–9, 10bβ, 15–18, 21aα*, 22–23, 26, 27aα*, 28–29.

29. Blum, *Studien*, 260; in n. 116 he lists the following passages as "unselbständig": 11:9–10; 12:1–20, 28, 37a(?), 40–42, 43–51; 13:1, 20.

30. J. L. Ska, *Bib* 72 (1991) 253–63; cf. R. N. Whybray, *The Making of the Pentateuch* (JSOTSup 53; Sheffield, 1987) 215.

31. Blum, *Studien*, 382.

may recall that Blum was a pupil of Rendtorff, but it is to the Rendtorff of the *Introduction to the Old Testament* and the yet-to-appear *Old Testament Theology*, with their canonical perspectives, that he is closest.[32] Secondly, the anti-Jewish polemic of Wellhausen's work is noticeably lacking, and Blum gives a sympathetic interpretation of the theologies of Kᴅ and Kᴘ, in which law and ritual can find a prominent place without discomfort.

The two "theses" that were identified at the beginning of this essay as comprising the heart of the newer accounts of Pentateuchal origins are logically independent. It is possible to hold to one without holding to the other, and some scholars have done so. For example F. M. Cross maintained that P was never an independent source-document,[33] but he has apparently not questioned the attribution of the older material to J and E (or at least to JE). On the other hand J. Blenkinsopp believes in an extensive "Deuteronomic-Deuteronomistic" editing of the Pentateuch, but equally clearly holds that P once existed as a separate source.[34] I propose to discuss Blum's arguments for the application of the two "theses" to Exodus separately and in reverse order. On a methodological level, it has been a long-standing principle that analysis should begin with the text that we possess, that is, the completed Pentateuch, and work backwards from there. Moreover, on this occasion I shall comment only briefly on Blum's conclusions about Kᴅ, leaving fuller evaluation for another study. I intend to focus attention here exclusively on Blum's own arguments and observations, rather than attempt a discussion of all those who have written in a similar vein about the Pentateuch; and I shall, for the sake of brevity, make only passing reference to the analysis of the other books of the Pentateuch, although I fully recognize that in the end a theory of Pentateuchal origins must be judged on its ability to provide an acceptable account of all the data.

First, then, let me deal with the Priestly Composition as "neither a source nor a redaction." Blum's discussion identifies three types of evidence in Exodus that, taken together, point to this conclusion: (1) passages, mostly quite short, that are customarily attributed to P and do not form a continuous narrative; (2) the fact that, when Moses is first mentioned in a P passage (6:2), he immediately takes center stage, without any introduction, which makes best sense if the P narrative was simply a supplement to the older stories about Moses in Exodus 1–5; (3) the character of three larger sections of P, which Blum investigates in more detail as "Fallbeispiele" (Exodus 6, 7–11, and 14). We will consider these points in turn, along with (4) the Sinai pericope (especially Exo-

---

32. For an indication of Rendtorff's approach to Old Testament Theology see R. Rendtorff, *Kanon und Theologie* (Neukirchen-Vluyn, 1991).

33. F. M. Cross, *Canaanite Myth and Hebrew Epic: Essays in the History of the Religion of Israel* (Cambridge, Mass., 1973) 293–325, esp. 324–25.

34. J. Blenkinsopp, *The Pentateuch: An Introduction to the First Five Books of the Bible* (New York, 1992) 78, 118–19, 143–44, 160, etc.

dus 25–31, 35–40), which Blum does not discuss in the analytical part of his study of K$_P$.[35]

(1) These passages are not listed by Blum in a single place, but the following list may be built up from what he says in various contexts: Exod 1:1–5, 7, 13–14; 2:23ab-25; 11:9–10; 12:1–20, 28, 37a(?), 40–42, 43–51; 13:1, 20; 15:19; 20:11; the references to Aaron, Nadab, and Abihu in 24:1 and 9; 31:18; 32:15–16; 34:29–35. The surprising thing, despite Blum's confident assertion to the contrary, is that most of these passages do form, with the longer passages discussed elsewhere, a coherent connected narrative. Blum himself acknowledges this for the verses from chaps. 1–2, if they are taken by themselves, but he finds the sudden introduction of Moses in 6:2 an obstacle to tracing any further coherence in the series (on this see below, p. 80). In general the connections are self-evident and do not need detailed discussion.[36] For the exceptional cases where verses or parts of verses are closely attached to non-P material an adequate explanation is generally available. Thus 12:37a and 13:20 should not be attributed to P at all. They form part of a long "itinerary-chain" extending through Exodus and Numbers (cf. Exod 15:22, 27; 16:1; 17:1abα; 19:2), which is probably composed of extracts taken from Num 33:1–49. Although it sometimes uses vocabulary typical of P, it can scarcely be part of P, since it exhibits doublets with P at Exod 19:1 and Num 10:12 (the latter being paralleled by 10:33, 11:35, and 12:16). The affinities of the "chain" in the later section of the wilderness narrative seem rather to be with the Deuteronomistic conception of the route.[37] Exod 15:19, on the other hand, certainly repeats what has already been said in much the same terms in 14:23, 28–29 (P) and so is scarcely likely to have formed part of an independent P narrative; its role is to integrate the "Song of Moses" into its present secondary context. Yet it is by no means clear that it could form part of a Priestly composition of the kind envisaged by Blum either. The "seam" on the other side of the Song of Moses (15:1aα) has its closest parallel in Num 21:7a, where there is no sign of Priestly authorship, and in both passages the insertion of the poems into their present contexts may have been made at a very late stage of the composition of the Pentateuch. The references to Aaron, Nadab, and Abihu in Exod 24:1, 9 at first sight do look likely to derive from P, as it is only in P that Nadab and Abihu are otherwise mentioned. Yet it would be very strange if the two sons of Aaron

---

35. These chapters do, however, receive detailed consideration in the treatment of the theology of K$_P$; see Blum, *Studien*, 293–312.

36. Even Exod 11:9–10, which Blum takes to refer to the preceding encounter between Moses and Pharaoh (11:4–8), makes good sense as a general conclusion to the Priestly plague-cycle on its own: לא ישמע may be iterative, not future, in meaning. While Blum says that these verses pick up the formulae of both sets of (what are for him) P plague-units, that is, I, II, III, VI (לא שמע) and VII, VIII, IX (לא שלח), it should be noted that in fact the שלח-formula in v. 10 corresponds verbatim only with those used in the prologue to the plague-cycle (6:11, 7:2).

37. For details, see G. I. Davies, "The Wilderness Itineraries and the Composition of the Pentateuch," *VT* 33 (1983) 1–13.

who according to P were disobedient (Lev 10:1–2) were privileged with this theophany experience, and not the two who became the ancestors of the legitimate priesthood, Eleazar and Ithamar.[38] It follows that the names Aaron, Nadab, and Abihu in Exod 24:1, 9 probably belong to the underlying older narrative (like the elusive Hur of Exod 17:12 and 24:14), as most commentators have thought. The only text in the list that poses a serious problem for the view that P was an independent source is Exod 20:11, which reinforces the Sabbath commandment in the Decalogue by a reference to the Priestly creation account in Gen 1:1–2.4a. P's concern for the observance of the sabbath is also evident in Exod 16:23–27, 31:12–17, and 35:2–3. It is certainly possible to attribute the insertion of Exod 20:11 to a comprehensive Priestly composition as envisaged by Blum, but it is also possible that it was added by a redactor who combined an independent P narrative with the older material.[39] The choice can only be made when other arguments have been considered.

A feature on which Blum lays frequent emphasis in relation to many of these passages is that they fit well in their present context, among the older material, and so would appear to have been composed with that context in mind. The smoothness of fit, however, need not be so surprising, since the subject-matter was the same and P may well have known the older version. It is just as likely that the smooth fit is due to such factors (and the work of a careful redactor) as that the Priestly author was composing these passages specifically to insert them into their present contexts.

(2) The "sudden" introduction of Moses into Exod 6:2 can be dealt with briefly. There is, first of all, no evidence that this was felt to be a problem in antiquity, as the contents and position of the passage that Blum cites to show this indicate that it was included chiefly to "introduce" Aaron.[40] Moses, on the other hand, needed no introduction: by the time of the Priestly writer at least his place in the story could be assumed to be well known, as it is also by the authors of Deuteronomy (cf. Deut 1:1, 4:44, and 5:1 for the various "beginnings" of that work).[41]

(3) With the three longer passages we come to evidence that Blum is able only with great difficulty to accommodate to his thesis. These passages, as he recognizes, exhibit two of the criteria that have played a central role in traditional source-criticism: contradiction and duplication of the parallel non-Priestly material. In his attempt to do justice to this situation while maintaining

---

38. The addition of אלעזר ואיתמר in the Samaritan text is no doubt due to sensitivity to this point. 4QpaleoExod[m] evidently had the same readings as the Samaritan here: see J. E. Sanderson, *An Exodus Scroll from Qumran: 4QpaleoExod[m] and the Samaritan Tradition* (HSS 30; Atlanta, 1986) 212–14.

39. J. A. Emerton has pointed out to me that the wording is not identical to Gen 2:2–3, which may favor the view that a different writer (that is, a redactor) was responsible for Exod 20:11.

40. Exod 6:14–25; E. Blum, *Studien*, 231.

41. Note also that Hosea is able to refer to Moses without even naming him (12:14).

his view of P as a supplementer of the older tradition, Blum makes some interesting new proposals about P's material and his method of composition, but their validity needs careful evaluation. First, he proposes that Exod 6:3 could have been designed to stand in the same narrative as the passages in Genesis that indicate familiarity with the name Yahweh on the part of the patriarchs (for example, Gen 28:13), because by means of Exod 6:3, "the whole preceding presentation, including its recalcitrant, 'unharmonized' components, is given a binding interpretation (*verbindlich interpretiert wird*); it appears, as it were, between brackets and with a new definition as a result of the Priestly 'key' (*Schlüssel*)."[42] It seems to me very doubtful whether such a strategy could have succeeded or have been expected to succeed by the Priestly author, especially when the "key" follows the texts that have to be so "interpreted." The combination of the new Priestly passages with the older material could not but serve to blur the important distinctions that the Priestly author wanted to make.[43] Secondly, to account for the coherence of the Priestly account at the beginning of Exodus, which forms a briefer but quite viable parallel to the older version, Blum argues that the Priestly author highlighted his own contribution to the tradition in the process of composition and that even perhaps "the compositional texts were not immediately written into the main text [namely, the older narrative] but were first *conceived* 'for themselves' (*für sich*) (of course with knowledge of the tradition that was to be reworked)."[44] If we consider the extent of the Priestly materials involved, not just in Exodus but also elsewhere in the Pentateuch, it is very difficult to believe that the Priestly author was able to do this entirely in his head, and a separate written composition becomes almost inevitable. Once this is granted, the considerations urged above against Blum's explanation of the contradiction with much of Genesis surely make it most probable that this separate written composition was not from the outset designed for combination with the older material but was intended to replace it as the standard written account of Israel's origins.

In the cases of the plague-cycle and the account of the sea-crossing, Blum acknowledges that his Priestly author was working with an already existing narrative: only so can he account for the extent of the Priestly material and its duplication of features of the older narrative.[45] This also fits much better the older source-critical view that a continuous Priestly version of the story existed first independently and then was interwoven with the older material. Apart from wider considerations, however, which clearly play a part in Blum's evaluation of the Exodus evidence, there are three features of these texts that

---

42. Blum, *Studien*, 235.

43. This has already been seen by R. W. L. Moberly (*The Old Testament of the Old Testament: Patriarchal Narratives and Mosaic Yahwism* [Minneapolis, 1992] 42 n.12), who also refutes older "harmonizing" explanations of Exod 6:3.

44. Blum, *Studien*, 241–42.

45. Ibid., 242–62.

seem to him to rule out such an explanation. These are (1) the fact that the "non-J" sections of plagues VII–IX, which, like Noth, he attributes to P, "lean on" the "J" material and so could not have existed independently; (2) the fact that the Priestly sections of Exodus 14 refer to Moses' rod (cf. v. 16), while the "proto-P"[46] sections of the plague-cycle (those in plagues I, II, III, and VI) speak of Aaron's rod;[47] and (3) the fact that the Priestly introduction to the plague-cycle (7:1–5) introduces a theme, the Egyptians' future recognition of Yahweh (7:5), which does not appear in the Priestly plague-stories, but only in the ones from KD. None of these features, however, provides a very secure basis for argument. In regard to (1) it must be noted that in a number of ways these passages differ from the pattern of the other plague-stories in P, for example, by the fact that Aaron is not involved in them. Blum attributes this to the development of the plot. But it is just as probable that these passages do not belong to P at all but to a layer of the older narrative (whether redactional or from a source need not be decided here). As for (2), Exod 14:16 is the only place in the Priestly section of the chapter (or anywhere in the chapter) where a reference is made to Moses' rod—in vv. 21, 26, and 27 (all P) only his "hand" is mentioned—and here there is an awkward duplication of "rod" and "hand." In fact elsewhere Moses' rod is found in the non-Priestly material. The alternation is particularly clear in Exod 7:14–19, where the older section (verses 15–18) refers to Moses' rod (with v. 15; cf. 4:1–5, not 7:8–13), while the P verse (v. 19) mentions Aaron's rod.[48] This makes it likely that the phrase הרם את מטך in 14:16 derives not from P but from the older narrative with which it was combined by a redactor. Nor is (3) a serious problem. For P Pharaoh is a lost cause: there is never any possibility that he will change his mind (see 7:3) and the recognition theme naturally only reappears in the sea-narrative (14:4, 18).[49] There is then no obstacle here to seeing the Priestly plague-story and the Priestly sea-narrative as parts of a continuous source.[50]

---

46. I use this expression to refer to the earlier plague-narrative that Blum holds was used by the Priestly author when formulating his supplements to the older material.

47. Blum, *Studien*, 261 n. 121.

48. Interestingly two of the disputed passages in Exodus 9–10 mentioned under (1) above make reference to Moses' rod (cf. 9:23, 10:13).

49. It has been argued that in other respects 7:1–5 only makes sense as an introduction to the combined "KD" and P plague-cycles; cf. Ska, "Les plaies d'Egypte"; J. Van Seters, *The Life of Moses: The Yahwist as Historian in Exodus–Numbers* (Louisville, 1994) 105–12. I am not convinced by this reading of the text, however, and I hope to return to it on another occasion.

50. The one link that is missing in the Priestly material in Exodus, it must be acknowledged, is an account of the slaying of the Egyptian firstborn. Exod 12:12 looks forward to it and 13:1–2 in all probability looks back to it. This account would need to include a judgment on the gods of Egypt (see 12:12), which actually prevents us from seeing the older account in 12:29ff. as being what 12:12 looks back to. In fact, by a surprising coincidence, a trace of the original Priestly account of the final plague can be seen in Num 33:3–4, which is (with vv. 38–39) one of the few places where the itinerary has been amplified with extracts from the *complete* Priestly narrative.

(4) A discussion of the Priestly component of Exodus would not be complete without some reference to the Sinai-pericope, which clearly dominates it both in size and in importance. It comprises thirteen complete chapters and a few introductory or transitional verses in Exodus as well as large parts of the two following books, Leviticus and Numbers. This is clearly the climax of the Priestly work, as Blum's theological discussion of it makes very clear.[51] It scarcely needs saying that this great complex is built up without reference to or dependence on the corresponding section in the older narrative. Indeed the fact has often been emphasized that P's provisions are contradictory to features of the older texts, so that once again it becomes very questionable whether P could have been written merely as a supplement to them. The case of the priesthood may serve as an example. According to P it is exclusively Aaron and his descendants who are to be priests in the full sense (Exodus 29; cf. Leviticus 8–10) and the Levites occupy an inferior position. In the older narrative Aaron is an idolater, and the Levites by their zeal for pure religion "ordain themselves for the service of the Lord" (Exod 32:1–6, 21–29).[52] It is surely inconceivable that P could have allowed this chapter to stand in the middle of the tabernacle chapters, in his "holy of holies," as it were.

The climactic role of the Sinai-pericope also helps to explain the fact, which proponents of the "supplementary" view of P have found so puzzling, that the Priestly narrative omits many of the episodes that are described in much detail in the older version(s). In the preliminary parts of its narrative the Priestly Work gives only the essentials, often transforming paradigmatic narratives into brief theological statements or legal provisions. Possibly even the amount of space available on a scroll was a factor in this abbreviation of the older tradition. In some cases omissions may be attributed to Priestly doctrine. In any case the lack of lively narrative material, for the most part, should not be regarded as something extraordinary to which there is no parallel in biblical literature. 1 Chronicles is not so dissimilar.[53]

To summarize my reactions to Blum's second thesis: I conclude that in Exodus there is no evidence that necessitates the view of P as a *Bearbeitung* or "reworking" of an older narrative, and evidence that *prima facie* favors the original composition of P as an independent source can only be accommodated within such a view by means of improbable hypotheses, if indeed it can be accommodated at all. It is perhaps understandable that Blum should have reached a different conclusion after beginning his study of the question in

---

51. Blum, *Studien*, 293–332.

52. The idiom used in 32:29 of the Levites, מלאו ידכם היום ליהוה, is exactly the same as the one used in 29:9 of Aaron and his sons alone.

53. M. Noth, *Überlieferungsgeschichtliche Studien I* (Halle, 1943) 206–11; Noth's observations on P's selection of subject matter are still illuminating, as is his insistence that, far from being a "supplement," the P material was the framework into which extracts from the older narrative were inserted (cf. idem, *Überlieferungsgeschichte des Pentateuch* [Stuttgart, 1948] 11–17).

Genesis. There, especially in the patriarchal narratives, the evidence for P is much smaller and more amenable to a "supplementary" interpretation.[54] But perhaps this is an issue where the more plentiful evidence in Exodus should be the starting point, and the data in Genesis should be understood in the way that makes the best sense of Exodus, rather than vice versa. A final consideration is the question of the date of P. Blum dates P in the Persian Period and relates the integration of older and newer legislation to Persian imperial policy, about which we are now better informed. As an account of the circumstances under which the last major step in the composition of the Pentateuch was taken, this is quite probable, but it is not at all clear that it is the most likely date for the composition of P. Haran has, of course, like some other scholars, argued for a preexilic date for the compilation of P.[55] While I do not accept his arguments as they stand, despite the learning with which they are presented, they do at several points seem to me to make a mid–sixth century date for P more likely than a date in the Persian Period, after the rebuilding of the temple in Jerusalem. The proportion of priests to Levites envisaged by the tithe law is a case in point. Linguistically and theologically, as well, the middle of the sixth century seems the most likely setting for P. This is probably too early for the reworking of a *D-Komposition* of the kind that Blum envisages[56] and not the most likely setting for the compromise that the final major compositional stage of the Pentateuch's formation represents.

As for Blum's first thesis, that of a comprehensive Deuteronomistic composition in Exodus, it is possible here to make only some brief preliminary comments.

(a) The exploration of a series of "strings" of texts in Exodus 1–14, all of them linked to the programmatic text in chaps. 3–4, offers the prospect of a quite new way of investigating the composition of the non-Priestly narrative in this section of the book. Of course it need not be the case that related texts are contemporary in origin, but at the very least Blum's approach sheds fresh light on the dominant themes of this material as a whole and promises a way out of the impasse of previous source-critical debates.

(b) Questions, however, still remain about the relationship(s) of this composition to the Deuteronomistic literature. For example, the formulaic parallel between Exod 14:13, 31 and 1 Sam 12:16–18 may be interpreted in more than

54. This is not to say that such an interpretation of the evidence is correct. For a restatement of the arguments for the original independence of P in Genesis, see J. A. Emerton, "The Priestly Writer in Genesis," *JTS* n.s. 39 (1988) 381–400.

55. See especially M. Haran, *Temples and Temple-Service in Ancient Israel* (Oxford, 1978 repr. Winona Lake, Ind., 1985); compare also the linguistic arguments in A. Hurvitz, *A Linguistic Study of the Relationships between the Priestly Source and the Book of Ezekiel: A New Approach to an Old Problem* (CahRB 20; Paris, 1982).

56. He himself dates KD to the "(early) post-exilic" or Persian Period (Blum, *Studien*, 164 n. 276).

one way; and the presentation of Moses as a prophet was not first introduced by Deuteronomy (cf. Hos 12:14).

(c) Blum is more cautious in this book than he was in his earlier one regarding the stage(s) of the tradition prior to K_D. Nevertheless his tentative conclusions point in most interesting directions. If I understand him correctly, he envisages an older basis to the "call of Moses" in Exodus 3–4 that had a connection with the tradition underlying Exodus 18, and also a *vita Mosis* that presumably provided a more substantial account of the Exodus story. This seems to be evidence of earlier versions of the Moses-story that were perhaps more selective in the episodes which they dealt with than was assumed for the supposedly parallel sources J and E.

(d) When it comes to the Sinai-narrative, Blum makes some perceptive comments, but one has the impression that we have not yet arrived at an altogether satisfactory solution to the difficult problems here. To begin as he does with Exodus 32–34 may prove to be better than starting with chaps. 19–24, but I find it very difficult to believe that Exod 34:11–26 was composed to fill out the reference to the "ten words" in v. 28. Surely everyone would know what the "ten words" were. It remains, in my opinion, most probable that v. 28 was added by a Deuteronomistic redactor to try to bring the Exodus account of the renewed (and therefore still valid) covenant into some conformity with the narrative in Deuteronomy 9–10. The attribution of the whole of the remainder of Exodus 33–34 to K_D and its use to make connections for the "composition strand" to earlier and later parts of the Pentateuch also seem rather imprecise. Much depends, of course, on what is being attempted, a synchronic or a diachronic analysis, but I have the impression that Blum is trying to do both, and for this more precision may be required.

SOME RECENT NON-ARGUMENTS CONCERNING
THE DOCUMENTARY HYPOTHESIS

Richard Elliott Friedman

FOR MORE THAN A CENTURY, the documentary hypothesis has been the basic model for scholars who study the origins of the first books of the Bible. Periodically we hear that the hypothesis is in question, but this is not really true. It remains the dominant model in which we work. For most scholars, it is sufficiently established as to be *assumed* in their research, and generally those who challenge it are really refining rather than attacking it: they question whether individual verses or passages are J or E, they consider the possibility that the works are themselves composite, they raise questions about the way in which the editors handled the sources, and they debate over when each was composed in the biblical world. But there are very few scholars on earth actively working on the problem today who would argue that the Pentateuch was written by any one person, and no other model has displaced the documentary hypothesis or even attracted a substantially large following among those who work in the field.

I refer to scholars who enter into exchange with other scholars through the usual professional channels of major journals, conferences, volumes such as this one, and so forth. In past generations there were scholars in these circles who represented the orthodox Christian and Jewish belief that one man wrote the Torah, but few have defended such a position since Umberto Cassuto in the 1930s (the notable recent exception being R. N. Whybray, whose work deserves a separate treatment).[1]

Still, I do not mean to represent our field as being single-minded on this point. Though the documentary hypothesis is the dominant model, arguments continue to be raised against this picture of several authors and editors. It must be said that frequently these arguments have appeared to be so ill-conceived or

1. R. N. Whybray, *The Making of the Pentateuch* (JSOTSup 53; Sheffield, 1987).

poorly defended that scholars have disdained to respond to them. I have sometimes felt the same way myself. But I would like to make an exception in this volume and refer to some of these ill-conceived arguments for three reasons. First, I think that it is healthy for the field to air these things. Second, I think that there are several things to be learned from this. Third, it strikes me as ironic that such arguments persist at the same time that a scholar such as Menahem Haran is pursuing serious, responsible scholarly inquiry in this area. Professor Haran has for years challenged the old notion in the field that the Priestly portions of the Torah were composed late in the biblical world and has continually argued that these texts were preexilic compositions. In recent years a number of scholars, including myself, have come to offer evidence and argumentation that are consistent with the view that Haran has long defended. These arguments have been linguistic, historical, archaeological, literary, and even architectural (in relation to the tabernacle and the temple). To me it is striking that, while the argument has reached this fairly advanced level of sophistication with regard to the date and identity of the biblical authors, there still appear these relatively simplistic arguments against the simplest form of the hypothesis, arguments that do not come to terms with the weight and complexity of the evidence on the other side.

The first of these arguments is an old one, namely, that no other works were ever composed in the manner that the documentary hypothesis attributes to the Pentateuch. The Torah of Moses, this argument goes, is being pictured as a "crazy patchwork," having a literary history that has no parallel in the ancient Near East or in subsequent ages.

Recently, this argument has been criticized in a collection of studies by Jeffrey Tigay and others in a volume entitled *Empirical Models for Biblical Criticism*.[2] Tigay's own contributions to this volume, in particular, provide a number of cases of demonstrable parallels in works from the ancient Near East. Notably, he reviews the stages of composition of the "Epic of Gilgamesh." These stages are documented, thanks to the existence of copies from several periods, and so the development of the work can be observed. Tigay and his fellow contributors (E. Tov, A. Rofé, Y. Zakovitch, and M. Cogan) also bring examples of conflation of stories in the Qumran scrolls (as in the case of the conflate text of the Decalogue in the *All Souls Deuteronomy Scroll*); in the Septuagint (as in the Bigtan and Teresh episode in the book of Esther); in the Samaritan Pentateuch; in postbiblical literature (as in the *Temple Scroll*); and even in modern works. They show that literary conflation in these texts results in inconsistencies and vocabulary variation like those in the Hebrew Bible. Tigay also includes G. F. Moore's classic study of Tatian's *Diatessaron*, the

---

2. Jeffrey H. Tigay (ed.), *Empirical Models for Biblical Criticism* (Philadelphia, 1985). Tigay refers to C. M. Mead's remark that "no example of such a 'crazy patchwork' can be found in all literature as the one alleged to have been discovered in the Pentateuch." He also quotes similar comments by M. H. Segal and K. A. Kitchen. See ibid., 2–3, for quotations and references.

work that merged the four Gospels of the New Testament in a manner similar to the merging of the four sources J, E, P, and D in the Torah.

Not only do these ancient works involve doublets and conflation of texts in the manner of the Torah, they involve the same editorial techniques. Tigay demonstrated, for example, cases of epanalepsis—also known as resumptive repetition or *Wiederaufnahme*—that is, cases in which an editor inserts material into a text and then resumes the interrupted text by restating the last line before the interruption. This is a well-known phenomenon in the Hebrew Bible as well. Tigay also found that "a comparison of [four different] stages [in the evolution of the "Gilgamesh Epic"] reveals a pattern of decreasing degrees of adaptation of earlier sources and versions." This, too, parallels the development of the Torah, in which the exilic Deuteronomist and the final Redactor can now be shown (in my own research and that of others) to have practiced substantially less adaptation of their sources than the earlier redactor of the J and E sources.[3]

These analyses provide the visible, empirically-documented parallels that the challengers of the documentary hypotheses asked. But the point that I want to make here is that, even before these new analyses came to light, this argument was really no argument at all. A lack of analogies to the Torah's literary history was never an argument against that history's reality. As Tigay put it, "The reluctance of these writers to contemplate the possibility of something unique in Israelite literary history does not commend itself."[4] Indeed it does not. A vast body of evidence led to the identification of distinct source works and layers of editing in the Five Books of Moses. Numerous lines of evidence converged to point in the same direction. This convergence of evidence is what made the hypothesis so compelling a century ago and at the present time. One cannot challenge such a body of evidence with a simple claim that other books were not written that way. The Tigay collection should bring this argument to an end, and it will not be missed. But really it never was an argument anyway.

One significant thing about this argument is that it was of a different type from most previous arguments against the hypothesis. Traditional responses to the hypothesis had been to argue the items of evidence one at a time. Each doublet was interpreted as complimentary rather than repetitious. Each change in the divine names was explained as reflecting different divine aspects. Each contradictory datum was defended as not being contradictory, or ascribed to prophecy, and so on. The modern analysis, meanwhile, explained virtually all of the data with a very few, consistent premises. The item-by-item approach

---

3. R. E. Friedman, "Sacred History and Theology: The Redaction of Torah," *The Creation of Sacred Literature* (ed. R. E. Friedman; Berkeley, 1981) 25–34; idem, "From Egypt to Egypt: Dtr[1] and Dtr[2]," *Traditions in Transformation: Turning Points in Biblical Faith* (Frank Moore Cross Festschrift; ed. Baruch Halpern and Jon Levenson; Winona Lake, Ind., 1981) 167–92.

4. Tigay, *Empirical Models*, 3.

never came to terms with the *convergence* of the evidence. The argument concerning analogous works at least was an argument against the *structure* of the hypothesis rather than a one-for-one series of responses that missed the forest for the trees.

Two other recent arguments have been made that attempted to deal with the hypothesis *in toto* rather than item-by-item. The first of these is based on literary structure. It has been claimed that texts regarded by critical scholars as composite are in fact so structurally unified as to cast doubt on the possibility of combination. One work that makes this claim is *Before Abraham Was*, by Kikawada and Quinn.[5]

The authors deal with the primeval history in Genesis, and they claim: "We offer a persuasive refutation of the documentary analysis of Genesis 1–11."[6] What is this refutation? They refer to analyses of the "Atrahasis Epic" by scholars such as Lambert and Millard. This analysis identifies five components in the structure of Atrahasis: Creation, First Threat, Second Threat, Final Threat, and Resolution. Kikawada then identifies the same five components in Genesis 1–11 and claims that we find "striking parallels" in the five major components and in several subdivisions of these components. The biblical account begins with the Creation, the First Threat is the Adam and Eve event, the Second Threat is Cain and Abel, the Final Threat is the Flood, and the Resolution is the Tower of Babel followed by Abraham's migration. He therefore concludes that "the author of Genesis 1–11 adapts the Atrahasis structure for his own purposes."[7] We might object that Kikawada stretches some of the biblical components here and elsewhere in his book to make them match the Near Eastern parallels. But even if we were to take his judgments as correct and stipulate the presence of an extraordinary parallel to the Atrahasis structure in Genesis 1–11, this would not argue against the fact that the biblical text was composed by combining two separate texts, J and P, into one. This is because Kikawada apparently failed to notice that all of the structural components in question are found in the J source: Creation, Adam and Eve, Cain and Abel, the Flood, the Tower of Babel, and Abraham's migration. P simply adds doublets of the steps that are in J anyway. The similarity of structure to Atrahasis and other ancient epics here sheds no light on the documentary hypothesis at all.

In another structural argument, Kikawada argues that the Noah story has a chiastic structure and that this indicates that it is a "coherent whole" and not a combination of two distinct works. First of all, we have known since Mowinckel that the author of P was following the J account and that the two were

---

5. I. M. Kikawada and A. Quinn, *Before Abraham Was: The Unity of Genesis 1–11* (Nashville, 1985).
6. Ibid., 125.
7. Ibid., 124.

subsequently combined.[8] This is not the least bit inconsistent with the emergence (or better, the preservation) of chiasm in the combined product. Second, Kikawada stretches the text beyond what is reasonable to obtain his chiasms. To make a chiasm, he says that the end of the story (Noah's drunkenness) and the beginning of the story (the sons of gods and human women) are both about procreation. What does drunkenness have to do with procreation? Kikawada says, "The wine was his way to rekindle *diminished sexual drive*."[9] The Hebrew text says that he was drunk בתוך אהלה. The word אהלה is spelled with a *he* mater lectionis, so Kikawada says that it means *her* tent—that is, Noah's *wife's* tent. Kikawada says, "We propose [this interpretation] not because we think we have presented decisive arguments in its favor, but only because it shows how the recognition of chiastic structure can shed light on the most obscure of stories."[10] I fear that the opposite is true. It shows how misleading—to the point of absurdity—it is to impose a false structure on a text, finding a chiasm where it does not exist, in order to argue unified design.

J. A. Emerton has examined five other analyses that sought chiasmus in the flood narrative, each of which had been used to maintain the unity of this narrative against source analysis. He found all of them to be deficient, often in the same areas as the Kikawada and Quinn analysis. Sometimes the chiasms were incorrectly identified, and sometimes the corresponding elements of the chiasms were both to be found within a single source, J or P, and so they presented no challenge to source analysis.[11]

Kikawada and Quinn make other claims about literary artistry as answers to arguments for the documentary hypothesis. Concerning the repetition of events in the story, they say that this is for emphasis. When Noah's family enter the ark twice, Kikawada says, "But could this repetition be for emphasis, as when the psalmist writes, 'The voice of the Lord breaks the cedars, the Lord breaks the cedars of Lebanon' (Ps 29:5)?"[12] This is incredible: comparing people going onto the same ark twice in a prose account of events to a case of poetic parallel. Likewise Kikawada compares the mixing of divine names in Genesis with the mixing of two names for deities in "Atrahasis," "Enuma Elish," and Ugaritic texts. But all of his examples are cases of poetic parallel, though he misleadingly refers to them as "narratives."[13] Concerning the consistent patterning of the names of the deity, Kikawada and Quinn say that Genesis 1–5 "might just have an author with a strong sense of decorum about the use of divine names."[14] Regarding Gen 7:16, a verse that scholars split between P and

8. Sigmund Mowinckel, *Erwägungen zur Pentateuch Quellenfrage* (Trondheim, 1964).
9. Kikawada and Quinn, *Before Abraham Was*, 102.
10. Ibid.
11. J. A. Emerton, "An Examination of Some Attempts to Defend the Unity of the Flood Narrative in Genesis," *VT* 37 (1987) 401–20, and *VT* 38 (1988) 1–21.
12. Kikawada and Quinn, *Before Abraham Was*, 89.
13. Ibid., 91.
14. Ibid., 14.

J, Kikawada and Quinn claim that this is "awkward . . . for the documentary analyst who, Solomon-like, must split it in half," as though they did not know that versification of the Bible was made centuries after the text was completed and has nothing to do with this at all. Concerning the fact that three genealogies in Genesis each have different forms, they explain this as an author's "literary dexterity," an author who "apparently invites us to take delight in his ability to create variety for its own sake." To "take delight" in *genealogies*?! Genealogies are useful, important, and interesting. But I suggest that it is an abuse of literary analysis of the Bible to look at two long, conflicting lists and call the result "brilliant artistry." It is a devaluation of all the *really* brilliant artistry in the Bible.

And, once again, *the most important argument for the documentary hypothesis is the convergence of the many lines of evidence*. Kikawada and Quinn take no account of this. They say that repetitions may be for emphasis, and they say that an author may vary divine names, but they do not come to terms with the fact that the repetitions *line up* with the different divine names, as well as with details, narrative flow, other terminology, and so on. This converging evidence, moreover, extends over a large body of material—that is, through the entire Torah (and some scholars, including Haran and me, would say even further). By treating only a small number of chapters, Kikawada is not really addressing the primary evidence supporting the hypothesis, yet he speaks as though he had struck a major blow against it.

This matter of overstatement leads us to the third recent argument against the documentary hypothesis: a computer study. There was considerable attention in the press when in 1981 a team at the Technion conducted a computer study of the authorship of Genesis. According to reports, this study had shown that the documentary hypothesis was "highly improbable." A news release from the Technion stated that "controversy over the unity of Genesis may once and for all be settled as a result of [this] research." [15] The research of the Technion team, Radday and Shore, and two other researchers was not published until four years later, in Italy. [16] Once it became available, we were able to examine the research to see if it really established what had been claimed. It did not.

As I have said, it was the convergence of many lines of evidence that was so persuasive. Of all the different types of evidence that contributed to this picture, probably the least persuasive was style. Since style is so very difficult to define, and since stylistic idiosyncracies are so difficult to pinpoint, differences of style were rarely, if ever, the most persuasive factor. I do not recall ever hearing any biblical scholar of my acquaintance speak of style as the element of evidence that first persuaded him or her of the accuracy of the

---

15. News release from the Technion, October 28, 1981.
16. Yehuda T. Radday and Haim Shore, *Genesis: An Authorship Study* (Rome, 1985).

documentary hypothesis. Rather, it is generally after one has already been convinced by the convergence of the more concrete types of evidence that one begins to address questions of comparative style. Even then, when such distinctions have been attempted, they have been most general. They often amount to little more than saying that P had an obviously distinctive style from J and E, but that J and E were exceedingly similar to each other. The notable exceptions, the scholars who have dealt with style more extensively, are Sean McEvenue and Meir Paran, though their main interest in style was not as a proof of the hypothesis or as a means of distinguishing between sources. As McEvenue said, "There may result some confirmation of source criticism, but the main value in stylistic study is that the individual text is revealed in its exact shape and colour." [17] As long ago as 1897, Driver pointed out that it was virtually impossible to distinguish J and E from each other on the basis of style. Since then, scholars have been working on the similarity of these two works, seeking to explain why they repeat and contradict each other and use different names for the same persons while writing so similarly in other respects. Possibly one was based on the other or both were based on a common forerunner.

In recent years, remarkable advances have been made, so that we have gone beyond the mere separation of the component works of the biblical books. Now we are actually looking into the world that produced each. We are dealing with questions such as: what was happening in the author's world that made the author tell the story this way and not another way? where did the author live? to what professional group or party did the author belong? whom did he favor? whom did he (or she) oppose? And we are at the point of studying the development of Biblical Hebrew through the stages that these works represent. [18]

Radday and his colleagues, meanwhile, are still questioning whether these works exist, and they do so on the basis of only one kind of evidence, the kind that was never crucial to the discussion anyway: style! Now, to their credit, they reject what is usually meant by "style," and they speak in terms of much more definable, measurable categories. Specifically, they identify 54 characteristics of the way individuals express themselves in writing, and they programmed a computer to count these specific characteristics. Radday calls this "language behavior." I am not sure that this is a better term than "style," but in any case he is trying to put his analysis on more quantifiable grounds than earlier scholarly discussions. [19] This is fine, but the larger point remains, namely

17. McEvenue, "A Comparison of Narrative Styles in the Hagar Story," *Semeia* 3 (1975) 64–77; idem, *The Narrative Style of the Priestly Writer* (Rome, 1971); idem, "The Elohist at Work," *ZAW* 96 (1984) 315–32.

18. R. E. Friedman, *Who Wrote the Bible?* (New York, 1987).

19. Radday explains the relationship between "style" and "language behavior" as he uses the terms in a section entitled "On Style" (*Genesis*, 14–16).

that his analysis was measuring an element of evidence that was not prominent in the discussion anyway. In fact, he made a point of saying that he was
not addressing all the other evidence (contradictions, doublets, and so forth).
He wrote, "the existence of problems, especially of repetitions and contradictions, is not denied in, nor explained by, our investigation. The discipline of
statistics has nothing to contribute to their solution. . . ." [20]

It must be understood, therefore, that this was not a study of the accuracy
of the entire documentary hypothesis. It was a study of "language behavior"
as evidence for the hypothesis. As I have said, the two sources J and E had
been regarded widely by biblical scholars as extremely difficult to separate
from each other on "stylistic" grounds but were separated by means of more
tangible evidence. It had always been easy, however, to separate the third
source, P, from them by its "style," that is, by its blatantly different language.
Radday's results were in agreement with this: J and E were not distinguishable
in "language behavior." P was blatantly distinguishable. Specifically, the probability of relationship between J and E was expressed as 82 percent. The probability of P being thus identified with J or E was expressed as 0.0000000.
Radday's results appeared to be manifestly consistent with standard scholarship and were a striking confirmation of the distinctiveness of P in particular.
How then did he come to be claiming that he had proven that the standard
view was "highly improbable"?

Radday said that the similarity of J and E indicated that they may well
have been written by the same person. But the difference between P and J/E, he
said, did not necessarily indicate that P was written by a different person. He
said that the difference could be accounted for by the fact that P and J/E were
different kinds of literature. He offered the analogy that if a man wrote tele-
phone books and also wrote love letters, the computer analysis of "language
behavior" would, likewise, not recognize the two as being by the same person.

A number of scholars, including me, wondered at this strange depiction of
his results. P tells stories, just as J and E do. In fact, most of P's stories are
about the same people and events as in J and E, including creation, the flood,
Abraham's and Sarah's migration to Canaan, Lot, the Abrahamic covenant, and
more. Why then was Radday picturing P as something as different from J and
E as a phone book is from a love letter? It turned out that he had entered the
wrong texts into his computer.

In a section of his book entitled "Which Documentary Hypothesis?" Radday states that since scholars differ over the assignment of various passages to
J, E, or P, he singled out one version of the source divisions for testing. He
says that he chose a version that was originally proposed by E. Sellin, and he
lists all of his assignments of verses to J, E, or P.[21] What reason does he give

20. Ibid., 190.
21. Ibid., 20.

for choosing this version? Amazingly, he gives no explanation or justification at all.[22]

This was a strange and unfortunate choice. Sellin's is not an identification of the sources that is generally used by scholars working in the field. Radday's chosen version identifies Genesis 22, the sacrifice of Isaac, as J, when this text is generally regarded as a classic example of E. Sellin's version attributes a number of passages that use the name Yahweh to E and P, when usage of this name is supposed to be an obvious sign of J. Sellin attributes a whole section of the flood story to E, whereas E is generally thought not to begin until many chapters later.

Radday then made changes of his own to this set of identifications. Genesis 14, the story of Abraham and the battle of the kings, is generally not regarded as part of any of the three main sourceworks of Genesis. Radday, however, simply decided to call it part of P. Why? In Radday's own words, "We put it, for the sake of convenience and for the lack of any better, into P."[23] For no good reason at all, he was studying the language of an author while including an entire chapter that, according to the hypothesis being tested, was by someone else.

Worse, he excluded the creation story in Genesis 1—probably the most famous passage in P—from the study altogether because, according to Radday, his was a study of prose, and Genesis 1 is poetry. But Genesis 1 is *prose*. It is beautiful, patterned prose, but this fact does not make it legitimate to call it poetry and exclude it from the analysis.

In all, I found errors in 29 of the 50 chapters of Genesis in Radday's source identifications. Most of the errors were serious enough to throw off the results of the analysis. The questionable verses, by my reckoning, total 350, which is about a fourth of the verses in the entire study, yet Radday says that if he were to test any other reckoning of the verses, "it may quite safely be assumed that results would not vary significantly. . . ."[24] Radday and his colleagues had given whole chapters of J to E, and E to J, and then came up with an 82-percent coalescence of J's and E's "language behavior"! What else could we expect? If you give whole chapters of Mark Twain to Herman Melville and Melville to Mark Twain, and then do a study of their "language behavior," Mark Twain and Melville are going to start looking strangely alike.

22. To complicate matters further, Sellin's original treatment, *Einleitung in das Alte Testament*, appeared in 1910 and then was reprinted in seven editions, with changes that Sellin made in each new edition. It went through further changes in two more editions, which L. Rost edited and revised. Radday chose the 1959 edition, edited by Rost, for his study. Again, he gave no reason for choosing this version. Moreover, he commented that this version is similar to a version of the sources that appears in an article by N. Sarna on Genesis in *Encyclopaedia Judaica*, but he gave no reason for this comment. In an earlier article on this study, Radday included a copy of the Sarna identifications rather than the Sellin-Rost identifications.

23. Radday and Shore, *Genesis*, 188.

24. Ibid., 19.

Radday may blame all of this on Sellin or on the disagreements among scholars about the identification of some texts, but that is not a satisfactory response. When you test a hypothesis, you test it in its *best* form and in the light of the most *current* information. You cannot choose an unlikely, incomplete version of the hypothesis. And you certainly cannot be silent about your reasons for choosing that unlikely version over all others.

Still, that is not the largest problem with the Raddy and Shore study. As I said earlier, scholars were aware of a similarity between J and E anyway, so Radday's findings, even had they not been so questionable, were not a challenge to the hypothesis on this point. The more serious problem was with the work known as P. In this case, Radday's comparison of P and J/E to phone books and love letters was still the problem. Simply put, Radday claimed that the P work was understood to be primarily genealogies and lists, while J and E were primarily stories. This, he said, accounted for the dramatic zero-percent likelihood of their being written by the same person.

But that is simply not true. The problem is that Radday's attribution of sources skews P's comparable passages to J and E on the creation (Radday leaves it out completely), the flood, the migration of Abraham, Lot, the birth of Isaac, and Joseph in Egypt. That is, Radday misidentified or simply eliminated a substantial amount of the P story material. To be sure, P has less total narrative in Genesis than J or E does. That appears to be visibly due to the fact that most of a *Priestly* author's interests start in the period when there first begin to be *priests* in the story, in the age of Moses and Aaron. And that begins in Exodus, where P's narrative in fact becomes more developed. But Radday's unusual source identifications took from P much of what narrative it *did* have in Genesis.

Meanwhile, Radday counted the genealogies of the *tôlĕdōt* Book as P, even though this attribution is extremely doubtful in the light of present scholarship. The lists of generations in Genesis 5 and 11 were long associated with P, but Frank Moore Cross argued nearly twenty years ago that these lists and a few other verses in Genesis were originally a separate document called The Book of Generations (*tôlĕdōt*). Cross showed that this was one of the documents that were used as editorial framing devices to connect the various stories into a continuous narrative. The Book of Generations may have been a Priestly archival document, but it should not be counted as actually having been composed by the author of P. Cross's treatment appeared in 1973, and it has been discussed in other works since then,[25] but Radday did not even consider it in a work that appeared in 1985. He was both eliminating much of the P narrative and mistakenly attributing nonnarrative material to P. And then he

---

25. Cross, "The Priestly Houses of Early Israel," *Canaanite Myth and Hebrew Epic: Essays in the History of the Religion of Israel* (Cambridge, Mass., 1973) 195–215. See also R. E. Friedman, *The Exile and Biblical Narrative: The Formation of the Deuteronomic and Priestly Works* (HSM 22; Atlanta, 1981) 77–89.

said that the zero-percent connection that his study showed between P and J/E was because P was not narrative like J and E!

Did it make a difference? Radday noted that one of the results of his computer analysis is that Genesis 5 and 11 "have absolutely nothing in common with other P Narrative samples." [26] But he also observed that, to his surprise, another P genealogical list in Genesis 36 is not like Genesis 5 and 11. Exactly right. That list in Genesis 36 is part of P (and J). The lists in Genesis 5 and 11 are not part of P; they are part of The Book of Generations. What this means is: (1) without meaning to, Radday found further confirmation of Cross's analysis; and (2) Radday was counting lists that came from another work as though they were P.

In short, the data that Radday was testing were poorly chosen to begin with. By intermingling hundreds of verses of J and E with each other, he was destined from the start to arrive at the conclusion that J and E were quite similar to one another. By eliminating a P narrative (Genesis 1), attributing another author's story to P (Genesis 14), and counting long lists (the *tôlĕdōt* Book) as P, he was destined to arrive at the conclusion that P was different from J and E. And even then, when his work came out consistent with the standard view of biblical scholarship, he claimed that he had shown that this view was "highly improbable."

And besides: if he was going to explain differences as merely resulting from different genres of literature, what was the point of doing the study? Why compare the two things if you do not believe that this can prove anything anyway? Radday himself offered the rule that "a comparison between two different literary types is meaningless in an authorship study, no matter whether it results in statistical significance or not." [27]

Radday added another element to the analysis, and said that he did so as an "afterthought." In addition to identifying the words of Genesis as J, E, or P, he identified the words of the biblical text according to another set of divisions. He distinguished three sorts of discourse: (1) quotations in which God is speaking; (2) quotations in which humans are speaking; (3) the words of the narrator. For example:

> And it was when they were in the field, and Cain rose against Abel his brother and killed him. And Yahweh said to Cain, "Where is Abel your brother?" And he said, "I don't know. Am I my brother's keeper?"

In this case, presumably, the words "Where is Abel your brother?" would be listed as (1) divine speech. The words "I don't know. Am I my brother's keeper?" would be listed as (2) human speech. And the words "And it was when they were in the field, and Cain rose against Abel his brother and killed

26. Radday and Shore, *Genesis*, 185.
27. Ibid., 189.

him. And Yahweh said to Cain . . . And he said . . ." would be listed as (3) the narrator's words. Radday chose new letter symbols for these three new categories: D for Divine speech, H for Human speech, and N for Narration.

Radday and his colleagues then observed the differences among these three categories (D, H, and N), just as they had observed the differences among J, E, and P. They found that there were substantial differences among them. In the case of vocabulary richness and vocabulary concentration, Radday concluded:

> As far as these two linguistic properties are concerned, assigning the words of the storyteller, the utterances of the story's personages, and those of the Deity each to a different writer is at least as justified as ascribing the text of the book to three different sources J, E, and P. . . .[28]

That is, Radday is saying that N, H, and D are just as different from one another as J, E, and P are; so if you claim that J, E, and P are by different authors, then you might just as well claim that the words "and he said" and the words "I don't know. Am I my brother's keeper?" are by two different authors.

This is upside down. *Of course* narration behaves differently from quotation. Consider this example from Steinbeck:

> . . . they saw him put his arms on the table and rest his head on his arms and go to sleep. "He was tar'd anyways," said Tom. "Leave him be."

Obviously the language ascribed to Tom behaves differently from the way the narrator speaks. But claiming that such differences show that the differences between J, E, and P are not evidence of separate authors is an absurd argument. When we read a story, we *expect* the "language behavior" of narrators to be different from that of the speakers. We do not expect the story itself to split into two complete, flowing versions in which each has a strikingly different "language behavior" from the other.

The proof of the pudding can be seen in Radday's results. He combines the NHD study with the JEP study, represented thus:

	P	E	J
N	NP	NE	NJ
H	HP	HE	HJ
D	DP	DE	DJ

---

28. Ibid., 214.

This way, it is possible to look at, for example, the "language behavior" of divine speech in P (DP), narration in J (NJ), and so forth. What sorts of things did Radday and his colleagues find by doing this? One notable example is: they found that the quotations of the deity in J were the most mixed category of all. In Radday's words, "Judged either by reliability measures or by correlations between forms, DJ is notably more heterogeneous than any other subcategory." This is no surprise. Radday had assigned Gen 8:1–22, which has a *P* quotation of God, to J. He had also assigned Gen 22:1–18, which has an *E* quotation of God, to J. And then he found that these J quotations of God were looking extremely "heterogeneous"!

In short, Radday's "afterthought" added a complicated dimension to an already problematic study. Ironically, an interesting result was that, in the case of "DJ," the study actually depicted statistically Radday's errors in identifying the sources J, E, and P. A proper statement of what Radday has shown, in my judgment, would be:

> In Sellin's identifications of the Pentateuchal sources, J and E cannot be distinguished from one another by the criterion of "language behavior," but P can be distinguished from them.

But here is the way Radday and his colleagues expressed their conclusions:

> The main thrust of the present enquiry is the non-significance between the E- and J-Documents: they may well have been written by the same person.[29]

> . . . the Documentary Hypothesis, if not discarded *in toto* in view of the above results, should be examined anew and possibly reformulated. . . .[30]

> . . . there is massive evidence that the pre-Biblical triplicity of Genesis . . . is actually a unity.[31]

This kind of overstatement only serves to undermine further an already problematic project.

There are still more problems. In everything that we have considered thus far, we have been assuming that Radday and his colleagues' *statistical* operations on these texts were correct. But even this has been questioned. Following the first presentation of these findings, a response was written by a statistician, Stephen L. Portnoy of the University of Illinois, and a biblical scholar, David L. Peterson of the Iliff School of Theology. They criticized the study both for misuse of statistical analysis broadly on Genesis and for making statistical errors. They said, "It is clear that the study includes errors of

29. Ibid., 51.
30. Ibid., 122.
31. Ibid., 190.

statistical terminology and methodology as well as a fundamental problem in
the application of statistics to (the analysis of) authorship.[32]

There is also the fact that other studies of language have produced blatantly different results. Radday did not take account of what Hurvitz, Polzin,
and others have indicated, namely that the biblical sources are written in the
Hebrew of several different periods.[33] This fact is devastating to Radday's
point. It cannot be explained on grounds of different subject matter or different
"sorts of discourse." [34] Yet he leaves it unanswered.

Overall, Radday's study has been a disappointment, poorly conceived and
poorly executed. Its chief value is as a demonstration of the potential of this
method. Hopefully, over the years there will be methodological refinements
and applications of the technology to other bodies of biblical text.

There is one more unfortunate aspect of these studies by scholars who
challenge the documentary hypothesis that must be mentioned here. In the
light of all that is questionable about these projects, it is especially disturbing
to read in them a number of misrepresentations and insults toward much of the
field of biblical scholarship. Kikawada says, "We propose a unitary reading of
Genesis 1–11 in the spirit of inquiry, not of polemic." [35] But later he says, "Unlike the documentary analyst, we cannot invoke a napping editor to remove an
unpleasant inconsistency."[36] Further, he states that in source identifications
"we have all the delusive comfort of an epistemologically closed world in
which scholars can while away their lives worrying about the attribution of this
or that half-verse." [37] No polemic here.

Radday depicts the field as being divided between two camps on the point
of authorship. In an unthoughtful choice of wording, he refers to these so-
called camps as "documentarians" and "unitarians"! He pre-accuses biblical
scholars of being unfair to his work once it appears. He refers to their subjective beliefs, in contrast to his own research, "which intends to be guided by
uncompromising objectivity." [38] He suggests that biblical scholars accepted his

---

32. S. L. Portnoy and D. L. Peterson, "Genesis, Wellhausen and the Computer: A Response,"
ZAW 96 (1984) 421–25.

33. Robert Polzin, *Late Biblical Hebrew: Toward an Historical Typology of Biblical Hebrew
Prose* (Atlanta, 1976); Gary Rendsburg, "Late Biblical Hebrew and the Date of P," *JANESCU* 12
(1980) 65–80; Ziony Zevit, "Converging Lines of Evidence Bearing on the Date of P," *ZAW* 94
(1982) 505–9; A. R. Guenther, *A Diachronic Study of Biblical Hebrew Prose Syntax* (Ph.D. diss.,
University of Toronto, 1977); Avi Hurvitz, *A Linguistic Study of the Relationship between the
Priestly Source and the Book of Ezekiel* (CahRB; Paris, 1982).

34. Radday and Shore, *Genesis*, 182.

35. Kikawada and Quinn, *Before Abraham Was*, 13.

36. Ibid., 56.

37. Ibid., 125.

38. Radday and Shore, *Genesis*, 191.

method earlier, when it was consistent with standard scholarship, and so now they are uncomfortably stuck with it. He says:

> One thing is certain: the method is sound. After it established, operating with the very same criteria and much to the satisfaction of the critical school, that Judges, Isaiah, and Zechariah are each not of one fabric, its trustworthiness cannot be questioned when it overturns deeply entrenched concepts, much to that school's discomfort.[39]

The method is hardly sound, it is not the same as his work on Isaiah and Zechariah, and there is no such thing as "the critical school." Radday refers to the fact that biblical scholars will not accept his conclusions as "dysfunction," and he speaks of scientists who "shut their eyes to data" that challenge them. This is outrageous. Radday has done his study no service by maligning responsible scholars.

Overall, it must be said that the very fact of resorting to such weak arguments is significant. It reflects the fact that the more visible, quantifiable evidence points to several authors. The fact of the overstatement of *implications* likewise reflects the weakness of the position. And the fact of the rudeness to reputable scholars is (a) another reflection of the the weakness of the position and (b) disgraceful. Perhaps Radday's and his colleagues' own concluding sentence depicts the situation best: "So Genesis will continue to be a rich field for research, and all the four of us researchers can look forward to is to have supplied it with some new fertilizer."

To return chiastically to my opening point, some may say that it is not even worth the effort to criticize such studies as these. But the fact is that, since Wellhausen, three major developments in our field have been: the opening up of ancient Near Eastern civilization, the increased concentration on literary artistry, and the introduction of computer analysis in our field. Already these studies have misconstrued these three potentially rich developments, and so it would seem to be worthwhile to identify the errors and then get back to our work.

---

39. Ibid., 217.

THE PRIESTLY ACCOUNT OF THE THEOPHANY
AND LAWGIVING AT SINAI

Baruch J. Schwartz

THE FOLLOWING STUDY is an attempt to demonstrate that the Priestly material in the Pentateuchal account of the lawgiving at Sinai comprises a complete, originally continuous narrative, entirely separate from and independent of the J, E, and D accounts of the Sinai events; further, to bring into focus the unique, distinctly Priestly view of the Sinaitic revelation expressed in this narrative and its place in the Priestly theology. It is hoped that this may constitute a modest contribution to the ongoing debate concerning the literary nature of P, strengthening the view that it is not a redactional layer but a literary source. In so doing, and in arguing for the inseparable integration of law and narrative in the P source as well as for the centrality of the Sinai pericope therein, this study is immeasurably indebted to the published works and oral teaching of Professor Menahem Haran, by whose inspired explication of the Pentateuchal literature the author has been guided in even more ways than are evidenced below.

P: The State of Inquiry

Scholarship long ago reached virtual unanimity on the existence of a Priestly stratum in the Pentateuch and on its general and particular stylistic features. Leaving aside the specific issue of the existence of the Priestly writings outside of the Pentateuch and the occasional idiosyncratic view of the scope of P within the Pentateuch, it may safely be asserted that basic agreement also exists concerning the identification of the Priestly material itself.[1] The basic features of

---

1. For an up-to-date comparative synopsis of scholarship, see P. P. Jenson, *Graded Holiness: A Key to the Priestly Conception of the World* (JSOTSup 116; Sheffield, 1992) 220–24; compare R. E. Friedman, *The Exile and Biblical Narrative: The Formation of the Deuteronomistic and Priestly Works* (HSM 22; Chico, Cal., 1981) 141–47.

the Priestly "world view" also remain uncontested, though here it should be noted that only recently, and in large part due to the ground-breaking studies of Haran, has this topic been taken up in any real detail and with adequate precision.[2] First among the issues surrounding the Priestly writings, concerning which debate, often fierce, continues to rage, is the question of date, both absolute and relative to the other Pentateuchal strata. The case for a preexilic date for all or most of the Priestly writings is no longer made, as it was a generation ago by a few loyal adherents of Kaufmann alone; it has instead become a respectable position in scholarship, though by no means the dominant one.[3] Other issues that remain controversial are often a function of the question of date. For instance, the interesting search for the "kerygma" of P remains among the unresolved issues. Yet the attempt to define the primary theological or didactic aim of the Priestly work is never, nor can it possibly be, divorced from the issue of the religio-historical situation in which it was composed and the audience for whom it was intended. Indeed, the question of "kerygma" is usually nothing more than the question of date in disguise.[4]

Another unresolved issue is of course the theological and aesthetic evaluation of P, and of P's world view in particular. Here, agreement is not likely ever to be reached, depending as it does upon the scholar's individual tastes as well as upon his willingness to penetrate the Priestly writings on their own terms. Still, it must be conceded that the predilection of some scholars to place them in the postexilic period has often engendered a negative evaluation (or vice versa), while the scholars favoring a preexilic date are more likely to be predisposed to discovering some more commendable sides of P's legal and ritual logic, theological depth, and literary art.[5] The opinion of scholarship (one

2. Haran's ground-breaking studies are synthesized in M. Haran, *Temples and Temple-Service in Ancient Israel* (Oxford, 1978; repr. Winona Lake, Ind., 1985). Recent works include F. H. Gorman, *The Ideology of Ritual: Space, Time and Status in the Priestly Theology* (JSOTSup 91; Sheffield, 1990); Jenson, *Graded Holiness* (for a summary of scholarship, see pp. 16–31); and Sections D through G of the introduction in J. Milgrom, *Leviticus 1–16* (AB 3; New York, 1991) 35–61. The systematic treatment of specific Priestly rituals is also a relatively recent phenomenon; see J. Milgrom, *Cult and Conscience* (Studies in Judaism in Late Antiquity 18; Leiden, 1976); idem, *Studies in Cultic Theology and Terminology* (Studies in Judaism in Late Antiquity 36; Leiden, 1983); D. P. Wright, *The Disposal of Impurity* (SBLDS 101; Atlanta, 1987); N. Kiuchi, *The Purification Offering in the Priestly Literature* (JSOTSup 56; Sheffield, 1987); B. Janowski, *Sühne als Heilsgeschehen: Studien zur Sühnetheologie der Priesterschrift und zur Wurzel KPR im Alten Orient und im Alten Testament* (WMANT 55; Neukirchen-Vluyn, 1982).

3. For a recent, thorough discussion, see Thomas M. Krapf, *Die Priesterschrift und die Vorexilische Zeit* (OBO 119; Freiburg/Göttingen, 1992) 3–66.

4. For discussion, and references to the discussions of Boorer, Bruggemann, Klein, Saebø, and others, see Jenson, *Graded Holiness*, 26–31.

5. The sympathetic treatment of P's ideology by those who favor a preexilic date is best exemplified by Haran; see also the writings of J. Milgrom; compare G. Wenham, *The Book of Leviticus* (NICOT; Grand Rapids, 1979). The opposite tendency is described by D. Damrosch, *The Narrative Covenant: Transformations of Genre in the Growth of Biblical Literature* (San Francisco,

can hardly say scholarly opinion) on P is no less a function of the historical question than is any other point of debate.

P as Source, Not Redaction

Here we shall address another matter, one with which Pentateuchal criticism has been continuously occupied in the last quarter of a century: the question of the literary character of the Priestly writings. Despite a wealth of scholarly publications dealing with this issue in recent years,[6] it would be inaccurate to state either that critics have reached an impasse or that they have arrived at a consensus; the situation is considerably more complex. It is not true that the classical view of the Graf-Wellhausen school, most clearly articulated by and traditionally associated with Noth,[7] has been rejected by modern scholarship—namely, that the Priestly writings are indeed a document that once existed independently and with which the J and E documents (whether earlier or later than P themselves) were eventually combined. Nor has the alternative view, primarily associated with the names of Cross, Rendtorff, and

---

1987) 261–62; Jenson, *Graded Holiness*, 16–20. The literary art of P is treated with admiration by M. Paran, *Forms of the Priestly Style in the Pentateuch* (Jerusalem, 1989) [Heb.]; the opposite is true, for instance, of S. McEvenue, *The Narrative Style of the Priestly Writer* (AnBib 50; Rome, 1971). An exception is B. A. Levine, who has consistently argued for a late date of P, yet has taken seriously its literary and theological complexity; see, for example, his "Priestly Writers" and "Priests" in *IDBSup* 683–90; idem, *Leviticus* (JPS Torah Commentary; Philadelphia, 1989); idem, *Numbers 1–20* (AB 4; New York, 1993)

6. For discussions and convenient summaries of the vast literature, see N. Lohfink, "Die Priesterschrift und die Geschichte," *Congress Volume, Göttingen 1977* (VTSup 29; Leiden, 1978) 196–200; R. E. Clements, "Pentateuchal Problems," in ed. G. W. Anderson, *Tradition and Interpretation* (Oxford, 1979), 102–4; R. W. Klein, "The Message of P," in *Die Botschaft und die Boten: Festschrift für Hans Walter Wolff zum 70. Geburtstag* (ed. J. Jeremias and L. Perlitt; Neukirchen-Vluyn, 1981) 57–58; D. A. Knight, "The Pentateuch," in *The Hebrew Bible and Its Modern Interpreters* (ed. D. A. Knight and G. M. Tucker; Philadelphia/Chico, Cal., 1985) 285–86; K. Koch, "P—Kein Redaktor! Errinerung an zwei Eckdaten der Quellenscheidung," *VT* 37 (1987) 446–56; E. Blum, *Studien zur Komposition des Pentateuch* (BZAW 189; Berlin, 1990) 229–32; M. Vervenne, "The 'P' Tradition in the Pentateuch: Document and/or Redaction," in *Pentateuchal and Deuteronomistic Studies* (ed. C. Brekelmans and J. Lust; BETL 94; Louvain, 1990) 67–76; Jenson, *Graded Holiness*, 21–25.

7. M. Noth's most important discussion of the issue, was the appendix to "The 'Priestly Writing' and the Redaction of the Pentateuch," which appeared in the second volume of his *Überlieferungsgeschichtliche Studien* in 1943. Unfortunately the English translation of this work appeared only in 1987 (in M. Noth, *The Chronicler's History* [JSOTSup 50; Sheffield, 1987] 107–47), as a result of which some English-speaking scholars seem not to have consulted it, relying instead on the briefer, and far less detailed, third and fifteenth chapters of Noth's *Überlieferungsgeschichte des Pentateuch* (1948) (Eng. trans., M. Noth, *A History of Pentateuchal Traditions* [Englewood Cliffs, N.J., 1972] 8–19, 234–47). For thorough surveys of the literature, see the works cited in the previous note.

most recently Blum,[8] gained the upper hand—namely, that there never existed a continuous Priestly source and that separate, unconnected Priestly writings (either preexisting ones or ones composed on the spot, or some combination of the two) comprise a redactional layer in the process of the composition of the Pentateuch. Rather, there appears to be a paradox: while the latter view is often presented—by its adherents as well as by its opponents—as if it were the accepted one, the criticisms leveled against it have not been rebuffed, and it has occasionally been maintained without substantiation, perhaps because it has the appeal of modernity or the weight of prominent scholars behind it. At the same time, while respondents for the former view have been numerous and persuasive, they have repeatedly taken up their position as if rallying to the defense of an obsolete, minority opinion.[9]

Towards rectifying this situation, we may begin by reviewing some of the main reasons why the classical, Nothian view remains the preferable, indeed, the only convincing one:

(1) In narrative after narrative, whenever the text shows evidence that Priestly and non-Priestly writings have been combined, the separation of the strands shows that two accounts have been combined, not one account and its supplement. In the passage to be discussed below, we shall add yet another example.

8. F. M. Cross, *Canaanite Myth and Hebrew Epic* (Cambridge, Mass., 1973) 294–319; R. Rendtorff, *Das überlieferungsgeschichtliche Problem des Pentateuch* (BZAW 147; Berlin, 1977); Blum, *Studien zur Komposition*, 229–85. On Blum, see the contribution of G. I. Davies in the present volume ("The Composition of the Book of Exodus: Reflections on the Theses of Erhard Blum," 71–85).

9. The Cross-Rendtorff-Blum approach, it should be noted, was represented in previous generations by such scholars as Eerdmans, Engnell, and Volz; see the discussions by Clements, "Pentateuchal Problems" and Vervenne, "The P-Tradition." Among its recent proponents are: T. Dozeman, *God on the Mountain: A Study of Redaction, Theology and Canon in Exodus 19–24* (SBLMS 37; Atlanta, 1989) 87–120; Gorman, *Ideology of Ritual*, 45–46; R. N. Whybray, *The Making of the Pentateuch* (JSOTSup 53; Sheffield, 1987) 108–11, 125–26; and Vervenne ("The P-Tradition"), who refers to additional adherents. The main defenders of the Nothian view are: Lohfink, "Priesterschrift"; Clements, "Pentateuchal Problems"; Klein, "Message of P"; E. Zenger, *Gottes Bogen in den Wolken: Untersuchungen zu Komposition und Theologie der priesterschriftlichen Urgeschichte* (Stuttgarter Bibelstudien 112; Stuttgart, 1983) 32–36; P. Weimar, "Struktur und Komposition der priesterschriftlichen Geschichtsdarstellung," *Biblische Notizen* 23 (1984) 81–134, and 24 (1984) 138–62; Koch, "P—Kein Redaktor!" 446–67; J. A. Emerton, "The Priestly Writer in Genesis," *JTS* 39 (1988) 381–400 (Emerton also provides important references to earlier scholarship); J. Blenkinsopp, *The Pentateuch* (AB Reference Library; New York, 1992) 185–86 (on his earlier position, see "The Structure of P," *CBQ* 38 [1976] 275–80); Jenson, *Graded Holiness*, 25–26; and most recently L. Schmidt, *Studien zur Priesterschrift* (BZAW 214; Berlin, 1993). Somewhat unique is Friedman, *Exile and Biblical Narrative*, 44–132. While accepting the position of Noth virtually in its entirety, Friedman, instead of speaking of the combination of the sources by a redactor who also supplied the connectives, refers to the redactional portions of the Pentateuch as a stage in the Priestly work, referring to them as "P²" rather than as "R." In this manner Friedman is able to appear to follow Cross, ostensibly admitting that P is a redaction, while at the same time agreeing with Noth that P is a source.

(2) The sheer scope of the Priestly material, and the large narrative blocks it contains (exclusively Priestly ones, not only ones that may be separated out of combined narratives) are uncharacteristic of redactional activity, while they are the natural features of a narrative source. Indeed, the response of the Cross-Rendtorff-Blum school to this elementary observation, namely, that the Priestly redactor has evidently availed himself of preexisting Priestly narratives and used them as redactional material, simply fails to hold water. Where have these narratives come from, if not from a distinctly Priestly tradition of the events? And what is meant by *redaction* if it includes the insertion of full blocks of narrative that compete with the material being redacted?

(3) To be sure, once the P-as-redaction school admits that P includes independent narratives, the only question remaining is: do they also comprise a continuous whole? The answer is in the affirmative. The Priestly narratives, though now dispersed throughout the Pentateuch, can taken together be read as a continuous narrative, most often without any need to supply even the connectives. Cross's claim that the narrative thus obtained is not parallel enough to the (J and E) epic tradition to be taken seriously, in particular because it lacks certain "essential" elements that no self-respecting Pentateuchal source would dare to omit,[10] is not only subjective in the extreme and based on what is missing rather than what exists, it was anticipated and convincingly refuted by Noth himself.[11] Recent critics remind us, moreover, that there is in theory no reason to assume that P has been preserved in absolute totality. Thus on the one hand even critics who point to an occasional lack of continuity in P can just as easily posit that an episode has been omitted as that the Priestly account is insufficient in scope;[12] on the other, "sufficient" is a matter of opinion and certainly cannot be defined as total correspondence with the other sources.[13]

(4) Cross's other claim is not compelling, namely, that a few brief narrative connectives that are Priestly in style disrupt the continuity of P and/or serve to introduce or conclude patently non-Priestly sections and thus are most readily explained as redactional.[14] To say that some, or even all, of the redaction of the Pentateuch is Priestly in style (and this has long been admitted) is not to say that the entire Priestly work is redactional. The main examples are formulae, such as אלה תולדות appearing at the head of non-Priestly sections of Genesis, ויחזק appearing at the conclusion of non-Priestly episodes in the plagues pericope, and itineraries of the ויסעו . . . ויחנו type used at the head of

10. Cross, *Canaanite Myth and Hebrew Epic*, esp. 301–8.

11. Noth, *Chronicler's History*, 135–37 and notes.

12. Emerton, "Priestly Writer," 385.

13. Koch, "P—Kein Redaktor!" 454–55.

14. Cross, *Canaanite Myth and Hebrew Epic*, 301–5, 308–18; see the discussions of Friedman, *Exile and Biblical Narrative*, 77–95, 98; etc.; Koch, "P—Kein Redaktor!" 452–54. Friedman (pp. 80ff.) assigns to P² all portions of the Priestly work that cause it to flow smoothly together, enabling him to accept Cross's idea that the original Priestly work (his "P¹") is not really quite as complete and continuous as might have been hoped and to speak instead of a "collection of accounts, lists, and legal materials" (p. 118)—thus again placing himself in both camps.

non-Priestly wilderness narratives. Yet even if some, or indeed all, of these are redactional, the great bulk of remaining Priestly material is of a different sort.

(5) The narrative obtained when the nonredactional Priestly material is taken as a whole is not only continuous; its parts exhibit remarkable interconnection on the ideational and structural levels far beyond what might reasonably be expected of redactional stages. Further, the work as a whole exhibits an overall structure that bespeaks its original coherence.[15]

(6) The interconnected stories, themes, motifs, ideas, and structures that inform the Priestly work as a whole are so irreconcilable with the non-Priestly material that they cannot logically be seen as redactional. When the Priestly material duplicates J and E rather than integrating with them, and certainly when it contradicts J and E rather than replacing them, its composition can in no wise be attributed to a redactional effort. The nature of redaction is that it synthesizes; P does not.

(7) Since the earliest days of Pentateuchal criticism it has been admitted that the Priestly laws are organically interconnected with the Priestly narrative. Indeed, one of the primary factors that enabled criticism to identify the Priestly narrative as Priestly at all was the fact that it reflects, and even mentions explicitly, the assumptions and the stipulations of incontestably Priestly legislation. This interconnection extends to areas of theology, but it begins at the level of story line, with such simple features as the underlying principle that most of the laws were imparted from the adytum after the tabernacle was built and the corollary notion that many significant laws were in fact imparted in advance, incorporated into the narratives to which they pertained or included in the building instructions.[16] In such cases law and narrative are inseparably interdependent.

Now, irrespective of how one conceives of the relationship of the Priestly law code to the non-Priestly corpora, that is, whether it is presumed to be independent of them or a legislative development that came about in response to them or even in order to supersede them, P's *law code* has never been considered "redactional." Whether it grew by increments or was composed as a whole, the final product as well as the individual parts are held by all critics to be thoroughly self-contained. Their distinctive locations within the Pentateuchal framework, especially the concentration of most of them in one narrative context (the tabernacle pericope in its fullest scope), are the surest indication. Even critics who claim to detect occasional Priestly "redaction" in the non-Priestly legal texts would never go so far as to suggest that the Priestly laws as a whole

15. On the internal coherence of P from both thematic and structural points of view, see Noth, *Chronicler's History*, 136–38; idem, *A History of Pentateuchal Traditions*, 234–47; Blenkinsopp, "The Structure of P," 275–92; Lohfink, "Priesterschrift," 204–8; Weimar, "Struktur und Komposition"; Emerton, "Priestly Writer," 386–92.

16. Gen 17:1–14; Exod 16:4–12, 16–30; 25:30; 27:20–21; 29:38–42a; 30:19–21, 31–33, 37–38; etc.

are in any sense "redactional." And if the law code is not redactional, neither is the narrative tradition with which it is inseparably connected.

(8) On the latter point, the analogy of the non-Priestly sources can be mustered as well. The Pentateuchal sources share a common *Gattung*: each one consists of a law code and a narrative framework (in the case of D, rhetorically constructed), the latter serving to explain the existence of, and the necessity of compliance with, the former. It may be argued a fortiori: if the epic sources, of which the law makes up a relatively small part, still recognize its centrality by devoting a significant portion of their narrative to providing the historical and theological rationale for it, and if even the Deuteronomic source, in which the law code could conceivably have stood alone, does the same, it is unimaginable that the Priestly code could ever have existed without its own law-focused narrative. The Priestly narrative confirms this logic. It telegraphs early events and rushes to Sinai, after which it slows down to a snail's pace and becomes a protracted tale of endless lawgiving. This is precisely the story in which one would expect the Priestly corpus to be encased. To explain it as a redaction of the non-Priestly narrative is to ignore its essential nature and to deny the Priestly law its natural, requisite literary setting.

P and the Non-Priestly Sources

Accepting the above arguments, both on their merits and because they have withstood the test of time even in the face of an interesting alternative, still leaves a number of questions unanswered. Given the fact that the Priestly narrative was once independent, was it originally separate from or of a piece with the Priestly law code? If the two were originally distinct, how and when did they come to be combined? Once the Priestly document as a whole was intact, how did it come to be combined with the non-Priestly sources: was the redaction solely a matter of the most reasonable chronological arrangement possible, or as Noth posited did P serve as "host"—as the frame-narrative into which the others were inserted?[17]

To these pressing questions we may add one more: that of P's reliance on the earlier sources. On this question there is less controversy. Almost all critics assume that the Priestly narrator must have been familiar with whatever Pentateuchal sources predated him (J, E, and D for most critics; only J and E for the followers of Kaufmann).[18] Those who view P as a redactional stratum, of

---

17. On these questions, see Lohfink, "Priesterschrift," 190–96; Zenger, *Gottes Bogen in den Wolken*, 27–32.

18. The possibility of P's having come into existence without actually relying on the J and E sources is suggested, interestingly enough, by Noth in the introduction to his commentary to Exodus; see M. Noth, *Exodus* (OTL; Philadelphia, 1962) 16. In his earlier writings he seems to take P's literary reliance on J and E for granted. Note the discussion by Koch, "P—Kein Redaktor!" 455–66.

course, have no choice in the matter. P could not have been created to redact that with which its creators were not familiar. But for those who maintain that P was a source, there is no a priori reason to assume that the P-narrative was based on the earlier ones. If scholars do so, it would seem to be because they have accepted uncritically the Hegelian view of Israel's narrative tradition as a linear development: whatever came later must be a response to what came earlier; all literary activity had access to all preceding literature. This acceptance comes dangerously close to the view of the opposing school: at least one critic admits that P's literary form was a document but supposes it was composed to complement, indeed, to be read along with, the (by now combined) J and E accounts—thus taking away with the left hand what he gave with the right.[19]

Here too, the literary question cannot be separated from the question of date. The prevailing opinion, that P is both the latest of the Pentateuchal sources to have been composed and also postexilic, has probably led to the automatic assumption that it must have had access to all earlier sources. How could a postexilic author not have been familiar with the Yahwistic, Elohistic and Deuteronomic Torahs? How could P be anything but a response to them? With this as an assumption, scholars have then proceeded to define the nature of the "response," each in accord with his own evaluation of P's correspondence with the non-Priestly tradition. The more conservative view is that it was "built upon" JE; the more radical view is that it was dissatisfied with JE and rejected it. If, however, it is allowed that P may be preexilic, perhaps more or less contemporary with D and not all that much later than the epic sources, then it becomes not only possible but actually probable that it was composed independently of them.

Following the lead of Zenger, Koch, Emerton, Weimar, and Schmidt,[20] I shall now attempt to substantiate further the view that there existed an independent Priestly document, by means of illustration from a particular narrative complex in the Priestly writings. At the same time, diverging from the general view, I will argue, at least in the passage to be analyzed, that the preferable conclusion is that the Priestly account was originally independent not only in the narrow sense of a self-contained literary document but in the wider sense as well. It was an alternative account, not a rewriting of or a response to (and certainly not a supplement to) the earlier sources, but a separate version, thoroughly uninfluenced by them and indeed unaware of them.

19. Blenkinsopp, "Structure of P," 275–80.
20. Zenger, *Gottes Bogen in den Wolken*: the Creation and Flood narratives, as well as their interrelationship with the remainder of the Priestly narratives; Koch, "P—Kein Redaktor!": the creation of man and the revelation of the divine name; Emerton, "Priestly Writer": the Genesis narratives; P. Weimar, "Sinai und Schöpfung: Komposition und Theologie der priesterschriftlichen Sinaigeschichte," *RB* 95 (1988) 337–85: the Sinai pericope and its interconnection with the Creation account; Schmidt, *Studien zur Priesterschrift*: the enslavement and exile; the wilderness complaint narratives.

The Lawgiving Pericope in Scholarship

The sample selected for analysis, namely, the account of the lawgiving at Sinai, is of particular interest for a number of reasons. First, the Pentateuchal Sinai traditions have been the topic of several recent studies.[21] Virtually all critics agree that the canonical version of the story as given in Exodus 19ff. cannot be read as a continuous account without insurmountable problems, and it is agreed that these can only be alleviated by recourse to the literary history of the text. Second, if the centrality of the lawgiving at Sinai (or Horeb) in the Pentateuchal traditions is admitted, and especially once it is recognized that it is the focal point of the Priestly narrative, the analysis of its unique form, content and message becomes a desideratum. This is even more the case if the integrity of law and narrative within P (whether original or not) is upheld, since the Sinai pericope is by far the most extensive, and most significant, literary unit in the combined Priestly document.

A third reason for my interest is that this portion of the Priestly narrative tends to be overlooked in scholarship, both in the discussion of P and in the discussion of the Sinai traditions. To be sure, this is only to be expected: when scholars arrive at the Sinai narratives, they naturally focus first on Exodus 19–24, where they find a lengthy narrative text. They note the paucity of Priestly material and the wealth of non-Priestly and proceed to examine the latter and ignore the former.[22] Those who move on to Exodus 25ff. discover a wealth of Priestly material, which they may examine in detail but not strictly as narrative, rather as cultic instruction or legislation. The tabernacle per se becomes the center of attention, and all sight of the narrative strand begun at Exod 19:1 is lost.[23] Studies of P in Leviticus tend to be exclusively legal; the brief nonlegal

---

21. Studies devoted specifically to this topic include: E. Zenger, *Die Sinaitheophanie* (Forschung zur Bibel 3; Würzburg, 1971) [including the history of earlier scholarship]); A. Toeg, מתן תורה בסיני (Jerusalem, 1977); J. Licht, "גילוי שכינה במעמד הר סיני," in *Studies in the Bible and the Ancient Near East Presented to Samuel E. Loewenstamm on His Seventieth Birthday* (ed. Y. Avishur and J. Blau; Jerusalem, 1978) 1.251–67; R. W. L. Moberly, *At the Mountain of God* (JSOTSup 22; Sheffield, 1983); Dozeman, *God on the Mountain*; see also Blum, *Studien zur Komposition*, 45–99.

22. This characterizes many of the studies surveyed by Zenger, *Sinaitheophanie* 13–45, as well as those of Zenger himself, of Moberly, and of Blum (*Studien zur Komposition*, 45–99), and all of the commentaries on Exodus.

23. This tendency is discernible in the only extant study devoted exclusively to the lawgiving in P: K. Koch, "Die Eigenart der priesterschriftlichen Sinaigesetzgebung," *ZTK* 55 (1958) 36–51, as well as in Weimar, "Sinai und Schöpfung." Special mention should be made of the discussions of the Sinai pericope in P found in Toeg, מתן תורה, 144–59; Dozeman, *God on the Mountain*, 90–120; and Gorman, *Ideology of Ritual*, 45–52. In all three, the priestly material is succinctly described in a way that makes its narrative and ideological tradition perfectly clear, yet all three authors present it as though it were a redactional effort, composed in order to be grafted to the JE account. They cannot bring themselves even to consider the far simpler conclusion, and the one that emerges naturally from their own discussions, namely, that the Priestly material comprises an independent, preexisting account. I believe this to be attributable to uncritical adherence to the view

portions of Leviticus are either treated as though they were legal texts (chaps. 8–9), intrusions (chap. 10), or both (24:10–23). In Numbers, commentators resume interest in the story line, but this interest is usually episodic rather than continuous, and in any case pertains in the main to events after the sojourn at Sinai. This same scholarly disinterest is characteristic of most attempts to argue the Cross-Rendtorff position of P-as-redactor, as well as of most attempts to defend the classical view of P-as-source: the narratives in Genesis have been the preferred samples, and the plagues and the sea narratives in Exodus have also been discussed, but the dramatic events at Sinai to which the Priestly narrative leads have not yet been given attention from this point of view.

Fourthly, the claim made by Cross and his followers, that unless P is treated as redactional it includes no Sinaitic covenant and that since this is inconceivable P must be redactional,[24] can be treated with the seriousness it requires only if the Priestly view of the Sinaitic events is considered in all of its distinctiveness and of course in its entirety.

Finally, while numerous events belonging to the Pentateuchal traditions are recounted by two or three sources, the Sinaitic lawgiving is one of the only events that all four Pentateuchal sources recount. Significant in its own right, this fact enables us to view the passage under discussion with its appropriate "controls": the parallel accounts in the other sources. Moreover, the danger, both of overlooking the distinctive features of a single source and of presuming the existence of some feature that actually emerges only from the combination of sources, becomes particularly great when all four sources "agree" on the basic event: that the laws were imparted by God to Israel through Moses at Sinai.

The Identification of P in Exodus 19ff.

The identification of the Priestly material in Exodus 19ff. can be accepted as virtually certain. The occasional suggestion that Exod 19:3–8 (with its reference to a "kingdom of priests and holy nation" in v. 6) betrays Priestly authorship[25] is rightly dismissed; nothing could be less Priestly than the notion that all Israel is as sacred as a priesthood,[26] even if intended as a rhetorical figure and not as an actual viewpoint. The recent suggestion that Exod 19:12–13a

---

of Cross, just as the positions of Friedman (nn. 9 and 14) and Blenkinsopp (n. 19) reflect a desire to pay at least lip-service to Cross's viewpoint.

24. Cross, *Canaanite Myth and Hebrew Epic*, 312–13, 318; see below note 58.

25. H. Cazelles, "Alliance du Sinai, Alliance de l'Horeb et Renouvellement de l'Alliance," in *Beiträge zur alttestamentlichen Theologie: Festschrift für Walther Zimmerli zum 70. Geburtstag* (ed. H. Von Donner, R. Hanhart, and R. Smend; Göttingen, 1977) 78. Cazelles' aim, of course, was to salvage some mention of a Sinai covenant in the Priestly source; see below, pp. 130–32.

26. M. Weinfeld, *Deuteronomy and the Deuteronomic School* (Oxford, 1972; repr. Winona Lake, Ind., 1992) 226–30.

and 19:20–25 are Priestly[27] betrays a serious misconception of the nature of the Priestly writings: it combines the naive and superficial assumption that only P used such words as "sacred" and "priests" and that anything even remotely ceremonial in the Pentateuch must be Priestly in origin, with the blaring contradiction to the firm Priestly claim that the priests were consecrated, and ceremonial worship begun, only after the tabernacle was erected.

The only persuasively argued case of Priestly writing in Exodus 20 is the motivational section of the Sabbath command in vv. 10–11.[28] Since this is evidently redactional, however, and in any case is not a narrative passage, we may omit it from the present discussion. The end of Exodus 24, with its description of the divine firecloud's arrival to rest on Mount Sinai and God's call to Moses to ascend, is clearly Priestly; it parallels and anticipates the concluding verses of Exodus 40 (vv. 34–35) and the opening verse of Leviticus.

Weimar's highly subjective and thoroughly unsubstantiated attempt to limit the tabernacle instructions and the account of their execution to an "original" story in which the tabernacle was designed to be both virtually unfurnished and thoroughly cult-less may also be passed over without serious comment.[29] It should be remarked, however, that even this extreme suggestion does not denude the tabernacle, or the account of its construction, of the feature that most clearly demonstrates its interconnection with the Sinai events: namely, the role of the tabernacle as earthly abode of the divine presence said to reside therein in splendid solitude. However, whereas Weimar has chosen to isolate one dimension of this belief in the resident, enshrined deity, the secure knowledge of God's constant company, the text, as we shall see, has not confined the matter to this element alone.

To be as brief as possible, all critics agree that (1) the tabernacle pericope in its entirety belongs to the Priestly writings, and (2) the general outline of the pericope has always included the instructions and their execution. Whether some portions of the pericope (even, as some would have it, most of the details of the execution account in Exodus 35–40[30]) are accretions or insertions to be attributed to later Priestly tradents, the tabernacle and everything related about it in the Pentateuch remains exclusively Priestly. Exod 25:1–31:18 and chaps.

---

27. J. Van Seters, "'Comparing Scripture with Scripture': Some Observations on the Sinai Pericope of Exodus 19–24," in *Canon, Theology and Old Testament Interpretation* (ed. G. M. Tucker; Philadelphia, 1988) 112–14. The same is true of Dozeman, *God on the Mountain*, 90–118, who arbitrarily assigns even more passages of no Priestly character whatsoever to the "P-redaction."

28. This is despite the tendency of the P-as-redaction school to assign the Decalogue in its entirety to P or to a Priestly revision. See Cross, *Canaanite Myth and Hebrew Epic*, 312–13; contrast Friedman, *Exile and Biblical Narrative*, 98. For a recent treatment, see W. Johnstone, "The Decalogue and the Redaction of the Sinai Pericope in Exodus," *ZAW* 100 (1988) 361–85.

29. Weimar, "Sinai und Schöpfung."

30. I. Knohl, (הדרממה מקדש [Jerusalem, 1993] 64, 66–67, 110 n. 12) assigns this entire section to H.

35–40 are therefore assigned with certainty to P and include no non-Priestly material at all.

The calf episode and related material (Exod 32:1–34:28), on the other hand, which separate the two main portions of the tabernacle account, are held by all to be a non-Priestly section, combining at least two narrative strands, J and E for most source-critics. An acknowledged Priestly passage does stand, however, at the conclusion of the pericope, namely, the description of Moses' shining face in 34:29–35, the phenomenology of which has recently been discussed by Haran.[31] We may confidently assume that this passage, beginning as it does with the words ויהי ברדת משה מהר סיני (34:29), was preceded directly by the words ויפן וירד משה מן ההר וְ . . . הָעֵדֻת בידו (32:15), which are undoubtedly the direct continuation of the words ויתן אל משה כְּכַלֹתו לדבר אתו בהר סיני . . . עֵדֻת in 31:18. We shall return to these verses (referring also to the words omitted here) below (pp. 126–27).

Thoroughly narrative texts in P almost disappear after Lev 1:1; strictly speaking they occur only in Lev 8:1–9:24 with the account of the consecration of the priesthood and dedication of the tabernacle and altar, which is of course suddenly interrupted by the Nadab and Abihu episode (10:1–7, 12–19). It has long been realized that these events are the narrative sequel to the tabernacle construction completed in Exodus 40, although, as we shall observe, Leviticus 1–7 is chronologically and literarily in place and should not be treated as an insertion. With this exception and that of the report of the blasphemer in Lev 24:10–23 (the connection of which to Sinai is more coincidental than intrinsic), the narrative of P is now a static one in which the only thing related time after time is that "the LORD spoke to Moses and said." Usually what is said is in the category of laws—that is, commands binding for all time. In Leviticus 26 what is said is the speech of "blessings and curses" and in much of Numbers 1–10 it is the census instructions and the order for marching and encampment. Still, all of these are contained in the divine speeches, the periodic occurrence of which is virtually the only action described by the narrative. When movement resumes, it is to leave Sinai (Num 10:11ff., introduced by 9:15–23).

The Giving of the Law as Recounted by P

Thus, the narrative material pertaining to the Sinai events that can safely be assigned to P consists essentially of: Exod 19:1–2a, 24:16–31:18, 32:15a, 34:29–40:38, and Lev 1:1ff. The story consists of three narrative types: (1) brief, strictly narrative passages; (2) "cultic" narratives, in which the construction of the tabernacle and the establishment of its forms of worship are described and detailed; (3) legal narratives, in which commands for the Israelite people as a whole are imparted. The interrelationship of the three types cannot be understated. Brief passages from the third category are included here and there

31. M. Haran, "כי קרן עור פני משה," in *Studies in Bible Dedicated to the Memory of U. Cassuto on the 100th Anniversary of His Birth* (ed. S. A. Loewenstamm; Jerusalem, 1987) 127–36.

among the second, and the cultic forms instituted in passages of the second type are regulated in passages of the third. The three types are still distinct, however, and occur in logical sequence. Dividing the narrative more precisely into its constituent parts, the following outline emerges:

(a) Exod 19:1–2a and 24:16–18a
(b) Exod 25:1–31:17
(c) Exod 31:18, 32:15, and 34:29–35
(d) Exod 35:1–40:33 (a more precise, eight-part breakdown would be: (1) 35:1–20, (2) 35:21–29, (3) 35:30–36:1, (4) 36:2–7, (5) 36:8–39:32, (6) 39:33–43, (7) 40:1–16, (8) 40:17–33)
(e) Exod 40:34–35 (and the parenthetical, proleptic 36–38)
(f) Lev 1–7
(g) Lev 8–9
(h) Lev 10:1–7 and 10:12–19
(i) Lev 11ff.

The story told by this account may be summed up as follows:[32]

(a) The Israelites arrive at Sinai in the third month after the Exodus. The divine firecloud, encasing the כבוד, takes up residence atop the mountain, covering it for six days, following which Moses is called to ascend. He ascends the mountain on the seventh day and enters the cloud, where he remains for some time. During this entire time the visible manifestation of the residing deity remains in full view of the people day and night.

(b) Throughout his stay on the mountain, Moses is addressed by God. Among the first things he is told is that at the end of the audience he will be given an עֵדוּת to place in the tabernacle ark that he is to make. At great length, the instructions for the building and furnishing of the tabernacle, the vestments and investiture of the priesthood, the consecration of the altar—all shown, as well as spoken—and the *kippurîm*-payment, as well as the appointment of Bezalel and Oholiab and the Sabbath-warning, are communicated to Moses. By way of necessary explanation of the use of objects mentioned, several of these matters are accompanied by their pertinent permanent legislation.[33] In the main, however, Moses is told (Exod 25:22) that the actual lawgiving will commence only after the instructions are carried out. Then, true to his promise, God concludes the session, presents Moses with the עדות, and dismisses him.

(c) Moses descends from the mountain with the עדות in his hands. When he comes into sight, unaware that the residual radiation of the divine reflection still shines from his face, he creates quite a stir, causing the people to flee. When he explains the source of his fearsome radiance to Aaron and the tribal chiefs, however, they coax the people to return and summon up the courage to

---

32. One of the only recent authors to summarize the continuous Priestly Sinai narrative is G. I. Davies, "Sinai," *ABD* 6.47–48; compare Friedman, *Exile and Biblical Narrative*, 98–100; "Koch, "Eigenart."

33. Exod 25:30; 27:20–21; 29:38–42a; 30:19–21, 31–33, 37–38; etc.

face Moses as he transmits to them the words of God, on the condition that thereafter he will cover his radiant face. Not only is this done immediately, in the proleptic and parenthetical 34:34–35 we read that Moses followed this practice thereafter, each time he participated in an audience with God.[34] Thus the story adheres consistently to what was adumbrated in 25:22 and 29:42–43. The ongoing, protracted process of lawgiving, accomplished by means of a series of divine meetings with Moses, will begin after the tabernacle is erected; the events of 34:29–33 merely set the precedent.

(d) The brief notice in 34:32b that before placing the veil over his face Moses in fact reported to the entire people everything he had been told by God on the mountain, is resumed, following the parenthesis, in 35:1. In section after section marked by varying degrees of verbal repetition, (1) Moses assembles the people and reports to them of the meeting on the mountain, ordering them to supply the needed materials; (2) the people comply; (3) Moses then appoints the artisans and calls for talented volunteers to join them, (4) charges them with their task, and presents them with the overabundant materials supplied by the people. (5) The workers carry out their task, manufacturing every item stipulated; (6) they then display the finished products to Moses for inspection, and once his approval is given, (7) God orders Moses to assemble the entire complex on the first day of the first month. (8) Thus, just ten months after arriving at Sinai, the Israelites complete their task of constructing the portable abode for the deity.

(e) As the second year begins, the deity takes up residence, arriving in full view of the entire people in the firecloud that descends from Sinai to the tabernacle, upon which it rests, proceeding then to fill the tent, and finally shrinking into the adytum, the divine throne-room. In characteristic Priestly style, we read parenthetically that this visual arrival of God was thereafter repeated each time camp was struck, and reversed each time the march was to recommence.

(f) Resuming after the parenthesis, the divine כבוד calls to Moses, and, true to the promise made in Exod 25:22, the process of lawgiving begins. The first laws to be imparted pertain to the types of sacrifices: how they are offered and their disposition. This is logical enough, considering the primacy of worship in P. It is also mandated by the flow of the narrative, since (g) the consecration of the priesthood and dedication of the tabernacle, instructions for which Moses received on the mountain, cannot take place until the types of sacrifice have been elucidated, and the manner in which each is handled has been stipulated. Here again, P's concern for flawless, logical continuity of narrative is unmistakable.[35]

---

34. Exod 34:29–35 is correctly assigned to P, but misread, by Friedman, *Exile and Biblical Narrative*, 99. Moses *uncovers* his face in order to communicate the laws to the people, covering it only when he is not engaged in this revelatory act.

35. See the interesting treatment by Damrosch, *Narrative Covenant*, 263–66. My own reading is similar to Milgrom's, in *Leviticus 1–16*, 494.

The sign that the now-resident deity is pleased to be enshrined among the Israelites is the only natural one: fire bursts forth from the adytum, where the firecloud has deigned to confine itself, and consumes the offerings of dedication. At this point, the sacrificial regulations having already been given and the tabernacle and priesthood having been consecrated by man and God, the long-awaited process of imparting the full body of laws pertaining to the totality of life may begin.

(h) At this pivotal moment, however, there is yet another delay: two sons of Aaron haughtily attempt to attract the divine fire to their own "alien coals."[36] In their attempt to channel God's presence and revelation to their own private censers, they presumptuously flout the exclusivity of the legitimate destination of the divine fire. Their punishment is swift. Following it, their father and surviving younger brothers are bidden to continue without batting an eyelash, and (i) the Priestly law code per se is finally unfolded, a section at a time, by the enshrined deity to Moses, by means of the voice speaking to him from inside the adytum between the wings of the cherubs, as he listens from without. When this is complete, and the wages of compliance/disobedience have been duly pronounced, the entire body of law is retroactively given the only title it could possibly receive: "the laws, rules, and instructions that the LORD commanded, through Moses on Mount Sinai, between Himself and the Israelite people" (Lev 26:46; compare 27:34).

Coherence and Continuity:
P versus the Canonical Account

The first thing to note about this narrative is its scope. The length and structural complexity are the clearest evidence that it is a story and not a redactional stratum or supplement to an existing account.

The second, and more important, point is that the narrative is thoroughly complete and coherent. Nothing is out of sequence, nothing is mentioned that has not properly been introduced, and nothing is introduced that is not developed to its logical conclusion, either within the confines of the Sinai pericope or later on in P. Further, not a word is missing: nothing in the story needs to be supplied mentally or inferred, and nothing in the text needs to be reconstructed or assumed. This remarkably continuous whole is simply here for the asking, and it is eminently readable the moment the non-Priestly verses are separated out of it. Indeed, such literary-critical problems as have been identified in this enormous block of Priestly writing all pertain to the substantive details of instruction and legislation, while the narrative structure remains intact.[37] Were

---

36. See the masterful treatment of Leviticus 10 in Milgrom, *Leviticus 1–16*, 595–640.

37. A good example is Toeg, (מתן תורה, 144), who takes the stratification for granted, though the only inconsistencies he adduces pertain to the laws. On the stratification of P in general, and the relationship of P to H, consult the standard works, and recently Knohl, מקדש הדממה and Milgrom, *Leviticus 1–16*, 1–3, 13–35, 61–63. To my mind, the only flaw in narrative logic in P's

we not accustomed to picturing the lawgiving at Sinai as containing such elements as thunder, lightning, the Decalogue, the Torah-book and the ceremonial conclusion of a "covenant," we would not imagine that anything was lacking here. There is therefore no just cause to do so.

The third aspect to be noted is the fact that when this account is broken down into a series of episodes and intertwined (artfully, to be sure) with the J and E material, the coherence and continuity disintegrate, and confusion and downright contradiction appear on the simplest, narrative level:

(1) In the combined account, when Moses ascends the mountain in 24:18, it is because he has been ordered to come and receive the tablets, the law and commandments, which God has already written down (24:12). When he arrives, however, it suddenly emerges that he has been summoned for an entirely different reason: to receive the tabernacle instructions, of which no prior notification has been given. But Moses is informed that at the end of his stay, as a parting gesture, he will receive something—not the tablets, nor law and commandment—but the עדות (25:16). If the עדות were identical to the "tablets, the law and commandments," this second notification, by way of afterthought, would be superfluous, and the use of a new name would be incomprehensible. This is the unavoidable result of the combination of two extant narratives, each of which referred to the object presented by God to Moses in its own way, not of the purposeful supplementation of one.

(2) Similarly, in the combined account, the covenant is made after the laws given to Moses have been proclaimed to the people, and they have expressed their willingness to comply. After this, however, the process of lawgiving continues, and indeed the bulk of the legislation is given. This results in manifest absurdity: the covenant—written, sealed, and accepted—turns out to have been made over a very small portion of the laws. The Priestly material here does not supplement or even amend; it contradicts.

(3) This confusion is compounded when the instructions for the ark, which comprise the first paragraph of the detailed tabernacle instructions (Exod 25:10–22), are considered. Practically the first thing Moses is told about the tabernacle (once he is informed that God will dwell in it, enthroned upon His ark and cherubs) is that it is to serve as the place from which God will speak to him, conveying to him "all that I have to command the Israelites" (25:22). In the combined account, Moses would be no less confused than the reader: has not God already communicated to Moses everything that He has to command the Israelites?

Taken together, the last two points indicate that not only is the Priestly law code distinct and independent; it is introduced by the narrative as *the* law code. The code that precedes it (Exod 20:19–24:33) is not presented as its prelude,

---

account of the Sinai events occurs in Exod 40:1: since Moses has descended from the mountain long before, and the tabernacle has not yet been set up, where is Moses and where is God when the order is given to erect the tabernacle on the first day of the first month?

nor is the Priestly code presented as a supplement to what preceded, nor are the codes that follow it (Exod 34:10–27 and the Deuteronomic code) presented as its supplement. The law codes are *narrationally* mutually exclusive. The Priestly view maintains that *all* the laws were given after the divine abode was built. This is not merely a matter of sequence but rather of principle: P cannot conceive of its happening any other way. Each of the non-Priestly sources maintains that *all* the laws were given to Moses on the mountain. When they are combined, it turns out that *all* the laws were given four times. Were the Priestly writer merely adding a redactional supplement to the earlier account, he might not have been able to solve the discrepancy, but he would not have compounded it.

(4) A further discrepancy can be detected here. When, following the theophany, the fright of the people necessitates that the actual law-giving not replicate the theophany but rather be done in private, Moses reascends the mountain and reenters the misty cloud (Exod 20:18), just as he did several times in preparation for the theophany (Exod 19:3, 8, 20). But if it is perfectly acceptable for Moses to return and meet with God again and again on the mountain, what need is there for the meeting-place to be shifted to the tabernacle at all?

Indeed, the number of ascents and descents gives pause. While in the Priestly version Moses climbs and descends Mount Sinai precisely as many times as necessary—once, since thereafter God will meet with him in the tabernacle—in the canonical version, Moses ascends and descends Mount Sinai at least eight times; this is plausible in the context of the calf episode or its Yahwistic counterpart, but it is not compatible with the Priestly idea of the tabernacle and its function as the Tent of Meeting.

(5) In 34:4, Moses again ascends the mountain in order for God to engrave the second set of tablets, which, unlike the first, Moses himself has made. When he returns, however, with the tablets in his hand, no mention is made of the fact that they are the replacement set that he has made himself and that they are treated differently from the first set; they are called simply שני לחת העדת. If the Priestly section in 34:29ff. had been composed as a sequel to the JE narrative, this omission would be incomprehensible.

(6) The passage recounts instead that Moses' arrival in the camp is greeted, rather than with jubilation at his having been successful in securing forgiveness, with dismay, the result of his fearsome radiance. Yet in the combined account, this is Moses' *eighth* descent from the mountain, following his *eighth* meeting with God. One rightly asks why the radiance was not noticed on the seven previous occasions, and why only this time, when an entirely different reaction is appropriate, did the people suddenly find it necessary to deal with it.

(7) The question grows more difficult when it is recalled that, while on previous occasions Moses has spoken to God face-to-face,[38] on this visit alone,

---

38. Only, of course, in the canonical account, where it appears that Exod 33:11 is indicative of the norm. Indeed, the placement of 33:6–11 would seem to be best explained in this context: the normal, face-to-face meeting provides the contrastive background for the one-time posterior view. Yet this is of course impossible, since 33:20 states clearly that no man may view God directly.

Moses has asked to see God's face but has been denied; he has been vouch-safed a view of the divine posterior only (Exod 33:18, 19–33)! If this is so, whence the radiance? And can this rear-view of the deity be, as the sequel emphasizes, the prototype of all future meetings (34:34–35)? None of this can have been composed as the supplement of the preceding; the entire passage indicates that the writer is speaking here of Moses' first—and only—descent from the mountain, and informing the reader that thereafter he met with God in the tabernacle (ובבא משה לפני ה׳ לדבר אתו; 34:34–35).

(8) If the Priestly writer had merely been supplementing an existing account, he would presumably have placed the tabernacle instructions in Moses' *first* meeting following the theophany (at Exod 20:18 in the canonical account) or even in one of the meetings that took place before the theophany, not in the meeting following the lawgiving. They have been placed there by a redactor because they were already part of a complete account, one which already contained the notification that the interview would end with the handing of the עדות (identified by the redactor with the tablets) to Moses.

(9) Finally, just as the Priestly law code is presented as *the* laws, the Priestly tabernacle is presented as *the* Tent of Meeting. The non-Priestly tent, as shown conclusively by Haran, is something else entirely, and the two cannot be reconciled.[39] If the Priestly writer had been composing a supplementary redaction, he could have phrased his own account so that the tabernacle and the non-Priestly tent would not have competed over the same name; at the very least he could have included in his own "redaction" some acknowledgment that the other tent was also called the Tent of Meeting. He has done neither, and this is because the two accounts are mutually unaware.

The continuous nature of the Priestly material when viewed alone, and the confusion created when it is viewed in the canonical version, lead to the conclusion that it was composed to stand independently, not as a redactional supplement to the other accounts. The compilation of materials so thoroughly incompatible with J and E is the work of an author; the combination of these same materials with others is that of a redactor. The two processes cannot be attributed to the same creative effort.

The Priestly Account's Non-reliance
on the Other Sources

Was this continuous account "based on" the earlier accounts? Was it even familiar with them, in which case it utterly rejected them and attempted to replace them, or was it unaware of them? To approach this question, we must con-

---

To be sure, the confusion has resulted from the juxtaposition of 33:6–11 [E] with the narrative in 33:12ff. [J].

39. See Haran, *Temples and Temple-Service*, 260–75.

sider a fourth feature of the Priestly version, namely, the extent to which it is analogous to yet not identical with most of the non-Priestly ones. As alluded to above, all of the sources show the same literary interaction of *Gattung* and *Ziel*. The overall purpose of the writers was to convey the substance of the laws themselves and to establish the need for compliance with them by explaining their origin. Yet they did so by composing not a "law code" but a narrative account, in which the laws are encased as divine speech. Clearly the law codes embedded in each document parallel each other in certain features of structure and, of course, in topics of the legislation and even its substance. What is more, they all concur on the centrality of the figure of Moses as receiver and conveyer of the laws, the Sinai location, and the moment in Israel's history at which the laws were given. Further, as noted by Toeg,[40] P's version, just as J, E, and D, begins with a public theophany (the firecloud's gradual descent from heaven to take up residence first on the mountain and finally in the tabernacle) in which the laws per se are not yet given, after which it proceeds to a more prolonged process of law-giving, in which Moses alone participates directly. In addition, all four sources speak of a "relic" deposited with the Israelites for safekeeping in perpetuity as a reminder of the Sinai experience: the tablets in E and D, the written record of the covenant in J, and the עדות in P.

Further, similar to J and E, P associates the theophany with the performance of ceremonial rites of a unique character. Just as J describes the self-sanctification of the people in preparation for the divine descent (Exod 19:10–12, 14–15, 20–24) and relates that the elders follow Moses and Aaron up the mountain to view God, after which they partake of festive food and drink (24:9–11), and just as E recounts the covenant sacrifice performed when Moses returns with the law (24:4–8), so P connects the climax of the theophany with the rites of inauguration and dedication of the tabernacle (Leviticus 8–10).

Another point of correspondence is the element of fear. Just as E and D speak of the fearful reaction of the people to the theophany (Exod 20:18–21; Deut 5:4–5, 22–27), so P's version of the events relates the fearful response of the people to the radiation emanating from Moses' face when he returns from what we now realize can only have been his first meeting with the deity.

Finally it should be noted that all four accounts relate that between the theophany and the lawgiving some terrible offense against the deity was committed, interrupting the process and indeed threatening to abort it. In E and D, of course, this was the calf episode, integrally connected to the lawgiving both by the reason for its occurrence and by the role of the tablets in the story. In J it appears that the dispute between Moses and God on the question of whether God will continue to accompany the Israelites on their journey (Exod 33:1–5,

---

40. In what follows, I am very much indebted to the late Arie Toeg, whose succinct discussion of the Priestly Sinai tradition was unfortunately impeded by the fact that, apparently influenced by Cross, he was unable to conceive of the Priestly account as independent. See Toeg, מתן תורה, 147–57.

12–16) presupposes a crisis brought on after the theophany in which God threatens to abandon the Israelites. In the wake of the dispute, it is necessary for Moses to reascend the mountain and be assured that God's "way" includes at least temporary forgiveness (33:17–23; 34:5–9), after which the covenant laws are finally given (34:10–26). P's parallel, of course, is the sin of Nadab and Abihu, also occurring at the moment of the public theophany.

The resemblances enumerated above are, first of all, additional evidence that P is not a redactional stratum or "supplement" to J and E. The very existence of a long series of functionally duplicate elements is the clearest evidence that we have before us a separate account and not a sequel to, or redaction of, the existing ones. A redactor combines and integrates; he does not append duplication. A sequel adds new elements in order to complete the existing narrative, not competing versions of it. The canonical version is in the nature of a redaction; the Priestly version is not.

Now it might appear that the resemblances are indications of a literary dependence. Yet, when careful comparison is made, the opposite conclusion becomes virtually inescapable. For while a number of similar "ingredients" are indeed present, their use in P is so thoroughly irreconcilable with their use in the other sources, that it is inconceivable that P was even familiar with the other accounts. Furthermore, other elements of the Pentateuchal tradition, unanimously associated with the Sinai events in J, E, and D, are either lacking in P or connected in it with other Pentateuchal traditions. Most logically, then, although the Priestly narrator and his non-Priestly colleagues recall and recount the same chapter in Israel's distant past, P draws directly on national memory and on tradition, not on the other sources. The similarity between them is on the level of *Gattung*, not of literary dependence.[41]

The fullest appreciation of the uniqueness of the Priestly Sinai tradition will emerge, therefore, from a consideration of the separate elements of P's account of the lawgiving at Sinai in contrast to their counterparts in the other Pentateuchal sources. We begin with the analogous elements mentioned above, which all or most of the sources associate with the Sinai pericope, after which we will note two further elements, which though they appear in P are not internally connected to the Sinai events.

(1) *The interaction of* Gattung *and* Ziel. The overall structure of the Priestly narrative is aimed at describing the gradual arrival of the immanent Presence of God to dwell upon earth in the midst of the Israelites. At the center of this tale is the construction of the divine abode and the actual arrival of the כבוד to dwell therein. Yet, once this has been told, the bulk of the Priestly document is still to come: the laws conveyed from the tabernacle. In this way, the process of lawgiving and the laws themselves become at least a primary aim, if not indeed the supreme purpose, of the very descent of the divine Pres-

41. Cf. Koch, "P—Kein Redaktor!" 455.

ence. As much as the law collection is a function of the tabernacle story, the tabernacle story is told in order to provide the only imaginable circumstances for the giving of the laws. It goes without saying that nothing in the non-Priestly tradition even approaches this conception and its literary execution.

(2) *Moses.* The character of Moses as developed by P cannot be reconciled with the other accounts. In P Moses merely receives the divine commands and conveys them to the people. No initiative, no prophetic intercession, and no impulsiveness are attributed to him.[42] He is the spokesman for the strict letter of the law in Leviticus 10, and when, later on in the Priestly narrative (Num 20:1–13), he strays (slightly, momentarily, and only once) from his instructions, he is severely punished. This Priestly view of Moses cannot be "based on" the non-Priestly one; it is not supplementary, nor has it in any way been redactionally integrated into the earlier account. The passive, obedient, legalist Moses of P belongs to an independent, already-extant Priestly document, which is why even in the redacted version he is still intact.

(3) *Sinai.* In addition to the well-known fact that the name Sinai appears in J and P only while E and D refer to Horeb,[43] in the Priestly version Mount Sinai is not the place of lawgiving. It is merely the place where the כבוד of God rested before the lawgiving commenced. The laws were given in the tabernacle; Sinai is simply the site where the tabernacle was first erected. This cannot be harmonized with the non-Priestly view, in which Sinai is no less than the mountain of God. No wonder that in E it is introduced in advance of the Israelites' arrival there (Exod 3:1, 12), that in J Moses discovers there the attributes of God (Exod 34:5–7), and that in D the mountain burns with fire (Deut 4:11; 5:5, 19, and so on)! In the non-Priestly accounts, God dwells on the mountain; in P the firecloud comes from heaven, settles temporarily on the top of the mountain, and finally takes up permanent residence among the Israelites.[44] Early commentators were perplexed by the words בהר סיני in Lev 7:38 and במדבר סיני in Lev 25:1, 26:46, and 27:34, taking them as inconsistent with the assumption that the laws were conveyed in the tabernacle.[45] There is no cause for this. In P "the wilderness of Sinai" and "Mount Sinai" indicate simply the geographic location of the tabernacle, which is where the laws are given.

As rightly observed by Wellhausen, the tabernacle in P supersedes and replaces, indeed dwarfs, the mountain.[46] The shrine is not a "portable Sinai," as

---

42. J. Wellhausen, *Prolegomena to the History of Ancient Israel* (Eng. trans.; New York, 1957) 346.

43. See Davies, "Sinai."

44. Compare Dozeman, *God on the Mountain*, 120–30. Dozeman's far-reaching inferences seem to me somewhat unwarranted.

45. See the traditional commentators, in particular, Ramban on Lev 25:1; and cf. A. Dillmann, *Die Bücher Exodus und Leviticus* (Leipzig, 1897), and B. Baentsch, *Exodus–Leviticus* (HKAT 1/2; Göttingen, 1903) on Lev 25:1. My view is close to the view of Toeg, מתן תורה, 153–54.

46. Wellhausen, *Prolegomena*, 353.

is the non-Priestly tent of Moses.[47] It is rather the portable abode of the deity, replacing not the mountain on which he temporarily rested during his descent to earth but rather his heavenly palace and throne-room. It seems that in this case as well, the Priestly writer has taken no notice at all of his "colleagues." He has his own, utterly unique conception of the role of Mount Sinai in the giving of the law.

(4) *The time.* Presuming that all of the sources consider the Sinai/Horeb theophany to have taken place shortly after the Exodus (though to be sure, only P gives precise dates), the duration of the lawgiving process as a whole is uniquely prolonged in P. For J the theophany occurred "on the third day" (Exod 19:11, 15–16aα) and cannot have lasted longer than a day. The second stage of private lawgiving (Exod 34:5–27) seems to have been over in a matter of moments. E and D also describe the theophany at Sinai as a brief affair, and the private meeting with Moses that followed immediately logically lasted only as long as it took God to proclaim the remaining laws to Moses. The motif of "forty days and forty nights" derives from the need to provide a reason for the people's uneasiness at Moses' delayed return with the tablets. It figures prominently in the appeals for forgiveness made after the calf episode and in explaining the time required for Moses to inscribe the second set of tablets, but is not inherently connected with the lawgiving.[48]

In P the first phase of the public theophany lasts six days; the second phase at least several more; and the third phase, the building of the tabernacle, throughout which the divine firecloud remains in full view, lasts until the year is out—several months more. Nor is this all. The lawgiving begins after the כבוד has made its descent and continues, in its first phase, for almost two months more (see Num 10:11). In its second phase, following the departure from Sinai, it continues intermittently for the remainder of the Israelites' sojourn in the wilderness, achieving completeness only after the last station in the journey, the plains of Moab, has been reached (Num 36:13).

(5) *The public theophany.* In E and D the public theophany is essentially an auditory one. It consists primarily of speech, horns and thunder. It is accompanied by lightning and, in D, fire. The speech consists of commands that the

47. The suggestive notion of the tabernacle as a "portable Sinai" has occasionally been associated with Ramban (see his introduction to Exodus 25) and with U. Cassuto (*A Commentary on the Book of Exodus* [Jerusalem, 1951] on Exod 25:1). Both, however, speak only of the necessity of providing a means for the divine Presence, or a symbol of it, to accompany the Israelites from Sinai, not of taking a reminder of the mountain with them. The first to speak of the tabernacle as a "portable Sinai" may have been B. Jacob, *The Second Book of the Bible: Exodus* (Eng. trans.; Hoboken, N.J., 1992) 759; see also Weimar, "Sinai und Schöpfung," 352. It is the non-Priestly tent that, as shown by Haran (*Temples and Temple-Service*, 267, 269), reproduces and permanently reflects the revelation on Mount Sinai.

48. The delivery of the laws to the people is delayed by D until just prior to the entry into Canaan, but it still does not seem to have been a long process. In any case, the actual duration cannot be any longer than it took to deliver the oration that includes the laws (Deut 5:1–26:19).

people can at least hear (if not, perhaps, discern). The content, the Decalogue, is not only recorded in the story, it is communicated by Moses to the people, written down on the tablets, and kept for posterity. Since these commands are not repeated to Moses privately, they function as an extract of the law code, and the moment they have been spoken they are considered to have been legislated. Thus, the essence of the public theophany in E and D is that it gives a sample of what is to come.[49] In J the public theophany is only visual and minimal: the people must stand at a distance, at the foot of the mountain, and when "the LORD descends to Mount Sinai in the sight of the whole people" (Exod 19:11, 18, 20), all they perceive is thunder and lightning, the mountain being conveniently covered by smoke.

P's idea of the public theophany is totally dissimilar to the theophany of E and D, and while it resembles J somewhat, it does not appear to be derived from it. In P no words are spoken, no Decalogue or other such sample of divine law is proclaimed. Further, nature does not participate: no thunder, lightning, horns, fire, or smoke are present. Rather, the divine firecloud, which has accompanied the Israelites from Egypt, descends from the heavens to the mountain, remaining there in full view of the people while Moses meets with God. It presumably remains there, still in full view of the people, while the instructions for the tabernacle are being carried out. After this, again in full view, it continues its descent, entering the shrine and taking up residence. The emergence of the divine fire from the adytum, at the sight of which the people shout for joy, climaxes this prolonged public theophany. Yet this is not the end. In the P account the periodic meetings between God and Moses also have their theophanic aspect: the residual radiance of the divine Presence beheld by the people each time Moses reports to them another set of commands. Thus only in P does the private stage of the lawgiving ultimately involve the repeated, vicarious participation of the people.[50] And while a sort of vicarious participation of the people in Moses' audiences with God is also reported by the non-Priestly tradition (Exod 33:8), this is decisively for ad hoc, oracular communication and not for the purpose of lawgiving.

Similar to this is the entry of the firecloud into the tabernacle, combined with its departure therefrom and its heavenly guidance of the Israelites through the wilderness. Together, these recurring events make the Priestly account one of unending public theophany. As in the other accounts, the appearance of God on the mountain leads to the private lawgiving, but in P the visible Presence of God does not depart; it remains with the Israelites forever. Indeed, the express function of the tabernacle is that God's Presence may continually abide therein, and the rituals of the tabernacle dramatize this notion perpetually.

---

49. M. Greenberg, "נסה in Exodus 20:30 and the Purpose of the Sinaitic Theophany," *JBL* 79 (1960) 273–76.

50. Cf. Toeg, מתן תורה, 155–57.

(6) *The private theophany.* In J the private theophany experienced by Moses, Aaron and the elders, and the rear view of the divinity vouchsafed to Moses at a later stage are primarily visual in nature, though the latter meeting, in which the laws are given, includes a verbal aspect. In E and D of course, the private audience consists entirely of speech. According to P, in Moses' first meeting with God on the mountain, he beholds the deity, gazing at length, at least long enough to absorb the glowing radiance visible on his descent. Moreover, this is repeated each time he meets with God. He also views the heavenly image of the divine abode, again gazing at length, so that he can study and internalize the picture thoroughly. As in J the spoken is combined with the visual, but in a way totally unique to Priestly tradition.

(7) *The residue.* Here too P appears to have its own independent tradition. At the beginning of their meeting, God informs Moses that at its conclusion he will entrust him with an עֵדֻת. In Exod 40:20 Moses takes this עדות, which he had received earlier, and places it in the magnificent ark constructed in the tabernacle, just as he was instructed (Exod 25:16, 21). Elsewhere in P as well, the ark, which functions primarily as the throne/footstool of the divine presence, is called the ארון העדות (Exod 25:22, 26:33–34, 27:21, and so on).[51] Nowhere is any indication given that this עדות is a document. Not only are we not told what is written in it, we do not know for a fact that it is written at all.[52] Only in three places does it seem that P refers to the "tablets" (Exod 31:18, 32:15, and 34:29). Each of these verses, however, occurs precisely where the Elohistic account, in which the tablets play a major role, has been inserted into

---

51. Similarly, it refers to the tabernacle as משכן העדות (Exod 38:21; Num 1:50, 53 [2x]; 10:11) and אהל העדות (Num 9:15; 17:22, 23; 18:2); compare פרכת העדת (Lev 24:3). See C. L. Seow, "The Designation of the Ark in Priestly Theology," *HAR* 8 (1984) 185–98; compare Haran, *Temples and Temple-Service*, 142, 255, 272–73.

52. On the meaning of the word עדות, see M. Parnas, "עֵדֻת', עֵדוֹת', עֵדְוֹת' במקרא על רקע תעודות חיצוניות," *Shnaton* 1 (1977) 235–46; Seow, "Designation of the Ark," 192–93; Knohl, מקדש הדממה, 136–38; all of whom connect the term with Akkadian *adê* and explain it as though it were P's replacement for ברית (following Cross, *Canaanite Myth and Hebrew Epic*, 296, 300). The use of עדות in P, however, does not parallel that of ברית in the other sources. Quite the contrary. All of the sources, including P, agree that the ברית is the relationship existing between Israel and God. P simply believes this to be the promise made to Abraham, not the obligations (upon which its duration and ultimate fulfillment are indeed dependent) imposed at the lawgiving. The latter, indeed, is not called ברית in P—but it is most certainly not called עדות either! Rather, the עדות in P is an object, presented by God to Moses in commemoration of the meeting on the mountain. In 2 Kgs 11:12 as well, an עדות would seem to be an evidentiary object, not a text. The collocation of ברית and עֵדֹת in Pss 25:10 and 132:12 notwithstanding, the mere fact that P has named the ארון after the עדות, which was, after all placed in it, while the other sources speak of הברית ארון, does not in any way imply that the עֵדֻת for P is what the ברית is for the other sources. Despite the evidence of the Akkadian, which may attest to the actual origin of the Hebrew word itself, it still seems that the Priestly writers have used the word in the sense of "material evidence," as though it were derived from ʿûd 'to testify' (which, to be sure, they have associated by popular etymology with yʿd [*Niphal*] 'to meet', referring to the tabernacle as אהל/משכן העדות and as אהל מועד (see Haran, *Temples and Temple-Service*, 255, 272).

the Priestly narrative. As argued above the three verses are originally contiguous, relating that when the audience had been concluded, the עדות was given to Moses, who then descended from the mountain, unaware that his face showed the divine reflection. The insertion of the calf story, comprised of successive episodes, required that this single descent be separated into two, and that between the handing of the tablets to Moses and the first descent, the initial stages of the calf pericope be introduced.

Taking the transitional role of these verses into account, there is reason to believe that in all three the words שני לוחות have been added by the redactor and that here too, as everywhere else (Exod 16:34; 27:21; 30:6, 36; Lev 16:13; 24:3; Num 17:19, 25), P spoke only of the עדות. In this case, it may be surmised that the P account read approximately as follows:

ויתן אל משה ככלתו לדבר אתו בהר סיני עֵדֻת
ויפן וירד משה מן ההר וְהָעֵדֻת בידו
ויהי ברדת משה מהר סיני וְהָעֵדֻת ביד משה ברדתו מן ההר
ומשה לא ידע כי קרן עור פניו בדברו אתו

Only E and D refer to tablets received from God. Since J does not admit that any words were spoken to the people, it is only natural that it knows of no written evidence of the public theophany. P again differs so radically from E and D that it cannot have been derived from them, and though P resembles J, it still seems independent of it.

Toeg, who did not view the Priestly material as an independent source, suggested that the de-emphasis of the tablets in P was designed to shift attention from the earlier tradition of tablets received from God, which served as the sign of the Sinaitic covenant, to the more significant residue of the theophany in the Priestly view: the divine Presence itself.[53] His suggestion can be modified if the Priestly account is viewed as independent. P has not "de-emphasized" the tablets; they are simply absent from it. If P were derived from the other accounts, it would be difficult indeed to explain why the tablets containing the Decalogue are obscured instead of simply identified with the עדות. It is precisely because P does not even conceive of the public theophany as consisting of speech and totally ignores the possibility that the Sinaitic events constitute the making of a covenant, and further because it has an entirely unique view of the function of the ark, that it knows of no tablets. It knows of an עדות, the nature and contents of which cannot even be guessed, and which in any case is never displayed or even seen by anyone but Moses: it is a relic of the private theophany. The residue of the public theophany is nothing less than the כבוד itself.

(8) *The people's fear.* In J not only is this element missing entirely, the distinct impression is given that the people were utterly without fear. If not for

---

53. Toeg, מתן תורה, 146, 149.

the measures taken to restrict their access, they would most likely have reck-
lessly stormed the mountain and then followed Moses, Aaron, and the elders
up to view the deity (Exod 19:12–13, 21–25; 24:1–2). P cannot have been
"based on" J in this matter either. Nor is it based on E, in which the fear of the
people is what leads to, or at least indicates the necessity of prophetic mediation
between God and the people. In P the people's fear is confined to the discomfort they feel when they confront Moses' shining face, and it is overcome as
soon as the proper explanation has been made and the compromise of the veil
has been proposed. It arises, and is dealt with once and for all, after the first set
of divine instructions is issued. It has no effect at all on the later process of receiving and conveying the commandments. For the Priestly writer, the signs of
divine immanence are initially unnerving but overcome immediately, because
the ever-Present divine כבוד is for P a matter of course.

(9) *The publication of the laws.* In the biblical conception, the publication of the laws is of the essence.[54] The sources seem to agree on this, though
they differ on the amount of explicit reference and emphasis the point is given.
There does not seem to be any J report of Moses' having conveyed the laws to
the people; E relates that he first proclaimed them aloud, then wrote them
down, and finally read the book to the people (Exod 24:3–7). D, while it delays
the publication until just prior to the death of Moses, goes to great pains to
stress that all of the people were assembled, no one was absent, and even commands that this general assembly be repeated once in seven years.[55] P is unique
not so much in its report that Moses assembled the entire community but in its
presumption that he did so again and again. One must envision not only intermittent meetings with God for the purpose of receiving the laws but also regular, full assemblies of the entire Israelite people.[56]

(10) *The rituals.* J speaks of rituals that accompany the public theophany,
and E tells of an altar erected at the foot of the mountain and of the covenant
ceremony made there. D has omitted all mention of this; for D the covenant
made at Horeb consists of the Decalogue alone, and the ceremony performed
over the lawgiving is that to be held at Shechem upon entering the land of
Canaan (Deut 27:1–8). P also includes this motif but could not be more unlike
the other sources in the manner in which it employs it. Obviously for P no
sacrificial ritual can be performed until the tabernacle has been constructed.
And since for P no covenant is made at Sinai, no ceremony affirming it is made
even after the tabernacle is completed. Instead, the public theophany is interrupted, its consummation made dependent on rituals. The descent of the divine
presence to enter its earthly abode takes place the moment the tabernacle is
complete, but the climax of the theophany, the self-manifestation of the God-

54. M. Greenberg, "שמות, ספר שמות," *Encyclopedia Miqraʾit* 8.99.
55. Deut 1:1; 4:45; 5:1; 27:9, 14; 29:1, 9. In 29:13–14 the publication is figuratively extended to future generations, and in 31:11–13 instructions are given to assure that this is in fact
carried out.
56. Compare Toeg, מתן תורה, 155–56.

head in the fire surging forth from the adytum to ignite the altar, is delayed until the inaugural, purificational, and dedicatory ceremonies of the Priesthood and tabernacle have taken place. These do not pertain directly to the process of lawgiving, but without them it cannot begin. Only after the divine abode and its furnishings are fit for dwelling, the household staff ready to perform its task, and the fixed regimen of service rehearsed, does the divine being manifest himself. This is the significance of the fact that the first seven chapters of Leviticus, containing the specific instructions for the several types of sacrifice, are positioned between the arrival of the כבוד and its appearance: the instructions are necessary in order for the inaugural rituals to be performed, and the כבוד will not make its appearance until this has been done. Thus in P ritual does not ratify, much less celebrate, the giving of the law. It is rather a precondition for it. Moreover, it is not the ritual of covenant-making, but the institution of the permanent ritual, on which the giving of the law depends. There is no covenant ritual in Priestly legislation.

(11) *The crisis.*   Last among the points of contact between P and the other sources is the motif of the crisis that follows closely upon the Sinai events. In the E and D accounts, of course, as the theophany opens with the prohibition of other gods, the crisis that ensues is the violation of this foremost command; the calf apostasy is presented in both sources. In the fragmentary J account, it can only be inferred that the crisis that has led to the threat of divine abandonment is something of a similar nature. In P the crisis is of course connected directly with the tabernacle cult, and the sin is committed not by the people but by priests. More significantly, it is not one of apostasy but of offense against the indwelling divine Presence. The sin of Nadab and Abihu, one of disobedience in the first degree, is in their attempt to deflect the divine fire to their own firepans, in which they have placed "unauthorized coals," thus seeking to channel the energy of the divine Presence away from its chosen altar and to their own unwarranted offerings.

Not only in the nature of the "original sin" does the Priestly version differ. In P no plea for mercy is issued, and no reprieve is granted. Disobedience in P, particularly in matters pertaining to the divine כבוד, is met with untempered justice; when the sacred is at stake, there is no room for any emotion other than righteous indignation. Here too, it seems most plausible that the barest kernel of the motif is held in common by all of the sources, but the Priestly account cannot possibly be derived from any or all of the others.[57]

---

57. The absence of the calf episode from the Priestly account is significant for another reason, pertaining more to the tabernacle and its cult than to the lawgiving per se. It is sometimes suggested, and not only by midrashic interpreters, that the establishment of the tabernacle cult, indeed the sacrificial worship of God in general, was somehow connected with the calf apostasy. Yet this is clearly not the case; indeed, even in the canonical account, the sequence indicates that the tabernacle and the cult were the a priori plan of the deity, not a reaction to human failings. The recognition that the account of the building of the tabernacle and the sacrificial laws has no knowledge of the calf episode confirms this and establishes further that none of the tabernacle rituals

(12) *The evidence of D.* As a corollary to the above, it must not be over-looked that the Deuteronomic tradition of the lawgiving, though it must be reconstructed from the discontinuous references to it in Moses' orations (Deut 4:5–15, 5:1–33, 9:7–10:5), shows no familiarity whatsoever with the Priestly material in Exodus 19ff. Nowhere does the Deuteronomic oration mention the tabernacle or any of its institutions or rituals, nor does it refer in any way to the indwelling כבוד and all that it implies or to the prolonged process of intermittent lawgiving that took place in the wilderness. Conventional criticism, which places P after D in any case, might of course simply take the absence from D of all knowledge of the incontestably Priestly traditions of the Sinai events as further evidence that the Priestly account is later than the Deuteronomic. But for those who place D after P, this fact at least corroborates what has been argued so far: that the Priestly account is an independent one, one that existed in isolation from the other sources.

The Covenant and the "Torah" in P

Finally, I want to make note of two central features of the lawgiving that are present in the non-Priestly Sinai traditions only. Though the Priestly document is not unfamiliar with them, it employs them in a way unconnected with the actual Sinai events.

(1) *The covenant.* As scholars have long recognized, the covenant in P consists of the promise of land and progeny made to the patriarchs. The fulfillment of the covenant is in two stages; a miraculous number of progeny is procreated in Egypt before Moses is born, whereas the possession of the land takes place after the Pentateuchal narrative ends, that is, after Moses dies. Thus the career of Moses in P spans the gap between the two stages. The reiteration of the promise of land to Moses at the outset of his career (Exod 6:2–8; see also 2:24) serves as the affirmation of the covenant: that which has not yet been fulfilled is still in force.[58]

Neither the theophany and lawgiving at Sinai nor any element of them is conceived of by P as a "covenant." The pronouncement of blessings and curses

---

including the "atonement" rituals in Leviticus 8–9, contains any element of commemoration of, or expiation for, the calf apostasy.

58. On the the Sinai covenant in P, see M. Noth, *The Laws in the Pentateuch and Other Studies* (Philadelphia, 1957) 91–92; W. Zimmerli, "Sinaibund und Abrahambund," *Theologische Zeitschrift* 16 (1960) 268–80; Cross, *Canaanite Myth and Hebrew Epic*, 312–13, 318; N. Lohfink, "Die Abänderung der Theologie des priesterlichen Geschichtswerks im Segen des Heiligkeitsgesetzes," *Karl Elliger Festschrift* (AOAT 18; ed. H. Gese and H. P. Rueger; Kevelaer, 1973) 129–36; Blenkinsopp, "Structure of P," 278–79; Cazelles, "Alliance du Sinai"; W. Gross, "Bundeszeichen und Bundesschluß in der Priesterschrift," *Trierer theologische Zeitschrift* 87 (1978) 98–115; Klein, "Message of P," 59–62; Y. Hoffman, יציאת מצרים באמונת המקרא (Tel Aviv, 1983) 129–33; Seow, "Designation of the Ark"; Emerton, "Priestly Writer," 394; Weimar, "Sinai und Schöpfung," 353–58; Knohl, מקדש הדממה, 135–39 (p. 137 and notes 79–80 for additional references and discussion of earlier scholarship).

in the Priestly lawgiving does not change this fact; at the very most it may indicate that the covenant form has influenced the literary structure (though if this were so, as many scholars believe, it would be difficult to understand why they have been placed at the end of a portion of the laws, those given before the departure from Sinai, instead of at the conclusion of the lawgiving process, after Numbers 36).[59]

P does find room to mention the covenant in connection with Sinai in the promises and threats of Leviticus 26. Here too, almost all of the references are to the fulfillment or abrogation by God of the covenant made with the patriarchs (emphatically in v. 42; also vv. 44–45), the only addition being that the Exodus is now seen as part of its fulfillment (v. 45). Only v. 15 would seem to differ, denoting failure to comply with the laws and statues of God as abrogation of his covenant. Still, as the phrase הפר ברית appears in v. 44 where it certainly refers to divine reversal of the land promise (in opposition to הקים ברית in v. 9), the peculiar use of v. 15 may be a rhetorical reflex. Along with the somewhat obscure threat of the "covenant vengeance" with which God characterizes his terrible swift sword (v. 25), this may indeed be a case of innovative, local rhetoric employed by H, rather than consistent terminology, which cannot be taken as being reflective of any overriding viewpoint.

Still, it is not true that P sees the laws given at Sinai as unconnected with the covenant. The evidence of Leviticus 26 attests to the fact that P acknowledges that the promise of land and progeny are contingent upon Israel's compliance with the laws and statutes given by God to Moses. This is corroborated by P's insistence that this is particularly true of compliance with the rules of purity, physical and moral (Lev 15:31, 16:16, 18:24–30, 20:22–24; and Num 5:3). Circumcision, the sign of the covenant, is a performative command; its neglect results in כרת—namely, at the individual level, exclusion from the promise of progeny (Gen 17:1–14).[60] Observance of the Sabbath, also a command, is the second sign of the covenant (Exod 31:12–17).[61] *The conditional nature of the promise is not disputed by P*; rather, the meaning of the word ברית. In P the ברית is only the promise, not the contractual relationship connected with it. Thus in the Priestly tradition no ברית was made at Sinai.

The most telling texts are the Priestly superscriptions at the end of the two stages of lawgiving: Lev 26:46 (and the resumptive repetition in 27:34), which sums up the lawgiving prior to the departure from Sinai, and Num 36:13,

---

59. As noted by Knohl (מקדש הדממה, 138), the blessings and curses are actually quite absent from the Priestly law code once the Holiness stratum is subtracted, further corroborating that the Sinai lawgiving is not, in the Priestly conception, a ברית.

60. M. V. Fox, "The Sign of the Covenant," *RB* 87 (1980) 557–96.

61. The role of circumcision and Sabbath observance as covenant signs is assigned by Knohl to H, as is Num 5:1–4 (מקדש הדממה, 23–26, 82, 96–97); so are Lev 18:24–30 and 20:22–24 by all critics. Yet in light of Lev 15:31 and 16:16 and the expiation procedures in general, even Knohl would have to acknowledge the conditionality of the divine indwelling and by extension, of Israel's survival, in P.

which sums up the lawgiving during the subsequent journey. The non-Priestly sources consistently use the term 'covenant' when they refer to the full body of legislation; P does not. The Priestly authors do not reject or depreciate the Sinai covenant; they are simply unfamiliar with it. For them, the word 'covenant' has an entirely different sense, and in connection with the Sinai theophany and lawgiving it is simply inapplicable.

(2) *The "Torah."*   All of the non-Priestly sources relate that the private stage of the lawgiving was preserved in written form. E and J presume that the writing took place soon after the laws were given to Moses, while D of course delays the writing until the laws have been transmitted to the people, just prior to the entry into Canaan.

P represents a singular departure from the other traditions: it has no reference to any written Torah at all. The term תורה in P means 'rule or instructions pertaining to a particular area of legislation', and it is part of the divine vocabulary. With one exception (Lev 7:37), only God uses the word 'Torah' in P, always referring to something he has just said or is about to say; not the narrator. As with the 'covenant', the non-Priestly sources speak of the entire body of legislation as 'the Torah'; P does not. In P, Moses is not believed to have committed any laws to writing at all; rather, he is believed to have written down, at God's dictation, the list of the starting-points of the stages of the wilderness journey (Num 33:2). P relates that Moses received the laws in a series of audiences with God and conveyed them verbatim to the people, but nowhere is he charged with writing them down, and nowhere is it related that he did so. Nowhere does the Priestly work itself claim to be 'the Torah'; like J and E, it is the account of an anonymous, omniscient, third-person narrator, who does not even claim to have been a witness to the events.

Here lies the simplest explanation for one of the most frequently noticed stylistic features of P, namely, its emphasis on verbal repetition and precise, to-the-letter execution of the divine commands. What the other sources call 'the Torah' is in the Priestly view an entirely oral body of instruction; no single collective noun is ever used to denote it. Precision in its oral transmission and, as noted, the widest possible publication are essential because nothing is written down. Nowhere in P is תורה a body of teaching or law, and nowhere is any "book" of laws mentioned in P.

Summary

The Priestly view of the Sinai lawgiving can thus be appreciated in all its uniqueness only against the background of the other sources, with due attention given to elements entirely lacking in P, to elements exclusive to P, and to the unique way in which elements common to the sources are employed by P.

P knows of no covenant made at Sinai or of any covenant ceremony. It knows of no theophanic upheaval of nature, no divine voice heard from the heavens, no holy mountain, and no Decalogue. Thus it knows of no tablets of the law or of any other written record of the theophany. Indeed, it does not even know of a written record of the laws given subsequently. The absence of the tablets is perfectly natural, since, because P is unaware of the worship of the golden calf or any other public apostasy, it has no need of broken or replaced tablets. It assigns no prophetic role to Moses or any role to the Sinai events in the foundation of the prophetic office. Thus it has no reason to attribute Moses' role as mediator to the people's fear; the motif of fear is all but lacking, and the necessity of the laws being communicated through Moses requires no explanation.

The infrastructure of the Sinai events in the Priestly view is provided by the arrival and descent of the divine כבוד to dwell permanently among the Israelites. The theophany and lawgiving are subordinate to and subsumed under this heading, as is everything else in the Priestly Sinai pericope and all of the Priestly ritual. Indeed, as long recognized, this is the aim and climax of the Priestly narrative as a whole. The tabernacle of God is the exclusive locus of divine communication with man, and practically the only instructions conveyed to Israel before it was constructed are those pertaining to its construction. The giving of the law depends not only on the divine indwelling; it is contingent upon the prior establishment and maintenance of the tabernacle cult and its permanent institutions.[62]

In the Priestly view, the theophany happened to occur at Sinai; it could have occurred anywhere, and its residue, the divine Presence, is portable. The mountain recedes into the distance long before the Israelites depart from it. Once the כבוד enters the divine abode the mountain disappears, having served only as a temporary resting-place.

The Priestly account emphasizes over and over again the immanence of the divine Presence. God's closeness is manifest in the lengthy, constantly visible process of the arrival of the כבוד, in the constant presence of the cloud hovering over the occupied adytum, and in the repeated arrival and departure of the כבוד during the journey from Sinai. It is also repeatedly felt in the physical contact made between the divine and the human spheres in the fire that bursts forth from before the LORD and in the experience of vicarious revelation, in which the people participate each time they gaze upon Moses' face as he proclaims an installment of the laws to them. Of course it is also at the root of most of the Priestly ritual. The Priestly tradition allows for no doubt and requires no leap of faith concerning the origin and authenticity of the laws:

---

62. The attempt by Koch ("Eigenart," 45–50) to present the Priestly legend as being aimed at extolling the grace of God in providing a means for man to atone for his sins (that is to say, the cult, which he sees as primarily expiatory) is not only overtly Christological in the extreme but is also inconsistent with P's view of the cult and its doctrine of sin and expiation. The overall function of the cult, as Haran's writings make clear (see above, p. 104 n. 2), is the honor and worship of the enshrined deity; the essence of atonement, as demonstrated in the writings of Milgrom (see above, p. 104 n. 2), is purification of the shrine from the defilement that wrongdoing causes to accumulate there. Koch, by postulating that the sanctuary was created in order that there be a means of atonement, places the proverbial cart before the horse.

though they were given through an intermediary, they were openly and indisputably given by the ever-present, indwelling deity.

In this prolonged and sublime process of lawgiving, only one momentary
impediment interferes: the crime of insult against the immanent divine Presence. It is immediately dealt with, however, and though its consequences become an object lesson for the future, it has no repercussions whatsoever. The
absolutely imperative nature of the commands is such that both Israel's life
and God's continued abiding Presence among the Israelites are said to be contingent on their meticulous observance. If they are kept to the fullest, these
benefits are guaranteed, and only then is there any room even to speak of God's
covenant—his promise of land and progeny.

The unique Priestly view of the connection between the giving of the law
and the presence of God in the tabernacle is of course a reflection of the Priestly
conception of the relationship between Israel and its God. Observance of the
laws, in particular the sacrificial cult, including the regular service of the deity
and the constant concern for the protection of the sacred and the elimination of
contamination from the divine abode, is after all what will ensure the enduring
Presence of God among the Israelites, upon which their national existence
depends. The fact that the giving of the laws is inextricably bound up with the
arrival and indwelling of the Presence is the clearest expression of this belief.

The tabernacle-lawgiving pericope, from Sinai to the plains of Moab,
comprises the bulk of the Priestly work and is indisputably its climax and focal
point, indeed its raison d'être. Our analysis opens wide a window to redefining
the work's literary genre. It is, as aptly phrased by Toeg, a myth.[63] Yet it is not
primarily the myth of the establishment of the deity's earthly resting-place,[64] or
a myth of revelation for its own sake.[65] For the authors, the immanent, regularly visible, localized, portable, divine Presence belonged to the realm of tradition or national memory. What remained in perpetuity was the temple (the
reminder of these sublime but long-distant events) and the law: the body of divine commands including, but not restricted to, the maintenance of the temple
and its cult. Compliance with the law would ensure survival and blessing, the
fulfillment of the ברית—the promise to Abraham. The Priestly work, generi-
cally speaking, was for its creators and earliest readers what the canonical
Torah became for Judaism: the myth of the giving of the law.

---

63. Toeg, מתן תורה, 158 n. 132. Though Toeg is speaking of the genre of the Pentateuch,
his conclusion rests primarily on the Priestly work (which, as noted, he takes as the redactional
stratum of the Pentateuch).

64. Ibid.

65. This is rightly stressed by Licht, "גילוי שכינה," 254. Though he pulverizes the Pentateuchal Sinai and lawgiving accounts into disconnected granules, Licht is the only recent writer
to have correctly sensed the obvious: that throughout the Pentateuchal tradition, the essence and
primary aim of the Sinai events was the lawgiving. Sincere thanks to Simeon Chavel and Shimon
Bar-On for their helpful comments.

SONS OF GOD(S), HEROES, AND *nephilim*: REMARKS ON GENESIS 6:1–4

J. A. Soggin

OUR TEXT IS ONE of the most controversial of the Hebrew Bible. C. Westermann[1] devotes some 27 pages to its exegesis, but there are many more items that cannot be explained than items that can be considered satisfactorily settled.

The first problem is to delimit the textual unit. Does it end at v. 4 ("The Nephilim were on the earth in those days, and afterwards as well, when the sons of the gods had intercourse with the daughters of men and bore children for them. These are the heroes who were in ancient times famous men")? Most authors hold this view. Or does it include vv. 5–7? Benno Jacob, in his commentary,[2] favors the latter and therefore considers the episode to be reporting the corruption of human beings in contrast with the righteousness of Noah. But he gives no reason for this combination of verses, which, as far as I can see, is not accepted as part of the unit by any modern commentary. That we are dealing with a self-contained episode ending at v. 4 seems relatively clear.

The meaning of single verses and of single words therein is also controversial. What does *něpilîm* (v. 4) mean? What is the meaning of *yādôn* and *běšaggam* in v. 3? And what kind of information does v. 3 want to convey to the reader? As far as v. 3 is concerned, there is a certain consensus among scholars that we are dealing with a late addition.[3] But if this is true, why is the passage so unclear? Could such an explanation not be an attempt to bypass the difficulties by ignoring them? Or could the meaning of v. 3 have been blurred on purpose by later redactors, in order to eliminate an unorthodox statement, as

1. C. Westermann, *Genesis* (BKAT 1/1; Neukirchen-Vluyn, 1974).
2. Benno Jacob, *Das Erste Buch der Tora, Genesis* (Berlin, 1934; repr. New York, no date).
3. Thus, already, Julius Wellhausen, *Die Composition des Hexateuchs* (3d ed.; Berlin, 1899) 307ff.; there is a full treatment by R. Bartelmus, *Heroentum in Israel und seiner Umwelt* (ATANT 65; Zurich, 1979) 15ff.; and cf. the latest analysis by L. Perlitt, *Riesen im Alten Testament* (Göttinger Akademie der Wissenschaften; Göttingen, 1990) 41–42.

G. Garbini has been suggesting lately for other cases?[4] A satisfactory answer to these questions has not yet been given and will hardly be given for some time to come, and so the scholar is left with an unsolved crux. Whether Gen 6:4 is a late or an early part of the text, its meaning cannot be adequately explained.

This leaves us with the word *nĕpilîm*. The term is rare: it appears only in Num 13:33 and in our text. A proposal to read the word also in Ezek 32:27, instead of the MT's *nōpĕlîm*[5] has been made in the past but has no textual backing. An etymology from the root *n-p-l* seems to be obvious but does not lead anywhere,[6] and thus it may be better to drop it altogether. The parallelism in Num 13:33 allows us to conclude that there the word means 'giants', as in 1QapGen (= 1Q20) II 1, and this is what one finds in the LXX of Gen 6:4: οἱ δὲ γίγαντες; Aquila has οἱ ἐπιπίπτοντες, again deriving the word from *nāpal*. The Targum goes in the same direction, but Symmachus reads οἱ βίαιοι 'the violent ones', and the same pattern is followed for *ʾanšê haššēm* at the end of the text, where Aquila has οἱ δύνατοι. The Vulgate has *gigantes* and *potentes*, respectively.

The last verse of our text states that "in those days" there were *nĕpilîm* "on earth," "when the sons of the gods had intercourse with the daughters of men"; but not, as in Numbers 13, where the word appears this time in parallelism with *haggibbōrîm*. It therefore seems rash to identify the *gibbōrîm* with the offspring of these marriages, even if it were from the point of view of history of religions and folklore the most obvious suggestion. *Gibbōrîm* in the Hebrew Bible are, except when the reference is to Yhwh, heroes in the sense of warriors, without any supernatural connotation. Although in Western languages the word can lend itself to mythical interpretations, such a rendering is impossible for the Hebrew word.

However, in later times the text was used in various ways. In the New Testament, Jude (v. 6) seems to interpret the Genesis 6 passage as referring to the fall of rebellious angels; apocalyptic, intertestamental literature appears to have been well aware of the Genesis text (see Enoch 6:1ff.), as were the Enoch fragments from Qumran published by J. T. Milik,[7] who even suggests that Genesis 6 is a summary (and an intentionally faulty one at that) of the original of the text in Enoch.

Be that as it may, the present function of the text is to show the increase of sin among human beings; and this increase is one of the prerequisites for the Flood. Therefore the exact meaning of the text seems not even to have been important to the author(s). What really matters was to show that humanity *deserved* the deluge, something that was inadequately stated in 6:5ff. And this could favor a connection with vv. 5–7.

4. G. Garbini, oral communication.

5. See W. Zimmerli, *Ezechiel* (BKAT 13/2; Neukirchen-Vluyn, 1969), vol. 2, ad loc.; R. S. Hendel, "Of Demigods and the Deluge: Towards an Interpretation of Genesis 6:1–4," *JBL* 106 (1987) 21–22.

6. See Perlitt, *Riesen im Alten Testament*, 39–40.

7. See J. Milik, *The Books of Enoch* (Oxford, 1974) 31.

THE SIGNIFICANCE OF THE END OF DEUTERONOMY (DEUTERONOMY 34:10–12)

Jeffrey H. Tigay

Never again did there arise in Israel a prophet like Moses, whom the Lord singled out, face to face, for the various signs and portents that the Lord sent him to display in the land of Egypt, against Pharaoh and all his courtiers and his whole country, and for all the great might and awesome power that Moses displayed before all Israel (Deut 34:10–12, NJPSV).

THE STATEMENT at the end of Deuteronomy that Moses was never equaled by another prophet has attracted relatively little attention. Perhaps scholars have implicitly agreed that this is Moses' "literary epitaph" and hence deserves no more attention than is usually paid to epitaphs.[1] But a moment's reflection should suffice to indicate that the passage is more than that. It is hardly stereotypical. Biblical biographies of other great leaders usually end with their burial and do not go on to evaluate their role in history.[2] As the final statement about Moses in a markedly ideological book, and as the book's own conclusion,[3] the passage is likely to have a significance that serves the ideological aims of the book as

Author's note: Menahem Haran is a scholar whom I have long admired for the thoroughness and depth of his magisterial contributions to scholarship and the keen intuition that has led him into areas of research that many others had not suspected could be so rewarding. It is a pleasure for me to take part in this expression of esteem and gratitude for his many personal courtesies and for all that I have learned from his work.

1. P. C. Craigie, *The Book of Deuteronomy* (NICOT; Grand Rapids, 1976) 406. G. A. Smith calls the passage "homage to [Moses'] incomparable rank as a prophet" (*The Book of Deuteronomy* [Cambridge, 1918] 378), while A. Bertholet calls it a "panegyric" (*Deuteronomium* [Freiburg, 1899] 113).

2. See, for example, Gen 25:9–10; 35:29; 49:33–50:13; 50:26; Josh 24:30, 33; Judg 8:32; 12:7; 16:31; 1 Sam 25:1; 31:13; 1 Kgs 2:10; 2 Kgs 13:20. The evaluation of Josiah in 2 Kgs 23:25 is modeled on Deut 34:10 and is not the final sentence in the account of his life.

3. The endings of biblical books are discussed by Isaac B. Gottlieb, "*Sof Davar*: Biblical Endings," *Prooftexts* 11 (1991) 213–24.

a whole. Like the Bible's declarations about the incomparability of YHWH, it may well have a polemical purpose.

Medieval Jewish writers were alert to the polemical possibilities of the passage. Combining it with Deut 4:2 and 13:1 ("You shall not add anything to what I command you or take any thing away from it"), they understood it as asserting the supreme authority of Moses' Torah, forestalling attempts by later prophets to contradict or supersede Moses' Torah.[4] These writers meant their interpretation as a rebuttal of Christianity and Islam, for which reason Maimonides held that belief in Moses' incomparability as a prophet is a dogma of Judaism.[5] More recently, S. Dean McBride, avoiding the anachronism, observed that in biblical times the incomparability of Moses would have had the effect of making his Torah "the measure of truth by which all subsequent prophetical revelations were to be assessed and interpreted."[6]

Both of these views agree that Deut 34:10–12 underscores the superiority of Moses as a prophet *of YHWH*; Moses' teachings are the most authentic expression of YHWH's will because YHWH favored him and dealt with him more directly than any other prophet (cf. Num 12:6–8). It goes without saying that Moses is also greater than prophets of other gods, but this is not the issue here (according to Deut 18:20, prophesying in the name of other gods is a capital crime). Here the aim of the text is to authenticate Moses' teachings against competing versions of *Yahwistic* revelation.

What competing versions might Deuteronomy have in mind? One possibility is suggested by the fact that the *waw* at the beginning of v. 10 could be adversative, meaning 'but', with the intention of contrasting Moses and Joshua; Joshua succeeded Moses but was not his equal. This would have the effect of subordinating the laws given by Joshua at Shechem (Josh 24:25–26) to those given by Moses. Another possibility is that the passage means to subordinate any aspects of later prophetic teachings that might be inconsistent with those of Moses, such as the classical prophets' critique of sacrifice.

These possibilities, however, are purely theoretical and do not correspond to Deuteronomy's express concerns. There is evidence, in Deuteronomy and

---

4. Seforno: "No other prophet ever reached his level of prophecy and thus it is clear that no prophet is permitted to institute new laws henceforth" (cf. *b. Šabb.* 104a; see R. Pelcovitz, *Sforno: Commentary on the Torah* [Brooklyn, 1989] 2.903); Gersonides, ad loc. and lesson 15; Crescas, אור ה' II, 4, 3 ([Vienna ed., 1859 45a [ref. courtesy of Daniel Lasker]; cited, with better reading [נצחותה, instead of בצחותה], by Abravanel, פירוש על התורה [Jerusalem, 1979] 354 col. ii).

5. Maimonides, Introduction to *Pereq Ḥeleq* (*m. Sanh.* 10).

6. S. Dean McBride, "Biblical Literature in Its Historical Context: The Old Testament," *HBC* (ed. J. L. Mays et al.; San Francisco, 1988) 23. In a paper presented to the Biblical Colloquium in October, 1992, McBride suggested that the passage would have the effect of relativizing Ezekiel's "Torah" (Ezekiel 40–48) and subordinating it to that of Moses. This is certainly what happened to Ezekiel's Torah in late Second Temple times. Talmudic sources state that because it contradicts Moses' Torah, the book of Ezekiel would have been withdrawn from circulation (*nignaz*) had it not been for one Hananiah ben Hezekiah who found ways to harmonize it with Moses' Torah (*b. Šabb.* 13b). In what follows, I attempt to explain the passage in the light of Deuteronomy's own emphases.

in books describing conditions around the time that it was discovered, that some parties claimed that YHWH authorized practices radically inconsistent with the fundamental principles of Deuteronomy. These parties were polytheistic Yahwists or, to borrow Morton Smith's term, "syncretistic Yahwists"[7] who claimed, among other things, that YHWH commanded Israelites to offer child sacrifices and to worship his subordinates, the heavenly bodies and other gods, in addition to himself. In the following discussion I shall refer to them as polytheistic when I refer only to their advocacy of worshiping many gods, and as syncretistic when I include as well their advocacy of what the Bible considers to be distinctively pagan practices, such as child sacrifice.

That some Yahwists believed that YHWH accepted human sacrifice is clear from the case of Jephthah and from other evidence to be cited below. It is also clear that there were polytheistic Yahwists in ancient Israel who worshiped YHWH along with other deities. Joash had a Yahwistic theophoric name and told his son Gideon about YHWH's wondrous deeds, but he also had a Baal altar and an *asherah*.[8] Ahab gave his children Yahwistic names but worshiped Baal as well.[9] Elijah's demand—characteristically monotheistic—that Israel stop "hopping on the two boughs" and choose between YHWH and Baal implies that his audience was likewise worshiping both simultaneously.[10] From the biblical point of view such polytheistic Yahwism is a contradiction in terms: worshiping other gods is by definition "abandonment" of YHWH. But this definition is a dogmatic hyperbole.[11] Polytheistic Yahwists would have rejected it because polytheists did not have to choose one god to the exclusion of others.

Evidence for syncretistic Yahwism is present in Deuteronomy itself and in sources describing conditions in the seventh century, when the book was developing. Although I have elsewhere expressed doubt that polytheism, including syncretistic Yahwism, was extensive in late monarchic times in Israel,[12] syncretistic Yahwism enjoyed royal support and was perceived by monotheists as theologically dangerous enough to require a strong response. Deuteronomy is aware of claims by syncretists that YHWH wants Israelites to worship other gods alongside of him. This is clear from 17:3, which describes "the worship of other gods . . . the sun or the moon or any of the heavenly host" as "something which I (YHWH) never commanded." The need to deny that YHWH made

7. M. Smith, *Palestinian Parties and Politics that Shaped the Old Testament* (New York, 1971) 27 and passim.

8. Judg 6:11, 13, 25.

9. 1 Kgs 16:32, 22:40; 2 Kgs 3:1, 10:18.

10. 1 Kgs 18:21.

11. Because the Bible demands exclusive loyalty to YHWH, it hyperbolically characterizes the worship of other gods as abandonment of him, since whatever relationship the idolater continues to maintain with Him is meaningless. Note how Isa 1:11–15 scolds Israel for lavishly (though hypocritically) maintaining YHWH's worship, while vv. 4 and 28 accuse them of "abandoning," "spurning," and "turning their backs on" him. Compare also Jer 2:4–13 and 17 with 7:9–10 and 14.

12. J. H. Tigay, *You Shall Have No Other Gods: Israelite Religion in the Light of Hebrew Inscriptions* (HSS 31; Atlanta, 1986).

such a command implies that others claimed that he did. Some commentators take "which I never commanded" as a case of litotes, a figure of speech in which a positive idea is expressed by negating its contrary, meaning "which I commanded not to do" (compare "not a few" meaning "many").[13] However, the same phrase appears several times in Jeremiah, where God describes child sacrifice as something "which I never commanded, never decreed, and which never came to my mind" (Jer 7:31; 19:5; 32:35). There the phrase is not a litotes ("never came to my mind" hardly means "came to my mind not to do") but a denial of something that others claimed was true. It appears from Ezek 20:25–26 that some people claimed that YHWH did require child sacrifice; this is the claim that Jeremiah is rejecting.[14] In Deut 17:3, therefore, "something I never commanded" is meant to deny claims that YHWH ordains the worship of certain other gods.[15] Just as human sacrifice had advocates in Jeremiah's time claiming divine authority, the polytheism rejected by Deuteronomy must have been supported by similar claims in the period preceding the book's composition. We do not know who made such claims, but they clearly included Manasseh and Amon, the kings of Judah who established the worship of other gods in the temple of YHWH.[16]

It would have seemed perfectly natural to polytheistic Yahwists that YHWH authorized the worship of other deities, conceived as his subordinates. Even the monotheistic text of the Torah states that God granted the heavenly bodies dominion (Gen 1:16, 18), and Deuteronomy acknowledges that he ordained the worship of the heavenly bodies by other nations (4:19).[17] An Israelite poly-

---

13. A. B. Ehrlich, מקרא כפשוטו (New York, 1969); S. R. Driver, *Deuteronomy* (ICC; 3d ed.; Edinburgh, 1902). Cf. Num 11:11; Isa 10:7.

14. M. Greenberg, *Ezekiel* (AB 22; Garden City, N.Y., 1983) 369–70; "Ezekiel 20 and the Spiritual Exile," עז לדוד (Studies . . . Ben Gurion; ed. Y. Kaufmann et al.; Jerusalem, 1964) 437 n. 3; and 1964 class lecture on Deuteronomy 17. Similarly Mic 6:7 and Deut 12:29–31, although they do not necessarily imply the existence of a heterodox view that YHWH commanded child sacrifice, imply at least the existence of a view that he would accept it.

15. Cf. *Sipre Deuteronomy* §148: This commandment "includes one who joins (YHWH's name to idols)," that is, who worships YHWH along with other gods (see D. Z. Hoffmann, ספר דברים [Tel Aviv, 1959] 2.300).

16. See 2 Kgs 21:3–7; 23:4, 11. Those behind the pagan practices in the temple described in Ezekiel 8 must have made similar claims (as Morton Smith observed: "The temple was the temple of Yahweh; such things could not have happened in it without the consent and cooperation of the priests of Yahweh. This proves that the cult of Yahweh was not conceived as exclusive by the priests of his principal temple. Those who did conceive of it as exclusive were not at the time the official representatives of the country's legally established religion" [*Palestinian Parties*, 26]). However, all or most of these practices likely reflect the time of Manasseh, not Ezekiel; see Kaufmann, *The Religion of Israel* (trans. M. Greenberg; Chicago, 1960) 405–8, 430–32; M. Greenberg, "Prolegomenon," in C. C. Torrey, *Pseudo-Ezekiel and the Original Prophecy, and Critical Articles by S. Spiegel and C. C. Torrey* (New York, 1970) xx–xxv; contrast M. Smith, "The Veracity of Ezekiel, the Sins of Manasseh, and Jeremiah 44:18," *ZAW* 87 (1975) 11–16.

17. See also Deut 32:8–9 (reading *bny ᵓlhym* in place of *bny ysrᵓl*, with 4QDeutʲ and LXX); Sir 17:17.

theist, even one who believed that YHWH was the supreme deity, might well believe that YHWH favored the worship of His "fellow gods" and lesser supernatural beings even by Israelites.[18]

Deut 13:2–6 confirms that Deuteronomy is concerned about advocates of polytheistic Yahwism who base their claims on an oracle from YHWH. There, the "prophet or dream-diviner" who advocates the worship of other gods is said to have *dibber sārâ ʿal YHWH* 'uttered falsehood about YHWH'. Many translations and commentators understand the Hebrew to mean 'he urged disloyalty to YHWH',[19] which would admittedly fit the context, but this translation is unlikely. It is not certain that *dibber sārâ* ever means 'urge disloyalty' in the Bible, but there are several passages where the idiom clearly means 'utter falsehood'. Most importantly, when describing the speech of prophets, *dibber sārâ ʿal YHWH*

18. Cf. M. Greenberg, "Religion: Stability and Ferment," *Culture and Society* (WHJP 4/2; Jerusalem, 1979) 104. For pagan gods ordaining the worship of other gods or spirits, see Enuma Elish VI 110–20 (E. A. Speiser, "Akkadian Myths and Epics," *ANET*, 69); and Akkadian letters *e* and *g* (W. L. Moran, "Akkadian Letters," *ANET*, 624). Even later monotheism at times made room for the worship of subordinate divine beings along with YHWH; Kaufmann notes the worship of saints and intercessors in Christianity and Islam and the rabbinic understanding of the scapegoat as a propitiatory offering to Sammael (*Religion of Israel*, 135–38; cf. Smith, *Palestinian Parties*, 218 n. 111). Note Josephus's description of the morning prayers to the sun by the Essenes (who were no polytheists): "as though entreating him to rise" (Josephus, *Jewish Wars* 2 §§128–29). The reasoning that might lead even a loyal worshiper of YHWH to think that the worship of the heavenly bodies and other gods in addition to himself was acceptable is spelled out by Maimonides in his explanation of the origin of paganism:

> In the days of Enosh, the people [reasoned]: "Since God created these stars and spheres to guide the world, set them on high and allotted to them honor, and since they are ministers who minister before Him, they deserve to be praised and glorified, and honor should be rendered them; and it is the will of God . . . that men should aggrandize and honor those whom He aggrandized and honored, just as a king desires that respect should be shown to the officers who serve him, and thus honor is shown to the king." [The people then began to honor these objects in order] to obtain the Creator's favor. . . . Their error and folly consists in imagining that this vain worship is [God's] desire. . . . Even if the worshiper is aware that the Eternal is God, and worships the created thing in the sense in which Enosh and his contemporaries did [i.e., as subordinates who manage the world under God's orders], he is an idolater.—[Maimonides, *Hilkot ʿAvodah Zarah* 1:1; 2:1 (translation slightly modified, from M. Hyamson, *The Mishneh Torah by Maimonides*, Book I (New York, 1937) 67a–b, and I. Twersky, ed., *A Maimonides Reader* (New York, 1972) 71–72. For other commentators writing similarly, see S. Fraade, *Enosh and His Generation* (Chico, Calif., 1984) 129 n. 53.]

Maimonides' comment refers to the worship of natural phenomena. Nachmanides suggests that even the worship of foreign gods might be rationalized in a similar way (comment to Deut 13:2); the real likelihood of such reasoning explains why the Torah so frequently repeats the prohibition of worshiping other gods.

19. Various translations and commentaries use terms such as 'disloyalty', 'rebellion', 'going astray', and 'apostasy': LXX; Vg.; *Tgs. Onqelos* and *Pseudo-Jonathan*; Ibn Janaḥ in his dictionary; Bekhor Shor; Ibn Ezra; Baḥya; KJV; Moffat; RSV; NJPSV, 2d and subsequent editions (since 1966); NEB; NAB; JB; Smith, *The Book of Deuteronomy*; ICC; Mayes; Craigie.

means 'to claim falsely that Y<small>HWH</small> said something'.[20] Since the prophet in Deuteronomy 13 has urged the worship of other gods, his falsehood about Y<small>HWH</small>
must have been a claim that he ordains the worship of those gods,[21] the claim
that we have seen is implied by 17:3. In other words, 13:2–6 does not refer to
a prophet of another god, but to a prophet of Y<small>HWH</small> who advocates the worship
of additional gods.

If Deut 34:10–12 is indeed aimed against syncretistic Yahwism, the medieval writers cited above were right to connect the passage with 4:2 and 13:1,
which forbid abrogating any of the laws taught by Moses or adding to them.
Although this prohibition is well known as a general principle,[22] in the context
of Deuteronomy it has a specific focus. Each time it appears it is connected
with warnings against adopting pagan practices.[23] In 13:1 it concludes a warning not to adopt Canaanite religious practices, particularly child sacrifice, for
the worship of Y<small>HWH</small> (12:29–31) and it introduces the prohibition against following a prophet who claims that Y<small>HWH</small> commands Israel to worship other
gods (13:2–6).[24] In 4:2 it precedes a reminder that all who worshiped another

20. Saadia; Rashi; Shadal here and at Isa 1:5; AT; NJPSV (1st ed.; 1962); Chaim Rabinowitz,
דעת סופרים, Deuteronomy (Jerusalem, 1957); A. B. Ehrlich, *Randglossen zur hebräischen Bibel:
Textkritisches, Sprachliches und Sachliches* (Hildesheim, 1968); E. Jenni, "Dtn 19,16: Sarâ 'Falsch-
heit,'" *Mélanges bibliques et orientaux en l'honneur de M. Henri Cazelles* (ed. A. Caquot and
M. Delcor; Kevelaer and Neukirchen-Vluyn, 1981) 201–11. As Shadal notes, *dibber sārâ* unques-
tionably means 'lie' in Jer 28:16, 29:32; and probably in Isa 59:13b, as does 'testify *sārâ*' in Deut
19:16 (cf. v. 18). The cognate Akkadian expression 'to speak *sartu* [or *sarratu, surratu*]' means both
to tell lies and to propose disloyalty. In Biblical Hebrew, however, there are no convincing cases
with the second meaning; in Jeremiah, the prophets are clearly not proposing rebellion against
Y<small>HWH</small>. If the idiom meant 'propose disloyalty' in Deut 13:6, it could have been used in v. 11, too.

21. Seforno; Nachmanides, paraphrasing *b. Sanh.* 90a top (see Rashi there); Maimonides,
הלכות יסודי התורה 9:5. Cf. B. Goff, "Syncretism in the Religion of Israel," *JBL* 58 (1939) 154:
"Even some prophets of Yahweh encouraged a syncretistic cult."

22. As a general principle, the first that Moses declares in Deuteronomy, this is a fitting introduction to the laws, expressing the completeness of Moses' teachings. Injunctions against adding and removing items appear in various genres of ancient literature, including treaties. Likewise,
the Laws of Hammurabi conclude with exhortations against changing them. See M. Weinfeld, *Deuteronomy* (AB 5; Garden City, N.Y., 1991) at 4:2; *Deuteronomy and the Deuteronomic School* (Oxford, 1972) 262 n. 3 (repr. Winona Lake, Ind., 1992). Cf. T. J. Meek, "The Code of Hammurabi,"
ANET, 178cd; N. Lewis and M. Reinhold, *Roman Civilization* (New York, 1951) 1.169.

23. Hazzekuni at Deut 4:2 (H. D. Chavel [ed.], חזקוני. פירושי התורה לרבינו חזקיה בר מנוח
[Jerusalem, 1988] 531).

24. The MT *parasha* division marks 13:1 as the conclusion of 12:29–31, from which
M. Greenberg inferred that it may be intended as a rejection of current claims that Y<small>HWH</small> wants
child sacrifice (Greenberg, "Ezekiel 20 and the Spiritual Exile," 437 n. 3). This does not negate the
fact that 13:1 is also an apt introduction to 13:2–6 (as implied by 4:2–3 and sensed by Maimonides,
הלכות יסודי התורה 8:3; 9:1), since prophets who would instigate Israel to worship other gods in addition to Y<small>HWH</small> would in effect be adding to his commandments or subtracting from them. Clauses
about not adding or subtracting often refer to prophets, scribes, and messengers who must faithfully report what they have been told (see Jer 26:2, Rev 22:18–19; Josephus *Ant.* 1.17; *Erra Epic*
5:43–44 [W. G. Lambert, "The Fifth Tablet of the Era Epic," *Iraq* 24 (1962) 122–23]; J. A. Wilson,

god (Baal-peor) perished. Evidently, then, these passages cite the prohibition in order to stress that one may not nullify the commandments banning the worship of other gods (such as the first commandment of the Decalogue)[25] and the adoption of pagan practices, or add commandments ordaining their worship or adoption of child sacrifice and other pagan practices.[26]

It is likely that various other practices forbidden by Deuteronomy were also defended with claims of prophetic validation by YHWH. For example, the priests of the local sanctuaries that are forbidden in chap. 12 probably claimed that their sanctuaries and the sacred posts and pillars used at them (forbidden in 16:21–22) were erected at YHWH's command, just as the tabernacle, Solomon's Temple, Jacob's altar at Bethel, and the copper serpent were.[27] Deut 34:10–12 would nullify the authenticity of any claims of this nature that are inconsistent with Mosaic prophecy.[28]

Seen in this light, Deut 34:10–12 possesses significance worthy of its place as the conclusion of Deuteronomy. True to the "pluralism" that is inherent in polytheism, the Israelite polytheism combated by Deuteronomy and the rest of the Bible was essentially a syncretistic form of Yahwism, and its adherents included prophets who claimed that this syncretism was desired by YHWH. By reminding the reader that Moses, who forbade the worship of other gods and the adoption of pagan practices, was the supreme prophet of YHWH and hence the final authority on His will, Deut 34:10–12 undercuts all such claims in a final effort to safeguard the uncompromising monotheism that is its primary message.

"Proverbs and Precepts," *ANET*, 413a; and idem, 'Observations on Life and the World Order," *ANET*, 434b). The placement of 13:2–6 after 13:1 implies that 13:1 was also understood as a warning against the falsification of God's message by prophets. Note also the *inclusio* that 13:1 forms with 13:19, calling on Israel to "obey *all* His commandments."

25. Ibn Ezra recognized that "You shall have no other gods beside Me" (Exod 20:3, Deut 5:7) rules out worshiping other gods *in combination with* YHWH, as was done by those who worshiped *malkat* [thus point] *haššāmayim* (Jer 44:18), the first Samaritans (2 Kgs 17:33), and Naaman (2 Kgs 5:18) (Ibn Ezra [introduction to Exodus 20] פירושי התורה לרבינו אברהם אבן עזרא [ed. A. Weiser; Jerusalem, 1976] 2.133). We may add that the phrase ʿal pānāy in the commandment may mean 'in addition to me'. Note the use of ʿal in Laban's demand that Jacob not "take other wives beside (ʿal) my daughters" (Gen 31:50).

26. This interpretation of 4:2 is consistent with the fact that 4:1–40 is primarily concerned with preventing the worship of other gods, not simply with the integrity of Deuteronomy as a legal code. In fact, throughout Deuteronomy 4–11 "the laws and rules" that Moses expounds are usually those against idolatry (note, for example, 4:14 and the subject to which Moses turns after it). For this reason, Deut 4:2 is an appropriate beginning for chaps. 4–11.

27. Exod 25–31, 2 Samuel 7, Gen 35:1, Num 21:8. In Mesopotamia, too, the building of a sanctuary required divine authorization revealed by divination. See the evidence gathered by T. Ishida, *The Royal Dynasties in Ancient Israel* (BZAW 142; Berlin, 1977) 85–88.

28. Strictly speaking, this passage emphasizes the authority of Moses, not of Deuteronomy, and would not by itself strengthen Deuteronomy's positions on matters where it disagreed with other *Mosaic* traditions in Exodus, Numbers, and Deuteronomy.

Part 3

The Prophets

THE AUTHENTIC SERMON OF JEREMIAH
IN JEREMIAH 7:1–20

Sa-Moon Kang

Introduction

THE PURPOSE OF THE PRESENT STUDY is to reconstruct an authentic sermon of Jeremiah from Jer 7:1–20,[1] whose authenticity together with the other 830 Masoretic verses was first rejected by B. Duhm in 1901.[2] He understood them as later additions throughout the history of transmission up to the second century B.C.E. According to him, most of these later additions have many similarities in both form and content with the Former Prophets, Joshua–Kings, which were composed by the Deuteronomistic *Ergänzer* during the exilic or the postexilic period.

It was S. Mowinckel who, in 1914, next called attention to the distinctiveness of these prose sermons.[3] He compared these autobiographical prose

---

1. Most scholars deal with Jer 7:1–15 as a literary unit. Cf. W. Eichrodt, "Right Interpretation of the Old Testament: A Study of Jer 7:1–15," *Teologisk Tidsskrift* 7 (1950) 15–25; G. Fohrer, "Jeremias Tempelwort 7:1–15," *TZ* 5 (1949) 401–17; H. G. Reventlow, "Gattung und Überlieferung in der Tempelrede Jeremias, Jer 7 und 26," *ZAW* 81 (1969) 315–52; H. Weippert, *Die Prosareden des Jeremiabuches* (BZAW 132; Berlin, 1973) 26–48; J. Bright, *Jeremiah* (AB 21; New York, 1965) 58–59. However, M. Haran has suggested that it is necessary to consider Jer 7:1–20 as a literary unit. The verses following 7:15 are a lyric "response" to the earlier announcement of calamity; cf. "From Early to Classical Prophecy: Continuity and Change," *VT* 77/4 (1977) 391. The formula לכן כה־אמר אדני יהוה 'therefore thus says the Lord YHWH' indicates the closing of the literary unit that began in v. 3 and consists of three small literary divisions: vv. 3–11, 12–15, 16–19. The next messenger formula indicating a new literary unit, כה אמר יהוה צבאות אלהי ישראל 'thus says YHWH of hosts, the God of Israel', occurs at v. 21.

2. B. Duhm, *Das Buch Jeremia* (Kurzer Hand-Commentar zum Alten Testament 11; Tübingen, 1901) xvi–xx. According to him, some 280 Masoretic verses are attributable as poetic oracles of Kinah meter to Jeremiah himself, while some 220 belong to Jeremiah's scribe, Baruch, as biographer of Jeremiah. In BHK, W. Rudolph counts the total verses of the Masoretic text of Jeremiah as 1364 verses like the Babylonian Codex, rather than the 1350 of Duhm.

3. S. Mowinckel, *Zur Komposition des Buches Jeremia* (Kristiania, 1914) 31–45. According to to him, these are called source C: 7:1–8:3; 8:9–14; 11:1–5; 18:1–12; 21:1–10; 25:1–11a; 32:1–2,

---

sermons in the first person, which are called source C, to the other two main
sources of Jeremiah, namely, source A (a collection of Jeremian poetic oracles)
and source B (a biography of Jeremiah by someone who lived in Egypt between
580 and 480 B.C.E.). Source C, according to him, was composed by the Deuteronomistic editors in Babylon or Palestine about 400 B.C.E. as a terminus a
quo.[4] Thus the authenticity of the Jeremian authorship of these prose sermons
was again denied; their origins were located in the Deuteronomistic literature.

    Although W. Rudolph, J. P. Hyatt, and M. Weinfeld have stood generally
in the same line as the above with respect to later Deuteronomic additions, they
have a different viewpoint about the later additions. They have suggested that
the later additions were grafted onto genuine words of the prophet Jeremiah. In
1947, Rudolph recognized these prose sermons as "eine Arbeit der exilischen
Deuteronomiker" but they are not all "freie Schöpfungen."[5] Rather, Rudolph
contended that the additions are based on the real Jeremian words, though he
still followed Mowinckel's system of three major sources. In 1951, Hyatt also
attributed these prose sermons to the work of the Deuteronomic editors who
lived during the Babylonian Exile, a date around 550 B.C.E.[6] He suggested that
not only is there no evidence of the D editor's work on Jeremiah at the end of
the Exile, but that there is also no evidence of the influence of Second Isaiah
or the early postexilic writers.[7]

    M. Weinfeld contended that these prose sermons were Deuteronomic,
composed during the second half of the sixth century B.C.E. He suggested that
as the Deuteronomic editor of Joshua–Kings appended his own prophetic orations to the original authentic prophecies, so the author of source C attached his
sermons to the brief but genuine prophecies of Jeremiah.[8] With this viewpoint,
one may believe that it is at least possible to discover some authentic words of
Jeremiah among the prose sermons of the Masoretic Text.

    J. Bright, who asserted the existence of two traditions, poetry and prose,
that were separated until their inclusion into the present book,[9] noted that the
style of the discourse units itself is definitely not characteristic of the late exilic
or postexilic period. According to him, it began to develop early in the prophet's

---

6–16, 24–44; 34:1–22; 35:1–19; 44:1–14; also, source D: 30:1–31:28. In 1946, however, Mowinckel somewhat modified his view, describing source C as a circle of tradition rather than a
source (*Prophecy and Tradition* [Oslo, 1946] 62–63).

    4. Mowinckel, *Komposition*, 56–57.
    5. W. Rudolph, *Jeremia* (3d ed.; HAT 12; Tübingen, 1968) xvii.
    6. J. P. Hyatt, "The Deuteronomic Edition of Jeremiah," *Vanderbilt Studies in the Humani-
ties* 1 (Nashville, 1951) 91.
    7. Ibid.
    8. M. Weinfeld, *Deuteronomy and the Deuteronomic School* (Oxford, 1972; repr. Winona
Lake, Ind., 1992) 28.
    9. While Bright asserts the existence of the two traditions, he does not sharply distinguish
the two.

own lifetime, for B (who was Jeremiah's contemporary) knew of, cited, and paraphrased C, was a tradent of C, and had a style like C.[10] The style is, however, characteristic of rhetorical prose of the seventh and sixth centuries B.C.E., a fact that suggests that these prose materials were given their fixed form shortly after the middle of the exilic period, thus within at most a few decades after Jeremiah's death.[11] Thus the style of these discourses, though indeed closely akin to that of the Deuteronomic literature, is a style in its own right with peculiarities and distinctive expressions of its own. It is by no means glibly to be classified as "Deuteronomistic."[12]

Recently, H. Weippert maintained that the *Prosarede* in Jeremiah is not from the hand of a later redactor, but a Kunstprosa that is a demetrification of the prophet's own words.[13] She supported the idea that the prose discourses represent a tradition that was nearer to Jeremiah. Thus, for example, 7:1–15 has priority over the same account in 26:4–6, which is an abbreviated form of the sermon: source C has priority over source B. She thus concluded, unlike E. W. Nicholson,[14] that the prose materials are not really sermons, but the parenetic portions of the Jeremian proclamation of Yhwh's words.[15]

In the same year as Weippert's claim concerning the prose sermons, however, W. Thiel supported the view of Duhm, Mowinckel, and Rudolph by formula studies,[16] asserting that the style of the prose sermons in the book of Jeremiah is the alternative preaching and question-answer style of the Deuteronomistic (Dtr), not the Deuteronomic school (Dtn).[17] The characteristic of this style is the conditional clause that begins with *kî ʾim* or *ʾim* 'surely if'. He claims that 7:1–15 and 17:19–27 have the common structure of Dtr, which predominated during the time of the Exile. Furthermore, he asserts that the question-answer style that consists of (1) a "why" question, (2) an answer to the question, and (3) judgment words, is also a special Dtr type that is found in Jer 22:8ff., Deut 29:23–27, and 1 Kgs 9:8ff. Thus one can see that there are basically three different points of view. The first (Bright, Weippert) accepts the authenticity of the prose sermons. The second (Duhm, Mowinckel) rejects their authenticity. The third view (Rudolph, Hyatt, Weinfeld, Thiel) represents a compromise between the first two viewpoints. Next I wish to

---

10. J. Bright, "The Prophetic Reminiscence: Its Place and Function in the Book of Jeremiah," *Biblical Essays, Proceedings of the 9th Meeting: Die Ou-Testamentises Werkgemeeskap in Suid-Africa* (Pretoria, 1966) 17.

11. Idem, "The Date of the Prose Sermons of Jeremiah," *JBL* 70 (1951) 15–35.

12. Idem, *Jeremiah*, lxxi.

13. Weippert, *Prosareden*, 27–48.

14. E. W. Nicholson, *Preaching to the Exiles* (New York, 1970) 136ff.

15. Weippert, *Prosareden*, 231–33.

16. W. Thiel, *Die deuteronomistische Redaktion von Jeremia I-25* (WMANT 41; Neukirchen-Vluyn, 1973) 290–300.

17. Ibid., 118.

examine Jer 7:1–20 in the three different exegetical stages, beginning with the
last exegetical stage: the post-Deuteronomistic exegesis of Jeremiah.

The Exegesis of the Post-Deuteronomistic Jeremians

The textual expansions were the work of the followers of the Deuteronomistic Jeremiah (DtrJer), who lived in the postexilic period. The cases and na-
tures of these additions, have been well analyzed by J. G. Janzen and E. Tov.[18]
They showed that these additions, representing texts that were reworked, clarified, and embellished, were produced through a long tradition of scribal activity
during the postexilic period. The additions, flowed mainly from the contents of
the same book, though some of them show a certain creativity in theological
and exegetical purpose. Thus they reflect the exegetical situation during the postexilic period. While we cannot determine the exact beginning of these additions, the Qumran documents 4QJer[a] and 4QJer[b] prove that most of the activity
was completed around 200 B.C.E. Thus additions and alterations were still possible, as the comparison of Jer-LXX and Jer-MT shows. But many additions
reflect the fact that the exegetical activities intended to clarify the theological
aspects of Yahwism were much later than the early postexilic period. The purpose of this exegesis was to provide contemporary theological interpretation for
the people in a different situation.

Verse 1 is an addition of Jer-MT that is absent in Jer-LXX. The introductory formula in v. 1, הדבר אשר היה אל־ירמיהו מאת יהוה 'the word that came to
Jeremiah from Yʜᴡʜ', suggests an effort to avoid the anthropomorphic expression and to emphasize the transcendence of Yʜᴡʜ God.[19] Otherwise, 1:1 in Jer-
LXX, דבר־יהוה אשר היה על 'the word of Yʜᴡʜ that came upon . . . ', was a way
of expressing in the exilic period the fact that God gave his words to prophets.[20] But the expression was changed in different ways in the postexilic period, such as: היה דבר־יהוה . . . . אל 'the word of Yʜᴡʜ . . . to . . .'[21] or אשר היה
דבר־יהוה אל 'that the word of Yʜᴡʜ came to . . . '.[22] These expressions show
that God speaks his words (similar to the words of Jeremiah [1:1] or Amos
[1:1]), while the introductory phrase (הדבר אשר היה אל־ירמיהו מאת יהוה)
avoids the anthropomorphic expression of the words of God. The Aramaic

18. J. G. Janzen, *Studies in the Text of Jeremiah* (HSM 6; Cambridge, Mass., 1973) 34ff.;
E. Tov, "The Textual Contribution to the Literary Criticism of the Book of Jeremiah," *Beth Miqraʾ*
3/50 (1972) 281–86.

19. P. K. D. Neumann, "Das Wort, das Geschehen ist: Zum Problem der Wortempfangster-
minologie in Jer 1–25," *VT* 23 (1973) 204–6. Thus, 11:1; 18:1; 21:1; 25:1; 30:1 (37:1); 32:1 (39:1);
34:1, 8 (41:1, 8); 35:1 (42:1); 40:1 (47:1).

20. Cf. ibid., 192 n. 1.

21. Hag 1:1, Zech 1:1. The terminus a quo is 520 B.C.E.

22. Jer 1:2, 14:1, 46:1, 47:1, 49:34. This is a superscription of judgment speeches that appear
only in Jer-MT (chaps. 1–25, 46–51); Neumann, "Das Wort, das Geschehen ist," 172.

translation clearly supports the view that the words came from before God (*min qĕdām Yw″y*).[23]

Thus the words that Jeremiah had spoken to the people were the ones that were committed from God to Jeremiah and so originated with God, not Jeremiah himself. However, with the destruction of the Jerusalem Temple, the people came to understand that God's existence was not confined to the Temple. Thus in the Dtr school, the dwelling place of God began to become abstract: לשכן שמו שם 'to make his name dwell there', לשום שמו שם 'to put his name there', or נקרא שמי שם 'my name has been called there'.[24] This theological tendency shows God as the transcendent one who lives in heaven, as is reflected in later apocalyptic literature. Thus the introductory formula in v. 1 indicates that God is transcendent above the limits of time and space.

Besides the biographical form with third person, there is an autobiographical form with first person, such as, ויהי־דבר יהוה אלי 'and the word of Yhwh came to me'. The formula begins with the prophet Jeremiah, though this occurs only nine times in the book of Jeremiah.[25] Outside of Jeremiah, the formula does not appear in the early prophetic writings, but it is common in the exilic literature.[26] Thus W. H. Schmidt maintains that the autobiographical form might be the prophet Jeremiah's own style of expression.[27] Moreover, the autobiographical formula consists of the *waw*-consecutive form, *wayĕhî* instead of *hāyâ*. The *waw*-consecutive form belongs to the classical style of Biblical Hebrew (BH), rather than the form that lacks *waw*-consecutive. E. Y. Kutscher points out that the system of the consecutive tenses was discarded in Mishnaic Hebrew (henceforth, MH), which began around the first century.[28] This tendency to discard is found in late Biblical Hebrew (LBH) and Qumran Hebrew as well.[29] Thus the opening formula of the temple sermon with the perfect form, *hāyâ*, is evidence of a later period than the autobiographical formula, which has the *waw*-consecutive form, *wayĕhî*.

However, there are biographical formulas with the *waw*-consecutive form, such as, ויהי־דבר יהוה אל־ירמיהו. This form does not appear in the early prophetic writings, but it is found in the exilic and postexilic writings.[30] It may be said that the biographical formula with *waw*-consecutive began after the time of the prophet Jeremiah. Note that this form is attested more than ten times in

---

23. A. Sperber (ed.), *The Bible in Aramaic* (Leiden, 1959–62) 3.152.

24. Y. Zakovitch, "To Cause His Name to Dwell There: To Put His Name There," *Tarbiz* 41 (1972) 338–40; Thiel, *Redaktion*, 112; M. Rose, *Der Ausschliesslichkeitsanspruch Jahwes* (BWANT 106; Stuttgart, 1975) 77.

25. Jer 1:4, 11, 13; 2:1; 13:3, 8; 16:1; 18:5; 24:4.

26. Thirty-seven times in Ezekiel and four times in Zechariah. BDB 182.

27. W. H. Schmidt, "דבר," *TWAT* 2.119.

28. E. Y. Kutscher, "Hebrew Language," *EncJud* 16 col. 1584–85.

29. A. Hurvitz, "The Date of the Prose Tale of Job," *HTR* 67/1 (1974) 28.

30. 1 Chr 17:3; 1 Kgs 12:22; 13:20; 16:1; 21:17, 28; Isa 38:4; Jonah 1:1; 3:1; etc.

Jeremiah.[31] Thus the above evidence shows that the introductory formula in 7:1 was edited by the Jeremian *Tradentenkreise* in the postexilic period and not by the Dtr redactors. So the formula is not the best criterion for source C of Mowinckel.

There are other grammatical elements that need to be considered. For instance, the introductory formula with third person in v. 1 has the relative pronoun ʾăšer. The word ʾăšer in BH is še everywhere in MH, except in quotations, early liturgical language, and semibiblical strains. In BH, še occurs six times in the North Israelite portions. But its use, under the influence of the Phoenician šer or še, the Akkadian ša and, perhaps also the Aramaic zi or di, must have supplanted entirely the longer ʾăšer in the language of the common people.[32]

Another element in this formula that needs to be considered is the orthography of *yirmĕyāhû*, the plene form with *waw*. As E. Y. Kutscher pointed out, these plene forms are the rule for the First Temple Period, whereas the defective forms without *waw* are rare in the literature of that period.[33] This is true for the Neo-Babylonian inscriptions of Nippur, for the Elephantine Papyri, and for the later biblical literature, that is, Ezra or Nehemiah. Thus *yirmĕyāhû* is an older form than *yirmĕyâ* in the Aramaic Targum. Therefore one may accept Neumann's suggestion that the terminus a quo of this introductory formula should be after 520 B.C.E., while the terminus ad quem is the formation of the Targum.[34]

Another issue is that while an introductory formula such as 7:1 appeared ten times in the LXX, it is omitted in 7:1 of the LXX.[35] Thus two things may be suggested: (1) The formula in v. 1 was not a creation of the editor of the MT but of the LXX in the postexilic period. (2) At first, the literary unit 7:1–20 did not belong to the same group as the others that have the introductory formula in the LXX, but later it was identified as the same literary group with the introductory formula. Therefore it was added by an editor.

In v. 2 the expression, except for יהודה כל יהוה־דבר שמעו 'hear the word of YHWH, all you of Israel', is not found in Jer-LXX. The expression of Jer-LXX belongs to the layer older than the rest of the expressions of Jer-MT. Thiel proposes that the *Prophetenbefehl* in v. 2—'stand and read' (go and say)—should

31. This formula occurs in Jer 28:12; 29:30; 32:26; 33:1, 19, 23; 34:12; 35:12; 36:27; 42:7; 43:8.

32. M. H. Segal, *A Grammar of Mishnaic Hebrew* (Oxford, 1927–70) 43.

33. E. Y. Kutscher, *The Language and Linguistic Background of the Isaiah Scroll (1QIsaᵃ)* (STDJ 6; Leiden, 1974) 4.

34. Neumann, "Das Wort, das Geschehen ist," 171–217. The writer suggests that the terminus a quo of this formula (Wortgeschehensformel B) is after 520 B.C.E. (p. 206), while WGF A, which was used as a superscription of the judgment speeches to the prophet's own or to foreign people, is also much later (p. 197).

35. Jer 11:1; 18:1; 21:1; 25:1; 30:1; 32:1; 34:1, 8; 35:1; 40:1. Jer 44:1 and 45:1 are the words which Jeremiah spoke to the people in Egypt (cf. 22:1).

be a formula of Dtr.[36] But this formula is on almost the same level with the introductory formula in v. 1, since the object of the verb *qārāʾ* is *haddābār hazzeh*, not *děbar-yhwh*. Thus the additional parts are also the post-DtrJer interpolation.

The interpolator understood from 26:2 that the addressees were people who came to worship YHWH. The similar phrases occur in Jer 17:20 and 22:2. The other exegetical additions in this stage are as follows: *şěbāʾôt* (MT, v. 3); *kî lōʾ yoʾilu lākem měʾuma* 'for they will not profit you nothing at all' (LXX, v. 4); *lěhāraᶜ lākem* 'to hurt you' (LXX, v. 9); *šām* 'there' (LXX, v. 11); *něʾum-yhwh* 'says YHWH' . . . *haškēm wědabbēr* 'to rise up early and speak'' (MT, v. 13), *ʾelay* 'to me' (LXX, v. 13); *baᶜădām* 'for them' (MT, v. 16); *ădōnāy* (MT, v. 20). Most additions above from the last exegetical stage in Jer-LXX and the MT were mainly for clarification of phrases. They were frequently paralleled with the verses in Jeremiah and in other books in the Old Testament. Thus these were the productions of scribal activities during the postexilic period. In the next section I will deal with the exegetical activities of the Deuteronomistic Jeremiah during the exilic period.

The Exegesis of the Deuteronomistic Jeremiah

The second compositional stage is Jeremian exegesis that had been influenced by the Dtn or the Dtr school. The Babylonian Exile was a period of religious awakening in the history of Israel. After that time, the so-called Deuteronomists began to formulate their theology to answer the question of the reasons for the destruction of Judah and Jerusalem. It was during this time that Jeremiah's words also began to be collected and arranged by his disciples. As time passed, the threat to the Yahwistic faith by foreign influence deepened, making the prophetic Yahwism necessary. It was not a simple repetition or imitation of tradition, but a creative interpretation for the people of the time. The people who responded to the requirements of this period composed their theology based on the Jeremian words. Their literary style and form were similar to those of Deuteronomic and Deuteronomistic literatures. They imitated not only the style and form of Dtn, Dtr, and Jeremiah, but also created their own literary devices throughout the entire period of their activities. The continuous exegesis is shown by the fact that they used idioms or phrases that are not found in Dtn, Dtr, and Jeremiah. P. Diepold calls these exegetes Deuteronomistic Jeremiah.[37] He maintains that DtrJer was influenced by DtrG (*Geschichte*), which was composed for the portion of history earlier than DtrJer in the exilic period.[38] W. Dietrich clarifies the date of Dtr composition: DtrG in 580, DtrN

---

36. Thiel, *Redaktion*, 291.
37. P. Diepold, *Israels Land* (BZAW 95; Stuttgart, 1972) 155–65.
38. Ibid., 193ff.

(Nomist) in 560, and DtrP (Prophetie) in between 580 and 560.[39] Thus it is supposed that DtrJer was contemporary with DtrP, for both showed prophetic concern to keep Yahwism for the people in that time. But DtrJer showed hope of salvation in the future, while DtrG and DtrP did not express any hope in the future.[40] One might label v. 1 (LXX), vv. 5–8, and some phrases of vv. 9–14 and 15–20 as DtrJer on the basis of the phrases or the contextual elements.

The expression, *šimĕʿû dĕbar-yhwh kol-yĕhûdâ* appears in v. 1 of the seventh chapter of Jer-LXX is v. 2 of the MT. Bright and Snaith have commented that the expression of Jer-LXX is closer to the authentic Jeremiah.[41] However, Mowinckel has pointed out that the whole passage of 7:1–2 is a product of the Deuteronomistic writer.[42] The conventional introductory formula, *šimĕʿû dĕbar-yhwh*, is used as a proclamation formula (*Hörbefehl*) that requires attention from the addressee: 'Hear, the words of Yhwh'. H. W. Wolff has pointed out that the expression as a *Rahmenformel* of the speech, the first time, appears about fifteen times in the book of Jeremiah and around ten times in Ezekiel.[43] The formula, attested in JE strands such as Num 12:6,[44] occurs approximately forty-five times in the Old Testament in the context of giving admonition. However, this expression rarely appears in the imperative form in the Pentateuch. The phrase, *šimĕʿû dĕbar-yhah* does not appear in the early prophetic oracles, such as Hosea, Amos, and Isaiah,[45] but is reshaped or expanded for a specific purpose by them, since the proclamation formula opens the whole oracle by stating the motivation for punishment. But the messenger formula introduces only the announcement of punishment (Amos 7:16). In other words, the combined usage (calling one to attention by using both *šmʿ* and *dĕbar-yhwh*) usually appeared in the exilic period. For example, the expression,

39. W. Dietrich, *Prophetie und Geschichte* (FRLANT 108; Göttingen, 1972) 134ff. But Weinfeld suggests that the Deuteronomic edition of Joshua–Kings was composed during the first half of the sixth century B.C.E., while the Deuteronomic prose sermons in Jeremiah were composed in the second half of the same century. He does not make a sharp distinction between Dtn and Dtr in Jeremiah, only for the author of Deuteronomy. See Weinfeld, *Deuteronomic School*, 4 n. 1, 7.

40. Dietrich, *Prophetie und Geschichte*, 104.

41. Bright, *Jeremiah*, 55; N. H. Snaith, *Notes on the Hebrew Text* (London, 1945) 17. Rudolph (*Jeremia*, 50–51) prefers Jer-MT in 7:2 and interprets Jer-LXX as a radical abbreviation. But it is more reasonable that Jer-LXX is original, because its short and compact form is found many times in other instances in the Old Testament. It is reported in Jer 44:24b that Jeremiah used the same conventional formula to address the people in Egypt.

42. Mowinckel, *Komposition*, 31.

43. H. W. Wolff, *Dodekapropheten 1: Hosea 2* (BKAT 14/1; Neukirchen-Vluyn, 1961) 82.

44. BDB 1033.

45. For Hosea, see: Wolff, *Hosea*, 82; v. 4:1 is a later addition. For Amos, see: Wolff, *Dodekapropheten 2: Joel und Amos* (BKAT 14/2; Neukirchen-Vluyn, 1961) 212–13, 379. Verses 3:1, 5:1, 7:16 all are unauthentic, for this formula is a Deuteronomistic phrase used toward those who refuse to accept Yhwh's words. For Isaiah, see: H. Wildberger, *Jesaja 1–12* (BKAT 10/1; Neukirchen-Vluyn, 1972) 33–34.

dĕbar-yhwh does not appear in the authentic oracles of Amos[46] but does appear thirteen times in the book of Jeremiah.[47] Of these thirteen occurrences, ten appear in prose style, while three are in poetic style (2:4, 21:11, 31:10); all are late additions except 21:11.

Because of its general nature, Jer 21:11b might have been delivered during the reign of any of the kings; perhaps it was delivered during the reign of Zedekiah who sent to Jeremiah to inquire of Yʜwʜ's wonderful deed for Nebuchadnezzar's withdrawal from Jerusalem while the siege of was upon the city. Hyatt has seen 21:11b as Dtr's rewriting, but Rudolph has seen it as authentic Jeremiah.[48] It is more reasonable to assume that 21:11b is a late addition of DtrJer, since it is difficult to believe that Jeremiah used it only here. At the same time, the combined usage, the *Aufmerkruf* and *Botenformel* does not appear in the early writings, but only in Kings, Jeremiah, and Ezekiel.[49] Thus it is more reasonable to consider that the expression *šimĕ^cû dĕbar-yhwh* was the rhetorical and didactic speech form of DtrJer. Instead of this formula, the phrase *šimĕ^cû bĕqōl yhwh*, as an imperative, usually occurs in the Pentateuch and Deuteronomy as a DtrN addition (Exod 18:19; 23:21; Deut 4:30; 8:20; 9:23; 15:5; 26:14, 17; 27:10; 28:1, 2, 15, 45, 62; 30:2, 8, 10, 20).[50] The verb *šm^c* is used in various situations such as: the opening form of the old songs (Judg 5:3, Gen 4:23), the instruction of an old man (Prov 7:24, Isa 28:23), the invocational situation in the cult (Deut 6:4; Ps 50:7, 81:9), an admonition in a courtroom (Prov 4:1, Job 13:6, Isa 49:1), and prayer petitions (Ps 4:2, 102:2). Frequently the opening formula of the wisdom literature pairs another word with *šm^c*, such as *šimĕ^cû* and *haqšîbû* 'Listen!' (Mic 1:2; Isa 28:23; Job 13:6, 33:31; Prov 4:1, 7:24, et passim) or *šimĕ^cû* and *ha^ɔăzînû* (Deut 32:1; Judg 5:3; Isa 1:2, 10; 28:23a; 32:9; Jer 13:15 et passim).[51] This opening formula had occurred already in the instruction of Amenemope in Egyptian wisdom literature: "Give thy ears, hear what he said, Give thy heart to understand them";[52] or in the prayer for help in the Egyptian law court: "O Amon, give thy ear to one who is alone in the law court. . . ."[53] This evidence shows that the didactic opening

46. Wolff, *Joel und Amos*, 362.
47. Jer 10:1 is a DtrN usage.
48. Hyatt, "The Deuteronomic Edition of Jeremiah," 83–84; Rudolph, *Jeremia*, 136.
49. 1 Kgs 22:19; 2 Kgs 7:1, 18:28, 19:6, 20:16. Ezek 6:3; 13:2; 16:35; 21:3; 23:5; 34:9; 36:1, 4; 37:4; cf. M. Weinfeld, *Deuteronomic School*, 176.
50. Dietrich, *Prophetie und Geschichte*, 89 n. 1; Rose, *Jahwes*, 44. Bright has shown that this formula is found fifty times in Dtr, eighteen times in Jeremiah prose, three times in Jeremiah poetry and twelve times in JE; it rarely occurs in the later prophets (only Isa 50:10, Hag 1:12, Zech 6:15) and never in P. This formula appears five times in Psalms, one time in Proverbs, and three times in Daniel. See J. Bright, "The Date of the Prose Sermons of Jeremiah," *JBL* 70 (1951) 35, appendix A, no. 46. Cf. Weinfeld, *Deuteronomic School*, 337, appendix A, V 18a.
51. Wolff, *Hosea*, 123.
52. J. A. Wilson (trans.), "Proverbs and Precepts," *ANET*, 421.
53. J. A. Wilson (trans.), "Egyptian Hymns and Prayers," *ANET*, 380.

formula of the wisdom tradition was adopted by biblical writers in the exilic period.

The phrase *kî ᵓim-*, which appears in Jer 7:5, is attested 134 times in the Old Testament.[54] The phrase performs various functions according to its context.[55] As a single conjunction, it can mean 'but'; as an opening for conditional clauses, it can mean 'surely if'. After a negative clause, *kî ᵓim-* means 'except'; in the emphatic context it can be translated 'unless', such as: לא אשלחך כי אם־ברכתני 'I will not let you go unless you bless me' (Gen 32:27). Usually, however, its meaning is adversative, for example, לא יעקב יאמר עוד שמך כי אם־ישראל 'your name shall no longer be called Jacob, but Israel' (Gen 32:29), ... לא־שבה אלי ... בכל־לבה כי אם־בשקר '... did not return to me with all her heart, but rather in falsehood' (Jer 3:10); or in the Siloam tomb inscription 1–2: אין (פ)ה כסף וזהב (כי) אם (עצמתו) 'here is no silver and gold but only (his bones)'.[56]

Verse 5 contains two protases: (1) *kî ᵓim-* which presents general statements, and (2) *ᵓim-*, which presents specific conditional statements having the emphatic and the deictic function, with the infinitive absolute of the same root preceding the finite verb. Verse 6 appears without *kî ᵓim-* or *ᵓim-* but continues the protasis begun in v. 5. The apodosis that describes the solution appears in v. 7. Thus vv. 5–8 consist of a protasis and an apodosis as a whole.

The use of *kî ᵓim-* + infinitive absolute + *ᵓim-* may be seen in the casuistic laws in the Book of the Covenant (Exod 21:2–6), in the Codex Hammurapi (nos. 278–82), or in the Lachish Letters (no. 3:6–13). An example from a Lachish Letter is as follows:[57] ... כי לב עבדך דוה ... אם נסה איש לקרא לי ספר לנצח אם קראתי אתה ראת מנהו כל מאומה 'if the heart of your servant has been sick ... no one has ever undertaken to call a scribe for me ... surely I did not call him, nor would I give anything at all for him!' Moreover, similar passages, *kîᵓim-* + infinitive absolute + *ᵓim-*, are found in Exod 22:22, 2 Sam 18:3, Prov 2:3, and Esth 4:9.

W. McKane asserts that Prov 2:2–5 (vv. 2–4 protasis, v. 5 apodosis) is not instruction style, but Babylonian omen style, since the conditional clause is used before the imperative in the instruction in order to define more precisely the circumstances in an "if ... then" type of construction.[58] The purpose of this style is to recommend, to exhort, and to preach. The tendency toward a preaching style in Proverb 2 may owe something to Deuteronomy, for the seam

---

54. Here I count only the form with a *maqqēp* after *ᵓim* such as *kî ᵓim-*.

55. GKC §163c and §113m; C. van Leeuwen, "Die Partikel אם," *OTS* 18 (1973) 42–43; J. Muilenburg, "The Linguistic and Rhetorical Usage of the Particle כי in the Old Testament," *HUCA* 32 (1961) 140–42.

56. J. C. L. Gibson, *Textbook of Syrian Semitic Inscriptions: Hebrew and Moabite Inscriptions* (Oxford, 1971) 1.24.

57. N. H. Torczyner, *Lachish I: The Lachish Letters* (London, 1938) 51.

58. W. McKane, *Proverbs* (OTL; London, 1970) 278–81.

between the original sense of the vocabulary in the protasis and the reinterpretation imposed by v. 5 is clearly visible. Exod 23:22 is a Dtr redaction in the conclusion of the Book of the Covenant.[59] Exod 22:22 [23] is not a part of the original legal section.[60] In this verse *ʾim-* precedes *kî ʾim-* such as: אם־ענה תענה אתו כי אם־צעק יצעק אלי שמע אשמע צעקתו 'If you surely afflict him, (and) if he surely cry out to me, I will surely hear his cry'. This verse is also recognized as a secondary addition of the Dtr editor. This evidence implies that the passages *kî ʾim-* + infinitive absolute + *ʾim-* were adopted as emphatic contexts by Dtr redactors in the Bible. This conditional promise was a dogma of the Dtr, who was active at the time of the fall of Judah and the exile.[61] Thus Jer 7:5–7 is an insertion of the DtrJer exegetes during the exilic period.

There are also some linguistic features of the exilic period in vv. 5–7 that need to be considered.

(1) The first feature is the use of the infinitive absolute, as seen in v. 5, to emphasize the importance of the fulfillment of the condition on which some consequence depends; it frequently appears in conditional sentences after *ʾim-*.[62] This linguistic phenomena which almost died out in LBH, especially in Chronicles, does not appear in EBH, especially in the early poetry.[63]

(2) The signs of the direct object, *ʾet* or *ʾōt* as a *nota accusativi*, are not written in preexilic Hebrew poetry.[64]

(3) Third, the formula, בין ובין in v. 5b is usually found in the early exilic writings, while the contrast formula to it, *bên . . . lĕ* is often attested in the postexilic time, such as: Gen 1:6; Deut 17:8 (3x); 2 Sam 19:36; 1 Kgs 3:9; Isa 59:2; Ezek 41:18, 42:20, 44:23 (2x); Jonah 4:11; Mal 3:18 (2x); 2 Chr 14:10.

(4) Next, the stereotype formula גר יתום ואלמנה 'the stranger, the orphan, and the widow' in v. 6a appears only nine times in Deuteronomy (14:29; 16:11, 14; 24:19, 20, 21; 26:12, 13; 27:19) and two times in Jeremiah (7:6, 22:3).[65] In Jer 22:3 the formula is used as an imperative before the *kîʾim- . . .* *ʾim- . . .* passage. This formula is a Deuteronomic creation of triple words, as

59. B. S. Childs, *The Book of Exodus* (OTL; Philadelphia, 1974) 486–87.
60. Ibid., 478–79; M. Noth, *A History of Pentateuchal Traditions* (trans. B. W. Anderson; Englewood Cliffs, N.J., 1972) 30–36.
61. M. Weinfeld, "The Covenant of Grant in the Old Testament and in the Ancient Near East," *JAOS* 90/2 (1970) 196.
62. GKC §113o–p/pp. 342–43.
63. R. Polzin, *Late Biblical Hebrew* (HSM 12; Missoula, Mont., 1976) 41.
64. Kutscher, *Isaiah Scroll*, 412–13.
65. The "double-noun" phrases, 'widow and orphan' and 'widow and stranger' are found: twice in Deut (10:18, 24:17); twice in Exodus (22:2a, 21); Isa 10:2; Ezek 22:7; Zech 7:10; Mal 2:5; Job 22:9, 24:3, 31:16–17; Ps 94:6, 146:9. The "double-noun" expression is found in the old tradition in Exod 22:20–21, but the "triple" expression appears from Deuteronomy. However, Weippert asserts that the "triple words" should be considered Jeremian, like Isa 1:17 (*ger* = *ḥāmôṣ*), while Thiel supports classifying the phrase as Deuteronomic. Finally, Rose accepts Thiel's view, citing the different usage of "double" and "triple" words. See Weippert, *Prosareden*, 42; Thiel, *Redaktion*, 110; Rose, *Jahwes*, 220.

Weinfeld points out, in which *yātôm wĕ³almānâ* has been added to *gēr* to make it conform with the Deuteronomic mold.[66] But the conception of the protection of the weak already existed in Egyptian, Mesopotamian, and Ugaritic literatures as the will of god and the duty of kings.[67] Of course, the concept was adopted in the Old Testament from early times as the will of Yʜᴡʜ, becoming an important ethical doctrine in the Old Testament. In addition, the three words *gēr yātôm wĕ³almānâ* suggest that Israel knew from her own experience what it was like to be a stranger in the exilic and the postexilic period.[68]

(5) The expression דם נקי אל־תשפכו 'do not shed innocent blood' in this context must be a Dtn or Dtr redaction, for all of its occurrences are found in Deuteronomy, Dtr, and Jeremiah (Deut 19:10; 2 Kgs 24:4; Jer 7:6; 22:3, 17). Thiel suggests that 7:6aβ could be a change by Dtr, from 22:17b, in which Jeremiah attacked Jehoiakim.[69]

(6) The formula הלך אחרי אלהים אחרים 'to go after other gods' (vv. 6, 9) may also be seen in Jeremiah or in the author of Deuteronomy,[70] since both are Yahwists and are opposed to the foreign gods.

(7) The phrase אשר לא ידעתם 'that you shall not know them' (v. 9) is a characteristic DtrJer expansion.[71]

(8) In this context, v. 6b will be seen as Dtr redaction along with the remaining part of v. 6 and vv. 5–8. In particular the usage of *³al* with the imperfect is a style that enforces the divine commands, such as *lō³ tignōb* 'you shall not steal' (Exod 20:15).[72]

(9) The expression in v. 7 למן־עולם ועד־עולם 'forever and ever' reflects the exilic situation, but it is not the language of the late postexilic period, which has the article *hā* before *ᶜôlām*, such as:[73] מן־העולם ועד העולם (Ps 106:48). It is a reflection of important grammatical change.

(10) The phrase אלהים אחרים in vv. 6b and 9b is a Dtr phrase. Some of the thirty-eight examples reflect strata of the material earlier than Dtr influence. But since the phrase occurs only three times outside this material, it is clear that the phrase enjoyed popular usage only in the Dtr and Jeremian prose.

(11) The phrase בארץ אשר נתתי לאבותיכם 'in the land that I gave to your fathers' in 7aβ occurs eight times in Jeremiah prose. There are at least ten occurrences in DtrG. There are only five other Old Testament occurrences. The use in Numbers may indicate earlier usage than Dtn, but certainly the clause gains in frequency in Dtr work.

66. Weinfeld, *Deuteronomic School*, 227; Thiel, *Redaktion*, 110.

67. F. C. Fensham, "Widow, Orphan, and the Poor in Ancient Near Eastern Legal and Wisdom Literature," *JNES* 21 (1962) 129–39.

68. Childs, *Exodus*, 478.

69. Thiel, *Redaktion*, 110.

70. Weippert, *Prosareden*, 215–22.

71. Rose, *Jahwes*, 220–21.

72. GKC §107.

73. A. Hurvitz, *The Transition Period in Biblical Hebrew* (Jerusalem, 1972) 158–59 [Heb.].

Thus 7:5–8 are generally recognized as a late Dtr expansion. In vv. 9–20 three elements need to be considered. First, v. 13b is parallel to Jer 35:14b, which belongs to Dtr prose speeches. Next, v. 16 is used in almost the same wording in Jer 11:14. The phrase *hassēk něsākîm* 'to pour out drink-offerings' in v. 18 is characteristic of the Jeremian prose. The root *nsk* is a favorite word in Dtn and Dtr books (thirty-three times). Verse 20 confirms a total destruction on the whole land, a theme of Dtr theology.

The prose speeches are sermons that were formed on the basis of the prophet's own speeches, which were remembered by the Dtr circle of Levitical preachers, as many parallels in phraseology and style show. The sermons were formed in the community assemblies for worship among the exiles in Babylon. The intention of the sermons is to encourage the exiles in Babylon and for the exiles to respond to Yhwh in obedience in order to avoid further disaster and to enjoy continued existence as the people of God in the land that he will give to them once again. This tradition of the prose sermons most probably was joined with other Jeremian strata of tradition toward the end of the exilic period after sources A and B were joined.

Conclusion

In the Jeremian stage, the prophet's *ipsissima verba* that were remembered, understood, and repeated in the circle of his followers (such as Baruch) are the main topic. The prose tradition of Jeremiah was in itself not late but was developed on the basis of his words and apparently was intended to present his message as his followers understood it.

(1) The phrase "Lord of hosts" in 7:3a is common in the prose sections of Jeremiah[74] (nineteen times), but it does not occur elsewhere in the Old Testament. While *yhwh ṣěbā'ôt* is used in Isaiah 40–66 (six times), it is not employed as an introductory formula there. It appears that this formula and its variations were rarely used in traditions earlier than the ones associated with Jeremiah, where the formula is quite characteristic. The combination of *'ělōhê yiśrā'ēl* + *ṣěbā'ôt* in v. 3aα occurs only in the Jeremian prose and is considered to have arisen during the exilic period. It is reasonable to assume that 3aαα and 3b belong to the speech delivered by Jeremiah to the people in the temple. In v. 3aβ, especially in the MT, the word of Yhwh was introduced in imperative form.

(2) The word *hêtîbû*, found in v. 3a, appears again in v. 5, and a parallel expression is given in Jer 18:11, 26:13, 35:15 as a D formula.[75]

---

74. The formula was used in 67 Yhwh speeches in 107 occurrences; C. Westermann, *Basic Form of Prophetic Speech* (trans. H. C. White; Philadelphia, 1966) 51.

75. Thiel, *Redaktion*, 108–9.

(3) The combination *hêtîb* and *derek* by D occurs in Jer 2:33. D considered this saying to be a high point, for the promise of the land was one of the main themes of Deuteronomic theology.

(4) Verse 4 is an authentic Jeremian speech that was a warning to people who depended on the false premise that the temple of Yhwh was a place of automatic divine protection.

(5) As shown before, v. 9b, like v. 6b, is a Dtr phrase. Thus v. 9a is an authentic Jeremian utterance.

(6) The phrase *niqrāʾ-šĕmî ʿālāyw* in vv. 10, 11, 14, and 30 occurs six times in the sermon. This phrase is characteristic of Dtr Jeremian prose material, and there is no indication of dependence on another body of the Old Testament tradition in this instance.

(7) Verse 10aα, which is parallel to Jer 26:2, is an authentic Jeremian utterance.

(8) Verse 11aβ, as we have seen, is a characteristic Dtr phrase. So vv. 11aα and b belong to authentic Jeremian speeches.

(9) Verse 12bβ is an interpretation by someone in the Dtr Jeremian circles, who explained the reason that Shiloh was destroyed. So vv. 12a and bα belong to an authentic Jeremian prose sermon. In v. 12 a call for the people to make pilgrimages to Shiloh was to show to the people what God had done before.

(10) Although v. 13b is in first-person style, it belongs to Dtr Jeremian phraseology. The word *ʾattâ* is an old rhetorical term used as a transition between the opening salutation and the subject matter.[76]

(11) As shown before, 14aβ is a characteristic Dtr phrase. The remaining words of v. 14 are Jeremian words.

As a result, I assign vv. 3aαa, 3aβ, b; 4; 9a; 10aα; 11aα, b; 12a, bα; 13aα; and 14aα, b to the authentic prose sermon of Jeremiah.[77] Therefore one may isolate the authentic prose sermon of Jeremiah as follows:[78]

v. 3: Thus says Yhwh: "Amend your ways and your deeds, so that I may dwell with you in this place.

v. 4: Do not put your trust in deceptive words, saying, "This is Yhwh's temple, Yhwh's temple, Yhwh's temple."

v. 9: Will you steal, murder, commit adultery, swear falsely, and burn sacrifices to Baal,

v. 10: and then come and stand before me and say, 'We are safe!'?

v. 11: A robber's hideout—is that what this house has become in your opinion? But look! I too am watching! This is Yhwh's word.

---

76. Weinfeld, *Deuteronomic School*, 175.

77. Rose assigns v. 8 to the Jeremian sermon but as a duplicate of v. 4 (*Jahwes*, 223–24). It is better, however, to assign v. 11 to the Jeremian sermon.

78. Bright, *Jeremiah*, 52–53.

v. 12: Yes, go, if you will, to my place that was in Shiloh, where I made my name dwell at first, and see what I did to it.

v. 13: And now, because you have done all these things,

v. 14: I will treat the house in which you place your trust just as I treated Shiloh."

Summary

Jer 7:1–20 as a unit is summarized in these three stages:

	Jer	DtrJer	post-DtrJer
Introduction	3aαa	2bα	1, 2bαa, b
	3aβ, b	3aαbβ	*ṣĕbāʾôt*—3aαb
	4	5–8	*kî mûmâ lōʾ*—4b (LXX)
	9a	9b	*yoᶜilu lākem*
Message	10aα	10aβ, b	*lĕhāraᶜ lākem*—9a (LXX)
	11aα, b	11a	*nĕʾum yhwh*—13aβb
	12a, bα	12b	*haškēm wĕdabbēr*—13bαa
	13aα	13b	*baᶜădām*—16b
	14aα, b	14a	*ʾădōnāy*—20a
Conclusion		15	
		16–20	

First of all, it is presupposed that the temple sermon was preserved and written down by the followers of Jeremiah, such as Baruch, after Jeremiah had spoken. The sermon was collated from the written or oral sources and then written down by some writer to preserve the message of Jeremiah. At this stage the sermon was a Jeremian message that the writer believed and thought to be in line with the given materials. Of course, it was not the real verbatim of Jeremiah but a message interpreted by the Jeremian writer. There is no way to distinguish the real words of Jeremiah from the message interpreted by the Jeremian writer. However, we cannot get closer to the original speech than the Jeremian judgment message. The activities of Jeremian composers presumably took place in the early exilic time or after the death of Jeremiah.

During the second stage, the DtrJer composers added their own message to the temple sermon by means of composition, in order to emphasize the message of Jeremiah in a different context. The principle of the DtrJer composition was that the destruction of the temple and land resulted from the religious and moral sin of the people, such as idolatry and social injustice. They believed that if people accepted the prophetic message, they could live in the land that God gave to their fathers. Thus the conditional sentence was their dogma.

During the last stage, the post-DtrJer composers continued their exegetical work during the Second Temple Period, up to the second century B.C.E. But our text already had a fixed form after the second stage. Thus there were not many changes in the basic structure of the text. The composers added some technical terms such as *ṣĕbā'ôt* or *'ădōnāy* in order to emphasize particular features of their theology. In this way, through the historical process of compositional activities our text was fixed in its present textual form.

LE CADRE ALPHABÉTIQUE DU "LIVRE DE JONATHAN" (1 SAM 16:14–2 SAM 1:27*)

François Langlamet

LE "LIVRE DE JONATHAN" n'est mentionné nulle part. Il subsiste pourtant, intact semble-t-il, dans le livre de *Samuel* canonique. Il n'en représente, il est vrai, que le septième, mais c'est précisément son intérêt: nous avons là un livre court qui peut nous renseigner sur les méthodes de composition des auteurs précanoniques.

Cette composition était soumise à des contraintes, même matérielles. A partir du texte lui-même, nous entreverrons donc le problème des rouleaux, des scribes (et des scribes-*éditeurs*) étudié depuis des années par le Professeur M. Haran. Cette esquisse lui est dédiée, en signe de reconnaissance et d'amitié. Ce n'est malheureusement qu'une esquisse, extraite d'un travail encore inachevé. Elle présuppose un texte que le lecteur n'a pas sous les yeux. Qu'il veuille bien excuser les inconvénients qui en résultent.

En 1989, à l'usage des étudiants de l'École Biblique, j'avais traduit le texte restitué du récit "David—Jonathan—Saül" ou "Livre de Jonathan" en y intégrant 2 Sam 2:1–7. Ainsi délimité, le "livre" comprenait 4201 mots.[1] Dérouté par ce nombre et par d'autres chiffres énigmatiques (dans un récit fondé par ailleurs sur des nombres traditionnels), j'ai cherché une solution dans l'arithmétique

---

Editor's note: On the use of the asterisk in scripture references in this article, see, e.g., J. Skinner, *Genesis* (ICC; Edinburgh, 1910) xx: "* Frequently used to indicate that a section is of composite authorship."

1. Dans le présent article, où les *chiffres* sont mis en relation avec les *mots*, il est souvent impossible de distinguer les chiffres-nombres des chiffres-références ou numéros d'ordre. J'écrirai donc habituellement, sans "petit blanc" ni point, "4201," etc., qu'il s'agisse de "4201 mots" ou du "mot 4201." Quelques exceptions s'imposent néanmoins, par exemple pour les additions, les multiplications ou les nombres à partir de 10,000. D'autre part, l'arithmétique alphabétique étant bel et bien de l'arithmétique, j'écrirai fréquemment les nombres en chiffres et non en lettres (les exceptions sont une affaire de goût).

alphabétique.[2] L'enquête m'a déçu. Les séquences de lettres qui jouent sur 4200/ 4201 n'étaient pas une caractéristique du "Livre de Jonathan": en *Samuel* même, on pouvait les retrouver dans "David et Goliath." Ce travail ingrat avait pourtant abouti à la construction d'un "rectangle alphabétique" qui pouvait expliquer la préférence de l'auteur pour 4201, 1006, etc.

Mais 4201 est-il bien le "chiffre" du livre? Si Fokkelman[3] a raison de présenter comme un ensemble le texte actuel de 1 Samuel 13–2 Samuel 1, est-il raisonnable de considérer 2 Sam 2:1–7 comme la conclusion du "Livre de Jonathan"? 2 Sam 2:1–4b conclut bien un récit. Ce récit n'est pas le "Livre de Jonathan." C'est le récit ancien de la "montée" de David à *Hébron*, jamais mentionnée dans "Jonathan." Le message de David aux gens de Yabesh (2:4c–7) présuppose 1 Sam 31:11–13, que le rédacteur de "Jonathan" avait intégré à son oeuvre. Mais, en 2 Sam 2:5–7, David ne se réfère au passé que pour assurer le présent et préparer l'avenir. L'"avenir" est évidemment le ralliement du Nord. Bref, à la fois conclusion et introduction, 2 Sam 2:1–7 est une *transition*: du Livre I au Livre II de l'histoire de David.

Dans un article rédigé en 1992,[4] j'hésitais encore à assigner 2 Sam 2:1–7 à un rédacteur défini. Il me semble clair aujourd'hui que l'éditeur du "Livre de Jonathan" qui, en 2 Samuel 1, avait repris et amplifié "David, fils de Jessé"[5] a procédé de la même manière en 2 Sam 2:1–4b. Aux vv. 4c–7, il "citera" (ou écrira lui-même) le message de David. Qu'en conclurons-nous? Que 2 Sam 2:1–7 fait encore partie du Livre I? Il me semble beaucoup plus vraisemblable que l'éditeur du "Livre de Jonathan" ait poursuivi, au Livre II, son travail de rédaction.

Le "Livre de Jonathan" n'a donc plus que 4082 mots. Dans un livre déjà rédigé comme un texte sacré, ce nombre est intelligible: $4082 = 157 \times 26$, et 26 est le "chiffre" du Tétragramme. 4082 peut-il encore s'expliquer dans le cadre du rectangle alphabétique? Si la réponse est affirmative, comment l'auteur a-t-il utilisé ce cadre? Comme une table quadrillée, qui pourrait ultérieurement servir de grille de contrôle, ou comme un plan d'architecte, qui lui fournirait les mesures à respecter dans l'agencement des épisodes?

---

2. François Langlamet, "Arithmétique des scribes et texte consonantique: Gen 46:1–7 et 1 Sam 17:1–54," *RB* 97 (1990) 379–409; Étienne Nodet, "Note complémentaire sur les calculs," *RB* 97 (1990) 409–13.

3. J. P. Fokkelman, *Narrative Art and Poetry in the Books of Samuel: A Full Interpretation Based on Stylistic and Structural Analyses*, vol. 2: *The Crossing Fates (I Sam. 13–31 and II Sam. 1)* (SSN 23; Assen: Van Gorcum, 1986); cf. F. Langlamet, "1 Samuel 13–2 Samuel 1? Fokkelman et le prêtre de Nob (1 Sam 21:2–7)," *RB* 99 (1992) 631–75.

4. F. Langlamet, "De 'David, fils de Jessé' au 'Livre de Jonathan': Deux éditions divergentes de l' 'Ascension de David' en 1 Sam 16–2 Sam 1?" *RB* 100 (1993) 321–57. On trouvera dans ce dernier article quelques indications bibliographiques. Une bibliographie sélective accompagnera ultérieurement la traduction du "Livre de Jonathan." L'objet très limité du présent article invitait à réduire les notes au minimum indispensable.

5. Sur cette question, voir l'article cité à la note précédente. La traduction du récit "David, fils de Jessé" a paru dans: F. Langlamet, "David, fils de Jessé: Une édition prédeutéronomiste de l' 'Histoire de la Succession,'" *RB* 89 (1982) 5–47.

Avant d'aborder ces questions, nous devrons jeter un coup d'oeil sur le récit lui-même et sa structure. Faute de texte publié, sans entrer dans le détail des scènes, je présenterai seulement le plan du livre en seize épisodes, en y ajoutant quelques mots de commentaire (§I). Nous étudierons ensuite les lignes 2 à 8 du rectangle alphabétique, non pas intégralement (le dossier est trop gros), mais pour en signaler les avantages (§II). Nous comparerons enfin (§III) les résultats du §II au texte lui-même et à sa structure (esquissée au §I).

I. La structure du "Livre de Jonathan"

Le plan ci-dessous indiquera, pour chaque épisode, le nombre des mots qui figurent dans le texte restitué. Dans la majorité des cas, ce texte "restitué" n'est autre que le texte actuel: le travail de restitution, difficile aux chap. 16–19, a consisté pour l'essentiel à démêler les récits concurrents. Je m'en suis expliqué ailleurs,[6] mais la publication du texte sera, je le crois, le meilleur plaidoyer en sa faveur.

1. 1 Sam 16:14–23: David au service de Saül (147 mots).
2. 18:1b–4: Jonathan fait alliance avec David (30 mots).
    18:10–12: Premier attentat manqué (42 mots).
    L'épisode 2, divisé en deux scènes, a, au total, 72 mots.
3. 19:1–4, 5–6, 6–7: Jonathan intervient pour David (111 mots).
4. 19:9–10c: Deuxième attentat manqué (27 mots).
5. 19:10de*; 20:1b–39; 21:1: Jonathan donne à David le signal du départ (649 mots).
6. 21:2–8: David à Nob (140 mots).
7. 22:1–4: David chef de bande (70 mots).
8. 22:6–19*: Le massacre des prêtres de Nob (255 mots).
    22:20–23: Abiatar (56 mots).
    Avec cette dernière scène, l'épisode 8 a 311 mots.
9. 23:1–15: David à Qeïla, avec Abiatar (230 mots).
    23:16–18: A Horesha, visite de Jonathan (46 mots).
    L'épisode 9 a, au total, 276 mots.
10. 23:19–24:1: La "Roche des Séparations": David échappe à Saül (167 mots).
11. 24:2–23: Le pan du manteau coupé, mais David épargne Saül (367 mots).
12. 25:2–21, 22* (*om.* "ennemis"), 23–43: David et Abigaïl (721 mots).

6. Langlamet, "De 'David, fils de Jessé,'" 348–54, 357.

13. 26:1–25: La lance et la gourde d'eau dérobées, mais David épargne Saül et lui rend sa lance (475 mots).
14. 31:1–10: Bataille de Gilboa. Mort de Saül et de ses trois fils (160 mots).
    31:11–13: L'initiative des habitants de Yabesh (42 mots).
    L'épisode 14 a, au total, 202 mots.
15. 2 Sam 1:2–16: David apprend la mort de Saül et de Jonathan (223 mots).
16. 1:17, 18*, 19–27: Élégie sur Saül et Jonathan (124 mots: 14 + 110).

Provisoirement, les seize épisodes du récit pourraient se répartir en quatre grandes sections:

Section 1 (épisodes 1–5).   David, à la cour de Saül, échappe par deux fois à la lance du roi. *Jonathan*, lié à David par une alliance, symbolisée par le don du manteau et des armes (18:4), intervient pour aider son ami, soit en plaidant sa cause, soit en le prévenant du danger qui le menace.

Section 2 (épisodes 6–9).   Ahimélek vient en aide à David et les prêtres de Nob le paient de leur vie. *Abiatar*, seul rescapé, rejoint David et sa troupe. Suivant les instructions de l'oracle, David libère Qeïla et quitte la ville avant l'arrivée de Saül. La dernière scène de l'épisode 9 relate une visite de *Jonathan*, venu encourager David.

Section 3 (épisodes 10–13).   C'est à l'épisode 10 que David et ses hommes courent le plus grand danger. A la "Roche des Séparations," l'arrivée inopinée d'un messager les sauve. Les épisodes 11 et 13, qui encadrent l'épisode 12, sont symétriques et relatent deux histoires analogues, mais il semble que notre "auteur" (rédacteur-éditeur) ait attaché une importance spéciale au symbolisme du manteau: 1 Sam 24:5—"*David se leva* et coupa furtivement le pan du manteau de Saül"—contient les deux mots médians (2041–42: *wyqm dwd*) de ce livre de 4082 mots.

Section 4 (épisodes 14–16).   Le rédacteur-éditeur reprend ici le récit de la bataille de Gilboa et, en l'amplifiant, la scène du messager qui annonce la mort de Saül. L' "épisode" 16 n'est pas un épisode, mais l'élégie de David sur Saül et Jonathan. Le rédacteur y retrouvait le respect, l'admiration de David pour le roi son maître, les armes de Saül et de Jonathan, l'amitié de David pour son "frère" Jonathan. C'était donc, pour l'ensemble du livre, une excellente conclusion.

Ces quatre sections sont de longueur inégale:

Section 1 (épisodes 1–5)	1006 mots (260 propositions)
Section 2 (épisodes 6–9)	797 mots (168 propositions)
Section 3 (épisodes 10–13)	1730 mots (400 propositions)
Section 4 (épisodes 14–16)	549 mots (132 propositions)

Les propositions jouent sur des nombres traditionnels, mais, dans quelques cas difficiles, les divisions adoptées restent hypothétiques. Mieux vaut donc s'en tenir aux mots, dont le total est clair (4082 = 157 × 26), mais le détail incompréhensible à première vue.

Quant à la longueur des épisodes, elle varie entre 27 et 721 mots: 27 mots (épisode 4), 70 (7), 72 (2), 111 (3), 124 (16), 140 (6), 147 (1), 167 (10), 202 (14), 223 (15), 276 (9), 311 (8), 367 (11), 475 (13), 649 (5), 721 (12). Si les nombres 70 (épisode 7), 72 (2) et 140 (6) sont bien traditionnels, le système d'ensemble ne saute pas aux yeux. Des multiples de 3 (27, 72, 111, 147, 276), voire précisément de 12 (72, 276), des multiples de 7 (70, 140, 147, 721), un multiple de 11 (649), de 19 (475) et de 31 (124, quatre fois *l'/ 'l*) ne constituent pas un système. L'"équilibre" des épisodes serait-il plus éclairant?

Additionnons les mots des épisodes symétriques:

	Mots				Total	
1.	147	16.	124	271	↓271	4082
2.	72	15.	223	295	566	3811
3.	111	14.	202	313	879	3516
4.	27	13.	475	502	**1381**	3203
5.	649	12.	721	**1370**	2751	2701
6.	140	11.	367	507	3258	**1331**
7.	70	10.	167	237	3495	824
8.	311	9.	276	587	4082	587↑

Nous constatons que les 8 épisodes des extrêmes (1381 mots), les épisodes 5 et 12 (1370 mots) et les 6 épisodes du centre (1331 mots) ont approximativement le même nombre de mots, mais le seul chiffre suggestif est **1331** (= 11 × 11 × 11). L'éditeur aurait-il voulu attirer l'attention sur les 6 épisodes du centre?

Les 2 épisodes médians (8 et 9) sont placés sous le signe des prêtres, d'Ahimélek et d'Abiatar. Il avait été question d'Ahimélek à l'épisode 6, mais les épisodes 10 et 11 ne mentionnent même plus Abiatar. La symétrie des épisodes 6 et 11 est-elle purement artificielle? Voudrait-elle insinuer que, sans l'aide du prêtre, on ne retrouvera jamais *haḥēṣî* (20:35–39), la *flèche*, qu'il faut aller chercher plus loin, ou le *milieu* du livre, qui est bien à l'épisode 11? Y aurait-il un lien secret entre les 140 mots de l'épisode 6 et le pan du manteau royal coupé par David (*dwd*) à l'épisode 11?

Quoi qu'il en soit, les 6 épisodes du centre (1331 = 11^3), plus encore que l'épisode de la "flèche" (649 mots = 59 × 11) ou le total général des mots à la fin des épisodes 3 (330 mots = 30 × 11) et 12 (3058 = 139 × 22), nous orientent discrètement vers une solution alphabétique. Mais laquelle?

II. Les lignes 2 à 8 du rectangle alphabétique

Dans *RB* 97 (1990) 402 (cf. supra, n. 2), j'ai présenté un des deux cas les plus simples du rectangle alphabétique, en 12 lignes et 11 colonnes.[7] Je préfère ce 1er cas au "2e cas" d'É. Nodet (ibid., p. 410), en 11 lignes et 12 colonnes, pour la simple raison que le rédacteur-éditeur du "Livre de Jonathan" l'avait lui-même adopté. Le voici pour mémoire:

	1	2	3	4	5	6	7	8	9	0	1
1.	ʾ	r	q	ṣ	p	ʿ	s	n	m	l	k
2.	b	š	y	ṭ	ḥ	z	w	h	d	g	y
3.	g	t	k	n	m	l	k	y	ṭ	b	ṭ
4.	d	ʾ	l	s	y	ṭ	ḥ	z	ḥ	ʾ	ḥ
5.	h	b	m	ʿ	k	r	q	w	z	t	z
6.	w	g	n	p	l	š	ṣ	h	w	š	w
7.	z	d	s	ṣ	m	t	p	d	h	r	h
8.	ḥ	h	ʿ	q	n	s	ʿ	g	d	q	d
9.	ṭ	w	p	r	š	t	ʾ	b	g	ṣ	g
10.	y	z	ṣ	q	r	ṣ	t	ʾ	b	p	b
11.	k	ḥ	ṭ	y	k	l	m	n	s	ʿ	ʾ
12.	l	m	n	s	ʿ	p	ṣ	q	r	š	t

Utilisées comme chiffres, les 22 lettres de l'alphabet nous donnent:

9 chiffres	pour les unités (1 à 9) dont la somme	=	45
9	pour les dizaines (10 à 90)	=	450
4	pour les centaines	=	1000
		Total	1495

Dans le rectangle alphabétique (6 fois l'alphabet), nous avons donc:

9 × 6 = 54 chiffres	pour les unités	=	45 × 6	=	270
9 × 6 = 54	pour les dizaines	=	450 × 6	=	2700
4 × 6 = 24	pour les centaines	=	1000 × 6	=	6000
			Total		8970

Si l'on compare les lignes 2–8 du rectangle aux lignes 1 + 9–12, on obtient:

	pour les lignes 2–8			*pour les lignes 1 + 9 – 12*		
unités	40 lettres	=	215	14 lettres	=	55
dizaines	26 lettres	=	1190	28 lettres	=	1510
centaines	11 lettres	=	2800	13 lettres	=	3200
Total	77 lettres	=	4205	55 lettres	=	4765

---

7. Ce module 1 contient 6 fois l'alphabet de 22 lettres. Le module 2 (23 lignes, 22 colonnes ou l'inverse) comporte déjà 23 alphabets, ce qui donne en valeur numérique: 1495 × 23 = 34,385. Cette somme dépasse déjà de plus de 10,000 le total des mots du livre de Samuel (en "L": 24,301).

Avec ses 40 lettres-chiffres désignant des unités, la section "4205" permet une analyse à la fois plus détaillée, plus sélective et plus révélatrice que celle qu'on pourrait entreprendre à partir des lignes 9–12, qui fournissent: 13 lettres pour les unités (valeur numérique: 54), 20 lettres pour les dizaines (= 1070) et 11 lettres pour les centaines (= 2900), 44 lettres au total dont la valeur numérique est de 4024. La somme n'atteint pas 4201, ni même 4082. Inconvénient supplémentaire (et nous verrons qu'il est grave): les lignes 9–12 n'ont pas de ligne médiane.

Dans le rectangle alphabétique, les lignes 2–8 ont tous les avantages: 40 lettres pour les unités; une colonne médiane (col. 6); une ligne médiane (la ligne 5 du rectangle); une valeur numérique de 4205.

En supprimant le *dalet* de la ligne 8, col. 11, on obtient une grille "4201." Supprimons encore, à la col. 11, le *ṭet* de la ligne 3 et le *yod* de la ligne 2, puis, à la col. 10, le *qop* de la ligne 8, nous avons notre grille "4082." Elle comprend:

unités	38 lettres	=	202	Ailleurs	16 lettres	=	68
dizaines	25 lettres	=	1180		29 lettres	=	1520
centaines	10 lettres	=	2700		14 lettres	=	3300
Total	73 lettres	=	4082		59 lettres	=	4888

Mais pourquoi le rédacteur-éditeur a-t-il opté pour cette grille de 73 lettres plutôt que pour les 77 lettres des lignes 2–8? Nous ne le saurons qu'après avoir étudié la grille de 73 lettres-chiffres. Pour plus de clarté, transcrivons les lettres en chiffres et numérotons de 1 à 7 les lignes 2 à 8 du rectangle (voir tableau p. 170).

Comment utiliser cette table? En additionnant successivement les lettres-chiffres, ligne par ligne ou colonne par colonne, dans l'ordre des lignes et des colonnes? C'est à première vue le procédé le plus simple, mais la présence de **1006** à la col. 6 semble indiquer que notre éditeur a calculé à partir du centre: à la fin de la proposition 260, c'est-à-dire au dernier mot de 1 Sam 21:1, son récit atteint 1006 mots. Faut-il donc opter pour une lecture à partir de la colonne médiane? Expérience faite, aucune méthode n'est à exclure. La grille se prête à 24 lectures "méthodiques" et nous verrons que le rédacteur-éditeur a tenu compte des résultats de ces 24 lectures. Mais, avant de comparer les lectures de la grille à la structure du récit, dressons la liste de ces lectures, en indiquant pour chacune d'elles le total obtenu à la lettre médiane (la 37e des 73 lettres additionnées successivement):

1. Lignes 1-7, dans le sens normal de la lecture (centre: 1421);
2. Lignes 1-7, lues à rebours (centre: 1804);
3. Lignes 7-1, dans le sens normal (centre: 2478);
4. Lignes 7-1, lues à rebours (centre: 2861).

A partir de la ligne médiane (ligne 4):

5. Lignes 4-3-5-2-6-1-7, dans le sens normal (centre: 2352);
6. Lignes 4-3-5-2-6-1-7, lues à rebours (centre: 1920);

	(1)	(2)	(3)	(4)	(5)	(6)	(7)	(8)	(9)	(10)	(11)		Total	
(1)	2	300	10	9	8	7	6	5	4	3		354.	↓354.	4082
(2)	3	400	20	50	40	30	20	10	9	2		584.	938.	3728
(3)	4	1	30	60	10	9	8	7	8	1	8	146.	1084.	3144
(4)	5	2	40	70	20	200	100	6	7	400	7	857.	1941.	2998
(5)	6	3	50	80	30	300	90	5	6	300	6	876.	2817.	2141
(6)	7	4	60	90	40	400	80	4	5	200	5	895.	3712.	1265
(7)	8	5	70	100	50	60	70	3	4			370.	4082.	370†
↑												↓		
	35	715	280	459	198	1006	374	40	43	906	26			
	35.	750.	1030.	1489.	1687.	2693.	3067.	3107.	3150.	4056.	4082.			
	4082.	4047.	3332.	3052.	2593.	2395.	1389.	1015.	975.	932.	26			

1006
1578
2077
2400
4021
4082

7. Lignes 4-5-3-6-2-7-1, dans le sens normal (centre: 2040);
8. Lignes 4-5-3-6-2-7-1, lues à rebours (centre: 2093).

A partir des extrêmes (lignes 1 et 7):

9. Lignes 1-7-2-6-3-5-4, dans le sens normal (centre: 1993);
10. Lignes 1-7-2-6-3-5-4, lues à rebours (centre: 2132);
11. Lignes 7-1-6-2-5-3-4, dans le sens normal (centre: 2182);
12. Lignes 7-1-6-2-5-3-4, lues à rebours (centre: 1780).

13. Colonnes 1-11, à partir du haut (centre: 1724);
14. Colonnes 1-11, à partir du bas (centre: 2147);
15. Colonnes 11-1, à partir du haut (centre: 2335);
16. Colonnes 11-1, à partir du bas (centre: 2388).

A partir de la colonne médiane (col. 6):

17. Colonnes 6-5-7-4-8-3-9-2-10-1-11, à partir du haut (centre: 2107);
18. Colonnes 6-5-7-4-8-3-9-2-10-1-11, à partir du bas (centre: 2207);
19. Colonnes 6-7-5-8-4-9-3-10-2-11-1, à partir du haut (centre: 2090);
20. Colonnes 6-7-5-8-4-9-3-10-2-11-1, à partir du bas (centre: 2086).

A partir des extrêmes (col. 1 et 11):

21. Colonnes 1-11-2-10-3-9-4-8-5-7-6, à partir du haut (centre: 2001);
22. Colonnes 1-11-2-10-3-9-4-8-5-7-6, à partir du bas (centre: 2001);
23. Colonnes 11-1-10-2-9-3-8-4-7-5-6, à partir du haut (centre: 1935);
24. Colonnes 11-1-10-2-9-3-8-4-7-5-6, à partir du bas (centre: 1995).

Lues 24 fois, les 73 lettres ne nous fournissent pas $24 \times 73 = 1752$ chiffres: toujours évidemment à la dernière lettre, mais ailleurs aussi dans un certain nombre de cas, deux ou plusieurs lectures coïncident. En synthétisant les résultats obtenus, on obtient une liste de 1164 chiffres, avec, au centre, 2033 et 2037 (n°s 582–83 de la liste). Elle figure au tableau 1.

Néanmoins, pour éviter de multiplier les tableaux, j'ai composé le tableau 1 en fonction du §III de cet article. Les nombres complémentaires y sont donc présentés sur la même ligne. Quatorze chiffres isolés entraînant de légers décalages, le lecteur ne retrouvera les deux nombres médians de la liste (2033 et 2037) qu'à proximité du centre (2040 et 2042). C'est un premier inconvénient.

Le second inconvénient concerne la limite des épisodes, indiquée au tableau 1 par des traits horizontaux. Pour ne prendre qu'un exemple, les 53 "références" aux épisodes 1 et 16 ne sont plus aussi "parlantes" quand 4082 (dépourvu de chiffre complémentaire) oblige à décaler d'une ligne les deux séries de 53 chiffres.

Enfin, si l'on regroupe les chiffres successifs, la liste "1164" ne comporte plus que 738 numéros. Aux numéros médians (369 et 370), figurent 2037–38 et 2040. Faute de place, j'omets cette seconde liste. Nous la retrouverons, résumée, au §III. Aussi bien, le tableau 1, tel qu'il est présenté ici, permet de retrouver facilement les groupes de chiffres successifs. Les séries qui dépassent

TABLEAU 1

Col.	1	24	2	23	3	22	4	21	5	20	6	19
1.		4082	77	4005	432	3650	741	3341	934	3148	1012	3070
2.	2	4080	83	3999	437	3645	745	3337	935	3147	1014	3068
3.	3	4079	117	3965	441		750	3332	936	3146	1015	3067
4.	4	4078	137	3945	443	3639	757	3325	938	3144	1018	3064
5.	5	4077	183	3899	450	3632	760	3322	941	3141	1020	3062
6.	7	4075	187	3895	460	3622	761	3321	942	3140	1021	3061
7.	8	4074	226	3856	465	3617	762	3320	943	3139	1026	3056
8.	9	4073	233	3849	467	3615	764	3318	945	3137	1030	3052
9.	11	4071	246	3836	476	3606	765	3317	946	3136	1032	3050
10.	12	4070	261	3821	491	3591	767	3315	947	3135	1033	3049
11.	13	4069	287	3795	515	3567	771	3311	952	3130	1039	3043
12.	14	4068	293	3789	520	3562	776	3306	953	3129	1040	3042
13.	15	4067	302	3780	526	3556	777	3305	954	3128	1041	3041
14.	18	4064	312	3770	531		779	3303	955	3127	1043	3039
15.	20	4062	321	3761	535	3547	780	3302	960	3122		3036
16.	21	4061	329	3753	537	3545	781	3301	961	3121	1049	3033
17.	25	4057	335	3747	541	3541	782	3300	962	3120	1051	
18.	26	4056	336	3746	546	3536	795	3287	964	3118	1052	3030
19.	27	4055	337	3745	561	3521	810	3772	966	3116	1054	3028
20.	28	4054	342	3740	571		820	3262	967	3115	1055	
21.	29	4053	347	3735	575		827	3255	968	3114	1056	
22.	30	4052	351	3731		3507	835	3247	969	3113	1060	3022
23.	31	4051	352	3730	580	3502	850	3232	970	3112	1062	3020
24.	32	4050	354	3728	584	3498	852	3230	971	3111	1064	3018
25.	33	4049	356	3726	587	3495	857	3225	972	3110	1067	3015
26.	34	4048	357	3725	641	3441	861	3221	973	3109	1075	3007
27.	35	4047	358	3724	647	3435	862	3220	975	3107	1076	3006
28.	37	4045	361	3721	664	3418	863	3219	976	3106	1079	3003
29.	40	4042	362	3720	672	3410	865	3217	978	3104	1080	3002
30.	41	4041	363	3719	682	3400	866	3216	979	3103	1084	2998
31.	42	4040	365	3717	691	3391	867	3215	980	3102	1085	2997
32.	43	4039	366	3716	699	3383	874	3208	981	3101	1089	2993
33.	44	4038	367	3715	706	3376	880	3202	982	3100	1091	2991
34.	46	4036	370	3712	711	3371	881	3201	986	3096	1096	2986
35.	47	4035	372	3710	712	3370	885	3197	987	3095	1104	2978
36.	49	4033	373	3709	716	3366	889	3193	989	3093	1114	2968
37.	50	4032	375	3707	717	3365	892	3190	990	3092	1126	2956
38.	52	4030	377	3705	720	3362	897	3185	993	3089	1127	2955
39.	53	4029	381		721	3361	898	3184	994	3088	1130	2952
40.	56	4026	382	3700	722	3360	900	3182	995	3087	1131	2951
41.	59	4023	388	3694	724	3358	905	3177	996	3086	1140	2942
42.	60	4022	395	3687	726	3356	908	3174	997	3085	1142	2940
43.	61	4021	403	3679	727	3355	916	3166	998	3084	1146	2936
44.	64	4018	407	3675	729	3353	917	3165	999	3083	1147	2935
45.	66	4016	412	3670	731	3351	925	3157	1000	3082	1149	2933
46.	67	4015	414	3668	732	3350	926	3156	1003	3079	1154	2928
47.	70	4012	420	3662	735	3347	927	3155	1006	3076	1156	2926
48.	73	4009	422	3660	736	3346	929	3153	1008	3074	1163	2919
49.	75	4007	425	3657	738	3344	930	3152	1009	3073	1165	2917
50.	76	4006	431	3651	740	3342	932	3150	1010	3072	1169	2913
Nos	49	1115	99	1066	148	1020	198	970	248	920	297	873

TABLEAU 1

Col.	7	18	8	17	9	16	10	15	11	14	12	13
1.	1172	2910	1379	2703	1539	2543	1668	2414	1795	2287	1950	2132
2.	1174	2908	1380	2702	1544	2538	1670	2412	1800	2282	1952	2130
3.	1182	2900	1382	2700	1547	2535	1672	2410	1804	2278	1958	2124
4.	1194	2888	1383	2699	1548	2534	1673	2409	1807	2275	1962	2120
5.	1196	2886	1388		1552	2530	1674	2408	1808	2274	1966	2116
6.	1197	2885	1389	2693	1562	2520	1676	2406	1812	2270	1971	2111
7.	1201	2881	1396	2686	1564	2518	1677	2405	1820	2262	1972	2110
8.	1204	2878	1404	2678	1567	2515	1678	2404	1824	2258	1975	2107
9.	1210	2872	1405	2677	1570	2512	1679	2403	1825	2257	1977	2105
10.	1219	2863	1409	2673	1571	2511	1682	2400	1828	2254	1978	2104
11.	1220	2862	1410	2672	1572	2510	1686	2396	1829	2253	1983	2099
12.	1221	2861	1414	2668	1573	2509	1687	2395	1832	2250	1984	2098
13.	1230	2852	1416	2666	1577	2505	1690	2392	1835	2247	1989	2093
14.	1237	2845	1418	2664	1578	2504	1691	2391	1838	2244	1990	2092
15.	1238	2844		2662	1579	2503	1692	2390	1844	2238	1992	2090
16.	1239	2843	1421	2661	1581	2501	1694	2388	1847	2235	1993	2089
17.	1246	2836	1426	2656	1582	2500	1695	2387	1848	2234	1995	2087
18.	1254	2828	1427	2655	1583	2499	1697	2385	1849	2233	1996	2086
19.	1255	2827	1428	2654	1585	2497	1703	2379	1855	2227	1988	2084
20.	1258	2824	1430	2652	1587	2495	1704	2378	1862	2220	2000	2082
21.	1260		1434	2648	1590	2492	1710	2372	1870	2212	2001	2081
22.	1264	2818	1435	2647	1593	2489	1712	2370	1871	2211	2002	2080
23.	1265	2817	1438	2644	1594	2488	1716	2366	1873	2209	2005	2077
24.	1267	2815	1444	2638	1596	2486	1718	2364	1874	2208	2008	2074
25.	1271	2811	1449	2633	1597	2485	1721	2361	1875	2207	2010	2072
26.	1274	2808	1458	2624	1600	2482	1724	2358	1879	2203	2012	2070
27.	1276	2806	1469	2613	1602	2480	1725	2357	1881	2201	2014	2068
28.	1287	2795	1470	2612	1603	2479	1727	2355	1882	2200	2017	2065
29.	1297	2785	1472	2610	1604	2478	1730	2352	1884	2198	2018	2064
30.	1299	2783	1480	2602	1606	2476	1733	2349	1886	2196	2020	2062
31.	1300	2782	1482	2600	1608	2474	1734	2348	1887	2195	2022	2060
32.	1305	2777	1488	2594	1609	2473	1735	2347	1888	2194	2023	2059
33.	1306	2776	1489	2593	1611	2471	1737	2345	1890	2192	2027	2055
34.	1308	2774	1491	2591	1612	2470	1738	2344	1892	2190	2028	2054
35.	1309	2773	1497	2585	1613	2469	1740	2342	1894	2188	2030	2052
36.	1310	2772	1498	2584	1614	2468	1741	2341	1900	2182	2033	2049
37.	1313	2769	1500	2582	1615	2467	1742	2340	1902	2180	2037	2045
38.	1315	2767	1504	2578	1618	2464	1747	2355	1905	2177	2038	2044
39.	1319	2763	1508	2574	1619	2463	1750	2332	1909	2173	2040	2042
40.	1320	2762	1509	2573	1621	2461	1752	2330	1918	2164		
41.	1324	2758	1513	2569	1622	2460	1755	2327	1920	2162		
42.	1325	2757	1518	2564	1627	2455	1757	2325	1932	2150		
43.	1326	2756	1520	2562	1629	2453	1765	2317	1933	2149		
44.	1338	2744	1521	2561	1630	2452	1767	2315	1934	2148		
45.	1346	2736	1522	2560	1635	2447	1768	2314	1935	2147		
46.	1354	2728	1527	2555	1637	2445	1774	2308	1936	2146		
47.	1355	2727	1528	2554	1639	2443	1780	2302	1937	2145		
48.	1363	2719	1530	2552	1640	2442	1782	2300	1941	2141		
49.	1370	2712	1534	2548	1660	2422	1784	2298	1945	2137		
50.	1374	2708	1537	2545	1667	2415	1785	2297	1947	2135		
Nᵒˢ	347	824	396	775	446	725	496	675	546	625	585	586

3 chiffres y sont imprimées en caractères gras: elles recèlent un secret que nous révéleront les prêtres (§III).

III. Le "Livre de Jonathan" et la section "4082" du rectangle alphabétique

Si nous comparons les seize épisodes du "Livre de Jonathan" aux 1164 chiffres qui figurent au tableau 1 (pp. 172-73), nous pourrons dès maintenant parler, non plus de chiffres, mais de "références":

Épisodes	Mots par épisode	Total	Références	Total par épisode
1. David au service de Saül	147	147	2–137*	**53**
2. Jonathan-David. Premier attentat	72	219	183, 187	2
3. Jonathan intervient pour David	111	330	226–329*	**10**
4. Deuxième attentat	27	**357**	335–**357***	**10**
5. Le signal de la flèche	649	**1006**	358–**1006***	170
6. David à Nob	140	**1146**	1008–**1146***	**45**
7. David chef de bande	70	1216	**1147**–1210*	16
8. Le massacre des prêtres de Nob	311	**1527**	1219–**1527***	86
9. David à Qeïla	276	1803	**1528**–1800*	106
10. David échappe à Saül	167	1970	**1804**–1966*	**53**
11. David épargne Saül	367	2337	**1971**–2335*	**136**
12. David et Abigaïl	721	3058	2340–3056*	226
13. David épargne Saül	475	3533	3061–3521*	**136**
14. Bataille de Gilboa	202	**3735**	3536–**3735***	**45**
15. Le messager	223	3958	3740–3945*	17
16. Élégie sur Saül et Jonathan	124	**4082**	3965–**4082***	**53**

Les épisodes 1 (147 mots), 10 (167 mots) et 16 (124 mots) ont, au total, 438 mots (= 73 × 6). Bien que de longueur inégale, ces trois épisodes correspondent respectivement, dans la liste du tableau 1 établie à partir des 24 lectures, à **53** références. Le fait est d'autant plus frappant que les épisodes 1 et 16 constituent l'*introduction* et la *conclusion* d'un récit dont l'épisode 10 est le *tournant narratif*: quand David monta "de là" (mot 1966)—c'est-à-dire de la Roche (mot 1962) des Séparations—pour demeurer dans les refuges d'Engadi (mot 1970), le danger était écarté (cf. supra, §I). David pourrait maintenant prouver au roi son innocence en lui montrant le pan de son manteau (épisode 11), en lui restituant sa lance (épisode 13).

Symétriques, les épisodes 11 et 13 ont respectivement 367 mots et (108 mots de plus) 475. Ils correspondent pourtant l'un et l'autre à **136** références dans la liste du tableau 1. La symétrie des épisodes 11 et 13, qui encadrent l'épisode 12, n'est donc pas le résultat fortuit de la présence dans le texte actuel de deux récits parallèles. Voulue, *calculée* par le rédacteur-éditeur, elle souligne une connexion entre les épisodes 11–13, qui développent, chacun à sa manière, le même thème de la vengeance, qui n'appartient qu'à Yʜwʜ (1 Sam 24:13–16; 25:24–34, 39; 26:10), et font annoncer à David son règne futur (24:21; 25:30; 26:25).

On pourrait signaler d'autres correspondances: les 10 références aux épisodes 3 et 4 (d'autant plus intéressantes que l'épisode 4 n'a que 27 mots); les 45 références aux épisodes 6 et 14; les 106 références à l'épisode 9, juste avant l'épisode 10 qui correspond à 53 références.

On notera également les 11 références exactes au premier ou au dernier mot d'un épisode: 358, 1147, 1528, 1804, 1971, d'une part; 357, 1006, 1146, 1527, 3725 et, bien entendu, 4082, d'autre part. Ailleurs, la liste nous renvoie, sinon au premier ou au dernier mot, du moins à la première ou à la dernière proposition de l'épisode: mots 2 (prop. 1), 226 (prop. 58), 335 (prop. 84), 1008 (prop. 261), 1219 (prop. 302), 3061 (prop. 720), 3536 (prop. 829), 3965 (prop. 940), d'une part; 329 (prop. 83), 1210 (prop. 301), 2335 (prop. 559), 3056 (prop. 719), d'autre part. La référence 1800 vise le dernier mot de la proposition 427 (23:18b: David demeura à Horesha) et 1966 le dernier mot de la proposition 470 (24:1a: David monta de là); 2340 renvoie à la proposition 561 (25:2b) et 3740 à la proposition 874 (2 Sam 1:2b). Autant dire que tous les épisodes, à l'exception de l'épisode 2 à peine signalé, s'insèrent parfaitement dans le cadre de la liste "1164" (tableau 1).

Mais ce chiffre est trop élevé pour ne pas inquiéter le lecteur, d'autant plus que nos 1164 "références" sont le résultat de 24 lectures de la grille, dans tous les sens compatibles avec une lecture "méthodique." Les "erreurs" de tir d'une lecture donnée, effectuée dans le sens normal de la lecture, sont corrigées par les "erreurs" de la lecture correspondante faite "à rebours." S'agit-il donc d'un jeu de hasard?

Avec l'auteur lui-même du "Livre de Jonathan" (cf. épisode 5), imaginons plutôt ce "jeu" comme un exercice de tir à l'arc. La "flèche" doit atteindre le "milieu" du récit, c'est-à-dire l'épisode 11, où figurent les deux mots médians (2041 et 2042). Elle doit atteindre cette cible précisément quand le lecteur-calculateur est parvenu à la lettre médiane, la 37e de chaque lecture.[8]

Les "jeunes gens" peuvent donc s'exercer sur les 73 lettres de la section "4082." Ils doivent viser 1971–2337 (épisode 11), voire, s'ils le peuvent, 2041–2042 (mots médians du livre). Aux six premiers essais, le tir est trop court (lectures 1 et 2), trop long (lectures 3 à 5), encore trop court, mais prometteur (lecture 6, où le centre se réfère à 1 Sam 23:26b: "David et ses hommes étaient de l'autre côté de la montagne"). Aux lectures 7 à 11, l'objectif est atteint. Aux lectures 12 et 13, le tir est de nouveau trop court; trop long à la lecture 16; trop court à la lecture 23. Aux lectures 14–15, 17–22 et 24, l'objectif est atteint. Quatorze lectures au total atteignent l'épisode 11 quand le lecteur est parvenu à la 37e lettre.

8. Le rédacteur-éditeur le suggère peut-être en 1 Sam 20:14–15, où il fait curieusement dire à Jonathan: "*wlʾ... wlʾ... wlʾ... wlʾ... wlʾ...*," mettant ainsi cinq fois "37" à la disposition de David, avant qu'Ahimélek ne lui donne les "cinq pains" (21:4).

Voici, classées selon les chiffres, les références médianes des 24 lectures:

N°	Lecture(s)	Référence	Proposition	1 Samuel	Mot correspondant
1.	1	1421	340*	22:17f	$^{\supset}znw$
2.	13	1724	409	23:13d	ky
3.	12	1780	*423	23:17d	$w^{\supset}th$
4.	2	1804	*429	23:19a	wy^clw
5.	6	1920	460	23:26b	$m\d{s}d$
6.	23	1935	462	23:26d	$^{\supset}n\check{s}yw$
7.	9	1993	*477	24:3b	$wylk$
8.	24	1995	477	24:3b	$^{\supset}t$
9.	21, 22	2001	477*	24:3b	hy^clym
10.	7	2040	485*	24:5d	b^cynyk
11.	20	2086	495	24:8a	$^{\supset}t$
12.	19	2090	496	24:8b	$lqwm$
13.	8	2093	496*	24:8b	$\check{s}^{\supset}wl$
14.	17	2107	501	24:9c	$^{\supset}\d{h}ry$
15.	10	2132	508*	24:10c	r^ctk
16.	14	2147	*511	24:11c	$wt\d{h}s$
17.	11	2182	520*	24:12f	lk
18.	18	2207	527	24:14c	$l^{\supset}$
19.	15	2335	559	24:23c	^clw
20.	5	2352	564	25:2e	$bgzz$
21.	16	2388	*573	25:5c	^clw
22.	3	2478	597	25:10e	$hmtpr\d{s}ym$
23.	4	2861	674	25:32c	$^{\supset}lhy$

Si 14 lectures sur 24 atteignent l'objectif, pourquoi faudrait-il tenir compte des 10 lectures qui le manquent? Ne sont-elles pas le lot des ignorants, auxquels les prêtres "n'ont pas révélé" leur secret (1 Sam 22:17f, centre de la lecture 1), voire de cet infâme Nabal, auquel se réfèrent, directement ou indirectement, les lectures 3, 4, 5 et 16?

Relevons les références attestées dans les 14 "bonnes" lectures. Nous obtenons une première liste de 781 numéros où la référence médiane (n° 391) est 2040. Une seconde liste, qui regroupe les chiffres successifs, ne comporte plus que 580 numéros (581 si l'on sépare 1146 de 1147), avec, au centre, 2037 et 2040.

Dans le cadre des seize épisodes du récit, comparons maintenant les résultats obtenus: aux données du tableau 1 (1164 références); aux 741 numéros qu'on peut extraire du tableau 1 en regroupant les chiffres successifs.[9]

___

9. A la fin du §II, j'avais mentionné 738 et non 741 numéros. La différence s'explique par le fait que 3 séries de chiffres successifs correspondent à la fin d'un épisode et au début de l'épisode suivant: 356–58 chevauchent les épisodes 4 et 5; 1146–47, les épisodes 6 et 7; 1527–28, les épisodes 8 et 9. Les chiffres 1146–47 figurant déjà dans la liste "781," les 580 numéros de la liste abrégée deviennent ci-dessous 581.

Dans le résumé qui suit, les chiffres indiquent pour chaque épisode: le premier et le dernier mot dans le texte; la première et la dernière référence dans les listes "1164" et "781"; le nombre des références recueillies dans les listes "1164" et "741" (établies à partir des 24 lectures), puis dans les listes "781" et "581" (fondées sur les 14 "bonnes" lectures).

	Texte	"1164"	"781"	"1164"	"741"	"781"	"581"
1.	1–147	2–137	2–137	**53**	**21**	48	**22**
2.	148–219	183, 187	183	2	2	1	1
3.	220–330	226–329	233–329	**10**	10	8	8
4.	331–**357**	335–**357**	336–354	**10**	6	7	5
5.	**358–1006**	**358–1006**	**358–1006**	170	106	101	75
6.	1007–**1146**	1008–**1146**	1008–**1146**	**45**	30	24	20
7.	**1147**–1216	**1147**–1210	**1147**–1210	16	15	12	11
8.	1217–**1527**	1219–**1527**	1220–1522	86	58	59	48
9.	**1528**–1803	**1528**–1800	**1528**–1795	106	66	69	54
10.	**1804**–1970	**1804**–1966	1807–1966	**53**	37	35	29
11.	**1971**–2337	**1971**–2335	**1971**–2335	**136**	94	108	85
12.	2338–3058	2340–3056	2340–3056	226	149	141	115
13.	3059–3533	3061–3521	3061–3521	**136**	75	84	56
14.	3534–**3735**	3536–**3735**	3536–**3735**	**45**	36	25	21
15.	3736–3958	3740–3945	3740–3945	17	15	10	9
16.	3959–**4082**	3965–**4082**	3965–**4082**	**53**	**21**	49	**22**
Lectures		24	14	24	24	14	14

Nous constatons que les listes "14" nous fournissent déjà, sur la structure numérique des épisodes, les références et les renseignements essentiels. Néanmoins, ce sont bien les listes "24" qui permettent de comprendre comment le rédacteur-éditeur a "mesuré" les épisodes du récit: la longueur de chaque épisode a été calculée de telle sorte qu'elle corresponde, dans les listes "24," à un nombre donné de références. Ne pouvant ici tout étudier, nous ne retiendrons que la liste "1164" (tableau 1), plus précisément, ses *quatorze chiffres isolés* et les *séries de nombres successifs qui dépassent trois paires de références.*

Le tableau 1, nous l'avons vu, présente sur la même ligne les nombres complémentaires. Complémentaires, ils le sont tous à 14 exceptions près: 381 (d'après la lecture 3), 441 (lecture 3), 531 (lecture 3), 571 (lecture 3), 575 (lecture 4), 1051 (lecture 3), 1055 (lecture 3), 1056 (lecture 18), 1260 (lecture 3), 1388 (lecture 19), 2662 (lecture 22), 3036 (lecture 23), 3507 (lectures 1 et 2), enfin 4082 (lectures 1 à 24). Où l'on voit que la lecture 3 (les lignes 7 à 1 lues dans le sens normal) nous fournit à elle seule 7 références isolées.

Le rédacteur-éditeur, qui a tout calculé, a bien dû remarquer les 14 chiffres isolés. Peut-être en a-t-il tiré parti. Cherchons donc dans le texte les mots correspondants.

Mot 381: *tmwt* (1 Sam 20:2c); 441: *wy²mr* (20:5a); 531: *wl²* (20,9d); 571: *whnh* (20:12d); 575: *wl²* (20:12e); 1051: *²lmwny* (21:3e); 1055: *tḥt* (21:4a);

1056: *ydk* (21:4a); 1260: *qšrtm* (22:8a); 1388: *ʾw* (22:15*c); 2662: *lw* (25:21c); 3036: *ʿl* (25:42c); 3507: *tgdl* (26:24a); 4082: *mlḥmh* (2 Sam 1:27b).

Si l'on additionne successivement les 51 lettres de ces 14 mots, on obtient: 8 références à l'épisode 5; 5 à l'épisode 6; 4 à l'épisode 7; 8 à l'épisode 8; 2 à l'épisode 9; 5 à l'épisode 11; 2 à l'épisode 12; 8 à l'épisode 13; 7 à l'épisode 15; 2 à l'épisode 16. A la 26e lettre (médiane), le total (1780) nous renvoie à 1 Sam 23:17d: "*C'est toi qui régneras sur Israël.*" Les autres références ne sont pas moins suggestives. Il s'agit manifestement d'une grille, mais elle est incomplète: elle nous mène seulement jusqu'à 2 Sam 1:17, mots 3960 (David) et 3965 (Saül).

Cette grille incomplète est en fait une "cachette" (cf. 1 Sam 23:23). Pour trouver la grille intégrale (4082), il faut dresser la liste des mots qui, dans le texte, correspondent aux 51 références fournies par notre "cachette." Voici cette liste: *hdbr. lk. ḥdš. ʾp. nʿwt. lbšt. ʿrwt. lhktw. drk. bkly. Yʜwʜ. wšmw. lšʾwl. ʾl. mh. ʾt. ʿmw. šmʿw. nʾ. bny. mkm. ʾhymlk. byt. ḥlylh. ky. wʾth* (1780). *wgm. yšpṭ. bk. hqdmny. ʾhry. ʾt. wtʾmr. ky. wnqh. wʾt. spḥt. wʾyn. ʾbnr. ʾbnr. zh. Yʜwʜ. šʾwl. wyʾmr. nqrʾ. ʾly. wgm. ʾy. ʾnky. dwd* (3960). *šʾwl* (3965).

C'est dans les 178 lettres de ces 51 mots qu'on trouvera la séquence 4082, conforme aux 4082 mots du récit. Elle commence à la première lettre du 6e mot et se termine à la seconde lettre du 21e mot. Elle va donc de la 16e lettre de la liste à la 68e. Elle comprend ainsi 53 lettres, 15 mots et un 16e incomplet.

Cette séquence de 53 lettres est une véritable grille, qui nous fournit 53 références à onze des seize épisodes:[10] 30 et 32 (1er épisode); 332 (2e mot de l'épisode 4); 732, 802 et 1002 (épisode 5); 1008 (2e mot de l'épisode 6); 1408, 1438, 1443 et 1463 (épisode 8); 1863, 1869 et 1873 (épisode 9); 2073, 2093, 2095, 2115, 2145, 2155, 2165, 2170, 2176, 2181, 2187, onze références à l'épisode 11, grâce à 11 lettres empruntées à l'épisode de Nob (6): -*rk bkly Yʜwʜ w*- (un don d'Ahimélek, si l'on en croit les 7 lettres qui suivent immédiatement la grille: -*m ʾhymlk*); 2487, 2527, 2533, 2563, 2863, 2864, 2870, 2900, 2901, 2931, 2971, 2976, 2977 (épisode 12); 3377, 3447, 3487, 3493 (épisode 13); 3793, 3833, 3903, 3909 (épisode 15); enfin, sept références à l'épisode 16, dont les trois premières visent le 1er, le 2e et le 4e mot de 2 Sam 1:17 (*wyqnn dwd . . . hqynh*), l'endroit précis où nous avaient laissé les lettres 50 et 51 de la *cachette*[11] (3960 et 3965): 3959, 3960, 3962, 4012, 4022, 4062, 4082.

Les quatorze références isolées méritaient, on le voit, quelques mots de commentaire. Dans la liste "1164," leur isolement est en fait un privilège. Si nous les mettons à part, il nous reste 575 paires de nombres complémentaires (x + y = 4082), 1150 références au total:

---

10. Ne pouvant étudier en détail la grille de 53 lettres, je signale seulement les textes où figurent les 16 mots qui la composent: *lbšt ʿrwt* (1 Sam 20:30c), *lhktw* (20:33a), *drk* (21:6e), *bkly* (21:6f), *Yʜwʜ* (21:8a), *wšmw* (21:8b), *lšʾwl* (dernier mot de l'épisode 6 en 21:8c), *ʾl* (22:1b), *mh* (22:3d), *ʾt* (22:4a), *ʿmw* (22:4b), *šmʿw nʾ bny* (22:7b), *mk-* (22:8c).

11. En parlant ci-dessus de "cachette" (avec référence à 1 Sam 23:23), je ne pensais pas si bien dire: la 12e lettre de la grille "53" nous renvoie précisément au mot 1863, aux "cachettes" (*hmḥbʾym*) de 1 Sam 23:23b.

239 paires de nombres complémentaires, soit 478 références;
79 séries de 2 paires de nombres complémentaires successifs, soit 316 références;
35 séries de 3 paires de nombres complémentaires successifs, soit 210 références;
13 séries (4/5/3/1) dépassant 3 paires de nombres complémentaires successifs (4 + 4; 5 + 5; 11 + 11; 5 + 5 / 4 + 4; 4 + 4; 8 + 8; 5 + 5; 8 + 8 / 4 + 4; 5 + 5; 4 + 4 / 6 + 6), 146 références au total (73 + 73).

Nos 1150 références sont donc la somme de 478 + 316 + 210 + 146. Ces deux derniers chiffres attirent l'attention: le dernier évoque les 73 lettres de la section "4082"; 210 est un multiple de 7 et de 3. Il faudrait donc étudier les 35 séries de 3 paires. Faute de place, je m'en tiendrai ici aux 13 séries de plus de 3 paires.

Ces 13 séries mettaient à la disposition du rédacteur-éditeur 26 points de repère et 146 références. Pouvait-il trouver mieux que le chiffre du Tétragramme (26) et deux fois le nombre des lettres de sa grille fondamentale pour fixer un texte sacré? Relevons les 26 passages et les 146 mots qui correspondent aux 146 références, en signalant: le numéro d'ordre; la "référence" indiquée par le tableau 1; la proposition[12] qui lui correspond dans le "Livre de Jonathan"; la référence biblique; le mot lui-même.

Nº	Réf.	Prop.	1 Samuel	Mot	Nº	Réf.	Prop.	2 Samuel	Mot
1.	2	1	16:14a	Yhwh	146.	4080	*960	1:27b	wyᵓbdw
2.	3	1		srh	145.	4079	959*		gbwrym
3.	4	1		mᶜm	144.	4078	959		nplw
4.	5	1*		šᵓwl	143.	4077	959	1:27a	ᵓyk
5.	11	*3	16:15a	wyᵓmrw	142.	4071	957*		mᵓd
6.	12	3		ᶜbdy	141.	4070	957		ly
7.	13	3		šᵓwl	140.	4069	*957	1:26b	nᶜmt
8.	14	3*		ᵓlyw	139.	4068	956*		yhwntn
9.	15	*4	16:15b	hnh	138.	4067	956	1:26a	ᵓhy
10.	25	6*		lpnyk	137.	4057	954		gbrym
11.	26	*7	16:16c	ybqšw	136.	4056	954		nplw
12.	27	7		ᵓyš	135.	4055	*954	1:25a	ᵓyk
13.	28	7		ydᶜ	134.	4054	953*		lbwškn
14.	29	7		mngn	133.	4053	953		ᶜl
15.	30	7*		bknwr	132.	4052	953		zhb
16.	31	*8	16:16d	whyh	131.	4051	953		ᶜdy
17.	32	8		bhywt	130.	4050	953		hmᶜlh
18.	33	8		ᶜlyk	129.	4049	953		ᶜdnym

12. Ici comme ci-dessus dans la liste des références médianes des 24 lectures, l'astérisque indique: le début de la proposition quand il est placé avant le numéro de la proposition; la fin de la proposition quand il est placé après. Les propositions qui n'ont qu'un seul mot sont marquées d'un astérisque avant et après leur numéro.

N°	Réf.	Prop.	1 Samuel	Mot	N°	Réf.	Prop.	2 Samuel	Mot
19.	34	8		rwḥ	128.	4048	953		ʿm
20.	35	8		ʾlhym	127.	4047	953	1:24a	šny
21.	40	10*	16:16f	lk	126.	4042	953		yśrʾl
22.	41	*11	16:17a	wyʾmr	125.	4041	*953	1:24a	bnwt
23.	42	11		šʾwl	124.	4040	952*		gbrw
24.	43	11		ʾl	123.	4039	*952	1:23c	mʾrywt
25.	44	11*		ʿbdyw	122.	4038	951*	1:23b	qlw
26.	779	*206	20:26e	ky	121.	3303	772	26:14b	hlwʾ
27.	780	206		lʾ	120.	3302	771*		lʾmr
28.	781	206*		ṭhwr	119.	3301	771		nr
29.	782	*207	20:27a	wyhy	118.	3300	771	26:14a	bn
30.	952	243*	20:36c	mwrh	117.	3130	731		hmqwm
31.	953	*244	20:36d	hnʿr	116.	3129	731		ʾt
32.	954	244*		rṣ	115.	3128	731		dwd
33.	955	*245	20:36e	whwʾ	114.	3127	*731	26:5c	wyrʾ
34.	966	246*	20:37a	yhwntn	113.	3116	728		ʾl
35.	967	*247	20:37b	wyqrʾ	112.	3115	728		šʾwl
36.	968	247		yhwntn	111.	3114	728		bʾ
37.	969	247		ʾhry	110.	3113	728		ky
38.	970	247*		hnʿr	109.	3112	*728	26:4b	wydʿ
39.	971	*248*	20:37c	wyʾmr	108.	3111	727*		mrglym
40.	972	*249	20:37d	hlwʾ	107.	3110	727		dwd
41.	973	249		hḥṣy	106.	3109	*727	26:4a	wyšlḥ
42.	978	250	20:38a	ʾhry	105.	3104	726		ky
43.	979	250*		hnʿr	104.	3103	*726	26:3c	wyrʾ
44.	980	*251*	20:38b	mhrh	103.	3102	725*		bmdbr
45.	981	*252*	20:38c	ḥwšh	102.	3101	725		yšb
46.	982	*253	20:38d	ʾl	101.	3100	725	26:3b	wdwd
47.	993	256	20:39a	lʾ	100.	3089	723*		zyp
48.	994	256		ydʿ	99.	3088	723		bmdbr
49.	995	256*		mʾwmh	98.	3087	723		dwd
50.	996	*257	20:39b	ʾk	97.	3086	723		ʾt
51.	997	257		yhwntn	96.	3085	723		lbqš
52.	998	257		wdwd	95.	3084	723		yśrʾl
53.	999	257		ydʿw	94.	3083	723		bḥwry
54.	1000	257		ʾt	93.	3082	723	26:2b	ʾyš
55.	1570	372	23:3c	ʾl	92.	2512	604		dwd
56.	1571	372		mʿrkwt	91.	2511	*604	25:13a	wyʾmr
57.	1572	372*		plštym	90.	2510	603*		hʾlh
58.	1573	*373	23:4a	wywsp	89.	2509	603	25:12d	hdbrym
59.	1611	384	23:6a	bn	88.	2471	595*		dwd
60.	1612	384		ʾhymlk	87.	2470	*595	25:10c	my
61.	1613	384		ʾl	86.	2469	*594*	25:10b	wyʾmr

Nº	Réf.	Prop.	1 Samuel	Mot	Nº	Réf.	Prop.	2 Samuel	Mot
62.	1614	384		dwd	85.	2468	593*		dwd
63.	1615	384*		$q^c ylh$	84.	2467	593	25:10a	$^c bdy$
64.	1676	395	23:10b	$q^c ylh$	83.	2406	580		lk
65.	1677	395		lšḫt	82.	2405	580		$^{\jmath}šr$
66.	1678	395		$l^c yr$	81.	2404	*580	25:6e	wkl
67.	1679	395*		$b^c bwry$	80.	2403	579*	25:6d	šlwm
68.	1932	462	23:26d	$^{\jmath}l$	79.	2150	*513	24:11e	$l^{\jmath}$
69.	1933	462		dwd	78.	2149	*512*	24:11d	$w^{\jmath}mr$
70.	1934	462		$w^{\jmath}l$	77.	2148	511*		$^c lyk$
71.	1935	462		$^{\jmath}nšyw$	76.	2147	*511	24:11c	wtḥs
72.	1936	462*		ltpśm	75.	2146	510*		lhrgk
73.	1937	*463	23:27a	$wml^{\jmath}k$	74.	2145	*510	24:11b	$w^{\jmath}mr$

Résumons la liste qui précède: voir tableau p. 182.

Les 26 points de repère nous renvoient globalement à 14 (7 + 7) passages du récit, précisément à 26 textes (13 + 13), à 146 mots (73 + 73), qui ont, au total, 560 lettres (288 + 272):

1.	YHWH srh $m^c m$ $š^{\jmath}wl$. $wy^{\jmath}mrw$ $^c bdy$ $š^{\jmath}wl$ $^{\jmath}lyw$ hnh. lpnyk	40
2.	ybqšw $^{\jmath}yš$ yd^c mngn bknwr whyh bhywt $^c lyk$ rwḥ $^{\jmath}lhy-$	80
3.	m. lk $wy^{\jmath}mr$ $š^{\jmath}wl$ $^{\jmath}l$ $^c bdyw$. ky $l^{\jmath}$ ṭhwr wyhy. mwrh $hn^c r$ r-	120
4.	ṣ $whw^{\jmath}$. yhwntn $wyqr^{\jmath}$ yhwntn $^{\jmath}hry$ $hn^c r$ $wy^{\jmath}mr$ $hlw^{\jmath}$ h-	160
5.	ḥsy. $^{\jmath}hry$ $hn^c r$ mhrh ḥwšh $^{\jmath}l$. $l^{\jmath}$ yd^c $m^{\jmath}wmh$ $^{\jmath}k$ yhwntn w-	200
6.	dwd $yd^c w$ $^{\jmath}t$. $^{\jmath}l$ $m^c rkwt$ plštym wywsp. bn $^{\jmath}hymlk$ $^{\jmath}l$ dw-	240
7.	d $q^c ylh$. $q^c ylh$ lšḫt $l^c yr$ $b^c bwry$. $^{\jmath}l$ dwd $w^{\jmath}l$ $^{\jmath}nšyw$ lt-	280
8.	pśm $wml^{\jmath}k$. $w^{\jmath}mr$ lhrgk wtḥs $^c lyk$ $w^{\jmath}mr$ $l^{\jmath}$. šlwm wkl $^{\jmath}š$-	320
9.	r lk. $^c bdy$ dwd $wy^{\jmath}mr$ my dwd. hdbrym $h^{\jmath}lh$ $wy^{\jmath}mr$ dwd. $^{\jmath}y$-	360
10.	š bḥwry $yśr^{\jmath}l$ lbqš $^{\jmath}t$ dwd bmdbr zyp. wdwd yšb bmdbr	400
11.	$wyr^{\jmath}$ ky. wyšlḥ dwd mrglym wyd^c ky $b^{\jmath}$ $š^{\jmath}wl$ $^{\jmath}l$. $wyr^{\jmath}$ dw-	440
12.	d $^{\jmath}t$ hmqwm. bn nr $l^{\jmath}mr$ $hlw^{\jmath}$. qlw $m^{\jmath}rywt$ gbrw bnwt yśr-	480
13.	$^{\jmath}l$. šny $^c m$ $^c dnym$ $hm^c lh$ $^c dy$ zhb $^c l$ lbwškn $^{\jmath}yk$ nplw gb-	520
14.	rym. $^{\jmath}hy$ yhwntn $n^c mt$ ly $m^{\jmath}d$. $^{\jmath}yk$ nplw gbrym $wy^{\jmath}bdw$.	560

Quel secret recèlent ces 560 lettres? En les additionnant successivement, selon le programme exposé dans RB 97 (1990) 383ss. mais cette fois à la recherche des séquences "4082," on y trouve d'emblée quatre grilles, puis quatre autres grilles qui chevauchent les précédentes (capitales = lettres médianes):

Grille 1, de la ligne 1, lettre 24, à la ligne 3, lettre 34 (lettres 24–114 = 91 lettres): -y $š^{\jmath}wl$ $^c lyw$ hnh. lpnyk ybqšw $^{\jmath}yš$ yd^c mngn bknwr whyh bhywT $^c lyk$ rwḥ $^{\jmath}lhym$. lk $wy^{\jmath}mr$ $š^{\jmath}wl$ $^{\jmath}l$ $^c bdyw$. ky lw ṭhwr wyhy. mwr-

Grille 2, de la ligne 3, lettre 38, à la ligne 5, lettre 25 (lettres 118–205 = 68 lettres): $-^c r$ rṣ $whw^{\jmath}$. yhwntn $wyqr^{\jmath}$ yhwntn $^{\jmath}hry$ $hn^c r$ $WY^{\jmath}mr$ $hlw^{\jmath}$ hḥsy. $^{\jmath}hry$ $hn^c r$ mhrh ḥwšh $^{\jmath}l$. $l^{\jmath}$ yd-

	Réf.	Nombre	Total	1 Samuel
1.	2–5	4	4	16:14–17*
2.	11–15	5	9	
3.	25–35	11	20	
4.	40–44	5	25	
5.	779–82	4	29	20:26–27*
6.	952–55	4	33	20:36–39*
7.	966–73	8	41	
8.	978–82	5	46	
9.	993–1000	8	54	
10.	1570–73	4	58	23:3–4*
11.	1611–15	5	63	23:6*
12.	1676–79	4	67	23:10*
13.	1932–37	6	73	23:26–27*

	Réf.	Nombre	Total	Samuel
26.	4077–80	4	73	
25.	4067–71	5	69	
24.	4047–57	11	64	
23.	4038–42	5	53	2 Sam 1:23–27*
22.	3300–3303	4	48	1 Sam 26:14*
21.	3127–30	4	44	
20.	3109–16	8	40	
19.	3100–3104	5	32	
18.	3082–89	8	27	26:2–5*
17.	2509–12	4	19	25:12–13*
16.	2467–71	5	15	25:10*
15.	2403–6	4	10	25:6*
14.	2145–50	6	6↑	1 Sam 24:11*

Grille 3, de la ligne 7, lettre 23, à la ligne 9, lettre 10 (lettres 263–330 = 68 lettres): *-wry. ᵓl dwd wᵓl ᵓnšyw ltpśm wmlᵓk. wᵓmr lhrGK wtḥs ᶜlyk wᵓmr lᵓ. šlwm wkl ᵓšr lk. ᶜbdy dwd*

Grille 4, de la ligne 11, lettre 7, à la ligne 12, lettre 37 (lettres 407–77 = 71 lettres): *wyšlḥ dwd mrglym wydᶜ ky bᵓ šᵓwl ᵓl. wyrᵓ dwd At hmqwm. bn nr lᵓmr hlwᵓ. qlw mᵓrywt gbrw bnwt*

Grille 5, de la ligne 4, lettre 5, à la ligne 6, lettre 9 (lettres 135–209 = 75 lettres): *-rᵓ yhwntn ᵓḥry hnᶜr wyᵓmr hlwᵓ hḥṣy. ᵓḥry hnᶜr Mhrh ḥwšh ᵓl. lᵓ ydᶜ mᵓwmh ᵓk yhwntn wdwd ydᶜw ᵓt*

Grille 6, de la ligne 7, lettre 30, à la ligne 9, lettre 15 (lettres 270–335 = 66 lettres): *-d wᵓl ᵓnšyw ltpśm wmlᵓk. wᵓmr lhrgk wtḥs CLyk wᵓmr lᵓ. šlwm wkl ᵓšr lk. ᶜbdy dwd wyᵓmr*

Grille 7, de la ligne 9, lettre 20, à la ligne 11, lettre 15 (lettres 340–415 = 76 lettres): *-d. hdbrym hᵓlh wyᵓmr dwd. ᵓyš bḥwry yśr ᵓl lbqš ᵓT Dwd bmdbr zyp. wdwd yšb bmdbr wyrᵓ ky. wyšlḥ dwd m-*

Grille 8, de la ligne 11, lettre 39, à la ligne 13, lettre 19 (lettres 439–99 = 59 lettres): *dwd ᵓt hmqwm. bn nr lᵓmr hlwᵓ. qlw mᵓrywt Gbrw bnwt yśrᵓl. šny ᶜm ᶜdnym hmᶜlh ᶜd-*

Les grilles 1–8 ont donc au total: 91 + 68 + 68 + 71 + 75 + 66 + 76 + 59 = 574 lettres, soit 14 lettres de plus que les passages qu'elles utilisent. Mais, en raison des chevauchements, elles laissent encore disponibles 144 lettres:

1. *Yₕwₕ srh mᶜm šᵓwl. wyᵓmrw ᶜbd- . -h hn- . ᵓl mᶜrkwt pl-*   36 lettres
2. *štym wywsp. bn ᵓhymlk ᵓl dwd qᶜylh. qᶜylh lšḥt*   72
3. *lᶜyr bᶜb- . my dw- . -y zhb ᶜl lbwškn ᵓyk nplw gbrym. ᵓ-*   108
4. *ḥy yhwntn nᶜmt ly mᵓd ᵓyk nplw gbwrym wyᵓbdw.*   144

Ce texte paraît étrange surtout si on l'examine en détail. Remarquons seulement que 53 lettres (12 mots et un 13ᵉ mot imcomplet) sont empruntées à l'épisode de Qeïla (1 Sam 23:3–10*), où intervient le "fils d'Ahimélek," et que la fin du texte "cite" l'élégie sur Jonathan (2 Sam 1:26–27). Abiatar et Jonathan n'auraient-ils rien à nous apprendre?

En additionnant les lettres, nous trouvons d'emblée une première grille, sur le *seuil* du fils d'Ahimélek, puis une seconde, qui chevauche la première et les deux mentions de Qeïla:

Grille 9 (79 lettres: lettres 227–62, 336–39, 500–538 du texte de 560 lettres): *-sp. bn ᵓhymlk ᵓl dwd qᶜylh. qᶜylh lšḥt lᶜyr bᶜb- . my dW- . -y zhb ᶜl lbwškn ᵓyk nplw gbrym. ᵓḥy yhwntn nᶜmt ly*

Grille 10 (82 lettres: lettres 245–62, 336–39, 500–559 du texte de 560 lettres): *-lh. qᶜylh lšḥt lᶜyr bᶜb- . my dw-. -y zhb ᶜl lbwškn ᵓyk nplW Gbrym. ᵓhy yhwntn nᶜmt ly mᵓd. ᵓyk nplw gbwrym wyᵓbd-*

Ici finit un "jeu" accessible à tout "bon élève." Les initiés pourront chercher d'autres grilles "cachettes" (cf. supra) qui leur donneront accès à de vraies grilles. J'ai trouvé deux "cachettes" qui méritent d'être signalées.

Pour accéder à la première, il faut partir des 15 références médianes recueillies dans les 10 grilles qui précèdent (où les lettres médianes figurent en capitales). On peut dresser ainsi une liste de 15 mots, correspondant aux références des grilles:

(4) 1414: *ydᶜw*; (9) 1958: *kn*; (8) 2007: *hdrk*; (3) 2097: *wylk*; 2117: *ᵓpym*; (10) 2161: *rᵓh*; 2164: *mᶜylk*; (5) 2262: *ky*; (1) 2327: *dwd*; (6) 2404: *wkl*; 2434: *wymṣᵓw*; (2) 2487: *wᵓt*; (7) 2488: *ᵓšr*; 2492: *wntty*; (2) 2497: *ᵓy*.

On additionne ensuite successivement les 53 lettres de ces 15 mots, à la recherche d'une séquence 4082 dans les mots correspondant aux sommes successives. Cette séquence existe: elle commence au mot 992 (total obtenu à la lettre 28) et se termine au mot 2990 (qui correspond à la lettre 52). Voici cette grille, composée de 25 mots, 90 lettres:

nᶜr. ᵓk. wyqm. hᶜyr. hkhn. wyᵓmr. hnmṣᵓ. ᵓyn. yš. lḥm. mlk. mwᵓb. dwD. Dwd. wᵓnšym. bᵓ. dwd. wyhy. lmh. hnh. wpšᶜ. hywtnw. brwk. ᶜbdw. ḥśk.

Le lecteur aura reconnu les passages utilisés, qui, dans le système de l'éditeur, constituent des textes clés: l'épisode de la flèche: 1 Sam 20:39a (Le *garçon* ne savait rien): 20:39b (seuls Jonathan et David connaissaient *haddābār*); 21:1a, c; l'épisode de Nob: 21:2a, 3c, 4b, 5cd, 7b; David chez le roi de Moab: 22:4ab; le massacre des prêtres: 22:6a; Qeïla: 23:7a; David s'éloignant de Saül: 23:26c; l'épisode central: 24:10bc, 12e; enfin l'histoire d'Abigaïl: 25:16, 39cd, où David bénit Yʜwʜ qui "a préservé son serviteur du mal" (v. 39cd). Nous retrouvons ici un des grands thèmes des épisodes 11–13: la vengeance humaine est un "mal."

Pour découvrir une 12ᵉ grille, on notera que, des 560 lettres fournies par les 26 textes-repères, 144 étaient restées disponibles après le repérage des 8 premières grilles et que les grilles 9 et 10 avaient utilisé 100 autres lettres. Il reste donc 44 lettres: Yʜwʜ *srh mᶜm šᵓwl. wyᵓmrw ᶜbd- . -h hn- . ᵓl mᶜrkwt plštym wyw- . -w* (le *waw* final).

En additionnant ces 44 lettres, nous n'obtenons qu'une grille incomplète, dont la dernière référence est 2832. Cette grille partielle est encore une "cachette": de la lettre 26 à la lettre 41, elle nous renvoie à 16 mots qui nous fournissent une nouvelle grille de 61 lettres. Voici ces mots, suivis simplement d'une référence:

ᶜlyhm lśr (22:2b); *mlk* (22:4a); *ytn* (22:7c); *wᵓt* (22:11a); *ybqš* (22:23c); *hgrnwt* (23:1c); *whkyty* (23:2c); *ky* (23:27d); *hnh* (24:5b); *1b* (24:6b); *ṣᵓnw* (25:2e); *bdmym* (25:26cc); *ᵓdny* (25:26d); *npšk* (25:29a); *ḥḥyy-* (25:29b).

Ces cinq derniers mots, on le voit, sont empruntés au discours d'Abigaïl: c'est YHWH qui vengera David.

Au point où nous en sommes, nous n'avons plus que 28 lettres disponibles: *YHWH srh m^{c}m š$^{\,?}$wl. wy$^{\,?}$mrw ^{c}bd-. -h h-. yw-. w.* Elles nous fournissent: 5 références à l'épisode 1 (1 Sam 16:14b, 15b, 16a, c, 19), 2 références à l'épisode 3 (19:4bc), 1 référence au 1er mot de l'épisode 4 (19:9a), 10 références à l'épisode 5 (20:2f, 5a, 24bc, 25a, 26d, 27a, d[*bis*], 29g), 9 références à l'épisode 6 (21:3d[*bis*], 7a[*bis*], 7b [*ter*], 8a, c), 1 référence au dernier mot de la 1re proposition de l'épisode 7 (22:1a: David partit *de là*, c'est-à-dire de Nob). La grille est incomplète. Voudrait-elle souligner qu'en quittant Nob avec les cinq pains dans son sac, David avait pour lui toutes les chances et ses "garçons" tous les "instruments" de travail qui leur permettraient d'accéder aux énigmes du texte sacré?

Quoi qu'il en soit, dans les "cachettes" ménagées par le rédacteur-éditeur, les disciples des prêtres ne trouveront rien d'autre que ce que le texte enseigne explicitement (par exemple, que la vengeance est à Dieu). Les couloirs souterrains du récit, qui en assurent les fondations, permettent aussi de s'exercer sur le texte, voire d'en vérifier le bon état de conservation. Ils ne recèlent aucune doctrine ésotérique. Ni franc-maçon, ni même cabaliste avant la lettre, le rédacteur-éditeur était un *architecte*.

Nous le savions déjà: le "Livre de Jonathan" est un édifice harmonieux (§I). Il est composé de seize épisodes et centré sur les épisodes 8 et 9, où les prêtres de Nob, Ahimélek et Abiatar, attirent à la fois l'attention et la sympathie du *visiteur*. La place centrale des épisodes 8–9 est soulignée, à la fin de l'épisode 9, par les encouragements de Jonathan à David. Ici pourtant, le *lecteur* n'a pas encore atteint le "tournant" du récit (épisode 10), ni le *scribe attentif* son centre arithmétique (épisode 11). La *structure numérique* du "Livre de Jonathan" ne recoupe exactement ni le *plan* de l'édifice, ni le *développement narratif*. Elle semble artificielle, mais où est l'artifice?

La longueur des épisodes est manifestement calculée: ce n'est pas par hasard, pour ne rappeler qu'un exemple, que les épisodes 6 et 7 ont respectivement 140 et 70 mots. Néanmoins, les chiffres traditionnels ne rendent compte que d'une partie des données. Certains détails orientent vers une explication alphabétique. Faudrait-il donc chercher la clé de l'énigme dans le "rectangle alphabétique"?

Les lignes 2 à 8 du rectangle (§II) nous offrent, à cet égard, un terrain privilégié. Réduites à 73 lettres, elles nous fournissent d'emblée une section "4082" qui correspond exactement au nombre des mots du livre. On peut lire cette section de 24 manières différentes et disposer ainsi de 24 grilles distinctes. Si l'on compare les indications de ces grilles à la structure du récit (§III), on s'aperçoit que 14 d'entre elles esquissent un plan concentrique comparable à la structure numérique du "Livre de Jonathan": à la lettre médiane (la 37e) de chacune d'elles, le total obtenu semble renvoyer le lecteur au mot correspondant de l'épisode 11, où figurent précisément les deux mots médians du livre (2041–42). Regroupés, les résultats de ces 14 lectures résolvent les énigmes que les chiffres traditionnels avaient laissées inexpliquées.

Néanmoins, la structure numérique du livre dans son ensemble n'apparaît clairement que si l'on compare les seize épisodes aux 1164 "références" recueillies dans les 24 grilles (tableau 1). On s'aperçoit alors que le rédacteur-éditeur a remanié et complété les récits dont il disposait de telle sorte que chaque épisode corresponde, dans les 24 grilles, à un nombre donné de "références": 53, par exemple, pour l'introduction et la conclusion du livre; 136, pour les récits "parallèles" de 1 Samuel 24 et 26.

Le rédacteur-éditeur a fait plus. Initié aux secrets des 73 lettres et des 1164 "références," il a joué sur 14 chiffres isolés et 575 paires de nombres complémentaires (x + y = 4082) pour créer de nouvelles grilles "4082," cette fois à partir des mots du texte lui-même. Ce système complexe, qui fixait un texte sacré, permettait aussi aux disciples de s'entraîner au maniement des lettres-chiffres en cherchant patiemment la solution des énigmes alphabétiques que recélaient les textes clés du "Livre de Jonathan." Textes clés du système, les passages en question ne sont pas très nombreux (les plus intéressants, étudiés ci-dessus, sont au nombre de vingt-six). Cependant, le système dans son ensemble a entraîné, un peu partout dans le livre, des amplifications, des remaniements de détail, voire de curieuses variantes orthographiques. La critique de *Samuel* a souvent "résolu" les difficultés qui en résultent soit en restituant le texte "primitif," soit en éliminant des gloses ou des ajouts rédactionnels. La critique n'a sans doute pas tort, mais, avant de toucher au texte, ne faudrait-il pas essayer de le comprendre? Il est plus savant qu'on ne le croit et, si le rédacteur-éditeur du "Jonathan" précanonique connaissait déjà les méthodes attestées dans le texte consonantique de 1 Samuel 13–2 Samuel 1, au nom de quel principe pourrions-nous déclarer "corrompu" le TM de *Samuel*?

Post-scriptum.—Depuis la rédaction de cet article, la traduction de 1989 (supra, n. 1) a été publiée dans: F. Langlamet, "'David—Jonathan—Saül' ou le 'Livre de Jonathan': *1 Sam* 16,14–*2 Sam* 1,27*," *RB* 101 (1994) 326–54 (328–47).

THE COMPOSITION OF JEREMIAH 30–31

William McKane

IN THE MODERN HISTORY of the exegesis of these chapters, there has been a transition from the theory that some words of the prophet Jeremiah are found scattered in them to the opinion that they consist substantially of his own words. The setting and composition of the chapters that are obtained differ greatly depending on which of these models is accepted. If the chapters are mostly from Jeremiah, with a few later additions, the main task will be to elucidate them in the context of the time and circumstances of his ministry, whatever greater precision or finer tuning may be sought in the discharge of this, whether Jeremiah's early period and his tender regard for Ephraim in the disintegration and exile that the people had suffered is the key or whether the composition consists also of oracles from the later part of his ministry and embraces Judah as well as Ephraim.

If, on the other hand, chaps. 30–31 contain only a scattering of words from Jeremiah himself, his words may not be highly significant in an analysis of the composition of these chapters. The words would *ex hypothesi* have been picked up as valuable fragments by later editors or redactors, but they would comprise only a small part of the whole and furnish no clue about the time and circumstances of the composition. With this in mind, one may ask whether Cornill's expression *Überarbeitung*[1] is not misleading when applied to everything in these chapters that is not attributable to Jeremiah. That the appellation originates in a critical concern to separate "genuine" words of Jeremiah from "nongenuine" is understandable, but if Cornill's analysis is correct, the term *Überarbeitung* is a case of the tail wagging the dog.

Should Duhm be correct in locating these chapters late in the postexilic period,[2] it is the setting, rather than the words of Jeremiah that have been attracted

---

Author's note: It is a privilege to write this small piece for Prof. Haran and to pay homage to his scholarship.

1. C. H. Cornill, *Das Buch Jeremia* (Leipzig, 1905) 323.
2. B. Duhm, *Das Buch Jeremia* (Kurzer Hand-Commentar zum Alten Testament 9; Tübingen, 1901) 237–60.

to the chapters, which is significant for the understanding of their composition. The prediction of restoration is then not a prediction that was projected by Jeremiah in the sixth century as much as a prediction that sustained Judah in the late postexilic period. To draw such a conclusion is, however, to uncover awkward complications, since 31:2–6 and 15–20, which refer to Ephraim and are acknowledged by Duhm and Cornill to be Jeremiah's words, do not seem to fit into the theory. Their original context would then be (according to Duhm and Cornill) some point, perhaps early in Jeremiah's ministry, but because there was, at a much later period, so much concern to embrace the former Northern Kingdom in a predicted restoration, these Jeremianic verses were conscripted into the composition as an expression of it.

It is now appropriate to reinforce the general outline that has been offered with some detail. Giesebrecht's conclusion was that, out of the contents of chaps. 30–31, only 31:2–6, 15–20, and 27–34 were probably attributable to Jeremiah.[3] The Jeremianic "kernel," according to Duhm, is 30:12–15 and 31:15–22.[4] Cornill describes chap. 30 as entirely an *Überarbeitung* and attributes 31:2–6, 15–20, and 27–34 to Jeremiah.[5] The change of opinion, observed above, may be seen in Volz and is continued in Rudolph, Weiser, and Bright.[6] Both Volz and Rudolph are guided by the assumption that chaps. 30 and 31 are essentially a prediction of restoration addressed to the exiled Northern Kingdom by Jeremiah and that references to Judah are secondary insertions (30:4, 17; 31:23–30, 38–40).[7] Weiser, though he deletes "Judah" (30:4) and "Zion" (30:17, a gloss), regards the references to Judah as intrinsic to chaps. 30 and 31; he appeals to a preexilic all-Israelite concept to which Jeremiah was attached and that was the *Leitmotiv* of the composition.[8]

Bright's explanation of the combination Ephraim and Judah is different, and it finds room for both of them in the composition of chaps. 30–31. He contends that concerns that emerged at different points in Jeremiah's career have been combined in chaps. 30–31: sayings addressed to Northern Israel that were uttered relatively early and later sayings that in some cases have been expanded in order to apply Jeremiah's prophecies more directly to the situation of the exiles in Babylon. In this connection he discerns the influence of Deutero-Isaiah (30:10–11, 18–22; 31:7–9, 10–14). He agrees that 30:18–22 is post-587 but holds that it may have been uttered by Jeremiah. In his perception of possible Deutero-Isaianic influence, he returns to a position that Giesebrecht stressed.

---

3. F. Giesebrecht, *Das Buch Jeremia* (HKAT 3/2; Göttingen, 1894; repr. 1907) 165.

4. Duhm, *Jeremia*, 240, 247.

5. Cornill, *Jeremia*, 323.

6. P. Volz, *Der Prophet Jeremia* (KAT 10; Leipzig, 1928); W. Rudolph, *Jeremia* (HAT 12; Tübingen, 1968) 188–89; A. Weiser, *Das Buch Jeremia* (ATD 20–21; Göttingen, 1969) 264–68; J. Bright, *Jeremiah: Introduction* (AB 21; New York, 1965) 284–87.

7. Redactional elements, according to W. Thiel, *Die deuteronomistische Redaktion von Jeremia 26–45* (Neukirchen-Vluyn, 1981) 20–28.

8. Weiser, *Jeremia*, 267 n. 7.

His estimate of the date of composition, not later than the middle of the exilic period, places it much earlier than Duhm.

Without depending on Weiser's postulated premonarchical covenant ideology, the equation of "Israel" with "all-Israel" rather than "Northern Israel" in chaps. 30–31 is a respectable hypothesis, and the contention that references to Judah in these chapters are secondary (Volz, Rudolph) may be resisted. Yet a special tenderness for Ephraim (31:4–6, 15–20) may be accounted for by the theorizing of an early concept and experience of solidarity that embraced both Ephraim and Judah in the future restoration of Israel. More particularly, if we turn to 30:3–4, we find a consensus (including Weiser but not Bright) that "Judah" (v. 3) and "to Judah" (v. 4) should be deleted, though this is unsupported by textual evidence. It may be that "Judah" (v. 3) and "to Judah" (v. 4) are additions, but there are at least two ways of explaining them. Either their purpose is to take account of other secondary references to Judah and Jerusalem (31:38–40) in chaps. 30–31, or else they are additions by a later glossator who had chaps. 30–31 in their extant form before him, who assumed that "Israel" meant the Northern Kingdom and who added "Judah" to harmonize vv. 3–4 with the references to Judah in chaps. 30–31.

There is a difference between these two explanations: according to the first, secondary references to Judah in chaps. 30–31 trigger the addition "Judah"; according to the second, "Judah" was triggered by a later reader's equation of "Israel" with the Northern Kingdom, combined with the perception that there are references to Judah in chaps. 30–31. If the second possibility is accepted, the allowance that "Judah" is secondary does not lead to the conclusion that the references to Judah in chaps. 30–31 are secondary, and it raises the question whether the equation of "Israel" with the Northern Kingdom in these chapters is everywhere a correct one. In particular, it should be questioned whether the association of Israel and Ephraim at 31:9 ("For I have become a father to Israel and Ephraim is my eldest son") is a firm indication that 31:7–9 are addressed to Ephraim. That "Jacob" is a prop for this argument will be questioned below and v. 9b need establish no more than that "Ephraim" is included in "Israel." Again, the deletion of "Judah" at 31:31 (Volz, Rudolph) without textual support should be resisted. It follows from the assumption that the promise of the new covenant is addressed exclusively to Ephraim and not also to Judah. The only argument that may be produced for this is the one that has already been weighed in the balance and found wanting, namely, that all the references to Judah in chaps. 30–31 are secondary.

At 30:3–4 the equation of "Israel" with "all Israel" (assuming that "Judah" is an addition) is slightly reinforced (only slightly) if the word-string means 'change the fortunes of my people Israel'.[9] The term *šbwt* or *šbyt* should then be

---

9. S. Böhmer (*Heimkehr und neuer Bund* [Studien zur Jeremia 30–31; Göttingen, 1976] 81) prefers 'to bring back from exile my people Israel', though he sometimes gives the sense as 'to change the fortune of my people Israel'.

derived from *šwb* not *šbh* and is cognate with the verb. It should be noticed that the match is between the *Qal* (*wšbty*) of the verb and *šbwt*, whereas the reference to bringing back from exile later in the verse features the *Hiphil* of *šwb* (*whšbtym*). Moreover, were the words "bring back from exile my people Israel and Judah" correct, the continuation of the verse if not redundant would have to be regarded as epexegesis of "And I shall bring back from exile my people Israel and Judah" rather than a particularizing of how this promise would be implemented. The verse predicts a radical turnaround of all-Israel's fortunes, as the Vulgate correctly indicates (*et convertam conversionem*) and, as a manifestation of this, their return to repossess the land that Yahweh gave to their fathers.

The assertion that "Israel" in chaps. 30–31 is to be identified with "all-Israel" has to take into account 31:15–20, where it may be concluded with certainty that the Northern Kingdom (Ephraim) is addressed. Moreover, it is the inhabitants of the Northern Kingdom returned from exile who are to plant vineyards on the hills of Samaria (v. 5) and who are invited or summoned to go up to Zion (v. 6). Even so the all-Israelite scope of 31:1–6, its acknowledgement of the centrality of Zion, and the inclusiveness of its concept of Israel are impressive. Verse 31:1 may not be originally integral to the poetry of vv. 2–6, but it should be noticed that Rudolph, who is a stout contender for the equation "Israel" = the Northern Kingdom, allows that the statement "God of all the families of Israel" (v. 1) has both the Northern Kingdom and Judah in view. Thiel judges that "all the families of Israel" is prior to D, whose phrase for "all Israel" is "Israel and Judah," but he supposes that 31:1 has the same meaning as "Israel and Judah" at 31:27.[10] At 31:12 there is a reference to pilgrims coming with shouts of joy to Zion's height, but there is no indication that they came from the Northern Kingdom, unless "Israel" (v. 10) and "Jacob" (v. 11) are taken to show this.

Use of the word "Israel" must be analyzed in combination with a consideration of the use of "Jacob" at 30:7, 10, 18; 31:7, 11. If the argument that chaps. 30–31 contain an address by Jeremiah to the Northern Kingdom cannot be sustained by an appeal to "Israel," much less can it win the day by an appeal to "Jacob,"[11] which is a more appropriate model for all-Israel (since Jacob was the "father" of the twelve tribes) than it is for Northern Israel. Further, the conclusion that 30:12–17 is addressed to Zion (v. 17), which the NEB and REB have reinforced by means of a gloss at 30:12 ('to Zion'), should not be called into question on the ground that vv. 12–17 are the continuation of an address to Jacob (30:7–10) that is, Northern Israel, so that 30:17 has to be emended. Volz makes vv. 16–17 secondary, while Rudolph follows the LXX at v. 17 and emends 'Zion' to 'our prey'.

10. Thiel, *Deuteronomistische Redaktion von Jeremia*, 22.
11. Agreeing with Böhmer, *Heimkehr und neuer Bund*, 82.

That 31:15–20 is addressed to Ephraim cannot be contested (see above, p. 190, on 31:1–6), but this should not lead to the conclusions that chaps. 30–31 are essentially an address to Ephraim and that all references to Judah are secondary. The allusion to Rachel weeping for her children at Ramah is agreeable with an Ephraim context, since her "children" were the Northern tribes, Joseph (Gen 30:24) and Benjamin (Gen 35:18). But a tender concern for Ephraim—a special mention of the tribe's penitence and remorse and of its participation in the restoration that is predicted—is compatible with the all-Israelite scope of chaps. 30–31.

The critical opinion that the composition of chaps. 30–31 is postexilic may be further probed with the help of the more recent books of Böhmer and Thiel. Thiel discerns post-Deuteronomistic intrusions in chaps. 30–31: at 30:22, where the second-person plural is formally jarring and the verse serves no useful purpose in the context; and at 30:23–24, which is similarly isolated, but whose subject (threat of judgment) makes a good stopgap in diverse contexts.[12] Further post-Deuteronomistic insertions are discerned at 31:38–40 and ("most probably") at 31:37. Thiel allows the possibility that there may be others.

The structure of chaps. 30–31 preferred by Thiel over the scheme discussed above may be seen clearly in relation to 30:3–4. In Thiel's view the term "Judah" in these verses is not merely secondary but is an integral redactional item.[13] In v. 3 the use of "Israel and Judah" is attributable to a framework supplied by D that is closed by 31:27–28. The remaining contributions by D to chap. 31 are vv. 29–30[14] and vv. 31–34, the pinnacle of his redaction.[15] At 31:31, "Judah" is an essential part of D's redaction and "Israel" at 31:33 = "all-Israel." Thiel's opinion that chaps. 30 and 31 are fundamentally addressed to Northern Israel follows Volz and Rudolph, but he identifies 30:8–9 as "Judean" though not attributable to D.[16] The other framework that he identifies (30:4, 31:23–25) is attributed to a Judean redactor and dated in the first half of the Exilic Period.[17] The purpose of the framework is to extend to Judah promises that had originally been addressed to Ephraim in the *Grundbestand* of chaps. 30–31.

With the assumption that there is a *Grundbestand* of chaps. 30–31 addressed to the Northern Kingdom, I have taken issue in the earlier discussion. Thiel equates "Jacob" (30:7, 10, 18; 31:7, 11) and "Israel" (31:2, 4, 7, 9, 10; parallel to "Jacob," v. 11) with the Northern Kingdom.[18] Thiel's definition of

12. Thiel, *Deuteronomistische Redaktion von Jeremia*, 28.

13. Ibid., 23; similarly, Böhmer, *Heimkehr und neuer Bund*, 82. Böhmer rejects the equation of Volz and Rudolph: Israel (31:33) = Northern Kingdom.

14. Thiel, *Deuteronomistische Redaktion von Jeremia*, 23.

15. Ibid., 27–28.

16. Ibid., 21.

17. Ibid.

18. Ibid.

the core of chaps. 30–31 follows Rudolph, which as far as I can see, would consist of 30:5–7, 10–11, 12–17 (this would require the deletion of "Zion" in v. 17), 18–24; 31:2–6, 7–14, 15–22. If the equation of "Israel" and "Jacob" with the Northern Kingdom is denied, this core disintegrates. Thiel further identifies D at 31:27–28 and 29–30.[19] At 27–28, the closing bracket of D's framework, Thiel discerns an exegesis of 1:10 that makes a sharper division between past and future than 1:10, a distinction associated with an antithetic opposition (the double use of *šqd*), the negative pole of which Thiel traces to 1:12.[20] In vv. 29–30 Thiel notices the influence of Ezek 18:2 (Lam 5:7), as well as the originality of D, who mediates between individual and collective responsibility, who is influenced by Deut 24:6 and 2 Kgs 24:6, but who also predicts a state of affairs in the future rather than describing a status quo.[21] Thiel questions whether D's prediction amounts to eschatology and supposes that fulfilment is expected in the proximate future.[22]

Böhmer agrees with Thiel that the new covenant is Deuteronomistic, but his analysis of the composition of chaps. 30–31 differs from Thiel's in important respects.[23] He assumes that the chapters contain verses attributable to Jeremiah (30:12–15, 23–24; 31:2–6, 15–20); however, it should be noticed that one of these passages (30:12–15) is a lament coupled with an indictment, another (30:23–24) is a threat of judgment, and only 31:2–6 and 15:20 embrace the main theme of chaps. 30 and 31, return and restoration.[24] Neither "Israel" nor "Jacob" appears in these verses (apart from "virgin Israel" in 31:4), and Böhmer dissents from the view held by Volz, Rudolph, and Thiel that verses referring to "Israel" or "Jacob" are evidence of an address by Jeremiah to the Northern Kingdom and contain the fundamental deposit of chaps. 30 and 31.[25]

Böhmer introduces a category of "post-Jeremianic" poetry that he supposes is exilic and to which he assigns the verses containing the words "Israel" and "Jacob."[26] "Israel" and "Jacob," in these passages, refer to "all-Israel" with perhaps the Babylonian Exile of Judah in mind. Hence Böhmer's core of Jeremianic verses compared to Thiel's (30:5–7, 10–11, 12–17, 18–24; 31:2–6, 7–14, 15–20) is much reduced. Böhmer's post-Jeremianic exilic poetry consists of 30:5–11, 16–17, 18–22; 31:7–14, 21–25.

Böhmer discusses the prose frameworks proposed by Mowinckel[27] (30:1–3/31:27–28 and 30:4/31:26). The first of these corresponds closely with the

19. Ibid., 22.
20. Ibid.
21. Ibid., 23.
22. Ibid., 28.
23. Böhmer, *Heimkehr und neuer Bund*, 83.
24. Ibid., 81.
25. Ibid., 82.
26. Ibid., 84.
27. Ibid., 84. Also, see S. Mowinckel, *Zur Komposition des Buches Jeremia* (Kristiana, 1914) 46–47.

opening and closing brackets identified by Thiel as the work of D, the posited Deuteronomistic redactor of the book of Jeremiah.[28] Thiel had also identified another prose framework (30:4/31:23–26), which he associated with a collection consisting largely of Jeremianic poetry that was Judean but not Deuteronomistic.[29] Böhmer questions Mowinckel's exegesis of 31:26 and doubts whether it is a candidate for the role of a closing bracket in a framework.[30] Mowinckel had supposed that v. 26 was a device used by a redactor to claim prophetic status for himself, whereas Böhmer thinks of it rather as an apposite snatch of poetry taken out of its context in another poem.

Böhmer entertains the idea that the Deuteronomistic redactor may have joined two separate collections, one on Israel's enemies (chap. 30) and the other on Israel's restoration (chap. 31).[31] Alternately he offers the hypothesis that the Deuteronomistic redactor may have combined Jeremianic and post-Jeremianic exilic poetry, supplied a prose framework (30:4/31:27–28), and reached the high point of his redaction at 31:31–34 (the new covenant). Böhmer classifies 31:23–26 and 31:38–40 as post-Deuteronomistic and the non-Deuteronomistic Judean redaction is identified in 30:7–8 (cf. 31:21) and 31:23–26.

Böhmer searches for hints about where the authors of chaps. 30 and 31 may have resided but finds it difficult to supply answers to his questions.[32] He suggests tentatively that the reference to exiles that came from the north (31:8) may indicate that the author had his domicile in Palestine (see 1:14), but he regards the phrases "from distant lands" (Isa 49:12) and "from the ends of the earth" (43:6) as possible support to the view that he may have resided in Babylon. Böhmer observes that the domicile of the Deuteronomistic redactor cannot be ascertained and that the final non-Deuteronomistic redaction is Judean. Only in the case of 31:38–40 does he offer the firm conclusion that its author has a strong Jerusalem connection.

Böhmer comes nearer than Thiel to the contention upheld earlier in the article that the concern of chaps. 30–31 is substantially all-Israelite and that "Israel" and "Jacob" refer to "all-Israel" not to the Northern Kingdom. Böhmer's analysis also supports the opinion that verses of poetry attributable to Jeremiah do not make up a substantial part of chaps. 30–31.

In general, I do not feel the need to modify my own analysis in the light of this examination of the work of Böhmer and Thiel. I have questioned the view that the *Grundbestand* of chaps. 30–31 consists of oracles addressed by Jeremiah to the Northern Kingdom in the early part of his ministry and that all references to Judah in these chapters are secondary. I have held that 31:15–20

---

28. Thiel, *Deuteronomistische Redaktion von Jeremia*, 21.
29. Ibid.
30. Böhmer, *Heimkehr und neuer Bund*, 84. For Mowinckel's argument, see *Zur Komposition des Buches Jeremia*, 46ff.
31. Böhmer, *Heimkehr und neuer Bund*, 85.
32. Ibid.

is addressed to Ephraim and that Ephraim is mentioned in 31:5–6, but I have argued that this is compatible with the all-Israelite context of chaps. 30–31 and does not necessitate the conclusion that all the references to Judah in them are secondary. The use of "Judah" (30:3) and "to Judah" (30:4) arises from the mistaken equation of "Israel" with the Northern Kingdom. I have urged that "Israel" and "Jacob" are, for the most part, to be equated with the Northern Kingdom and Judah, not with the Northern Kingdom only. "Virgin Israel" at 31:4 and 31:21 may refer to Ephraim.

LE CANTIQUE DE DÉBORA ET SES RELECTURES

R. J. Tournay

Traduction

[1]Ce jour-là, Débora et Baraq, fils d'Avinoam, chantèrent en disant:[1]

[2]Quand les chevelures s'échevelaient en Israël,
quand le peuple s'engageait, bénissez Yhwh!
[3]Écoutez, rois, prêtez l'oreille, princes:
moi, pour Yhwh, moi, je vais chanter,
je psalmodie pour Yhwh, le Dieu d'Israël.

[4]Yhwh, quand tu sortis de Séir,
quand tu partis du plateau d'Edom,
la terre trembla, même les cieux ruisselèrent,
les nuées aussi ruisselèrent en eaux;

---

1. *Bibliographie choisie*: M.-J. Lagrange, *Le livre des Juges* (Études Bibliques; Paris, 1903); R. Tournay, "Le psaume LXVIII et le livre des Juges," *RB* 66 (1959) 358–68; A. Caquot, "Les tribus d'Israël dans le cantique de Débora (*Juges* 5, 13–17)," *Sem* 36 (1986) 47–70 (bibliogr. 47–48); J. Bottéro, *Naissance de Dieu: La Bible et l'historien* (Paris, 1986) 139–54; Cesare Lepre, *Il Canto di Debhorah* (Storia e Testi 6; Naples, 1987) bibliogr. 9–14; J. A. Soggin, *Le livre des Juges* (Commentaire de l'A.T. 5b; Genève, 1987) 54–92 (bibliogr. 73–74); B. G. Welb, *The Book of Judges: An Integrated Reading* (JSOTSup 46; Sheffield, 1987); T. Amit, "Judges 4: Its Contents and Form," *JSOT* 39 (1987) 89–111; L. R. Klein, *The Triumph of Irony in the Book of Judges* (JSOTSup 68; Sheffield, 1988); U. Bechmann, *Das Deboralied zwischen Geschichte und Fiktion: Eine exegetische Untersuchung zu Richter 5* (Dissertationen; Theologische Reihe / Band 33; St. Ottilien, 1989) bibliogr. 217–58; A. Brenner, "A Triangle and a Rhombus in Narrative Structure: A Proposed Integration Reading of Judges IV and V," *VT* 40 (1990) 129–38; D. Naᵓaman, "Literary and Topographical Notes on the Battle of Kishon (Judges IV–V)," *VT* 40 (1990) 423–36; H. Schulte, "Richter 5, Das Debora-Lied: Versuch einer Deutung," *Die Hebräische Bibel und ihre zweifache Nachgeschichte: Festschrift Rolf Rendtorff* (Neukirchen-Vluyn, 1990) 177–91.

5les montagnes fondirent devant la face de Yhwh [c'est le Sinaï],
devant la face de Yhwh, le Dieu d'Israël.

6Aux jours de Shamgar, fils d'ᶜAnat,
aux jours de Yaël, on renonçait aux caravanes;
en prenant des sentiers, on prenait [en caravanes] des détours.
7On renonçait à la campagne, on y renonçait en Israël
jusqu'à ce que je me lève, Débora,
jusqu'à ce que je me lève, mère en Israël.

8On choisissait des dieux nouveaux:
alors pour 'cinq villages',
un bouclier, en voyait-on, ou une lance,
pour quarante mille en Israël?

9Mon coeur est pour les commandants d'Israël:
ceux qui s'engagent parmi le peuple, bénissez Yhwh.
10Vous qui montez des ânesses rouanes,
vous qui siégez sur des tapis,
vous qui cheminez, soyez attentifs.

11Par la voix des préposés aux points d'eau,
là, on redit les bienfaits de Yhwh,
les bienfaits de sa campagne en Israël:
Alors le peuple de Yhwh descendait aux portes.

12"Éveille-toi, éveille-toi, Débora,
'réveille les multitudes du peuple',
éveille-toi, éveille-toi, exécute un chant.
Lève-toi, Baraq, capture ceux qui t'ont capturé, fils d'Avinoam."

13Alors le rescapé descend vers les notables,
le peuple de Yhwh descend pour moi, avec les braves.
14D'Éphraïm, les 'officiers' sont dans la 'plaine'.
"Derrière toi, Benjamin est parmi tes troupes."

De Makir, ils descendent, les commandants,
de Zabulon, ceux qui se déploient avec le bâton de scribe.
15Les chefs en Issachar sont avec Débora,
et 'Nephtali' [ainsi Baraq], dans la plaine, s'est lancé sur ses pas.

Dans les clans de Ruben, grandes résolutions!
16Pourquoi es-tu assis entre les deux murets
en écoutant siffler les troupeaux?
Dans les clans de Ruben, grandes réflexions!

[17]Galaad demeure au-delà du Jourdain.
Et Dan, pourquoi prend-il passage sur des navires?
Asher est resté au bord de la mer,
il demeure auprès de ses criques.

[[18]Zabulon, un peuple qui risque sa vie jusqu'à la mort,
Nephtali de même, sur les hauteurs de la région.]

[19]Arrivent les rois, ils combattent,
alors ils combattent, les rois de Canaan,
à Ta[c]anak, aux Eaux de Mégiddo,
sans en retirer aucun profit d'argent.

[20]Du haut du ciel, les étoiles combattent,
de leur orbites, elles combattent Sisara.
[21]Le torrent du Qishôn les balaye, [le torrent],
il les 'recouvre', le torrent du Qishôn:
tu peux marcher, ô mon âme, hardiment!
[22]Alors retentissent les sabots des chevaux,
au galop, au galop des coursiers.

[23]Maudissez Méroz, dit le messager de Yhwh,
maudissez, maudissez ses habitants:
ils ne sont pas venus au secours de Yhwh,
au secours de Yhwh, avec les braves.

[24]Bénie soit parmi les femmes Yaël
[femme de Héber le Qénite],
parmi les femmes, sous la tente, qu'elle soit bénie!
[25]Il demandait de l'eau, elle donne du lait,
dans la coupe des princes, elle offre de la crème.

[26]Elle tend la main vers le piquet,
et sa droite, vers le marteau des tâcherons;
elle martèle Sisera, lui brise la tête,
elle frappe et lui fracasse la tempe;
[27]à ses pieds il s'écroule, il tombe, il gît,
[à ses pieds il s'écroule, il tombe]
c'est là qu'il s'écroule, qu'il tombe, terrassé.

[28]Par le treillis, elle se penche et se lamente,
la mère de Sisera, à travers le grillage:
"Pourquoi son char tarde-t-il à venir,
pourquoi traîne-t-elle, la marche de ses chariots?"

²⁹Les plus avisées de ses dames lui répondent,
elle-même se redit ses propres paroles:
³⁰"Sans doute ils recueillent, ils partagent le butin:
une jeune fille, deux jeunes filles par tête de guerrier,
[ ] pour Sisera, un butin d'"étoffe teinte', de deux étoffes teintes,
une broderie [d'étoffe teinte], deux broderies pour 'mon' cou [en butin]."

³¹Qu'ainsi périssent tous tes ennemis, Yʜwʜ!
Que ses amis soient comme le soleil à son puissant lever!

Commentaire

Le Cantique de Débora est souvent considéré comme le plus ancien poème de
la Bible hébraïque; cet hymne triomphal serait proche de la bataille qu'il
décrit et qui aurait eu lieu vers 1125 av. J.-C. Il n'est pas nécessaire de redire
que cette date est très incertaine,[2] comme aussi le temps de composition du
poème. Celui-ci renferme un certain nombre de mots rares que la Septante n'a
pu traduire et s'est contentée de transcrire. On a signalé depuis longtemps des
contacts avec les textes d'Ugarit,[3] ce qui n'implique aucunement une datation
ancienne, étant donné, d'une part, que le poème semble issu du nord de la Palestine, et que, d'autre part, bien des ugaritismes figurent dans des écrits tar-
difs.[4] Une lecture attentive du poème suppose que les Hébreux habitaient dans
des villages avec des portes fortifiées, et que le harcèlement des Philistins, en-
travant le transit caravanier, existait depuis un certain temps, avec des escar-
mouches comme le suggèrent 12b et 13a qui parlent de prisonniers et de
rescapés. Surtout, la structure complexe et savante de ce long poème, ainsi
que son style épique supposent une longue tradition littéraire antécédente.

On est en effet frappé par l'abondance des procédés de style: anaphores,
chiasmes, mérismes, antithèses, anadiplosis (rythme graduel). Les répétitions
de mots ne sont pas rares; mais elles sont parfois la conséquence de ditto-
graphies et de doublets qu'il importe de supprimer, si l'on veut avoir une idée
des cadences rythmiques et de la strophique du poème dans son état ancien,
avant les relectures qu'il a subies. Le parallélisme synonymique est partout bien
marqué. La plupart des stiques obéissent au grand rythme épique de 2 + 2 accents toniques, qu'on a comparé à notre alexandrin; le rythme ternaire de trois
accents, ailleurs si fréquent, subsiste parfois. Les stiques se groupent en dis-
tiques pour former des couplets ou des triades; il y a quelques tristiques. Ainsi,

---

2. Cf. R. de Vaux, *Histoire ancienne d'Israël: La période des Juges* (ÉBib; Paris, 1973) 2.103.
3. Ainsi on rapproche "les étoiles combattent de leur orbites" (v. 20), de "la pluie qu'ont
versée les étoiles." Cf. A. Caquot et alii, "Mythes et légendes," *Textes Ougaritiques* (LAPO 7;
Paris, 1974) 2.161, 172.
4. Cf. Soggin, *Le livre des Juges* (Genéve, 1987) 87; R. Tournay, *Seeing and Hearing God
with the Psalms* (JSOTSup 118; Sheffield, 1991) 20.

la troisième strophe ou triade (6–7) comprend deux tristiques. Le v. 8 comprend un stique (8a) suivi d'un tristique. Le v. 10 est un tristique, suivi d'un autre tristique (v. 11), complété par un stique (11d). Le v. 21 est un tristique (deux stiques suivis d'un autre stique). Ces derniers cas manifestent la souplesse de la structure strophique de notre poème.

Le texte du Cantique de Débora a été transcrit d'une façon spéciale dans les manuscrits, comme pour Exode 15, Deutéronome 32, 2 Samuel 22 et Psaume 18. La Massore appelle cette disposition: demi-brique sur demi-brique, et brique sur brique. Une telle mise en page avait l'inconvénient de disloquer les phrases et de provoquer des corruptions textuelles, comme ce fut sans doute le cas pour le v. 30. On compte 21 stiques (3 × 7) du v. 2 au v. 8, du v. 9 au v. 15, du v. 16 au v. 22, et du v. 23 au v. 31. La symbolique du nombre a pu jouer ici un certain rôle.[5]

Une lecture globale du poème permet d'en dégager une suite de thèmes antithétiques. Après l'exorde de ton liturgique (2–3), le poète décrit une théophanie de Yʜwʜ (4–5), maître du cosmos, dans des termes analogues aux préludes de Deutéronome 33 et de Habacuc 3; ce prélude est repris par le Ps 68:8. Aux bouleversements de la nature s'oppose l'impuissance d'Israël (6–8), bloqué sur place, malgré les recours aux faux dieux (cf. Jug 10:14, etc.). D'où le nouvel appel (9–10) adressé cette fois par Débora aux chefs et aux combattants (9b reprend 2b). Ils doivent bénir Yʜwʜ et être attentifs à l'évocation des hauts faits de Yʜwʜ. Alors le peuple se mobilise sous la conduite de Débora et de Baraq. Les clans d'Ephraïm (dont Débora fait partie), de Benjamin, de Makir (fils de Manassé), de Zabulon, d'Issachar et de Nephtali (mot restitué; voir ci-après) convergent dans la plaine, près du Tabor. Mais les quatre clans isolationnistes de Ruben, Galaad (Gad), Dan et Asher sont absents du combat. Les pluies violentes et le débordement du Qishôn auront raison de Sisera et de ses chars.

Le poète oppose ensuite la malédiction du clan de Méroz (sans doute Khirbet Marous, au sud de Qédesh de Nephtali) à la bénédiction de Yaël, femme de Héber le Qénite. A la description du meurtre de Sisera par la bédouine Yaël s'oppose l'attente de sa femme qui ne pense qu'au butin. Enfin, au v. 31, l'épilogue oppose le sort des ennemis à celui des amis de Yʜwʜ.

*   *   *

Il ne peut être question de présenter ici un commentaire détaillé du Cantique de Débora. D'autres l'ont déjà fait. Mais il a paru utile de revoir certaines interprétations et d'en discuter le bien-fondé. C'est ainsi qu'on notera dès le v. 2

5. Cf. P. Hyvernant, "Le langage de la Massore, B: Lexique massorétique," *RB* (1904) 526; T. Piatti, "Una nuova interpretazione metrica, testuale, esegetica del Cantico di Dèbora," *Bib* 27 (1946) 69.

l'accord général sur la traduction de la "figure étymologique" d'après Deut 32:42 et les textes qui parlent de la chevelure du nazir (Samson, Samuel, etc.). Une coutume analogue est signalée par A. Jaussen[6] chez les Bédouins partant pour la razzia. Il s'agit d'un rite sacré, au moment de partir pour la guerre sainte, de la part des chefs (cf. G^A). Pour Soggin, suivi par Schulte,[7] ce rite signifie que le peuple regagne sa liberté. Comme Débora le rappelle encore au v. 9, le peuple est étroitement uni à ses chefs, et tous doivent bénir Yhwh, le Dieu d'Israël (cf. Ps 68:27) qui les mènera jusqu'à la victoire.

Du point de vue rythmique, *běhitnaddēb* avec l'accent conjonctif *ṭarḥa*, comparable au *maqqep*, peut être considéré comme proclitique avec trois syllabes atones (la *něsigâ* étant impossible), ce qui est le maximum entre deux accents toniques. L'accent portant sur ^{c}*am*, le stique a 2 + 2 + 2 accents, et non 3 + 3 accents. Le rythme binaire de 2 + 2 accents prévaut au v. 3, si l'on ne retranche rien (avec LXX).

Le v. 3a est un exorde classique qui rappelle Prov 14:28 (texte d'époque monarchique) et Hab 1:10 (cf. Ps 2:2, etc.). Le verset 3b rappelle l'exorde d'Ex 15:1 (d'époque monarchique) et a été imité par Ps 68:5, 33. Am 5:23 (d'époque monarchique) a aussi le verbe *zāmar*, verbe "psalmique" par excellence qui signifie chanter avec un accompagnement musical. La fin de cette strophe, "Yhwh, le Dieu d'Israël," revient à la fin de la strophe suivante (5b). Le mot "Israël" achève les deux strophes suivantes (7c, 8d), ainsi que 11c. Ces répétitions indiquent qu'il s'agit d'un hymne théocentrique qui suppose l'Alliance entre Dieu et Israël. C'est Dieu qui sauve son peuple et lui rend justice, comme on aime à le redire en Israël (v. 11).

Comme dans l'hymnologie suméro-akkadienne, la strophe 4–5 débute par un rappel du passé, la théophanie qui a sauvé Israël: de violentes pluies d'orage, venues du sud de la Palestine, ont inondé le pays et provoqué le débordement du Qishôn (v. 21). Yhwh est ainsi "sorti" pour la guerre sainte (Jug 4:14; cf. 1 Sam 8:20; 2 Sam 5:24; Hab 3:13). Le tonnerre ébranle la terre, tandis que la pluie "ruisselle," verbe répété deux fois (TM à garder). C'est après coup qu'on a pensé ici, d'après le parallèle Deut 33:2, à la grande théophanie sinaïtique et qu'on a ajouté la glose "c'est le Sinaï, ou celui du Sinaï" (relecture reprise dans le Ps 68:9). Mais le seul contact entre le récit des deux théophanies

---

6. A. Jaussen et R. Savignac, *Mission archéologique en Arabie*, Supplément au Vol. 2: *Coutumes des Fuqarâ* (Publications de la Société française des fouilles archéologiques; Paris, 1914) 73; P. Bordreuil, "A propos du papyrus de Wen Amon," *Sem* 17 (1967) 35; T. Kronholm, "*pāra^c*," *TWAT* 6 col. 759; J. G. Janzen, en s'appuyant sur Deut 32:42, "The Root pr^c in Judges V 2 and Deuteronomy XXXII 42," *VT* 39 (1989) 403, traduit: "Quand les rebelles rejettent la contrainte en Israël."

7. On ne peut donc en conclure, comme Schulte ("Richter 5, Das Debora-Lied," 180), que ce couplet serait d'origine judéenne et aurait été inséré ici. En Palestine, toute pluie provient du sud-ouest. Séir et Edom sont souvent nommés dans les sources égyptiennes avec les Bédouins Shasou. R. Giveon cite le texte: "Yahvé (du) pays des Shasou" ("Toponymes ouest-asiatiques à Soleb," *VT* 14 [1964] 244).

est que "la montagne (Ex 19:18) / la terre (Jug 5:4) trembla (deux verbes différents)." Selon le TM, les montagnes fondirent (cf. Ex 15:8). LXX aura lu *nazollû* "sont secouées, vacillent," comme dans Is 63:19 et 64:2. Mais le contexte favorise le TM. On notera le rythme graduel, bien en situation.

La mention de Shamgar, fils d'ᶜAnat, au v. 6, a soulevé beaucoup d'hypothèses, étant donné que la notice (3:31) sur le "juge" Shamgar est interpolée entre 3:30 et 4:1. Au lieu d'un nom d'origine hourrite (*šimigi-ari* 'le soleil a donné'), on a pensé à un nom théophore cananéen dérivé de la racine *mgr*, selon un sceau récemment publié.[8] On a supposé que la mention de Yaël a été ici suggérée par Jug 4:17, et le v. 24; on a proposé de lire *bîmê-ᶜol* 'aux jours du joug' (Sellin, Soggin, Schulte). Le mot *pĕrāzôn*,[9] repris au v. 11 (transcrit *phrazôn* par Gᴬ) peut s'expliquer par les mots apparentés; *pĕrāzôt* 'villes ouvertes' (Ez 38:1); *pĕrāzî* 'pays ouvert' (Deut 3:5; 1 Sam 6:18); d'où le sens de 'campagne' ou de 'campagne guerrière'. Les voies normales de communication, comme la plaine d'Esdrelon, sont devenues impraticables aux caravanes que pillent les Cananéens. On peut citer des parallèles plus anciens.[10] Pour 8b, corrompu, la meilleure conjecture est *lĕḥāmēš ᶜarîm* 'pour cinq villes'.[11] Cette situation d'infériorité et d'oppression n'est pas sans rapport avec le syncrétisme des Israélites qui oublient Yʜᴡʜ et choisissent de nouvelles divinités (cf. Deut 32:17), impuissantes à les sauver, comme il est dit dans Jug 10:14.

Le verbe *šaqqamtî*, répété deux fois en anaphore, peut être une première personne 'je me lève' ou une deuxième personne 'tu te lèves'. Beaucoup de traducteurs[12] optent pour la deuxième personne. C'est alors le poète anonyme qui évoque Débora, surnommée 'mère en Israël'. Mais dans ce cas, ce n'est plus Débora qui 'chante' (3b, 12c) ici, ni non plus aux vv. 3, 9a, 13b ('pour moi'), et 21c. Les vv. 9 et 21c seraient des réflexions secondaires comme Gen 49:18, et on s'explique mal la suite. C'est pourquoi il faut mieux traduire 'je me lève'.[13] Dans 9b, Débora exhorte les commandants à bénir Dieu (ce qui reprend 2b), à

---

8. Sur ce sceau, cf. Soggin, *Le livre des Juges*, 55; P. Bordreuil et A. Lemaire, "Nouveaux sceaux hébreux, araméens, et ammonites," *Sem* 26 (1976) 61 no. 33. Pour l'origine hourrite du nom de Shamgar, *šimigi-ari* 'le soleil a donné', voir E. Laroche, *Glossaire de la langue hourrite* (Paris, 1980) 52 et 232.

9. Voir *HALAT* 908b; Cf. Zach 2:8; Deut 3:5; Est 9:19. On a *przytᵓ*, *przyᵓ* 'faubourg', dans la "Description de la Jérusalem nouvelle" (5Q; *Les "Petites Grottes" de Qumrân* [DJD 3; Oxford, 1962] 187 [Je dois cette référence à É. Puech]). Cf. arabe *baraz* 'sortir sur une vaste plaine'.

10. Voici un passage de l'inscription d'Utu-Hegal (2123–2113): "(Le roi de Gutium) a pillé en bas les champs de Sumer; en haut, il a pillé les caravanes. Sur les routes du Pays, il a laissé l'herbe croître haut" (E. Sollberger et J.-R. Kupper, *Inscriptions royales sumériennes et akkadiennes* (LAPO 3; Paris, 1971) 130.

11. Déjà Lagrange; Soggin, *Le livre des Juges*, 81; cf. Tournay, "Recension de Richter, *Traditionsgeschichtliche Untersuchung zum Richterbuch* (1963)," *RB* 72 (1965) 125. On a proposé des conjectures plus compliquées où interviendraient des 'démons'; cf. J. K. Cathcart, "The 'Demons' in Judges 5:8a," *BZ* n.s. 21 (1977) 111.

12. Avec la Bible du Rabbinat, la Bible de la Pléiade, Lepre (*Il Canto di Debborah*), etc.

13. Bechmann, *Das Deboralied*, 173.

être attentifs (10c) à l'action passée de YHWH combattant pour Israël; cette intervention va se reproduire, comme on se le répète aux points d'eau où le peuple se rassemble (cf. Nomb 21:17).

On notera ici qu'il s'agit de chants répétés (cf. Ps 8:2) ou alternés, comme dans Ex 32:19c; l'Orient a pratiqué de tout temps la psalmodie "responsoriale" (cf. Psaume 136). On peut se demander si l'on n'est pas ici en présence d'un texte dramatique, pouvant être récité ou chanté avec chœurs et solistes, dans un spectacle.[14] Averti par des orateurs professionnels, le peuple de YHWH se mobilise et commence à descendre aux portes (11d). Ainsi se prépare l'apostrophe adressée aux deux chefs, Débora et Baraq, qui doivent diriger l'action militaire; cette sorte d'antienne populaire, avec ses redites (cf. Cant 7:1), est un appel au combat. On complète le distique 12ab d'après G^A. En suivant le Syriaque et l'Arabe, on traduit à la fin du v. 2: 'capture ceux qui t'ont capturé' (cf. Is 14:2), au lieu de 'prends tes prisonniers', leçon du Grec et du TM (mot mal vocalisé). On a ainsi en fin de strophe un stique de 2 + 2 + 2 accents, de rythme binaire accéléré.

Sans nous arrêter sur un certain nombre de détails, nous insisterons ici sur les versets 13 à 18 qui ont fait l'objet d'un article important de A. Caquot.[15] En réponse aux appels populaires, Débora reprend la parole. Le survivant ou le rescapé[16] qui avait fui les attaques des gens de Sisera redescend vers les notables. Ainsi, dit Débora, le peuple de YHWH descend *pour moi*, et s'en va rejoindre les braves. D'Éphraïm, tribu de Débora, les chefs donnent l'exemple et sont déjà 'dans la plaine'.

Cette dernière traduction suppose une correction du texte massorétique, 'leur racine est en Amaleq'. Affirmation malveillante (cf. Nomb 14:20; Deut 25:17) qui a suscité bien des conjectures. La solution la plus simple semble être de supposer ici une double correction tendancieuse, antisamaritaine, postérieure à la traduction de la Septante.[17] En effet, G^A a la leçon *bāᶜēmeq* 'dans la plaine', comme dans 15b; il suffisait d'ajouter un *lamed* pour obtenir le nom d'Amaleq (ce nom a été à moitié effacé dans le TM de Jug 1:16; cf. Deut 25:19). 'Leur racine', dans le TM, serait due à une vocalisation péjorative de *sārîsîm* 'officiers' (nommés avec les *śarîm* 'chefs' dans Jér 34:19, 41:16).

Alors les Éphraïmites interpellent Débora: "*Derrière-toi*, Benjamin est parmi tes troupes." La petite tribu, la plus méridionale, est même accourue pour ren-

---

14. Cf. Schulte, "Richter 5, Das Debora-Lied," 183, 190.

15. Caquot, "Les tribus d'Israël dans le cantique de Débora," 47–70. Il est suivi par Naᶜaman, "Literary and Topographical Notes," 426.

16. Cf. *HALAT* 1264a. Naʾaman ("Literary and Topographical Notes," 425) reprend l'hypothèse d'un village, Sarid (cf. Jos 19:10, 12, TM, texte incertain), situé à moins de 10 km au sud de Taᶜanak; mais le village est dans la plaine; on n'en descend pas!

17. Cf. R. Tournay, "Quelques relectures bibliques antisamaritaines," *RB* 71 (1964) 507–11. On a tenté de retrouver des traces d'une occupation des Amalécites (cf. Jug 12:15; 2 Sam 1:8, 13) sur le territoire d'Israël cf. H. Cazelles, "Déborah (Jug. 5,14), Amaleq et Makîr," *VT* 24 (1974) 235–38; E. A. Knauf, "Zum Text von Ri 5,14," *Bib* 64 (1983) 428.

forcer Éphraïm. Quand le prophète Osée dénoncera la guerre fratricide du début du VIIIᵉ siècle, entre le roi Amasias d'Israël et le roi Joas de Juda (2 Rois 14), il citera seulement les deux mots "Derrière toi, Benjamin!" (Os 5:8), formule elliptique qui peut nous fournir un bon *terminus ad quem* pour le Cantique de Débora. Osée parle ensuite, dans un contexte aussi "tribal," d'Éphraïm, des tribus d'Israël et des chefs de Juda. Le monologue de Débora devient ainsi au v. 14 un début de dialogue avec ceux qui l'ont interpellée au v. 12.

La strophe suivante mentionne quatre tribus: Makir, Zabulon, Issachar et Nephtali (restitué dans 15b). Makir, le "mercenaire," premier des clans de Manassé, en tient lieu; il sera absorbé plus tard par Manassé qui se déplacera en Transjordanie, entre le Jabboq et le Yarmuk. Makir descend au combat avec ses commandants (cf. déjà au v. 9; Gen 49:10; Nomb 21:18; Is 33:22). Zabulon se déploie (cf. 4:6, 7; 20:37) avec "le bâton de scribe," expression obscure qui peut faire allusion à la logistique militaire du temps.

Le v. 15 mentionne deux fois Issachar qui n'en méritait pas autant, alors que Nephtali, tribu de Baraq, joue avec Zabulon le rôle le plus important, d'après 4:6, 10. Ce doublet et l'absence de Nephtali ont obligé les rédacteurs à rappeler ici le rôle de Baraq, de Qadesh en Nephtali, en ajoutant "ainsi Baraq," addition qui trouble le rythme du stique. (Baraq a été aussi ajouté au v. 1; le verbe 'chanta' est au singulier.) C'est aussi, selon nous, la raison d'être du v. 18 qui célèbre Zabulon et Nephtali seulement *après* les quatre tribus périphériques et isolationnistes: Ruben, Galaad (= Gad), Dan, et Asher. Ce vers-distique isolé (plusieurs couplets le précèdent) n'obéit à aucun rythme (binaire ou ternaire); il est "d'un tout autre ton," comme l'écrit justement A. Caquot.[18] Mais celui-ci considère les vv. 14–17 comme une insertion secondaire, sorte de pastiche de Genèse 49, destinée à discréditer les tribus du Nord.

Nous ne pensons pas qu'il en soit ainsi, tout en reconnaissant que le seul lien du v. 18 avec le dit d'Asher qui précède est la ressemblance entre 17cd et le dit de Zabulon dans Gen 49:13. Le v. 18 est donc une relecture inspirée par le récit en prose du chapitre 4 qui ne met en scène que Nephtali et Zabulon. C'est aussi l'opinion de H. Schulte.[19]

Le passage sur Ruben a été imité par le Ps 68:14. Contentons-nous de rappeler ici l'interprétation du mot *mišpĕtayîm* ou *šĕpātayîm*.[20] Ce mot est au duel, car il s'agit des *deux* murets convergents vers l'entrée resserrée du corral ou parc à troupeaux. Cet aménagement d'un double muret est abondamment attesté en Transjordanie; on a relevé les dessins qui le représentent et dont le plus ancien figurerait sur la palette du roi Narmer, vers 3,000 av. J.-C.[21] Le poète consacre toute une strophe à la tribu de Ruben, alors qu'il ne nomme Gad que par le nom

---

18. Cf. Caquot, "Les tribus d'Israël dans le cantique de Débora," 68.
19. Cf. Schulte, "Richter 5, Das Debora-Lied," 186.
20. Cf. *HALAT* 1511a.
21. Cf. Tournay, "Le psaume LXVIII et le livre des Juges," 361; Caquot, "Les tribus d'Israël dans le cantique de Débora," 65 n. 64.

de Galaad. Il a pu exploiter un jeu de mots entre le nom de Ruben, l'indécis, et *re⁾û bên* 'voyez entre', préposition reprise ensuite ('*entre* les deux murets'). On est ici à une époque antérieure à celle que supposent les "Bénédictions de Moïse," quand la paix et la prospérité l'emportaient partout dans le Nord sous le règne de Jéroboam II.[22] Le Cantique de Débora est plus ancien que ces Bénédictions auxquelles il serait intéressant de le comparer en détail, comme aussi avec Genèse 49. Mais ce n'est pas le propos de cet article.

Avant d'examiner la relecture du v. 21, notons le grand chiasme de 19ab, ainsi que, dans 19c, le nom du site où fut défait Sisera: à Taᶜanak, aux Eaux de Megiddo, là où passe le torrent du Qishôn. C'est donc une forte pluie, déjà évoquée aux vv. 4–5, qui va faire sortir de son lit le torrent et provoquer la défaite de Sisera. L'événement prend ici une dimension cosmique; ce sont les étoiles qui, de leurs orbites, combattent les chars cananéens. Ce thème épique est repris ailleurs, en particulier dans le poème ougaritique de Baᶜal et de ᶜAnat où l'on parle de "la pluie qu'ont versée les étoiles."[23] H. Schulte[24] a supposé que, du v. 19 au v. 30 (sauf 23) où il est question des Cananéens et de Sisera, on aurait un ancien texte d'origine non israélite réutilisé par l'auteur du Cantique. Cette hypothèse ne s'impose pas.

Le premier stique du v. 21 est clair: "Le torrent du Qichôn les balaye (*gĕrafam*, verbe araméen)." Mais la suite est obscure et peut résulter d'une mauvaise relecture du texte primitif: "le torrent des anciens (jours?; G^A transcrit le mot sans le traduire), le torrent du Qishôn: avance, mon âme, hardiment." Beaucoup corrigent *qĕdûmîm* en *qiddĕmam* 'les affronte' (cf. Ps 18:6, 19). Mais la version syriaque qui semble avoir lu un nom propre, *dqrmyn*, nous suggère de restituer le verbe araméen *qĕramam* 'les recouvre'.[25] En plus du chiasme, il y a une allitération entre les deux verbes araméens. Un scribe aura confondu un *reš* et un *dalet*—faute classique—puis il a ajouté un doublet 'le torrent' avant le verbe défiguré. Le sens correspond exactement à Ex 15:5, 10: "Les abîmes / l'eau les recouvrent." Alors la suite s'éclaire, car Débora s'écrie: "Avance, mon âme (c'était "mon coeur" au v. 9), hardiment / en force." Autrement dit: "Piétine

---

22. Cf. R. Tournay, "Le psaume et les bénédictions de Moïse," *RB* 65 (1958) 191–202. H. Seebass pense au règne d'Achab ("Die Stämmeliste von Dt. XXXIII," *VT* 27 [1977] 168). La migration des Danites (Juges 18) est un fait accompli.

23. Voir note 3. Cf. déjà de Vaux, "Recension de C. Virolleaud, *La déesse Anat* (1938)," *RB* 48 (1939) 596. *Les Rituels accadiens* (F. Thureau-Dangin [Paris, 1921]) 138, ligne 306 mentionnent "l'astre Gud (Mercure) qui fait pleuvoir la pluie." A. Erman (*La Religion des Égyptiens* [Paris, 1937] 250) cite le texte suivant: "Le ciel pleut, les étoiles combattent." Voir M. Weinfeld, "Divine Intervention in War in Ancient Israel and in Ancient Near East," dans *History, Historiography, and Interpretation: Studies in Biblical and Cuneiform Literatures* (ed. H. Tadmor et M. Weinfeld; Jerusalem, 1983) 124–31.

24. Cf. Schulte, "Richter 5, Das Debora-Lied," 188.

25. Voir déjà R. Tournay, "Recension de Richter, *Traditionsgeschichtliche Untersuchung*," 125. Cf. Ezek 37:6, 8; Sir 43:20. Même verbe en arabe.

sans crainte les cadavres et les chars cananéens couverts de boue." La plaine d'Esdrelon se trouve enfin libérée de l'armée de Sisera.

Ce tristique épique est suivi d'un distique fort suggestif: "Alors martèlent les sabots des chevaux, au galop (cf. Nah 3:3), au galop des coursiers." Le reste des attelages cananéens s'enfuit rapidement. Cette galopade effrénée est évoquée par les trois anapestes de 22b: *middaḥărôt, daḥărôt ʾabbîrayw*. L'auteur du Psaume 68 imite une fois de plus notre Cantique avec la même harmonie imitative et en usant de voyelles sourdes: "Les rois des armées *yiddōdûn, yiddōdûn* / détalaient, détalaient" (ou: 'se débandent, se débandent', si l'on veut retrouver de semblables sonorités).

La suite du poème met en scène deux femmes, Yaël la Qénite, qui tue Sisera, et la mère du chef cananéen, qui attend en vain le retour triomphal de son fils, qu'elle croit chargé de butin. La triple malédiction, au v. 23, de Méroz (peut-être Khirbet Marous, à 12 km de Qédesh de Nephtali) forme une antithèse avec la double bénédiction de Yaël (noter le chiasme) par le messager de YHWH. Le poète en profite pour mettre en relief, grâce au rythme graduel, le caractère sacré de cette guerre sainte, menée par YHWH lui-même. Au v. 24, un rédacteur a ajouté la glose explicative 'femme de Héber le Qénite', tirée de 4:17.

La description de la mise à mort de Sisera diffère quelque peu de celle du chapitre 4. On notera que la suite des verbes, dans 26b, fait une paronomase. Le v. 27 est surchargé; il devrait n'y avoir que deux stiques de 4 accents. Dix-huit manuscrits omettent la dittographie *kāraᶜ nāpāl*; huit autres omettent *šākāb* qui proviendrait de Nomb 24:9 (Nombres 24 reprend souvent les expressions de Juges 5). Vingt-six manuscrits omettent *šādûd*. L'expression "*là où* il s'écroule" est rapprochée de Gen 21:17 (tradition "élohiste").

Le couplet (28) et la triade (29–30) qui concernent la mère de Sisera ont été rapprochés des *Perses* d'Eschyle (lignes 159 à 214), drame représenté pour la première fois au printemps 472. Le chiasme du v. 28ab met en relief le motif de la femme à la fenêtre, souvent représentée sur les ivoires syro-cananéens, et auquel font allusion Prov 7:6; Sir 42:11. Il s'agit parfois d'Ishtar *kilili*, la reine des fenêtres (Aphrodite *parakuptousa*)[26] et plus généralement de la prostituée qui guette son client. Il faut ici garder le verbe araméen hapax du TM 'elle se lamente', sans le corriger d'après le grec (*wattabbeṭ*); car il prépare les "pour-quoi" éplorés de la mère de Sisera, interrogations dans le style des lamentations. Quant au participe *bōšēš*, il figure dans Ex 32:1 (texte "élohiste"; cf. Tob 10:2).

L'ironie du poète[27] apparaît, au début du v. 29, dans l'épithète "les plus sages" des dames et dans l'interrogation exprimée par la mère de Sisera, laquelle

26. Cf. R. Giveon, *The Impact of Egypt on Canaan* (OBO 20; Freiburg/Göttingen, 1978) 41; A. S. Dalix, *Astarté à la fenêtre* (CahRB; Paris, Gabalda), à paraître.

27. Cf. Klein, *Triumph of Irony*, 40, 47.

attend naïvement le précieux butin fait par son fils: une fille, deux filles pour chacun des guerriers. L'hébreu *raḥam* 'fille' se trouve à la ligne 17 de la stèle de Mésha (vers 850, date sans doute peu éloignée de celle de notre cantique), ainsi qu'à Ougarit. L'expression "partager le butin" (Gen 49:27) est reprise par le Ps 68:13. Le mot *ṣebaᶜ* 'étoffe teinte ou de couleur" est araméen. Les tissus bariolés ainsi que les broderies (*riqmâ*) ont toujours été fort appréciés en Canaan (cf. Gen 37:3, 23; Jug 8:26; 2 Sam 1:24).

Dans 30cd, on attendrait deux stiques comme dans 30ab, et une séquence analogue (un/deux) pour les filles, les étoffes et les broderies. C'est pourquoi il est indiqué d'omettre au début, comme un doublet: 'un butin de deux étoffes teintes', et de remplacer ensuite *ṣalal* par *ṣebaᶜ*, mot décalé après *riqmâ*. Ce qui donne, avec une structure en chiasme et la correction *lĕṣawwāʾrî* 'pour mon cou' (d'après le grec pour les deux derniers mots):

> Pour Sisera, un butin d'étoffe teinte, de deux étoffes teintes,
> une broderie, deux broderies pour mon cou.

Le verset 31 est la conclusion du poème; il en exprime l'enseignement dans une antithèse que souligne la paronomase (en hébreu) des deux mots "tes ennemis" et "ceux qui l'aiment" (cf. 1 Mac 4:33). On passe de la deuxième personne à la troisième, ce qui est fréquent en poésie; 2 MSS, Syr. et Vulg. ont cependant la deuxième personne dans le second stique. Le rythme de ce distique est de 4 + 4 accents, rythme bien attesté précédemment. Le dernier mot, *gĕburâ*, apparenté à *gibbôr* (vv. 13, 23) et *geber* (v. 30), se trouve dans Ex 32:18, texte de tradition "élohiste." Il s'agit ici de la puissance du soleil levant, si majestueux quand on l'aperçoit du sommet du mont Tabor. Le dieu soleil des Sémites est un guerrier (assyrien *quradu*; hébreu *gibbôr*; cf. Ps 19:6). La lumière solaire appartient à l'imaginaire de la Bible.[28]

On souligne dans ce distique le style "psalmique," comme au v. 3, et la mention de l'amour pour Dieu, thème essentiellement deutéronomique (Deut 5:10, 6:5; Ex 20:6, etc.): ce qui interdirait d'assigner une date ancienne au Cantique de Débora si le v. 31 est authentique, ou au contraire obligerait à considérer ce verset (ainsi que les vv. 2–3 et 9) comme une relecture, addition liturgique postérieure.[29] Mais, comme l'écrivait le P. Lagrange en 1903: "Il n'est pas prouvé qu'on ne pouvait parler au temps de Débora de l'amour de

---

28. 2 Sam 23:4 (cf. R. J. Tournay, "Les 'dernières paroles de David' (II Samuel XXIII, 1–7," *RB* 88 [1981] 495); Prov 4:18, Mal 3:20, Dan 12:3, Sag 3:7, Luc 1:78. Voir la représentation en bronze, d'origine élamite, du *ṣit šamši* ('lever du soleil'), dans *ANEP*, 619 [203].

29. Parmi d'autres exégètes, W. Moran accepte l'antiquité de ce verset ("The Ancient Near Eastern Background of the Love of God in Deuteronomy," *CBQ* 23 [1963] 8). Cf. Tournay, "Le psaume et les bénédictions de Moïse," 450. Par contre, B. Lindars, par exemple, considère les vv. 2–5, 9–11, et 31 comme des additions liturgiques ("Debora's Song: Women in the Old Testament," *BJRL* 65 [1983] 158–59).

Iahvé, il fallait l'aimer pour se dévouer à sa cause."[30] Effectivement, beaucoup d'exégètes ont souligné que le Cantique suppose l'existence de Alliance entre YHWH et son peuple, tout dévoué à sa cause comme en témoignent les vv. 2, 9, 11cd, 13b, 23c (et 31). On s'est même demandé si ce Cantique ne fut pas utilisé dans le royaume du Nord pour les fêtes célébrant l'Alliance, au IXe siècle avant J.-C., avant les oracles du prophète Osée sur le *ḥesed* ('bonté, amour'); d'après 14b, Osée dépendrait du Cantique (voir ci-dessus). On aurait donc là l'un des premiers textes où Israël affirme son amour pour YHWH, son Dieu. Ainsi, la victoire des tribus du nord de la Palestine aura été avant tout celle du Dieu d'Israël, dont on célèbre ici les hauts faits en faveur de son peuple.

---

30. Lagrange, *Le livre des Juges*, 104.

Part 4

The Writings

THE CONCEPT OF ABOMINATION IN
THE BOOK OF PROVERBS

R. E. Clements

A WIDELY RECOGNIZED feature of the book of Proverbs is its concern to define the "way" of wisdom as a path of virtue that is exemplified in daily life and that conforms to the realities of actual human experience. In pursuing this aim, the book of Proverbs appeals strongly to the order given to the world at its creation as a governing principle that binds together the natural and moral realms.[1] Good conduct leads to prosperity and happiness, whereas bad conduct leads to disappointment and ruin. It is in this context that a good deal of attention has been drawn to the idea of retribution, especially in bringing punishment to bear upon bad conduct. An appeal to the inevitability of the hurt that will befall the wrongdoer is used quite extensively as a basis for moral appeal. Wrongdoers will ultimately get their just deserts.[2]

How this will come about is not always made clear. Sometimes it is openly asserted that God ensures that this is the case; at other times, the sage affirms that the bad conduct itself is ultimately ruinous in its consequences. This is true, for instance, of the often cited sentence instruction:

1. The literature on this point is now extensive; cf. R. E. Clements, *Wisdom in Theology* (Grand Rapids, 1993) 15 and the articles cited there.
2. Cf. especially J. Fichtner, *Die altorientalische Weisheit in ihrer israelitisch-jüdischen Ausprägung* (BZAW 62; Berlin, 1933) 62ff.; K. Koch, "Is There a Doctrine of Retribution in the Old Testament?" *Theodicy in the Old Testament* (ed. J. L. Crenshaw; London, 1983) 57–87. Following Fichtner and B. Gemser (*Sprüche Salomos* [HAT 16; Tübingen, 1963] 6–7), Koch sees the usage in Proverbs as exemplary of a doctrine that the natural order ensures an act-consequence relationship: "A wicked action . . . inevitably results in disastrous consequences" (p. 58). A more extended treatment of the distinctive formulations of the problem in Proverbs is found in L. Boström, *The God of the Sages: The Portrayal of God in the Book of Proverbs* (ConBOT 29; Stockholm, 1990).

> Whoever digs a pit will fall into it,
> and a stone will come back on the one who starts it rolling.
>
> Prov 26:27

Here it is claimed that the very nature of bad conduct is such that the hurt it unleashes will ultimately fall on the one responsible for it. No doubt instances of such deserved self-inflicted hurt could be found, but the assertion is clearly not wholly based on experience. It is, in part, a didactic device to encourage good behavior and positive, responsible attitudes. Qoheleth could not have been alone in noting that the wisdom teaching on this point did not match the facts of real life (8:10–15). While partially drawn from a sense of poetic justice, in an ethical context, there is an evident desire to link the ultimate responsibility for good and evil to human beings and their behavior. This assignment of responsibility represents a part of the distinctive humanizing and moralizing tendency of the Israelite wisdom tradition.

Abomination as Abhorrent Behavior

The concern of the present study is not with the appeal made by the authors of wisdom to ideas of retribution as a moral sanction but rather with the use they have made of a different concept—the sense of moral outrage occasioned by bad conduct. This outrage is expressed by describing certain objects or actions as "an abomination" and, in a significant number of cases, as "an abomination to the Lord." Elsewhere in the Hebrew Bible, "abomination" terminology has either a natural or cultic significance rather than the specifically ethical connotation prominent in Proverbs. Both spheres have moral overtones, but those of natural or cultic significance lack the forceful, ethical character that many of the instances in Proverbs show. There are several reasons for examining the wisdom use of the concept of abomination; most conspicuous is the point that in spite of the prominence given to feelings of moral outrage as a basis for condemnation, there is the awareness that bad actions do often go unpunished. The wrongdoer may often appear to "get away with it," since no harmful consequences ensue from wicked actions. Moreover, as Koch points out, there arises an inherent paradox in emphasizing that retribution follows naturally on bad actions, since human intervention to enforce retribution forms the basis of any juridical system, which the wise of Israel clearly did not intend to set aside.[3]

Since the authors of wisdom teaching sought to strongly justify their distinctions between good and bad conduct, the idea of the inevitability of retribution evidently had its limitations. It would then have been natural to appeal to other deeply traditional concepts, each with a strongly psychological con-

---

3. Koch, "Retribution," 59.

nection that Israel's religion afforded. The feeling of shame comes readily to mind;[4] yet, surprisingly, this widely experienced sense of personal and social humiliation is not given great prominence in wisdom's appeal. In the book of Proverbs such humiliation is mentioned almost exclusively in regard to other members of a household, such as a wife or child whose behavior causes shame (Prov 10:5; 17:2; 19:26; 29:15—a son who brings shame; 12:4—a wife who brings shame to her husband; and in 14:35—a slave who shames his owner).

Even less prominent than the appeal to a sense of shame is the concern for holiness, which scarcely provides a sufficient basis of appeal as a motive for good conduct (only Prov 20:25 in regard to vows; otherwise, as a divine title—Prov 9:10; 30:3). Similarly Qoheleth (5:1–6) follows Prov 20:25 in asserting that a proper respect for vows and holy places is a mark of the virtuous person. In the wisdom tradition, holiness appears to be treated as a concept that defines a special sphere of activities and places rather than a broad concept that obtrudes into everyday life.[5] This limited sphere is a far cry from the repeated and comprehensive appeals to holiness that characterize the Pentateuchal material and that penetrate a wide range of social and domestic actions.

In contrast to this seeming lack of interest in social psychological feelings as a motive for conduct in the book of Proverbs, the assertion that certain actions constitute an 'abomination' (Heb. *tôʿēbâ*) is surprisingly prominent. Since elsewhere in the Hebrew Bible the concept of abomination is almost wholly applied to objectionable and non-Israelite cult practices or to deviant forms of sexual conduct, this distinctive wisdom usage is especially interesting. In our own present day legislative concerns, the idea of public outrage is much discussed. With the obsolescence of notions of blasphemy and deep concerns about what is appropriate for theater, film, and public displays, the concept of what is socially outrageous is still a matter of great public interest.

The fact that in the book of Proverbs certain objectionable forms of conduct or objects that imply objectionable behavior are repudiated as an "abomination" indicates that public abhorrence provided a significant basis for reproof. In addition, human feelings of outrage and abhorrence possessed a more ultimate significance because they could also be regarded as being felt by God; the assertion of God's outrage at bad human conduct then becomes a form of extreme reproof.

We may begin by noting that the noun *tôʿēbâ* and the verb *t-ʿ-b* describe something or some activity that is repulsive, abhorrent, and strongly undesirable.[6] Our study will concentrate on the use of this vocabulary in the book of

---

4. Cf. M. A. Klopfenstein, *Scham und Schande nach dem Alten Testament* (ATANT 62; Zurich, 1972); H. Seebass, "*bôš*," *TDOT* 2.50–60.

5. Contra J. G. Gammie, *Holiness in Israel* (Minneapolis, 1990) 126ff.

6. Cf. P. Humbert, "Le substantif *toʿeba* et le verbe *tʿb* dans L'Ancien Testament," *ZAW* 72 (1960) 217–37; idem, "L'Etymologie du substantif *toʿēbā*," *Verbannung und Heimkehr:*

214 R. E. Clements

Proverbs where it is evident that the sages have employed this terminology to serve their purposes by expressing a strong measure of reproof. While "abomination" has been used to define a range of activities either in a general, comprehensive way or in a more particular way for specified persons, such as fools or kings, our special interest lies in those sayings that extend this idea of abomination to condemn activities that are so bad as to constitute 'an abomination to the Lord' (Heb. *tôʿăbat YHWH*).

This usage in Proverbs is heightened by a number of observations regarding its occurrence elsewhere in biblical texts. Most striking is the fact that the specific phrase "an abomination to the Lord" is found most frequently in the book of Deuteronomy (16 occurrences), along with the synonymous *tôʿăbat ʾĕlōhîm*. The noun occurs more frequently in the book of Ezekiel (43 occurrences), where it is used to describe a variety of actions and alien cult objects that the prophet strongly repudiates as abhorrent. It is closely paralleled in the language of this prophet by the noun *šiqqûṣ* (Ezek 5:11; 7:20; 11:18, 21, etc.; cf. Jer 16:18).

Both in Deuteronomy and Ezekiel, the expression predominantly defines alien cult objects and practices (images of gods—Deut 7:25f.; child sacrifices—Deut 12:31; unacceptable sacrificial animals—Deut 17:1; prostitutes' fees—Deut 23:19; unnatural sexual practices—Ezek 22:11; cf. Lev 18:22, 26, 27, 30; 20:13). This conforms with later usage, which retained the expression primarily in reference to alien cult objects and unnatural sexual practices. However, both J. L'Hour[7] and M. Weinfeld[8] have suggested that the term *tôʿăbat YHWH* was a distinctive development of the Israelite wisdom tradition, from whence it was adopted by the Deuteronomists. Such a conclusion does not fit comfortably with the very different activities that are condemned in the respective literary contexts. There may, however, be some support for such a conclusion, since a comparable condemnation of bad behavior as abominable is found in the Egyptian Wisdom of Amenemope.[9]

My special concern is not so much to trace a particular pattern of semantic or form-critical development that, at best, appears to be rather uncertain,

---

FS W. Rudolph (Tübingen, 1970) 157–60. D. L. Christensen (*Deuteronomy 1–11* [WBC 6A; Dallas, 1991] 168) refers to A. S. Yahuda (*The Language of the Pentateuch in Its Relation to Egyptian* [Oxford, 1933] 75, 95) for the claim that the origin of the Hebrew word is to be found in ancient Egyptian. E. Gerstenberger ("*t-ʿ-b*," *THAT* 2.1051–55) notes the wide range of reference in the biblical usage. In his commentary, W. McKane, *Proverbs* (OTL; Philadelphia, 1970) passim, usually translates the term by the verb 'to loath'.

7. J. L'Hour, "Les Interdits *toʿeba* dans le Deuteronome," *RB* 71 (1964) 481–503.

8. M. Weinfeld, *Deuteronomy and the Deuteronomic School* (Oxford, 1972; repr. Winona Lake, 1992) 267ff., 323–24; idem, *Deuteronomy 1–11* (AB 5; New York, 1991) 376.

9. Cf. J. B. Pritchard, *ANET* (3d ed.) 505. Amenemope xiii 15, xv 20; cf. also v 7; vii 11; Miriam Lichtheim, *Ancient Egyptian Literature* (Berkeley, 1976) 2.154–55. Amenemope xiv 1 reads: "God hates the falsifier of words / He greatly abhors the dissembler" (Lichtheim's translation). The usage in Amenemope especially concerns the condemnation of deception and hypocrisy.

but rather to draw attention to the considerable importance the Israelite sapiential tradition gave to the notion of "outrage, abhorrence" as a basis for moral sanction. From a purely linguistic point of view, it would seem most probable that the notion of abhorrence was primarily attached to unnatural and repugnant features of the world; many of these had a perfectly natural origin, such as decaying carcasses of animals, bad smells, and the like. Accordingly, this notion defined objectionable realities that possessed little, if any, religious or moral significance. That this concept of abomination should then have extended further to include features that had additional significance of this kind is perfectly understandable. Deviant sexual practices and foreign cult objects could readily have been included under aspects of the social world that were abhorrent, especially since they may sometimes have gone hand in hand. Therefore, it is not difficult to understand how the idea of abomination took on a degree of moral significance; we do not need to suppose that there was a narrowly unilinear line of semantic development from one sphere to the other. The special significance of the development of the concept of abomination in the book of Proverbs seems to be that "an abomination to the Lord" focused on conduct that could not easily be repudiated by appeal to some other sanction. The extent to which the concept was taken to imply that certain actions that offended God would inevitably be punished appears overstated.

Abhorrent Behavior in the Book of Proverbs

The noun *tôʿēbâ* is found a total of twenty-one times in the book of Proverbs, twelve of these in the formulation *tôʿăbat YHWH*. The range of activities dealt with in these latter instances suggests that, in each case, the intention behind the saying is the assertion that conduct that arouses a feeling of outrage and abhorrence in human beings is similarly repudiated by God. In other words, the social sanction present in human feelings of abhorrence and the sense of grievance at the suffering of moral injury are feelings also shared by the deity. If this is the case, then it would point toward the conclusion that there was a qualitative, rather than a fundamental, distinction between those actions repudiated as a *tôʿēbâ* to human beings and those that are *tôʿăbat YHWH*, so far as the compilers of the book of Proverbs were concerned.

The claims of J. L'Hour and M. Weinfeld that the Deuteronomists borrowed the formula from the wisdom tradition may perhaps be valid, but they certainly appear questionable. The use of the concept in Amenemope, which was certainly known in the Israelite wisdom tradition, could have provided a point of origin. Yet, against this, the feeling of "revulsion, abhorrence" is a perfectly natural human emotion when faced with certain unpleasant objects or situations. The application to forbidden cult materials would then have been a simple transfer to this very sensitive sphere; similarly, the application of the term to objectional sexual behavior is readily explicable. The case is doubtful, therefore, whether the biblical occurrences can be made to fit any uniform pattern. The activities condemned by the term in the Deuteronomic legislation show more connection with cultic than wisdom usage.[10] In examining the usage in Proverbs, the primary focus of attention should surely rest on the particular objects and actions that are said to cause abhorrence to God rather than on the similarities of the formulations employed. We certainly find greater similarity between the usage in Ezekiel and Deuteronomy concerning the activities and objects that are said to cause abhorrence to God than between Deuteronomy and the book of Proverbs. Whereas in the former case it is consistently cultic or deviant sexual conduct that is reproved, it is uniquely bad moral conduct of a social kind in the case of Proverbs. In particular, this usage is employed to condemn conduct that would appear to have readily eluded other forms of control. Just as the Dodecalogue of curses in Deut 27:11–26 sought to outlaw activities that were difficult to control through the processes of law, so the wisdom teachers developed their own distinctive categories of moral valuation and methods of reproof.

In ancient Israelite society in general, the repudiation of activities and objects as causing feelings of abhorrence was wide-ranging. It is therefore not surprising to find that the term could be used in a quite general fashion in the book of Proverbs to describe the instinctive dislike of one type of person for another. Good people dislike bad people, and vice versa:

> The unrighteous are an abomination to the righteous,
> and good people are an abomination to the wicked.
>
> Prov 29:27

This simple portrait of contrasting personalities seems to have been designed to draw attention to the awareness that good and bad conduct relate usually to good and bad persons and that these contrasting lifestyles will quickly reveal themselves. In a related fashion, the lifestyle of the arrogant, abusive person (Heb. *lēṣ*) is declared to be "an abomination" to everyone (Prov 24:9). Over against this, those undesirable persons who have chosen folly and evil as a way of life regard the abandonment of such a lifestyle as an abomination (Prov 13:19). All of this fits closely with the broader wisdom teaching that bad actions are usually the outworking of a badly nurtured and badly directed attitude within a person; those who embrace antisocial attitudes and who fail to control selfish and arrogant desires will find themselves continually launching forth into bad actions. To depart from such an ingrained habit of mind and personality itself then becomes so undesirable as to constitute an "abomination."

---

10. G. von Rad (*Studies in Deuteronomy* [London, 1956] 18) suggests that behind the Deuteronomic usage there may at one time have existed a liturgically formulated list of "abominations to the Lord."

When a person has become a personal enemy, then only hostile actions and intentions are to be expected. The cautious and observant pupil of wisdom is accordingly warned against being "taken in" by gracious and friendly words from such a person:

> When an enemy speaks graciously
>> do not believe it,
> for there are seven abominations
>> concealed within;
> though hatred is covered with craftiness,
>> the wickedness of the enemy will be
>> revealed in public assembly.
>
> Prov 26:25–26

From the point of view of understanding the significance of "abomination" in such a context, it clearly does not matter that the noun is not defined more fully. Bad and hurtful conduct and feelings of all kinds were to be expected in the situation envisaged. We find present here a feature that characterizes much of the sentence instruction of the wise concerning "abomination"; attention is drawn to the conduct that causes a feeling of outrage, that is antisocial in nature, and that leads to violence and physical hurt. Yet it is not in itself necessarily criminal behavior, but merely an attitude or action that causes offense. The dissimulation and craftiness of the enemy who hides enmity behind a show of graciousness is similar to the bad behavior of the liar (Prov 12:22). In this case, "lying lips" constitute "an abomination to the Lord," but this is not significantly different from saying simply that they are an "abomination."

We can note that the idea of abomination, with its connotations of outrage and repudiation, has as its direct antonym the noun *rāṣôn* (= 'favor, acceptability'). Like *tôʿēbâ*, *rāṣôn* can be applied to both cultic and social realms of conduct. In Prov 12:22 and 16:12–13 there appears to be a play on this contrast. Where the former denotes what is acceptable and, therefore, favorably applauded, the latter denotes revulsion and rejection. Social acceptability is thereby shown to be a relevant criterion for judging conduct, but not in a merely superficial fashion. Some conduct is reprehensible and therefore destructive to good relationships and good order in society; other patterns of conduct evoke good feelings and good relationships and serve to promote the general well-being of society. This correlation between conduct and relationships is brought out further in the speech of Lady Wisdom on the virtuous nature of her gifts in Prov 8:1–36. In this discourse, deceitful, ill-intended speech of all kinds is classified as an "abomination" (Prov 8:7). It is the exemplary practioner of wisdom who, when tempted to speak hurtful words, recognizes immediately that they are reprehensible and outrageous. Hence the feelings of horror and outrage that are experienced by the wise person when confronted with bad behavior act as a kind of "conscience" to control conduct.

To whom is this kind of bad behavior outrageous? To the victim? Or to God? The answer is that both victim and God are ultimately thought to be involved. The feeling of abhorrence, which is the primary factor, gains added forcefulness through the notion that grossly bad behavior is abhorrent to God also.

I would therefore contend that the formal distinction between behavior that constitutes "an abomination to the Lord" and that which is simply repudiated as "an abomination" without further definition is not major. Perhaps to make such a distinction is even misleading because it is the abhorrent nature of certain actions, as sensed by fellow human beings, that serves to alert the reader to the potential that such activites may also be abhorrent to God. In this way, the idea of "revulsion, outrage" takes on a strongly moral tone that appears to be precisely what the teachers of wisdom intended.

We may later take up the broader issue of the significance of this sapiential development of the notion of popular outrage as a moral sanction. It is sufficient for the moment to note that it represents one, albeit a rather extensive one, of the ways in which the wisdom tradition of ancient Israel has endeavored to offer "natural" and "this worldly" explanations for the nature of evil. We have already pointed out that considerable attention has been given to the idea of retribution as a form of act-consequence arguments. Yet, as is clear, this did not always conform to perceived realities. Moroever, the act-consequence arguments left indeterminate how punishment for bad actions was to be implemented. Appeal to the harmful consequences of bad actions provided the sages with a rhetorical didactic technique as much as a recognized cautionary observation.

The significance of a degree of openness in the concept of abomination regarding who exactly feels outrage and abhorrence at the behavior described is particularly prominent in regard to the king. In a much-cited piece of sentence instruction, the wise affirms:

> It is an abomination to kings to do evil,
>   for the throne is established by righteousness.
>   Prov 16:12

Following McKane,[11] we should take this text to imply that monarchs, by virtue of their royal office, uphold righteous conduct and therefore repudiate and abhor the evil conduct of others. While this view no doubt presents a rather warmly tinted view of kingship, it must be what is intended, since this is a view that is widely present in the teaching of the wise with regard to the king. The king was in the eyes of the wise a pivotal figure of the social and political order (cf. 1 Kgs 3:3–14). The sayings that follow in Prov 16:13–15 conform

11. McKane, *Proverbs*, 235, 491–92.

to this line of interpretation. The kingly office, by virtue of its role as the foundation of justice, must instinctively oppose all that is unjust and evil. Less plausible would be an interpretation in a more absolute sense, suggesting that the concept of abomination implies activities that are abhorrent to God.

Conduct Abhorrent to God

What is distinctive in the teaching of Proverbs is precisely its concern with classifying certain activities as an abomination to God. It may well be that the background for such teaching is to be traced to the cultic usage of similar vocabulary where unclean, unsafe, or undesirable cultic materials are branded as "abominations." If this is so, then the wise have adapted and moralized a prominent and necessary feature of cultic life. That such a cultic background was fully apparent to the teachers of wisdom is suggested by the two pieces of sentence instruction preserved in the book of Proverbs that make reference to sacrifical rites:

> The sacrifice of the wicked is an
> abomination to the Lord,
> but the prayer of the upright is a delight to him.
> Prov 15:8

> The sacrifice of the wicked is an abomination;
> how much more when brought in pretence.
> Prov 21:27

McKane's translation of the final line of 21:27, 'with evil intent' (Heb. *zimmâ*),[12] is followed by the NRSV and is in line with earlier English renderings. This translation suggests that the act of piety is a cloak for some secret and nefarious purpose. However, since it is not clear what this might be, such a rendering may not capture the true meaning of what is envisaged. Either the notion of harboring ill-feelings toward another is what is meant or it refers to participating in formal cultic activities in the full knowledge that the worshiper's life-style is contrary to what God requires. The meaning may be simply "with the intention of deceiving (fellow-worshipers) by a display of piety." The overall impression is that it refers to participating in any kind of cultic activity where outward appearance and inward feeling are in conflict.

More interesting, from the perspective of the present study, is the lack of any real distinction between the undefined notion of "abomination" in 21:27 and the more narrowly defined "abomination to the Lord" of 15:8. The very idea of abomination has taken on a kind of absolute quality that implies that such actions are contrary to the very order of life and creation as a whole.

12. Ibid., 244, 560.

This adds support to my contention that our understanding of the distinctive "abomination to the Lord" sayings of the book of Proverbs is linked to the other less distinctive sayings about "abomination" rather than separate from them as a uniquely distinctive group.

The broader, general character of "abomination" attached to the idea of "abomination to the Lord" would then be consonant with the usage found in Prov 15:9, where it is "the way of the wicked" that is declared to be abhorrent to God. This is then also in line with the assertion that "evil plans" (literally "thoughts, calculations") constitute "an abomination to the Lord" (Prov 15:26). Prov 11:20 also bears the same all-inclusive character, insisting that "perverse minds" are abhorrent to God. None of these admonitions clearly detail what such perverse minds are thinking or planning. The balancing line in 11:20 refers to personal integrity (lit., "wholeness of way;" NRSV "blameless ways"). This suggests that it is a lack of integrity, or at least of good intention, that draws forth the teacher's condemnation.

The same all-encompassing range of condemnation is found in another summarizing affirmation:

> for the perverse are an abomination to the Lord,
> but right-acting persons are in his confidence.
> Prov 3:32

The kind of ill-motivated and corrupt behavior included under the heading of 'perverse' (Heb. *nālôz*) does not need to be spelled out in detail. The admonitory instruction is aimed at encouraging worthy aims and ideals and at avoiding the harboring of hurtful desires and plans of various kinds. Good intentions will lead to good behavior.

All of this serves to support the contention that what makes certain attitudes and activities abhorrent to God is to be traced back to their hurtful and hostile nature. It is not that such activities or plans can be denounced as illegal or even contrary to the welfare of the kin-group, regarded as the primary social unit, but rather that they intend to inflict harm by deceiving, by humiliating, or even by defrauding another person. While they offend good order in a deeper way, they cannot readily be dealt with by any other means of social sanction than reproof. These attitudes and activities can be warned against, but they cannot readily be acted against.

This certainly appears to be the case in the categorization of dishonest trading activities that are summed up in three separate "abomination to the Lord" sayings:

> A false balance is an abomination to the Lord,
> but an accurate weight is his delight.
> Prov 11:1

Diverse weights and diverse measures
are both alike an abomination to the Lord.

Prov 20:10

Differing weights are an abomination to the Lord,
and false scales are not good.

Prov 20:23

Clearly, all these sayings describing physical objects (weights and measures) as an abhorrent feature are intended as strong reproof of dishonest trading practices. Such practices were clearly illegal; their inclusion in the list of the sapiential abomination sayings may be accounted for by recognizing that it was extremely difficult to obtain proof of such practices and to prevent them by legal inspection and subsequent punitive action. This kind of crime was well-nigh impossible to detect and take action against.

The recognition that there were simple ways of cheating and defrauding that often escaped punitive action through normal processes of law undoubtedly caused problems for ancient lawmakers. This recognition rendered many ancient legal administrations defective. When we consider the development of ancient Near Eastern law codes in a broader spectrum, the significance of this realization becomes more apparent. The Near Eastern law codes amply testify to their close alliance with the promotion of efficient trading ventures. The concerns to secure capital, to inflict severe penalties for non-payment of debt, and to make trading deals binding all served to support the contention that law in the ancient Near East emerged as part of a large and ambitious sociopolitical and mercantile order. Whatever undermined this, in however minor a fashion, undermined the entire system. It is not surprising, therefore, that even relatively small-scale cheating in the market place called forth a very sharp and powerful reproof from the composers and compilers of the instructions of wisdom.

If this was true of such relatively minor offenses, how much more was it true of more major ones? In particular, what would be the reaction to the entire legal system becoming corrupt? It is just such a situation, where the legal system itself is used corruptly, that is condemned as an "abomination to the Lord:"

The person who justifies the wicked
and one who condemns the innocent
are both alike an abomination to the Lord.

Prov 17:15

The notion that particular attitudes and types of behavior are thoroughly reprehensible and are to be dealt with and opposed by education rather than by other social means is then brought out in its most comprehensive form in the number-saying of Prov 6:16–19:

> There are six things that the Lord hates,
> seven that are an abomination to him:
> arrogant looks, a lying tongue,
> and hands that shed innocent blood,
> a mind that thinks out wicked schemes,
> feet that hasten after evil,
> a lying witness who gives false evidence,
> and one who sows discord in a family.
>
> Prov 6:16–19

Not only is it instructive to find that condemnation here is provided by the classification of bad behavior patterns as constituting "abominations to the Lord," but the list itself is informative. Bad attitudes are condemned as much as bad actions, since the former lead to the latter. Overall, the concern is to promote good social awareness and to outlaw ill-intended behavior of all kinds, whether it falls foul of the legal system or not. This listing represents a real attempt to establish a concept of moral action based on informed and prudent attitudes that can be regarded as right in a comprehensive way. Wrongdoing and wrongful desires are condemned, not because they will elicit inevitable retribution when their consequences are finally complete, but because they conflict with the human (and divinely willed) social order. We have here broken out of a merely self-preserving, prudential morality and out of one based on claims of inevitable retribution, however realistically or ideally conceived. What is wrong is wrong *in itself* and is recognized by the feelings of outrage that it engenders. In contrast, what is right is right *in itself* and is recognized by the acceptability of such conduct to the community at large.

Conclusion

The idea that morally reprehensible behavior can be condemned and, hopefully, outlawed by appeal to the comprehensive category of what amounts to "an abomination to the Lord" provided the wisdom teachers with an instructive moral sanction. Whether or not the case that it took its origin from earlier cultic ideas relating to actions or things that were unacceptable in the worship of God can be substantiated, the use in wisdom is markedly different. "Abomination" in wisdom provided an intelligible category for moral argument that had genuine social and personal significance. It targeted two special areas of concern: those practices for which legal redress was difficult to obtain and those underlying, antisocial attitudes which led to objectionable and often criminal behavior.

Bad attitudes are warned against in the full recognition that they could not normally be acted against by the resources of the legal system. It may be argued that this is to claim too much for the notion of abomination; after all, what is felt to be an "abomination" is essentially a matter of an emotional, rather than a purely intellectual, response to a situation. In this regard, it is arguable that the notion of abomination, with its connotations of outrage and repudiation, serves as a contrast to the notion of conduct that is "fitting" (Heb. *nā'weh*). This contrast in concepts dominates the various negative images of Prov 26:1–12.[13] All the gifts and help that wisdom could offer—respect, reproof, instruction and insight—are of no use at all to the fool, because they are not appreciated and therefore not acted upon. These gifts of wisdom serve no enlightening or improving purpose to the person whose mind is set against wisdom. Accordingly, not only are they not "fitting" for such a person, they may even become a cause of danger, if the likeness to an incompetent archer who injures everybody (26:10) is taken seriously. In contrasting fashion, conduct that constitutes an "abomination" offends natural human feelings and sensitivities, offends God, and is against good sense and good order.

If this is the case, then it supports our overall contention that the formal distinction between what constitutes "an abomination to the Lord" and what is simply repudiated as "an abomination" without further definition should not be taken as particularly significant. Assigning significance to the distinction is yet another instance of over-attention to questions of formal presentation; so-called "form criticism" has been allowed to override far more significant features of content. It is the abhorrent nature of certain actions, as sensed by fellow human beings, that is appealed to in order to enable the reader to recognize that such activities are abhorrent to God. Moreover, the actions that are repudiated in this fashion, or more frequently the attitudes and life-style that are so condemned, could not readily be rejected by appeal to other, more familiar modes of rebuttal. The concept of abomination provides the teachers of wisdom with an effective and easily understood category of moral sanction.

So the concept of horror and outrage takes on a strongly moral tone, which would appear to be precisely what the teachers of wisdom intended. When an action or an attitude is labeled "an abomination to God," it represents a category of value that is intrinsic to the activity or life-style itself rather than one that requires the idea of punitive consequences to justify its badness.

Summary

In the first place, it is worth reiterating that the use of the argument that certain attitudes, actions, or objects implying actions, constitute "an abomination to the Lord" is a distinctive feature of the moralizing rhetoric of the book of Proverbs. Sayings containing this formulation stand close to others that simply brand certain attitudes or actions as "an abomination." The primary purpose in

---

13. Cf. R. C. Van Leeuwen, *Context and Meaning in Proverbs 25–27* (SBLDS 96; Atlanta, 1988) 87ff.

adding the phrase "to the Lord" appears to be to lend a more urgent and extreme form of condemnation to the reproof; it is akin to the argument of D. Winton Thomas that in Hebrew the clause "to God" (Heb. *lēʾlōhîm*) could convey a superlative sense.[14] Similar condemnation of certain types of activity as "an abomination to God" are to be found in the Egyptian *Teaching of Amenemope*; these teachings have been suggested as a possible source of the Israelite usage in Proverbs.

However, we have noted that the expression "an abomination to the Lord" also occurs several times in the book of Deuteronomy, but the expressions there relate to very different objects and activities. More frequent still is the use of the noun "abomination" in the book of Ezekiel to delineate certain actions and objects that offend the purity of the Israelite cultus. The implied condemnation of prostitution as an "abomination" in Deut 23:19 links social condemnation with rejection for cultic use, suggesting that the dividing line between what was socially abhorrent and what was cultically unacceptable was probably a difficult one to draw.

Scholarly argument hitherto has tried to link the usage in the book of Proverbs with that of the book of Deuteronomy because of the marked distinctiveness of the shared phrase "an abomination of the Lord." Yet the subjects covered in the respective books are very different; there is greater connectedness between Ezekiel and Deuteronomy in regard to the cultic nature of what is claimed to be abhorrent "to the Lord" than with the usage of the book of Proverbs.

My argument is primarily that all attempts to trace a particular line of form-critical development are uncertain and probably misleading; they tend to obscure the more important features of the use of the phrase in Proverbs, namely to condemn certain types of behavior and attitudes. Such sayings recognized that it is pointless to suppose that any sort of legal redress could be obtained against those who adopted a scornful and broadly antisocial attitude. At the same time, it was important to affirm the need for discouraging such behavior and for recognizing its far-reaching consequences on the health of society as a whole. The repudiation of some activities as "an abomination to the Lord" also served to highlight certain types of criminal behavior, such as the use of fraudulent weights and measures, that must have been difficult to control by other means. Similarly, hypocritical conduct is rebuffed by this concept.

Lastly, it seems important to note that the appeal on the part of the teachers of wisdom to the idea of a divine sense of outrage at bad human conduct reflects an awareness that the more frequent appeals to the bad consequences of bad behavior were unrealistic. These act-consequence arguments could only

---

14. D. Winton Thomas, "A Consideration of Some Unusual Ways of Expressing the Superlative in Hebrew," *VT* 3 (1953) 209–24.

be upheld as true in a broad sense, and only then as vaguely true in the long term. Moreover, they were flawed by their failure to distinguish where it was necessary to introduce human punishments rather than simply let events take their inevitable course. On the positive side, there is a broader ethical significance in the use in Proverbs of the phrase "an abomination to the Lord" in that it reveals a valuable concern to relate fundamental moral concepts to experienced social realities. Instead of resorting to a straightforward reaffirmation of claims that God has commanded human beings to behave in a particular fashion, these sayings bind together the sense of an ultimate divine authority with the felt needs and responses of human beings acting in a context of social reality. As such, they mark a noteworthy step in the integration of ethical and social concepts, seeing in an educative principle a path to virtue.

THE SOCIAL LOCATION OF
THE BOOK OF PROVERBS

Michael V. Fox

THE BOOK OF PROVERBS is manifestly, and by its own testimony (Prov 22:17, 24:23, 30:1, 31:1), a collection of diverse sayings from many sources, for the most part assembled with little concern for topical or formal organization. At the same time it presents itself (1:1) as a unity, and indeed it manifests a fair degree of homogeneity in literary character, presuppositions, and message. Can we reconstruct the process of the book's formation in such a way as to accommodate both its centrifugal and its centripetal forces? This task calls for a

Author's note: My work on Wisdom Literature began with the dissertation I wrote under Professor Haran's guidance. My interest in the subject has continued ever since. Some of Professor Haran's ideas on Wisdom Literature have impressed themselves deeply in my thinking. His gracious academic and personal mentoring has been a mainstay of my career.

Reference to Egyptian texts is according to the following editions and uses their unit numbering:

Old Kingdom:
Djedefhar (or Hordjedef): W. Helck, *Die Lehre des Djedefhor* . . . (KÄT [Kleine Ägyptische Texte]; Wiesbaden, 1984).
Kagemeni: A. H. Gardiner, "The Instruction Addressed to Kagemni and His Brethren," *JEA* 32 (1946) 71–74.
The Kemit ['The Compilation']: G. Posener, *Ostraca hiératiques littéraires de Deir el Médineh* (FIFAO 18; Cairo, 1951), pls. 1–21; Winfried Barta, "Das Schulbuch Kemit," *ZÄS* 105 (1978) 6–14.
Ptahhotep: Z. Žába, *Les Maximes de Ptahhotep* (Prague, 1956) [Middle Kingdom dating possible].

Middle Kingdom:
Amenemhet: W. Helck, *Der Text der "Lehre Amenemhets I. für seinen Sohn"* (KÄT; Wiesbaden, 1969).
Duachety: W. Helck, *Die Lehre des Dw3-Htjj* (2 vols.; KÄT; Wiesbaden, 1970).
The Loyalist Instruction: G. Posener, *L'Enseignment loyaliste* (Geneva, 1976).

227

combination of form criticism, which inquires into the social location of the literary types found in the book, and redaction history, which traces the process of development that produced a particular form of the book.[1] The present essay does not undertake this task in its entirety, but rather discusses the principal components of a theory that could guide this reconstruction. I will focus on chaps. 10–29, which are the locus of current controversy.

School or Farm?

Since the 1960s there has been a dichotomy in scholarly approaches to the social location of the proverbs between what we may call the "folk school" and the "school school."

The school school, associated with Hermisson, locates the origin of the sayings of the book of Proverbs in schools connected with the royal court. Wisdom Literature was supposedly composed for use in the "Weisheitsschule," which trained children of courtiers and the upper class for the royal bureaucracy.[2] While Hermisson grants that the book probably does incorporate some folk sayings, the collections are essentially literary texts. The folk school is represented by Westermann, Golka, and, for the most part, Whybray.[3] On the basis of a thematic analysis of the proverbs, Westermann asserts that the middle collections

---

New Kingdom:

Anii: E. Suys, *La Sagesse d'Ani* (Rome, 1935).

Amenemope: H. O. Lange, *Das Weisheitsbuch des Amenemope* (Copenhagen, 1925).

Amennakhte: G. Posener, "L'Exorde de l'instruction éducative d'Amennakhte," *RdE* 65 (1955) 61–72; G. Posener, *Catalogue des ostraca hiératiques littéraires de Deir el Médineh* (Cairo; Vol. 1 [1938]; Vol. 2 [1951]; Vol. 3 [1977–80 = FIFAO 20]).

Pap. Chester Beatty IV: A. H. Gardiner, *Hieratic Papyri in the British Museum* (Third Ser.; London, 1935) pls. 37–44.

The Teaching according to Ancient Writings: *HO*: J. Černý and A. H. Gardiner, *Hieratic Ostraca* (Oxford, 1957) pl. 88.

For translations and further bibliographical information on Egyptian Wisdom texts, see H. Brunner, *Altägyptische Weisheit* (Zurich, 1988) and M. Lichtheim, *Ancient Egyptian Literature* (3 vols.; Berkeley, 1973–80).

1. The focus is almost always on the Masoretic form, as is the case in this study, but this choice is not inevitable.

2. H. J. Hermisson, *Studien zur israelitischen Spruchweisheit* (WMANT 28; Neukirchen-Vluyn, 1968). The idea is earlier. Paul Volz identified the scribal schools in Egypt as "Weisheitsschulen" and for Israel pictured a "geistliche Schule" alongside the "Berufsschulen," the latter training scribes, the former concerned with the "religiös-sittlichen Kenntnisstand" and "inner Erziehung" (*Hiob und Weisheit* [Göttingen, 1921] 103).

3. Westermann, *Wurzeln der Weisheit* (Göttingen, 1990; see my review of this book in *JBL* 111 [1992] 529–32); F. W. Golka, "Die israelitische Weisheitsschule oder 'der Kaisers neue Kleider,'" *VT* 33 (1983) 257–70; idem, "Die Königs- und hofsprüche und der Ursprung der israelitischen Weisheit," *VT* 36 (1986) 13–36; R. N. Whybray, *Wealth and Poverty in the Book of Proverbs* (JSOTSup 99; Sheffield, 1990). Golka's articles are incorporated in his book, *The Leopard's Spots* (Edinburgh, 1993).

of Proverbs (chaps. 10–29) comprise mainly oral folk sayings that originated in the daily life of "simple folk"—smallholding farmers, craftsmen, laborers, slaves, and housewives in preexilic times.[4] Whybray locates the proverbs among the smallholding farmers, neither rich nor poor. There were, he says, numerous scholastic additions, and chaps. 1–9 are entirely postexilic and didactic.[5]

The School?

The debate about the existence of scribal schools in preexilic Israel has proceeded with no real evidence on either side.[6] To be sure, lack of evidence does not prove the negative; after all, there is no direct evidence of schools in *post*exilic Judea before the time of Ben Sira, but no one claims that *he* invented them. But for purposes of locating Wisdom's *Sitz im Leben*, the question of the existence of schools may be set aside, for there is no sign that Proverbs was composed *for* them. Education, which obviously is the goal of Wisdom, is not identical with schooling.[7]

The theory of the scribal-school *Sitz* was derived by analogy from Egyptian Wisdom Literature, but the analogy is wrong. In fact, it may work the other way, because Egyptian Wisdom Literature, though used in the schools, shows no signs of having been composed within and for them.

First of all, we should not confuse the issue by calling the scribal school the "Wisdom School." The scribal school in Egypt was not a Wisdom School, either in the sense of an intellectual circle or in the sense of an academy that specialized

---

4. Westermann, *Wurzeln*, 27 and passim.

5. Related to this trend is C. R. Fontaine's emphasis on the oral origins of wisdom and on the family as the setting of instruction, which was shared by mother and father ("The Sage in Family and Tribe," in *The Sage in Israel and the Ancient Near East* [ed. John G. Gammie and Leo Perdue; Winona Lake, Ind., 1990] 155–64). Fontaine does not deny the subsequent formulation of this wisdom within schools.

6. The arguments for the existence of schools in Israel are exhaustively presented by Hermisson, *Studien zur israelitischen Spruchweisheit*, 97–136; and A. Lemaire, *Les Écoles et la formation de la Bible dans l'ancien Israel* (Freiburg, 1981) and "Sagesse et écoles," *VT* 34 (1984) 270–81. Lemaire gives special attention to abecedaries as evidence for schools, an argument that M. Haran ("On the Diffusion of Literacy and Schools in Ancient Israel," *Congress Volume: Jerusalem, 1986* [VTSup 40; ed. J. A. Emerton; Jerusalem, 1988] 81–95) has decisively countered. Golka argues the contrary, proposing instead that education took place in a "famulus" or apprentice system ("Die israelitische Weisheitsschule"). R. N. Whybray (*The Intellectual Tradition in the Old Testament* [BZAW 135; Berlin, 1974]) argues that nothing in the Bible points to a professional class of wise men called *ḥăkāmîm*. He largely disproves the hypothesis of a Wisdom *School* in the sense of an ideological-political faction.

7. Nili Shupak ("The Book of Proverbs and Wisdom Literature," *RB* 94 [1987] 99–119) argues that Proverbs contains semantic equivalents of terms in Egyptian Wisdom Literature and that this shows that the book of Proverbs too was connected with education "*in either an official context or a private and familial one*" (p. 104; italics mine). I agree entirely with the latter alternative. We may grant that Wisdom Literature was indisputably "connected" with education "in an official context," for it was extensively copied (alongside other types of literature) in the schools.

in the teaching of Wisdom.[8] Wisdom Literature was indeed extensively taught and copied in the scribal schools, but so were math, geography, administrative correspondence, and many other types of texts relevant to the future occupations of the pupils. We might just as well call the scribal school the "Magic School" because scribes wrote magical texts and scribal students copied them.

The authors of Wisdom instructions were not, as far as we can tell, school teachers. The books are ascribed to men from a variety of professions, from king and vizier to ordinary scribes. Some ascriptions are probably fictitious,[9] but some certainly are not, for their authors are too individualized and unillustrious to be likely candidates for typological fiction; Duachety, Amenemope, and Anii are examples. They are scribes of respectable station but not the sort likely to be retained in historical memory. The details, especially in the case of Amenemope (who gives his wife's and his son's titulary as well) leave little doubt about the accuracy of the ascription, for they are highly specific and have no literary or rhetorical function that would justify their fabrication. Nor are their sons men of the sort whose mention—along with priestly and professional titles—would have importance in itself.

In any case, ascriptions, fictional as well authentic, show whom an Egyptian reader could be expected to envision as an author of Wisdom and who the expected and appropriate audience is. The ascriptions show no predisposition to see teachers as the authors or scribal students as their audience. The ostensive, and often true, authors are men from various walks of life who are speaking to their actual sons. Ptahhotep addresses his "staff of old age," who is his biological son (lines 29 and 52). Amenemope writes his book for his youngest son only, out of all his children, a narrowing of audience that would have no fictional function and does not belong to the generic formulae. His son, Horemma^ckher, has various functions appropriate to an adult, not a schoolboy. Anii is a scribe of the palace and his son Khonshotep is himself a scribe (9, 13).

Various maxims in the Wisdom Instructions speak of passing this wisdom on to one's own children,[10] never to one's pupils.[11] Furthermore, there are sev-

8. The ambiguity of the word *school* causes considerable confusion. Even if Wisdom Literature were composed for scribal schools, this fact would not imply the existence of a special intellectual faction along the lines of the Greek philosophical "schools." Conversely, a Wisdom School in this sense might theoretically exist independently of the scribal schools.

9. King Amenemhet apparently speaks from the afterlife, and the teacher of Kagemeni is, from the standpoint of the epilogue, deceased. In the case of a prominent figure such as Prince Djedefhar, we do not know whether the preserved instruction is a result or a cause of his fame. He is, however, remembered among the immortal authors listed in Pap. Chester Beatty IV. A more complex case is the stele of Sehetepibre^c, which incorporates part of the "Loyalist Instruction." The tomb owner, an actual individual, appropriated a version of an older instruction, while maintaining the formal setting of father-child instruction. The instruction addresses the speaker's children in the plural. The attribution as such is not fictional because Sehetepibre^c is delivering the words as his own teaching.

10. Cf. Ptahhotep (lines 30–32, 590–96); and Duachety (XXXg; Pap. Sallier II, 11, 4).

11. In one case Amennakhte, the recipient of the instruction is, according to one ostracon, the apprentice (*ḥry-^c*) of the author, though according to another ostracon, he is his son (*s^ꜣ*). The original

eral references, early and late, to fathers instructing sons in different skills. The author of the Kemit had an instructor but also was educated in the writings by his father. The scribe Hori in Pap. Anastasi I declares that his father instructed him "in all that he knew," including horsemanship.

Apart from the supposed Egyptian analogy, there is nothing in Proverbs to point to a school origin.[12] The father-son discourse is maintained throughout Proverbs. In chaps. 10–31 it is indicated only sporadically,[13] but in chaps. 1–9 it is consistently in the foreground. It is widely assumed that 'father' means 'teacher' in Wisdom Literature. But even if 'father' was an epithet for teacher in the postulated Israelite school, there is no reason to think that the word 'father' *means* 'teacher' in the Wisdom Instructions (it does not in Egypt).[14] In Prov 4:3, the father's reminiscence of the education he received from his own father clearly envisions family, not school, education.[15] The issue in 4:3–4 is not whether the speaker's mother delivered the teaching quoted in 4:5ff. (the passage makes no such claim), but whether it was the speaker's father or his teacher who spoke the teaching. If the speaker's 'father' were not his actual father, the parallel in 4:3 would be warped, as if to say, "I was a pupil to my teacher // tender and alone before my mother."

The mention of the mother's teaching in Prov 1:8 and 6:20 is significant, for 'mother' can hardly mean schoolmarm. Moreover, Prov 30:1–9 is an example of a Wisdom instruction attributed to a woman, Lemuel's mother. It is true that, as Haran has shown, the needs of parallelism may engender an "automatism" in which one term of a parallel pair becomes semantically otiose.[16] In my view, the mention of 'mother' is otiose insofar as the particular teachings quoted are the father's words alone,[17] but the concept of 'mother's teaching' cannot be dismissed. The mother's teaching is spoken of in the same terms as the father's; the two persons are of the same order. The authenticity of the ascription is

---

text probably had "his son his apprentice" (Posener, "L'Exorde," 61–72). Amennakhte was a scribe in the House of Life (a scribal center in the temple that included a library and, possibly, a school), but he does not call himself a schoolteacher (*sbꜣw n pr ꜥnḫ*). The literary letter of Menena is addressed to "his son his apprentice" (W. Gugliemi, "Eine 'Lehre' für einen reiselustigen Sohn," *WO* 14 [1983] 149–59).

12. The likeliest allusion to schools is Prov 5:13, "And I did not listen to the voice of my instructors (*môrāy*), and did not incline my ear to my teachers (*mĕlammĕday*)." These could be various people in life who tried to teach him moral behavior, especially his father and mother, though the plural is suggestive of schoolteachers. The existence of schoolteachers does not, however, prove that Proverbs, not even its postexilic sections, was written *for* schools.

13. Prov 19:27; 23:15, 19, 26; 24:13–14; 27:11; cf. 31:1–4.

14. The word was used thus in the Sumerian school, but the speaker in the Instruction of Suruppak is a father, not a teacher, speaking to his son (B. Alster, *The Instructions of Šuruppak* [Copenhagen, 1974]).

15. Thus Whybray (*Intellectual Tradition*, 42).

16. M. Haran, "The Graded Numerical Sequence and the Phenomenon of 'Automatism' in Biblical Poetry," *Congress Volume* (VTSup 22; Leiden, 1972) 238–67.

17. Thus ibid. 248.

unimportant; what is significant is the author's *image* of a mother delivering Wisdom teachings. This image would make no sense if the 'father' he had in mind were only a schoolteacher. We may also note that Duachety concludes his instruction with the words, "Praise God for your father and your mother, who set you on the way of the living. See these things which I have set before you and your children's children" (XXXf–g). Both parents set the child on 'the way of life', which is precisely the goal of Wisdom Literature.[18] Within the text of Duachety, however, the speaker is the auditor's biological father. We may say that the substance of the teaching comes from both parents, but, in almost all cases, the formulation is the father's.[19]

Some Wisdom books may have been composed for schools, but this is not the way they present themselves. The self-presentation of Wisdom Literature is as paternal teaching. If the ostensive setting really is just a cloak for a teacher-pupil school setting, why are the schoolteachers, for a period of some 2600 years, so determined to hide the instructor's role in Wisdom authorship?

A strong analogy to the ancient Wisdom Instructions is the medieval Jewish ethical testament. Ethical testaments are instructions written by men in their maturity for the religious-ethical guidance of their sons and, sometimes, daughters. (These texts are, in fact, descendants of ancient Wisdom Literature, since they use Proverbs as a model.) The testaments are family wisdom but nonetheless literary.[20] The father addresses his son (or sons) and through him speaks to a larger reading audience. The form became popular and was sometimes used as a fictional literary setting, but other testaments were written for an author's actual children.

The Farm?

If the collections of Proverbs, like Egyptian Wisdom Instructions, were not written as school textbooks, were they folk literature? This has been claimed for the earlier layer of the book. (Chaps. 1–9 and various proverbs in the rest of the book are relegated to the postexilic school.) Westermann locates the bulk of the middle collections among the "einfache[s] Leute"[21] in the small agrarian village at a preliterate stage of culture.[22] On the basis of the proverbs

18. Cf. 'to guide one in the way of life' (Amenemope 1,7).
19. There is a late reference to a woman's *written* wisdom that describes the woman Renpetnefret as 'expert with (her) mouth, sweet in speech, excellent in counsel in her writings' (G. Lefebvre, *Le Tombeau de Petosiris* [Cairo, 1923–24] 1.101; 2.35).
20. J. Bergman ("Gedanken zum Thema 'Lehre-Testament-Grab-Name,'" in *Studien zu altägyptischen Lebenslehren* [ed. E. Hornung and O. Keel; OBO 28; Freiburg, 1979] 74–103) and E. von Nordheim (*Die Lehre der Alten* [Leiden, 1985] vol. 1) have compared Egyptian Wisdom Instructions with the ethical testament genre and connected it with the testaments in the apocrypha and pseudepigrapha. A selection of medieval ethical testaments is found in Israel Abrahams, *Hebrew Ethical Wills* (Philadelphia, 1948).
21. Westermann, *Wurzeln*, 45; see p. 75 and passim.
22. Ibid., 10.

(or proverb-parts) that he considers folk sayings, he draws an idyllic picture of village society—a "nüchterne, solide, bürgerliche Welt."[23] The folk sayings express a communitarian, egalitarian ethic.

Many of the sayings in Proverbs are doubtless folk sayings, and some of them may well have originated in small villages. This setting does not, however, dominate the book or even the individual proverbs. Westermann extracts evidence for a village setting from sayings such as 27:21: "For the silver the smelter and for the gold the oven; but for man reputation is decisive."[24] This, he believes, reflects the background of "a relatively small neighborhood," in which everyone knows everyone else and in which one achieves a good reputation not by wealth or connections but by proving worthy in personal trials.[25] Such inferences, however, are guided by a network of stereotypes; they are not based on any real sociological data, or even, so far as I can tell, on casual personal observation. To the extent that this adage is true, it is true everywhere. Ben Sira makes a similar observation (27:7), and he was an urban sophisticate. In any case, a royal court too is "a small neighborhood," and even urban dwellers live in social groupings smaller than the city in its entirety. The folk school also tends to slight the diversity of sources by overlooking clues to an urban setting, such as references to goldsmiths and messengers, which have no place in the small village. Most problematically, Westermann's approach reflects a romanticism that allows him to extract a communitarian ideal from proverbs (*some* proverbs) and then to spin a reality out of the ideal and identify *that* with life in a small, egalitarian village. Similar romanticism is displayed by Whybray's belief that references to drunkenness, gluttony, and licentiousness "may be an indication of an urban setting."[26] Presumably such things don't happen in small towns.

Some adages do seem to have an agrarian setting because they offer advice relevant only to agriculturalists and seem to speak from within, and not only about, this background. Many of these adages address well-to-do landowners rather than smallholders. Prov 11:26 is redolent of agribusiness more than Old MacDonald: "As for him who withholds grain—the nation (*lĕʾōm*) will curse him; but blessings come upon him who distributes food" (*mašbîr*). A small farmer, working just to feed his family, could not affect the market on his own, and we cannot imagine a cartel of small farmers. A *mašbîr* is a major distributor—a central grain distributor; Joseph (Gen 42:6), Sihon (Deut 2:28; verb), and the greedy rich men in Amos (8:5) are *mašbirîm*. Moreover, the withholder of grain in this proverb is cursed by the *lĕʾōm*, which always refers to a nation as a whole, not just one's neighbors or the residents of a town. Hence the proverb speaks about, and holds a lesson for, men who control central granaries, either

---

23. Ibid., 27.
24. ". . . über den Mann aber entscheidet der Ruf" (*wĕʾîš lĕpî mahălālô*); ibid., 19.
25. Ibid.
26. *Wealth and Poverty*, 90.

as owners or as royal officials.[27] Similarly, when slaves are mentioned, it is from the perspective of owners, people who are concerned with efficient discipline of slaves (29:21).

The Court and Environs

Most significantly, a fair number of proverbs bespeak a setting in the royal court, describing kings and governors and giving advice to their servants and ministers. Chaps. 28–29 in particular seems to comprise a sort of manual for a future monarch.[28] Do these kinds of sayings point to a court setting?

Golka cites African proverbs at length to show that sayings about kings may originate among the folk, far from the court.[29] Of course they may; however, the evidence for the setting lies not merely in the topic of a proverb, but in its point of view, the implied audience, and the purpose of each proverb. These considerations point to a court setting (see below, pp. 235–36). The folk school finds criticism of the king in any saying that implies even the possibility of royal imperfection and assumes that such criticism cannot issue from the court; for example: "Remove wickedness from before the king, and his throne will be established in righteousness" (25:5). Golka thinks that this is a "hofkritischer Text,"[30] but not even Louis XIV would have trouble with it. Moreover, its message pertains first of all to people directly in the royal service and to the king himself; for others, it is an abstraction.

We should be wary about drawing conclusions from African parallels. First of all, the African proverbs Golka cites bear little resemblance to Israelite proverbs, most being brief remarks, usually cynical, about the effects and benefits of power, with no reference to a king; for example: "Authority is the tail of a water-rat"; or "The turtle cannot climb up on a stump; someone has to put it there." Moreover, African sayings that do speak from a courtier's perspective may well come from courtiers. Africa has known innumerable kings and courts, court officials, bureaucracies, and professional poets. Furthermore, the communities from which the parallels are taken were not preliterate—certainly not in the 20th century, when most of the sayings were recorded—and they do

27. We may note that the vizier Ptahhotep has advice for farmers (§9), formulated in such a way that one might think that the reader might do the labor himself ("If you plow and there is growth in the field . . ."). The "Loyalist Teaching" (Posener, *L'Enseignement*), which is largely devoted to extolling the royal power and which was appropriated for the stele of the high official Sehetepibre[c], has much to teach about farming (§§ 9–13). It speaks to the concerns of large estate owners.

28. U. Skladny, *Die ältesten Spruchsammlungen in Israel* (Göttingen, 1962) 58–62; B. Malchow, "A Manual for Future Monarchs," *CBQ* 47 (1985) 238–45; G. Bryce, *A Legacy of Wisdom* (Lewisburg, Pa., 1979) 135–55.

29. Golka, "Königs- und hofsprüche," passim.

30. Ibid., 31.

not necessarily offer insights into preliterate use of proverbs. An African parallel, no matter how close, is no evidence that an Israelite saying originated among "simple folk."[31] A further complication is the fact that if the parallel is *too* close, we must suspect biblical influence, not a minor factor in modern African traditions.

I will not go through the court sayings in Proverbs and rebut the folk school reinterpretations. My basic contention is that the sayings in question speak not only *about* kings and courtiers, but *to* and *for* them. Here are three examples:

- "The king's anger is angels of death, but a wise man can assuage it"(16:14). This is relevant only to someone who might experience the king's anger firsthand and attempt to assuage it.[32]
- "Do not put on airs before the king; do not stand in the place of the mighty. It is better that he say to you, 'Come up here,' etc." (25:6–7). This is not pertinent to a simple farmer. It is germane, however, to a man working in an administrative hierarchy, and it closely resembles the numerous counsels of etiquette found in Egyptian Wisdom.[33]
- "Entscheidung (durch Orakel . . .) ist auf den Lippen des Königs / sein Mund spricht nicht fehl im Gericht" (16:10; Golka's trans.[34]). This is pure courtly flattery, as Golka unintentionally shows by comparing it with the words of the wise woman of Tekoa (2 Sam 14:19–20).

Why strain to assign such proverbs to "simple folk" rather to the royal scribes, such as are mentioned in 25:1, or at least to men who know how to act when near the king?

The motive for such straining may well be that the presence of courtly sayings undermines the strong form of the folk school hypothesis by showing

31. For informants in his valuable study of proverb performance in Akan rhetoric, Kwesi Yankah used *akyeame* (sing. *okyeame*), which he translates 'chief's spokesman', an official who is the chief's confidant, spokesman, and advisor, and who is considered a repository of traditional wisdom (*The Proverb in the Context of Akan Rhetoric* [Bern, 1989] 82–86). Compare Hezekiah's men! One of Yankah's informants was the *okyeame* Antwi Boasiako. It turns out that he is also a paremiologist, having published a book of Akan proverbs (p. 85). Again we may compare Hezekiah's men. The threads of oral and written, folk and courtly traditions are inextricably tangled.

32. The same may be said of the dubious parallel that Golka quotes: "A fierce sovereign makes afraid / a gentle sovereign makes ashamed" ("Königs- und hofsprüche," 29).

33. This advice is reiterated in Egyptian Wisdom Literature, where it is clearly a matter of practical concern; e.g.: "If you are in the antechamber, stand and sit as fits your rank, which was assigned you the first day. Do not trespass—you will be turned back, etc." (Ptahhotep §13; lines 220–31). "When you walk behind high officials, walk at a distance behind the last of them" (Duachety, XXIVa). "You should not sit while another stands who is older than you or stationed higher in his office. . . . Walk the accustomed path each day. Stand according to your rank, etc." (Anii, 6, 10–13). "Attend to your position, whether low or high; it is not good to push forward. Go in accordance with your rank" (ibid., 8, 10–11). "Do not sit before one greater than you" (Pap. Chester Beatty IV, verso 4, 6).

34. Golka, "Königs- und hofsprüche," 28.

members of the royal court at the apex of the creative activity of Wisdom Literature. The courtly sayings are more than late, disruptive fillers in an anthology of folk sayings. They constitute a prominent theme throughout chaps. 10–29, though partly clustered in certain places. Together with the reference to the editorial work by the men of Hezekiah in 25:1 (and surely this credible heading refers to more than mechanical copying), they show that the court was the decisive locus of creativity. Everything we have was channelled to the court and through it; the flow cannot be supposed to move in the other direction.

Following the usage of Prov 25:1,[35] which calls the compilers of chaps. 25–29 "Hezekiah's men," we may designate the authors and redactors *the king's men*. This term is preferable to the usual *courtier*, which connotes wealth and nobility. The royal service would include clerks and officials of high and low degree, much like the men whom Ben Sira addresses and to whose class he belonged. When Ben Sira says, "Among the great, do not act as their equal . . . " (32:9; Greek), he is speaking to men who may come into contact with grandees but are not *of* them.

Ben Sira is an example of the kind of person who could write Wisdom Instructions. He was a scholar with the leisure to study and write. He speaks about the rich and the poor in a way that suggests that he saw himself as neither, but his suspicion of the rich and powerful suggests that he knew them, uncomfortably, firsthand. This critical stance does not make him one of the "simple folk." It is likely that Ben Sira himself served before rulers (39:4) and travelled in their service (34:10–11). (There is no evidence that he was a schoolmaster; his *bet midraš*, mentioned in the much misunderstood 51:23, is the book itself.)[36] He was a *sofer*, which should be translated 'scholar' or better, 'clerk' in the medieval sense, rather than 'scribe', for being a *sofer* was not in itself a profession, but a qualification for various professional opportunities. In all regards, Ben Sira resembled the authors of Egyptian Wisdom.

The king's men had their hand in the formation of Proverbs, and they reached deep. What did they do? Surely they did not undertake paremiological field work in the villages, gathering and publishing folk sayings. Ben Sira gives us a glimpse into the way that folk proverbs could come into learned collections:

> If you are willing, [you will receive knowledge]. Incline your ear that you may gain discipline. [Stand in the company of the elders, and attach yourself to whosoever is wise.] Desire to hear every discourse (*śîḥâ*), and let no perceptive proverb (*māšāl bînâ*) escape you."
>
> (6:33–35)[37]

---

35. Cf. 1 Kgs 10:8 (MT) (*ʾănāšeykā // ʿăbādeykā*).

36. The passage concludes the book and recommends it to the reader. Through it, one may gain wisdom "without money" (v. 25).

37. From Hebrew MS A, supplemented (in brackets) from the Greek.

This advice (written by a scholar to a reading audience) shows appreciation for oral discourse as a source of wisdom.[38] A scholar should listen to and absorb intelligent conversation and perceptive proverbs. It is a small step from doing so to recalling them, along with written proverbs one has read, and embedding them in one's own creations.

Such a process accounts for the great diversity and the even greater unity in Proverbs. The diversity comes from the varied sources, the unity from the redactors' own creative activity. The redactors' intervention was radical and determinative, going far beyond "later addition" to existing proverbs. They did add, but, most important, they *selected*. They chose what to include and what to ignore, and what they chose, they reshaped. In such a process, the very notions of original and additional, of authorial and redactional, intertwine inextricably.

Thus the book of Proverbs does not give us a random or representative sampling of Israelite sayings but a selection made by individuals for their own purposes. Skladny, while exaggerating the ideological unity of each collection, showed that the central collections in the book of Proverbs differ in ideological character, formal preferences, and areas of emphasis.[39] This in itself witnesses to creative selectivity on the part of individual redactors, as does the clustering of certain types of proverbs in certain collections. G. Bryce and R. Van Leeuwen have gone further and shown that the Hezekian collection includes some well-arranged proverb-poems as well as thematic clusters.[40]

Good field-paremiologists will try to subordinate their own beliefs and preferences to the material they gather and to preserve its integrity. The redactors of Proverbs were not paremiologists. They were closer to authors or collage artists, and they preserved proverbs that served *their* purposes. It would be more accurate to think of the redactors as *incorporating* folk sayings than as collecting them. Observe that Ben Sira does not urge the pupil to remember proverbs but to remember *wise* proverbs. All proverbs preserved must meet the redactor's, not the "folk's," notion of wisdom. A fair portion of the folk proverbs found elsewhere in the Bible would not have qualified as wisdom and been enshrined in proverb collections. "The fathers have eaten sour grapes and the children's teeth stand on edge" (Ezek 18:2) is a self-serving gripe that shifts the

---

38. As does Ptahhotep, who says that fine discourse is to be found even with the maids at the grinding stones (§1).

39. Skladny, *Die ältesten Spruchsammlungen*, 32.

40. R. Van Leeuwen (*Context and Meaning in Proverbs 25–27* [SBLDS 96; Atlanta, 1988] passim) argues for the existence of "proverb poems" in 25:2–27, 26:1–12, 26:17–28, and 27:23–27; and for a "proverb miscellany" in 27:1–22. G. Bryce (*Legacy*, 138–62) identifies a royal instruction in Prov 25:2–27.

There is evidence for the technique of composing poems from older proverbs in Egypt. This is implied by the title to the fragmentary text: "Beginning of the Educational Teaching according to Ancient Writings" (*HO*, pl. 88). This means that earlier writings were drawn upon to form this new Instruction. This title may belong to O. Petrie 11 (*HO*, pl. 1–1A); if not, it belongs to a very similar text, as the line following the title shows.

blame to father; "He who puts on his armor should not boast like one who takes it off" (1 Kgs 20:11) is a bellicose taunt.

Wisdom Literature is the work of literati, and it is *their* notion of wisdom we are reading. The lovely background picture the folk school derives from the proverbs—the gentle, egalitarian, village society based on finely tuned human relations—is to a degree accurate, not as a depiction but as an ideal. This is the ideal that the author-redactors of Proverbs—the king's men—*want* us to derive. It is a deliberate and programmatic construal of reality.

The image that the king's men have constructed for our edification is a society in a harmonious stasis operated by self-regulating mechanisms. The social order is presided over by the king, who is *ex officio* righteous and wise, even though individual rulers may be oppressive. The social order is guaranteed, never modified, by God. In this ideal world, crises are preventable by individual moderation and good sense. If they break out because of folly or venality, they may be resolved through decency and judiciousness. Laziness and folly cause poverty, though not all poverty comes from these defects. Some poverty just *is*, but it requires mercy and mitigation, not reform. This society needs no constitution, no Torah, no prophetic correctives. The rules are out there and need merely be learned, absorbed, and applied. I doubt that any society, village or urban, is truly this smooth and tidy. On the contrary, the prophetic perception of Israelite society, although itself a heavily ideological construction, must be weighed against the sages' picture.

The didactic nature of Proverbs justifies the assumption that the redactors' image of society was programmatic. In David Shapiro's apt characterization of Proverbs, it is an anthology of utopian, and, paradoxically, materialist idealizations.[41] This is not to reduce these idealizations to propaganda. The program does not seem to be insidious or cynical; it at least gives the impression of being the authors' own viewpoint, not a picture fabricated for public consumption. Nor does the image seem to be polemical, an ideology advanced against a contrary viewpoint.[42] But it *is* didactic; it is the way the compilers of the proverbs wished their readers to view the world and their own role within it.

For a comparable process of idealization through selective vision, consider the way Norman Rockwell promulgated a sentimentalized, heavily didactic ideal of white, middle-class, small-town America, with its family values and love for honest work and self-reliance, an America where tolerance means recognizing homogeneity beneath the surface rather than in accepting true variance. This not unworthy—but certainly subjective—vision was created not by distortion but by selection. It is not a vision imposed from above; farmers and small-town shopkeepers might share it as a flattering self-image and others

41. D. Shapiro, "Proverbs," *Congregation* (ed. David Rosenberg; New York, 1987) 324.
42. Fools are not an opposition group. Even they would publicly embrace the book's social values; they would simply assert (and believe) that *they* are not fools.

enjoy its sentiments. Any one of Rockwell's pictures could be a reality, but as a corpus they convey a message that is grossly idealized and didactic. This is not to say *bad*; ideals hold valid lessons and useful encouragement. But they are not a mirror of reality.

Perhaps the folk sayings in Proverbs reflect a desired self-image of village folk. But even if we could identify sayings with a village provenance, we would not know which kinds of sayings were excluded. Hence we cannot give an undistorted description even of the social *idealization* of folk wisdom, let alone of the social realities underlying it. The redactional process of memory, selection, addition, and subtraction has buried that stage beyond the reach of literary archaeology.

Learned clerks, at least some of them the king's men, were the membrane through which principles, sayings and coinages, folk and otherwise, were filtered. The central collections of Proverbs are their filtrate, an essentially homogeneous one. In the end, it is *their* work and *their* idea of wisdom that we are reading, and it is, not surprisingly, quite coherent.

The generations of readers who interpreted Proverbs as the wisdom of one man, Solomon, went too far, but they were going in the right direction.

A FORENSIC UNDERSTANDING OF THE
SPEECH FROM THE WHIRLWIND

Edward L. Greenstein

Prologue

THE ULTIMATE SENSE of the book of Job will remain elusive. This inevitability derives, in large part, from the commonly held view that the key to the book's understanding lies locked in the divine speeches from the whirlwind[1] and from the widespread conclusion that those speeches remain at best equivocal.[2] The God speeches have indeed been interpreted in antithetical ways, both as evidence of divine providence[3] and as evidence of divine indifference.[4] Any interpretation of the Lord's speeches must be based, as Hoffman has put it, not on what is said but on what is not.[5]

In the present study I am seeking to interpret the YHWH speeches within one of the book's literary frameworks, the lawsuit, in which Job challenges God's

Author's note: Preparation of this study has been assisted by the Maxwell Abbell Research Fund of the Jewish Theological Seminary of America. It was researched and written while I enjoyed the hospitality of the Institute of Jewish Studies, Hebrew University of Jerusalem, and was supported by fellowships from the National Endowment for the Humanities, the John Simon Guggenheim Memorial Foundation, and the Memorial Foundation for Jewish Culture. I am very grateful to all the above. I also thank Alice Bach of Stanford University for assistance in researching the Greek versions. An abridged version of this paper was presented at the 1994 Mid-Atlantic Regional Meeting of the Society of Biblical Literature.

1. See, e.g., James G. Williams, "Deciphering the Unspoken: The Theophany of Job," *HUCA* 49 (1978) 59–72, esp. 60.

2. See, e.g., Athalya Brenner, "God's Answer to Job," *VT* 31 (1981) 129.

3. See, e.g., Marvin H. Pope, *Job* (AB 15; Garden City, N.Y., 1965) lxxv–vi; Gerhard von Rad, *Wisdom in Israel* (trans. J. D. Martin; London, 1972) 225.

4. E.g., Walter Kaufmann, "Suffering and the Bible," *The Faith of a Heretic* (Garden City, N.Y., 1961) 165; Matitiahu Tsevat, *The Meaning of the Book of Job and Other Biblical Studies* (New York, 1980) 1–37.

5. Yair Hoffman, "Irony in the Book of Job," *TeᶜudaΡ* 2 (*Bible Studies: Y. M. Grintz in Memoriam*; ed. Benjamin Uffenheimer; 1982) 167 [Heb.]. Hoffman gives a concise summary of prevailing interpretations of the divine speeches on pp. 167–68.

justice toward him in particular and toward humanity in general (see esp. chaps. 21 and 24). My forensic reading of the speeches from the whirlwind will, like all other readings, necessarily be selective in its focus on particular passages, rhetorical modes, and verbal nuances. The whirlwind discourse, like the poetry that precedes it, is far too complex and ambiguous to be captured by a single line of interpretation. My forensic interpretation does, however, possess its own advantage, which I shall indicate in conclusion.

Job's Complaint

The poetic speeches of Job are laced with legal rhetoric and shaped to express the hero's mounting desire to meet his God in a court of law.[6] At first Job, like Jeremiah (12:1),[7] considers bringing charges of injustice against the deity. Jeremiah refrains from actually suing (ʾārîb) YHWH because in litigation with the deity, God, who is also supreme judge, 'would be the victor' (ṣaddîq). Similarly, Job, who has been advised by Eliphaz to lay his complaint before the divine magistrate (Job 5:8),[8] hesitates to press his case in the knowledge that a human being cannot win (yiṣdaq) a legal contest (rîb) against God (9:2–3).[9] Even if he were able to muster a case, he does not trust the deity to hear him out (9:14–17).[10] Moreover, Job is convinced that the deity would find him

6. Cf., e.g., B. Gemser, "The *RÎB-* or Controversy-Pattern in Hebrew Mentality," *Wisdom in Israel and in the Ancient Near East Presented to Professor Harold Henry Rowley* (VTSup 3; ed. M. Noth and D. W. Thomas; Leiden, 1955) 120–37, esp. 134–35; Heinz Richter, *Studien zu Hiob: Der Aufbau des Hiobbuches, dargestellt an den Gattungen des Rechtslebens* (Berlin, 1959); J. J. M. Roberts, "Job's Summons to Yahweh: The Exploitation of a Legal Metaphor," *ResQ* 16 (1973) 159–65; Norman C. Habel, *The Book of Job: A Commentary* (OTL; Philadelphia, 1985) 54–57; Sylvia H. Scholnick, *Lawsuit Drama in the Book of Job* (Ph.D. diss., Brandeis University, 1977); idem, "The Meaning of Mišpāṭ in the Book of Job," *JBL* 101 (1982) 521–29; idem, "Poetry in the Courtroom: Job 38–41," *Directions in Biblical Hebrew Poetry* (JSOTSup 40; ed. Elaine R. Follis; Sheffield, 1987) 185–204; Tsevat, *Meaning of Job* 5–8; Claus Westermann, *The Structure of the Book of Job: A Form-Critical Analysis* (trans. C. Muenchow; Philadelphia, 1981) 105; Bruce Zuckerman, *Job the Silent: A Study in Historical Counterpoint* (New York, 1991) 104–17.

7. See, e.g., Scholnick, *Lawsuit Drama*, 124–25. The book of Job would seem to be dependent literarily on the poetry of Jeremiah; in addition to the present instance, compare Job 3:3–26 and 10:18–19 with Jer 15:10 and 20:14–18; Job 6:15–21 with Jer 15:18; and Job 6:22–23 with Jer 15:10. For the relation of Job 3 to Jeremiah 20, see now: E. Greenstein, "The Loneliness of Job," in *Job in the Bible, Philosophy, and Art* (ed. Lea Mazor; Jerusalem, 1995) 43–53 [Heb.].

8. See S. M. Paul, "Unrecognized Biblical Legal Idioms in the Light of Comparative Akkadian Expressions," *RB* 86 (1979) 235–36.

9. For a list of works on the procedures and vocabulary of ancient Hebrew jurisprudence, as well as on *rîb*, see appendix A.

10. I would render Job 9:17 as follows: 'He would strike me on the head (lit., hair), and would multiply my wounds for no cause'. For *śēʿârâ/śaʿărâ* 'hair' see Job 4:15 and, for example, Lev 13:4, 1 Sam 14:45, 2 Sam 14:11, 1 Kgs 1:52. For a discussion of Job 9:17 and its symbolic meaning, see appendix B.

guilty even if he were in the right (9:20).[11] Contrary to what Bildad had asserted (8:3), Job does not believe that God would afford him a fair trial (9:30–31). Accordingly, he initially forgoes any attempt to vindicate himself juridically (9:28). He would venture such an effort "only were there an arbitrator" between his opponent and himself, some neutral party who would maintain due process and prevent God from overwhelming him with his awesomeness (9:33–34).[12] Only then would Job state his case without fear (9:35–10:1).[13]

Job steps up his hypothetical challenge to an actual one, however, apparently in reaction to the provocative words of Zophar (11:5–6). Zophar expresses his certainty that Job is suffering on account of some sin that he committed, and that were God to appear, he would reveal this sin to Job and thereby convince him of divine justice. Job reacts to Zophar's sadistic enthusiasm with characteristic irony. Mocking Zophar's pseudo-wisdom (chap. 12), Job goes on to mimic him and boldly to announce that he will sue the deity. Zophar had said, "Rather, if only God would state his case" (11:5a). Job echoes: "Rather, I will state my case to Shaddai" (13:3a). The juridical import of his pronouncement is made even clearer in the following clause: "I desire to litigate with God."[14]

Although interpreters typically understand Job's lawsuit as a "metaphor,"[15] it is figurative only if one defines the legal process as a purely human affair. In the book of Job, the human hero regards his litigation with God as altogether real; he pursues it deliberately at the highest personal risk (e.g., Job 13:13–14). Job literally goes through the stages of making a legal claim against another party, in this case, God. I will contend in this study that Yhwh's speeches from the whirlwind may be interpreted as the deity's response to the suit. In order to lay the foundations for the forensic interpretation of the whirlwind response, it will be necessary to spell out my understanding of certain earlier passages in some detail.

In ancient Near Eastern jurisprudence in general and in Israel in particular a litigation may begin when witnesses bring charges. Under such circumstances,

---

11. Reading *pî(y)w* 'his mouth', instead of *pî* 'my mouth'; see, e.g., Gerhard Fohrer, *Das Buch Hiob* (KAT; Gütersloh, 1963) 199; contrast D. J. A. Clines, *Job 1–20* (WBC; Waco, Tex., 1989) 218. That Job condemns himself is the argument of Eliphaz (Job 15:5–6), not Job.

12. Reading *lû*; see, e.g., Clines, *Job 1–20*; so already Samuel David Luzzatto, *S. D. Luzzatto's Commentaries on Jeremiah, Ezekiel, Proverbs and Job* (Lemberg, 1876) 201 [Heb.].

13. For *dibbēr* in the forensic sense of stating a case, see Scholnick, *Lawsuit Drama*, 215–27. For *ᶜāzab śîaḥ* in the forensic sense of preparing an argument, see Mitchell Dahood, "The Root עזב II in Job," *JBL* 78 (1959) 305.

14. For *hôkîaḥ* in the sense of 'litigate', see, for example, Gemser, "The RÎB- or Controversy-Pattern," 124–25 n. 4; I. Leo Seeligmann, "On the Terminology of Legal Procedures in the Lexicon of Biblical Hebrew," *Studies in Biblical Literature* (ed. A. Hurvitz, S. Japhet, and E. Tov; Jerusalem, 1992) 258–59 [Heb.].

15. So, e.g., Roberts, "Job's Summons"; Michael B. Dick, "The Legal Metaphor in Job 31," *CBQ* 41 (1979) 37–50; G. B. Caird, *The Language and Imagery of the Bible* (Philadelphia, 1980) 157–58; Habel, *Book of Job.*

witnesses serve the prosecutorial function.[16] Job, who will serve an indictment on the basis of his own testimony, summons his three companions not as a tribunal but as the requisite quorum of citizens that lends a transaction or procedure legal status.[17] In accordance with the rules of testimony in Exod 23:3, he instructs his companions to refrain from favoring the defendant and perjuring themselves on his behalf, since God, who must ironically act as judge, must, in line with the rules of adjudication in Exod 23:7, reject false testimony (Job 13:7–10). Job opens the proceedings with the conventional formula, "Hear ye!" (13:6 and cf. v. 17)[18] and declares his suit against God: "I charge him with his ways" (13:15b).[19] He summons the deity to join him in the litigation (v. 19a) and asks only that God respond to the charges and refrain from suppressing him through power and terror (v. 21). Respectfully, if not reverently, Job offers God the privilege of explaining himself first, that is, the privilege of formally initiating a complaint (v. 22). In the absence of a divine reply, Job continues by pressing his particular charges:

> How many are my crimes and sin?
> My sin and my transgression[20]—let me know (them)!
> Why do you hide your face,
> and count me as your enemy? . . .
> (Why) do you mark my feet with lime[21]
> so you can observe all of my tracks,
> and pursue my footsteps?
>
> (vv. 23–24, 27)

---

16. Cf., e.g., Gemser, "The *RÎB-* or Controversy-Pattern," 130 n. 1; Roland de Vaux, *Ancient Israel: Its Life and Institutions* (trans. J. McHugh; London, 1961) 156; Moshe Greenberg, "Witness," *IDB* 4.864; Hans J. Boecker, *Law and the Administration of Justice in the Old Testament and Ancient East* (trans. J. Maiser; Minneapolis, 1980) 38. For a similar situation in Mesopotamian jurisprudence, see, e.g., Johannes Renger, "Wrongdoing and Its Sanctions: On 'Criminal' and 'Civil' Law in the Old Babylonian Period," *The Treatment of Criminals in the Ancient Near East* (ed. Jack M. Sasson; Leiden, 1977) 73 with n. 21.

17. Compare the functions of the Hittites in Genesis 23 and the Bethlehemites in Ruth 4. Contrast, for example, Scholnick (*Lawsuit Drama*, 138–39), who regards the companions as a tribunal.

18. Cf., e.g., Frank M. Cross Jr., "The Council of Yahweh in Second Isaiah," *JNES* 12 (1953) 275 n. 3; Scholnick, *Lawsuit Drama*, 137.

19. Reading *darkô* 'his way' for *děrākay* 'my ways'; see Job 21:31 and compare, for example, N. H. Tur-Sinai, *The Book of Job: A New Commentary* (rev. ed.; Jerusalem, 1967) 225; Seeligmann, "On the Terminology of Legal Procedures," 258–59.

20. This is a formula indicating formal legal charges; see Gen 31:36 and cf. Charles Mabee, "Jacob and Laban: The Structure of Judicial Proceedings (Genesis XXXI 25–42)," *VT* 30 (1980) 192–207, esp. p. 203.

21. For an enumeration of the philological possibilities and for the basis of this rendering, see Clines, *Job 1–20*, 321–22.

Job bases his complaint on his earlier conclusions about the divine nature and the human condition (note especially chap. 7). God finds fault with human beings for simply being human—yet: "Even on such a one you train your eyes; and me you bring into litigation with you!" (14:3). Humans are so frail and ephemeral (14:1–2) that they cannot possibly deserve to be punished for the peccadiloes that are nothing more than the natural by-products of human nature (see the balance of chap. 14). This is Job's case. In subsequent responses to his critical companions, Job simply elaborates these charges. Because Job believes that the divine injustice to him is one that is common to all of humanity, Job serves the dual role of personal plaintiff and public prosecutor.

It is important for our interpretation of the God speeches in chaps. 38–41 to underscore the fact that Job rests his case on his own testimony. Job has introduced his intention to prosecute God by claiming to possess the requisite knowledge to pursue his action:

> Since my eye has seen all,
> my ear heard and gained understanding,
> What you know, I know, too;
> I (know) no less than you.
>
> (13:1–2)

From a forensic perspective, Job is here asserting his legal status as witness. The key biblical text that characterizes or defines what it is to be a witness is Lev 5:1. This verse condemns anyone who possesses testimony concerning a certain case and does not come forward when a proclamation calling for testimony is sounded.[22] According to this verse, a 'witness' ($^c\bar{e}d$) is someone who 'has seen' ($r\bar{a}^{\jmath}\hat{a}$) or 'had personal knowledge' ($y\bar{a}d\bar{a}^c$).

The same language is used to describe firsthand testimony in 1 Sam 24:8–22, where David invokes the deity to adjudicate between Saul and himself. David presents his contention in juridical terms by calling his case a *rîb* (v. 16 [15]). David has demonstrated to Saul that he has no intention of killing him, offering the shorn hem of Saul's robe as material evidence. He calls to Saul to 'see' this evidence and deduce from it ('see and know') that he is innocent (v. 12 [11]). David refers to Saul's witness to the testimony of the entire proceeding as sight ('your eyes have seen', v. 11 [10]) and to the divine magistrate's examination of the testimony as seeing ('he saw', v. 16 [15]). In Jer 29:23 YHWH describes his role as the accusing witness or prosecutor as *hayyōdēa^c* [Qere]

---

22. Cf. Baruch A. Levine, *Leviticus* (JPS Torah Commentary; Philadelphia, 1989) 26; Menahem Bula, *The Book of Leviticus* (Da^cat Miqra^ʾ; Jerusalem, 1991) 72–73 [Heb.]; Jacob Milgrom, *Leviticus 1–16* (AB 3; Garden City, N.Y., 1991) 292–94. Contrast Ze^ʾev W. Falk, *Hebrew Law in Biblical Times* (Jerusalem, 1964) 70; Martin Noth, *Leviticus: A Commentary* (OTL; London, 1965) 44.

wāʿēd 'the one who knows and bears witness'.[23] In addition to seeing and knowing, Job also claims to have 'heard' pertinent evidence (13:1).[24]

Job is fully aware that unless the deity formally recognizes the suit, it has no standing. Consequently, he presses for God to respond:

> I would lay my case before him,
> I would fill my mouth with accusations,
> That I might know the words he would answer me,
> That I might perceive what he would tell me .
>
> (23:4–5)

Seeing that God does not (yet) respond, Job adopts a legal tactic that would seem calculated to force his adversary's hand and induce him to appear in court. In order to appreciate its force, we must bear in mind that while Job takes the offensive tack of prosecuting the deity, he at the same time perceives himself as being prosecuted by God.[25] Accordingly, within his legal prosecution of God, Job seeks the bill of particulars on whose basis God is, to Job's mind, prosecuting him (for example, 13:23, quoted above, and 23:4–5, cited here).

Toward the end of his final speech, Job enumerates the many sins he has not committed (chap. 31). Beginning every few verses with the negative oath-particle ʾ*im*, Job swears to his innocence. This oath of innocence has often been taken to represent the last resort of a defendant to exculpate himself.[26] Comparison with the so-called Egyptian "Book of the Dead" would seem to reinforce such an interpretation.[27] The confession is said to be spoken "on reaching the Broad-Hall of the Two Justices, absolving [so-and-so] of every sin which

---

23. Cf., for example, Gemser, "The *RÎB*- or Controversy-Pattern," 124. Several commentators prefer to reconstruct the text, based on the Ketiv, as *hûʾ[?] yôdēaʿ*; for example, Ferdinand Hitzig, *Der Prophet Jeremia* (KHAT; 2d ed.; Leipzig, 1866) 226; Bernhard Duhm, *Das Buch Jeremia* (KHAT; Tübingen, 1901) 233; Arnold B. Ehrlich, *Randglossen zur hebräischen Bibel* (7 vols.; Leipzig, 1912) 4.316. Others dismiss the word, which is not reflected in the Greek, as a dittography; for example, A. W. Streame, *The Book of the Prophet Jeremiah Together with Lamentations* (Cambridge, 1913) 177; Robert P. Carroll, *The Book of Jeremiah* (OTL; London, 1986) 555; William L. Holladay, *Jeremiah 2* (Hermeneia; Minneapolis, 1989) 134. However, as Gemser indicates, the phrase 'knower and witness' would seem to reflect traditional usage. Compare the phrase *šībī mūdī ḫulqim* 'witnesses who know the lost article' in the Code of Hammurapi (law 9: lines 14–15, 25, 33–37; law 11: lines 61–63); cf. G. R. Driver and John C. Miles, *The Babylonian Laws* (2 vols.; Oxford, 1955) 2.17; and see their remarks in 1.154.

24. This may refer to the words of the apparition in Job 4:12–21, which gave his 'ear' a 'fright' (*šēmeṣ*). For the attribution of the speech to Job, see appendix C.

25. See, e.g., Dick, "Legal Metaphor," 40 n. 17.

26. Cf., e.g., Sheldon H. Blank, "An Effective Literary Device in Job XXXI," *JJS* 2 (1950–51) 105–7; Falk, *Hebrew Law*, 60, 64; Boecker, *Law and Administration*, 35.

27. Cf., e.g., William B. Stevenson, *The Poem of Job: A Literary Study with a New Translation* (London, 1947) 27; Michael B. Dick, "Job 31, the Oath of Innocence, and the Sage," *ZAW* 95 (1983) 45–48.

he has committed, and seeing the faces of the gods." [28] It is meant to enable the deceased to enter eternal life. The numerous protestations of innocence formulated therein have clear parallels in Job 29–31. Although many scholars emphasize that the Egyptian texts deal with cultic and ethical purity rather than legal innocence, which is the subject of Job, [29] the "Book of the Dead" uses an undeniably forensic framework. [30] For example, in approaching the "Two Justices" the deceased is to say, among other things: "I have come here to testify to justice and to bring the scales to their (proper) position in the cemetery." [31]

The specific function of Job's "negative confession" is, however, as Dick has shown, [32] not simply exculpatory. Job asks for an impartial magistrate to hear his case, a $\check{s}\bar{o}m\bar{e}a^c$ (Job 31:35; compare, for example, with Judg 11:10 and 2 Sam 15:3). [33] Job, who, as was said, understands himself to be the defendant in God's case, as well as the initiator of a countersuit against God, supports his request for an independent hearing by an oath declaring his own innocence. This practice follows Near Eastern custom. Dick cites, for example, an Assyrian text in which a magistrate requires a plaintiff to prove his case or drop it, because the defendant has come forward and sworn to his own innocence of the charges. [34] Dick further cites Mesopotamian legal records in which officials formally authorize an investigation of wrongdoing on the basis of a sworn complaint. [35] Such a practice was known in ancient Israel as well, as Dick has also shown. [36] The appeal of a wronged harvester is supported by the assertion that he can produce witnesses to his claim and by a personal oath of innocence. [37]

Job would therefore seem to have completed the necessary steps to bring the deity to trial. He presents a written complaint and calls on his co-litigant to present the bill of particulars that he has demanded (Job 31:35). If God fails to respond to the suit, he might, in accord with Near Eastern practice, lose by default. [38]

28. John A. Wilson (trans.), "The Protestation of Guiltlessness," *ANET*, 34a.

29. Cf., e.g., Robert Gordis, *The Book of God and Man* (Chicago, 1965) 64; Georg Fohrer, "The Righteous Man in Job 31," *Essays in Old Testament Ethics* (ed. James L. Crenshaw and J. T. Willis; New York, 1974) 10.

30. Cf., e.g., Stevenson, *Poem of Job*, 27; Nili Shupak, "A New Source for the Study of the Judiciary and Law of Ancient Egypt: 'The Tale of the Eloquent Peasant,'" *JNES* 51 (1992) 11.

31. Wilson, "Protestation," 36a.

32. Dick, "Legal Metaphor"; idem, "Job 31."

33. Cf. Scholnick, *Lawsuit Drama*, 188–201.

34. Dick, "Legal Metaphor," 42–43.

35. Ibid., 43.

36. Ibid., 43–44.

37. *KAI* no. 200, lines 10–12; see Dick, "The Legal Metaphor," 44 n. 32, for this most plausible interpretation.

38. Boecker, *Law and Administration*, 23; compare Fohrer, "Righteous Man," 5–6; James G. Williams, "Deciphering the Unspoken: The Theophany of Job," *HUCA* 49 (1978) 63–64; Westermann, *Structure of the Book of Job*, 105.

Yнwн's *Reply*

Yнwн does, of course, respond to the suit. And he does so in an extraordinarily belligerent fashion. This is evident even apart from the combative tenor of the questions he puts to Job. Most obviously, the divine challenge "Gird your loins like a man!" (38:3; 40:7) belongs to the militant ordeal of belt-wrestling[39] or perhaps more generally to preparation for battle.[40] They are literally fighting words. Less obviously, but just as clearly, Yнwн's appearance in a storm (38:1, 40:6) evokes the popular image of the storm-god warrior.[41] The deity himself highlights his martial persona when, in his first speech, he depicts the storehouses of snow as an arsenal (38:22–23). In line with this image, wind often serves a destructive purpose in biblical literature.[42] Yнwн, therefore, confronts Job in battle gear.

It may be understood that the deity's hostile demeanor has been provoked, though not without reason. Job ends his final speech (chaps. 29–31) in a subtly but discernibly aggressive tone. He has felt all along that God had been assaulting him.[43] He had imagined God as an archer, shooting poisoned arrows at him (6:4, 7:20, 16:12–13), as a swordsman spilling his innards on the ground (6:9, 16:13–14), and as a commander surrounding his tent with an entire military machine (19:11–12). He had felt as though God were treating him like the monster of chaos, God's arch enemy from primeval times (7:12). In 13:24 Job interprets his own name, *ʾiyyôb*, to mean *ʾôyēb* 'enemy' of God.[44]

---

39. Cyrus H. Gordon, *Ugaritic Literature* (Rome, 1949) 134; idem, "Belt-Wrestling in the Bible World," *HUCA* 23 (1950–51) 131–36 with plates I–IV; cf., e.g., Georg Fohrer, "Gottes Antwort aus dem Sturmwind (Hi 38–41)," *Studien zum Buche Hiob (1956–1979)* (2d ed.; BZAW 196; Berlin, 1983) 126–27.

40. E.g., Edwin M. Good, *In Turns of Tempest: A Reading of Job with a Translation* (Stanford, 1990) 341.

41. See, e.g., Fohrer, "Gottes Antwort," 124; see, in general, e.g., Leonard Greenspoon, "The Warrior God, or God, the Divine Warrior," *Religion and Politics in the Modern World* (ed. Peter H. Merkl and Ninian Smart; New York, 1983) 205–31; and, most recently, Marc Brettler, "Images of Yнwн the Warrior in Psalms," *Semeia* 61 (*Women, War, and Metaphor*; ed. Claudia V. Camp and Carole R. Fontaine; 1993) 135–65.

42. Cf. John Wright, "Spirit and Wilderness: The Interplay of Two Motifs within the Hebrew Bible as a Background to Mark 1:2–3," in *Perspectives on Language and Text: Essays and Poems in Honor of Francis I. Andersen's Sixtieth Birthday* (ed. Edgar W. Conrad and E. G. Newing; Winona Lake, Ind., 1987) 278–80.

43. Cf., e.g., Samuel Terrien, "The Book of Job," *Interpreter's Bible* (New York, 1954) vol. 3, cols. 875–1198, at 899; Norman C. Habel, "In Defense of God the Sage," *The Voice from the Whirlwind: Interpreting the Book of Job* (ed. Leo G. Perdue and W. Clark Gilpin; Nashville, 1992) 28–30.

44. Compare, for example, Ken Frieden, "Job's Encounter with the Adversary," *Response* 47 (1985) 3–15. This possibly paronomastic etymology has a sound linguistic basis. Hebrew *ʾiyyôb* 'Job' is ultimately derived from **ʾayyāb* 'enemy'; cf. Akkadian *ʾayyābu*.

In response to a perceived attack by God, Job insinuates into the language of his legal challenge a bellicose shade of meaning. After asking for a written catalog of the assumed divine charges against him, Job goes on to say (31:37):

> *mispar ṣĕ'āday 'aggîdennû / kĕmô nāgîd 'ăqārăbennû*
> A count of my steps would I affirm to him,
> Like a leader would I approach him.[45]

Three levels of meaning may be discerned in the verse.[46] On the surface, it simply states that Job would cooperate with God in tracking his every (mis)step (see 13:27, 14:16, 31:4); he would produce such potentially damning information without diffidence. On another level, Job formulates his language juridically. The verb *higgîd* has the forensic sense of delivering testimony;[47] and the verb *qārēb*, used intransitively as it is here,[48] is employed to indicate an approach to litigation.[49] On yet another level, the diction suggests an offensive action. The noun *nāgîd*, which presence in the verse is highlighted by the fact that it is peculiar in context and is reinforced by a wordplay with the verb *'aggîdennû* in the preceding colon,[50] has the primary sense of military commander.[51] Its apparent etymology, related to the preposition 'in front of, opposed to' connotes 'opponent'. The verb in the phrase *'ăqārăbennû* 'I shall approach him' is sometimes used of a military assault[52] and can hardly but evoke the noun *qĕrāb* 'battle'.[53] In light of such diction, the word *ṣĕ'āday* 'my steps' may also be understood in a military sense, indicating a march.[54] Interpreted on this third level, the verse means: 'I will announce to him the count of my marching-steps; like a commander will I attack him'.

God's belligerent response to Job may have been prompted, therefore, by the aggressive nature of Job's challenge. The series of rhetorical questions that

45. In analyzing the verse philologically, I follow the constraint advised, for example, by Eduard Dhorme (*A Commentary on the Book of Job* [trans. H. Knight; Nashville, 1984] 471) that the two pronominal suffixes *-ennû* be interpreted similarly. Moreover, since the entire verse focuses on what Job would do vis-à-vis God ('him'), I interpret the phrase *kĕmô nāgîd*, initially glossed here 'like a leader', to refer to Job.
46. Polysemy is a hallmark of Joban poetry; see, for example, David Yellin, "On Biblical Rhetoric," *Selected Writings* (2 vols.; Jerusalem, 1959) 2.103–6 [Heb.]; Yair Hoffman, "The Use of Equivocal Words in the First Speech of Eliphaz," *VT* 30 (1980) 114–18.
47. For example, Lev 5:1, 1 Sam 24:19, and Prov 29:24b; see, for example, Seeligmann, "On the Terminology of Legal Procedures," 254; and see further below, p. 253.
48. For the transitive use of *q-r-b* in the *Piel* conjugation, see, for example, Ezek 36:8.
49. For example, Isa 50:8, Mal 3:5; see Yair Hoffman, "The Root QRB as a Legal Term," *JNSL* 10 (1983) 67–73.
50. Cf., e.g., Habel, *Book of Job*, 439.
51. E.g., 1 Sam 9:16, 2 Sam 7:8–9, 2 Chr 32:21.
52. E.g., Deut 2:19, 37; 20:10.
53. E.g., 2 Sam 17:11, Zech 14:3, Ps 78:9, Job 38:23.
54. E.g., Judg 5:4, 2 Sam 5:24, Hab 3:12, Ps 68:8.

make up most of the divine speeches, however, may be taken to serve a distinctly juridical purpose. From 40:2, in which YHWH refers to Job as 'the one serving a suit (*rîb*) on Shaddai', 'the one indicting God', it is evident that God perceives Job to be prosecuting him. God is also aggravated by Job's resort to offense as a defense, clearing himself by condemning the deity (40:8).

Other scholars also have interpreted the speech from the whirlwind as the divine response to the indictment by Job.[55] Of the most recent, Scholnick and Zuckerman have provided the most specific forensic interpretations. For Scholnick, God replies to particular charges that Job has leveled, mainly that the deity has misappropriated Job's property (her interpretation of ^{c}-*š*-*q* in 10:3). I do not share her reading. For one thing, in order to argue her case she diminishes the importance of the best-known charges Job makes: that God governs the world unjustly and, indeed, perverts justice; and that God prosecutes him for trivial transgressions that are nothing more than the intractable consequence of being human.[56] For another thing, Scholnick must interpret the contents of the speeches from the storm in what strikes me as a highly forced manner.

Zuckerman maintains that YHWH seeks to rid Job of the notion that he can find justice by appealing to some other authority.[57] I, however, do not accept the interpretation of the Job speeches according to which the existence of another judge or advocate is suggested,[58] nor do I see any particular evidence for this specific sense in the God speeches.

In my reading, YHWH does not answer any charges. He will not submit to litigation in which he as supreme judge would be virtually compelled to show bias and acquit himself. Were he to do so, he would merely corroborate Job's accusations in chap. 9 that God would fail to give him a proper hearing and would dismiss his case without cause (see "Job's Complaint," pp. 242–47 above). Nor does YHWH need to dispel Job's alleged illusion that he can judge God.[59] Job has repeatedly acknowledged that he requires a nonpartisan arbitrator (for example, 9:33–34).

---

55. See above, n. 6.

56. Cf. Johannes Pedersen, *Israel: Its Life and Culture* (2 vols.; London, 1926–40) 1.366: "It is arbitrariness, lawlessness, of which Job accuses God. . . . What [Job] demands is therefore proper judgment, a settlement between him and God, through which it is proved whether he himself has vitiated his righteousness, or whether God has taken it by violence, so that Job may take it back."

57. Cf. John B. Curtis, "On Job's Witness in Heaven," *JBL* 102 (1983) 549–62.

58. Compare Job in 10:7: "You have knowledge that I am not in the wrong, and that there is no deliverer (*maṣṣîl*) from your hand (i.e., power)." The term *maṣṣîl* here is virtually synonymous with the more commonly employed term, *môšîa^c* 'forensic advocate'; see John Sawyer, "What was a *môšîa^c*?" *VT* 15 (1965) 475–86. The enigmatic 'redeemer' (*gō$^{\jmath}$ēl*) of Job 19:24 is probably the same divine advocate; cf. Norman C. Habel, "'Only the Jackal Is My Friend': On Friends and Redeemers in Job," *Int* 31 (1977) 235.

59. Cf., e.g., Gordis, *Book of God and Man*, 119–20; Zuckerman, *Job the Silent*, 116.

In the present forensic reading, YHWH displays a sophistication even greater than is shown by Job in chap. 31. Job may have had experience as a magistrate (Job 29:7–16), but he is no match for YHWH, whose expertise in law includes legislation (the Torah), litigation (as prosecutor in the covenant lawsuit and defender of the disadvantaged), and adjudication (as high judge, for example, Gen 18:25). The Lord adopts a tactic, the force of which is to throw Job's case out of court for cause. In bringing his suit, Job had presented himself as a witness to God's behavior (see "Job's Complaint," above). Job's entire case rests on the strength of this testimony. It is YHWH's obligation as magistrate and his right as a defendant to interrogate Job and cross-examine his deposition. In the speeches from the whirlwind YHWH fulfills this judicial duty and/or exercises his right as a defendant.

Deut 19:18 enjoins judges to examine the depositions of witnesses most carefully. In this verse the technical term for interrogation is the verb *dāraš*, but elsewhere the term most commonly used is *ḥāqar*.[60] It is a duty of the king as magistrate to investigate the validity of a legal case (*ḥāqar dābār*, Prov 25:2b), and Job himself, as a leading citizen, claims to have carried out this function (*rîb . . . ᵓehqěrēhû*, Job 29:16b).[61] Indeed, Job takes the cross-examination of witnesses for granted and—ironically, as it turns out—warns his companions that they ought to fear a divine interrogation (13:9).

The sequence of testimony followed by cross-examination is represented in Prov 18:17:

ṣaddîq hārîᵓšôn běrîbô / ûbāᵓ [Qere] rēᶜēhû waḥăqārô

The one in the right is first in his litigation;
Then his companion comes and cross-examines him.

This sequence is reflected, perhaps not accidentally, in the overall structure of the book of Job: the righteous Job (compare 1:1, 8), the one who sees himself in the right (*ṣaddîq*, 32:1), first makes his complaint (chap. 3), and his companions (*rēᶜê ᵓiyyôb*, 2:11) cross-examine him;[62] then, at the conclusion of Job's suit, the deity cross-examines Job.

---

60. Note that *ḥāqar* is used in conjunction with *dāraš* to denote a criminal investigation in Deut 13:15. Rashi, in his commentary on Deut 19:18, glosses *dāraš* 'to seek' with *bādaq* 'to examine' and *ḥāqar* 'to investigate', in accord with rabbinic usage; for example, *m. Sanh.* 3:6; 5:1, 2; and passim.

61. Compare, for example, Gemser, "The *RÎB*- or Controversy-Pattern," 124. The interrogation of witnesses is well attested in ancient Mesopotamian documents; see, for example, Arthur Ungnad, *Babylonian Letters of the Hammurapi Period* (Philadelphia, 1915), no. 7 (pp. 27–29 with plate V); see also the Old Babylonian document translated in A. Leo Oppenheim, *Letters from Mesopotamia* (Chicago, 1967) 88–91.

62. Elihu claims to have waited for the others to finish speaking: 'while you were examining the words' (*taḥqěrûn millîn*, 32:11). That 'to examine words' is an expression denoting the interrogation of witnesses is clear enough from a comparison to, for example, the Code of Hammurapi, law 9: 'The judges shall examine (lit., see) their (viz., the witnesses') words' (*dayyānū āwātišunu īmarū*).

While the interrogation of witnesses is thus well attested in the Hebrew Bible in theory, the act of interrogation is, apart from Job 38–41, not described therein in practice. It is depicted, however, in postbiblical Jewish literature. In the book of Susannah the false accusations of two witnesses (satirically, professional judges!) are thwarted by the young, divinely endowed Daniel, who confronts the assembly and asks: "Have you condemned a daughter of Israel without examination and without learning the facts?" (v. 49, RSV). The Greek term used to convey 'to examine', *anakrinein*, is used in the Septuagint to translate Hebrew *ḥāqar* at 1 Sam 20:12, where it means 'to investigate'.

Daniel examines the witnesses by separating them and interrogating each individually, a practice that is also enjoined in the Mishna (*m. Sanh.* 3:6, 5:3–4).[63] He asks each witness to identify the type of tree under which the alleged transgression was to have occurred (vv. 54, 58). The Mishna (*m. Sanh.* 5:1) delineates a series of seven questions concerning both the place and time of the alleged events. The most fundamental question that a witness is asked, according to *m. Sanh.* 3:6, concerns the basis of his knowledge: "Say: How do you know . . . ?" The Mishna seeks to ascertain whether or not a witness possesses firsthand knowledge of the matter to which he is to testify.

It is Job's claim to firsthand knowledge of the divine behavior that YHWH challenges. In his testimony, Job had claimed to have full knowledge (13:1–2; see pp. 245–46 above). The divine interrogation aims to confute this notion and invalidate Job's testimony. YHWH characterizes Job's deposition as "words without knowledge" (38:2, 42:3). Job is not one who brings truth to light, but one who 'darkens/conceals counsel'.[64] The term 'counsel' (*ʿēṣâ*), which ordinarily refers to wisdom or a plan in general, may well have a forensic nuance here,[65] as it does in 10:3[66] and probably in 29:21, as well. The resultant sense might then be paraphrased: Who is this who builds a case on ignorance?!

The battery of questions that YHWH puts to Job, especially in the first of the two long speeches (chaps. 38–39), seeks to demonstrate that Job has not been at a vantage point of time (creation) or place (the far reaches of the world) that would position him to bear witness to God's activities. Consider, for example, such questions as: "Where were you when I laid the foundations of the land?" (38:4); "Have you ever reached the sources of the sea? Walked around the recesses of the deep?" (38:16); "Have you ever reached the storerooms of the

---

63. For bibliography on the central role of cross-examination in the book of Susannah, see Seeligmann, "Terminology," 255 n. 37.

64. The verb 'to darken' (*heḥšîk*) has the sense of covering up, as it does in Ps 139:12. It may have been chosen to introduce Job 38 in order to anticipate the motif of the lights of creation; compare with Robert Alter, *The Art of Biblical Poetry* (New York, 1985) 97.

65. So, for example, Good, *In Turns of Tempest*, 348; contrast, for example, Veronika Kubina (*Die Gottesreden im Buche Hiob* [Freiburger, 1979] 122–23 with n. 41), who more typically interprets it as divine providence.

66. So, e.g., Clines, *Job 1–20*, 221.

snow? Or have you seen the storerooms of the hail?" (38:22). From the fact that Job has not been at the right time and place to witness God's activities, it follows that he lacks the detailed knowledge of the created world that is entailed by the balance of the questions.

Repeatedly YHWH interrogates Job concerning his (lack of) knowledge, harping on the verb 'to know' (*yāda^c*; 38:4, 5, 18, 21, 33; 39:1, 2).[67] One of these instances is cruelly sarcastic:

> You must know, for you were born then;
> The number of your days is many!

For good measure, YHWH throws in another use of *yāda^c*, the *Piel* verb 'to appoint', in 38:12.

Job, who had earlier affirmed his knowledge, had asked for the one bit of information he sorely lacked: the bill of particulars held against him. Job had demanded that God inform him of the charges he presumed were hanging over him (10:2, 13:23). Mockingly, YHWH turns the tables: "I shall ask you questions, and you will inform me (lit., let me know)" (38:3b, 40:7b, 42:4b).

The verb repeated in YHWH's mock call for information, *haggēd* 'Tell (if you know . . .)!' (38:4, 5), also sustains the juridical tenor of the proceedings. It will be recalled that *higgîd* 'to tell' is a technical term for delivering testimony. It is precisely the language we would expect of a litigant drawing testimony out of a witness in cross-examination. The verb *higgîd* is functionally equivalent to *^{x}ĕmōr* 'Say!' in *m. Sanh.* 3:6 and may well lie behind the Greek *eipein*, used in Susannah 51: "Now then, if you really saw her, *tell* me this!" Although this verb does not ordinarily translate *higgîd* in the Septuagint, it does render *higgîd* at Isa 41:22 and Job 15:18. In any event, the forensic nuance of *higgîd* is manifest in Job 38.

Job acknowledges that from a juridical standpoint, God has won.[68] Job is indeed an incompetent witness. He admits that he has nothing to reply and signifies the propriety of his silence by placing his hand over his mouth (40:4; cf. 21:5). In response to YHWH's second speech, which deals more pointedly with divine power, Job confesses his incompetence explicitly. More precisely, he acknowledges what he thought he knew but does not; and what he thought he knew and does in fact know. What he did not know are the specific, divinely delineated areas of esoteric lore:

---

67. That knowledge (of some kind) is the key issue in the God speeches has been suggested by other interpreters; see, for example, Nahum N. Glatzer, "Introduction: A Study of Job," *The Dimensions of Job: A Study and Selected Readings* (ed. Glatzer; New York, 1969) 1–48, esp. at 7; and recently, John T. Wilcox, *The Bitterness of Job: A Philosophical Reading* (Ann Arbor, 1989) 122–28, 173–88.

68. Hence, in my interpretation Job does not retract his suit, as Scholnick ("Meaning of Mišpaṭ," 521), following Richter (*Studien zu Hiob*, 126), suggests. Job has lost his case because his testimony could not stand up under interrogation.

> Indeed, I have testified without understanding,
> Things far beyond me without knowledge (42:3).

What he did know, and what has been reiterated in no uncertain terms before his very eyes (42:5), is that God's knowledge is incomparable and his power boundless:

> I know that you are able to do all,
> And that no scheme of yours can be blocked (42:2).

The confession of this knowledge in no way evinces admiration for the deity and may possibly suggest the very opposite.[69] Verse 2b (*wĕlō⁾ yibbāṣēr mim-mĕkā mĕzimmâ*) is an almost verbatim quotation of Gen 11:6b, the words YHWH uses to express contempt for the builders of Babel (*wĕ⁽attâ lō⁾ yibbāṣēr mēhem kōl ⁾ăšer yāzĕmû la⁽ăśôt* 'And now there will be no blocking them in all they have schemed to do').[70] Job may not be satisfied with God's answer. But he has been shown that even in the forensic forum, the only recourse he thought he might have, the divine contender can defeat him.

That the purpose of YHWH's speeches, and the first in particular, is to demonstrate Job's incompetence as a witness can be further supported form-critically. The litigious aspect of the discourse shares many features with the prophetic lawsuit, and numerous parallels may be drawn with the disputational sections of so-called Second Isaiah[71] and Job 38–41.[72] The most specific Near Eastern parallel to the rhetoric of the divine speeches in Job is the parallel afforded by Papyrus Anastasi I, the so-called "Satirical Letter."[73] In this literary text, a favorite among Egyptian scribes, the scribe Amenemopet responds to a letter from a royal scribe named Hori, who had written his colleague "to instruct [him], like a friend teaching one greater than himself. . . ." Hori, in a manner reminiscent of Job, allows that he is "not in dread before" Amenemopet, despite his colleague's apparent attempt to intimidate him.[74]

---

69. It is commonly held that Job 42:6 expresses Job's acceptance of the divine lesson in chaps. 38–41; see, however, John B. Curtis, "On Job's Response to Yahweh," *JBL* 98 (1979) 497–511.

70. For *mĕzimmâ* as a divine plan, see Jer 23:20; for the comparison in general, compare, for example, Tur-Sinai, *Book of Job*, 577.

71. See Ludwig Köhler, *Deuterojesaja (Jesaja 40–55) stilkritisch untersucht* (BZAW 37; Giessen, 1923) 110–20.

72. E.g., Isa 40:12–18, 21, 25–28; 41:2–3, 21–23; 42:21–23; 42:23–24; 43:9–10; 48:14, 16; cf., e.g., Kubina, *Die Gottesreden im Buche Hiob*, 137. Note also the similarities of Isa 40:27 to Job 3:20 and of Isa 41:21–23 to Job 31:37.

73. John A. Wilson (trans.), "A Satirical Letter," *ANET*, 475–79; cf. Gerhard von Rad, "Job XXXVIII and Ancient Egyptian Wisdom," *Studies in Ancient Israelite Wisdom* (ed. James L. Crenshaw; New York, 1976) 274; Fohrer, "Gottes Antwort," 128. Obviously, the papyrus has a scholastic, not a forensic, setting. I am comparing it, however, for its purpose in exposing a rival's incompetence.

74. Wilson, "A Satirical Letter," 475b.

Amenemopet, in turn, refers to Hori sarcastically, saying, "there is nothing which he does not know,"[75] a remark strongly parallel to Yhwh's ironic speech to Job. Amenemopet, however, unlike Yhwh, explains to his colleague the purpose of the interrogation through which he puts him; he seeks to test his rival's mettle:

> Let us see what thy hand can do. I shall explain for thee the nature of a *mahir* (i.e., expert scribe)[76] and let thee see what he has done.[77]

The speaker continues by enumerating the many places his colleague has not been, the many phenomena he has not seen, the many things he cannot do. He frequently formulates his challenge in the sort of sarcastic questions that typify Yhwh's discourse to Job. Compare the following characteristic excerpt:

> Thou hast not gone to the land of Hatti, thou hast not seen the land of Upi. . . . On which side of it is the city of Aleppo? What is its stream like?[78]

These questions, like Yhwh's to Job, presuppose that the subject of the interrogation lacks the requisite experience that would enable him to answer them. They are purely rhetorical, in short, a put-down.

The Egyptian scribe endeavors to prove his colleague's incompetence and his own superiority. Yhwh also, if the comparison holds, seeks to prove his contender's incompetence—as a litigant with God, and a plaintiff at that. Job's relative ignorance disqualifies him from bearing witness against the deity, whom he had deigned to call 'the man of my suit', a co-litigant, a peer under subpoena (31:35). Amenemopet closes his letter on a defiant, triumphant note:

> Now how will this end? Should I withdraw? Behold, I have arrived! Submit thou![79]

The upshot of Yhwh's speeches is hardly different.

Epilogue

As I said at the outset, the present reading has of necessity interpreted the Lord's words from the whirlwind within a specific literary framework, paying special attention to the forms of discourse that belong to the designated pattern. The forensic interpretation nevertheless succeeds more than some others in handling one of the book's profoundest perplexities. How is it that, after overwhelming Job, or worse, in the speeches from the whirlwind, God can

---

75. Ibid., 475a.
76. A West Semitic loanword, as has been widely noted; compare Hebrew *sôpēr māhîr* 'skilled scribe' (Ps 45:2, Ezra 7:6).
77. Wilson, "Satirical Letter," 477a.
78. Ibid.
79. Ibid., 478b.

still approve of Job's discourse in 42:7? The juridical angle provides a solution. Y_HWH's demonstration of Job's incompetence to bear witness, and consequently to prosecute God, is a matter of legal form, not substance. In disqualifying Job's status as a witness, Y_HWH implies no quarrel with the content of Job's charges. Job had chosen to present his charges in a legal forum. God undermined Job's standing in that forum without in any way responding to the charges themselves. The answer to Job, if there is one, has not been rendered.

Appendix A: Ancient Hebrew Jurisprudence

For the procedures and vocabulary of ancient Hebrew jurisprudence, see, for example:

Johannes Pedersen, *Israel: Its Life and Culture* (2 vols.; London, 1926–40) 406–10.

Ludwig Köhler, *Deuterojesaja (Jesaja 40–55) stilkritisch undersucht* (BZAW 37; Giessen, 1923) 110–20.

Idem, "Justice in the Gate," *Hebrew Man* (trans. P. R. Ackroyd; London, 1956) 149–75.

B. Gemser, "The *RÎB*- or Controversy-Pattern in Hebrew Mentality," *Wisdom in Israel and in the Ancient Near East Presented to Professor Harold Henry Rowley* (VTSup 3; ed. M. Noth and D. W. Thomas; Leiden, 1955) 120–37.

Roland de Vaux, *Ancient Israel: Its Life and Institutions* (trans. J. McHugh; London, 1961) 143–63.

Ze'ev W. Falk, *Hebrew Law in Biblical Times* (Jerusalem, 1964).

Donald A. McKenzie, "Judicial Procedure at the Town Gate," *VT* 14 (1964) 100–104.

J. J. M. Roberts, "Job's Summons to Yahweh: The Exploitation of a Legal Metaphor," *ResQ* 16 (1973) 159–65.

S. Scholnick, *Lawsuit Drama in the Book of Job* (Ph.D. diss., Brandeis University, 1977).

Hans J. Boecker, *Law and the Administration of Justice in the Old Testament and Ancient East* (trans. J. Maiser; Minneapolis, 1980).

Charles Mabee, "Jacob and Laban: The Structure of Judicial Proceedings (Genesis XXXI 25–42)," *VT* 30 (1980) 192–207.

I. Leo Seeligmann, "On the Terminology of Legal Procedures in the Lexicon of Biblical Hebrew," *Studies in Biblical Literature* (ed. Avi Hurvitz, S. Japhet, and E. Tov; Jerusalem, 1992) 245–68 [Heb.].

On the *rîb* in particular, see also, for example:

Herbert B. Huffmon, "The Covenant Lawsuit in the Prophets," *JBL* 78 (1959) 285–95.

Julien Harvey, *Le plaidoyer prophétique contre Israël après la rupture de l'alliance* (Bruges, 1967).

James Limburg, "The Root ריב and the Prophetic Lawsuit Speeches," *JBL* 88 (1969) 291–304.

Marjorie O'Rourke Boyle, "The Covenant Lawsuit of the Prophet Amos: III 1–IV 13," *VT* 21 (1971) 338–62.

Kirsten Nielsen, *Yahweh as Prosecutor and Judge: An Investigation of the Prophetic Lawsuit (Rib-Pattern)* (JSOTSup 9; Sheffield, 1978).

Appendix B: Translation of Job 9:17

I would render Job 9:17 as follows: 'He would strike me on the head (lit., hair), and would multiply my wounds for no cause'. For *śaᶜărâ* 'hair', see Job 4:15 and, for example, Lev 13:4, 1 Sam 14:45, 2 Sam 14:11, 1 Kgs 1:52. Clines also interprets *śĕᶜārâ* as 'hair' but only because he construes it in "synonymous" parallelism with *bĕḥinnām* 'for nothing' (David J. A. Clines, *Job 1–20* [WBC; Waco, Texas, 1989] 218); hence, he translates 'for a trifle'. Others interpret *śĕᶜārâ* here as 'storm, tempest'; for example, S. R. Driver and G. B. Gray, *A Critical and Exegetical Commentary on the Book of Job* (ICC; Edinburgh, 1921) 91; M. H. Pope, *Job* (AB 15; Garden City, N.Y., 1965) 68; Amos Hakham, *The Book of Job* (Daᶜat Miqraʾ; Jerusalem, 1984) 72 [Heb.]. However, although the homonymous word for 'storm' is written *śᶜrh* in Nah 1:3 and the verb 'to blow by storm' is spelled *śᶜr* in Job 27:21, it is noteworthy that in Job 38:1 and 40:6 'storm' is written with *samek*, not *śin*. Once God (in the end) speaks to Job from the storm, it is possible to reinterpret Job 9:17 in retrospect and render it 'He would strike me in a storm', understanding it as a premonition of what is to come; compare, for example, James G. Williams, "'You Have Not Spoken Truth of Me': Mystery and Irony in Job," *ZAW* 83 (1971) 245. For seeing the same wordplay in *śĕᶜārâ* 'storm' in Job 38:1, see, for example, Moshe Greenberg, "Reflections on Job's Theology," *The Book of Job: A New Translation according to the Traditional Hebrew Text* (Philadelphia, 1980) xix.

Compared to ancient Near Eastern evidence, Job 9:17 would appear to refer to a symbolic gesture by which a legal complaint is rejected. In seventeenth-century Alalakh, for example, King Yarimlim of Yamḫad is asked to smite the head of a woman whose claim against the king is rejected, and to do so in the presence of witnesses (*qaqqada maḫāṣu* in AT 11, lines 14, 20–21); for discussion and bibliography, see Donald J. Wiseman, *The Alalakh Tablets* (Occasional Publications of the British Institute of Archaeology at Ankara 2; London, 1953) 38; idem, "Alalakh," in *Archaeology and Old Testament Study* (ed. D. W. Thomas; Oxford, 1967) 128 with 134 n. 49. One may also compare the following difficult line in the commentary to *Ludlul bel nēmeqi*, line m: *muttutu ammašid abbuttu appašir* 'I was struck on the forehead, my slavemark removed'

(W. G. Lambert, *Babylonian Wisdom Literature* [Oxford, 1960] 54; but read and translated according to CAD M 352a; and Benjamin R. Foster, *Before the Muses* [2 vols.; Bethesda, 1993] 322). In this instance, the gesture would seem to symbolize the dismissal of charges.

Wiseman sees a likely connection in Ps 141:5. The verse is difficult, particularly on account of its obscure third clause. I would follow Qimḥi and Hakham and render the first two clauses: 'Were a person in the right to smite me—it would be a kindness; were such a one to charge me—it would be oil for the head (i.e., a beneficence)': David Qimḥi, *The Complete Commentary on Psalms* (ed. A. Darom; Jerusalem, 1967) 106 [Heb.]; Amos Hakham, *The Book of Psalms* (Daᶜat Miqraɔ; 2 vols.; Jerusalem, 1981) 547 [Heb.].

Appendix C: The Attribution of Job 4:12–21

As noted above in the body of the paper, in 13:1 Job claims to have 'heard' pertinent evidence. This may refer to the words of the apparition in Job 4:12–21 that gave his 'ear' a 'fright' (*šēmeṣ*). For the attribution of this speech to Job rather than Eliphaz, as it is in the received text, see N. H. Tur-Sinai, *The Book of Job: A New Commentary* (rev. ed.; Jerusalem, 1967) 88–91; H. L. Ginsberg, "Job the Patient and Job the Impatient," *Congress Volume, Rome, 1968* (VTSup 17; Leiden, 1969) 98–107; cf. Gary V. Smith, "Job IV 12–21: Is It Eliphaz's Vision?" *VT* 40 (1990) 453–63. (Ginsberg unnecessarily attaches v. 21 to Eliphaz's speech, following 5:5; see p. 96.) Among the various arguments that Job 4:12–21 resumes Job's speech in chap. 3, the one that is decisive is that in 15:13 Eliphaz introduces a variant of 4:17–21 as the 'words' of Job, the words that are to Eliphaz no less than blasphemy. (On criteria for identifying quotations in biblical discourse, see Michael V. Fox, "The Identification of Quotations in Biblical Literature," *ZAW* 92 [1980] 416–31.) Bildad also repeats these to him in 25:4–6, but this chapter is obviously no more than a torso of the original text. As Ginsberg observes, that Eliphaz is in chap. 15 quoting, or paraphrasing, an earlier speech is evident in the fact that in 15:16 the possessive suffixes otherwise have no antecedent.

In addition to the arguments adduced by Tur-Sinai and Ginsberg, one may note that when one removes 4:12–21 to form the conclusion of Job's first speech, a beautiful *inclusio* appears. The complaint begins, "Perish the day . . . !" (3:3), and it would nearly end: ". . . they perish forever" (4:20). Comparative evidence also supports the attribution of 4:12–21 to Job. In one of the closest Near Eastern parallels to Job, the Babylonian *Ludlul bel nēmeqi*, it is the sufferer who sees a series of apparitions (tablet III, lines 9ff.). Job, of course, is the one who in the book of his name complains of frightening dreams (7:13–14). (On the similarities between Job's initial complaint and Ludlul, compare, for example, Norman H. Snaith, *The Book of Job: Its Origin and Purpose* [London, 1968], esp. p. 26.)

CHRONICLES AND THE PRIESTLY TORAH

Rolf Rendtorff

THE CHRONICLER SEVERAL TIMES RECORDS cultic events and activities. In a number of cases he does so on the basis of his source or *Vorlage*; in other cases he formulates his texts himself. In order to learn something about the Chronicler's own ideas and concepts of cultic matters, it would be interesting to compare texts of both types, those with parallels and those without. Related to this is the question of which sources the Chronicler uses for cultic matters; in other words, how does he relate to the different texts of the Pentateuch.

But first, a warning. I believe we should not think too strictly in terms of literary dependence. I imagine that persons like the authors of the books of Chronicles knew a great deal about their people's national and religious tradition without having constantly to consult written documents. In some cases, of course, they used written material; in others, they might have drawn from their own knowledge gained through experience and education, for authors of texts like Chronicles must have had an excellent education. Hence, in every case, we should seek to identify the authors' sources from among the texts that are extant; if we cannot, we might then ask how we could interpret the tradition behind these utterances.

I do not believe that the books of Chronicles were written or composed by a single author. But because this question does not bear on my present concern, to simplify matters I will use the singular. Also for simplicity's sake I will use the term *Priestly Texts* to refer to the Priestly layers of the Pentateuch, whether P or H.

I begin by comparing two texts in the books of Chronicles where the author speaks about sacrifices: one text for which the author had a source in the book of Kings, the other where he had none. The first deals with Solomon's

Author's note: This is a revised version of a paper read at the 1992 Annual Meeting of the Society of Biblical Literature in San Francisco.

sacrifices in the recently established temple (2 Chronicles 8), the other one with Hezekiah's cultic reform (2 Chronicles 29–31). This comparison will reveal some relevant features of the Chronicler's use of Pentateuchal texts.

For the report on Solomon's regular cult in the just-completed temple in 2 Chr 8:12ff. we have a source in 1 Kgs 9:25. One difference between these two texts is visible at first glance; in 1 Kings there is only one verse, but in 2 Chronicles 8 there are five. The greater part of the addendum refers to the functions of the Levites, which I will leave aside for the moment. I want to concentrate on the sacrifices.

The text in 1 Kings begins: "Three times a year Solomon offered *ʿōlôt* and *šĕlāmîm* upon the altar he had built for the Lord." The Chronicler takes up this text, but he makes some substantial changes. First, he begins by saying in a more general way that Solomon offered *ʿōlôt* on the altar he had built. In this first sentence he does not speak about specific occasions, nor does he mention the *šĕlāmîm* (to deal with the latter point unfortunately would go beyond the scope of this paper).

Then the author continues to specify the occasions for sacrifices. Again, he begins with a more general statement: Solomon offered 'what was due for each day' (*dĕbar-yôm bĕyôm*) and he did it *kĕmiṣwat mōšeh* 'according to the commandment of Moses'. The latter expression looks like a reference to a written collection of *miṣwôt*, but the formulation *miṣwat mōšeh* is unique in the Hebrew Bible and so does not help identify the reference. Then the Chronicler continues, saying, 'for the sabbaths and the new moons and the festivals' (*laššab-bātôt wĕlehŏdāšîm wĕlammôʿădôt*). This formula is found several times in Chronicles[1] and also in Nehemiah (10:34); except for 2 Chronicles 8, the formula always has *môʿădîm*, not *môʿădôt*. The formula seems specifically to express the Chronicler's idea of the regular sacrificial cult.[2] We find it also in the report of Hezekiah's reform in 2 Chr 31:3. But in 2 Chronicles 8, it is most interesting that the Chronicler continues quoting his source by saying "three times a year." Thus he combines his own formula, "for the sabbaths, the new moon, and the festivals," with the quotation from his source, "three times a year."

This puts the Chronicler in somewhat of a dilemma. The term *môʿădîm* is also used in the Priestly cultic calendars in the Pentateuch in Leviticus 23 and Numbers 28–29. These calendars, however, do not limit the feasts to a triad arrangement; they recognize more than three feasts, and the number three is not mentioned. The Chronicler seems to feel that it is necessary to explain which triad he means, and therefore he adds *bĕḥag hammaṣṣôt ûbĕḥag haššābuʿôt ûbĕḥag hassukkôt* 'at the Festival of Unleavened Bread and at the Festival of Weeks and at the festival of Booths'. Obviously these three feasts are what is meant in 1 Kings, too, because the formula *šālôš pĕʿāmîm baššānâ* is regularly

---

1. 1 Chr 23:31; 2 Chr 2:3, 8:13, 31:3.
2. Similar formulations are found in Ezek 45:17; 46:3, 9. The combination of these three expressions we find also in Isa 1:13–14, arranged in two pairs: *ḥōdeš wĕšabbāt* (v. 13) and *ḥod-šêkem ûmôʿădêkem* (v. 14).

used for this triad. These three ancient feasts are mentioned by different names in the Hebrew Bible. The naming here is the same as in Deut 16:16—the Festival of Unleavened Bread, the Festival of Weeks, and the Festival of Booths. The names for these three annual feasts appear somewhat differently in the lists of feasts in Exodus 23 and 34. This shows that the Chronicler is quoting one version of the tradition as it has been transmitted by Deuteronomy. This is not to say that he is citing Deuteronomy as a written document. It is also possible that he is just quoting from the tradition he is familiar with.

Before we continue to reflect on this alternative, let us look at the other text in question, the story about the cultic reform of King Hezekiah in 2 Chronicles 29–31. Here we find a brief remark about the sacrifices for which the king paid from his own budget (31:3). The text speaks only about *ʿōlôt*: first the daily ones, in the morning and in the evening; then follows the formula *laššabbātôt wĕleḥŏdāšîm wĕlammôʿădîm* 'for the sabbaths and the new moons and the appointed times', without any further explanation. This can be read as being in full accordance with the Priestly calendar of sacrifices in Numbers 28–29. This text begins with the daily offerings (28:3–8). Next come the offerings on the Sabbath (28:9–10), then those on the new moon (28:11–15), and finally those on the rest of the festivals. In 2 Chronicles 31 there is no reference either to the traditional triad or to specific ones that would define the number of *môʿădîm* as in 2 Chronicles 8. Instead we have the more developed list of feasts, including Pesaḥ (28:16–25), the Festival of Weeks (28:26–31), and the series of three feast days in the seventh month, whose names are not explicitly mentioned: the new moon of the seventh month, later called Rosh Hashana (29:1–6); the tenth day of the seventh month, elsewhere called the Day of Atonement (29:7–11); and finally the series of eight days of the festival elsewhere called Sukkot (29:12–38). At the end of the whole calendar, the term *môʿădîm* is used in the final subscription: *ʾēlleh taʿăśû l-YHWH bĕmôʿădêkem* 'these shall you perform for the Lord at your appointed festivals' (29:39). One could conclude that in this case, where the Chronicler was free to choose his own formulation, he expressed things in accordance with the Priestly sacrificial calendar.

But there are discrepancies among the Priestly calendars as well. Numbers 28–29 seems to represent the most developed stage of the cultic calendar. The word *môʿădîm* is only used once in the final paragraph. Leviticus 23 is obviously much less uniform. The expression *môʿădîm* we find several times, in the introduction as well as in the final remarks. In the introduction it is surprising to find it in two places. First at the very beginning in v. 2, God says to Moses:

> *dabbēr ʾel bĕnê yiśrāʾēl wĕʾāmartā ʾălēhem môʿădê Yhwh ʾăšer tiqrĕʾû ʾōtām miqrāʾê qōdeš ʾēlleh hēm môʿădāy.*

Here we find the word *môʿădîm* twice, seemingly as an introductory term for all the following events. Then follows a paragraph on the sabbath (v. 3), after which the text continues in v. 4:

ᵓēlleh môᶜădê Yʜwʜ *miqrāᵓê qōdeš ᵓăšer tiqrĕᵓû ᵓōtām bĕmôᶜădām.*

Here we have the word *môᶜădîm* a second time in a special introduction to the chapter on feasts that are called *môᶜădîm* in a more specific sense. Obviously there is some diachronic reason for this double introduction, as we will see later.

After the second introduction, the first festival mentioned is the combined feast of Pesaḥ and Unleavened Bread. The latter is explicitly named *ḥag hammaṣṣôt*. So we are in accordance with the explanation in 2 Chronicles 8 where the list of the three main feasts begins with *ḥag hammaṣṣôt*. In Leviticus 23, sacrifices are mentioned as well, but in a nonspecific way, just by the term *ᵓiš-šeh*, which does not mean 'offerings by fire' but 'gift', as we now know from the Ugaritic.[3]

In Leviticus 23 there follows a paragraph (vv. 9–14) on the bringing of the firstfruits that is not a feast with a fixed time and therefore not a *môᶜēd*. Next is the Festival of Weeks (vv. 15–21). While the name *šābûᶜôt* does not appear, the description speaks of the seven weeks that are to be counted off making the identification clear. The bringing of the *ᶜōlâ* is explicitly mentioned in v. 18, together with other sacrifices. This is in accordance with the list of feasts in 2 Chronicles 8 as well.

Next there is a doublet within Leviticus 23. First we have the same series of three feast days to be celebrated in the seventh month as in Numbers 28: the first day of the month (vv. 23–25), the Day of Atonement (vv. 26–32), and finally the Festival of Sukkot for eight days (vv. 33–36). But at the end of the chapter the Festival of Sukkot is mentioned a second time in another special paragraph that adds more details (vv. 39–43). This double mention of Sukkot goes together with a double subscription in vv. 37–38 and 44, one of them before, the other after the second paragraph on Sukkot, with both of them using the term *mōᶜădîm*. Whatever the diachronic reasons for this doubling might be, it shows the particular role of the Feast of Sukkot independently of the series of the high festivals in the seventh month. At the same time it shows a specific relevance of the term *mōᶜădîm*.

Thus in the calendar of festivals in Leviticus 23, we can determine two layers of tradition with regard to the number and sequence of feasts. One of them can be seen to be in accordance with the triad of festivals named in 2 Chronicles 8. This means that the Chronicler refers to a tradition that is still recognizable in Leviticus 23 but does not represent the last stage of literary development in the calendar. The last stage in Leviticus 23 is close to Numbers 28–29.

The comparison of the two texts in Chronicles shows a difference that clearly depends on the question of whether or not the Chronicler had a source text. In the second case, 2 Chronicles 31 where he had none, his list of occa-

---

3. Compare my commentary, *Leviticus* (BKAT 3/1; Neukirchen-Vluyn, 1985) 63–65; and J. Milgrom, *Leviticus 1–16* (AB 3; New York, 1991) 161–62.

sions for sacrifices is in accordance with the most developed stage of the Priestly sacrificial calendar as found in Numbers 28–29. In the first case, 2 Chronicles 8, however, he follows his source text in speaking about three feasts a year. The question arises as to why he did not leave this aside as he often does elsewhere. Perhaps he could not; perhaps he did not because it was a commonly known tradition that Solomon offered three times a year. Besides, the formula "three times a year" appears three times in non-Priestly texts (which is to say, earlier texts in the Pentateuch), so it must have been very well known to the Chronicler's readership. But why does he go beyond his source, naming the three feasts, statements that are not in accordance with the final stage in the Priestly texts? Several answers are possible. First, he may be citing Deut 16:16 as his authoritative source. Second, he may suspect that his readers did not know exactly which festivals are meant. Third, he may feel this to be in accordance with the contemporary cultic tradition represented in the earlier layer within Leviticus 23. Perhaps other answers are possible. My concern is to point out the difference in the Chronicler's relations to the Priestly texts depending on whether he had a source text or not.

Let us return to the story of Hezekiah's cultic reform. In 2 Chronicles 29, after the cleaning of the temple, a great celebration of sacrifices takes place. According to v. 24 it comprises *ʿôlâ* and *ḥaṭṭāʾt*. In v. 21 the animals are specified: first a group of seven bulls, seven rams, and seven lambs, which obviously are meant for *ʿôlôt*, even if the word itself is not used in this verse. For the last group of seven male goats, it is explicitly said that they are intended for *ḥaṭṭāʾt*. Because the text speaks about an ad hoc celebration rather than a regular feast, we cannot compare this list of animals with any particular Priestly text. But nowhere else in the Hebrew Bible do we find a list of four times seven animals. Seven lambs are mentioned several times in Numbers 28–29; seven bulls are mentioned only once in the descending number of bulls at the seventh day of Sukkot in Num 29:32. The Balaam story (Numbers 23) and Job 42:8 both include seven bulls and seven rams. Seven rams are mentioned as an illegal presentation to the priests in 2 Chr 13:9. So this combination of four groups of seven animals seems to be a product of the Chronicler's imagination.

The same is true for the number of seven male goats, which we find nowhere else in the Hebrew Bible. The *ḥaṭṭāʾt* usually requires but one goat, and only on the Day of Atonement (Leviticus 16) are there two. The elders of the tribes bring twelve (Num 7:87), as do the returnees with Ezra (Ezra 8:35). But a reference to seven male goats is unique. Furthermore, the Chronicler is inconsistent in his terminology. For the male goat he first uses the word *ṣāpîr* (2 Chr 29:21), which is never used in Priestly texts (it also appears in Ezra 8:35); then he changes to the regular cultic expression *śāʿîr* (v. 23). Apparently the exact terminology of the Priestly texts either was unknown or of less importance to the Chronicler. Nor is the Chronicler in accordance with the Priestly texts in the terminology of bringing sacrifices. Throughout, he uses the verb *heʿĕlâ*, which is never used in the Priestly texts. Conversely, the Chronicler very rarely uses the most frequent Priestly term, *hiqrîb* (only 1 Chr 16:1 and 2 Chr 35:12).[4]

The description of the performance of the sacrifices in 2 Chronicles 29 is more or less in accordance with the Priestly texts. The king orders the priests to execute the sacrifices upon the altar. They do this according the rules written in Leviticus 1: they slaughter the animals and dash (*wayyizrĕqû*) the blood against the altar (v. 22). Here we find an interesting detail (2 Chr 29:22): before dashing the blood, it is said that the priests 'received' (*wayĕqabbĕlû*) the blood. This act is not mentioned in Leviticus 1. Yet in Lev 1:5, between the slaughter and dashing the blood, it is said: "The sons of Aaron . . . bring (*wĕhiqrîbû*) the blood." In order to bring it, they must have taken or received it before in some kind of vessel. In Exod 29:16 it is said that Moses shall take (*wĕlāqaḥtā*) the blood and 'dash' it.[5] In Leviticus 9 it is said that Aaron slaughtered the sacrifices, and his sons presented or passed the blood to him (*wayyaqribû* [v. 9], *wayyamṣiʾû* [vv. 12, 18]). But nowhere in the Priestly texts do we find the term used by the Chronicler, *qîbbēl*; this detail seems to come from his own knowledge or memory.

The Chronicler does not say from whom the priests received the blood (2 Chr 29:22). Later in the Passover ritual it is said: "The priests dashed the blood from the hand of the Levites" (*miyyād halĕwiyyîm*), which can only mean that they received the blood from the Levites (compare also 2 Chr 35:11). But here the case is different because it is the Passover, and in slaughtering the animals the Levites are acting on behalf of the laymen who did not sanctify themselves. Here we are entering another field of problems because in the Priestly texts we have no rituals for the Passover, and it is never mentioned together with sacrifices. Nevertheless, in our context it is interesting that the text speaks about a separate act of taking or receiving the blood.

In the succeeding verses of 2 Chronicles 29, the Chronicler makes a clear difference between the *ʿôlâ* and the *ḥaṭṭāʾt*. The description of the latter begins with a report of the bringing of the victim (2 Chr 29:23). Here the Chronicler uses the word *wayyaggîšû*, which is not used in the priestly rituals[6] but does appear in the story about the consecration of the priests in Lev 8:14. In this text, the individual acts are related in the following order: Moses had the *ḥaṭṭāʾt*-bull brought (*wayyaggēš*), Aaron and his sons laid their hands on the head of the bull (*wayyismōk*), Moses slaughtered it (*wayyišḥāṭ*; v. 15). The same sequence appears in the Chronicles text: they brought (*wayyaggîšû*) the goats, laid their hands (*wayyismĕkû*) on them, the priests slaughtered them (*wayyišḥāṭûm*; 2 Chr 29:23–24).

4. In 1 Chronicles 16 the source in 2 Sam 6:17–18 uses *heʿĕlâ*. In 2 Chronicles 35 there is no source text, but the Chronicler adds *kakkātûb bĕsēper mōšeh*.

5. Similarly it is said in Exod 24:6, 8, "Moses took (*wayyiqaḥ*) the blood and dashed it."

6. An exception is the *minḥâ* in Lev 2:8; however, an animal is not used.

In 2 Chr 29:23, the laying-on of hands is performed by the king and the assembly (*qāhāl*), which again is in accordance with the ritual of the *ḥaṭṭāʾt* of the "whole congregation Israel" in Lev 4:13ff., where the elders of the congregation lay their hands on the head of the victim (v. 15).

For the blood ritual, the Chronicler uses the word *wayĕḥaṭṭĕʾû*. This term is never used in that meaning in the Priestly texts. We find the word *ḥiṭṭēʾ* only once in a broader sense of executing a *ḥaṭṭāʾt* in Lev 6:19, but not with specific reference to the blood ritual. The Chronicler's following remark *lĕkappēr ʿal-kol-yiśrāʾēl* is again in accordance with the Priestly terminology. In Numbers 28–29, the formula *lĕkappēr ʿălêkem* is used several times and expresses the Priestly understanding of the *ḥaṭṭāʾt* as a means to *kîppēr*, whatever the exact meaning of this word might be—'atonement' or 'purification', or whatever else.

But at this point we find a remarkable inconsistency in the Chronicler's theology. In chap. 30 there follows the story about the great Passover that Hezekiah had organized. It is told that many participants had not sanctified themselves and thus had eaten the Passover in an incorrect manner (*bĕlōʾ kakkātûb*, v. 18). But King Hezekiah prayed that the Lord might 'make atonement for them' (*yĕkappēr bĕʿad*); the Lord heard Hezekiah and healed the people (*wayyirpāʾ ʾet-hāʿām*). I must confess that I do not understand what the Chronicler means, but in any case this use of *kîppēr* is incompatible with any priestly theology. It is amazing that the Chronicler presents two totally different concepts of *kîppēr* so close to each other.

I want to add one final observation: the Chronicler has no specific interest in the *ḥaṭṭāʾt*. Only in 2 Chronicles 29 does the *ḥaṭṭāʾt* appear at all.[7] Interestingly enough, this is a text that the Chronicler invented and composed himself. Obviously in this case he felt it necessary to have a *ḥaṭṭāʾt* as an integral part of the cultic reform of King Hezekiah, which was of special importance to him. But even in this context, everything is focused on the huge quantity of *ʿōlôt* and the great joy evoked by them. Here the music of the Levites seems to be even more important than the sacrifices.

In several cases the Chronicler formulates the duties of the priests.[8] In 1 Chr 16:40, after having brought the ark to Jerusalem, their duties are described as "to offer *ʿōlôt* to the Lord on the altar of *ʿōlôt* regularly, morning and evening, according to all that is written in the law of the Lord that he commanded Israel." This sounds like a reference to the sacrificial calendar of Numbers 28–29, but only to the first paragraph about the daily *ʿōlôt*. In 2 Chr 23:18,

---

7. The same is true for the book of Ezra where the *ḥaṭṭāʾt* appears only once, upon the return of Ezra and his crew in Ezra 8:35. But the summary at the end of the verse subsumes all the sacrifices under the term *ʿōlâ*. In Neh 10:34 the *ḥaṭṭāʾt* is mentioned in the list of tributes for the temple cult.

8. 1 Chr 6:34 is somewhat problematic. The duties of the Aaronides are described as "sacrificing (*maqṭîrîm*) on the altar of burnt offering and making atonement (*ûlĕkappēr*,) for Israel, according to all that Moses the servant of God had commanded."

Jehoiada entrusted the "levitical priests"—or rather the Levites *and* the priests (reading *hakkōhănîm* [*wĕ*]*halĕwiyyim*)—"to offer *ʿōlôt* to the Lord, as it is written in the law of Moses, with rejoicing and singing, according to the order of David." Other texts could be added. The *ʿōlâ* is the central cultic duty of what is commanded in "the law of the Lord" as well as in "the law of Moses." The question of what exactly is meant by these two expressions goes beyond the scope of this paper. But it is interesting that even in these quotations the Chronicler does not use the terminology of the Priestly texts, but instead says *lĕhaʿălôt* *ʿōlôt* rather than *lĕhaqrîb* *ʿōlôt*.

This examination of the Chronicler's ideas of the sacrificial cult and his use of cultic language in 2 Chronicles 29–31 has shown that the Chronicler, on the one hand, has a good knowledge of the sacrificial service in the temple, more or less in accordance with the Priestly texts of the Pentateuch. In at least one case, however, he mentions a detail not recorded in the Priestly texts, the receiving of the blood. On the other hand, he usually does not seem to quote directly from Pentateuchal texts or to be too eager to use exact cultic terminology. In one case he shows a totally non-Priestly use of a central Priestly word, namely *kippēr*. Thus the relations to the Priestly texts of the Pentateuch are rather ambiguous. In certain cases, one would better understand the Chronicler not in terms of literary dependence but in terms of personal knowledge and experience with the cultic reality of his own time.

ON THE CANONICITY OF
THE SONG OF SONGS

Magne Sæbø

THE OLD DICTUM *libelli sua fata* seems to be particularly appropriate to the biblical book of שִׁיר הַשִּׁירִים, *the Song of Songs, Canticum canticorum* (Cant). The interpretations of it through the ages, as well as modern critical discussion of its problems, have differed more widely than for nearly any other book of the Hebrew Bible. This state of affairs is, first of all, related to the highly variegated *Wirkungsgeschichte* and *Rezeptionsgeschichte* of the Song of Songs; through the centuries, scholars tended to be especially attracted to these later (or postbiblical) stages of the history of the book.[1] During the last two centuries, on the other hand, questions of the book's preliterary and literary character have been frequently and differently focused upon by modern critical scholarship. As for these *earlier* stages of the history of the book, scholars often discussed the background and origin of its individual songs and units, their specific genres and composition; further, they debated issues such as the possible opposition of popular versus art poetry and the secular versus sacred character of the songs.[2]

---

1. See C. D. Ginsburg, *Song of Songs* (1857; repr. New York, 1970); H. H. Rowley, "The Interpretation of the Song of Songs," in his *The Servant of the Lord and Other Essays on the Old Testament* (2d rev. ed.; Oxford, 1965); U. Köpf, "Hoheliedauslegung als Quelle einer Theologie der Mystik," *Grundfragen christlicher Mystik* (ed. M. Schmidt; Stuttgart, 1987) 50–72; D. Lerch, "Zur Geschichte der Auslegung des Hohenliedes," *ATK* 54 (1957) 257–77; F. Ohly, *Hohelied-Studien: Grundzüge einer Geschichte der Hoheliedauslegung des Abendlands bis um 1200* (Wiesbaden, 1958); M. H. Pope, *Song of Songs* (AB 7C; Garden City, N.Y., 1977) 89–229 (extended bibliographies 233–88).

2. See recently R. E. Murphy, *The Song of Songs* (Hermeneia; Minneapolis, 1990) 57–91, and the reviews by C. Kuhl, "Das Hohelied und seine Deutung," *ThR* n.s. 9 (1937) 137–67; E. Würthwein, "Zum Verständnis des Hohenliedes," *ThR* 32 (1967) 177–212; also Pope, *Song of Songs*, 21–85; H. Graf Reventlow, "Hoheslied. I. Altes Testament," *TRE* 15.499–502.

In contrast to these historical perspectives on the Song of Songs, the specific problems of the process of its *canonization*—being actually in between what might be called the *Vorgeschichte* and the *Nachgeschichte* of the book— seem not to have received as much attention.[3] When the issue of canonization was brought up, it was often related to the later interpretations of the book, especially the allegorical one. Nevertheless, I would maintain, *the foundation was laid for the book's canonization in different ways in the final stages of redaction.* It may enhance our understanding of the book to locate the question of its canonization, particularly, in the final traditio-historical and redactional process of the book. After all, current scholarship tends to view the canonization of the Hebrew Bible as less localized, rejecting the older connection with the so-called "council" of Jamnia, at the end of the first century C.E. Instead it is viewed as a longer formative and traditio-historical process.[4]

As already stated, the canonicity of the Song of Songs has often been assumed to require a prior allegorical reading and interpretation of the book, and occasionally this may even seem to have been made a *conditio sine qua non* for its canonization.[5] But the contrary is apparently the case. After having critically reviewed the Jewish and the Christian allegorical view, as well as different

---

3. For example Pope gives little more than one page to the questions of canonicity in the very long introduction of his commentary (*Song of Songs*, 15–288), which otherwise has a broad discussion of many aspects of the book, especially of its religio-historical context.

4. See first W. M. Christie, "The Jamnia Period in Jewish History," *JTS* 26 (1925) 352–56, esp. 356: "There never seems to have been a formal canonizing of any portion of the Old Testament . . . by any judicial authority. The books gradually made their way to universal acceptance . . . , and in these disputes on the part of individuals or schools we see the process in operation"; and then P. Katz, "The Old Testament Canon in Palestine and Alexandria," *ZNW* 47 (1956) 191-217; J. P. Lewis, "What Do We Mean by Jabneh?" *JAAR* 32 (1964) 125–32; J. C. H. Lebram, "Aspekte der alttestamentlichen Kanonbildung," *VT* 18 (1968) 173–89; D. Barthélemy, "L'État de la Bible juive depuis le début de notre ère jusqu'à la deuxième révolte contre Rome," *Le canon de l'Ancien Testament: Sa formation et son histoire* (ed. J. E. Kaestli and O. Wermelinger; Geneva, 1984) 25–36. Cf. also S. Zeitlin, *An Historical Study of the Canonization of the Hebrew Scriptures* (Philadelphia, 1933) 9–21, 37; M. Haran, "מבעיות הקנוניזציה של המקרא" [Problems of the Canonization of Scripture], *Tarbiz* 25 (1956) 259–62; A. Jepsen, "Zur Kanongeschichte des Alten Testaments," *ZAW* 71 (1959) 131-32; S. Z. Leiman (ed.), *The Canon and Masorah of the Hebrew Bible* (New York, 1974) 113–282; M. Sæbø, "Vom 'Zusammen-Denken' zum Kanon: Aspekte der traditionsgeschichtlichen Endstadien des Alten Testaments," *JbBiblTh* 3 (1988) 115–33.

5. See, inter alia, R. Gordis, *The Song of Songs and Lamentations* (rev. ed.; New York, 1974) 2, 43; A. Bentzen, "Remarks on the Canonisation of the Song of Solomon," *Studia orientalia Ioanni Pedersen . . . dicata* (Copenhagen, 1953) 41-47; A. Lacoque, "L'insertion du Cantique des Cantiques dans le Canon," *Revue d'histoire et de philosophie religieuses* 42 (1962) 38–44; cf. the critical remarks by Rowley, "Interpretation of The Song of Songs," 198–215; B. S. Childs, *Introduction to the Old Testament as Scripture* (London, 1979) 578; Murphy, *Song of Songs*, 5–7; and especially G. Gerleman, *Hohelied* (BKAT 18; Neukirchen-Vluyn, 1965) 51: "Als Voraussetzung seiner [i.e., Cant's] Aufnahme in den Kanon pflegt man ziemlich unreflektiert die allegorische Auslegung anzugeben. Die Deutung der Lieder auf Jahwe und Israel habe dem Büchlein die erforderte religiöse Legitimierung gegeben und es für den Kanon fähig gemacht."

forms of a dramatic theory,[6] the modern wedding-cycle theory,[7] and also the cultic theory of an Adonis-Tammuz liturgy,[8] Rowley asserts that he "finds in it nothing but what it appears to be, lovers' songs, expressing their delight in one another and the warm emotions of their hearts," and he adds, "all of the other views find in the Song what they bring to it."[9] Be that as it may, Rowley has regrettably not confronted his view with the problem of canonization.[10] This problem represents an even harder challenge when one assumes, as Rowley does, that the songs have an exclusively "secular" character and background.[11]

The history of interpretation of the Song of Songs shows that a proper point of departure and direction of argumentation is crucial to the general understanding of the book. For this reason, it is most appropriate not to start with some interpretation within the book's *Nachgeschichte* and move "backward" to the book itself, nor to start with an alleged religio-historical or cultic *Vorgeschichte*, but to take the book's own literary character and composition as the point of departure, a procedure that has become increasingly customary.[12] Childs is surely right when, in his search for "the canonical shape" of the book, he seeks "the particular stamp which the collectors of Israel's scripture left as a key for its interpretation,"[13] and also when he focuses on the role of Solomon in the book. But when he relates (rather one-sidedly) the mention of Solomon to the realm of "wisdom" and states that "the Song is to be understood as wisdom literature," he is making a dubious claim, although the book seems to have some contact with wisdom.[14] While "the particular stamp" of the "collectors" was not related exclusively to Solomon, there are good reasons for starting with the role of Solomon in the Song.

6. So recently R. J. Tournay, *Quand Dieu parle aux hommes le langage de l'amour* (CRB 21; Paris 1982); M. V. Fox, *The Song of Songs and the Ancient Egyptian Love Songs* (Madison, 1985) 253–66; for recent criticism, cf. O. Keel, *Das Hohelied* (Zürcher Bibelkommentare 18; Zürich, 1986) 24–27.

7. Cf., inter alia, Gordis, *Song of Songs*, 17–18; W. Rudolph, *Das Buch Ruth, Das Hohelied, Die Klagelieder* (KAT 17/1-3; Gütersloh, 1962) 101-6, 140–42; Würthwein, "Zum Verständnis," 202–6, 209–12; idem, *Ruth, Das Hohelied, Esther* (HAT 1/18; 2d ed.; Tübingen, 1969) 31-33; Fox, *Song of Songs*, 330–32.

8. Subsequently broadly expanded by Pope, *Song of Songs*; cf. a critical review by Würthwein, "Zum Verständnis," 196–201.

9. Rowley, *Interpretation of the Song*, 243.

10. Cf. Childs, *Introduction*, 571, who holds that "the simple recounting" of the history of different views, as by Ginsburg and Rowley, "has failed to make clear the exact nature of the hermeneutical problems at stake."

11. Cf. the scrutiny of Rudolph, *Hohelied*, 82–109.

12. Recently also structural aspects have been focused on; cf. J. C. Exum, "A Literary and Structural Analysis of the Song of Songs," *ZAW* 85 (1973) 47–79; R. Alter, *The Art of Biblical Poetry* (New York, 1985) 185–203; F. Landy, "The Song of Songs," *The Literary Guide to the Bible* (ed. R. Alter and F. Kermode; Cambridge, 1987) 305–19.

13. Childs, *Introduction*, 573.

14. Ibid., 574; cf. J. P. Audet, "Le sens du Cantique des Cantiques," *RB* 62 (1955) 203–7.

It has long been registered that the figure of Solomon seems to have special significance in the Song of Songs.[15] But it should not be overlooked that the various references to Solomon (1:1, 5; 3:7, 9, 11; 8:11-12), as well as the anonymous mention of a "king" (1:4, 12; 7:6[5]; cf. 4:4), differ in character and function. This fact may have a bearing on various issues, including the question of "royal travesty" in some of the individual songs, and on the Song as a whole.

In the superscription of the book in Cant 1:1 (שיר השירים אשר לשלמה), the mention of Solomon seems to indicate his *authorship* of the Song. Traditionally it was understood in this way, but the majority of modern scholars do not regard it so.[16] It is, by the way, most remarkable that the Vulgate leaves out the name of Solomon, starting the book after the title, with v. 2 as v. 1 (compare with 8:11). Modern scholars have challenged actual Solomonic authorship, arguing on the basis of a historical perspective, as well as reasons internal to the book; some have sought to explain the role of Solomon in the Song as being other than the role of author. In all this, the question of canonicity of the Song has been made more complicated.

We should also raise the critical question of whether the mention of Solomon in Cant 1:1 is intended not so much as an expression of authorship as an expression of authority.[17] For in this way, the Song of Songs seems to have been "laid under" or "covered by" the authority of King Solomon. Hermeneutically and traditio-historically, a "borrowed" authority of this kind may be understood as a typical precanonical (or protocanonical) phenomenon. For it may be argued that before a biblical book had reached the canonical status of being a holy and authoritative entity, it was provided with the authority of some past personage of undisputable authority, such as the Law of Moses with Moses and the Psalms of David with David.[18]

It was surely not mere chance that Solomon, of all the important people in the past, became the "front figure" of the Song, its tutelary genius; there are various reasons for this. First, there are references elsewhere in the book to both Solomon and to "the king." These references, occurring predominately at the beginning and the end (as perhaps younger sections) of the collections of the Song, may have been effective links.[19] Second, commentators usually connect Cant 1:1 with 1 Kgs 5:9–14 [MT; NJPSV = Eng. 4:29–34], where Solomon is portrayed as the wisest king. Indeed, 1 Kgs 5:12 [4:32] says (in a partly uncertain Hebrew text [see BHS]) that he had "composed (וידבר) three thousand proverbs (משל), and *his songs* (שירו) numbered one thousand and five" (NJPSV).

---

15. See especially Gordis, *Song of Songs*, 18–23.

16. Cf. Childs, *Interpretation* 573–78.

17. The syntactic and translation problems of the formulation cannot be discussed here; but see M. H. Segal, "The Song of Songs," *VT* 12 (1962) 481; Gerleman, *Hohelied*, 93; Keel, *Das Hohelied*, 47; Murphy, *Song of Songs*, 119–22; H. P. Müller, *Das Hohelied* (ATD 16/2; 4th rev. ed.; Göttingen, 1992) 11.

18. Sæbø, "Zusammen-Denken," 128–33.

19. See Rudolph, *Hohelied*, 121.

In the following verse, however, there are many references to nature, as in the wisdom literature, but not to human love and marriage, the specific content of the Song. Third, Solomon is also associated elsewhere with wisdom: (a) at the beginning of Proverbs; (b) in Prov 10:1 and 25:1; (c) as well as (somewhat cryptically) at the beginning of Qohelet (1:1, קהלת בן־דוד מלך בירושלם; compare the "royal travesty" in 1:12, 16). This state of affairs has important consequences for a canonical perspective, but in evaluating these circumstances, one must be very cautious.

It is noteworthy that the Song of Songs is regularly located together with Proverbs and Qohelet in some canon lists, especially in the supposedly oldest "Hebrew-Aramaic list" that might have originated in a Jewish milieu at the end of the first century C.E.[20] This triad of "Solomonic" books with the Song of Songs in the third place[21] may not, however, be regarded so much in terms of a Solomonic authorship as in the terms of securing the books' authority through association with the name of a person of authority. This order should not lead one to attach a basic wisdom character to the Song of Songs. It is not because of its alleged wisdom character that it has been attributed to Solomon, but the other way round.

In the remaining instances of the Song where Solomon is mentioned, Solomon never speaks. There are only references to him, directly by his name and indirectly, if the term "the king" (see above) may be judged a reference to him. Interpreting these references to Solomon continues to be a matter for discussion.

With regard to the name "Solomon" in Cant 1:5b, the Hebrew text may not be in order. Because of the parallelism between "like the tents (כאהלי) of Kedar" and "like the curtains (כיריעות) of Solomon" (so the NRSV), some scholars—starting with Winckler and Wellhausen—have found "Solomon" to be an inadequate parallel to "Kedar," a tribe of northern Arabia (see Gen 25:13 and others); they have proposed to read שַׁלְמָה Shalma (see BHK), a south Arabian tribe, instead of שְׁלֹמֹה,[22] but without any support from the versions. The

20. J. P. Audet, "A Hebrew-Aramaic List of Books of the Old Testament in Greek Transcription," *JTS* n.s. 1 (1950) 135–54; idem, "Le sens de Cantique des Cantiques," 202; see, however, the critical remarks by Katz, "Old Testament Canon," 204–8, and Jepsen, "Zur Kanongeschichte," 114–32; see further Zeitlin, *Historical Study of Canonization*, 9–15, 15–21; H. B. Swete, et al., *An Introduction to the Old Testament in Greek* (Cambridge, 1902; repr., New York, 1968) 197–219, 226–29; also Barthélemy, "L'État de la Bible," 20, 22–30; É. Junod, "La formation et la composition de l'Ancien Testament dans l'Église grecque des quatre premiers siècles," in *Le canon de l'Ancien Testament: Sa formation et son histoire* (ed. J. D. Kaestli and O. Wermelinger; Geneva, 1984) 114, 118–20, 135–38, 144–51.

21. As for the books' present order in the Hebrew Bible, Pope, *Song of Songs*, 18 says: "This order may be a secondary development since the Talmud (Baba Bathra 14b, 15a), some Spanish MSS, and the Massora indicate that the older order was Proverbs, Ecclesiastes, Song of Songs, putting the putative Solomonic compositions together."

22. For 'Shalma', among recent commentators, see Rudolph, *Hohelied*, 123; Gerleman, *Hohelied*, 99; Würthwein, *Hohelied*, etc., 39–40; Pope, *Song of Songs*, 319–20; Müller, *Hohelied*, 14; also the NEB and REB. 'Solomon' is kept by Gordis, *Song of Songs*, 46. 'Solomonic hangings'

Masoretic is preferable. The form might be understood as a reference by the girl, competing with "the daughters of Jerusalem," to some fine, royal "curtains" in parallel to "exotic" ones from the distant Kedar.[23] Alternatively, "Solomon" might be a redactional rereading intended to strengthen the Solomonic element in the songs. So, when Murphy finds "a certain 'historicizing' interest" in the mention of Solomon in Cant 1:1, the same may be the case in 1:5b as well.[24]

Something similar may be said of Cant 8:11-12. In v. 11 there is a narrative style and what might be called a "historical" reference to Solomon: "Solomon had a vineyard in Baal-hamon. He gave . . ." (the place remains unidentified). The Vulgate, in this instance, does not quite omit the royal name as it does in 1:1 but translates the alleged sense of the noun as 'Vinea fuit Pacifico' (v. 11a) and 'tui Pacifici' (v. 12). In this, it may be influenced by the postcanonical allegorical understanding of the Song as a whole, which may have weakened the role of the "historical" Solomon in the Song. Regarding the allegorical approach of the Targum, referring the Song to the history of Israel, consult Rudolph and Pope.[25] However, in Hebrew the reference to Solomon here is surprisingly ambiguous. The male lover (possibly the groom), who may be the speaker in this small unit,[26] at first introduces Solomon and his great and unsurpassed richness (cf. 1 Kgs 10:14–29) in a positive and literal way. Then, however, he employs the immense richness of Solomon as a contrast, making use of the double entendre of the word 'vineyard', both in a literal sense (v. 11) and as a metaphor for his beloved (v. 12).[27] Through this shift—its "ironische Wirkung," as Müller says—the speaker expresses the unique preciousness of his own girl, and the comparison of his "own vineyard" with that of the incomparable king gives expression to the incomparability of his beloved and possible bride. This subtle way of using the wealth of Solomon has, to some extent, made the king a type-figure, a *typos,* in the framework of the literary composition. In this and other respects, the song may be understood as a multileveled literary composition.[28]

The composition of Cant 3:6–11, which has a threefold mention of Solomon (vv. 7, 9, and 11) that is different and more positive than Cant 8:11–12, may be considered to be the most important unit with respect to the Solomonic aspect of the Song. Gordis even regards it as the oldest part of the book, deriving

---

is rendered by Ginsberg, *The Five Megilloth and Jonah* (2d rev. ed.; Philadelphia, 1975) 5; and Murphy, *Song of Songs,* 124–26: 'the pavilions of Solomon'; G. Krinetzki, *Hoheslied* (Würzburg, 1980) 9: 'wie Salomos Decken'.

23. Murphy, *Song of Songs,* 128

24. Ibid., 120.

25. Rudolph, *Hohelied,* 184; Pope, *Song of Songs,* 21, 689, 692.

26. Rudolph, *Hohelied,* 185; Sæbø, "Zusammen-Denken," 313; Müller, *Hohelied,* 88.

27. Fox, *Song of Songs,* 211; Müller, *Hohelied,* 88.

28. Müller, *Hohelied,* 88–89; and see especially idem, *Vergleich und Metapher im Hohenlied* (OBO 56; Fribourg/Göttingen, 1984) .

it from the time of Solomon, and "as the nucleus for the tradition attributing the entire book to Solomon." [29] Be this as it may, the Solomonic element is definitely stronger here than in other parts of the Song, and there might well be a historical Solomonic kernel in it. However, the unit's complexity, being more conspicuous than its unity, refers not only to the many lexical, text-historical, and syntactical problems of the verses, but also to the complex relation between "her" (doubtless present in v. 6, because of the verbal forms, possibly also in vv. 7–8), "him" (possibly in v. 7 and certainly in vv. 9–11), and "them," the "daughters of Jerusalem" parallelled by the "daughters of Zion" (only in v. 11). [30]

The place and function of vv. 9–10 in the present context of Cant 3:6–11 is problematic; it is difficult to pronounce with any certainty the prehistory of the complex unity of this text because of the literary incoherence. Verse 11b provides the song's only instance of *direct* reference to a wedding situation, יוֹם חֲתֻנָּתוֹ 'the day of his marriage', [31] referring to King Solomon. Further, he is "crowned" by "his mother," which also is unique to this verse. It is likely that v. 11 should be combined with vv. 6 and 7–8, where also the marriage setting is the most probable one, regardless of how the individual elements of vv. 6–8 are to be explained. In these verses, the colorful description of a wedding situation is marked by a participial and nominal style. It gives an impression of something present, something that is currently happening; so also in v. 11, in spite of one verb form in the suffix conjugation (עִטְּרָה). Verses 9–10, however, present a remarkable shift of attention. Through the narrative style and the past tense verbs in v. 9, the attention is abruptly directed to the past and, moreover, is focused on a single object rather than the whole festive situation; this single object is a "palanquin (אַפִּרְיוֹן) that King Solomon made for himself (עָשָׂה לוֹ) from Lebanon wood" (v. 9). Attention is first of all drawn to the way in which it had been made (v. 10). The point of departure for this puzzling digression is, in all probability, the word מִטָּה 'bed'/'litter' (compare 1 Sam 19:13ff., 2 Sam 3:31), which belongs to the opening phrase of v. 7: "Look, it is the litter of Solomon!" (NRSV). Some commentators, however, delete v. 7aα as a gloss occasioned by v. 9. [32] But this proposal has "no valid cause." [33] On the contrary,

---

29. R. Gordis ("A Wedding Song for Solomon," *JBL* 63 (1944) 266–70; idem, *Song of Songs*, 18–23) says: "It is at present the oldest datable unit in the book. By contributing to the growth of the tradition of Solomonic authorship, it helped to win inclusion for the entire Song of Songs in the canon of Scripture" (p. 23).

30. One should not be deluded by the late verse division or by any alleged metrical rule to delete the first vocative in v. 10bβ (cf. BHK), but let the chiastic parallelism in vv. 10bβ–11aα remain (cf. BHS; and recently Murphy, *Song of Songs*, 148, 150).

31. But see also 4:8–11, 12; 5:1; and 8:8–10; cf. Fox, *Song of Songs*, 230–32, 314; see also n. 7 above.

32. The argument of Rudolph is *metri causa* (*Hohelied*, 138–39); cf. Müller, *Hohelied*, 36; BHS.

33. See Pope, *Song of Songs*, 432.

the first line of v. 7a is most likely related to the preceding verse and has in this context "an articular and emphatic function."[34] Since vv. 9–10, on the other hand, hark back to v. 7aα, with its older and more common word מִטָּה, by means of the late (probably Greek) loanword אַפִּרְיוֹן 'palanquin',[35] this reference to Solomon differs from those elsewhere in the unit. In v. 11, as well as v. 7, Solomon is referred to as a bridegroom. There is some ambiguity about whether this is the historical King Solomon or a literary fiction, a "royal travesty," representing any groom as "king" in Israel. Because of the link of v. 9a to v. 7a, King Solomon might be regarded as a groom even in vv. 9–10, likewise with the same ambiguity between reality and fiction.

However, it may be more significant hermeneutically that the narrative style and the detailed "technical" description in vv. 9–10, primarily related to the past, seem to point in another direction. Just the "technical" character of the two verses, besides leaving the impression of being an insert,[36] makes it more probable that the intent of the verses is to focus upon the historical Solomon, the rich and illustrious *roi du soleil* of ancient Israel. The final aim of Cant 3:9–10, therefore, may be the same as was revealed in 1:1 and possibly also in 1:5b: in what might be called a "historicizing interest," it will focus upon the picture of King Solomon as the exalted figure of authority in the book.[37]

The mention of Solomon, then, is relatively distinct, but the mention of a "king" (Cant 1:4, 12 and 7:6[5]) seems to be indefinite. Possibly also "the king" refers to Solomon, at least in the present shape of the book. Whether a relation to him was intended originally is doubtful; but at the same time, this matter is less relevant to the final form of the book.

Still, if these three instances are treated separately and seen in their respective contexts they certainly turn out to be very different, yet they have in common the fact that "the king" in all of them is described as the lover/beloved of the young girl (in 1:4, 12 by the girl herself; in 7:6 by others). This description, however, may easily be understood as a "literary fiction,"[38] being the girl's effusive praise, in a festive style, of her lover/beloved (or groom). In this way, he is depicted in the guise of a "king" in a "royal travesty."[39] Müller calls it a royal lyric "Travestie-nach-oben."[40] Fox, who is critical to some current uses of the term 'travesty', also rightly grants that

34. See Murphy, *Song of Songs*, 149.

35. Compare, inter alia, F. Rundgren, "אפריון 'Tragsessel, Sänfte,'" *ZAW* 74 (1962) 70–72; M. Görg, "Die 'Sänfte Salomos' nach HL 3,9f," *Biblische Notizen* 18 (1982) 15–25; Pope, *Song of Songs*, 412, 441–42 ('litter'); Murphy, *Song of Songs*, 148–50 ('carriage').

36. Also the present problematic transition from v. 10 to 11 (cf. BHS) confirms the impression that vv. 9–10 were inserted into an existing composition; cf. n. 33 above.

37. Murphy, *Song of Songs*, 120.

38. See, among others, ibid., 47, 83, 127.

39. Rudolph (*Hohelied*, 123) sees in Cant 1:4 an "Anspielung an die Hochzeit"; and Gerleman (*Hohelied*, 98), the "Verkleidung eines Königs"; compare also Pope, *Song of Songs*, 303, 347, 630.

40. And Müller goes on to say: "weil für eine vordemokratische Gesellschaft im Königtum die klassische Wunschrolle liegt" (*Hohelied*, 13; see 89 on Cant 8:11).

there is a "royal disguise" in Canticles, namely in 1:4, 12 and 3:7–11, where the girl speaks of her lover as if he were a king. This disguise is not an attempt on the characters' part to escape their social situation, but a way of expressing their emotional exaltation, their joy in their current state.[41]

When, finally, these references to "the king" are compared with the references to "(King) Solomon," it seems (somewhat unexpectedly) that the differences between them are more prominent than their common ambiguity. On the one hand, contributing to this ambiguity, there is a link between the "royal disguise" of the "king" references and the possible aspect of a similar disguise in some of the Solomon references (namely, Cant 3:6–8, 11 and 8:11-12; perhaps also 1:5b). On the other hand, the most conspicuous trait in the Solomon references is the "historicizing interest" (primarily in Cant 1:1 and 3:9–10; possibly also in 1:5b), focusing on the historical King Solomon as the wisest and richest man of old. This differs from the use of the "king"-phrase, which should be assessed as an integral part of the "love language" of the songs. So, the "king"-references and the Solomon references are not as similar as one might have expected them to be; therefore, they should be kept properly apart and not be mixed together uncritically.

The *Solomonic element* in the Song, then, seems to have a dual character; there are two "lines" that apparently run contrary to each other. Both of them may have been significant to the canonization and later understanding of the book, but in different ways. At one line, Solomon as a *king* is part of the sophisticated "literary fiction" that is found as "royal travesty" in some songs, partly in the framework of a wedding situation; this element may have "prepared" for a later allegorical understanding and interpretation of the book. At the other line, Solomon as the unique King *Solomon*, a man of indisputable authority in ancient Israel,[42] is focused upon in a most specific "historicizing interest." His honor, status, and authority seem to have contributed decisively to the status and authority of the collection of songs now constituting the Song, and may have been a primary cause for the upcoming process of "sacralization" and canonization of the book; in due time, his authority was like a shield against attack on it. "The Song must have been regarded as in some way part of the national religious literature *before* it was read allegorically."[43]

It may be beyond any dispute that it was the complex Solomonic element in the Song (see above, p. 270) that had the primary significance for the process of "sacralization" and canonization as part of the final stages in the tradition and redaction history of the book, when the collection of old love and marriage songs became the Song of Songs. But as a result of this process, there are also other "particular stamps" that "the collectors of Israel's scripture left as a key

41. Fox, *Song of Songs*, 292–94; quotation from p. 293.
42. This may have validity in spite of the Deuteronomistic criticism of his "love affairs" in 1 Kgs 11:1-8 (9–13).
43. Fox, *Song of Songs*, 250.

for its interpretation."[44] In the end, some of them may be briefly commented on. Partly they belong to what Müller has called "versprengte Fragmente" (1:12, 13–14; 2:6–7, 15; 4:8; 7:11, 14) and "redaktionelle Rahmenverse" (5:9, 16b; 6:1). He did not fully recognize, however, their function in the concluding redactional process, which had a bearing on the later canonization of the book.[45]

There has been much discussion about the character and function of the utterance in Cant 2:7, which returns in nearly the same form in 3:5 and 8:4. It is particularly hard to explain their respective locations. They are thought either to be out of place or to express a request not to disturb the lovers.[46] But these explanations may be regarded as missing the aim of these particular words. Nor are they some sort of "refrain."

Nevertheless, the observation that some commentators have made that these utterances are out of place may well be correct, even though the commentators' explanation turns out to be faulty, for the words' respective places are not accidental. On the contrary, it is most noteworthy that in all three instances the call "I adjure you, O Daughters of Jerusalem, . . . Do not arouse, do not stir up love, until it be ready!"[47] follows upon the most intimate descriptions of sexual intercourse that are to be found in the songs, especially 2:6 and 8:3, but also 3:4b indirectly. Therefore, the point may be made with good reason that the three statements are to be understood as moral *admonitions* that are purposely set in sharp contrast to the directly preceding description. Otherwise, they may have been on the edge of what was morally tolerable. In this way, these three statements of contrast may be understood positively as some sort of theological "safeguarding" of the understanding of a "daring" love description. Thus, the admonitions of Cant 2:7, 3:5, and 8:4 may have fostered the coming canonization of the Song.

In the light of this explanation of Cant 2:7, 3:5, and 8:4 (see above, p. 270), some other instances may be better understood in an ethical or theological perspective that otherwise is not distinctive in the Song. First of all, the reason that the seemingly unrelated verse Cant 2:15 is "enigmatic" and "obscure"[48] is probably because it is a *moral reminder*, placed between the strongly hortative descriptions in 2:8–14 and 2:16–17. Perhaps also the "rather solemn air about the announcement of the brothers concerning their little sister"[49] in Cant 8:8–9

44. Childs, *Introduction*, 573; see above, p. 268.
45. Müller, *Hohelied*, 7; Sæbø, *Fortolkning til Salomos ordsprak, Forkynneren, Høysangen, Klagesangene* (Oslo, 1986) 266–67.
46. For views of these being out of place, compare Rudolph, *Hohelied*, 131; Würthwein, *Hohelied*, 44. For the second opinion, cf. Gerleman, *Hohelied*, 120; cf. also Müller, *Hohelied*, 26.
47. So Murphy, *Song of Songs*, 130, 144, 180.
48. Ibid., 141.
49. Ibid., 198.

should be reckoned to the efforts to "safeguard" the text of the Song.[50] For obvious reasons, little can be said with certainty in this respect; nevertheless, a certain pattern of redactional procedure seems to have been operative in these instances.

Finally, a most difficult item may be brought up, namely the divided text tradition in Cant 8:6b. Here the Ben Asher text reads: שַׁלְהֶבֶתְיָה, whereas the Ben Naphtali tradition as well as many manuscripts and editors (BHK) have שלהבת־יָה, with the short form of the holy name of God of Israel.[51] Is this divided text tradition a witness of a deep theological disagreement regarding the theological "safeguarding" of the Song? As is well known, there is no mention of any of the names of God in the Song. However, it may well be that among some Jewish sages there was a wish to set the stamp of the name of God on the Song, but the wish was rejected by other sages, and their wishes determined the most authoritative text tradition, the Ben Asher text. And with this echo of disagreement, one may be at the border of the ancient discussion of the canonicity of the Song of Songs.

The problem of the canonicity of the Song of Songs is much more complex, and the process of its canonization may have started much earlier than is usually stated in the handbooks. There may be good reasons to maintain that the early stages of the canonization of the book, starting with some sort of "sacralization," were interwoven with the final stages of the tradition and redaction history of the Song. In this center point between the *Vorgeschichte* and the *Nachgeschichte* of the book, the present collection of old love and marriage songs in Israel became the Song of Songs.

50. Also compare with Gen 24:29ff.; Judg 21:22.
51. See, inter alia, Fox, *Song of Songs*, 170 and the major commentaries.

NOTES ON THE USE OF THE DEFINITE ARTICLE IN THE POETRY OF JOB

Nahum M. Sarna

THE DATING OF BIBLICAL HEBREW poetry is an exceedingly difficult task,[1] but it is common knowledge that one of the distinctively characteristic features of the early compositions is the absence or sparse use of the prefixed definite article *ha-*. This contrasts strongly with its frequent occurrence in prose texts. Freedman has pointed out that the morpheme occurs about six to eight times more frequently in prose passages than in poetic ones.[2] This phenomenon is to be explained by the tendency of poetry to imitate the older forms of the language, and there is general agreement about the comparatively late appearance of the article in Northwest Semitic languages. Ugaritic, Syriac, and Aramaic[3] possess no prefixed article, nor is it present in the fourteenth century B.C.E. Canaanite dialects that underlie the language of many of the Akkadian Amarna texts. Ethiopic also has no definite article, nor has Akkadian. Moabite more or less follows the pattern of Biblical Hebrew, as does Ammonite,[4] but the use of the definite article in Phoenician is quite erratic, since there are no discernible rules governing its presence or omission.[5]

---

1. See D. A. Robertson, *Linguistic Evidence in Dating Early Hebrew Poetry* (SBLDS 3; Missoula, Mont., 1972).

2. D. N. Freedman, *Pottery, Poetry and Prophecy: Studies in Early Hebrew Poetry* (Winona Lake, Ind., 1980) 3.

3. Aramaic and Syriac, of course, expressed definiteness by the suffixed article *-â*, which later lost its meaning; see S. Moscati, *An Introduction to the Comparative Grammar of the Semitic Languages* (Wiesbaden, 1964) 98, §12.74.

4. See *KAI* 1.3, no. 181, lines 1, 3, 4, 9, 11, 12, 15, 21–26, 29, 31. For examples of the definite article in Ammonite, see W. E. Aufrecht, *A Corpus of Ammonite Inscriptions* (ANETS 4; Lewiston, N.Y., 1988) 66, texts 27:2, 66:2, 68, 78:4:1.

5. J. Friedrich and W. Röllig, *Phönizisch-Punische Grammatik* (Rome, 1970) §300; cf. G. A. Cooke, *A Text-Book of North-Semitic Inscriptions* (Oxford, 1903) 21; Z. S. Harris, *A Grammar of the Phoenician Language* (New Haven, Conn., 1936) 66; cf. M. Dahood, "Canaanite-Phoenician Influence in Qoheleth," *Bib* 33 (1952) 30–52, 191–221. In rebutting Dahood's general conclusions,

279

Cross and Freedman connect the innovation of the definite article with the loss of case endings in Canaanite, a development that Albright dated to around the fourteenth century[6] and Cross and Saley to between the thirteenth and tenth centuries B.C.E.[7] The first appearance of the article itself in Canaanite is said to have occurred, according to Cross and Freedman, in the tenth century B.C.E.[8] Parallel with the sparse use of the article in biblical poetry is the equally rare occurrence of the *nota accusativi* *ʾet*, which also appears very frequently in prose texts.[9] It is generally hard to tell whether the two characteristic features of Hebrew poetry are indicators of genuinely archaic compositions or of an archaizing tendency.[10] Either way, a very puzzling phenomenon is the strikingly contrasting, apparently vocalized determination of the inseparable prepositions *b-*, *k-*, and *l-*, which is a common occurrence.[11]

Thus, in Gen 49:1–27 the article as the determinator of a noun appears only twice,[12] whereas the received punctuation of the inseparable prepositions *b-*, *k-*, *l-* implies another six examples.[13] Most revealing is the situation in Exod 15:1–19. Other than the editorial prose introduction in v. 1, the song does not feature a single usage of the definite article *ha-* with a noun; nevertheless, there are eight seeming instances of the phenomenon with the prepositions.[14] Some other biblical poetic texts exhibit greater consistency.

The Oracles of Balaam in Numbers 23–24 contain only one noun with the prefixed *ha-*[15] and two cases of a preposition vocalized as though with the ar-

---

H. L. Ginsberg (*Koheleth* [Tel Aviv, 1961] 42–49, [Heb.]) does not relate to the issue of the erratic use of the definite article. R. Gordis (*Koheleth: The Man and His World* [3d aug. ed.; New York, 1968] 60, 416–17) also refutes the Phoenician hypothesis and explains the irregular use of the definite article as being due to Aramaic influence.

6. W. F. Albright, "Review of Pfeiffer, *Introduction to the Old Testament,*" *JBL* 61 (1942) 117. On the development of the definite article, see Thomas O. Lambdin, "The Junctural Origin of the West Semitic Article," in *Near Eastern Studies in Honor of William Foxwell Albright* (ed. Hans Goedicke; Baltimore, 1971) 315–33.

7. F. M. Cross and R. J. Saley, "Phoenician Incantations on a Plaque of the Seventh Century B.C. from Arslan Tash in Upper Syria," *BASOR* (1970) 48.

8. F. M. Cross and D. N. Freedman, "Some Observations on Early Hebrew," *Bib* 53 (1972) 418–19.

9. The *nota accusativi* occurs three times in Job without a following definite article: 13:25, 36:7, 41:26. On its rarity in Hebrew poetry in general, see GKC §117a; A. M. Wilson, "The Particle את in Hebrew," *Hebraica* 6 (1889–90) 139–50, 212–24; J. Hoftijzer, "Remarks concerning the Use of the Particle *ʾt* in Classical Hebrew," *OTS* 14 (1965) 1–99.

10. As Robertson (*Linguistic Evidence,* 57 n. 1) observes, arguing for an early date from the absence of the article *h-* is an argument from silence.

11. See GKC §126h, n fn. 2.

12. Gen 49:14–15. In vv. 17, 21 the articles function as a relative attached to participles.

13. Gen 49:4, 11 (3x), 27 (2x).

14. Exod 15:1, 4, 6, 7, 10, 11 (2x), 16.

15. Num 24:3, 15. W. F. Albright ("The Oracles of Balaam," *JBL* 63 [1944] 216 n. 55) maintains that *ha-geber* is "the only case where the article is obviously original in these poems; it still has a clear, demonstrative force." However, in regard to *hā-ʿayin*, he accepts the emendation of Wellhausen, reading *še-tammah ʿayin*.

ticle (23:9, 24:21). On the other hand, the Song of Moses in Deut 32:1–43 twice uses the definite article with vocative force in v. 1 and perhaps also in v. 4 and has no determined prepositions. The Testament of Moses in Deuteronomy 33 shows the article once as a relative with a participle (v. 9) and once with a noun (v. 12), while there are two instances of apparent determination of prepositions (v. 24). The Song of Deborah in Judges 5 exhibits a single instance of the article as a relative (v. 9) and five usages with a noun (vv. 16, 20, 24, 28, 31), while there are four cases of a preposition vocalized as with an article (vv. 13, 15, 23, 26).

Psalm 78, which Eissfeldt, Albright, and Freedman date to preexilic times,[16] possibly as early as the period of the united monarchy, fully illustrates the problem. In this long composition the definite article is used only twice (vv. 14, 53), whereas what appears to be the same with a preposition occurs no less than twenty-two times.[17] A thorough scrutiny of the Psalms would abundantly detail the enormous disproportion between the two forms. The present study, however, must be limited to the Hebrew of Job.

Almost one hundred years ago, both E. König and M. Lambert took note of the puzzling contrast between the scarcity of the definite article *ha-* and its apparent frequency in elided form, as indicated by the Masoretic vocalization of the prepositions *b-*, *k-*, and *l-*.[18] König produced a phonetic theory, which Lambert easily showed could not be sustained, because the indefinite preposition is extensively prefixed to nouns in the pre-tone and before gutturals. Lambert himself explained the situation by assuming that, where the consonantal text permitted, the vocalization of prose style (in which the definite article is much more frequently used) had been introduced into poetry. Accordingly, he decided that the present vowels of these prepositions are not original. Gesenius claimed that when the article *ha-* is omitted after a prefix, "the vowel of the article is often retained after the prefix even in poetry." However, this remark is modified in a footnote to the effect that the vowel of the prefix might "be merely due to the masoretic punctuation," but he adds that "there is however, no reason to doubt the correctness of the tradition."[19]

W. G. E. Watson notes that the article does not appear in the poetry of Num 12:6–8, and he decides that in v. 6 the vowels of the prepositions that presuppose the article are "secondary."[20] Freedman similarly rules that while the

16. O. Eissfeldt, *Das Lied Moses Deuteronomium 32:1–43 und das Lehrgedicht Asaphs Psalm 78 samt einer Analyse der Umgebung des Mose-Liedes* (Berlin, 1958); W. F. Albright, "From the Patriarchs to Moses, II: Moses out of Egypt," *BA* 36 (1973) 52–53; D. N. Freedman, ("Review of J. Sanders, *Torah and Canon*," *JBL* 92 [1973] 118) dates the psalm to the 11th–12th centuries B.C.E.

17. Verses 14–16, 19, 26, 33 (2x), 40, 46 (2x), 47 (2x), 48 (2x), 50, 52 (3x), 60–62, 64.

18. E. König, *Historisch-comparative Syntax der hebräischen Sprache* (1897) §292n. M. Lambert, "L'Article dans la Póesie hebraique," *REJ* 37 (1898) 203–9.

19. GKC §126h, n fn. 2.

20. W. G. E. Watson, *Classical Hebrew Poetry: A Guide to Its Techniques* (Sheffield, 1984) 54 and n. 110.

scribes did not tamper with the existing text, when it came to vocalization "they followed a uniform pattern marking the presence of the article indiscriminately in prose and poetry wherever it seemed grammatically appropriate."[21] This explanation requires modification, however, because, as will be shown below, there are many inconsistencies.

As stated, the present study is restricted to the book of Job, the morphological, syntactical, and linguistic peculiarities and difficulties of which are well known. In Job, the inconsistencies and erraticisms in the use of the article abound. Its dual function as a relative with a participle and as the determination of a noun features glaring incongruities in both instances. Thus the article is present in 9:5–7 but absent in 9:8–10. Similarly the participle is defined in 5:10a but not in 5:9, 13. The following instances, which include the article, 3:8, 14, 15, 21, 22; 6:16; 22:17; 30:3–4, may be contrasted to this series, which omits it, 12:17, 19–24; and 26:7–8. The conclusion seems to be unavoidable that the presence or absence of the article in a participial construction is a mere stylistic device for which, just as in Phoenician, no controlling conditions may be discovered.

With respect to the full form of the definite article with a noun, as distinct from its apparently elided form with a preposition, its most frequent appearance is in a cliché, especially of the kind composed of two nouns in construct relationship. There are eight such with *ʾereṣ* as the nomen rectum. Of these, five are determined and three are not: 5:22, 25; 12:24; 28:24; 37:3; 38:13; in contrast to 14:19; 24:4, 18; and 35:11. Compound phrases with *yām* occur five times; in two cases *yām* is defined, 12:8 and 36:30, while it remains undefined three times, 6:3, 9:8, 38:16. Another example is the occurrence of compounds with *šāmayim*. Of the eight, only one takes the article in each of its three appearances, namely, the phrase *ʿôp ha-šāmayim*: 12:7, 28:21, 35:11. Otherwise, the article is omitted: 11:8; 22:12, 14; 26:11; 38:29, 33, 37. Finally, comparison between Job and other books is instructive: Job 3:3 has *yōʾbad yôm*, whereas Jer 20:14 has *ʾārûr ha-yôm*; Job 14:19 has *ʿăpar ʾāreṣ*, but Isa 40:12 reads *ʿăpar hā-ʾāreṣ*; Job 22:14 features *ḥûg šāmayim* as opposed to Isa 40:22 *ḥûg hā-ʾāreṣ*. On the other hand, *ʾereṣ ha-ḥayyîm* in Job 28:13 appears as *ʾereṣ ḥayyîm* in Isa 53:8.

How is this erraticism to be explained? König suggested that in two parallel clauses, the presence of the article in the first clause also determines the second.[22] In Job, however, the evidence is against this interpretation, for in the majority of instances in the book the article is present in the second clause but omitted in the first. Thus, it is found in the first clause and not in the second only three times, 28:12–20, 37:9, and 38:29, but the reverse situation occurs nine times: 3:3, 5:22, 12:7, 28:21, 33:30, 35:11, 38:12 (*Qere*), 39:15, 40:20. In fact, the article is actually present in both members of the parallelism only four times: 3:4, 6; 5:23; 28:24; 37:3. The foregoing evidence unmistakably demon-

21. Freedman, *Pottery, Poetry and Prophecy*, 4.
22. König, *Historisch-comparative Syntax*; and see Lambert, "L'Article," 206.

strates once again that the presence or absence of the article defies systemiza-
tion and that König's rule cannot be substantiated.

There are no nonsyncopated forms of prepositions with the article in Job.
Even the shortened form of the preposition *min* with which the article never
elides, namely *me-ha-*, does not appear. This confirms the view that those who
supposedly "normalized" the vocalization did not tamper with the consonantal
text in order to bring it into line with the prose usage. That the punctuators did
not blindly vocalize the prepositions is evidenced by the punctuation of *šĕˀôl*.
This term never takes the definite article in Biblical Hebrew. Significantly, although it appears with the prepositions *b-* (Amos 9:2, Ps 6:6, Job 14:13, Qoh
9:10), *k-* (Hab 2:5, Prov 1:12, Song 8:6), and *l-* (Pss 16:10, 31:18, 49:15, 88:4),
these too never feature the defined forms. This phenomenon indicates a con-
sciousness on the part of the punctuators of the perpetually undefined, absolute
form of *šĕˀôl*. Those scholars did not unthinkingly follow the regular prose usage as in the case of other nouns.

Another peculiar feature of the language of Job is the presence of many
nouns that never take the definite article in this book, but which seem to do so
with an affixed preposition. Examples are *ˀebyôn*, *ˀôr*, *ˀēl*, *bînâ*, *ḥōšek*, *māwet*,
māyim, *ˤāb*, *ṣēl*, *šĕḥāqîm*, *šāḥat*, *mišpāṭ*.[23] Each of these nouns occurs with a
preposition vocalized as though defined, but in most cases there are other
examples of the same word used elsewhere in the book but with undefined prepositions. Most puzzling of all are numerous instances of nouns in parallelism in

---

23. *ˀebyôn*—Job 5:15, 24:14, but it is defined in 29:16, 30:25, 31:19.

ˀôr—The word is undefined in Job 3:16, 20; 12:25; 17:12; 18:6; 22:28; 24:13, 16; 26:10;
28:11; 31:26; 36:32; 37:21; 38:19, 24; 41:10. It appears with an undefined preposition in 18:18
and 30:26 but with a defined one in 12:22, 24:14, 33:28.

ˀēl—This noun appears 43 times in the absolute form: 5:8; 8:3, 5, 13, 20; 9:2; 12:6; 13:3, 7;
15:4, 11, 13, 25; 16:11; 18:21; 19:22; 20:15; 22:13; 23:16; 25:4; 27:2, 9, 11, 13; 31:14, 23; 32:13;
33:4, 14, 29; 35:5, 12, 23, 31; 35:13; 36:5, 22, 26; 37:5, 10, 14; 40:19. Nevertheless, it occurs 9
times with a determined preposition, 13:8; 21:14; 22:17; 31:28; 33:6; 34:10, 36; 40:9; but only
twice with an undetermined one: 21:22, 22:2.

bînâ—This noun occurs 6 times in the absolute form: 28:12, 20, 28; 34:16; 38:4, 36; but the
sole example with a preposition is defined: 39:17.

ḥōšek—This term occurs 20 times, but not once with the article: 3:4, 5; 5:14; 10:21; 12:22,
25; 15:22, 23, 30; 17:12; 18:18; 19:8; 20:26; 22:11; 23:17; 26:10; 29:3; 34:22; 37:19; 38:19.
Nevertheless, each of its three appearances with a preposition is vocalized as though defined:
17:13, 24:16, 28:3.

māwet—This word occurs 4 times in the absolute form, 7:15, 18:13, 30:23, and 38:17, but
twice with a defined preposition: 3:21; 27:15.

māyim—This word is featured 17 times in the absolute form: 5:10; 8:11; 14:9, 11, 19; 22:7,
11; 24:18; 26:5, 8, 10; 28:25; 29:19; 36:27, 37:10; 38:30, 34. It does not occur with an undefined
preposition but occurs 5 times with a defined one: 3:24, 12:15, 15:16, 27:20, 34:7.

ˤāb—The absolute form occurs 4 times, 22:14; 36:29; 37:11, 16; twice with a defined preposition, 20:6, 38:34, and once with an undefined one, 30:15.

ṣēl—This noun is featured 4 times, twice in absolute form, 7:2 and 8:9, and twice with a
defined preposition: 14:2, 17:7.

which the defined and undefined forms of the prepositions alternate[24] or in which one noun is in the absolute form and the other possesses a defined preposition.[25]

From all the foregoing it would seem to be certain that what appears to be the definite article with prepositions in poetic texts is not that at all, just as Lambert had suspected. However, might the vocalization have some explanation other than the capriciousness of the Masoretic punctuators, who supposedly, mindlessly and inconsistently, imposed prose forms on the poetry? I would suggest an alternative theory.

It is worth considering that the form of the inseparable prepositions with a *patah* may well preserve an earlier, pre-Masoretic, nondetermined vocalization, rather than being due to the elision of the definite article. It is significant that in the second column of the Hexapla, which featured the transliteration of the Hebrew biblical text into Greek letters, Origen transcribed the preposition *b-* by *ba-*, even when our received Hebrew Text bears a *šewaᵓ*.[26] Thus, the extant Psalm 30 from this column has in v. 6 βααφφω, βαρσωνω, and in v. 8 βαρσωναχ. Similarly, in Ps 89:50, Origen has βαεμουναθαχ.[27] It is reasonable to assume that this vocalization of the preposition reflects Palestinian Jewish pronunciation in the first half of the third century c.e. Sperber pointed out that more than 100 years later Jerome generally transliterated *b-*, *k-*, *l-* by βα-, χα, λα, and this even when the Hebrew wholly precludes any possibility of a definite article, as for instance, in the case of Hebrew *be-yah*, which appeared as βάια, *be-kaᶜas* as βαχας, and *bilbabam* as βαλβαβαμ.[28] In this connection, it is also worth noting that in Ethiopic the prepositions *b-* and *l-* are pronounced *ba-* and *la-* respectively, and in Arabic *k-* is vocalized *ka-*. Further, Gordon points out that Ugaritic vocalization of *l-* as *la-* "is likely from comparative evidence."[29]

To sum up, it may not be the *patah* form of the prepositions that has been influenced by the prose form, but only the *dageš* in the succeeding consonant. The vocalization with the *patah* may be original.

šĕhāqîm—This noun occurs 3 times in absolute form, 35:5, 36:28, 38:37, once with an undefined preposition, 37:18, and once with a defined one, 37:21.

šahat—The absolute form occurs in 33:18, 24, 30, and with defined prepositions in 9:31; 17:14; 33:22, 28.

mišpāt—The absolute form appears in 8:3; 13:18; 19:7; 23:4; 32:9; 34:4, 12, 17; 36:17; 37:23. It occurs 3 times with undefined prepositions, 9:19, 14:3, and 35:2, and 3 times with a defined preposition, 9:32; 22:4, 34:23.

24. These are 11:17, 14:2, 24:24, 29:23, 30:15, 39:21.

25. These are 3:21–22; 9:6–7 (cf. vv. 8, 9); 12:7, 22; 18:10; 24:5; 26:6; 28:25, 26; 29:7; 30:19; 31:19, 24, 32; 33:18; 37:9; 39:17.

26. On this see A. Sperber, "Hebrew Based upon Greek and Latin Transliterations," *HUCA* 12–13 (1937–38) 103–274, esp. 137–38, 194.

27. P. Kahle, *The Cairo Geniza* (2d ed.; New York, 1960) 163, 171.

28. Sperber, "Hebrew Based upon Greek," 194.

29. C. H. Gordon, *Ugaritic Textbook* (Rome, 1965) 97, §10.10.

Part 5

Language and Writing

THE MEANING OF צלמות 'DARKNESS': A STUDY IN PHILOLOGICAL METHOD

Chaim Cohen

IN COMPARATIVE SEMITIC PHILOLOGY, two main theories vie to replace the old etymological approach. The first method is that of James Barr, especially as described in his book, *Comparative Philology and the Text of the Old Testament*.[1] The alternate method is that of the late Moshe Held, as presented in my article, "The Held Method for Comparative Semitic Philology."[2] The purpose of the present study is to apply the "Held method" to the meaning and origin of the word צלמות and to compare the results with Barr's results in his 1974 article "Philology and Exegesis," where he deals at length with the same term.[3]

Barr's major conclusions concerning the meaning and origin of the term צלמות are as follows:

> [The problem of צלמות] is . . . one in which several different levels of explanation can be and must be held together in the mind at one time. It is at least possible that the total history involves: (a) forms from a root ṣ-l-m 'dark'; (b) an idiom where 'shadow' plus 'death' meant 'deep shadow'; (c) a name of the type 'may Mot give protection'. *The eventual standardization of 'shadow of*

Author's note: This paper was first delivered in an abbreviated Hebrew version at the Eleventh World Congress for Jewish Studies (Jerusalem, June 23, 1993). It is a great pleasure for me to include this more complete version in the present Jubilee Volume as a token of friendship and esteem for one of the most prominent Israeli biblical scholars, Prof. Menaham Haran.

1. J. Barr, *Comparative Philology and the Text of the Old Testament* (1st ed.; Oxford, 1968; repr. with additions and corrections: Winona Lake, Ind., 1987; [henceforth *CPTOT*]).

2. C. Cohen, "The Held Method for Comparative Semitic Philology," *JANES* 19 (1989) 9–23.

3. See J. Barr, "Philology and Exegesis," in *Questions disputées d'Ancien Testament: Méthode et théologie* (ed. C. Brekelmans; Gembloux, Belgium, 1974) 39–61 = Barr, *CPTOT*, 362–87. The pages having to do with צַלְמָוֶת are *CPTOT*, 375–81. Barr originally wrote this article as a methodological response to M. J. Dahood's review of *CPTOT* with specific reference to examples taken from Job 3 (see *CPTOT*, 362).

death' would then be not an artificial invention, but a universalization over the entire usage of that which had earlier belonged only to a part. The phonetic form preserved in MT is not an artificial invention but has real foundations in the history of the term.[4]

Barr further maintains that this understanding of the "total history" of צלמות warrants the following methodological conclusions:

> The case is an example, then, of the complexity of the strata of tradition and understanding with which we have to deal in the analysis of a Hebrew text, *and the improbability that simple philological parallels will prove to be in themselves decisive. In particular, philological information from cognate languages is something that is to be taken into account, but does not in itself provide a decision; and the provision of a "correct translation" cannot be a correct representation of the dimensions of the tradition.*[5]

Before pursuing the specific analysis of צלמות according to the "Held method," a general remark is in order concerning Barr's failure even to mention the important and often-suggested comparison between צלמות and Akkadian *ṣalmu* 'black' and *ṣalāmu* 'to be dark'.[6] There is no justification whatsoever for the

---

4. *CPTOT*, 380.

5. Ibid., 380–81. See also Barr, "Hebrew Lexicography: Informal Thoughts," in *Linguistics and Biblical Hebrew* (ed. W. R. Bodine; Winona Lake, Ind., 1992) 139–40. In regard to this latter, most recent article, it should also be noted that the work of N. H. Tur-Sinai on Job is philologically on a much higher level than G. R. Driver's in the NEB or M. J. Dahood's on Psalms (see, e.g., n. 16 below).

6. Barr's attitude in this particular case was strongly influenced by the opinion of T. Nöldeke in "צלמות und צלם" (*ZAW* 17 [1897] 183–87), where according to Barr (*CPTOT*, 375), Nöldeke defended "both the traditional pronunciation and the sense 'shadow of death'." Nöldeke further "denied the existence in Hebrew and Aramaic of the root *ṣ-l-m* 'dark'." Barr (*CPTOT*, 375–76 n. 30) claims to have distanced himself somewhat from Nöldeke in that he doubts any "connection with an Arabic *ṣ-l-m* 'cut off'—a suggestion made by him [Nöldeke—C. C.] only hesitatingly in any case," and he (Barr) now gives "hesitant favor to the derivation from *ṣ-l-m* 'dark' of the two instances in the Psalms (39:7[6], 73:20). . . ." The only other reference made by Barr to other Semitic languages is in *CPTOT*, 379–80 n. 40: "I merely mention, for the sake of information, the pair of apparent names *ġlmt* and *ẓlmt* in CTA 4 vii 54–55 (p. 30), Gordon UT 51 VII 54. These may be relevant, but I am not sure how *ẓl* 'shadow' is well established in Ugaritic, but *ẓlm* 'darkness' is not; this may be relevant to the question whether it ever existed in Hebrew" (contrast n. 67 below in the present study). Thus, Barr mentions no positive evidence whatsoever for a root *ṣlm* or *ẓlm* in any Semitic language with the meaning 'to be dark'. This is quite difficult to justify given the fact that Barr cites quite favorably (*CPTOT*, 378 and n. 34) D. Winton-Thomas, "צלמות in the Old Testament" (*JSS* 7 [1962] 191–200), where on pages 193–94, "Akkadian *ṣalāmu*, Arabic *ẓlm* IV, and Ethiopic *ṣalma*, in the same sense" are specifically referred to and accepted as meaning 'to be dark' (even through Winton-Thomas himself opts for a different etymology; see suggested etymology b, p. 304, below). Finally, note the more recent study of W. L. Michel, "ṢLMWT, 'Deep Darkness' or 'Shadow of Death'" (*Biblical Research* 29 [1984] 5–20), where the above cognates are cited (p. 14 n. 1) but are deemed irrelevant because of a statement by Barr in *CPTOT*, 381 n. 41 (the first footnote referring to Barr's discussion of *the next phrase*, כמרירי יום, also in Job 3:5): "The Hebrew dictionaries tend to give an impression that the sense 'black' is basic in Syriac. My impression is that the sense 'be sad' (of personal emotion) is much more central than that of colour;

overall negative attitude displayed by Barr in this particular case. With all the critical reservations that may be expressed against the extreme suggestions of such scholars as G. R. Driver and M. J. Dahood, it should still be remembered that the purpose of methodology in comparative Semitic philology is to posit clear rules both for new sound proposals and for differentiating between previous comparisons that are acceptable and previous comparisons that must be rejected. By not even mentioning this important comparison, Barr has neglected comparative philological evidence important for the proper understanding of צלמות. Furthermore, as will also be demonstrated below, the semantic comparison with other Akkadian terms for 'darkness' is no less significant in this case and will provide additional crucial evidence.

According to the "Held method," one must first investigate the Biblical Hebrew usage of the word in question and determine its semantic range according to its various occurrences in different contexts. This investigation must be undertaken *without any etymological consideration whatsoever* (in fact, it is best during this stage to relate to the word in question as X). Furthermore, it is this investigation "by means of the inductive method" that takes precedence over any etymological evidence.[7] Such a semantic investigation of the biblical usage of צלמות yields the following results: (a) the substantive חוֹשֶׁךְ 'darkness' (or the verb חש״ך 'to be dark') is attested together with צלמות in twelve of its eighteen occurrences in the MT, four times together as the hendiadys חוֹשֶׁךְ וצלמות (Ps 107:10, 14; Job 3:5; 10:21); three times in synonymous parallelism with צלמות as the B-word (Isa 9:1; Job 12:22, 34:22); and five times within the same context (Jer 13:16; Amos 5:8; Job 24:16–17 [twice], 28:3); (b) of the remaining six occurrences, in one case צלמות occurs in synonymous parallelism with אֹפֶל 'darkness' (Job 10:22); while in the other five attestations, none of the regular terms relating to the semantic field of 'darkness' is present (Jer 2:6; Ps 23:4, 44:20; Job 16:16, 38:17); (c) among the thirteen attestations that include terms relating to the semantic field of 'darkness', the term צלמות also occurs in opposition to the words אוֹר 'light' and בֹּקֶר 'morning' (Isa 9:1; Jer 13:16; Amos 5:8; Job 12:22, 24:16–17 [twice]) and in parallelism or in the same context with אֹפֶל 'darkness' (Job 10:21–22, 28:3) and ערפל 'darkness' (Jer 13:16).[8] This evidence based on "poetic usage and parallelism" should be

---

for the colour *black* the Syriac uses primarily other words, especially the root ᵓkm." While this statement by Barr did not at all refer to Barr's discussion of צלמות, it was used by Michel to arrive at the following completely untenable etymological conclusion (p. 13): "the supposed root ṣlm is very rare in Hebrew (or does not even exist at all) and probably does not mean 'to be dark, black,' but 'to be sad.'"

7. Cohen, "Held Method," 10–11 ("principle one").

8. For 'darkness' as the basic meaning of ערפל, see my article "The Basic Meaning of the Term עֲרָפֶל 'Darkness' " (*Hebrew Studies* 36 [1995] 7–12). For the present, note that the fifteen attestations may be semantically divided up according to the following four usages: (1) *a general usage of 'darkness' (without any specific connection to clouds)*—only Isa 60:2, Jer 13:16; (2) *a specialized usage (sometimes cosmological) referring to God's heavenly presence or abode being*

considered decisive in establishing positively (at least in regard to the aforementioned thirteen occurrences) that the term צלמות has approximately the same semantic range as the term חושך.[9]

It is also possible to determine differences in usage between חושך and צלמות. The occurrence of צלמות in poetic contexts only, the fixed order of the parallelism חושך//צלמות, and the four attestations of the hendiadys חושך וצלמות are firm indications that צלמות is basically a poetic B-word to the more generally used חושך.[10] This relationship is similar to the relationship between חושך and its other poetic B-words: אופל (e.g., Amos 5:20; Isa 29:18 [reverse order]; Job 23:17; cf. together with צלמות—Job 3:4–6, 10:21–22, 28:3), אפלה (e.g., Exod 10:22; Isa 58:10, 59:9) and ערפל (Isa 60:2; cf. together with צלמות —Jer 13:16).[11] Particularly noteworthy is the comparison of the hendiadys חושך וצלמות (Ps 107:10, 14; Job 3:5; 10:21) with its semantic equivalent חושך (ו)אפלה (Exod 10:22, Joel 2:2, Zeph 1:15).

Up to this point, the usage of צלמות has been examined only in the thirteen occurrences for which a clear connection with the semantic range of חושך 'darkness' can be definitely established. Barr maintains that this evidence is not at all decisive because it does not take into consideration the five remaining attestations. Barr labels three of the five "places where the generally accepted sense 'darkness' does not fit very well" and further contends as follows:

> I do not wish to claim too much for these examples; but it is only right that they should be set alongside the well-known cases where *ṣalmawet* stands in parallel with words for "darkness" like *ḥoshek* or in opposition to words for "light" such as *ʾor*.[12]

The "Held Method" diametrically opposes such an assertion. *It can hardly be expected that every occurrence of the word in question will appear in a clear parallelistic structure that can help us in determining the sought-after meaning or semantic range.* As stated above, one must first utilize all such attestations in order to determine the semantic range of the word. Then, the remaining con-

---

conceived of in the form of a cloud (without any specific connection to darkness)—only 1 Kgs 8:12 = 2 Chr 6:1; Ps 97:2; Job 38:9; (3) *a combination of the first two usages where the cloud in usage b is enveloped in darkness*—e.g., Deut 4:11, Joel 2:2; (4) *the technical weather phenomenon of "darkness in the sky," i.e., dense fog involving thick cloud formations*—only Job 22:13–14, the key usage that explains the connection between the three other usages as derived from the basic meaning 'darkness'. Etymologically, this term must be connected with its Ugaritic cognate *ǵrpl* 'dense fog' (KTU 1.107:7–10, 12–13, 19–20) and therefore dissociated from Ugaritic *ʿrpt* 'cloud' (= Akkadian primary noun *erp/betu* 'cloud' and Biblical Hebrew ערבות in Ps 68:5). Biblical Hebrew ערפל / Ugaritic *ǵrpl* must then be connected with the Akkadian verb *erēpu* 'to be dusky, dark' used esp. with respect to weather phenomena (CAD E 279–80).

9. Cohen, "Held Method," 12–13 ("principle three").

10. For "B-words," see ibid., 13 and note esp. the bibliography listed there in n. 28.

11. In regard to ערפל, see n. 8 above.

12. Barr, *CPTOT*, 377–78.

texts should be checked to see if the determined meaning fits them, as well. Where it does not (presumably in a relatively small percentage of cases), the possibilities of homonyms or scribal errors should be thoroughly investigated. *Under no circumstances, however, should the unclear attestations be utilized as a counterweight in order to neutralize the crucial evidence provided by parallelism in those occurrences where the parallelistic structure is clear.* It should also be stressed that, aside from the above quotation, Barr never again refers to the crucial evidence provided by thirteen of the eighteen occurrences of the term צלמות.

The next part of this study deals with the remaining five occurrences of the term צלמות in Biblical Hebrew. They will be examined in the following order: Jer 2:6, Ps 44:19–20, Ps 23:4, Job 16:16, and Job 38:17. The main issue to be determined is: does the meaning 'darkness' fit in each of these passages, or are there other meanings that may be more appropriate? Since the Bible itself does not provide sufficient evidence in all of these cases, it will also be necessary to gather evidence from the ancient Semitic languages (in this particular case, Akkadian). The most important principle that will guide us in the utilization of comparative evidence is the principle of interdialectal distribution.[13]

The Akkadian interdialectal equivalents to the Biblical Hebrew substantive חֹשֶׁךְ 'darkness' and the Biblical Hebrew root חשׁך 'to be dark' are as follows: *da'ummatu, i/ekletu,* and *eṭūtu,* all meaning 'darkness'; their corresponding verbs *da'āmu, ekēlu,* and *eṭû* and the verb *ṣalāmu,* all meaning 'to be dark'.[14] The first Akkadian verb *da'āmu* 'to be dark' and the noun derived from it *da'ummatu* 'darkness' occur quite often in astronomical and astrological contexts and with reference to technical weather phenomena.[15] This technical usage in Akkadian is paralleled by the Biblical Hebrew technical usage of the verb קדר 'to be dark' and the noun derived from it קדרות 'darkness'.[16] The "Held method" calls for

---

13. Cohen, "Held Method," 13–14 ("principle four").

14. For *da'ummatu* and *da'āmu,* see the many examples listed in CAD D 1 and 123; AHw 146a, 166a, and 1549a; see also n. 16 below and my forthcoming study on ערפל referred to in n. 8 above. For *i/ekletu* and *ekēlu,* see CAD E 64; CAD I/J 60–61; AHw 193b–194a, 195b, and 1552b. For the Biblical Hebrew semantic and etymological equivalents חכלילי (Gen 49:12) and חכללות (Prov 23:29), see Cohen, "Held Method," 15–16, example 2; and see nn. 33–34, 39 below. For *eṭūtu* and *eṭû,* see CAD E 412–13; AHw 266 and 1555b; and see the discussion concerning Job 38:17 in the text of the present study. For the verb *ṣalāmu,* see CAD Ṣ 70–71; AHw 1076; see also Cohen, "Held Method," 15–16, example 2; and see nn. 18, 35 below and the extended discussion concerning Job 16:16 in the text of the present study.

15. See the corresponding references to the Akkadian dictionaries in the previous note.

16. The key to a proper semantic analysis of the Biblical Hebrew root קדר was first suggested by H. Torczyner (N. H. Tur-Sinai) more than 75 years ago (*Die Entstehung des semitischen Sprachtypus* [Vienna, 1916] 210). See also his הלשׁון והספר: כרך הלשׁון [Jerusalem, 1954] 385; idem, *The Book of Job* [Jerusalem, 1967] 100–101). Tur-Sinai's main conclusion was as follows: (*The Book of Job,* 100): ". . . the root קדר, wherever so spelt in the Bible, has not been recognized by the Masorah. In the masoretic text, the verb is preserved only in the shorter forms of the future:

such a distinction between general and technical usage.[17] On the other hand, it should be emphasized already at this stage that Akkadian *ṣalāmu* is the most well attested of the previously mentioned verbs meaning 'to be dark', even though no substantive meaning 'darkness' was apparently ever derived from it.[18] We will now deal with each of these five passages in turn, first and foremost according to the internal biblical philological evidence, and then, *only when necessary*, additional philological evidence will be considered from the ancient Semitic languages.

Jeremiah 2:6: ‏במדבר בארץ ערבה ושוחה בארץ ציה וצלמות . . .‏

With respect to this verse, Barr contends that " 'darkness' does not fit" in such a natural description of the desert, "parallel with terms suggesting its quality of waste and dryness."[19] The appropriateness or inappropriateness of the meaning 'darkness' in the present context, however, is *not dependent on what appears to be more natural or less natural according to the logic of the modern researcher* but rather may be determined in this case on the basis of the existence of a clear precedent for this usage with one of the Biblical Hebrew terms for 'darkness' discussed above. Surely no precedent would be more suitable than the one found later on in the very same chapter, in Jer 2:31, where the semantically identical parallelism ‏ארץ מאפליה // מדבר‏ 'desert // land of deep

---

‏יקד‏ etc., while everywhere else it has been misread as ‏קדר‏." The real proof for this view is the correspondence between Biblical Hebrew ‏הלך קדרנית‏ (Mal 3:14) and Akkadian *qaddiš / qaddāniš / qadadāniš alāku* (see, e.g., the passages listed in CAD Q 44 and 47) 'to walk bowed down'. Just as this idiom is connected to Akkadian *qadādu* 'to bow, to bend down' (cf. CAD Q 44–45), so the Biblical Hebrew corresponding idiom must be connected with the Biblical Hebrew cognate verb ‏קדד‏. Once it is accepted that ‏קָדַדְנִית‏! must be read in Mal 3:14, it then follows that all cases of ‏הלך‏ ‏קֹדֵר‏ (Ps 35:14, 38:7, 42:10, 43:2) must be likewise emended to ‏קֹדֵד‏! The only exception is Job 30:28, for which see C. Cohen, *Beer-Sheva* 3 (1988) 79 (#11) and esp. 102 n. 84 [Hebrew]. On this Biblical Hebrew–Akkadian correspondence and the semantic conclusions that derive from it, see esp. M. Held, "Pits and Pitfalls in Akkadian and Biblical Hebrew," *JANES(CU)* 5 [1973] 177 n. 45. The further emendation to ‏קדד‏ in Jer 8:21, 14:2; Job 5:11 then follows as a matter of course. Both the fact that the Masora recognized the verb ‏קדר‏ only for those forms where a single ‏ד‏ was present (e.g., ‏וַיָּקְדּוּ‏) and the fact that in the majority of these cases, the verb ‏קדר‏ occurs as an A-word to the verb ‏השתחוה‏ 'to bow down' is further corroboratory evidence. According to this view, the root ‏קדר‏ 'to be dark' originally existed in Biblical Hebrew only in the following eleven passages: ten times as a verbal form (1 Kgs 18:45; Jer 4:28; Ezek 31:15; 32:7, 8; Joel 2:10; 4:15; Mic 3:6; Job 6:16; 30:28) and once as a substantive ‏קַדְרוּת‏ 'darkness' (Isa 50:3). The outstanding semantic characteristic demonstrated by the usage of this root within these eleven passages is that in all of the nine *clear* passages (only Ezek 31:15 and Job 6:16 are *unclear*), the contexts in which the verb ‏קדר‏ 'to be dark' occurs are all concerned with the darkening of the sky, the stars, the sun or the moon, and various related weather phenomena. The darkening of the sky was also understood metaphorically as a symbol of mourning (Jer 4:28, Isa 50:3). Contrast, for example, the philological analysis of the usage of this root in A. Brenner, *Colour Terms in the Old Testament* (Sheffield, 1982) 163.

17. See Cohen, "Held Method," 14 ("principle five").

18. See the list of derivatives of the verb *ṣalāmu* in CAD Ṣ 70 and AHw 1076b. See also n. 14 above with additional bibliography.

19. Barr, *CPTOT*, 377.

darkness' occurs within the first two clauses of a triple rhetorical question:[20] המדבר הייתי לישראל אם ארץ מאפליה מדוע . . . 'Have I been like a desert to Israel, / Or like a land of deep darkness? Then why . . . '. Thus the parallelism in Jer 2:31 clearly provides the precedent needed to demonstrate that the meaning 'darkness' for צלמות is quite appropriate for the context of Jer 2:6, whatever the ancient rationale for relating the concepts 'desert' and 'darkness'.[21]

Psalm 44:20: כי דכיתנו במקום תנים ותכס עלינו בצלמות

Barr claims the following concerning this passage:

> In Ps. 44.20 there seems to be a parallel between "in the place of *tannim*" (probably to be read, or understood, as referring to the *tannin* or dragon) and בצלמות. "You have covered us with darkness" seems rather lame and thin after a previous half-verse which talks of crushing "in the place of dragons." It is perhaps because of this consideration that NEB renders with "Yet thou hast crushed us as the sea-serpent was crushed and covered us with the darkness of death"—in other words, the recognition of *death* as a semantic element in the sentence gives it a proper balance.[22]

In fact, however, the word תנים 'jackals' in this verse should not be understood as, or emended to, תנין 'dragon'.[23] The resultant phrase *מקום תנין has no

20. Concerning the phenomena of double and triple rhetorical questions in Biblical Hebrew and Ugaritic, see esp. M. Held, "Rhetorical Questions in Ugaritic and Biblical Hebrew," *ErIsr* 9 (1969) 71–79; Y. Avishur, "The Doubled and Tripled Rhetorical Question Patterns and Their Variations in the Bible and in Ugaritic," זר לגבורות (Zalman Shazar Jubilee Volume; Jerusalem, 1973) 421–64 [Hebrew].

21. For this semantic connection between Jer 2:6 and 2:31 and the general relationship between the concepts of 'desert' and 'darkness', see already J. Pedersen, *Israel: Its Life and Culture I–II* (London, 1926) 464–65; Y. Amir, "מדבר," *Encyclopedia Miqraʾit* (1962) vol. 4, col. 674; S. Talmon, "Wilderness," *IDBSup* 946b. Note, however, that both Amir and Talmon refer to the intermingling or "blending" of two otherwise disparate realms, those of the desert and the netherworld. This seems quite exaggerated and unwarranted contextually, at least in Jer 2:6, 31. While there certainly are some verses where 'darkness' is mentioned as a major feature of the netherworld and even some contexts where terms for 'darkness' serve as epithets of that realm (see the discussion concerning Job 38:17 in the text of the present study), all such passages are clearly otherwise identifiable as dealing with the netherworld. Jer 2:6, 31 refer only to the 'desert'. See also Winton-Thomas, "צַלְמָוֶת," 198 n. 1 (and the additional bibliography cited there); A. van Selms apud J. A. Loader, "The Concept of Darkness in the Hebrew Root ᶜRB/ᶜRP," in *De fructu oris sui* [A. van Selms Festschrift; Leiden, 1971) 105–6. For the term מאפליה 'deep darkness', see towards the end of the text of the present study and n. 61 below.

22. Barr, *CPTOT*, 377.

23. C. A. Briggs, *The Book of Psalms I* (ICC; Edinburgh 1906] 376, 381–83. See also BDB 1072a; *HALAT* 1619b (contra *HALAT* 593a). Contrast most modern translations and commentaries, which emend תַּנִּים to תַּנִּין, e.g., BHS 1127, 20a; Ps 44:20, NJPSV, note b-b. While תַּנִּים must indeed be emended to תַּנִּין in Ezek 29:3 and 32:2, those contexts clearly warrant such an emendation as opposed to the present context. For the confusion in the MT between תַּן 'jackal' and תַּנִּין 'snake, dragon', see C. Cohen, "The Other Meaning of the Biblical תַּנִּין: 'Snake' or 'Crocodile'," *H. M. I. Gevaryahu Memorial Volume II* (Jerusalem 1991) 75 n. 1 [Hebrew].

precedent either in Biblical Hebrew or in Ugaritic.[24] It is also impossible to understand Biblical Hebrew בְמקוֹם as meaning 'like, as' (contra NEB quoted above), since its prepositional meaning can only be 'instead of' (like the preposition תחת).[25] On the other hand, the phrase מקוֹם תנים 'habitat of jackals' (cf. Jer 4:7 for a similar usage with respect to lions) may be accepted as a variant of the regular phrases מעוֹן תנים 'den of jackals' (Jer 9:10, 10:22, 49:33, 51:37) and נוה תנים 'abode of jackals' (Isa 34:13, 35:7). Note that in Isa 35:7 (cf. also 43:20), the phrase נוה תנים occurs together with שרב 'parched earth' and צמאוֹן 'scorched land' in a description of dangers of the desert similar to the description in Jer 2:6 (see immediately above). Thus both מקוֹם תנים 'habitat of jackals' and צלמות 'darkness' (cf. Jer 2:6) are appropriate semantically in a context dealing with dangers of the desert, and this is the best way to understand Ps 44:20. As in Jer 2:6, there is surely no need in such a context to add "death as a semantic element."

Psalm 23:4: גם כי אלך בגיא צלמות לא אירא רע כי אתה עמדי

The meaning 'darkness' for צלמות may be accepted in the present context only if a valid contextual precedent is located, that is, a context parallel to Ps 23:4 including one of the aforementioned Biblical Hebrew terms for 'darkness' instead of the term צלמות. Such a parallel context would ideally consist of the following elements: walking confidently in the darkness in a topographically treacherous area because God is with you. Such topographically treacherous areas would include הר 'mountain'; גבעה 'hill'; בקעת/עמק/גיא 'valley'. The only verse that incorporates all these elements (although only through inference by referring to the opposite situation) is Jer 13:16 (which includes the term הר 'mountain' and three 'darkness' terms, the verb חשך and ערפל//צלמות).[26] Without the topographic element, however, there are many contextually parallel verses such as Isa 9:1 and Ps 107:10, 14;[27] Isa 42:16; 59:9; Mic 7:8; Job 29:2–3.[28] Isa 50:10 is especially worthy of comparison:

24. For a complete semantic study of תנין, see Cohen, "תנין," 75–81.

25. Cf., e.g., BDB 880; *HALAT* 592a.

26. Jer 13:16 was already referred to above as one of the thirteen occurrences of צלמות for which the meaning 'darkness' is beyond any doubt. For the comparison between Jer 13:16 and Ps 23:4, see, e.g., W. McKane, *Jeremiah I–XXV* (ICC; Edinburgh, 1986) 301–2; and esp. W. L. Holladay, *Jeremiah 1* (Hermeneia; Philadelphia, 1986) 407.

27. Isa 9:1 and Ps 107:10, 14 were already discussed above as three of the thirteen occurrences of צלמות for which the meaning 'darkness' is certain.

28. Here too might conceivably belong Ps 39:7 (were צֶלֶם to be derived from the same root as צלמות 'darkness' and Akkadian *ṣalāmu* 'to be dark'): אך בצלם יתהלך איש ... ולא ידע ... 'Man walks about in utter צֶלֶם ... and he knows not. . . .' Those favoring this derivation usually compare esp. Ps 82:5: לא ידעו ולא יבינו בחשכה יתהלכו 'They neither know nor understand, but (rather) walk about in darkness'. This comparison, however, does not take into consideration the wider context of Ps 39:5–7, which deals with the shortness and futility (הֶבֶל) of the human condition and lifespan (יָמַי). The NJPSV translation 'Man walks about as a mere shadow' (based presumably on understanding the מ of the word צלם as enclitic) is more appropriate in this wider context since the term

Who among you reveres the Lord, obeying the voice of his servant?
Though he walk in darkness, having no light
(אשר הלך חשכים ואין נגה לוֹ),
He may trust in God's name and rely upon his God
(יבטח בשם ה׳ וישען באלהיו).

Thus, the meaning 'darkness' for צלמות in Ps 23:4 is contextually appropriate and there is no need here to seek alternative nuances.[29]

צל 'shadow' is used similarly elsewhere (e.g., Ps 102:12, 144:4; Job 8:9, 14:1–2; 1 Chr 29:15), while the aforementioned Biblical Hebrew terms for 'darkness' are not. Cf. esp. Ps 144:4: אדם להבל דמה ימיו כצל עובר 'Man is akin to futility / His days are like a transient shadow'. For the two main views regarding the difficult usage of כַּצֵּל in both Qoh 6:12 and 8:13, see H. L. Ginsberg, קוהלת (Jerusalem, 1977) 39–41, 95, 110; M. V. Fox, *Qohelet and His Contradictions* (Sheffield, 1989) 223, 225, 249, 252, and in general 155. The other alleged occurrence of צֶלֶם 'darkness' in Ps 73:20 is contextually obscure and devoid of any semantic elements occurring together with the aforementioned Biblical Hebrew terms for 'darkness' (see, e.g., BDB 854a; BHS 1155; *HALAT* 963–64; NJPSV, note a-a). Contrast, e.g., Barr, *CPTOT*, 375–76, where צלם is accepted as meaning 'darkness' in both verses with "hesitant favour." Many scholars accept this meaning in Ps 39:7 but reject it in Ps 73:20, e.g., Rashi (citing Dunash ben Labrat, who understood צלם in Ps 39:7 as "לשון צלמות"); Radaq; Yona ibn Janach in ספר השרשים (ed. W. Bacher; Berlin, 1896) 430–31; Winton-Thomas, "צלמות," 193; S. Paul, "צלמות," *Encyclopedia Miqraʾit* (1971) vol. 6, cols. 735–36. Note finally the "etymological" treatment of D. J. A. Clines ("The Etymology of Hebrew ṢELEM," *JNSL* 3 [1974] 22–25), who etymologically concludes that צלם in both Ps 39:7 and 73:20 should be derived from the regular Biblical Hebrew substantive צֶלֶם 'image' and be understood in both verses as 'an (unsubstantial) image' (this view is also listed in *HALAT* 963–64). Biblical Hebrew צל"ם 'to be dark' has been suggested in two other verses, Ps 68:15 (בְּצַלְמוֹן; first proposed in *b. Ber.* 15b) and Ps 88:7 (suggested reading: בְּצַלְמָוֶת! for MT בִּמְצֹלוֹת, as clearly supported by the LXX and Peshiṭta). See, e.g., Winton-Thomas, "צלמות," 193; Paul, "צלמות," col. 736. Neither suggestion is persuasive. For Ps 68:15, see W. F. Albright, "A Catalogue of Early Hebrew Lyric Poems (Psalm LXVIII)," *HUCA* 23 (1950–51) 23; "צלמון .2," *Encyclopedia Miqraʾit* (1971) vol. 6, col. 735. This proposal could only be accepted if a clear textual precedent could be found for an ancient mountain-name derived from a Biblical Hebrew (or ancient Near Eastern) term for 'darkness'. Regarding Ps 88:7, the suggested metathesis בְּצַלְמָוֶת should only be adopted as the preferred reading if it fits the context *better than* MT בִּמְצֹלוֹת 'in the depths'. While the previous term בְּמַחֲשַׁכִּים 'in the darkest places' and the immediate context of Ps 88:7 fit the term צלמות 'darkness' quite well, the same could be said about מְצוּלָה/מְצֹלוֹת/מְצֹלוֹת 'depths'. For in the wider context of Psalm 88, the term מחשכים 'darkest places' serves as an epithet of שְׁאוֹל 'the netherworld' (see esp. vv 4–6). Just as צלמות is used elsewhere as the same epithet (see the discussion concerning Job 38:17 in the present study), so also is the term מְצוּלָה (see esp. Jonah 2:3–4 and cf. N. J. Tromp, *Primitive Conceptions of Death and the Nether World in the Old Testament* [Rome 1969] 56–58). The term מְצֹלוֹת in Ps 88:7, however, fits the wider context better because of the use of the term מִשְׁבָּרֶיךָ 'Your (God's) waves, breakers' in the next verse, occurring together with מְצוּלָה in a similar context in Jonah 2:3–4 (cf. Zech 10:11, Ps 107:24–25), while the terms מִשְׁבָּר/גַל 'wave, breaker' (see H. R. [Chaim] Cohen, *Biblical Hapax Legomena in the Light of Akkadian and Ugaritic* [Missoula, Mont., 1978] 25–26 [hereafter *BHL*]) never occur together with צלמות or any other Biblical Hebrew term for 'darkness'.

29. It is for this reason that one cannot accept D. Pardee's attempt to analyze Ps 23:4, 6 as containing "two antonymic pairs distributed distantly: 'evil//good' [טוב//רע—C. C.] and 'death//life' [מות/חיי—C. C.] (both sets in vv. 4a, 6a) . . . if *ṣlmwt* consists of *ṣl+mwt*" (see D. Pardee, "Structure and Meaning in Hebrew Poetry: The Example of Psalm 23," *Maarav* 5–6 [1990] 251 and n. 23).

Job 16:16: פְּנַי חֳמַרְמְרָה מִנִּי בֶכִי וְעַל עַפְעַפַּי צַלְמָוֶת

The parallelism in this verse is based on two parallel physiological reactions of the face and the eyes to weeping.[30] Since there is still no consensus among biblical scholars concerning the meaning of חֳמַרְמְרָה,[31] the only recourse in determining whether the meaning 'darkness' is appropriate for צַלְמָוֶת in this verse is to seek out contextual precedents among the aforementioned Biblical Hebrew and (if necessary) Akkadian terms for 'darkness'. In Biblical Hebrew the most important precedent is Lam 5:17:

עַל זֶה הָיָה דָוֶה לִבֵּנוּ עַל אֵלֶּה חָשְׁכוּ עֵינֵינוּ

On account of this, our hearts are sick;
Because of these, our eyes are darkened.[32]

In addition, it should be noted that the Akkadian verb *ekēlu*, one of the previously mentioned semantic equivalents of Biblical Hebrew חשׁך, has a Biblical

---

As has been demonstrated in the present study, the basic meaning of צַלְמָוֶת in Ps 23:4 must be 'darkness'. There is also no precedent whatsoever for the use of צֵל 'shadow' in such a context (see n. 56 below). At the very most, one might accept Pardee's alternate suggestion of a distant "punning parallelism, for the last part of *ṣalmāwet* is, according to the Masoretic tradition, vocalized like *māwet* 'death' " (ibid.). But even if this secondary midrashic pun is accepted as originally intended by the author of Psalm 23, it could surely just as well be based on an original vocalization צַלְמֻות* (see below, pp. 306–8).

30. The Biblical Hebrew term עַפְעַפַּיִם 'eyes' is a clear example of a B-word of the regular term עֵינַיִם 'eyes'. Of its ten occurrences, six are in synonymous parallelism with עֵינַיִם 'eyes' as the A-word (Jer 9:17; Ps 11:4, 132:4; Prov 4:25, 6:4, 30:13). For A-words and B-words, see Cohen, "Held Method," 12–13 ("principle three"). Thus, as in the case of the term צַלְמָוֶת, this parallelism determines absolutely the semantic range of the term עפעפים in those six passages. As for the other four passages (including Job 16:16), a determination must be made separately for each one (based mainly on the usage of the regular term עינים), whether or not the meaning 'eyes' is appropriate. In Job 16:16, the two notions that relate to עפעפים are בֶכִי 'crying' (which occurs in the first stich but stands for both stichs) and being covered by צַלְמָוֶת. A precedent for the first notion occurs in Jer 9:17 (one of the six verses where עפעפים is parallel to עינים; see above), while for the second notion, the two key verses are Lam 5:17 and Prov 23:29–30 as discussed immediately above in the text of the present study. Concerning the other three passages (Prov 6:25; Job 3:9, 41:10), Ugaritic ʿpʿp, and the etymology of this term, I intend to deal with all these issues in a separate article.

31. The main problem in determining the meaning of the verb חמרמר is its occurrence in two additional passages (besides Job 16:16) with respect to מֵעַיִם 'belly, inner digestive organs' (Lam 1:20, 2:11). See esp. R. Gradwohl, *Die Farben im Alten Testament* (Berlin, 1963) 16–18, 27; Brenner, *Colour Terms in the Old Testament*, 126 and esp. 131–32; *HALAT* I, 316b–17a; H. Ringgren, "חמר," *TDOT* 5.1–2. Once again, usage rather than etymology must be the prime consideration in dealing with this problem. Furthermore, the possibility of two separate roots (either with ḥ and ḫ or two true homonyms) seems most unlikely in view of the extremely rare verbal form *qṭlṭl*.

32. Ps 69:24 and Qoh 12:3 have not been taken into consideration here because there is no emotional physiological reaction in either case. In the former verse, what is involved is a curse of blindness: "May their eyes grow dark (תֶחְשַׁכְנָה עֵינֵיהֶם) so that they cannot see." In the latter verse the context has to do with the natural process of aging: "When the 'guards of the house' [i.e. the arms] are unsteady, . . . and the 'peerers through the windows' [i.e. the eyes] grow dark."

Hebrew semantic and etymological parallel, the *dis-legomenon* חכל 'to be dark'.[33] While the first occurrence חכלילי 'dark' (Gen 49:12) is best understood as referring to the color of Judah's eyes' being darker than wine,[34] the second attestation חכללות 'darkness' (Prov 23:29–30) is in fact particularly pertinent to the present discussion since it deals with a physiological reaction of the eyes as a result of inebriation (each clause of v. 29 describes a different manifestation of drunkenness):

> Who cries, "Woe!" who, "Alas!"?
> Who has quarrels, who complaints?
> Who has wounds without any reason?
> Who has darkness of the eyes (למי חכללות עינים)?
> Those whom wine keeps up late,
> Those who assemble to drain the cups.

Finally, it should be emphasized that this usage of Biblical Hebrew צלמות 'darkness' has a well-attested parallel Akkadian usage for the aforementioned verb *ṣalāmu* 'to be dark' with regard to emotional physiological reactions of both the face and the lips.[35] For example, both the goddess Ereshkigal, Queen of the Netherworld (in the composition "The Descent of Ishtar to the Netherworld"), and the divine messenger Namtar (in the composition "Nergal and Ereshkigal") display the same emotional physiological reaction of anger in their response when each one is informed that an unwelcome guest is waiting at the gate of the Netherworld, seeking permission to enter:

> *kīma nikis bīni eriqū/īr(i)qū panūša/panūš*
> *kīma šapat/šapti kunīni iṣlimā šabātuša/šaptāšu*

> Her/His face grew pallid like a cut-off tamarisk,
> Her/His lips darkened like the edge of a *kunīnu*-bowl.[36]

---

33. For the comparison between Akkadian *ekēlu* and Biblical Hebrew חכל (both meaning 'to be dark') and their respective usage, see C. Cohen and A. Demsky, "חכלילי עינים מיין" *Encyclopaedia ᶜOlam Hatanakh: Genesis* (Ramat-Gan, 1982) 250ab; Cohen, "Held Method," 15–16. See also n. 39 below.

34. חכלילי עינים מיין in Gen 49:12 means either 'his eyes are darker than wine' (as best fits the parallelism and overall positive context of the verse) or, less likely, 'his eyes are dark from (drinking) wine' (which best fits the second occurrence of the root חכל in Prov 23:29–30, where the context, however, is negative). See, for example, NJPSV, note c-c to Gen 49:12.

35. See, for example, CAD Ṣ 70, meanings 1a, 1d, and 2b; AHw 1076a, meaning 1e. Compare also the Old Assyrian phrase *ṣulum panī* 'anger, angry face' (e.g. CAD Ṣ 240–41, meaning 1c; AHw 1110b, meaning 4).

36. *BAL*², 97:29–30; *AnSt* 10 (1960) 116:21–22. The translation here follows, for example, CAD K 539b; CAD Š/1 484a. On these two passages, see E. Reiner, *Your Thwarts in Pieces, Your Mooring Rope Cut* (Michigan, 1985) 38: ". . . Ereshkigal's reaction to the news of Ištar at her gate implies that Ištar's arrival forebodes no good. Her immediate reaction—her face grew pallid (literally, yellow) like a cut-off tamarisk, her lips turned black (or purple) like a *kunīnu*-plant (a plant not otherwise identifiable)—is described in terms of her physical symptoms, drawn upon an imagery

It is difficult to determine today precisely which physiological reactions of the body, real or imaginary, are being depicted in both the biblical and the Akkadian passages. It is abundantly clear, however, that in all of the above passages in both Biblical Hebrew and Akkadian, we are dealing with verbs with the basic meaning 'to be dark', and to this group of verses we may now add the present case of צלמות in Job 16:16 as discussed above.

Job 38:17: הנגלו לך שערי מות ושערי צלמות תראה

Barr understands this usage of צלמות as follows:

> In Job 38:17 the parallel is with *mawet* "death." Hehn maintained that "darkness" was impossible here. Even if this is going too far, the sense "shadow of death" seems a strong contender. Note also that *ṣalmawet* is in this case a *place*, a place with doors (or doorkeepers—so NEB with its "the doorkeepers of the place of darkness").[37]

This context and Job 10:21–22 are the only two passages in which צלמות 'darkness' refers to the Netherworld. In the latter passage, the phrase ארץ חושך וצלמות 'the land of darkness and gloom' is clearly used as an epithet of שאול 'the Netherworld'. In that same passage, the words בטרם אלך ולא אשוב 'before I depart, never to return' are best understood as a reflex of the Mesopotamian epithet of the Netherworld, Akkadian *erṣet lā târi* 'the land of no return'. A parallel allusion to the same Mesopotamian designation occurs in Prov 2:19 (comparing the house of the "foreign woman" to the Netherworld):

כל באיה לא ישובון ולא ישיגו ארחות חיים

All who enter her (house) cannot return,
They will never again find the paths of life.

This verse is clearly reminiscent of the first eleven lines of the Akkadian version of "The Descent of Ishtar to the Netherworld,"[38] which include the epithet of the Netherworld *bītu eṭû* 'the dark house':

> *iškunma mārat Sîn uzu[nša] ana bīti eṭê šubat Ir[kalla]*
> *ana bīti ša ēribūšu lā āṣ[û] ana ḫarrāni ša alaktaša lā tār[at]*

---

used elsewhere too to depict emotions, fear as well as anger" (cf. also p. 56). Reiner does not provide any evidence for her understanding of *kunīnu* as a plant rather than a type of bowl (other than the obvious parallelism with the term *bīnu* 'tamarisk'). This, however, does not affect her point that the same emotional reaction of anger and fear is described in both texts in terms of "physical symptoms."

37. Barr, *CPTOT*, 377.

38. For the Mesopotamian tradition involved and a discussion of several biblical literary allusions to it (although without specific reference to Prov 2:19 and the aforementioned first four words of Job 10:21), see M. Held, "Pits and Pitfalls," 178–81 and esp. nn. 53 and 56. See generally Reiner, *Your Thwarts in Pieces*, 29–49. See also nn. 36 above and 40 below.

> The daughter of Sîn did indeed direct (her) attention
> To *the dark house*, the abode of Irkalla,
> To the house from which those who enter it do not exist,
> To the road whose course does not turn back.[39]

M. Held has written the following concerning this epithet and its biblical parallels:

> ... the Hebrew idiom closest to our *bītu eṭû* (=*bīt ekleti* in Gilg. VII, iv:33) would seem to be ארץ חושך וצלמות in Job 10:21–22. . . . For darkness as a characteristic of the netherworld, cf. particularly CT 15, 45:7–9 (Descent of Ištar) = Gilg. VII, iv:36–39 and LKA, 62 r. 15–17 (MA version of the Descent of Ištar . . .). In light of this tradition, it is hardly surprising to note that, according to the Babylonian lexicographers (Landsberger, *MSL* III [1955], 138:101–2; cf. CAD, G, 43b, sub *ganzir*), *ekletu/eṭūtu* 'darkness, gloom' may come to denote the netherworld itself. So, too, in Hebrew, חושך and צלמות are not only B-words of שאול and מות, respectively (Job 17:13; 38:17; cf. Ps 88:7, 13), but חושך and מחשך alone come to denote 'netherworld' (cf. I Sam 2:9; Ps 143:3; Job 18:18; Lam 3:6).[40]

Among the biblical evidence cited by Held, Job 17:13 is particularly significant as a clear precedent (שאול 'Netherworld'//חושך 'darkness') for the use of צלמות 'darkness' as an epithet for the Netherworld in both Job 10:21–22 and 38:17:

> אם אקוה שאול ביתי בחושך רפדתי יצועי
>
> If I must look forward to the Netherworld as my home,
> And make my bed in the 'dark place'.[41]

There is obviously no difference between the parallelism צלמות//מות in Job 38:17 and the parallelism שאול//חושך in Job 17:13.[42] Finally, note that the use of the phrase שערי צלמות 'gates of the "dark place"'[43] in Job 38:17 has as its

---

39. CT 15, 45:3–6 (= *BAL*², 95–96:3–6). The translation is quoted from Held, "Pits and Pitfalls," 179–80. The epithet *bītu eṭû* 'the dark house' occurs in line 4. Note the parallel epithet *bīt ekleti* 'the house of darkness' [= 'the dark house'] which occurs in the quotation of these lines in "Gilgamesh" VII iv:33–39a. For Biblical Hebrew חכל, the Biblical Hebrew semantic and etymological equivalent of Akkadian *ekēlu*, see nn. 33–34 above. On the grammatical genitival construction interpreted adjectivally, see Cohen, *BHL*, 139–40; Reiner, *Your Thwarts in Pieces*, 48 n. 2.

40. Held, "Pits and Pitfalls," 179 n. 53.

41. The translation here is almost identical with that of the NJPSV at Job 17:13.

42. For all these terms as epithets of the netherworld, see Tromp, *Death and the Nether World*, passim, but esp. 21–23, 95–97, and 140–44. It is quite difficult to understand why Tromp understands all Biblical Hebrew occurrences of מָוֶת referring to the Netherworld as cases of personification. On this entire issue, see n. 44 below. In Job 38:17, there can be no doubt whatsoever that both מות and צלמות are epithets of שאול to be translated 'Netherworld' and 'the "dark place"' respectively.

43. The NEB reading שֹׁעֲרֵי צלמות 'gatekeepers of the "dark place"' referred to by Barr in the aforementioned quote is by no means excluded. Aside from the obvious advantage of avoiding repetition of the same word within two parallel stichs, the NEB reading has clear Akkadian precedents

Biblical Hebrew precedent not only the parallel phrase שַׁעֲרֵי מָוֶת 'gates of the Netherworld'[44] in the very same verse, but also the other three verses where this imagery is found—שַׁעֲרֵי מָוֶת/שְׁאוֹל 'gates of the Netherworld' (Isa 38:10; Ps 9:14, 107:18). While this biblical evidence is certainly sufficient, some additional Akkadian evidence from the above-mentioned composition, "The Descent of Ishtar to the Netherworld," may also be cited. The Akkadian term *bābu* 'gate', the interdialectal equivalent[45] of Biblical Hebrew שַׁעַר occurs no less than 23 times in the 138 preserved lines of this composition, in all cases referring to the (seven) gate(s) of the Netherworld.[46] In view of this abundance of evidence both from Biblical Hebrew and from Akkadian, there should be no doubt whatsoever that Job 38:17 must be understood as an additional biblical literary allusion to the widespread Mesopotamian tradition concerning the Netherworld. Rather than contending that "darkness is impossible here," צַלְמָוֶת 'darkness' should be understood in this Netherworld context, as a bonafide epithet of the Netherworld meaning 'the "dark place"' just as is the case with its semantic equivalents Biblical Hebrew חוֹשֶׁךְ and Akkadian *eṭūtu*.

---

and perhaps even some Biblical Hebrew support. The Akkadian term *atû*, the interdialectal equivalent of Biblical Hebrew שׁוֹעֵר 'gatekeeper', occurs in "The Descent of Ishtar to the Netherworld" thirteen times with reference to the gatekeeper of the Netherworld (lines 13, 14, 21, 25, 37, 39, 43, 46, 49, 52, 55, 58, 61; for the phrase "seven gates of the Netherworld", see the end of the present note and n. 46 below). In four cases (lines 13, 14, 37, 39), *bābu* 'gate' is specifically mentioned (see also n. 46 below), while in line 14, the construct *atî bābi* 'the keeper of the gate' is found. Thus, the NEB reading שַׁעַר 'gate' // שֹׁעֵר 'gatekeeper' in Job 38:17 on the basis of this Akkadian usage is certainly plausible (even if not absolutely necessary). Note also that the vast majority of the cited cases of *atî* 'gatekeeper' in CAD A/2 516b–517a refer to the gatekeeper of the Netherworld. Finally, note that although Biblical Hebrew שׁוֹעֵר 'gatekeeper' in its 37 attestations never occurs referring to the Netherworld, Isa 38:10, one of the four cases of שַׁעֲרֵי מָוֶת/שְׁאוֹל (the other three are Ps 9:14, 107:18; Job 38:17), may best be read בְּשֹׁעֲרֵי שְׁאוֹל פֻּקַּדְתִּי (instead of MT בְּשַׁעֲרֵי) 'I was consigned [*qal*-passive] to the gatekeepers of the Netherworld'. This reading is based on the following similar Akkadian usage of *paqādu* (= Biblical Hebrew פקד) in *AfO* 19, 117:24 (cf. CAD A/2 517a): *lipqidkunūši ana 7 atê* [*ša*] *Ereškigal* 'May he consign you (pl.) to the seven gatekeepers of the netherworld'.

44. It is very difficult to fathom on what basis Barr assumes that שַׁעֲרֵי 'the gates of' *cannot* occur with the abstract noun צַלְמָוֶת 'darkness' in the second stich of Job 38:17 but *can* occur with the abstract noun מָוֶת 'death' in the first stich of that verse. Surely Barr's reasoning ("צַלְמָוֶת is in this case a *place*, a place with doors") applies equally to the abstract noun מָוֶת 'death' (see Barr, *CPTOT*, 377). In fact, the term מָוֶת is often used as an epithet for the location of the Netherworld (e.g., Ps 6:6, 9:14, 107:18; Prov 5:5, 7:27), sometimes in personified form (e.g., Isa 28:15, 18; 38:18; Hos 13:14; Hab 2:5; Job 28:22). Therefore, just as צַלְמָוֶת and חוֹשֶׁךְ must be understood in such contexts as 'the "dark place"', so מָוֶת must be similarly understood (in its nonpersonified form) as 'the "death place"'. See already BDB 560 ('state of death' is incorrect; 'place of death' is correct); *HALAT* II, 534b (meaning 4: 'Totenreich'). See also n. 42 above.

45. See n. 13 above and the corresponding text of the present study.

46. CT 15, 45 (= *BAL*[2], 95–103): lines 12, 13, 14, 15, 16, 37, 39, 42, 45, 48, 51, 54, 57, 60, 93, 94, 119, 120, 121, 122, 123, 124, 125.

This concludes the two semantic analyses undertaken in this study: for the first, concerning thirteen occurrences of צלמות, a clear connection has easily been established with the semantic range of חוֹשֶׁךְ 'darkness'; for the second, with regard to the remaining five attestations, it has been philologically demonstrated that the semantic range of 'darkness' is most appropriate. Thus, the overall semantic conclusion regarding this term is that of the medieval Jewish commentator Rashi in his comment on Ps 23:4 (in the name of Dunash ben Labrat): כל צלמות לשון חשך 'every occurrence of צלמות is semantically connected to 'darkness'.

Barr makes two further claims concerning the philological analysis of the term צלמות that warrant a response here. The first additional claim is as follows:

> Even if we accept that "darkness" is the right meaning, this can hardly be the end of the matter. The understanding as "the shadow of death" is very old: out of the 18 or so cases in the Hebrew, about ten or 11 are rendered with σκιὰ θανάτου in Greek. These include not only some in the Writings, such as in Job itself and in the Psalms, but also two in the Major Prophets (Isa 9:1 and Jer 13:16). Since, on quite other grounds, Job may be a somewhat late book, at least in its final form, no very great distance in time may separate its completion from the Septuagintal interpretation of this word. It is thus quite possible that the sense "the shadow of death" was already understood by the final redactor of the canonical text of Job, or was known to him and influenced his thinking, even if it was not intended by the earliest composer of ch. 3.[47]

Certainly all renderings of the ancient versions are a legitimate object of scholarly scrutiny. It is valid to analyze each version in order to reconstruct the factors (conscious or subconscious) that influenced the translator(s) to translate in one particular way and thus to utilize the translation itself as a sort of ancient commentary to the original Hebrew text. However, such a scholarly endeavor is not the job of the biblical philologist. The philological evidence that may be derived from such an effort is no more valid than a reconstructed commentary on a particular verse based on how that verse is understood in rabbinic literature (for example, Mishnaic, Talmudic, or early Midrashic exegesis). In biblical philological research, there is only one certain value in studying the ancient translations. The value is in the confirmation of the consonantal Hebrew text (the *Vorlage*) that served as the translator's source.[48] Thus in the present case, it makes little difference to the philologist whether the LXX translated 'shadow of death' or 'darkness', since the *Vorlage* in either case would be the unvocalized term צלמות. As long as the semantic investigation of the biblical usage of

---

47. *CPTOT*, 376. See also, for example, Winton-Thomas, "צלמות," 191–92 and n. 1; Michel, "ṢLMWT," 7; Paul, "צלמות," 735–36.

48. See most recently E. Tov, *Textual Criticism of the Hebrew Bible* (Minneapolis, 1992) 121–33 and the bibliography cited there.

this term does not yield a single context for which 'shadow of death' is more appropriate than 'darkness', all speculation about whether "the sense 'the shadow of death' was already understood by the final redactor of the canonical text of Job, or was known to him and influenced his thinking, even if it was not intended by the earliest composer of ch. 3" is philologically irrelevant in regard to the basic meaning of this term.[49]

Barr's second additional claim concerns the etymology of the term צלמות, the final aspect to be discussed in the present study:

> As we have seen, it is usual to say that the word should be read as *ṣalmût*, with the abstract noun-ending *-ût*. But is it really probable that the tradition took a word which had previously always been pronounced as *ṣalmût* and altered its pronunciation to *ṣalmāwet*, purely in order to support a midrashic-etymological explanation, and without any justification whatever in the current phonetics of the word?[50]

Four different etymologies have been suggested for the term צלמות:[51]

(a) צֵל (שֶׁל) מָוֶת 'shadow of death'—in accordance with the MT vocalization and through comparison with the PN בְּצַלְאֵל[52] and the construct form קַן (for example, Deut 22:6) of the substantive קֵן 'nest'. This etymology is accepted by most Jewish commentators and grammarians of the Medieval Period (e.g., Saᶜadya, Ibn Janach, and Radaq)[53] and is considered a reasonable possibility by

---

49. Obviously such speculation must be taken into consideration when investigating the origins of this midrashic understanding 'shadow of death' as reflected by the MT vocalization צַלְמָוֶת. It is even possible that this early midrash originated prior to the LXX and was known to some or all of the biblical authors. It might have even influenced their choice of צלמות as a B-word to חוֹשֶׁךְ 'darkness' in certain contexts (Job 10:21–22 and esp. Job 38:17) as preferable to other B-words such as אוֹפֶל or אפלה. Under no circumstances, however, should we allow such speculations to affect our understanding of the basic meaning of this term 'darkness', based on its Biblical Hebrew usage. See also nn. 53 and 56 below.

50. Barr, *CPTOT*, 376. It should again be emphasized that the extensive semantic investigation undertaken here was carried out independently, without any reliance whatsoever upon etymological considerations. It is only during the current final stage of the investigation, when the semantic conclusions have already been drawn, that an appropriate etymology must be sought that corresponds to those conclusions.

51. See, in general, the excellent summary in Paul, "צלמות," 735–36.

52. The PN בְּצַלְאֵל means literally 'in the shadow (i.e., under the protection) of God' (cf. esp. Ps 91:1). For this PN and the many parallel PNs in Akkadian such as *Ina-ṣilli-ᵈNergal* and *Ina-ṣilli-ᵈNabû* (based on the cognate Akkadian substantive *ṣillu* 'shadow'), see, for example, Y. M. Grintz, "Bezalel," *EncJud* 4.786–87; *HALAT* 1.141; J. J. Stamm, *Die Akkadische Namengebung* (Darmstadt, 1968) 276. This is further corroboratory evidence of the positive usage of the term צל meaning 'protection'. See also n. 56 below.

53. For the views of Saᶜadya and Radaq, see J. H. R. Biesenthal and F. Lebrecht (eds.), ספר השרשים לרבי דויד בן יוסף קמחי הספרדי (reprint: Jerusalem, 1967) 313b (note, however, that Saᶜadya never translates צלמות as 'shadow of death', but rather always by Judaeo-Arabic גבס,

many modern scholars as well.[54] One main conclusion of the present study is that this etymology must be rejected because the resultant meaning contradicts the two major results of the extensive semantic investigation undertaken here, namely that every occurrence of צלמות is semantically connected to 'darkness' and that the principal usage of this term is as a B-word to חוֹשֶׁךְ 'darkness'. It may be added that the two components of this etymology, צל 'shadow' and מות 'death', are also semantically inappropriate on an individual basis. The term מות 'death' fits only the Netherworld contexts of Job 10:21–22 and 38:17 where, as already shown, 'darkness' is no less appropriate.[55] Moreover, the more than fifty Biblical Hebrew occurrences of צל 'shadow, protection' may be divided into four basic usages, *none of which is semantically appropriate for any of the occurrences of* צלמות.[56]

---

which, according to Y. Qapach, "is a synonym of חוֹשֶׁךְ"; see Y. Qapach (ed.), איוב עם תרגום ופירוש רס"ג [Jerusalem, 1973] 78). For the view of Ibn Janach, see Ibn Janach, ספר השרשים, 430–31 (note that Ibn Janach chose the best possible verse in support of this etymology, Job 38:17; it is here suggested that the choice of צלמות as a B-word to חוֹשֶׁךְ in this context may have been made with this popular etymology in mind—see n. 49 above, n. 56 below, and the extensive discussion of Job 38:17 on pp. 298–300.

54. Barr, *CPTOT*, 375–81; BDB 853b; H. Bauer and P. Leander, *Historische Grammatik der hebräischen Sprache* (repr. Hildesheim, 1965) 506 (§ui); Clines, "ṢELEM," 23–25; D. N. Freedman, *Pottery, Poetry and Prophecy: Collected Essays on Biblical Hebrew Poetry* (Winona Lake, Ind., 1980) 292; L. L. Grabbe, *Comparative Philology and the Text of Job* (Missoula, Mont., 1977) 27–29; J. Hehn, *MVAG* 22 (= *Orientalische Studien Fritz Hommel zur sechzigsten Geburtstag . . . gewidmet*; 1918) 79–90; Michel, "ṢLMWT," 5–20; T. Nöldeke, "צלמות und צלם," *ZAW* 17 (1897) 183–87; Pardee, "Psalm 23," 251 n. 23; J. F. A. Sawyer, *Semantics in Biblical Research* (London, 1972) 14, 40, 90; idem, "Review of W. L. Holladay, *A Concise Hebrew and Aramaic Lexicon of the Old Testament*," *JSS* 17/2 (1972) 257–59; Tromp, *Death and the Netherworld*, 140–42.

55. See the extensive discussion concerning Job 38:17 and appendix A at the end of this study.

56. The four basic usages of the Biblical Hebrew term צל are as follows: (1) *'shadow', in a natural graphic sense, often in connection with the time of day*—Judg 9:36 (cf. v. 34); 2 Kgs 20:9, 10 (twice), 11; Isa 38:8; Jer 6:4; Ps 80:11 (figurative); Cant 2:17; 4:6. (2) *'shade' provided by trees or the like, as protection from the heat of the sun (both literal and figurative, occasionally implied only)*—e.g., Jonah 4:5, 6 (lit.); Ezek 31:6, 12, 17 (fig.); Job 7:2 (implied). (3) *'protection' in general without reference (even through implication) to protection specifically from the heat of the sun*—Gen 19:8; Num 14:9; Isa 16:3; 30:2, 3; 49:2; 51:16; Jer 48:45; Ps 17:8; 36:8; 57:2; 63:8; 91:1; Lam 4:20. (4) *'shadow' as a symbol of the frailty and transitoriness of mortal life, often referring specifically to the brevity of the human life-span*—Ps 39:7! (see n. 28 above); 102:12; 109:23; 144:4; Job 8:9; 14:1–2; 17:7; 1 Chr 29:15. For the PN בצלאל (according to basic usage [3]), see n. 52 above. For a discussion of basic usage (4) as well as the unclear occurrences in Qoh 6:12 and 8:13, see n. 28 above. For the two additional unclear cases of בְּצֵל in Qoh 7:12, see Ginsberg, קוהלת, 97; Fox, *Qohelet*, 231. Note that the above semantic range of Biblical Hebrew צל is nearly identical with the usage of the Akkadian cognates ṣillu/ṣulūlu (the Akkadian cognates have some additional meanings not attested for צל, while basic meaning (4) above seems to be unattested in Akkadian) together with their partial synonym andullu in the meaning 'protection'. See, for example, CAD A/2 114–15; CAD Ṣ 189–92, 242–43; AHw 50, 1101, and 1111. Note also the Akkadian personal names with andullu/ṣillu/ṣulūlu 'protection' and cf. Biblical Hebrew

(b) מָוֶת (שֶׁל) צֵל 'very deep shadow, thick darkness'—first suggested by
D. Winton-Thomas in 1962.[57] This etymology understands the component מות
not as 'death', but rather as an indication of the superlative, citing such precedents as the usage of Greek θάνατος and such English phrases as '*deadly dull*'
or '*bored to death*'. In Biblical Hebrew, such equivalent phrases as 1 Sam 5:11
(מהומת מות 'a deadly destruction') with 1 Sam 5:9 (מהומה גדולה מאד 'a very
severe destruction') have been compared.[58] Winton-Thomas concludes his proposal by remarking, "If indeed צלמות does mean '(a) very deep shadow, thick
darkness', nothing is to be gained by reading צַלְמוּת, and a great deal is lost
since a specific Hebrew idiom goes unrecognized."[59] This etymology is likewise unacceptable because it is based on equating semantically the component
צל 'shadow' with חוֹשֶׁךְ 'darkness'. It must be emphasized that even if מות could
be used as an indication of the superlative, the term צַלְמָוֶת could only mean
'thick darkness' if צל 'shadow' could be shown also to mean 'darkness'. In fact,
Winton-Thomas had noted in his previous research (following Radaq and
other medieval Jewish commentators) that Biblical Hebrew divine appellatives
such as אלהים, אל, and יה (either as separate terms or as final elements of compound terms) could also be used in certain cases as an indication of the super-

---

בצלאל. See n. 52 above and see CAD A/2 115a; AHw 50b; Stamm, *Namengebung*, 211 and n. 3.
It is thus absolutely clear that the semantic range of Biblical Hebrew צל is totally different from
that of Biblical Hebrew חוֹשֶׁךְ 'darkness'. No occurrence of צלמות fits any of the four basic usages
of צל listed above; neither does Biblical Hebrew צל ever occur in construct with מות or any other
term having to do with death or the Netherworld, nor is צלמות ever used in any context where the
term צל would be appropriate. This is the correct response to Nöldeke's claim "that it depends on
the object that casts the shadow. The shade given by death would certainly be differently perceived than the shade of a rock." See Michel, "ṢLMWT," 7, summarizing Nöldeke, "צלמות und
צלם," 184; and see esp. S. R. Driver and G. B. Gray, *The Book of Job* ([ICC; Edinburgh, 1921]
18–19). The sole context I was able to find where any of the three Akkadian terms ṣillu, ṣulūlu,
or *andullu* occurs together with any of the Akkadian terms for 'darkness' mentioned in the present
study is the Akkadian version of the bilingual text BIN II, 22:i:31–32, as cited, for example, in
CAD Ṣ 189a; CAD E 64, 279; and CAD N/2 347b: *urrup ṣillašu ukkul ina zumrišu nūr[u] ul
ibašši* 'he (the *utukku*-demon) is dark, his shadow is dark, within his body, there is no light' (this
passage includes Akkadian ṣillu 'shadow' together with *ekēlu* 'to be dark' [see nn. 14, 33, 34
above] and *erēpu* 'to be dusky, dark' [see n. 8 above]. This isolated apparently atypical, Akkadian
passage is surely insufficient (as opposed to all the contrary evidence) basis for the claim that the
semantic range of Biblical Hebrew צל corresponds in any way to that of חוֹשֶׁךְ 'darkness'. It might
serve, however, as further evidence (from the popular genre of demonology) for the *popular etymology* of מָוֶת + צֵל discussed above in nn. 49 and 53.

57. Winton-Thomas, "צלמות," 196–200. Dahood, *Psalms I*, 147.

58. See Winton-Thomas, "צלמות," 196–97 for this and other examples. See also idem, "A
Consideration of Some Unusual Ways of Expressing the Superlative in Hebrew," *VT* 3 (1953)
221; idem, "Some Further Remarks on Unusual Ways of Expressing the Superlative in Hebrew,"
VT 18 (1968) 120–24 (note that צלמות is not mentioned in these two latter studies).

59. Winton-Thomas, "צלמות," 197.

lative.[60] One of the examples cited (following Radaq and Mezudat Zion) is מַאְפֵּלְיָה 'deep darkness'.[61] It is this term that serves as the exact precedent for the structure required in this case, for in order for such a term to mean 'deep darkness', its first element must be one of the Biblical Hebrew terms for 'darkness', just as מַאְפֵּל 'darkness' (cf. Josh 24:7) is the first element of מַאְפֵּלְיָה.

(c) צַלְמוּת* 'darkness'—apparently first mentioned (in a negative way for the purpose of refutation) by Ibn Janach in the eleventh century[62] and subsequently adopted by most modern biblical scholars to this day.[63] The reconstructed form of the substantive צַלְמוּת* follows the same pattern as קַדְרוּת 'darkness' (Isa 50:3),[64] מַלְכוּת 'kingship' (for example, Ps 145:13), and הוֹלֵלוּת 'madness' (Qoh 10:13), namely with the suffix תו- for abstract nouns.[65] The root צלם (< ẓlm) 'to be dark' is cognate with Akkadian ṣalāmu, Arabic ẓalima and Ethiopic ṣalma/ ṣalama.[66] Ugaritic ẓlmt/ǵlmt and ǵlm have also been suggested as cognates, but these comparisons are presently quite uncertain because the extant Ugaritic contexts (KTU 1.4:VII:54–56; 1.8:7–9; 1.14:I:19–20) are all still

---

60. Examples for such a superlative usage of אֵל and אֱלֹהִים as separate terms include הררי אל 'the great mountains' (Ps 36:7), ארזי אל 'the mighty cedars' (Ps 80:11) and נפתולי אלהים 'a fateful contest' (Gen 30:8). For the superlative usage of יָה as a final element in a compound term, see, for example, שלהבתיה 'a blazing flame' (Cant 8:6), and see the above discussion concerning מאפליה 'deep darkness' (Jer 2:31). For these and other cases, see Winton-Thomas, "Superlative," 210–19 (note esp. the contribution of the medieval Jewish commentators to this research discussed on p. 211 and nn. 1–8); idem, "Some Further Remarks," 120–22.

61. See Radaq's commentary on 1 Sam 26:12, Jonah 3:3, and Jer 2:31 (cf. Winton-Thomas ["Superlative," 211 n. 6], who mistakenly added Ps 36:7 and omitted Jer 2:31); and the commentary of Mezudat Zion on Jer 2:31 as correctly cited by Winton-Thomas ("Superlative," 211 n. 8). For this term, see also the discussion of Jer 2:6 above (pp. 292–93).

62. Ibn Janach, ספר השרשים, 430–31. This is apparently the answer to Michel's query concerning "the first scholar who proposed the root ṣlm for ṣlmwt." See Michel, "ṢLMWT," 14 n. 2.

63. For example, E. Ben-Yehuda, מילון הלשון העברית (repr. New York, 1960) 6.5501a n. 1; Brenner, *Colour Terms in the Old Testament*, 163; Briggs, *Psalms I*, 211–12, 383; A. Chacham, ספר איוב (Jerusalem, 1984) 19b; idem, ספר תהלים (Jerusalem, 1990) 125a; Driver and Gray, *Job* (Philological Notes), part 2, 18–19; GKC 103 n. 1; R. Gordis, *The Book of Job* (New York, 1978) 33; HALAT 963 and 964b; W. R. Harper, *Amos and Hosea* (ICC; Edinburgh, 1905) 115, 117; A. van Selms apud Loader, "Concept of Darkness," 105–6 and esp. 106 n. 1; Tur-Sinai, *Job*, 53. For further bibliography, see also Winton-Thomas, "צלמות," 193 n. 7.

64. See n. 16 above.

65. On this early suffix, which is not to be attributed to late Aramaic influence, see my work *BHL*, 79–80 n. 170 (argument #3 and response #3).

66. For ṣalāmu, see nn. 14, 18, and 35 above. For ẓalima, see, for example, E. W. Lane, *An Arabic-English Lexicon* (repr. Lebanon, 1968), part 5, 1921–22; H. Wehr, *A Dictionary of Modern Written Arabic* (New York, 1961) 582–83 (the relevant form of the verb is verbal form #4). See also Winton-Thomas, "צלמות," 193–94 and 194 n. 3. For ṣalma/ṣalama, see, for example, T. O. Lambdin, *Introduction to Classical Ethiopic* (Missoula, Mont., 1978) 437: "G (yeṣlam/yeṣlem) to grow dark, be black; of eyes: to grow blind; ṣalma gaṣṣu he became angry. CG ᶜaṣlama caus. ṣelum dark, obscured, blinded. ṣalim (f. ṣalām) black. ṣelmat m.f. darkness; . . . "

unclear.[67] This etymology is basically accepted here because it is supported by valid evidence and is in accord with the semantic conclusions arrived at previously. Yet, Barr's objection that this etymology does not satisfactorily explain the Masoretic vocalization צַלְמָוֶת remains to be considered.

(d) צַלְמוֹת* 'darkness'—first suggested by J. Barth in 1894.[68] This etymology is based on the same root as in the previous suggestion, namely *ẓlm* > צלם 'to be dark'. The reconstructed form צַלְמוֹת*, however, is not with abstract suffix וּת-, but rather with the less frequently attested abstract suffix וֹת- (perhaps of Phoenician origin).[69] This feminine singular suffix[70] occurs with such abstract

---

67. See the extensive bibliography listed in *HALAT* 963a. I currently still lean toward H. L. Ginsberg's first explanation of KTU 1.14:I:19–20 ("The Legend of King Keret," 34; contrast idem, "Ugaritic Myths, Epics, and Legends," *ANET*, 143), namely that the numerical forms in lines 16–21 are fractions and that the verbal form *ǵlm* with subject *ym* 'the sea' means here semantically 'covered over', based on such verses as Exod 15:5, 10; Ezek 26:19b; Ps 106:11. Note further that the semantic range of 'to hide' also includes 'to cover' (see, e.g., Gen 18:17 versus 2 Kgs 4:27) so that Ugaritic *ǵlm* in this context may well be cognate to Biblical Hebrew העלים 'to conceal, hide'. On these lines and Ugaritic fractions in general, see now D. Sivan, דקדוק לשׁוֹן אוגרית (Jerusalem, 1993) 63, 169 [Hebrew] with further bibliography. For a completely different understanding, see also A. Caquot et al., *Textes ougaritiques* (Paris, 1974) 1.506, 506–7 note o. Finally, note that KTU 1.4:VII:54–56 and 1.8:7–9 are so contextually obscure that the parallelism *ẓlmt/ǵlmt* cannot provide any comparative evidence whatsoever. Contrast, for example, the three contradictory interpretations suggested in *ANET*, 135 (proper names), J. C. L. Gibson, *Canaanite Myths and Legends* (Edinburgh, 1977) 66 ('obscurity'//'darkness') and B. Margalit, *A Matter of Life and Death* (Neukirchen-Vluyn, 1980) 68, 71–72 and 72 n. 1 ('the maiden'//'darkness'). For J. Barr's view concerning these contexts, see n. 6 above.

68. J. Barth, *Die Nominalbildung in den semitischen Sprachen* (reprint Hildesheim, 1967) 411 n. 3: "Vermuthungsweise möchte ich eine alte Abstractform auf ות in dem Wort צלמות 'Finsterniss' suchen, das durch Volksetymologie in צַלְמָוֶת 'Todesschatten' umgewandelt worden ist. Die Umbildung wird eher erklärlich, wenn das Wort ursprünglich צַלְמוֹת (צֵל-מוֹת), als wenn es צַלְמוּת gelautet hat." See also, for example, Chacham, ספר תהלים, 125 n. 3; Harper, *Amos and Hosea*, 117; Paul, "צלמות," 736; Winton-Thomas, "צלמות," 194 n. 4.

69. For the possible Phoenician origin of the abstract ending ות- with specific reference to the etymology of the term צלמות 'darkness', see H. L. Ginsberg, *LKK*, 45; idem apud Paul, "צלמות," 736. In general, see also idem, "Ugaritico-Phoenicia," *JANES(CU)* 5 (1973) 134 n. 19; idem, *The Israelian Heritage of Judaism* (New York, 1982) 36; J. Friedrich, *Phönizisch-punische Grammatik* (Rome, 1951) 30 (§78b); J. Friedrich and W. Röllig, *Phönizisch-punische Grammatik* (2d ed.; Rome, 1970) 30 (§78b); S. Segert, *A Grammar of Phoenician and Punic* (Munich, 1976) 74 (§36.46), 87 (§43.412.1), and 115 (§52.52).

70. On this Biblical Hebrew suffix, see esp. Barth, *Nominalbildung*, 411 (§259c); GKC 241 (§86 l). Recently, some doubts have been expressed regarding the likelihood of an additional ות- fem. suffix for abstract nouns in the singular (alongside the regular fem. pl. suffix וֹת-). B. K. Waltke and M. O'Connor have claimed that "An *abstract noun* is frequently expressed by a plural. . . . Such plurals may refer to *qualities*" (B. K. Waltke and M. O'Connor, *An Introduction to Biblical Hebrew Syntax* [Winona Lake, Ind., 1990] 120–21 [§7.4.2a]). In T. Muraoka's new edition of P. Joüon's Biblical Hebrew grammar, the contention is that "חָכְמוֹת Wisdom, treated as a singular in Prov 1:20; 9:1, seems to be some kind of plural of majesty. . . . The word הוֹלֵלוֹת madness (Qoh 1:17; 2:12; 7:25; 9:3) alongside הוֹלֵלוּת (10:13) is suspect. . . ." (P. Joüon, *A Grammar of*

nouns as חָכְמוֹת 'wisdom' (Prov 1:20),[71] בִּינוֹת 'understanding' (Isa 27:11)[72] and הוֹלֵלוֹת 'madness'.[73] It is this form that provides the appropriate answer to Barr's second objection. Surely it is easier to understand how an original form צַלְמוֹת*
was transformed into MT צַלְמָוֶת under the midrashic influence of the "popular etymology" צֵל מוּת (שֶׁל) 'shadow of death', since מוּת- (the construct form of מָוֶת; cf. תּוֹךְ-תָּוֶךְ)[74] could certainly be understood midrashically as standing for מוּת 'death'. Only one question remains regarding this final etymology. Is there a precedent for the use of abstract suffix ־וֹת with any of the aforementioned Biblical Hebrew terms for 'darkness', such as there is for the usage of abstract suffix ־וּת with the term קַדְרוּת 'darkness'? Such a precedent occurs only once in the Bible, but this evidence is sufficient to determine that this last etymology is to be preferred over all others and does indeed provide the appropriate answer to Barr's previously mentioned final objection. The relevant term is אֲפֵלוֹת 'darkness' in Isa 59:9:

Biblical Hebrew [trans. and rev. T. Muraoka; 2 vols.; Subsidia Biblica 14/1, 2; Rome, 1991] 1.265–66 [§88Mk] and 2.500–501 [§136d]). Here it must be emphasized that abstract nouns do not generally have plural forms (except for a few expressing periods of time such as מַלְכֻות 'reign'). For example, the only Biblical Hebrew term for 'darkness' discussed in this study that occurs in the plural is מַחְשָׁךְ 'dark place' because it is not an abstract noun (four out of seven occurrences are in the plural—Ps 74:20, 88:7, 143:3; Lam 3:6). On the other hand, all 80 Biblical Hebrew occurrences of חוֹשֶׁךְ, 9 occurrences of אפל, 10 occurrences of אפלה (including אפלות in Isa 59:9 discussed at the conclusion of the present study), 15 occurrences of ערפל, 18 occurrences of צלמות, and the single occurrence of קדרות are exclusively in the singular. Therefore it is clear that the Biblical Hebrew suffix ־וֹת cannot be taken as feminine plural in the cases cited above and below, but rather must be understood as an archaic feminine singular suffix for abstract nouns (see also n. 75 below).

71. The verbal form תָּרֹנָּה 'cries aloud' (Prov 1:20) must be interpreted as 3d feminine singular תָּרֹן+נָה with the so-called "nun-energicum" suffix, with which compare Judg 5:26 (תִּשְׁלַח+נָה) and see, for example, Joüon and Muraoka, *Grammar of Biblical Hebrew*, 172–73 (§61f) with further bibliography. Note also the parallel stich in the singular בָּרְחֹבוֹת תִּתֵּן קוֹלָהּ 'raises her voice in the squares' and the 3d feminine singular paraphrase in Prov 8:1–3 (where the regular feminine singular form חָכְמָה occurs together with תָּרֹנָּה). Singular חָכְמוֹת also occurs in Prov 9:1 and probably in Prov 14:1 (read חָכְמוֹת for MT חַכְמוֹת—see, e.g., Barth, *Nominalbildung*, 411; BHS 1292 n. 1a). Finally, note that there is an Akkadian precedent for a substantive meaning 'wisdom' occurring both as a regular noun and as an abstract noun (parallel to the usage of Biblical Hebrew חָכְמוֹת/חָכְמָה). The two forms are *igigallu/igigallūtu* 'wisdom'. For these two Akkadian terms, see CAD I/J 39b–40b; AHw 366b, 1563a; R. F. G. Sweet, "The Sage in Akkadian Literature: A Philological Study," in J. G. Gammie and L. G. Perdue, ed., *The Sage in Israel and the Ancient Near East* (Winona Lake, Ind., 1990) 48 (§1.4) and 49 (§§3.4 and 3.5).

72. Out of the 37 occurrences of בִּינָה 'understanding', the form בִּינוֹת occurs only here. For semantic parallels to this phrase, see Deut 4:6; 32:6, 28–29; Isa 29:14.

73. As noted already by Barth (*Nominalbildung*, 411), there is no difference in meaning or usage between הוֹלֵלוּת 'folly' (Qoh 10:13) and הוֹלֵלוֹת 'folly' (Qoh 1:17, 2:12, 7:25, 9:3).

74. For the comparison with תּוֹךְ-תָּוֶךְ, see Paul, "צלמות," 736.

That is why redress is far from us,
And vindication does not reach us.

נקוה לאור והנה חשך
לנגהות באפלות נהלך

We hope for light—but behold darkness;
For radiance—but we must walk in gloom.[75]

In conclusion, I would quote Barr, who has claimed that the following trend exists among the scholars who have dealt with the term צַלְמָוֶת in a comprehensive manner:

> The case of this word is a curious one, in that the majority opinion in modern times has certainly been in favor of the form *ṣalmût* and the sense 'darkness' (root *ṣ-l-m*), but among scholars who have devoted full independent studies to the word the trend has been in the opposite direction.[76]

It is my fervent hope that the present "full independent study" will mark the beginning of the reversal of that trend.

---

75. The translation adopted here is similar to that of the NJPSV for Isa 59:9. Note that not only is אֲפֵלוֹת 'gloom' (// חוֹשֶׁךְ 'darkness') a feminine singular noun with abstract וֹת-suffix, such is also the case as regards the adjoining noun נְגֹהוֹת 'radiance' (// אוֹר 'light'). Just as the former occurs in its present form only in this verse and is the only Biblical Hebrew noun with abstract וֹת-suffix meaning 'darkness' (see n. 70 above), such is also precisely the case with the latter term, which also occurs only here and is the only Biblical Hebrew noun with the abstract וֹת- suffix meaning 'light'. For example, the regular term אוֹר 'light' occurs 122 times in Biblical Hebrew, never in the abstract form אוֹרוֹת*. Just as is true in the case of abstract terms for 'darkness' (see n. 70 above), אוֹרוֹת* also never occurs as a plural form. The plural form אוֹרִים does occur once (Ps 136:7), but is not there an abstract noun (it is equivalent there to מְאוֹרוֹת meaning 'heavenly luminaries').

76. Barr, *CPTOT*, 378.

Appendix: Semantic Classification of the Eighteen Biblical Hebrew Occurrences of צלמות

1. *Cosmological contexts describing God's awesome power*
   Amos 5:8; Job 12:22, 28:3
2. *Contexts referring to darkness as an appropriate time for crime*
   Job 24:13–17 (twice), 34:21–22
3. *Contexts describing the dangers of darkness unless God is present*
   Jer 13:16; Ps 23:4
4. *Contexts describing the dangers of darkness in the desert*
   Jer 2:6 (cf. v. 31); Ps 44:19–20
5. *Contexts referring to dwelling in darkness as a period of punishment*
   Isa 60:1; Ps. 107:10–14 (twice)
6. *Contexts in which darkness occurs as an epithet for the Netherworld*
   Job 10:21–22 (twice), 38:17
7. *Cursing the day of one's birth (isolated context)*
   Job 3:3–6
8. *The dark color of the eyes as part of an emotional physiological response (isolated context)*
   Job 16:16

A PAPYRUS RECORDING A DIVINE LEGAL DECISION AND THE ROOT *rḥq* IN BIBLICAL AND NEAR EASTERN LEGAL USAGE

Frank Moore Cross

A Legal Papyrus

RECENTLY PIERRE BORDREUIL AND DENNIS PARDEE published a small, but important papyrus.[1] It is well preserved, complete in fact, and written in an elegant professional hand. Few questions of material reading or of interpretation remain to be resolved. I should transcribe and translate the brief legal text as follows:

1. kh .ʾmrw . ʾlhn . lgrʾ² . lk . hmrzḥ . whrḥyn . wh
2. byt . wyšᶜ³ . rḥq . mhm . wmlkʾ . hšlš

1. Thus saith the godhead[3] to Geraʾ: "The *marzēḥ* (*symposion*), and the millstones, and the

---

1. P. Bordreuil and Dennis Pardee, "Le Papyrus du marzeaḥ," *Semitica* 38 (Hommages à Maurice Sznycer; 2 vols.; 1990) 1.49–69, pls. VII–X.

2. Bordreuil and Pardee read *srʾ* here, a unique name. The putative *samek* they read is of the Aramaic form found for example in the Nimrud Ostracon (much too early for this papyrus) or of the Phoenician form found in late Phoenician and Punic, for example in the Cyprus Tariff (late fifth century B.C.E.) (too late for this papyrus). The tradition of the script of the papyrus, as we shall see, is that of Hebrew and its daughter scripts: Moabite, Edomite, and Hebreo-Philistine. In these scripts, where *samek* is extant, it bears no resemblance to the letter in question in our papyrus. I believe that the letter is a *gimel* of the type found in the Hebrew cursives of the mid- and late seventh century (e.g., in the Yabneh-yam Letter). The *gimel* has been confused with *samek* owing to the running of ink in the fibers of the papyrus at the left of the upper stroke of *gimel*. The name Gēraʾ and its analogs, Gēray, Gērbaᶜl, Gēr-yāḥ, that is *gēr* 'client' plus DN or hypocoristic suffix *-aʾ* or *-ay*, are well known in Northwest Semitic.

3. I have translated *ʾlhn* as a singular despite the plural verb form *ʾmrw*. Evidence that the plural of the divine name in extrabiblical contexts is sometimes to be taken as singular in reference, at least in translation, continues to increase. The usage of *ʾlm* in Phoenician of a single god (or

311

2. house are thine. As for Yišᶜaᵓ,[4] he is without claim on them (lit., is far
from them); and Malkaᵓ is the depositary."

The papyrus records a divine decision, presumably a case brought to a
sanctuary owing to circumstances that make an ordinary legal decision difficult or impossible. Claims to property—what sort of claims we do not
know—were adjudicated by the god, presumably through the instrumentality
of a priest of the sanctuary's patron god, using lots, divination, or some similar
means of manipulating the deity. The precise origin of the papyrus is unknown. It may be of Transjordanian Israelite provenience or of Moabite or
Edomite provenience, a question we shall return to in discussing its language
and script. In each of these cases, we should expect the decision to be made
by the national god. The states of the southeast, originating in tribal leagues,
are characterized by the dominance of a patron god: Yahweh, Milcom (ᵓEl),
Chemosh (ᵓAštar), and Qaws, respectively, as is evidenced by the onomastica
of the several states.[5]

The script of the papyrus is of special interest. We have seen no script before with its peculiar combination of Hebrew and Transjordanian features.
When T. C. Mitchell sent me a photograph of the papyrus, I replied that I had
no real doubts about the authenticity of the document. The script, while combining elements in a unique style, was, nevertheless, the work of a professional hand, the mode of penning letters and their stance sure.[6] Certain letter
forms derive from a cursive Hebrew tradition; some have their closest analogs
with Edomite and Ammonite. Unhappily we have no Moabite cursives with
which to compare the script.

ᵓAlep is made in the mode of the seventh-century Hebrew cursive from
Judah,[7] the Edomite cursive of the early sixth century from the ostracon from

goddess!) is well known. An unpublished Phoenician *ex voto* of the end of the sixth century dedi-
cates a bowl to "our lord ᵓAštrm" clearly a reference to (singular) ᵓAštar (see Friedrich and Röllig,
Phönizisch-punische Grammatik [Rome, 1970] §306). That plural agreement with verbs or adjectives survives in Hebrew with ᵓĕlōhîm, despite the tendency to revise to singular agreement, is
well known. See for example, Gen 20:13, 31:53; and 2 Sam 7:23 (with plural verbs); and Deut
5:26[23] and Josh 24:19 (with plural adjectives). The use of anarthrous ᵓelōhîm with plural verbs
in legal contexts as in this papyrus is noteworthy (see especially Exod 22:8b and 1 Sam 2:25
[reading û-pillû ᵓĕlōhîm]). The view that ᵓĕlōhîm means 'judges' on occasion should be firmly rejected. Cf. Bordreuil and Pardee, "Papyrus," 52–53.

4. I prefer to take yišᶜaᵓ as a *casus pendens* and rḥq as a finite verb.

5. See provisionally, F. M. Cross, "The Epic Traditions of Early Israel: Epic Narrative and
the Reconstruction of Early Israelite Institutions," *The Poet and the Historian: Essays in Literary
and Historical Biblical Criticism* (ed. Richard Elliott Friedman; HSS 26; Chico, Cal., 1983) 35–
37; and especially "Kinship and Covenant in Ancient Israel," in F. M. Cross, *Biblical Essays:
From Epic to Canon* (forthcoming).

6. Mitchell's letter of June 5, 1984, and my reply of June 16, 1984.

7. See the discussion of these cursive scripts and the script chart in F. M. Cross, "Epigraphic
Notes on Hebrew Documents of the Eighth–Sixth Centuries B.C., II: The Murabbaᶜât Papyrus and
the Letter Found near Yabneh-yam," *BASOR* 165 (1962) 34–46 and fig. 1.

Ḥorvat ᶜUza[8] and Ostracon 6043 from Tell Ḥeleifeh.[9] It does not show the Aramaizing form found in the Ammonite texts that date from the end of the seventh century through the first half of the sixth century and later. The latter type of *ʾalep* is drawn with the elements on the right side of the vertical drawn as a "check," the point of which meets the vertical. The Ammonite cursives of this period are now known from Tell Mazār in the north to Tell Hisbān (Heshbon) in the south, that is, over the whole range of the lands into which the Ammonites expanded in this period.[10]

The letter *he* is surprising in featuring a form with precise parallels only in the late eighth-century Israelite cursive, notably in the Barley Check of Samaria.[11] It exhibits a lower horizontal that curves up (usually) to touch the top

8. See Itzhaq Beit-Aryeh and Bruce Cresson, "An Edomite Ostracon from Ḥorvat ᶜUza," *Tel Aviv* 12 (1985) 96–101. I should read the ostracon as follows:

1. *ʾmr . lmlk . ʾmr . lblbl*	1. Utterance of LMLK: Say to BLBL
2. *hšlm . ʾt . whbrktk*	2. Are you well? May you be blessed
3. *lqws . wᶜt . tn . ʾt . hʾkl*	3. by Qaws! Now: give the grain
4. *ʾšr . ᶜmdy ⌈.⌉ ⟨l⟩ʾhʾmh . ⌈yᶜl⌉*	4. which is in my care to Aḥ-ʾimmā. Let
5. *whrm. šʾl . ᶜl mz[bḥ . qw]s*	5. Saul bring up and offer on Qaws' altar
6. *ᶜmr . hʾkl*	6. a sheaf of grain.

I am under the impression that the reading *ᶜmdy* is certain, the expression being used in the sense 'to be in one's care, possession'. The reading *yᶜl* is more adventuresome, suggested by context but not excluded by the traces.

9. Ostracon 6043 was first published by Nelson Glueck in his paper "Ostraca from Elath (Continued)," *BASOR* 82 (1941) 3–10. Albright and later Naveh made advances in reading the ostracon: W. F. Albright, "Ostracon 6043 from Ezion-Geber," *BASOR* 62 (1941) 11–15; and J. Naveh, "The Scripts of Two Ostraca from Elath," *BASOR* 183 (1966) 27–30. The best photograph is published by Glueck, "Some Ezion-Geber: Elath Iron II Pottery," *ErIsr* 9 (1969) pl. XI:2. My own reading of the ostracon differs little from that of Naveh: (1) *rᶜ ʾl*, (2) *bdq[ws]*, (3) *šlm*, (4) *qwsb[nh]*, (5) *pgᶜqw[s]*, (6) *ndb-*, (7) *škk*, (8) *rpʾ*, (9) *pgᶜqws*, (10) *qwsn-*. For a useful review and bibliography of Edomite epigraphic material, see Felice Israel, "Miscellanea Idumea," *Revista bíblica* 27 (1979) 171–203.

10. The Heshbon Ostraca in Ammonite cursive script include Heshbon A1 (IV) from about 600, A2 (XI) from the early sixth century, and A3 from ca. 550–525 B.C.E. See F. M. Cross, "An Unpublished Ammonite Ostracon from Ḥesbān" (*The Archaeology of Jordan and Other Studies Presented to Siegfried H. Horn* [ed. Lawrence T. Geraty and Larry G. Herr; Berrien Springs, Mich.: 1986] 475–89), where the Ammonite scripts are discussed, as well as the transition from the national scripts (Ammonite, Hebrew, Edomite) to the Aramaic chancellery hand towards 500 B.C.E. The Tell Mazār Letter (Inscription No. 3) falls in date between Heshbon Ostracon A1 and A3, thus in the first half of the sixth century B.C.E., and this date is confirmed by the archaeological locus of the find (early sixth century B.C.E.). See Khair Yassineh and Javier Teixidor, "Ammonite and Aramaic Inscriptions from Tell El-Mazār in Jordan," *BASOR* 264 (1986) 45–50, esp. 47–48. I am less concerned here with the lapidary or formal scripts in Ammonite; this typological series is fairly well dated thanks to the seals of "servants" of Ammonite kings, including the seal of the servant of Baᶜl-yašaᶜ (biblical Baᶜlay [Baᶜlîs]), who flourished about 580 B.C.E., following the ᶜAmminadab of the Tell Sirān Bottle Inscription. See L. G. Herr, "The Servant of Baalis," *BA* 48 (1985) 169–72; and F. M. Cross, "Notes on the Ammonite Inscription from Tell Sirān," *BASOR* 212 (1973) 12–15.

11. The *editio princeps* is that of S. A. Birnbaum in J. W. Crowfoot, G. M. Crowfoot, and Kathleen Kenyon, *The Objects from Samaria* (London, 1957) 11–17 and pl. I:1.

horizontal (but not the short middle horizontal). It also has the characteristic Hebrew "breakthrough" of the top horizontal to the right as an invariable feature of the letter. The Judean cursive occasionally shows a tendency to draw the lower horizontal curving upward, but not so dramatically as the script of the papyrus.[12] Forms with these two features are not found in the Aramaizing forms of Deir ᶜAllā or in later Ammonite scripts (notably Tell Mazār). It is noteworthy, however, that the Moabite seal script exhibits a form with the top horizontal "broken through" to the right and a lengthened lower horizontal.[13]

The letter *waw* in the script of the papyrus with its *hamza*-shaped head has parallels only with the Israelite and Judaean cursive *waw* and with what may be called the Hebreo-Philistine cursive.[14] Ammonite and Edomite cursives have an "Aramaizing" form: a curved stroke on the left connected with a vertical, no element on the right of the vertical.

Zayin is damaged on the papyrus, but its form is clear enough. It is not the *z*-form of Aramaic and Ammonite; rather, it is like an occasional form in Judaean cursives and especially like the *zayin* in the recently discovered ostraca from Beth Shean.[15]

Ḥet in the papyrus is penned with two horizontal strokes. Bordreuil and Pardee compared the *ḥet* of the Meshaᶜ Stone and a Moabite seal. They might have added the semiformal Sirān *ḥet*, the cursive and semiformal *ḥet*s widely used in the ᶜArad Ostraca and on bowls from Hebron and Beth-shemesh, as well as the *ḥet* of the Edomite Ostracon from Ḥorvat ᶜUza. All of these have two-bar *ḥet*s, and the ᶜArad specimens stand closer to the forms in the legal papyrus than do the older Moabite exemplars. Actually, the *ḥet* has other features which are unusual: the short, high downstroke on the left and the unattached lower horizontal. It gives the impression of standing halfway typologically between the Deir ᶜAllā *ḥet* and the cursive Ammonite "reversed-*n*" form.

12. See, for example, the letter *he* in the Beit Lei inscriptions and my comments in "The Cave Inscriptions from Khirbet Beit Lei," *Near Eastern Archaeology in the Twentieth Century: Essays in Honor of Nelson Glueck* (ed. James A. Sanders; Garden City, N.Y., 1970) 299–306 and fig. l.

13. See the excellent photographs of the seals of ᵓmṣ hspr and kmšᶜm bn kmšᵓl hspr published by Bordreuil and Pardee, "Papyrus," pl. IX. Cf. the Judean form on seals like that of yᵓznyhw ᶜbd hmlk.

14. Joseph Naveh was the first to recognize this peculiar style or national script. Its close filiation with Hebrew has caused it to be overlooked. See his paper "Writing and Scripts in Seventh-Century B.C.E. Philistia: The New Evidence from Tell Jemmeh," *IEJ* 35 (1985) 8–21 and plates 2–3. The ostracon from Tel Seraᶜ (Tell eš-Šarîᶜah) presents a form of *waw* identical with that of the papyrus. Ashkelon is also producing epigraphic material in Hebreo-Philistine, which I will be publishing presently.

15. Amihai Mazar showed me these fragmentary ostraca found in 1990. Their script departs in a number of ways from the early and late eighth-century scripts from Samaria. Its *zayin* does not have the final downward tick on the lower right that usually marks the Israelite (and Judaean) script. Of some interest is the fact that of the eight personal names preserved on the ostraca, five are hypocoristica in -aᵓ: *zimmaᵓ*, *ᵓēlaᵓ*, *ᵓabaᵓ*, *ᶜuzzaᵓ* and *dōdaᵓ*. Their popularity in this period— compare *gēraᵓ*, *yišᶜaᵓ*, and *malkaᵓ* in the legal papyrus—is remarkable.

Kap, mem, and *nun* in the papyrus script have long legs, curling strongly leftward at the foot. This is a Hebrew trait, surviving in the cursives of Israelite, Judaean, Edomite, and Hebreo-Philistine. In Ammonite cursives, the legs of their letters tend to be straight, curving slightly if at all, and this verticality is even more apparent in Ammonite seal scripts. The head of *mem* in the papyrus most resembles eighth–seventh century cursive forms and survives in the archaizing palaeo-Hebrew script of the Qumran biblical manuscripts. It is not as developed as the sixth-century cursive form with the lowered right shoulder found in Judaea.[16]

Three letters, *bet,* *ᶜayin,* and *reš,* tend to open at the top. This trait is shared with the Ammonite cursives from Tell Mazār and Heshbon. It is also found in the Edomite cursive. This feature spread through the Ammonite and Edomite cursive scripts in the seventh century; by the end of the seventh century, it had invaded the formal scripts. The Deir ᶜAllā script of ca. 700 shows little or no sign of the tendency. The relation of the opening of the tops of *bet,* *ᶜayin,* and *reš* in Ammonite and Edomite to the opening of the tops of *bet,* *dalet,* *ᶜayin,* and *reš* in the Aramaic chancellery cursive is not clear. The phenomenon is fully developed in Aramaic in the eighth century, a century before it appears in the Transjordanian scripts. It may be noted that in Ammonite and Edomite, contrary to Aramaic, the *dalet* remains closed well into the sixth century. Certainly national scripts of Transjordan are not part of the Aramaic development of this stylistic feature. It may be that the Ammonite and Edomite scripts are secondarily (a century after the Aramaic shifts) and selectively influenced by the Aramaic cursive style in the case of *bet,* *ᶜayin,* and *reš*—but not *dalet.*

Taw exhibits a form, the vertical lengthened beyond that of the Hebrew *taw,* and the crossbar shifted to the right. The Deir ᶜAllā *taw* shows the beginning of this development, and it is fully developed in the Ammonite and Edomite cursives. As in the case of *bet,* *ᶜayin,* and *reš* discussed in the preceding paragraph, this feature is found also in the Aramaic cursive, where contrary to the case with *bet,* *ᶜayin,* and *reš,* the development of the new form of *taw* seems to take place in the Aramaic cursive and in the Transjordanian cursives at roughly the same time, suggesting direct influence.

Since the script of the papyrus combines features of the Hebrew cursives and characters of the Transjordanian cursives,[17] it is not easy to date. Ordinarily the paleographer wishes to date in a typological sequence of a known national script; otherwise, he is easily misled by the survival of archaic features in related national scripts or by innovation creating similar features at different times in two filiated script traditions. Still we can describe the date of

16. See the discussion in Cross, "Epigraphic Notes."
17. I use the term *Transjordanian* to include the Edomite cursive, although the best exemplars are from Cis-Jordan.

Hebrew features of the papyrus script in the sequence of Hebrew cursives, Israelite, Judaean, and Hebreo-Philistine. In the Hebrew sequence they would
fall in the second half of the seventh century. Similarly we can describe the
place of the Transjordanian elements of the papyrus script in the sequence of
Transjordanian scripts. They are later than the Deir ᶜAllā hand of ca. 700
B.C.E., earlier than the script of the Heshbon Ostraca of ca. 600–550, and earlier than the early sixth-century Edomite hands. This suggests strongly that we
must date the papyrus to the mid- or late seventh century B.C.E.[18]

Bordreuil and Pardee have argued that the script of the bulla appended to
the papyrus has striking traits in common with the script of Moabite seals. It
does indeed. However, I know no way of differentiating the form of the letters
preserved on the sealing from the forms of letters on contemporary Edomite
seals and sealings.[19] I note, too, that on the sealing of Qawsᶜanal, servant of
the king, the letters *bet* and ᶜ*ayin* are open and the *dalet* closed, precisely as in
the script of the legal papyrus.[20] The scripts of the bulla and the papyrus can
be assigned either to a Moabite or to an Edomite provenience.

In seeking out a provenience for the legal papyrus, Bordreuil and Pardee
suggest the hypothesis that the bulla is to be read *lmlk* / ᵓ*k*ᵀ*t*¹[ ], and that we
are to interpret it to mean 'Appartenant au roi de ᵓKT[-]'. Further, they propose
that the element in second register, ᵓ*k*ᵀ*t*¹[?], is to be identified with the place
name Iktanu, a site alongside the Wâdī Ḥesbān on the west of ancient Heshbon. There are many problems with this hypothesis, and in my judgment it
must be discarded. First of all it is probable, I think, that the single seal on the
papyrus should be the seal of the Malkaᵓ who is depositary, listed at the end
of the papyrus. To read the seal, *lmlk/*ᵓ*,* running over from the first to the second register constitutes no problem; it happens frequently on seals (including
Moabite seals). The place-name often written *Iktanu* is properly ᵓ*Iktanwah*
(variant ᵓ*Uktanweh*).[21] ᵓ*Iktanwah* can hardly be taken as a Moabite (or North-

18. The sealing associated with the papyrus is of little help in dating. The seal scripts of Hebrew, Edomite, and Moabite show very slow evolutionary changes in the seventh and early sixth
centuries. For excellent photographs of Moabite seals, see the splendid volume of Pierre Bordreuil,
Catalogue des sceaux ouest-sémitiques inscrits (Paris, 1986) 57–62.

19. See for example the form of the letters *lamed, mem, kap,* and ᵓ*alep* on the following
Edomite seals or sealings: *lmlkl/b*ᶜ ᶜ*bd/hmlk* (seventh century, from Buserah), *lqwsg*[*br*]*/mlk* ᵓ[*dm*]
(seventh century, from Umm el-Biyara), and *lqws*ᶜ*nl/*ᶜ*bd/hmlk* (beginning of the sixth century, from
Tell Ḥeleifeh). For bibliography, see Israel, "Miscellanea Idumea"; and L. Herr, *The Scripts of Ancient Northwest Semitic Seals* (HSM 18; Missoula, Mont., 1978) 161–70. The best photograph of
the Qawsᶜanal sealing is found in Glueck's paper, "Ezion-Geber," pl. VI: 1–2.

20. I have examined several of the original sealings in the Harvard Semitic Museum and
confirm this reading of the letter-forms.

21. My colleague Wolfhart Heinrichs has confirmed this reading on the basis of references in
The Hashemite Kingdom of Jordan, Archaeological Map, Scale 1:25000, Sheet 1: Amman, and
Official Standard Names Gazetteer: Jordan (Washington, D.C., 1971) 175. He suggests further
that a misreading of the Arabic ᵓ*ktnwh* as Iktanūh (> Iktanū) is responsible for the confusion in
the spelling of the name. Another of my colleagues, James Sauer, *facile princeps* of American

west Semitic) place name, and in any case cannot be fitted onto the lower register of the seal. One may question whether there is room for another letter after the damaged *taw*; certainly there is no room for more than one letter.[22] More serious, the site of *ʾIktanwah* was little occupied, if at all, in the late seventh and early sixth centuries B.C.E.[23] In the Iron II Period there was a small fort, but the length of its duration is uncertain.[24] Finally, it is clear that the site of *ʾIktanwah,* in the Ḥesbān Valley, is not in Moabite territory in this period, but in the Ammonite orbit. This is clear from both this distribution of Ammonite pottery and of the Ammonite scripts, lapidary and cursive.[25] In any case this outpost, insignificant in the period of the papyrus, surrounded by large Ammonite sites, is hardly the seat of an independent king.[26]

The little papyrus bearing a divine decree appears to be either Moabite or Edomite. There appear to be no paleographical arguments presently available that can decide the issue. Nor are there grammatical elements that can aid us. The masculine plural ending in *-n* (i.e., *-īn*, known in Moabite and in at least one Hebrew dialect) is not decisive. We do not know the form in Edomite. The preservation of diphthongs (at least *-ay*) is not decisive against a Moabite identification, since the evidence for the contraction of diphthongs found in the Meshaᶜ Stone may be the result of a court dialect and not characteristic of the popular dialect.[27] I am inclined to speculate that the papyrus comes from a cave in one of the great wadis that feed into the Dead Sea in Moabite or Edomite territory in Transjordan or in Edomite territory in the south of Cis-Jordan. It is only

---

archaeologists of Jordan, tells me that, being curious about the odd place name, he sought out the local inhabitants of the region and found that invariably they pronounced the name of the site as *ʾIktanwah (*and not *ʾIktānwah, ʾIktanū,* or *ʾIḫtanū,* variants scattered through the literature). The name obviously has no easy explanation as a Canaanite or Aramaic name and most probably is Arabic.

22. I have no suggestion for a reading. It may preserve a rare patronymic. Cp. the names *kt* 'Slim' in Safaitic and Nabataean *ktytw*. Or it may preserve an abbreviation of a title.

23. James Sauer, who has carried out systematic surface exploration of the site, has provided me with this information and given me permission to quote him.

24. Cf. the discussion of Kay Prag, "Preliminary Report on the Excavations at Tell Iktanu, Jordan, 1987," *Levant* 21 (1989) 33–45, esp. 40–45. She concludes, "Only the north tell appears to have been re-occupied in the Iron Age, apparently in the Iron I period. The construction of a fort, perhaps to be identified as Beth-Haram, is not yet dated but its use may have extended into the Persian/?Hellenistic periods."

25. See the discussion of Ammonite expansion north, west, and south in this period in the study of James Sauer, "ᶜAmmon, Moab, and Edom," *Biblical Archaeology Today: Proceedings of the International Congress on Biblical Archaeology, April, 1984* (Jerusalem, 1985) 212–13.

26. Bordreuil and Pardee offer, as a parallel to their reading of the bulla, the Phoenician seal reading *lmlk ṣrpt* 'belonging to the king of Sarepta'. The parallel is not a good one. Phoenicia is characterized in the period in question by a city-state system. This is not the case in the Ammonite, Moabite, and Edomite realms in this time. They are organized as nation states, so we should expect references to royalty to read: *mlk ᶜmn, mlk mwᵓb, mlk ᵓdm,* as is in fact the case of other extant seals mentioning a king from these regions.

27. See the discussion in F. M. Cross and D. N. Freedman, *Early Hebrew Orthography* (AOS 36; New Haven, 1953) 35–44, esp. 42.

in such a locale that we can expect papyrus to be so beautifully preserved. Moreover, we know that bedouin, notably the enterprising Taᶜamireh, continue their searches in dry caves of the Jordan rift on both sides of the Dead Sea.

The Root *rḥq*

The use of the root *rḥq* 'to be far' (in the legal sense, 'to relinquish claims' or 'to forfeit rights') found in our papyrus is well known in the Aramaic papyri from Elephantine. For example, in a document recording the settlement of a debt by the conveyance of a house, we find the following formulae: *zk byt⁾ yhbth lk⟨y⟩ wrḥqt mnh dylky hw* . . . 'As for this house, I gave it to you and for-feit/relinquish (all) claim to it. It is yours'.[28] Yohanan Muffs, in his exemplary study of the Elephantine legal papyri, discusses several types of documents that use these technical formulae: the deed of sale that records the relinquishment (*rḥq*) and transfer of property, the deed of cession or forfeiture (*spr mrḥq*) that records the cession of goods through their transfer to a second party, and the deed of forfeiture (*spr mrḥq*) that records the forfeiture of claims upon decision by judges after litigation.[29] The new papyrus belongs generally in this last category, being distinct from it only in that the godhead replaces human judges.

Among the most common formulae in the operative clauses of these docu-ments are the formula of cession, *rḥqt mnh* ('I relinquish/forfeit claims to it', lit-erally, 'I am far from it') and the formula of investiture, *zylk hw* ('It is yours'). Comparable usage is found in Akkadian in the use of *rêqu* ('forfeit/relinquish rights', literally, 'to be far, withdraw') and *qerêbu* ('to have/press a claim', lit-erally, 'to be near, approach').[30] Demotic deeds also exhibit an identical idiom: *sh n wy* ('deeds of being far/cession') and *iw.y wy.k(wy)* ('I am far/ relinquish claim').[31]

The use of *rḥq* in its special legal sense has hitherto not been detected in Biblical Hebrew. I am persuaded, however, that several passages in the book of Ezekiel, where the usual translation of *rḥq* 'to be far' has been the occasion for difficulty or puzzlement, yield sense when the legal idiom is recognized.[32]

Ezekiel 8:6

The setting of the oracle is in the temple complex, whether in the inner court, as the Masoretic Text reads, or in the outer court as many moderns sug-

28. A. E. Cowley, *Aramaic Papyri of the Fifth Century B.C.* (Oxford, 1923) P 13:15–16.

29. Yohannan Muffs, *Studies in the Aramaic Legal Papyri from Elephantine* (Leiden, 1969) 17, 24, 48–50, 118–20, 158–62, 177–78. Cf. R. Yaron, *The Law of the Aramaic Papyri* (Oxford, 1961) 81–82; J. J. Rabinowitz, "The Susa Tablets, the Bible, and the Aramaic Papyri," *VT* 11 (1961) 74ff.; and E. Y. Kutscher, "New Aramaic Texts," *JAOS* 74 (1954) 238.

30. Muffs, *Studies,* 177–78.

31. Ibid., 160.

32. Often the problem in the text has been finessed by what I may call emendation by skewed translation.

gest.[33] Ezekiel is called upon to view the abominations committed there, notably the *"semel* of jealousy" on its podium, and asked, "Do you see what they are doing . . . here *lrḥqh mᶜl mqdšy.*" Interpreters divide between taking the latter phrase to mean 'to be far from my sanctuary', that is, 'to distance themselves from my sanctuary', or taking it to mean 'so that I (the deity) am far from my sanctuary', in other words, 'so that I distance myself from my sanctuary'. The second alternative, already found in Jerome, runs counter to biblical and Ezekielian usage of *rḥq mᶜl* and may be dismissed.[34] However, the first alternative is awkward, as is generally recognized. Why is it that by committing abominations they 'distance themselves' from the sanctuary? Certainly *physical* distance cannot be meant. Those engaged in abominable practices could scarcely be closer to the sanctuary, and they obviously regard their activities as adjuncts to the temple cultus.

The solution, I believe, as will have been anticipated, is to recognize Ezekiel's use of a legal idiom. The phrase *lrḥqh mᶜl mqdšy* means 'to forfeit (any) claim on my sanctuary', or, to forfeit the right to participate in the temple cult and in particular to receive its benefits.[35]

Ezekiel 44:10

In his vision of the new temple, the seer asserts that the Levites, because they led Israel astray, are rejected from the (full rights of) priesthood and are to serve only as temple attendants, as a second-level clergy: "But the Levites *ᵓšr rḥqw mᶜly* . . . shall be punished, becoming attendants in my sanctuary. . . ." The phrase *ᵓšr rḥqw mᶜly* (literally 'who were far from me' in light of legal usage) is to be translated, 'who forfeited rights to me', in other words, rights to the priesthood. The passage, Ezek 44:10-16, reflects the ancient struggle between the Zadokite house and the Levitic house for dominance in the priestly office, in which the Zadokite house was finally successful.[36] In Ezek 44:10, as in Ezek 8:6, there is no question of physical distance from Yahweh or his sanctuary. The question is rather of lost rights or privileges.

---

33. Compare M. Greenberg, *Ezekiel 1–20* (AB 22; Garden City, N.Y., 1983) 168; and W. Zimmerli, *Ezekiel* (Hermeneia; Philadelphia, 1979) 1.238. See also the discussion of Susan Ackerman, *Under Every Green Tree: Popular Religion in Sixth-Century Judah* (HSM 46; Atlanta, 1992) 53–55.

34. Greenberg, *Ezekiel 1–20*, 169.

35. The Ezekielian idiom, *rḥq* followed by *mᶜl*, differs slightly from the Aramaic *rḥq mn* and *rḥq m-* of the papyrus. It should be noted that the compound preposition *mᶜl* in Hebrew is dominated, so to speak, by the element *m(n)*. With *rḥq* it may carry the added nuance of 'from attachment to' or simply mean 'from'. On the contrary, in Aramaic (and sometimes in Late Hebrew), the compound *mn ᶜl* (Late Hebrew *mᶜl*) is dominated by the element *ᶜl*, usually meaning 'above', and is unsuitable for use with *rḥq*.

36. For the prehistory of the rivalry between the priestly houses in Israel, see my discussion in *Canaanite Myth and Hebrew Epic* (Cambridge, 1973) 195–215; and in my paper "Reuben, First-Born of Jacob," *ZAW* 100 Supplement (1988) 46–65.

Ezekiel 11:15–17

This passage is perhaps the most interesting of the three on which I shall comment. Here, if I am not mistaken, there is evident play on the two meanings of *rḥq*: the ordinary meaning of *rḥq* 'to be distant' (and *hrḥyq* 'to send far away') and *rḥq* 'to forfeit/lack claim'. Ezekiel and his companions in exile are addressed by the surviving inhabitants of Jerusalem as follows: *rḥqw m*ᶜ*l yhwh lnw hyᵓ ntnh hᵓrṣ lmwršh*. We may translate literally, 'They (the exiles) are far from Yahweh;[37] it (the land) is ours; the land is given (to us the inhabitants of Jerusalem) as an inheritance'. The passage is rather elliptical. We may paraphrase, "The exiles are far from Yahweh (and his land). The land is thus awarded to us, given as an inheritance." At the same time, the legal formulae of forfeiture and investiture are used by the prophet: "They have forfeited (all) claim upon Yahweh (and his land). It (the land) is ours." Often scholars have removed the pronoun *hyᵓ*, in the phrase *lnw hyᵓ*, by emendation. In my view, this is wholly wrongheaded. The expression *lnw hyᵓ* is the formula of investiture, comparable to *zylk hw* in Aramaic law, to *lk hmrzḥ* . . . in the papyrus. Its use makes it clear that the prophet is playing on the literal and the legal meaning of the term *rḥq*. The exiles are distant from/forfeit the land.

In verses 16 and 17, the two levels of meaning, legal distance and ordinary distance, persist: "Although I have removed them far away (*hrḥqtym*) among the nations . . . yet I have become for them (*lhm*) a sanctuary. . . ."[38] That is, they *still* have a claim on, or the right to worship, Yahweh. Furthermore, in verse 17 we read, "I will give to you (the exiles), *ntty lkm*, the soil of Israel."

In other words, the Jerusalemites claim that they have been invested with the land, *lnw hyᵓ*, and assert that the exiles have forfeited privileges to worship Yahweh. The exiles have no claim on him or his land. Yahweh replies that while he has "distanced" the exiles, they have not lost the right to worship. He is a sanctuary (or small sanctuary) to the exiles. A fortiori, he will invest the exiles with the land (*ntty lkm),* repudiating the claims of the inhabitants of Jerusalem. The exiles may be "distant" in space; they are not distant in law. Their rights persist while in exile; their claims on the soil of Israel will be upheld when the Lord restores them to Zion.

---

37. I have read *rḥqw* as a perfect form, not as a *Qal* imperative with the Masoretic pointing. In this I follow most commentators. The imperative is by no means impossible: 'renounce claim'. But this reading removes the play on meanings, since 'be far, distance (yourselves)', the ordinary meaning, ill fits the circumstances of the distant exiles. Moshe Greenberg comments that *rḥqw m*ᶜ*l yhwh* (which he translates 'remove yourselves from Yʜᴡʜ') "carries a demand to renounce the privileges of Yʜᴡʜ worship" (*Ezekiel 1–20*, 189). Thus he comes very close to recognizing the legal force of the expression.

38. The Masoretic Text reads *mqdš m*ᶜ*ṭ* 'a sanctuary, a little', presumably 'a little sanctuary', but the expression is odd, and *m*ᶜ*ṭ* may be a gloss in the interest of the primacy of the Jerusalem temple.

ARE THERE EXAMPLES OF ENCLITIC *mem* IN THE HEBREW BIBLE?

John A. Emerton

THE DECIPHERMENT of the Ras Shamra tablets and the reading of their contents have shed much light on the religious and literary world in which the people of ancient Israel lived. The discoveries have also added considerably to our knowledge of the Northwest Semitic background of the language in which the Hebrew Bible was written. At the same time, not every suggested new interpretation of the biblical text has stood the test of time, and it can scarcely be denied that all such theories need to be subjected to rigorous examination before they deserve to be accepted.

The purpose of the present article is to examine one theory that Moran claimed "has cleared up scores of grammatical and logical inconcinnities of the Hebrew text,"[1] and that has won wide acceptance, namely, the theory that Classical Hebrew, like Ugaritic, had an enclitic *mem* of which examples may be found in the Hebrew Bible.

The letter *m* is added at the end of some words in Ugaritic, including even nouns in the construct state. The function of this *m* is uncertain, but its presence is undeniable. A comparable phenomenon has been "found in Mari names . . . and in a variety of uses in Amarna,"[2] as well as in Epigraphic South Arabian.[3] It has, therefore, seemed plausible to suppose that there may be traces of it in the Hebrew Bible, especially in early Hebrew poetry. As long ago as 1936,

Author's note: It is a pleasure to dedicate this essay to Prof. Menahem Haran, a friend of many years' standing.

1. W. L. Moran, "The Hebrew Language in Its Northwest Semitic Background," *The Bible and the Ancient Near East: Essays in Honor of William Foxwell Albright* (ed. G. E. Wright; London, 1961; repr. Winona Lake, Ind., 1979) 60.

2. Ibid.

3. A. F. L. Beeston, *A Descriptive Grammar of Epigraphic South Arabian* (London, 1962) §57.3–4.

H. L. Ginsberg claimed to have found an example in Ps 29:6, and since then many other alleged instances have been detected.

In 1957, H. D. Hummel published an article in which he discussed enclitic *mem*, collected all the examples that he could find of suggestions that had been made, and advanced some further suggestions of his own or of his teachers and friends. He wrote:

> it can now be considered as established beyond any reasonable doubt that enclitic *mem* was once a prominent feature of literary Hebrew, especially in poetry, just as in Ugaritic. Some of these enclitics survived later editings and revisions until the time came when it was sacrilege to alter the consonantal text.[4]

He thought that "this now useless feature of the language was discarded . . . about the time of the Exile."[5]

It was thus maintained that the evidence was sufficient to show that the theory was "established beyond any reasonable doubt." But not everyone agreed. The year before the publication of Hummel's article, G. R. Driver had claimed that "all the examples cited can be otherwise explained or the text may be suspected."[6] Moran commented:

> After H. D. Hummel's completely convincing study on the subject, a skepticism which prefers to suspect the text rather than accept a linguistic feature attested in Amorite, Ugaritic, and Amarna (Jerusalem!) should be virtually impossible.[7]

To this he added a reference to Driver that showed at whom his remarks were directed. Nevertheless, some years later, Driver remained skeptical and described the alleged phenomenon as "growing like a weed in the M.T." and claimed that "all the supposed instances of this -*m* can be explained within the rules of Semitic grammar or Hebrew palaeography."[8] He doubtless also continued to suspect the text in some places.

In seeking to reach a conclusion about the presence of enclitic *mem* in the Hebrew Bible, it is necessary to distinguish between two types of alleged examples. First, there are examples on the basis of which it may be argued that the phenomenon existed in Hebrew. If there are "grammatical and logical inconcinnities" (to borrow Moran's phrase) in the MT that are more satisfactorily solved by postulating enclitic *mem* than by any other theory, then they are positive evidence in its support. Second, if the first type of example can establish

---

4. H. D. Hummel, "Enclitic *Mem* in Early Northwest Semitic, Especially Hebrew," *JBL* 76 (1957) 106.

5. Ibid., 104 and 106.

6. G. R. Driver, *Canaanite Myths and Legends* (Edinburgh, 1956) 129–30.

7. Moran, "Hebrew Language," 60.

8. G. R. Driver, "Review of M. Dahood, *Proverbs and Northwest Semitic Philology*," *JSS* 10 (1965) 112–17.

the probability that enclitic *mem* existed in Hebrew, then there may be other places where the theory is helpful even though they do not have strong evidential value themselves. It is the first type of example, and only the first type, that we must find if we are to be confident that traces of enclitic *mem* are to be detected in the Hebrew Bible. An examination of the evidence must therefore discard all examples in which the MT is defensible. Some other considerations also need to be borne in mind.

First, where there is evidence in the ancient versions or the Samaritan text for the omission of a *mem* that is present in the MT, it must be remembered that there may be more than one way of accounting for the evidence. Hummel says of וַיַּכְשִׁלוּם in Jer 18:15: "we probably should follow the context and point the verb as *niphal* plus enclitic *mem*, as LXX, Syriac, and Vulgate evidently all did."[9] But it is not evident that the translators responsible for the versions had before them a *mem*, recognized it to be enclitic, and therefore ignored it in their translations. Indeed, such a view is difficult to reconcile with Hummel's dating of the discarding of enclitic *mem* in Hebrew "perhaps about the time of the Exile." Is it likely that it was still remembered several centuries later? It is conceivable that at an earlier date some scribe still knew of enclitic *mem* and so failed to copy what he knew to be an anachronism, and that the later translators had before them a text without it. It is also possible that the *mem* had been omitted accidentally, or that the translators had a text with the *mem* but found it difficult to translate and so ignored it, or that the *mem* in the MT is itself the result of corruption and that the versions are based on a superior *Vorlage*. The fact that the versions ignore a *mem* that is in the MT is not necessarily evidence in support of the theory that it is enclitic.

Second, if Hummel were right in supposing that enclitic *mem* ceased to be used during the Exile, it would be implausible to postulate its presence in passages written long after the middle of the sixth century. Yet he refers to alleged examples in Qoh 10:15, 18,[10] which most scholars would probably date two or more centuries later. It is true that some scholars believe that enclitic *mem* continued to be used after the sixth century, but part of the apparent plausibility of Hummel's formulation of the theory is the characterization of enclitic *mem* as an archaic survival that left only traces in the Hebrew Bible. The later its continued use is dated, the greater the difficulty in explaining why it was misunderstood in the tradition behind the pointing of the MT and why it was not taken up by the men responsible for attempting to write Classical Hebrew in the Qumran texts.

Third, in evaluating the theory of enclitic *mem* in a particular verse, it must be asked whether it alone suffices to account for a difficulty in the text or whether it needs to be supplemented by additional emendation. Some of Hummel's

9. Hummel, "Enclitic *Mem*," 104.
10. Ibid., 94.

examples involve emendation of the consonantal text and so—even according to him—the text is *ex hypothesi* suspect. The case for the presence of enclitic *mem* is weakened in such instances.

Fourth, to suggest that a *mem* is enclitic is not itself always sufficient to solve the problem even when Hummel does not mention a change of the consonantal text. In some places where the MT has a masculine plural noun (e.g., צדיקים in Isa 5:23), he thinks that the noun was originally singular and that the *mem* was enclitic. Presumably, he regards the MT's *yod*, which is a mater lectionis, as an addition made when the noun was thought to be plural and when it was usual to write it plene. It is a reasonable hypothesis, but it is, nevertheless, a supplementary one.

Fifth, a number of Hummel's examples postulate the use of enclitic *mem* after a vowel letter (e.g., לנו-ם in Ps 137:3) or the *yod* representing a diphthong or vowel as the ending of the construct state of the dual (for example, מתני-ם in Deut 33:11) or masculine plural (for example, אלהי-ם in Ps 59:6). But there are sometimes difficulties. In supposing that מקום in Gen 1:9 was once מקוה followed by enclitic *mem*, he puts square brackets round the letter *he*, which is not in the MT. He perhaps thinks that it was lost at some stage, and so he must resort to a supplementary hypothesis. In Deut 33:3 he supposes that עמים was originally עמו-ם. Before the Exile, however, the third-person masculine singular pronominal suffix was regularly written with *he*, not *waw*, and so we should have expected עמה-ם. Further, the letter *waw* was unlikely to be confused with *yod* until the adoption of the square script—after the time when Hummel supposes that enclitic *mem* had ceased to be used. Perhaps Hummel would appeal to the theory of Cross and Freedman that the Blessing of Moses in Deuteronomy 33 was composed in the eleventh century and written down in the tenth, when Israelites, like Phoenicians, still used a purely consonantal script and no final matres lectionis were in use. Here the theory of enclitic *mem* needs, not just one, but two supplementary hypotheses: first, that so early a date for the chapter is correct, a theory that is not accepted by all scholars; and second, the view of Cross and Freedman that final vowel letters were not written in Hebrew until the tenth century. The latter hypothesis relies heavily on the judgment that the Gezer Calendar is Israelite rather than Canaanite, as some suppose, and that it is possible to generalize from this one inscription. In any case, whatever view is held about the date and original orthography of Deut 33:3, the same explanation scarcely fits Isa 3:13, where עמים is thought by Hummel to have been originally עמו-ם, but where עמה-ם would have been expected at the time. Finally, if בהרם in Gen 14:6 was originally בהרי-ם, it is necessary to explain the loss of the letter *yod* in the MT.

It would be a difficult task to collect all the alleged examples of enclitic *mem* in the Hebrew Bible, and for the present purpose it is unnecessary to try. Hummel believed that he had found sufficient examples to establish the existence of the phenomenon, and Moran agreed. Hummel's examples are certainly numerous: he lists 31 that had previously been suggested and adds a further 76 (indeed, a few more if we count references made in passing). If the theory is true, it should be possible to prove it on the basis of the examples listed by Hummel. In the following, therefore, I will limit the discussion to the evidence given in his article.

Thirteen Examples in Which the Masoretic Text Makes Good Sense

We begin our investigation of Hummel's evidence by examining the 31 examples that had been suggested by previous scholars. In the following discussion I note (sometimes in parentheses) the numbers allotted to the examples by Hummel in his list. In 13 of the 31, the MT makes good sense as it stands without recourse to the theory of enclitic *mem*, and so they cannot serve as evidence for its existence in Hebrew.

Although it is no. 12 in Hummel's list, it is appropriate to begin with Ps 29:6, the verse in which Ginsberg first suggested in 1936 the presence of enclitic *mem* in the Hebrew Bible,[11] and v. 6 needs to be considered together with v. 5:

5. קול יהוה שבר ארזים
וישבר יהוה את־ארזי הלבנון:

6. וירקידם כמו־עגל
לבנון ושרין כמו בן־ראמים:

In v. 6, considerations of metrical balance lead many scholars to attach לבנון to the first part of the verse against the traditional accents. If the *mem* at the end of וַיַּרְקִידֵם is regarded as enclitic, then Lebanon and Sirion become the direct objects of the verb. Some scholars had earlier suggested that the *mem* should be deleted, and Ginsberg now offered an explanation of its origin.

Ginsberg's suggestion is attractive, but before accepting it we must ask whether the MT can be satisfactorily explained as it stands, or whether Hummel is justified in saying that the received text "is almost impossible in the context."[12] Driver suggests that "this may be an instance of the suffix anticipating the object."[13] There are some examples of such an anticipatory suffix in the Hebrew Bible, either as the direct object of a verb or after a preposition.[14] The construction is not common, and there is evidence in the Samaritan Pentateuch or the versions that casts doubt on the originality of the text in some verses. Still, there is probably sufficient reason to accept the possibility of Driver's explanation.

11. H. L. Ginsberg, *The Ugarit Tablets* (Jerusalem, 1936) 130 [Heb.].
12. Hummel, "Enclitic *Mem*," 93.
13. Driver, *Canaanite Myths*, 130.
14. GKC §131 m, n, o; G. Khan, *Studies in Semitic Syntax* (Oxford, 1988) 76–77.

Another possibility is that v. 6 does not speak of the mountains dancing (despite Ps 114:4, 6), but the 'cedars of Lebanon' mentioned in v. 5, which would be the antecedent of the suffix at the end of וירקידם. There would be no difficulty in supposing that a poetic text such as v. 5 does not imply that every cedar was shattered, and in understanding v. 6 to refer to other cedars (quite apart from the possibility that even broken cedars might be said to dance). The question then arises how 'Lebanon and Sirion' in v. 6 are related to the verb with the suffix. It is possible that 'Lebanon' denotes, not the mountain itself, but the trees on it, as in Isa 10:13, 40:16.[15] If the suffix has an antecedent in v. 5, there is no difficulty in supposing that 'Lebanon and Sirion' are in apposition to that suffix. Further, it is possible that there is an ellipsis of ארזי before לבנון ושרין. This way of understanding the text follows the MT's accentuation, which has the principal internal pause at עגל. The psalm is not metrically uniform, and some other verses have a second part that is longer than the first (for example, vv. 5, 10, 11). Thus, Ginsberg's suggestion about Ps 29:6 does not amount to proof of the theory of enclitic *mem*, though it is one of the best examples.

Number 1 in Hummel's list is Gen 1:9, where God commands that the waters should be gathered into one place. It is suggested, however, that instead of מקום 'place', we should read מקוה, 'a gathering, pool of water', as in v. 10; and in v. 9 the LXX has εἰς συναγωγὴν μίαν. It is possible that the LXX translators associated the Hebrew word before them in v. 9 with the root קוה, but it is by no means certain that their Hebrew reading was different from the MT; it may be significant that מקוה in v. 10 is translated by a different Greek word.[16] The MT makes sense, and it is not self-evident that the same Hebrew noun must originally have been used in both verses. Verse 9 expresses the idea of gathering by the verb יקוו and has no need to use the cognate noun, whereas that verb does not appear in v. 10. On the other hand, if there was a reading מקוה in v. 9 in the LXX's *Vorlage*—which is questionable—it may have arisen under the influence of the verb. Further, the hypothesis seems to presuppose the improbable view that the translators recognized enclitic *mem* as late as the time of the LXX. Moreover, as we have seen, there is the problem of knowing what happened to the letter *he* of מקוה.

In Exod 15:9 (no. 3) it was suggested by Albright, followed by Cross and Freedman,[17] that the suffixes on תמלאמו and תורישמו should be regarded as relics of enclitic *mem*. Yet the MT yields good sense as it stands, and the fact that the nearby cola do not have pronominal suffixes is not proof that there were once none in v. 9. Further, the theory that these two examples of *mem* are enclitic requires an additional change to the consonantal text, for the *waw* that follows each of them must be deleted.

15. See F. Baethgen, *Die Psalmen* (Göttingen, 1892) 82–83.
16. I shall not discuss the further problem of the longer Greek text in v. 9.
17. F. M. Cross and D. N. Freedman, *Studies in Ancient Yahwistic Poetry* (Missoula, Mont., 1975) 51, 60; most of the material in this book was earlier published in articles.

Nor is there any difficulty about the prepositions in Num 24:17 (no. 5): דרך כוכב מיעקב וקם שבט מישראל. The only reason given by Albright for detaching the two examples of *mem* from 'Jacob' and 'Israel' was:

> The *mem* belongs clearly with the preceding, not with the following word, in view of the common Canaanite insertion of enclitic -*mi* between the nominative and the genitive of a construct chain.[18]

The word "clearly" thus seems to be based on no more than the fact that an *m* is often (though not invariably) found in Ugaritic at the end of a noun in the construct state. This is not evidence for enclitic *mem* in Hebrew. It is, rather, an arbitrary tinkering with a text that makes good sense in Hebrew and does not need to be brought into line with a different Semitic language.

Deut 33:11 (no. 9) was described by Albright as a "very pretty example" of an enclitic *mem*:[19] מחץ מתנים קמיו. If the *mem* at the end of מתנים is enclitic, the word may be repointed as a dual in the construct state: 'Smite the loins of his foes'.[20] The Samaritan Pentateuch lacks the *mem*, but this has no necessary bearing on the theory under discussion.[21] It is possible, however, to explain the MT without change if we follow the older analysis of the text as found, for example, in GKC §117 ll. The word קמיו can be understood as the direct object of the verb, and מתנים as "the second accusative . . . more closely" determining "the nearer object by indicating the part or member specially affected by the action." Admittedly, מתנים is not the "second accusative" in the sense of the second to appear, and קמיו would have come before it if the word order had been the same as in, for example, Ps 3:8. Nevertheless, there is often some flexibility in Hebrew word order; and this is a verse that may have been influenced by considerations of what sounded right to the Israelite ear. At any rate, the MT is defensible.

Ps 18:16 (no. 10) contains the phrase אפיקי מים. The theory that the *mem* at the beginning of the second word was originally enclitic at the end of the first has been suggested, not because the MT is difficult, but in order to explain its relation to the parallel passage in 2 Sam 22:16, which has אפקי ים. This is not, however, the only way that the relationship may be explained. As well as having two consonants in common, the words for 'sea' and 'water' have closely related meanings (and may occur in close proximity or even in parallel: for example, Isa 50:2; Ps 78:13, 93:4), and either makes sense in the context. The two words are thus explicable as variants.[22] It is not unknown for copyists, or

18. W. F. Albright, "The Oracles of Balaam," *JBL* 63 (1944) 219.
19. W. F. Albright, "The Old Testament and Canaanite Language and Literature," *CBQ* 7 (1945) 23.
20. Ibid., 24.
21. Contrary to Hummel, "Enclitic *Mem*," 93.
22. Cf. S. Talmon, "The Textual Study of the Bible: A New Outlook," *Qumran and the History of the Biblical Text* (ed. F. M. Cross and S. Talmon; Cambridge, Mass., 1975) 338ff., especially 340–41, 370–73, 377–78.

whoever else transmitted the poems, to make such minor (and often probably unconscious) changes. This example has no evidential value for the theory of enclitic *mem*.

In 1950–51, Albright suggested that in הרים גבנים in Ps 68:17 (no. 14), the first word was once in the construct state and followed by enclitic *mem*.[23] The second word appears in v. 16 after a noun, הר, in the construct state, but it does not necessarily follow that the same construction was used in both verses; in v. 17 גבנים may be used as an adjective or as a noun in apposition to the preceding word.

In זרמו מים עבות in Ps 77:18 (no. 16), it is suggested that the verb is intransitive and that 'water' is in the construct state with enclitic *mem*: 'The waters of the clouds pour down'.[24] It is not clear what is thought to be wrong with the MT if the verb is regarded as transitive.

O'Callaghan also suggests that an enclitic *mem* is to be found in Ps 125:1 (no. 18) at the end of the first of the following words: הבטחים ביהוה כהר־ציון לא־ימוט לעולם ישב. But the sentence makes good sense with the plural (the singular verb in the second part is in a relative clause referring to Mount Zion).

Ps 141:4 (no. 19) contains the rare plural אישים, and it is suggested that the noun is singular and the *mem* enclitic. The same suggestion is made by Hummel for Isa 53:3 in his list of suggestions not published previously.[25] Yet he grants that the same plural should stand in Prov 8:4, and he notes that a similar plural is found in Phoenician. But if the plural is original in one place, why should it be rejected in others?

In Isa 10:1 (no. 24), הוי החקקים חקקי־און ומכתבים עמל כתבו, Ginsberg suggests the reading מכתבי־ם עמל,[26] and Hummel comments: "Poetic parallelism is better preserved" if that reading is accepted.[27] But again the MT makes sense: 'and the writers who write what is evil'.

Isa 10:2 (no. 25), להטות מדין דלים. If the *mem* at the beginning of the second word were originally enclitic, then the phrase could be translated 'to pervert the cause of the poor'. But there is no difficulty in the MT, and the suggestion is superfluous.

Hab 3:8 (no. 31) asks whether the Lord's anger was against the rivers (בנהרים) and the sea. It is suggested that a singular 'river' followed by enclitic *mem* would "better fit the context, full of mythological allusions, than MT's plural."[28] The reference is presumably to Yammu (the enemy of Baal in the Ugaritic texts), who is also called 'Judge River'. But it is questionable whether

23. W. F. Albright, "A Catalogue of Early Hebrew Lyric Poems (Psalm LXVIII)," *HUCA* 23/1 (1950–51) 14, 24, 37.

24. R. T. O'Callaghan, "Echoes of Canaanite Literature in the Psalms," *VT* 4 (1954) 171.

25. Hummel, "Enclitic *Mem*," 101.

26. H. L. Ginsberg, "The Ugaritic Texts and Textual Criticism," *JBL* 62 (1943) 115.

27. Hummel, "Enclitic *Mem*," 94.

28. Ibid., 95.

we should assume that no difference appeared in Hebrew allusions to mythology. In Ps 24:2, 74:15, 93:3; and Isa 44:22, some of whose contexts are comparable, we have the plural נהרות, whose ending cannot be regarded as an enclitic *mem*.

Eighteen Examples in Which the Masoretic Text is Difficult

The remaining 18 examples in the list of the items published before Hummel wrote his article all involve difficulties, and it is not easy to make sense of the MT as it stands. In seeking to evaluate the theory of enclitic *mem*, it is necessary to weigh it against other proposed solutions to the problems.

In Gen 14:6 (no. 2), where the MT has בהררם שעיר, the Samaritan Pentateuch has בהררי שעיר, which is obviously easier. The LXX, Vulgate, and Peshiṭta all translate the verse as though their *Vorlagen* agreed with the Samaritan text, although it is possible that they were simply attempting a meaningful translation of a text identical with the MT. Moran suggested that another example of enclitic *mem* is to be found here.[29] It is strange, however, that he says of both the Samaritan and the two versions that they "*seem* to read only the construct plural" (my italics). The Samaritan is a Hebrew text and in fact reads, and does not merely seem to read, the construct plural. This passage is prose and does not easily fit the theory that traces of enclitic *mem* are to be found in early verse, unless one is to maintain the dubious hypothesis that "this chapter represents a prose version of an old poetic saga."[30] Some have also doubted whether this passage may be dated sufficiently early to meet Hummel's view of the period during which enclitic *mem* remained in use. Further, it was noted above that there is a need to explain what became of the *yod* at the end of the construct plural, which is not in the MT. It is at least as likely that the *mem* is the result of a scribal *lapsus calami*, and that the Samaritan Pentateuch preserves the original text.

Num 23:22 (no. 4) has אל מוציאם ממצרים. Num 24:8 repeats these three words (and the three that follow them), except that it has מוציאו. Albright's article did not, as one might have expected, explain the *mem* at the end of the participle in the former passage as enclitic;[31] rather, he regarded it as the result of dittography. But he argued that the verse should have a verb in the perfect instead of a participle, and so he moved the *mem* at its beginning to the preceding word and added the letter *he* by conjecture; אל-ם הוציאו ממצרים. His theory thus involved a conjectural emendation. In any case, a participle is possible here, as Gray argued convincingly.[32]

29. W. L. Moran, "The Putative Root ᶜTM in Is. 9:18," *CBQ* 12 (1950) 154.
30. Ibid.
31. Albright, "Oracles of Balaam," 215.
32. G. B. Gray, *A Critical and Exegetical Commentary on Numbers* (Edinburgh, 1912) 354.

In Num 24:19 (no. 6), וירד מיעקב is difficult. Albright's solution to the problem involves, not only postulating the presence of enclitic *mem*, but also a rearrangement of the order of words.[33] Where the text is so uncertain, and where the solution departs so far from the MT, the example cannot serve as evidence for the existence of enclitic *mem*. Cross and Freedman are not as radical in their treatment of ואתה מרבבת קדש in Deut 33:2 (no. 7), where they suppose that the text was originally ‹את-ם רבבת קדש›ם and that את-ם 'with him' later became אתה-ם.[34] But they have to add a *mem* after קדש and make other changes to the text of the verse, and they admit that they have no solution to one of its problems. Here, too, it would be unsafe to base a case for enclitic *mem* on the testimony of a problematic verse.

The words ישא מִדַּבְּרֹתֶיךָ in Deut 33:3 (no. 8) appear in a verse with several textual problems (like 33:2, which was considered above). The least of the difficulties is that the last word is a hapax legomenon, for it appears to be a form of a familiar root. Cross and Freedman suppose that the *mem* was originally enclitic and (probably rightly) that the verb should be plural (and the Samaritan Pentateuch has a *waw* at the end of the verb, though its first letter is *waw*, not *yod*).[35] Their translation yields sense: 'They carry out thy decisions'. On the other hand, the verb may mean 'to receive'; the view that the *mem* is a preposition and is to be understood partitively, as in Isa 2:3 and Mic 4:2, may be correct. It is thus possible to make sense of the MT of this part of the verse. In any case, once again, textual problems in these verses in Deuteronomy make this word an unsuitable basis for establishing the theory of enclitic *mem*.

Ps 18:28 (no. 11) is not difficult in itself: ועינים רמות תשפיל. The problem is to relate it to ועיניך על־רמים תשפיל, the corresponding verse in 2 Sam 22:28, and to discover the original text. Cross and Freedman postulate an original עיני-ם רמים תשפיל.[36] This, however, is purely hypothetical and does not account for all the consonants.

Ps 42:5 (no. 13) אדדם. The suggestion that the *mem* is enclitic and that the verb, when revocalized, means 'I move' might be more convincing if the meaning of the hapax legomenon סך with the preposition ב immediately before אדדם were known for certain.

Albright suggested that in אלפי שנאן in Ps 68:18 (no. 15) the second word should be emended to שנן and explained with the help of Ugaritic.[37] Originally אלפים was read, but "the final *mem* may have been erroneously considered as enclitic and dropped." It is impossible to ascribe evidential value to such a string of conjectures, in a verse in which the *mem* (which was *ex hypothesi*, not really enclitic) does not actually appear in the Hebrew text.

33. Albright, "Oracles of Balaam," 221.
34. Cross and Freedman, *Studies in Ancient Yahwistic Poetry*, 99, 105–6.
35. Ibid., 99, 109.
36. Ibid., 136, 150.
37. Albright, "Catalogue of Early Hebrew Lyric Poems," 14, 25.

The first pronominal suffix is difficult in שיתמו נדיבמו in Ps 83:12 (no. 17). It is suggested that the verb was originally שית, followed by enclitic *mem*. The suggestion fails, however, to account for the *waw* that follows the *mem*. The alternative solution to the problem, namely, that the ending of the first word was assimilated to the ending of the second, seems satisfactory.

It was observed above that Qoh 10:15 (no. 20) and 10:18 (no. 21) come from a book that is too late to fit Hummel's dating of the discontinuing of the use of enclitic *mem*. It was also noted that, in both verses, Hummel must postulate that the letter *yod* was later added to the text.

The plural צדיקים does not fit ממנו with a singular suffix in Isa 5:23 (no. 22), and it has been suggested that the *mem* is enclitic. The alternative explanation is that the plural ending is a scribal error, perhaps resulting from an unthinking and inappropriate assimilation to the plural verb יסירו. While this alternative explanation is far from certain, it is at least a possibility.

Isa 9:18 (no. 23): נעתם ארץ. The fact that the verb appears to be masculine is not an insuperable problem, for it comes before the feminine subject.[38] The difficulty is that the verb עתם is not attested elsewhere. Moran suggested that the *mem* is enclitic, and that נעת is the archaic form of the third-person feminine singular of the *Qal* of נוע: 'the earth reeled'.[39] This is probably the best example of enclitic *mem* to be suggested, but it is not certain. Not every hapax legomenon must be made to conform to a root that is otherwise attested in Hebrew, and the verb עתם may have existed in ancient times but has left no other trace in the Bible. Blau notes that medieval Jewish scholars explained it from Arabic *ᶜatama* 'to become dark', and he compares ותחשך הארץ in Exod 10:15, והחשכתי לארץ in Amos 8:9, and ארץ עיפתה כמו אפל, in Job 10:22.[40] Attractive though Moran's suggestion is, it is not the only reasonable explanation of the difficult verb.

Isa 10:5 (no. 26): ומטה־הוא בידם זעמי. Ginsberg suggested that the *mem* of בידם is enclitic and that the noun is in the construct state: 'in the hand of my rage'.[41] This suggestion solves the problem of the last two words when they are seen on their own, but it does not solve all the problems of the verse. The parallel שבט אפי suggests that זעמי belongs in sense with ומטה, rather than with יד: it is the staff that is the instrument of God's anger, rather than the hand that is angry. Driver therefore plausibly suggested that זעמי has been misplaced and should be restored to a position after ומטה.[42] If so, there is the problem that Assyria is here regarded as plural in the third-person masculine plural suffix but

---

38. GKC §145 o.

39. Moran, "Putative Root," 153–54.

40. J. Blau, "Etymologische Untersuchungen auf Grund des palästinischen Arabisch," *VT* 5 (1955) 342–43.

41. Ginsberg, "Ugaritic Texts," 115.

42. G. R. Driver, "Studies in the Vocabulary of the Old Testament, VI," *JTS* 34 (1933) 383; see the NEB.

is construed as singular in the following verses. While such a change is not impossible in Hebrew, it is a problem. Driver sought to solve it by emending the text to read בידמו and understanding the suffix here to be singular.[43] Alternatively, בידים might be read. Admittedly, the moving of זעמי and the emendation of בידם are conjectural, and they go further from the MT than Ginsberg's suggestion. Nevertheless, Driver has drawn attention to a genuine difficulty in the present order of the words. This is another of the better examples of enclitic *mem*, but doubt about the text remains.

בעים רוחו in Isa 11:15 (no. 27) is difficult. Hummel says, "Dahood makes the plausible suggestion that we read the infinitive absolute בע(ה)-ם (in the sense of 'boiling up of water'), followed by enclitic *mem*."[44] The verb תבעה in Isa 64:1 has been thought to mean 'cause to boil up', and an Arabic verb meaning 'swell' has been compared.[45] But Dahood must postulate the substitution of *yod* for the letter *he*; this example is too obscure to have value as evidence.

The third-person plural pronominal suffix in זרעם of Isa 33:2 (no. 28) contrasts with the first-person plural endings elsewhere in the verse; the Vulgate, Peshiṭta, and Targum all translate the word as though the first-person plural suffix were present here too. If the *mem* is enclitic, there is no suffix, but the force of the first-person suffix later in the verse may serve this noun as well. Weiss, however, objects that "it would be harsh to say היה זרוע לבקרים אף ישועתנו...."[46] He favors a different account of the text. His article draws attention to a number of passages in which a textual problem may be solved by postulating scribal confusion between the letters final *mem* and *nun* plus *waw*. If he is right—and the case he makes for the confusion is a strong one—then זרעם here may be a mistake for זרענו. His theory also offers a satisfactory solution to the problem of חטאותם in Mic 7:19 (no. 30), where the first-person plural suffix is expected.[47] He again criticizes the theory that the difficult *mem* is enclitic: "it is not usual for the language to say כל חטאת ...עונותנו יכבש."

Joel 1:17 (no. 29) has נהרסו ממגרות, but in Hag 2:19 the word for 'granary, storehouse' is מגורה. It is therefore suggested that the first *mem* in Joel was originally enclitic and attached to the end of the preceding word. It may also be explained, however, as a dittograph. Further, the probable postexilic date of the passage is difficult to reconcile with Hummel's view of the time when enclitic *mem* disappeared from use.

The strength of the examples in Hummel's list of suggestions published before he wrote his article varies considerably from verse to verse. Some are extremely weak. Yet even the strongest of them (perhaps Isa 5:23, 9:18, 10:5; as well as Ps 29:6) scarcely amount to proof. If we could be sure on other grounds

43. Cf. GKC §103 f, n. 3.
44. Hummel, "Enclitic *Mem*," 94–95.
45. BDB 126.
46. R. Weiss, "On Ligatures in the Hebrew Bible (נו = ם)," *JBL* 82 (1963) 191.
47. Ibid., 192.

that enclitic *mem* existed in Hebrew, they would have something to commend them, but they cannot serve as a secure foundation on which to establish the theory. We must, however, also consider Hummel's further examples to see whether they may offer stronger support for the theory.

Seventy-Six Additional Examples

Hummel acknowledges that among his 76 additional examples, "there are relatively few cases in which we can be absolutely certain that a genuine enclitic *mem* has been found,"[48] and it is unnecessary to discuss all his examples separately. There is, for example, no need to examine the seven verses in which he seeks to get rid of "intensive" or abstract plurals; Isa 19:4; Jer 8:19, 13:19; Hos 12:15; Isa 53:12, and 61:5, and my comments above on Ps 141:4 are relevant to his dislike of אישים in Isa 53:3, which Hummel strangely lists among "intensive plurals."[49] Hummel says that he does "not suggest that intensive plurals were unknown in ancient Hebrew" (and he says nothing about ones with feminine plural endings, to which enclitic *mem* would be irrelevant), "but we seriously suspect that they were not used as widely as the Masoretes have led us to believe."[50] His only reason appears to be that this "construction is relatively rarer in other Semitic languages than in Hebrew . . . ," which is scarcely a convincing argument. It is also surprising that he appears to object to the preformative *mem* of מפעל in Ps 46:9 and to the use of the construct state before a preposition in Isa 28:9 (does he find the other examples in the Hebrew Bible unacceptable?).

In many other verses, the MT makes sense, at least as far as the relevant *mem* is concerned: Isa 1:6; 17:9, 13; 19:9, 12; 24:18, 22; 29:4; 33:21, 23;[51] 40:17; 62:10; 65:20; Jer 10:4, 10;[52] 22:6; 46:5; 50:26; Hos 7:5; Jonah 2:9; Ps 21:2;[53] 22:16; 29:1; 38:20; 58:12; 60:11; 65:10; 72:15; 74:12; 77:6; 78:3; 88:7; 89:10; 107:39; 109:13, 15;[54] 147:20; Job 28:9; Prov 28:1;[55] 30:13.[56] Since sense can be made of the MT without postulating the presence of enclitic *mem*, it is unnecessary to consider further the above examples.

In some verses in which a difficulty has been found, the theory of enclitic *mem* must compete with other explanations that involve no change to the

---

48. Hummel, "Enclitic *Mem*," 96.
49. Ibid., 101.
50. Ibid., 96–97.
51. There are problems here, but the antecedent of the third-person masculine plural suffix is חבליך.
52. The word אמת may be used adverbially as in Jer 23:28 and Ps 132:11.
53. Where Hummel has to delete the letter *he*.
54. In both verses, the plural suffixes refer to the evildoer's offspring, and Hummel has to add a *waw* before each supposed enclitic *mem*.
55. The verb in the singular is in a relative clause referring to כפיר.
56. Where Hummel has to delete the letter *he*.

consonantal text. Sometimes a supposed difficulty may really be no problem at all. Thus, in Isa 25:10,[57] מתבן is not necessarily to be rejected because the word for 'straw' elsewhere lacks a preformative *mem*. As Wildberger points out,[58] there may be a play on words with מדמנה later in the verse.[59] The difficulty of the plural suffix of תפלתם in Ps 102:18 disappears if its antecedent ערער is regarded as a collective noun.[60] Similarly, if שוא in Jer 18:15 is understood as a collective noun denoting idols,[61] they may be the subject of ויכשלום, and the people may be the object.

In some verses the difficulties may be solved by changing the vocalization, though not the consonantal text: for example, לחמם in Isa 47:14; if ותזנח in Lam 3:17 is pointed as a *Niphal*, the *mem* at the beginning of the next word is not difficult. In Isa 30:27 the problem of וכבד משאה is solved by Hummel by postulating an original כבדו-ם שאה 'his liver raging'.[62] He thus needs to add a *waw*. But if the first word is vocalized as an adjective and the second as משא, followed by the letter *he* serving as the third-person masculine singular suffix, even that small change to the consonantal text may be avoided.[63] In Ps 7:7, ועורה אֵלי משפט צוית, Hummel reads אֵל-ם, treats שפט as a participle, and emends the text to read צוה: 'Awake, O God; O Judge, command'.[64] It is a disadvantage that he has to emend צוית and delete the *yod* in אלי. If, however, the pointing is changed to אֱלִי, the words may be translated: 'And awake, O my God, who hast commanded justice'. It has been doubted whether מָרֹום can mean 'proudly' in Ps 56:3: כי-רבים לחמים לי מרום. Hummel dismisses the LXX's ἀπὸ ὕψους, which he understands to presuppose מְרֹום, as "no better" and suggests *mâra-m* 'bitterly'.[65] But the vocalization of the Hebrew presupposed by the LXX may have meant 'from pride', which appears to fit the context.

In other verses where Hummel seeks to solve problems by recourse to the theory of enclitic *mem*, different solutions have also been proposed, and it is not self-evident that his solutions are the right ones. In Isa 3:12, Hummel regards as enclitic the *mem* at the beginning of the last word of עמי נגשיו מעולל and reads נגשיו-ם. An alternative suggestion is that נגשים עוללו should be read; the *waw* in the suffix in the MT has arisen through confusion between *waw* and *yod* accompanied by dittography, and the plural ending of the verb is derived from the following word by postulating haplography. The suggestion that a *mem* serving as a suffix was lost by haplography after השיבות in Ps 85:4 is an

---

57. Which, in any case, some would date too late to fit Hummel's theory.

58. H. Wildberger, *Jesaja* (3 vols.; Neukirchen-Vluyn, 1972–82) 2.970.

59. One may ask if the prophet chose the less common word for that reason.

60. Here Hummel must add a *waw* to the singular suffix.

61. See W. McKane, *A Critical and Exegetical Commentary on Jeremiah I* (ICC; Edinburgh, 1986) 428, 433.

62. Hummel, "Enclitic *Mem*," 100.

63. See Wildberger, *Jesaja*, 3.1208.

64. Hummel, "Enclitic *Mem*," 101.

65. Ibid., 105.

alternative to Hummel's theory that the *mem* of מחרון was once enclitic and attached to the end of the preceding word. On the other hand, dittography may account for the *mem* at the beginning of משחר in Ps 110:3, though perhaps the possibility of a form with preformative *mem* alongside the usual form without it should not be excluded. In any case, there are several textual difficulties in this psalm, and it would be unwise to build much on one word in it. Hummel suggests that the awkward *mem* of אכן לשקר מגבעות in Jer 3:23 is enclitic, but it is also possible to read the plural לשקרים,[66] though it must be granted that it is necessary to add the letter *yod*. In Ps 12:8 the problem of the difference between the suffixes of תשמרם and תצרנו can be solved on Weiss's hypothesis of confusion between final *mem* and *nun* plus *waw*.[67]

The quotation from the Book of the Wars of the Lord in Num 21:14 contains the words הנחלים ארנון. As they stand in the MT, they are perhaps to be understood as an elliptical form of expression: "*the valleys*, namely the valleys *of Arnon.*"[68] Hummel is confident about what should be done: "Undoubtedly, we should point the text נחלי-ם ארנון."[69] His solution to the problem involves more than regarding the *mem* as enclitic; he also has to delete the definite article, which would be impossible before a noun in the construct state. But if the text is *ex hypothesi* corrupt, then the *mem* may be part of the corruption. In any case, the quotation does not constitute a complete sentence, and there are other obscurities in this passage.

In Deut 33:3 and Isa 3:13, it is highly probable that עמו should be read in place of the MT's עמים; the meaning is understood to be 'his people' in the LXX of the former verse, and in the LXX and Peshiṭta of the latter. It was noted above that Hummel thinks that the *mem* was originally enclitic. It was also noted that the theory encounters the difficulty that the third-person masculine singular suffix was written with the letter *he* before the exile and that Hummel has not accounted for its loss. Further, there are other textual problems in Deut 33:3. In both verses, it is possible that a scribe wrote the plural under the influence of Ps 7:9, 96:10; Job 36:31, where the verb דין has עמים as its object; compare also Ps 9:9 and 110:6, where it is followed by לאמים and בגוים, respectively.

The *mem* at the beginning of the third word of כי שמת מעיר לגל in Isa 25:2 is probably due to an error, and Hummel believes that it was once enclitic and attached to the end of the preceding word. It is also possible, however, that an original עיר was assimilated to מעיר later in the same verse. In any case, many scholars date this passage too late to fit Hummel's theory.

Isa 28:1 contains the words אשר על ראש גיא־שמנים הלומי יין. Hummel suggests that the final *mem* of שמנים is enclitic: 'which is on the head of the rich

66. See McKane, *Jeremiah I*, 81.
67. R. Weiss, "Ligatures in the Hebrew Bible," 192.
68. GKC §127 f.
69. Hummel, "Enclitic *Mem*," 97.

valley of those overcome by wine'. His suggestion does not free the verse from all difficulty, however, and he grants that the meaning is "still rather obscure."[70] The verse begins, "Woe to the proud (or, majestic) garland of the drunkards of Ephraim," and the figure of speech is thought to refer to Samaria. According to this figure, the later part of the verse should say that the garland is on the head of 'those overcome by wine', not of 'the rich valley'. Some scholars have thought that the text has been expanded. Perhaps the phrase הלומי יין or שמנים גיא is an addition. It is also possible that we should adopt the reading גאי, which is found here (and in v. 4) in 1QIsaᵃ. The reference would then be to 'those proud of rich fare' or 'unguents', to which the phrase הלומי יין would be in apposition. To speak of pride in rich fare or in unguents is perhaps unusual, but the garland is said to be of גאות and the phrase is not impossible. Driver's suggestion that גאי שמנים means "streaming with unguents" or "perfumes" is attractive, but the semantic development that he postulates is too conjectural to be convincing.[71]

In Jer 48:32 the reference to the sea is puzzling in עד ים יעזר נגעו, and it is not found in Isa 16:8, where the other words appear. Hummel thinks that the *mem* is enclitic and that the *yod* is the ending of the preposition: עד-ם. In Isa 16:8, however, the preposition lacks *yod*, and Hummel's theory presupposes that it must have been lost at some stage. An alternative explanation of ים is that it is a scribal error due to the appearance of the same word earlier in the verse immediately before עד.

The word מאד is difficult in הייתי חרפה ולשכני מאד, in Ps 31:12, and so Hummel adopts the suggestion of M. J. Dahood and W. F. Albright that we should read לשכני-ם איד 'calamity to my neighbors'.[72] But it may be doubted whether איד is entirely satisfactory as a parallel to חרפה or פחד. The suggestion that we should read מנוד 'a shaking', with ellipsis of 'head', seems more appropriate to the context. In Ps 44:15, מנוד־ראש is parallel to משל, and v. 14 contains the words חרפה לשכנינו, as well as לעג וקלס.

Hummel finds two examples of enclitic *mem* in Psalm 49. In v. 15 the *mem* of מזבל is difficult. Hummel suggests that it is enclitic, 'Sheol will be his dwelling place', though he admits that "the entire verse is quite obscure."[73] He fails to say, however, that the treatment of the last clause does not solve the problem of plural suffixes earlier in the verse. If they were also to be regarded as enclitic, he would still have the problem of the plural suffixes in v. 14, not all of which may be accounted for by postulating the presence of enclitic *mem*. Hummel's suggestion that נפשם in v. 9 was once either נפש-ם or נפשו-ם is more plausible, although the second restoration involves the supplementary hypothe-

---

70. Ibid., 98.

71. G. R. Driver, " 'Another Little Drink': Isaiah 28:1–22," *Words and Meanings: Essays Presented to David Winton Thomas* (ed. P. R. Ackroyd and B. Lindars; Cambridge, 1968) 48–50.

72. Hummel, "Enclitic *Mem*," 99.

73. Ibid., 102.

sis that a *waw* has been lost. Certainly v. 8 leads us to expect the singular here. However, it is widely believed that there are a number of textual difficulties in this psalm, as Hummel's comments on v. 15 recognize, and it would be incautious to base much on this verse. The poet changes from plural to singular several times in the psalm, and a scribe could easily have become confused.

The words אלהים צבאות in Ps 59:6 are difficult, and the *mem* is an obvious candidate for the label "enclitic." But this part of the verse is metrically overloaded, and it is likely that the original text has been expanded. Further, this psalm belongs to the so-called Elohistic Psalter, and it may be suspected that part of the difficulty, at least, arose as the result of a clumsy attempt to substitute אלהים for the Tetragrammaton without deleting the latter and without putting the substituted word in the construct state. Something similar seems to have happened in Psalm 80.

Hummel's suggestion for ועז מלך משפט אהב in Ps 99:4 is that we should read עז-ם לך as 'Thou hast strength', and he compares Ps 62:12–13.[74] Several other solutions to the problem have been proposed. The best is perhaps the suggestion that ועז should be vocalized as an adjective and attached to the end of v. 3: 'holy is he and strong'. The word מלך in v. 4 is then understood to be vocative: 'O king, who lovest justice'.

In Ps 137:3, שירו לנו משיר ציון, Hummel attaches the *mem* to the preceding word: 'Sing us Zion's song'.[75] There were, however, a number of songs from Zion, not just one, and the versions have the plural. Perhaps a *yod* has dropped out between *reš* and *ṣade* (which are preceded and followed, respectively, by *yod*), and the *mem* is partitive: 'Sing us one (or, some) of the songs of Zion'.

We come last to Hummel's best example. It has long been held by scholars that the second word of כל־רבים עמים in Ps 89:51 should be emended to ר(י)בי. Hummel seeks to explain the corruption of the text by the hypothesis that the *mem* was originally enclitic: 'the controversies of the peoples'.[76] Without the theory of enclitic *mem*, it might be claimed, it would not be as easy to explain how the final letter came into the text. It would not, however, be impossible.[77] If Hummel had other examples as convincing as this one, his case would be much stronger. As it is, one example is not a sufficiently strong foundation for the theory.

Conclusion

I do not claim to have proved that enclitic *mem* can never have existed in Hebrew or that no relics of it can possibly lie in the present text of the Hebrew Bible. The question is whether there are enough convincing examples

74. Ibid.
75. Ibid., 105.
76. Ibid., 98.
77. Possible explanations include scribal carelessness and the influence of the next word, which ends in *yod* plus *mem*.

in the evidence collected by Hummel to establish as probable the theory of its existence. I have sought to show that the overwhelming majority of his examples are unconvincing or, at best, no better than alternative solutions to the problems of the text. Although some of the 31 examples in Hummel's first list are better than others, none of them is strong enough to constitute proof. Perhaps it may be argued that the large number of suggested examples have a cumulative force that is lacking in any individual example. Against that view, a large number of doubtful cases do not add up to certainty or even a respectable degree of probability. Hummel has performed a useful service in collecting so many examples of the alleged phenomenon, but they fail to prove his case. If scholars are to continue to maintain that enclitic *mem* has left traces in the Hebrew Bible, they need to advance a case based on a sufficient number of strong examples.

NOISY AND YEARNING: THE SEMANTICS OF שקק AND ITS CONGENERS

Moshe Greenberg

MENAHEM HARAN is distinguished among his Israeli colleagues not only by his erudition, but also by the elegance and precision of his Hebrew style. It is a pleasure for me to offer him a tribute in the form of a word study that, aiming to clarify one Hebrew verb, touches upon a metonymic usage common to several languages.

1. Translations old and new differ in their renderings of בָּעִיר יָשֹׁקּוּ in Joel 2:9:

LXX:	'they attack the city'
Vulgate:	'they enter the city'
Syriac:	'they go up in(to) the city'
Targum:	'they arm themselves in the city'
AT:	'they rush upon the city'
RSV:	'they leap upon the city'
NAB:	'they assault the city'[1]
NEB:	'they burst into the city'
NJPSV:	'they dash about in the city'

Clearly there is no real tradition of the meaning of this verb, and a glance at KB[3] shows that there is also no agreed etymology for it.[2]

2. The verb parses as imperfect *Qal* of the root שקק, a root the derivatives of which seem to go in two directions, according to the words with which they are paired. On the one hand we have the idea of making a loud sound/noise: ארי נוהם ודב שוקק Prov 28:15, glossed nicely by Rashi: "נהימה goes with a lion as שקיקה goes with a bear, and both signify a crying sound." The Aramaic

---

1. KB[3]: *anstürmen, überfallen*.
2. Ibid., 4.1519 s.v. שקק I.

versions anticipated him: Tg., מצריח 'cry' and Syr., יהבת קלא 'raise voice'. We render the Proverbs phrase accordingly, 'a roaring lion and a growling bear'.[3]

3. The *Pilpel* form of the root appears in Nah 2:5, ישתקשקון ברחובות, which the Targum renders 'the noise of the clanging of their weapons (קל נקוש זייניהון) is heard in the squares of the city'. This rendering seems to associate ישתקשקון with נקש 'knock against' on the one hand, and with נשק 'arms' on the other; but it supports the view that loud noise is referred to (קל). (Some association with נקש likely underlies LXX 'they shall lock together [in combat]' = Vg 'collide'). Render: 'they raise a din in the squares', taking the *Pilpel* (= *Piel*) form to mean the same as the *Qal* (as, for example, געש = התגעש 'heave' [intransitive, Ps 18:8]).[4]

4. However, the LXX renders שוקק (דב) in Proverbs by *dipsōn* 'thirsty, longing' = Vg *esuriens* 'hungry, desirous', which seems to point in another direction. In support of this meaning one may adduce the parallelism, in Ps 107:9, of נפש שוקקה with נפש רעבה 'thirsty [=parched] gullet[5] // hungry gullet', and in Isa 29:8 of ריקה נפשו . . . עיף ונפשו שוקקה "his gullet is empty . . . he is faint, and his gullet is thirsty'.

Can these two meanings be connected?

5. Let us return to the growling bear. In Isa 59:11 a bear's growling is rendered by המה—נֶהֱמֶה כַדֻּבִּים—a synonym of נהם, from which we may establish the synonymy of המה 'make noise (growl, groan, roar, a commotion)' with שקק. Now, מֵעַי הָמוּ עָלָיו (Cant 5:4), literally, "my guts groaned / were in a commotion on his account' = 'my heart yearned for him' (AT);[6] so too המו מעי לו (Jer 31:20) = 'my heart yearned for him' (NJPSV). But if groaning / turbulent guts can signify yearning, the synonymous נפש שוקקה, literally, 'growling, groaning gullet' can express hunger or thirst (physical and spiritual), hankering, yearning. By metonymy these affective states are denoted by the vocal phenomena (roaring, groaning) associated with them.[7]

---

3. Most modern scholars, ignoring the parallelism with שואג 'roar', take שוקק variously as, for example, 'prowling' (NJPSV), 'charging' (RSV), 'ravenous' (AT, NAB). The NEB's 'thirsty' reacts on its parallel, making the lion 'starving'. See §4, below. Rashi follows Dunash ben Labrat; see §8.2, below.

4. On the morphology of ישתקשקון, see I. Yannay, "Augmented Verbs in Biblical Hebrew," *HUCA* 45 (1974) 71–95, esp. 81–82. My preference for associating this verb with ישקק < שקק is based on the similar contexts of the two verbs (action of invaders).

5. KB[3] 3.672b s.v. נפש, def. 1.

6. See M. Pope's earthy discussion in his *Song of Songs* (AB 7c; Garden City, N.Y., 1977) 519.

7. I have left out of consideration ותשקקה of Ps 65:10, for its context, 'enrichment' of the earth through a 'channel of God full of water', suggests a connection with שוק instead (KB[3] a by-form of שקק) the *Hiphil* forms of which in Joel 2:24, 4:13 mean 'overflow'. In the Psalms passage the *Polel* form will mean something like 'make it overflow' (AT), 'irrigate' (NJPSV), 'watered' (NAB), and so on. Regarding כְּמַשָּׁק גֵּבִים שׁוֹקֵק בּוֹ in Isa 33:4, we are in no better state than was A. Ehrlich eighty years ago when he wrote: "But what שקק and its derivative משק mean in our passage cannot be said, because the meaning of גבים is not clear" (*Randglossen zur hebräischen Bibel*

6. In biblical idiom the affected part of the body is, poetically, the sub-ject of the verb: the gullet growls in hunger or thirst;[8] the guts—the seat of emotion—are in commotion when one yearns. In Tannaitic Hebrew שקק ap-pears in the *Hitpolel* verb form, in the sense of 'hanker after, desire strongly', and its subject is, prosaically, a person: דברים שהאשה משתוקקת עליהם—ומאי (כתובות סה ע״א) תכשיטים? נינהו 'things that a woman hankers after—what are they?—ornaments' (*b. Ketub.* 65a). The verb המה also continues to serve me-tonymously for 'yearn', with a person as subject: שכל מי שהוא הומה ומהמה אחר ממון וקרקע אין לו מה הנאה יש לו 'for whoever yearns and hankers after money but owns no real estate, what benefit has he?' (*Qoh. Rab.* 5:9).

7. We may now render בעיר ישוקו of Joel 2:9, 'they clamor in the city', referring to the triumphant war cries of the invader. For a similar expression, see Ps 74:4: 'Your foes roar (שאגו) inside your meeting-place (= sanctuary?) . . . (v. 23). Do not ignore the shouts (קול) of your foes, the din (שאון) of your enemy that ascends all the time'.

8. Support for this harmonization of the two senses of שקק 'make a noise, clamor', and so forth, and 'hanker' comes from semantic parallels.

8.1. Consider the verb in Ps 42:2: 'As the hind תערג on/by/for (על) water-courses, so my soul תערג for you, God; my soul thirsts for God, the living God'. The LXX translates the verb 'yearns'; Syr., 'bellows' (געי); Tg., 'desires'. In Joel 1:20, 'Even the beasts of the field תערוג to you, for watercourses have dried up', the LXX translates the verb 'look up'; Syr., 'bellow'; Tg., 'hope on'. The early translators thus divide into those who understand the verb to mean utter a cry and those who take it as denoting a feeling.[9]

8.2. *Midraš Psalms* (ca. tenth century) understood the verb in Ps 42:2 to mean 'cry': 'As the hind, in giving birth, is in pain and cries out (עורגת) to God, and he answers her, so the sons of Korah called (קראו) on God in their distress and he answered them'.[10] Similarly, the Spanish Jewish grammarian Dunash ben Labrat (end of tenth century) maintained that the verb referred to a sound:

. . . and the עריגה of the hind is her cry (קול). It is also used with other beasts, while other verbs of crying are common to birds and beasts—e.g., הגה serves for lions and

---

[Leipzig, 1912] 4.118). njpsv, 'It was amassed as grasshoppers [see KB³] are amassed' is based on reading קשש . . . כמקש (H. L. Ginsberg's proposal in "Some Emendations in Isaiah," *JBL* 69 [1950] 57).

8. Tur-Sinai (in Ben-Yehuda 7448b n. 1) drolly compares the rumble of bowels.

9. E. Ullendorff (*Ethiopia and the Bible* [London, 1968] 129), compares Ethiopic and Ara-bic ᶜrg[/j] 'to ascend' and renders, 'As the deer goes up to the water brooks, so my soul rises to thee, O God'. But aside from the strangeness of going upward to a brook, why should so general a motion as going up (shared by a deer and a soul) require a rare term when ᶜlh 'go up' was avail-able? And can the Joel passage possibly mean 'the beasts of the field go up to [God]'?

10. מדרש תהלים, המכונה שוחר טוב [*Midraš Psalms*] (ed. S. Buber; New York, 1947) 265 [reprint].

doves. Animal cries are distinguished by different terms: שואג for a lion, עורג—a hind, שוקק—a bear, נוהק—a wild ass, צורח—a warrior, נובח—a dog, תגעה—a cow, תפעה—a woman in labor.[11]

Dunash's view (in which he followed his teacher Saadya Gaon, who translated the verb in Psalms by 'bleat'[12]) was adopted by Ibn Janaḥ, Rashi, and Qimḥi.[13] It was challenged by Rashi's grandson Jacob Tam, who opted for the alternative, 'yearn, desire'. On the Psalms verse he writes:

> Its meaning is: "As the soul of a hind yearns for (תהיה שוקקה אל) watercourses, so my soul תערג, that is, yearns for you." [So too the Joel passage:] . . . the beasts of the field yearn for you, because watercourses have dried up and their soul yearns; . . . toward you is their yearning (תשוקתם).[14]

Modern translations remain divided; for example:

	Psalms	*Joel*
AT	longs for	cry out
RSV	longs for	cry
NEB	longs for	look up
NAB	longs for	cry out
NJPSV	crying for	cry out

I conclude that ערג is best understood as basically denoting an animal sound but is used metonymically to refer to a state of mind or an emotion expressed by the sound.

9. Another semantic parallel seems to be the Tannaitic base געגע, hence the noun ג(י)עגועים 'yearnings', as in the following anecdote:

> An infidel once said to Rabban Gamaliel, "I know what your God does and where he dwells." [Gamaliel made as if] he grew faint and sighed. The other said, "What's the matter?" He answered, "I have a son across the sea and I have yearnings for him (יש לי גיעגועין עליו); I ask that you tell me about him." He replied, "Do I know where he is?" [Gamaliel] then said, "You don't know what is on earth; what is in heaven you do know?" (*b. Sanh* 39a).

---

11. A. Saenz Badillos (ed.), *Tešubot de Dunaš ben Labrat: Edición crítica* (Granada, 1980) 31* = Z. Filipowski (ed.), תשובות דונש בן לברט, עם הכרעות רבינו יעקב תם (London, 1851) 18.

12. Y. Kafah (ed.), תהלים עם תרגום ופירוש הגאון רבינו סעדיה בן יוסף פיומי זצ״ל (Jerusalem, 1966) 123 (Arabic: יתׂגי).

13. W. Bacher (ed.), ספר השרשים [מאת] יונה בן גנאח [תרגם מערבית] יהודה בן תבון (Berlin, 1896) 385; Rashi, as cited in §2 above; J. H. R. Biesenthal and F. Lebrecht (ed.), ׳ספר השרשים לר דוד בן ר׳ יוסף קמחי (Berlin, 1847) col. 556.

14. Filipowski, passage cited in n. 11. The derivation of תשוקה is presumably from שוק, a byform of שקק (KB³). A. Ehrlich (*Die Psalmen* [Berlin, 1905] 95) argues that in Joel 1:20 only 'cry out' fits, for, "while lions 'roar to God' in Psalms 104:21 and seek their food from him, a beast that yearns for God is inconceivable." This argument would be persuasive, were we not dealing with poetry.

Elsewhere we read of 'a son who had געגועין for his father' (*b. Šabb.* 66b). Rashi explains: "he longs for him (מגעגע עליו)—the verb in this sense is an invention of Rashi[15]), and cannot be parted from him."

9.1. For the etymology of געגועין, A. Kohut compared Arabic *jaᶜjaᶜa* 'roar, shout, clamor, explode in anger' and referred to the two senses of ערג, cry and yearn.[16] It so happens that KB adduces the same Arabic word in the etymology of געה 'low (of cattle)'. The word געה in scripture refers to cows separated from their young (1 Sam 6:12; compare with Rabban Gamaliel's pretended situation) and to hungry oxen (Job 6:5). (In Tannaitic Hebrew געה בבכיה 'broke out in loud weeping' [of humans] is a commonplace.) J. Levy suggests that געגועין may be derived from געה, and then יש לי ג' על will be semantically parallel to המו מעי על[17] (§5 above). In view of the evidence that words for crying, roaring, and so on, serve for emotions expressed by such sounds, this is an attractive suggestion. To round out the argument for this derivation it remains only to show that the reduplicated noun pattern occurs with final-weak roots; תעתועים 'deception, delusion' from תעה 'go astray' is a morphological analogue.[18]

10. Other languages show an analogous metonymy: the associated emotion or feeling is included in the semantic range of words denoting giving voice. We take our cue from the anecdote concerning Rabban Gamaliel and the infidel. Gamaliel sighed and then expressed his longing for his absent son. Now English uses the vocal verb *sigh* to mean "yearn," as in "long have I sighed for a calm" (Tennyson).[19] Note especially the combination of vocal verbs in this citation from Spenser: "I was belou'd of many a gentle Knight. . . . Full many a one for me deepe groand and sight [= sighed]." And if we take up the thread of *groan* and pursue its range in the *OED*, we find that (1) it once had a specialized, now obsolete meaning, "Of a buck: to utter its peculiar cry at rutting time" (compare with ערג); (2) ". . . to yearn or long as if with groans"; an example: "It is now harvest time, our Corn . . . is in the field groaning for the sickle."

10.1. Rashi glosses געגועין 'yearnings' in *b. Šabb.* 66b by Old French 'bramors', evidently denoting an emotional state.[20] Contrast Modern French

---

15. According to Y. Avinery, היכל רש״י: כרך ראשון: אוצר המלים (Jerusalem 1979) col. 240. See below, §10.1.

16. A. Kohut, *Aruch Completum*, 2.331–32.

17. J. Levy, *Chaldäisches Wörterbuch über die Targumim*, 1.150b.

18. With Ibn Janaḥ s.v. תעה, and Qimḥi s.v. תעתע (works cited in n. 13 above); Tur-Sinai in Ben-Yehuda s.v. תעתע (7841 n. 1). KB³ 4.1629 follows other modern scholars in postulating an unattested root תעע (the Arabic verb cited for support is far removed from the required sense of the Hebrew verb).

19. *OED* s.v. "sigh" 2a.

20. According to M. Katan (שבפירושי רש״י על התלמוד) אוצר הלעזים . . . שבפירושי רש״י [Jerusalem, 1984] 18, no. 269), dictionaries of Old French do not record this word. Katan glosses it by Modern Hebrew 'desire, yearning'; this is confirmed by Rashi's comment to נה in Ezek 7:11: "drawn to me, yearns (מגעגע), sets his heart on me."

bramer 'of a stag: to bell [make the rutting cry]'. The Italian cognates neatly divide the two senses between them: *bramire* 'to bell(ow)' and *bramare* 'to desire intensely, hanker after'.[21]

11. To sum up: the difficulty in defining satisfactorily the senses of שקק is ameliorated by recognizing the metonymic relation of certain usages to the basic sense: emotions (for example, 'yearnings') are denoted by vocal terms associated with them ('cry, groan'). The case of שקק is but one example of this phenomenon, which, as we have seen, recurs again and again in Hebrew and elsewhere.

21. From D. Bloch and W. von Wartburg, *Dictionnaire étymologique de la langue française* (Paris, 1975) s.v. *bramer*: Germanic **brammōn* 'low, bellow' > Provencal *bramar* > French *bramer*; from the same Germanic word > Italian *bramare* 'desire intensely'. Add, from M. Cortelazzo and P. Zolli, *Dizionario etimologico della lingua italiana* (Bologna, 1979) vol. 1, s.v. *bramire*: from this verb is derived *bramito* "a loud, mournful cry, characteristic of wild animals, especially stag and bear" (cf. איל עורג, דב שוקק).

BILINGUALISM AND THE BEGINNINGS
OF TRANSLATION

William W. Hallo

*To Menahem Haran
in friendship and respect*

Introduction

"AND ALL THE EARTH was (of) one tongue and (of) uniform speech" or, in the rather free translation of the New English Bible, "Once upon a time all the world spoke a single language and used the same (or: few) words" (Gen 11:1). Thus begins the tale (in the NEB version, we might almost say, the fairy tale) of "the confusion of tongues" and, we should add, the dispersion of peoples from their original home in lower Mesopotamia. The tale is found near the end of the primeval history that makes up the first eleven chapters of Genesis—set between the so-called Table of Nations (Genesis 10) and the "line of Shem" (Gen 11:10–26). It is a *locus classicus* for an early awareness of linguistic issues, albeit an ambiguous one, given the problem of translating the plural of the numeral one, which recurs only four times in the Bible, mostly in the plain sense of 'a few (days)'[1] and which is translated above variously by 'uniform, same, or few'.

In an unpublished paper,[2] Aaron Shaffer has suggested a novel understanding of the passage as referring more specifically to the Mesopotamian situation where, by the beginning of the second millennium, all were of one tongue but of two written languages, Sumerian and Akkadian, with each word

---

1. So in Gen 27:44a, 29:20b; and Dan 11:20b. For Ezek 37:17b, the NEB has: 'then they will be a folding tablet (*lᵊḥdym*) in your hand'.

2. Delivered in New Haven, November 1977 (and elsewhere); but see the quotation of the relevant portion in F. Staal, "Oriental Ideas on the Origin of Language," *JAOS* 99 (1979) 1–14 (p. 5).

in the vernacular Akkadian corresponding to one in the learned Sumerian. These correspondences were eventually fixed in long lexical texts. Shaffer accordingly proposed to translate the Genesis passage: 'All the earth was of one speech and corresponding words'.

This situation was also presumably described in a Sumerian epic known by its modern title as "Enmerkar and the Lord of Aratta."[3] Although ostensibly concerned with more or less historic events, the epic also includes an aetiology on the confusion of tongues in the guise of a 'spell (NAM.ŠUB) of Nudimmud'.[4] The proper translation of this pericope is almost as widely debated as that of the biblical passage.[5] In line 142, for example, the initial EME.ḪA.MUN[6] has been variously translated by 'harmony-tongued(?)',[7] '(of) mutually opposed tongues',[8] '(of) different tongue',[9] 'whose languages (originally) were opposed (to that of Sumer)',[10] 'contrasting tongues', and most recently even 'bilingual'.[11]

What is *not* in dispute is that Mesopotamia is a parade example—and the earliest one documented anywhere—of bilingualism.[12] It is literally the land between the rivers (originally within the great bend of the Euphrates; Greek Mesopotamia is a loan-translation from Akkadian *birît nārim*)[13] or the land of

3. Latest translation by T. Jacobsen, *The Harps that Once . . . : Sumerian Poetry in Translation* (New Haven, 1987) 275–319.

4. Ibid., 288–90, lines 135–56. Nudimmud is a deity equated with Enki.

5. See especially Samuel N. Kramer, "Man's Golden Age: A Sumerian Parallel to Genesis 11:1," *JAOS* 63 (1943) 191–94; idem, " 'The Babel of Tongues': A Sumerian Version," *JAOS* 88 (1968) 108–11; J. van Dijk, "La 'Confusion des langues': Note sur le lexique et sur la morphologie d'Enmerkar, 147–155," *Or* 39 (1970) 302–10; B. Alster, "An Aspect of 'Enmerkar and the Lord of Aratta,' " *RA* 67 (1973) 101–10; O. Gurney, "A Note on 'The Babel of Tongues,' " *AfO* 25 (1974–77) 170f.; and Samuel N. Kramer and John Maier, *Myths of Enki, the Crafty God* (New York, 1989) 88–89.

6. Equated with Akkadian *lišan mithurti* in later lexical and bilingual texts (cf. CAD M/2 137), but this does not resolve the ambiguity. Cf. also W. von Soden, *BiOr* 16 (1959) 132, cited by Åke W. Sjöberg, *The Collection of the Sumerian Temple Hymns* (Texts from Cuneiform Sources 3; Locust Valley, N.Y., 1969) 83.

7. Samuel N. Kramer, *Sumerian Mythology* (Memoirs of the American Philosophical Society 21; Philadelphia, 1944) 107. Cf. idem, "The Babel of Tongues," 109.

8. T. Jacobsen, "Sumerian Mythology: A Review Article," *JNES* 5 (1946) 128–52, esp. 147–48; reprinted in idem, *Toward the Image of Tammuz* (HSS 21; Cambridge, Mass., 1970) 104–31, 353–65, esp. 364–65, n. 32.

9. Sjöberg, *Collection of the Sumerian Temple Hymns*, 83.

10. Alster, "Enmerkar," 103 with n. 2.

11. Jacobsen, *Harps that Once . . .* , 289.

12. See especially Wolfram von Soden, *Zweisprachigkeit in der geistigen Kultur Babyloniens* (Österreichische Akademie der Wissenschaften, phil.-hist. Klasse, Sitzungsberichte 235/1, 1960). For a more recent treatment see T. J. H. Krispijn, "Tweetalige teksten in de oudere Mesopotamische Literatuur," in *Literatuur en Tweetaligheid: 22–23 Januari 1990* (ed. W. J. Boot; Leiden, 1990).

13. J. J. Finkelstein, "Mesopotamia," *Journal of Near Eastern Languages* 21 (1962) 73–92; originally, "that territory surrounded on three sides by the great bend of the Euphrates" (p. 82).

the two rivers (Egyptian *naharina*, Hebrew (Aram) *naharaim*) meaning, originally, Euphrates and Balih or Euphrates and Habur and later Euphrates and Tigris, but figuratively it is the land of two linguistic and cultural streams, the older Sumerian one and the younger Semitic one—whether in Akkadian guise, Amorite, Aramaic or, ultimately, Arabic.

It is not for nothing that modern examples of linguistic and cultural symbiosis have appealed to Mesopotamian precedent, for example, when Franz Rosenzweig entitled his essays on German Jewry (too optimistically as it turned out) "Zweistromland."[14] The allusion to this renowned theologian (1886–1929) is not coincidental, for he is one of the first systematic writers on the subject, not only of bilingualism, but of translation, as was duly noted by George Steiner's more recent classic on the theory of translation.[15] I have dealt elsewhere with this aspect of Rosenzweig's work[16] and will forego reviewing his theories of translation or the problems posed by applying them to his own writings. Instead, I will address some questions of translation in the context of ancient Near Eastern bilingualism.

The Early Bronze Age

My survey begins, not in Mesopotamia proper (in any of its senses), but in western Syria, where the Italian excavations at Ebla have revealed the existence of a prosperous and literate culture that owed much to Mesopotamia and to Egypt as well but that had developed along lines of its own to a degree previously unsuspected, and this as early as the third quarter of the third millennium.[17] The native language of Ebla was a form of Semitic (indeed the earliest form now known), combining features of grammar and lexicon later divided between East Semitic and (North)west Semitic and therefore best described as "North Semitic."[18] But the thousands of large-sized and well-preserved tablets recovered from its royal archives and library employed the cuneiform of lower

14. William W. Hallo, "German and Jewish Culture: A Land of Two Rivers?" *Shofar* 7/4 (1989) 1–10.

15. George Steiner, *After Babel: Aspects of Language and Translation* (New York, 1975); cited hereafter from the New York edition of 1977.

16. William W. Hallo, "Notes on Translation," *ErIsr* 16 (H. M. Orlinsky volume; 1982) 99*–102*; idem, "Franz Rosenzweig Übersetzt," *Der Philosoph Franz Rosenzweig (1886–1929)* (ed. W. Schmied-Kowarzik; Freiburg, 1988) 1.287–300.

17. For the latest discussion of Ebla chronology, see Michael C. Astour, "The Date of the Destruction of Palace G at Ebla," *New Horizons in the Study of Ancient Syria* (BiMes 25; ed. Mark K. Chavalas and John L. Hayes; Malibu, Calif., 1992) 23–39. For my own view in the same volume, see "The Syrian Contribution to Cuneiform Literature and Learning," 69–88, esp. 70.

18. Wolfram von Soden, "Das Nordsemitische in Babylonien und Syrien," *La lingua di Ebla* (ed. L. Cagni; Naples, 1981) 355–61. For the even newer concept of "Central Semitic," see Rainer M. Voigt, "The Classification of Central Semitic," *JSS* 32 (1987) 1–21.

Mesopotamia, which was primarily designed to write Sumerian. As a result, the bulk of each tablet, perhaps as much as 90%, was simply written in Sumerian, with only an occasional word or morpheme from the native Semitic language written in syllabic script, together with a large number of native personal and other proper names.[19]

Whether the Sumerian portions of the texts were read off in Sumerian or Semitic is not entirely clear.[20] What is clear is that the native scribes mastered the foreign script and languages with the help of very extensive lexical lists in which the basic stock of Sumerian words was listed in a fixed sequence, with or without translations into the native Eblaite equivalents.[21] Where the equivalents are given, we thus have bilingual lexical lists that provide the first examples in history of systematic translation. Most notable in this regard is the text that has been suitably given the modern title of "The Vocabulary of Ebla (VE)."[22] It includes nearly 1500 entries, represented by as many as nine different exemplars each,[23] that often enough exhibit variant spellings or translations, and together provide a substantial data-base.[24] Let me illustrate.

VE 572	BALAG	=	*gi-na-ru$_{12}$-um*	(*kinārum*)
			gi-na-rum	"
			gi-na-lum	"
VE 531a	ŠU.ŠU.RA	=	*ma-ḫa-ṣí i-da*	(*maḫāṣ idān*)
(0411)			*ta-ba-um*	(*ṭabāḫum*)
VE 179	EME.BAL	=	*a-ba-lu-um*	(*appālum*)
(079)			*a-ba-um*	"
			a-bí-lu-um	(*āpilum*)
			tá-da-bí-lu	(*tatappilu*)

19. For the personal names, see Alfonso Archi, *Eblaite Personal Names and Semitic Name-Giving* (Archivi Reali di Ebla, Studi 1; Rome, 1988); and Manfred Krebernik, *Die Personennamen der Ebla-Texte: Eine Zwischenbilanz* (= Berliner Beiträge zum Vorderen Orient 7; Berlin, 1991). For geographical names see Michael C. Astour, "Toponymy of Ebla and Ethnohistory of Northern Syria," *JAOS* 108 (1988) 545–55; for divine names, see F. Pomponio, "I nomi divini nei testi di Ebla," *UF* 15 (1983) 141–56.

20. Miguel Civil, "Bilingualism in Logographically Written Languages: Sumerian in Ebla," *Il bilinguismo a Ebla* (Istituto Universitario Orientale; ed. Luigi Cagni; Naples, 1984) 75–97, esp. 75–76.

21. W. Hallo, "Syrian Contribution," 74–76 with notes 44–68. Previously H. J. Nissen, "Bemerkungen zur Listenliteratur Vorderasiens im 3. Jahrtausend," *La lingua di Ebla* (Istituto Universitario Orientale; ed. Luigi Cagni; Naples, 1981) 99–108.

22. Giovanni Pettinato, "I vocabolari bilingui di Ebla," *La Lingua di Ebla* (Istituto Universitario Orientale; ed. Luigi Cagni; Naples, 1981) 241–77 and pls. 1–2; idem, *Testi lessicali monolingui della Biblioteca L. 2769* (Materiali Epigrafici di Ebla 3; Naples, 1981); idem, *Testi lessicali bilingui della Biblioteca L. 2769* (Materiali Epigrafici di Ebla 4; Naples, 1982) 115–343.

23. E.g., VE 118 and 126 in Pettinato, *Testi lessicali bilingui*, 210–11.

24. Luigi Cagni (ed.), *Il Bilinguismo a Ebla* (Istituto Universitario Orientale; Naples, 1984).

The first two examples help illustrate the lexical affinities of Eblaite to both (North)west Semitic[25] and East Semitic,[26] an impression confirmed by the morphology. The third example testifies to the existence of a professional translator at Ebla, his role sufficiently important or institutionalized to enter the "Vocabulary of Ebla,"[27] as well as the standard unilingual list of professions (EDLuE) that Ebla shared with contemporary Mesopotamia,[28] where unilingual lists of Sumerian words and toponyms go back to the very beginnings of writing at the end of the fourth millennium.[29]

Ebla was visited and probably destroyed by Sargon. The great conqueror was at pains to unite the disparate parts of his growing empire. His daughter Enheduanna used her outstanding command of Sumerian, probably literally her mother tongue, to create a body of poetry intended to celebrate her father's achievements and make them theologically acceptable to the Sumerian-speaking South.[30] He himself raised Akkadian to the status of an official court language and had his royal inscriptions composed in Akkadian. But in at least two cases, he provided them with translations into Sumerian;[31] they are known to us from parallel versions copied in Old Babylonian times by the scribes and student scribes of Nippur and Ur[32] on the basis of the original monuments then

25. Sumerian BALAG 'lyre' or 'harp', rendered in Akkadian by the Sumerian loanword *balaggu*, is rendered in Eblaite by a cognate of Hebrew *kinnôr*.

26. Sumerian ŠU.ŠU.RA, literally 'strike the (two) hands', is rendered in Eblaite by a cognate of Akkadian 'striking (of) the two hands' and, alternatively, by a cognate of 'to slaughter' occurring equally in Akkadian and (North)west Semitic.

27. P. Fronzaroli, "Gli equivalenti di eme-bal nelle liste lessicali eblaite," *Studi Eblaiti* 2 (1980), 91–95, esp. p. 92; Alfonso Archi, "Les Textes lexicaux bilingues d'Ebla 1980," *Studi Eblaiti* 2 (1980) 81–89, esp. p. 88. For the form of *tatappilu*, see Karl Hecker, "Doppelt t-erweiterte Formen oder: der eblaitische Infinitiv," *Il bilinguismo a Ebla* (Istituto Universitario Orientale; ed. Luigi Cagni; Naples, 1984) 205–23, esp. p. 217; Burkhart Kienast, "Nomina mit t-Präfix und t-Infix in der Sprache von Ebla und ihre sumerischen Äquivalente," *Il Bilinguismo a Ebla* (Istituto Universitario Orientale; ed. L. Cagni; Naples, 1984) 225–55, esp. p. 228.

28. Pettinato, *Testi lessicali monolingui*, 27 no. 6:11, 30 no. 7:11; compared with Miguel Civil, *The Series lú = ša and Related Texts* (MSL 12; Rome, 1969) 17, no. 1.53:11.

29. Nissen, "Bemerkungen zur Listenliteratur Vorderasiens" (cf. esp. the table on 106–7). Of the earliest (Uruk) lexical texts, some 10% go back to Uruk IV date, the rest are of Jemdet Nasr date (p. 101).

30. William W. Hallo and J. J. A. van Dijk, *The Exaltation of Inanna* (Yale Near Eastern Researches 3; New Haven, Conn., 1968) esp. chap. 1; Tasia Chatzē, Ενχεντουάννα: η εποχη, η ζοη, και το εργο της (Athens, 1988); Joan Goodnick Westenholz, "Enheduanna, En-Priestess, Hen of Nanna, Spouse of Nanna," *DUMU-E₂-DUB-BA-A: Studies in Honor of Åke W. Sjöberg* (Occasional Publications of the Samuel Noah Kramer Fund 11; ed. H. Behrens, D. Loding, and M. T. Roth; Philadelphia, 1989) 539–56.

31. Hans Hirsch, "Die Inschriften der Könige von Agade," *AO* 20 (1963) 1–82, esp. 34–39; I. J. Gelb and B. Kienast, *Die altakkadischen Königsinschriften* (Freiburger Altorientalische Studien 7; Stuttgart, 1990) 157–67. Cf. now Douglas Frayne, *Sargonic and Gutian Periods (2334–2113 BC)* (The Royal Inscriptions of Mesopotamia: Early Periods 2; Toronto, 1993) 9–12, 27–29.

32. For information demonstrating that such "field trips" were part of the curriculum of the Old Babylonian scribal schools, see Åke W. Sjöberg, "The Old Babylonian Eduba," *Sumerological*

still in place, most likely in the open spaces before the palaces and temples of those cities.[33] Together with a comparable inscription by Sargon's son and successor, Rimush,[34] these early Sargonic royal inscriptions constitute the first true bilinguals known from Mesopotamia proper.

The Sargonic Period also provides the first evidence of the existence of professional translators outside the lexical lists.[35] They were still designated by the Sumerian term EME.BAL, literally 'language-turner', or its later replacement INIM.BAL, literally 'word-turner',[36] but the latter were eventually equated with an Akkadian term *targumannu* (or *turgumannu*), of uncertain origin but first attested in Old Assyrian and perhaps derived from Hittite *tarkummai-* 'to announce, interpret, translate'.[37] The meticulous bookkeeping of the outgoing third millennium informs us of specialists in 'turning the languages' of the Gutians and of Meluhha (the Indus Valley?) during the Sargonic Period, and of Marhashi (in Iran) and Amurru (in Syria) in the subsequent Ur III Period, when there was also a 'traveling interpreter' (EME.BAL KASKAL.LA) for good measure.[38]

The Middle Bronze Age

By the beginning of the second millennium, Sumerian was ceasing to serve as a spoken language anywhere, except perhaps near the head of the Persian Gulf. Monumental texts continued to employ it, but true bilinguals, in the sense of a single monument bearing both Sumerian and Akkadian versions, were confined to stone statues or steles with narratives extolling royal triumphs,[39] or

---

Studies in Honor Of Thorkild Jacobsen (AS 20; ed. S. L. Lieberman; Chicago, 1976) 159–79, esp. p. 166 and nn. 26–27; Jacob Klein, "On Writing Monumental Inscriptions in Ur III Scribal Curriculum," *RA* 80 (1986) 1–7; note the reservations of Mamoru Yoshikawa, "maš-dàra and sag-tag," *Acta Sumerologica* 11 (1989) 353–55.

33. Giorgio Buccellati, "Through a Glass Darkly: A Reconstruction of Old Akkadian Monuments Described in Old Babylonian Copies," *The Tablet and the Scroll: Near Eastern Studies in Honor of William W. Hallo* (ed. M. E. Cohen, Daniel C. Snell, and David B. Weisberg; Bethesda, Md., 1993) 58–71.

34. Hirsch, "Die Inschriften," 68–69; Gelb and Kienast, *Die altakkadischen Königsinschriften*, 215–17. Cf. now Frayne, *Sargonic and Gutian Periods*, 67–69.

35. Above, nn. 27–28.

36. Åke Sjöberg, "Der Examenstext A," *ZA* 64 (1975) 152–56. The replacement occurs after Ur III times: p. 153 n. 4.

37. I. J. Gelb, "The Word for Dragoman in the Ancient Near East," *Glossa* 2 (1968) 92–103, esp. pp. 101–2; cf. W. G. Lambert, "A Vocabulary of an Unknown Language," *MARI* 5 (1987) 409–13, esp. 410–11. Differently, Frank Starke, "Zur Herkunft von Akkad. *ta/urgumannu(m)* 'Dolmetscher'," *WO* 24 (1993) 20–38.

38. Sjöberg, "Der Examenstext A," 153 n. 4. Cf. Lambert, "Vocabulary of an Unknown Language," 409–10.

39. Douglas R. Frayne, "Historical Texts in Haifa: Notes on R. Kutscher's 'Brockmon Tablets,'" *BiOr* 48 (1991) 378–409, esp. col. 407 and n. 157. See also below, Postscript.

what may be called "triumphal inscriptions,"[40] and then only from the time of Hammurapi on.

But Sumerian continued to function as the language of learning and liturgy. In scribal schools and temples, it thus survived for another two millennia, much like Latin in postclassical Europe. The unilingual lists of words and names[41] were gradually provided with one or more explanatory columns that exploited to the full the technique of organizing knowledge in lists, a technique that was characteristic of Mesopotamian learning, its so-called "Listenwissenschaft."[42] Ordinarily, the explanatory column involved translation into Akkadian, but other equivalences were also introduced as the genre evolved: for example, syllabic spellings to indicate the exact pronunciation of the Sumerian lemma written logographically, a dialectal equivalent in Sumerian or, where divine names were concerned, a description of the deity's function, relationship to other deities, and so forth.

Like these lexical lists, bilingual literary texts sometimes employed the column format. This was true of some mid-second millennium texts from the Hittite capital at Hattusha[43] and some slightly later texts from Assur, such as the great prayer of Tukulti-Ninurta I.[44] But other formats were also experimented with, at least initially, for example: occasional glosses above or more often below the Sumerian line,[45] enclosing both versions in a single case,[46] or separating them by a *Glossenkeil*, with the Akkadian in the middle between two half-lines of Sumerian.[47] There were even two instances of putting the Sumerian on the obverse and the Akkadian on the reverse.[48] By the first millennium, however, one format became almost universally favored for literary bilinguals,

40. G. Van Driel, "On 'Standard' and 'Triumphal' Inscriptions," in *Symbolae Biblicae et Mesopotamicae Francisco Mario Theodoro de Liagre Böhl Dedicatae* (ed. M. A. Beek et al.; Leiden, 1973) 99–106.

41. See above, n. 29.

42. Wolfram von Soden, "Leistung und Grenze sumerischer und babylonischer Wissenschaft," *Die Welt als Geschichte* 2 (1936) 411–64 and 509–57, esp. 425; reprinted with Benno Landsberger, *Die Eigenbegrifflichkeit der babylonischen Welt* (Darmstadt, 1965) 21–133 with additions, esp. 35.

43. Jerrold S. Cooper, "Bilinguals from Boghazköi," *ZA* 61 (1971) 1–22; *ZA* 62 (1972) 62–81. See 1971–2:6 and 11 (no. 7). Three columns were used for trilinguals (Sumerian-Akkadian-Hittite): ibid., 8–9 (nos. 1 and 2). See also below, Postscript.

44. KAR 128–29. Cf. William W. Hallo, "Review of Marie-Joseph Seux, *Hymnes et Prières aux Dieux de Babylonie et d'Assyrie*," *JAOS* 97 (1977) 582–85, esp. 585. Cf. also KAR 97, a hymn to Ningirsu/Ninurta.

45. E.g., Claus Wilcke, "Die akkadischen Glossen in TMH NF 3 Nr. 25 . . . ," *AO* 23 (1970) 84–87.

46. E.g., Miguel Civil and R. D. Biggs, "Notes sur les textes sumériens archaïques," *RA* 60 (1966) 1–16.

47. E.g., CT:13:35–38, "The Founding of Eridu." Translation in Alexander Heidel, *The Babylonian Genesis* (Chicago, 1942) 49–52; (reprinted, 1951) 60–63.

48. Vincent Scheil, "Contraste féminin," *RA* 24 (1927) 34–37; Felix E. Peiser, *Urkunden aus der Zeit der dritten babylonischen Dynastie* (Berlin, 1905) 4–5 (a prayer in the form of a school-text).

the interlinear one, in which each Sumerian line was followed by its literal translation into Akkadian.[49]

One format that is conspicuous by its rarity is the case of straight translation into Akkadian in the *absence* of the Sumerian original.[50] Apart from some proverbs, this case is most notably illustrated by the twelfth tablet of the canonical "Gilgamesh Epic," which has long been recognized as a late addition to the epic[51] based on the second half of the Sumerian composition variously known as "Gilgamesh, Enkidu and the Netherworld" or "Gilgamesh and the *huluppu*-tree."[52] But whatever the format, the bilingual tradition in Mesopotamia was characterized by a slavish fidelity to the received Sumerian text and a literalness of translation into Akkadian that extended to every morpheme and sometimes actually did violence to the meaning of the original—or what we today regard as its intended meaning. This characterization applies in the first place to the literary texts but could be extended as well to the lexical texts and is perhaps best illustrated by a genre occupying a position in some sense midway between the two, the grammatical texts.[53]

The Old Babylonian grammatical texts graphically illustrate the list system of organizing knowledge in cuneiform. They are arranged in double columns, and each entry registers a Sumerian form in the left column and its Akkadian equivalent in the right column. Horizontal dividing lines group the entries in a strict taxonomy according to person, number, mood, and other considerations. The paradigm of the verb 'to go' alone runs to over 300 entries. And while it is the longest of the paradigms, it is by no means the only one, because it only illustrates one verbal type, the simple intransitive verb. There are at least three

---

For all the preceding see Jerrold S. Cooper, *Sumero-Akkadian Bilingualism* (Ph.D. diss., University of Chicago, 1969).

49. Joachim Krecher, "Interlinearbilinguen," *RLA* 5.124–28.

50. William W. Hallo, "Disturbing the Dead," *Minhah le-Nahum: Biblical and Other Studies Presented to Nahum M. Sarna in Honour of His 70th Birthday* (JSOTSup 154; ed. Michael Fishbane and Marc Brettler; Sheffield, 1993) 183–92, esp. 183–84 n. 5, with previous literature; cf. Krecher, "Sumerische Literatur," *Altorientalische Literaturen* (Neues Handbuch der Literaturwissenschaft 1; ed. W. Röllig; Wiesbaden, 1978) 100–150, esp. 102.

51. For a recent dissenting opinion, see Simo Parpola, "The Assyrian Tree of Life," *JNES* 52 (1993) 192–96; and now Nicola Vulpe, "Irony and Unity in the Gilgamesh Epic," *JNES* 53 (1994) 275–83.

52. Hallo, "Disturbing the Dead," 183–84, with previous literature.

53. Dietz Otto Edzard, "Grammatik," *RLA* 3.610–16; Thorkild Jacobsen, "Very Ancient Texts: Babylonian Grammatical Texts," in *Studies in the History of Linguistics: Traditions and Paradigms* (ed. Dell Hymes; Bloomington, Ind., 1974) 41–62; Jeremy A. Black, *Sumerian Grammar in Babylonian Theory* (Studia Pohl: Series Maior 12; Rome, 1984); for additions to the corpus see especially Oliver Gurney, *Middle Babylonian Legal Documents and Other Texts* (Ur Excavation Texts 7; London, 1974) nos. 97–102. For unilingual forerunners see Franco D'Agostino, "The Study of Sumerian Grammar at Ebla, Part I," *Acta Sumerologica* 13 (1991) 157–80; T. J. Krispijn, "The Early Mesopotamian Lexical Lists and the Dawn of Linguistics," *Jaarbericht . . . Ex Oriente Lux* 32 (1991–92) 12–22.

others almost as long for other sorts of verbs, and other grammatical texts as well. What they all have in common is the careful grouping and ordering of the entries, the desire to enter every possible form, whether attested in the literature or made up on the basis of analogy, and finally the morpheme-for-morpheme equation with Akkadian forms.

The Late Bronze Age

Our survey of ancient Near Eastern translation next takes us back to the "periphery," that great swatch of the Fertile Crescent that surrounds the core area of the Sumero-Akkadian homeland of the cuneiform traditions. By the second half of the second millennium, Akkadian was becoming the lingua franca of the Near East, especially for diplomatic purposes, and scribal schools on the Mesopotamian pattern sprang up in a great arc from Amarna in Egypt, via Ugarit and other cities of the Levant, to Hattusha the Hittite capital in Anatolia. (In Susa, the Elamite metropolis of southwestern Iran, they had existed for some time already.) West of the Jordan, cuneiform texts have been found at Hazor, Megiddo, Taanach, Shechem, Aphek, and Gezer, and invariably included among the finds were school-texts. The lone exception is Hebron. Along the Euphrates, the city of Emar yielded remarkable numbers of traditional Sumero-Akkadian canonical texts in native versions, often expanding on the received texts with sentiments borrowed from a more western tradition. Another innovation of these western texts is their tendency to add additional translations into the local vernacular—at Hattusha Hittite, and at Ugarit Hurrian or Ugaritic (if we may regard the abecedary in Ugaritic with Akkadian pronunciation in this light). The message of Ludingira to his mother will illustrate this feature; though found at Ugarit, it clearly derives from Hattusha, for it comes in no less than four versions: Sumerian, syllabic Sumerian, Akkadian, and Hittite, all written in parallel columns.[54]

Not all this translation activity in the west was confined to the schools. Here as in Mesopotamia the schools stood under the patronage of church and state, or rather temple and palace, and their alumni served these patrons. Thus we encounter the phenomenon of bilingualism on the highest levels, as for example in the drawing up of international treaties, a common enough requirement in the era of internationalism and cosmopolitanism known as the Amarna Age (ca. 1350–1275). Among the numerous treaties preserved from this age there are some in Hittite with more or less verbatim equivalents in Egyptian or Akkadian which, although recovered in separate documents from Egypt and Hattusha respectively, nevertheless qualify as bilinguals of sorts.[55] Much the

---

54. See Hallo, "Syrian Contribution," 80–86, with full documentation.
55. J. A. Wilson (trans.), "Egyptian and Hittite Treaties," *ANET*, 199–205; A. Goetze (trans.), "Egyptian and Hittite Treaties," *ANET*, 529–30.

same could already be said of the "Annals of Hattushili I" (ca. 1640), preserved on separate tablets, in Akkadian and Hittite respectively, from Hattusha.[56]

The Iron Age

The balance of power characteristic of the outgoing Bronze Age came to a precipitous end under the onslaught of the great migrations of the thirteenth century. But bilingualism survived into the Iron Age that dawned in the twelfth century. Indeed it was encouraged by the attendant relocation of whole ethnic entities and the resultant phenomenon of "languages in contact."[57] Thus for example the collapse of the Hittite Empire in Anatolia drove the surviving speakers of Hittite across the Taurus into Cilicia and northern Syria, where they came in contact with speakers of Aramaic, themselves perhaps newly arrived from the Syrian Desert. Together these totally unrelated ethnic groups evolved a so-called Aramaeo-Hittite or Syro-Hittite symbiosis, among whose distinctive features was a reliance on writing systems derived either from Hittite or from the newer "alphabetic" script of the Phoenicians. A parade example is the royal inscription of Azitawadda, king of the neo-Hittite Danunite (Danaoi?) discovered in 1946–47, in Karatepe (Cilicia) on the Çeyhan River. This monumental inscription was recorded at least four times on the statues, orthostats, and gateway of the citadel and city of Azitawadda: three times in Phoenician and once in Luwian, a dialect of Hittite written in the Hittite Hieroglyphic script.[58]

From the same approximate time (the late ninth century), though much farther east and hence closer to Assyria, comes a more recently discovered bilingual monument, that of Tell Fekherye, ancient Sikannu, in northern Syria. The double inscription was discovered on the statue of a king or governor (MLK/šaknu) of ancient Guzana, the biblical Gozan, and is written once in Aramaic and once in the neo-Assyrian dialect of Akkadian. The Akkadian text is written vertically on the skirt of the statue, instead of horizontally in the manner adopted for cuneiform, even of the monumental sort, almost a millennium earlier (and for cursive canons and archives probably well before that). This was then a deliberate case of archaism, perhaps based on the notion that alphabetic script was expected to run perpendicular to the traditional cuneiform script.[59]

56. H. C. Melchert, "The Acts of Hattušili I," *JNES* 37 (1978) 1–22.

57. U. Weinreich, *Languages in Contact* (The Hague, 1962); G. Haayer, "Languages in Contact: The Case of Akkadian and Sumerian," in *Scripta Signa Vocis: Studies about Script, Scriptures, Scribes, and Languages in the Near East Presented to J. H. Hospers by His Pupils, Colleagues, and Friends* (ed. H. L. J. Vanstiphout et al.; Groningen, 1986) 77–84.

58. F. Rosenthal (trans.), "Canaanite and Aramaic Inscriptions," *ANET*, 653–54.

59. Stephen A. Kaufman, "An Assyro-Aramaic *egirtu ša šulmu*," in *Essays on the Ancient Near East in Memory of Jacob Joel Finkelstein* (ed. Maria de Jong Ellis; Memoirs of the Connecticut Academy of Arts and Sciences 19; Hamden, Conn., 1982) 124 n. 44; W. W. Hallo, "Review of *Cuneiform Brick Inscriptions*, by C. B. F. Walker," *JCS* 34 (1982) 114.

Modern Theories

Returning to the core area of Assyria and Babylonia, it is enough to characterize the bilinguals of the first millennium in two broad strokes: (1) they settled on the interlinear format as the preferred method of presentation, and (2) they adopted an almost slavish literalism in translation from Sumerian to Akkadian. The latter characterization could apply equally well to certain ancient versions of the Bible, especially some of the translations into Aramaic.[60] The Bible is no doubt the most translated book of all time, but not, as the foregoing has amply demonstrated, the first, though both superlatives have sometimes been claimed for it in the same breath, even by such an authority as Rosenzweig.[61]

Nor, by the same token, is the Greek version of Aquila the first example of literal translation, though no less a scholar than James Barr makes this claim for it, and even suggests as a reason that Aquila's attention to the text's Hebraic properties is distinctively Jewish.[62] At most we may, following Edward Greenstein, consider the *meturgeman* the first practitioner of "simultaneous translation" and hold him responsible for the resultant literalism of some of the targumim.[63] (His European namesake, the dragoman, would be a later example of the same tradition.)[64]

Finally, we must reject the claim that the concept of an "interlinear version" is original with Bible translation, even though it has been put forward by none other than Johann Wolfgang Goethe, often regarded as the first systematic modern theoretician of translation, as well as a lifelong practitioner of the art.[65] In the *Noten und Abhandlungen* to his *West-östlicher Divan* (1819),[66] he briefly sketched out a tripartite typology of translation according to whether the source language is simply transferred into the target language, or whether the source language is transformed into the target language, or whether the source language and target language are somehow made equivalent. The first approach does violence to the target language, the second to the source language. Only the third may claim true fidelity to both, and only it therefore qualifies for the designation of interlinearity.[67]

60. Etan Levine, *The Aramaic Version of the Bible: Contents and Context* (BZAW 174; Berlin, 1988).

61. Hallo, "Franz Rosenzweig übersetzt," 293 with n. 14; idem, "Notes on Translation," 103* with n. 30.

62. James Barr, *The Typology of Literalism in Ancient Bible Translations* (Mitteilungen des Septuaginta-Unternehmens 15; Göttingen, 1979) 46, as paraphrased by E. L. Greenstein, "Theories of Modern Bible Translation," *Prooftexts* 3 (1983) 9–39 (see p. 19).

63. Ibid., 20.

64. Gelb, "The Word for Dragoman."

65. Steiner, *After Babel*, 256–60.

66. "Übersetzungen," in *Sämtliche Werke* (Hamburger Ausgabe 1949–67, 12th ed.; Munich, 1981) 2.255–58; translated in Goethe, "Three Types of Translation," *Delos* 1 (1968) 188–90.

67. Steiner, *After Babel*, 256–60. For the concepts of *source* and *target language*, see Hallo, "Notes on Translation," 101*; idem, "Franz Rosenzweig übersetzt," 289.

Goethe described the second and third of these types of translation as "parodistic" and "metamorphic" in the etymological sense of these words. He perhaps could have characterized the first as "metathesis," since simply to "transfer" from source to target language is literally to "translate," the older English rendering of the Greek *metathein*[68] in connection with Enoch in the Septuagint (Gen 5:24), Apocrypha (Sir 44:16), and New Testament (Heb 11:5).[69]

In his praise of the "interlinear version" of translation, Goethe was rejected a century later by Franz Rosenzweig[70] but followed about the same time by Walter Benjamin, whose one brief essay on translation has had an impact far beyond its size. "Die Aufgabe des Übersetzers" was originally prefaced to his translation of Baudelaire's *Tableaux Parisiens* of 1923, but frequently reissued[71] and translated.[72] According to Benjamin, "in some degree, all great writings, but the Scriptures in the highest degree, contain between the lines their virtual translation. The interlinear version of the Scriptures is the archetype or ideal of all translation."[73]

Goethe was preceded by Dryden (1631–1700), who preferred "paraphrase" to either "metaphrase" or "imitation" in translation.[74] In another sense, however, he was already anticipated by the Tannaim and Amoraim of the rabbinic tradition. Rosenzweig had argued that "the Bible must surely be the first book to be translated and then held equal to the original text in the translation."[75] On the contrary, Levine points out that, according to the rabbis, the Targum (Aramaic translation) was *not* held equal to the Torah. Moreover, "The *meturgeman*[76] was expected to exercise caution in not misleading the assembled populace, either by verbatim literalism which would distort the sense of scripture, or by free paraphrase which would be blasphemous."[77] Or in the words of the Talmud, "He who translates a verse verbatim is a liar! And he who alters it is a villain and a heretic!"[78] By implication, only a third alternative, like Goethe's, is able to avoid both pitfalls.

---

68. Admittedly, Latin transfero/-ferre/-tuli/-latus is the calque of Greek *metapherein*; cf. Steiner, *After Babel*, 77.

69. Hallo, "Notes on Translation," 103*–4*.

70. Ibid., 103* with n. 27 for his "subtle polemic against Goethe."

71. Walter Benjamin, *Schriften*; repr. as *Illuminationen: Ausgewählte Schriften* (Frankfurt, 1955, 1961, 1971, 1977). See specifically 1955: 40–54; 1961: 56–69; 1977: 50–62.

72. W. Benjamin, "The Task of the Translator," *Delos* 2 (1968) 76–99 [cf. Steiner, *After Babel*, 63 n. 1]); idem, "The Task of the Translator," *Illuminations* (ed. Hannah Arendt; New York, 1968, 1969, 1973) 69–82.

73. Benjamin, *Schriften* (1955: 54; 1968: 88; 1973: xx). Cited by Steiner, *After Babel*, 65, 308.

74. John Dryden, "Three Kinds of Translation," *Delos* 2 (1968) 167–70; cf. Steiner, *After Babel*, 253–56.

75. Cited in Hallo, "Notes on Translation," 103*; idem, "Franz Rosenzweig übersetzt," 293.

76. Translator; see above, p. 350, on Akkadian *targumannu/turgumannu*.

77. Levine, *Aramaic Version*, 11 and nn. 18–19.

78. Talmud *b. Qidd.* 49a; cited in Levine, *Aramaic Version*, 11, n. 21.

Perhaps the typology is inherent in the enterprise of translation. In the very latest statement of the case, Nicholas de Lange speaks of the translator as either a copyist, a servant, or a creative artist, leaving no doubt that he prefers the last characterization.[79] Indeed he "would liken the translator to a performing musician,"[80] though one might prefer Steiner's analogy with the composer putting a poem or narrative to music.[81]

In summary, many cultures know of a Babel, a legend about the pristine unity of human speech, of the first confusion of languages and dispersion of peoples over the earth.[82] But only on the soil of Babylonia itself, and of the surrounding countries exposed to its influence, are we able to document the historic efforts to deal with bilingualism or multilingualism by means of translation.

Postscript

To n. 39 above: True bilinguals are also represented in what may be called "date-formula proclamations" of the Old Babylonian Dynasty, for which see, e.g., F. E. Peiser, "Zur altbabylonischen Datierungsweise," *OLZ* 8 (1905) 1–6.

To n. 43 above: For a two-column bilingual from Mari, see Dominique Charpin, "Les malheurs d'un scribe ou de l'inutilité du Sumérien loin de Nippur," in *Nippur at the Centennial: Papers Read at the 35ᵉ Rencontre Assyriologique Internationale, Philadelphia, 1985* (ed. Maria de Jong Ellis; Occasional Publications of the Samuel Noah Kramer Fund 14; Philadelphia, 1992) 7–27.

79. Nicholas de Lange, *Reflections of a Translator* (Cincinnati, 1993).

80. Ibid., 6.

81. Steiner, *After Babel*, 416–24; for Steiner as a music critic, see his review of Charles Rosen, *The Romantic Generation* in *The New Yorker* (July 24, 1995) 85–88.

82. Arno Borst, *Der Turmbau von Babel: Geschichte der Meinungen über Ursprung und Vielfalt der Sprachen und Völker* (Stuttgart, 1957–63).

THREE BIBLICAL EXPRESSIONS FOR BEING MERCIFUL IN LIGHT OF AKKADIAN AND ARAMAIC

Victor Avigdor Hurowitz

מורי ורבי, Prof. Menahem Haran, has always demonstrated an exegetical sensitivity to fine distinctions in nuance between words and idioms of superficially similar meaning or usage. This article in his honor examines three formulas for arousing and displaying mercy. The first occurs in Akkadian, Aramaic, and Hebrew texts particularly from the Neo-Assyrian to Persian Periods.[1] The second formula is found in Hebrew and Akkadian but not in Aramaic. The third is attested in Aramaic and late Biblical Hebrew but not in Akkadian. The formulas to be investigated here resemble each other in vocabulary but are distinct in syntax and meaning. They seem to have been subject on occasion to interchange, possibly inadvertent, by biblical authors and modern scholars alike. It is appropriate, therefore, that they be examined together and sorted out. In the

Author's note: I dedicate this article to Professor Haran in deep gratitude for the countless kindnesses he has extended to me since I came to Jerusalem to study under him a quarter of a century ago.

1. F. M. Fales ("Aramaic Letters and Neo-Assyrian Letters: Philological and Methodological Notes," *JAOS* 107 [1987] 451–69) has presented a lengthy discussion of the formulaic and topical-literary patterns common to the Neo-Assyrian letters and to the Aramaic letters from Elephantine, which are several centuries younger. Although the similarities between the Elephantine letters, especially Cowley 30 and 31, and the Aramaic portions of the biblical book of Ezra are well known (see especially B. Porten, "The Archive of Jedaniah Son of Gemariah of Elephantine: The Structure and Style of the Letters [I]," *ErIsr* 14 (Ginsberg Volume; ed. M. Haran; 1978] 165–77 [Heb.]), Fales is not particularly concerned with them in this study. Connections between the Assyrian and Aramaic epistolary corpora on the one hand, and the Hebrew sections of the Bible on the other, interest him just as little. At one place (p. 459) he refers to *šaʾal lěšālōm* in Jer 15:5 as a possible parallel to cognate expressions in the documents under discussion. Although he points out a parallel between several wishes for a thousandfold increase of blessing found in the two letter collections (p. 457 n. 32), he makes no mention of Moses' wish that YHWH increase Israel's numbers a thousand times in Deut 1:11, a passage certainly dating to the Neo-Babylonian Period (see M. Weinfeld, *Deuteronomy 1–11* [AB 5; New York, 1991] 137 on v. 11).

course of identifying the formulas and determining their precise meanings, I will also attempt to elucidate three somewhat difficult biblical passages in which they appear.

Cowley 30:1–3 (= 31:1–3)

In Cowley 30:1–3 (= 31:1–3),[2] Jedaniah and the priests of Elephantine greet Bagohi as follows:

שלם מראן אלה שמיא ישאל שגיא בכל עדן ולרחמן ישימנך קדם דריוהוש
מלכא ובני ביתא יתר מן זי כען חד אלף

May the God of Heaven look after our lord greatly at all times, *and may he place you for mercy*[3] before Darius the king and the palace officials a thousand times more than now . . .

As early as 1915, the Gesenius-Buhl lexicon cites this passage as a parallel to no less than four Biblical verses containing the words נתן X לרחמים לפני Y.[4] This comparison has been repeated most recently in the fourth volume of *HALAT* with acknowledgment to Gesenius-Buhl.[5] The relevant biblical texts are:

ונתתם לרחמים לפני שוביהם
and you shall give them for mercy before their captors (1 Kgs 8:50);

ויתן אותם לרחמים לפני כל-שוביהם
and He gave them for mercy before all their captors (Ps 106:46);

ויתן האלהים את-דניאל לחסד ולרחמים לפני שר הסריסים
and God gave Daniel for kindness and mercy before the chief courtier (Dan 1:9);

ותנהו לרחמים לפני האיש הזה
and give him for mercy before this man (Neh 1:11).

The similarity between these passages is striking. In each instance, God is asked or said to 'give' (*ntn/śym*) the person or persons being blessed or prayed about for 'mercy' (*lĕraḥămîm*) 'before' (*lipnê/qdm*) a superior or someone with power (*šôbêhem / śar hassārîsîm / hā²îš hazzeh / drywhwš mlk²*). In other

---

2. A. Cowley, *Aramaic Papyri of the Fifth Century B.C.* (Oxford, 1923).

3. For the sake of convenience, I have translated the Semitic root *rḥm* throughout this study as 'mercy' or 'pity', even though the various contexts, as well as considerations of eloquence in English, might suggest other renditions, such as 'favor', 'kindness', and so on. In order to echo faithfully the original Semitic idiom under discussion, I have consistently used the awkward, verbatim rendition 'to give X for mercy', even though this collocation makes little sense in English. 'To give X for mercy' means 'to cause X to be regarded mercifully'.

4. F. Buhl, *Wilhelm Gesenius' Hebräisches und aramäisches Handwörterbuch* (16th ed.; Leipzig, 1915) 755b s.v. *rḥm*.

5. See also Porten, "Archive of Jedaniah," 167.

words, God is asked to inspire one person or persons to be merciful to someone else. Although the passage from Psalms 106 (a historical confession) is most likely dependent on the Deuteronomistic passage 1 Kgs 8:50, there is no reason to regard any of the other passages as interdependent. It is obvious that, apart from these two particular verses, all the passages cited reflect an accepted prayer formula rather than an interbiblical tradition.

The four biblical passages mentioned above are cited verbatim in later rabbinic texts of midrashic nature. But, in addition to such fossilized quotations, the formula lives on independently, appearing again in only slightly different forms in several recommended prayers that have no biblical precedents.[6] These prayers have entered Jewish liturgy in forms diverging only little from the way they occur in the rabbinic sources.

The prayer recommended for the wayfarer contains the words: ... ותנני לחן ולחסד ולרחמים בעיניך ובעיני כל רואי 'and give me for favor, kindness, and mercy in your eyes and in the eyes of all who behold me' (*b. Ber* 29b).

After washing one's face in the morning, one is to say a lengthy benediction containing the words ותנני היום ובכל יום לחן ולחסד ולרחמים בעיניך ובעיני כל רואי 'and give me today and everyday for favor, kindness and mercy in your eyes and in the eyes of all who behold me' (*b. Ber* 60b).

The rabbinic formula is, of course, expanded in comparison with its biblical antecedents. The book of Daniel had already extended the formula by adding the word *lĕḥesed*, and the rabbis follow suit by introducing *lĕḥēn*. They have also changed the adverbial phrase *lipnê X* or *qdm X* to *bĕ cênê X*, and the new preposition now has as an object, not only a third party, but God himself.[7] Thus, the meaning of the original formula has been altered. No longer is it only a wish that God cause a person to be merciful to the supplicant, but it now asks God himself to be merciful to him. In a certain sense, a formula originally involving three parties now involves four, with God being both a subject and an object; and an active, causative formula now has a reflexive element introduced.

This expanded form has entered the Midrash as well. According to *Midraš Tanḥuma* (Warsaw ed.; *Vayyeshev*, chap. 8), Joseph, before waiting on Potiphar, used to say:

Master of the Universe, you are my trust and my patron,
תנני לחן ולחסד ולרחמים בעיניך ובעיני כל רואי ובעיני פטיפר אדוני
give me for favor, kindness, and mercy in your eyes and in the eyes of all who behold me and in the eyes of Potiphar my master.

---

6. Ibid., 167.

7. For the interchange of לפני and בעיני in a similar formula (not investigated in this study), cf. Sir 3:18, where one Hebrew manuscript reads לפני אל תמצא רחמים, while the parallel passage in a different manuscript reads ובעיני אלהים תמצא חן. See The Historical Dictionary of the Hebrew Language, *The Book of Ben Sira: Text, Concordance, and an Analysis of the Vocabulary* (Jerusalem, 1973) 3.

To the Hebrew and Aramaic material adduced so far, we may now add two Akkadian texts from the Sargonid Period. In a newly edited letter, this one from a certain Hunni to Sargon II, we read (CT 53 43 obv. 10–13 = SAA I no. 134):

šarru bēlī [xx]
[a]tta lu ekurru ša šarrāni
ammar napištišu ina kitti [šēpēka] išakkanuni
u ṭabatka inaṣṣaruni
ilānika ana rēme ina pānika issakunūšu
ki ša ūmē anni tulabbaš taka[rrabšu]

O king, my lord, may you be the temple of kings! Each and everyone who truly lays down his life under [your feet] and keeps your treaty, *your gods will place him for mercy / favorably before you*,[8] and you will dress him (in purple) and [bless him] as today . . .

In a highly emotional petition to the crown prince (Ashurbanipal), the beginning of which is no longer extant so that the sender's identity is unknown, we read:

anniu riksu ša dabābi gabbu
ina pān mātāti gabbu labki
memeni ša libbu isakkannini lašša
ana kaša adaggalka ša bēli attani
ina pānika abtiki
šumma ilānika ina pānika ana rēme issaknunni
diᵓatija šakkil
ula qibiᵓa ma alik mutu [lal]lik lamūt

This is the entire quotation of the report. I have cried to the entire world. There is no one who will pay attention to me. I turn to you, for you are my lord. I cry before you. *If your gods place me in mercy / favorably before you*, take away my tears, or say to me, "Go! Die!" and I will go away and die (ABL 1149 rev.).

The words *ilānika ina pānika ana rēme issaknūnni*, found in both of these documents, are the exact Akkadian equivalent of the Aramaic and Hebrew formulas described above.

Although the basic language is identical, the use of the formula varies from one occurrence to the other. In the second Assyrian letter, the formula is

---

8. Parpola translates this line 'will be pardoned in your presence by your gods'. CAD Š/1 149b s.v. *šakānu* 6g10′ translates the other passage, 'if your gods have moved you to pity for me'. CAD D 147b s.v. *dimtu* 1a gives the same expression in the next text a more literal, less idiomatic rendition, '. . . if your gods make me find mercy in your eyes . . . '. Since we are dealing with a fixed formula, it seems as though the last translation should be adopted for both texts, for it suits all the circumstances in which the formula is employed.

part of a petition to the king, included in the body of the letter. It is in essence a prayer formula. This is the way the formula is used in the prayers of Solomon (1 Kgs 8:50) and Nehemiah, as well as the rabbinic sources. The difference, of course, is that in the biblical passages and Jewish prayers God is being addressed, so that he need not be mentioned explicitly in the formula. In the first Assyrian letter the formula appears in the highfaluting, obsequious salutation that makes up most of the document. This is the way it functions in the opening lines of Cowley 30 and 31, which are also highly poetic. In Ps 106:46 and the book of Daniel, the formula is absorbed into the narrative to describe the way a captor behaves toward his captive. These variant uses make it clear that the formula was not specifically an epistolary expression but had wider currency. More precisely, it seems to be a prayer formula used secondarily in letters and narrative rather than an epistolary turn of speech adapted for liturgical and narrative use.

The existence of such a formula in Assyrian texts obviously forestalls any suggestion that the Elephantine formula might reflect traditional Israelite usage. The formula develops in Jewish literature more than elsewhere, but it is not of Judean or Israelite origin. We may thus safely add this formula to the collection of stock phrases characteristic of the cosmopolitan, cultural symbiosis of the Assyrian-Persian Period. Whether the formula is originally Aramaic or Akkadian cannot be determined.[9]

Isaiah 47:6

In Isa 47:6, a poetic text from the Persian Period, God chastises Chaldean Babylon saying:

חללתי נחלתי	קצפתי על־עמי
לא שמת להם רחמים	ואתנם בידך
הכבדת עלך מאד	על־זקן

I raged against my people	I desecrated my possession
I delivered them into your hand	*You gave them no mercy*
Upon the elderly	you made your yoke very heavy.

9. Borrowing of words and expressions can and does go in both directions. For Akkadian influence on Aramaic, see S. A. Kaufman, "The Akkadian Influences on Aramaic," *Assyriological Studies* 19 (Chicago, 1974). For Aramaic influence on Akkadian, see, inter alia, H. Tadmor, "The Aramaization of Assyria: Aspects of Western Impact," *Mesopotamien und seine Nachbarn* (ed. H. J. Nissen and J. Renger; Berliner Beiträge zum Vorderen Orient 1; Berlin, 1982) 2.449–70; idem, "On the Use of Aramaic in the Assyrian Empire: Three Observations on a Relief of Sargon II," *ErIsr* 20 (Yigael Yadin Memorial Volume; ed. A. Ben-Tor et al.; 1989) 249–52; A. R. Millard, "Assyrians and Arameans," *Iraq* 45 (1983) 101–7; F. M. Fales, *Aramaic Epigraphs on Clay Tablets of the Neo-Assyrian Period* (Studi Semitici n.s. 2 = Materiali per il lessico aramaico 1; Rome, 1986). For literary topoi shared by the Bible and a Neo-Assyrian letter, see V. A. Hurowitz, "ABL 1285 and the Hebrew Bible: Literary Topoi in Urad-Gula's Letter of Petition to Assurbanipal," *SAAB* 7 (1993) 9–17.

The middle line of this passage contains the expression *lōʾ śamt lāhem raḥă-mîm*. [10] The literal meaning of *śām raḥămîm lĕ-X* is 'to give/display mercy to someone', in other words, 'to be merciful toward someone'. God is accusing Babylon of not being kind to his people. The expression is identical to the one found in Deut 13:18 save that *nātan* is used rather than *śām*:

ונתן לך רחמים ורחמך והרבך

> He (Yʜᴡʜ) will give you pity [that is, be merciful to you], and when he will pity you he will increase you (Deut 13:18[17]).

The word *śām* is used in Isa 47:6b because *nātan* appears in the previous, parallel stich. [11] Both of these expressions are Hebrew interdialectical equivalents of an Akkadian phrase *rēmam šakānum ana X* found in numerous sources ranging from the Old Babylonian to the Neo-Babylonian Periods. Here are but a few examples in chronological order: [12]

> *išratku ṭudum u šakinku rēm[um]*
>
> The way is straight for you, mercy is accorded you (*RB* 59 [1952] 246 VIII 8). [13]
>
> *mâdutu ša ana šarri bēlija iḫṭû u šarru rēmu iškunūšunūtimma*
>
> There are many who have sinned to my lord, the king, but the king has given mercy towards them (ABL 530 rev.).
>
> *šumma kalbu ana bīt ili īrub ilāni ana māti rēma ul išakkanū*
>
> If a dog entered the temple, the gods will not be merciful to the land (*RAcc* 36 rev. 3).

As noted above, the expressions *nātan/śām raḥămîm lĕ-X* and *rēmam iškun ana X* or *rēmam iškun* + dative pronoun suffix all mean 'he was merciful toward X'. They differ from the first expression discussed in a very basic man-

---

10. The middle line contains an example of "antonymous parallelism," juxtaposing *nātan* and *lōʾ śām*. The last line may contain an example of a "pivot phrase," with the word *hikbadt* to be read in the deep structure as belonging to both cola. The passage was studied by Y. Avishur, "לא שמת להם רחמים [Isaiah 47:6]: Biblical Style or Translated Idiom?" *Shnaton* 5–6 (1982–83) 91–99 [Heb.]. His division of the verse into five cola ignores these well-known stylistic phenomena and is incorrect, as is his preference for the suggestion that the verse contains an Akkadian calque.

11. Contra Avishur ("לא שמת להם רחמים," 91–99), who prefers to explain it as an Akkadian calque, even though he himself musters more than ample convincing evidence for the interchangeability of *nātan* and *śām*.

12. See AHw 970b s.v. *rēmu*.

13. For a new edition of this text, see W. G. Lambert, "A Further Attempt at the Babylonian 'Man and His God,'" *Language, Literature, and History: Philological and Historical Studies Presented to Erica Reiner* (AOS 67; ed. F. Rochberg-Halton; New Haven, 1987) 187–202. He translates, 'Your path is straight and compassion is bestowed upon you'. In this passage, the expression appears in a passive form, and a dative pronominal suffix appears bound to the verb instead of an independent dative phrase with a preposition.

ner. The first expression is a causative one involving three parties; to be precise, a deity causes or is asked to cause one person to be regarded mercifully by another person. It is not the god who is merciful but the person of a superior rank who is under the god's influence or control. The second expression is active but not causative and refers simply to one party (god or person) who is being merciful (giving/showing mercy) toward another.

We will see below that on certain occasions this distinction seems either to have been distorted by ancient scribes or misunderstood by modern exegetes.

Cowley 38:2–3

Cowley 38:2–3 contains the following greeting:

שלם מרא[ן]י אלה שמיא ישאל שגיא שגיא בכל עדן ו[ן]לרחמן הוו קדם אלה שמיא

May the [God of Heaven ask mightily for the] well-being of my lord [at all times] and *may you (my lord) be for mercy before* the God of Heaven.

The Aramaic expression *hwy lrḥmn qdm DN* is similar but not identical to the two expressions examined thus far. Moreover, it may have a biblical counterpart as well, although this potential counterpart has hitherto gone unnoticed. In this passage only two parties—a king and God—are involved, and it is asked that the one will be favorably regarded by the other. This turn of speech is essentially a passive form of the two expressions discussed above. Although by using *lrḥmn qdm*, the phrase is closer in formulation to the first, it is actually nearer in meaning to the second.

An identical expression may be uncovered in 2 Chr 30:9.[14] Hezekiah admonishes the people he wishes to invite to celebrate the Passover in Jerusalem as follows:

כי בשובכם על־יהוה אחיכם ובניכם לרחמים לפני שוביהם

For through your returning to YHWH, your brothers and your children for mercy before their captors (2 Chr 30:9).

The similarity between this statement and the first and third formulas studied here is obvious. It is particularly close to the example of the formula in Solomon's prayer in 1 Kgs 8:50 (a line that, incidentally, is not present in Chronicle's version of Solomon's prayer, 2 Chr 6:39). However, this passage is missing a verb, as the verbatim and awkward translation given above makes clear. In light of the first formula, it would be worthwhile to consider restoring *yittēn*, giving us 'may YHWH give your brothers and children for mercy before their captors'.[15] Nonetheless, an ancient deletion of *yittēn* would be hard to

14. Porten ("Archive of Jedaniah," 167) states that this formula has no biblical parallel but compares it with the talmudic formula mentioned above. However, as we have seen above, the talmudic formula is identical not with this one, but with the first formula discussed!

15. Cf. E. L. Curtis and A. A. Madsen, *Chronicles* (ICC; Edinburgh, 1910) 474.

explain, and no direct support could be given from the versions for this particular restoration. However, BHS has already suggested restoring the word
yihyû 'they will be', in accordance with the Septuagint reading (*esontai*), explaining the loss of the word as a haplography with the Tetragrammaton that
precedes it (**yhwh yhyw > yhwh*).[16] If this were true, the verse would contain
an exact Hebrew equivalent of the third formula that is in Aramaic. The existence of the formula in a contemporary document obviously speaks strongly in
favor of the suggested restoration and shows the Septuagint reading to be more
than just an attempt by a translator to smooth out a bit of choppy syntax.[17]

Genesis 43:14

Bearing in mind these three expressions and the clear distinction between
them, it is possible to shed some light on a well-known passage in the Joseph
story. Before sending his remaining sons back to Egypt to buy more food and
pick up Simeon, Jacob utters the desperate prayer:

ואל שדי יתן לכם רחמים לפני האיש . . .

And may El Shaddai give you mercy before the man . . . (Gen 43:14).

On the face of it, this passage clearly includes the second of the expressions discussed above, *nātan raḥămîm lĕ-X*, meaning 'to be merciful to X'. As such it has
little to do with the first formula. Nonetheless, the words *lipnê hā-ʾîš* with which
the prayer concludes are nowhere else used in association with *nātan raḥămîm
lĕ-X* and seem superfluous. On the other hand, they are quite at home with the
first expression and, in fact, an integral part of it. Furthermore, although older
Bible translations (KJV, RSV, JPSV 1917) render this passage quite literally as 'may
God Almighty give you mercy before the man . . . '. Moffatt and the more recent
versions (Speiser,[18] NJPSV, NEB, NAB) render it 'and may El Shaddai dispose/
move this man to mercy towards you . . . '. This interpretive translation is
clearly wrong, given the difference between the two expressions under consideration. To be precise, rendering it in a causative manner imposes on the second
formula something of the meaning of the first. Nonetheless, it reflects what the
translators (rightly!) feel must be the plain meaning and intention of the text.[19]

I suggest that the expression נתן רחמים ל-PN has through confusion or for
some theological consideration supplanted the proper נתן את PN לרחמים and
that below the extant form of the verse we should read ואל שדי יתן אתכם
לרחמים לפני האיש . . . , 'and may El Shaddai place you for mercy before the

---

16. See also W. Rudolph, *Chronikbucher* (HAT 21; Tübingen, 1955) 300 ad loc., but with
no reference to the Septuagint.

17. I am grateful to Zippora Talshir for discussing the Septuagint reading with me.

18. E. A. Speiser, *Genesis* (AB; Garden City, N.Y., 1964).

19. Cf. A. B. Ehrlich, *Randglossen zur Hebräischen Bibel* (Hildesheim, 1968 [orig., 1908]),
vol. 1, ad loc.

man'. Restoration of a formula at home in the parlance of the Neo-Assyrian to Persian time span would accord quite well with the presence in the Joseph story of other elements having similar chronological background.[20]

Jeremiah 42:12

A similarly problematic passage is Jer 42:12. The MT reads:

ואתן לכם רחמים ורחם אתכם והשיב אתכם אל אדמתכם

I (YHWH) will give mercy to you and he (the king of Babylon) will be merciful to you and he (the king of Babylon) will return you to your land.

The understanding of the prophecy reflected in this translation yields a prediction corresponding in structure to Jacob's prayer. In both instances, God is to be merciful to someone (the brothers, the Judeans), and as a result someone else (Joseph, the king of Babylon) will also be well disposed toward them and will do something beneficial, namely, release a captive. They both contain the expressions *nātan raḥămîm l-X* and *whšb*. What is missing from Jeremiah's words is the crucial expression *lipnê melek Bābel*, or the like, to correspond with *lipnê hā ˀîš*.

The Septuagint, on the other hand, reads the second and third verbs in this sentence as though God were the subject of them, as well ('*I* will give you mercy, and *I* will be merciful to you, and *I* will return you / cause you to dwell in your land'). Scholars have already explained the variation in person by suggesting that the LXX regards these verbs not as third-person masculine singular finite verbs, but as infinitive absolutes,[21] thus obviating the need to make inexplicable changes in the consonantal Vorlage. These same scholars see the MT as primary and do not suggest emending the text to first person.

These opinions notwithstanding, the Septuagint's understanding of the prophecy in which all the verbs have the same subject is more in keeping with the meaning of *nātan raḥămîm lĕ-X*, which, as we have seen, is not a causative expression. Moreover, this passage can hardly be separated from and may well be derivative of Deut 13:18, which reads:

ונתן־לך רחמים ורחמך והרבך . . .

He (YHWH) will give you mercy, and he will act mercifully to you, and he will increase you.

Deut 13:18 corresponds precisely to what we find in the LXX to Jer 42:12! In both cases, a promise to give mercy to someone is followed by a promise to be

---

20. Despite the use of the divine name El Shaddai, scholars have been reluctant to attribute this verse to P. The combination of the typically Priestly divine appellative and a formula from no earlier than the Neo-Assyrian Period would indicate just such an attribution!

21. See B. Duhm, *Das Buch Jeremia* (KHAT 11; Tübingen, 1901) 322.

merciful to him (*Piel* of *rḥm* with direct second-person object) and finally a promise to do something beneficial for the party being pitied. Most important, in both verses, the subject of each of the verbs is the same, namely God.

Paradoxically, both readings are equally difficult but also equally sensible. This seems to be a situation in which a consonantal text has been understood in the two textual/exegetical traditions according to different semantic patterns or textual paradigms. The MT understands the Jeremian wish as though it resembled Jacob's prayer, while the LXX has interpreted it in light of the similarly sounding promise from the book of Deuteronomy. Given the dependence of Jeremiah on Deuteronomy, it may be argued that the LXX's interpretation is probably the authentic one. Nonetheless, the MT's understanding is not lacking in sense and may have been influenced by the precedent of attested biblical idiom.

POLYSEMOUS PIVOTAL PUNCTUATION: MORE JANUS DOUBLE ENTENDRES

Shalom M. Paul

To Menahem:
Friend and Colleague

Isaiah 49:7

IN ISA 49:7 THERE APPEARS a vivid depiction of the radical metamorphosis that is to take place in Israel's fortunes. The prophet, comforting the enslaved nation, proclaims that in the future kings will rise in their presence and nobles will prostrate themselves before them, "because of the Lord who is faithful, the Holy One of Israel who has chosen them." Their present state, described by a triad[1] of couplets, is, however, extremely pathetic, for they are:

1. בְזֹה נפש, which according to almost all commentators (medieval and modern alike), should be understood as בְזוּי נפש[2] 'one whose being is despised', a reading now supported by 1QIsa^a;

Author's note: I have written on the phenomenon of Janus parallelism in the Bible in: "Polysensuous Polyvalency in Poetic Parallelism," in *"Sha^carei Talmon": Studies in the Bible, Qumran, and the Ancient Near East Presented to Shemaryahu Talmon* (ed. M. Fishbane, E. Tov, and W. W. Fields; Winona Lake, Ind., 1992) 147–63. This poetic device has now been identified in Akkadian literature as well. See S. Noegel, "A Janus Parallelism in the Gilgamesh Flood Story," *Acta Sumerologica* 13 (1991) 419–21; see now W. Horowitz and S. Paul, "Two Proposed Janus Parallelisms in Akkadian Literature," *N.A.B.U.* (1995) 11–12, with additional bibliography.

1. Triads are one of the most characteristic devices of Second Isaiah's poetic style.

2. All commentators, whether they (1) assume that the Masoretic pointing is based on the vocalization of the Aramaic passive participle בְּזֵה (e.g., Dan 2:23, 3:19; Ezra 5:11; see S. D. Luzzatto, *Il Profeta Isaia* [Padua, 1855] 523; cf. already the comment of Ibn Bal^cam, in M. Goshen-Gottstein, *R. Judah Ibn Bal^cam's Commentary on Isaiah* [Ramat Gan, 1992] 199 [Heb.]); or (2) regard it as an adjective (cf. *Tg. Jonathan*, Rashi, Ibn Ezra); or (3) consider it a *Qal* infinitive construct (cf. Ibn

369

2. מְתָעֵב גוי, repointed by most as מְתֹעַב גוי [3] 'abhorred of nations';[4]

3. עבד מֹשְׁלִים 'slave of rulers'.

The middle stich, 'abhorred of nations', correlates well with the following, 'slave of rulers', since both substantives, גוי and מֹשְׁלִים, are well-attested political terms.[5] It is here suggested, moreover, that גוֹי may also be revocalized גֵּ(יְ)וֹ 'back', 'body'.[6] Of the six occurrences of גֵּו (Isa 38:17, 50:6, 51:23; Prov 10:13, 19:29, 26:3), note should be made in particular of Isa 51:23, where the substantives נפש and גֵּו appear in close conjunction: 'I will put it (i.e., the cup of God's wrath) in the hands of your tormentors, who have commanded you (לְנַפְשֵׁךְ), "Bow down that we may walk over you." So you made your back/body (גֵּוֵךְ) like the ground, like a street for passers-by'. Compare, too, this same meaning for גֵּו in Job 20:25: 'It (the arrow from the 'bow of bronze') is drawn forth and runs through his body (reading מִגֵּוֹה for Masoretic מִגֵּוָה);[7] its blade, through his gall, strikes terror in him'. When revocalized, the expression מתעב גֵּ(יְ)וֹ would mean 'whose body is detested' and would thus be analogous to the previous description, בְּזוּי נפש 'whose being is despised'.

Hebrew גו(י) thus functions as a *double entendre* in a pivotal role. When pointed גוֹי 'abhorred of nations', it complements the following expression, 'slave of rulers', and when pointed גֵּ(יְ)וֹ 'whose body is abhorred', it correlates with the previous בזה נפש 'whose being is despised'—in true Janus-like fashion.

Ganah, ספר הרקמה [Jerusalem, 1994] 323–24; C. R. North, *The Second Isaiah* [Oxford, 1967] 190; see also E. Y. Kutscher, *The Language and Linguistic Background of the Isaiah Scroll* [Jerusalem, 1959] 267 [Heb.]) still interpret it as being equivalent to בְּזוּי, the *Qal* passive participle.

3. Cf. LXX. See Y. Ratzaby, *Saadya's Translation and Commentary on Isaiah* (Jerusalem, 1993) 111 [Hebrew and Judeo-Arabic]; Ibn Ganah, ספר הרקמה, 325; Ibn Bal‛am, *Commentary*, 199; Luzzatto, *Il Profeta Isaia*, 523; and all modern exegetes. For 1QIsaᵃ מתעב, see the suggestion by P. Skehan, "The Text of Isaias at Qumrân," *CBQ* 17 (1955) 158.

4. Heb. גוי is a collective.

5. See E. A. Speiser, " 'People' and 'Nation' of Israel," *JBL* 79 (1960) 157–63, repr. in *Oriental and Biblical Studies: Collected Writings of E. A. Speiser* (ed. J. J. Finkelstein and M. Greenberg; Philadelphia, 1967) 160–70. His comment in the latter (p. 164) is worth noting: "A word, like a person, is sometimes typified by the company he keeps." Regarding גוי, compare its other correlates: ממלכה: Exod 19:6; 1 Kgs 18:10; Jer 18:7, 9; 2 Chr 32:15; אֻמִּים: Ps 149:7; and especially מלכים: Jer 50:41.

6. This may be a case of metathesis, גֵּיו > גוי, though גֵּו is never written with a *yod*. It is of interest to note that Aramaic גֵּו 'belly, innermost' is sometimes written גֵּיו; see M. Jastrow, ספר מלים: *Dictionary of the Targumim, Talmud Babli, Yerushalmi and Midrashic Literature* (repr., New York, 1971) 216. This possibility was independently suggested by N. H. Tur-Sinai, פשוטו של מקרא (Jerusalem, 1957) 3/1.126. See also R. J. Clifford (*Fair-Spoken and Persuading: An Interpretation of Second Isaiah* [New York, 1984] 147 n. 3), who follows the suggestion of the NJPSV that *gôy* be repointed *gĕwîyyâ* 'body'. Compare also the other biforms of גו, meaning 'body': גֵּב: 1 Kgs 14:9, Ezek 23:35, Neh 9:26; גַּב: for example, Ezek 10:12, Ps 129:3; and גּוְּיָה, which refers to both a living 'body', for example, Gen 47:18, Neh 9:37; and a dead 'body', for example, 1 Sam 31:10, 12; Nah 3:3.

7. Thus many of the modern commentaries to Job.

Isaiah 49:17

In another pericope in this same chapter, Isa 49:14ff., the Lord announces his incontrovertible decision never to abandon Zion (personified as a mother) and proclaims her forthcoming rebuilding, restoration, and repopulation. The transition from present destruction to future reconstruction is succinctly depicted in v. 17: מהרו בניך מהרסיך ומחריביך ממך יצאו. The pivotal word that functions as a *double entendre* here is בניך. As vocalized in the Masoretic Text, בָּנָיִךְ, the verse may be translated, 'Swiftly your children (בָּנָיִךְ) are coming. Your destroyers and those who laid you waste shall depart from you'. This reading is supported by Symmachus, the Peshiṭta, and one version of the Aramaic Targum (בניכי). It is also substantiated contextually by the children motif used throughout the literary unit: v. 15, "Can a woman forsake her baby (עוּלָהּ), a young woman[8] the child of her womb (בן-בטנה)?"; v. 20, "The children of your bereavement (בני-שכוליך) shall yet say in your hearing . . ."; v. 21, "And you will say to yourself, 'Who bore these for me. . . . By whom, then, were these raised?'" The next pericope also continues this same theme: v. 22, "And they shall bring your sons (בניך) in their bosoms and carry your daughters (בנותיך) on their shoulders"; v. 23, "Kings shall be your foster-fathers; their queens shall be your nurses. . . ."

It is well known, however, that according to another tradition the word was interpreted as being vocalized בֹּנָיִךְ 'your builders'.[9] This is the way it was understood by Aquila, Theodotian, the Vulgate, and a version of the Aramaic Targum (יבנון); compare also LXX οἰκοδομηθήσῃ 'you will be built', and this is now attested in 1QIsaᵃ, בוניך.[10] Contextual support for such a reading may

---

8. For this interpretation of Heb. מרחם, see the studies of M. I. Gruber: "Will a Woman Forget Her Infant . . . ?" *Tarbiz* 51 (1982) 491–92 [Heb.]; idem, "The Motherhood of God in Second Isaiah," *RB* 90 (1983) 355–56, now reprinted in *The Motherhood of God and Other Studies* (Atlanta, 1992) 3–15; idem, "Feminine Similes Applied to the Lord in Second Isaiah," *Beer Sheva* 2 (1985) 81 [Heb.]; and those of R. Gordis: "Studies in the Book of Amos," *American Academy for Jewish Research Jubilee Volume* (Jerusalem, 1980) 1.211; idem, "On mrḥm bn bṭnh in Isaiah 49:15," *Tarbiz* 53 (1983) 137–38 [Heb.]; and E. Qimron, "A Note to מרחם = Women, Mother," *Tarbiz* 52 (1982–83) 509 [Heb.].

9. This is also accepted by some medieval commentators, for example, Saadiyah and Ibn Ḥafni. It is cited but rejected by Ibn Balᶜam, *Commentary*, 200; and Luzzatto, *Il Profeta Isaia*, 525.

10. Many modern exegetes prefer the Qumran reading; cf., e.g., J. L. McKenzie, *Second Isaiah* (AB 20; Garden City, N.Y., 1968) 110; C. Westermann, *Isaiah 40–66* (OTL; Philadelphia, 1969) 217; R. N. Whybray, *Isaiah 40–66* (NCB; Grand Rapids, 1981) 144; North, *Second Isaiah*, 195; Tur-Sinai, פשוטו של מקרא, 127; A. Ehrlich, *Mikra ki-Pheschuto* (New York, 1969) 3.118 [Heb.]; idem, *Randglossen zur hebräischen Bibel* (Leipzig, 1912) 4.180. For a discussion of this passage, see H. M. Orlinsky ("Studies in the St. Mark's Isaiah Scroll, vii," *Tarbiz* 24 [1954] 4–8 [Heb.]), who cites earlier scholars who emended to בֹנַיִךְ before the discovery of the *Isaiah Scroll* but who himself still accepts בָנַיִךְ as the original reading. D. Flusser ("The Text of Is. 49:17 in the DSS," *Textus* 2 [1962] 140–42) concludes that the reading of the Septuagint is based on the vocalization reflected in the *Isaiah Scroll* and this, in turn, was paraphrased in the *Epistle of Barnabas* 16:3. Accepting

372   *Shalom M. Paul*

be drawn from the second stich of this very same verse: 'Swiftly your *builders*
(בָּנָיִך) are coming. Your *destroyers* and *those who laid you waste* shall depart
from you'. 'Your builders' stands in sharp contrast to 'your destroyers' and 'those
who laid you waste'.

Thus the prophet employs the substantive בניך in a skillful Janus-construc-
tion. Within the context of the repeated imagery of children that appears in the
preceding verses, the vocalization בָּנַיִךְ 'your children' is most apt. However, in
direct conjunction with the second half of this verse, which pertains to the theme
of destroyers, בֹּנַיִךְ 'your builders' is also very fitting. Pivoting both ways, Zion's
returning 'children' are to be her future 'builders'.

This very same *double entendre* (though not a Janus polysemy) is also
present in Isa 54:13, וכל בניך למודי ה׳ ורב שלום בניך, where according to the
Masoretic Text the word is twice vocalized בָּנַיִךְ 'And all *your children* shall be
disciples of the Lord and great shall be the prosperity of *your children*'.[11] However, in the second occurrence of this substantive in 1QIsaᵃ a suspended *waw*
has been appended between the *bet* and *nun*, בו׳ניך, that is, 'your builders'.[12]
Here, too, both readings are perfectly suitable. On the one hand, the repetition
of the same substantive in both stichs, בָּנַיִךְ, is a feature of biblical poetry, and,
on the other hand, בֹּנַיִךְ fits admirably well into the present context. It is first
preceded in vv. 11–12 by a description of the future rebuilding of Zion, depicted
in terms of her "building stones," "foundations," "battlements," and "gates."
Then it is immediately followed in v. 14 by the phrase בצדקה תכונני 'you shall
be established in righteousness', where the root כון constitutes the second half
of a set-pair poetic parallelism with בנה (compare with Num 21:27, Hab 2:12,
Prov 24:3). This reading, בֹּנַיִךְ, is also reflected in a statement recorded in
b. Ber. 64a:[13]

אמר ר׳ אליעזר אמר ר׳ חנינא: תלמידי חכמים מרבים שלום בעולם, שנא׳: "וכל בניך למודי
ה׳ ורב שלום בניך"; אל תקרי "בניך" אלא "בוניך"

---

also the reading מהורסיך (*Qal* participle preceded by *mem*) in the scroll (for Masoretic מהרסיך, *Piel*
participle) as a "classical example of a *lectio difficilior*," Flusser concludes that the "rebuilding
will be accomplished even more quickly than the destruction," that is, מהרו בֹּנַיִך מהורסיך 'Your
builders outstrip (lit., make more haste than) your destroyers'. So, too, RSV and Whybray, *Isaiah
40–66*, 144. Compare with the NEB, 'Those who are to rebuild you make better speed than those
who pulled you down'. For pertinent objections to this interpretation, see Kutscher (*Language and
Linguistic Background*, 391), who still accepts בָּנַיִךְ.

11. Though the Septuagint translates the dual בניך by two different nouns, υἱούς and τέκνα
respectively, both have the same meaning and were only employed for internal Greek variation.

12. It is of interest to note that some exegetes have read בֹּנַיִך for the first בָּנַיִךְ; compare
S. Krauss, ספר ישעיהו (Budapest, 1904) 110; and North (*Second Isaiah*, 67), who incorrectly
states, however, that, "Qᵃ has בוניכי ('Your builders') for the first . . ." (p. 251).

13. Cf. also *Yalkut Shimoni*, §579, on Isa 54:7.

Rabbi Eliezer said in the name of Rabbi Hanina: "The students of the sages increase peace in the world, as it is said: [Isa 54:13 is cited here]." Do not read בָּנַיִךְ, 'your children', but בּוֹנַיִךְ, 'your builders'.[14]

Song of Songs 7:6

The final *waṣf* that appears in the Song of Songs depicts the female body from foot to head (7:2ff.).[15] Verse 6, which provides the description and portrayal of the woman's head and hair, abounds, however, in difficulties, especially replete in the final clause. Attention here will focus only on the first two cola of this verse: "Your head (ראשך) upon you is like כרמל; the locks of your hair (ראשך) are like purple." The comparison to כרמל, usually understood to mean Mount Carmel (so the LXX and Vulgate), is related to the ambiguous meaning of ראשך, either 'your head' or 'your head of hair' (as in the second stich).[16] Those who favor the former would tend to translate the stich in the manner of the NEB, 'You carry your head like Carmel', thus denoting and connoting the height, stateliness, and majesty of the image. Those who accept the latter apply the forested mountain region to the luxuriant growth of her thick tresses. There are, on the other hand, exegetes who favor revocalizing כַּרְמֶל to כַּרְמִל 'crimson' (a late borrowing into Biblical Hebrew from Sanskrit, appearing also in 2 Chr 2:6, 13; 3:14), which would then apply to either the color, dye, or brilliant sheen of her hair.[17]

It is here suggested that the author had both meanings in mind and thereby created a very effective Janus *double entendre*. If the substantive were vocalized כַּרְמֶל, Mount Carmel would provide an apt sequence to the names of the other northern locales immediately cited in the previous verse (v. 5): Heshbon, Lebanon, and Damascus. And when interpreted as כַּרְמִל 'crimson', it creates a very fine parallel with ארגמן 'purple'[18] in the following colon.[19]

---

14. For a similar paronomasia, see *Midr. Exod. Rab.* 23:10, on Song of Songs 1:5: שחורה'" "אני ונאוה בנות ירושלים' אמרו רבותינו: אל תהי קורא 'בנות ירושלים' אלא 'בנות ירושלים'".

15. There are some commentators who think that this is part of an overall description drawn from the model of a sculpture. See G. Gerleman, *Ruth: Das Hohelied* (Neukirchen-Vluyn, 1965) 69–71; H. P. Müller, *Vergleich und Metapher im Hohenlied* (OBO 56; Göttingen, 1984) 23, who follows, in general, W. Hermann, "Gedanken zur Geschichte des altorientalischen Beschreibungsliedes," *ZAW* 75 (1963) 176–97. The latter still interprets it as Mount Carmel.

16. For both opinions, consult the medieval and modern commentaries.

17. For כרמל, see A. Brenner, *Colour Terms in the Old Testament* (JSOTSup 21; Sheffield, 1982) 24–25, 138, 144; E. Bilik, "כרמל," *Encyclopedia Biblica* 4.322–23; R. Pines, "צבעים," *Encyclopedia Biblica* 6.1669. For its etymology, see C. Rabin, "Indian Words," *Leshonenu LeAm* 14.241–42 [Heb.].

18. For ארגמן, see Brenner, *Colour Terms*, 145. For Akkadian *argamannu*, which means both 'red purple wool' and 'tribute', see CAD A/2 253. The latter is also its meaning in Ugaritic, *argmn*. See, for example, D. Pardee, "The Ugaritic Text 147(90)," *UF* 6 (1974) 277–78. There are, however,

some scholars who think that the Ugaritic word also occasionally designates 'red purple wool'. For the various opinions concerning the expression *riš arg*[*mn*] in KTU 1.87:4–5, see M. Dietrich, O. Loretz, and J. Sanmartín, "Die Texteinheiten in RS 1.2 = CTA 32 and RS 17.100 = CTA Appendice I," *UF* 7 (1975) 145; J. Sanmartín, "*RIŠ ARGMN* in den Ug. Ritualen," *UF* 10 (1978) 455–56. As tempting as it may appear, there is no connection between Heb. ‏(דלת) ראשך כארגמן‎ and Ugaritic *riš argmn*.

19. Some ancient translations, Aquila, Symmachus, Vulgate, Peshiṭta, as well as modern commentators, attach the next word in the verse, ‏מלך‎, to ‏ארגמן‎ and translate 'royal purple'. See, for example, Gerleman, *Ruth*, 194, 199, 200; Y. Feliks, *Song of Songs* (Jerusalem, 1974) 109 [Heb.]; Brenner, *Colour Terms*, 145. See, in general, L. B. Jensen, "Royal Purple of Tyre," *JNES* 22 (1963) 104–18.

PARTICIPIAL FORMULATIONS:
LAWSUIT, NOT WISDOM—
A STUDY IN PROPHETIC LANGUAGE

Henning Graf Reventlow

Analysis of the Passages

SINCE H. W. WOLFF IN HIS FAMOUS ESSAY "Hoseas geistige Heimat"[1] and later in his book *Amos' geistige Heimat*[2] declared wisdom to be the intellectual background of prophetic thinking, the problem has not yet found a final solution. I have sometimes expressed my doubts as to whether this assumption could stand the test of a closer inspection of the respective prophetic utterances. As a global thesis, it might be difficult to collect reasons pro and con, but there are some concrete prophetic texts where it seems to have reached its limit as a working hypothesis. The most noticeable indication that this is the case seems to be that Wolf has sometimes had to resort to altering the Masoretic Text in order to maintain his stance when confronted with such passages. My renewed discussion of one of these cases is not intended to bring back to life a half-forgotten difference of opinion. The real motive is that the respective passages can better be explained when the text is left unaltered, thereby putting the understanding of the prophetic message as a whole on firmer ground.

We shall begin with Amos 5:7:

ההפכים ללענה משפט　　　　　　וצדקה לארץ הניחו

At first glance, a clause beginning with a participle looks awkward. Therefore, the "correction" first proposed by G. Smith[3] of putting a הוי at the beginning

---

1. H. W. Wolff, "Hoseas geistige Heimat," *TLZ* 81 (1956) 83–94; idem, *Gesammelte Studien zum Alten Testament* (ThB 22; Munich, 1964) 232–50.
2. H. W. Wolff, *Amos' geistige Heimat* (WMANT 18; Neukirchen-Vluyn, 1964).
3. G. Smith, *The Book of the Twelve Prophets* (ExpB; London, 1902) 1.166 n. 4.

375

of the clause has found many followers.[4] But this solution should only be used in cases where the text cannot be understood as it stands. Observing that there are other instances in which the same construction occurs at the beginning of a sentence can serve as a warning against being too hasty in text critical operations. In the book of Amos, two other occurrences of the same *asyndeton* construction can be found: Amos 2:7[5] and 6:13.[6] Simply denying that such a construction is possible[7] is not a solution.

To begin with, it appears as though Amos 5:7 is a fragment; v. 10 seems to be its continuation,[8] a fact that may shed light on the form of the whole. The fragmentary preservation of the material in the book of Amos is a well-known fact. This does not mean, however, that v. 7 itself has been damaged. Our task will be to show how the special form of expression encountered here can be explained within the frame of the prophetic message.

The Masoretic Text will be the basis of our analysis. The Greek version has a completely different form in which κύριος is the subject.[9] Verse 10 begins with an asyndetic perfect that can be explained as explicating v. 7; in other words, v. 7 speaks in a general way about the behavior of the addressees, and v. 10 adds the details.

For an evaluation of the asyndetic participle in v. 7, it is important to observe that the participle appears elsewhere in similar contexts. The next occurrence is v. 12b, which in the present context is introduced by the phrase in v. 12a as an address to God and can be recognised as an independent sentence by the third-person singular at the end. The perfect form seems to be the standard continuation of the foregoing participles. In 2:7 the construction looks less

---

4. Including H. W. Wolff, *Dodekapropheton 2: Joel und Amos* (BKAT 14/2; Neukirchen-Vluyn, 1969) ad loc.; and, most recently, F. I. Andersen and D. N. Freedman, *Amos* (AB 24A; New York, 1989) ad loc. Against this reading, see G. Fleischer, *Von Menschenverkäufern, Baschankühen und Rechtsverkehrern* (BBB 74; Frankfort, 1989) 110–11 (mentioning earlier authors sharing the same standpoint).

5. Where a הוי is likewise added by many commentators.

6. In 6:13 few would add a הוי (L. Köhler, *Amos* [SThZ 34; 1917] ad loc.; V. Maag, *Text, Wortschatz und Begriffswelt des Buches Amos* [Leiden, 1951] ad loc.; K. Elliger, BHS, app.). The suggestion that the beginning of the prophetic utterance might have been broken off (H. W. Wolff, *Joel und Amos*, 332) has been rightly repelled by Fleischer, *Von Menschenverkäufern*, 109 n. 74. Andersen and Freedman (*Amos*, ad loc.) explain this as a woe oracle by reading the whole text from 6:1 on as a single utterance. But this seems to overlook the shortness of most of Amos's utterances. The problem of whether or not the sentence should be regarded as genuine, which some deny, is here out of the question.

7. Cf. Fleischer, *Von Menschenverkäufern*, 109, who, however, argues that a *casus pendens*–construction is conceivable in 6:13.

8. Thus, after many others recently, Fleischer, *Von Menschenverkäufern*, 112. A total isolation of v. 7 is not necessary (against T. H. Robinson, *Die Zwölf Kleinen Propheten: Hosea bis Micha* [2d ed.; HAT 14; Tübingen, 1954] ad loc).

9. J. D. W. Watts, *VT* 4 (1954) 215–16, proposes a reconstruction of the text on this basis, but it is not convincing.

offensive, because the verse seems to be a continuation of v. 6. In 6:13 the context is similar, if one is prepared to see in v. 13 a continuation of v. 12, but this is not very likely.[10] It is better to regard the verse as a fragment. Amos 6:3–6 is an especially impressive example, because the participles appear in a whole series. Wolff's opinion that the הוי of v. 1 still rules the text,[11] is not likely if one is not prepared to explain with him v. 2 as a later addition to the text.

Occasionally the participial form fits so well into the grammatical construction, as in Amos 4:1 beginning with שמעו (*šimᶜû*), that one is misled to believe it is directly caused by the context. But since the other two passages introduced by the same phrase (Amos 3:1–2 and 5:1ff.) go on in quite another manner, the connection is not original. Therefore, the use of the participles in 4:1b is to be seen on the same level as in the other cases.

We encounter the same form also outside the Amos tradition. A quite similar model may be found in Mic 3:1–4. The participles in v. 2 are separated from the שמעו in v. 1. A question put between, interrupts the connection. After the three participles in v. 2, the accusation is continued in vv. 3–4 by a relative clause and finite verbs. This allows a look at the form background in Mic 3:9ff.: here the participle appearing in v. 9b at first seems to be grammatically connected with the שמעו in the opening of the verse. But this connection has been linked at a later stage. In v. 9b already a finite verb had been used in the parallel semicolon in the usual manner; v. 10a, however, begins again with a participle.[12] There the connection with the beginning in v. 9 has already been interrupted.

Other cases of participial formulations in prophetic condemnations are:

(1) Hos 5:11[13] is a genuine parallel, if one is prepared to abandon the political interpretation of A. Alt[14] in favor of an understanding that takes the wording in its original sense, meaning deceitful acts in rural circumstances.[15] Then it is a prophetic condemnation, not a complaint.

---

10. Cf. K. Elliger's arrangement of the text in BHS.

11. H. W. Wolff, *Amos' geistige Heimat*, 12; idem, *Joel und Amos*, 314ff. Similarly, Andersen and Freedman, *Amos*, ad loc., who are even more adventurous in adding *woe*s in vv. 3a, 4a, 4b, 5a, 6a.

12. Perhaps the participle singular has to be changed to a participle plural; cf. BHS, app. ad loc.

13. Here the LXX reads the active form of the participles: κατεδυνάστευσεν Εφραιμ τὸν ἀντίδικον αὐτου κατεπάτησε κρίμα: 'Ephraim suppressed its enemy, trampled down justice'. This version, though preferred by earlier commentators, has to be rejected as *lectio facilior*.

14. A. Alt, "Hosea 5:8–6:6: Ein Krieg und seine Folgen in prophetischer Beleuchtung," *NKZ* 30 (1919) 537–68; idem, *Kleine Schriften zur Geschichte des Volkes Israel* (4th ed.; Munich, 1978) 2.163–87.

15. Cf. Henning Graf Reventlow, "Zeitgeschichtliche Exegese prophetischer Texte? Über die Grenzen eines methodischen Zuganges zum Alten Testament (am Beispiel von Hos 5,8–14)," *Prophetie und geschichtliche Wirklichkeit im alten Israel* (S. Herrmann Festschrift; Stuttgart, 1991) 155–64, esp. 157.

(2) A similar piece is Isa 1:23, belonging to a fragment composed of vv. 21–23 in the collection of prophetic utterances in the first chapter of the book. The word occurs now in the second-singular feminine form, as an address of the prophet to the personified city of Jerusalem. But beginning with v. 23aβ, the sentences are in the third person, interestingly, first as a participial formulation in the singular, but in v. 23b obviously a fixed poetic verse in the form of synonymous parallelism has been quoted.[16] Verse 23aβ gives the impression of having been molded according to a traditional form of utterance, which we now can better identify in the light of the aforementioned parallels.

(3) Jer 7:17–19 may also be mentioned, though in the present text there are little more than remains of the participial form to be detected. But in this speech, which has been formed in a Deuteronomistic style, the participial formulations are still indicating concrete transgressions of an order that is willed by God but has been disregarded by the people spoken about.

(4) Coming to postexilic prophecy, some passages in the book of Malachi are relevant. The first is Mal 1:7. The context is a dispute[17] between God (through the mouth of the prophet) and the priests. In v. 6bδ, the addressees (namely, the priests) ask how they had despised the name of God, as they had been accused earlier in v. 6bγ. The answer follows in v. 7aα. But why is the direct address in the second-person plural now dropped in favor of a participial formulation? Obviously because a fixed form of speaking stands in the background, a form the prophet used under special conditions. And again, it is a concrete offense against a fixed rule that is spoken about, in this case an offense of the priests against special duties of their office (the offering of holy bread).[18]

(5) The last passage that might be considered is Mal 3:5.[19] Here also the context is important.[20] It is striking that again the utterance begins with a direct address in the second-person plural in v. 5aα but continues with participial forms in v. 5aβ–bα. Again, this shape of the text is not by mere chance but depends upon pre-fixed modes of speech which are part of the prophet's tradition.

Lastly, C. Westermann points out the possibility that sometimes the regular sequence of the prophetic sentence of judgement can be reversed.[21] In such cases, the sequence would begin with the announcement of punishment. Then a participial formulation is used in the (now succeeding) condemnation forming the proof for the judgment proclaimed before.[22]

16. The meter seems to be 3 + 3 (or 3 + 4).

17. Cf. E. Pfeiffer, "Die Disputationsworte im Buche Maleachi (Ein Beitrag zur formgeschichtlichen Struktur)," *EvT* 19 (1959) 546–68.

18. One can also compare Mal 1:12, but the form is not as clear there.

19. This does not mean that all possible texts are exhausted. I did not systematically check the whole bulk of prophetic literature.

20. Especially the catchwords משפט and עד are important, indicating juridical language.

21. C. Westermann, *Grundformen prophetischer Rede* (Munich, 1960) 127. English translation of this work: *Basic Forms of Prophetic Speech* (Philadelphia, 1967).

22. Such cases are: Jer 2:26–28 (v. 27); Amos 9:8–10 (v. 10b); Hos 9:7–9 (v. 8).

Basic Insights

The result of this short overview leads to some basic insights. The first is that the participial formulation does not always belong to a "Woe"-oracle. The passages that we inspected more closely showed the contrary. On the other side, a הוֹי can be inserted before an already existing participial formulation to fit it into a new context altering the form. Examples of this type of alteration can be found at several places that begin with a שִׁמְעוּ, such as Amos 4:1, beginning with the address in v. 4a, to which the participles in v. 4b are added seemingly without a seam. A second example would be Mic 3:1–2 and 3:9–10. That the call שִׁמְעוּ is, however, an independent form, can be seen in its occurrence in quite different contexts.[23]

The same can be said regarding the הוֹי, which has its particular form. In Mic 2:1–4, only the opening clause in v. 1a is formulated in participles; the rest of the verse is composed of finite verbs. The same can be said about the series of *woes* in Isa 5:8ff. and Isa 10:1–3. See also Isa 29:15, 30:1, 31:1, 33:1; Jer 22:13,[24] 23:1;[25] and Hab 2:6, 9, 12, 15, and 19. It can also be seen that the הוֹי is not originally and inseparably connected with the participles in the numerous cases where it occurs in quite different connections.

These results allow some further conclusions regarding the *Sitz im Leben* of the prophetic message. Wolff's basic hypothesis was that the prophets Amos and Hosea were stamped by the traditions of Wisdom.[26] The use of "Woe"-oracles by Amos is one of Wolff's proofs for showing this.[27] The problem is connected with the old discussion about the origin of the "Woe"-oracles.[28] We cannot dwell upon it in our context. Suffice it to say that Wolff's objection to the derivation of the "Woe"-oracles from the curse-formula, that it can be based on only *one* text (Deut 27:15ff.) as a parallel,[29] seems to be convincing. But against the Gerstenberger/Wolff hypothesis concerning the Wisdom-origin of the "Woe"-oracles, G. Wanke's proof about the difference between אוֹי and הוֹי is

---

23. For instance Amos 3:1, 5:1.

24. In the Masoretic Text, v. 14 has a repetition of the participle, which seems to take up the הוֹי of v. 13. But the LXX has the second-person singular. It is difficult to decide which might be the more original version.

25. No continuing clause; what follows is the לָכֵן, introducing the judgment.

26. He wrote about these two, but the thesis might be regarded valid also for other prophets, such as Micah and Isaiah. On the latter, it has often been maintained for other reasons.

27. See nn. 1 and 2. The thesis in this special form was developed by E. Gerstenberger, "The Woe-Oracles of the Prophets," *JBL* 81 (1962) 249–63.

28. There are two alternatives. Either the "Woe"-oracles belong to the sphere of Wisdom (cf. ibid.), or they are the opposite of salvation-oracles and are to be connected with the אָרוּר-formulations (cf. Westermann, *Grundformen*, 137ff.). Both alternatives are decribed by H. W. Wolff, *Joel und Amos*, 284–87.

29. Wolf, *Amos' geistige Heimat*, 14f.; idem, *Joel und Amos*, 285.

likewise important.[30] If Wanke is right in maintaining that אוֹי is a cry of fear or lament in a situation of disaster and came from there to be used in a prophetic announcement of calamity, whereas הוֹי, originally used in the lament about a deceased person[31] and as a summons-cry normally[32] introduces a prophetic sentence of blame,[33] the whole argument becomes rather feeble.

If the origin of the participial formulations cannot be located in the הוֹי oracles, are there other reasons for identifying them as typical Wisdom language? The mere use of participles in Wisdom texts has never been adduced for claiming Wisdom as their birthplace. While participles are used sometimes in Wisdom-sentences,[34] this does not mean that they are typical for Wisdom-language. The utility of participles for expressing timeless proverbs about man and the connection between his deeds and his fate is obvious. The sages love to oppose two different forms of acting by the same type of man; the participle is a fitting form for that. But we seldom observe a tendency of forming a series of such sentences. All in all, participial formulations are but *one* form of expression in a context that is constructed out of rather different forms of sentences.

Having excluded Wisdom as a likely place of origin of the participial formulations in the prophets, our next task will be to look for another possible solution. The prophetic utterance of Amos 5:7 can be a suitable starting-place for finding our way to this aim.

The first observation is that Amos uses two central juridical terms in his reproach of his hearers: מִשְׁפָּט and צְדָקָה stand in synonymous parallelism. The difference and connection between the two terms can perhaps best be decribed by saying that מִשְׁפָּט is more the formal aspect, whereas צְדָקָה means the content of the same idea. It is not our intention here to enter into the long debate about the sense of these expressions, but the result has been that the terminology belongs to the idea of order ruling the world, which is willed and guaranteed by God as the creator and highest judge.[35] Also for Amos, the conduct of Israel in relation to its God and the conduct of the Israelites amongst one another has to be measured by the rules of צֶדֶק and צְדָקָה. Whoever despises 'justice' between individuals destroys communion with God; thereby he falls out of the order of שָׁלוֹם.

---

30. G. Wanke, "אוֹי und הוֹי," *ZAW* 78 (1966) 215–18. Cf. also W. W. Weir, *The Nature and Origin of the Woe-Speeches of the Prophets* (Diss. Abstr. Int. 32; 1971–72) 1096–A; H. J. Zobel, "הוֹי," *TWAT* 2.382–88.

31. Cf. also J. G. Williams, "The Alas-Oracles of the Eighth-Century Prophets," *HUCA* 38 (1967) 75–91.

32. Except in Isa 29:1, Zeph 2:5.

33. In his commentary (*Joel und Amos*, 284f.), H. W. Wolff has acknowledged the correctness of Wanke's arguments.

34. A cluster can be found in Prov 11:26–29; cf. also 12:1, 11, 20; 13:3, 24; 14:2, 31; 15:32— to take just the collection Proverbs 10–15.

35. Cf. the summary of H. Ringgren and B. Johnson, "צָדַק," *TWAT* 6.898–924 (bibliography).

But where is the original *Sitz im Leben* of these terms? Wolff again tried
to find it in Wisdom-language.[36] Some sentences in the book of Proverbs that
also juxtapose מִשְׁפָּט and צְדָקָה are his prooftexts.[37] But, though one could
observe that the idea of order is typical for Wisdom thinking,[38] there is no reason for seeing in both words terms that are typical for Wisdom language. Their
occurrence is rather scarce, given the many variations of expression to be
found there.

A way to the solution of the difficulties is opened when one regards again
the participial formulation of Amos 5:7 and similar cases. That Amos uses the
third person for addressing his hearers appears curious if one does not recognize the special background of such a form. Such language is normally used in
lawsuits, where both sides try to persuade the judges of the guilt of the contra-
hents and the innocence of their own sides;[39] before and after the impeachment is pleaded before the judges, both sides can also address one another
directly in second person. The indictment can be formulated in different ways.
From the cases Boecker uses for his study, the lawsuit against the disobedient
son (Deut 21:18–21)[40] is of special interest. Boecker calls our attention to the
correspondence between the introduction of the case in v. 18 and the following impeachment speech of the parents that is cited verbally. In the introduction we read:

כי יהיה לאיש בן סורר ומורה איננו שמע בקול אביו ובקול אמו

The impeachment corresponds to this formulation (v. 10):

בננו זה סורר ומרה איננו שמע בקלנו

The impeachment is formulated in a fixed form: the participle is used for describing not a single deed, but the continuous behavior of the accused son. It is
his habit not to obey his parents, to be obdurate and rebellious. But there seems
to be still another intention for this styling: the parents draw upon well-known
facts suggesting to the judges a preconceived decision.

We can attach an additional consideration. Among the forms of Israelite
law, the formulation using a protasis in the participle[41] has been much debated.
A. Alt subsumed this form under the apodictic law.[42] Since one has learned to

---

36. Wolff, *Amos' geistige Heimat*, 40ff.; cf. *Joel und Amos*, ad loc.

37. Prov 16:8 and 21:3; cf. also the late superscriptions 1:3 and 2:9.

38. Wolff does not argue in this way.

39. For the procedure, cf. L. Köhler, *Der hebräische Mensch* (Tübingen, 1953) 143–71; H. J.
Boecker, *Redeformen des Rechtslebens im Alten Testament* (WMANT 14; Neukirchen-Vluyn, 1964;
2d ed. 1970).

40. Ibid., 75–76.

41. The form with a relative clause is similar.

42. A. Alt, "Die Ursprünge des israelitischen Rechts," *Kleine Schriften zur Geschichte des
Volkes Israel* (2d ed.; Munich, 1953) 1.278–332. English translation: idem, *The Origins of Israelite
Law: Essays in Old Testament History and Religion* (Garden City, N.Y., 1967) 101–71.

distinguish between this form and the second-person direct address,[43] the different intentions of the divergent formulations have also become discernible. The
participle is used as the form describing the continuing state of an incriminated
person or group, which can be legally defined so that the appropriate punishment
is obvious.

Conclusions

The foregoing observations enable us to get to some conclusions regarding
the use of participial forms in some condemnations directed by Amos and other
prophets against their hearers. The people are not addressed directly but spoken
about in third person, because the real addressee is the divine judge who is
looking down upon the transgressors threatening to punish them. Or—if we detect behind the prophet as his speaker the judge himself, who is personally one
of the combatants in the lawsuit according to the rules of Israelite law[44]—God
announces that he has seen very well the behavior of the people and will punish
them according to the rules of the law he has proclaimed for his people.

With this, we return to the well-known patterns of prophetic speech. The
announcement of doom is normally introduced by the word לכן; this shows the
narrow connection between the evil of the people and the fate proclaimed to
them. As Westermann already saw clearly, the prophetic speech has close relations to juridical language.[45] This fact obviously depends on the way in
which the relations between God and the people can be seen to be guided by
law. The will of God is decisive; if it is disobeyed, the whole order of life for
the people is disturbed. The prophet is the speaker of God who has the duty to
proclaim this situation to the people.

We have arrived at well-known facts. That we *did* arrive there seems to
show that we were correct in seeking the background for the participial formulations in Amos 5:7 and similar prophetic passages not in Wisdom, but in the
sphere of the lawsuit. This answer also places prophecy with its different forms
of speech into the role it had to fulfill in the history of Israel's God with his
people.

43. There is a good summary with short bibliography recently in R. Sonsino, "Forms of Biblical Law," *ABD* 4.251–54.

44. Cf. Köhler, *Amos*, passim.

45. C. Westermann, *Grundformen*, 27f.

SCRIBAL PRACTICES REFLECTED IN THE DOCUMENTS FROM THE JUDEAN DESERT AND IN THE RABBINIC LITERATURE: A COMPARATIVE STUDY

Emanuel Tov

A COMPARATIVE STUDY of scribal practices in two partially contemporary bodies of literature, documents from the Judean Desert and the instructions for the copying of such documents in the rabbinic literature, is valid in its own right. In the course of such an investigation certain links are revealed between the instructions in the rabbinic literature and a segment of the texts found in Qumran, to the exclusion of another segment found there.

This paper is an investigation of *scribal practices* in relation to the copying of the Bible. When speaking about such scribal practices in relation to the Bible, I refer to the different aspects of the procedure of copying biblical texts: the script, material, size, and scope of the scroll, its sheets, columns, margins, patching, and stitching; furthermore, there are the issues of spacing between books, ruling of the manuscript, correction procedures, and the stichometric arrangement of the text.[1] The investigation also refers to some elements within the text itself, such as spacing, mistakes, and their corrections, final versus nonfinal letters, supralinear letters, and scribal marks.

An understanding of the approach of the scribes, consistent or not, to these practices is an integral component of a study of the textual transmission of the Hebrew Bible. All these aspects of the writing activity are necessarily reflected in the documents from the Judean Desert, and many of them are also referred to in the vast body of rabbinic literature. However, when comparing the

Author's note: This article is dedicated to Menahem Haran, who has contributed much to the area covered by this paper. The paper was presented to the Qumran research group at the Annenberg Research Institute, Philadelphia (February, 1993).

1. For a major study in this area, see M. Martin, *The Scribal Character of the Dead Sea Scrolls* (Bibliothèque du Muséon 44–45; Louvain, 1958), vols. 1–2. See further C. Kuhl, "Schreibereigenthümlichkeiten: Bemerkungen zur Jesajarolle (DSIᵃ)," *VT* 2 (1952) 307–33.

documents from the Judean Desert and the rabbinic literature, by definition we analyze two different entities. The rabbinic literature contains discussions of and prescriptions for the writing of sacred texts, while the actual documents found in Qumran reflect the writing practices themselves. One of our interests is to find out the relation between these documents and the abstract prescriptions in the rabbinic literature. Naturally we will never know to what extent and in which circles the prescriptions of the rabbis were adhered to. But when studying the Qumran scrolls we see the reflection of at least some of these rules. Indeed, realizing that several of the writing habits reflected in the Qumran scrolls coincide with rules laid down in the rabbinic literature, some scholars noted that scrolls presumably written by the Qumran covenanters agree with the Pharisaic writing practices, or with writing practices of so-called normative Judaism.[2] But an investigation of this kind is actually rather complex, since it is now clear that not all the Qumran scrolls were copied by the Qumran scribes, and the Qumran documents should therefore not be taken as reflecting a single scribal tradition. Indeed, the Qumran documents derived from various circles and were composed at different times.[3] Moreover, the body of texts under investigation in this article is more extensive than the Qumran finds, since I refer to all of the documents from the Judean Desert, although not all documents have actually been consulted. It is my intention to investigate the relation between the documents found in the Judean Desert and the rabbinic regulations, realizing that some documents may be closer to these regulations than others.

A few remarks are in order.

2. See S. Talmon, "Aspects of the Textual Transmission of the Bible in the Light of the Qumran Manuscripts," *Textus* 4 (1964) 96: "That the Qumran Scrolls indeed exhibit scribal conventions and techniques which were generally prevalent in Jewry of the Second Commonwealth is easily proved from the fact that the sectarian scribes in many details followed rules which tally with those laid down by the Rabbis for Torah-scribes of the 'normative' community" (repr. in *The World of Qumran from Within* [Jerusalem/Leiden, 1989] 71–116). J. P. Siegel, "The Employment of Palaeo-Hebrew Characters for the Divine Names at Qumran in the Light of Tannaitic Sources," *HUCA* 42 (1971) 159–72, esp. 159: "It is my purpose to examine, in the light of certain Tannaitic sources, the corpus of Qumran texts which exhibit the phenomenon of palaeo-Hebrew Divine Names, and to show how a significant theological consideration was translated into a scribal convention by both 'normative' and 'sectarian' Jewish scribes." For similar remarks by J. P. Siegel, see his dissertation *The Scribes of Qumran: Studies in the Early History of Jewish Scribal Customs, with Special Reference to the Qumran Biblical Scrolls and to the Tannaitic Traditions of Massekheth Soferim* (Ph.D. diss., Brandeis University, Waltham, Mass., 1972) 27–28. The discussion below shows that I do not disagree with these statements, but the situation is more complicated than implied by them.

3. See my "Orthography and Language of the Hebrew Scrolls Found at Qumran and the Origin of These Scrolls," *Textus* 13 (1986) 31–57; idem, "Hebrew Biblical Manuscripts from the Judaean Desert: Their Contribution to Textual Criticism," *JJS* 39 (1988) 5–37; idem, "Groups of Hebrew Biblical Texts Found at Qumran," in *A Time to Prepare the Way in the Wilderness: Papers on the Qumran Scrolls by Fellows of the Institute for Advanced Studies of the Hebrew University, Jerusalem, 1989–1990* (ed. D. Dimant and L. H. Schiffman; STDJ 16; Leiden, 1995) 85–102; idem, "*Tefillin* of Different Origin from Qumran?" *J. Licht Memorial Volume*, in press.

(1) At an earlier stage of my research of scribal habits, the point of departure for the identification of scribal practices was that of the Dead Sea Scrolls only. For the present purpose, however, such scribal practices were researched not only on the basis of these newly found documents, but also, independently, on the basis of references in the rabbinic literature. In that literature, instructions for writing occur with regard to single issues, but more frequently they are grouped into compilations dealing with various matters, such as *b. Menaḥ.* 29b–32b; *b. Meg.* passim; *b. Šabb.* 103a–105a; *y. Meg.* 1.71d–72a. Another significant block of traditions has been laid down in *Masseket Soperim*.[4] Although this tractate is post-Talmudic (ninth century), it is based on *Masseket Seper Torah*,[5] as well as on several early sources, and thus preserves earlier traditions that go back to the Talmud and the Talmudic period. The rabbinic instructions pertain to such matters as writing materials, skins and their preparation, scribes, measurements of sheets, columns, lines, and margins, correction of errors, the writing of divine names, matters of storage, and the reading of the books. Many references to the relevant discussions in rabbinic literature are quoted in the valuable monograph by L. Blau.[6]

(2) The rabbinic literature is extensive, dating from different periods, and accordingly the conclusions below may have to be made more specific by paying attention to the different persons to whom the statements are attributed in the rabbinic literature and their respective chronological backgrounds.

(3) Many of the data mentioned below are based on their description in the published documents from the Judean Desert. As more documents are analyzed in detail, the description of the scribal habits will have to be updated.

We now turn to the details themselves, in which the writing practices reflected in the Qumran documents are compared with what is known from rabbinic sources.

Scribal Practices Reflected in the Qumran Texts Agreeing with Rabbinic Sources

(1) *Ruling.* The ruling of the empty columns (*dĕlātôt* 'columns' according to Jer 36:23, and *dapîm* 'pages', in talmudic terminology) that are found at the

---

4. See the edition of M. Higger, מסכת סופרים ונלוו עליה מדרש מסכת סופרים בא (New York, 1937; repr. Jerusalem, 1970).

5. See the edition of M. Higger, *Seven Minor Treatises: Sefer Torah, Mezuzah, Tefillin, Ẓiẓith, ʿAbadim, Kutim, Gerim* (New York, 1930).

6. L. Blau, *Studien zum althebräischen Buchwesen und zur biblischen Literatur und Textgeschichte* (Strasbourg i. E., 1902). For a still earlier study, see S. Krauss, *Talmudische Archäologie* (Leipzig, 1912) vol. 3. For later studies, see Siegel, *The Scribes of Qumran*; M. Bar-Ilan, "Scribes and Books in the Late Second Commonwealth and Rabbinic Period," in *Mikra: Text, Translation and Interpretation of the Hebrew Bible in Ancient Judaism and Early Christianity* (ed. M. J. Mulder; Compendia Rerum Judaicarum ad Novum Testamentum 2/1; Philadelphia and Assen/Maastricht, 1988) 21–38.

end of several Qumran scrolls, both in the square "Assyrian" script and in the "early" Hebrew script (1QpHab, 11QpaleoLevᵃ, 11QPsᵃ, 11QTᵃ) shows that scribes marked out the columns on the sheets before copying. Prior to writing, most scrolls were ruled horizontally (indicating lines) and vertically (indicating the beginnings and sometimes also the ends of columns). This ruling was usually done with a pointed instrument, producing the so-called blind ruling, but sometimes with ink, and it is known from most of the Qumran texts.[7] It is likewise known from manuscripts of the Sam. Pent. and from medieval Masoretic sources.[8]

This technique is also mentioned in talmudic sources, according to which the ruling of the lines was called *syrṭwṭ* (*b. Šabb.* 75b; *b. Meg.* 18b). In Palestinian texts it is referred to as *msrglyn bqnh* 'one rules with a reed' (*y. Meg.* 1.71d; *Sop.* 1.1).

(2) In the Qumran scrolls the *upper margin* is usually smaller than the bottom margin.[9] This difference between the top and bottom margins is also prescribed by *b. Menaḥ.* 30a:

שיעור גליון מלמטה טפח מלמעלה ג׳ אצבעות ובין דף לדף כמלא ריוח רוחב
שתי אצבעות ובחומשין מלמטה שלש אצבעות מלמעלה שתי אצבעות ובין
דף לדף כמלא ריוח רוחב גודל.

The width of the margin below shall be one handbreadth, above three fingerbreadths, and between one column and the other the space of two fingerbreadths ⟨in all the books of the Bible⟩. In the books of the Torah the margin below shall be three fingerbreadths, above two fingerbreadths, and between one column and the other the space of a thumbbreadth.

Different measures are mentioned in the following sources, in which however, there is a similar difference between the top and bottom margins: *y. Meg.* 1.71d and *Sop.* 2.5 mention for the books of the Bible, except for the Torah, a margin of two fingerbreadths above the text and three below. The discussion in these places also mentions the view of Rabbi prescribing for the Torah three fingerbreadths above the text and a handbreadth below the text.

---

7. For a partial description, see the data collected by Martin, *Scribal Character of the Dead Sea Scrolls*, 1.98–101. A full study of the ruling and other scribal aspects of the Qumran documents is still in order, and this pertains also to the other documents from the Judean Desert. According to the description by S. Talmon, MasLev and MasDeut are not ruled ("Fragments of Two Scrolls of the Book of Leviticus from Masada," *ErIsr* 24 [Malamat Volume; 1993] 99–110).

8. See M. Glatzer, "The Aleppo Codex: Codicological and Paleographical Aspects," *Sefunot* 4 (1989) 210–15 [Heb. with Eng. summary].

9. Details are provided in an unpublished seminar paper by W. W. Fields presented to the Hebrew University, "Qumran Scribal Practices and the Size of the Column Block in the Scrolls from the Judean Desert" (1987). For example, for the top and bottom margins of the following texts these figures are provided by Fields: 1QIsaᵃ 2.0–2.8 cm and 2.5–3.3 cm; 4QDanᵃ 1.2 and 1.7; 4QJerᵃ 2.2 and 2.6; 4QpaleoExodᵐ 2.7 and 4.3.

(3) *Supralinear correcting additions* of a single letter or letters, a word or words to elements in the text are found in many texts, among them 1QIsaª.[10] Such additions between the lines occasionally continue into the margins and also vertically, alongside the text (1QIsaª, cols. XXX, XXXII, XXXIII), and even below the text, upside down (4QJerª, col. III). A few examples of added letters have also been preserved in the MT in the form of *suspended letters*. At present it is not known whether certain Qumran texts contain more suspended letters than others.

The system of adding letters above the line is mentioned in *y. Meg.* 1.71c:[11]

תולין בספרים אין תולין לא בתפילין ולא במזוזות.

One may hang ⟨the letter above the line⟩ in scrolls, but one may not hang ⟨the letter above the line⟩ in *tefillin* or *mezuzot*.[12]

Likewise, *b. Menaḥ.* 30b (cf. also *Sop.* 5.4) approves of the erasure or correction of a word and the writing of the divine name in its stead or above the line:

הטועה בשם גורר את מה שכתב ותולה את מה שגרר וכותב את השם על
מקום הגרר. דברי רבי יהודה. רבי יוסי אומר אף תולין את השם. רבי יצחק אומר
אף מוחק וכותב. ר״ש שזורי אומר כל השם כולו תולין מקצתו אין תולין . . .
הלכה כר״ש שזורי.

If ⟨the scribe⟩ omitted the name of God ⟨and had already written the next word⟩, he should erase the word that was written and insert it above the line, and should write the name upon the erasure. This is the opinion of R. Judah. R. Jose says: "He may even insert the name above the line." R. Isaac says: "He may even wipe away ⟨the word that was written⟩ and write ⟨the name in its place⟩." R. Simeon of Shezur says: "He may write the whole name above the line but not a part of it. . . ." The *Halakah* is in accordance with R. Simeon of Shezur.

(4) *Spaces between the books.*   In scrolls containing more than one biblical book, spaces are left between the books. Thus in MurXII,[13] the equivalent

---

10. For a complete list for 1QIsaª see E. Y. Kutscher, *The Language and Linguistic Background of the Isaiah Scroll (1QIsaª)* (STDJ 6; Leiden, 1974) 522–31, 555–58.

11. On the other hand, *Sop.* 5.10 notes: הטועה את השיטה אינו תולה מנגד השיטין אלא נגד הטעות. גורר אחת וכותב שתים. שתים וכותב שלש ובלבד שלא יגרור שלש. 'If he omits a line in error, he may not suspend it between the lines but insert it in close proximity to the place of the error by erasing one ⟨adjacent line⟩ and writing two in its place or ⟨by erasing⟩ two lines and writing three, provided only that he does not erase three lines'. However, this dictum probably refers to omissions recognized by the original scribe, while in the cases under review the omissions were added by later scribes. In the case of 4QJerª the corrector probably had little choice but to act as he did, that is to add three lines in small letters between the original lines, four lines in the left margin and one line in the space under the text.

12. See, however, the discussion in *b. Menaḥ.* 29b and *y. Šabb.* 16.15b concerning the validity of a relatively large number of such additions.

13. See, M. Baillet, J. T. Milik, and R. de Vaux (eds.), *Les 'petites grottes' de Qumrân* (DJD 3; Oxford, 1961) 182, 192, 197, 200, 202, 205, and plates lxi, lxvi, lxix, lxxi, lxxii.

of three lines has been left between various books of the Minor Prophets, that is, between Jonah and Micah, Micah and Nahum, and Zephaniah and Haggai. In 8HevXIIgr, six lines are left empty in the middle of the column between Jonah and Micah.[14] Three blank lines have been left in the middle of the column between the beginning of Exodus and what looks like the last line of Genesis in 4QpaleoGen–Exod[l], preceded by at least one sheet of written text.[15] Exodus in 4QGen–Exod[a] and 4QExod[b] begins more than halfway down the column and may have been preceded by such spaces.[16]

Similar instructions are reflected in the rabbinic literature. According to the instructions of *b. B. Bat.* 13b:

בין חומש לחומש של חומש של תורה ארבעה שיטין וכן בין כל נביא לנביא ובנביא של
שנים עשר ג׳ שיטין.

Between each book of the Torah there should be left a space of four lines, and so between one prophet and the next. In the Twelve Minor Prophets, however, the space should only be three lines.

For similar statements, see *y. Meg.* 1.71d and *Sop.* 2.4. See further below, p. 391.

(5) The division of the text of the biblical and nonbiblical Qumran texts into content units reflects in general terms the system of *parašiyyot* that was later also accepted in the MT: a space in the middle of a line to denote a minor subdivision, *parašah sĕtumah* in the terminology of the Masoretes, and a space extending from the last word in the line to the end of the line, *parašah pĕtuḥah*, to denote a major subdivision.

Although the medieval manuscripts continue the tradition of the proto-Masoretic texts from Qumran in general, they often differ with regard to the indication of individual section breaks. The studies by Oesch and Maori concerning 1QIsa[a] show that in 80 percent of the cases it agrees with the medieval manuscripts of the MT (MSS A, C).[17] Likewise, 4QJer[a] and 4QJer[c], otherwise very close to the medieval text of the MT, often differ from the MT in *parašiyyot*, since they contain more section divisions than the medieval texts.[18]

---

14. See E. Tov (ed.), *The Greek Minor Prophets Scroll from Naḥal Ḥever (8HevXIIgr)* (DJD 8; Oxford, 1990) 33 and pl. iv.

15. Indirect evidence for the joining of books is further available for Mur 1, probably containing Genesis, Exodus, and Numbers (see DJD 3.75–78 and plates xix–xxi) and 4QLev–Num[a]. However, in neither of these texts has the actual join between the two books been preserved.

16. Most texts reflect the Masoretic family.

17. J. M. Oesch, *Petucha und Setuma: Untersuchungen zu einer überlieferten Gliederung im hebräischen Text des Alten Testaments* (OBO 27; Freiburg/Göttingen, 1979); idem, "Textgliederung im Alten Testament und in den Qumranhandschriften," *Henoch* 5 (1983) 289–321; Y. Maori, "The Tradition of *Pisqaʾot* in Ancient Hebrew Manuscripts: The Isaiah Texts and Commentaries from Qumran," *Textus* 10 (1982) 1*–50* [Heb.].

18. See my "4QJer[c] (4Q72)," in *Tradition of the Text* (ed. G. J. Norton and S. Pisano; OBO 109; Freiburg/Göttingen, 1991) 249–76, esp. 274–76.

A similar system is mentioned in the rabbinic literature and is required by *b. Šabb.* 103b (compare with *b. Ber.* 12b):

פרשה פתוחה לא יעשנה סתומה. סתומה לא יעשנה פתוחה.

An open section may not be written closed, nor a closed section open.

Likewise *Sop.* 1.15:

פתוחה שעשאה סתומה. סתומה שעשאה פתוחה. הרי זה יגנז.

If an open section was written as closed or a closed section as open, the scroll must be stored away.[19]

See further *Sipre* 36 on Deut 6:9.

(6) Several of the poetic texts from the Judean Desert are arranged sticho-metrically. Three main systems are recognizable in these texts, but their distri-bution and even the use of any system at all can only be analyzed after the publication of all the scrolls. In several texts only one stich or two hemistichs (without spaces separating the hemistichs) are written per line (4QPs[b], 1QPs[a], 4QPs[g,h], 5QPs, 11QPs[a] [in the latter five in Psalm 119], 4QDeut[q], and probably also 4QDeut[c] [both Deuteronomy 32]). Probably 4QpaleoJob was written in the same system as well. In other texts two hemistichs are written per line with spaces between them (1QDeut[b], 4QDeut[b], 4QpaleoDeut[r] [all Deuteronomy 32]; 2QSir, 4QLam, 8QPs, 5/6ḤevPs, MasSir). Interestingly enough, Deuteronomy 32 is transmitted in both systems. Texts belonging to a third system have spaces after a hemistich or a group of two or three words, but unlike in the first two systems, these spaces occur at different places in the line. This applies to MasPs[b] and 4QProv[a,b] as well as to 4QRP[c] (4Q*365* frg. 6b); the latter text con-tains clusters of 2–4 words in Exodus 15, separated by spaces.

With some exceptions, the texts from the Judean Desert reflect the system described in rabbinic literature and executed in the medieval Masoretic manu-scripts.[20] The stichometric arrangements have become part and parcel of the traditional way of writing the text, so that *Sop.* 1.11 says:

האזינו שעשאה שירה, שירה שעשאה האזינו . . . אל יקרא בה.

If *haʾăzînû* was arranged like the "Song of Moses" or if the "Song of Moses" was arranged like *haʾăzînû* , . . . the scroll may not be used for the lection.

---

19. The fact that the scrolls were considered unfit for use if they were imprecise with regard to open and closed sections was in a way unrealistic, since all known texts, including the Masoretic family, differ internally.

20. One system of stichometric arrangement in the MT is "a half-brick, אריח, over a whole brick, לבנה, and a whole brick over a half-brick"; in other words, an unwritten part (that is, a space) placed over a part that is written in the following line and vice versa. According to *b. Meg.* 16b (see also *b. Menaḥ.* 31b; *Sop.* 1.11), this system was used for all poetic texts contained in nonpoetic

The Qumran manuscripts can be compared with the rabbinic regulations only with regard to three texts. The "Song of Moses" in 4QDeut[q] is not written according to the rabbinic regulations since it has one hemistich per line, while according to the rabbinic regulations and later Masoretic practice, this song should be written in two columns (see n. 20). Interestingly enough, 4QDeut[q] does not belong to the Masoretic family, but it has close affinities to the LXX and also has independent features. On the other hand, 1QDeut[b] and 4QpaleoDeut[r], following the rabbinic rule for the writing of Deuteronomy 32, could be Masoretic, since they reflect the MT and the Sam. Pent. equally well. Third, the "Song of the Sea" in 4Q*365* frg. 6b (4QRP, based on a pre-Samaritan biblical text; Qumran practice) is not written according to rabbinic prescriptions, and it thus also differs from the MT. The arrangement in the fragment (preserving Exod 15:16–19) somewhat resembles the arrangement of the Sam. Pent., but at the same time differs from it. In this song, the MT is arranged according to the system of "a half-brick, אריח, over a whole brick, לבנה, and a whole brick over a half-brick," while 4Q*365* arranged the text in hemistichs as a running text. In a way, the Qumran text resembles the Sam. Pent. more than the MT, but the resemblance is only partial. What the Qumran text and the Sam. Pent. have in common is that they arrange the Song in groups of words consisting of two to three words, thus amounting to a hemistich. But these hemistichs are presented in parallel layout in the Sam. Pent., and as a running text in 4Q*365*.

(7) According to *Sop.* 2:11,

צריך שיהא משייר מלמעלן ומלמטן כדי שלא יקרע.

A space should be left ⟨unstitched⟩ at the top and at the bottom ⟨of the sheets⟩ in order that the scroll be not torn ⟨in use⟩.

See *b. Meg.* 19b. Similarly, in various instances, the sheets of several texts were stitched in accord with the rabbinic instruction, not at the very end of the leather but somewhat below the top edge or above the bottom edge: 4QNum[b], col. XV; 11QT[a] cols. XLIX, LIII, LVII, LXI, LXIV, and LXVII. On the other hand, in 1QIsa[a] and 1QS the stitching reaches to the very end of the leather. A more detailed study is in order.

---

books, for example, in the "Song of the Sea" in Exod 15:1–18 and the "Song of Deborah" in Judg 5:2–30, with the exception of the list of the kings of Canaan in Josh 12:9–24 and the list of the sons of Haman in Esth 9:6–9. Another method used was "a half-brick, אריח, over a half-brick and a whole brick, לבנה, over a whole brick," that is, an unwritten part above another unwritten part in the following line with the written text appearing above the written text in the following line. According to *b. Meg.* 16b, the list of the kings of Canaan in Josh 12:9–24 and the list of the sons of Haman in Esth 9:6–9 are written in this way. The "Song of Moses" in Deut 32:1–43 is also written thus. See further Oesch, *Petucha und Setuma*, 121–22.

Scribal Practices Differing from Rabbinic Sources

We now turn to the details in which writing practices reflected in some or all Qumran documents differ from what is known from rabbinic sources.

(1) A subdivision into small text units (*verses*) is reflected by the accents in the MT, according to which each unit ending with a *silluq* is considered a *verse*. A similar division is known in the Talmud, where the number of verses of some of the books is mentioned, thus implying that at that time verses formed a distinct unit:

תנו רבנן חמשת אלפים ושמונה מאות ושמונים ושמונה פסוקים הוו פסוקי ס״ת.
יתר עליו תהלים שמונה. חסר ממנו דברי הימים שמונה.

Our rabbis taught: There are 5888 verses in the Torah. The Psalms exceed this by eight, while ⟨Daniel and?⟩ Chronicles are less by eight (*b. Qidd.* 30a).

Likewise, *Sop.* 11.1ff. speaks about the reading of individual verses (*pĕsuqim*).

A similar division was indicated by distinctive marks in manuscripts of the Sam. Pent. and in a few Greek biblical texts, 8HevXIIgr, P. Fouad 266, P. Ryl. Gk. 458, probably representing early revisions of the Greek Bible. On the other hand, in the great majority of the Hebrew biblical texts from the Judean Desert (as well as in medieval liturgical Masorah scrolls) no verse division is used, although two or three Qumran texts appear to have a spacing system: 4QDan[a,d] (4QDan[a] is independent from a textual point of view) and possibly 1QLev (insufficient information).

(2) *Y. Meg.* 1.71d:

וצריך שיהא גומר באמצע הדף ומתחיל באמצעיתו ובנביא גומר בסופו ומתחיל
בראשו ובנביא של שנים עשר אסור.

⟨In the Torah⟩ one has to finish in the middle of a page and to commence in the middle of ⟨the same⟩ page. In the Prophets one finishes at the end and begins at the top of a page, but in the Dodekapr_he_ton this is forbidden.

For the Torah this regulation is adhered to in 4QpaleoGen–Exod[l] (see above; character of the MT), 4QGen–Exod[a] (character of the MT) and 4QExod[b] (probably independent character), where Exodus starts in the middle of a column.[21] However, this rule is not adhered to in 4QLev[c] (MT / Sam. Pent.), which begins

---

21. This custom is probably also followed in 4Q*365*, a (nonbiblical) manuscript of 4QReworked Pentateuch (hereafter 4QRP), where in frg. 26a–b the first verse of Numbers is preceded by what looks like a paraphrastic version of the last verse of Leviticus, followed by an empty line. See further above with regard to spaces left between books.

at the top of a column, or in 11QpaleoLev[a] (independent character) ending in the middle of a column but not followed by Numbers. Since the latter scroll contained a single biblical book only, the aforementioned prescription would not pertain to it.

(3) Various methods were used in the Qumran manuscripts for the *correction of errors*, in the text itself, in the margin, or between the lines. The following methods used in the Qumran texts are *not* mentioned by *Masseket Soperim* chaps. 4–5 as legitimate correcting procedures:

(a) *A marking of cancellation dots* in the Qumran scrolls above, below, or both above and below the letters, or (in the case of added words) on both sides of the word, was used to omit letters or words already written.[22]

The custom of canceling letters or words by means of dots has also been preserved in the *puncta extraordinaria* in the MT. These dots in the MT are explained in various ways in the Talmud and midrashim, but not as cancellation dots,[23] and they are not mentioned in *Masseket Soperim* as a correction technique. As for the Qumran texts, it is important to realize that with one exception these cancellation dots have been spotted so far in 22 texts that reflect the Qumran practice of orthography and morphology, among them: 1QIsa[a], 1QS, 1QM, 1QH[a], 1QpHab, all of them sectarian; 4QCatena[a] (*177*) line 15; 4QD[a], 4Q*365* (4QRP; pre-Samaritan), 11QT[a] XLV 18. Similar dots are found in 4QIsa[d] and 4QJer[a] 14:6 (col. IX, part 2).[24]

(b) *Reshaping letters.* In attempting to correct a letter or letters, a scribe would sometimes change the form of a letter into another one. Examples of remodeled letters have been given by Martin for the major sectarian texts from Cave 1: 1QIsa[a], 1QpHab, 1QH[a], 1QM, 1QS.[25]

(c) *Parenthesis Signs.* Omissions of words by enclosing them within scribal signs are known from the Greek scribal tradition as *sigma* and *antisigma*[26] and from the Masoretic tradition as inverted *nunim.*[27] In the Qumran texts these signs have been spotted only in a few texts: in 11QpaleoLev[a] (independent) the notation of a *sigma* and *antisigma* serves to indicate verses written in the wrong place (Lev 20:23–24 written in the middle of 18:27). Similar notations are found in 4QJer[a] col. XII, 4QQoh[a] (Qumran practice), and in the sectarian texts 1QM III 1 and 1QS VII 8.

22. See Martin, *Scribal Character of the Dead Sea Scrolls*, 1.154–70; Kutscher, *Language and Linguistic Background*, 531–36; S. Talmon, "Prolegomenon" to R. Butin, *The Ten Nequdoth of the Torah or the Meaning and Purpose of the Extraordinary Points of the Pentateuch (Masoretic Text)* (Baltimore, 1906; repr. New York, 1969). See further E. Tov, *Textual Criticism of the Hebrew Bible* (Minneapolis, 1992) 214.

23. See A. Shinan, "Ten Dots in the Torah," in *The Bible in the Light of Its Interpreters: Sarah Kamin Memorial Volume* (ed. S. Japhet; Jerusalem, 1994) [Heb.].

24. This scroll reflects the textual tradition of the MT, but because of its extensive scribal activity it differs from the other texts belonging to the Masoretic family.

25. Martin, *Scribal Character of the Dead Sea Scrolls*, vol. 2, passim.

26. Cf. E. G. Turner, *Greek Manuscripts of the Ancient World* (Oxford, 1971) pls. 15, 25.

27. See Tov, *Textual Criticism of the Hebrew Bible*, 54–55.

(d) *Crossing out a word with a horizontal line* has been spotted in some 15 texts, among them 1QIsaᵃ, 4Q*491* (Mᵃ), 4Q*501* (all written in the Qumran practice); and 4QDanᵃ (independent). This practice is probably not mentioned in rabbinic literature.[28]

(4) *Biblical texts written in the Paleo-Hebrew Script.* At Qumran, fragments of 11–14 biblical texts written in the Paleo-Hebrew script have been found. These texts, rather than preceding the use of the square "Assyrian" script, were actually written at a relatively late period, as a natural continuation of the earlier tradition of writing in the "early" Hebrew script. They were concurrent with the use of the square script, as can also be proved by a paleographical examination of the Paleo-Hebrew script.[29]

Use of this script for biblical texts was forbidden according to various statements in the Talmudic literature, for example, *b. Sanh.* 21b:

אמר מר זוטרא ואיתימא מר עוקבא בתחלה ניתנה תורה לישראל בכתב עברי
ולשון הקודש. חזרה וניתנה להם בימי עזרא בכתב אשורית ולשון ארמי. בירדו
להן לישראל כתב אשורית ולשון הקודש והניחו להדיוטות כתב עברית
ולשון ארמי.

Mar Zuṭra or, as some say, Mar ᶜUkba said: "Originally the Torah was given to Israel in Hebrew characters and in the sacred ⟨Hebrew⟩ language; later, in the time of Ezra, the Torah was given in the Assyrian script and the Aramaic language. ⟨Finally,⟩ Israel selected the Assyrian script and the Hebrew language, leaving the Hebrew characters and Aramaic language for the ordinary people" (cf. *b. Meg.* 9a; *t. Sanh.* 5.7; *y. Meg.* 1.71b–c).

Likewise, *m. Yad.* 4.5:

תרגום שכתבו עברית ועברית שכתבו תרגום וכתב עברית אינו מטמא את
הידים. לעולם אינו מטמא עד שיכתבנו אשורית על העור ובדיו.

28. On the other hand, this system may be referred to in *Soperim*, depending on one's understanding of the terminology used and the variants listed in Higger's edition. With regard to the double writing of the divine name, the formulation of *Sop.* 5.1 is מקיים את הראשון ומעכב את האחרון '. . . he retains the first and *erases* the latter'. The word used for 'erases' is מעכב, and the variant readings in the edition of the Gaon from Wilna and in the parallel section in *Masseket Seper Torah*, מחטב and מחטיב, are explained by Ben-Yehuda's *Thesaurus* as 'to cross out with a line'. The term used for the erasing of the divine name should be contrasted with the erasing of nondivine names written twice, for which *Soperim* used the term מוחק 'erases' (with one of the techniques of erasing, such as with a sharp instrument). Because of the uncertainty concerning the readings in *Soperim* and their meaning, the relevance of this detail for the present discussion is not clear.

29. See M. D. McLean, *The Use and Development of Palaeo-Hebrew in the Hellenistic and Roman Periods* (Ph.D. diss., Harvard University, 1982) 41–47; R. S. Hanson *apud* D. N. Freedman and K. A. Mathews, *The Paleo-Hebrew Leviticus Scroll (11QpaleoLev)* (Winona Lake, Ind., 1985) 20–23. For an earlier discussion, see L. Blau, "Wie lange stand die althebräische Schrift bei den Juden im Gebrauch?" in *Gedenkbuch zur Erinnerung an David Kaufmann* (ed. M. Brann and F. Rosenthal; Breslau, 1900) 44–57.

If an Aramaic ⟨portion of Scripture⟩ was written in Hebrew, or if ⟨Scripture that is in⟩ Hebrew was written in an ⟨Aramaic⟩ version, or in Hebrew script, it does not render the hands unclean. ⟨The Holy Scriptures⟩ render the hands unclean only when they are written in Assyrian characters, on leather, and in ink (cf. *b. Šabb.* 115b).

It is hard to determine the provenance of the Paleo-Hebrew texts that have been found at Qumran.[30] One of the texts is of an independent textual character (11QpaleoLev^a), another one pre-Samaritan, clearly without the Samaritan features (4QpaleoExod^m), but the majority of the texts seem to belong to the Masoretic family, although a decision is difficult since some are equally close to the MT and Sam. Pent. (1QpaleoLev [equally close to the Sam. Pent.]. 1QpaleoNum, 4QpaleoGen–Exod^l [with independent features], 4QpaleoDeut^r [equally close to the Sam. Pent.]).[31] It is thus not easy to explain the nature of these Paleo-Hebrew texts of Masoretic character against the background of the negative remarks in the rabbinic literature on the use of the Paleo-Hebrew script. It should also be remembered that these texts are very carefully transmitted, with virtually no scribal intervention, as opposed to various degrees of such intervention in the texts written in square characters. It is therefore suggested here, by way of elimination, but also because of the traditional nature of the Sadducean priestly families and their reverence for the ancient script, that these texts were of Sadducean origin.[32]

(5) The use of Paleo-Hebrew characters for the *Tetragrammaton*, as well as oftentimes for אל(הים) and צבאות,[33] with/without prefixes and suffixes is used

---

30. Possibly the main reason for the disallowance of the rabbis' use of the "early" Hebrew script is the fact that the Samaritans used this script for their biblical text as well as for other forms of writing. Indeed, the term 'ordinary people' in the dictum in *b. Sanh.* 21b is explained as 'Samaritans' by Rab Ḥisda in the continued discussion, but it is not clear whether only the Samaritans continued to write in the "early" Hebrew script.

31. For a discussion, see E. Ulrich, "The Palaeo-Hebrew Biblical Manuscripts from Qumran Cave 4," in *A Time to Prepare the Way in the Wilderness: Papers on the Qumran Scrolls by Fellows of the Institute for Advanced Studies of the Hebrew University, Jerusalem, 1989–1990* (ed. D. Dimant and L. H. Schiffman; STDJ 16; Leiden, 1995) 103–29.

32. See my article, "The Socio-Religious Background of the Paleo-Hebrew Texts Found at Qumran," *Festschrift M. Hengel*, in press. Note that the connection between the Qumran Paleo-Hebrew texts and the Sadducees was first made by D. Diringer, "Early Hebrew Script versus Square Script," in *Essays and Studies Presented to Stanley Arthur Cook* (ed. D. W. Thomas; London, 1950) 35–49, esp. 48–49. According to Diringer it was the Sadducees who influenced the Maccabees in their decision to revive the ancient script.

33. For a detailed analysis of the writing of the different divine names in Paleo-Hebrew, see K. A. Mathews, "The Background of the Paleo-Hebrew Texts at Qumran," in *The Word of the Lord Shall Go Forth: Essays in Honor of David Noel Freedman in Celebration of His Sixtieth Birthday* (ed. C. Meyers and M. O'Connor; Winona Lake, Ind., 1983) 549–68; P. W. Skehan, "The Divine Name at Qumran, in the Masada Scroll, and in the Septuagint," *BIOSCS* 13 (1980) 14–44; E. Ulrich, in his forthcoming DJD edition of 4QIsa^c.

in 23 different Qumran texts, of which the majority are nonbiblical.[34] As for the background of the writing of the divine names in Paleo-Hebrew characters, it was shown by Siegel that this practice secured their permanence in the manuscripts by the use of a special script. Since the divine names should not be erased according to *y. Meg.* 1.71d,[35] a system was devised to ensure that it would not happen. Apparently the writing in Paleo-Hebrew characters gave the words a higher degree of sacredness in certain religious and/or scribal circles prohibiting their erasure.[36]

No explicit remarks against this scribal habit are found in the rabbinic literature, but one may conclude that since the use of Paleo-Hebrew script was forbidden for complete biblical texts, the proscription would by implication include individual words.

At the same time, the concept of the sanctity of the divine names that is behind the writing in Paleo-Hebrew characters is in agreement with the aforementioned statements in *y. Meg.* 1.71d (cf. *Sop.* 4.1ff.) forbidding the erasing of the various divine names. Even though the use of Paleo-Hebrew characters for divine names is not mentioned in the rabbinic literature, the practice is thus not opposed to the spirit of the rabbinic regulations.[37] In their wish to preserve the sanctity of the divine names, the Qumran scribes simply went one step further; they were in fact more strict than the rules laid down in the rabbinic literature.[38]

(6) In many of the Qumran texts *nonfinal letters* are written in final position.[39] A lack of consistency in the use of these letters is reflected in biblical and nonbiblical texts from Qumran written in the Qumran practice of orthography and morphology (called Qumran practice). In these texts both final and nonfinal forms are written at the ends of words.[40] This lack of distinction is

---

34. Nonbiblical texts: 1QpMic, 1QpHab, 1QpZeph, 1QMyst, 1QH[a], 4QpPs[a], 4QpIsa[a], 4Q*180*, 4QS[d], 4Q*183*, 6QD, 6QHymn, 11QPs[a], as well as the fragmentary 3Q*14*. Biblical texts: 1QPs[b], 2QExod[b] (probably a rewritten Torah text, see n. 21), 4QIsa[c], 3QLam, 11QLev[b]. To these, 4QExod[j], 4QDeut[K2], and 4QLev[g] should now be added.

35. See Siegel, "The Employment of Palaeo-Hebrew Characters for the Divine Names at Qumran."

36. For a fuller discussion, see my "The Socio-Religious Background" (n. 32 above).

37. The Qumran texts differ internally with regard to the details of the use of Paleo-Hebrew characters. 4QIsa[c] also writes the prefixes to the divine names with Paleo-Hebrew characters, while 11QPs[a] does not. That the scribe of 4QIsa[c] should not be considered detached from the rules laid down in the Talmud is shown by the fact that only this text treats צבאות as a divine name, writing it with Paleo-Hebrew characters, and in this regard it agrees with the main view presented in *y. Meg.* 1.71d.

38. This detail may again point to the Sadducees (see n. 32).

39. In the "early" Hebrew script, no distinction was made between the final and nonfinal forms of any letters, and presumably in the first biblical scrolls written in the Assyrian ("square") script, no distinction was made. During the Persian Period final forms of the letters *mem, nun, ṣade, pe,* and *kap* gradually developed but were not used consistently.

40. Most of the instances in which nonfinal letters are written at the ends of words occur in monosyllabic words such as גמ, אמ, נאמ. See J. P. Siegel, "Final *Mem* in Medial Position and Medial *Mem* in Final Position in 11QPs[a]: Some Observations," *RevQ* 7 (1969) 125–30.

known also from other texts, but among the known texts it is especially frequent in the texts written according to Qumran practice.[41]

Traditions concerning a lack of consistency in the writing of the final forms of letters have also been preserved in the Talmud.[42] This nondistinction between the two types of letters was not allowed in rabbinic sources. See *b. Šabb.* 103b–104a:

> שלא יכתוב . . . סתומין פתוחין פתוחין סתומין . . . הרי אלו יגנזו.
>
> That one should not write . . . closed letters as open or open as closed . . . such scrolls should be stored away.

For further comparison, see *y. Meg.* 1.71d (quoted in n. 42), *Sipre* 36 on Deut 6:9, and *Sop.* 2.20:

> כל האותיות הכפולים באלפא ביתא, כותב את הראשונים בתחילת התיבה ובאמצע התיבה, ואת האחרונים בסוף ואם שינה פסול.
>
> In the case of the double letters of the alphabet the first ones are written at the beginning and in the middle of the word and the second at the end. If this is reversed, the scroll is disqualified.

Because of this situation the texts that often use nonfinal letters in final position were not tolerated by the rabbis. Among the known biblical texts, this pertains to all texts written in the Qumran practice of morphology and orthography.

(7) While most of the Qumran scrolls were written on leather, a few were written on papyrus: 4QpapIsa[p], 6Q*3* (Deuteronomy?), 6Q*4* (Kings), 6Q*5* (Psalms?), and 6Q*7* (Daniel).

The use of papyrus was not allowed for scripture, according to the Talmud.[43] For example, *m. Meg* 2.2:

41. A similar lack of distinction between final and nonfinal letters is visible in the Torah scroll from the synagogue of Severus (see Tov, *Textual Criticism of the Hebrew Bible*, 119–20), and one instance is preserved in the MT: Neh 2:13, 𝔐[K] הַמפרוצים 'that-were-breached', MT[Q] הֵם פרוצים. There is also one instance of a final form of *mem* in the middle of a word: Isa 9:6 MT[K] לםרבה 'of the increase of . . . ', MT[Q] למרבה.

42. See *y. Meg.* 1.71d: "In the case of the double letters of the alphabet, one writes the first ones at the beginning and middle of a word, and the second ⟨final forms⟩ at the end. If one did otherwise, the scroll is invalid. In the name of R. Mattiah b. Heresh they have said, '⟨The letters⟩ *m*, *n*, *ṣ*, *p*, *k* ⟨that appear in two forms⟩ were revealed to Moses at Sinai.' . . . The men of Jerusalem would write 'Jerusalem' as 'to Jerusalem' (that is, ירושלימ) and ⟨sages⟩ did not scruple in this regard. Along the same lines, צפון 'north' was written 'to the north' (that is, צפונ) and תימן 'south' was written 'to the south' (that is, תימנ)." Compare also *b. Šabb.* 104a; *b. Meg.* 2b. A similar use of writing nonfinal letters in final position is reflected in the tradition of the three scrolls of the Law found in the temple court, since one of the books was called the "*ma*ᶜ*on* scroll" after one of its prominent characteristics, namely, the absence of a final *nun* in *ma*ᶜ*on* and apparently in other words as well.

43. Likewise, writing *tefillin* and *mezuzot* on paper (papyrus) is forbidden (compare *b. Sanh.* 48b, *Menaḥ.* 42b, *Sop.* 1.1). On the other hand, liturgical texts were written on papyrus (see the Nash papyrus containing the Decalogue).

הייתה כתובה בסם ובסקרא ובקומוס ובקנקנתום על הניר ועל הדפתרא לא יצא
עד שתהא כתובה אשורית על הספר ובדיו.

If it was written with caustic, red dye, gum, or copperas, or on paper
(papyrus) or *diftera*, he has not fulfilled his obligation; but only if it
was written in Assyrian writing, on parchment and with ink.

Likewise *y. Meg.* 1.71d:

הלכה למשה מסיני שיהו כותבין בעורות.

It is an oral prescription delivered to Moses at Sinai that one would
write on skins.

In the Qumran caves the great majority of the texts were on leather, and this
pertains also to the finds in Massada, although they include a large number of
ostraca. On the other hand, the great majority of the documents from the other
sites are on papyrus. This different use of material is related to the content of
the documents. Most of the texts of literary content were written on leather,
which accounts for the contents of the corpora of texts from Qumran and Massada, while papyrus was used for personal documents such as letters and documentary texts, found at the other sites. At the same time, the background of
the papyrus copies of literary works is less clear. Papyrus was less expensive,
and it was probably used for personal copies.[44]

In view of this situation an examination of the textual character of the papyrus fragments is in order. While several of the fragments are too small to determine their character, the larger fragments of 1–2 Kings, and possibly also
Daniel, may be characterized as non-Masoretic, more specifically as independent, which could mean that these texts did not derive from Pharisaic circles.

(8) *Patching.* The writing on a patch is forbidden by *Sop.* 2.17:

ולא כותבין על גבי המטלית.

. . . nor is it permitted to write on a patch.

However, the text continues in the following way:

אמר ר׳ אלעזר משום ר׳ מאיר שדובקין בדבק וכותבין על גבי המטלית אבל אין
תופרין במקום הכתב מבפנים ותופרין הכתב מבחוץ.

R. Simeon b. Eleazar said in the name of R. Meir: "⟨A torn sheet⟩ may
be joined with glue, and it is permitted to write on the patch. It is forbidden, however, to do the sewing on the written side, but it must be
done on the outside."

---

44. Thus M. O. Wise, *Thunder in Gemini, and Other Essays on the History, Language and
Literature of Second Temple Palestine* (JSPSS 15; Sheffield, 1994) 103–57, esp. 125ff.

It is therefore relevant to note that the one text in which writing on a patch has been spotted does not belong to the family of the MT: 4QpaleoExod[m] (pre-Samaritan).[45] In this text a segment of the scroll was replaced with a round patch stitched onto col. VIII.[46]

(9) *Stitching.* According to *b. Menaḥ.* 31b stitching was permitted in the following case:

אמר רב זעירא אמר רב חננאל אמר רב קרע הבא בשני שיטין יתפור. בשלש אל יתפור.

R. Zeira said in the name of R. Hananel who said it in the name of Rab: "If a rent ⟨in a scroll of the Law⟩ extended into two lines it may be sown together; but if into three lines it may not be sewn together."[47]

See also *Sop.* 2.17 (main opinion; for the view of R. Simeon see above):

אין דובקין בדבק ולא כותבין על גבי המטלית ולא תופרין במקום הכתב.

⟨A tear in a parchment sheet of a Torah scroll⟩ may not be joined with glue, nor is it permitted to write on a patch, nor may ⟨the sheets⟩ be sewn together on the written side.

On the other hand, several small rents in 1QIsa[a] (Qumran practice) as well as a long rent over the length of col. XII were stitched after it had been written on. The stitching before the writing, such as col. XXI of 4QJer[c] (proto-Masoretic), is not relevant to this regulation, but the stitching over the writing in at least three lines of col. XXIII of this scroll would not be acceptable to the rabbis.

(10) *Scribal markings*, not all of which are understood, are found almost exclusively in the margins of compositions written in the Qumran practice of orthography and morphology. The largest number of signs is found in 1QS-1QSa-1QSb (written by the same scribe who also corrected 1QIsa[a]), in 4Q502–511, 4QpIsa[c] and in 4QCant[b] (probably an abbreviated text), all different from

45. Patches have also been found on manuscripts of the Sam. Pent.

46. That patch displays an orthography different from the remainder of the scroll (ʾhrn is spelled defectively in the patch).

47. In the continuation of this text the Talmud mentions certain circumstances, the relevance of which can no longer be examined in the preserved texts:

א״ל רבה זוטי לרב אשי הכי אמר רבי ירמיה מדיפתי משמיה דרבא הא דאמרינן בשלש אל יתפור לא אמרן אלא בעתיקתא אבל חדתתא לית לן בה ולא עתיקתא עתיקתא ממש ולא חדתתא חדתתא ממש אלא הא דלא אפיצן הא דאפיצן.

Rabbah the younger said to R. Ashi: "Thus said R. Jeremiah of Difti in the name of Raba: 'The rule that we have laid down, namely, that if it extended into three lines it may be sewn together, applies only to old scrolls; but in the case of new scrolls it would not matter. ⟨That is, it may always be sewn together.⟩ Moreover "old" does not mean actually old, nor "new" actually new, but the one means prepared with gall-nut juice and the other means not so prepared.' "

each other.[48] Furthermore, in two Paleo-Hebrew texts (4QpaleoExod[m] [pre-Samaritan] and 11QpaleoLev[a] [independent]), a large *waw* was written in the spaces between the paragraphs, when the first word of the following paragraph would have started with a *waw*. In such cases the new paragraph now begins with a word without *waw*. It is also found in the margins of a few texts written in the square "Assyrian" script: 4QPs[b] (independent), 1QIsa[a] VI 22, and 1QS V 1, at the beginning of a new section.

Rabbinic literature does not explicitly forbid scribal marks, but they would probably be disallowed by the stringent laws of copying.

(11) *Paragraphing.* Most of the vertical lines, named παράγραφος in Greek sources, written between two lines at the beginning of the line in 1QIsa[a] and a long list of nonbiblical texts,[49] denote a content division of the text, which was also indicated in such cases by means of spaces, that is, the so-called closed and open sections. The same content division is intended by a sign similar to the character X[50] and by a sign resembling a Mexican hat in 1QIsa[a].[51] In several instances in 4QNum[b] (probably indicating new sections) and in 2QPs (the first two lines of Psalm 103)[52] divisions are indicated by writing with red ink, similar to earlier nonbiblical documents.[53]

As in the case of scribal markings, rabbinic literature does not explicitly forbid the use of paragraph signs, but it would probably be disallowed by the stringent laws of copying.

(12) In some Qumran texts, single *guide dots* ('points jalons') were written before the beginning of the first lines of the sheet and after the last lines, guiding the drawing of these lines, but sometimes also in the middle of a sheet (4Q*365* = 4QRP[c], frg. 12a). Such dots, not mentioned in rabbinic sources, are preserved in several texts, for example: 4QGen–Exod[a] (proto-Masoretic), 2QpaleoLev, 4QpaleoExod[m] (pre-Samaritan), 4QNum[b] (pre-Samaritan), 1QDeut[a] (Qumran practice), 2QDeut[c] (Qumran practice), 4QDeut[n] (pre-Samaritan), 4QJer[d] (LXX), 4QXII[c] (Qumran practice), 4QPs[b] (independent), 2QSir, MasSir V; 4Q*365* (= 4QRP[c]). While the great majority of the biblical Qumran texts reflect the MT,[54] only one of the texts in which the guide dots are found belongs to this group. This

48. Certain scribal markings found in 1QIsa[a], 1QS, and 1QSa are not known from other texts, because the latter two and the corrections in the former were produced by the same scribe.

49. E.g., 1QpHab, 1QMyst (27), 1QS, 1QSa and b, 4QpIsa[c], 4QTest (*175*), 4Q*502* ("rituel de mariage"), 4Q*503* (daily prayers), 4QDibHam[a] (*504*), *509* (PrFetes[c]), and *512* ("rituel de purification").

50. E.g., 1QS, 1QIsa[a], and 4QCatena[a] (*177*).

51. This sign occurs six times in the second part of 1QIsa[a], always coinciding with an open or closed section.

52. DJD 3.70.

53. For similar usages of red ink in Egyptian, Greek, and Roman documents, as well as references to usages mentioned in the Talmud, see the discussion in DJD 3.70 and in *Qumran Cave 4, VII: Genesis to Numbers* (DJD 12; ed. E. Ulrich and F. M. Cross; Oxford, 1994) 221–22.

54. See my "Groups of Hebrew Biblical Texts."

custom must have been used in particular outside of the circle of Masoretic texts, as well as in some 15 nonbiblical texts written in the Qumran scribal practice.

(13) According to rabbinic prescription, sheets of scrolls are to be joined by sinews of ritually clean cattle or wild animals. See *Sop.* 1.1:

והלכה למשה מסיני שכותבין על עורות בהמה טהורה ועל עורות חיה טהורה
ותופרין בגידן.

It is an oral prescription delivered to Moses at Sinai that ⟨all these⟩ shall be written on the skins of ritually clean cattle or ritually clean wild animals, and be sewn together with their sinews. . . .

On the other hand, Poole and Reed, upon investigation of "stitching material" say: "but examination showed that these were all of vegetable origin and most probably derived from flax."[55] It is now known, however, which texts were examined for this purpose. In his edition of 4QNum[b] (pre-Samaritan, Qumran practice), N. Jastram likewise concludes that the unraveling of the thread before col. XV suggests that it consists of flax rather than sinews.[56] Furthermore, the stitching material in 1QIsa[a] (Qumran practice) is described by Burrows[57] as "linen thread." A thorough investigation of the stitching material should be carried out, in order to find out which ones are made of animal sinews and which of flax, in the latter case in disagreement with rabbinic custom. The two texts quoted above that deviate from the rabbinic custom are non-Masoretic: 4QNum[b] and 1QIsa[a].

Conclusions

An investigation of the amount of (dis)agreement between individual scribal habits reflected in the Qumran scrolls and the rabbinic sources is valuable in its own right, and the relevant material has been presented above. It is now in order to attempt to distinguish between the *individual* Qumran texts with regard to their relation to the rules laid down in the rabbinic literature. My general conclusion is that texts of the Masoretic family adhere more closely to these rules than other texts, which in previous studies have been characterized as "Qumran practice," pre-Samaritan texts, texts close to the Septuagint, and nonaligned or independent texts. This conclusion is reached on the basis of negative evidence. That is, the evidence concerning Qumran texts that disagree with rabbinic regulations comes from non-Masoretic texts, while the evidence from texts that agree comes from the entire collection of the Qumran texts.

55. J. B. Poole and R. Reed, "The Preparation of Leather and Parchment by the Dead Sea Scrolls Community," in *Technology and Culture: An Anthology* (ed. M. Kranzberg and W. H. Davenport; New York, 1972) 143–68. The quotation is from p. 164.

56. DJD 12.217.

57. M. Burrows, *The Dead Sea Scrolls of St. Mark's Monastery* (New Haven, Conn., 1950) 1.xiv.

This conclusion has been reached without resorting to circular reasoning, since the characterization of the various groups of texts has been made previously on the basis of different (namely, textual) criteria.

My assumption concerning the two groups of texts thus suits hypotheses expressed previously about the background of the different texts of the Bible: the texts of the Masoretic family presumably derive from Pharisaic circles and would therefore be more likely than other texts to reflect the rabbinic prescriptions for copying texts. The other texts do not derive from Pharisaic circles and hence are expected to reflect only a certain amount of the prescriptions laid down in the rabbinic literature.

On the basis of the preceding analysis, I shall now list the (dis)agreements between individual Qumran texts and the rabbinic prescriptions. In most cases a remark on the textual character of the text is added in parentheses.[58]

Disagreement with Rules Prescribed by the Rabbinic Literature or Rules Not Mentioned in This Literature

(1) *Crossing out a word with a horizontal line* has been spotted in some 15 texts, among them 1QIsa[a] (Qumran practice) and 4QDan[a] (independent), as well as in the nonbiblical 4Q*491* (M[a]) and 4Q*501* (both written according to Qumran practice). This practice, known from Greek sources, is probably not mentioned in rabbinic literature.

(2) *Stichometric* arrangement: the Song of Moses in 4QDeut[q] (LXX and independent) and the Song of the Sea in 4Q*365*, frg. 6b (pre-Samaritan; Qumran practice) are not written according to the rabbinic regulations. See below concerning 1QDeut[b].

(3) *Guide dots* are found in several texts, for example: 4QGen–Exod[a] (proto-Masoretic); 2QpaleoLev; 4Qpaleo-Exod[m] (pre-Samaritan); 4QNum[b] (pre-Samaritan); 1QDeut[a] (Qumran practice); 2QDeut[c] (Qumran practice); 4QDeut[n] (pre-Samaritan); 4QJer[d] (LXX); 4QXII[c] (Qumran practice); 4QPs[b] (independent); 4QPs[f] (Qumran practice); 2QSir; MasSir V; and 4Q*365* (= 4QRP[c]). While the great majority of the biblical Qumran texts reflect the MT, only one of the texts in which the guide dots are found belongs to this group. This custom must have been used in particular outside of the circle of Masoretic texts.

(4) *Cancellation dots* are mentioned in rabbinic sources but with a different explanation. Such dots are found in several texts that reflect the Qumran practice of orthography and morphology: 1QIsa[a] as well as a long series of nonbiblical texts. Similar dots are found in 4QJer[a] (proto-Masoretic).

(5) *Parenthesis signs* have been spotted in 11QpaleoLev[a] (independent), 4QQoh[a] (Qumran practice), and in the sectarian texts 1QM and 1QS. This practice is not mentioned in rabbinic literature and probably is disallowed.

---

58. The characterizations are based on my article "Orthography and Language of the Hebrew Scrolls Found at Qumran" and on my monograph *Textual Criticism of the Hebrew Bible* (pp. 114–17).

(6) The following *papyrus* fragments have been preserved at Qumran: 4QpapIsa^p and 6Q*3–5, 7* containing fragments of Deuteronomy (?), Kings, Psalms (?), and Daniel. Several of the fragments are too small to determine their textual character, but the larger fragments of 1–2 Kings, and possibly also Daniel, are characterized as independent. The use of papyrus was not allowed for scripture according to the Talmud.

(7) Contrary to the rabbinic prescription, several *rents* in 1QIsa^a (Qumran practice) and 4QJer^c (proto-Masoretic) were stitched after the leather had been written on.

(8) *Writing on patching*, disallowed by rabbinic prescriptions, is spotted in 4QpaleoExod^m (pre-Samaritan).

(9) *Scribal markings* are found almost exclusively in the margins of compositions written according to the Qumran practice of orthography and morphology: 1QIsa^a, 4QCant^b (probably an abbreviated text), and a long list of nonbiblical texts. Furthermore, in two Paleo-Hebrew texts (4QpaleoExod^m [pre-Samaritan] and 11QpaleoLev [independent]), a large *waw* was written in the spaces between the paragraphs. It is also found frequently in a few texts written in the square "Assyrian" script: 4QPs^b (independent), 1QIsa^a, and 1QS. Rabbinic literature does not explicitly forbid scribal marks, but they would probably be disallowed by the stringent laws of copying.

(10) Use of *paragraph* indicators of different types in 1QIsa^a and in a long list of nonbiblical texts written in the Qumran practice of orthography and morphology. No such system is mentioned in the rabbinic literature.

(11) In 23 Qumran texts written in the square script, the Tetragrammaton and occasionally other divine names were written in the *Paleo-Hebrew* script. No explicit remarks against this scribal habit are found in rabbinic literature, but one may conclude that since the use of the Paleo-Hebrew script was forbidden for complete biblical texts, by implication individual words would also be excluded. At the same time, the concept of the sanctity of the divine names, which is behind the writing in Paleo-Hebrew characters, is in agreement with *y. Meg.* 1.71d (compare *Sop.* 4.1ff.).

(12) The *remodeling* of letters found in 1QIsa^a (Qumran practice) and in several sectarian texts (1QpHab, 1QH^a, 1QM, 1QS) is not mentioned in *Soperim* as a legitimate correcting procedure.

(13) The writing of *nonfinal* letters in final position, found mainly in texts written according to the Qumran practice of orthography and morphology, was not allowed according to rabbinic sources.

Agreement with Rules Prescribed in Rabbinic Literature

(1) *Spaces* were added between the biblical books in accordance with rabbinic regulations in MurXII, 4QpaleoGen–Exod^l, and possibly also in 4QGen–Exod^a (all three Masoretic family), and 4QExod^b (probably independent character). However, this rule is not adhered to in 4QLev^c (MT / Sam. Pent.),

which begins at the top of a column, or in 4QpaleoLev[a] (independent character) ending in the middle of a column but not being followed by Numbers. On the other hand, if the latter two scrolls contained a single biblical book only, the aforementioned prescription does not pertain to them.

(2) The stichometric arrangement of 1QDeut[b] and 4QpaleoDeut[r] follows the rabbinic rule for the writing of Deuteronomy 32. Both fragments reflect the text of both the MT and the Sam. Pent.

The great majority of the instances in which a scribal custom in the biblical Qumran texts can be identified as disagreeing with the rabbinic instructions are in texts that for other reasons have been labeled non-Masoretic. It should be remembered that the largest identifiable group of manuscripts from Qumran is Masoretic (some 40 percent).[59] At the same time, positive evidence for linking specific Qumran texts with the rabbinic prescriptions is very scanty at the level of scribal habits.

This temporary conclusion, which should be scrutinized further as more texts are analyzed, has a bearing on many aspects of the study of the Qumran texts. At the same time, the conclusion lends further support to the view that the Qumran scrolls should be subdivided into two main groups, texts copied by the Qumran community and texts copied elsewhere.[60]

---

59. For the statistics see the article quoted in n. 53.

60. See further my forthcoming article, *"Tefillin* of Different Origin from Qumran?" in *J. Licht Memorial Volume* (Jerusalem, in press). In this article an attempt is made to distinguish between *tefillin* written in the Qumran scribal system, probably reflecting the sectarians' *tefillin*, and *tefillin* agreeing with the rabbinic prescriptions in content.

ENGLISH ABSTRACTS OF HEBREW ESSAYS

King Solomon's Designation for Kingship in Biblical Historiography

Shmuel Aḥituv

King Solomon was neither David's firstborn son nor the senior surviving son after the death of Amnon and Absalom. Yet it was Solomon who succeeded David. In this study the author examines the various attitudes in biblical historiography towards the concept of Solomon's designation for kingship.

This concept developed in stages. The vision of the prophet Nathan in 2 Samuel 7 makes no mention of Solomon's designation. The first stage is discerned in the story of the death of David and Bath-sheba's illegitimate child, a story that ends with the birth of Solomon and disregards the three other sons born to Bath-sheba before Solomon (1 Chr 3:5). However, the story makes no reference to Nathan's vision.

The first reference to Nathan's vision is probably 1 Kgs 2:15a, 24. A further stage can be seen in the description of Solomon's kingship as an act of divine grace towards David, "You dealt most graciously with your servant my father David. . . . You have continued this great kindness to him by giving him a son to occupy his throne as is now the case" (1 Kgs 3:6), which is an elaboration of 2 Sam 7:15, "But I will never withdraw my favor from him."

The divine designation of Solomon as David's successor is expressed more explicitly in the deuteronomistic scriptures. It is retrospectively made clear that Solomon is the offspring spoken of in Nathan's vision. While this Deuteronomistic elaboration remains on the rationalistic level, the Chronicler depicts Solomon as being chosen for kingship from the womb, which is his interpretation of Nathan's vision.

Implicit Redaction and Latent Polemic in the Story of the Rape of Dinah

Yairah Amit

The story of the rape of Dinah and the subsequent bloody encounter between the sons of Jacob and the Shechemites provides for an interesting meeting of modern approaches to exegetical difficulties in a biblical narrative text.

The first part of the article contains a summary of the various approaches,
presenting their contribution to the implicit redaction method. The second part
deals with the latent polemic woven into this story. In the third and last part, an
attempt is made to prove the late date of this composition and its affinities to
the Holiness School.

The Date and the Meaning of the Prophecy against "Those Who Live in These Ruins in the Land of Israel" (Ezekiel 33:23–29)

Gershon Brin

The article deals with various issues concerning the above-mentioned
prophecy, tackling the problems of the date and the message of the unit
through analysis of its structure and idioms. The prophecy expresses Ezekiel's
attitude towards the inhabitants of Israel after the Exile of 587/586. The exact
date of this piece is established by comparing it with the parallel prophecy in
Ezek 11:14–21 on the one hand, and with the other prophecies in chap. 33 on
the other.

The succeeding prophecy in chap. 33 (vv. 30–33) deals with the attitude of
Ezekiel's audience in Babylon towards the prophet. By comparing the two
neighboring prophecies (vv. 23–29 and 30–33), one can evaluate the prophet's
relations with the two groups: those who are with him in the Exile and those who
remained in the land of Israel after the Exile.

The Origins and Development of the Expression מְגִלַּת סֵפֶר: A Study in the History of Writing-Related Terminology in Bibilical Times

Avi Hurvitz

The idiom מְגִלַּת סֵפֶר presents interesting problems on two linguistic levels.
First, as far as its *structure* is concerned, it is noteworthy that the components

of the idiom (סֵפֶר, מְגִלָּה)—each of which carries, semantically, the same basic notion of writing material on the one hand and the text written on it on the other—are combined, by means of the construct-state pattern, into a single expression. Secondly, as far as the *frequency* and *distribution* pattern are concerned, it is instructive to observe that the number of biblical occurrences is remarkably small (4×) and that they are attested in only three books: Jeremiah (2×), Ezekiel (1×), and Psalms (1×). These facts call for comment, since references to writing materials and written texts abound throughout the *entire* corpus of biblical literature. One may wonder, therefore, what the specific linguistic-historical background is behind the emergence of מְגִלַּת סֵפֶר and under what circumstances it found its way into biblical literature.

In an attempt to answer these questions, סֵפֶר and מְגִלָּה are first separately examined and the combined expression מְגִלַּת סֵפֶר is then discussed. Our basic argument is that סֵפֶר—widely taken as the standard West-Semitic lexeme for '(any written) document'—is replaced in Biblical Hebrew, in certain cases and under certain conditions, by its more recent competitor, מְגִלָּה. The word מְגִלָּה was extensively used in the Aramaic-speaking milieu, whence a whole set of similar terms related to writing and writing-materials were borrowed by Hebrew, particularly in the exilic/postexilic period (אִגֶּרֶת, דָּת, כְּתָב, etc.). It stands to reason, therefore, that מְגִלָּה in Biblical Hebrew is likewise a loanword from Aramaic (note that Arabic كَلّ is also considered to be of Aramaic origin). Chronologically speaking, however, the word מְגִלָּה seems to have been borrowed slightly earlier than אִגֶּרֶת, דָּת, and so forth, since it is already attested in Jeremiah, that is, at the end of the preexilic period. This conclusion, based on innerbiblical data, is supported by extrabiblical sources. Akkadian *magallatu* (also attributed by Assyriologists to Aramaic influence) first appears in documents that belong (roughly) to this historical period.

Accordingly, two conclusions may be suggested with regard to the origins and development of the biblical expression מְגִלַּת סֵפֶר: (1) The appearance of the lexeme מְגִלָּה on the biblical scene is only one case, among many others, reflecting the intensive impact of the rich Aramaic formulary in the sphere of writing-related terminology in biblical times, a formulary whose imprints may be found far beyond the narrow boundaries of the biblical corpus at our disposal; (2) the usage of the lexeme מְגִלָּה within Biblical Hebrew, whether standing alone or combined with the (semi-) synonymous סֵפֶר by means of a construct-state pattern, is indicative of a relatively late stage in the history of Biblical Hebrew. If the further suggestion is accepted that this "pleonastic" (or tautological) construct-state pattern is indicative of lateness as well, then our *lexicographical* analysis is also supported by *stylistic* considerations.

"And I Will Tell of All Your Work":
Faith and Belief in Psalm 77

Meir Weiss

In this study, the author argues that Psalm 77, the literary unity of which has often been disputed by scholars, is in fact an organic whole. The Psalm embodies an internal struggle in which the memory of a glorious past, arising in the psalmist's mind as a result of his present distress, undergoes a gradual transformation. First, it causes the psalmist to doubt whether God's providential care still exists, casting a growing darkness on the already-dim present. Thereafter, however, as he continues to ponder the past, the psalmist arrives at the conclusion that although divine providence exists eternally, its ways are utterly incomprehensible to man.

The Book of the Covenant Interprets the Book of the Covenant: The "Boomerang Phenomenon"

Yair Zakovitch

The "boomerang phenomenon" is the name I have given to a phenomenon that occurs in a variety of biblical texts and literary genres whereby a biblical text is interpreted by another biblical text, and the interpretation finds its way back to the original text, where it effects changes.

The Book of the Covenant—the oldest collection of laws in the Pentateuch—served as a foundation for later biblical law-collections, as interpreters found themselves having to reshape the ancient laws in order to meet the needs and ideologies of their own times. Towards the end of the process of the editing of the Pentateuch, the different law collections ended up side by side in the same book. Changes sometimes had to be introduced in order to overcome disagreements and contradictions between the ancient laws and their interpretations. The "boomerang phenomenon" points to one type of change, whereby the interpretations of the laws in the Book of the Covenant found in the newer law collections were then introduced back into the original laws. The present article discusses five examples of this phenomenon.

A Calendrical Scroll from Qumran Cave 4:
Mišmarot B^b (4Q321^a)

Shemaryahu Talmon and Israel Knohl

In this paper we publish a calendrical composition from Qumran, seven fragments of which were discovered among the Cave 4 finds. Drawing upon the known structure of the solar calendar of 364 days to which the Covenanters' community adhered and upon a more extensively preserved parallel scroll (4Q*321*) miš B^a, the text of eight columns of 4Q*321*^a miš B^b under review here can be confidently restored in its entirety.

The ancient author records seriatim two dates in every single month of the solar calendar over a period of six consecutive years. One date is fixed by the specification of the day in the week of service of a given priestly course, משמר, and the day in the solar month with which it coincides. We designate it X. The other date is similarly riveted to the משמרות roster and to the revolution of the solar year. But in addition it is also identified by the designation דוקה ,דוקו, or דוקה. We propose to derive this hitherto unknown term from דקק 'to become thin', rather than from דיק, a root that expresses 'exactitude' or 'precision', and take it to designate the night in the middle of the lunar month in which the moon begins to wane. X pertains to the night of the moon's total eclipse at the end of the month.

It should be stressed that calendrical documents like the one published here are not intended to provide overall "synchronization tables" between the solar and the lunar year, as is sometimes maintained. Rather, the specification of the moon's monthly "dark" phases and their equivalent dates in the solar calendar are intended to provide the *yaḥad* members with a means for avoiding, to the best of their ability, the "negative" dates in the moon's revolution that spell evil and potential disaster.

Towards the Structure of the Book of Kings:
Formulaic Synchronism and Story Synchronism
(1 Kings 12–2 Kings 17)

Zipora Talshir

The article discusses the structure and composition of the synchronized part of the book of Kings (1 Kings 12–2 Kings 17). A review of the studies, particularly of commentaries on the book of Kings, shows no little chaos regarding the identification of text units within this section. (Every scholar designates units as he sees fit, whether for reasons of content or on grounds of form criticism.) The research is characterized by a patent disregard for the structure imposed by the author of Kings himself. This attitude may be due to the conception of the author as a "mere" editor or compiler, rather than as the one responsible for the present form of the book.

The structure of this section was meticulously planned by its author. The synchronization between the kingdoms of Israel and Judah has been accomplished through two methods: first, by means of synchronizing formulae that impose a very clear technical structure on the material, rendering the description of each reign a self-contained literary unit; second, by interweaving the stories of the kingdoms in the instances where their history converges in a special fashion. The latter method is used for the reigns of Jehoram, king of Israel, Jehoram and Ahaziah, kings of Judah, and Jehu, king of Israel (2 Kgs 3:1–10:36), as well as for reigns of Jehoash, king of Israel, and Amaziah, king of Judah (13:10–14:22).

The author of this synchronized structure had access to the sources, and it is he who *combined* the different kinds of sources, both the archival material and the prophetic stories, within the "kingly" framework that he created for the book.

Cushan-Rishathaim (Judges 3:8–11): An Implicit Polemic

Bustenai Oded

The paper is an attempt to explain the hitherto enigmatic story about Cushan-rishathaim, its historiographic and historical aspects. From the historiographic point of view, the Cushan episode is an unrealistic story, compiled of vocabulary and phrases typical of the book of Judges. It was added by a compiler to the original work, which began with the Benjaminite story about the judge Ehud (Judg 3:12–20). The pro-Davidic/Judahite orientation detected in the Cushan story is complemented, I believe, by an implicit polemic against the house of Saul.

From the historical point of view, the story is based on a vague reminiscence about hostilities between Judahite/Kenizzite clans and a nomad tribe in southern Judah.

Complementary Fragments from the Cairo Genizah

Michael L. Klein

The arbitrary distribution of manuscripts from the Cairo Genizah to individual collectors and eventually to major libraries on three continents during the latter half of the nineteenth century is well known. This resulted in the fragmentation of many manuscripts into individual leaves or groups of pages dispersed over Oxford, Cambridge, St. Petersburg, Budapest, New York, Philadelphia, and elsewhere.

The present article presents newly discovered fragments from the collections of the Cambridge University Library and the Library of the Jewish Theological Seminary (New York) that contain complementary portions or variant versions of several Aramaic (targumic) poems that were part of the ancient Palestinian liturgical tradition or that served as introductory compositions for the Torah readings during the festivals.

Ruth 4:11 LXX: A Midrashic Dramatization

Alexander Rofé

A characteristic of Jewish Aggadah is its tendency to reshape biblical narratives by attributing distinct roles to heroes that had been represented in the Bible as acting in concert. A series of instances is quoted from: *t. Soṭa* 9:3–9; *b. Mak.* 23b; *Mek. de Rabbi Ishmael*, Tractate *Wayeḥi* §2 (end). The last instance has a parallel in Pseudo-Philo's *Antiquitates Biblicarum* (10:3) and the Samaritan *Memar Merqa* (4:8). The three sources describe the Israelites, when overcome by the Egyptians at the Reed Sea, as dividing into three factions: one resolved to commit suicide, another intending to capitulate to the Egyptians, and a third calling for resistance and fighting. The widespread diffusion of this particular legend and the wealth of the other material suggest that the said Aggadic quality developed relatively early, perhaps already in Hellenistic or Hasmonean times.

In Ruth 4:11 (MT) one reads: "All the people who were at the gate and the elders said: 'We are witnesses. May the Lord make the woman who is coming into your house like Rachel and Leah. . . .'" The Greek (LXX) version states: "All the people who were at the gate said: 'We are witnesses.' And the elders said: 'May the Lord make the woman who is coming into your house like Rachel and Leah. . . .'"

Which is the primary text? Ehrlich, Joüon, Kahana, and Robinson preferred the Greek; Bertholet, Nowack, Haller, Campbell, and Zakovitch opted for the MT. Now that the differentiation of roles has been established as an Aggadic quality, we can assert that the Greek of Ruth 4:11, with its distinction between the people who witness and the elders who bless, attests to a secondary Hebrew text that incorporated a Midrashic expansion in the course of the Second Commonwealth.

The Joseph Story: Legend or History?

Nili Shupak

A renewed treatment of the Egyptian features in the story of Joseph (Genesis 37–50) in the light of recent research shows that most of them relate to the New Kingdom Period. In particular, one of the most important of these features, the position of Joseph at Pharaoh's court, suggests that the original Joseph story was based on the autobiography of an Egyptian official of foreign (Semitic) origin. This individual rose to prominence at the court of one of the Eighteenth Dynasty kings, probably during the Amarna Period.

With the rise of the Northern Kingdom, this ancient Joseph story was reworked by a Hebrew writer, whose purpose was to legitimize the emergence of a king from the House of Joseph, to wit, Jeroboam son of Nebat.

INDEX OF AUTHORITIES

INDEX OF SCRIPTURE

423

Deuterocanonical Literature

New Testament

מִקְדָּשׁ, מִקְרָא, וּמָסוֹרֶת

מִנְחָה לִמְנַחֵם הָרָן

בעריכת

אבי הורביץ

אביגדור הורוויץ

מיכאל פוקס

מיכאל קליין

ברוך יעקב שורץ

נילי שצ'ופק

עריכה לשונית:

רות פידלר

התקנה והבאה לדפוס:

אמיתי שפיצר

סדר מחשב על ידי דעץ, ירושלים

Hebrew section typeset by *Daatz*, Jerusalem

תוכן העניינים של החלק העברי

רשימת המשתתפים

שמואל אחיטוב	אוניברסיטת בן־גוריון בנגב
יאירה אמית	אוניברסיטת תל־אביב
ג'ון אמרטון	אוניברסיטת קמבּרידג'
גרשון ברין	אוניברסיטת תל־אביב
משה גרינברג	האוניברסיטה העברית בירושלים
אליעזר גרינשטיין	בית המדרש לרבנים באמריקה
גרהם דיוויס	אוניברסיטת קמבּרידג'
ר"ו האלו	אוניברסיטת ייל
אבי הורביץ	האוניברסיטה העברית בירושלים
אביגדור הורוויץ	אוניברסיטת בן־גוריון בנגב
מאיר וייס	האוניברסיטה העברית בירושלים
יו ג"מ ויליאמסון	אוניברסיטת אוקספורד
ציוני זביט	האוניברסיטה למדעי היהדות, לוס אנג'לס
יאיר זקוביץ	האוניברסיטה העברית בירושלים
עמנואל טוב	האוניברסיטה העברית בירושלים
ריימונד ז'ק טורניי	אקול ביבליק, ירושלים
יעקב חיים טיגאי	אוניברסיטת פנסילבניה
שמריהו טלמון	האוניברסיטה העברית בירושלים
צפורה טלשיר	אוניברסיטת בן־גוריון בנגב
שרה יפת	האוניברסיטה העברית בירושלים
מרדכי כוגן	אוניברסיטת בן־גוריון בנגב
חיים כהן	אוניברסיטת בן־גוריון בנגב
פרנסואה לנגלמה	אקול ביבליק, ירושלים
קרול מיירס	אוניברסיטת דיוק
וויליאם מק־קיין	אוניברסיטת סנט אנדריוס
ג' אלברטו סוג'ין	סמינר וולדנסיאני, רומא
מגנה סיבו	הפקולטה החופשית לתיאולוגיה, אוסלו
נחום סרנה	אוניברסיטת ברנדייס
בוסתנאי עודד	אוניברסיטת חיפה
שלום פאול	האוניברסיטה העברית בירושלים
מיכאל פוקס	אוניברסיטת ויסקונסין, מדיסון
ריצ'רד אליוט פרידמן	אוניברסיטת קליפורניה, סן־דיאגו
סא־מון קאנג	סמינר פרסבטריאני, קוריאה
יעקב קוגל	אוניברסיטת הרוורד
מיכאל קליין	היברו יוניון קולג', ירושלים
רונלד קלמנטס	אוניברסיטת לונדון
ישראל קנוהל	האוניברסיטה העברית בירושלים
פרנק מור קרוס	אוניברסיטת הרוורד
הנינג גרף רוונטלוב	אוניברסיטת רוהר, בוכום
אלכסנדר רופא	האוניברסיטה העברית בירושלים
רולף רנדטורף	אוניברסיטת היידלברג
ברוך יעקב שורץ	אוניברסיטת תל־אביב
נילי שצ'ופק	אוניברסיטת חיפה

פרסום ספר זה נתאפשר בסיועם האדיב של:

נשיא האוניברסיטה העברית בירושלים

הקרן לחקר המקרא ע"ש פיליפ ופלורנס דבורסקי

המכון למדעי היהדות, האוניברסיטה העברית בירושלים

הפקולטה למדעי הרוח, אוניברסיטת חיפה

דר' ש"ז אברמוב וגב' אילה זקס אברמוב

קרן מוריה

דר' סא מון קאנג

הקדמה

ספר זה הוא ציון לדרכו רבת הפעלים של פרופסור מנחם הרן. בדברינו כאן נעמוד על מקצת שבחו של האדם; ואילו בדברי ההערכה, המופיעים בחלק הלועזי של הכרך, יסקרו הישגיו המדעיים.

מנחם הרן החל בלימוד המקרא כנער ברוסיה הסובייטית, כשהוא לומד תורה בסתר מפי מורה פרטי ששכר אביו. לאחר עליית המשפחה ארצה בשנת תרצ"ג, גדל מנחם בתל-אביב. הוא נלחם במלחמת תש"ח והמשיך את שירותו הצבאי כקצין מודיעין בצה"ל. מנחם הוכתר בשלושת התארים האקדמיים – בוגר, מוסמך, ודוקטור – על ידי האוניברסיטה העברית בירושלים. למוסד זה הוא הקדיש את חייו ובו פעל כל שנותיו, אם כי מעת לעת שימש גם כפרופסור אורח באוניברסיטאות שונות ברחבי תבל. בין הכא להתם השתתף מנחם גם בייסודם של החוגים למקרא באוניברסיטאות האחרות בארץ: אוניברסיטת תל-אביב, אוניברסיטת חיפה, ואוניברסיטת בן-גוריון בנגב.

זכינו אנחנו, חברי המערכת, להימנות על תלמידיו – ואחר כך עם עמיתיו – של מנחם ולפעול במחיצתו. הוא היטיב להדריך את צעדינו הראשונים בדרך החתחתים של עולם המחקר בחום לב ובמסירות, ואנו אסירי תודה לו על כך עד עצם היום הזה.

גם מנחם וגם רעיה אשתו הם נצר לשושלות של תלמידי חכמים, והם עצמם בנו בית נאמן למורשת זו. ביתם הוא בית ועד לחכמים, והם ידועים בירושלים במידת הכנסת האורחים שלהם. בחדר האורחים של רעיה זכינו להסתופף מאז היותנו תלמידים, ולהכיר שם רבים מטובי המלומדים בארץ ובעולם.

עוד כתלמידים ידענו להעריך את דבקותו של מנחם בכללי המשמעת שהעיסוק המדעי מחייב ואת יושרו האינטלקטואלי. תביעתו לבהירות הניסוח ולסברה ישרה באות לביטוי בכל הרצאותיו וכתביו. ידיעותיו בחקר המקרא מרשימות בהיקפן; ועם זאת, דומה מנחם לאותה נפה, שמוציאה את הקמח וקולטת את הסולת. איננו רץ לכל חידוש, ואת השיטות החדשניות ההופכות לאופנה בודק הוא בשבע בדיקות. דרישותיו המדעיות אכן היו לנו למופת. גם אהבתו העזה לימוד דבקה בנו. פרופסור הרן הצליח להחדיר אהבה זו, יחד עם תחושת חשיבותו של העמל בשדה המקרא, בקרב מאות סטודנטים לתואר הראשון, השני והשלישי ששהו במחיצתו.

ועוד ידו נטויה. במלוא כוחו מתמסר פרופסור הרן בימים אלה למפעלו החדש, בבקעה שהוא עצמו מצא והתגדר בה. בפרסום תוצאות מחקר זה, עתיד פרופסור הרן להטביע שוב את חותמו המיוחד על חקר המקרא – הן בארץ הן מחוצה לה. יהי רצון שנזכה ללמוד תורה מפיו וליהנות מידידות נפשו לאורך ימים טובים.

העורכים

ייעודו של שלמה למלכות בהיסטוריוגראפיה המקראית

שמואל אחיטוב

שלמה לא היה בכור בניו של דויד, אף לא הבכיר בבנים שנותרו לאחר מותם של אמנון
ואבשלום. בכל זאת שלמה הוא שעלה על כס דויד אביו, ובו ובצאצאיו נמשכה שושלת בית
דויד. במאמר זה נעשה נסיון לברר את הגישות השונות לעניין זה המשוקעות במקורות
ההיסטוריוגראפיים שבמקרא, ואת ההתפתחות הניכרת בהם.

א. חזיון נתן (שמ"ב ז 1–17)

הדיון דלקמן באחדותו או במורכבותו של חזיון נתן בשמ"ב ז בא לברר את השאלה האם נזכר
בחזיונו של נתן הנביא, או אף נרמז בו, ששלמה הוא יורשו המיועד של דויד, ובו תתקיים
הבטחת השושלת האמורה בחזיון.[1]
אחדותו הספרותית של שמ"ב ז היא אחדות שההיסטוריון המשנה-תורתי כפה על מקורותיו.[2]
אף קשה לראות בחזיון נתן יחידה אחידה מבחינת תוכנו וצורתו. נות מצא בו שלושה עניינים
שונים: בניין המקדש, ההכוונה האלוהית של תולדות ישראל והבטחת נצחיותה של שושלת
בית דויד.[3] ואילו קרוס, המוצא שבצורתו הנוכחית חזיון נתן משקף עיבוד משנה-תורתי, מפרק
אותו לשלושה חלקים: 'החזיון הקדום' (פסוקים 1–7), ההבטחה האלוהית (פסוקים 11ב–16),
וקטע קישור משנה-תורתי (פסוקים 8–11א).[4]

1   חוקרי המקרא הגיעו למסקנות שונות ואף מנוגדות בנוגע לאחדותו או מורכבותו של החזיון ולזמנו:
ולהאוזן ראה בו תוצר ספרותי של ימי יאשיהו; J. Wellhausen, *Die Composition des*
Hexateuchs und der historischen Bücher des Alte Testament[3], Berlin 1899 (repr.
1963), p. 255. לדעת רוסט, זהו חיבור מורכב, שנתלקט ונתלכד בתהליך ממושך סביב שני יסודות
מימי דויד; L. Rost, *The Succession to the Throne of David*, Sheffield 1982, pp. 35-
36. נות סבר שבשמ"ב ז משוקעת תעודה בת זמנו של דויד, אלא שנוספו לה תוספות שונות; M.
Noth, 'David and Israel in II Samuel', *The Laws in the Pentateuch and Other*
Studies, Philadelphia 1967, pp. 250-259. קויפמן ראה בשמ"ב ז פרק קדום מימי דויד, שאין
בו עיבודים משנה-תורתיים; ראה: י' קויפמן, תולדות האמונה הישראלית, ירושלים ותל-אביב
תרצ"ז–תשכ"ז, ב, עמ' 360, 369; 'הסיפורים על דוד ושלמה', מכבשונה של היצירה המקראית,
תל-אביב תשכ"ו, עמ' 178; 'נתן הנביא בחצר המלך', שם, עמ' 181. וייזר טען שפרשתנו היא יצירה
ספרותית אחידה מימי שלמה; ראה A. Weiser, 'Die Tempelbaukrise unter David', *ZAW*
77 (1965), p. 156

2   ראה F.M. Cross, *Canaanite Myth and Hebrew Epic: Essays in the History of the*
Religion of Israel, Cambridge Mass. 1973, p. 252

3   נות (לעיל, הערה 1), עמ' 250–251.

4   קרוס (לעיל, הערה 2), עמ' 254. 'החזיון הקדום' הוא פרוזה משנה-תורתית, לדעת קרוס, אלא שכאן
הוא מוצא גם חומר קדום, כולל שרידי חרוזים הניתנים לשחזור: 'אנכי ישב בבית ארזים // וארון ישב

נראה שיש בחזיון רק שני עניינים עצמאיים ושתי חטיבות עצמאיות: בניין המקדש ונצחיות
השושלת. נושא הכוונה האלוהית של תולדות ישראל אינו עומד בפני עצמו. הוא בא רק כדי
לנמק את סירובו של ה' לתוכניתו של דוד לבנות לו בית (פסוקים 5–7), והרי הוא משני. דברי
נתן אינם איסור חדמשמעי על בניין הבית. את האיסור יש להסיק מסקירת תולדות ישראל למן
יציאת מצרים ואילך. הסקירה מדגישה שה' התהלך באוהל ובמשכן, ומעולם לא ציווה לבנות לו
בית. בניין הבית פותח עניין ומסיים אותו. פסוק 7 חותם את עניין בניית בית ארזים לה'.
פסוק 8 פותח בעניין אחר, במלכות דויד ונצחיות שושלתו (פסוקים 8–16), שגם בו זרועים
רמזים לתולדות ישראל ולהכוונתו על ידי האל. גם כאן אין הרמיזות לתולדות ישראל עומדות
בפני עצמן. אי אפשר לעקרן מתוך הרצאת הדברים בלי שתהיינה תלושות ופורחות באוויר.

התיאור ההיסטורי אינו עקבי ורצוף, אף שלכאורה הוא נראה כך. אין כאן תיאור של תולדות
ישראל למן יציאת מצרים ועד לימי דויד המבקש לבנות בית לה', אלא שני נושאים נפרדים:
הראשון, נדודי ה' באוהל ובמשכן מיציאת מצרים ועד היום הזה (פסוקים 6–7), והשני,
הבחירה בדויד ובשושלתו, שבהשוואה לתקופת השופטים ושאול היא תחילתה של תקופת
מנוחה לישראל (פסוק 8 ואילך). המעבר מנושא לנושא ניכר לא רק מבחינה עניינית אלא גם
מבחינה צורנית. הרישא של פסוק 8 מפסיקה את שטף ההרצאה העוסקת בבניין בית לה'
ועוברת לדן בדויד וביתו.

מקובל במחקר לחבר את שני העניינים שבחזיון נתן על ידי הקבלת הכתובים 'האתה תבנה לי
בית לשבתי' (5ב) ו'בית יעשה לך ה' ' (11ב), ולפרשם כבריח המחבר את שני החלקים. אומרים
כביכול: לא אתה תבנה לי בית אלא אני אבנה לך בית. נות סירב לראות את שני הכתובים
הרחוקים זה מזה כמשלימים רעיון אחד.[5] ואכן, שני פעלים שונים משמשים בשני הכתובים,
בנ"ה לעומת עש"ה (בעל דה"י שינה מהמטבע המקורי והשתמש בלשון בנ"ה בשני המקומות).
יתר על כן, בעוד שבכתוב הראשון הנושא המודגש הוא תיבת 'אתה', בכתוב השני מודגשת
תיבת 'בית' במשמע בית מלוכה, שושלת. לוא היה כאן רעיון אחד היה הכתוב השני צריך
להדגיש את ה' כנושא.[6]

כנגד הכתוב 'האתה תבנה לי בית לשבתי' (5ב) נכון להקביל את הכתוב בפסוק 13א: 'הוא יבנה
בית לשמי'. שני הכתובים מדברים בבית המקדש, ואף הנושאים של שני הכתובים מקבילים
ומקומם בכתובים זהה מבחינת מיקומם התחבירי.[7] אלא שעוד יש לברר אם פסוק 13א הוא בן
זמנו של פסוק 5ב, ומה משמעותו של פסוק 5ב (וראה לקמן).

אחת מאבני היסוד להנחת אחדותה של הפרשה היתה השערתו של הרמן, ששמ"ב ז שייך
מבחינת הצורה והתוכן לסוג של ה'נובלה המלכותית' (Königsnovelle) המצרית, שבה האל
מתגלה למלך בחלום ומצווה עליו לבנות לו מקדש וכיוצא בזה. המלך הנפעם מקיץ משנתו,
מתייעץ בפומבי בחצרניו, ואלה מחזקים את ידיו למלא את מצוות האל.[8] אבל כאן חסרים כמה
מיסודותיו של הסוג הספרותי הנזכר: האל אינו מתגלה למלך בחלום ודורש לבנות לו מקדש.
אדרבה, דויד הוא היוזם, ולא כתוצאה מחלום אלא מהיקש הגיוני: 'אנכי יושב בית ארזים

בתוך יריעה' (שם, עמ' 255); אבל להבחנה של קרוס בין קטע הקישור המשנה-תורתי ובין ההבטחה
האלוהית אין אחיזה מספקת, לא מצד התוכן ולא מצד הסגנון המשנה-תורתי של כל הפסקה (פסוקים
8–16).

5   נות (לעיל, הערה 1), עמ' 251.
6   ראה נות, שם.
7   W. Caspari, *Die Samuelbücher* (KAT), Leipzig 1962, p. 428
8   S. Herrmann, 'Die Königsnovelle in Ägypten und Israel', *Wissenschaftliche Zeitschrift der Karl-Marx-Universität, Leipzig, Gesellschafts- und Sprachwissenschaftliche*, Reihe III (1953/4), Heft 1, pp. 51-62

וארון האלהים ישב בתוך היריעה' (פסוק 2). גם אם נאמר שנתן הוא נביא חצר, כלומר חצרן,
עודנו חסרים את ההתייעצות הפומבית עם החצרנים. לעומת התיאור של בניין מקדש ב'נובלה
המלכותית' המצרית, כאן האל דוחה את יוזמתו של המלך. הרי זה ניגוד גמור לז'אנר המצרי.
עוד זאת, התגלות האל שבה הוא דורש לבנות לו מקדש אינה בלעדית למצרים ונודעה גם
ממסופוטמיה.[9]

אין אפוא שום ראיה של ממש לאחדותו של חזיון נתן, לא מבחינת התוכן אף לא מבחינה
צורנית. אם נכונה ההשערה שפסוק 8א הוא המחבר את שני עניייני החזיון, ושאין פסוק 11ב
השלמה עניינית של פסוק 5ב, אולי יש לחלק את החזיון לשני חזיונות נפרדים. סברה זו ניתן
לאוששה גם על ידי בחינת סגנונה השונה של חטיבת הפסוקים 1–7 לעומת הפסקה 8–16:
החטיבה הראשונה כתובה בפרוזה ומתייחדת בשאלות רטוריות (פסוקים 5ב, 7), ואילו בחטיבה
השנייה ניתן למצוא שרידים של משקל ותקבולת.[10]

בחטיבה הראשונה של חזיון נתן אינגו מוצאים רמז להבטחת השושלת. את השאלה הרטורית
בפסוק 5ב: 'האתה תבנה לי בית לשבתי', אין לפרש: לא אתה תבנה לי בית לשבתי אלא איש
אחר יבנהו, כמו שנתפרש בפסוק 13א המאוחר. משמעות זו אינה יוצאת מדבריו נתן בפסוקים
6–7. משתמע מהם שנתן העמיד את רצונו של דויד לבנות לה' בית ארזים כמנוגד למסורת
הקדומה של האל השוכן בתוך היריעה.[11] אין בדברי נתן בחטיבה זו רמז להסכמה לבניין בית
לה' במועד מאוחר יותר, בניגוד למה שנאמר בחטיבה השנייה, שמכאן ואילך תתואר כחזיון
השני של נתן.

החזיון השני של נתן מתקשר לחזיון הראשון בהבטחה שזרעו של דויד אשר יצא ממעיו 'הוא
יבנה בית לשמי' (13א). אלא שכתוב זה נראה כמאוחר,[12] ופוגם באחדותה של היחידה. מובנו של
המונח בית בפסוק 11ב, 16א (וגם בתפילת דויד, שהיא תגובה על החזיון השני, בפסוקים 18–19,
25, 26–27, 29) הוא שושלת. הרי זה הרעיון העיקרי בחזיון השני – הבטחת השושלת
ונצחיותה. ואילו בפסוק 13ב בית הוא בית מקדש. בניגוד ללשון הסירוב שבחזיון הראשון,
'האתה תבנה לי בית לשבתי' (פסוק 5ב), שמאחוריה תפיסה מעין אנתרופומורפית של האל
היושב כביכול בבית שיבנו לו, נוקט פסוק 13א בלשון של עידון וזיכוך: 'הוא יבנה בית לשמי'.
שימוש מעודן זה הוא משנה-תורתי מובהק.[13] אישוש מה להשערה שפסוק 13א הוא תוספת
אפשר למצוא בהעדר כל התייחסות אליו בתפילת דויד. קשה להניח שפסוק 13א היה נותר ללא
התייחסות בתפילת דויד אילו היה מגוף דברי נתן. נראה שהפסקת רצף ההרצאה על ידי
התוספת המשנה-תורתית (פסוק 13א) גרמה לחזרה 'והכינתי את ממלכתו... וכוננתי את כסא
ממלכתו עד עולם' (פסוקים 12ב, 13ב).

אם נכון לראות בפסוק 13 תוספת משנה-תורתית, הרי שנונתקה החוליה המקשרת היחידה בין

---

9   לדוגמאות ראה מ' ויינפלד, עיונים בספרות נביאים ראשונים ובעריכתה, ירושלים תשכ"ו, עמ' 13
    ואילך; T. Ishida, *The Royal Dynasties in Ancient Israel: A Study on the Formation
    and Development of Royal-Dynastic Ideology* (BZAW 142), Berlin 1977, pp. 83-
    92. נימוקים נוספים לדחיית רעיון ה-Königsnovelle מביא קרוס (לעיל, הערה 2), עמ' 247–
    248, ולאחרונה V.A. Hurowitz, *I Have Built You an Exalted House*, (JSOTSup 115)
    Sheffield 1992, pp. 38-39, 57-58, 61-62, 82, 84-85, 86, 87, 88

10   H.P. Smith, *Samuel* (ICC), Edinburgh 1899, pp. 247f.

11   ראה G. von Rad, *Old Testament Theology*, I, London 1963, p. 61; W.V. Rabe,
    'Israelite Opposition to the Temple', *CBQ* 29 (1967), pp. 228-230

12   ראה ולהאון (לעיל, הערה 1), עמ' 257.

13   השווה M. Weinfeld, *Deuteronomy and the Deuteronomic School*, Oxford 1972, p.

שני חזיונותיו של נתן: חזיון הסירוב לבניין בית מקדש וחזיון שושלת בית דויד; ובשניהם אין שלמה מוזכר. החזיון הראשון כלל אינו עוסק בעניין השושלת, ואילו השני, המדבר בעיקר בשושלת בית דויד ובנצחיותה, אף אינו רומז לשלמה.

העדר רמז מפורש לשלמה בחזיון השני אומר דרשני. קויפמן טען שהפרשה קדומה, ויסודה ורובה מימי דויד: מלכות דויד מופיעה כאן כראשיתה של תקופה חדשה, כתקופת זוהר שתימשך לעולם; תיפסקנה הצרות של תקופת השופטים; המלכות וחסד ה' לא יסורו מבית דויד לעולם. אין בפרשה רמז לצרות של סוף ימי שלמה ולפילוג המלוכה.[14]

אופיו הקדום של החזיון השני עולה מהחשיבות הרבה המיוחסת בו להבטחת המלוכה לזרע דויד. הבטחת המלוכה לזרע המלך חשובה ביותר בעת עליית שושלת חדשה חסרת מסורת וביסוס. חריפותה של בעיית המשכיות השושלת בולטת בהדגשת המונח 'בית' = שושלת, ובהבטחת כינון הכיסא 'עד עולם' בחזיון השני, וכמותו בתפילת דויד. אלא שאי אפשר לפרש את החזיון לימי דויד, וכנראה גם לא לימי שלמה. יש מקום לסברה שפסוקים 14ב–15 כבר מושפעים מהמאורעות של פילוג המלוכה.[15] אף יש מקום לקשור את נבואת אחיה לירבעם במל"א יא 31–39 עם החזיון השני מבחינה עניינית וסגנונית. מבחינה סגנונית אפשר לגלות סימנים לתלותה של נבואת אחיה בחזיון נתן (ראה בייחוד מל"א יא 38א: 'ובניתי לך בית נאמן כאשר בניתי לדויד'), ואילו שמ"ב ז 14ב–15 רומזים כנראה לנבואת אחיה, או אף מבוססים עליה. אלא שאין הדברים יוצאים מגדר השערה.

ההנחה בדבר קדמותו של החזיון השני תתחזק יותר אם נקבל שאינו אחיד אלא מורכב. יש מקום להשערה שהגרעין המקורי של החזיון הוא פסוקים 8–9 העוסקים בדויד עצמו. פסוק 10 מניח לדויד ופונה לישראל. התיבות 'ולמן היום אשר צויתי שפטים על עמי ישראל' בפסוק 11 תלושות ואינן מתקשרות אל מה שלפניהן ואל מה שאחריהן. זליגמן סבר שהן וריאנט של פסוק 7א: 'הדבר דברתי אל אחד שבטי ישראל אשר צויתי לרעות את עמי את ישראל', שנשתרבבו משולי הגליון למקום לא מתאים.[16] התיבות 'והניחתי לך מכל איביך', שבהמשכו של פסוק 11, אינן מתקשרות אל 'והגיד לך ה'' וגו'. נראה ששיעורו של הכתוב היה 'והניחתי לך מכל איביך ואגדלך',[17] ואינו אלא וריאנט משנה-תורתי של הנוסחה הראשונית של פסוק 9: 'ואכריתה את כל איביך מפניך ואגדלך', ותיבת 'ואגדלך' נתרחבה אל 'ועשתי לך שם גדול כשם הגדלים אשר בארץ'. פסוק 12 נראה כמקורי (אבל התיבות 'אשר יצא ממעיך' יכולות להיות הרחבה משנית של 'את זרעך') והוא מתקשר אל פסוק 9. פסוק 13א הוא משנה-תורתי, והסיפא של הפסוק נתבררה למעלה כוריאנט של הסיפא של פסוק 12. פסוקים 14–15 נחשדו כמושפעים מהמאורעות של פילוג המלוכה (כאמור לעיל). פסוק 16 יכול היה להיחשב כמקורי אלמלא נחשד כמשנה-תורתי (השימוש במונח 'נאמן').

הפרשה כולה מורכבת אפוא משתי חטיבות ברורות, משני חזיונות, שהראשון נראה כקדמון ואף אחיד בעיקרו. לעומתו החזיון השני, העוסק בשושלת בית דויד, נראה כמורכב ומגובב. גרעינו המקורי נראה כנראה פסוקים 8–9, 11ב ('בית יעשה לך ה'' או כיוצא בו) ופסוק 12 (להוציא התיבות 'אשר יצא ממעיך'). ואם נניח שהחזיון מאוחר לימי שלמה, הרי שגם פסוקים 14–15 הם מגוף

---

14 י' קויפמן, תולדות האמונה הישראלית, ב, עמ' 170, 369; קויפמן אמנם מודה באפשרות שפסוקים 12–13 הם מימי שלמה, אבל במקום אחר טען שגם פסוק 13 נאמר קודם להולדת שלמה ('הסיפורים על דוד ושלמה' [לעיל, הערה 1], עמ' 178), ואין דבריו נראים.

15 השווה מ"צ סגל, ספרי שמואל, ירושלים תשכ"ז, עמ' רפ.

16 י"א זליגמן, 'סימנים לשינויים ולעיבודים עריכתיים בנוסחת המסורה ובתרגום השבעים', מחקרים בספרות המקרא, ירושלים תשנ"ב, עמ' 327.

17 זליגמן, שם, עמ' 327–328.

החזיון. מפסוק 16 אפשר לקיים את הרישא או את הסיפא שעניינם זהה, אבל לא את שניהם. רמיזה לשלמה כיורש, בונה המקדש, מצוינו רק בתוספת המשנה-תורתית, פסוק 13א: 'הוא יבנה בית לשמי'.

ב. שמואל ב יב, והיחס הכרונולוגי בינו לבין שמואל ב ז

זמנם של המאורעות המוזכרים בשמ"ב יב מעוגן במסגרת כרונולוגית ברורה, המלחמה בעמון. לעומת זאת המסגרת הכרונולוגית של שמ"ב ז מעורפלת. סמיכות הפרשיות בין שמ"ב ז לפרשת העלאת הארון בשמ"ב ו עניינית וסבירה. משהתבסס שלטונו של דוד בירושלים והעלה אליה את ארון האלוהים, ביקש גם לבנות לו בית ארזים. ואילו שמ"ב ז 1ב: 'וה' הניח לו מסביב מכל איביו', אינו אלא נוסחה משנה-תורתית שאין להיאחז בה. הרי שיש סיבה לאחר את שמ"ב יב לשמ"ב ז. יתר על כן, אין בחזיון נתן שבשמ"ב ז זכר לאירועים המוזכרים בשמ"ב יב. אין בהבטחת השושלת שבחזיון אף רמז לחטאו של דוד בבת-שבע, גם לא בפסוקים 14ב–15, הנראים כמאוחרים (ראה לעיל).

נראה שהגרעין המקורי של תוכחת נתן הוא בפסוקים 7–10. הקללה שבפי נתן קרובה לנבואות קדומות אחרות: לקללת בית עלי (שמ"א ב 31, 33; ג 14), לקללת בית יואב (שמ"ב ג 29) ולקללה לגיחזי ובניו (מל"ב ה 27). ראיה נוספת לקדמותה של הנבואה היא שלא נתקיימה. אין זו נבואה למפרע. פסוקים 11–12 נכתבו כנראה בהשפעת מעשה אבשלום בפילגשי אביו (שמ"ב טז 20–22). הרעה קמה על דוד מתוך ביתו, כדברי הכתוב כאן 'הנני מקים עליך רעה מביתך' (פסוק 11א), ובפומבי: 'ואני אעשה את הדבר הזה נגד כל ישראל' (פסוק 12), להתאים להתקוממותו של אבשלום ולמעשה המביש שעשה 'לעיני כל ישראל' (שמ"ב טז 22ב).

נבואת התוכחה החריפה של נתן והעונש: 'ועתה לא תסור חרב מביתך עד עולם' (פסוק 10א), אינם מתיישבים עם האמור בחזיון נתן על נצחיותה של שושלת בית דוד, ועל היחס בין האל ליורשו של דוד. לא היה זה מקום לחזיון האופטימי לאחר הקללה שבתוכחת נתן. על כרחך חזיון נתן אינו יודע על התוכחה והקללה, והסדר הכרונולוגי שנקבע בספר הוא אכן הסדר הנכון.

הסיפור על מות ממזרו של דוד מביא אף את הקורא למסיבות הולדתו של שלמה. לפי שמ"ב יב נולד שלמה לאחר מות בן הנאפופים של דוד ובת-שבע. לעומת עדות זו, שניתן לחשוד בה במגמתיות, בנסיון לטהר את שלמה,[18] להראות שלעומת הילד הראשון שמת בחטא הוריו, הורתו ולידתו של שלמה היו בטהרה (השווה פסוק 15: 'ויגף ה' את הילד אשר ילדה אשת אוריה לדוד' אל פסוק 24: 'וינחם דוד את בת-שבע אשתו ויבא אליה וישכב עמה ותלד בן' וגו'), מצויה עדות אחרת. עדות זו משיחה לפי תומה, ולכן עדיפה. בדה"א ג 5 נאמר: 'ואלה נולדו לו בירושלים שמעא ושובב ונתן ושלמה ארבעה לבת-שוע בת עמיאל. מסתבר שיש גרעין עובדתי בסיפור על מות הילד הראשון והולדת שלמה. גרעין זה הוא כנראה מות שלושת בניה הראשונים של בת-שבע, דבר שאיפשר את עלייתו של שלמה, אחרון בניה. שלמה נולד כנראה כמה שנים לאחר המלחמה בעמון, והיה הרביעי בבני בת-שבע.

מכל האמור לעיל עולה שמבחינה כרונולוגית יש להקדים את שמ"ב ז לשמ"ב יב. לפיכך לא יכול להיות בחזיון המקורי של נתן שום רמז לשלמה. את ראשיתו של התהליך המכשיר את שלמה למלכות אפשר למצוא בטיהורו של שלמה, שנולד מבת-שבע אשת דוד. המספר פוסח בסיפורו על הבנים האחרים שנולדו לבת-שבע קודם להולדת שלמה, כדי להציג את שלמה כראשון בניה של בת-שבע, ולייחס אליו את שבועת דוד לבת-שבע.

---

18   ראה א' אוארבך, המדבר וארץ הבחירה, תל-אביב תשי"ח, עמ' 233, הערה 46.

מיד עם סיפור הולדת שלמה מכריז המספר 'וה' אֲהֵבו' (פסוק 24), ומסמיך לכך את קריאת
שלמה בשם ידידיה ביד נתן הנביא (פסוק 25). כך השלים המספר את המעגל של טיהור מעשה
דויד והכשרת שלמה. נתן, שבא אל דויד להוכיחו על מעשהו באוריה ובת־שבע, הוא הסוגר את
המעגל וקורא לשלמה בן דויד ובת־שבע בשם ידידיה 'בעבור ה' ' (פסוק 25). המספר מנצל את
שמו השני של שלמה כדי לתארו כמי שמתאים למלכות. אם את השם שלמה לא דרש, הרי את
השם ידידיה דרש כידיד ה', אהובו, שנקרא כן 'בעבור ה''.

ג. התמלכות שלמה (מל"א א–ב)

קולמוסים הרבה שברו כל מי שעסקו במהימנותה של שבועת דויד לבת־שבע. האם באמת נשבע
דויד לבת־שבע שבנה שלמה ימלוך אחריו, או שמא ערמומיותו של נתן היא שהושיבה את
שלמה על כסאו של דויד הזקן? והרי נתן הוא הדמות היוזמת והמפעילה את בת־שבע בסיפור
ההמלכה, כאמור: 'ועתה לכי איעצך נא עצה... לכי ובאי אל המלך דוד ואמרת אליו הלא אתה
אדני המלך נשבעת לאמתך לאמר כי שלמה בנך ימלך אחרי והוא יֵשֵׁב על כסאי' וגו' (מל"א א
13–12).

השאלה כאן אינה רק מה מידת המהימנות ההיסטורית של שבועת דויד לבת־שבע, אלא בעיקר
כיצד ראה אותה המספר. האם האמין בה או שחשבה להמצאה, מתכניו של הנביא החרצן? אף
שניסוח הדברים מאפשר פירוש כזה, הרי רוח החיבור האוהד את שלמה, והעדר כל ערעור על
השבועה מאיזה צד שהוא, מקרבים את ההנחה שהמחבר האמין בשבועה זו.

חשוב יותר לציין, שבעת המאבק בין אדניהו לשלמה על ירושת הכיסא לא נזכר אף לא נרמז
חזיון נתן על שושלת דויד.[19] אכן חזיון נתן אינו יכול לשרת אף צד בעימות, שכן אפשר להסב
אותו על כל אחד מיורשי דויד.

את ראשיתה של הפרשנות לחזיון נתן כמוסב על שלמה ניתן לראות כבר בדברי אדוניהו במל"א
ב 15ב: 'ותסב המלוכה ותהי לאחי כי מה' היתה לו'. אבל את דברי אדניהו מוטב לפרש כראייה
לאחור: אכן נתברר 'כי מה' היתה לו', מאחר ששלמה הוא שאליו נסבה המלוכה. לא כן הדברים
בשבועת שלמה במל"א ב 24: 'ועתה חי ה' אשר הכינני ויושיבני (קרי) על כסא דוד אבי ואשר
עשה לי בית כאשר דִּבֵּר' וגו'. דברי שלמה תלויים בשמ"ב ז 11ב ומפרשים אותם.[20] רושם זה
מתחזק עוד נוכח קושי מסוים בדברי שלמה. הניסוח 'ואשר עשה לי בית' קשה, שהרי בשום
מקום לא נאמר שה' יעשה בית (=שושלת) לשלמה, ודאי שאין לדברים אלה מקום בשלב
מוקדם כל כך במלכות שלמה. אם נגרוס 'ואשר עשה לו (=לדויד) בית', הכל אתי שפיר,
והתלות בחזיון נתן ברורה. גם אם נניח ששבועת שלמה (מל"א ב 24) היא תוספת,[21] תגדל הסבירות של
תלותה בחזיון נתן, אלא שאז צריך יהיה ליחס את התלות לעורך ולא למספר הראשון.

ד. שלמה בגבעון (מל"א ג 4–15א)

הסיפור על ביקור שלמה וחלומו בבמה הגדולה אשר בגבעון מורכב, חלקו בעל אופי משנה־תורתי
וחלקו קדום יותר. החלק הקדום יותר והנוגע לבחירת שלמה הוא פסוקים 4–13, 15.[22] אופיו

---

19   ראה י' קויפמן, תולדות האמונה הישראלית, ד, עמ' 453–462.

20   ראה ש' זלבסקי, עליית שלמה למלוכה, ירושלים תשמ"א, עמ' 27.

21   כך, למשל, T.N.D. Mettinger, *King and Messiah*, Lund 1976, p. 30

22   ראה S.R. Driver, *An Introduction to the Literature of the Old Testament*, [1897],

הקדם-משנה-תורתי בולט כשמשווים אותו אל התוספות המשנה-תורתיות (פסוקים 2–3, 14).
המקור הקדם-משנה-תורתי מספר על הליכתו של שלמה לזבוח בבמה הגדולה אשר בגבעון,
ורואה את חלומו של שלמה כהתגלות אלוהים של ממש, בלי לחוש שיש פגם כלשהו במעשיו
של שלמה. לא כן התפישה המשנה-תורתית, הרואה חטא בקיום הבמות ומתייחסת בשלילה
לחלומות כאמצעי מאנטי. עורך מן האסכולה המשנה-תורתית הוסיף את פסוק 3, דברי
התנצלות והסבר להליכתו של שלמה לגבעון[23] (בעל דה"י מפתח את ההתנצלות: 'כי שם היה
אהל מועד האלהים אשר עשה משה עבד ה' במדבר' [דה"ב א 3]). גם תוכנו של החלום, והקשר
שלו לסיפור משפט שלמה (מל"א ג 16 ואילך) מלמדים על המקור הקדם-משנה-תורתי שלו. הוא
שייך לאותן סיפורים על חכמת שלמה ותפארתו (מל"א ה 9–14).[24]

חידושו של המקור הקדם-משנה-תורתי הוא בתפישת מלכות שלמה כחסד אלוהי לדויד, כמו
שנאמר: 'ויאמר שלמה אתה עשית עם עבדך דוד אבי חסד גדול... ותשמר לו את החסד הגדול
הזה ותתן לו בן יושב על כסאו כיום הזה' (מל"א ג 6). נראה שרעיון זה קשור במה שנאמר
בשמ"ב ז 15: 'וחסדי לא יסור ממנו' וגו', ושני הכתובים מוצאם מחוג אחד. כבר נאמר לעיל
(סעיף א) ששמ"ב ז 14ב–15 מושפעים כנראה מהמאורעות של פילוג המלוכה. מכל מקום,
כתובים אלו מעמידים במרכז לא את ברית ה' לדויד אלא את החסד שבשמירת הברית לדויד
ובניו (על חסד בהקשר של שמירת ברית, ראה שמ"א כ 8, וכן יהו' ב 12, 14; שופ' א 24).
הצגתה של ירושת כיסא דויד על ידי שלמה כחסד האל לדויד היא כנראה שלב ביניים בין
התפישה הרציונאלית של מל"א א–ב בעניין ירושת הכיסא, לבין התפישה הרואה בשלמה את
יורשו של דויד עוד קודם להיוולדו, ותולה את מלכות שלמה בהיותו בונה המקדש.

נסיון לקשור את סיפור שלמה בגבעון בייעודו למלכות עוד קודם שנולד, תוך הסתמכות על
דברי שלמה 'ואנכי נער קטן לא אדע צאת ובא' (פסוק 7ב), וייחוסו של הסיפור לסוג הספרותי
של ה'נובלה המלכותית' המצרית,[25] אינם עולים יפה. הדבר המשותף היחיד לסיפור על שלמה
בגבעון ול'נובלה המלכותית' המצרית הוא החלום. אבל חלום שלמה, שלא כקרוביו המצריים,
אינו מופיע במסגרת של כינוס חצרנים ואין עניינו במפעל בנייה מלכותי וכיו"ב. דברי שלמה
'ואנכי נער קטן' וגו', אינם כי אם דברי ענווה. שלמה מוצג כאן כמי שלא כמלך שליט ואדון לעמו, כי
אם כשליח הנושא את מעמסת העם (פסוקים 8–9). את דבריו נכון יותר להשוות לדברי
המנהיגים המבקשים להשתמט מעול המנהיגות: משה (שמ' ד 10 ואילך), גדעון (שופ' ו 15)
וירמיהו (יר' א 6); או אף אל אל ענוונותו של שאול (שמ"א י 22). אין כאן אפוא שום רמז או הד
לתפישה ששלמה נבחר למלוכה מבטן.

ה. ייעודו של שלמה למלכות

בתפישה המשנה-תורתית הקטעים המשנה-תורתיים הנוגעים לנושא הם: התוספות המשנה-
תורתיות לשמ"ב ז (עיין לעיל, סעיף א), מכתב שלמה לחירם (מל"א ה 16–19), וברכת שלמה
בעת חנוכת המקדש (מל"א ח 14–21).

גם אם יש רקע היסטורי מהימן לחליפת המכתבים של שלמה וחירם, וקשה לפקפק באפשרות

Meridian Books Edition, New York 1956, p. 191; M. Noth, *Könige* I (BK),
Neukirchen-Vluyn 1968, p. 46

23   פסוק 2 נראה כתוספת מיד אחרת, אולי מאוחרת יותר, ראה, למשל, *J. Gray, I & II Kings*
(OTL), London 1964, pp. 113-114, 116

24   ראה י' ליוור, 'ספר דברי שלמה', חקרי מקרא ומגילות מדבר יהודה, ירושלים תשל"ב, עמ' 83–92.

25   הרמן (לעיל הערה 8).

זו,[26] הרי המכתבים עצמם לא נשמרו. המכתבים כמו שהם לפנינו עברו עיבודים
משנה-תורתיים. גרעין ממכתבו של שלמה שרד כנראה במל"א ה 20, וגרעין מתשובתו של חירם
בפסוקים 22–23 שם. אבל גם אלו כנראה אינם כי אם תקצירים של המכתבים המקוריים.

העיבוד המשנה-תורתי של מכתבו של שלמה עולה מההנמקה הניתנת בו להימנעותו של דויד
מבניין המקדש: 'מפני המלחמה אשר סבבהו' (מל"א ה 17). ולעומת זאת שלמה יכול לגשת
לבניין הבית, כי 'עתה הניח ה' אלהי לי מסביב אין שטן ואין פגע רע' (פסוק 18). הרי זה אותו
נימוק שהעלתה התוספת המשנה-תורתית בשמ"ב ז 1ב לרצונו של דויד לבנות בית לה'.

על פי דעה נפוצה במחקר, תלוי תוכנו של מכתב שלמה לחירם בשמ"ב ז.[27] הקשר בין שמ"ב ז
13א למל"א ה 19 בולט לעין. נראה ששניהם יצאו מאותו חוג והם בני אותו זמן.

בכתובים המשנה-תורתיים אנו מוצאים את ראשיתה של התפישה הרואה את שלמה כמי
שנועד למלכות מבטן. אמנם הדברים אינם מפורשים, אלא בנוסח של 'הוברר הדבר למפרע'. כך
בשמ"ב ז 13ב, ובמל"א ה 19: 'והנני אמר לבנות בית לשם ה' אלהי כאשר דבר ה' אל דוד אבי
לאמר בנך אשר אתן תחתיך על כסאך הוא יבנה הבית לשמי'. כך גם בחזרה המילולית כמעט
על שמ"ב ז 13ב בנאום חנוכת המקדש: 'רק אתה לא תבנה הבית כי אם בנך היצא מחלציך הוא
יבנה הבית לשמי' (מל"א ח 19). השינויים נובעים רק משינוי המסיבות. פסוק 20 מחדש חידוש
גדול לגבי חזיון נתן. החידוש אינו בכך ששלמה מציג את עצמו כמי שבו מתקיים החזיון
(המעובד), כמי שבו נתקיימו דברי ה' בפי נתן הנביא, שהרי הדברים נאמרו כבר בשבועת שלמה
(מל"א ב 24; וראה לעיל, סעיף ג), אלא בהצגה המפורשת והנחרצת של הדברים: 'ויקם ה' את
דברו אשר דבֵּר וָאָקֻם תחת דוד אבי וָאֵשֵׁב על כסא ישראל כאשר דבר ה' ואבנה הבית לשם ה'
אלהי ישראל' (מל"א ח 20). כאן מתגלה בצורה תמציתית התפישה, שהורחבה בספר דה"י, בדבר
הועדתו של שלמה למלכות מבטן.

חשיבות רבה יש לייחס לכך שהמחבר כורך את בחירת שלמה בבחירת ירושלים ובבחירת דויד.
פסוק 16 מדבר בבחירת ירושלים כעיר שבה יבנה הבית, ובבחירת דויד לנגיד על ישראל (הנוסח
העדיף הוא של דה"י ב ו 5–6 והשבעים).[28] אבל בימי דויד עוד לא הושלמה מטרת הבחירה, שכן
הבית לא נבנה (פסוק 17), תפקיד זה נדחה לימי יורשו שבנה את הבית לה'. בניית המקדש
משתלבת בבחירת ירושלים — 'המקום אשר יבחר' — ומביאה את תהליך הבחירה לתכליתו,
הקמת הבית לה'. לא לחינם הזכיר כאן המחבר המשנה-תורתי את יציאת מצרים. הוא מתייחס
לחזיון נתן לאחר שעיבדו לצרכיו. לעומת הרעיון שה' לא ציווה לו לבנות לו בית מאז יציאת
מצרים ועד היום הזה, הוא מעמיד ניסוח אחר. הניסוח החדש אמנם דבוק מבחינה סגנונית
בנוסח הקדום של חזיון נתן, אבל מובנו נשתנה. המחבר המשנה-תורתי טוען שעד ה' לא
בחר בעיר מכל שבטי ישראל לבנות בה את הבית. עתה, משבנה שלמה את הבית והשכין בו את
הארון ובתוכו 'ברית ה' אשר כרת עם אבתינו בהוציאו אתם מארץ מצרים' (פסוק 21), קשר
את ברית סיני בבחירת ירושלים ובמלכות שלמה.

26 השווה J.A. Montgomery, *The Books of Kings* (ICC), Edinburgh 1951, p. 133
27 ראה מונטגומרי, שם.
28 התיבות 'ולא בחרתי באיש להית נגיד על עמי ישראל ואבחר בירושלים להיות שמי שם' נשמטו
מחמת שוויון הסיומות (הומיוטלאוטון); חסרונם בנוסח של מל"א מותיר את הפסוק קטוע. ראה
H.G.H. Williamson, *1 and 2 Chronicles* (NCB), Grand Rapids-London 1982,
p. 216

ו. שלמה בספר דברי הימים: המיועד מבטן

בעל ספר דה"י פיתח את הרמז המשנה-תורתי על ייעודו האלוהי של שלמה למלכות קודם
להיוולדו והדגישו חזור והדגש. על תפישתו יש ללמוד לא רק ממה שכתב בפירוש אלא גם מתוך
מה שבחר להשמיט ממקורותיו, מספרי שמואל ומלכים.

בעל דה"י השמיט מסיפורו את מסיבות הולדתו של שלמה. המחבר דילג על פרשת דויד
ובת-שבע, ואין בספרו אף רמז למעשה. הטעם לכך כפול: להעלים את חטאו של דויד בחיר ה'
ומשיחו (זה כנראה ראשיתו של התהליך המתבטא בדרשה המטהרת את דויד מחטאו: 'אמר ר'
שמואל בר נחמני אמר ר' יוחנן כל האומר דויד חטא אינו אלא טועה' [שבת נו ע"ב]) ולסכל כל
אפשרות למצוא פגם בשלמה בגלל מוצאו וממילא בכל השושלת. המחבר השמיט גם את סיפור
עליית שלמה למלכות שבמל"א א. הסיפור על התמלכות שלמה בגלל שבועת דויד לבת-שבע
עשוי היה לסתור את שיטתו בדבר ייעודו של שלמה למלכות מבטן.

המחבר, המעריץ את דויד, היה חייב לנמק בצורה חותכת ומשכנעת את העובדה שדויד לא בנה
את הבית לה'. הוא השמיט את הכתוב בשמ"ב ז, 1ב: 'וה' הניח לו מסביב מכל איביו', שהרי דויד
עוד נלחם הרבה אחר כך,[29] וסידר את כל פרשת מלחמות דויד בצורה שונה מזו של ספר
שמואל.[30] אבל לא הסתפק בכך, אלא העלה ממכתבו של שלמה לחירם את הכתוב 'מפני
המלחמה אשר סבבהו' (מל"א ה 17א), ופירשו לפי דרכו: דויד, שהיה איש מלחמות ושפך דם
לרוב, לא היה האיש המתאים לבנות מקדש לה', שכן ידיו היו מגואלות בדם (דה"א כב 8; כח
3).[31] ברור שאין לדבריו אחיזה בהשקפות התיאולוגיות של הדורות הקדמים, ודאי לא באלו
של תקופת דויד. דבריו מעידים על השקפתו שלו. הוא מתעלם לחלוטין ממלחמותיו של שלמה
ומכך שאף שלמה שפך דם, גם אם הוא לא כדויד אביו. הטשטוש והשכתוב באו לטהר את שלמה
ולהעמידו, תוך דרישת שמו (דה"א כב 9), כניגוד לדויד איש המלחמות.

בעל דה"י מפרש את חזיון נתן לשיטתו, ומשנה מן המקור שהיה לפניו. אמנם במקבילה
לשמ"ב ז בדה"א יז אין למצוא שינויים רבי משמעות, חוץ משינוי מגמתי אחד. את סירובו של
נתן לבניין הבית: 'האתה תבנה לי בית לשבתי' (שמ"ב ז 5ב), שפירושו: האתה, בן-תמותה,
תבנה בית לאלוהים, שעה שאני (ה') בחרתי לשכון באוהל, משנה בעל דה"י יז 4ב: 'לא אתה
תבנה לי הבית לשבת'. לעומת הלשון ההחלטית שבמקור, לשונו של בעל דה"י החלטית
פחות.[32] ואין המדובר ב'בית' אלא ב'הבית', הוא הבית שיבנה שלמה.[33] פירושו של בעל דה"י
לכתוב הוא: לא אתה תבנה את הבית אלא בנך. לבעל דה"י, הרואה את הדברים ממרחק, ברור
היה שאת חזיון נתן בשמ"ב ז יש לפרש על שלמה, ורק עליו.

בעל דה"י מפרש את הדברים בפאראפראזות של חזיון נתן שהוא שם בפי דויד: בצוואתו לשלמה
(דה"א כב 6 ואילך) ובנאומו לפני ראשי העם (דה"א כח 1 ואילך): באלו שמו של שלמה נזכר
במפורש. בעל דה"י דואג שששלמה ייזכר בהזכרות של חזיון נתן, ולא יהיה ספק כי שלמה הוא מי
שנועד למלוך ולבנות את בית המקדש (דה"א כב 9, 11; כח 6-5; השווה גם כט 1, 19).[34]

29 ראה P.K. McCarter, *II Samuel* (AB), New York 1984, p. 191; וכן ויליאמסון, שם, עמ'
134.
30 עיין W. Rudolph, *Chronikbücher* (HAT), Tübingen 1955, pp. 129, 139
31 ראה רודולף, שם, עמ' 131; ויליאמסון (לעיל, הערה 28), עמ' 134.
32 ראה A.C. Welch, *The Work of the Chronicler*, London 1938, p. 19
33 רודולף (לעיל, הערה 30), עמ' 131-129; ויליאמסון (לעיל, הערה 28), עמ' 134.
34 ראה R.L. Braun, 'Solomonic Apologetic in Chronicles', *JBL* 92 (1937), p. 507

בחירת שלמה, שרמז לכריכתה בבחירת ירושלים ובבחירת דויד מצינו בעיבודים המשנה-
תורתיים, מובעת כאן בפירוש ובהחלטיות. בעוד שבחירת ירושלים כבר היתה נתון שאין
צריכים להזכירו, שב בעל דה"י להזכיר את בחירת דויד מכל בית אביו ואת בחירת שלמה מכל
בני דויד (דה"א כח 4–5). אף אמר על שלמה על פי שמ"ב ז 14: 'שלמה בנך... כי בחרתי בו לי
לבן ואני אהיה לו לאב' (דה"א כח 6).

סיכום

ייעודו של שלמה למלכות הוא רעיון מתפתח בהיסטוריוגראפיה המקראית. חזיון נתן בשמ"ב ז
אינו יודע דבר על ייעודו של שלמה למלכות. שלב ראשון בתהליך אפשר למצוא בסיפור על מות
ממזרו של דויד, סיפור המסתיים בהולדת שלמה, תוך דילוג על שלושת בניה האחרים של
בת־שבע שנולדו לפני שלמה (דה"א ג 5). אבל עוד אין כאן התייחסות לחזיון נתן. התייחסות
ראשונה לחזיון נתן ניתן ניתן לגלות אולי במל"א ב 15ב, 24. שלב נוסף נרמז כנראה בתפישת מלכות
שלמה כחסד האל לדויד, 'אתה עשית עם עבדך דוד אבי חסד גדול... ותתן לו בן ישב על כסאו
כיום הזה' (מל"א ג 6), תוך תלייתו בכתוב בשמ"ב ז 15: 'וחסדי לא יסור ממנו'.
הדברים מתפרשים יותר בכתובים המשנה־תורתיים, אבל עודם בתחום הראציונאלי. למפרע
מתברר ששלמה הוא הבן שעליו דובר בחזיון נתן. לעומת זאת בעל דה"י כבר רואה את שלמה
כמי שנועד למלוכה מבטן, כמי שאליו נתכוון חזיון נתן.

עריכה מובלעת ופולמוס סמוי בפרשת אונס דינה

יאירה אמית

1. מבוא

פרשת אונס דינה (בר' פרק לד), המתארת את המפגש האלים בין בני יעקב לבין אנשי שכם,
מהווה נקודת מפגש מעניינת של גישות פרשניות עכשוויות להבנת טקסט הלקוח מן הסיפורת
המקראית, ולפתרון קשיים שעולים מתוכו. פרשה זו מעסיקה הן את אנשי הגישה
הפילולוגית־היסטורית, הן את החוקרים המזוהים עם הגישה שמקובל לכנותה ספרותית,[1] והן
את אלו השמים דגש על מעשה העריכה.

1.1 עיקר עניינם של בעלי הגישה **הפילולוגית־היסטורית** הוא שחזור התעודות המקוריות
המרכיבות את הפרשה, או חשיפת המסורות שהשפיעו על עיצובה, ומעקב אחר
תולדות הטקסט. את הכלים לשחזור מספקים ביקורת הנוסח וניתוח תופעות בכתוב, כגון:
כפילויות, ריבוי סגנונות ואי־התאמות מסוגים שונים.[2] בתהליך השחזור קובע החוקר את
הרקע ההיסטורי לכתיבת התעודה על תוספותיה ואלו חוגי יוצרים הותירו בה את חותמם.
ואולם התבוננות במצב המחקר של סיפור אונס דינה הוא דוגמא מאלפת למסקנות השונות
במחלוקת של הגישה הביקורתית, שלא הצליחה להכריע אם הפרשה משקפת מקור אחד,
ששולבו בו תוספות מאוחרות,[3] או שהיא תוצאה של שילוב שני מקורות או שתי

מסורות,[4] ואף לא השכילה לזהות את רכיבי הפרק.[5] ראוי לציין כי במקרים רבים שיטה זו
מסתייעת בכלים, שמדע הספרות מגדירם כטכניקות פואטיות, דוגמת: תשומת לב לסדר
מסירת הפרטים ולדחיית מתן אינפורמציה, מעקב אחר חלקן של הדמויות, אחר שינוי הדובר
ושינוי בנקודת התצפית או בסגנון, שימוש בחזרות ובכינויים, הופעת דברי שיפוט מטעמו של
המספר, ועוד. ואמנם כמה וכמה מן התופעות הנזכרות הוצגו כקשיים בפרשת אונס דינה. עם
זאת אצל חוקרים שונים התעוררה התחושה, כי במקרים רבים הקשיים שהוצגו הינם
מאולצים ומלאכותיים, וכי העלאתם נועדה לבסס את פירוק השלם למרכיביו. על רקע זה
צמחה הביקורת, הטוענת כי יש ופירוק הכתוב לרכיביו מגלה לא רק התעלמות מטכניקות
מעצבות, אלא גם העדר רגישות פסיכולוגית למגוון ההתרחשויות המרכיבות מציאות כלשהי.

1.2 חסידי **הגישה הספרותית**, לעומת זאת, טורחים לתאר בקפידה את דרכי העיצוב שהופעלו
בעיבוד הפרשה. נקודת המוצא שלהם היא, שהפרשה אחידה ואינה מהווה שילוב של מקורות.
לפיכך כל מה שהוגדר כקשיים או כזרויות, כגון אי–התאמות, חזרות וכדומה, הם רואים כחלק

---

4 כאמצעי מרמה, כבר מראשית המשא ומתן; ראה: A. Kuenen, 'Beiträge zur Hexateuchkritik. VI: Dina und Sichem', in *Gesammelte Abhandlungen zur biblische Wissenschaft*, Freiburg und Leipzig 1894, pp. 255-276. לרוב מייחסים החוקרים את הסיפור המקורי ל-J ומצטיעים על קדמותו. ראה, למשל, בפירוש של פון–ראד (A — *Genesis* ,G. von Rad [OTL], tr. by J.H. Marks, London 1961, pp. 325-330 (*Commentary* ושל שפייזר (E. Meyer,). לדעת מייר E.A. Speiser, *Genesis* [AB], New York 1964, pp. 266-268) הסיפור המקורי דן (*Die Israeliten und ihre Nachbarstämme*, Halle a. S. 1906, p. 420 בשמעון ובלוי בלבד, והתוספת מערבת את שאר האחים. זקוביץ Y. Zakovitch, 'Assimilation' in Biblical "Narratives" ', in J.H. Tigay [ed.], *Empirical Models for Biblical Criticism*, Philadelphia 1985, pp. 185-192), לעומת זאת, סבור, כי נקמת שמעון ולוי דוקא היא תוספת לסיפור הראשוני, לפיו אהב שכם את דינה, הגיע להסכם עם אחיה, אך הם רימו, רצחו ובזזו. לסיפור זה נוספו המוטיב המשני של האונס, שנועד לנמק את התנהגות האחים ולהפליל את אנשי שכם, ונקמת שמעון ולוי, התורמת להדגשת הממד המוסרי בהתנהגות האחים. ודומה לכך דעתו של סנדמל (S. Sandmel, *The Hebrew Scriptures*, New York 1963, pp. 365-366).
לעניין זה ראה לאחרונה: פירושו של וסטרמן (A — *Genesis 12-36* ,C. Westermann [*Commentary*, tr. by J.J. Scullion, London, 1985 [1981¹]], pp. 532-545); ואולם אין החוקרים תמימי דעים באשר לזהות בעלי המקורות. סקינר (J. Skinner, *Genesis* [ICC], Edinburgh 1930², pp. 417-418), שסיכם את התחבטות המחקר בנושא, פתר את הבעיה בקביעה שמדובר ב-J^X ו-E^X, שנערכו בידי P. מקורות אלו קרובים למקורות המוכרים, אך אינם חלק מהם. הוא מזכיר את דילמן (A. Dillmann, *Die Genesis* [KHAT], Leipzig, 1892⁶,) ואת דרייבר (S.R. Driver, *The Book of Genesis* [WC], London 1926¹²,) pp. 351-355 (pp. 302-308) כמי שאינם מהססים ליחס ל-P את המקור שאחרים מייחסים ל-E. וסטרמן, בעקבות ולהוזן, מסתייג לחלוטין מליחס את שני הסיפורים למקורות הקלאסיות או לקרובים להם. הוא מפריד בין הסיפור המשפחתי של A, שבמרכזו שמעון, לוי ושכם, השייך לתקופת האבות, לבין הדיווח השבטי של B, שבמרכזו בני יעקב וחמור, השייך לתקופת הכיבוש. רק שלב האיחוי של הסיפורים מאוחר ואין להקדימו לתקופת הגלות. לשלב זה אחראי מחבר שכבר הכיר את השקפת דב' ז והיה קרוב ללשון P. מעניינו שגם להמינג (S. Lehming, 'Zur Überlieferungsgeschichte von Gen 34', *ZAW* 70 [1958], pp. 228-250), הנאמן לחקר הסוגים, מבחין בתשתית הסיפור, שהועלה על הכתב בידי J, שני סיפורים פרימיטיביים, שאוחדו כבר בשלב שבעל פה באמפיקטיוניה של שכם.

5 סקירה שיטתית וממצה של המחקר הביקורתי מביא קוורס, המדגיש בדברי הסיכום הביקורתיים שלו, כי המחקר נכשל הן בנסיון לשחזר בפרק שני סיפורים שלמים ומובחנים זה מזה, והן בהבחנת התוספות לסיפור המקורי. לשיטתו, בר' לד 1–26 מהווה אחדות ספרותית כמעט שלמה. אחדות זו מתקיימת בתנאי שהתיבה 'שני' והשמות 'שמעון' ו'לוי' יוצאו מפסוק 25. ראה: P. Kevers, 'Étude Littéraire de Genese XXXIV', *RB* 87 (1980), pp. 38-46

מן התכסיסים הרטוריים והתחבולות המעוצבות שנקט אותם הכותב.[6] נשאלת אפוא השאלה: האם ניתוח בשיטה זו אינו חוטא באותה מלאכותיות שחטאו בה קודמיו. הם הניחו מראש של כל הסיפור כולו אינו אחיד וראוי לחצותו לשניים, ואילו הוא מניח מראש את אחדות הסיפור ומתעלם מן התוספות שכן דבקו בו, ומתאמץ להצדיק גם את זרויותיו הנובעות מחוסר האחדות'.[7] סוגיה נוספת, שנראית לי לא פחות משמעותית, נוגעת להתעלמות – האופיינית לבעלי שיטה זו – מהרקע ההיסטורי–החברתי של שלב העיצוב. כך, למשל, ספק אם עקרון מאחד של העדר איזון בין שני מעשי אלימות הטריד מבחינה מוסרית, וממילא גם פואטית, את הכותב המקראי; שהרי לדידו הריגת חיים – שבלשון הקורא המודרני תכונה: 'רצח עם' – יכולה להתפרש כמצווה וכהיענות לצו האל.[8] השאלה העקרונית היא אפוא: האם הפרשנות שמציעים בעלי גישה זו הולמת את החשיבה הקדומה על ערכיה ועל האסור והמותר שבה.

1.3 בעלי הגישה השלישית, המתחקים אחר **מעשה העריכה**, יוצרים מעין סינתזה בין הקטבים הנזכרים. הם מניחים, כי לעורכים הקדומים היה מעמד של מחברים וכי עורכים אלה, במקרים רבים, לא הסתפקו בצירוף מקורות ובשילוב הערות. פעמים עיצבו את החומרים שהגיעו לידיהם על פי עיקרון אחדות מרכזי, שמעניק משמעות ליצירה על מרכיביה; ופעמים יצרו חומרים שהשלמו את צורכיהם. מטבע הדברים, ככל שעבודת העורכים היתה יסודית וטובה, כך נמנעת מקורא היצירה החדשה האפשרות לשחזר את מקורותיה המשוערים. מחד גיסא, הנחה זו מהווה בלם בפני מסקנות הגישה הפילולוגית–היסטורית, שבנסיון לשחזר את תולדות הטקסט מצליחה לפורר יצירות, שאין עילה לפקפק באחדותן, ומאידך גיסא, בעלי גישה זו אינם

6   השווה: מ' שטרנברג, 'איזון עדין בסיפור אונס דינה: הסיפור המקראי והרטוריקה של היצירה הסיפורית', הספרות ד (1973), עמ' 193–231. לטענתו, הפרק מסופר בדרך שתיצור בקורא תגובה מאוזנת כלפי אונס דינה וכלפי נקמת האחים, שכן על סמך העובדות לבדו 'לא יהיה מנוס מהרשעה בוטה של האחים על הדיספרופורציונאליות המחרידה של תגובתם' (שם, עמ' 195). האיזון העדין הוא העקרון שמאחד את הסיפור ומסביר את כל זרויותיו, וצורכי האיזון אף הכתיבו את עיצוב דמות יעקב כ'פחות סימפאטית', ואת בידולם של שמעון ולוי מהדמות הקולקטיבית של האחים (שם, עמ' 214–215). ניתוחו מאיר את אותם מקומות דווקא, שקודמיו הציגו כעדויות מכריעות לקשיים ולאי-התאמות, כביטוי למערך האסטראטגיה הרטורית. מחקרו היה מניע לכמה וכמה מחקרים, המטעימים את הגישה הספרותית. כך אררט, המצביע על עקרון אחדות שונה, הנובע מתחום שונה של הפרשה: בר' לג 18–לה 8. לדעתו, סיפור דינה הוא חוליה בהצגת ה'עוקב' ההופך ל'ישורון', שמשמעו: עיצוב דמות המאמין של יעקב, המטוהר מכל עורמה ומרמה (נ' אררט, 'קריאה על-פי ה"סדר" בסיפור המקראי: לאיזון הקריאה בפרשת דינה', הספרות 27 [1978], עמ' 15–34). גישה ספרותית נוספת, המטעימה את הדינאמיקה של תהליך הקריאה ואינה נוטלת מן הסיפור את אחדותו, מציג מ"א כספי, 'מעשה דינה – מקרא, קורא ומדרש', בית מקרא צד (תשמ"ג), עמ' 236–255. ואילו ביקורת ברוח פמיניסטית על פרשנותו של שטרנברג, ראה לאחרונה אצל: .D.N. Fewell & D.M Gunn, 'Tipping the Balance: Sternberg's Reader and the Rape of Dinah', *JBL* 110 (1991), pp. 193-211. זו נענתה בתגובה החריפה של: ,M. Sternberg, 'Biblical Poetics and Sexual Politics: From Reading to Counter-Reading', *JBL* 111 (1992), pp. 463-488

7   י' זקוביץ, 'על מצב המחקר – סקירה על המחקר הספרותי של המקרא בישראל', ידיעון האיגוד העולמי למדעי היהדות, כ (תשמ"ב) עמ' 27.

8   רגישות לנושא הנורמאטיבי הראתה ח' נסים, 'הערות על ניתוח הסיפור המקראי למאמרו של מאיר שטרנברג "איזון עדין באונס דינה"', הספרות 24 (1977), עמ' 136–143. נסים מדגישה, כי הרגשת האיזון בסיפור נובעת מקובעות הגישות שהמספר מציע, וזו מותירה את הקורא כשלבו חלוק בין שתי מערכות נורמאטיביות. הקורא בן זמננו רשאי, לדעתה, לתת את מלוא אהדתו ליעקב, לדינה, לשכם, או לאחים כרצונו.

מתכחשים לאפשרות קיומם של מוקדי מתח, שחדרו ליצירה במהלך שנות מסירתה וטרם התקדשותה, ואינם מגייסים תחבולות פואטיות, כדי להצביע על אחדות במקום של ריבוי. כמו כן, אין הם מתעלמים מן האתגר לשחזר את הרקע ההיסטורי של עיקר מעשה החיבור והעריכה.[9]

בחלקו הראשון של המאמר אאיר את תרומת הגישה המתמקדת במעשה העריכה להבנת הפרשה ולפתרון קשייה.[10] בחלקו השני — אצביע על פולמוס סמוי הגלום בפרשה זו, ובחלק השלישי אתמקד בשאלה: 'ומי כתבן', ואעלה השערה באשר לבית המדרש האחראי לעיצובה של הפרשה.

2. עיון בפרשת אונס דינה לאור הנחותיה של העריכה המובלעת

פירוש הסיפור על פי השיטה המניחה קיומה של עריכה מובלעת קובע כנקודת מוצא כי מרכיביו השונים של הסיפור קשורים זה בזה ובהצטרפותם נועדו לבטא את מעשה העריכה. לפיכך עם ההתקדמות בקריאת הרצף המספר מתגלה עקרון האחדות המרכזי, שהוא העקרון המונח בתשתית מעשה החיבור, והוא שהנחה את העריכה לדורותיה. מצד אחר, יש רמה גבוהה של סבירות, כי במהלך השנים חדרו לטקסט ודבקו בו גם זרויות, שאין לראות בהן חלק אינטגרלי ממשמעותו. לכן, גילויי נתונים שאינם משתלבים עם עקרון האחדות המרכזי מצריך לנסות ולהבין את המימצאים בטקסט הנתון. יתרה מזאת, ההתמקדות בשאלת העריכה תובעת התייחסות לא רק לרכיבים השונים הבונים את הסיפור ולאינטגרציה הקיימת ביניהם, אלא גם להשתבלות הסיפור בהקשר הקרוב (הספר או מחזור הסיפורים) ובהקשר הרחב (ההיסטוריוגראפיה המקראית).

2.1 בדיקת ההקשר הקרוב מורה, כי שהותו של יעקב ליד שכם והאירועים הקשורים לאותו מרחב ולאותה יחידת זמן נכללים ביחידה: לג 18–לה 5, וכי סיפור האונס והנקמה (פרק לד) מהווה יחידה מובחנת. הפסוקים העוטפים את סיפור האונס (לג 18–20 ו-לה 1–5) קושרים אותו עם ההקשר הקרוב של נדודי האבות. פסוקי מסגרת אלו מטעימים, כי מסעות יעקב הם חזרה על מסעות אברהם. יעקב בא למקומות שבהם שהה אברהם ועושה מעשים דומים: בונה מזבחות ואף קונה אדמה, כך שהשיבה למקומות אלו ממממשת את הכלל: 'מעשה אבות סימן לבנים'.[11] הנושא המרכזי של קטעים אלו הוא: היחסים שבין האב הקדמון לאלוהיו. ואילו בסיפור המובחן, שעניינו אונס דינה ותוצאותיו, שם ה' אפילו אינו נזכר, ובמרכז הבמה ניצבים בני יעקב מול שכם וחמור. אפשר אפוא לראות בפרק לד יחידה מובחנת, ששולבה בתוך מסעות האב הקדמון יעקב.

---

9   הצגה מפורטת של השיטה ראה בספרי: ספר שופטים — אמנות העריכה, ירושלים, תשנ"ב; ועיין במיוחד בעמ' 3–24.

10   ראוי לציין, כי לצד שלושת דרכי הפתרון שהצגתי היו גם גישות איזוטריות, שטענו כי בר' לד הוא יחידה מקורית שלמה ואחידה, שאפשר לנמק את הקשיים הקיימים בה בהנחות שונות, כגון: סיפור ארוך שקוצר, סיפור שמשקף את הפסיכולוגיה של מחברו, סיפור שבעיות סוציולוגיות או אנתנולוגיות גרמו לקשיים הקיימים בו, ועוד. ראה אצל קוורס (לעיל, הערה 5), עמ' 44–45.

11   עיקרון שחזור בפרשנות של קאסוטו לספר בראשית. וראה למשל: מ"ד קאסוטו, פירוש על ספר בראשית, ירושלים, תשכ"ה[4], עמ' 205; הנ"ל, 'בראשית', אנציקלופדיה מקראית, ב, ירושלים תשי"ד, עמ' 328, 332.

2.2 עלילת **היחידה המובחנת** מורכבת מכמה וכמה אירועים, הקשורים זה בזה בקשר של סיבה ומסובב. הסיפור פותח באונס ובנסיון לכפר עליו באמצעות נישואים, ומסיים בנקמה אכזרית על מעשה האונס, למרות נכונות האשם למלא אחר כל תנאי הנישואים שהוצגו לפניו. התבוננות בעלילה מנקודת מוצא זו, של אונס ותוצאותיו, מצביעה על היותה מורכבת מחמישה שלבים. השלב הראשון עוסק בהצגת הבעיה: דינה בת יעקב, שיצאה 'לראות בבנות הארץ', נאנסה. האפשרות לפתרון נראית מיידית וקרובה, כי הנסיך שאנס התאהב בנערה, דיבר על לבה ואף הצהיר באוזני אביו על רצונו לקחתה לו לאשה (פסוקים 1–4). השלב השני מתאר את הדרך להשגת הפתרון: הצדדים נפגשים ומנהלים משא ומתן בנושא הנישואים (פסוקים 5–19). מבחינת הקורא, המשא ומתן מסתבך, כי המספר מודיע לו שהצד הנפגע, בני יעקב, אינו מתכוון לכבד את ההסכם שיושג ואת המשתמע ממנו, ומדיניותו אינה אלא מרמה (פסוק 13). בשלב השלישי נעשה צעד נוסף להשגת הפתרון. צעד זה תורם להעמקת הסיבוך ומצעידו לקראת משבר, כי תושבי שכם כולם מלו עצמם כמתחייב מן ההסכם (פסוקים 20–24). בשלב הרביעי מתברר לקורא, כי הדרישה לימול שימשה תכסיס לביצוע הנקמה הקשה והאכזרית באנשי שכם (פסוקים 25–29). שלב הנקמה נפתח בתיאור מעשה שמעון ולוי, שביצעו את הרצח ושחררו את אחותם. האחים האחרים עסקו בביזה ובלקיחת שבויים. בשלב החמישי והאחרון מוכיח יעקב רק שניים מבניו, את שמעון ואת לוי, על שהרגו כל זכר בשכם. שמעון ולוי, לעומת זאת, משוכנעים בצדקת דרכם (פסוקים 30–31).

2.3 התבוננות ברצף העלילתי מעוררת אצל הקורא תהייה, וזו יכולה להצביע על **מוקד מתח עלילתי**, שראשיתו בשלב הרביעי והוא כולל גם את השלב החמישי: מדוע רק שמעון ולוי תקפו את העיר ושחררו את אחותם? לא זו בלבד שהתכנית היתה משותפת לכלל האחים והשניים פעלו מכוח החלטה קולקטיבית, אלא שלפעולת נקם מסוג זה היה ראוי לגייס כוח גדול ככל האפשר. יש אף מקום להמשיך ולשאול: מה עשו כל האחים בשעה ששניים מהם הרגו כל זכר בעיר ושחררו את אחותם? האם המתינו להודעת שמעון ולוי, כדי שאפשר יהיה לפתוח בשלב הביזה? מדוע הפנה יעקב את תוכחתו רק כלפי שמעון ולוי ולא כלפי כל האחים – הרי תכנית הנקמה באמצעות מילה היתה משותפת לכולם, ואין היא מבטאת את רצונם של שמעון ולוי לבדם? לפיכך, התוכחה של השלב החמישי, המופנית רק כלפי שניים אלה, יוצרת מוקד מתח מקומי. אין לפתור קושי זה בטענה, שיעקב פנה רק לאחראים על ההתרחשות, שהרי אם שמעון ולוי לא היו רוצחים את תושבי העיר, אין משתמע מכך שכל האחים האחרים לא היו בוזזים, או רוצחים ובוזזים. מה עוד, שאין ולו רמז להסתייגות האחים מן הרצח האכזרי. יתרה מזאת, די בחלקם של האחים בביזה חסרת המעצורים כדי להוכיחם, שהרי זו מספקת כדי להבאיש את ריחו של יעקב בקרב יושבי הארץ. וכן, האם העובדה, שבנוסף על הביזה שבו האחים גם את הנשים והטף, אינה חמורה ורואיה לתוכחה? התיאור הגדוש של המספר (פסוקים 27–29), המפרט את הביזה ומזכיר את לקיחת הנשים והטף, מאלץ את הקורא להתייחס לחלקם בנקמה ולכך שאין לנקות את האחים מאשמת 'הבאשה', ולטעון שהביזה אינה אלא תוצאה של הרצח. אפשר אפוא לסכם ולומר, כי הרצח והביזה הם צדדים שונים של אותה נקמה, שהתאפשרה בזכות תכנון מרמת המילה, שבה היו שותפים כל האחים.[12]

---

12 לרמב"ן, המניח כי גם יעקב היה שותף למרמת המילה, יש השגות נוספות: 'ויש כאן שאלה, שהדבר נראה כי ברצון אביה ובעצתו ענו, כי לפניו היו, והוא היודע מענם, כי במרמה ידברו, אם כן למה כעס? ועוד: שלא יתכן שיהיה רצונו להשיא בתו לכנעני אשר טימא אותה. ורבים ישאלו: ואיך עשו בני יעקב הצדיקים המעשה הזה לשפוך דם נקי'. ראה פירושו לפסוק 13, וראה גם נ' ליבוביץ, עיונים בספר בראשית, ירושלים, תשכ"ו, עמ' 264–269.

מוקד מתח זה מועצם גם על ידי ההקשר. מן ההמשך למדים, שיעקב לא הסתפק בתוכחה המיידית ולפני מותו גזר על שמעון ולוי להיות שבטים חסרי נחלה (בר' מט 5–7). קישור 'ברכת יעקב' עם הסיפור מעורר תמיהה באשר לתמיכת האל. מרצף המסופר אפשר להבין כי האל תמך במעשה בני יעקב, כולל במה שעשו שמעון ולוי. הוא הזים את חשש האב הקדמון, ויושבי הארץ לא רדפו אחרי יעקב ובניו (בר' לה 5); מצד אחר, ההיסטוריוגרפיה המקראית מצביעה על תמיכה אלוהית שונה, שהרי 'ברכת יעקב' התממשה, והשבטים שמעון ולוי לא זכו בנחלה.

לאור כל האמור לעיל נראה כי בעיית זהות הנוקמים והקשר בין הנקמה לתוכחה היתה נעלמת, לו בני יעקב היו מופיעים כגוף אחד, ובשום שלב לא היה המספר מבדל את שמעון ולוי; וכן, לו היתה ברכת יעקב נבחנת לעצמה ובלא כל קשר לסיפורנו. לפיכך משכנעת הטענה, כי הקושי בסיפור נובע מהוצאת שמעון ולוי מכלל האחים ומהצגתם כאשמים יותר. הסיפור מתקדם ברצף הגיוני עד פסוק 25 (ראה לעיל, הערה 5), והבעיות השונות עולות בשלב הנקמה והתוכחה. לפיכך, השמטת התיבה 'שני' והשמות 'שמעון ולוי' (ראה פסוק 25 ופסוק 30), יכולה לסייע לארגון חומרי העלילה לרצף נמשך, שאין עמו מוקד מתח עלילתי. מסקנה זו אינה מצביעה על גילוי סיפור קדום, המשקף מאורע היסטורי כלשהו,[13] אלא על העובדה, שהוצאת מוקד המתח מאפשרת הצעת מסגרת פרשנית, שבכולתה לנמק את פרטי הסיפור.

2.4 בדיקת המסגרת הפרשנית היא מציאת עקרון האחדות המרכזי, שהוא הקו המנחה של העריכה בסיפור זה. נראה לי, כי כל חומרי הטקסט, חוץ מסטיית העריכה הקשורה בשמעון ולוי, מתארגנים סביב קו מנחה אחד, המנמק את הקשיים שהציגו הפרשנים השונים (ראה לעיל, הערה 2), והוא, כניסוחו של אהרליך, בהקדמתו לפירוש הפרק: 'פרשת דינה כתובה בתורה להודיעך כמה היו האבות נזהרים מהתחתן בכנענים, שאפילו זו שנבעלה לא נתנה לבעל לאשה.'[14]

2.4.1 קו מנחה זה מנמק בראש ובראשונה את חומרי התשתית של העלילה: אונס ונישואים כפתרון. חשוב לציין, כי העלילה אינה מתמקדת באונס. האונס נזכר רק בשלב האקספוזיציה, כמניע עלילתי, ואילו הסיפור כולו מוקדש לבחינת הנישואים כפתרון, או להבהרה, כי יש לדחות פתרון זה על הסף, למרות יתרונותיו.

נבדוק אפוא את יתרונות הצעת הנישואים במקרה שלפנינו:

א. פתרון מקובל במקרה אונס: '...ולו תהיה לאשה אשר ענה תחת אשר ענה לא יוכל שלחה כל ימיו' (דב' כב 28–29).[15]

ב. פתרון שבמקרה מסוים זה יש לו יתרון, כי הנישואים אינם נכפים על האנס, היות שזה התאהב בקורבנו. כמו כן, הנישואים מבטלים את בעיית שילוח האשה.

13 מרבית הפרשנים מוצאים בסיפור זה הד היסטורי לכיבוש ישראלי מוקדם של שכם, או למגעים בין
    העברים לכנענים לפני כיבוש הארץ. כך למשל נילסן: -E. Nielsen, Shechem — A Traditio
    Historical Investigation, Copenhagen 1955, pp. 259-283; G.E. Wright,
    Shechem — The Biography of a Biblical City, New-York 1965, pp. 19-135. מ' הרן
    ('פרקי שכם', ציון לח [תשל"ג], עמ' 1–31) טוען, כי הפרשה אינה אלא 'סיפור נובליסטי', שאין בו
    גרעין היסטורי של מאורע אלא יחסי האיבה בין הישראלים לעיר הכנענית, שאפיינו את התקופה
    שקדמה לאבימלך. תפישת הסיפור כפאראדיגמה הציע לאחרונה נ' נאמן, 'פרשת "כיבוש הארץ" בספר
    יהושע ובמציאות ההיסטורית', בתוך: נ' נאמן וי' פינקלשטיין (עורכים), מנוודות למלוכה — היבטים
    ארכיאולוגיים והיסטוריים על ראשית ישראל ירושלים תש"ן, עמ' 343–344.

14 א"ב, אהרליך, מקרא כפשוטו, ב, ניו־יורק 1969 (1899–1901), עמ' 95.

15 השווה שמ"ב יג 11–16. גם תמר רואה בנישואים פתרון לאונס, ובשילוחה — רעה גדולה יותר.

ג. יתרון הפתרון אף מועצם כאשר מדובר ביורש העצר ובאביו, 'נשיא הארץ', המוכנים למלא אחר כל תנאי שהצד הנפגע וחסר הזכויות יטיל עליהם.

ד. פתרון מועדף, כאשר מדובר בפיתויים כלכליים של אזורי סחר, בטחון מדיני ובאפשרות להגיע אל המנוחה ואל הנחלה. כך עתידים בני יעקב לזכות בחבל ארץ שיוכלו להיאחז בו, ולא להסתפק בחלקת השדה שאביהם קנה מחוץ לעיר (בר' לג 19).

נמצא, כי נישואים, שהם ציר מרכזי בעלילה זו, והם פתרון מעוגן בחוק במקרה רגיל של אונס, אינם אפשריים במקרה שלפנינו, חרף כל היתרונות הטמונים בהם. משום שהפעם מדובר בחיוי, הנמנה עם שבעת עמי כנען, שעליהם נאמר: 'ולא תתחתן בם' (דב' ז 3).[16]

מסקנה נוספת של ניתוח זה היא: אין מקום לטענה כי מוטיב האונס משני הוא, שהרי מוטיב זה מהווה עילה להצעת הנישואים, דהיינו, הוא מניע את עלילת הסיפור כולו.

2.4.2   כדי לחדד את בעיית האונס שלא ניתן לכפר עליו בנישואים, מקפיד המחבר בבחירת הכינויים; הוא חוזר ומדגיש כי דינה היא **בת לאה אשר ילדה ליעקב** (פסוק 1), והיא **בת יעקב** (פסוק 3). לחזרה יש אפוא מגמה להדגיש את המוצא. למספר חשוב להודיע, כי דינה היא צאצא 'טהור' של משפחת בית האב, ולא בת אחת הפילגשים. מבחינת הקורא, המודע לנורמות המקראיות בנושא הנישואים עם כנענים (וראה להלן, סעיף 2.4.7), התחיל הסיבוך כבר עם הדיווח על האונס. קורא זה מבין, כי מוצא הגיבורים אינו מאפשר פתרון של נישואים. המספר מפנה את תשומת לב הקוראו לסוגיית הנישואים עם יושבי הארץ, שהם הכנענים, גם על ידי החזרה על המלה 'ארץ' בצירופים האלה: 'בנות הארץ' (פסוק 1), ו'נשיא הארץ' (פסוק 2), ותושבים אלה הם חיוים. בהמשך נזכר גם 'ישב הארץ' (פסוק 30), שהם הכנעני והפריזי.[17]

2.4.3   הקו המנחה המוצע אף מבהיר מדוע מוקדש זמן הסיפֵּר הארוך יחסית לסצינת המשא ומתן, ובה מציעים חמור ושכם את הנישואים כפתרון, שמשמעו התמזגות של שתי האוכלוסיות זו בזו (פסוקים 5–19), ועיין גם בדברי השכנוע של חמור ושכם לבאי שער עירם פסוקים 20–24). נראה, כי הסיבה לדיספרופורציה זו קשורה בחשיבות הניתנת בפרשה לבחינת ההיבטים השונים של נושא הנישואים. המספר מתגבר מסגרת הֶקשר זו בדרך של חזרה; יש דמיון בין דברי חמור (פסוקים 9–10) לבין דברי בני יעקב (פסוק 16), ולדברי חמור אל אנשי עירו (פסוק 21). החזרות, המרחיבות את מסגרת זמן הסיפור המוקדש לנושא הנישואים, מצביעות על הקשר שבין מבנה הסיפור לבין משמעו.

2.4.4   גם המילה, שהיא חלק אינטגרלי מהתפתחות העלילה, משרתת את הקו המנחה. ביצוע תנאי המילה אפשר לבני יעקב, לדברי יעקב, שהיו, לדברי המספר, 'מתי מספר', לנקום ביושבי העיר הכואבים ולבטל את עסקת הנישואים. כמו כן, פיתוח עלילתי זה ממחיש את הרעיון, כי נישואים אלה פסולים מכל וכל. אפילו נכונות אנשי שכם להיכנס בבריתו של אברהם אבינו אינה מקנה לגיטימציה לנישואים עם חיוי. לתכסיס המילה יש אפוא משמעות תימאטית מכרעת. המילה מסבכת את שאלת הנישואים ומחדדת את המסר: איסור הנישואים עם יושבי הארץ חל גם על אלו שנימולו. המספר מתגבר את ביקורתו על רעיון הנישואים בין דינה לבין

---

16   התעלמות מעיקרון זה של הסיפור מוצאים בדברי לוצאטו: 'והיו דבריהם נגד השכל, כי אמר שהיה לוקח אותה לאשה, לא היה כבודם מזולזל אלא מתרבה...'; ש"ד לוצאטו, פירוש שד"ל על חמשה חמשי תורה, תל-אביב תשכ"ה, עמ' 141.

17   ראוי לציין, כי התיבה 'ארץ' חוזרת בהמשך בהקשר של נישואים שיש עמם הבטחה לישיבה בארץ (פסוקים 10, 21).

שכם הנימול, בשימו בפיהם של בני יעקב דווקא את הבקשה, הבלתי אפשרית מבחינת התפיסה המקראית: להיות 'לעם אחד' (פסוק 16).[18]

2.4.5   דחיית האינפורמאציה בדבר מקום הימצאה של דינה מבהירה בדיעבד לקורא, כי בשלבי המשא ומתן הוחזקה דינה בביתו של שכם (פסוק 26). מידע זה במקום שיבוצו מעצים אצל הקורא את התחושה, כי המילה שימשה מוצא של אין ברירה, תכסיס בידי החלשים כנגד החזקים מהם, המחזיקים באחותם.

2.4.6   התערבויות המספר חיוניות לחידוד הקו המנחה:

א. המחבר, המעוניין שקוראו יפרש את המסופר לא רק כמקרה ספציפי, אלא כפרדיגמה ליחסי ישראל והכנענים, מנמק את כעסם של בני יעקב באמצעות משפט אנאכרוניסטי מחושב: 'כי נבלה עשה בישראל' (פסוק 7, והשווה לשמ"ב יג 12–13; שופ' כ 6, 10; דב' כב 21 ויהו' ז 15). אזכור שמו הלאומי של יעקב, ישראל, רומז לכלליות הבעיה ומפקיע אותה מן המסגרת המשפחתית.

ב. במהלך המשא ומתן, לאחר שחמור סיים לתאר את הפיתויים הנלווים אל הצעת הנישואים, מתערב המספר, והוא מקדים ומודיע לקוראו, כי אין בני יעקב עתידים להתפתות להצעה זו, וכי הצעת המילה אינה אלא תכסיס של מרמה (פסוק 13). ההודעה המקדימה היא הבעת דעה עקיפה של הכותב, שאפשרות זו אינה קיימת, והיא יכולה לשמש אך ורק כתכסיס. התערבות זו חיונית אפוא להכוונת הקורא בתהליך הקריאה ולחידוד המסר.

ג. המחבר, המעוניין לרכך ביקורת אפשרית על השימוש במילה כתכסיס של מרמה, מוסיף את שיפוטו, כי בנסיבות הקיימות יש הצדקה לדרך המרמה: 'אשר טמא את דינה אחתם' (פסוק 13; וראה גם פסוק 27).

2.4.7   גם בדיקת מידת ההתאמה של העקרון המנחה את עריכת הסיפור (עריכה מובלעת) עם קווי העריכה של הספר (ההקשר הקרוב) מעלה, כי לפנינו נושא שחוזר ונשנה לאורך ספר בראשית. הוא עולה לראשונה בבר' כד: '...אשר לא תקח אשה לבני מבנות הכנעני אשר אנכי יושב בקרבו' (פסוק 3ב), ולאחר מכן בדברי יצחק ליעקב: 'ויצו עליו לאמר לא תקח אשה מבנות כנען...' (בר' כח 6). הוא אף משתמע מהתנהגות עשו, שבשלב ראשון נשא לנשים את יהודית בת בארי החתי ואת בשמת בת אילן החתי, והן היו 'מרת רוח ליצחק ולרבקה' (שם, כו 34– 35; וראה גם: כז 46). ואמנם בהמשך מסופר: 'וירא עשו כי רעות בנות כנען בעיני יצחק אביו; וילך עשו אל ישמעאל ויקח את מחלת בת ישמעאל בן אברהם אחות נביות על נשיו לו לאשה' (כח 8–9). לנישואי האבות ובניהם יש אפוא משמעות אידיאולוגית מכרעת.

2.4.8   המספר מבטא את ביקורתו על פתרון הנישואים, שמציעים שכם וחמור אביו, גם באמצעי העקיף של ציטוט והרמזה ללשון החוק והתוכחה, האוסרים נישואים עם כנענים;[19] והשווה לכתובים:

בר' לד 9:   בנתיכם תתנו לנו ואת בנתינו תקחו לכם.

שמ' לד 16:   ולקחת מבנתיו לבניך וזנו בנתיו אחרי אלהיהן והזנו את בניך אחרי אלהיהן.

דב' ז 3:   ולא תתחתן בם; בתך לא תתן לבנו ובתו לא תקח לבנך.

שופ' ג 6:   ויקחו את בנותיהם להם לנשים ואת בנותיהם נתנו לבניהם ויעבדו את אלהיהם.

---

18   בפסוק 22 נאמרים הדברים מפיהם של חמור ושכם. בנוסח השומרוני ובתרגום השבעים מקדימה את הצירוף 'עם אחד' כ"ף הדמיון. אין ספק, שנוסח המסורה מחריף את הבעייתיות.

19   השווה: עז' ט 1–2, 12; י 2, 10–17; נחמ' י 31; יג 25; וכן: מל' ב 10–12. בכתובים אלה, שעניינם נישואים עם נוכרים, הניסוחים קרובים.

כתובים אלו מורים, כי לביטול הנישואים יש משמעות תימאטית עמוקה גם בהקשר הרחב של מערכת החוק וההיסטוריוגראפיה המקראית.

נתונים מצטברים אלו מבססים את המסקנה, כי **העקרון המובלע**, שמנחה את העריכה המעוצבת, **הוא הזהרה מפני נישואים עם יושבי הארץ הכנענים**. השערה זו מהווה מסגרת הֶקשר אינטגראטיבית, שמנמקת הן את רוב חלקי הטקסט והן את אופן עיצובם.

2.5 עד הנה עסקתי בחלקו האינטגראטיבי של הטקסט הנתון. עתה עולה ביתר חומרה שאלת מוקד המתח העלילתי: מה גרם להבלטת חלקם של שמעון ולוי בפרשת הנקמה? במלים אחרות, מה גרם לעורך כלשהו להחדיר לסיפור מרכיב שמפר את האינטגראציה של המסופר? נראה, כי הפתרון לשאלה זו קשור בצורך לנמק את ברכת-קללת יעקב בבראשית מט 5–7 (הקשר הקרוב). כבר שד"ל טען, כי 'הסיפור הזה נכתב להבנת דברי יעקב בברכותיו...'. טענתי היא שיש לישם את דבריו לא על הסיפור כולו, אלא על שילוב שמעון ולוי בלבד.[20]

2.5.1 טענה זו נשענת על ההקשר הרחב, דהיינו על הצורך לנמק את מעמדו המיוחד של שבט יהודה לאורך ההיסטוריה, משמע – בהיסטוריוגראפיה המקראית. כידוע, בסדר לידת השבטים ובברכת יעקב מופיע יהודה במקום הרביעי, אך במציאות זכה שבט זה בבכורה המעשית. מטבע הדברים מצאה העריכה לנכון לנמק את גורל השבטים שנדחו מן הבכורה, וחיפשה סיפור להיתלות בו.[21] הפתרון שנמצא לראובן, בכור לשבטים, הוא פרשת ראובן ובלהה (בר' לה 21–22). נותר אפוא למצוא סיפור, שיענה על השאלה: כיצד איבדו גם שמעון ולוי את זכות הבכורה, וזו הועברה לבן הרביעי – יהודה. לפיכך נראה שעורך מאוחר כלשהו מצא בפרשת אונס דינה תשובה על השאלה.

2.5.2 עורך זה בחר לקשור את דברי יעקב דווקא עם סיפור אונס דינה, משום שאפיינו אותו סממנים של נקמה, המלווה בכעס רב, מרמה, שימוש אכזרי בחרב ותוכחה. אלו יכלו להתפרש כקשורים במעשה הנקמה, הנשקף מן המסורת המיוצגת ב'ברכה', משום הופעת הביטויים: 'כלי חמס', ו'כי באפם הרגו איש', ומשום העמדה המסויגת של יעקב: 'בסודם אל תבא נפשי'.[22] הקישור בוצע על ידי הבלטת חלקם של שמעון ולוי בתיאור הנקמה ובידולם מהדמות הקולקטיבית של האחים (פסוקים 25, 30). מטבע הדברים יצר מעשה השילוב בעיות בהמשך הסיפור, כמו, למשל, ההפרדה בין רוצחים לבוזזים, או תיאור שאר האחים כמי שמגיעים רק לאחר שהראשונים יצאו.[23]

2.5.3 יתרה מזאת, העיון בתוכחת יעקב (פסוקים 30–31) והמרת הפנייה לשמעון ולוי בפנייה לכלל האחים תורמים גם לעיצוב העימות האנאלוגי של הדמויות הפועלות: חמור ובנו מול שכם מול יעקב ובניו. חמור מופיע לאורך כל הסיפור לצד שכם, בנו, ואף אפשר להבחין במעין חלוקת

---

20 שד"ל (לעיל, הערה 16), עמ' 139. והשווה: זקוביץ (לעיל, הערה 4), עמ' 175–196.

21 ראה גם: בר' כט 31–35. בספר בראשית מקבל צורך זה את ביטויו גם בשילוב פרשת יהודה ותמר (פרק לח) במסגרת סיפור יוסף, וכן בעיצוב המקנה לאורך הסיפור עדיפות לדמות יהודה על זו של ראובן. בעל דה"י מתמודד עם סוגיה זו באופן שונה, והשווה דה"א ה 1–2.

22 על רופפות הקישור אפשר, למשל, ללמוד מן העובדה, שבסיפורנו אין רמז לעיקור שוורים.

23 פרשנים שונים עמדו על הקשיים בטקע זה. דילמאן (לעיל, הערה 4, עמ' 374–375) רואה בפסוקים 27–29 שרבוב מאוחר. גם סקינר (לעיל, הערה 4, עמ' 421) שוקל אם פסוקים אלו הוחדרו בידי מי שהכיר את במ' לא 9–11. פון-ראד (לעיל, הערה 3, עמ' 325) – בתגובה על פסוק 27 – שואל אם לא מדובר בגרסה חלופית, שסיפרה על ההתקפה על כל בני יעקב. לאחרונה הציע קווֶר (לעיל, הערה 5) לחתום את הסיפור בפסוק 26.

תפקידים בין האב לבן: הדברים השקולים נאמרים מפי האב, המבוגר, ואילו הדברים המוגזמים ('הרבו עלי מאד מהר ומתן', פסוק 12) וההתנהגות חסרת המעצורים, שראשיתה באונס ואחריתה במילה ('ולא אחר הנער לעשות הדבר', פסוק 19), מיוחסים לבן. יעקב, לעומת זאת, אינו ניצב לצד בניו. מיד עם ראשית הופעתו הוא מתואר כמחריש, ואילו הבנים מתוארים כבעלי כושר החלטה, תכנון וביצוע. אין הוא נזכר בשום שלב של המשא ומתן, ורק כשנודע לו על מעשה בניו בשכם, הוא חושש ומוכיח. הבנים, לעומת זאת, מתגלים כמי שמוכנים להגן על כבודם ועל עקרונותיהם בכל דרך אפשרית, ממרמה עבור לנקמה וכלה במחאה על התוכחה: 'הכזונה יעשה את אחותנו' (פסוק 31), שהרי ביטול הנישואים מותיר את כבוד דינה מחולל. נמצא כי הוצאת שמעון ולוי מסיפורנו, לא זו בלבד שפותרת קושי עלילתי ומאירה באור חדש את שלב הנקמה, אלא גם תורמת לאפיון השיטתי של הדמויות לאורך הסיפור.

נוכל אפוא לסכם ולומר, כי עיבוד המסופר כסיפור שבמרכזו אונס, המסתיים בנקמה ולא בנישואים, משרת את עקרון האחדות המרכזית של העריכה המובלעת: התבדלות מאנשי שכם, יושבי הארץ. ואילו הצגת שמעון ולוי כנוקמים עיקריים היא חותם של עריכה מאוחרת, שהתאימה את המסופר לצורכי ההקשר הרחב.

3. פולמוס סמוי בפרשת אונס דינה

לדעתי, פרשת אונס דינה היא בעת ובעונה אחת גם פולמוס סמוי עם תופעת הנישואים של תושבי יהודה עם תושבי פחוות שומרון, העתידים להיקרא שומרונים. הפולמוס הגלוי נוגע בכנענים, ואילו ברובד הסמוי הכוונה היא לעמי הארצות היושבים מצפון. פולמוס זה העסיק, כנראה, את השבים מבבל עד שנקבעה המדיניות הרשמית בידי עזרא ונחמיה וננקטה עמדה מפורשת וגלויה בסוגיית הנישואים עם עמי הארצות.

ההכרעה בדבר קיומו של פולמוס סמוי נסמכת על ההגדרה שהגדרתי סוג זה של סיפורים, ועל הכללים הנוקשים שהצבתי לגילויו.[24] לשיטתי, סיפורים שיש בהם פולמוס סמוי הם סיפורים, שבדרכים מרומזות בלבד (סמנים), ולא בדרכים ישירות, ננקטת בהם עמדה בנושא כלשהו, שקיימות לגביו דעות שונות בספרות המקרא (עילת פולמוס). אחד המסרים החשובים של סיפורים אלו הוא הגינוי הסמוי או ההמלצה העקיפה. מכיוון שהסכנה בהגדרה זו היא היותה פתח לאין סוף פרשנויות, שפעמים עשויים לדרוש את הסיפור, להתעלם מכוונת מחברו ולהתרחק מן המשמעות הסמויה המובנית בו, יש להעמיד את הסיפור במבחן של ארבע אמות המידה המפורטות להלן:

3.1 הימנעות מאזכור מפורש של התופעה שהמחבר מעוניין לגנותה או להמליץ עליה. סיפורנו מרחיק עדותו ודן בנישואים עם חיים, הנמנים עם שבעת עממי כנען, ולא נזכרים בו במפורש נוכרים או עמי הארצות ובוודאי שלא שומרון ותושביה.

3.2 הימצאותם של סמנים, בינתים אף זרויות או קשיים, שבאמצעותם מכוון המחבר לפולמוס. כך, למרות שנושא הפולמוס אינו נזכר מפורשות, מוצא הקורא די ציוני דרך לגלותו. דוגמא לסמן, המייצג זרות או קושי, היא: הימנעות שיטתית מציון שמו של מקום בסיפור שמרבים להיזכר בו שמות מקומות. הקורא בפרשת פסל מיכה (שופ' יז–יח) אינו יודע מה שם היישוב

24 ראה: י' אמית, 'פולמוס סמוי בסיפור כיבוש דן (שופטים יז–יח)', בית מקרא קכו (תשנ"א), עמ' 267– 278; וכן: הנ"ל, 'פרשת פילגש בגבעה כפולמוס סמוי נגד מלכות שאול ואוהדיה (שופטים יט–כא)', בית מקרא קכט (תשנ"ב), עמ' 109–118.

שבו התגורר מיכה ואליו הגיע הלוי (ראה יז 1, 8; יח 2, 13), אך הוא יודע מה שם עירו של
הלוי (יז 7, 8), מאין הגיעו המרגלים (יח, 2, 11), לאן פניהם מועדות (יח 7, 27–29), היכן הם
חנו (יח 11–12), ועוד. טיפוס אחר של סמן, שאינו זרות או קושי, יכולה להיות העדפה
פואטית כלשהי, הנוגעת למבנה הסיפור, או לעיצוב הדמויות, או לתיאור המרחב, ועוד. כך
למשל, בעל פרשת פילגש בגבעה (שופ' יט–כא) בחר להדגיש כי הלוי התארח בבית לחם יהודה
(יט 1–10), נמנע ממלון בירושלים, 'אשר לא מבני ישראל', והעדיף עליה את 'הגבעה אשר
לבנימין' (ראה יט 11–14). הדגשת ההעדפה אינה מקרית, שכן אירוע שמתרחש במרחב של
שבט בנימין ובעיר גבעה דווקא, שהיא עירו של שאול, כשברקע נזכרות ערים הקשורות
בתולדות דוד, עשוי לרמז לשאול. ההכרעה אם אמנם קיימת בסיפור הרמיזה המשוערת
מותנית בקיומם של מספר סמנים ולא רק בעיצוב המרחב. נמצא, שכדי לבסס את השערתו,
חייב הפרשן לגלות כמה סמנים, ואין הוא יכול להסתפק בסמן אחד. כאשר מובאים בחשבון כל
הסמנים, מתגלה הפולמוס הסמוי, שמהווה בעת ובעונה אחת פרשני לתופעות שונות
בסיפור. להלן פירוט הסמנים בסיפורנו:

3.2.1 **בחירת המספֵּר בשכם דווקא** כרקע לפרשת האונס. נקודות ציון בתולדות העיר יכולות
לנמק את הבחירה בשכם כייצוג של בעיית תושבי הר שומרון ופתרונה: התנתקות מעמי
הארצות היושבים מצפון. א. שכם מאופיינת כעיר שאוכלוסייתה מעורבת, גרים בה כנענים,
אנשי חמור, אבי שכם (שופ' ט 28). כידוע, גם אוכלוסיית שומרון לאחר הגלות היתה מעורבת
(מל"ב יז 24; עז' ד 2, 9–10),[25] וגם בימי עזרא הוגדרה אוכלוסייה זו, באופן אנאכרוניסטי,
ככנענית (עז' ט 2). שכם המעורבת מתאימה אפוא ליצג את חשש ההתבוללות בעמי הארצות.
ב. שכם מציינת את פילוג הממלכה ואת הניתוק מאוכלוסיית הצפון, משום שבה הוכרז המרד
בבית דוד והיא שימשה בירה ראשונה לירבעם (מל"א יב 1, 25). לפיכך ההתייחסות לשכם
רומזת לקרע ההיסטורי (הקיים והרצוי) בין יהודה לבין הצפון, משמע בין ירושלים לשומרון,
בירת ישראל הצפונית ומרכז הפחווה האשורית.[26] ג. במסגרת הסיפור שלפנינו (בר' לה 1–5)
נזכרת שכם כמקום שלידיו טמן יעקב את כל אלוהי הנכר: 'ויתנו אל יעקב את כל אלהי הנכר
אשר בידם ואת הנזמים אשר באזניהם ויטמן אותם יעקב **תחת האלה אשר עם שכם**' (שם,
פסוק 4). קישור שכם עם הטמנת אלילים ולא עם שרפתם או ניפוצם (השווה התוספת
בתה"ש לפסוק 4) רומז לעבודה הזרה שהמשיכה להתקיים במקום. לאורך ההיסטוריה של
ממלכת הצפון, שומרון ולא שכם[27] מאופיינת כמקום עבודת אלילים: 'ויקם מזבח לבעל בית
הבעל אשר בנה בשמרון' (מל"א טז 32 ואילך). עבודת אלילים התקיימה בערי שומרון גם לאחר
הגלות: 'ואת פסיליהם היו עבדים גם בניהם ובני בניהם כאשר עשו אבתם הם עשים עד היום
הזה' (מל"ב יז 41). נראה, כי מוטיב הסרת אלוהי הנכר, מעשה שיעקב לא נצטווה עליו כל

---

25   מציאות זו אף נלמדת מן האנאלים של סרגון, ראה: ח' תדמור וש' אחיטוב, 'שמרון', אנציקלופדיה
     מקראית, ח, ירושלים תשל"ב.

26   אין תימה, שבמהלך ההיסטוריה הפכה עיר זו, שלה מסורות קדושה מתקופת האבות ומימי יהושע
     (בר' יב 6, לג 18–20; יהו' ח 30, כד 25–27, 32), אתר מקודש לשומרונים. קדושה זו קיבלה את
     אישורה הפורמאלי בתורה השומרונית. בנוסח השומרוני לעשרת הדיברות בשמות ובדברים נמצא, לפי
     שיטת מניינם, דיבר עשירי, המצווה לבנות מזבח אבנים בהר גריזים. כמו כן, בנוסח השומרוני לדב' יא
     29ב–30 מודגש, כי הר גריזים הוא הר הברכה: 'ונתת את הברכה על הר גריזים ואת הקללה על
     הר עיבל. הלוא הם בעבר הירדן אחרי דרך מבוא השמש בארץ הכנעני הישב בערבה מול הגלגל אצל
     אלוני מורא מול שכם'.

27   לאחר עליית אבימלך לשלטון, בסיוע כספי בית בעל ברית (שופ' ט 4), אין רמז לעבודת אלילים
     בשכם. שכם אינה קשורה לא בחטאות ירבעם ולא בחטאות אחאב.

(בר' לה 1), הוא משני ולקוח מיהו' כד 23.28 החדרת מוטיב זה למקומנו נועדה לשרת את הפולמוס נגד שכם, העולה מן הסיפור, ועתה אף ממסגרתו. אך השאלה הנשאלת היא: מדוע לנהל פולמוס דווקא נגד עיר, שאינה מאופיינת בעבודת אלילים או בפולחן סינקרטיסטי, ולא נגד עיר דוגמת בית-אל, שמרבה להופיע בספר בראשית כאתר מקודש? הפתרון לשאלה זו הוא הבנת המסופר לא רק כפולמוס גלוי נגד שכם החיווית, אלא גם כפולמוס סמוי נגד מה שמיוצג בשכם. שכם מייצגת את אוכלוסיית הצפון, ואלו אינם אלא עמי ארצות ועובדי עבודה זרה.

3.2.2 הגדרת תושבי שכם כחיים: לרוב נזכרים החיווים כמי שיושבים בצפון (יהו' יא 3; שופ' ג 3; שמ"ב כד 7). באזור המרכז נאמר על הגבעונים שהם ממוצא חיווי, ואולם שכם אינה נמנית עם ערי הגבעונים (יהו' ט 7, 17). מצד אחר, הקשר עם פרשת הגבעונים מתהדק אף באמצעות החזרה על עניין המרמה: מרמת בני יעקב מול מרמת הגבעונים (השווה את בר' לד 13 ליהו' ט 22, וראה גם פסוק 3). בשיוך חמור ושכם לחיווים דווקא יש אפוא רמז לברית עם החיווי, שתוצאותיה - ישיבתם במקדש 'עד היום הזה' (יהו' ט 27). לפי המסורת המשנה תורתית לא הוחרמו החיווים, ומכוחה של ברית ושבועה הם הפכו חלק מן החברה הישראלית והשתלבו בפולחנה. האנלוגיה לפרשת הגבעונים-החיווים רומזת אפוא לפולמוס של שבי ציון עם עמי הארצות בשאלת הפולחן, שהרי עמי הארצות היו מעוניינים ליטול חלק בפולחן הירושלמי: 'נבנה עמכם כי ככם נדרוש לאלהיכם...' (עזרא ד 2).

3.2.3 הימנעות מהורשת החיווים: הנושא של מניעת כל מגע אפשרי עם הכנענים ותרבותם קשור בהורשתם (שמ' לד 11–16; דב' ז 1–6; יהו' כג 7–13; ועוד). והנה בסיפורנו, אף על פי שנוצרו התנאים המתאימים להורשה, היא לא נעשתה. תיאור הנקמה אמנם נפתח בהריגת כל זכר, אך מהמשכו עולה כי בני יעקב שבו ונשים וטף, משמע - הותירו נשים וזכרים שבטף. קושי זה אף מועצם עם השוואת תיאור הביזה בסיפורנו (פסוקים 27–29) לתיאור נקמת ישראל במדיינים (במ' לא; ראה לעיל, הערה 23). הדמיון בולט הן מצד המבנה התחבירי - ריבוי מלית החיבור 'ואת' - והן מצד אוצר המלים, שמצביע על מעשה נקמה דומה: '...ויהרגו **כל זכר**; ואת מלכי מדין הרגו על חלליהם...; וישבו בני ישראל את **נשי** מדין ואת **טפם** ואת כל בהמתם ואת כל מקנהם ואת כל **חילם בזזו**' (במ' לא 7–9). עם זאת, מן הסיפור בספר במדבר עולה כי כותבו היה מודע לקושי שבשביית נשים וטף, ולכן הוא מציע פתרון, לפיו יש להרוג את כל הנשים שידעו משכב זכר ואת כל הזכרים שבטף (שם, 11–19, וראה גם שופ' כא 9–12). לעומת זאת, בסיפורנו, לא זו בלבד ששביית הנשים והטף אינה עולה בקנה אחד עם הדרישה להרוג כל זכר, אלא שמעשה זה מותיר שאלה פתוחה באשר לנשים ולילדיהן, שגורלם עשוי להתקשר עם בני יעקב. יתר על כן, למרות התלות הספרותית האפשרית שבין שני תיאורי הנקמה, אין סיפורנו מתאר את שרפת העיר (השווה במ' לא 10). נראה, כי הפתרון למוקד מתח זה, יותר משהוא כרוך בהקשר הרחב הוא תוצאה של הפולמוס הסמוי. העורך אמנם ראה לנכון להתאים את המסופר לכתובים אחרים, המניחים כי שכם לא נכבשה (ראה יהו' ח-יב) וכי נמשך קיומה כעיר שבה יסוד כנעני חזק מצאצאי חמור אבי שכם,[29] אך לשם כך לא היה עליו לתאר שבייה של הנשים והטף, שמשמעה - צירופם למחנה. התיאור הקיים, הנמנע מאופציית ההורשה ורומז למציאות של קשר של ישראל בין ישראל לשכמים, הוא כנראה סמן של מציאות, שבה לא

---

28 על משניות בר' לה 2בב, 4, עמד לאחרונה י' זקוביץ, 'מגמתו של מעשה הטמנת האלילים בשכם (בראשית ל"ה, ב, ד)', בית מקרא כה (תש"ם), עמ' 30–37; וכן: הנ"ל, מבוא לפרשנות פנים-מקראית, אבן יהודה תשנ"ב, עמ' 30–33.

29 ראה: מ' הרן (לעיל, הערה 13), עמ' 1–31.

היה ניתן להעלות על הדעת הורשה של אנשי פחוות שומרון, וברור שקיימת זיקה בין שתי קבוצות האוכלוסין.

3.2.4 השימוש במוטיב המילה כלפי אוכלוסייה כנענית: סביר להניח, שתושבי שכם הקדומים, בדומה לכנענים, שהספרות המקראית אינה מציגה אותם כערלים, נהגו למול עצמם.[30] ולכן ההתייחסות לשכמים כמי שלא נהגו להמול אינו רומז לתקופה הכנענית ולמוצאם החיווי, שאינו שמי–מערבי, או לימי ממלכת ישראל, אלא לתקופה מאוחרת יותר. המילה מייצגת את הברית עם אלוהי ישראל, וגם תושבי הממלכה הצפונית היו שותפים בה. סביר להניח שברית זו נשמרה ברוב המקרים גם לאחר גלות שומרון ולאחר ששולבו באוכלוסיית הצפון יסודות אתניים שונים מרחבי האימפריה האשורית. מסקנה זו נסמכת הן על רצון התושבים החדשים ללמוד את משפט אלוהי הארץ (מל"ב יז 25–28), והן על העובדה ש'צרי יהודה ובנימין', שהם כנראה תושבי פחוות שומרון, ביקשו להשתלב בעבודת ה': 'נבנה עמכם כי ככם נדרוש לאלהיכם ולא (קרי: ולו) אנחנו זבחים מימי אסר חדון מלך אשור המעלה אתנו פה' (עז' ד 2; וראה גם פסוק 10).[31] נראה כי נושא המילה העסיק את אוכלוסיית הצפון רק לאחר הגלות, משהגיעו אליה קבוצות מן המזרח שלא נהגו להמול. השימוש במוטיב המילה רומז אפוא לאוכלוסיית הצפון מן התקופה שלאחר הגלות.

3.2.5 השימוש במוטיב של נישואים לצד החזרה על התיבה 'ארץ' דווקא (פסוקים 1–3, 8–10, 21, 30):[32] כך מכוון המספר את קוראו לצירופים 'עמי הארץ' או 'עמי הארצות', השכיחים בעזרא ונחמיה בהקשר של נישואים דווקא: 'ואשר לא ניתן בנתינו לעמי הארץ ואת בנתיהם לא נקח לבנינו' (נחמ' י 31; וראה גם עז' ט 1–2, 12, י 2; נחמ' יג 25). מן הראוי לציין כי בימי הבית הראשון היו נישואים של בני המעמד העליון עם נוכריות חלק בלתי נפרד מהמציאות המדינית, והגינויים בנושא זה מאוחרים הם ומייצגים את גישת האסכולה המשנה תורתית, שאומצה בידי עזרא ונחמיה (נחמ' יג 26). בעזרא מודגש, כי 'יד השרים והסגנים היתה במעל הזה ראשונה' (עז' ט 2), ומנחמיה למדים, כי משפחת הכוהנים הגדולים היתה מחותנת ובכבדי השומרונים בדרך של נישואים מדיניים: 'ומבני יוידע בן אלישיב הכהן הגדול חתן לסנבלט החרני...' (נחמ' יג 28). נראה אפוא, כי העלאת האופציה של נישואים בין שכם, בנו של נשיא הארץ, לבין דינה, שיצאה 'לראות בבנות הארץ', נועדה לרמוז לתקופת שיבת ציון ולאחת הבעיות המרכזיות שאפיינו אותה: טיהור 'עם ישראל', 'זרע הקדש', מנשים מבנות עמי הארץ.

3.2.6 הפיכת מקרה אונס לבעיה לאומית: האנס אינו אחד מנערי שכם, אלא נסיך העיר, שכם בן חמור, ואילו הנאנסת אינה רק בת יעקב אלא בת בישראל, כך שלאירוע אופי של 'נבלה עשה בישראל'. נמצא, כי השימוש באנאכרוניזם 'ישראל' נועד לשרת את מערכת הסמנים. יתרה מזאת, ההתייחסות לקשר עם הכנענים כמעשה של כפייה ואלימות מצדם אינו הולם את תיאורי תקופת הכיבוש, המפנים את כל חצי הביקורת כנגד ישראל, המעוניין בקשר זה ומטעמים שונים נמנע מלהוריש את הכנענים. לעומת זאת, הקשר עם הכנענים, עמי הארצות, מוצג בספרי עזרא ונחמיה כלחץ כפייתי וכבד של עמי הארצות.

---

30   י"ש ליכט, 'מילה', אנציקלופדיה מקראית, ד, ירושלים תשכ"ב, עמ' 894–901.

31   ראה, למשל, פירושו של: L.B. Batten, *The Books of Ezra and Nehemiah* (ICC), Edinburgh 1961 (1913), pp. 125ff. המקור הכוהני מדגיש כי המילה היא תנאי לשיתוף בפולחן: שמ' יב 47–48; במ' ט 13–14.

32   העובדה שבתרגום בר' לד 1 בחרו מתרגמי השבעים והפשיטתא בביטוי המצמצם 'תושבים' תמורת 'ארץ' שבנוסח המסורה, מחזקת את הטענה, שבבחירת התיבה 'ארץ' יש משום רמיזה לבעיה העקרונית של נישואים עם יושבי הארץ, ולא רק לתושבי העיר שכם.

3.2.7 **פרופורציות של מעטים מול עוינות הרבים**: אפיון זה של תקופת האבות מודגש רק בפרשתנו. בסיפורי האבות בולטת הנטייה לפאר את מצב אבות האומה ואפילו לתארם כעם (ראה, למשל, בר' יג 5–7, לב 8, 11 ועוד). לעומת זאת, בסיפורנו עומדים זה מול זה בני משפחת יעקב, שהם 'מתי מספר', כנגד כל יוצאי שער שכם ויושב הארץ הכנעני והפריזי. ולכן, ההצעה להיות 'לעם אחד' מתפרשת כסכנת טמיעה, והאיום של יושב הארץ – כסכנת השמדה (בר' לד 30). ראוי לציין, כי החשש מן הצמצום הדמוגראפי מאפיין את הספרות המאוחרת, של סוף ימי הבית הראשון.[33] נראה אפוא, כי תיאור זה בא לרמוז לאוכלוסיית השבים לציון, שהיתה מעטה בהשוואה לאנשי פחוות שומרון, ונאלצה להתמודד עם קבוצה רחבה יותר של 'צרי יהודה' (וראה, למשל, נחמ' ד 1–2).

3.2.8 **הצגת יעקב כבעל עמדה שונה מעמדת בניו**: בסיפורנו יעקב מחריש וירא מסביבתו, בניגוד לבניו, המייצגים עמדה קיצונית, גאה וערכית, שזוכה גם לתמיכה אלוהית (שם, לה 5). עיצובו הפאסיבי לאורך הסיפור מתגלה בסיומו כנקיטת עמדה עקרונית, מתפשרת, פרגמאטית, השונה מעמדת בניו, והיא באה לביטוי בנזיפתו בהם. לקיום שתי העמדות יש משמעות על רקע הפולמוס עם עמי הארצות. נראה, כי עמדת הבנים מהווה ביקורת עקיפה על עמדות שמסתייגים מעקרון הבדלנות, ונציגיה היו ממנהיגי היישוב – משפחת הכהן הגדול. בעיצוב פרקנו ניתנה עדיפות לעמדה הבדלנית המובהקת, הרואה במדיניות הנישואים ביטוי של פחדנות ושל פשרה מיותרת.

נמצא, כי שמונה סמנים מכוונים לכך שסיפורנו לא נועד רק לתאר את מערכת היחסים עם הכנענים, שאותם היה ראוי להחרים, אלא הוא כוון בעיקר למערכת יחסים מורכבת יותר, עם החיים, הקשורים עם ישראל ביחסים של ברית. ונראה לי, כי חיים אלה אינם אלא עמי הארצות, היושבים בשומרון, ושמפני ההיטמעות בהם חששו השבים מבבל.

3.3 **הופעת נושא הפולמוס בכתובים מקראיים נוספים**: היחסים עם יושבי הר שומרון, לאחר שיבת בני הגולה לירושלים בחסות הצו של כורש, היו נושא מרכזי בספרות התקופה. סכסוך זה עולה ממל"ב יז 24–41, ומעידים על כך ספרי עזרא ונחמיה (עז' ד; נחמ' ב 10, ג 33–38, ד, ו, יג 28).[34] משני הספרים האחרונים אפשר אף ללמוד על הנטייה להכללת הבעיה ולתפישת תושבי הצפון כחלק מעמי הארצות. לפיכך האיסור על נישואים עם עמי הארצות חל ממילא עליהם (ראה גם: מל' ב 10–12).

3.4 **הופעת הנושא הסמוי של הפולמוס במסורת הפרשנית**: לבראשית לד מקום מרכזי בספרות החיצונית ובספרות היהודית-ההלניסטית. בספר היובלים (ל 1–26) משרת פרקנו פולמוס גלוי וקשה עם נישואים לנוכרים (והשווה גם: יהודית ט 2–4). בצוואת לוי (ה–ז 3) מוצגת שכם כעיר עוינת מימי אברהם. הרמיזה לזמנו של הכותב, משמע לפולמוס המתמשך עם השומרונים, נמצאת בכינוי הגנאי שניתן לה: 'כי מהיום תקרא שכם עיר הכסילים' (שם, ז 2; השווה בן-סירא נ 25–26, המכנה את השומרונים כ'גוי נבל הדר בשכם').[35] מקור נוסף הוא שירו האפי של

---

33 הביטוי 'מתי מספר' מופיע בספר דברים ובספרות מאוחרת לו, וראה: דב' ד 27; יר' מד 28; תה' קה 12; דה"א טז 19. ביטוי קרוב, 'מתי מעט', מופיע בדב' כו 5, כח 62.

34 ראה: אמית (לעיל, הערה 9), עמ' 8–9; וראה גם: יוסף בן מתתיהו (קדמוניות היהודים, יא, 84), המזהה את ה'צרים' לשבט יהודה ובנימין' עם השומרונים.

35 הציטטות לקוחות ממהדורות כהנא (הספרים החיצוניים, א–ב, תל-אביב, תשט"ז). קוגל דן בהרחבה בעניין מקומו של סיפור דינה בצוואת לוי, ומפרש את הכינוי 'עיר הכסילים' כרמיזה ברורה לשומרונים; ראה: J. Kugel, 'The Story of Dinah in the Testament of Levi', *HTR* 8 (1992), pp. 23-25

תיאודוטוס, הדן בפרשת דינה וחורבן שכם בידי שמעון ולוי. החוקרים חלוקים בשאלה אם תיאודוטוס היה שומרוני או יהודי.[36] מכל מקום, הכול סבורים כי אפוס זה שימש כלי בפולמוס היהודי–שומרוני של המאה השנייה לפסה"נ, ויש גם מי שהגדיר את בראשית לד כ'מאגנה כארטה' של המאבק היהודי בשומרונים, מאבק שתפקידו להסביר מדוע השומרונים אינם אלא נוכרים.[37] לאחרונה אף הוצע לראות בחלק מן הספרים החיצוניים את המשך הפולמיקה עם השומרונים בדבר קדושתה של שכם.[38] נראה אפוא, כי פרקנו הלם את צורכי הוויכוח של סוף ימי הבית השני, משום שהוא שירת באופן סמוי ויכוח דומה בראשית ימי הבית השני.[39]

3.5 מדוע הועדפה טכניקת הפולמוס הסמוי? נראה לי, כי המאבק בעמי הארצות שמצפון ליהודה נוהל, עד ימי עזרא ונחמיה, גם באופן סמוי, מסיבות מדיניות–חברתיות ומסיבות רטוריות:

3.5.1 בנסיבות המדיניות שמימי עזרא ונחמיה התגבשה מדיניות רשמית אנטי–שומרונית, שהלכה והחריפה. סביר אפוא להניח, כי בתקופה שקדמה לימיהם, היה היחס לתושבי הצפון שנוי במחלוקת. היו חוגים שמתחו עליהם ביקורת, כפי שניתן ללמוד ממל"ב יז 24–41, והיו חוגים כוהניים, בעלי עצמה מדינית, שנטו לקשור עמם קשרים. מצב זה של העדר הכרעה הוא רקע מתאים לקיומו של פולמוס סמוי.

3.5.2 מבחינה רטורית יש יתרון לפולמוס כשהוא סמוי, משום שהוא יכול לשמש אמצעי עקיף, הנוטל מן המסופר את ההתנגדות הראשונית, שמטבעו פולמוס עשוי לעורר. עם זאת, הפולמוס הסמוי יוצר משקע מצטבר אצל הקורא, משקע שמטרתו לנווט עמדות. כך תורם סיפורנו, באופן עקיף, לפולמוס שמנהלים תומכי הגישה הבדלנית.

4. בית מדרשה של העריכה המעצבת

למן ראשית המחקר בפרשה ועד ימינו נוטים החוקרים לקשור את עיצוב הפרשה עם עריכה כוהנית בשלב כלשהו (ראה לעיל הערות 3–5). מסקנה זו נשענת על סגנון הכתוב, העשיר בביטויים שמאפיינים את האסכולה הכוהנית, כמו: 'נשיא' (פסוק 2), 'טמא' (פסוקים 5, 13, 27), 'נאחז' (פסוק 10), 'המל לכם כל זכר' (פסוקים 15, 22, וראה גם פסוק 24), 'קנין' ו'בהמה' (פסוק 23). עם זאת, חשוב לציין כי משום תוכן המסופר, מרבית החוקרים מהססים מליחס

36 סקירה מסכמת ראה: R. Pummer, 'Genesis 34 in the Jewish Writings of the Hellenistic and Roman Periods', *HTR* 75 (1982), pp. 177-188. וראה גם: ג' גוטמן, 'האפוס על שכם', בתוך: הספרות היהודית–ההלניסטית, א: היהדות וההלניות לפני תקופת החשמונאים, ירושלים תשי"ח, עמ' 245–261; ולאחרונה אצל: J.J. Collins, 'The Epic of Theodotus and the Hellenism of the Hasmoneans', *HTR* 73, 1980, pp. 91-104

37 ראה: H.G. Kippenberg, *Garizim und Synagoge*, Berlin 1971

38 כספי (לעיל הערה 6), עמ' 255 הערה 49. כספי אף מצביע על השתמרות שרידי מסורת פולמוסית זו בספרות הבבלאדית של יהוד ספרד.

39 לדעת דיבנר חוברה הפרשה במאה השנייה לפסה"נ, ראה: B.J. Diebner, 'Gen 34 und Dinas Rolle bei der Definition "Israels"', *DBAT* 18 (1984), pp. 59-76. ביקורת על קביעת הזמן של דיבנר, ובעת ובעונה אחת קבלת תפישתו העקרונית, ראה אצל נ' נאמן, 'שכם וירושלים בימי גלות בבל ושיבת ציון', ציון נח (תשנ"ג), עמ' 30. נאמן מטעים כי בר' לד, בדומה לטקסטים נוספים – כמו: דב' יא 26–30; יהו' ח 30–35, כד – נתחברו במסגרת הפולמוס הגלוי עם אתר הפולחן של שכם, דהיינו 'על רקע המתיחות בין מרכזי הפולחן של שכם וירושלים בימי הבית השני' (הציטוט לקוח מעמ' 30, אך ראה המאמר כולו, עמ' 7–32).

את הסיפור למקור הכוהני, ומצביעים על זיקתו ההדוקה גם למקורות הקדומים (יהוויסטי ואלוהיסטי). לי נראה, כי גורמים מספר מאששים את המסקנה, שסיפור זה חובר ועוצב בידי עריכה מאוחרת, הקשורה בבית המדרש הכוהני, ואלה הם:

4.1   סימני האיחור אינם נשענים על הלשון הכוהנית, שהרי זו יכולה ליצג גם את ימי הבית הראשון,[40] אלא על התופעות הבאות:

4.1.1   העריכה שלפנינו מכירה את המשנה הקדם־דויטרונומיסטית והדויטרונומיסטית על שתי תביעותיה הכרוכות זו בזו: לא להתחתן בכנענים אלא להורישם או להחרימם.[41] לפיכך מדגישה העריכה את היות שכם חויי ואת העובדה שלפנינו מקרה של נישואים עם תושב הארץ, נישואים שיש למנוע בכל מחיר. ואולם, למרות סיטואציית הלחימה שמעוצבת בסיפור, אין המספר טורח לגנות או להצדיק את אי־הורשת כל תושבי שכם. נראה אפוא, כי הפרספקטיבה ההיסטוריוגרפית של מחבר סיפורנו מאפשרת לו להבחין בין תיאור תקופת הכיבוש והתקופות שלאחריה (ההיסטוריוגרפיה דויטרונומיסטית) לבין תיאור התקופות שקדמו לה, שאז לא היה צורך בהנמקות להותרת כנענים (ההיסטוריוגרפיה קדם־דויטרונומיסטית). במקרה שלפנינו נראה, כי כותב הפרשה הכיר את פרשת הגבעונים־חיים ביהושע ט, ובסיפורו אף דאג שתושב לגבעונים מרמה כנגד מרמה. כמו כן נטל הכותב את שמות חלק מגיבוריו משופטים ט 28 (ראה גם יהו' כד 32, וכן לעיל סעיפים: 3.2.2; 3.2.3).

4.1.2   העריכה שלפנינו מכירה גם את סיפור הנקמה במדיינים, מבית המדרש הכוהני,[42] והיא קשורה אליו בקשר סגנוני ורעיוני (ראה סעיף 3.2.3 לעיל). הסיפור הכוהני שימש לה אפוא מודל חיקוי, אך משום האילוצים ההיסטוריוגרפיים (שופ' ט) והפולמוסיים היא העדיפה להסתייג ממנו.

4.1.3   השימוש במוטיב המילה כתנאי להווית של 'עם אחד' הוא מאוחר. ידוע, כי מנהג המילה אפיין את מרבית עמי קדמת המזרח התיכון הקדום (ראה יר' ט 24–25), וכי המפגש בגלות עם התרבות המסופוטאמית, ההשתלטות הפרסית, ואחר כך היוונית, הפכוהו לסממן המאפיין את האוכלוסייה הנמנית עם ישראל, ואף הולידו את ההסתייגויות מסממן זה (ראה סעיף 3.2.4). בסיפורנו המילה אינה מוטיב משני; היא חלק בלתי נפרד מהתפתחות העלילה. היא קשורה במרמה, שמשמעה ביטול הנישואים, ובתכסיס שמאפשר את נצחון המעטים על הרבים. ובמלים

---

40   דיון ביקורתי שיטתי כנגד שיטה ולהוויזן ובעד הקדמת זמנו של המקור הכוהני, ראה: י' קויפמן, תולדות האמונה הישראלית, א, ירושלים ותל־אביב, תשכ״ד, עמ' 113–184; וראה גם תרומתו של הרן לנושא זה: מ' הרן, 'הריפורמות הפולחניות וזמנו של ס״כ', בתוך: תקופות ומוסדות במקרא, תל־אביב תשל״ב, עמ' 175–190. חיזוק בתחום הלשוני נמצא אצל הורביץ: A. Hurvitz, 'The Evidence of Language in Dating the Priestly Code', *RB* 81 (1974), pp. 25-55; idem, *A Linguistic Study of the Relationship Between the Priestly Source and the Book of Ezekiel*, Paris 1981 ועוד.

41   על ההבחנה בין היסטוריוגראפיה קדם־דויטרונומיסטית לדויטרונומיסטית, ראה: אמית (לעיל, הערה 9), עמ' 331–353; ולאחרונה: א' רופא, 'החיבור האפרתי כנגד החיבור המשנה־תורתי', בית מקרא קלב (תשנ״ג), עמ' 14–28. רופא מבחין בין חיבור אפרתי לבין חיבור משנה תורתי.

42   על שייכות של פרשה זו למקור הכוהני אין עוררין, וראה הפירושים הביקורתיים לספר במדבר. לאחרונה הוצע לראות בה חיבור מבית מדרשה של אסכולת הקדושה, ראה: י' קנוהל, מקדש הדממה: עיון ברובדי היצירה הכוהנית שבתורה, ירושלים תשנ״ג, עמ' 92–93. מן הראוי לציין, שחיבור זה מבסס את הטענות כי אסכולת הקדושה כוללת לא רק את ספר הקדושה (וי' יז–כו), אלא גם פרשיות נוספות בתורה, וכי היא מאוחרת לתורת כוהנים.

אחרות, אם המילה היא מאבני היסוד של הסיפור, ואם ההתייחסות אליה כאל סממן שמבדל את ישראל משכניו היא מאוחרת, הרי שהסיפור כולו עוצב בתקופה מאוחרת למדי.

4.1.4   אם נכונה המסקנה, שלסיפור מגמה בדלנית והוא נועד למתוח ביקורת על קשרי נישואים עם נוכרים, הרי גם מגמה זו מלמדת על איחור המסופר, שכן אין היא עולה בקנה אחד עם המציאות של ימי הבית הראשון.[43]

4.2   ההתייחסות לעריכה מאוחרת שיש בה סגנון כוהני מעלה את האפשרות שלפנינו סיפור מבית מדרשה של 'אסכולת הקדושה', משמע סיפור מאוחר לאסכולה הכוהנית (ראה סעיף 4.1.2). שייך סיפור זה לבית מדרשה של אסכולת הקדושה, שאולי אף עיצבה את ספרות התורה, יכול ללמדנו על דרכי פעולתה בתקופת שיבת ציון.[44]

4.2.1   אסכולה זו, יותר מהאסכולה הכוהנית, קשורה לחומרים הספרותיים הקדומים (היהוויסטי, האלוהיסטי והדייטרונומיסטי), שאליהם מגלה סיפורנו קירבה. פתרון זה מסביר אפוא את ערבוב הסגנונות, שכה הקשה על המחקר הפילולוגי–היסטורי.[45]

4.2.2   אסכולת הקדושה מתרכזת, כידוע, גם בשאלות הנוגעות לסדרי החברה ולא רק בנושאים הקשורים בפולחן, ואמנם פרקנו עוסק בסוגיה חברתית מובהקת.[46]

4.2.3   מסימניה הברורים של אסכולת הקדושה הוא שוויון הגר והתושב (וי' יט 33–34).[47] בסיפורנו מבוסס המשא ומתן על אופציה שוויונית זו. בני יעקב הזרים עתידים להפוך שווים ליושבי הארץ, ובדומה לכך עם קיום המילה תושבי שכם עתידים להפוך שווים לישראל. ואולם, באסכולה זו נשמעת גם התביעה להורשת יושבי הארץ (במ' לג 52–56), להתקדשות ולהתבדלות. גישה אמביוואלנטית זו, של שוויון לצד התבדלות, עולה גם מפרקנו.

4.2.4   העמדה הננקטת בסיפורנו בנושא המילה שונה מזו של בית המדרש הכוהני, המתיר לגרים שנימולו להשתתף בפולחן (ראה שמ' יב 43–49; במ' ט 14). סביר אפוא להניח, כי גרים נימולים נקשרו לישראלים בקשרי נישואים.[48] ואולם בית המדרש הכוהני, שבמרכז ענייני עמדה הקדושה הריטואלית, לא הזהיר מפני נישואים עם אוכלוסייה נכרית–נימולה. לעומת זאת, בית המדרש של אסכולת הקדושה, המרחיב את תחום הקדושה, מגלה גישה קיצונית יותר, התובעת

---

43   השווה לדברי ויינפלד: 'אין צריך לומר, שהעלאת איסור החיתון כתנאי ראשון במעלה לקיום הלאומי תואמת את מפעלו של עזרא: סילוק הנשים הנוכריות והיבדלות עדת הגולים מבני נכר'. מ' ויינפלד, 'ירושת הארץ – זכות וחובה: תפיסת ההבטחה במקורות מימי בית ראשון וימי בית שני', ציון מט (תשמ"ד), עמ' 124.

44   קנוהל (לעיל, הערה 42), עמ' 15, 96–98, 207. לדעת קנוהל, אסכולת הקדושה היתה אחראית למפעל הגדול של עריכת התורה. לא זה המקום להרחיב, אך לא נראית לי טענתו בדבר המסגרת ההיסטורית, המקדימה את אסכולת הקדושה לימי אחז–חזקיה, ואני מקווה שתימצא לי ההזדמנות להרחיב בנושא זה.

45   קנוהל, שם, עמ' 13.

46   קנוהל, שם, עמ' 13, 165–169, ועוד.

47   קנוהל, שם, עמ' 28, 171.

48   אין תימה, שגישה ברורה זו הפכה בסיס לחוקי הגיור של ההלכה; וראה: ש' יפת, אמונות ודעות בספר דברי הימים ומקומן בעולם המחשבה המקראית, ירושלים, תשל"ז, עמ' 290–295. מילגרום מבחין בין טמיעה עקב נישואים, בתקופה הקדומה, לבין טכניקות מאוחרות של גיור. :J. Milgrom 'Religious Conversion and the Revolt Model for the Formation of Israel', *JBL* 101 (1982), pp. 169-176

התבדלות מגרים ומצאצאיהם (ו' כה 45–55), לצד תביעה להתייחס אליהם בנושאים
מסוימים כאל אזרחים שווים, ואזהרה להתרחק מתועבות הגויים (ו' יז 10–16, יח 26, כ 2).

נראה אפוא, כי אסכולת הקדושה היא בית המדרש שעיצב את סיפורנו. אסכולה זו רצתה לחדד
את סוגיית הקשר עם הגרים, ולהדגיש כי גם קיום מצוות המילה אינו מתיר נישואים. כך
שילבה אסכולה בדלנית זו את החוקים הכוהניים עם הבדלנות הדייטרונומיסטית. אם נכונה
ההשערה, כי אסכולת הקדושה משקפת ביקורת על הכהונה,[49] אזי אפשר למצוא בסיפורנו
ביקורת סמויה על האריסטוקרטיה הכוהנית של ימי שיבת ציון, ועל מגעיה עם נכבדים
היושבים בהר שומרון.

5. סיכום

בדיון זה ניסיתי להראות, כי פרשת אונס דינה הוא סיפור שחובר ועוצב בראשית ימי הבית
השני, והוא משרת מאבק חברתי קשה נגד נישואים עם נוכרים ועם עמי הארצות, העתידים
להיקרא 'שומרונים', ובעד קיום חברה שונה ונבדלת. אמנם תיאור זה שולל את האפשרות
לפרש את הפרשה כהד למציאות ההיסטורית קדומה של האלף השני לפסה"נ, אך מצד אחר, הוא
מעשיר את הכרת אווירת התקופה של ימי שיבת ציון, שידיעותינו עליה כה דלות. לפי הגישה
שהוצגה במאמר זה, פרקנו משרת את הפולמוס הבדלני, ואף הופך בסיס לפולמוס האנטי-
שומרוני. קיומה של ספרות מסוג זה מבהיר את הרקע להתפתחותן של מגמות פולמוסיות
מנוגדות, המבטאות גישה חיובית לנוכרים ולעמי הארצות שמצפון כאחד.[50]

49 קנוהל (לעיל, הערה 42), עמ' 190–197.

50 יפת (לעיל, הערה 41, עמ' 286–299) מוצאת בספר דה"י פולמוס פרו-שומרוני. לאחרונה מאיר
    זקוביץ את ספר רות כפולמוס נגד גירוש הנשים הנוכריות: 'היקפה הרחב של תופעת נישואי
    התערובת מעיד כי לא הכל היו תמימי דעים כי יש פסול בנישואים אלה. הדרישה לגירוש הנשים
    הנוכריות עוררה מן הסתם התנגדות חריפה שמגילת רות מבטאת אותה....'. ראה: י' זקוביץ, רות עם
    מבוא ופירוש, מקרא לישראל, תל-אביב וירושלים תש"ן, עמ' 19. על המגמה הבדלנית ועל המגמה
    לפתיחות הקיימות זו לצד זו בראשית ימי הבית השני, ראה: מ' וינפלד, 'המגמה האוניברסליסטית
    והמגמה הבדלנית בתקופת שיבת ציון', תרביץ לג (תשכ"ד), עמ' 228–242 [=ליקוטי תרביץ, א:
    מקראה בחקר המקרא, ירושלים תשל"ט, עמ' 117–146].

זמנה ועניינה של הנבואה על 'ישבי החרבות' (יחזקאל לג 23–29)

גרשון ברין

יחזקאל לג כולל מספר נבואות שיש להן מקבילות בחלקי הספר האחרים, כגון נבואת הצופה (לג 1–9 // ג 17–21 ועוד); פרשת הגמול (לג 10–20 // יח); פרשת האלם (לג 21–22 // ג 22–27 ועוד), והנבואה נגד יושבי החרבות (לג 23–29 // יא 14 ואילך). גם מיקומו של הפרק במערך המבנה של ספר יחזקאל, מיד אחר נבואות הגויים ולכאורה בתוך גוש נבואות הנחמה שבפרקים לד ואילך, מעורר שאלה האם שייך החומר שבו לתוכחה או לנחמה.

אקדים ואציג עתה קצת דברים על המסקנות המתקבלות מצירוף כלל מרכיבי הפרק:

1. לכל הקטעים או לרובם (פרט, אולי, לנבואה האחרונה, על השוואת דברי הנביא לשיר עגבים, פסוקים 30–33) יש מקבילות בפרקים א–כד.
2. ניתן להוכיח שבכל זוג מקבילות, הנבואה שבפרק לג היא המאוחרת יותר.
3. המכנה המשותף לכל הנבואות שבפרק זה הוא בזמן – ערב החורבן והתקופה שלאחריו, ובעניין – בירור נושאים הקשורים לעבר מחד גיסא, והכשרת הלבבות לקראת העתיד מאידך גיסא.
4. ניתוח ענייני של מרכיבי מגילת הנבואות שבפרק לג מלמד, שצירופם נועד לשמש הכנה ומבוא לגאולה, הנושא העיקרי בשליחותו של יחזקאל לאחר החורבן.

המאמר הנוכחי מתמקד בנבואה אחת מתוך מגילה זו (לג 23–29). היא כוללת תוכחה קשה כנגד הנשארים בארץ, המכונים 'ישבי החרבות האלה על אדמת ישראל'. בכוונתי לבדוק את מבנה הנבואה ואת המסר הנבואי שבה. לנבואה זו מקבילה מוקדמת יותר בקורות שליחותו של יחזקאל: יא 14–21, שכוונה לנשארים בארץ אחר גלות יהויכין, ומעניין יהיה לבדוק את הנושאים המשותפים לשתי הנבואות ואת ההבדל ביניהן. כן נשאל האם יחס הנביא לאוכלוסייה הנשארת זהה בשני המקרים, או שחלה בו התפתחות כלשהי. בהמשך נדון גם בשאלת זמן הנבואה וביחסה לקבוצת הנבואות האחרות שקובצו באותה מגילה – פרק לג.

א. מבנה הנבואה על יושבי החרבות (לג 23–29)

פתיחה	פסוק 23
ציטוט דברי הנשארים	פסוק 24
חטאי הנשארים	פסוקים 25–26
העונש ונוסחת הסיום	פסוקים 27–29

מן המבנה עולה התמונה המקובלת של נבואות תוכחה: נוסחת פתיחה ובעקבותיה פירוט של

חטא ועונש. נמצא, שיחזקאל בונה את הנבואה הנדונה לפי המתכונת שבה השתמשו נביאי הכתב האחרים ואף הוא עצמו בנבואות אחרות.[1]

ב. אשמות יושבי הארץ ועונשיהם, והזיקה לשאלת זמנה של הנבואה

טענת הנשארים היא שהם היורשים הלגיטימיים של ירושת אברהם ה'אחד', וזאת משום מוצאם מאב קדמון זה. יתרה מזו, הם סבורים שזכויותיהם עולות על זכויותיו של אברהם, משום שהוא היה אחד ואילו הם רבים. הנביא תוקף את טענותיהם, בהדגישו את חולשותיהם המוסריות-חברתיות של הנותרים בארץ לאחר הגלות.

חידוש גדול יש כאן: בספרות הנבואה שעד יחזקאל מופיע בקביעות רעיון הפרימאט המוסרי בזיקה לפולחן (היינו, העדפת המוסר על הפולחן), ואילו בנבואה הנדונה פונה העקרון של הפרימאט בכיוון שונה, היינו, העדפת המוסר על פני זכויות האבות, וכדומה.

מתוכחת הנביא עולה, שלדעתו זכות הירושה דינה להישלל, גם ממי שזכאי לה על פי קריטריונים כאלה ואחרים. משמע, הקריטריון המוסרי חשוב ועדיף על כל שיקול אחר של זכות כלשהי.

החטאים נבנים בנבואה בצורת **רשימה**, הדומה לרשימות המצויות בשני טיפוסי יצירות: (1) פרקי הגמול, כגון אלה שבפרק יח, שם יש רשימה של תכונות חיוביות ושליליות – בתיאורי הצדיק כבתיאורי הרשע. (2) פרשיות בספרות החכמה ובחלקי המקרא המושפעים ממנה, שיש בהן הגדרות של תכונות הצדיק, הרשע וכדומה (והשווה תהילים פרקים טו ו־כד). יש לציין, שעם שיחזקאל משתמש כאן בדגם קבוע ומוכן של **רשימות** חטאים (ככל הנראה בהשפעת ספרות החכמה), הרי הוא מכוון אותן לצרכים ספציפיים. הרלוואנטיות לעניין הנדון באה לידי ביטוי בכך שכל אחת מקבוצות החטאים (היינו, פסוקים 25–26) מסתיימת בשאלה הריטורית: 'והארץ תירשו'?! המתייחסת ישירות לנושא הראשי של הנבואה: רצונם של 'יושבי החרבות' **לרשת** את כל הארץ על חשבון אחיהם הגולים. השווה 'אחד היה אברהם **ויירש** את **הארץ** ... הארץ **למורשה**'. אותו צירוף ממש מופיע בתמיהת הנביא: 'והארץ תירשו'?![2] נפנה עתה להרכב הרשימה:

להלן נבדוק את תיאור החטאים,[3] את משמעם, את סדר הופעתם ואת זיקתם לרשימות מקבילות בספר יחזקאל ומחוצה לו.

1. רשימת החטאים (פסוקים 25–26)

רשימת החטאים[4] מחולקת, כאמור, לשתי קבוצות, שבסוף כל אחת מהן באה השאלה החוזרת: 'והארץ תירשו' ?! בקבוצה הראשונה (פסוק 25) נמנו חטאים אלה:

1   למבנים כאלה השווה: C. Westermann, *Basic Forms of Prophetic Speech*, Philadelphia 1967, pp. 169-189. לדעת ג'ויס, עמ' 42, הנבואה בנויה לפי המתכונת של יב 21–25; ראה: P. Joyce, *Divine Initiative and Human Response in Ezekiel*, Sheffield 1989, p. 42

2   רד"ק מוצא נקודת קישור נוספת לעניין אברהם, והיא, שגם ביחס אליו הכתוב השתמש בלשון יר"ש בהקשר לירושת הארץ על ידיו (בר' טו 7–8).

3   פסוקים 25–26 חסרים בתרגום השבעים, ולפי צימרלי ההשמטה נוצרה עקב הומויטלויטון; W. Zimmerli, *Ezekiel* (Hermeneia), Philadelphia 1983, ad loc.

4   ר' אליעזר מבלגנצי, פירוש יחזקאל ותרי עשר, ורשא 1909, בפירושו לכתובנו, מוסיף על יד כל חטא את המלים: 'ועדיין אתם חוטאים כך וכך'. ללמד, כנראה, שלמרות שנענשו וגלו, וכתוצאה מכך נשארו במקום רק דלת הארץ, בכל זאת ממשיכים אלה בחטאי העבר של העם.

על הדם תאכלו
ועינכם תשאו אל גלוליכם
ודם תשפכו

מלת 'דם' באה בראש הרשימה ובסופה, ואפשר שהיא מצביעה על אחד המוקדים של הנבואה.
יש הבדל בין ההאשמה הראשונה – אכילה על הדם – לבין שפיכת דם, באשר הראשונה
עניינה קרוב להיות דתי–פולחני,5 ואילו האחרונה היא עבירה מוסרית–חברתית, רצח. נשיאת
עיניים אל הגילולים ברור שהיא עבירה דתית–פולחנית. עולה מזה, ששתיים משלוש העבירות
מכוונות לעניין דתי, ואילו האחרונה לעניין חברתי מובהק.
הקבוצה השנייה (פסוק 26) מונה חטאים אלה:

עמדתם על חרבכם
עשיתן תועבה
ואיש את אשת רעהו טמאתם

קבוצה זו פותחת במה שסיימה הראשונה, אך בניסוח שונה 'עמדתם על חרבכם' (//דם
תשפכו'). הלשון השני: 'עשיתן תועבה' מנוסח בלשון כללי, שיכול להתפרש לכיוון חברתי ודתי
כאחד. אמנם 'תועבה' שכיח בטקסטים כוהניים העוסקים בטומאה וטהרה (השווה, למשל,
ויקרא כ 13 ועוד), ואפשר שכאן הוא משמש כבן זוגו המקביל של הביטוי האמצעי בקבוצה א'
('ועינכם תשאו אל גלוליכם'). העבירה המינית, טימוא אשת הרֵע, הריהי עבירה חברתית
ודתית גם יחד.
נמצא, שלעומת קבוצת החטאים הראשונה (פסוק 25), הנעה מן הכיוון הדתי–פולחני ('על
הדם תאכלו') אל הכיוון החברתי–מוסרי ('ודם תשפכו'), פותחת הרשימה השנייה (פסוק 26)
בעבירה מוסרית–חברתית ('עמדתם על חרבכם') ומסתיימת בחטא דתי–חברתי ('ואיש את
אשת רעהו וגו').
בשתי הקבוצות גובר כמותית היסוד הדתי (2:1 1:2). אמנם, כאמור, ההאשמה האמצעית
בקבוצה השנייה, 'עשיתן תועבה', עשויה להתפרש בגלל אופיה הכללי גם בכיוון חברתי, אך
הלשון 'תועבה' מכוון יותר לכיוון הדתי.
האברים בשתי הקבוצות מסודרים, אפוא, באופן מעין כיאסטי, ליתר דיוק: האֵבר הראשון
בקבוצה השנייה מקביל לאֵבר האחרון בקבוצה הראשונה.

עמדתם על חרבכם	c		על הדם תאכלו	a	
עשיתן תועבה6	b		עינכם ... גלוליכם	b	
ואיש את אשת רעהו טמאתם	a		דם תשפכו	c	

מרשימת החטאים עוברת התוכחה לתיאור העונש. מבנה הדברים בנבואה ערוך, אפוא, כך:

<hr>

5   רש"י ורד"ק: נצטוו על כך בתורה ולא מילאו אחר הצו. רד"ק מוסיף על כך, שהם עושים מעשי
    אלילות כאלה שבגללם סולקו הכנענים מן הארץ. לדעת קרלי מדובר כאן באכילת דם בניגוד לדין
    הכוהני, אבל אולי הגירסה המקורית כוונה לאכילה על ההרים, כמו ב–יח 6, והוא מנהג אלילי;
    K.W. Carley, *Ezekiel* (CBC), Cambridge 1974, ad loc. וכן סבר קוק, המזהה את המנהג
    עם חגי פולחן שנחוגו בבמות; G.A. Cooke, *A Critical and Exegetical Commentary on*
    the Book of Ezekiel (ICC), Edinburgh 1936, ad loc. כך כבר פירש ר"א מבלגנצי את
    הלשון 'על הדם' בפסוקנו: 'שהיו זובחים לשעירים, כמו שפירשנו בא‏חרי מות'.
6   רד"ק מציין שחל כאן חילוף מ"ם בנו"ן, או שהנביא מכוון את האשמתו כנגד נקבות. רש"י מפרש,
    שמדובר במשכב זכור.

1. תיאור מאוויהם — ירושת הארץ
2. תלונה על חטאיהם — ותמיהה: 'והארץ תירשו'?
3. תיאור העונש

הרעיון המבוסס על המבנה הנדון הוא, שלא זו בלבד שציפייתם לרשת את כל הארץ לא תתממש, אלא יתרה מזאת, הם ייענשו על מעשיהם הרעים. יש בכך עונש כפול לכל הנותרים בארץ לאחר חורבן הבית והגלות.

2. תיאור העונש (פסוקים 27–29)

הפתיחה לתיאור העונש אינה מפתיעה: 'אשר בחרבות בחרב יפלו'. אמירה זו נאה לה לפתוח את פסקת העונש, משום ש'חרב' מתייחסת לאמור ברשימת החטאים: 'עמדתם על חרבכם', ונוהג רגיל הוא בסגנון המקראי, שהעונש מנוסח בלשונות של 'מידה כנגד מידה' ביחס לחטא. בכך הצבענו על הקשרים שבין שני המרכיבים האחרונים בנבואה: התלונה על החטאים (מרכיב 2 לעיל) ותיאור העונש (מרכיב 3 לעיל). אולם בלשון זה ניתן גם למצוא קשר בין החלק הראשון והשני בנבואה: המלה 'חרבות' (פסוק 27) רומזת ל'ישבי החרבות האלה על אדמת ישראל' (פסוק 23).[7] הנביא רצה לרמוז באמצעותה על אשמתם ועל גאוותם של 'ישבי החרבות'.

בנבואה יש, אפוא, ארבע הופעות של הצירוף חר"ב (בשורשים שונים) — ישבי **החרבות**, עמדתם על **חרבכם**, אשר **בחרבות בחרב** יפלו — הנשזרות יחד, ויש בהן נוסף על האפקט של צליל קבוע ולשון נופל על לשון גם שימוש של מעין 'מלה מנחה'. שיבוצן של המלים החוזרות הללו בחלקים השונים של הנבואה, מפתיחת הנבואה ועד קרוב לסיומה, גורם לליכודה הן מבחינה ספרותית-סגנונית והן מבחינה רעיונית. ברור, אפוא, שהקטע על העונש (פסוקים 27– 29) בא לסגור את התיאור שבקטעים הקודמים.

בתיאור העונש נזכרה, כאמור, החרב כראשונה בין שאר האמצעים של העינשה האלהית. נעמוד עתה על כל מרכיבי העונש של הפסקה:

> כה אמר אדני ה' חי אני אם לא
> אשר בחרבות **בחרב** יפלו
> ואשר על פני השדה **לחיה** נתתיו לאכלו
> ואשר במצדות ובמערות **בדבר** ימתו
> ונתתי את הארץ שממה ומשמה...מאין עובר
> וידעו כי אני ה' בתתי את הארץ שממה...
> על כל תועבתם אשר עשו

חרב, חיה רעה ודבר שייכים למכלול מונחים סטריאוטיפיים, המשמשים לתיאור עונש אלוהי: חרב, רעב, דבר וחיה רעה (השווה, למשל, רשימת העונשים שבאה בפרק יד 12–21).[8] הופעת המונחים הללו בפסקת העונש מעלה את המסקנות הבאות:

1. יחזקאל משתמש כאן ברשימה סטריאוטיפית של מכות אלהיות החוזרת במקומות שונים במקרא. על כן נראה שהוא בקיא במסורות הללו ורגיל אצלן, באשר הוא משתמש בהן גם בנבואות אחרות.

---

7   רש"י, ד"ה 'אשר בחרבות': 'שסופן להיות חריבים'.

8   לפי רש"י יש 'דירוג' מסוים בתיאור העונש: בד"ה 'ואשר במצדות' הוא אומר: 'במחבא להטמן מן החרב — אשלח בם את הדבר'. גם מלבי"ם בפירושו לפסוק 27 מדבר בסוגי העונש: בחרב, בחיה ובדבר, בהתאמה למקום מחבואם. ר"א מבלנצ'י: במצדות ובמערות: 'שלא תבואהו חרב וחיה'.

2. השימוש ברשימה בנבואה הנדונה אינו מלא, שכן עונש ה'רעב' אינו מופיע. ושמא כוונת מכוון יש בזה: בסיום הנבואה יחזקאל מתאר מצב של שממה טוטאלית של הארץ, ולפיכך הוא בחר לדבר על שלשה סוגי עונשים הגורמים להיעלמות מיידית של האנשים מן הארץ, ולא בעונש הרעב, הגורם סבל לעם אך לא לנטישה מיידית של הארץ.

3. בפרק יד באות המגפות הללו בשתי שיטות סידור:

א. בפסוקים 12–20 — רעב, חיה רעה, חרב, דבר
ב. בפסוק 21 — חרב ורעב וחיה רעה ודבר

נמצא, הסדר בנבואה הנדונה הוא לפי המסורת השנייה (יד 21), ואפשר שהיא מסורת שהיתה מקובלת יותר על יחזקאל.

גם ב־ו 11, 'אשר בחרב ברעב ובדבר', הסדר זהה למקומנו בשינויים מסוימים, שם 'רעב' בא במקום 'חיה'. ב־ה 17 נזכרו רעב, חיה רעה ודבר. יש בכך קרבה למקומנו בשינוי של 'רעב' במקום 'חרב', הבאה בטקסט זה כמכה אחרונה ולאחר הפסקה מעטה. סדר שונה בא ב־ז 15: (a) 'חרב דבר ורעב — (b) חרב רעב ודבר'. a שונה ממקומנו בזה שהוא כולל את לשון 'רעב' במקום 'חיה רעה', וכן בכך שסדר האברים השני והשלישי שונה מזה שב־ג, ואילו ב־b יש רק הבדל אחד ביחס למקומנו: 'חיה רעה' בא 'רעב'.

קטע העונש בנבואה נחלק לשני חלקים: בחלק הראשון (פסוק כז) יש מקבילה לרשימה הסטריאוטיפית של המגפות: חרב, דבר וכו' (ראה לעיל), ובחלק השני (פסוקים כח–כט) דברי סיום לעונש האופייניים ליחזקאל: 'וידעו כי אני ה''. הסיום בשני החלקים יוצר מסגרת מתאימה בגלל לשונות זהים או קרובים הבאים בהם:

פסוק 28: 'ונתתי את הארץ שממה ומשמה ... ושממו מאין עובר'
פסוק 29: בתתי את הארץ שממה ומשמה'.

בין שתי פסקאות העונש יש מעין חלוקת תפקידים: בראשון, פסוק 27, ברשימת המגפות, יש הודעה על מיני מגפות שתושבי הארץ ייענשו בהן, בשני, פסוקים 28–29 — עונש הארץ עצמה. אף נראה, שהחלק השני הוא תוצאת האמור בחלק הראשון, שהרי שממת הארץ באה על שום חטאי התושבים ('על כל תועבותם אשר עשו') והיא תהיה שממה 'מאין עובר'. ללשונות 'שממה ומשמה' צליל קרוב, החוזר כאן מספר פעמים: שממה ומשמה...ושממו (28) שממה ומשמה (29), וגם הלשונות האחרים יוצרים תמונה קרובה לזה ('מאין עובר'). נוסף לקשרים שציינתי לעיל, קיים גם קשר בין קטע החטא (פסוקים 25–26) לחלק השני של פסקת העונש (פסוק 28–29). בכך מביע הנביא את הרעיון הפשוט: כל העונשים החמורים שאים על העם יבואו — 'על כל תועבתם אשר עשו' (29). כלומר, העם ייענש בעונש הראוי להם בגלל חטאיהם.

ג. קווים סגנוניים ורעיוניים בנבואת יחזקאל על יושבי הארץ

יחזקאל מכנה את הקהל של יושבי הארץ שלאחר גלות צדקיהו, שאליו מכוונת נבואתו: 'ישבי החרבות **האלה**'.[9] בכך הוא מבטא את יחסו השלילי אליהם, יחס העולה גם מנבואות נוספות.

---

9   לפי צימרלי (לעיל, הערה 4), בפירושו לכתוב, 'האלה' נוספה לטקסט המקורי כמקבילה מבארת
     לפסוקים 21–22 (יצוין, שהיא חסרה בתרגום השבעים ובווטוס לאטינה). לפי קרלי (לעיל, הערה

אציין בזה קווים סגנוניים–רעיוניים לשימוש הלשון 'חרבות' ביחזקאל:

ראשון – מלת 'חרבות' באה ביחזקאל תשע פעמים, וזה יותר מבכל ספר מקראי אחר. יתרה מזו, שימוש זה מהווה למעלה משליש מכלל ההופעות של צורת הרבים של שם זה במקרא. אם נצרף לכאן גם את צורת היחיד (חורבה) יתוספו לנו 5 הופעות, זאת כאשר כלל ההופעות במקרא – פרט ליחזקאל – הוא 11 פעמים. השימוש ביחזקאל הוא, אפוא, למעלה ממחצית מכל שאר הופעות הצורה ברבים (16/9) ומעט פחות ממחצית שימושו בצורת היחיד בשאר הספרים (11/5).

השימוש בצורת היחיד והרבים של השם בולט בעיקר בספרות של שלהי ימי הבית הראשון ואילך (כך ירמיה, מלאכי, ישעיה השני, דניאל, עזרא, ודברי הימים).

השימוש ב'חרבה' נעשה גם בטקסטים שונים, בויקרא ובקצת מזמורי תהילים, שאולי הם מאוחרים. ושמא לפנינו מלה שצמחה בעקבות האיום הממשי לחורבן ירושלים, והשימוש בה התרחב בעקבות החורבן.

עתה נסקור את הכתובים הכוללים את הצורה 'חרבה'/'חרבות', במגמה להסביר את שימושי יחזקאל בצורה האמורה.

הנביא מכנה את הנמענים בנבואה הנדונה: 'ישבי החרבות' (פסוק 24), והוא תואר שלילי, המתאר את הארץ שלאחר החורבן. מאידך בא בנבואות גוג ארץ המגוג צירוף קרוב לזה אולם במשמעות חיובית, שהרי אמור שם 'להשיב ידך על חרבות נושבת' (לח 12), היינו, חורבות הארץ שנושבו מחדש בזמן הגאולה, בניגוד ל'ישבי החרבות', המסתופפים בארץ אחר חורבנה. השווה גם בדברים המצוטטים בספר מלאכי 'ונשוב ונבנה חרבות' (א 4). יחזקאל, הרגיל לתאר את הארץ בחורבנה בלשונות 'חרבה' (ביחיד) ו'חרבות' (ברבים), משתמש, כאמור, בלשון זה גם כדי לתאר את ישועת הארץ. כך לו 10, 'ונושבו הערים והחרבות תבנינה', והוא היפוך האמור בפסוק 4 'ולחרבות השממות'.

חשיבות הכינוי 'ישבי החרבות' בנבואה הנדונה עולה מן ההשוואה שבינה לבין יא 15–14. גם שם עולה שאלת היחסים שבין יושבי הארץ לבין הגולים, אולם היחס המספרי שונה: בעת ההיא, גלות יהויכין, אוכלוסיית הנותרים בארץ היתה גדולה לעומת אוכלוסיית הגולים. בנבואה ההיא כונו הנשארים 'ישבי ירושלים', בתואר החיובי או לפחות הניטרלי, ואילו עתה הם מכונים בתואר השלילי: 'ישבי החרבות'.[10]

אלה הם הגורמים המכתיבים, אפוא, את הכינוי השונה: המועד השונה ושינוי היחס המספרי, היקף הגלות וגודל החורבן.

'(על/אל) אדמת ישראל' – צירוף לשון זה מופיע רק בספר יחזקאל (שבע עשרה פעמים). ונראה, שהוא לשון שהומצא על ידי הנביא לצרכיו הרעיוניים.

---

5), תפקיד הנבואה להצביע על כך שלמרות החורבן שבא על העם ועל הארץ לא חל כל שינוי לטובה בעם. מאידך סבור ג'ויס (לעיל, הערה 1), עמ' 44, שההתקפה על יושבי ישראל אינה משקפת את מגמת הגולים. אולם אחרת לחלוטין סבר אייכרודט. לדעתו, הנבואה כנגד יושבי הארץ היתה בעלת חשיבות גדולה ליושבי הגולה, באשר ההתנגדות ליושבי הארץ היתה טבעית בקרבם; W. Eichrodt, Ezekiel (OTL), London 1970, ad loc. לדעתי, הלשון 'האלה' מביע סלידה ובוז לנשארים, והשווה: 'כי נאצו האנשים האלה את ה'' (במ' טז 30); 'החטאים האלה בנפשתם' (במ' יז 3); 'לא יטפו לאלה' (מיכה ב 6); 'פן יבאו הערלים האלה' (דה"א י 4).

10 לדעת בות, כל יחידות הנבואה שבפרק לג רומזות לנבואות שונה שבמכלול הפרקים א–כד; L. Boadt, 'The Function of the Salvation Oracles in Ezekiel 33-37', HAR 12 (1990), pp. 7f. בהמשך הוא הולך ומצביע על המקבילות לכל אחת מן הנבואות שבפרק. כך, למשל, בעמ' 7–8 הוא מצביע על המקבילות לנבואה הנדונה: ה 17,16,12,11,9; ו 11–12; ה 19; ו 14; יא 14–21, ועוד.

במקרה דנן, תפקיד לשון זה (בצד הכינוי 'האלה') הוא להצביע על ריחוק: אתם, שם בארץ ישראל, בהשוואה אלינו, הנמצאים בבבל. הוא משלים, אפוא, את 'האלה' (ואת 'ישבי החרבות'), במגמה לציין את אלה שסברו להיבנות מחורבנם של אחרים, רק עתה תבוא גם עליהם המכה הכואבת.

'אחד היה אברהם ... ואנחנו רבים' – טיעון של הסתמכות על האבות ניתן למצוא בנבואת ישעיהו השני, יש' סג 16: 'כי אתה אבינו כי אברהם לא ידענו וישראל לא יכירנו אתה ה' אבינו גאלנו מעולם שמך'. בשני הכתובים אברהם מוצג באור נחות בהשוואה לדמויות אחרות. בישעיה סג נאמר, ש'האב' אברהם אינו (עוד) מעוז ומבטח לבני הדור, אלא רק הא הוא האב הראוי, ואילו בנבואת יחזקאל (פסוק 24) הנותרים בארץ מצביעים על זכותם לרשת את הארץ כעדיפה על זו של אברהם, כי הם הרבים.[11]

הלשון 'לנו נתנה הארץ למורשה' מובא כציטוט של דברי הנשארים בארץ, ונראה שהוא משקף אמרה אמיתית של בני הארץ, והיא מופיעה גם בנבואה המקבילה על אנשי הארץ (יא 14–15 [וראה לעיל על הלשון 'ישבי החרבות']): 'לנו היא נתנה הארץ למורשה' (יא 15). מסתבר שאחר הגליית חלק מן העם בגלות יהויכין נסתמנה מגמה כזאת של טענה לירושת כל הארץ. עתה, כשרוב הארץ נעזבה, התחזקה מגמה זו אצל הנשארים המעטים.

עוד יש לציין, כי מלת 'מורשה' היא כמעט בלעדית ליחזקאל (שבע פעמים, לעומת פעמים בשאר ספרי המקרא). שבע ההופעות עניינן זהה: הכרזה על נחלה כשייכת לעם פלוני. כך בנבואות הנחמה (לו 3) יחזקאל מתריע על המצב בהווה, שבו ישראל נתונים בידי הגוים ('להיותכם מורשה לשארית הגוים'), והשוואה גם בדברי הגוים ב-לו 2. וכן בא שימוש זה גם על אומות אחרות ב-כה 4, 10.

יש בכך כדי לאשש את המסקנה, שיחזקאל שמע – מכלי שני – טיעון מפורש כזה של הנשארים, או שהוא מצא את לנכון לנסח אמרה עממית, או הלוך רוח עממי, במלים משלו ('מורשה' וכו').[12]

האמירה הזהה בשתי הנבואות משמשת לניסוח תפיסות שונות של מחשבות הנשארים לגבי הטענה, שהארץ ניתנה להם למורשה: בפרק יא 14–16 טענתם מיוסדת על הרעיון, שהעובדה שחלקם נשארו בארץ בשעה שאחיהם, גולי יהויכין, הורחקו ממנה, היא בגדר סימן לכך שהאל בחר בהם להיות יורשי הארץ. על כך משיב יחזקאל, שריחוקם הפיסי של הגולים מן הארץ אין פירושו שהם רחוקים מן האל, אלא להפך. הלוך המחשבה ב-לג 23–29 שונה לחלוטין. לא עוד טענה לעגינה כנגד הגולים ש'רחקו מעל ה'', אלא קביעה הנשענת על זכותם של הנשארים מכח החזקה, שהם יושבים בארץ ועל היותם בני אברהם, האב הקדמון, ועוד שהם רבים לעומת אברהם ה'אחד'. בפעם הזאת לא הועלתה כל טענה כלשהי על חולשת זכויותיהם של הגולים. לשון אחר: בנבואה יא שבפרק עיקר הטיעונים שמשמיעים הנשארים בארץ הוא **כנגד הגולים**, ואילו כאן, עיקר הטיעון הוא **בזכות הנשארים.**

11 קרליי, בפירושו לכתוב (לעיל, הערה 5), סבור שיש בזה התייחסות להבטחה לאברהם; ראה דב' ט 5; ל 20. אלה שנשארו בארץ אחרי 587 לפנה"ס התפארו בהיותם בחירי האל. על אברהם כאביהם של ישראל, ראה מתי ג 9; לוקס ג 8; יוחנן ח 39.

12 כפי שהראיתי בפרק: הציטוט – קו סגנוני-רעיוני בנבואות יחזקאל, בספרי, עיונים בספר יחזקאל, תל אביב תשל"ה, עמ' 18–52.

ד. סיכום

הנבואה על 'ישבי החרבות' שובצה במגילת הנבואות שבפרק לג מאותו הטעם ששובצו בה שאר
הנבואות. מקום הנבואה הנדונה הוא לאחר הנבואה על בוא הפליט (לג 21–22). תאריכה של
האחרונה רשום במפורש, ועוד בולט בה ביסוד הזמן, באשר היא עוסקת בנושא שעניינו זמן
מסוים לאחר החורבן. ניתוח תוכנה ורעיונה של הנבואה על 'ישבי החרבות' מלמד, אפוא,
ששיבוצה בסמוך ולאחר הנבואה על בוא הפליט והפסקת האלם משקף נכונה את כוונת
יחזקאל.[13]

בכלל הדברים נראה לי, שבפרק לג ריכז עורך הספר קבוצת נבואות, שזמנן ועניינן הם
המאורעות של **סביבות** החורבן. הנבואה הקדומה במגילה (נבואת הצופה, פסוקים 1–9; או
נבואת הגמול, פסוקים 10–20) היא מכשנה לפני חורבן ירושלים, ואילו האחרונה (השוואת
נבואת יחזקאל לשיר עגבים, פסוקים 30–33) היא בבירור זמן מה לאחר החורבן. היחידות
המאוחרות במגילה מבטאות את השאננות של בני הגולה, שלמרות שנבואות התוכחה הקדומות
של יחזקאל נתקיימו, הם בכל זאת ממשיכים במעשי ההוללות שלהם, שמגיעים לשיאם בכך
שגם דבר ה' שבפי הנביא נהפך להם לגורם של שחוק ובידור (לג 30–33).

מן העיון בחמש הנבואות שבמגילה עולה, ששתיים מהן מתאימות לשעה המיידית שלאחר
החורבן והגלות: השלישית – פרשת סיום האלם (פסוקים 21–22), והרביעית – הנבואה על
יושבי החורבות (פסוקים 23–29).

ועוד: כפי שאני מראה בדיון אחר,[14] קיימת זיקת של השוואה בין הנבואה הנוכחית על יושבי
החורבות (=ארץ ישראל) לבין הנבואה על יחס בני הגולה (=בבל) אל הנביא (לג 30–33).[15]
נמצאת אומר, שהנביא אמר עתה[16] את דבריו כדי להראות ב**מקביל** את יחסו לאלה הרחוקים
(=הנשארים בארץ) ולאלה הקרובים (=שכניו בבבל).[17]

13 והיות והזיקה בין הנבואות הללו היא שקופה וברורה, הרי שיבוצן בסדר הנתון נועד להצביע על יחסו
    של יחזקאל גם לחלק זה של העם. תאריכה המוקדם ביותר של הנבואה הנדונה הוא שנת 586
    (כלומר, לא לפני שמלאו שש שנים לשליחות יחזקאל).

14 ראה מאמרי, 'הנבואה על "שיר העגבים" (לג ל–לג) ומקומה בספר יחזקאל', ספר ליכט (בדפוס).

15 לדעת קרוגר, T. Kruger, *Geschichtskonzepte in Ezechielbuch*, Berlin 1989, p. 323
    אותה מגמה עריכתית (ואותו חוג עורכים) שעמדה בבסיס יא 14–21 באה לידי ביטוי גם בעריכת לג
    23–29. לפי אייכרודט (לעיל, הערה 9) הכותרת לנבואה גרמה לכך, שהעורכים הביאו את שתי
    הנבואות (פסוקים 23–29 ופסוקים 30–33) ברצף אחד, אולם יש לבדוק אם בשיבוץ זה עשו
    העורכים את הראוי לפי רוח הנבואות הללו.

16 מאידך סבר רד"ק, שמדובר במלכות צדקיהו, היינו, לפני החורבן והגלות של 587/6.

17 לדעת ח' תדמור, 'הזיקה בין עם ישראל לארצו גלות בבל ושיבת ציון', גלות אחר גולה, ספר
    חיים ביינרט, ירושלים תשמ"ח, עמ' 50–55, יש בנבואה הנדונה משום פיתוח הרעיון של השארית
    שארית. אלא שאצל יחזקאל וירמיהו, בחזון שני דודאי התאנים (יר' כד), בניגוד לישעיהו, מדובר על
    רעה. תושבי ירושלים הסתמכו על נבואות עתיקות, שלפיהן הם, הנשארים, ממשיכים גרעין של
    ישראל שבעתיד. אזכור אברהם הוא על כל שום עניין ירושת הארץ. מן הדמיון לסיפורי אברהם, שם
    מופיע יר"ש, וכן לדב' ד 37–38; ט 4–6, שגם בהם בא שימוש ב-נת"ן, יר"ש ומלת ארץ, נראה שדברי
    העם מושרשים בספרות ספרותית העתיקה. לפי העולה מעדות ספר עזרא, נראה שהוא תומך בגולים החוזרים
    ורואה ב**הם** את השארית הטובה.

לתולדות צמיחתו של הביטוי 'מגלת־ספר' —
פרק בהתפתחות מינוח הכתיבה בתקופת המקרא

אבי הורביץ

א

הביטוי המקראי 'מגלת־ספר' מעורר כמה סוגיות לשוניות מעניינות — הן מבחינת הרכבו, הן
מבחינת שימושו. אשר להרכבו, מאלף הדבר, כי שתי מלים ('מגלה', 'ספר') — שביסוד כל אחת
מהן עומדת, מבחינה סימאנטית, אותה משמעות בסיסית (חומר הכתיבה עצמו, מחד, והטקסט
הנכתב עליו, מאידך) — חָברוּ כאן זו לזו, כשהן מופיעות יחדיו בתוך צירוף של סמיכות
('מגלת־ספר'). אשר לשימושו, ראויה לתשומת לב העובדה, כי תפוצת הביטוי מצומצמת למדי,
והיא מוגבלת אך ורק לספרים ירמיהו, יחזקאל ותהלים (סך הכל ארבע היקרויות: יר' לו 2, 4;
יח' ב 9; תה' מ 8). השאלה הנשאלת אפוא היא: מהו הרקע הלשוני של ביטוי זה, ומהו מקומו
במסגרת ההיסטוריה של העברית המקראית?

הפרשנים ומחברי המילונים המקראיים המקובלים אינם מרחיבים את הדיבור על טיבו
ומשמעותו של הביטוי הנדון, ואין הם נכנסים לבירור השאלה באילו נסיבות נטבע צירוף יוצא
דופן זה ומהם התנאים הלשוניים שהכשירו את לידתו.[1] נושא זה הוא שיעמוד כאן במרכז
ענייננו, וללבונו מוקדש הבירור שלהלן. במסגרת זו נבחן, תחילה, את המלים 'ספר' ו'מגלה', כל
אחת **כשהיא לעצמה**, ולאחר מכן ננסה לעמוד על טיבו הלשוני של **הצירוף** 'מגלת־ספר' ועל
ההשלכות המתבקשות מכך לגבי הנושא העומד פה לדיון.

שמח אני להביא דברים אלה בספר היובל לפרופ' מ' הרן, מורי בעבר ועמיתי בהווה, משום
שנוגעים הם במישרין לנושא של דרכי כתיבת ספרים ומגילות בעת העתיקה — נושא לו
מקדיש לאחרונה בעל היובל מחקרים רבים וחשובים מפרי עטו.

ב

המלה 'ספר' שגורה ביותר בספרות המקראית, והיא עשויה לציין הן את חומר הכתיבה עצמו
והן את מה שנכתב עליו. כגון:[2]

---

1. מילון KB, למשל, בערך 'מגלה', איננו מוצא אפילו לנכון להזכיר את הצירוף 'מגלת־ספר'. מראי
    המקומות ל'מגלת־ספר' ול'מגלה' מובאים בו יחדיו, ללא שום הבחנה ביניהם (עמ' 493; וכך גם
    במהדורתו המחודשת של המילון, HALAT, ב, עמ' 517). גם י' ליכט (בערך: 'מגלה', אנציקלופדיה
    מקראית, ד, טור 671–672) איננו מבחין בדיונו בין 'מגלה' לבין 'מגלת־ספר'.
2. ראה, למשל, י' ליכט, 'ספר', אנציקלופדיה מקראית, ה, טורים 1080–1081.

איוב יט 23–24: מי יתן אֵפוֹ וְיִכָּתְבוּן מִלָּי
מי יתן **בספר** וְיֻחָקוּ
[=חומר כתיבה / כתובת]3 ...לָעַד בְּצוּר יֵחָצְבוּן

מל"ב ה 5: ויאמר מלך ארם לֶךְ־בֹּא
ואשלחה **ספר** אל מלך ישראל [=מכתב, איגרת]

דב' כד 1: כי יקח איש אשה ובעלה
והיה אם לא תמצא חן בעיניו...
וכתב לה **ספר** כריתֻת [=שטר (גירושין), גט]

שמ"ב א 17–18: ויקֹנן דוד את
הקינה הזאת... הנה כתובה על
ספר הישר [=קובץ של יצירות פיוטיות]

מל"א יא 41: ויתר דברי שלמה וכל
אשר עשה וחכמתו הלוא הם כתֻבים
על **ספר** דברי שלמה [=חיבור היסטוריוגרפי]

נחמ' ז 5: ... וָאֶקְבְּצָה את החרים
ואת הסגנים ואת העם להתיחש
וָאֶמְצָא **ספר** היחשׂ [=רשימת יוחסין, גיניאלוגיה]

יהו' א 8: לא ימוש **ספר** התורה הזה
מפיך והגית בו יומם ולילה [=תורת משה]4

המלה 'ספר' משמשת בגֹוני משמעות דומים גם בדיאלקטים השונים של השמית הצפון–
מערבית (אוגריתית, כנענית–פֹניקית, ארמית [עתיקה וממלכתית]).5 השווה:

---

3 התקבֹלת 'בספר'//'בצור' מקרבת להניח שמדובר כאן 'על החומר שהיו כותבים בו או עליו' (נ"ה
טור–סיני, איוב, תל־אביב תשי"ד, עמ' 183); וראה גם: M. Pope, *Job*3 (AB), Garden City,
New York 1979, pp. 143 f. (הוא מתרגם את המלה 'ספר' על ידי 'stela'). לפירוש 'ספר' =
'כתובת', ראה, למשל: G.R. Driver, *Semitic Writing* (The Schweich Lectures), London:
1948, p. 83, n. 10 (אולם בעמ' 241 יש הסתייגות מפירוש זה); י' קוטשר, מלים ותולדותיהן,
ירושלים תשכ"א, עמ' 67; *HALAT*, ג, עמ' 723.
4 אמנם אינֵנו יודעים ודעים מהו היקפֹ וטיבֹ המדויק של 'ספר התורה' שמדובר בו.
5 לגבי האוגריתית, ראה: J. Aistleitner, *Wörterbuch der ugaritischen Sprache*, Berlin:
1963, p. 223; לגבי הכנענית והארמית, ראה: Ch.-F. Jean – J. Hoftijzer, *Dictionnaire des
inscriptions sémitiques de l'ouest*, Leiden 1965, pp. 196 f. נֹסח הכתובות הכנעניות
והארמיות מובא להלן על פי ספרם של H. Donner–W. Röllig, *Kanaanäische und
aramäische Inschriften*3, 1, Wiesbaden 1971 (=*KAI*); ומכתבי יב, ממהדורתו של קאולי:
A. Cowley, *Aramaic Papyri of the Fifth Century B.C.*, Oxford 1923 (=Cow.).

אוגריתית
(UT 1005:8-9): נקמד מלכ אֻגרת כתב ספר הנד
('נקמד מלך אוגרית כָּתַב ספר זה')   [=מכתב[6

(UT 1161:1-3): ספר ערבנמ דת ערב במתנ
('ספר הערֵבים אשר ערבו למתן')[7]   [תעודה/רשימה[8

אחירם
(KAI 1:2): תחתספ חטר משפטה תהתפכ
('יִשָּׁבֵר חוטר משפטו יֵהָפֵךּ')

כסא מלכה... והא ימח **ספרה**
(כסא מלכותו... והוא יִמְחֶה ספרו')   [=כתובת אפיגרפית]

כלמו
(KAI 24:13-14): ומי בבני אש ישב תחתנ
('ומי מבני אשר יֵשֵׁב תחתי')

ויזק **בספר** ז...
(ויגרום נזק לספר זה...')   [=כתובת אפיגרפית/
מצבה]

ספירי
(KAI 222 C 17): מלי **ספרא** זי בנצֺבא זנה
('מלות הספר אשר על המצבה הזאת')   [=כתובת אפיגרפית]

יב
(Cow. 14:3-4): ...כספ... ונחש ופרזל כל
('...כסף... ונחשת וברזל כל')

נכסן וקנין **וספר** אנתו
(נכסים וקנין וספר אישוּת')   [=שטר (אישוּת); מעין
כתובה]

ספר מרחק זי כתב...
('ספר מרחק אשר כָּתַב...')   .[=שטר (ויתור/הרחקה)]

הטקסטים האוגריתיים מצוטטים על פי C.H. Gordon, *Ugaritic Textbook*, Rome 1965
(UT=); במהדורת KTU הם מופיעים כ־KTU 2·19 ו־KTU 3·3, בהתאמה.
אפשר שניתן להוסיף לרשימת המקורות שלהלן גם את כתובת דיר־עלא ('[זנה] סֺפֺר [ב]לֺעֺמֺ');
אולם קריאה זו מבוססת, כמובן, על שחזור גרידא (השווה לאחרונה :M. Weipert, 'The Balaam
Text from Deir ʿAllā...', in: J. Hoftijzer – G. van der Kooij (eds.), *The Balaam Text
from Deir ʿAlla Re-evaluated*, Leiden 1991, p. 153

6 אייסטלייטנר, שם: 'Schrift, Brief'; גורדון (שם, עמ' 451) מתרגם את 'ספר' 'any
" document" '
7 א"פ רייני, מבנה החברה באוגרית, ירושלים תשכ"ז, עמ' 108.
8 אייסטלייטנר (לעיל, הערה 5): 'Aufzählung, Liste; Zahl'.

תפוצתה הנרחבת של המלה 'ספר' בכל המקורות הללו ורציפות השימוש בה במשך כל תקופת המקרא מצדיקות בהחלט את המסקנה, כי יש לראות בתיבה זו מונח שמי–מערבי מובהק.[9] לעומת זאת, אופי השימוש בתיבה 'מגלה' משקף מציאות לשונית שונה לחלוטין. בניגוד ל'ספר', המשמש כאמור בכל המקרא כולו,[10] אין 'מגלה' מתועדת לא בחומש, לא בספרי נביאים ראשונים ולא בכתבי הנבואה הקלאסית של המאה השמינית לפסה"נ. הופעתה הברורה[11] הראשונה של 'מגלה' בספרות המקראית מצויה בספר ירמיהו – היינו, בשלהי ימי הבית הראשון – ומחוץ לירמיהו (x14)[12] היא מופיעה בספרי המקרא העבריים ביחזקאל (x4),[13] בזכריה (x2)[14] ובתהלים (x1).[15] דרך משל:

 יר' לו 28: שוב קח לך מגלה אחרת וכתב עליה את כל הדברים הראשנים אשר היו על המגלה הראשנה אשר שרף יהויקים מלך יהודה

יח' ג 1:   ויאמר אלי בן אדם... אכול את המגלה הזאת ולך דבֵּר אל בית ישראל

זכ' ה 1:   ואשוב ואשא עיני ואראה והנה מגלה עפה.

כמו כן מתועדת 'מגלה' בארמית המקראית:

עז' ו 1–2: ... בקרו   בבית ספריא...   והשתכח באחמתא...
           ('וערכו ביקורת   בבית הספרים...   ונמצאה באחמתא...)

מגלה   חדה   וכן כתיב   בגוה   דכרונה
(מגילה   אחת   וכך כתוב   בתוכה   הזכרון') [=תזכיר].[16]

נתונים אלה, המצביעים על כך שהופעתה של 'מגלה' על הזירה הלשונית של הספרות המקראית היא מאוחרת למדי,[17] עולים בקנה אחד עם העדויות שמספקים לנו המקורות החוץ–

9   ראה: Y. Muffs, *Studies in the Aramaic Legal Papyri from Elephantine* (Studia et Documenta ad Iura Orientis Antiqui Pertinentia, 8), Leiden 1969, pp. 196, 207 (אמנם, דבריו של מופס מתייחסים לשימושה **המשפטי** של 'ספר', שהוראתה 'שטר' או 'תעודה'). מוצאה של המלה שנוי במחלוקת. הדעה המקובלת במחקר היא כי מקורה של 'ספר' ב–*šipru* האכדית במשמעות 'שליחות' (ראה, למשל: S.A. Kaufman, *The Akkadian Influences on Aramaic* (AS, 19), Chicago–London 1974, p. 29. השווה גם קוטשר (לעיל, הערה 3), עמ' 67. מופס מתנגד לגזרון זה; ראה בספרו, עמ' 207). מכל מקום, גם מבלי להיכנס לשאלת ה'פריהיסטוריה' של המלה, הרי אין ספק בדבר כי מן האלף השני לפסה"נ יש בידינו תיעוד רצוף של השימוש ב'ספר' כמלה רגילה ומקובלת באוצר המלים של השפות השמיות הצפון–מערביות (השווה קאופמן, שם, עמ' 28).

10   השווה לעיל, עמ' 2. חשוב לציין כי המלה מופיעה גם בחרסי לכיש; ראה, למשל, ז'אן–הופטייזר (לעיל, הערה 5).

11   השווה להלן, הערה 17.

12   כל ההיקרויות מרוכזות בפרק אחד, בפרק לו: 'מגלה' – בפסוקים 6, 14 (פעמיים), 20, 21, 23, 25, 27, 28 (פעמיים), 29, 32; 'מגלת־ספר' – בפסוקים 2, 4.

13   'מגלה' – ג 1, 2, 3; 'מגלת־ספר' – ב 9.

14   'מגלה עפה' (ה 1, 2).

15   'מגלת־ספר' (מ 8)

16   'memorandum'=; ראה: BDB, עמ' 1088; KB, עמ' 1066.

17   ראה: BDB, עמ' 166 – 'late' (זמנו של מזמור מ' איננו ידוע, ועל כן אין ללמוד ממנו דבר ברור לעניננו).

מקראיים.[18] על פי עדויות אלה מתברר, כי 'מגלה' איננה מופיעה לא באוגריתית ולא בכנענית (שתי לשונות שבהן נשתמרו רבות מן התכונות המאפיינות את לשון התקופה המקראית הקדומה);[19] ומאידך, התיבה רווחת ביותר בלשון חכמים ובדיאלקטים הארמיים (שלשונם מצטרפת, בדרך כלל, ל־milieu הלשוני של התקופה המקראית המאוחרת).[20] יתר על כן, יש בידינו עדויות ברורות המצביעות על כך, שהתיבה 'מגלה' 'פולשת', בתקופה המאוחרת, לתחומה של 'ספר' הקדומה ותופסת את מקומה. השווה:

(1) ספרות התנאים[21]

משנה יב' ד, יג: אמר ר' שמעון בן עזיי מצאתי **מגילת** יוחסים בירושלם וכתוב בה...

נחמ' ז 5: וָאמצא ספר היחש... ואמצא   כתוב בו
(וראה גם בר' ה 1: ספר תולדֹת)[22]

משנה סוטה ב, ד: ואינו כותב לא על הלוח ולא על הנייר ולא על הדיפתרא אלא **במגילה**,
שנאמר [במ' ה 23]: בספר

מכילתא לשמות יז 14: 'כְּתֹב זאת זכרון בספר' וגו':
... 'בספר' – מה שכתוב **במגלה**

(2) התרגומים הארמיים

במ' ה 23: וְכָתַב את האלֹת האלה הכהן בספר   ומחה...
פס' יונתן:[23] ויכתוב ית לווטייא האילין כהנא על **מגילתא**   וימחוק...

---

18 ראה, למשל, HALAT, ב, עמ' 517.

19 באוגריתית מצאנו את הצירוף לח(ת) ספר (=לוּחַ סֵפֶר), הבנוי במתכונת הביטוי 'מגלת־ספר' במקרא (השווה: M. Dahood, *Psalms*, 1 (AB), Garden City, New York 1965, p. 246). למשמעות הצירוף האוגריתי ראה גם: K. Galling, 'Tafel, Buch und Blatt,' in: H. Goedicke (ed.), *Near Eastern Studies in Honor of W.F. Albright*, Baltimore–London 1971, p. 211, n. 13. אולם 'מגלת־ספר' (וכן גם, כאמור, 'מגלה' כשלעצמה) אין בה.

20 לאחרונה נתפרסם מקור נוסף לתיעודה של המלה בארמית של התקופה הפרסית; ראה: E. Bresciani, 'L'attività archeologica dell'Università di Pisa in Egitto: 1977–1980', *Egitto e Vicino Oriente* 3 (1980), p. 16 (על מראה מקום זה חייב אני תודה לידידי פרופ' ב' פורטן).

21 המשנה מצוטטת כאן על־פי כ"י קאופמן, והמכילתא על־פי מהדורת ח"ש האראוויטץ – י"א רבין, מכילתא דרבי ישמעאל[2], ירושלים תש"ל.

22 'ספר יחש' = 'ספר תולדות'. (השימוש בשורש 'יחש'/'יחס' הוא מסממני לשונה של תקופת הבית השני, ובכיתוי הנידון מחליף הוא את השורש הקלאסי 'ילד'; השווה: A. Hurvitz, 'The Evidence of Language in Dating the Priestly Code', *RB* 81 (1974), pp. 26-29. דוגמא נוספת להחלפת המונח המקראי הקדום 'ספר' במונח חדש יותר – שאף הוא בא מתחום הארמית – ניתן למצוא בנחמ' ו 5, המדבר על 'אגרת פתוחה'. נראה כי היפוכו של מושג זה מופיע ביש' כט 11: 'ספר חתום' ('חתום' כנגד 'פתוח'); אבל במקום 'אגרת' המאוחרת משמש בו עדיין 'ספר' הקדום (רש"י בפירושו לפסוק זה מישעיהו, אכן 'מתרגם' את הביטוי 'ספר חתום' ל'אגרת חתומה'! [אולם אינטרפרטאציה זו ליש' כט 11 איננה בטוחה. ל' בלאו, למשל, מפרש כאן 'ספר'=Buch'; ראה: L. Blau, *Studien zum althebräischen Buchwesen*, Budapest 1902, p. 36

23 השווה משנה סוטה ב, ד, אשר הובאה לעיל (נוסח התרגום הוא על פי מהדורת E.G. Clarke, *Targum Pseudo-Jonathan...*, Hoboken, New Jersey 1984

יהו' יח 9:... וַיַּעַבְרוּ בָאָרֶץ וַיִּכְתְּבוּהָ לֶעָרִים לְשִׁבְעָה חֲלָקִים עַל סֵפֶר
פשיטתא:... ועברו בארעא וכתבו אנין לקוריא שבע פלגון על **מגלתא**

ישע' לד 4: ... וְנָגֹלּוּ   כַּסֵּפֶר הַשָּׁמִים
פשיטתא: ... ונתכרכון[24] שמיא איך **מגלתא.**

הדוגמא מישעיה לד מאלפת במיוחד לעניינו. אף על פי שמופיע בה פועל הנגזר מן השורש
'גלל' ('נָגֹלּוּ') – המעיד כמאה עדים על כך, שהשמים משולים כאן ל־'roll' / 'scroll' (היינו,
שניתן ל'גוֹלֵל' אותם) – אין הפסוק נזקק בהקשר זה למלה 'מגלה' (שאף היא גזורה, כמובן, מן
השורש 'גלל') אלא ל'סֵפֶר'! פירושו של דבר הוא, כי למרות מה שמבחינת הריאליה ב'מגלה'
(מתקפלת)[25] עסקינן, הרי הטרמינולוגיה המקראית משמרת כאן עדיין את המונח הקדמון 'סֵפֶר'
– אשר שימש, מלכתחילה, כמונח כללי ל'כל דבר כתוב, ממצבה חקוקה (ישעיה ל, ח; איוב יט,
כג–כד) ועד אגרת [ישעיה] לז, יד ועוד).'[26]

אמת שמצאנו את המלה גם באכדית (magallatu) ובערבית (مَـجَلَّة); אלא שבשתי הלשונות
הללו מתפרשת היא, על ידי המומחים לדבר, כ'ארמאיזם' מאוחר![27] במלים אחרות, הקורלאציה
שמצאנו בין הנתונים המקראיים לבין הטקסטים החיצוניים מאשרת בצורה ברורה את
המסקנה, כי התיבה 'מגלה' משתייכת לשכבה לשונית צעירה, יחסית, בתולדותיה של העברית
המקראית.[28]

24 'כרך' משמעו 'סבב', 'גלל', ומכאן גם 'כֶּרֶךְ' = '(roll (of a book. ראה מילון בן־יהודה בערכו, כרך
ה, עמ' 2517; וכן בלאו (לעיל, הערה 22), עמ' 46. לשימוש דומה של 'כרך' (='גלל') בזיקה ל'ספר'
ראה גם בנוסח הסורי של לוקס ד, 17–20: 'וַיָּתֵּן לוֹ סֵפֶר ישעיה הנביא ויפתח את הספר [בסורית:
'ופתח ישוע ספרא'] וימצא את המקום אשר היה כתוב בו: "רוח ה' עלי..."] ויגלל את הספר [בסורית:
'וכרך ספרא'] ויתנהו לַשַּׁמָּשׁ, וילך וישב'. פעולת ה'כריכה' (=גלילה) הנזכרת כאן מלמדת, כמובן,
שה'ספר' שמדובר בו לא היה אלא 'מגלה'. וכך, כידוע, גם בספרות חז"ל; דרך משל, משנה עירובין י,
ג: 'הקורא בספר על האיסקופה, נתגלגל הספר מידו גוללו אצלו' (השווה: בלאו [לעיל, הערה 22], עמ'
40–41).

25 בין שהיא עשויה מפאפירוס, ובין שהיא עשויה מעור; השווה: דרייבר (לעיל, הערה 3), עמ' 84. וראה
גם את הדיונים המקיפים והמפורטים בסוגיה זו אצל מ' הרן, 'מלאכת הסופר בתקופת המקרא –
מגילות הספרים ואביזרי הכתיבה', תרביץ נ (תשמ"א), עמ' 65–87; 'מגילות הספרים בתחילת ימי
בית שני – המעבר מפפירוסים לעורות', ארץ־ישראל טז (ספר צ"מ אורלינסקי), ירושלים תשמ"ב,
עמ' 86–92.

26 מ' וינפלד, ספר בראשית (מהדורה מחודשת ומתקנת' של פירוש ש"ל גורדון), תל־אביב תשל"ה, עמ'
26 (דבריו נאמרים בהקשר לצירוף 'סֵפֶר תּוֹלְדֹת אָדָם' [בר' ה 1], שבו 'ספר' = 'רשימה כתובה'). וראה
גם דרייבר, שם, עמ' 83. כתוב נוסף שבו מתפרשת המלה 'סֵפֶר' באופן דומה הוא מל"ב יט 14 // ישע'
לז 14): 'וַיִּקַּח חִזְקִיָּהוּ אֶת הַסְּפָרִים מִיַּד הַמַּלְאָכִים וַיִּקְרָאֵם... וַיִּפְרְשֵׂהוּ חִזְקִיָּהוּ לִפְנֵי ה''. 'פרישת'
הספרים (=מכתבים) מעידה, שוב, כי הם כתובים על חומר רך ומתקפל; ראה: גלינג (לעיל, הערה
19), עמ' 220.

27 לגבי הערבית, ראה: S. Fraenkel, *Die aramäischen Fremdwörter im Arabischen*, Leiden
1886 [Hildesheim 1962], pp. 247 f. לגבי האכדית, ראה: .W. von Soden, 'Aramäische
Wörter in neuassyrischen und neu- und spätbabylonischen Texten...', *Orientalia*
וראה גם N.S. 35 (1966), pp. 15; 46 (1977), p. 189; *CAD* M1, Chicago 1977, p. 31a
בדיונו המקיף של: H. Tadmor, 'The Aramaization of Assyria: Aspects of Western
Impact', in: H.-J. Nissen–J. Renger (eds.), *Mesopotamien und seine Nachbarn*
(Berliner Beiträge zum Vorderen Orient, 1), Berlin 1982, p. 454

28 השווה BDB, שם (לעיל, הערה 17). מעניין כי המילונים האחרים (GB, KB, *HALAT*, בן־יהודה)
אינם מסווגים את 'מגלה' כמלה מאוחרת או כארמאיזם. 'מגלה' איננה נידונה גם בספריהם של .E

ג

לאחר שעמדנו על משמעותן של התיבות 'ספר' ו'מגלה', כל אחת **כשהיא לעצמה**, מגיעים אנו
עתה לבירור טיבו של **צירוף הסמיכות** 'מגלת־ספר'. כפי שהזכרנו לעיל,[29] עצם הזיווג של 'מגלה'
ו'ספר' לביטוי אחד הוא בחזקת תופעה שיש לתת עליה את הדעת; ומסתבר שהיא משקפת
חריגה מסוימת מדרכי הביטוי המקובלות בעברית, הן בלשון המקרא והן בלשון חכמים.
בספרות המקראית מוצאים אנו ביטויים לא מעטים בהם משמשת 'ספר' כנסמך למלה אחרת.
דרך משל,[30] 'ספר כריתות', 'ספר דברי שלמה', 'ספר התורה'. גם בספרות חז"ל משמשים ביטויים
דומים, כאשר בהם מופיעה 'מגילה' כחוליה הראשונה בצירוף הסמיכות, כגון, 'מגילת יוחסים',
'מגילת סתרים', 'מגילת אסתר'. הצד השווה בכל צמדי הסמיכויות הללו הוא שרק המלה
הראשונה בהם ('ספר', 'מגלה') מציינת את **חומר הכתיבה** אשר עליו נכתב הטקסט שמדובר בו,
ואילו המלה השנייה מציינת לעולם את **תוכן הכתוב** או את **שמו**. דרך משל: במקרא — 'ספר
כריתות', שהוא השטר (=ספר) אשר תוכנו מתייחס להליך הגירושין (=כריתות), או 'ספר
התורה', שהוא הספר המכיל בתוכו את תורת משה;[31] ובספרות חז"ל — 'מגילת יוחסים', שהיא
מגילה אשר יש בה חומר גניאלוגי, או 'מגילת אסתר', שהיא מגילה עליה נכתב סיפור המעשה
המקראי הקרוי על שם אסתר המלכה. 'מגלת־ספר', לעומת זאת, הוא ביטוי **ששני** רכיביו
מציינים, בסופו של דבר, את חומר הכתיבה עצמו; ומבחינה זו ניתן בהחלט לראות בצירוף
הנידון ביטוי מגובב ('פליאונאסטי'), שיש בו (על כל פנים מידה מסוימת של) כפל לשון
('טאוטולוגיה').[32]
אם מאמצים אנו תפיסה זו, הרואה ב'מגלת־ספר' ביטוי טאוטולוגי,[33] הרי מתוסף לדיוננו ממד

Kautzsch, *Die Aramaismen im Alten Testament*, Halle 1902; M. Wagner, *Die
lexikalischen und grammatikalischen Aramaismen im alttestamentlichen
Hebräisch* (BZAW 96), Berlin 1966

29   ראה עמ' 37.

30   ראה מילון בן־יהודה בערכו, כרך ח, עמ' 4180–4181; והשווה לעיל, עמ' 38.

31   השווה לעיל, הערה 4.

32   עניין זה בולט מאוד ביר' לו 2: 'קח לך מגלת ספר וכתבת אליה את כל הדברים...'. מלשון הציווי
'קח... **וְכָתַבְתָּ**' אתה שומע שהדברים האמורים להיכתב במגילה עדיין אינם רשומים עליה; כלומר,
הרכיב 'ספר' שבצירוף 'מגלת־ספר' אינֶנו יכול לציין בהקשר זה טקסט (שהוא **כבר**) כתוב, אלא חייב
הוא להתפרש — בדומה לתיבה 'מגלה' הצמודה אליו — כחומר הכתיבה אשר עליו **עתיד** ירמיהו
לרשום את הדברים שנצטווה (והשווה: בלאו [לעיל, הערה 22], עמ' 37: 'מגלת־ספר' = 'Die
unbeschriebene Rolle'). אשר לנסיבות לידתו של הצירוף המקראי 'מגלת־ספר' (אשר אין לו
תיעוד של שימוש לשון חי בספרות חז"ל), הרי יש לשקול את האפשרות שיסודו בהתלבטות מסוימת
שהורגשה עם הופעתה של המלה 'מגלה'. התלבטות מעין זו עשויה היתה להצמיח את הנסיון
(הבלתי־מודע?) לדבוק, מחד, במונח הישן 'ספר' — משום שהוא מייצג את סגנון הכתיבה הקלאסי
ולאמץ, מאידך, את המלה החדשה 'מגלה' — משום שהיא משקפת בצורה ברורה יותר את המציאות
הלשונית ששרוי בה הכותב. מסתבר שבדרך זו ניתן לפרש גם את הצירוף 'כְּתָב הַנִּשְׁתְּוָן' — אף הוא
מתחום הכתיבה — עזרא ד 7 *ktāb hanništwañ* amounts to a tautology meaning "the)
document" '; J. Lewy, *HUCA* 25 [1954], p. 175, n. 24 (ואולי גם את הצירוף 'כתב תקף'
(= **כְּתָב תֹּקֶף**') בנבטית, המשמש בלא הבחנה ברורה בינו לרכיביו העצמאיים 'כתב', מחד,
ו'תקף' מאידך (השווה: ח"י גרינפלד, 'מחקרים במונחי משפט בכתובות הקבר הנבטיות', ספר זיכרון
לחנוך ילון, בעריכת י' קוטשר, ש' ליברמן ומ"צ קדרי, רמת גן–ירושלים תשל"ד, עמ' 73–74).

33   כך כבר י' בן ג'נאח, ספר השרשים, ברלין תרנ"ו (מהדורת ד"ז באכער), ערך 'גוש', עמ' 89 ('וענינם [=
של 'ספר' ו'מגלה' בצירוף 'מגלת־ספר'] אחד. כי זה ממנהג העברים, ר"ל כשיתקבץ לדבר שני שמות
חלוקים במבטאם איפשר שיסמכו האחד לשני [= ישתמשו במבנה הסמיכות]'). הפנייה אל בן ג'נאח
בהקשר זה נמצאת בספריהם של אבישור וניצן הנזכרים להלן (הערות 34 ו־36, עמ' 90, הערה 165
ועמ' 91, הערה 18 בהתאמה).

חדש, העשוי לסייע לנו בבירור שאלת מוצאו המשוער של הצירוף הנידון. כידוע, מצויה בספרות
המקראית שורה של דוגמאות, שבהן מלים נרדפות, או נרדפות למחצה, מצטרפות אחת לשנייה
בתוך מבנה של סמיכות; כדרך משל, 'עב הענן' (שמ' יט 9), 'עון אשמה' (וי' כב 16), 'עד שלל'
(יש' לג 23), 'קבעת כוס' (התרעלה'; יש' נא 17), 'מטר גשם' (זכ' י 1), 'שמחת גילי' (תה' מג 4),
'צוף דבש' (מש' טז 24), 'אדמת עפר' (דנ' יב 2), 'עושי מלחמה ב]כח חיל' (דה"ב כו 13).
התופעה הסגנונית שמדובר בה נדונה בהרחבה על ידי אבישור.[34] אחת ממסקנותיו בהקשר זה
היא, 'שברוב המקרים מצויה הסמיכות בספרות **מאוחרת** בזמנה... הרושם הוא שהסמיכויות
הללו הן שלב **מאוחר** של התפתחות במליצה הפיוטית'; 'תופעת הסמיכויות של הנרדפים היא
דרך צימוד **מאוחרת**'.[35] מסקנה כרונולוגית דומה עולה גם ממשלל הדוגמאות המגוון אשר הביא
בנדויד ממגילות מדבר יהודה, ואשר אף בהן מצאנו שפע של סמיכויות שהן בבחינת 'הרכבי
נרדפים שאינם אלא כפל דברים';[36] כגון, 'אבל יגון' (סה"י ד 13), 'גוית בשרו' (פשר חב' ט 2),
'חסדי רחמים' (סה"י א 22), 'כנור נבלי' (שם י 9), 'כעס חמתו' (פשר חב' יא 5‑6), 'מזמת
ערמה' (סה"י יא 6), 'משכב יצועי' (שם י 14).[37]

נתונים אלה, המצביעים על שגירותה הכללית של תופעת 'סמיכויות הנרדפים' – **כתופעה
סגנונית** – בתקופה המאוחרת, עשויים להצביע על כך שבפרק זמן זה ניתן לחפש גם את בית
היוצר הלשוני אשר שימש לטביעתו של הצירוף הספציפי 'מגלת‑ספר' בו דנים אנו כאן. אולם,
יש להטעים כי גם ללא הנחה זו[38] עדיין עומדת בעינה – **מבחינה מילונאית** – עובדת איחורה
היחסי של התיבה 'מגלה', המשמשת כרכיב בתוך צירוף הסמיכות 'מגלת‑ספר'; ופשיטא, שאם
אחד מרכיבי הסמיכות שמדובר בה מאוחר הוא, הרי גם הצירוף כולו חייב להיות מסווג
כמאוחר.[39]

---

34   י' אבישור, סמיכויות הנרדפים במליצה המקראית, ירושלים תשל"ז.

35   שם, עמ' 99 ו‑124 בהתאמה. אמנם, אבישור מכנה סמיכות זו 'גוזמתית‑**פיוטית**'; אולם הוא עצמו
      קובע כי היא רווחת מאוד גם 'ביצירות **הפרוזאיות** שמימי הבית השני' (אסתר, דניאל, דברי
      הימים) – בניגוד לפרוזה המקראית הקדומה (עמ' 96 ו‑97 בהתאמה; וראה גם עמ' 100. ההדגשה
      בכל הציטוטים היא שלי, א"ה).

36   א' בנדויד, לשון מקרא ולשון חכמים, כרך א, תל‑אביב תשכ"ז, עמ' 90. וראה גם י' ליכט, מגילת
      הסרכים, ירושלים תשכ"ה, עמ' 32; ח' ילון, מגילות מדבר יהודה – דברי לשון, ירושלים תשכ"ז, עמ'
      71 ('סגנון מסה"י [=מגילת סרך היחד'] הרי הוא בעיקרו סגנון המקרא, אלא שהוא מפריז ביותר
      במליצות על דרך "כפל ענין במלים שונות". הוא מרדף אחרי סינונימים והקבלות... וכאילו הוא מחזר
      אחרי כל מיני ביטויים למושג אחד'); ב' ניצן, מגילת פשר חבקוק, ירושלים תשמ"ו, עמ' 90‑91.

37   כאמור (השווה דברי ילון בהערה הקודמת), התופעה רווחת מאוד בעיקר במגילת סרך היחד.

38   ככלות הכל, בספרות המקראית עצמה התופעה מתועדת – במידה בלתי מבוטלת – גם בטקסטים
      שלשונם רחוקה מלהיות 'מאוחרת' (כך אף אבישור [לעיל, הערה 34], עמ' 96 [לפי דבריו, בספרים
      ישעיהו ותהלים 'מצויים כ‑50% מכלל הסמיכויות במקרא'!]); ועל כן דומה כי מוטב שלא למתוח
      יתר על המידה את תוקפה הכרונולוגי של התופעה (והשווה: א' הורביץ, ניתוח בלשני של לשון
      השירה במקרא [עבודת גמר בחוג ללשון העברית של האוניברסיטה העברית בירושלים], 1961, נספח
      II: 'גבוב מלים', עמ' 96).

39   י' ליכט (לעיל, הערה 1), טור 671, קובע כי הספרות המקראית משתמשת בדרך כלל בשם העצם
      'ספר', וכי היא נוקטת בשמות 'מגלה' או 'מגלת‑ספר' 'רק בכתובים שיש בהם טעם מיוחד להסב את
      תשומת לבו של הקורא לדמותו החיצונית של החפץ המתואר'. הבחנה זו בין 'ספר' לבין 'מגלה'
      (ו'מגלת‑ספר') אפשר שיש בה ממש, במקרים מסומים, במישור הפרשני; אולם באופן ניסוחה אצל
      ליכט מתעלמת היא מן הנתונים הכרונולוגיים שהתבררו לנו לעיל במישור הבלשני. מנתונים אלה,
      שראינו, יש להסיק, כי האופוזיציה לבחור בין 'מגלה' לבין 'ספר' עמדה לרשותם של הסופרים
      המקראיים רק בתקופה מאוחרת, יחסית – לאחר שהשלמה 'מגלה' חדרה לשימושה הלשוני המקובל של
      העברית המקראית; היינו, בשלהי ימי הבית הראשון (שים לב כי על פי האינטרפרטאציה של ליכט

ד

לסיום מבקשים אנו לבחון את המונח 'מגלה' – אשר לצורך דיוננו הוא הוא המהווה, כמובן,
את מלת המפתח בצירוף הסמיכות 'מגלת־ספר' – לאור נתונים מתחום מינוח הכתיבה
שמספקת לנו הארמית המקראית. בעזרת נתונים אלה ניתן להשקיף על החומר המקראי אשר
נידון לעיל מתוך פרספקטיבה רחבה יותר, ובכך מסייעים הם להבהיר את התמונה הלשונית
שאנו מנסים לעמוד כאן על טיבה.

הפרקים הארמיים בספרי דניאל ועזרא עשירים במונחים שונים המציינים את מהותו (או
צורתו) של חומר הכתיבה ואת טיבו (או תוכנו) של הטקסט הכתוב עליו; השווה:[40] 'אִגְּרָא',
'אִגַּרְתָּא' (='letter'), 'אֱסָר' (='inhibition'),[41] 'דִּכְרוֹן' (='record'; 'memorandum'), 'דָּת' (=
'[royal] order'; 'public law'), 'טְעֵם' (='account'), 'כְּתָב' (='command'; 'report'; 'account'=
'writing'; 'document and its contents'), 'מִגְלָה' (='scroll'), 'נִשְׁתְּוָן' (='official=
'document'; 'decree' (document),*'סְפָר' (='book'), 'פַּרְשֶׁגֶן' (='copy'), 'פִּתְגָם' (='report'; 'account'=
'decree'), 'קְיָם' (='statute').[42] שפע המונחים הללו מרשים במיוחד לאור היקפם המצומצם
של קורפוס הארמית המקראית שבידינו (כעשרה פרקים בסך הכול!); והוא נותן ביטוי מוחשי
למידת חשיבותה של מלאכת הכתיבה – ולדרגת מורכבותה המקצועית של פעילות סופרי
החצר – בימי שלטון פרס. הלשון ששימשה לצרכים אלה היתה, כידוע, 'הארמית הממלכתית',
שהארמית המקראית היא חלק ממנה; ואין ספק כי שורת המונחים הארוכה אשר הובאו לעיל
– בין שהם ארמיים מקוריים, ובין שהם הגיעו אליה מלשונות כמו האכדית או הפרסית[43] –
משתייכים לטרמינולוגיה הלבלרית' שהיתה מקובלת בכתבי התקופה.

חלק הגון ממינוח ארמי זה חדר גם לעברית המקראית – ורובו ככולו מתועד בטקסטים
מאוחרים (או חשודים כמאוחרים).[44] במקביל לכך ניתן להצביע גם בספרות חז"ל על התרחבות

אין להבין מדוע נקט מחבר יש' לד 4 [השווה לעיל, עמ' 42] במלה 'ספר' ולא העדיף להשתמש
ב'מגלה'. לשיטתו של ליכט, 'דמותו החיצונית של החפץ המתואר' (שם) ביש' לד 4 – 'scroll' –
בהחלט 'מזמינה' כאן את השימוש במלה 'מגלה' דווקא. מבחינה זו יש להשוות את אי הופעתה של
'מגלה' ביש' לד 4 לאי הופעתה של 'אגרת' במל"ב יט 14 (ראה לעיל, הערה 26) – ואולי גם ביש' כט
11 (ראה לעיל, הערה 22).

40　　התרגומים לאנגלית שיובאו להלן לקוחים כולם ממילון KB.

41　　דנ' ו 10: 'מלכא דריוש רְשַׁם כְּתָבָא וֶאֱסָרָא'. כלומר, האיסור (=אֱסָר') – שיצא מטעם המלך – הוא
　　S. Paul, 'Dan 6, 8: An :בדומה ל'כְּתָב' הנזכר כאן לידו. והשווה (='רשום') – בחזקת מסמך כתוב
　　(דיון) Aramaic Reflex of Assyrian Legal Terminology,' Bib 65 (1984), pp 108-110
　　בביטוי 'לְתַקָּפָה אֱסָר').

42　　המדובר הוא ב'קִיָם מַלְכָּא' (דנ' ו 8) – 'צַו מלכותי', היינו, 'Edikt' (GB, עמ' 923) המתפרסם בכתב.
43　　'A[ramaic] played the role of clearing house between Orient and Occident' (E.Y.
　　Kutscher, 'Aramaic,' in: T.A. Sebeok [ed.], Current Trends in Linguistics, 6, The
　　Hague–Paris 1970, p. 384)

44　　'אגרת' – אסתר, נחמיה ודברי הימים; 'דת' – אסתר ועזרא ('decree, edict, commission') –
　　BDB, עמ' 206); 'טעם' – יונה ('decision, decree') – שם, עמ' 381); 'כְּתָב' – יחזקאל, אסתר,
　　דניאל, עזרא, נחמיה ודברי הימים; 'נשתון' – עזרא; 'פרשגן' – עזרא (וכך גם 'פתשגן' – אסתר);
　　'פתגם' – אסתר וקהלת; ואולי גם 'תֹקֶף' שבאסתר ט 29 (במשמעות 'legally valid document';
　　ראה פאול [לעיל, הערה 41], עמ' 108, הערה 27). בדומה לשורת מונחים זו, אף 'מגלה' הגיעה
　　מתחום הארמית אל העברית המקראית, כפי שראינו לעיל, רק בתקופה היסטורית מאוחרת יחסית.
　　אולם, שלא כמו 'אגרת', 'דת' וחברותיהן – אשר השימוש המקראי בהן הוא בגדר סימן היכר מובהק
　　לספרי הבית השני דווקא – הרי הופעתה של 'מגלה' על הזירה המקראית מתועדת, כאמור, כבר
　　בשלהי ימי הבית הראשון (ירמיהו, יחזקאל). וראוי לציין, כי זוהי (פחות או יותר) התקופה שבה

משמעותית בהיקפו של אוצר המלים המשמש בתחום הכתיבה; א' בנדויד, למשל, מונה חמישה 'תחליפים' חז"ליים ל'ספר' המקראית: 'אגרת', 'כְּתב', 'שטר', 'גט', 'פתק'.[45] לאור כל הנתונים הללו ברור, אפוא, כי את השימוש המקראי בתיבה 'מגלה' (בין כאשר המלה מופיעה לעצמה, ובין כאשר נסמכת היא ל'ספר'), יש לראות כחלק ממורשת **הארמית בתחום מינוח הכתיבה** – מורשה אשר הותירה את רישומיה הרחק מעבר לגבולותיו המצומצמים של הקורפוס המקראי שבידינו.

מתחילה להופיע גם *magallatu* באכדית! (מלה זו היא אחת מן הדוגמאות שמביא תדמור [לעיל, הערה 27] במאמרו על תהליך 'הארמיזציה של אשור').

45 בנדויד (לעיל, הערה 36), כרך ב, תל-אביב תשל"א, עמ' 880–881. 'אגרת' ו'כתב' נדונו לעיל (עמ' 45); 'שטר' ו'גט' הן אכדית-שומריות במקורן (השווה קוטשר [לעיל, הערה 3], עמ' 54), 'פתק' יוונית היא (ראה: מילון בן-יהודה בערכה, כרך יא, עמ' 5332, הערה 3); ומסתבר שכולן הגיעו אל העברית באמצעות הארמית.

'והגיתי בכל פעלך' — אמונות ודעות בתהילים עז

מאיר וייס

על פי עניינו, בנייניו ומארגו של תהילים עז ניתן לקבוע במידה ניכרת של סבירות, שהמזמור
בדמותו הנתונה אינו מעשה מרכבה, הרכב של מזמורים או קטעי מזמורים נפרדים, כדעה
שעדיין מובעת במחקר,[1] אלא מלאכת מחשבת של יצירה ספרותית אחידה. במאמרי זה, המוגש
עם ברכת בכל מכל כל לאיו"ש לחברי הפרופ' מנחם הרן נ"י, רצוני לנתח את המזמור לפי שיטת
האינטרפרטציה הכוללית, כדי לאשש מסקנה זו, ובעיקר כדי להעמיד על דיוקם פרטים לא
מעטים, וכך לעמוד על מלוא משמעותו של המזמור.
למבט ראשון זוהי דמות המזמור:

.2	קוֹלִי אֶל־אֱלֹהִים וְאֶצְעָקָה	קוֹלִי אֶל־אֱלֹהִים וְהַאֲזִין אֵלָי
.3	בְּיוֹם צָרָתִי אֲדֹנָי דָּרָשְׁתִּי	יָדִי לַיְלָה נִגְּרָה וְלֹא תָפוּג
	מֵאֲנָה הִנָּחֵם נַפְשִׁי	
.4	אֶזְכְּרָה אֱלֹהִים וְאֶהֱמָיָה	אָשִׂיחָה וְתִתְעַטֵּף רוּחִי סֶלָה
.5	אָחַזְתָּ שְׁמֻרוֹת עֵינָי	נִפְעַמְתִּי וְלֹא אֲדַבֵּר
.6	חִשַּׁבְתִּי יָמִים מִקֶּדֶם	שְׁנוֹת עוֹלָמִים
.7	אֶזְכְּרָה נְגִינָתִי בַּלַּיְלָה	עִם־לְבָבִי אָשִׂיחָה
	וַיְחַפֵּשׂ רוּחִי	
.8	הַלְעוֹלָמִים יִזְנַח אֲדֹנָי	וְלֹא־יֹסִיף לִרְצוֹת עוֹד
.9	הֶאָפֵס לָנֶצַח חַסְדּוֹ	גָּמַר אֹמֶר לְדֹר וָדֹר
.10	הֲשָׁכַח חַנּוֹת אֵל	אִם־קָפַץ בְּאַף רַחֲמָיו סֶלָה
.11	וָאֹמַר חַלּוֹתִי הִיא	שְׁנוֹת יְמִין עֶלְיוֹן
.12	אֶזְכּוֹר [קרי] מַעַלְלֵי־יָהּ	כִּי־אֶזְכְּרָה מִקֶּדֶם פִּלְאֶךָ
.13	וְהָגִיתִי בְכָל־פָּעֳלֶךָ	וּבַעֲלִילוֹתֶיךָ אָשִׂיחָה
.14	אֱלֹהִים בַּקֹּדֶשׁ דַּרְכֶּךָ	מִי־אֵל גָּדוֹל כֵּאלֹהִים
.15	אַתָּה הָאֵל עֹשֵׂה פֶלֶא	הוֹדַעְתָּ בָעַמִּים עֻזֶּךָ
.16	גָּאַלְתָּ בִּזְרוֹעַ עַמֶּךָ	בְּנֵי־יַעֲקֹב וְיוֹסֵף סֶלָה

1 מן החוקרים במחצית השנייה של המאה סבורים כך, למשל, מק'קולו (W.S. McCullough, *The*
Book of Psalms [The Interpreter's Bible 4], New York, Nashville 1955, pp. 408-
414); קראוס (H.-J. Kraus, *Psalmen* [BKAT 15], I, Neukirchen-Vluyn 1960, pp. 530-
534); ג'פרסן (H. Jefferson, 'Psalm LXXVII', *VT* 13 [1963], pp. 87-91)

17. רָאוּךָ מַּיִם אֱלֹהִים רָאוּךָ מַּיִם יָחִילוּ
אַף יִרְגְּזוּ תְהֹמוֹת

18. זֹרְמוּ מַיִם עָבוֹת קוֹל נָתְנוּ שְׁחָקִים
אַף־חֲצָצֶיךָ יִתְהַלָּכוּ

19. קוֹל רַעַמְךָ בַּגַּלְגַּל הֵאִירוּ בְרָקִים תֵּבֵל
רָגְזָה וַתִּרְעַשׁ הָאָרֶץ

20. בַּיָּם דַּרְכֶּךָ וּשְׁבִילְךָ [קרי] בְּמַיִם רַבִּים
וְעִקְּבוֹתֶיךָ לֹא נֹדָעוּ

21. נָחִיתָ כַצֹּאן עַמֶּךָ בְּיַד־מֹשֶׁה וְאַהֲרֹן

ובכן, במזמור מזדקרות מלים חוזרות. על עובדה זו כבר עמד קסלמן, ובעיקר בה הוא מוצא סימוכין לתפיסתו שהמזמור הוא 'יצירה ספרותית של משורר אחד'.[2] ואכן, מלים חוזרות אלה מקשרות בין חלקי המזמור מבחינה חיצונית, אך הן גם רומזות להתייחסויות הפנימיות, כפי שיתברר מהתבוננות מדויקת במזמור.

המזמור מתחלק לשני חלקים ראשיים: (א) פסוקים 2–10, קינה על המצב בהווה; (ב) פסוקים 11–21, שבח לה' על נפלאותיו עם עמו בימי קדם. בחלק (א) ניתן להבחין בין שני חלקי משנה: [a] פסוקים 2–7, הלך רוחו של בעל המזמור; [b] פסוקים 8–10, הרהוריו על יחסו של ה'. בחלק משנה [a] שני בתים, כל אחד בן שלושה פסוקים: (1) פסוקים 2–4; (2) פסוקים 5–7.

פסוק 2: 'קולי אל אלהים'. משפט קטוע. בהיות הדיבור המקוטע סימן אופייני ומובן להתרגשות, הוא מבטא אפוא נאמנה את המיית הלב ומתיחות הנפש של בעל המזמור. — 'ואצעקה'. לפי ההקשר ושימושיה של צורת העתיד המוארך, מתבטא כאן עידוד עצמי.[3] מן המשפט הקודם בהיותו קטוע, ניתן להבין שבעל המזמור מתקשה להשמיע את קולו אל אלוהים. לכן, בהרגישו בהכרחיות הדבר, הוא מעודד ומזרז את עצמו לצעוק אליו. ואולם במקום לעשות מה שקיבל על עצמו, הוא חוזר על המשפט שאמר זה עתה: 'קולי אל אלהים'. בחזרה זו הוא שב לעודד את עצמו. ובכן, מצבו הנפשי המזועזע נותן את אותותיו מיד עם פתיחת דבריו. אחר העידוד העצמי השני אומר בעל המזמור: 'וְהַאֲזִין[4] אלי'. לפי התפיסה הסבירה ביותר, שהיא גם המקובלת כיום, אין 'וְהַאֲזִין' כמו 'וְהַאֲזֵין', היינו ציווי, אלא כמו 'וְהַאֲזִין', היינו צורת וְקָטַל הרגילה בהפעיל בפעלים שפ"א הפועל שלהם אות גרונית, במיוחד בבואם עם ו"ו ההיפוך.[4] הפועל בצורת וְקָטַל אחרי פועל בצורת יקטל מציין כאן את תכלית הפעולה המצוינת בפועל הקודם.[5] בחפצו העז שיעלה בידו להרים את קולו אל אלוהים מבהיר אפוא בעל המזמור לעצמו את מטרת חפצו: למען יאזין ה' אלי.

פסוק 3: 'ביום צרתי אדני דרשתי'. הפועל 'דרש' מורה על פנייה בשאלה או בבקשה, כהוראתו כשמשושאו הוא אלוהים.[6] צורת קטל מציינת פעולה מתמדת.[7] בהקדמת המושא לנשוא מטעים בעל המזמור שאל 'אדני' הוא פונה ביום צרתו. — 'ידי לילה נגרה ולא תפוג'. הפועל 'נגר' משמעותו: נשפך. כנשוא ל'יד', הוא משמש במובן: היה פרוש.[8] המשפט 'ידי לילה נגרה' כוונתו

2 J.S. Kselman, 'Psalm 77 and the Book of Exodus', *JANES* 15 (1983), p. 57
3 W. Gesenius & E. Kautzsch, *Hebräische Grammatik*27, Leipzig 1902, §108b
4 ראה שם, 630§ — כבר ראב"ע מעיר: י"א "והאזין" היה ראוי להיות "וְהַאֲזֵן" כמו "לא האמין" פועל עבר'. לפי מנחת שי: 'בדפוס ישן כתוב: "וְהַאֲזֵין".
5 שם, 112m§.
6 KB: 'דרש'.
7 גזניוס-קאוטש (לעיל, הערה 3), 106g§.
8 זו הדעה המקובלת היום. ראה: KB: 'נגר'.

אפוא: בלילה ידי פרוסה כלפי מעלה, כפי שנהוג בתפילה.[9] 'ולא תפוג'. הוראת הפועל: היה חלש. צורת יקטל מציינת פעולה בו זמנית עם זו המציינת בצורת קטל של 'נגר' ותלויה בה.[10] 'ולא תפוג': אינה נחלשת. היינו, תפילתי אינה נפסקת. — 'מאנה הנחם נפשי', אך נפשי מסרבת להירגע, ככל הנראה הואיל ועל אף היותה בלתי פוסקת נשארה התפילה מנותקת מאלוהים.

פסוק 4: 'אזכרה אלהים ואהמיה'. רוצה אני לזכור את האלוהים, ולכן עלי להשמיע קול אנחה. — 'אשיחה'. פועל זה, המופיע עוד פעמיים במזמורנו (בפסוקים 7, 13), מציין דיבור טעון אמוציה. כאן, על פי ההקשר, הוא מציין תלונה. — 'ותתעטף רוחי', נחלשה רוחי, מתייאשת מרוב יגוני, צערי שעלי להתלונן עליו.

פסוק 5: 'אחזת שמרות עיני'. אתה מחזיק בעפעפי שלא ייסגרו, שלא אישן. עד פסוק זה, וכן בפסוקי החלק הראשון הבאים (פסוקים 8–10), הדיבור הוא על ה', בגוף שלישי. המעבר הפתאומי לדיבור אל ה', בגוף שני, ומיד שוב לדיבור בגוף שלישי, משקף את המתרחש בנפשו של בעל המזמור, אחר נסיון השווא בלילה למצוא קשר עם האלוהים. כשנודדת ממנו השינה שבייאושו הוא עורג לה, הוא מרגיש לפתע בנוכחות האלוהים, שהוא המונע את השינה מעיניו בכוח ובכוונה. אולם פנייתו לאלוהים אין בה קריאה מפורשת, והדבר מעיד על טיב הרגשתו את נוכחות האלוהים. — תגובתו על הרגשה זו: 'נפעמתי ולא אדבר'. אני מזועזע, נרגש, איני יכול לדבר, איני מסוגל להמשיך לדבר אל האלוהים.

פסוק 6: 'חשבתי ימים מקדם שנות עולמים'. 'חשב' בפִעֵל — הרהר בדבר, שקל, בחן.[11] הביטוי 'שנות עולמים' בוודאי מקביל ל'ימים מקדם'. עם זאת יש לשים לב למשמעות המיוחדת הצפונה במלה 'עולמים' שאינה ב'מקדם', המשמעות המשנית הסמויה: 'עולמים', היינו: נעלמים, אינם עוד. — אחר שלא הצליח לעודד עצמו בפנייה אל האלוהים, נמלט בעל המזמור בהרהוריו לעבר. אין הוא חושב על 'ימים מקדם, שנות עולמים' אלא מחשב, מהרהר בהם. הוא שוקל, חוקר ומבקש להבין, לתפוס אותן 'שנות עולמים', את הזמן שנעלם — את תעלומת העתים. חישוביו יתבררו על פי דבריו בפסוקים 8–10, אבל כבר לפי הנאמר כאן, מובן שהבעיה המציקה לו היא הניגוד בין 'ימים מקדם, שנות עולמים' לבין ההווה.

פסוק 7: 'אזכרה נגינתי בלילה'. ההרהורים בעבר מעלים בזכרונו של בעל המזמור את ימיו הטובים, את הימים שבהם שרתה עליו רוח השירה, בניגוד ללילה הזה, שבו שורה עליו רוח יגון ואנחה. שני פירושים הוצעו למובנו התחביר של המשפט: (א) 'בלילה' מתייחס ל'אזכרה' כתיאור זמן, היינו, מתאר את זמן הזכירה;[12] (ב) 'בלילה' — לוואי ל'נגינתי', היינו מתאר את זמן הנגינה.[13] דומה שהפירוש הראשון הוא המתאים יותר. בעל המזמור אינו מתכוון לומר מתי ניגן אלא מתי זכר שניגן. בלילה הוא זוכר זמן שבו לא נאלץ להשמיע את קול המיתו, אלא שבו השמיע את קול נגינתו. זוהי אחת המשמעויות של ההבדל שבין: 'אזכרה... ואהמיה...' (פסוק 4

9   כגון: שמ' ט 29, 33; מל"א ח 22, 54; יש' א 15; תה' כח 2, מד 21, ועוד.
10 D. Michel, *Tempora und Satzstellung in den Psalmen*, Bonn 1960, §14, 5
11 ש"א ליונשטם, 'י בלאו (מ"צ קדרי), אוצר לשון המקרא (להלן אל"ה); KB: 'חשב'.
12 רש"י, ראב"ע (בפירושו השני), רד"ק. כך גם בעל הביאור ובעלי הטעמים. בין החוקרים מפרש כך טייט (M.E. Tate, *Psalms 51-100* [WBC 20], Waco 1990), ואילו האחרים בדרך כלל מקבלים כנוסח המהימן את המשתקף בתרגומי השבעים והפשיטתא: '(ו)הגיתי' במקום 'נגינתי'. לדעתם שימש 'אזכרה', ביתר דיוק: 'אזכר, כנשוא למשפט שבפסוק 3ב (וראה BHK).
13 ראב"ע (בפירושו הראשון), המאירי (פירוש לספר תהלים, חברו רבי מנחם ב"ר שלמה המאירי, הוצאת מקיצי נרדמים², ירושלים תשל"א).

לבין: 'אזכרה... נגינתי...' (פסוק 7). – 'עם לבבי אשיחה'. בעל המזמור משוחח עם לבבו. –
'ויחפש רוחי'. ורוחי מחפשת, מן הסתם, פתרון לבעיה.
בפסוק 7 מסתיים, כאמור, תיאור הלך רוחו של בעל המזמור. על המשתקף בסיום ניתן לעמוד
מהשוואת לשונו של פסוק 7, פסוקו האחרון של הבית השני בתיאור, ללשונו של פסוק 4
המסיים את הבית הראשון, וליתר דיוק – מההבדלים שביניהם.

פסוק 4: **אזכרה** אלהים ואהמיה   **אשיחה** ותתעטף **רוחי**   סלה
פסוק 7: **אזכרה** נגינתי בלילה   עם לבבי   **אשיחה** ויחפש **רוחי**

שני הפסוקים מקבילים זה לזה במידה ניכרת: בעניין, במבנה ובלשון. בשניהם מדבר בעל
המזמור על זכרונות, בשניהם הוא משיח ובשניהם מסתיימת הזכירה והשיחה במצב רוחו.
בשניהם נושא המשפטים הראשונים הוא ה-'אני', ואילו נושא המשפט האחרון – 'רוחי'. עובדה
זו מראה שכל אחד מן הפסוקים הללו מסכם שלב אחד בתיאור הלך רוחו של בעל המזמור. אם
בפסוק 4 ממוקדת זכירתו של בעל המזמור באלוהים, הנה בפסוק 7 היא ממוקדת בעצמו. הבדל
זה בין שני הפסוקים משקף הבדל בולט בין שני חלקי התיאור, המוצא ביטוי מובהק גם
בתפוצת שם האלוהות: בחלק הראשון מופיע השם ארבע פעמים (שלוש פעמים 'אלהים'
[פסוקים 2, 4], פעם אחת 'אדני' [פסוק 3]), בחלק השני הוא אינו נזכר ולו פעם אחת, אף לא
במשפט הפונה אל אלוהים (פסוק 5א). הדבר מסתבר ממה שעבר על בעל המזמור מאז גרמה
זכירתו את האלוהים ל'ואהמיה' (פסוק 4). הדרך אל האלוהים נתגלתה כחסומה בפניו, והוא
הסתגר בעצמו: 'עם לבבי אשיחה'. בסוף השלב הראשון (פסוק 4) הפועל 'אשיחה' מובנו, כאמור,
תלונה; ואילו בסוף השלב השני 'אשיחה' מובנו דיבור. הדיבור אל הלב מנחם, מרגיע ומשקיט,
וככל שמרבה המשורר שיחה עם לבבו, כך מתעוררת שוב רוחו. זהו אפוא המעבר מ'ותתעטף
רוחי' ל'ויחפש רוחי'.
חיפוש רוחו של בעל המזמור מתבטא בשש השאלות על האלוהים שהוא מציג לעצמו בפסוקים
8–10. הן משקפות את מאבקו הנפשי, כפי שמראה העין בהן.

פסוק 8: 'הלעולמים יזנח אדני'. שאלה זו, הראשונה, מדגישה ביותר את הסתר הפנים של
האלוהים בהיותו מתואר בה במפורש כזונח, היינו: כנוטש, כמתרחק,[14] כדוחה[15] או ככועס,[16]
בכל אופן: כפעיל, כמתרחק. – השאלה השנייה: 'ולא יסיף לרצות עוד'. 'לרצות' בלשון המקרא:
לחפוץ ב-, לנטות ל-, לקבל ברצון. ניסוחה השלילי מתאר את ה' כבלתי פעיל, כלא מתקרב. ובכן,
השאלה השנייה אינה חמורה כראשונה, שכן היא לפחות מייחסת לאלוהים עתות רצון בעבר.
אם השאלה הראשונה מותירה בנו את רושם כעסו של אלוהים, השנייה מותירה רושם של
עתות רצון מצד אלוהים.

פסוק 9: 'האפס לנצח חסדו'. האם תם לנצח חסדו? – 'גמר אמר לדר ודר'. את המכוון במשפט
אין לקבוע אלא בלשון אולי. שכן לפי ההקשר, את הפועל 'גמר' ניתן לפרש כפועל יוצא או
כפועל עומד,[17] והשם 'אמר' יכול לציין דיבור טוב או דיבור רע.[18] האפשרות היותר סבירה היא

14   אל"ה (לעיל, הערה 11): 'זנח I'.
15   KB: 'זנח II'.
16   R. Yaron, 'The Meaning of ZANAḤ', VT 13 (1963), pp. 237-239; M. Dahood,
    Psalms II (AB), New York 1968; וכן: קסלמן (לעיל, הערה 2), עמ' 55, הערה 15; טייט
    (לעיל, הערה 12) סבורים שהוראת הפועל 'זנח': כעס.
17   ראה אל"ה (לעיל, הערה 11), KB: 'גמר'.
18   אל"ה (לעיל, הערה 11): 'אמר, אומר I'.

שכוונת 'גמר אמר' היא כמו 'גזר אומר' (איוב כב 28), היינו: גזר גזירה קשה.[19] אם זו אכן כוונת הצירוף, אזי יש בין שני חלקי הפסוק הקבלה רעיונית: היפסקות ה'חסד', היינו 'היחס שלפנים משורת הדין,[20] גוררת גזר דין חמור.

פסוק 10: 'השכח חנות אל'. בדרך כלל מסכימים כי 'חנות' צורה מיוחדת מאוד מן השורש חנ"ן, הגזורה לפי פעלי ל"ה.[21] — 'אם קפץ באף רחמיו. סלה'. 'קפץ' – סגר, חתם.[22] השאלה הנשאלת כאן האם 'סגר באפו רחמיו שלא יפתחו [...] עוד'.[23] אף ה' הוא ניגדו של חסד ה' (מי' ז 18; השווה יש' נד 8),[24] שמידת הרחמים היא אחת מתוצאותיו הקונקרטיות. שלוש המידות שבעל המזמור שואל בדבר נטישתן, 'חסד', 'חנות' ו'רחמים', קשורות לשדה סמאנטי אחד, ו'חסד' הוא מושג כולל.[25] ובכן, ארבע השאלות האחרונות ממחישות את השתיים הראשונות שבפסוק 8, ועוסקות במידות ה', היינו חסד, חנינה ורחמים, שבהן אין ה' נוהג בהווה. תואר הפועל 'באף' רומז כנראה למידה נוספת מעין אלה: המידה של 'ארך אפים'. כפי שהכירו כבר, בשאלות אלה מהדהדת הכרזת 'שלוש עשרה מידותיו' של הקב"ה (שמ' לד 6).[26] סמך להנחה שלכך מתייחס בעל המזמור נמצא בהשוואת הסדר של הזכרת המידות בשני הכתובים.

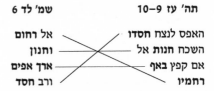

שמ' לד 6	תה' עז 9–10
אל רחום	האפס לנצח **חסדו**
וחנון	השכח **חנות** אל
ארך אפים	אם קפץ **באף**
רחמיו	**רחמיו**
ורב חסד	

ובכן, המידה הראשונה והמידה האחרונה במזמור מקבילות לאותן המידות שבספר שמות בסדר כיאסטי, שהוא, כידוע, סימן להתייחסות מודעת ומכוונת. בעל המזמור שואל אפוא על ארבע מידות, הכלולות, לפי אמונתו, ב'שלוש עשרה מידותיו' של ה', שהוא עצמו הכריז עליהן בעברו על פני משה (שמ', שם). לכן העובדה, שבהווה ה' אינו נוהג בהן, מציקה לו, גורמת לבעיה קובה שלפתרונה הוא נאבק עם נפשו. כלום ייתכן שה' אינו מקיים מה שהבטיח?!

פסוק 11: 'ואמר חלותי היא שנות ימין עליון'. פסוק זה פותח חטיבה שאווירתה שונה מאוד מאווירת קודמתה;[27] זהו, כאמור, חלקו הראשי השני של המזמור. סימן לכך ניתן לראות גם בפועל 'ואמר', הואיל ולפעמים[28] הוא מסמן מפנה פנימי, הכרה חדשה או מסקנה שנתברֶרה, נתלבנה, ומקבלת עתה את ניסוחה המפורש. — 'חלותי'. על שורש הפועל, על מובנו ואף על

---

19 שם: 'גמר. – מקדמונינו מפרשים כך רש"י וראב"ע.

20 כך ניתן להגדיר את הוראת היסוד של המושג 'חסד'. ראה אל"ה (לעיל, הערה 11): 'חסד'.

21 גזניוס-קאוטש (לעיל, הערה 3), 67r§. – לפי סברה אחרת, הפועל הוא מן השורש חנ"ה, צורת משנה לשורש חנ"ן (ראה אל"ה [לעיל, הערה 11]; KB: 'חנה II').

22 KB: 'קפץ'.

23 רד"ק.

24 H.-J. Zobel, 'חסד *ḥæssed*', *TWAT* III, p. 61

25 H.J. Stoebe, 'Die Bedeutung des Wortes ḤĀSĀD im Alten Testament', *VT* 2 (1952), pp. 247f.

26 קסלמן (לעיל, הערה 2), עמ' 55; טייט (לעיל, הערה 12).

27 השוני באווירה משמש יסוד לטענת חוקרים אחדים (לעיל, הערה 1), כי חטיבה זו אינה ממתכונתו הראשונית של מזמורנו.

28 כגון: תה' נה 7, קלט 11; איכה ג 18.

מהימנות גירסתו המסורה חלוקות דעות הפרשנים.[29] סביר ביותר להבינו כגזור מן השורש חל"ה (לשון מחלה), בצורת מקור בפָעל עם כינוי מושא של מדבר.[30] בעלי תפיסה זו מפרשים על פי רוב את הצירוף 'חלותי היא': המביא מחלה לי = מחלתי, כאבי, עצבי הוא.[31] המלה 'היא' נתפסת בדרך כלל כאוגד המכוון לטור הבא: 'שנות ימין עליון'.[32] על המלה 'שנות' רווחת הדעה שהיא צורת מקור בבניין קל של הפועל 'שנה', לשון שינוי,[33] אשר לצירוף 'ימין עליון', הוא אחד ההדים של שירת הים במזמורנו:[34] השם 'ימין' בקשר לה' מופיע שם שלוש פעמים (שמ' טו 6, 12) כמטאפורה המצוינת: כוח, גבורה. 'עליון', כידוע, כינוי לה'.[35] ובכן, לפי הפירוש המקובל ביותר, אומר בעל המזמור בפסוקנו שכאבו וסבלו הוא על כי ה' שינה את ימינו, והיא אינה עוד מה שהיתה 'בימים מקדם' (פסוק 6), היא אינה עוד היד החזקה, המושיעה. במלים אחרות, בעל המזמור מגיע להכרה שהגורם לעצבו הוא שינוי יחסו של ה'. נתבררה לו התשובה לשאלות שהציג בפסוקים 10–8: האם באופן סופי הפסיק ה' לנהוג באותן המידות שהודיען למשה? מסתבר שבעל המזמור הגיע לתשובה חיובית. ואולם פירוש זה מעורר קושי: הרי בהמשך אין מדובר בשינוי אצל 'ימין עליון', אלא בשינוי אצל בעל המזמור. אם כן, על אף ההתחשבות הדרושה בהתבטאותו הלירית של הלך המחשבה, קשה להסביר את המעבר ממסקנה זו למה שנאמר בהמשך. ואכן, המייחסים משמעות זו לפסוק נאלצים להסבירו בדוחק רב, אם לא באמצעות שינוי הנוסח המסור או בשלילת הקשר האורגאני שבין חטיבה זו של המזמור לקודמתה. נמצא, שפירוש הרבים לפסוק אינו פשוטו כל וכלל.

לכן נראה לי לשקול את האפשרות כי המלה 'שנות' היא נסמך בריבוי של השם 'שנה',[36] הנזכר באותה צורה בפסוק 6, והצירוף 'שנות ימין עליון' מתייחס למשפט שם, 'חשבתי... שנות עולמים'. בעל המזמור אומר להבין, לחקור 'שנות עולמים'. לפי הצירוף במשפטנו, השנים הן של 'ימין עליון': השנים ש'ימין עליון' היא השולטת עליהן, והאדם, אין לו שליטה עליהן ואינו יכול לתפוס אותן. ממשמעות זאת של הטור השני מתבקשת ההנחה שהפועל 'חלה' שבטור הראשון מורה, כמו בכמה כתובים אחרים,[37] על חולשה, רפיון.[38] ובכן, פירוש המשפט: 'ואמר', נתברר לי, כי חולשתי, טעותי 'היא'; זאת אומרת, עמדתי, כפי שהתבטאה במזמור עד כה, היא טעותי: התיימרתי לפענח את הנעלם, את 'שנות עולמים' שהינן 'שנות ימין עליון', בזהותי את דרכו של ה' עם דרך בני אדם. כתוצאה מכך התעצמה תחושתי בתהום שבין העבר הזוהר לבין ההווה החשוך, והיא הביאה למסקנה כי ה' השבית את מידותיו. נמצא, אחרי שבעל המזמור מבטא בפיו את המידות שה' גילה, מתבררת לו טעותו. חולשתו היא שהכשילתו בגישתו אל הבעיה שהציקה לו.

29 ראה את סקירתו של טייט (לעיל, הערה 12).

30 אל"ה (לעיל, הערה 11): 'חלה'. — הטעם מלעיל בגלל נסוג אחור.

31 אל"ה, שם; טייט (לעיל, הערה 12).

32 מפרשינינו הקדמונים סבורים כך, למשל, רש"י וראב"ע. תפיסה זו מתבטאת גם בתרגום הארמי וגם בביאור.

33 כך כבר בגרסה הראשונה של התרגום הארמי, בתרגום השבעים, ברש"י ובביאור. מן האחרונים ראה, למשל, קראוס (לעיל, הערה 1); קסלמן (לעיל, הערה 2), עמ' 52; טייט (לעיל, הערה 12).

34 קסלמן (לעיל, הערה 2), עמ' 52–53.

35 ראה: H.-J. Zobel, 'æljôn', *TWAT* VI, pp. 131-151

36 כך מתורגם בגרסה השנייה של התרגום הארמי ומפורש על ידי ראב"ע, רד"ק, וכן: F. Delitzsch, *Commentar über den Psalter*, I, Leipzig 1859; C.A. Briggs & E.G. Briggs, *The Book of Psalms* (ICC), II, Edinburgh 1907

37 כגון, שופ' טז 7, 11; שמ"א ל 13; יש' נז 10.

38 זהו מובן המלה על פי תרגומי עקילס והוולגטה.

פסוק 12: 'אזכור [קרי; כתיב: 'אזכיר'] מעללי יה'. הנשוא משתלב בהקשר, בין שהוא בהפעיל (כתיב) ובין שהוא בקל (קרי). – מה שבעל המזמור מקבל עליו לעשות, 'אזכור מעללי יה', הוא עושה: 'כי אזכרה מקדם פלאך'. הוראתה הסבירה כאן של המלית 'כי': אכן.[39] 'מקדם' מתייחס אל 'פלאך'; בעל המזמור זוכר את הפלא המציין את מעללי ה' 'מקדם', מאז. כדי לחזק, להוכיח לעצמו את מסקנתו, שטעה בהסיקו שיחסו של ה' בהווה מנוגד ליחסו בעבר, הוא ישוב ויעלה בזכרונו את העבר.

על השינוי בגישתו של בעל המזמור ועל מלוא משמעותם של הפסוקים 12–13 ניתן לעמוד מתוך השוואתם לפסוקים בחלקו הראשון של המזמור, הנוקטים אותן מלים:

פסוק 4: **אזכרה** אלהים <u>ואהמיה</u>
פסוק 12: **אזכור** <u>מעללי יה</u>

אם בפסוק 4 העיקר הוא תוצאותיה הכאובות של זכירת בעל המזמור את האלוהים ('ואהמיה'), הנה בפסוק 12 העיקר הוא עצם הזכירה – לא זכירת האלוהים בכלל, אלא 'מעללי יה' בפרט. ובזכרו את 'מעללי יה' הרבים הוא מתרשם מדבר אחד: כולם 'פלאך'. המעסיק מעתה את מחשבתו הוא הפלא שב'מעללי יה'. בשלב זה של הרהורים ב'מעללי יה' – 'פלאך', הוא גם קובע עליהם כאיוב: 'נפלאות ממני ולא אדע' (מב 3)? זאת ועוד.

פסוק 7: **אזכרה**   נגינתי   בלילה עם   <u>לבבי</u> **אשיחה**
פסוק 12: **אזכרה** מקדם פלאך פסוק 13: ובעלילותיך **אשיחה**

השוואה זו מציינת את העתקת ההתבוננות מן ה־אני האנושי אל ה־אתה האלוהי. גם העתקה זו אינה אלא תוצאתה המובנת מאליה של ההכרה שמצאה את ביטויה בפסוק 11. תחילה ביקש ה־אני לחשב 'ימים מקדם, שנות עולמים' (פסוק 6), והנה נוכח, כי 'שנות ימין עליון', אלוהים בלבד שולט על השנים. מכאן מובן שההתבוננות, אשר בחלקו הראשון של המזמור התרכזה באדם, ב־אני, נעתקה בחלקו השני וממוקדת עתה באלוהים, ב־אתה האלוהי. הדיבור אל ה' בגוף נוכח מעיד על הקשר שנוצר אתו.

פסוק 13: 'והגיתי בכל פעלך'. מן ההקשר מתברר שהפועל 'הגה' משמש כאן במובן הרהור בדבר, עיון, התעמק בו.[40] הפעם אפוא בעל המזמור אינו רק זוכר דבר, כמו בפעמים הקודמות (פסוקים 4, 7) אלא גם מתבונן, מתעמק, 'בכל פעלך'. – 'ובעלילותיך אשיחה'. לפועל 'אשיחה' כאן אין עוד האסוציאציה השלילית שבהופעותיו בפסוקים ההם.[41] מצוינת בו מדיטאציה של שבח.[42]

פסוק 14: 'אלהים בקדש דרכך'. 'קדש', לפי ההגדרה הנראית כהולמת ביותר, הוא 'ביטוי למהותו הנעלמת של האל',[43] לטרנסצנדנטיותו. המסקנה שבעל המזמור מסיק מהתבוננותו בכל פעלו ובעלילותיו של ה' היא אפוא: כמהות ה' כן דרכו, הנהגתו היא נעלמת, טרנסצנדנטאלית, כמוסה. – מסקנתו זו גוררת את התפעלותו המובעת בהכרזה שבפסק 14ב: 'מי אל גדול כאלהים'.

פסוק 15 א: 'אתה האל עשה פלא'. דברי פנייה זו אינם אלא ניסוחה של מסקנת ההתבוננות

39   לשימוש זה במלית 'כי', ראה KB: 'כי' II, 1.
40   אל"ה (לעיל, הערה 11): 'הגה'.
41   ראה לעיל, דיונינו בפסוקים 4, 7.
42   KB: 'שיח'.
43   י"ש ליכט, 'קדש, קדוש, קדושה', אנציקלופדיה מקראית, ז, ירושלים תשל"ו, טור 62.

שבפסוק 14א 'בלשון הדיוט'. רבים כבר העירו על כך, שבפסוקים 14, 15א מהדהד פסוק משירת
הים (שמ' טו 11).[44]

תה' עז 14, 15א: אלהים **בקדש** דרכך מי **אל** גדול כאלהים אתה האל **עשה פלא**

שמ' טו 11: מי כמכה **באלים** ה' מי כמכה נאדר **בקדש** נורא תהלת **עשה פלא**

בין תה' עז 14 לפסוק משירת הים יש הקבלה כיאסטית, המראה, כאמור, התייחסות מכוונת.
על פי הקבלה זו, וכן על פי השימוש באותו ביטוי, 'עשה פלא', במשפט הסמוך, אפשר להניח
במידה ניכרת של סבירות שקריעת ים סוף עמדה לנגד עיניו של בעל המזמור באמרו: 'אזכרה
מקדם פלאך' (פסוק 12), בהתבוננו 'בכל פעלך ובעלילותיך' (פסוק 13) ובהסיקו מזאת את
מסקנתו 'אלהים בקדש דרכך' (פסוק 14), ו־'אתה האל עשה פלא' (פסוק 15). הנחה זו מוצאת
אישוש נוסף בהמשך, כאשר בעל המזמור מדגים את מסקנת התבוננותו, ביתר דיוק, את
קביעתו האחרונה על ה' שהוא 'עשה פלא', הנמצאת גם בשירת הים. קריעת ים סוף הינה פרט
הבא ללמד על הכלל.

פסוק 15ב: 'הודעת בעמים עזך'. במלה 'עז' מוגדר מעשה ה' גם בשירת הים (שמ' טו 13).[45]
במה הודיע ה' בעמים את עוזו?

פסוק 16: 'גאלת בזרוע עמך, בני יעקב ויוסף – סלה'. הוצע שמזמורנו הוא אחד 'הכתובים
המתארים את קריעת ים סוף, בלי להיזקק לעניין המצרים'.[46] ואולם, שימוש הפועל 'גאל'
כנשוא המשפט רומז לשעבוד, מן הסתם, לזה שבמצרים. (אגב, האם לשון המשפט אינה מזכירה
את דברי ה' אל משה: '**וגאלתי** אתכם **בזרוע** נטויה' [שמ' ו 6[?]] הרמז משקף את התפיסה שמן
העבדות במצרים נגאל העם רק אחר שעבר את הים: ה' 'עשה פלא' בכך שהעביר את העם בים
סוף ולא שהוציאו מארץ מצרים. – המכוון במלה 'עמך' ברישא מוגדר בסיפא בביטוי 'בני יעקב
ויוסף'. יש הסבורים שהצירוף 'בני יעקב ויוסף' מתכוון לשני חלקי האומה.[47] ברם להגדרה כזו
אין שום טעם בהקשר. יש הרואים באזכור שמו של 'יוסף' סימן למוצאו של המזמור.[48] מכל
מקום, הזכרת 'משה ואהרן' בפסוק 21 נראית כמצדיקה את ההנחה שכאן 'יעקב ויוסף' לפי
פשוטם מציינים את שמותיהם הפרטיים של שניים מאבות האומה – כפי שסבורים אחדים
מן הפרשנים הראשונים[49] והאחרונים.[50] ואשר לכוונה בכינויו של העם 'בני יעקב ויוסף', יש
מקום להניח שגם עליה בא ללמד המכוון בנאמר שם על 'משה ואהרן'. ב'משה ואהרן' מדבר
הכתוב בדבר חלקם ביציאת בני ישראל ממצרים, ב'יעקב ויוסף', כנראה, בגלל חלקם בירידתם
מצרימה ובשהותם שם. זאת אומרת, 'יעקב ויוסף' מציינים את תחילת התהליך, וכנגדם 'משה
ואהרן' את סיומו. נשאלת השאלה: מהו הרעיון המומחש בציונו של השעבוד במצרים בהוספת
הכינוי 'יעקב ויוסף' למלה 'עמך'? הואיל והנושא הדידוקטי בפסוק 16: אתה, אלוהים, משתמע

44   כגון, ג'פרסון (לעיל, הערה 1), עמ' 89; ש"א ליונשטם, מסורת יציאת מצרים בהשתלשלותה,
ירושלים תשכ"ה, עמ' 115; קסלמן (לעיל, הערה 2), עמ' 51; טייט (לעיל, הערה 12), עמ' 274.

45   לפי שמ' טו 14–15, גם נודע לעמים מה שעשה ה' בעוזו. שם גם נמסר על תגובתם לכך, בהתאם
לעניינה של השירה.

46   ליונשטם (לעיל, הערה 44), עמ' 105.

47   M. Noth, *Überlieferungsgeschichte des Pentateuchs*, Stuttgart 1948, p. ראה, למשל,
231, n. 571

48   ליונשטם (לעיל, הערה 44), עמ' 105, הערה 9; טייט (לעיל, הערה 12), עמ' 274; וכן: .A. Weiser
Die Psalmen (ATD), Göttingen 1966, p. 361

49   ראב"ע, רד"ק. כך נדרש הביטוי כבר באגדה (ילקוט לשמ"א קכ"ט) ומתורגם בתרגום הארמי.

50   כגון, ג'פרסון (לעיל, הערה 44), עמ' 105; R. Kittel, *Die Psalmen* (KAT 13)[5-6], Leipzig 1929; קסלמן (לעיל, הערה 2), עמ' 52,
הערה 6.

בהוספת הכינוי כי מה שנעשה על ידי יעקב ויוסף בעצם אלוהים עשהו. וכוונת הפסוק: מי שגאל את 'בני יעקב ויוסף' ממצרים הוא שהוריד את יעקב ויוסף מצרימה. זאת אומרת: אלוהים הנהיג את העולם ביד בני אדם.[51]

פסוק 17: 'ראוך מים אלהים ראוך מים יחילו אף ירגזו תהמות'. בפסוקנו נפתח תיאור של 'רעדת הטבע בשעת הופעת ה''.[52] כפי שהראה ליונשטם,[53] היתה זו מסורת רווחת בישראל. המיוחד בתיאור שלפנינו (פסוקים 17–19),[54] שגם עליו עמד ליונשטם,[54] היא ההבלטה של תגובת המים על התיאופאניה. נזכרות כאן שמונה תגובות: האחרונה מהן היא של הארץ (פסוק 19ב), האחרות הן של גופי המים ('מים', 'תהמות', [פסוק 17], 'מים עבות' [פסוק 18א×b] ושל תופעות הקשורות לגשם ('קול רעמך', 'ברקים' [פסוק 19א×]). מסתבר שהסיבה להבלטה זו נעוצה בכך, שקריעת ים סוף (לפי מזמורנו, הנציג המובהק של פלאי ה' 'מקדם') היתה זעזועו של הים, כאחד מגופי המים שבעולם, למראה ה'. תפיסה זו מוצאת את ביטויה גם בלשון שבה מתואר פסוקנו כיצד 'מים', היינו מימי העולם בכלל, הגיבו כש'ראו' את האלוהים; הלשון שאולה מפסוק 14 בשירת הים[55] (שהשפעתה משתקפת, כאמור, גם בפסוק 15), כפי שנראה מהשוואת שני הפסוקים זה לזה:

תה' עז 17: ... ראוך מים **יחילו**   אף **ירגזו** תהמות
שמ' טו 14: שמעו עמים **ירגזון**   **חיל** אחז ישבי פלשת

ההקבלה אפוא כיאסטית, שהיא, כידוע, ביטוי להתייחסות מכוונת. דרך אגב יוער, כי המלה 'תהום', שהוראתה במקרא, ככל הנראה, שטף,[56] משמשת בשירת הים (פסוק 5, 8) כינוי לים סוף, בצורת הריבוי, 'תהמות'; כך גם ביש' סג 13; תה' קו 9; וביחיד, 'תהום' — ביש' נא 10.

פסוק 18: 'זרמו מים עבות'. צורת הפועל ניתנת לפירוש, ואכן היא מפורשת כפוֹעַל או כפוּעַל עם מושא.[57] צורת הריבוי 'עבות', במקום זו היותר שכיחה 'עבים', מופיעה במקרא עוד פעם (שמ"ב כג 4). היא נושא המשפט. פירוש נושא המשפט: עננים שפכו בעוז של זרם מים או נשטפו במים. – 'קול נתנו שחקים אף חצציך יתהלכו'. 'חצציך' – צורת ריבוי חד פעמית של של 'חץ', תחת הצורה הרגילה 'חצים', דוגמת 'הררי' (דב' א 9) לעומת 'הרים' (נחם' ט 22) לעומת 'עמים'. 'חץ' כאן הוא מטאפורה לברק, כמו בשמ"ב כב 15; תה' יח 15, צא 5, קמד 6, וכן: 'אור חצך' (חב' ג 11). המשפט האחרון מתאר התרחשות בו זמנית למתואר בשני המשפטים הקודמים בפסוק: כשקרה הנמסר בהם אז הלכו ברקים אנה ואנה.

פסוק 19: 'קול רעמך בגלגל'. המכוון במלה 'גלגל' שנוי במחלוקת. סביר ביותר לפרשה על פי יח' י 2, כמכוונת לגלגל המרכבה האלוהית, שבו מקור הברקים והרעמים.[58] נראה שבעל הביאור

51 ראה פסוק 21.
52 הגדרת תופעה זו בעקבות ש"א ליונשטם, 'רעדת הטבע בשעת הופעת ה'', עז לדוד, ירושלים תשכ"ד, עמ' 508–520.
53 שם, עמ' 508; ולעיל, הערה 44, עמ' 108.
54 ליונשטם (לעיל, הערה 52), עמ' 508, 510; ולעיל, הערה 44, עמ' 107–108.
55 כבר קסלמן (לעיל, הערה 2), עמ' 53, הערה 9, מעיר שפסוקנו מזכיר את לשונו של הפסוק ההוא בשמ' טו.
56 C. Westermann, *Genesis* (BKAT) I, Neukirchen-Vluyn 1974, p. 145
57 גזניוס-קאוטש (לעיל, הערה 3), §55b; KB: 'זרם'.
58 ליונשטם (לעיל, הערה 52), עמ' 513, הערה 14; ולעיל, הערה 44, עמ' 107, הערה 14.

קלע לפשוטם של משפט זה והבא אחריו, 'האירו ברקים תבל'. לפי פירושו, שני משפטים אלה
באים להבהיר ולהשלים את שני המשפטים האחרונים בפסוק הקודם. 'קול נתנו שחקים' הוא
'קול רעמך בגלגל'; 'אף חצציך יתהלכו', היינו: 'האירו ברקים תבל'. ה'ברקים' קשורים ל'תבל',
ליבשה, בהאירם אותה. ובכן, מבין תגובות איתני הטבע שבמרומים על הופעת ה' נקשרת זו
של ה'ברקים' עם יסוד הבריאה של מטה.

כבר שמו לב לכך, שבתיאור התיאופאניה 'קול' כפול (פסוקים 18, 19) ובתיאור הלך רוחו של
בעל המזמור 'קולי' כפול (פסוק 2א, ב). אולי רומזת התופעה הסטרוקטוראלית-סגנונית
להתייחסות רעיונית: תחילה הביע בעל המזמור את הרגשתו שקולו אינו נשמע על ידי ה',
ואילו עתה מתבטאת הכרתו שיש ל'קולי' תשובה ב'קול' רעמו של ה'.[59]

התיאור המתחיל באיתני הטבע של מטה ('מים', 'תהמות'), ממשיך לתאר איך הגיבו אלה של
מעלה ('עבות', 'שחקים'); לאחר מכן הוא שב דרך ה'ברקים' לתגובות של מטה, ומסיים בהן:
'רגזה ותרעש הארץ'. – לתפיסת סיומו של תיאור התיאופאניה במלוא משמעותו יש לשים לב
לשלושה מענייני לשון: (א) הפועל הראשון, 'רגזה', המציין את תגובת 'הארץ', מגדיר גם את
תגובת 'תהמות' (פסוק 17); (ב) הפועל השני, 'רעש', משמש לרוב כנשוא ל'הארץ', כמו כאן, או
למקושרים עמה,[60] ולפעמים – לנושאים אחרים,[61] אך אף פעם לא למים; (ג) השם 'ארץ' יש
שמציין רק את היבשה (בר' א 1, 2), היינו נרדף ל'תבל', שזוהי הוראתה הבלעדית, ויש שכולל
גם את 'מקוה המים', 'ימים', היינו את כל כדור הארץ. זהו שימושה של מלת 'ארץ' לא פעם,
וכל אימת שהיא מקבילה ל'תבל', כמו כאן. על פי הערות אלה נראה להניח, שמשתי התגובות
של 'הארץ' המתוארות במשפט הנדון, זו המצוינת בפועל 'ותרעש' היא תגובת היבשה, ואילו
הפועל 'רגזה' מגדיר את תגובת ה'ימים', בדומה ל'תהמות' בפסוק 17. דרך אגב יוער, שהשם
'תהום' מציין לפעמים ימים (איוב לח 16; מש' ח 27, 28). נמצא, כשם ששני המשפטים
הקודמים בפסוק 19 מתייחסים אל המתואר לפני כן, כך גם משפטנו. ביתר דיוק, הוא מתייחס
אל פסוק 17, תוך חזרה חלקית על לשונו והשלמתה מצד התוכן, וכך הוא מסכם את התגובות
למטה ומסיים את תיאור זעזועי הטבע בפני ה'. מבנה התיאור מאשש מסקנה זו:

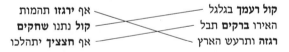

אחר שתיאר מזכרון העבר את תגובות הטבע של הופעת ה', עובר בעל המזמור אל הופעת ה'
עצמה.

פסוק 20: 'בים דרכך ושבילך במים רבים'. המשפט נתפס על ידי חז"ל, הפרשנים הראשונים
והאחרונים, כמכוון לקריעת ים סוף. ואכן, תפיסה זו מסתברת, לא רק מן העובדה שדברי שירת
הים מהדהדים בכל חלקי המזמור, אלא גם מידוע השם 'בים', ומהעמדתו מול 'מים רבים'
שבצלע המקבילה, המשלימה, ואף מן הפסוק הבא. עם זאת, בהימנעותו מכינויו המפורש של
ה'ים', מתבטאת התפיסה שמה שקרה את ים סוף קרה גם את ה'מים רבים'.[62] מה קרה לא
נאמר; פרט זה אינו רלוואנטי למכוון בתיאור. שכן, ענייננו הבלעדי של הפסוק הוא בדרכו,
בהופעתו של ה'. לפיכך, 'דרכך' כמובן אינה הדרך שהכין ה' למעבר העם, כפי שמפרשים בעיקר

59   קסלמן (לעיל, הערה 2), עמ' 57.
60   'מוסדי ארץ' (יש' כד 18), 'ההרים' (יר' ד 24; ועוד), 'האיים' (יח' כו 15).
61   כגון: 'הספים' (עמוס ט 1), 'דגי הים ועוף השמים וחית השדה וכל הרמש... וכל האדם' (יח' לח 20),
      'הסוס' (איוב לט 20).
62   לפי חז"ל 'כל מים שבעולם נבקעו' (מכילתא לשמ' יד 22).

קדמונינו,[63] אלא הדרך בה הלך ה' עצמו. הלך ולא הוליך. ברם, הנתיב 'במים רבים' מכונה 'שביל' ואילו הנתיב 'בים' מכונה 'דרך', היינו נתיב רחב; שמא התחשב בכל זאת המשורר בעובדה שבזה האחרון הלך גם העם, ולא רק ה'? – 'ועקבותיך לא נודעו'. בין הפרשנים הראשונים והאחרונים מוסכם שהנקבע במשפט הוא 'בעבור שוב הים מיד לאיתנו',[64] כפי שמסופר בשמ' יד 26–28. ואולם, בלשון המשפט אין כל רמז לכך שהמסופר בו קרה לאחר המסופר בשני המשפטים הקודמים. כשם שבמשפטים הקודמים, בדיבור על דרכו, על שבילו של ה', לא נרמז שאם חל שינוי במצב הרגיל של הים ושל 'מים רבים'. כפשוטו של הפסוק עדיף אפוא הפירוש שאמנם דרכו של ה' היתה 'בים' ושבילו 'במים רבים', אך לאחר ההליכה רשמי צעדיו לא ניכרו, כי כיסו עליהם מי הים. המכוון בקביעה זו נרמז כבר בפסוק 14: 'בקדש דרכך', היינו: דרך ה' טמירה ואין הדעת משיגתה. כדברי איוב (ט 11): 'הן יעבר עלי ולא אראה, ויחלף ולא אבין לו'.

פסוק 21: 'נחית כצאן עמך ביד משה ואהרן'. בעל המזמור עובר מתיאור אוניברסאלי, סתמי, של הנהגת העולם על ידי ה' לתיאור יותר קונקרטי של ההנהגה וגילויה בדברי ימי ישראל. המעבר מסתבר מאמונתו של בעל המזמור, שקיימת גם דרך אחרת בהנהגת ה' מלבד זו המתוארת בפסוקים הקודמים. כמו כן מובן מאליו שלקיומה של הדרך ההיא מביא בעל המזמור הוכחה מדברי ימי עמו. הרי ראינו שגם בתיאור האוניברסאלי מהדהדת שירת הים. העם המונהג על ידי ה' משול כאן לצאן, שהוא הברייה הזקוקה ביותר להדרכה ולהנחיה. במשל זה, השכיח במקרא,[65] מומחשת הנהגת ה', שהיא אחראית, קפדנית ופרטית.[66] הוספת איפיונה של ההנהגה מתבקשת מכך שאינה פעולתו הישירה של ה', אלא מבוצעת 'ביד משה ואהרן', היינו בידי אדם. בפסוקנו מדובר בפירוש על דרך עקיפה זו, ואילו פסוק 16 רומז אליה, כאמור, בהתייחסו אל גאולת 'בני יעקב ויוסף'.[67] שם הכוונה, ככל הנראה, להוצאת העם ממצרים, כאן – למסעם במדבר. כך מניחים רוב הפרשנים, ובדין. מסייעים להנחה זו כמה נתונים: (א) הופעת הביטוי 'ביד משה ואהרן' בקשר למסעיהם של יוצאי מצרים: 'אלה מסעי בני ישראל אשר יצאו מארץ מצרים... ביד משה ואהרן' (במ' לג 1); (ב) העובדה שפסוקנו ממשיך את פסוק 20, שבו נרמז המעבר בים סוף; (ג) הקשר של פסוקנו עם פסוק 16, קשר שעליו מעידים הן העניין והן הסגנון של שני הפסוקים. כבר העירו על כך,[68] שהנשואים במשפטי הפסוקים 16, 21 משמשים כך גם באחד מפסוקי שירת הים (שמ' טו 13). הופעתם במזמורנו בסדר כיאסטי לעומת הפסוק משירת הים מאששת את ההנחה שמדובר בהתייחסות מכוונת.

תה' עז 16: **גאלת** בזרוע **עמך**, בני יעקב ויוסף ← שמ' טו 13: **נחית** בחסדך
21: **נחית** כצאן עמך ביד משה ואהרן ← עם זו **גאלת**

נמצא, לפי בעל המזמור עז, שה' 'עשה פלא' בהנהגת העולם, הן כאשר פעל פעל בעצמו, בבטלו את חוקי הטבע, שהוא השליט בבריאה, והן כאשר פעל פעל ביד אדם בתוך סדר העולם הקבוע. בכך מסתכמת מסקנתו של בעל המזמור ממעשי ה' בימי קדם. זכרון מעשים אלה הביא אותו לידי ההכרה שקושייותיו על הנהגתו של ה' בטעות יסודן. ניתן להניח, כי עיצוב המסקנה גרר

---

63 כגון, ראב"ע, רד"ק. ראה גם הביאור.
64 ראב"ע.
65 כגון, יש' מ 11; יר' לא 10; יח' לד 11 ואילך; במזמורי אסף אחרים: עח 52, פ 2. ישראל הוא צאנו של ה', למשל, תה' עד 1, עט 13; ועוד.
66 השווה יש' מ 11.
67 ראה הדיון בפסוק 16, לעיל.
68 קסלמן (לעיל, הערה 2), עמ' 52.

הירגעות נפשית וחיזוק האמונה בקיומה של ההשגחה; אך מכאן עוד רחוקה הדרך עד לסברה,
שבמסקנתו של בעל המזמור משתמעת תקווה לגילוי מחודש של פלאי ההשגחה בעתיד. סברה
זו רווחת בפירוש מזמורנו אצל החוקרים הרואים בחטיבת הפסוקים 11–21 חלק אורגאני של
המזמור.[69] אלה תופסים את החלק השני של המזמור כתשובה על השאלות שבחלק הראשון
וכיישוב הקושייה המתבטאת בהן. וייזר, למשל, 'רואה בהיגד "ועקבותיך לא נודעו" את הדי
שאלתו של בעל המזמור אשר אף הוא חיפש לשווא את עקבות ההנהגה האלוהית. הוא מתנחם
עתה בכך שנבצר מאדם מאד להכיר את עקבות אלוהיו בקורות העמים'.[70]

ואולם תפיסה זו אינה מתיישבת עם לשונו של החלק השני: בחלק הראשון שואל בעל המזמור,
האם הופסקה ההשגחה לתמיד? האם בוטלו מידות החסד של ה'? בחלק השני הוא אומר,
בפנותו אל ה', שמעשי ה' בעבר היו פלאים. מקביעה זו אפשרית, הגיונית, מתחייבת המסקנה,
שאין להקשות על דרכו של ה' בהווה, ואין לשאול, למשל, 'הלעולמים יזנח אדני' (פסוק 8);
אבל מסקנה זו אינה מובעת. שמא היא אינה מובעת האויל והיא מובנת מאליה? על כך יש
להשיב, כי דרך זו מתאימה אולי לאדם שההגיון בלבד שולט במהלך מחשבתו; אך ספק אם היא
מתאימה להלך הנפש המשתקף במזמור, היינו לאדם אשר הגיע לפתרון בעייתו החמורה לאחר
מאבק קשה.

מכל מקום, ההתחשבות בדמות חלקו השני של המזמור מחייבת אותנו לדחות את התפיסה
הרווחת, הרואה בו מענה לשאלות שבחלק הראשון. לפשוטטו של הקשר שבין שני חלקי המזמור
מכוון בעל הביאור בצייֵנו: כיוון 'שיתחיל המשורר בצעקה על ענין צרותיו, ומיד כשיתחיל
מעט לדבר בימין ה' ומעלליו, הנם הם ימלאו כ"כ את נפשו ורעיונותיו ע"י תקפם וגדלם, עד
שיעבירו אותו מן הענין הראשון והוא יעזוב אותו לגמרי ויפרוט בענין האחר אשר עלה עתה
על רעיונו, והוא גם כן מתולדות ההתפעלות, ויורה בשיר בפרט שלפנינו על עוצם נחמתו
באלהיו, כי כבר שכח את צרותיו ולא ידבר בהם עוד'. ובכן, בעל המזמור נזכר כי 'שנות ימין
עליון' (פסוק 11), ומכאן ממשיך הוא לדבר על אופיים הפלאי של 'מעללי יה', ובתוך כך ממלא
הדבר יותר ויותר את תודעתו עד שמשתלט על הלך נפשו ורוחו.

69 מן החוקרים בדורנו, למשל, וייזר (לעיל, הערה 48), עמ' 362–363; קסלמן (לעיל, הערה 2), עמ' 55;
    טייט (לעיל, הערה 12), עמ' 273, הערה 2.
70 A. Weiser, 'Ps. 77. Ein Beitrag zur Frage nach dem Verhältnis von Kult und
    Heilsgeschichte', *TLZ* 72 (1947), p. 140

ספר הברית מבאר את ספר הברית — תופעת הבומראנג

יאיר זקוביץ

א

לראשונה נקרע לי צוהר אל מהותו ומחקרו של ספר הברית בהיותי תלמיד לתואר ראשון בחוג
למקרא, וזאת מקריאת הערך 'ספר הברית' באנציקלופדיה המקראית, אשר כתבו מורי, בעל
היובל, בסגנון בהיר ומלוטש היטב, כדרכו.[1]

בספר הברית — כמו בכל חטיבה ספרותית אחרת במקרא — חלו ידיהם של מסדרים ופרשנים,
שהותירו בכתובים את חותמם בבואם לפתור קושי כלשהו, וזאת על ידי השמטות, תוספות או
שינויים (היינו, המרת מלה, צירוף או משפט באחרים).

במאמר קצר זה נדגים אך סוג אחד של פירושים: ספר הברית, הקדום בקובצי החוקים שבתורה,
שימש, כידוע, יסוד לקובצי החוקים המאוחרים ממנו, הנוהגים לבאר את חוקיו ולהתאימם
למציאות זמנם ולעולם האמונות והדעות של החוג בקרבו הם נוצרו. כאשר, בסופו של תהליך
גיבוש התורה, מצויים ספר הברית ושאר קובצי החוקים בשכנות זה לזה, בספר התורה, ניכרים
מתחים וסתירות בין ספר הברית לבין הקבצים שחוברו בעקבותיו. שינויים–ביאורים ששולבו
בספר הברית כדי להתאים את דיניו את דיניו לדינים שינקו ממנו, ידונו להלן. את התופעה שתודגם כאן
אנו מכנים 'תופעת הבומראנג': טקסט א' משמש מצע לטקסט ב', אשר מצידו שב ומשפיע על
טקסט א'. תופעת הבומראנג אינה מיוחדת כמובן ל'ספר הברית'. קודם שנעבור לבחינת ביטוייה
של התופעה בספר הברית, נציג אפוא שתי דוגמאות מחטיבות ספרותיות אחרות, האחת
מתחום ההיסטוריוגראפיה והשנייה מתחום החוק.

1. בסיכום תולדות המלך אסא ולפני אזכור מותו מציין בעל ספר מלכים: 'רק לעת זקנתו חלה
את רגליו' (מל"א טו 23). מלת '(ו)רק' ניצבת לעתים קרובות בראשן של תוספות (ראה לדוגמא
שמ' ח 5; מל"א טו 5). ואכן, דומה כי הדיווח על מחלת אסא חדר לכתוב בהשפעת המסופר
עליו בספר דברי הימים (שדיווחו מושתת כמובן על ספר מלכים). בעל דברי הימים מרבה
במדרשים סמויים של שמות המלכים.[2] כך הוא דורש את שמו של המלך אסא — אסיא בארמית
רופא — על דרך הארמית, לשון הדיבור הנוהגת בימיו: 'ויחלא אסא בשנת שלושים ותשע
למלכותו ברגליו עד למעלה חליו וגם בחליו לא דרש את ה' כי ברפאים' (דה"ב טז 12).[3] ראוי

1 מ' הרן, 'ספר הברית', אנציקלופדיה מקראית, ה, ירושלים תשכ"ח, טורים 1087–1091.
2 ראה: י' זקוביץ, כפל מדרשי שם (עבודת גמר לתואר מוסמך בחוג למקרא), ירושלים תשל"א, עמ'
166–179.
3 על מדרש שמו של אסא ראה M. Friedlaender, *Die Veränderlichkeit der Namen in dem Stammlisten der Buches der Chronik*, Berlin 1903, p. 38

לציין כי בנוסח לוקיאנוס של תרגום השבעים התוספת הכרוניסטית בספר מלכים ארוכה יותר: לאחר המלים 'רק לעת זקנתו' מוספות שם המלים 'עשה את הרע ו' כהצדקה לחליו של המלך.

2. בחוק העבד שבספר דברים (טו 12–18) נזכרת האמה פעמים, וניכר שאזכוריה תלושים מגוף החוק: הופעתה הראשונה בפסוק 12 קוטעת את הדיבור בעבד: 'כי ימכר לך אחיך העברי או העבריה ועבדך...' (הפעלים בזכר הולמים את העבד). האמה נזכרת שנית בסופו של הדין בדבר עבד עולם: 'ואף לאמתך תעשה כן' (טו 17).

והנה, גרסת ספר דברים לחוק העבד מצוטטת בדברי הזעם של ה' לירמיהו על העם, אשר לא שחרר את עבדיו בשנה השביעית: 'אנכי כרתי ברית את אבותיכם ביום הוצאי אותם מארץ מצרים מבית עבדים לאמר. מקץ שבע שנים תשלחו איש את אחיו העברי אשר ימכר לך ועבדך שש שנים ושלחתו חפשי מעמך' (יר' לד 13–14). אף הפתיחה לציטוט 'מקץ שבע שנים' שאולה מלשונו של דברים טו. זוהי הפתיחה לחוק השמיטה הסמוך לחוק העבד (טו 1). בציטוט החוק שבירמיה לד האמה אינה נזכרת, ראיה נוספת לכך שאין היא יסוד אורגאני של החוק. עם זאת, דווקא פרשנות החוק המשוקעת בירמיה לד גרמה בסופו של דבר להוספת האמה בחוק שבספר דברים! בירמיה לד מובעת התפיסה שהן העבדים והן השפחות ראויים לשחרור: ראה פסוק 9: 'לשלח איש את עבדו ואיש את שפחתו העברי והעבריה חפשים'; פסוק 16: וַתָּשֻׁבוּ איש את עבדו ואיש את שפחתו אשר שלחתם חפשים לנפשם ותכבשו אתם להיות לכם לעבדים ולשפחות'. פרשנות החוק חזרה אפוא אל החוק והפכה לחלק אינטגראלי ממנו.

ב

נעבור עתה לתופעת הבומראנג בחוקי ספר הברית:

1. חוק המזבח שבראש ספר הברית (שמ' כ 24–26) דיבר מלכתחילה בצורת פולחן פשוטה ביותר, במזבח אדמה, שיכול אדם מישראל להקים כל אימת שליבו חפץ להקריב קורבן ובכל מקום שיחפץ: 'בכל המקום (=בכל מקום; ראה בר' כ 13, ועוד דב' יא 24) אשר אזכיר את שמי אבוא אליך וברכתיך' (שמ' כ 24). הפשיטתא, וכן התרגום הארמי של הנוסח השומרוני (נוסח A) משמרים את הנוסח המקורי של צורת הפועל: 'תזכיר'. לנוסח זה מכוונת, כפי הנראה, המשנה (אף שעתה מופיע בה הכתוב כצורתו בנוסח המסורה):[4] '...עשרה שיושבין ועוסקין בתורה שכינה שורה ביניהם... ומנין אפילו אחד, שנאמר "בכל המקום אשר אזכיר את שמי אבוא אליך וברכתיך"' (אבות ג,ו).[5] תיעוד מפורש של גרסה זו מופיע בדרשת אל תקרי: 'בכל המקום אשר אזכיר את שמי, בכל מקום שהצדיקים מתפללים שכינה עמהם, אל תקרי אזכיר אלא תזכיר' (מדרש מאור האפלה).[6] האדם הוא אשר מזכיר את שם אלוהיו (ראה לדוגמה יש' סב 6; תה' מה 18). השינוי מגוף שני לגוף ראשון, 'אזכיר', נובע מהתחשבות בחוקי ריכוז הפולחן שבספר דברים, ונועד למנוע את סתירתם. ה' הוא אשר יבחר מקום (אחד) לשכן את שמו שם, ראה דב' יב 11 ואילך,[7] ובמיוחד פסוק 13 שם, המנוסח כנגד החוק הנדון שבספר הברית: 'השמר לך פן תעלה עלתיך בכל מקום אשר תראה...'.

4   לריכוז דוגמאות לפער בין נוסח הכתוב המצוטט לבין זה המשתקף בדרשה, ראה V. Aptowitzer,
     Das Schriftwort in der Rabbinischen Literatur, I-IV, Wien 1906-1919

5   ראה N. Sarna, *Exodus* (JPS Torah Commentary), Philadelphia 1991, p. 251

6   על פי מ"מ כשר, חומש תורה שלמה, טז, ניו-יורק תשט"ו, עמ' קס"ו.

7   הנוסח השומרוני גורס בפסוקנו 'אזכרתי' במקום 'אזכיר', משום שלדידם של השומרונים כבר קבע ה' את המקום, וזאת בדיבר העשירי שבנוסחתם: 'והיה בעברכם את הירדן תקימו את האבנים האלה אשר אנכי מצוה אתכם היום בהר גריזים. ובנית שם מזבח לה' אלהיך מזבח אבנים...' (כך גם בנוסחה שבשמ' כ וגם בזו שבדב' ה).

בעקבות השינוי באה גם תוספת: אם במזבח אחד עסקינן, לא יהא זה מזבח אדמה אלא מזבח אבנים: 'ואם מזבח אבנים תעשה לי לא תבנה אתהן גזית כי חרבך הנפת עליה ותחללה' (שמ' כ 25). כתוב זה נוסף בהשראת דב' כז 5–6: 'ובנית שם מזבח לה' אלהיך מזבח אבנים לא תניף עליהם ברזל. אבנים שלמות תבנה את מזבח ה' אלהיך' (ראה עוד מילוי הצו של דב' כז כו ביהו' ח 31). הצירוף 'מזבח אבנים' אינו בא עוד במקרא כולו! איסור העלייה במעלות על המזבח (שמ' כ 26) הוא, כמובן, חלק מן התוספת שעניינה מזבח האבנים.[8]

2.   בחוק העבד שבספר הברית (כא 2–6) שלושה שינויים הנובעים מהשפעתם של קובצי החוקים היותר מאוחרים, המתייחסים לחוק הקדום ומבארים אותו (וי' כה 39–46; דב' טו 12–18).[9]

(א) תחת מלת 'יעבד' (שמ' כא 2) מצוי בנוסח השומרוני, בתרגום השבעים, בפשיטתא ובוולגטה הנוסח 'יעבדך'. דומה שנוסחם עדיף,[10] באשר הוא הולם את פתיחת החוק המדברת בזיקת האדון לעבדו בגוף שני: 'כי תקנה עבד עברי...'. גרסה זו אף משתקפת בחוק שבספר דברים: 'ועבדך שש שנים' (דב' טו 12); '...עבדך שש שנים' (טו 18); וכן בציטוטו ביר' לד 14, שנדון כבר לעיל. אף בחוק העבד שבספר הברית גופו, בציינו זיקתו של עבד עולם אל אדוניו, נאמר 'ועבדו לעולם' (כא 6). השינוי מ'יעבדך' ל'יעבד' כוון לתפיסת החוק שבספר ויקרא: 'כי עבדי הם אשר הוצאתי אתם מארץ מצרים לא ימכרו ממכרת עבד' (כה 42); 'כי לי בני ישראל עבדים עבדי הם אשר הוצאתי אתם מארץ מצרים...' (כה 55). ואכן בפסוק 40 שם נאמר 'יעבד עמך' ולא 'יעבדך'!

משהו מתפיסה זו ניכר גם בחוק שבספר דברים. מחברו של חוק זה התקשה בפתיחה הבוטה של החוק הקדום: 'כי תקנה עבד עברי' (שמ' כא 2), ועל כן המירה במלים: 'כי ימכר לך אחיך העברי' (דב' טו 12), כאילו לפתע ובעל כורחו מוצא מישראל אדם והוא אדון לאחד מאחיו.

(ב) חוק העבד בספר שמות מדבר מדבר ביציאת עבד עברי לחופשי בשנה השביעית (שמ' כא 2). שלושה סעיפי משנה של החוק מדברים במקרים פרטיים ההולמים את הכלל: 'אם בגפו יבא בגפו יצא. אם בעל אשה הוא ויצאה אשתו עמו. אם אדניו יתן לו אשה וילדה לו בנים או בנות האשה וילדיה תהיה לאדניה והוא יצא בגפו' (כא 3–4). סעיף המשנה הרביעי – סעיף חריג שעניינו בעבדות עולם – כרוך בקודמו: 'ואם אמר יאמר העבד אהבתי את אדני את אשתי ואת בני לא אצא חפשי. והגישו אדניו אל האלהים' (כא 5–6). אהבת העבד לאשתו ולבניו מובנת ומעוגנת בסעיף המשנה השלישי. אך מה עניין אהבתו לאדוניו? ונטולה מחוק העבד שבספר דברים. חוק זה האחרון מונע מן היווצרות נסיבות מעין אלה המתוארות בספר שמות, היינו שעבד עברי יוותר על זכותו לצאת לחופשי בשל אהבתו לאשתו ולבניו; שהרי, כפי שראינו לעיל, מורה חוק זה לשחרר גם אמה עברייה בשנה השביעית, כמו עבד, ואילו נישואין לאמה כנענית אינם בגדר האפשר לפי תפיסת ספר דברים, המקפיד על טוהר העם. לפיכך טעם יחיד בעטיו יהפוך 'אחיך העברי' לעבד עולם הוא: 'והיה כי יאמר אליך לא אצא מעמך כי אהבך כי טוב לו עמך' (דב' טו 16).

8   בנוסח השומרוני לפסוק 26 מופיעה המלה 'אליו' תחת 'עליו'. דומה כי הגרסה השומרונית עיקר (השווה יח' טז 37: 'וגליתי ערותך אלהם'), והשינוי הוא מעין תיקון סופרים, שכוונתו לשמור על כבוד ה'.

9   לזיקותיהם של החוקים המאוחרים אל חוק העבד שבספר הברית, ראה ש' יפת, 'חוקי שחרור עבדים ושאלת היחס בין קובצי החוקים שבתורה', מחקרים במקרא ובמזרח הקדמון מוגשים לשמואל א' ליונשטם במלאת לו שבעים שנה (ערכו י' אבישור, י' בלאו), א, ירושלים תשל"ח, עמ' 231–249.

10   כך סבור, לדוגמה B.S. Childs, *Exodus* (OTL), London 1974, p. 447

(ג) בספר הברית ניכרת כפילות באשר למקום עריכתו של הטקס המציין את היותו של העבד לעבד עולם: 'והגישו אדניו אל האלהים', מול 'והגישו אל הדלת או אל המזוזה' (שמ' כא 6).[11] מלכתחילה הופיע בחוק אך המשפט הראשון: 'והגישו אדניו אל האלהים'. ספר דברים, אשר ביקש להוציא את החוק מתחום הקדושה בשל הקושי שמעורר ביצועו נוכח המציאות החדשה של ריכוז הפולחן,[12] המיר הגשה אל האלוהים בהגשה אל הדלת, לצורך רציעה: 'ונתתה באזנו ובדלת' (דב' טו 17). בהשפעת מלים אלה הורחב החוק בשמות;[13] דומה כי מטרת השאילה מספר דברים היתה להמיר את 'והגישו...' הראשון בשני, וכך להתאים את תפיסת החוק בספר הברית לזו של ספר דברים; אך מי שהכיר את הנוסח המקורי השיב את ה'אבדה' אל מקומה.[14]

3. בשמות כא 12–17 מצוי קובץ קצר בן ארבעה חוקים אפודיקטיים המסתיימים באותו האופן, בעונש: 'מות יומת'. הקובץ מובנה היטב:

'מכה איש...' (12); 'ומכה אביו ואמו...' (15)
'וגנב איש...' (16); 'ומקלל אביו ואמו...' (17)

בולטת בקובץ זה חריגה בעלת היקף ניכר – הרחבת דין הרוצח בשני כתובים שעניינם בהבחנה בין רוצח בשגגה לרוצח במזיד: 'ואשר לא צדה והאלהים אנה לידו ושמתי לך מקום אשר ינוס שמה. וכי יזד איש על רעהו להרגו בערמה מעם מזבחי תקחנו למות' (כא 13–14).[15] האבחנה בין שני סוגי הרוצחים וקביעת הצורך במקום אליו ינוס הרוצח בשגגה נובעות שתיהן מדיני עיר המקלט בבמדבר לה ובדברים יט, אשר השלימו את החסר בספר הברית. השורש צד"ה (כא 13) מופיע בספר במדבר (לה 20, 22), הצירוף 'נוס שמה' (כא 13) מופיע הן בספר במדבר (לה 6, 15) והן בספר דברים (ד 42; יט 3, 4). מי שהכיר את חוקי עיר המקלט ביקש למנוע את התמיהה העולה למקרא החוק בשמות – התעלמותו מדיני הרוצח בשגגה – והוסיפם. רבים טעו לחשוב שה'מקום' בפסוק 13 מכוון אל 'מזבחי' שבפסוק 14,[16] ולא היא. פסוק 13 רומז לעיר מקלט (וראה "ושמתי לך מקום" אלו ערי מקלט' [מדרש אגדה]),[17] אך 'אינו קורא לילד בשמו', מפני שעניין זה יפורט די הצורך בחומשים במדבר ודברים. פסוק 14 בא להוסיף על קודמו ולהזהיר שרוצח במזיד לשווא יחפש בעיר המקלט הגנה מפני הדין היאה לו, ואף המזבח לא יקנה לו חסינות (זאת בהשפעת הכתובים מל"א א 50–53; ב 28–35).[18]

11 על הכפילות עמד .E. Meyer, *Die Israeliten und ihre Nachbarstämme*, Halle 1906, p 475, n. 2

12 ראה M. Weinfeld, *Deuteronomy and the Deuteronomic School*, Oxford 1972, p. 233

13 אף הוא מניח .J. Morgenstern, 'The Book of the Covenant II', *HUCA* 7 (1930), p. 9 כפל בכתוב, אך לדידו המלים 'והגישו אל הדלת...' הינן גלוסה קדם דויטרונומיסטית, המכוונת לטקס הנערך במקדש כלשהו ולא עוד בבית.

14 המקבילות לעדות לפני האלוהים בשער המקדש שמביא פנשאם (F.C. Fensham, 'New Light on אינן (Exodus 21₆ and 22₇ from the Laws of Eshnunna', *JBL* 78 [1959], pp. 160-161 מחייבות את הנחת אחדות הכתוב בשמות.

15 למשניות פסוקים אלה ראה, לדוגמה M. Noth, *Exodus* (OTL), London 1962, p. 170

16 ראה לדוגמה S.R. Driver, *Exodus* (CB), Cambridge 1911, p. 215; M. Greenberg, 'The Biblical Conception of Asylum', *JBL* 78 (1959), pp. 125-132; נות, שם, טוען בצדק ש'המקום' הוא עיר מקלט.

17 על פי מ"מ כשר (לעיל, הערה 6), יז, עמ' ע"ו.

18 בקובץ קצר זה חריגה נוספת מן הסגנון הקצוב: 'ונמצא בידו' (שמ' כא 16). מלים אלה אינן מוצאות מקבילה בחוק שבספר דברים המבואר דין זה (דב' כד 7), וניכר כי הינן תוספת (ראה D. Daube, *Studies in Biblical Law*, New York 1969, p. 95). דומה כי הוספתן היא כורח הנובע

4. 'ואנשי קדש תהיון לי ובשר בשדה טרפה לא תאכלו לכלב תשלכון אתו' (שמ' כב 30). מלת 'בשדה' אינה מתועדת בתרגומים העתיקים, ונסחם אכן חלק יותר מנוסח המסורה. בודה מניח אפוא שהמלה נוספה עקב שגגה כפולה של מעתיקים: (א) דיטוגרפיה: תן דעתך לדמיון הגרפי בין 'בשר' לבין 'בשדה'. (ב) הפרדת תיבות מוטעית: הה"א שבסוף מלת 'בשדה' נשתייכה במקורה, לדעת בודה, למלה הבאה: 'הטרפה' (והריהו משווה לפסוק 12 שם: '...הטרפה לא ישלם').[19] באשר לה"א, טענתנו מפוקפקת, שהרי ליידיע יש מקום בפסוק 12 – הטריפה נזכרת קודם לכן בכתוב: 'אם טרף יטרף...', ואילו במקומנו אין הדבר כך, והיידוע אינו הולם. נציע אפוא הסבר אחר לחספוס שבכתוב: נוסחו המקורי של הפסוק היה לדעתי: 'ואנשי קדש תהיון לי ובשר בשדה לא תאכלו'. רעיון קדושתם של בני ישראל מוצא את מקבילותיו המובהקות ביותר בספר הקדושה (כגון וי' יט 2; כ 7–8). דומה שהכתוב הנדון – שאינו מן הקדומים בחוקי ספר הברית – אכן מיוסד על תפיסותיו של ספר הקדושה. אכילת בשר בשדה מתבארת על פי ספר הקדושה כזביחה 'על פני השדה', היינו ללא הבאת הבהמה השחוטה אל פתח אהל מועד: 'למען אשר יביאו בני ישראל את זבחיהם אשר הם זבחים על פני השדה והביאם לה' אל פתח אהל מועד אל הכהן וזבחו זבחי שלמים לה' אותם' (וי' יז 5).

שמ' כב 30 בנוסחו המקורי המשוחזר – וכמוהו ויקרא יז 6, המחייב את זריקת הדם על המזבח – נמצא סותר לחוק ריכוז הפולחן בדברים יב 15–16, המאפשר שחיטת חולין ושפיכת הדם על הארץ כמים. פרשן שביקש למנוע את הסתירה העניק אפוא פירוש שונה לחוק שבספר הברית. לפי פירושו, אכילה בשדה היא אכילת טריפה, ובהתאם לכך הוא מוסיף הן את מלת 'טרפה'[20] והן את הסיום 'לכלב' תשלכון אתו, ומשמיט את מלת 'בשדה'. ההשמטה אכן מתועדת בתרגומים, אלא שבסופו של דבר הושבה 'האבדה' אל נוסח המסורה, וכך נשתמרו בו שתי הגרסות החלופיות.[21]

5. 'ושש שנים תזרע את ארצך ואספת את תבואתה. והשביעית תשמטנה ונטשתה ואכלו אביני עמך ויתרם תאכל חית השדה כן תעשה לכרמך לזיתך' (שמ' כג 10–11). דומה כי ארבע המלים האחרונות, המרחיבות את תחולת החוק על הכרם והזית, הן תוספת,[22] ביטוי לפרשנות מרחיבה.[23] הכרם הוסף ברוחו ובהשפעתו של חוק השמיטה שבספר ויקרא: 'שש שנים תזרע שדך ושש שנים תזמר כרמך... ובשנה השביעית שנת שבתון יהיה לארץ... שדך לא תזרע וכרמך לא תזמר. את ספיח קצירך לא תקצור ואת ענבי נזירך לא תבצר...' (וי' כה 3–5). אשר למלת 'לזיתך', יושם אל לב כי היא אינה חבורה אל קודמתה, שלא כבכמה כתבי יד עבריים, בחומש השומרוני, בפשיטתא ובוולגטה הגורסים 'ולזיתך'. אפשר אפוא שנוסח המסורה משקף תוספת על גבי תוספת: תחילה הוסף הכרם בהשפעת ויקרא כה ולאחריו הזית לשם הרחבה והשלמה.

משילוב החוק בספר הברית, ללמד שבמקרה של גניבת אדם אין הבחנה דומה לזו הקיימת בגניבת בהמה בין המחזיק בבהמה (שדינו לקולה) לבין מוכרה (שדינו לחומרה): 'כי יגנב איש שור או שה וטבחו או מכרו חמשה בקר ישלם תחת השור וארבע צאן תחת השה... אם המצא תמצא בידו הגנבה משור עד חמור עד שה חיים שנים ישלם' (שמ' כא 37–כב 3).

19 ראה K. Budde, 'Bemerkungen zum Bundesbuch', ZAW 11 (1891), p. 113

20 תחת 'לכלב' גורס החומש השומרוני 'השלך', ותן דעתך לדמיון הגרפי בין שתי המלים. עם זאת, השינוי בשומרוני מכוון ומיוסד על פרשנות מרחיבה, המבקשת למנוע את הרושם המוטעה שחייבים להשליך את בשר הטריפה לכלב דווקא (על סוג זה של שינויים-פירושים בנוסח השומרוני ראה ר' ויס, 'על סוג אחד של עיבודים בחומש השומרוני', בתוך: מחקרי מקרא, בחינות נוסח ולשון, ירושלים תשמ"א, עמ' 199–205).

21 לתופעה דומה ראה מה שהעירונו על הכפילות 'והגישו... והגישו...' (שמ' כא 6), לעיל, עמ' 62.

22 ראה M. Fishbane, Biblical Interpretation in Ancient Israel, Oxford 1985, p. 179

23 להרחבות נוספות בנוסחת פתיחה זו ממש, ראה שמ' כב 29; דב' כ 15; כב 3.

ג

הדוגמאות שהובאו לעיל מעידות, כי היותו של ספר הברית לחלק מספרות התורה חייבה את
עיבודו והתאמתו לכתוב בקובצי החוקים האחרים, קבצים המיוסדים עליו ומפרשים אותו. ככל
תהליך פרשני–עריכתי במקרא, תהליך זה אינו שיטתי; נותרו אי התאמות רבות בין חוקי ספר
הברית לבין שאר קובצי החוקים. עם זאת, ניכר כי בספר הברית הונחו יסודות ראשונים של
מדרש ההלכה המפשר בין דינים שונים. מודעות לתופעת הבומראנג בתחום החוק עשויה אפוא
לשנות את תפיסתנו בדבר תולדותיהם של חוקים ומוסדות בישראל של תקופת המקרא.
חשיפת התופעה בסוגים ספרותיים נוספים, שונים ומגוונים, תעמיק את ידיעותינו אודות
תולדות ספרות המקרא ודרכי גיבושה.[24]

---

24   אני מקווה להקדיש בקרוב מחקר מקיף לתופעת הבומראנג בספרות המקרא לסוגיה.

קטעי מגילת לוח ממערה 4 בקומראן — משמרות B^b (4Q 321^a)

שמריהו טלמון וישראל קנוהל

אנו מפרסמים בזאת קטעי מגילת לוח מקומראן. במגילה מצוינים צמדי ימים מיוחדים בלוח השנה. הימים מתוארים על פי חלותם בחודשי שנת החמה וכן על פי היום בשבוע השירות של משמר כהונה פלוני או אלמוני. המניין לשבועות משמרות הכוהנים מעיד על חיוניות סדרי משמרות הכהונה בקרב עדת היחד. שמחים אנו להגיש מאמר זה לבעל היובל, פרופ' מנחם הרן, שבספריו ובמחקריו הפיח חיים במורשת הכהונה הישראלית.

א. תיאור הקטעים

התעודה מורכבת משבעה קטעים בגדלים שונים, שאפשר לשבצם בשמונה טורים משוחזרים של המגילה המקורית, כפי שיתבאר להלן:

קטע 1, השני בגודלו מבין הקטעים, רוחבו 5.8 ס"מ וגובהו 4.7 ס"מ. בצידו הימני של הקטע נשתמרו שרידים מן הקצה השמאלי של השורות 4–6, 8 בטור א. צבעו של חלק זה של הקטע כהה מאוד ומרביתו אינה קריאה. החלק השמאלי של הקטע בהיר יותר וקריא. נשתמר בו הצד הימני של שורות 1–8 בטור ב.

קטע 2 גובהו 4.6 ס"מ ורוחבו המקסימאלי 2.8 ס"מ. צבע הגוויל בחלקו העליון כהה ובחלקו התחתון חום בהיר. הקטע מכיל את הקצה הימני של שורות 2–8 בטור ד.

קטע 3 גובהו 1.2 ס"מ ורוחבו 1.0 ס"מ. צבע הגוויל חום כהה. על פי השערתנו, מקומם של שרידי המלים שנשתמרו בקטע זה הוא בפינה הימנית של שורות 4–5 בטור ד.

קטע 4 גובהו 2.0 ס"מ ורוחבו 1.5 ס"מ. צבע הגוויל חום בהיר. אנו משערים כי שרידי המלים שנשתמרו בקטע, נותרו מן החלק האמצעי של שורות 7–9 בטור ד.

קטע 5 רוחבו 2.2 ס"מ וגובהו 2.3 ס"מ. צבע הגוויל חום כהה. בצידו הימני ניכרות שתי נקודות זו מעל לזו, אשר שימשו ככל הנראה את הסופר כסימנים לרישום שורות. השוליים הימניים של טור מטורי המגילה תופסים את רוב הקטע. האותיות שנשתמרו הן מן הקצה הימני של שלוש שורות. אנו מציעים לשבץ את הקטע בטור ו שורות 6–8. אולם, בשל מיעוט האותיות שנשתמרו, אין הצעה זו יוצאת מגדר השערה.

קטע 6 גובהו 1.5 ס"מ ורוחבו 2.0 ס"מ. צבע הגוויל חום כהה. בצידו הימני ניכרים סימנים של חורי מחט. שרידי המלים שנשתמרו הם, על פי השערתנו, מן החלק האמצעי של שורות 8–10 בטור ו.

קטע 7 הוא הגדול בקטעים שנשתמרו: גובהו 5.9 ס"מ ורוחבו 7.2 ס"מ. צבע הגוויל חום נוטה לכהה. בצידו הימני ניכרים חורי מחט. בקטע נשתמר רוב החלק הימני של השורות 1–10 בטור ז.

ב. נוסח התעודה

שחזור התעודה מבוסס על העקרונות המונחים ביסוד לוח השנה של קומראן וסדרי משמרות הכוהנים במקדש. ידיעת עקרונות אלה מאפשרת לנו למלא חללים בטקסט שנותר, ואף לשחזר טורים חסרים. השחזור נתמך על ידי הנוסח של תעודה תאומה, שממנה השתמרו חלקים גדולים יותר.[1] הגהות והשלמות בטקסט המקורי שהן מידי הסופר צוינו בסוגריים זוויתיים < >. אותיות שבורות סומנו בנקודה עילית ושרידי אותיות סומנו בעיגול עילי. כדי להבליט את היקף הטקסט שנשתמר לעומת הטקסט המשוחזר, הדגשנו את המלים שנשתמרו. ואילו ההשלמות שהוצעו על ידינו נתונות בין סוגריים מרובעים [].

טור א

[1] ....
[2] [השנה הראשונה החודש הראשון בחמשה]..............[2]
[3] [בידעיה בשלושים בחודש ודוקו בששה במעוזיה בשבעה עשר **בוא**]
[4] [שבת בקוץ בשלושים בשני ודוקו באחד במלכיה בשבעה עשר]³ **בוא**
[5] [באחד באלישיב בתשעה ועשרים בשלישי ודוקו בשנ]**ים בישוע ב**[ששה]
[6] [עשר בוא   בשלושה בבלגא בשמונה] **ועשרים ברביעי**
[7] [ודוקו בארבעה בחופה בחמשה עשר בוא]⁴ [
[8] [בארבעה בפתחיה בשבעה ועשרים בחמישי ודוקו בחמשה בחזי]**ר**
[9] [בארבעה עשר בוא   בששה בדליה בשבעה ועשרים בששי]
[10] [ודוקו שבת בגמול בארבעה עשר בוא   ]
[11] [שבת בשעורים בחמשה ועשרים בשביעי ודוקו באחד בידעיה בשנים]
[12] [עשר בוא   בשנים באביה בחמישה ועשרים בשמיני ודוקו]
[13] [בשלושה במימין בשנים עשר בוא   בשלושה ביקים]

טור ב

[1] **בארב**[עה ועשרים בתשיעי ודוקו בארבעה בשכניה]
[2] **באחד עשר** [בוא   בחמשה באמר בשלושה ועשרים]
[3] **בעשירי ו**[דוקו בששה בישבאב בעשרה בוא   [
[4] **בששה ב**[יחזקאל בשנים ועשרים באחד עשר החודש ודוק]ו
[5] **שבת בפתחיה** [בתשעה בוא   באחד ביריב בשנים]
[6] **ועשרים בשנים עש**[ר החודש ודוקו בשנים בדליה בתשעה]

---

1   ראה, ש' טלמון וי' קנוהל, 'קטעים של מגילת לוח מקומראן – משמרות Bᵃ (4Q321)', תרביץ ס (תשנ"א), עמ' 505–521.

2   מספר השורות בטור זה, וכן בטורים האחרים, שוחזר על פי ההתאמה של שרידי המלים שהשתמרו בשורות 4–6 של טור א עם אותן שורות בטור ב. מכוח התאמה זו הותרנו בראש טור א המשוחזר פער של שורה ומחצית השורה, שהכילה, ככל הנראה, מעין כותרת של התעודה (בפער מעין זה הבחנו אף בתעודה התאומה, ראה טלמון-קנוהל, שם, עמ' 507, 513).

3   לפני המלה 'בוא' ניכרים שרידי אותיות נוספות. כמו כן אפשר להבחין בשרידי אותיות לפני המלה 'בישוע' שבסיום שורה 9. אולם שרידים אלה אינם ניתנים לקריאה, שכן במקום זה צבע הגוויל שחור לחלוטין.

4   הסופר שייר כאן רווח כדי להתחיל את רישום ימי הבא בשורה הבאה. בהתאם לכך הותרנו להלן מרווחים דומים בשורה 10 וכן בטורים הבאים.

[7] **בוא**[5]

[8] [**השני**]ת החודש הראשון בשנים במלכיה בעשרים בוא ודוקו]

[9] [בשלושה בחרים בשבעה בוא   בארבעה בישוע בעשרים]

[10] [בשני ודוקו בחמשה בקוץ בשבעה בוא   בחמשה]

[11] [בחופה בתשעה עשר בשלישי ודוקו בששה באלישיב בששה בוא]

[12] [שבת בפצץ בשמונה עשר ברביעי ודוקו באחד באמר בחמשה]

[13] [בוא   באחד בגמול בשבעה עשר בחמישי ודוקו בשנים]

טור ג

[1] [ביחזקאל בארבעה בוא   בשלושה בידעיה בשבעה עשר]

[2] [בששי ודוקו בארבעה במעוזיה בארבעה בוא   בארבעה]

[3] [במימין בחמשה עשר בשביעי ודוקו בחמשה בשעורים בשנים]

[4] [בוא   בששה בשכניה בחמשה עשר בשמיני ודוקו שבת]

[5] [בישוע בשנים בוא   שבת בבלגא בארבעה עשר בתשיעי]

[6] [ודוקו באחד בחופה באחד בתשיעי בשלושה בחזיר בשלושים]

[7] [ואחד בוא דוקו שנית[6] בשנים בפתחיה בשלושה עשר בעשירי]

[8] [וד]וקו בארבעה ביכין בתשעה ועשרים בוא   [

[9] [בשל]ושה בדליה בשנים עשר בעשתי עשר החודש ודוקו בששה]

[10] [ב]ויריב בתשעה ועשרים בוא   בחמשה בחרים בשנים עשר]

[11] [בשנים עשר החודש ודוקו שבת במימין בשמונה ועשרים בוא]

[12] [השלישית החודש הראשון בששה בקוץ בעשרה בראשון ודוקו]

[13] [בשנים בשכניה בשבעה ועשרים בוא   באחד ביקים]

טור ד

[1] [בעשרה בשני ודוקו בשלושה בישבאב בששה ועשרים בוא   [

[2] [בשנים באמר בתשעה בשלישי ודוקו בחמשה בפצץ בששה וע]**שרים**

[3] [בוא בארבעה ביחזקאל בשמונה ברביעי ודוקו בששה ב]**גמול**

[4] [ב]**ארבעה** ו[עשרים בוא   בחמשה במעוזיה בשבעה] **בחמישי**

[5] **וד**וק[ו]**ה**[7] **באח**[ד בחרים בארבעה ועשרים בוא   [**ש**]**בת במלכיה בשבע**[ה]

[6] [בששי   ודוקו בשנים בקוץ בשלושה ועשרים בו]**א**

[7] [באחד בישוע   בחמש]ה **בש**[ביעי ודוקו בארבעה באלישי]**ב בשנים ועש**[ר]**ים**]

[8] [בוא   בשלושה בחופה] **בחמש**[ה בשמיני ודוקו בחמשה ב]**בלגא**

[9] [באחד ועשרים בוא בארב]**עה בחזי**[ר בארבעה בתשיעי ודוקו]

[10] [שבת ביחזקאל באחד ועשרים בוא   בששה ביכין בשלושה בעשירי]

[11] [ודוקו באחד במעוזיה בתשעה עשר בוא   שבת בידעיה בשנים]

[12] [בעשתי עשר החודש ודוקו בשלושה בשעורים בתשעה עשר בוא   [

[13] [בשנים במימין בשנים בשנים עשר החודש ודוקו בארבעה באביה בשמונה]

---

5   כאן שייר הסופר רווח של שורה כמעט שלמה, כדי להתחיל את רישום הימים בשנה השנית בשורה
     חדשה. בהתאם לכך שחזרנו אף להלן את רישום תחילות השנים הבאות בשורה חדשה (ראה: טור ג
     שורה 12, טור ה שורה 2, טור ו שורה 6, טור ז שורה 9).

6   לעניין פירוש המונח 'דוקו שנית', ראה טלמון–קנוהל (לעיל, הערה 1), עמ' 515 ולהלן, הערה 9.

7   כאן ניכר מעין קיפול בגוויל.

טור ה

[1]　[עשר בוא　　　　　　　　　　　　[

[2]　[הרביעית החודש הראשון בארבעה בשכניה באחד בראשון בחמשה]

[3]　[בישבאב בשלושים בוא השנית8　　　　　　ודוקו בששה ביקים בשבעה]

[4]　[עשר בוא　　　　　　שבת בפתחיה בשלושים בשני ודוקו באחד בחזיר]

[5]　[בשבעה עשר בוא　　　　באחד בדליה בתשעה ועשרים בשלישי ודוקו]

[6]　[בשנים ביכין בששה עשר בוא　　　בשלושה בחרים בשמונה ועשרים]

[7]　[רביעי ודוקו בארבעה ביורייב בחמשה עשר בוא　　　בארבעה]

[8]　[בקוץ בשבעה ועשרים בחמישי ודוקו בחמשה במלכיה בארבעה עשר בוא]

[9]　[בששה באלישיב בשבעה ועשרים בששי ודוקו שבת בשכניה בארבעה]

[10]　[עשר בוא　　　　　שבת באמר בחמשה ועשרים בשביעי ודוקו באחד]

[11]　[בישבאב בשנים עשר בוא　　　בשנים ביחזקאל בחמשה ועשרים]

[12]　[בשמיני ודוקו בשלושה בפצץ בשנים עשר בוא　　　בשלושה]

[13]　[במעוזיה בארבעה ועשרים בתשיעי ודוקו בארבעה בגמול באחד]

טור ו

[1]　[עשר בוא　　　　בחמשה בשעורים בשלושה ועשרים בעשירי]

[2]　[ודוקו בששה בידעיה בעשרה בוא　　　בששה באביה בשנים]

[3]　[ועשרים בעשתי עשר החודש ודוקו שבת בקוץ בתשעה בוא　　[

[4]　[באחד בחופה בשנים ועשרים בשנים עשר החודש ודוקו בשנים　[

[5]　[באלישיב בתשעה בוא　　　　　　　[

[6]　ה[חמישית בשנים בחזיר בעשרים בראשון ודוקו בשלושה בבלגא]

[7]　בשב[עה בוא　　　　　　　　בארבעה ביכין]

[8]　ב[עשרים בש[כ]ני ודוקו ב[חמשה בפתחיה בשבעה בוא　　[

[9]　[בחמשה ביורי]רב [בתשעה עשר בשלישי ודוקו בששה בדליה בששה]

[10]　[בוא　　　[ש]בת במימין בשמונה עשר בארבעי ודוקו באחד]

[11]　[בשעורים בחמשה בוא　　　באחד בשכניה בשבעה עשר]

[12]　[בחמישי ודוקו בשנים באביה בארבעה בוא　　　　[

[13]　[בשלושה בישבאב בשבעה עשר בששי ודוקו בארבעה ביקים בארבעה]

טור ז

[1]　[בוא　　　　　בארבעה בפ[צץ ב]חמשה עשר בשביעי ודוקו]

[2]　[בחמשה באמר בש[נ]ים בוא　　[בש]שה בגמול בחמשה עשר בשמיני ודוקו]

[3]　[שבת ביכי]ן בשנים בוא שבת ב[חרי]ם בארבעה ע[שר בתשיעי ודוקו באחד]

[4]　[ביורי]ב באחד בוא　　　בשלושה במלכיה בש[לושים ואחד בו דוקו שנית]9

[5]　בשנים בקוץ בשלושה עשר בעשירי ודוקוה10　[בארבעה בישוע בתשעה]

[6]　[ועשרים בוא　　　בשלושה באלישיב ב[שנים עשר באחד עשר החודש ודוקו]

8　לעניין הציון 'השנית', ראה טלמון–קנוהל (לעיל, הערה 1), הערה 23.

9　הסופר ציין כאן שני ימי דוקו החלים בחודש אחד, ראה להלן עמ' 71; וכן טלמון–קנוהל (לעיל, הערה 1), עמ' 515 והערה 8 בעמ' 508.

10　הקצה השמאלי של האות שבור, אך אין כל ספק בקריאתה כ־הֵא.

[7] **בששה בחופהא בתשעה ‹ועשרים› עשר[11] בוא**   [בחמשה בבלגא בשנים עשר]

[8] **בשנים עשר החודש ודוקו שבת** [בפצץ בשמונה ועשרים בוא   [

[9] **הש[ש]י[ת](?) [בש]שה בפתחיה בעשרים[12]** [בראשון ודוקו בשנים בגמול בשבעה]

[10] [ועשרים בוא   [בֿאֿחֿד בֿ](?)מעוזיה בעשרה בשני ודוקו שלושה בידעיה]

[11] [בששה ועשרים בוא   בשנים בשעורים בתשעה בשלישי ודוקו בחמשה]

[12] [במימין בששה ועשרים בוא   בארבעה באביה בשמונה ברביעי ודוקו]

[13] [בששה בשכניה בארבעה ועשרים בוא בחמשה ביקים בשבעה בחמישי]

טור ח

[1] [ודוקו באחד בבלגא בארבעה ועשרים בוא   שבת בחזיר בשבעה]

[2] [בששי ודוקו בשנים בפתחיה בשלושה ועשרים בוא   באחד ביכין]

[3] [בחמשה בשביעי ודוקו בארבעה בדליה בשנים ועשרים בוא   [

[4] [בשלושה ביוריב בחמשה בשמיני ודוקו בחמשה בחרים באחד ועשרים]

[5] [בוא   בארבעה במלכיה בארבעה בתשיעי ודוקו שבת באביה באחד]

[6] [ועשרים בוא   בששה בישוע בשלושה בעשירי ודוקו באחד ביקים]

[7] [בתשעה עשר בוא   שבת בישבאב בשנים באחד עשר החודש ודוקו]

[8] [בשלושה באמר בתשעה עשר בוא בשנים בפצץ בשנים בשנים]

[9] [עשר החודש ודוקו בארבעה ביחזקאל בשמונה עשר בוא   [

ג. הכתיב

התעודה כתובה בכתיב המלא האופייני לכתבי קומראן 'בוא'=בו (טור א שורה 4, טור ב שורה 7, טור ז שורות 2,3,4,6,7).[13] כתיב זה נוהג אף בשמות המשמרות כגון 'חופהא' (טור ז שורה 7).[14] כמו בתעודת התאומה, 4Q321, בא כאן הכתיב 'בלגא' (טור ד שורה 8)[15] תחת 'בלגה' שבמקרא. לעומת זאת גורסת התעודה שלנו 'מלכיה' (טור ד שורה 5, טור ז שורה 4) ככתיב שבנוסח המסורה. בכך היא נבדלת מן התעודה התאומה (4Q321), שבה נוהג הכתיב 'מלאכיה'.[16]

לציון מיוחד ראוי הכתיב של המונח הייחודי 'דוקו'. בתעודה התאומה הוא בא אך ורק בצורה 'דוקה'. על פי קריאתנו ושחזורנו משמש המונח בתעודתנו בשלושה אופנים שונים: בטור ז

---

11   הסופר טעה וכתב תחילה 'בתשעה עשר'. משעמד על טעותו סימן נקודות מעל למלה 'עשר' לציון
         מחיקתה, ותלה את המלה 'ועשרים' מעל השורה. לעניין השימוש בנקודות מעל למלה כסימן מחיקה,
         ראה: אבות דרבי נתן, נוסח א, פרק לד (מהדורת שכטר, נא, א); נוסח ב, פרק לז (שם, מט, ב); וכן
         ש' ליברמן, יוונית ויוונות בארץ ישראל, ירושלים תשכ"ג, עמ' 182, הערה 51; R. Butin, The Ten
         Nequdot of the Torah or the Meaning and the Purpose of the Extraordinary Points
         of the Pentateuch Text, Re-issued New York, 1969 ('Prolegomenon' by S.
         Talmon)

12   גם כאן טעה הסופר במה שכתב 'בעשרים' תחת 'בעשרה', אלא שלא השגיח בטעותו, ולפיכך לא
         תיקנה.

13   לעניין הכתיב המלא 'בוא', ראה י" קוטשר, הלשון והרקע הלשוני של מגילת ישעיהו, ירושלים תשי"ט,
         עמ' 129–131; E. Qimron, The Hebrew of The Dead Sea Scrolls, (HSS 29), Atlanta,
         Georgia 1986, pp. 20-21

14   לעניין השימוש ב־הֶא כאם קריאה לסימון התנועה â בסוף תיבה, ראה קוטשר, שם, עמ' 139.

15   כתיב זה בא גם בספרות חז"ל; ראה: טלמון–קנוהל (לעיל, הערה 1), הערה 19.

16   כאמור מיוחד כתיב זה לאותה תעודה (טלמון–קנוהל, שם, הערה 18).

שורה 8 השתמר בשלמותו הכתיב 'דוקו'.[17] שלוש שורות קודם לכן נוכל לשחזר בוודאות את הכתיב 'דוקה',[18] ואילו בטור ד שורה 5 נראה ששימש הכתיב 'דוקה'.[19] מגוון הצורות מחזק את הסברה כי לפנינו מונח בלשון זכר,[20] שכן הכתיב 'דוקו' הוא, ככל הנראה, דוגמה של סימון התנועה ô באמצעות 'ה'.[21] סעד להשערה זו בא מן הצורה 'דוקוה' שהיא כנראה כתיב מלא של 'דוקה'.[22]

ד. מבנה המגילה ומשמעותה

המגילה מחזיקה רשימה של תאריכים המסודרים במחזור של שש שנים על פי חודשי לוח החמה. ציינו בעקיבות שני מועדים בכל חודש: מועד אחד סומן באמצעות נקיבת חלותו – ביום פלוני בשבוע של משמר פלוני, החל ביום כך וכך לחודש החמה. המועד האחר צוין באותו אופן, אך בנוסף לכך כונה בכינויו 'דוקו', דוקה או 'דוקוה'.[23] לשם הדגמה נחזור ונציג כאן שתי שורות שנשתמרו חלקית בטור ז:

{5}   ...בשנים בקוץ בשלושה עשר בעשירי ודוקוה [בארבעה בישוע בתשעה]

{6}   ..ועשרים בוא   בשלושה באלישיב ב[שנים עשר באחד עשר החודש ודוקו]

ציון כאן צמד מועדים בחודש העשירי (של השנה החמישית). אזכור הצמד מתחיל בתחילת שורה 5 ומסתיים באמצע שורה 6. המועד הראשון בצמד חל אפוא ביום שני בשבוע שבו משרת משמר הקוץ, שהוא היום השלושה עשר בחודש העשירי מחודשי החמה. המועד השני בצמד, שכינויו 'דוקוה', חל ביום רביעי בשבוע שירותו של משמר ישוע, שהוא היום העשרים ותשעה בחודש העשירי.

כאמור, מציין המחבר בכל חודש תחילה את המועד שאין לו כינוי מיוחד (לצרכינו נכננו מעתה X), ולאחר מכן את המועד שכונה 'דוקו', 'דוקה' או 'דוקוה'. בחלק הראשון של הרשימה, X יחול בסוף חודש החמה, ו'דוקו' יחול באמצע החודש, שלושה עשר יום לפניו. בהמשך, X הולך ונסוג לאמצע החודש, ויחד עמו נסוג המועד של 'דוקו' לראשית החודש. אחר ציון ה'דוקו' החל בראשית החודש התשיעי של השנה השנייה (טור ג שורות 7-6) מתהפך הסדר הכרונולוגי של שני המועדים: מעתה 'דוקו' חל ששה עשר יום, ולעתים שבעה עשר יום, אחר X. בחלק האחרון של הרשימה (טור ז שורה 4 ואילך) הסדר חוזר ומתהפך (טור ה שורה 3, טור ז שורה 4), אולם מרווח הזמן שבין שני המועדים נשמר תדיר: יום X יחול שלושה עשר יום אחר 'דוקו', או יקדם לו בששה עשר, או בשבעה עשר יום.[24]

לדעתנו, יש לבאר את המונח 'דוקו', 'דוקה' או 'דוקוה' כמציין את הירח בלילה שבו הוא מתחיל

---

17   כתיב זה בא ככל הנראה גם בטור ו שו' 8, אך הקריאה שם מסופקת.

18   ראה לעיל, הערה 10.

19   ראה לעיל, הערה 7.

20   בעניין משמע המונח, ראה להלן.

21   ראה טלמון-קנוהל (לעיל, הערה 1) עמ' 520.

22   על 'וה' כאימות קריאה לתנועה ô בסוף תיבה, ראה קוטשר (לעיל, הערה 13) עמ' 137–139; קימרון (לעיל, הערה 13), עמ' 21, 137.

23   בשחזור הטקסט נקטנו תמיד בצורה 'דוקו', אולם יש להניח שהכתיבים השונים באו בכל חלקי התעודה.

24   נראה שמניין זה מבוסס על השיטה שלפיה מחצית חודשי הירח הם בני עשרים ותשעה יום ומחציתם בני שלושים יום (השווה חנוך, עח, טו–טז).

להתמעט, ואילו X מציין את מועד הכיסוי המלא של הירח בלילה שבסוף חודש הלבנה.[25] מן
המועד שבו מתחילה הלבנה להתמעט ועד ליל כיסויה המלא חולפים שלושה עשר יום; ומליל
הכיסוי עד לראשית התמעטות הלבנה בחודש שלאחר מכן – ששה עשר או שבעה עשר יום.
לאור זאת נפרש את צמדי הימים המנויים במגילה באופן הבא: 'בשנים בקוץ בשלושה עשר
בעשירי ודוקה [בארבעה בישוע בתשעה] ועשרים בוא' (טור ז שורות 5–6), פירושו: הירח
מתכסה בלילה שלפני היום השני בשבוע שבו משרת משמר הקוץ, שהוא היום השלושה עשר
בחודש העשירי מחודשי החמה; ו'דוקוה', היינו ההתמעטות של הירח החדש, מתחילה בלילה
שלפני היום הרביעי בשבוע שירותו של משמר ישוע, שהוא העשרים ותשעה באותו חודש חמה.
על פי שחזורנו צוינו בטור ז שורות 3–4 שני ימי 'דוקו' בחודש אחד:[26]

{3} [שבת ביכי]ן בשנים בוא שבת ב[חרי]ם בארבעה ע[שר בתשיעי ודוקו באחד]

{4} [בייירי]ב באחד בוא   בשלושה במלכיה בש[לושים ואחד בו דוקו שנית]

בלוח החמה בן 364 יום, החודש התשיעי הוא בן שלושים ואחד יום. כאשר חל 'דוקו' באחד
בחודש זה, X יחול שלושה עשר יום לאחריו, כלומר בארבעה עשר בתשיעי. ה'דוקו' הבא יחול
שבעה עשר יום לאחר X, בשלושים ואחד בתשיעי. כך מתבאר הציון 'דוקו שנית'.[27]
כזכור, ביקשנו לראות בהבלטת מניין המועדים שבהם מתכסה הלבנה ומתמעטת ביטוי
לפולמוס שבין אנשי עדת היחד, הדבקים בלוח השמש וקובעים על פיו את זמני המועדים וימי
הקודש, ובין יריביהם, הקובעים את מועדיהם על פי לוח הלבנה.[28] בהקשר זה ראוי לציין כי
בניגוד למגילה התאומה (4Q321), בה מצויה אחר רשימת זמני ה'דוקה' גם רשימת מועדי
קדש,[29] הרי בתעודה שלפנינו לא נותר שריד מרשימה מעין זו. בשל מיעוט הקטעים שנשתמרו,
קשה להכריע אם במקורה הכילה אף תעודה זו רשימת מועדים שאבדה ללא זכר, או שמא
מעיקרה לא כללה אלא את רשימת הצמדים של זמני 'דוקו' ו־X.*

25 ראה טלמון–קנוהל (לעיל, הערה 1), עמ' 518–519, ובמיוחד האסמכתא שהבאנו שם להשערה זו מן
התעודה Miš A 4Q320.

26 כיוצא בזה שחזרנו שני ימי 'דוקו' בטור ג שורה 7 (ראה לעיל, הערה 6) ואילו בטור ה שורות 2–3
שוחזרו שני ימי X (ראה לעיל, הערה 8).

27 בתעודה התאומה (טור 2 שורות 5–6) קודם הציון 'ודוקה שנית' לציון היום בחודש, ואילו כאן הוא
בא אחריו; ראה טלמון–קנוהל, שם, עמ' 508.

28 ראה טלמון–קנוהל, שם, עמ' 520–521.

29 צימוד דומה יש בתעודה הנזכרת (לעיל, הערה 25), המחזיקה רשימת ימי X ובצדה רשימת מועדים.

* ברצוננו להודות לגב' דליה עמארה על הסיוע שהגישה לפרופ' טלמון בשלב הראשון של הכנת
התעודה לפרסום.

למבנה ספר מלכים — סינכרוניזם נוסחתי וסינכרוניזם סיפורי (מל"א יב–מל"ב יז)

צפורה טלשיר

א

החטיבה מל"א יב–מל"ב יז מוקדשת לתולדות מלכויות ישראל ויהודה למן הפילוג ועד חורבן ממלכת הצפון. החומר מסודר מנקודת מוצא היסטורית: מלכות רודפת מלכות בסדר כרונולוגי, על פי עקרון קבוע של שילוב סינכרוניסטי בין מלכויות ישראל ויהודה. עקרון השילוב הוכר מימים ימימה;[1] הוא מתבסס על שני יסודות: ראשית, כדי שהסיפור לא ינדוד מממלכה לממלכה בפרקי זמן משתנים, על פי צורכי כל עניין ועניין, קבע המחבר שפרק הזמן המינימאלי המתואר מתחילה ועד סוף הוא פרק מלכותו של מלך אחד. שנית, היות שאין הנסיבות ההיסטוריות מאפשרות סידור לסירוגין, קבע לו המחבר כלל: הוא מתאר את מלכותו של מלך פלוני מישראל מראש ועד סוף. אם החלה בימי המלך הזה מלכותו של מלך מיהודה, הוא יעבור אליו. בעקבותיו יבואו בזה אחר זה הדיווחים על המלכים מיהודה שמלכותם החלה בימי אותו מלך מישראל. עם תום אלה יחזור הסיפור למלכות ישראל ולמלך ישראל הבא. עתה יתוארו מלכי ישראל שראשית מלכותם בימי מלך יהודה האחרון שתואר, וכן הלאה.[2] התוצאה החד-משמעית של הסידור העניייני הזה היא שיחידה ספרותית בספר מלכים היא מלכותו של מלך אחד. היחידות הספרותיות מוגדרות היטב במערכת הנוסחתית המעטרת את מלכויות המלכים; נוסחת פתיחה בראש, המציגה קודם לכול את הקשר הסינכרוניסטי שבין מלכויות ישראל ויהודה, ונוסחת סיום, הסוגרת על כל מלכות ומלכות. מתמיה שהכרה זו לא הטביעה את רישומה על המחקר בן ימינו. המבנה שבחר בעל ספר מלכים לתת לספרו נזנח לטובת תפיסה אחרת, צורנית או ספרותית, עניינית או רעיונית — כל חוקר ומפרש ותפישתו שלו.

S.R. Driver, *An Introduction to the Literature of the Old Testament* [9], Edinburgh 1913, p. 189: 'In the arrangement of the two series of kings a definite principle is followed by the compiler. When the narrative of a reign... has once been begun, it is continued to its close... When it is ended, the reign or reigns of the other series, which have synchronized with it, are dealt with; the reign overlapping it at the end having been completed, the compiler resumes his narrative of the first series with the reign next following, and so on'   [1]

הברכה שבסידור הסכימאטי הזה עולה יפה כאשר עוקבים אחר ניסיונותיו הבלתי נלאים של יוסף בן מתתיהו להשיג סינכרוניות עניינית מלאה יותר בין המלכויות האחיות; כך, למשל, קדמוניות היהודים ח, 298: 'כך היו פני העניינים, בהם היה נתון אסא מלך שני השבטים. אחזור (עתה) אל עם ישראל ואל בעשא מלכם, שהרג את נדב בן ירבעם ותפש את השלטון'; וכך גם שם, 393: 'כל זה אירע לאחאב. (ועכשיו) הריני חוזר אל יהושפט מלך ירושלים...'.   [2]

הרקע לצמיחת המבנים השונים שהעמידו החוקרים לספר מלכים מצטייר בשלושה קווים:
ראשון, הואיל ומושכל ראשון בפרשנות הוא קביעת היחידה הספרותית, וזו לעתים קרובות אין
גבולותיה ברורים, לפיכך זכות מוקנית היא לחוקר המקרא לחפש אחר ראיות שבצורה ובתוכן
כדי לקבוע את היקף היחידות ואף להכתירן בשם, שיביע את עיקר עניינן. שני, חקר הסוגים
מדגיש את החומרים הספרותיים העומדים ביסוד ספר מלכים ומחפש אחר היחידות שהגיעו
לידי המחבר ממקרורותיו לסוגיהם. ממילא מתקפח חלקה של היצירה שנבנתה מחומרי היסוד
הללו. שלישי, הביקורת הספרותית-היסטורית הגדירה את בעל ספר מלכים עורך או מסדר, לא
מחבר, ולפיכך המאמץ היצירתי שהשקיע בספר לא נחשב בעיני החוקרים, והתכנית הברורה
שהתווה לו היתה להם כקליפה עריכתית חיצונית.[3]

נדגים את הדבר בכמה פירושים על ספר מלכים, כולם משנות השמונים, אם כי שיטותיהם
אינן שונות באופן מהותי מן הפירושים הישנים יותר.

דוגמה בולטת, אם כי לא אופיינית, לשרירותיות שבקביעת היחידות ובהכתרתן בשם המגדיר
את תוכנן, היא השיטה הנקוטה בידי הובס.[4] הוא מעמיד את החלוקה הרשמית לפרקים כבסיס
לסידור פירושו, ונותן לכל פרק כותרת האמורה לבטא את תוכנו, משל החלוקה לפרקים אינה
רק טכנית, אלא גם משמעותית למהלך הספר.[5] תמיהה היא כיצד מכלכל הפרשן את החלק
המוקדש בפירושו ל-Setting/Structure/Form כאשר זהו מבנה היסוד.

נהוג מקובל הוא לתחום בספר מלכים יחידות מקיפות, כדרך שעושה קיל.[6] למשל: 'דברי ארבעה
בתי המלכות בישראל שהתחלפו בימי אסא'. התחלפות המלכים בממלכת ישראל בימי אסא היא
עובדה כרונולוגית, ואין לה נגיעה למבנה הספר. מחבר הספר לא כיוון לתחום בו יחידות כאלה.
המצע המחקרי ביסוד דרכי החלוקה שלהלן שונה, אך התוצאה אינה כל כך שונה בטיבה: נות,
לשיטתו, אמור היה להתחשב ביתר שאת בתכניתו של המחבר הדויטרונומיסטי, יהיו מקורותיו
אשר יהיו, ואף על פי כן גם הוא מתעלם מן הסידור הסכימאטי שהניח את מחבר ספר מלכים,
וממיר אותו בחלוקה ענייניית.[7] כך, דרך משל, נותן נות למל"א יד 1–18, סיפור ילדו החולה של
ירבעם, כותרת מתאימה, פחות או יותר: 'ירבעם והנביא אחיה'. אך כתוצאה מכך נותרים
הפסוקים הסמוכים, המחזיקים את דברי הסיכום של מלכות ירבעם (פסוקים 19–20), תלושים,
ונות נאלץ לצרפם אל היחידה הבאה שהוא תוחם: 'מלכי יהודה וישראל עד אסא–אחאב (מל"א
יד 19–טז 34)'. סופה של יחידה זו תמוה לא פחות מראשיתה: הרי מלכות אחאב מתחילה ב-טז
29; זוהי נוסחת הפתיחה של מלכותו! אלא, כדי ש-יז 1 ואילך יוכל להתייחד לאליהו, נשארים

---

3 מדברים על העורך (the redactor), או על המסדר (the compiler) שהעמיד חומרים קיימים
   במסגרת הנוסחתית הקבועה. אמנם אחרי נות (M. Noth, *Überlieferungsgeschichtliche*
   Studien, Halle 1949) וההשפעה הגדולה שהיתה לתיזה שלו בדבר מחבר אחד האחראי ליצירה
   הדויטרונומיסטית המקיפה (דברים עד מלכים), ניכרת נטייה גדולה יותר לדבר על מחבר או מחברים
   (deuteronomistic author or authors), אך עדיין מכנים את חיבורו של אותו מחבר the
   deuteronomistic compilation וכיוצא בזה, כלומר פרי עבודתם של מי שקיבץ חומרים קיימים
   תחת קורת גג אחת. אף א' רופא, סיפורי הנביאים, ירושלים תשמ"ג, עמ' 85–91, נוקט מינוח כגון:
   'עריכת ספר מלכים', 'העורך הראשון של ספר מלכים', אף על פי שענייניית הוא מתאר את חיבור ספר
   מלכים ואת דרך עבודתם של מחבריו.
4 T.R. Hobbs, *2 Kings* (WBC), Waco 1985
5 לדוגמה, מל"ב יג, המספר על מלכות יהואחז מלך ישראל (פסוקים 1–9) ומלכות יואש (לא עד תומה,
   פסוקים 10–25), מוגדר בכותרת הבלתי משמעותית: 'דיכוי ארמי ומות אלישע', ופרק יד, המציג שני
   עניינים שאינם קשורים זה לזה, מלכות אמציה ומלחמתו ביואש (פסוקים 1–22) ומלכות ירבעם
   (פסוקים 23–29), זוכה לכותרת אחת המקשרת ביניהם: 'אמציה וירבעם השני'.
6 י' קיל, ספר מלכים (דעת מקרא), ירושלים תשמ"ט.
7 M. Noth, *Könige*² (BKAT), Neukirchen-Vluyn 1983

פסוקי הפתיחה של מלכות אחאב (טז 34-29) בלא בית, ונדחקים, כמו פסוקי הסיום של
ירבעם, ליחידה בלתי אפשרית, הפותחת בסיום (של מלכות ירבעם) ונסגרת בפתיחה (של
מלכות אחאב).

דומה שיטתו של וירתוויין.[8] אמנם אין הוא מספח את פתיחת מלכות אחאב (מל"א טז 34-29)
ליחידה הקודמת, אך משאיר אותה בבדידות מזהרת, תחת הכותרת: 'אחאב מישראל – נוסחת
פתיחה'. וכל כך למה? שוב, למען היחידה הבאה: מל"א יז 1-מל"ב א 18, שכותרתה: 'אליהו'. לא
ברור מה למלחמות אחאב (מל"א כ; כב 38-1) בארמים או למלכות יהושפט (כב 51-41)
ולכותרת זו.

אותם הקווים מנחים את ג'ונס.[9] הוא מתעלם לגמרי ממחבר ספר מלכים ובונה לו מבנה עצמאי
משלו. כך הדבר כאשר הוא תוחם את מל"א יב 33-יד 18 כיחידה אחת, תחת הכותרת 'ירבעם
והנביאים'. הרווח, המתבטא בריכוז החומר הנבואי בכפיפה אחת, יוצא בהפסד גדול, באשר
נצטרפו לו יחד שתי יחידות שאין להן דבר זו עם זו – מעשה איש האלהים מיהודה (מל"א יג)
וסיפור ילדו החולה של ירבעם (יד 18-1). עקב כך נותרת נוסחת הסיום של מלכות ירבעם
(פסוק 20-19) כסרח עודף, והוא מצרפה ליחידה הבאה; זו מקיפה את יד 31-19, וכינויה: 'סיום
מלכויות ירבעם ורחבעם'. אין זו יחידה כלל ועיקר; אלא, פסוקים 20-19 הם סיום מלכות
ירבעם ושייכים ליחידה הקודמת, ואילו פסוקים 31-21 הם יחידה לעצמה המתארת את מלכות
רחבעם בין נוסחאות פתיחה וסיום.

בפירוש של כוגן ותדמור יש נטייה לפתור את רגבוניות החומר על ידי חלוקה ליחידות
קטנות.[10] הדבר לא מנע מסיפורי הנביאים להטיל מהומה גם בסידור הפירוש הזה. מל"ב ב 19-
ח 15 זוכה לכותרת המכלילה: 'מחזור אלישע', ואילו ח 17-16 מתכנה: 'חזרה לממלכה
המפולגת'. האם ב'מחזור אלישע' לא היינו בממלכה המפולגת? הרי ב 1 מציין את עליית יהורם
לכס המלכות בישראל. וכי אין מלכות יהורם מסתיימת רק אחרי מחזור אלישע? היחידות
הקטנות, מעין 'מלכות המלך פלוני', גם הן אינן מבטאות את המבנה של ספר מלכים, אלא
כאשר המבנה הוא סכימאטי. אך קביעת יחידה מעין ח 29-25 מותירה את מלכות אחזיה ללא
סופה, ואילו יד 22-1 אינה מוקדשת למלכות אמציה בלבד, שהרי היא כוללת גם את נוסחת
הסיום של יואש מלך ישראל (פסוקים 16-15).

לונג[11] אמנם תיאר את ספר מלכים במבנה הכרונולוגי-סינכרוניסטי שטבע לו מחברו, אך גם
דרכו אינה נעדרת קשיים: מן הצד האחד, אף הוא מקבץ תחת גג אחד שורת מלכויות, כגון:
'מלכות הצפון מסוף ירבעם ועד עליית עמרי', כותרת לא מוצלחת ליחידה טו 1-טז 28, באשר
לא ברור מה מקום למלכות אסא (טו 24-9) במסגרת הזאת; או: 'תהפוכות בממלכת הצפון',
כותרת מתאימה למלכויות אֵלָה, זמרי, עמרי (טז 28-8), ועם זאת, אין יחידה כזאת בספר
מלכים, שמחברו בנה אותו מלכות מלכות. מן הצד האחר, נתפס לונג לסכימטיזאציה יתרה,
וערך טבלה בשני טורים, המציגים זה מול זה את מלכויות ישראל ויהודה על פי העקרון
הסינכרוני. האפשרות הזאת עומדת כל עוד מחבר ספר מלכים שומר על הסידור הטכני המנחה
אותו. אך מתברר שאין הוא רק עורך המסדר את החומרים שבידו בתוך מסגרת סכימאטית
קבועה. הוא בונה את ספרו כיוצר עצמאי, והמערכת הסינכרונית נמצאת חיה תחת ידיו ומשנה
פנים לפי צורך הסיפור.

8   E. Würthwein, *Die Bücher der Könige* (ATD 11,1/2), Göttingen 1977, 1984
9   G.H. Jones, *1 & 2 Kings* (NCB), I, London 1984, pp. 83f.
10   M. Cogan & H. Tadmor, *II Kings* (AB), New York 1988
11   B.O. Long, *I Kings* (FOTL IX), Grand Rapids 1984, pp. 13f., 23

ב

מחבר ספר מלכים בוודאי צד של עורך או של מסדר יש בו, באשר הוא יוצר על יסוד
חומרים נתונים. אך אין לשכוח, דווקא מפני עושר מקורותיו וגוניהם, שמוטלת עליו משימה
כבדה – ליצור מכל אלה יצירה חדשה. ככזה הוא בלא ספק מחבר, שלקח על עצמו אחריות
כוללת של עיצוב יצירה חדשה. אין אנו רשאים לכנות את בעל ספר מלכים 'עורך', אלא אם כן
אנו מגדירים מחדש את המונח 'עריכה', על דרך המונחים המקבילים redaction/Redaktion,
כפי שהם משמשים בחקר ספרויות עתיקות כגון המקרא או הברית החדשה:[12] אם 'עריכה'
אינה רק סידור מקורות קיימים זה בצד זה אלא עיצוב מחדש של מקורות אלה; אם 'עריכה'
היא עיבוד מודע של חומרים עתיקים יותר כדי שיתאימו לצרכים ספרותיים ואידיאולוגיים
חדשים; אם 'עריכה' היא יצירת חיבור חדש בעל חיים משלו; אם כך מגדירים 'עריכה', הרי
בעל ספר מלכים הוא עורך; אך אם זאת ההגדרה, אין לי כל סיבה שלא לקרוא לו בכינוי הראוי לו:
מחבר ספר מלכים.[13]
ביסוד ספר מלכים בוודאי עומדים מקורות מגוונים, אך כל אלה נוצקו לתוך מסגרת מתוכננת
היטב. ואין הדברים סותרים, אולי אפילו אינם עומדים על מישור אחד: אין סיבה לחתור תחת
מבנהו של ספר מלכים, כפי שמחבר הספר תכנן אותו, כדי לחשוף את המקורות שהוא בנוי
עליהם.
שלד החטיבה מל"א יב–מל"ב יז בנוי על נוסחאות הפתיחה והסיום. מן הצד האחד, ייתכן
שהנתונים המרכיבים את הנוסחאות, ואף חלק מן הדגמים שהנתונים הללו קבועים בהם,
מקורם בחיבור קדום יותר, אנאליסטי או היסטורי–ספרותי.[14] אולי ראיה לדבר באותם מקרים,
בודדים אמנם, שנוסחה מופיעה במקום לא לה.[15] מן הצד האחר, המערכת הנוסחתית בצורתה
הנוכחית היא דויטרונומיסטית – הלוא חטא הבמות יסוד מוסד בה. שתי ההערכות האלה אינן
מוציאות מידי מחבר ספר מלכים: (1) גם אם הוא לקח חלק מן החומר הנוסחתי ממקורות
קודמים, עדיין המערכת הנוסחתית היא היסוד המארגן שבאמצעותו הוא בונה את חיבורו.
(2) הציביון הדויטרונומיסטי אינו מעלה ואינו מוריד: מחבר ספר מלכים הוא מן האסכולה
הדויטרונומיסטית. אין דין הנוסחאות כדין תוספות חיצוניות של עורך על חומר נתון, אלא
אמצעי הן ביד מחבר הספר – הלוא הוא המחבר הדויטרונומיסטי, שהעמיד, בין היתר, את
החיבור הסינכרוניסטי המקיף על תולדות ישראל ויהודה.

12   J.A. Wharton, 'Redaction Criticism, OT'; R.T. Fortna, 'Redaction Criticism, NT',
     IDBSup, Nashville 1976, pp. 730, 733

13   כדברי מ' הרן, 'מבעיות הקומפוזיציה של ספר מלכים ושל ספרי נביאים ראשונים', תרביץ לז
(תשכ"ח), עמ' 4: 'בבחינה זו היו הסופרים הדבטרונומיסטיים לא עורכים בלבד, אלא ממש מחברים,
לפי המשמעות העברית המדוייקת הנודעת לשם זה. הם צירפו את קטעי המקורות זה לזה, חיברו
אותם לאחד ועשאום קומפוזיציה ספרותית רצופה'. המבוכה הגדולה בהגדרת המונחים הללו
ובשימוש בהם בולטת כאשר מעניקים לבעל ספר דברי הימים את התואר 'עורך', ומייחסים את
הפרקים הרבים שכתב בעצמו ל'עריכה'; כך י' אמית, ספר שופטים – אמנות העריכה, ירושלים–
תל־אביב תשנ"ב, עמ' 3–7. והרי הוא יצר חיבור חדש בעל צביון יחודי משלו, גם אם שילב בחיבורו
פרקים רבים מתוך מקורותיו.

14   ראה המקור הסינכרוניסטי קצר היריעה שמעמיד יפסן ביסוד ספר מלכים: A. Jepsen, Die)
     Quellen des Königsbuches, Halle 1953, pp. 30-40; ראה גם :S.R. Bin-Nun,
     'Formulas from Royal Records of Israel and of Judah', VT 18 (1969), pp. 419-
     422, והביקורת של נלסון: R.D. Nelson, The Double Redaction of the
     Deuteronomistic History, Sheffield 1981, pp. 30f

15   מל"ב ט 29//ח 25; יג 12–13//15–16 (ראה להלן).

חלקו של המחבר בעיצוב המבנה הסינכרוניסטי ניכר עוד בפן אחר: פעם בפעם מתגלית חיותו
של הדגם הסינכרוניסטי, הפועל כחלק אינהרנטי ברקמת הספר. אכן, ברגיל, הקשר
הסינכרוניסטי מוצג בדגם קבוע בנוסחאות הפתיחה.[16] אך יש שהשימוש במטבע הסינכרוניסטי
גולש אל מחוץ לנוסחאות, לתוך הסיפור, ויש שהמארג הסינכרוניסטי אינו מושג בנוסחאות
הקבועות אלא באמצעים אחרים. במקרים הללו התיאור הסינכרוניסטי פושט את מדיו
הרשמיים ולובש מחלצות אחרות, סיפוריות.

(א) לרוב השילוב הסינכרוניסטי נשמר בצורתו הסכימאטית: אביה ואסא מיהודה עלו על כס
המלכות עוד בימי ירבעם, על כן מלכותם מתוארת מיד לאחר מלכות רחבעם, והסיפור יחזור
לנדב בן ירבעם רק אחרי תום מלכות אסא. בימי אסא מיהודה התחלפו בישראל מלכים רבים:
נדב בן ירבעם, בעשא, אלה בנו, זמרי, עמרי, בנו אחאב. כל אלה עלו לשלטון בעוד אסא מולך
ביהודה ועל כן מלכויותיהם מתוארות בזו אחר זו, ועל הקורא להתאזר בסבלנות רבה עד
שהסיפור יחזור למלכות יהודה עם ימי יהושפט, שמלכותו החלה לאחר עליית אחאב. בימי
עזריה מלך יהודה עלו לשלטון בישראל המלכים זכריה, שלום, מנחם, פקחיה ופקח בן רמליהו,
ושוב, מלכויותיהם מתוארות בזו אחר זו, והמחבר מחזירנו ליהודה רק עם יותם, שעלה למלוכה
בימי פקח. כל אחת מן המלכויות הללו מוגדרת היטב במסגרת הנוסחתית, ומהווה יחידה
ספרותית לעצמה.

השיטתיות של התיאור הסינכרוניסטי מתבררת בצורה חדה כאשר תיאור זה מתנגש עם הסדר
הכרונולוגי. כך הדבר, דרך משל, במלכות אסא מלך יהודה. זו התחילה בעוד ירבעם מולך
בישראל; לפיכך סמוך תיאור מלכות אסא לתיאור מלכות אביו אביה, נוסחה בראשו ונוסחה
בסופו, כרגיל (טו 9–24). במרכז מלכות אסא עומדת מלחמתו בבעשא מלך ישראל (טו 16–22).
העובדה שבעשא לא הוצג עדיין אינה מפריעה למחבר. סיפור המלחמה מתואר מנקודת ראותו
של אסא מלך יהודה, ועל כן מקומו בתיאור מלכות אסא, יהי מלך ישראל אשר יהי. עליית
בעשא תבוא בהמשך, בהתאם לשיטה, שהרי בעשא עלה לשלטון בימי אסא (טו 33).
בפרשת יהושפט מזדקרים ביתר שאת אילוציה של השיטה שקבע לעצמו המחבר. מלכות
יהושפט פותחת רשמית בנוסחת הפתיחה (מל"א כב 41).[17] אך, כמו במקרהו של בעשא, אין זו
הפעם הראשונה שיהושפט נזכר בתיאור המאורעות. הלוא כבר השתתף במלחמת רמות גלעד,
לאורך פרק כב. מאחר שנקודת המוצא של הסיפור היא במלך ישראל, הוא מסופר במסגרת
תולדות אחאב, ואין המחבר נטרד מן העובדה שעליית יהושפט על כס המלכות תתפוס את
מקומה רק אחר כך. מעניין עוד יותר לשיטת מחברנו סיפורה של מלחמה אחרת שיהושפט
השתתף בה, מלחמת יהורם בן אחאב במואב (מל"ב ג). נדמה שהשיטה השתלטה על החומר
במידה כזאת, עד שאיננו חשים כל קושי בהופעתו של יהושפט בסיפור זה, אף על פי שסוף
מלכותו ומותו תוארו זה מכבר (מל"א כב 51).[18] כמו במלחמת רמות גלעד, הסיפור מסופר

---

16 ואף באלה אין לשלול מן המחבר את זכות הגיוון וההתאמה לצורכי העניין, כדרך שעושה בן-נון
(לעיל, הערה 14), עמ' 418, הנוטה ליחס את הגיוון להבדלים שהמחבר מצא במקורותיו. וראה:
B. Halpern & D.S. Vanderhooft, 'The Editions of Kings in the 7th-6th Centuries
B.C.E.', *HUCA* 62 (1991), pp. 179-244. חוקרים אלה מעמידים הבחנות בין מחברי הספרים
השונים על פי צורתם המדויקת של מרכיבים מסוימים בנוסחאות.

17 בתרגום השבעים מתוארת מלכות יהושפט במקביל לנוסח המסורה, אך משתקפת בו גם גרסה אחרת.
על פי גרסה זו מלכות יהושפט באה אחרי מל"א טז 28, בין מלכות עמרי למלכות אחאב, שכן בגרסה
זו מלך יהושפט בשנה האחת עשרה לעמרי. מלכות יהושפט מקבלת אפוא מקום חדש על פי הנתון
החדש, אך עדיין בהתאם לשיטה הסינכרוניסטית.

18 ייתכן שזה אשר גרם לבעל דה"י 'לאבד' את הפרק הזה מתולדות יהושפט. למרות שהוא נוהג להביא
בספרו את הפרשיות המשותפות למלכי ישראל ויהודה, אין לפרק הזה פרק מקביל בספרו. ייתכן גם

מנקודת הראות של מלך ישראל, ואין מלך יהודה המשתתף בו קובע את מקומו של הסיפור, אלא מלך ישראל.

השיטתיות של מחברנו בולטת גם בשילוב חומר המקורות שהיה בידיו. כך בנוגע לסיפורי הנביאים. עם מות עמרי עולה אחאב למלוכה, עדיין בימי אסא. תיאור מלכותו משתרע על פני פרקים רבים (טז 29–כב 40). הסיבה לרוחב היריעה נעוצה בשילוב סיפורי אליהו. נוסחת הפתיחה של מלכות אחאב (טז 29–30) זורמת באופן טבעי לתוך המשך תיאור חטאות אחאב (טז 30: 'ויעש הרע...', טז 31: 'ויהי הנקל לכתו בדרכי ירבעם... ויקח אשה את איזבל... ויעבד את הבעל...'). כך מכין המחבר את הרקע להתערבות אליהו, כלומר לשילוב סיפורי אליהו. ייתכן שהיה בידי המחבר מחזור סיפורי אליהו, או, להלן, מחזור סיפורי אלישע; אך בספר מלכים אין יחידות מעין 'סיפורי אליהו' או 'סיפורי אלישע'.[19] אין ספק שסיפורי אליהו מבקשים להם מסגרות משל עצמם. אך אין לעוות את המבנה העיקרי לשם כך. מעמדם העצמאי יבוא לידי ביטוי, במידה האפשר, בחלוקה משנה. במבנה היסוד נשמרת המסגרת של מלכות אחאב – נוסחת הפתיחה בראש ונוסחת הסיום בסוף. תיאור מלכות יהורם בן אחאב משתרע אף הוא על פני פרקים רבים, ממל"ב ג 1 ועד הרצחו בידי יהוא (מל"ב ט 26), וגם כאן המסגרת הקובעת היא המסגרת המלכותית. אם יש בעיות בקביעת גבולות היחידה הספרותית של מלכות יהורם אין הן נובעות משילוב סיפורי אלישע, אלא משילוב המסגרות המלכותיות, כפי שנראה להלן. מחבר ספר מלכים שעבד אפוא את סיפורי הנביאים ל'מסגרות המלכותיות': מלכות אחאב, ובה משולבים סיפורי אליהו, מלכות יהורם, ובה משולבים סיפורי אלישע. כך בנה המחבר את ספרו, מנקודת המוצא של המלכים, ולא של הנביאים, גם אם סיפורי הנביאים מהווים את רוב בניינם של תיאורי ימי המלכים הללו.

(ב) בכמה פרשיות משנה המחבר את דגם השימוש בנוסחאות מכורח הסיפור. בולט הדבר כאשר מלך עולה לשלטון בנסיבות מיוחדות, בייחוד עקב מרד. מן הצד האחד, אנו מוצאים שימוש מורחב בדגם הסינכרוניסטי. כך מזדרז המספר לציין בסוף ימי אחזיה: 'וימלך יהורם תחתיו בשנת שתים ליהורם בן יהושפט... כי לא היה לו בן' (מל"ב א 17).[20] וכך בהפיכות, למרות שהמידע מופיע בנוסחאות, מציין המחבר: 'וימתהו בעשא בשנת שלש לאסא מלך יהודה וימלך תחתיו' (מל"א טז 28); 'ויבא זמרי ויכהו וימיתהו בשנת עשרים ושבע לאסא מלך יהודה וימלך תחתיו' (טז 10). בפרשת המרד בזמרי משתלבים הנוסחה בסיפור והסיפור בנוסחה: 'בשנת עשרים ושבע שנה לאסא מלך יהודה מלך זמרי שבעת ימים בתרצה והעם חונים על גבתון... ויעלה עמרי... ויהי כראות זמרי... וימת. על חטאתיו אשר חטא לעשות הרע בעיני ה'...' (טז

שדי היה לו בסיפור אחד (מל"א כב 1–38), או שניים (כב 49–50), של התקשרות-חטא בין מלך יהודה למלך ישראל, ועל כן ויתר ביודעין על הסיפור הנוסף הזה. ואפשר שבבואתו של מל"ב ג משתקפת בדה"ב כ. ראה M. Noth, 'Eine palästinische Lokalüberlieferung in 2. Chr. 20', *ZDPV* 67 (1944-1945), pp. 45-71

19   כדרך שמחלק ג'ונס (לעיל, הערה 9) את מל"א יז 1–מל"ב י 63 (ממלכות אחאב ועד מרד יהוא), לשלושה חלקים: (א) אליהו וזמנו; (ב) אלישע וזמנו; (ג) מרד יהוא. החלוקה הזאת חותרת תחת אשיות המבנה שבנה המחבר: ראשית, מה למלכויות יהושפט, יהורם ואחזיה מלכי יהודה תחת הכותרות 'הישראליות' הללו? וכאמור, יז 1 אינו פותח יחידה; מלכות אחאב מתחילה ב-טז 29, ושם מתחילה היחידה. נקודת המוצא היא מלכות אחאב ולא אליהו, יהיה מעמדו של אליהו מרכזי ככל שיהיה.

20   על פי מל"ב א 17 יהורם מלך ישראל עולה בשנה השנייה ליהורם בן יהושפט, ואילו על פי ג 1 הוא עולה בשנה השמונה עשרה ליהושפט. אין דרך לפשר בין הנתונים בלי להיזקק למערכת הנחות של עוצרות (קורגנטיות) הן ביהודה והן בישראל. ראה תיאורו של ח' תדמור, 'כרונולוגיה', אנציקלופדיה מקראית, ד, ירושלים תשכ"ג, עמ' 289–299.

למבנה ספר מלכים

15–19). תיאור ההתקוממויות בדגמים שבעיקרם מאפיינים את נוסחאות הפתיחה מפקיע את הסינכרוניזמים מן המסגרת. המחבר עושה בהם שימוש חי במהלך ספרו.

מן הצד השני, יש שסיפור המרד דוחק לגמרי את פני הדברים בתיאורי מלכויותיהם של ירבעם ויהוא. לשתי המלכויות אין נוסחאות פתיחה, והן משתלבות לתוך הספר עם סיפורי ההתקוממות שהובילו לכינונן.²¹ תוצאת לוואי היא שנתונים אופייניים לנוסחאות הפתיחה, כמו משך מלכותו של המלך, נדחו אל נוסחת הסיום. כך בירבעם (מל"א יד 20), וכך ביהוא (מל"ב י 36).²² הדבר מראה בעליל שהמבנה והנוסחאות המהוות לו שלד הם כחומר ביד היוצר – מחבר ספר מלכים.²³ תוצאה עיקרית היא, שקשה לקבוע את נקודת הפתיחה של היחידות הספרותיות המוקדשות למלכויות ירבעם ויהוא, שהרי סיפורי ההתקוממות מתרחשים כאשר המלך הקודם עדיין יושב על כס הממלכה. היכן מתחילה מלכות ירבעם? מל"א יב 1, פתיחת המשא ומתן בשכם, היא נקודת הפתיחה היחידה האפשרית. דבר המלכתו נמסר בפסוק 20: 'ויהי כשמע כל ישראל כי שב ירבעם וישלחו ויקראו אתו אל העדה וימליכו אתו על כל ישראל, לא היה אחרי בית דוד זולתי שבט יהודה לבדו'. אך כתוב זה הוא תוצאה של המשא ומתן, ולא התחלה של יחידה חדשה שעניינה מלכות ירבעם. מעשה שמעיה בפסוקים יב 22–24 מבקש לפרשה יב 1–24 מעמד משל עצמה וכותרת מעין: 'פילוג הממלכה'. בקטע זה מצטייר הפילוג מזווית הראייה של מלכות הדרום, המתעצבת באותה ההזדמנות, ומתקבל הרושם שכל הפרשה עניינה היווצרותן של מלכויות ישראל ויהודה.²⁴ פסוקים אלו נחשבים, מטעמים שונים לגמרי, ככתובים מאוחרים מבחינת המינוח, התוכן ועולם המושגים, ומפריעים את ההקשר באופן ברור ביותר.²⁵ ואכן, גם מבחינת המבנה יוצרים פסוקים אלה קושי מסוים. הפסוקים יב 22–24 מהווים מעין קו סיום, ובכך אין כל קושי. אלא שהדבר מעניק לי־יב 25 ('ויבן ירבעם את שכם...') מעמד של פתיחה. זהו הדיווח הראשון הנוגע למלכות ירבעם ממש, אך הוא בוודאי אינו התחלה, אלא המשך, וככל הנראה המשך של פסוק 20: ירבעם הומלך,

21   מחבר דה"י, לשיטתו, משמיט את מלכות ירבעם. לפיכך, מתקבל רצף אחד של מעשה הפילוג (דה"ב י
      1–יא 4 // מל"א יב 1–24) ומלכות רחבעם (דה"ב יא 5 ואילך). עקב כך נדחית נוסחת הפתיחה של
      מלכות רחבעם, בדומה למה שבספר מלכים לא נמצא מקום לנוסחת הפתיחה של מלכות ירבעם,
      ונתוניה באים רק סמוך לפני נוסחת הסיום של מלכות רחבעם (דה"ב יב 13–14) ואינם משתלבים
      בקלות יתרה במקומם.
22   הערכת יהוא כאמת המידה הפולחנית, יסוד קבוע נוסף בנוסחאות הפתיחה, אף היא מופיעה דווקא
      סמוך לסוף מלכותו; ראה מל"ב י 31.
23   השווה גם בעניין דויד ושלמה, מל"א י 11; יא 42. קשה לקבל את דבריה של בן־נון (לעיל, הערה
      14), עמ' 422, שזהו דגם שנשאל ממקורותיו של בעל הספר, שמצאו רק ברישומים של מלכי ישראל.
      האם דויד ושלמה הם לצורך זה מלכי ישראל? ואם הדגמים נולדו בירושלים, מדוע הם ממשיכים
      להתקיים בצפון, ורק בירבעם וביהוא? זוהי בפירוש בחירה של בעל הספר: מן הצד האחד, דמות
      החומר הכתיבה לו ויתור על נוסחת פתיחה, ומן הצד האחר, לא רצה לוותר על הנתון החיוני של
      אורך שנות המלכות, ולכן שילבו בנוסחת הסיום.
24   מצטרפות לכך תוספות אחרות בפרשה: 'עתה ראה ביתך דוד' (פסוק 16); 'ובני ישראל הישבים בערי
      יהודה וימלך עליהם רחבעם' (פסוק 17).
25   הטענה העיקרית נוגעת ליחידה המדינית המיוחסת לרחבעם באפיזודה הזאת, דהיינו יהודה ובנימין.
      זהו מושב זר לספר מלכים, ואילו בדה"י, עזרא ונחמיה הוא משמש כדבר מובן מאליו. ועוד: הן בדברי
      האל אל שלמה (יא 11–13), הן בדברי אחיה אל ירבעם (יא 29–39), והן ב־יב 20, הסמוך לפני הקטע
      הנדון, המושב המרכזי בכל הנוגע לבית דויד הוא השבט האחד, יהודה לבדו, ולא יהודה ובנימין. ראה,
      בין היתר: R. Kittel, *Die Bücher der Könige* (HKAT), Göttingen 1900; J.A.
      Montgomery & H.S. Gehman, *The Books of Kings* (ICC), Edinburgh 1951 וכן נות
      (לעיל, הערה 7); וירתוויין (לעיל, הערה 8); צ' טלשיר, המסורת הכפילה על פילוג המלוכה,
      ירושלים תשמ"ט, עמ' 194–195, 221–222.

ועתה הוא מבצר את הערים המרכזיות, כצעד ראשון לביסוס ממלכתו. פרשת הפילוג היא אפוא
סיפור המעשה המכין את עליית ירבעם על כס הממלכות, סיפור היוולדה של ממלכת הצפון. אי
אפשר אלא לראות ב־יב 1–יד 20 יחידה אחת, שנושאה: הפילוג וממלכות ירבעם.
כאלה הם פני הדברים גם בממלכות יהוא; ראשיתה בסיפור המרד (מל״ב ט 1 ואילך), למרות
ששלטון יהוא יחל באופן מסודר רק אחרי מות קודמו. אין נקודת התחלה לממלכות יהוא אחרי
תיאור הוצאתם להורג של יהורם מלך ישראל ואחזיה מלך יהודה (המסתיים ב־ט 28). הסיפור
ממשיך בהעלם אחד בשאר מעלליו של יהוא.
מלכות ירבעם וממלכות יהוא הן דוגמאות למידת החופש שנטל המחבר לעצמו בעיצוב מהלך
ספרו. למרות שכפה על יצירתו מערכת נוקשה למדי של נוסחאות, כאן ויתר על הדגם ונתן
לסיפור לעשות את שלו: הוא מבליע את עליית ירבעם ואת מהלך יהוא במהלך השוטף של
סיפורי ההתקוממות.
נזכיר בסוגיה זו גם את פרשת עתליה. במל״ב יא מתוארת ההפיכה והפיכת הנגד
שהעלתה את יואש בן אחזיה על כס הממלכות. למרות שנמשכה כשבע שנים, אין מלכות עתליה
זוכה למסגרת רשמית כלשהי. הנתון הסינכרוני ברור, שהרי ראשית שלטונה מקביל לראשית
שלטון יהוא, ומספר שנותיה בשלטון ניתן בעקיפין: 'ויהי [יואש] אתה [עם יהושבע] בית ה'
מתחבא שש שנים ועתליה מלכת על הארץ' (יא 3). עתליה עולה ויורדת עם הסיפור.[26]

(ג) בשתי פרשיות שינה המחבר ממנהגו הקפדני וויתר על ההפרדה הסכימאטית הקבועה בין
ממלכויות ישראל ויהודה; מדובר בממלכת יהורם בישראל ואחזיה ביהודה, ובמלכות יואש בישראל
ואמציה ביהודה. בפרשיות הללו תולדות שתי הממלכות משתלבות לא רק באירועים
היסטוריים, אלא גם במבנה הסיפורי.
(1) במל״ב ג 1 מתחילה מלכות יהורם בן אחאב.[27] כאמור, הרכב תיאורה יוצא דופן מפני סיפורי
אלישע, התופשים בו חלק נכבד, אך זו אינה הסיבה לשבירת מתכונת הדיווח הקבועה. על פי
הסדר הרגיל אנו מצפים לנוסחת הסיום של מלכות יהורם, ולאחריה נוסחת הפתיחה של מלך
יהודה. ולא היא. הנה, מבלי שתבוא נוסחת סיום למלכות יהורם מלך ישראל, מופיעה נוסחת
פתיחה חדשה, למלך יהודה: 'ובשנת חמש ליורם בן אחאב... מָלַך יהורם בן יהושפט...' (ח 16–
17). האם נשמטה נוסחת הסיום של מלכות יהורם מלך ישראל בטעות? במהרה יתברר שלא כן.
הקו המנחה של התיאור הסינכרוניסטי נמשך, אלא שהוא פושט את צורתו הסכימאטית ולובש
צורה שונה, סיפורית.
במל״ב ח 16–24 מופיעה אפוא מלכות יהורם בן יהושפט, כמקובל, בין נוסחת פתיחה לנוסחת
סיום. מיד אחר כך נפתחת מלכות אחזיה בן יהורם מלך יהודה בנוסחה הקבועה: 'בשנת שתים
עשרה שנה ליורם בן אחאב מלך ישראל מלך אחזיהו בן יהורם מלך יהודה...' (ח 25–27). נדמה
שחזרנו לשגרת התיאור הסינכרוניסטי, חוץ מחסרונה של נוסחת הסיום למלכות יהורם מלך
ישראל. אך העיון בהמשך תולדות אחזיה מלך יהודה מגלה במהרה שאף מלכותו אינה חותמת
בנוסחת סיום. אחרי נוסחת הפתיחה של מלכות אחזיה אין אלא דבר מלחמתו המשותפת עם
יורם מלך ישראל: 'וילך את יורם בן אחאב למלחמה עם חזהאל מלך ארם ברמת גלעד ויכו

---

26 שלא כבן־נון (לעיל, הערה 14), עמ' 423, הסבורה שמקורותיו של מחברנו לא המציאו נוסחאות
לעתליה מפני שלא היתה שליטה לגיטימית.

27 בתרגום השבעים מופיעה נוסחת הפתיחה של מלכות יהורם בסוף מל״ב א, מלבד גרסה מקבילה
לנוסח המסורה, בראש פרק ג. משמע, על פי אחת הגרסאות המשתקפות בתרגום השבעים גם סיפור
עלייתו של אליהו השמיימה (מל״ב ב) כלול במסגרת מלכות יהורם, ואינו חורג מן המסגרת, כפי
שקורה בנוסח המסורה.

ארמים את יורם. וישב יורם המלך להתרפא ביזרעאל מן המכים אשר יכהו ארמים ברמה בהלחמו את חזהאל מלך ארם ואחזיהו בן יהורם מלך יהודה ירד לראות את יורם בן אחאב ביזרעאל כי חלה הוא' (ח 28–29).

תחילה מן הראוי לציין את ההבדל הניכר בין התיאור הזה ובין תיאור שתי המלחמות הקודמות שמלך יהודה השתתף בהן לצד מלך ישראל. מלחמת אחאב ויהושפט בארם (מל"א כב) ומלחמת יהורם ויהושפט במואב (מל"ב ג) תוארו בהרחבה, מנקודת המוצא של מלכי ישראל ובמסגרת מלכויותיהם. המלחמה הזאת היא במתכונת דומה: אחזיה מלך יהודה הולך עם יורם מלך ישראל במלחמתו בחזהאל מלך ארם. המלחמה היא בוודאי מלחמה 'ישראלית', ושורת ההיגיון היא שסיפורה יבוא במסגרת מלכות יורם מלך ישראל. והנה היא מופיעה במהלך תיאור מלכות אחזיה מלך יהודה. זאת ועוד, אין תיאור ממשי של מלחמה זו. יש רק דיווח תמציתי שכל כולו מוביל לפגישתם של יהורם ואחזיה ביזרעאל. בכך מתבררת היטב מידת התערבותו של מחבר החיבור הסינכרוניסטי בחומר שלו. אין הוא רק עורך המכוון את החומר שבידיו לתוך המסגרות ולתוך הסכימה הכרונולוגית שעיצב; במקרה שלנו הוא מחליט לא רק על ה'היכן' אלא גם על ה'איך'. עיצוב הסיפור של מלחמת יהורם ואחזיה הוא פרי עבודתו של מחבר החיבור הסינכרוניסטי. ייתכן שהיה קיים סיפור מלא על המלחמה הזאת, והוא ויתר עליו ובחר להציג את תמציתו במסגרת מלכות אחזיה מלך יהודה. אולם נראה יותר, שהכרעתו נבעה ממצב החומר שהיה בידו; כלומר, לא היה בידו כל סיפור על מלחמת יהורם ואחזיה בחזהאל, וכל המידע בא לו למחבר ספר מלכים ממקור שנגע במלחמה זו רק בעקיפין. מקור כזה אכן נמצא בידינו; הרי ניכר במחבר שלצורך תיאור המלחמה במסגרת מלכות אחזיה מלך יהודה הוא השתמש בפיסת המידע המופיעה בסיפור מרד יהוא, המתארת את נסיבות הימצאותם של מלך ישראל ומלך יהודה ביזרעאל (ח 28–29// ט 14–16).

כל התמיהות שתמהנו על החומר הזה פתרון אחד להן. הן חסרונה של נוסחת הסיום ביהורם מלך ישראל, הן צורתה של מלחמת יהורם ואחזיה בחזהאל, והן קטיעותה של מלכות אחזיה בסופה, הם פרי תכננו של מחבר החיבור הסינכרוניסטי. המחבר מגלגל את תולדות יהורם מלך ישראל על פני כל סיפורי אלישע עד המלכת חזהאל (ח 7–15). העצירה בסיפור התמלכות חזהאל משרתת היטב את תווי הספר. מצד התוכן: חזהאל מתמלך כאן, והרי יהורם ואחזיה עתידים להילחם בו יחדיו. מצד המבנה: הסיום 'וימלך חזהאל תחתיו' (ח 15) שומר למראית עין על הסכימה הנוסחתית, ונוצרת אתנחתא לפני המעבר אל נוסחת הפתיחה של מלכות יהורם ביהודה (ח 16). עתה מתוארת אפוא מלכות יהורם ביהודה (ח 16–24), ולאחריה, בתורה, מלכות בנו אחזיה (ח 25–29). זו נעצרת בנקודת פגישתם של אחזיה ויהורם ביזרעאל (ח 29). כך סלל המחבר לעצמו דרך חזרה אל מלכות ישראל. ואכן סיפור משיחת יהוא יהוא עומד בשער (ט 1–31). יהוא קושר נגד אדונו, יהורם (ט 14א). והיכן נמצא יהורם? 'ויורם היה שמר ברמת גלעד הוא וכל ישראל מפני חזאל מלך ארם' (ט 14ב–15א). יהוא שם פניו ליזרעאל 'כי יורם שכב שמה ואחזיה מלך יהודה ירד לראות את יורם' (ט 16). וזהו אפוא המצב שיהורם ואחזיה ימצאו בו את סופם, עניינית וספרותית. המחבר השאיר את סיפור יהורם ואת סיפור אחזיה בלא סיום — כאן נקשרים הקצוות. תיאור מלכות יהורם נסגר, לא בנוסחה אלא עם הסיפור, סיפור הריגתו בידי יהוא. אחרי שחיסל את יהורם, שם יהוא פניו אל אחזיה שהזדמן ליזרעאל, רודף אחריו וממית אף אותו (ט 27).[28] גם מלכות אחזיה מסתיימת עם הסיפור ולא

28 'ואחזיה מלך יהודה ראה וינס דרך בית הגן וירדף אחריו יהוא ויאמר גם אתו הכהו אל המרכבה במעלה גור אשר את יבלעם וינס מגדו וימת שם'. הכתוב אינו קולח: אי אפשר שיהוא יאמר היכן להכות את אחזיה. במקום שישיגוהו שם יכוהו. ייתכן שניכר כאן מעשה החיבור בין הסיפור לבין

בנוסחה, אם כי זכר הנוסחה מתגנב לסיפור במשפט המסיים: 'וירכבו אתו עבדיו ירשלמה ויקברו אתו בקברתו... בעיר דוד' (ט 28).[29] בפרשת יהורם ואחזיה שגורלותיהם אחוזים זה בזה, יצר המחבר מבנה מיוחד. בניגוד למה שהורגלנו בו, המלכויות חותכות זו את זו ועושות יחד כברת דרך, בפרשת מרד יהוא. יוצא שמרד יהוא (ט 1–28), הוא הן הן סוף למלכות יהורם, הן סוף למלכות אחזיה והן התחלה למלכות יהוא. ביחידה הגדולה ג 1–י 36, קשה אפוא לתחום גבולות ליחידות ספרותיות נפרדות המוקדשות למלכויות השונות. מצד המערכת הסינכרוניסטית הגענו לנקודת שיווי זמן. כשם שמלכויות רחבעם וירבעם החלו בערך באותו הזמן, כך מלכות יהורם מישראל ואחזיה מיהודה הסתיימו באותו הזמן. המחבר לקח את הדבר הזה בחשבון, ובנה את דבריו לקראת התלכדות קו הסיום.[30]

שמנו את הדגש על כך שהמחבר מותר כאן על הדגם הקבוע, ונותן לסיפור למלא את מערכת הקשרים בין מלכויות ישראל ליהודה. אך למעשה אין הוא מותר על האמצעי הנוסחתי, אלא משלב בין המלכויות, הן באמצעות הדגם הקבוע והן באמצעות הסיפור השוטף. את סיפור יהורם מישראל השאיר פתוח כדי לחזור אליו אחר כך בסיפור יזרעאל. אך, בינתיים, כיצד עבר מיהורם למלכי יהודה שמלכו בימיו אם לא באמצעות הנוסחאות הקבועות? תחילה מופיעה, על פי צורכי המערכת הסינכרוניסטית ובדגמיה הקבועים, מלכות יהורם מיהודה, שאינה רלוונטית לסיפור יהורם מישראל המחכה להמשכו. אחר כך נפתחת, שוב על פי השיטה ובדגמיה, מלכות אחזיה מיהודה, ורק אז בא תורו של הסיפור שיוביל אותנו ליזרעאל וחזרה אל יהורם מלך ישראל. השיטה הסינכרוניסטית יוצאת אפוא אל הפועל בשילוב חי של הדגמים הקבועים עם הסיפור השוטף. סיפורים, כגון סיפור יהוא, אפשר שבאו לידי מחבר ספר מלכים ממקורות נבואיים או עממיים, אבל אין ספק שהוא עיצב אותם כך שיוכל לצקת אותם לתוך המערכת הסינכרוניסטית שלו.

(2) בדומה לפרשת יהורם מלך ישראל ואחזיה מלך יהודה בנויה גם פרשת יהואש-אמציה. מלכות יהואש בן יהואחז — כל כולה, כך דומה במבט ראשון, מורכבת מנוסחת הפתיחה ומנוסחת הסיום (מל"ב יג 10–11; 12–13).[31] דבר זה כשלעצמו מוזר משהו. אמנם יש עוד תיאורים קצרי יריעה. אך אין עוד כדבר הזה, שנוסחת הפתיחה נושקת לנוסחת הסיום ואין מלבדן ולא כלום. נוסף על כך, מיד אחרי נוסחת הסיום עומדות שתי אפיזודות, שיהואש לוקח

הידיעה ההיסטורית המשמשת אותו (ראה גם להלן, הערה 33). הידיעה ההיסטורית דיווחה על המקום שאחזיה הוכה בו: במעלה גור אשר את יבלעם. הסיפור שם את הידיעה הזאת בפי יהוא. ואולי חסרה חוליה, מעין: 'ויאמר גם אתו הכהו. ויכהו אל המרכבה במעלה גור אשר את יבלעם', ונפלה מלת 'ויכהו' מחמת דמיונה למלה הקודמת.

29 ב"ט 29 מופיעה נוסחת הפתיחה של מלכות אחזיה, בלא ספק מחוץ למקומה, ובלא כל טעם. היא חוזרת על הנאמר ב"ח 25, בהבדל של שנה: 'בשנת אחת/שתים עשרה שנה ליורם בן אחאב מלך ישראל מלך אחזיהו בן יהורם מלך יהודה'. אפשר שזהי גרסה שונה של אותה נוסחה, שנכתבה בשוליים ונשתלבה מחוץ למקומה. ראה גם להלן על יג 12–13.

30 כאן מתבררת חולשת הסידור של לונג (לעיל, הערה 11). לדידו, מלכי ישראל בימי יהושפט, אחזיה ויהורם מתוארים ביחידה מל"א כב 51(52)–מל"ב ח 15. וכי ח 15 מסיים את מלכות יהורם, ספרותית או ענייני? ובוודאי קשה להבין מדוע קבע לונג שבימי יהורם מלך ישראל מולך ביהודה יהורם, ושמלכותו מתוארת במל"ב ח 16–ט 28. ראשית, היחידה הזאת כוללת גם את אחזיה מלך יהודה (ח 25–29). ועוד, היא כוללת את מרד יהוא (ט 1–28), שאין מקומו ביחידה העוסקת במלכי יהודה. בסיכום של לונג יוצא שמלכות יהוא מתחילה בנקודה מוזרה מאוד — מל"ב ט 30 (הריגת איזבל). וזאת, יש להניח, משום שרק בנקודה זו בא הקץ על מלכות קודמו. אך, התניה זו פועלת בשיטה הנוסחתית הקפואה, ולא בשיטה הסיפורית החותכת את הקווים. המבוכה שמטיל החומר בשיטה של לונג באה לידי ביטוי פשוט בכך שאין ביכולתו לומר בימי איזה מלך מיהודה מלך יהוא.

31 ראה, למשל, קוגן ותדמור (לעיל, הערה 10).

חלק פעיל בשתיהן: מות אלישע (יג 14–21) ויחסי ארם-ישראל (יג 22–25); הן קשורות ביניהן קשר של אות והתגשמות: 'שלש פעמים תכה את ארם' (יג 19) – 'שלש פעמים הכהו יואש' (יג 25). ולמה לא באה נוסחת הסיום של מלכות יואש אחרי פרשה זו? אין כל סיבה נראית לעין לכך שהפרשה תעמוד מחוץ לתחום מלכותו.[32] ובכן, שמא בטעות נתגלגלה נוסחת הסיום למקומה הנוכחי ויש להעבירה למקומה הראוי לה, לסוף פרק יג? תיקון כזה מתבקש גם נוכח ההמשך. הלוא פרק יד פותח במלכות אמציהו מלך יהודה, שעלה לשלטון בימי יואש מישראל. כך היה מתקבל המבנה הסטריאוטיפי, והכל היה בא על מקומו בשלום: נוסחת הסיום של מלכות יהואש מלך ישראל נושקת לנוסחת הפתיחה של מלכות אמציהו מלך יהודה. ואף על פי כן, העתקת נוסחת הסיום למקום אחר אינה מהפתרון לבעיית הסידור בפרשה זו. הן החומר עצמו והן לקחה של פרשת יהורם ואחזיה מצביעים לכיוון אחר.

פרק יד פותח, אמנם, את מלכות אמציה מלך יהודה בנוסחה הקבועה (יד 1 ואילך: 'בשנת שתים ליואש... מלך אמציהו...'), ומסיימה בנוסחה הקבועה (יד 18 ואילך: 'ויתר דברי אמציהו...'). אבל בתוך המסגרת הזאת, אחרי ידיעות הנוגעות למדיניות פנים (יד 5–6) ולמדיניות חוץ (יד 7),[33] מתוארת ההתנגשות בין יהואש מלך ישראל לאמציה מלך יהודה (יד 8 ואילך). היזמה היא של מלך יהודה, והסיפור מסופר מנקודת הראות שלו, ולפיכך הוא נכלל במסגרת מלכותו. לשיטתו, יכול היה לחתום את מלכות יהואש תחילה ואחר כך לספר על המלחמה בינו לבין אמציה. אך המקרה הזה שונה, שהנה עם תום מלחמת יהואש-אמציה (יד 14) מופיעה שנית נוסחת הסיום של מלכות יהואש. וכאן מקומה קבוע היטב: הכתוב ממשיך ויוצר קשר בין מות יהואש למות אמציהו (יד 17), והופך את נוסחאות הסיום, הן זו של יהואש והן זו של אמציהו, לחלק בלתי נפרד מן הסיפור (יד 15–22).

הנה יצא החומר ללמד על עצמו. טענו לחריגותה של נוסחת הסיום של מלכות יהואש (יג 12–13), הן משום סמיכותה לנוסחת הפתיחה, והן משום שאחריה בא חומר המספר למעשה על מלכות יהואש (יג 14–25). והנה נוסחת הסיום של מלכות יהואש חוזרת ומופיעה אחרי מלחמתו באמציה (יד 15–16), ארוגה היטב בסיפור, ומיותרת לחלוטין את זו הראשונה, המוקשה ממילא. לא ברור כיצד נקלע העתק הנוסחה למקום לא לו. השינויים בין הטקסטים המקבילים קטנים מכדי לייחס להם ערך של מראינטים שנקלעו למקומות שונים. ייתכן שלנוסחאות הללו היו חיים עצמאיים שהוליבו אותן לעתים למקומות מוזרים משהו. במקרה זה נראה שהלכה נוסחת הסיום אחר נוסחת הפתיחה והטילה מבוכה במבנה הפרשה.[34] כיצד בנויה אפוא פרשת מלכות יהואש מלך ישראל ומלכות אמציהו מלך יהודה? בדומה לפרשת

---

32 אפשר לשער שהמחבר כיוון להוציא את סיפור מותו של אלישע אל מחוץ לתחומן של המסגרות המלכותיות, על דרך סיפור עליית אליהו השמימה, מל"ב ב. שתי הפרשיות אמנם קשורות בעצם העניין – מות הנביא, כמו גם במוטיב: 'אבי אבי רכב ישראל ופרשיו' (מל"ב ב 12; יג 14), אבל דרכיהן נפרדות בנקודה מרכזית לענייננו: בסיפור אליהו אין מלך ישראל נוטל חלק. זהו סיפור נבואי על העברת סמכות נבואית. לעומת זאת, בסיפור מותו של אלישע ממלא יהואש תפקיד נכבד.

33 יש לנו כאן דוגמה יפה של שעבוד ידיעה היסטורית לסיפור 'היסטורי'. ב'יד 7 באה ידיעה היסטורית, בדגם שמחבר ספרנו בחר לו להציג ידיעות כאלה (ראה להלן, הערה 41): 'הוא הכה את אדום בגיא מלח עשרת אלפים ותפש את הסלע במלחמה ויקרא את שמה יקתאל עד היום הזה'. והנה, הידיעה הזאת משמשת את הסיפור ההיסטורי על מלחמת החוח והארז: 'הכה הכית את אדום ונשאך לבך הכבד ושב בביתך...' (יד 10). אין להוציא מכלל אפשרות שהידיעה ההיסטורית לחוד, והסיפור, כולל הרמז למאורע ההיסטורי של הנצחון על אדום, לחוד. עם זאת, קשה לנתק בין השניים הסמוכים במקום ובעניין. ראה גם לעיל, הערה 28, וראה השימוש הכפול של 'ומלחמה היתה בין... כל הימים' (להלן).

34 ראה גם לעיל, הערה 27, וכן הערה 15.

יהורם מלך ישראל ואחזיה מלך יהודה: המחבר פתח במלכות יהואש, כמקובל, וסיפר בה עד נקודה מסוימת, בלי לסיים אותה באופן רשמי (יג 10–25, ללא פסוקים 12–13). אחר כך עבר אל מלכות אמציה, בפתיחה המקובלת (יד 1 ואילך), ותיאר במסגרתה את מלחמתו ביהואש (יד 8–14). כך נפגשו קורות שני המלכים ונוצרה ההזדמנות אף לסיים את מלכויותיהם זו בצד זו, בשילוב הנוסחאות בסיפור (יד 15 ואילך). משמע, אין בידינו לתחום יחידות נפרדות למלכות יהואש ולמלכות אמציה: הן מתוארות במשולב במל"ב יג 10–יד 22.[35]

נמצא אפוא שמחבר החיבור הסינכרוניסטי שולט בחומר המקורות שבידיו ומארגן אותו על פי תוכנית מחושבת היטב, בדרך כלל במסגרת הנוסחתית הקבועה, ולעתים על ידי שילוב סיפורי המלכויות זה בזה.

ג

חלקו של מחבר החיבור הסינכרוניסטי מתברר עוד מן הדרך ששיבץ ידיעות ארכיוניות קצרות וחסרות הקשר בדברי ימי המלכים, ובייחוד אלו המשתלבות בתוך הנוסחאות או נספחות בשוליהן, מאחר שהמסגרת היא השלד של יצירתו. כך חוזרת בנוסחאות הסיום ידיעה על מלחמה מתמשכת בין הצפון לדרום לאחר הפילוג: 'ומלחמה היתה בין רחבעם ובין ירבעם כל הימים' (מל"א יד 30), 'ומלחמה היתה בין אביה ובין ירבעם' (טו 7), בלי שסופר על כך דבר במסגרת מלכויותיהם של רחבעם או אביה. מאלפת ההופעה הכפולה של אותו נוסח בנוגע לאסא ולבעשא: פעם אחת משמשת הידיעה פתיחה למלחמת אסא–בעשא ברמה (טו 16), ופעם אחרת היא עומדת תלושה אחרי סיום תולדות נדב ולפני תחילת תולדות בעשא (טו 32); אמנם הכפילות צפויה בידיעה חסרת הֶקשר שהמחבר מחפש לה מקום במהלך דבריו. אך נראה שאין זו כפילות בעלמא, אלא שני שימושים שונים באותו נתן עצמו. הידיעה תלוית ההקשר (טו 16) מגלה את ידו המכוונת של מחבר הספר, הבונה את דבריו תוך כדי שילוב שני סוגי חומר: הדיווח הלאקוני על מצב המלחמה בין ישראל ליהודה, וסיפורה של מלחמה אחת.[36] מקומה המוזר של הידיעה בין תולדות נדב לתולדות בעשא (טו 32) אף הוא אינו יוצא דופן; גם במקרים אחרים באה ידיעה על מלך פלוני אחרי שהלה נזכר כיורשו של המלך הקודם ובטרם יתחיל באופן רשמי תיאור מלכותו שלו.[37] כך נוהג המחבר, למשל, בידיעה על הכאת תפסח[38] בידי מנחם מלך ישראל; בתיאור מלכות שלום בן יביש מתואר הקשר שקשר עליו מנחם בן גדי (מל"ב טו 14), אחריו בא הסיום הרשמי של מלכות שלום (טו 15), ומיד אחר כך באה הידיעה על מנחם: 'אז יכה מנחם...' (טו 16); וזה למרות שמלכות מנחם עצמו תתואר מיד בהמשך (טו 17 ואילך). כן יש לציין שהמחבר יודע לנצל את הרווח שבין נוסחת סיום לנוסחת פתיחה לעניינים שזהו מקומם הטבעי, כמו מעשה תבני–עמרי (טז 21–22).[39]

באותן דרכים עצמן מעוצבות ידיעות על מפעלי בנייה של המלכים. הידיעה על קניית שומרון נבנתה כהמשך של נוסחת הפתיחה למלכות עמרי: 'בשנת שלשים ואחת שנה לאסא מלך יהודה

35 ממילא הגדרת היחידה יד 1–22 בפשטות כמלכות אמציה — כך לונג (לעיל, הערה 11) — מטשטשת את מערך החומר המשלב בין מלכות יהואש ומלכות אמציה.

36 בדומה לכך משמש המקביל למל"א טו 7 בספר דה"י כפתיחה למלחמה מסוימת בין אביה לירבעם (דה"ב יג 2 ואילך).

37 בניגוד לדעה המקובלת, שזיהוי תוספת שלא במקומה; ראה, למשל, דברי וירתויין (לעיל, הערה 8), עמ' 19, הערה 1.

38 תפוח שבשומרון? ראה: K. Elliger, 'Die Grenze zwischen Ephraim und Manasse', *ZDPV* 53 (1930), pp. 292-293

39 וראה גם מל"ב כד 7: 'ולא הסיף עוד מלך מצרים לצאת מארצו...'.

מלך עמרי על ישראל שתים עשרה שנה בתרצה מלך שש שנים ויקן את ההר שמרון מאת
שמר... ויבן את ההר ויקרא את שם העיר אשר בנה על שם שמר אדני ההר שמרון' (מל"א טז
24–23). על הקורא להבין מעצמו שביתר שש שנותיו ישב בשומרון. ממש כך סוכמה מלכות
דויד: 'והימים אשר מלך דוד על ישראל ארבעים שנה; בחברון מלך שבע שנים, ובירושלם מלך
שלשים ושלש שנים' (מל"ב ב 11). גם בנוסחת הסיום לשלטון אחאב נרשמה ידיעה בלעדית על
מפעלי הבנייה שלו: 'ובית השן אשר בנה וכל הערים אשר בנה' (כב 39). אחרי הסיום של
מלכות אמציה, ובו תיאור הקשר נגדו והמלכת בנו עזריה תחתיו (מל"ב יד 18–21), נאמר על
עזריה: 'הוא בנה את אילת וישבה ליהודה אחרי שכב המלך עם אבתיו' (יד 22). התיאור הרשמי
של מלכות עזריה מתחיל מאוחר יותר (טו 1 ואילך), ובמסגרתו לא נזכר פועלו של עזריה
באילת כלל וכלל. אך מן הכתוב עצמו ברור שלא קנה לו את מקומו בטעות, שהנה המחבר מגלה
מודעות למקומו המיוחד: 'אחרי שכב המלך עם אבתיו'.[40] ובמלכות יהושפט – יותר נתונים
שולבו בנוסחת הסיום מאשר מחוצה לה (מל"א כב 46–51).

נוסחאות הסיום שימשו למחבר מקום טבעי לשלב דיווח על הנסיבות האלימות שאיפיינו את
סוף מלכותם של מלכים אחדים; כך נהג המחבר ביחס ליואש (מל"ב יב 22–20), לאמציה (יד
18–21), ואף תיאור מותו של יאשיהו מידי פרעה נכו הובלע במסגרת (כג 28–30). עוד הוא
מספר במסגרת נוסחת הסיום למלכות הסיום יותם על התפתחויות מדיניות שתימשכנה בימי המלך
הבא: 'בימים ההם החל ה' להשליח ביהודה רצין מלך ארם ואת פקח בן רמליהו' (טו 36–38).
נוסח כזה כבר הופיע במלכות יהוא, גם כן בסמיכות לחומר הנוסחאי: 'בימים ההם החל ה'
לקצות בישראל ויכם חזאל...' (י 32–33).

ידיעות בנוסח זה, על הפתיחות המיוחדות אותן ('הוא בנה...', 'אז יכה...'), תוארו במחקר
כידיעות שנשאלו הישר מן הארכיון המלכותי.[41] אם כך, עולה נקודה מעניינת בעניין תהליך
חיבורו של ספר מלכים. אילו היו ידיעות אלו בעלות תכנים אחרים, הגותיים למשל, אזי מעמדן
החריג בהקשר היה ודאי מקנה להן תואר של גלוסות עריכתיות או כיוצא באלה.[42] אך הידיעות
הנזכרות – טעם של נתונים היסטוריים מהימנים יש בהן. ומדוע קנו להן שביתה בין לבין,
במקום לא להן? למרות שהמסגרות הנוסחתיות מאוחרות לידיעות הללו, ולו רק מפני שהן
ביטוי לחיבור השלם, נראה הדבר שהמסגרת עיקר ובתוכה משובצות הידיעות ההיסטוריות,
ולא שהידיעות ההיסטוריות הן החומר הנתון והמסגרת נכפתה עליהן מעשה עורך. מקומן של
ידיעות אלה מצביע על כך שהמחבר אשר ארגן את החומר תחת מכבש השיטה הסינכרוניסטית,
היתה לו גישה אל החומר הארכיוני, והוא ששזר את הנתונים הללו במקומות שונים בספרו, אם

---

40   ושוב, נגד ההערכה הרווחת. וירתוויין (לעיל, הערה 8), עמ' 374–373, אומר על הכתוב במל"ב יד 22
     שנכנס למקום לא לו. ועם זאת, הוא מצביע על כך שיש עניין בהערה על אילת בהקשר לתולדות
     אמציה שהיכה את אדום.

41   דרייבר (לעיל, הערה 1), עמ' 203–202, מגדיר: The following modes adopted by the'
     בימי, הוא מונה את: compiler for introducing historical notices are observable'
     בימים ההם, בעת ההיא, הוא, אז, וממשיך ואומר בנוגע ל'אז': '...the notices introduced by it
     lack any definite point of attachment in the preceding narrative: at the same
     time, their directness of statement and terseness of form suggest the inference
     that they may be derived immediately from the contemporary annalistic records.
     J.A. :ראה זו נקודה לפיתוח .The same may be the case with some of the other notices'
     Montgomery, 'Archival Data in the Book of Kings', *JBL* 53 (1934), pp. 46-52

42   בקאטגוריה כזאת יכול להיחשב הכתוב החוזר על נבואת יהוא בן חנני, מל"א טז 7 (מלבד מיקומו,
     מתמיהה התפיסה הבאה לידי ביטוי במלים הסוגרות: 'ועל אשר הכה אתו'. אם משמעו שבעשא ראוי
     לעונש על שהיכה את בית ירבעם, הרי זו תפישה זרה לספר מלכים). בדומה באה נוסחת התגשמות
     הנבואה ליהוא אחרי תום נוסחת הסיום של מלכות המלך האחרון לבית יהוא (מל"ב טו 12).

במקומם הטבעי, אם, לעתים, במקום שנראה כבחירה שלאחר מעשה – יהי זה בתוך נוסחאות הסיום או לאחריהן.[43]

***

אין בדברינו על מל"א יב–מל"ב יז תשובה חד-משמעית לשאלה המונסרת בחקר ספר מלכים בדבר שלבי חיבורו וזמנם.[44] עם זאת, ניתוח מבנה החטיבה מעלה תרומה להבנת תהליך התהוותו של הספר. המבנה הקוהרנטי מקרב אל הדעת שהחטיבה הזאת היא בעיקרה פרי תכננו של מחבר אחד, שיצא לבנות חיבור סינכרוניסטי על מלכויות ישראל ויהודה, תוך שימוש במקורות ארכיוניים, נבואיים, מקדשיים ואחרים, שהיתה לו גישה אליהם. הוא פעל בוודאי לאחר ימי חזקיהו, אך אפשר שמעמד ריכוז הפולחן בתפישת עולמו מלמד על ימים שאחרי הרפורמה של יאשיהו. אין כוונתנו לומר שלא התערבו בחומר הזה ידיים מאוחרות יותר, אך התערבות זו משנית היא, מעשה עיבוד המשנה הדגשים ומעמיד את הדברים בפרספקטיבה של הגלות, ואינו מערער את המבנה כפי שמחבר החיבור הסינכרוניסטי העמידו. אם אכן היו המקורות בידיו, קרוב אל הדעת שפעל בימים של טרם גלות. בכיוון זה מצביעה גם הרוח המנחה את המחבר ליצור יצירה המשלבת את ישראל ויהודה לכדי מכלול אחד, אורינטציה שהיתה יכולה לצמוח באופן טבעי לאחר חורבן ממלכת הצפון, ובייחוד על רקע מעשיו של יאשיהו ודבריו של ירמיהו.

---

43 התופעה הזאת של ידיעות קדומות, שמעמדן בהקשר משל היו גלוסות, באה לידי ביטוי באופנים שונים במקומות אחרים בספר מלכים. הידיעה האותנטית על גזר, שניתנה כשילוחים לבת פרעה, עומדת כנטע זר במקומה, ומסומנת בחזרה מקשרת בתוך רשימת הערים שבנה שלמה (מל"א ט 16); ורשימת הערים עצמה, שבוודאי נסמכה על מקור רשמי, פורצת את מבנה הדברים על המס שהעלה שלמה (פסוקים 15–22). ראה צ' טלשיר, 'נוסחת הפירוט "וזה הדבר" ', תרביץ נא (תשמ"ב), עמ' 29–32. אין ספק שהנאום הפרוגראמאטי על מוצא עובדי הכפייה הוא המסגרת המאוחרת, ורשימת הערים שוקעה בו, כשם שהידיעה המיוחדת על גזר שוקעה בתוך רשימת הערים. עם זאת, הידיעות הקדומות הן שמשולבות בחומר המאוחר, ואין החומר המאוחר בבחינת חומר עריכתי שנכפה על חומר קדום נתון בשלב שני. הידיעה על הרמונו של שלמה (מל"א יא 3 אא) שוברת את רצף הדברים על נשיו הנוכריות המטות את לבבו אחרי אלוהים אחרים, ועם זאת, אין היא גלוסה מאוחרת אלא ביטוי לבעיות שנתקל בהן מחבר מאוחר, המרצה את רצף דבריו ומשלב בהם ידיעות קדומות שהיו עמו. ראה צ' טלשיר, 'לדמותה של מהדורת ספר מלכים המשתקפת בתרגום השבעים', תרביץ נט (תש"ן), עמ' 268–271. בקנה מידה גדול יותר יש לשיטה הזאת מהלכים אצל מסדר ההיסטוריוגרפיה הדויטרונומיסטית, כאשר חומרים קדומים נדחקים לתוך מסגרות של נספחים; כך נספחו לספר שמואל (שמ"ב כא–כד), כך בנספח לספר יהושע (שופ' א).

44 ראה לאחרונה מאמרם של הלפרן ואנדרהופט (לעיל, הערה 16), ובו ציטוט וסיכום הביבליוגרפיה הקודמת הרלוואנטית.

לוח מסכם: מבנה מל"א יב–מל"ב יז

ישראל		יהודה	
הפילוג וירבעם (מל"א יב 1–יד 20)		רחבעם	(יד 21–31)
		אביה	(טו 1–8)
נדב	(טו 25–32)	אסא	(טו 9–24)
בעשא	(טו 33–טז 7)		
אלה	(טז 8–14)		
זמרי	(טז 15–20/22)		
עמרי	(טז 23–28)		
אחאב	(טז 29–כב 40)	יהושפט	(כב 41–51)
אחזיה	(כב 52–מל"ב א 18)		
הסתלקות אליהו (מל"ב ב)			

יהורם מלך ישראל (ג 1–[ט 26]),

יהורם מלך יהודה (ח 16–24), אחזיה מלך יהודה (ח 25–[ט 27])

יהוא	([ט 1]–י 36)	עתליה	(יא 1–20)
יהואחז	(יג 1–9)	יהואש	(יב 1–22)

יהואש מלך ישראל ואמציה מלך יהודה (יג 1–יד 22)

ירבעם	(יד 23–29)	עזריה	(טו 1–7)
זכריה	(טו 8–12)		
שלום	(טו 13–15/16)		
מנחם	(טו 17–22)		
פקחיה	(טו 23–26)		
פקח	(טו 27–31)	יותם	(טו 32–38)
הושע	(יז 1–6)	אחז	(טז 1–20)

נאום הסיכום על חורבן מלכות הצפון (יז 7–41)

כושן רשעתיים – פולמוס סמוי

בוסתנאי עודד

לאחרונה הופיעו מחקרים המבקשים להראות בעליל שספר שופטים הוא חיבור מורכב, המקפל
בתוכו רבדי עריכה וספיחים מאוחרים והטבוע בחותם המגמתיות והסכמאטיות. בספרות זו
המטען האידיאולוגי–דתי והמגמה הפוליטית הם העיקר ולא הכוונה להנציח מאורעות כפי
שקרו באמת.[1] ואכן, מקובל ומוסכם על החוקרים שספר שופטים עבר תהליך ארוך של עריכה
על ידי סופרים שהטביעו את תפיסותיהם, אם בגלוי ואם בסמוי, במסורות קדומות על קורות
שבטי ישראל בתקופה שקדמה למלוכה.[2] כך, לדוגמא, נוספו מידי מחבר/עורך[3] פרטים אחדים
ואף קטעים שלמים המציגים אידיאולוגיה 'פרו יהודאית' ו'אנטי בנימינית'. הוא העמיד את
התוספות, כעין מסגרת לחיבור שמצא לפניו, בראשית הספר ובסופו.[4]

לאור הדברים האמורים, מן הראוי לבחון שוב את הסיפור על כושן רשעתיים, הפותח את
מחזור הסיפורים על השופטים המושיעים, בשופ' ג 7–11. הפרשנים שדנו בסוגיה זו[5] תמימי
דעים שהסיפור כפי שהוא כתוב אינו היסטורי; אלא שהם חלוקים בינהם בשאלה האם לפנינו
סיפור מלאכותי מתחילתו ועד סופו ללא קורטוב של היסטוריה, או שמדובר בעיבוד מגמתי של
פרשה קדומה בדבר זר פולש זר ששיעבד את שבטי ישראל בעידן השופטים.[6] לדידם של הנוקטים

1   M. Brettler, 'The Book of Judges: Literature as Politics', *JBL* 108 (1989), pp. 395-
418. ש' שניצר, 'תעמולה פוליטית בשופטים יט–כא', בית מקרא לה (תש"ן), עמ' 20–31; י' אמית,
'פולמוס סמוי בסיפור כבוש דן (שופטים יז–יח)', בית מקרא לו (תשנ"א), עמ' 267–278.

2   על שחזורים משוערים ורובדי עריכה של מקורות ספר שופטים וזמנם (קדם–דויטרונומיסט,
דויטרונומיסט, או בתר–דויטרונומיסט), ראה הפירושים לספר שופטים, כגון: K. Budde, *Das
Buch der Richter*, Freiburg 1897; W. Beyerlin, 'Gattung und Herkunft des
Rahmens im Richterbuch', in: E. Würthwein & O. Keiser (eds.), *Tradition und
Situation*, Göttingen 1963, pp. 1-29 א' מלמט, ישראל בתקופת המקרא, ירושלים תשמ"ג,
עמ' 81–85 והספרות שם בהערות 1–12; י' אמית, ספר שופטים: אמנות העריכה, ירושלים תשנ"ב,
בעיקר עמ' 66–84; י' זקוביץ ושי' ליונשטאם, 'שופטים, ספר שופטים', אנציקלופדיה מקראית, ז,
טורים 587–598, ושם ספרות.

3   אין הכוונה לסופר מסוים אלא לאסכולה רעיונית שדגלה בבית דוד.

4   על א 1–ב 5 ועל יט–כא, שאינם חלק אינטגראלי של ספר שופטים אלא נספחים מגמתיים משלב
מאוחר, ראה אמית, שופטים (לעיל, הערה 2), המדברת על העורך המספח ועל סטיית עריכה; מ'
וינפלד, מיהושע ועד יאשיהו, תשנ"ב, עמ' 67–70; A.G. Auld, 'Judges I and History: A
Reconstruction', *VT* 25 (1975), pp. 261-285

5   ראה ספרות אצל אמית, שופטים (לעיל, הערה 2), עמ' 152 הערה 56; J.A. Soggin, *Judges*
(OTL), London 1981, p.45

6   ראה סיכום הנימוקים לעמדות השונות אצל: J. Gray, *Joshua, Judges, Ruth*, Grand Rapids:
1967, pp. 197-198; J.D. Martin, *The Book of Judges*, Cambridge 1975, pp. 41-
44; J.M. Miller-J.H. Hayes, *A History of Ancient Israel and Judah*, Philadelphia
1986, pp. 105-106

את העמדה הראשונה הבעיה אינה היסטורית אלא טקסטואלית, ואילו הנוקטים את העמדה
השנייה מבקשים לחשוף את הגרעין ההיסטורי של הסיפור ואת דרכי העיבוד והעריכה של
המסורת על אותו מאורע קדום. אלה גם אלה סבורים, שאין לבקש שליט הנושא את השם
כושן שמלך בארם נהריים, אשר השתלט על ארץ כנען ושיעבד את ישראל שמונה שנים. דמות
כזו אינה ידועה מן ההיסטוריה של מסופוטמיה במאות ה־יב–יא לפנה"ס, לא כל שכן התואר
'רשעתים', שערכו ההיסטורי אינו עולה על אלה של 'ברע' ו'ברשע' בספר בראשית (יד 2),
'אישבשת' בספר שמואל, 'טָבְּאֵל' בישעיהו (ז 6) או 'שקוץ (מ)שומם' בספר דניאל (יא 31; יב
11).[7] לכל היותר משקף התואר את יחסו השלילי של הסופר לאויב זה, והסיומת הזוגית
(רשעתים) באה להדגיש יחס זה. גם 'ארם נהרים' אינו אלא אנאכרוניזם, כשמדובר בתקופת
השופטים.

אלה השוללים את הסיפור מכול וכול רואים בו סיפור מלאכותי, פארודיה ספרותית,
פאראדיגמה או אלגוריה פוליטית מעשה מאוחר, נסמכים על העובדה שאין בסיפור
יסודות קונקרטיים וייחודיים של מאורע שהתרחש באמת (הנסיבות, פרטים על המלחמה
ומהלכה). כאמור, שם הלוחץ העלום ותואריו המוזר אינם נחשבים יסודות כאלה; משך השעבוד
אין בו ממש, והוא מושפע בצורה כלשהי מן המספר שמונה עשרה (שופ' ג 14; י 8) או מן הציון
הכרונולוגי לפיו מלך דוד בחברון שבע וחצי שנים (שמ"ב ה 5);[8] שֵם המושיע לקוח מיהו' טו 17
ומשופ' א 13. כל הפרטים האחרים אינם אלא מארג של נוסחאות טיפוסיות השאולות מן
הפראזיאולוגיה של ספר שופטים בעניין השופטים המושיעים.[9] הסיפור הוא איפוא תוספת
למחרוזת העלילות של השופטים המושיעים, מחרוזת שנפתחה במקורה בפרשת אהוד, שהושיע
את ישראל מידי עגלון מלך מואב (שופ' ג 12 ואילך).[10] המחבר ריכז את כל הנוסחאות של ספר
שופטים כמבוא ללקט הסיפורים על השופטים המושיעים.[11]

לעומת השוללים לגמרי את האפיזודה על כושן כיצירה דמיונית ומגמתית, נמצאו חוקרים
הסבורים שהעורך, אשר היה מעוניין להוסיף שופט מיהודה, עיבד, בעזרת נוסחאות אופייניות
לספר שופטים, מסורת קדומה על מאורע שאכן התרחש בתקופת השופטים. מסורת זו סיפרה
על שליט זר, אשר שיעבד אוכלוסייה ישראלית ששכנה ביהודה ובנגב, ועל אישיות מיהודה
ששחררה את האוכלוסייה מן המשעבד. אף שהמסורת המקורית דיברה בשבט יהודה בלבד, או
אולי בבית האב של הקנזי, הרי במעשה העריכה 'הולאם' המאורע והגיבור הפך למושיע לאומי
ולמנהיג כלל שבטי, בדומה לשאר השופטים המושיעים, שאף דמויותיהם עברו, לדעת רבים,
תהליך של עריכה ספרותית דומה. את הסברות השונות ביחס לרקע ההיסטורי של הפרשה
ולזהותו של המשעבד ניתן למיין לשתי קבוצות, על פי אזור מוצאו המשוער של האויב.
המסתמכים על השם 'ארם נהרים' מבקשים אויב שבא מצפון, ואילו הפרשנים הרואים את

7 על תופעה זו ראה: ,W.H. Shea, 'Mutilation of Foreign Names by Biblical Writers'
‏Andrews University Seminary Studies 23 (1985), pp. 111-115. לגבי שלשת הכינויים
האחרונים, מדובר בשיבוש מכוון של השמות המקוריים.

8 באותו פרק זמן מלך אשבעל בן שאול על ישראל. הציון 'ושתים שנים מלך' בשמ"ב ב 10 הוא שיבוש
(אולי מכוון) משמ"א יג 1.

9 אמית (לעיל, הערה 2), עמ' 148–151; י' זקוביץ, 'העקרון האסוציאטיבי בסידור ספר שופטים
ושימושו כמכשיר לאבחנת שלבים בגיבוש הסֵפר', בתוך ספר יצחק אריה זליגמן (עורכים י' זקוביץ
וא' רופא), ירושלים תשמ"ג, עמ' 176.

10 E. Täubler, 'Cushan Rishataim', HUCA 20 (1947), pp. 138-142. לדעתו, פרשת כושן
רשעתיים אינה אלא פיקציה. ריכטר מתחיל את ניתוח ספר שופטים בפרשת אהוד, ג 13; ראה .W
‏Richter, Die Bearbeitungen des 'Retterbuches' in der Deuteronomischen Epoch,
Bonn 1964, p. 3

11 אמית (לעיל, הערה 2), עמ' 148–151; A.D.H. Mayes, Judges, Sheffield 1985, p. 27.

המושיע עתניאל כעיקר מחפשים את האויב בדרום, בהניחם ש'ארם' עשוי להיות שיבוש מ'אדם' (השווה שמ"ב ח 12; מל"א יא 25; מל"ב טז 6; יח' טז 57; דה"ב כ 2).[12]

אכן, לנו נראה שפרשתנו היא סיפור מלאכותי, שגרעינו מאורע היסטורי כלשהו מעצם ימי השופטים, ושהמחבר השתמש במסורת קדומה, וכנראה גם עמומה, על מאורע זה כחומר ביד היוצר כדי ליצור סיפור מגמתי, הנשען על הפראזיאולוגיה של ספר שופטים.

הדעה שהסיפור כנתינתו הוא מגמתי ואינו משקף מאורע היסטורי נסמכת על השיקול הבא:
(א) הסיפור מורכב ממאגר של נוסחאות ללא יסודות של אירועים ונתונים מיוחדים. המלים 'רשעתיים', 'נהרים' אינם שאובות ממציאות היסטורית אלא משוכות מעטו של הסופר. מכאן שמדובר בתוספת ולא בחלק אינטגראלי של מחזור הסיפורים על השופטים המושיעים. (ב) דרכה של תוספת שאינה באה לשמה אלא לשרת מגמה.[13] לפיכך, הסיפור הנדון, שהוא תוספת, טעון מגמה מסוימת. (ג) מצויים בספר שופטים סיפורים אחרים, שזוהתה בהם מגמה גלויה או סמויה מלבד המגמה הכללית הפראגמאטית של הספר. בחלק מסיפורים אלה (כמו הסיפור על פילגש בגבעה) נושא הפולמוס הוא האיבה בין יהודה לבנימין (ושבטי הצפון). בספרי יהושע, שופטים ושמואל ובמזמורי תהילים נושא הפולמוס, כולל הצדקת הבחירה בבית דוד, מובע בגלוי ובסמוי.[14] לפיכך סביר לבקש את המגמה של הסיפור הנדון בתחום הפולמוס ההוא.

את המגמה הסמויה של פרשת כושן רשעתיים ניתן להוציא לאור בעזרת הבחנות שנעשו לגבי הפרק הראשון של ספר שופטים ועל פי הפרשה האחרונה בו. חוקרים רבים כבר עמדו על כך שבספר שופטים פרקים א, יט–כא ניכרות שתי מגמות: (א) לפאר את שבט יהודה (ב) להכתים את בנימין ואת בית שאול.[15] לפיכך מן הראוי לברר האם המגמות ה'פרו-יהודאית/דודית' וה'אנטי–בנימינית/שאולית'[16] קיימות גם בסיפורנו. זאת ננסה לעשות בעזרת 'סימנים',[17] רמיזות ושיקולים שונים.

---

12 על ההצעות השונות לזיהוי כושן רשעתיים ולקביעת זמנו, ראה: א' מלמט, 'כושן רשעתיים והרקע ההיסטורי של זמנו', ארץ ישראל ג, תשי"ד, עמ' 85–91, ושם ספרות. מלמט מציע לזהות עם ירסו מארץ חארו, הנזכר בתעודה מצרית (פאפירוס האריס א). לעומתו קורא H. Goedicke את השם Sw וקושר אותו (כשם מקוצר) עם שאול: 'This Sw is the historical prototype of Saul of the Israelite monarchy', H. Goedicke, WZKM 71 (1971), pp. 1-17. על התעודה ראה גם: דוסין הציע לראות M. Liverani, Prestige and Interest, Padova 1990, pp. 137-138 ב'כושן' שיבוש מכוון מן השם גוזן, ואת 'רשעתים' הוא גזר בדרך מדרשית מ־KUŠ=mašku=עור, הקרוב בצלילו ל־masku=רע, רשעי. ראה: G. Dossin, 'Kushan Rishʿatayim, roi de l'Aram Naharayim', in: Zikir Šumim (F.R. Kraus Vol.), 1982, pp. 9-11: על קשירת הפרשה עם אדום ראה: J.R. Bartlett, Edom and the Edomites, Sheffield 1989, pp. 93-94.

13 אמית (לעיל, הערה 2), עמ' 152–154 מדברת על הסיפור כמוקד של עריכה ועל 'שיקולים בלבדיים של עריכה'. אך נראה שהמגמה הפרו–יהודאית נותנת לתת את הבכורה ליהודה. קביעת הסיפור בראש מחזור הסיפורים על השופטים מטרתה לתת את הבכורה ליהודה; וראה בהמשך. דוגמאות נוספות לחיבורים שנכתבו במגמה פרו–יהודאית מביא נ' נאמן, מנוחדות למלוכה, ירושלים 1990, עמ' 336, הערה 232.

14 חאת 'עילת הפולמוס', כהגדרתה של אמית. על המשכיות של הפולמוס ושל המסורות הקדומות הקשורות בבית שאול, ראה: ש' אברמסקי, 'שיבה למלכות שאול במגילת אסתר ובדברי הימים', מלאה א (תשמ"ג), עמ' 39–63. בפרקים יז–יח מצוי פולמוס בענייני מקדש דן.

15 ראה: ברטלר (לעיל, הערה 1), עמ' 401–402, 411–412 ויינפלד (לעיל, הערה 2), עמ' 61–71, 83–84; אמית (לעיל, הערה 2), עמ' 315–324; הנ"ל, 'פרשת פילגש בגבעה כפולמוס סמוי נגד מלכות שאול ואוהדיה (שופטים יט–כ)', בית מקרא לז (תשנ"ב), עמ' 109–118, ושם ספרות; שניצר (לעיל, הערה 1), ושם ספרות.

16 כבר חז"ל וכן רש"י קשרו בקשר כרונולוגי את כושן רשעתיים עם מעשה פילגש בגבעה. ראה זקוביץ (לעיל, הערה 9), עמ' 171, וראה גם להלן (הערה 21), בעניין 'כוש בן ימיני' (תה' ז 1).

17 ראה: אמית (לעיל, הערה 15), עמ' 110–114. מדובר בסימנים, ברמיזות ובשיקולים שונים, שכולם ביחד מהווים משקל שיש להתחשב בו.

א. הסיפור נוסף למחרוזת עלילותיהם של השופטים המושיעים במגמה ברורה להעמיד שופט גם משבט יהודה.[18] כשם שהציב העורך את שבט יהודה בראש הספר כמי שעלה בתחילה להלחם בכנעני במצוות האל (שופ' א 1–20), כך העמיד כראשון בין השופטים המושיעים את עתניאל מיהודה דווקא, במקום את אהוד משבט בנימין, שעמד במקום זה קודם לכן. עתניאל בן קנז, המתייחס על שבט יהודה, הוא אותו איש הנזכר ביהו' טו 17 ובשופ' א 13.

ב. בתואר הגנאי 'רשעתים' עולה הד לנאמר על שאול 'ובכל אשר יפנה ירשיע' (שמ"א יד 47). בשני המקרים עשה המחבר שימוש קאקופוני במלים מקוריות, אם אכן היו מלים כאלו לפניו.[19] את עתניאל בן קנז, לעומת זאת, מצא המחבר לנכון לציין כ'אחי כלב הקטן ממני' (פסוק 9). שתי המלים האחרונות אינן ביהו' טו 17, ואפשר שכוונו לרמוז לנאמר על דוד, יריבו המובהק של שאול, בשמ"א יז 14: 'ודוד הוא הקטן' (ואילו אליאב הוא 'אחיו הגדול', פסוק 28; והשווה ל'אחי כלב' ביהו' טו 17, שופ' א 13).

ג. 'כושן' מזכיר את 'קיש' אבי שאול.[20] מובן שהקשר אינו אטימולוגי או סמאנטי, אלא פונולוגי אסוציאטיבי. רמז לקשר כזה וראיה מסייעת לכך שנעשה שימוש מקראי בדמיון הצליל קיש/ כוש/כושן מצויים, ככל הנראה, בתה' ז 1, 'כוש בן ימיני' (והשווה 'קיש איש ימיני', אס' ב 5). במזמור זה, המיוחס לדוד, מופיעים כמה ביטויים — 'רשעים', 'מושיע' וכן הקריאה 'שפטני ה' כצדקי' (ז 9–11) — המקבילים אל דברי דוד הנרדף לשאול הרודף, 'והיה ה' לדין ושפט ביני וביניך' וגו' (שמ"א כד 16). מבחינת התוכן עשוי אפוא המזמור להתאים לפרשת היחסים שבין דוד לשאול. פרשנות זו משתקפת, מכל מקום, בתרגום הארמי לביטוי 'על דברי כוש בן ימיני' שבכותרת המזמור: 'על תבירא דשאול בר קיש דמן שבט בנימין'.[21]

ד. 'שאול מרחובות הנהר' ברשימת מלכי אדום (בר' לו 37). כאמור, פרשנים רבים סבורים ש'ארם' בפרשת כושן רשעתים הוא שיבוש מ'אדם', וכי המאורע ההיסטורי שביסוד הפרשה קשור בפלישה אל יהודה מכיוון אדום (ראה להלן). אם אכן 'אדם' היא הגרסה המקורית, אזי נראה לנו שאין כאן טעות סופרים גרידא (אדם–ארם) אלא שינוי מכוון, במסגרת הפולמוס הסמוי של הסוגיה כולה. '(ה)נהר' סתם הוא נהר פרת (השווה בר' לא 21; שמ' כג 31; במ' כב 5; מל"א ח 1; שם, יד 15; יר' ב 18; והשווה עם בר' טו 18).[22] כך הוא נזכר (על פי הכתיב) ביחס לדוד שהגיע עד נהר פרת לאחר שהכה את ארם.[23] השינוי 'ארם' במקום 'אדם' עשוי, אם כן, להיות רמז נוסף לדוד שהכה את ארם; ואילו הוספת התיבה 'נהרים' אפשר שכוונה לשאול מרחובות הנהר (וראה גם להלן)[24] ולא רק לחריזה עם 'רשעתים'.

ה. אין זה מקרה שמחבר המעשייה השתמש במאורע קדום הקשור לאדום כדי להקים שופט מיהודה. שכן אדום, הסמוכה ליהודה, היא מלכות הרשעה (השווה מל' א 4) השנואה על אנשי

18 סוג'ין (לעיל, הערה 5), עמ' 47, ושם ספרות; G. Wallis, *Geschichte und Überlieferung*, Berlin 1968, pp. 13-14; 38-39; מאייס (לעיל, הערה 11), עמ' 27–28. לדעת אמית (לעיל, הערה 2), עמ' 345, עיצוב פרשת עתניאל מעיד על עריכה יהודאית בעלת מגמות בדלניות.

19 הפרשנים נוטים להניח שבמקור היה כתוב 'יושיע' והמחבר/עורך שיבש את המילה ל'ירשיע'.

20 לעניין 'קיש' ו'איש ימיני', ראה: ש' אברמסקי, (לעיל, הערה 14), עמ' 39–42.

21 ראה: י' ליוור, ערך 'כוש', אנציקלופדיה מקראית, ד, טורים 64–65. והשווה גם 'מיכל בת כושי היתה' (עירובין צר, ע"א), ופירושו של רש"י המסתמך על המזמור הנ"ל.

22 י' אפעל וי' נוה, 'כתובות השלל של חז"אל', שנתון למקרא ולחקר המזרח הקדום, י (תש"ן), עמ' 41–42.

23 שמ"ב ח 3–13; י, 6; ו'ארם נהרים' בתה' ס 2; דה"א יט 6.

24 השווה גם אמית (לעיל, הערה 2), עמ' 153. לדעת עתניאל הוא 'בבחינת רמיזה לדוד, שעתיד לשלוט על שטחים סמוכים לארם נהרים'. על הזיקה הספרותית בין שאול המלך ל'שאול מרחובות הנהר', ראה: A.M. Honeyman, 'The Evidence for Regnal Names Among the Hebrews', *JBL* 67 (1948), pp. 13-25

יהודה,[25] בדומה לשנאה שרחשו חוגים ביהודה לבנימין, המשתקפת בסיפור על הפילגש בגבעה.
אפשר אפוא שהמחבר בחר באויב אדומי כפולמוס סמוי נגד בנימין ושאול וכהשלמה למגמתו
הפרו–יהודאית. השינוי המאוחר והמכוון מ'אדם' ל'ארם נהרים' נגרר מן האמור לעיל (ד). מלבד
זאת, ארם מייצג אויב לא פחות טיפוסי לישראל מאשר אדום, ומלך (מלך ארם–דמשק),
שעוצמתו עולה על זו של מלכי המדינות הקטנות השכנות לישראל,[26] שעמם התמודדו
השופטים משבטי ישראל האחרים. בכך ביקש המחבר לומר שהשופט מיהודה היכה את האויב
החזק ביותר.

ו. המחבר נתלה באדום וברשימת מלכי אדום גם מכיוון שברשימה יש רמיזה לשאול. הרשימה
פותחת במשפט 'ואלה המלכים אשר מלכו בארץ אדום לפני מלך מלך לבני ישראל' (בר' לו 31).
לפי פשוטו מכוון הפסוק לשאול, הוא המלך הראשון על ישראל. הקשר האסוציאטיבי בין שאול
לאדומים על רקע המאבק בין שאול לדוד מתחזק לאור המסורת על דואג האדומי, אביר הרועים
אשר לשאול, שהרג את כוהני נב.

אכן, הפולמוס בדבר בנימין ושאול הוא סמוי למדי, זאת בניגוד למצב בפרק א בשופטים או
בפרשת הפילגש בגבעה. הטעם לכך הוא שיצירת פרשת כושן רשעתיים מגמתה היתה בראש
ובראשונה פרו–יהודאית/דוידית, דהיינו, העמדת שופט מיהודה בראש רשימת השופטים, כשם
שפרק א הוא פיצוי על נחיתות יהודה במחזור הסיפורים על השופטים המושיעים. המגמה
האנטי–בנימינית היא תוצר לוואי, משלים ומשני למגמה העיקרית, והיא באה לידי ביטוי
בעצם הקדמתו של הסיפור על עתניאל מיהודה לעלילה המדברת באהוד מבנימין.

לסיכום, נראה לנו לצדד בהשערה שבסיפור על כושן רשעתיים חבוי זיכרון מעורפל של מאורע
היסטורי, שעניינו פלישה מכיוון אדום והערבה אל דרום יהודה שהתרחשה בתקופת
השופטים.[27] מנקודת ראות זו עדיף לגרוס 'אדם', הסמוכה ליהודה, על 'ארם נהרים' הרחוקה.
המחבר הפרו–יהודאי שרצה להעמיד שופט מיהודה בראש על כל ישראל, עשה שימוש בפרטים
עתיקים ועמומים גם לצורך פולמוס סמוי נגד בנימין ובית שאול.[28] דבר זה עולה בקנה אחד עם
המגמה הכפולה, כפי שציינו בראשית דברינו. גם המסורת על מלכי אדום (בר' לו) שימשה מאחז
הולם למגמתו הכפולה של המחבר. אמנם העתקת הרקע הגאוגרפי מאדום לארם נהרים אינה

25   הבסיס ההיסטורי לכך הוא פלישות אדומיים של יסודות אדומיים ששכנו סמוך לנגב הצפוני ולהר יהודה. אין
זה מן הנמנע שהערבה נחשבה על ארץ אדום, או לפחות כנתונה לשליטת אדום, לפני מלוך מלך
בישראל. ראה: N. Na'aman, Tel Aviv 19 (1992), pp. 71-93; והשווה לעניין זה י'
פינקלשטיין, 'אדום בתקופת הברזל א', ארץ ישראל כג (ספר בירן), תשנ"ב, עמ' 224-229. כמובן
שלאור חיזוק האחיזה המצרית בחבל הדרומי של כנען בימי הפרעונים מן השושלות הי"ט-כ, אפשר
לראות באחד ממלכי מצרים את הדמות המסתתרת מאחורי 'כושן רשעתים', שכן כוש הוא גם כינוי
למצרים. לדעת נאמן, ביסוס האחיזה המצרית בעת ההיא נועד 'בראש ובראשונה לרסן את כוחן
הגובר של קבוצות הנוודים והמתנחלים ולהגביר את הפיקוח עליהם'; ראה נאמן, 'הסטוריה מדינית
של ארץ ישראל בימי השושלות הי"ט-כ' ', בתוך ההסטוריה של ארץ ישראל (י' אפעל, עורך), א:
התקופות הקדומות, ירושלים תשמ"ב, עמ' 250.

26   ראה ברטלר (לעיל, הערה 1), עמ' 404-405 על השינוי מ'אדם' ל'ארם'. לדעת טויבלר (לעיל,
הערה 10), במקור היה מדובר על כושן–מדין, וסופר מאוחר שינה לכוש–בבל. לדעתי, הסיפור על
כושן רשעתיים משקף איבה לאדום ולבבל בתקופת הגלות ולאחריה.

27   הפעולות העוינות בין בני אדום ליהודה, שראשיתן בתקופת ההתנחלות והשופטים (השווה תה' פג 7),
נמשכו גם בימי דוד ולאחר מכן. ראה נאמן (לעיל, הערה 25), עמ' 75-79. באופן דומה, מוצאים
פרשנים עיבוד מאוחר (דויטרונומיסטי בעיקר) של חומר קדום גם בפרשיות אחרות שבספר שופטים:
כגון: בסיפורים על אהוד, יפתח, בסיפור פילגש בגבעה ואף בשירת דבורה. ראה מלמט (לעיל, הערה
2), עמ' 125-127; A. Caquot, Semitica 18 (1986), pp. 47-70

28   אם בכל זאת מדובר במושל סורי צפוני או מיסופוטאמי ששיעבד את ישראל, אזי נראה שהמשתעבד
עשה שימוש בשם Sw כפולמוס נגד שאול ובנימין. ראה גדיקה (לעיל, הערה 12).

תואמת למציאות ההיסטורית, אבל נמצאה יפה ומתאימה למלא את הפונקציות המרכזיות שלשמן נוצר הסיפור.

נמצא שמבחינה היסטורית אין ערך של ממש לסיפור על כושן רשעתיים. הסיפור מבוסס על זיכרון היסטורי בדבר מאורע קדום, שטיבו המדויק אינו נהיר ואינו ניתן לשחזור. מבחינה היסטוריוגרפית לפנינו חיבור הבנוי על אוסף נוסחאות האופייניות לספר שופטים והמיוסד, כל הנראה, על מסורת קדומה בדבר פלישה של בני אדום אל הר יהודה. כן נעשה כאן שימוש במסורת על מלכי אדום שמלכו לפני מלוך מלך בישראל. מבחינה אידיאולוגית מדובר בהאדרת שבט יהודה ובית דוד הגובלת בפולמוס עם שוחרי בנימין ובית שאול. תיארוך הפרשה קשור בבעיות הסבוכות של תיארוך פרק א' בספר שופטים, סיפור הפילגש בגבעה והעריכה האחרונה של ספר שופטים. אם אכן פולמוס סמוי יש כאן, הרי פרק הזמן שבו נתחברה הפרשה הוא בין ימי דוד לחורבן שומרון (722 לפסה"נ).[29] פרק זמן חלופי הוא התקופה הפרסית, אם אכן ייחוסו של מרדכי היהודי דווקא ל'קיש איש ימיני' הוא הד למתיחות בין אנשי יהודה לאלה שהתייחסו על בנימין.[30]

אכן 'כושן רשעתיים' לא נברא, והמעשה של הכאת 'ארם נהרים' על ידי איש מדרום יהודה לא היה, אלא הכל משל היה.

29 ראה אמית (לעיל, הערה 2), עמ' 339–340. לדעתה, ספר שופטים קדם לספרות המשנה תורתית.
30 בדבר אידיאולוגיה פרו–שאולית שנמשכה גם בתקופה שלאחר הגלות, ראה: ברטלר, שופטים, (לעיל, הערה 1), עמ' 415–414; אמית (לעיל, הערה 15), עמ' 117, ושם ספרות בהערה 23. על ריהביליטציה של מלכות שאול והאדרת משפחת קיש וברמזים בתקופת פרס, כפי שהדבר בא לידי ביטוי במגילת אסתר, ראה אברמסקי (לעיל, הערה 14), עמ' 55–61.

השלמות לכתבי יד מגניזת קאהיר

מיכאל קליין

אוספי הגניזה
'עניים במקום אחד
ועשירים במקום אחר'

תולדות גניזת קאהיר ידועות לכל בר בי רב, ובהן בייחוד סיפור חלוקתם של כתבי היד בין
אספנים שונים במחצית השנייה של המאה ה-י"ט, וגלגולם לספריות הגדולות ברחבי אירופה
וארה"ב. טלטולים אלה היו מקריים ושרירותיים, וכך אירע לא פעם שכתב יד פוצל לשניים
שלושה חלקים או יותר, כאשר קבוצות של דפים מוצאות דרכן לספריות שונות במקומות
שונים בעולם. קורותיו של כתב יד E של התרגום הארצישראלי לתורה הן דוגמה בולטת
לתופעה הנפוצה הזאת: שרידיו פזורים כיום בארבע ספריות על פני שתי יבשות –
בקיימברידג' ובאוקספורד שבאנגליה, בסנט פטרסבורג שברוסיה ובניו יורק שבארה"ב.

מקרה אופייני זה מאלף במיוחד מבחינת השלכותיו על גילוים מחדש ופרסומם של כתבי היד
מגניזת קאהיר, שכן כתב יד E פורסם בהמשכים על ידי שלושה חוקרים שונים במשך כשישים
שנה. בשנת 1930 פירסם פאול קאלה שנים עשר דפים ממנו, מתוך אוספי קיימברידג', אוקספורד
ולנינגרד;[1] עשרים וחמש שנה לאחר מכן הוציא לאור אלחנדרו דיאז מאצ'ו ארבעה דפים
נוספים מספריית בית המדרש לרבנים בניו יורק;[2] ואילו בבחינת ליקוטי בתר ליקוטי גיליתי
אנוכי שני דפים נוספים של אותו כתב יד בסדרה הנוספת (Additional Series) בקיימברידג',
אותם פרסמתי בשנת 1989.[3]

מתברר, שככל שהופכים בהם, מוסיפים אוספי הגניזה לגלות את אוצרותיהם הבלומים. במאמר
זה אבקש לפרסם השלמות לשלושה כתבי יד המוכרים לנו מתוך קטעים שפורסמו זה מכבר. מכל
השלושה זוהו לאחרונה קטעים נוספים, המאפשרים להשלים את הטקסט, אם במלואו ואם
בחלקים נוספים.

P. Kahle, *Masoreten des Westens*, II, Stuttgart 1930 [Hildesheim 1967], pp. 29-48   1

A. Diez Macho, 'Nuevos Fragmentos del Targum Palestinense', *Sefarad* 15 (1955), pp. 31-39   2

M.L. Klein, 'New Fragments of Palestinian Targum from the Cairo Genizah', *Sefarad* 49 (1989), pp. 123-133   3

א

במאמרו 'ראש ראשי חדשים', שהופיע לפני כעשרים וחמש שנה, פרסם עזרא פליישר קטע
משיר ארמי קדום על פי כתב יד מגניזת קאהיר, הנמצא כיום באוסף הגניזה של אוניברסיטת
קיימברידג' (C.U.L. T-S H12.11).[4] מאז זכה הקטע להתפרסם פעמיים נוספות, על ידי יוסף
היינימן[5] ועל ידי הכותב הנוכחי.[6]

מדובר בשיר 'אליסון', מה משבח הדין ירחא', המשבח את חודש ניסן 'דביה איתפרקו אבהן
ובנין'. ייתכן ששיר זה נועד לפתיחתא לקריאת התורה בשבת פרשת החודש לפי מנהג ארץ
ישראל, שכן פרשה זו מתחילה במלים 'החודש הזה לכם ראש חדשים' (שמות יב 2). השיר הוא
אקרוסטי, והכיל אפוא לפחות עשרים ושתיים שורות, כמספרן של אותיות האלפבית. בזמנו
הצטערנו על שלא נשתמרו אלא שלוש השורות הראשונות (אותיות אל"ף, בי"ת וגימ"ל).

לאחרונה סקרתי את אוספי קיימברידג' לשם הכנת קטאלוג של כתבי היד התרגומיים
שביניהם.[7] במהלך הסקירה נתגלו יצירות חדשות שהיו בלתי ידועות עד כה ואף קטעים
משלימים ליצירות ידועות. בין אלה האחרונים נמצא דף נייר שחום, המכיל עותק שני של
השיר הנזכר 'אליסון' וכו', אמנם מקוטע אף הוא. להלן תיאורו ונוסחו המלא של כתב היד:

C.U.L. T-S AS 116.453

דף נייר אחד שמידותיו 13.7x6.6 ס"מ, ארבע עשרה עד שש עשרה שורות לעמוד. קרוע ושחוק
במקצת. הכתיב מזרחי מרובע עם ניקוד טברני חלקי. רווח כפול או משולש לפני כל אות
שבאלפבית. כתב היד מכיל כותרת.

recto (לוח 1)

1. יקאל? לילה ראש חדש ניסן
2. ///אל אלקדוש?
3. [אליסון] מה משבח הדין   [א]
4. [ירחא] דביה אתפרקו אבהן
5. [ובנין ב]פלגיה דלילי [את]   [ב]
6. את[גלי] קיריס וימינ[ה]
7. פש[י]ט[א] על ישראל
8. גיבריהון דמצראי לחוד   [ג]
9. [רב]ריביהון נפקו מיללין ב[] ל
10. [ו]עיילין   דנין לפרעה טרוד   [ד]
11. עמא הדין דלא יתאחרון
12. וה[ון] כולם מיתין   הא   [ה]
13. בכ[ורינ]ן כולהון קטילין

4   ע' פליישר, 'ראש ראשי חדשים', תרביץ לז (תשכ"ח), עמ' 265–278; השיר מופיע שם בעמ' 272.

5   י' היינימן, 'שרידים מיצירתם הפיוטית של המתורגמנים הקדומים', הספרות ד (תשל"ג), עמ' 362–
375, ובעיקר עמ' 356.

6   M.L. Klein, *Genizah Manuscripts of Palestinian Targum to the Pentateuch*,
Cincinnati 1986, I, pp. 191f.; II, plate 172

7   M.L. Klein, *Targumic Manuscripts in the Cambridge Genizah Collections*,
Cambridge 1992

14. ואין [ית]עכבון אנן מתקטלין

15. ופרעה [קם] וקרא למשה   [ו]

16.   ולאהרן

verso (לוח 2)

1. קומו פוקו לכון [מגו עמי]

2. זיווהון דישראל [[[ז]

3. [וחינא וחסדא הוא ש]

4. חייהון דמצראי [אתעבדו]   [ח]

5. לשמא חולף די שע[בידו ית]

6. עמא בחירא   ט[עינו] כל   [ט]

7. דאית להון על עננ[ין] ושאלין

8. [כ]ל דאיתרעון חולף בגדיהון

9. יומא הוה מתח שעו[הי] ח[ד]   [י]

10. בכפלא: עד די ישאלון כל

11. צרכיהון   כל אצוותהון   [כ]

12. טענון בשושפיהון [[

13. גיף ימא עבדו פק[   ]ין

14. לא[   ]   חמא [[ל]

לשם השוואה, הנה שלוש השורות שנשתמרו בכתב יד קיימברידג׳ C.U.L. T-S H12.11:

1. אליסון מה משבח הדין ירחא דביה איתפרקו אבהן ובנין:

2. בפלגות ליליא איתגלי קיריס וימניה פשוטה על ישראל:

3. גיברי דמצראי איתעבדו לשמא חולף דשעבידו ית עמא

הדמיון הרב בין שתי הגרסאות מצביע על כך שאכן מדובר באותה יצירה. ואם נתגלה שוני
מהותי לכאורה בשורות של האות גימ״ל, הרי מדובר בהעתקת קטע ממקום למקום בלבד. החסר
בכתב היד החדש באות גימ״ל נמצא בו באות חי״ת: [אתעבדו] לשמא חולף די שע[בידו ית]
עמא בחירא׳. דומה, כי מדובר בטעות סופר בשל מלה מובילה זהה ׳דמצראי׳, היינו עקב שווי
ההתחלה (ex homoio archon).

תרגום

C.U.L. T-S AS 116.453

recto [הושענא] כמה משובח [החודש] הזה אשר בו נגאלו אבות [ובנים]

[ב]חצות הלילה נת[גלה] האדון וימינ[ו] נטויה על ישראל

גיבוריהם של המצרים ואף [ש]ריהם יצאו מייללים ב[קו]ל וצורחים(?)

דרשו מפרעה גרש את העם הזה שלא יתמהמהו ויהיו כולם מתים

הנה בכ[ורינו] כולם מתים ואם [ית]עכבו [גם] אנחנו נמות

ופרעה [קם] וקרא למשה ולאהרן verso קומו צאו לכם [מתוך עמי]

זיום של ישראל [   ]   וחן וחסד הוא [[

חייהם של המצרים [נעשו] לשמה מפני ששיע[בדו את] העם הנבחר

ט[ענו] כל אשר להם על עננ[ים](?) ושאלו [כ]ל אשר רצו בתמורה(?) לבגדיהם

היום משך את שעותיו פי שניים עד אשר שאלו כל צורכיהם

[שפת הים עשו]   [כל משארותם נשאו בשמלותם]
[   ] לא

ב

לפני כשלושים וחמש שנה פרסם פייר גרלו (Grelot) קטע ליטורגי מאוסף הגניזה שבספריית
קיימברידג' (C.U.L. T-S B8.9), שהכיל תפילת 'סליחה' לראש השנה ותרגום ארצישראלי
מורחב – מעין תוספתא תרגומית – לבראשית כב, המשמש, כידוע, קריאת התורה לראש
השנה.[8] והנה לאחרונה נתגלו שלושה קטעים נוספים של אותו כתב יד, שניים בסדרה החדשה
בקיימברידג' (C.U.L. T-S NS 271.183; C.U.L. T-S NS 138.79) והשלישי בספריית
בית המדרש לרבנים בניו יורק (J.T.S. NS ENA 42.27). ראוי לציין שהקטע שפורסם על
ידי גרלו הינו המשך ישיר של הקטע שנתגלה עכשיו בניו יורק: '...ואמר לתרין עולימוהי...'.

להלן תיאורו ונוסחו המלא של כתב היד: חמישה דפי נייר, שניים מהם מחוברים יחדיו (T-S
B8.9). מידותיהם 16.5 x 12.6 ס"מ בממוצע, אחת עשרה עד שלוש עשרה שורות לעמוד. דף
אחד קרוע ושחוק במקצת. כתיב מזרחי רהוט למחצה עם ניקוד טברני חלקי.

J.T.S. NS ENA 42.27

recto (לוח 3)

לית]	1. ש[י]ר]
[	2. אלה בר מ[נ]ך]
[	3. קודמוהי ארבעה]
ך]	4. שלם נטרתא ליה ק]
	5. גזרתא עמיה תל[תא גזיר]ין(?)
ניסיו[נין ובכל]הון	6. ניסיתיה בעש[רה] ניסיו[
	7. אישתכח מהימן ובסוף [ע]שרה
	8. ניסיו[נין] אמרת ליה סב ית ב[ר]ך
]לטור	9. ית יחידך לאת[ר]
	10. פולחאנא לא סר[ב] למימרך
	11. ולא עבר על פיתגמ[ך]

verso (לוח 4)

[לס[בא] סיב	1.]
אישתא ו[סכינא ושוי	2.]
[ית אעיא] על כתף בריה וצלח	3.]
[ת דעתא ואזלו [ת]	4.]
	5. ת[ריהון כ]חדא בשלימותא
	6. ואתו לא[תר]א דאמרת להון
	7. ואחזתיה ענן יקרך כד בעא

8   P. Grelot, 'Une Tosephta targoumique sur Genèse XXII dans un manuscrit
liturgique de la Geniza du Caire', *REJ* N.S. 16 (1957), pp. 5-27. הטכסט פורסם שוב:
קליין (לעיל, הערה 6), א, עמ' 34–35; ב, לוח 106.

8. למיזל ול[א] ידע [בהי]דין [א]

9. אתרא [ ] עד ד]חמא ליה ענן

10. [י]קרך ב[ ] ואמר לתרין

C.U.L. T-S B8.9, folio 1

recto

1. עולימוהי חמן אתון מידעם

2. בעלמא ואמרו ליה לית אנן

3. חמן מדעם בעלמא מתיב

4. ואמר ליצחק בריה את חמי

5. מדעם אמר ליה הא אנא חמי

6. עמ'דא דעננא מרקיעא

7. לארעא בההיא שעתא ידע

8. סבא דיצחק אתבחר לעלתא

9. מתיב ואמר לעולימוהי עמא

10. דמתילין בחמרא אוריכו לכון

11. הכא עם [ע] חמרא **שבו לכם** וג'   (בר' כב 5)

12. נסיב אעיא ושוי על יצחק בריה

verso

1. ואישתא וסכינא נסיב הוא

2. בידיה ואזלו [תריה] תרויהון

3. כחדא מאן דמטו לאתרא [מ]

4. משאיל יצחק לאבוהי במטו

5. מינך אבא הא אישתא ואעיא

6. ואן אימרא לעלתא מתיב

7. עקדא ואמר לעקדא קודם י'י

8. גלי אימרא לעלתא ברי לא אבא

9. עכיב והרהר ולא ברא סריב

10. עליה תרויהון בליבא שלמא

11. ובדעתא שלמתא למעבד

12. רעותך מרי עלמא ובנא

13. מדבחא בחדותא ברא

C.U.L. T-S NS 138.79

recto (לוח 5)

1. [ ] [תא רתיתא? ובע] [תא]

2. [אתבעית מן קודמך רבון

3. עלמא' בה שעתא כד חזו מלאכי

4. מרומא דיצחק על גבי מדבחא

5. ואבוהי שליף סכיניה למיכס יתיה

6. קטרו מספדא ואבלא ובכיא והכין

7. אמרו קדמך אלה שמיא אם

8. יצחק מתנכיס ואזיל מן יימר
9. קדמך עזי וזמרת יה אם יצחק   (שמ' טו 2)
10. מתנכיס ואזיל מן יימר י"י איש
11. מלחמה אם יצחק מתנכיס   (שמ' טו 3)
12. ואזיל מן יימר קדמך מי כמוכה
13. באלים י"י אם יצחק מתנכיס   (שמ' טו 11)

verso (לוח 6)

1. מן יי[מר] קודמך י"י י[מל]וך   (שמ' טו 18)
2. והכין מפרש בכ[ת]בך הן אר[אלם]
3. צעקו חוצה מלאכי שלום מר
4. יבכיון' בה שעתא שלחתא   (יש' לג 7)
5. ליה מלאכא מן שמיא ואמרת
6. ליה אברהם אב' וכן כתיב ויקרא
7. אליו מלאך י"י מן השמים וג' תר[י]ן
8. זמנין קראתה יתיה לא תושט
9. ידך בעולימא כמה דכת' אל
10. תשלח ידך אל הנער ואחיתתה
11. עליה טלא מן שמיא וחיית
12. רוחיה ואיתקיימת נשמתיה
13. ואמר קודמך תושבחתא

C.U.L. T-S NS 271.183

recto (לוח 7)

1. ברוך מחיה המתים' אשתבעתא
2. ליה שבועתא דלעלם דלית את
3. משני במימרך ולית את מבטל
4. שבועתך ' כמה דכת' ויאמר בי
5. נשבעתי נא' י"י וג' אמרת ליה לסבא
6. רחימך דאנא מברך על זרעיה
7. לעלם ומדכר [א] עקידה לעלם כמה
8. דכת' כי ברך אברכך וג' אחזיתא
9. ליה דיכרא לעלתא דאיתברי מן
10. שיתת ימי בראשית וקריב יתיה
11. חולף יחידיה וצלי ואמר קדמך
12. הכא יהון פלחין דריא וקבע[ת] עקידת
13. יצחק דוכרנא לעלם ואמרת

verso (לוח 8)

1. להון לעקדא ועקודא כד בניכון
2. קיימין בעקתא ידכרון קדמאי
3. עקידותא ואנא מרחם עליהון'
4. רח'[מנא] אידכר לן עקידת יצחק ורחם
5. עלן ונתחשב קדמך כקורבנא
6. דעלתא רח' אי[ס]תכל בעקידותיה

7.   ור^חם עלן דהא אנן בעקתא רבתא
8.   רח' ולא יבטל סיברן מינך ולא
9.   תיחוד תרעך באנפן' ולא תנזוף
10. בן ולא תגעור בן ולא [ת]הוי
11. אויב דילן דאת אוהב דילן ורחים'
12. דאבהתן בזכות עקידה בהר
13. המוריה אגין עלן הב עינך בן

תרגום

J.T.S. NS ENA 42.27

recto [   ] אין] אלהים חוץ ממך [   ] לפניו ארבעה [   ] שלם שמרת לו [   ] כרת
עמו שלו[נות] נסיו[נות ובכול]ם נמצא נאמן ובסוף עשרת
הנסיו[נות] אמרה לו קח את ב[נ]ך את יחידך למקו[ם   ] להר הפולחן לא סירב לאימרתך ולא
עבר על דבר[ך] verso [   ] לז[קן] לקח [את האש ו]המאכלת ושם [את העצים [על כתף בנו
וחצה [   ] הדעת וילכו [שניהם י]חדיו בשלמות ובאו למ[קו]ם שאמרת להם והראית לו ענן
כבודך כאשר ביקש ללכת ולא ידע [לאי]זה מקום [עד ש]ראה את ענן כבודך ויאמר אל שני

C.U.L. T-S B8.9

recto נעריו הרואים אתם דבר כלשהו ויאמרו לו אין אנחנו רואים שום דבר חזר ושאל את
יצחק בנו הרואה אתה דבר כלשהו אמר לו הנני רואה עמוד ענן מהרקיע [ועד] לארץ באותה
שעה ידע הזקן שיצחק נבחר לעולה וכך אמר לנעריו עם המשולים לחמור המתינו לכם פה עם
החמור שבו לכם וגו' לקח את העצים ושם על יצחק בנו verso והאש והמאכלת לקח הוא בידו
וילכו שניהם יחדיו משהגיעו למקום שאל יצחק את אביו בבקשה ממך אבא הנה האש והעצים
ואיה השה לעולה ענה העוקד ואמר לנעקד לפני ה' גלוי השה לעולה בני לא האב עיכב והרהר
ולא הבן סירב לו שניהם [הלכו] בלב שלם ובדעה שלמה לעשות רצונך אדון העולם ובנה את
המזבח בחדווה הבן...

C.U.L. T-S NS 138.79

recto [...   ] חרדה(?) ובקשה נתבקשה מלפניך רבון העולם. באותה שעה כאשר מלאכי המרום
ראו שיצחק [נמצא] על גבי המזבח ואביו שלוף סכין לשחוט אותו קשרו מספד ואבל ובכי וכך
אמרו בפניך אלוהי השמים אם יצחק הולך ונשחט מי יאמר לפניך 'עזי וזמרת יה' אם יצחק
הולך ונשחט מי יאמר 'ה' איש מלחמה' אם יצחק הולך ונשחט מי יאמר לפניך 'מי כמוך באלים
ה'' אם יצחק נשחט verso מי יא[מר] לפניך 'ה' י[מל]וך' וכך [כתוב] במפורש בכ[ת]בך 'הן
אר[אלם] צעקו חוצה מלאכי שלום מר יבכיון'. באותה שעה שלחת לו מלאך מן השמים ואמרת
לו אברהם אב[רהם] וכן כתוב 'ויקרא אליו מלאך ה' מן השמים' וגו' פעמים קראת לו אל
תשלח ידך אל הנער כמו שכתוב 'אל תשלח ידך אל הנער' והורדת לו טלה מן השמים וחיה
רוחו והתקיימה נשמתו ואמר לפניך תשבחה

C.U.L. T-S NS 271.138

recto 'ברוך מחיה המתים'. נשבעת לו שבועה אשר לעולם לא תשנה את אימרתך ולא תבטל
את שבועתך. כמו שכתוב 'ויאמר בי נשבעתי נא[ום] ה'' וגו' אמרת לו לזקן אהובך שאני מברך
את זרעו לעולם וזכור את העקידה לעולם כמו שכ[תוב] 'כי ברך אברכך' וגו' הראית לו איל
לעולה אשר נברא בששת ימי בראשית והקריב אותו תחת יחידו והתפלל ואמר לפניך כאן יהיו
הדורות עובדים [את האלהים] וקבעת את עקידת יצחק לזכרון עולם ואמרת verso להם
לעוקד ולנעקד כאשר בניכם יהיו בצרה יזכירו לפניי את העקידה ואני ארחם עליהם. הרח[מן]

זכור לנו עקידת יצחק ורחם עלינו וניחשב לפניך כקרבן עולה הרח[מן] הסתכל בעקידתו ורחם
עלינו כי אנחנו בצרה גדולה הרח[מן] ואל תתבטל תקוותנו ממך. ואל תנעל שערך בפנינו. ואל
תנזוף בנו ואל תגער בנו ואל תהיה אויבנו כי אתה אוהבנו ואהובם של אבותינו בזכות העקידה
בהר המוריה הגן עלינו ושים עינך עלינו...

הדף השני של כתב יד קיימברידג׳ C.U.L. T-S B8.9, שפורסם גם הוא על ידי גרלו, מכיל
תפילת סליחה, שאינה קשורה כלל לפרשת העקידה או לתרגום הארמי לתורה. כדי להשלים את
ההקשר הליטורגי של כתב היד נציג אותו כלשונו, בלי הערה או תוספת כלשהי.

C.U.L. T-S B8.9, folio 2

recto
1. מסכי לאיתפראקה וכל
2. דמתאסר מצפה דנפיק
3. [תא וכל דנחית מחמד　　]
4. דהוי ליה מסקאנא· אנחנא
5. לית דמסיק יתנא מעומקא
6. לית דשארי איסורן מינן לית
7. דפריק לן מן שיעבודן אנחנא
8. דחלין דעוייאתן סגן לחדא
9. וגרמו לן לאתנשאה מן קדמך
10. חובן לא שבקן לאשכאחא
11. אסו ועוייתן לא שבקן

verso
1. לאשכאחא תיובתא· אם
2. בתיובתא תליא אסותן [מ}
3. מטעינן לא שביק לן דנתיב
4. לדחלתך הא מטעי יתן
5. מאורחתך הא ליבא טפשא
6. דאית בן לא יילף למדע
7. דחלתך אף אנחנא בטלותא? [או: בפולגתא?]
8. לא הוי לן אסו· אנן מחשבין
9. נכלין/ אנן מחשבין בישן
10. חד על חבריה· צבינא
11. מומתא דשיקרא· במה

ג

תוספתות תרגומיות ופיוטים ארמיים רבים נתחברו לפרקים יד-טו ו־י״ט-כ בספר שמות,
המשמשים לקריאת התורה בשביעי של פסח ובחג השבועות. לעתים הועתקו יצירות אלו
בחוברות נפרדות, כאוספים בפני עצמם, ולעתים הוכללו במחזורים של תפילות לחגים ושולבו
לתוך סדרי קריאת התורה.[9]

9　ראה היינימן (לעיל, הערה 5).

אחד הפיוטים הקדומים והנפוצים ביותר הינו 'אזיל משה', אשר העתק קדום ביותר ממנו, כתוב על פאפירוס, פורסם על ידי יוסף יהלום.[10] יהלום תיארך את הפאפירוס למאה החמישית לסה"נ לכל המאוחר, והראה שמבחינה טקסטואלית, כתב היד מצטיין בנוסחו הפשוט והשוטף ובקצבו החלק. אשר לגלגולי הטקסט המאוחרים יותר, הוא מציין ש'קרוב-ביותר לנוסח הפאפירוס נוסח הגניזה בלבד', והכוונה לכתב יד אוקספורד Heb e25, שנתגלה על ידי פלישר והוזכר במאמרו של היינימן. מאז פורסם כתב יד נוסף מגניזת קאהיר עם נוסח שונה של הפיוט.[11] מכיוון שהפאפירוס מקוטע ושחוק במידה רבה ונשתמרה בו פחות ממחצית הטקסט, חשיבותן של נוסחאות הגניזה נשארה בעינה. גם יהלום נזקק לכתב יד אוקספורד הנזכר על מנת לשחזר ולהשלים את נוסח הפאפירוס.

והנה לאחרונה נתגלו קטעי גניזה נוספים בספריית בית המדרש לרבנים בניו יורק. קטעים אלה מכילים שלושה פיוטים ארמיים, ובהם נוסח נוסף ל'אזיל משה'. ביניהם משובצים גם תוספתא תרגומית לשמות טו 12 ותרגום ארצישראלי לשמות טו 13–15.

הפיוט הראשון הוא 'מאן כוותך' לשמות טו 11, אשר פורסם לראשונה בשנת 1900 על ידי משה גינזבורגר על פי כתב יד דה רוסי.[12] בפיוט זה מקלסים משה והמלאכים את האלוהים לסירוגין. בכתב היד נשתמרו רק האותיות עי"ן עד ת"ו מהאקרוסטיכון, ואין בו חילופין משמעותיים. גם התוספתא לפסוק 12 מקוטעת היא, וההבדלים בינה לבין הנוסחאות בניאופיטי, בקטעי הגניזה האחרים ובתרגום הקטעים אינם נראים כחשובים במיוחד.

הפיוט השני הוא כאמור 'אזיל משה', שנשתמר כמעט במלואו עם כותרת 'אל[פ]ביט [כך!] דויושע'. השוואת הנוסח החדש עם אלה הידועים כבר, מראה שהוא שייך דווקא לקבוצת המאוחרים, בניגוד לפאפירוס ולכתב יד אוקספורד Heb e25. ובכל זאת יש בו חילופין מעניינים הראויים לציון, כגון 'ומצראי דחקין מן בתריהון' במקום 'שנאיהון רדפין...' (אות ה"א), ו'קלפוני דקיריס' במקום 'דבירה' או 'קל רוח דקודשא' (אות שי"ן).

הפיוט השלישי הוא 'אנגלי מרומא' לשמות יט 25, המוכר אף הוא מהמחזורים ואשר פורסם לראשונה על ידי גינזבורגר,[13] ושוב על ידי דודזון והיינימן.[14] הנוסח שלפנינו מסומן בכותרת 'אלפבית דויד משה' והוא מורכב משני חלקים, האחד הוא ויכוח בין משה לבין מלאכי מרום המתנגדים לכניסתו לכניסתו השמימה: 'פתחון לי דניעול...לית אנן פתחין', ואילו השני הוא סירובו של משה לרדת ארצה בטרם יקבל את התורה: 'לית אנא נחית עד אורייתא אסב'. יש להצטער רק על כך שכתב היד מקוטע ונוסחו משובש. לאור הערות אלו נציג את הטקסטים של כתב יד זה כלשונם ובלי הרחבה כלשהי.

תיאור כתב היד: שני דפי קלף, שמידותיהם 14.2 x 14 ס"מ בממוצע, שלוש עשרה עד ארבע עשרה שורות לעמוד. קרוע במקצת. כתיב מזרחי רהוט למחצה. ניקוד טברני ספורדי.

10 י' יהלום, '"אזל משה" בפאפירוס', תרביץ מז (תשל"ח), עמ' 173–184.

11 ראה קליין (לעיל, הערה 6), עמ' 237–238. נוסח אחד הוא זה שהוזכר, ואילו השני, הדומה יותר לזה של המחזורים, גם הוא מספריית הבודלי באוקספורד, ציונו Heb c74-75.

12 M. Ginsburger, 'Aramäischer Introductionen zum Thargumvortrag an Festtagen', ZDMG 54 (1900), pp. 122f.

13 M. Ginsburger, 'Les Introductions Araméennes a la Lecture du Targum', REJ 73 (1921), pp. 15-16

14 י' דודזון, אוצר השירה והפיוט, ניו יורק, תרפ"ה, א, 6374; היינימן (לעיל, הערה 5), עמ' 365. היינימן מציין שהוא מסתמך על הנוסח של א' רוזנטל, 'הפיוטים הארמיים לשבועות', עבודת גמר בחוג ללשון עברית, האוניברסיטה העברית, ירושלים תשכ"ו, עמ' 103.

J.T.S. ENA 2752.18

recto (לוח 9)

1. עונה עלובין דהוון מושפלין אמ[רין] מל[אכיא] מן כות[ך] פונה וחובש אמ[ר]
2. מש[ה] צדקה לובש ונקמה מתלבש אמ מל מן כותך קרב לעובדך
3. אמ מש רברבין עובדך וכולא ע[ובד]א ידך אמ מל מן כות
4. שליט באיכסוסייא אמ מש וע[בד] נסיא לעמוסיא. אמ מל
5. מן כות תקוף בארא לים. אמ מש לשמך מהללים מי כמוך
6. באלים אמ מל מן כותך באילי מרומא יי מן כותך הדור
7. [בלבושך ד]חיל בתושבחתא עביד נסין ופליאן לעמיה בית יש:
8. //// [ימא וארעא הוון מדיי[נין כחדא ואמרין ימא הות
9. א[מ]ר[א] וארע]א הות אמרא לאנא קבל
10. ת[ביעא יתהון ולא ארעא] קטילך [ ]
11. הות בעיא //// [ ] קדמך ארכנת ידך בשבועה
12. ואשתבעת לא[רעא דלית את תב]ע יתהון מיניה לעלמא
13. דאתי הא בכן פתחת ארע[א ית פ]מה ובלעת יתהון: (13) נחית
14. דברת בחסדך עמא האי[לין די] פרקתא ותאחסן יתהון בטור

verso (לוח 10)

1. אחסנותך מבית שכינת קדשך– (14) שמעו שמעו אומיא
2. אתרגזון רתיתא אחדת יתהון כל דירי ארעא דפלשתאי–
3. (15) אז הא בכן אתבהילו ר[בר]באי אדומאי תקיפי מואבאי
4. רתיתא אחדת יתהון אתמ[סי] בלבביהון כל דירי ארעא דכנענאי
5. [אל]פביט(!) דויושע– איזל משה וקום על ימא ואמר לימא
6. זע מן קדמוי– בשמי תיזיל ותימור לימא שלוחיה אנא
7. ליוצר בראשית גלי ארחך שעה זעירא עד דיעברון
8. בגוף פריקוי דקיריס– דע[מא דיש שר]ין בעקא
9. דשנאיהון רדפין מן בתר[יהון– הא ימא] מן קדמיהון
10. ומצראי דחקין מן בתרי[הון– ואזל מ[שה וקם על ימא ואמ
11. לימא זע מן קדם אל [זע ימא מן] קדם משה כד חמא בידיה
12. חטר נסייא– חימה ורו[גזא עלת] לימא והוה מתרברב למחזור
13. לבתריה– טעו הי לך בר[י]ה ד[עמרם דאנא מתכבש מן
14. ילוד דאיתה– יומין תלתא אנא רב מנך– והיך את יכול

J.T.S. ENA 2752.19

recto (לוח 11)

1. למכבוש יתי– כד חמא משה לימא מסרהב וגללוהי מתרברבין
2. עלוהא לית שעתא דא שעת דינא האת לקבלי ואנא לקבלך–
3. מתיב משה ואמר לימא דאנא שלוחיה ליוצר בראשית–
4. נתהפך ימא כד שמע למילתיה וקם ליה למעבד רעותיה–
5. סוף מליא אמ (מש) ימא למש לית אנא מתכבש מן יליד דאתא–
6. ענה משה ואם לימא רב מ'ני ומנך יכבוש יתך– פתח
7. משה פומיה בשירה הכדין שבח בתושבחתא צלותיה
8. דמש עלת בבעו ובתחנונים אמר מילתיה– רבונו דעלמא

9. לא תמסור עמך בי[דיה דפרעה] רשיעא– שמע ימא קלפוני

10. דקיריס˙ דהוה ממלל [עם משה] מן גו נורא הכדין אמרת

11. לי בספר דאוריתא. כען ת[חמי ית דא]יעבד לפרעה. תב ימא

12. מן גללוהי ועברו בגוה בני י[שראל] – **אלפבית דוירד משה**˙

13. אנגלי מרומא פתחון לי דניעול˙ אם משה אנן לא פתחין

verso (לוח 12)

1. ולא שליטין למפתח˙ אמרו מלאכיא למשה נבייא– ביה אנא צווח

2. אורנוס פתחון לי˙ אמר משה ביה צווח קדם קירוס למצוח. אם

3. מל למש נבייא. [א]ין (את סליק [ ] סופך) אתון לא פתחין סופיכון למפתח.

4. אם מש [א]ין את סליק סופך לנחית˙ אמרו מלאכיא למש נבייא˙

5. ואמר משה למלאכיא˙ לית אנא נחית עד אוריתי אסב

6. ועד אצבע גבורתי (א)\כתב. עד אסב כלתי ואיזיל˙ עד אסב [א–]

7. אוריתי ואיחות˙– לית אנא נחית עד בריוני נחמה ועד––

8. בלוחות נירמה. עד אסב כלתי עד אסב אוריתי ואיחות–

9. לית אנא נחית עד גבור נש[   ] נתכון בקרני אנגח.

10. עד אסב כלתי ועא אז: [   ]תי אי/ופה(?) ועד דאימלל

11. פה אל פה˙ עד אסב כלת[י   ו]עא או: לאן עד השופרין

12. תוקעין˙ ועד אומה ביתבע[ע]ד אסב כלתי ואזיל˙ עאאו˙

13. לאן עד ונוריד יקרה ועד לב/כניס(?) יקרא עד אסב כלתי ו...

לוח 2. C.U.L. T-S AS 116.453v
באדיבות הספרייה של אוניברסיטת קיימברידג'

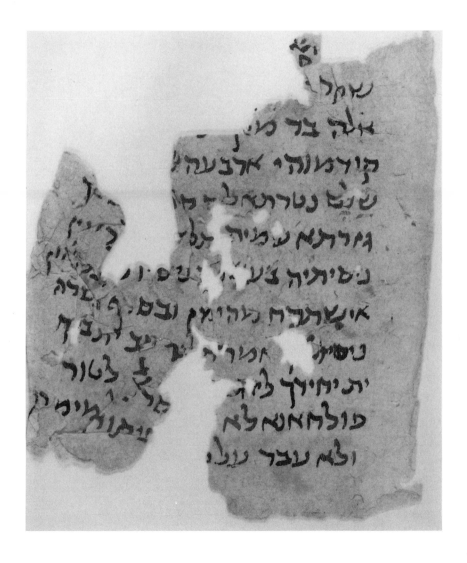

לוח J.T.S. NS ENA 42.27r .3
באדיבות הספרייה של בית המדרש לרבנים, ניו־יורק

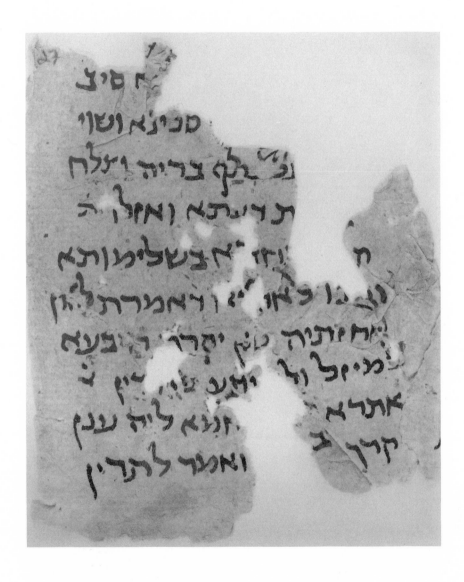

לוח 4. J.T.S. NS ENA 42.27v

באדיבות הספרייה של בית המדרש לרבנים, ניו־יורק

לוח 5. C.U.L. T-S NS 138.79r
באדיבות הספרייה של אוניברסיטת קיימברידג'

מן יייך תורמן נית
והכין מפרש בכו בך הן או
צעקו חוצה מלאכי שלום מר
יבכיון . נה שעתא צלחתא
כיה מלאכא וין שכייא . אמרג
ליה אבריום יאב ותן כתיב ויקרא
אליו מלאך י מן השמים ונ תרין
זמנין קרא אתו . יתיה לא תושט
ידך צעולימא כמה דכת אכ
תשלח ידך אל ה נער ואוזית תה
עליה כ יא מן שמיא וחיית
רוחיה ואיתקיימת נשמתיה
ואמר קורמי . תושבחתא

ברוך מחיה המתים ׳אשתבעתא
ליה שבועתא דלעלם דלית את
משע במימרך ולית את מבטל
שבועתך ׳ נמוה דכה ויאמר בי
נשבעתי ש׳ כ וג אמרתליה לקבא
רחימך דאנא מברך על זרעיה
לעלם ומדכר א עקיוה לעלם כמה
דכה לי ברך אצריכך א אחזיתא
ליה דיכראל׳ לתא דאיתגברי מן
שיתתקימי בראשית וקלי בימה
חולף יחידריה וגב ואמר קדמך
הכא יהון פלחין דריא וקבעד קטילו
יצחק דוכרנא לעלם ואמרית

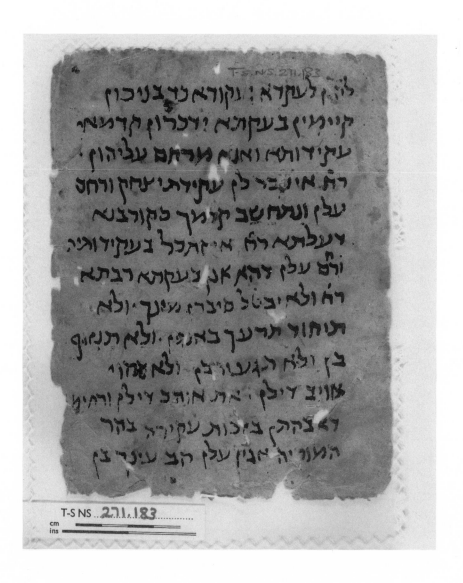

לוח 9. J.T.S. ENA 2752.18r
באדיבות הספרייה של בית המדרש לרבנים, ניו־יורק

לוח 11. ‏J.T.S. ENA 2752.19r
באדיבות הספרייה של בית המדרש לרבנים, ניו־יורק

תרגום השבעים לרות ד 11 — דראמאטיזאציה מדרשית

אלכסנדר רופא

שחזור הנוסח איננו דיסציפלינה העומדת בפני עצמה. להוציא כמה כללים הנוגעים לשגיאות
הנפוצות בקולמוסם של מעתיקים, הוא ניזון ממיגוון של תחומים שגובלים בו במדעי הרוח.[1]
הוא הדין בשחזור נוסח המקרא: הוא מתפרנס מתולדות הלשון העברית ולשונות התרגומים, מן
ההיסטוריה על כל ענפיה (מדינית, משפטית, חברתית, יישובית וכו'), מתולדות האמונות
והדעות ומתולדות הספרות. על כל אלה מנצחת חכמת הפרשנות, השוקלת את האפשרויות
השונות ובוררת — בהליך סובייקטיבי מאוד — את היותר מתקבלת על הדעת.
מאמר קצר זה מבקש להאיר נוסח משוער אחד בספר רות בעזרת תולדות הספרות
היהודית שלאחר המקרא, ביתר דיוק — בעזרת תכונה מתכונותיו של מדרש האגדה. אולם יחד
עם ברירת הנוסח — איזה קודם ואיזה משני לו — תעלה כאן עדות חשובה בדבר התחלותיו
של המדרש, הופעתו הראשונה בימי בית שני וחדירתו לתוך כתבי היד של ספרי המקרא.
ברות ד 11 אנו קוראים:

ויאמרו כל העם אשר בשער והזקנים: 'עדים; יתן ה' את האשה הבאה אל ביתך כרחל
וכלאה' וגו'.

תרגום השבעים מציע כאן לעומת זאת:

καὶ εἴποσαν πᾶς ὁ λαὸς οἱ ἐν τῇ πύλῃ Μάρτυρες. καὶ οἱ πρεσβύτεροι
εἴποσαν Δῴη κύριος τὴν γυναῖκά σου τὴν εἰσπορευομένην εἰς τὸν
οἶκόν σου ὡς Ραχηλ καὶ ὡς Λειαν κτλ.

ובתרגום חזרה ללשון המקרא:

ויאמרו כל העם אשר בשער: 'עדים'. והזקנים אמרו: 'יתן ה' את אשתך הבאה אל ביתך
כרחל וכלאה' וגו'.

במסגרת המאמר הזה נזדקק להבדל היותר נכבד שבין נוסח המסורה (=נוה"מ) לתרגום השבעים
(=תה"ש): בעוד נוה"מ מצרף יחדיו את העם ואת הזקנים למקהלה אחת, תה"ש מפריד בין
תפקידיהם — העם אמרו 'עדים', והזקנים הוסיפו עליהם וביִרכו את רות ואת בועז. השאלה
נשאלת: האם תה"ש משקף נוסח עברי שהיה לפניו? ואם כך, האם יש להעדיף נוסח משוער זה
על פני נוה"מ? אפשר ששאלה זו איננה מכריעה להבנת המסר של מגילת רות, אך בירורה עשוי
לגלות לנו טפח מן ההליכים של מסירת נוסח המקרא או תרגומיו בתקופת בית שני.

---

1   דברים הולמים בעניין זה כתב ח"ב רוזן במאמרו: 'האם היה הירודוטוס מודע לריטוריקה? תועלתם
    של ניתוחים בלשניים להכרה מעמיקה יותר של ההיסטוריוגראפיה', ספר יצחק אריה זליגמן, ב,
    ירושלים תשמ"ג, עמ' 499–508.

אחדים מטובי החוקרים ביכרו את תה"ש על פני נוה"מ בכתוב זה. עמהם אפשר למנות במאה הזאת את אהרליך, ז'ויון, כהנא ורובינסון.[2] אמנם חלקם לא נתנו טעם לדבריהם, אך מותר לשער, שהם נמשכו אחרי התמונה החיונית בתה"ש, לפיו קהל הנוכחים מתחלק לשתי מקהלות: העם מעידים והזקנים מברכים.[3]

גם המחזיקים בנוה"מ לא תמיד נצרכו לנמק את עמדתם. כך למשל נהגו ברתולט, נובאק והאלר.[4] קמפבל, לעומתם, הצביע על כך שבנוה"מ הזקנים וכל העם יחדיו הם נושאי פניותו של בעז לפני כן (פסוק 9), ולא עוד אלא באים הם בסדר הכיאסטי החביב על מליצת המקרא: 'ויאמר בעז לזקנים וכל העם' — 'ויאמר כל העם אשר בשער והזקנים'...[5] זקוביץ סבר ש'המעבר הישיר בין נוסחת העדות לבין הברכה הפריע לכמה מן התרגומים. השבעים פיצלו אפוא את יושבי השער לשני גופים, האחד מעיד ומשנהו מברך...'.[6] יש כאן אפוא שיקולים לכאן ולכאן:

לנוה"מ יש הארמוניה כיאסטית, אך מאידך יש בו מעבר פתאומי כלשהו. תה"ש גם יותר חלק גם יותר חיוני; אך האם אלה הן תכונותיו של הטקסט המקורי או תוצאה של עיבוד שנעשה אחריו בכתב יד עברי או מעשה ידי המתרגם? תיקו.[7]

והנה נראה לי שניתן בכל זאת להגיע למסקנה מוצקה למדי בסוגיה זו, והיא תהיה כדלקמן: תה"ש משקף כאן נוסח עברי שהיה מצוי בימי בית שני, אלא שזה היה נוסח משני. את ההוכחה לכך תספק השוואת תכונותיו עם אחת ממידותיו של המדרש.

תופעה חוזרת היא במדרש האגדה, שמעשירים את העלילה המקראית על ידי חלוקת המאמרים בין גיבורים שונים. בדרך זו מתרבים הקולות ומופיעות מגמות מגוונות ואף מנוגדות. התוצאה בכללה היא שכלול העלילה ליתר חיוניות וחריפות, במילה אחת — לדראמאטיזאציה.

המקום הקלאסי שבו פותחה תכונה זו הוא בתוס' סוטה ט, ג–ט, שם באו לא פחות משמונה דוגמאות של דרשת כתובים זו.[8] דיינו שנביא שתיים מהן:

A.B. Ehrlich, *Randglossen zur hebräischen Bibel*, VII, Leipzig 1914 [Hildesheim 1968], p. 28; P. Joüon, *Ruth: Commentaire philologique et exégétique*, Roma 1924 [Roma 1986], ad. loc.; א' כהנא, רות (תנ"ך עם פירוש מדעי), תל-אביב תר"ץ, על אתר; רובינסון ב-BHK וב-BHS.   2

'D'après le TM, tout le peuple, avec les anciens, formule le :משלי הנמקה נותן ז'ויון souhait. Mais il est difficile que ce souhait d'allure poétique, avec allusions savantes à Rachel et Lia à Pèrès et Tamar, soit prononcé par le peuple' נראה לי שהפרשן מעמיד כאן לפני הטקסט דרישות סופר-ריאליסטיות, ועל כן – בלתי לגיטימיות.   3

A. Bertholet, *Das Buch Ruth* (HKAT), Tübingen 1898, ad. loc.; W. Nowack, *Richter, Ruth etc.* (HKAT), Göttingen 1902, ad. loc.; M. Haller, *Die fünf Megilloth* (HAT), Tübingen 1940, ad. loc.   4

E.F. Campbell, *Ruth* (AB), Garden City, NY 1975, ad. loc.; בכיוון זה כבר רמז רודולף: W. Rudolph, *Das Buch Ruth etc.* (KAT), Gütersloh 1962, ad. loc.   5

י' זקוביץ, רות (מקרא לישראל), תל-אביב תש"ן, על אתר; ובכיוון זה פירש גם ירלמן: G. Gerleman, *Ruth; Das Hohelied* (BK), Neukirchen–Vluyn 1965, p. 35: 'LXX schreibt sehr gekünstelt die Bejahung nur dem Volk, und die Glückwünsche nur dem ältesten'.   6

ממילא לא חסרו גם הצעות אוריגינאליות. גרסמאן למשל מחק את 'העם' גם בפסוק ט וגם בפסוק 11. השווה: H. Gressmann, *Die Anfänge Israels*[2] (SATA I/2), Göttingen 1922, p. 267; ושם בנספח, עמ' 12.   7

השווה ליברמן (מהדיר), תוספתא על פי כתב יד וינה וכו', נויארק תשל"ג, עמ' 210–213; וכן: ש' ליברמן, תוספתא כפשוטה, באור ארוך לתוספתא, נויארק תשל"ג, עמ' 716–717. אני מודה לעמיתי ד"ר א' שנאן, שהעיר לי על הכתובים הללו.   8

כיוצא בדבר אתה אומר: 'באנו אל הארץ אשר שלחתנו' (במ' יג 27) — אמר יהושע; כלב
אמר: 'עלה נעלה וירשנו אתה' (שם, פסוק 30); מרגלים אמרו: 'אפס כי עז העם היושב
בארץ' (שם, 28), שלושה דברים זה בצד זה — מי שאמר זה לא אמר זה, ומי שאמר זה לא
אמר זה. – – – כיוצא בדבר אתה אומר, 'אוי לנו, מי יצילנו מיד האלים האדירים' (שמ"א
ד 8) — אמרו כשרין שבהן; רשעים שבהם אמרו: 'אלה הם האלים המכים עשר מכות,
ושלמו מכותיו במדבר'; גבורין שבהן אמרו: 'התחזקו והיו לאנשים פלשתים' (שם, פסוק 9);
שלושה דברים זה בצד זה וכו'.

על עתיקותה היחסית של דרשת כתובים זו מלמדים, ראשית כול, הפיתוחים השונים שהיא
זכתה להם. שהרי הם מוכיחים, שהדרשה הבסיסית היתה מוכרת ונפוצה, עד כי החלו לעבדה
בצורות שונות ולצרכים חדשים. פיתוח אחד הוא עצם יצירתן של סדרות של דרשות בעלות
צורה אחידה — שמונה בתוספתא, כפי שראינו, או שלוש בבבלי מכות, שנראה להלן. פיתוח
אחר, המוסיף על הדראמאטיזאציה, הוא כאשר אחד התפקידים ניתן לקב"ה עצמו. כך למשל
בבבלי מכות כג ע"ב:[9]

א"ר אלעזר: בג' מקומות הופיע רוח הקודש — בית דינו של שם ובבית דינו של שמואל
הרמתי ובבית דינו של שלמה. בבית דינו של שם, דכתיב: 'ויכר יהודה ויאמר: צדקה ממני'
(בר' לח 26); מנא ידע? דלמא כי היכי דאזל איהו לגבה, אזל נמי אינש אחרינא ל[גבה]? יצאת
בת קול ואמרה: 'ממני יצאו כבושים'. בבית דינו של שמואל, דכתיב וכו'.

כתוב אחר, שבו מיוחס לקב"ה אחד התפקידים, הוא בדרשת הכתובים מאלה שהזכרנו
בתוס' סוטה ט, ג, שיש לה מקבילה מפורטת יותר במשנה סוטה ט, ו, כדלקמן:

זקני אותה העיר רוחצין ידיהן במים במקום שלעגלה עריפתה ואומרים: 'ידינו לא שפכה
את הדם הזה, ועינינו לא ראו' (דב' כא 7). – – – – – – והכהנים אומרים: 'כפר לעמך ישראל
אשר פדית ה', ואל תתן דם נקי בקרב עמך ישראל' (שם, פסוק 8). לא היו צריכים לומר
'ונכפר להם הדם' (שם, שם), אלא רוח הקדש מבשרתן: אימתי שתעשו ככה, הדם מתכפר
לכם.

כאן אנו רואים התחלה לפיתוח מסוג אחר, פיתוח הלכתי. על ידי יחוס המאמרים לקולות
שונים, בחינת 'מי שאמר זה לא אמר זה', מסדירים חכמים את טקס עריפת העגלה בנחל. מעתה
ברור, לא רק מה זקני ירושלים וזקני אותה העיר עושים (שם, משניות א, ה), אלא גם הכהנים
בני לוי (דב' כא 5), שלפי התיאור המקראי חסרו כל תפקיד של ממש, מוצאים מעתה את
מקומם במעמד חגיגי זה.

הרושם הוא שהדרשה המחלקת תפקידים מושרשת במדרש האגדה, שבו היא מרבה להופיע,
והיא הועברה אל מדרש ההלכה, שבו היא מצויה באופן ספוראדי, בתהליך משני. רושם זה אף
מתגבר לנוכח הדיון ההלכתי לקמן, שבו יחוס התפקידים נעשה בצורה הרבה יותר מאולצת,
באחיזה רופפת בכתוב. זוהי ברייתא בתוס' סנהדרין ד, ה:

ר' אלעזר ברבי יוסי אומר: זקנים שאלו כהלכה, שנאמר 'תנה לנו מלך לשפטינו' (שמ"א ח
6), אבל עמי הארץ חזרו וקלקלו, שנאמר 'והיינו גם אנחנו ככל הגוים, ושפטנו מלכנו, ויצא
לפנינו, ונלחם' וגו' (שם, פסוק 20).

הדרשה מתרצת את הקושייה, 'אם כן, למה נענשו בימי שמואל', שנשאלה כלפי דעת רבי
יהודה, שסבר שמינוי המלך הוא אחת משלוש מצוות שנצטוו ישראל בביאתן לארץ. והתירוץ

_____

9   אף כתוב זה ציין לי דר' א' שנאן בטובו.

הוא, ששאילת המלך הועלתה שלא כהוגן. הקלקול נמצא במלים 'ככל הגוים', הבאות בסוף פסוק
5: 'עתה שימה לנו מלך לשפטנו ככל הגוים'. את הקלקול הזה מייחסת הדרשה לעמי הארץ, תוך
שהיא סומכת על פסוק 19–20: 'וימאנו העם... ויאמרו... והיינו גם אנחנו ככל הגוים'. לעומת
זאת, טוענת הדרשה, הזקנים שאלו כהלכה, והיא סומכת על ציטוט הבקשה בפסוק 6: 'תנה לנו
מלך לשפטנו'. האופי המאולץ של הדרשה ניכר הן בכך שהיא מחלקת משפט אחד בפסוק 5 לשני
קולות, הן מהישענותה (לגבי השאלה החיובית של הזקנים) דווקא על פסוק 6, הפותח: 'וירע
הדבר בעיני שמואל כאשר אמרו תנה לנו מלך לשפטנו', הן משחזור תפקידו של העם (עמי
הארץ) מסוף הסיפור, בפסוק 19–20, אחרי שכבר באה תשובתו הכעוסה והמאיימת של שמואל.
ואולם ראיה מעולה לעתיקותה של דרשת הכתובים המחלקת תפקידים יש בהופעתה במכילתא
דרבי ישמעאל, מסכתא דויהי בשלח, סוף פרשה ב:[10]

ארבע כיתות נעשו ישראל על הים. אחת אומרת ליפול אל הים, ואחת אומרת לשוב
למצרים, ואחת אומרת לעשות מלחמה, ואחת אומרת 'נצווח כנגדן'. זאת שאמרה ליפול אל
הים נאמר להם: 'התיצבו וראו את ישועת ה'' (שמ' יד 13); זו שאמרה לשוב למצרים נאמר
להם 'כי אשר ראיתם את מצרים...' (שם, שם). זו שאמרה 'נעשה מלחמה' נאמר להם 'ה'
ילחם לכם' (שם, 14). זו שאמרה 'נצווח כנגדן' נאמר להם 'ואתם תחרישון' (שם, שם).

יוסף היינימן דן באגדה זו ובירר שלכתחילה היו כאן שלוש כיתות בלבד, שהרי הרביעית, 'נצווח
כנגדן', רק כופלת את השלישית, 'נעשה מלחמה'.[11] כמו כן, הצביע על שתי מקבילות לאגדת
שלוש הכיתות על הים, במימר מרקה השומרוני[12] ובקדמוניות המקרא, שיוחס לפילון.[13] בזה
האחרון אף בא פירוט נוסף: ראובן, יששכר, זבולון ושמעון אמרו לזרוק עצמם לים; גד, אשר, דן
ונפתלי (בני השפחות!) אמרו לשוב לעבדות; לוי, יהודה, יוסף ובנימין (הנכבדים שבשבטים)
ביקשו לאחוז בנשק ולהשיב מלחמה. כיוון שקדמוניות המקרא נתחבר בסוף המאה הראשונה
לסה"נ, הריהו מעיד על האגדה היהודית שבפני הבית. מכאן מתברר היסוד העתיק שבמדרש
שהבאנו מן המכילתא. ויתרה מזו: כך גם מתברר אופיין העתיק יחסית של הדרשות המעובדות
אפיזודות מקראיות, על ידי חלוקת 'תפקידים' בין גיבוריה.

אם נשוב עתה לרות ד 11, תתבקשנה המסקנות הבאות. נוה"מ הוא עיקר; בספר זה, שנתחבר
אמנם בימי בית שני,[14] אך ביקש לחקות עד כמה שאפשר את דרכי ההבעה הקדמוניות, עוד לא
'חולקו התפקידים' בין הזקנים והעם הנוכחים בשער. תה"ש נתן גירסה משנית, לפי דרכו של
המדרש המאוחר יותר מימי בית שני. ואולם כיוון שהמדרש הזה הוא מעיקרו עברי
וארציישראלי, אין גירסת תה"ש מעשה ידי המתרגמים, אלא צמחה, ככל הנראה, במצע העברי

10 ח"ש האראוויטץ (מהדיר), מכילתא דרבי ישמעאל², ירושלים תש"ך, עמ' 96.

11 יוסף היינימן, אגדות ותולדותיהן, ירושלים 1974, עמ' 93.

12 היינימן, שם, עמ' 92; השווה מימר מרקה ד, ח; ז' בן-חיים, מימר מרקה, מקור, תרגום ופירוש,
ירושלים תשמ"ח, 274–278; J. Macdonald, *Memar Marqah*, edited and translated
(BZAW 84), Berlin 1963, I, pp. 100f.; II, p. 167

13 בפרק י, סעיף 3; השווה G. Kisch, *Pseudo-Philo's Liber Antiquitatum Biblicarum*,
Notre Dame, Indiana 1949, p. 141; תרגום אנגלי אצל M.R. James, *The Biblical
Antiquities of Philo*, London 1917, p. 104; תרגום עברי אצל א"ש הרטום, ספר
קדמוניות המקרא, מתורגם לעברית, תל-אביב תשכ"ז, עמ' 37. האב ברנאר דיפוי (Bernard
Dupuy) מפאריס העיר לי בטובו על מאמרו של אוליאן: S.M. Olyan, 'The Israelites
Debate Their Options at the Sea of Reeds etc', *JBL* 110 (1991), pp. 75-91. אוליאן
רואה את התחלת המדרש על הכיתות על הים ב'קדמוניות המקרא' דווקא. אבל לא הביא בחשבון
כי יש כאן תכונה מדרשית כללית ונפוצה.

14 השווה ע' ברנר, אהבת רות, תל-אביב תשמ"ח, עמ' 119–163.

שהיה לפניהם — נוסח עברי משני. והדבר ראוי לתשומת לב: יסודות של מדרש חדרו לכתב יד עברי של מגילת רות לפני שהספר תורגם ליוונית. יש כאן עדות מהימנה להתפתחות מוקדמת של מדרש האגדה ולחדירתו אל תוך כתבי היד של ספרי המקרא.

עדויות נוספות לתהליך זה מצויות בספרי מקרא אחרים ובעדי נוסח נוספים. כך, במגילת שמואל שנמצאה בקומראן (4QSam[a]), הועתק סיפור מלחמת נחש העמוני ביבש גלעד על ידי תיאור נרחב, כיצד נהג נחש לנקר עין ימין לכל בני גד וראובן; התיאור שובץ בתוך שמ"א י 27ב, והוא בא להטעים, ברוח המדרש, את תכונות איבתו ואכזריותו של נחש העמוני.[15]

במל"א כב 28ב, לפי נוה"מ, מסיים מיכיהו בן ימלה את דבריו במלים 'שמעו עמים כלם'. משפט זה אינו מיוצג בכתבי היד הטובים של תה"ש.[16] ומצד שני, המשפט איננו מתקשר לדבריו הקודמים של מיכיהו, אך חוזר מלה במלה בתחילת ספר מיכה (מי' א 2). מסתבר שהוא נתחב כאן במגמה מדרשית לזהות את מיכיהו בן ימלה, הנביא מימי אחאב, עם מיכה המורשתי, שניבא בימי יותם, אחז וחזקיהו (מי' א 1).[17] מגמת המדרש לזהות אישים מקראיים זה בזה כבר הוכרה היטב בידי יצחק היינמן.[18] אחת הדגמאות הבולטות שלה, הקרובה לענייננו, היא הזיהוי של עובדיהו 'אשר על הבית' בימי אחאב (מל"א יח 3–16) עם הנביא עובדיה, בעל הספר בתרי עשר.[19]

אסיים בשתי מסקנות כלליות. ההרחבות המדרשיות שראינו אינן אופייניות לעד נוסח אחד; הן באות בעדי נוסח שונים, שהשתייכו לטיפוסי נוסח נבדלים. בשמ"א י 27 באה ההרחבה בכתב היד 4QSam[a]; במל"א כב 28 היא מופיעה בנוה"מ; ברות ד 11 היא משתקפת בתה"ש. הווי אומר, זוהי תופעה רחבה למדי. מסתבר שבתקופה מסוימת בימי בית שני נהגו מעתיקים 'להעשיר' את הכתוב בדברי אגדה. פרי עבודתם נותר בעדי הנוסח השונים, אחד המרבה ואחד הממעיט. ותפוצתה של התופעה, במקומות שונים בעדי–נוסח שונים, מלמדת על קדמותה היחסית. יש לשער שאירעה כאשר ספרי המקרא עדיין הועתקו בצורה חופשית למדי, כנראה לפני התקופה החשמונאית.[20]

---

15 השווה -A. Rofé, 'The Acts of Nahash according to 4QSam[a]', *IEJ* 32 (1982), pp. 119- 133; ובגירסה עברית מורחבת: א' רופא, 'נחש מלך בני–עמון על פי מגילת שמואל מקומראן', בית מקרא לא (תשמ"ה), עמ' 456–462.

16 השווה: A.E. Brooke, N. McLean & H.St.J. Thackeray, *The Old Testament in Greek*: II/II, Cambridge 1930, ad. loc.

17 על המגמה המדרשית במל"א כב 28ב העיר לא פעם פרופ' י"א זליגמן ז"ל. הסבר זה עדיף בעיניי על דעתו של בול (E. Ball, 'A Note on 1 Kings XXII. 28', *JTS* N.S. 28 [1977], pp. 90-94). לדעתו, המשפט הנדון נוסף בידי עורך משנה תורתי, שביקש להטעים את הרציפות ממיכיהו עד מיכה.

18 י' היינמן, דרכי האגדה[2], ירושלים תשי"ד, עמ' 28–30.

19 השווה בבלי סנהדרין לט ע"ב: 'חזון עובדיהו: כה אמר ה' אלהים לאדום וגו'; מאי שנא עובדיה לאדום? אמר רבי יצחק, אמר הקדוש ברוך הוא: יבוא עובדיהו הדר בין שני רשעים [אחאב ואיזבל] ולא למד ממעשיהם, וינבא על עשו הרשע, שדר בין שני צדיקים [יצחק ורבקה] ולא למד ממעשיו'.

20 ואמנם התרגום היווני למגילת רות הוא מאוחר, שהרי יש לו מגעים עם אסכולת אקווילס (הוא מתרגם 'שדי' = ἱκανός ברות א 20, 21) ועם פרוטו–תיאודוטיון ('גם' מתורגם ב־καίγε ב־א 5; ב 16, 21, 15; ג 12; ד 10); אף על פי כן, מן השיקולים שהבאנו יש לקבוע את עתיקותה היחסית של ההרחבה בתרגום היווני של רות ד 11. אני מודה לד"ר פ"ג בורבונה (.P.G Borbone), מטורינו (איטליה), שדן עמי בסוגיה זו. וראה: M. Harl, G. Dorival & O. Munnich, *La Bible grecque des Septante*, [Paris] 1988, pp. 83-111.

* * *

מאמר זה הושלם בראשית ניסן תשנ"ג. והנה, בשבתי לקרוא בהגדה של פסח נתחוור לי, שדרשה
המחלקת מאמרים בין גיבורים שונים מצויה בעוד מקום אחד, והוא המפורסם מכולם, בברייתא
על ארבעה בנים. שהרי ברייתא זו נוטלת ארבעה כתובים המתארים שיחה עם הבנים ומייחסת
כל אחד מהם לבן בעל תכונה שונה. אם נחזיק בנוסח הברייתא שבהגדה של פסח, השאלה 'מה
העדות והחקים והמשפטים אשר צוה ה' אלהינו אתכם', בדב' ו 20, יוחסה לחכם; השאלה 'מה
העבדה הזאת לכם', בשמות יב 26, ניתנה לרשע; השאלה 'מה זאת', בשמות יג 14, הושמה בפי
התם; ואילו המאמר שלא קדמה לו שאלה, 'והגדת לבנך ביום ההוא', בשמות יג 8, נתפס כהסבר
האב לבן שאינו יודע לשאול. נוסחים שונים במקצת באים במכילתא דרבי ישמעאל ובמסכת
פסחים שבירושלמי.[21]

והנה נדמה לי, שלמסקנותינו עד כאן יש השלכות לגבי תולדותיה של הברייתא על ארבעה
בנים. כבר שיערו חכמים, שלכתחילה היה בה המדרש על שלושה בנים בלבד — חכם, תם
(טיפש) ושאינו יודע לשאול, ואילו הרשע נגרר אליה מהקשר אחר.[22] הרי 'הבן הרשע' אינו שייך
לסדרה העוסקת בתכונות האינטלקטואליות של הבנים, אלא משלב כאן הערכה מוסרית. על
עצמאותו מן הסדרה מעידות גם המכילתאות, משום שבהן הוא נזכר לבדו במקום אחר.[23]
ועכשיו, אם צדק היינימן במה שהראה, שמדרש מקורי על שלוש כיתות של ישראל על הים
הורחב למדרש על ארבע כיתות, הרי שיש ממנו ראיה נוספת, בדרך האנאלוגיה, לכך שמדרש על
שלושה בנים הורחב למדרש על ארבעה בנים.

באשר לזמנה של הברייתא על הבנים, יש שהקדימו אותה לימים שלפני מרד המקבים,[24] ויש
שאיחרו אותה לסוף ימי התנאים.[25] אין ביכולתי להכניס ראשי בין המחלוקת. אולם מן העיון
בתה"ש לרות ד 11 נתחוור, כי חלוקת התפקידים' היא תכונה מדרשית עתיקה ביחס,
שהופיעה ככל הנראה בתחילת התקופה ההלניסטית. נמצא, שלפחות מבחינת תכונותיה,
הברייתא על ארבעת (שלושת) הבנים משתייכת לרובד עתיק למדי ביצירה המדרשית.[26]

21 ד' גולדשמידט, הגדה של פסח, מקורותיה ותולדותיה במשך הדורות, וכו', ירושלים תש"ך, עמ'
   22–23.

22 D. Hoffmann, 'Die Baraita über die vier Söhne', *MWJ* 13 (1886), pp. 191-202;
   L. Finkelstein, 'Pre-Maccabean Documents in the Passover Haggadah', *HTR* 36
   (1943), pp. 8-18

23 מכילתא דרבי שמעון בן יוחai, פרשת בא, לשמ' יב, כו; י"ז אפשטיין וע"צ מלמד (מהדירים),
   ירושלים תשט"ו, עמ' 26; מכילתא דרבי ישמעאל (לעיל, הערה 10), עמ' 66. וראה גולדשמידט
   (לעיל, הערה 21), עמ' 25, שערך את הכתובים זה כנגד זה.

24 פינקלשטיין (לעיל, הערה 22), עמ' 8–18.

25 גולדשמידט, שם, עמ' 28.

26 ולולי דמסתפינא הייתי אומר שגם המדרש הנפרד על הבן הרשע, כפי שנשתמר במכילתא דרשב"י
   (לעיל, הערה 23), יש בו סימני עתיקות: 'והיה כי יאמרו אליכם בניכם — עתידין לומר לכם מה
   העבודה הזאת לכם. זה בן רשע שהוציא את עצמו מן הכלל...'. האם לא משתקפת כאן מחלוקת
   'האבות' ו'הבנים' המוכרת לנו ממלאכי ג 24 ומספר היובלים כג 9–32? וראה: א' רופא, 'ראשית
   צמיחתן של הכיתות בימי בית שני', קתדרה מט (תשרי תשמ"ט), 13–22, בעמ' 19–22.

סיפור יוסף – בין אגדה להיסטוריה

נילי שצ׳ופק

מבוא: הבעיה והכלים לפתרונה

סיפור יוסף, בראשית לז–נ, מהווה יחידה עצמאית בספר בראשית. סיפורי האבות, פרקים יב–
לו, הם סיפורים בודדים ללא רציפות עלילתית, ואילו סיפור יוסף הוא סיפור רצוף, שכל פרק בו
מהווה חוליה הממשיכה את קודמתה.[1] הרקע הגיאוגרפי של הפרקים הקודמים, העוסקים
בתולדות משפחת האבות, הוא צפוני, ואילו סיפור יוסף מתרחש בעיקרו בדרום, במצרים.
שאלות שונות עולות בקשר לסיפור זה: האם קורות יוסף מעוגנות במציאות היסטורית
מסוימת או שמא לפנינו יצירה ספרותית פיקטיבית?[2] לאיזו תקופה מתייחסת עלילת הסיפור?
אימתי הועלה הסיפור על הכתב? מהי מטרתו? ניסיון להשיב על שאלות אלו מתוך המקרא
עצמו, דהיינו, באמצעות תאריכים המופיעים בתורה ובהיסטוריוגראפיה המקראית, מעלה חרס.
אף השימוש בכלי המחקר המודרני, כגון שיטת המקורות, אין בו אלא כדי לקבוע terminus a
quo להעלאת הסיפור על הכתב – תקופת המלוכה.[3]
הכלי שנותר בידי החוקר הוא בדיקת הרישומים המצריים בסיפור יוסף. אמנם גם כלי זה אינו
מבטיחנו פתרון מוחלט לבעיה; שכן, גם אם קיים כאן רקע מצרי אותנטי ולא גוונים מצריים
כלליים חסרי זמן ומציאות, אזי תישאל השאלה, האם ניתן לתלותו במסגרת כרונולוגית

---

1 להוציא את סיפור תמר (לח) וברכת יעקב (מט), שהוכנסו על ידי יד מאוחרת.

2 לדיון רחב בהיבט הספרותי של סיפור יוסף ראה בעיקר: W.L. Humphreys, *Joseph and his
Family: A Literary Study*, University of South Carolina Press 1988; B.D.
Redford, *A Study of the Biblical Story of Joseph (Genesis 37-50)*, VTSup 20,
Leiden 1970, pp. 66ff. וכן, H. Gunkel, 'Die Komposition der Joseph-Geschichten'
ZDMG 76 (1922), pp. 55-71; A. Meinhold, 'Die Gattung der Josephgeschichte
und des Estherbuches, Diasporanovelle I, II', *ZAW* 87 (1975), pp. 306-324; *ibid.*,
88 (1976) pp. 72-93

3 לפי שיטת המקורות נארג סיפור יוסף בדרך של קישור ושילוב קטעים מתוך המקורות E, J, ור־P. ראה
J. Skinner, *Genesis* (ICC), Edinburgh 1963², pp. 438-442; G. von Rad, למשל,
Genesis (OTL), London 1976³, pp.348ff.; S.R. Driver, 'Joseph', in *Dictionary of
the Bible*, ed. J. Hastings, pp. 767-770 השווה גם ויברי, הסבור שמדובר בסיפור הומוגני
הנטול ממקור אחד, הוא R.N. Whybray, 'The Joseph Story and Pentateuchal
Criticism', *VT* 18 (1968), pp. 522-528 ובדומה: G.W. Coats, *From Canaan to Egypt*,
Structural and Theological Context for the Joseph Story, Washington 1976, pp.
72-68. לאחרונה רבו המסתייגים מיישום שיטת המקורות הקלאסית לסיפור יוסף; ראה, למשל,
רדפורד (לעיל, הערה 2), עמ' 106–186, המפריס (לעיל, הערה 2), עמ' 198–199 ומיינהולד (לעיל,
הערה 2), עמ' 311. לדיון ברקע המצרי של סיפור יוסף החלוקה למקורות איננה מעלה או מורידה:
הרישומים המצריים מופיעים הן בפסוקים המיוחסים למקור J והן באלו השייכים למקור E.

מסוימת. ואף אם תזכה שאלה זו לתשובה חיובית, עדיין אין בכך כדי לאשר את ההיסטוריות של הסיפור; שהרי המחבר העברי יכול היה להשתמש ברישומים מצריים אותנטיים כדי ליצור סיפור פיקטיבי–מגמתי.

על כל פנים, הרישומים המצריים שזורים לאורכו של סיפור יוסף, והמנסה להסיר ביותר בידו שלד עלילה חסרת רוח חיים. חוקר העוסק בסיפור יוסף לא יכול שלא להתייחס לגווניו המצריים. בהקשר זה הועלו שתי דעות עיקריות: (א) הרישומים המצריים כלליים ומעורפלים ואינם שייכים לתקופה ולמציאות מסוימות. (ב) הרישומים המצריים (ולו בחלקם) אותנטיים ומעוגנים בפרק זמן מסוים בתולדות מצרים.[4]

למעלה מעשרים שנה חלפו מאז ראו אור המחקרים ההשוואתיים המקיפים בנושא זה, של ורגוט (Vergote 1959), רדפורד (Redford 1970) וחוקרים אחרים.[5] אולם, בשנים האחרונות נתפרסמו מחקרים חדשים התורמים רבות לשחזור המבנה הכללי של מצרים והמנגנון המנהלי של תקופת הממלכה החדשה וכן להבנת האונומאסטיקון והאיקונוגראפיה המצרית.[6]

מטרת דיון זה היא אפוא: (א) לבחון מחדש, לאור מחקרים אגיפטולוגיים אלה האחרונים, את הרישומים המצריים בסיפור יוסף; (ב) לברר את השלכותיהם של הרישומים הללו על הבנת תהליך יצירתו של הסיפור.

הרישומים המצריים בסיפור יוסף

סיפור יוסף כולל מוטיבים ויסודות מצריים מובהקים, שניתן להסבירם אך ורק לאור הרקע המצרי. ואלו הם:

(1) טקס העלאת יוסף לגדולה – טקסים דומים מצויים אמנם בממלכות אחרות, כגון, בבל (דנ׳ ה 29) ופרס (אס׳ ו 11; ח 2, 15);, אולם הטקס בבראשית מלווה בגינונים ובמונחים מצריים המעידים על מקורו המצרי: הענקת רביד, טבעת ובגדי שש (ראה להלן).

(2) משרות ומוסדות בחצר פרעה – אשר על הבית, פה פרעה ואב לפרעה (ראה להלן) וכן בית הסוהר.

4   בדעה הראשונה אוחזים: O. Eissfeldt, *OLZ* 55 (1960), pp. 39-45; J.L. Thompson, in *Israelite and Judean History*, eds. J.H. Mayes and J.M. Miller, London 1977, pp. 149-166; ולאחרונה: המפריס (לעיל, הערה 2), עמ׳ 20, 22, 154–175; M. Görg, 'Das Ägypten des Alten Testaments bei Thomas Mann' *BN* 66 (1993), pp. 59-82; H. H. Rowley, *From Joseph to Joshua,* London 1950, pp.158-164; J.M.A. Janssen, 'Egyptological Remarks on the Story of Joseph in Genesis', *JEOL* 14 (1955-56), pp. 63-72; P. Montet, *L'Egypte et la Bible*, Neuchatel 1959, pp. 15-23; K.A. Kitchen, 'Joseph', in *The New Bible Dictionary*, ed. J. O. Douglas, pp. 656-660; idem, *JEA* 47 (1961), pp. 158-164; R. de Vaux, *The Early History of Israel*, Philadelphia 1978, pp. 291-320; רדפורד (לעיל, הערה 2) וי"מ גרינץ, יחידו וקדמותו של ספר בראשית, ירושלים תשמ"ג, עמ׳ 97–119. הדעה השנייה מקובלת על: J. Vergote, *Joseph en Egypt*, Louvain 1959

5   ראה מחקריהם של ורגוט, רדפורד, ינסן, קיטשן (לעיל, הערה 4).

6   J.J. Janssen, 'Prolegomena to the Study of Egypt's Economic History during the New Kingdom', *SAK* 3 (1975), pp.127-185; A. Kadry, *Officers and Officials in the New Kingdom*, Studia Aegyptiaca 8, Budapest 1982; A. R. Schulman, 'On the Egyptian Name of Joseph', *SAK* 2 (1975), pp. 235-243; idem, *Ceremonial Execution and Public Rewards*, (OBO 75), Freiburg-Göttingen 1988; G.A. Gaballa, *Narrative in Egyptian Art,* Mainz 1976

(3) הרפורמה האגררית — מוטיב הרעב, העיקרון של ליקוט ואיסוף תבואה לצורך חלוקתה מחדש, מתן זכויות יתר לכוהנים.

(4) חלומות השרים ופרעה — סוג החלום (חלום אלגורי-סמלי, המושתת על משחקי מלים), תפישת החלום (כאמצעי למניעת רעות), פותרי החלום (חרטומים) והרקע הגיאוגראפי-דתי של החלום (יאור, אחו — מונחים מצריים; שבלים, פרות — סמלי פוריות הכרוכים בדת ובמיתוס המצריים).

(5) מנהגי לוויה וקבורה — חניטה, קבורה בארון מתים, הרופאים-החונטים, ואורך החיים האידיאלי מאה ועשר שנה.

(6) מונחים וביטויים מצריים — פרעה, אחו, יאור, אברך, חרטומים, סוף, טבעת, שש.

(7) שמות פרטיים מצריים — צפנת פענח, אסנת, פוטיפר/ע.

(8) שמות מקומות במצרים — ארץ רעמסס, און, גושן.

דיון רחב במוטיבים אלו מן הראוי שייעשה במקום אחר. נסתפק כאן בכמה נתונים מספריים: מדובר בשלושים ושניים פריטים, אשר שנים עשר מהם שייכים לתקופת הממלכה החדשה (1500‏–1000 לפסה"נ), ואילו ששה עשר מהם קיימים כבר לפני תקופת הממלכה החדשה, אך ממשיכים בקיומם גם בתקופה זו.[7] עשרים ושמונה רישומים שייכים, אם כן, לתקופת הממלכה החדשה, ומתוכם שמונה שייכים לתקופת השושלת ה-יח.

רקע הסיפור הוא, לפיכך, תקופת הממלכה החדשה. אנו מניחים כי המציאות המתוארת כאן היא עלייתו לגדולה של פקיד שמי בימי הממלכה החדשה, השושלת ה-יח (1580‏–1320 לפסה"נ), קרוב לוודאי תקופת עמארנה (1400‏–1360 לפסה"נ בקירוב).[8]

כיוון שקצר המצע מהשתרע, ננסה להוכיח מסקנה זו על ידי ניתוח אחד מהמוטיבים המרכזיים בסיפור, והוא תפקיד יוסף בחצר פרעה. מוטיב זה רחב ומפורט יותר מכל רישום מצרי המופיע בו. לכאן שייכים לא רק תאריו של יוסף וטקס מינויו אלא אף מעשיו וביצועיו במסגרת תפקידו החדש.

תפקידו של יוסף בחצר פרעה

תפקידו של יוסף מתואר בספר בראשית פעמיים:

(1) מא 40‏–44 (מקור E):

אתה תהיה על ביתי ועל פיך ישק כל עמי רק הכסא אגדל ממך... ראה נתתי אותך על כל ארץ מצרים. ויסר פרעה את טבעתו... ויתן אותה על יד יוסף וילבש אותו בגדי שש וישם רבד הזהב על צוארו. וירכב אתו במרכבת המשנה אשר לו ויקראו לפניו אברך ונתן אותו על כל ארץ מצרים.

---

7   המונח 'ארץ רעמסס', השייך לתקופה הרעמסית, חדר כנראה לספר בראשית משמות א 11. המונחים המאוחרים 'סריס', 'ארץ העברים', והשבועה 'חי פרעה' (מן המאות 9‏–5 לפסה"נ), לא נכללו בשקלול שהובא לעיל, מאחר ומוצאם המצרי מוטל בספק. בהקשר זה מעניין להזכיר את שם המקום yšpir, המופיע ברשימת הטופונימים של תחותמס השלישי (השושלת ה-יח) באזור בקעת הלבנון. היה מי שקשר מקום זה עם השם יוסף, דהיינו, יסף-אל. ראה: .S. Aḥituv, *Canaanite* *Toponyms in Ancient Egyptian Documents*, Jerusalem and Leiden 1984, pp. 201-202. אולם קיטשן (לעיל, הערה 4), עמ' 656, כבר הצביע על כך ש-/ש/ש במצרית איננה האקוויוואלנט הרגיל של /ס/ ס/ בעברית (השווה גם ראולי [לעיל, הערה 4], עמ' 36‏–37, הערה 6).

8   בדעה זו אוחזים אף ורגוט וראולי (לעיל, הערה 4).

יוסף ממונה על בית פרעה, הוא יהיה פה לעמו (תואר מצרי הנרמז בבטוי 'על פיך ישק כל עמי', ראה להלן) ומושל על כל ארץ מצרים. רק פרעה יעלה עליו בשררתו.

(2) מה 8 (מקור J) חוזר על אותם פרטים במלים אחרות:

וישימני (האלהים) לאב לפרעה ולאדון לכל ביתו ומושל בכל ארץ מצרים.

החידוש היחיד כאן הוא, כי יוסף יהיה 'אב לפרעה' (השווה תה' קה 21: 'שמו אדון לביתו ומשל בכל קנינו').

מהו תפקידו של יוסף? עיון בטקס העלאתו של יוסף לגדולה, שהובא לעיל, מורה כי הוא בעל דמיון רב לטקסי מינוי או הענקת גמול, המופיעים במצרים החל מימי תחותמס הרביעי, בן השושלת ה-יח, וכלה בימי רעמסס התשיעי, בן השושלת ה-כ (1429–1123 לפסה"נ). אולם הוא שכיח והופך לדגם של קבע בקברי הפקידים באל עמארנה בתקופת פרעה אמנ-חותפ הרביעי, אח'-נ-אתון (1379–1362 לפסה"נ).[9] באיורי קברים אלו מופיעות במרכז דמויות המלך והמלכה, היושבים בקיוסק קטן, או משקיפים החוצה בעד חלון הארמון. למטה בצד עומד הפקיד המאושר, המרים את ידיו מעלה בהודיה כשצווארו עטוי רבידים ומשרתיו עסוקים בעיטורו בתכשיטים נוספים. סדרת התכשיטים כוללת רבידים, צמידים ולעתים אף שמלה. יש והמענק עשיר יותר וכולל, מלבד סדרת התכשיטים הקבועה, כלי קרמיקה, סרטים, טבעות חותם ואף זוג כפפות (כמו במקרה של אי ואשתו). לא תמיד כללה ההענקה טבעת חותם, אך מסירתה סמלה מתן סמכות לפקיד עם מינויו לתפקיד חשוב; במקרה של יוסף, מינוי ל'אשר על הבית' (ראה להלן).[10] בתום הטקס נראה לעתים הפקיד המאושר נישא במרכבה, כיוסף.[11] בטקסטים המלווים את האיורים מופיעים דברי המלך, המסביר את הסיבה להענקה, ודברי התודה של המקבל. תיאור זה חוזר ונשנה (35 דוגמאות) בקבריהם של בעלי שררה שונים (נושאי משרה צבאית, כוהנים, בעלי תפקיד מנהלי [אשר על ההרמון, אשר על האוצר, אשר על הבית], סופר ורופא).[12] לפיכך, אין בו כדי להשליך אור על תפקידו של יוסף בחצר פרעה. לכל היותר, יש בו כדי להעיד על הגבול העליון של המסגרת הכרונולוגית של הסיפור, דהיינו, המאה ה-יד לפסה"נ[13]

9 אין הבדל בין התיאורים של טקסי העלאה לגדולה לאלה של טקסי העניקת גמול השכיחים בקברי אל עמארנה. הטקסט, המלווה את האיורים, מסייע להבהיר את נסיבות המענק. אולם, לרוע המזל, לא תמיד השתמר הטקסט, וכשהוא השתמר, לעתים איננו מובן. על כל פנים, לפחות שלושה מהטקסטים הללו הם בבירור טקסי העלאה בדרגה: טוטו מונה ל'נביא הראשון במקדש אתון ב-אח'ת-אתון' (,*EA* VI pp.12-14; pls. XIX-XX); מרי-רע היה לכוהן אתון (*ibid*., I, pp. 20-23 pls. VI-IX); ואילו חויה קיבל תפקיד משולש של ה'מפקח על ההרמון המלכותי, אשר על האוצר ואשר על בית אם המלך' (*ibid*., III, pp. 12-13, pl. XVI), ראה גם: גבלה (לעיל, הערה 6), עמ' 64–62, 72–78, 91–93, 129–130; שולמן (לעיל, הערה 6), עמ' 116 ואילך. לאור זאת יש לדחות את טענתו של רדפורד (לעיל, הערה 2), עמ' 213 ואילך, כי הטקס המופיע באל עמארנה מציין העניקת גמול ולא מינוי, ולכן אין להשוותו לתיאור העלאתו לגדולה של יוסף אלא למקבילות ממצרים של המאה השביעית לפסה"נ.

10 ראה: *LÄ*, IV, p. 264. ה'טבעת' בטקס מינויו של יוסף היא רישום מצרי, מאחר שהמונח העברי מקורו במצרית db'.t. מונח זה, המציין במצרית טבעת חותם, שימש עד תקופת הממלכה החדשה; מתקופה זו ואילך ממיר אותו המונח htm.t.

11 חשובה לענייננו העובדה שמרכבה אינה מופיעה באיקונוגרפיה המצרית לפני ימי השושלת ה-יח. התמונה של שיבת הפקיד הגבוה, כשהוא נישא במרכבה, מופיעה בקברי פא-רנ-נפר, מרי-רע השני וטוטו באל עמארנה. ראה: EA, II, pl. 36; VI. pls. 5, 20

12 ראה: EA, I-VI, *passim*; H.A. Schlögel, *Amenophis IV, Echnaton*, Hamburg 1986, pp. 53-57

13 אמנם כבר לפני תקופת השושלת ה-יח ואף אחריה קיים המנהג של מתן מענק לאזרחים ולאנשי

ננסה להכריע בשאלה מתוך ניתוח מעשיו של יוסף בתוקף תפקידו, דהיינו, הרפורמה האגררית המיוחסת לו בפרקים מא 57–47 ר׳מז 13–26.

בשבע שנות השבע יוסף אוסף את התבואה באסמי הערים ובשנות הרעב הוא מוכרה. תחילה הוא מוכר תמורת ממון, אחר – תמורת מקנה, וכשתמו מקורות אלו הוא קונה באוצר המלך את כל אדמות מצרים. כך הופכת כל אדמת מצרים לרכוש המלך, מלבד אדמת הכהונה. לאחר מכן מחכיר יוסף לעם את אדמת המלך תמורת חמישית מהיבול.

בין שמצב בעלות הקרקעות במצרים הקדומה ושיטת גביית המסים בה מתוארים כאן במדויק ובין שלא[14] ברור לאור קטעים אלו כי:

א. יוסף מונה על ידי פרעה לפתור את בעיית הרעב בשעת חרום ומצוקה, כמשתקף מדברי פרעה אל עמו, הצועק ללחם: ׳ויאמר פרעה לכל מצרים לכו אל יוסף אשר יאמר לכם תעשו׳ (מא 55).

ב. יוסף עושה ברכוש המלך כברכושו שלו. הוא קונה בכסף המלך את קרקעות המדינה (מז 14, 20).

ג. יוסף מתפקד כ׳שר חקלאות׳ בן ימינו: הוא אוסף את התבואה באסמים (מא 35) וגובה מס מהתוצרת החקלאית (מא 34: ׳וחמש את ארץ מצרים׳; השווה מז 24).

מעשיו של יוסף תואמים להפליא את הסמכויות הנכללות בשלושה מהתארים שהוזכר בהם: ׳אשר על הבית׳ (השווה מא 40), ׳פה מצרים׳ (השווה שם) ו׳אב לפרעה׳ (השווה מה 8).

׳אשר על הבית׳, המקביל לתואר המצרי m r pr wr, הוא תפקיד המופיע במצרים החל מתקופת הממלכה התיכונה. pr–בית, במובנו כאן: ׳רכוש׳. ׳אשר על הבית׳ הוא אפוא הממונה על רכוש המלך, המנהל את מקורות ההכנסה שלו, דהיינו, בתיו, שדותיו, אסמיו, בקרו וכו׳. בין היתר, תפקידו לגבות מסים מהתוצרת החקלאית של אדמות המלך ולאגור תבואה באסמי המלך. ובכן, יוסף, העושה ברכוש המלך כברכושו שלו, מתפקד כאן כ׳אשר על הבית׳.

׳פה׳, ניתן להסביר תואר זה לאור המקורות המצריים בשתי צורות, ושתיהן מתאימות לעניינינו: (א) ׳הפה של מלך מצרים העליונה׳ (r ni sw.t) או ׳הפה המרגיע את כל הארץ עד קצותיה׳ (r sʿhrrw t3 nb r dr.f), הוא תואר המציין את תפקידו של הפקיד הגבוה כיועץ המלך בעניינים שונים הכרוכים בשלטון. תואר זה מתחבר יפה לכינוי נוסף הנכרך ביוסף – ׳אב לפרעה׳, המקביל ל־it ntr, ׳אב האל׳ במצרית. תואר כבוד זה הוענק על ידי המלך לפקידים מקורבים לו, בדרך כלל אנשים בעלי ניסיון, באים בימים, ומשמעותו נדרפת ל׳פה מלך מצרים׳. (ב) פה עליון (r hry) הוא תואר הניתן לפקיד, הממונה בשעת מצוקה על מפעלים שונים מטעם המלך. החל מימי הממלכה החדשה משמש תואר זה לציון ׳אשר על הבית׳, מנהל רכוש המלך.[15] לאור הסבר זה של ׳פה׳, יוסף, המשמש כ׳אשר על הבית׳ בזמן של שגרה, משמש כ׳פה עליון׳ בשעת החרום של מצוקת רעב.

הצבא (ראה: LÄ, I, pp. 581-582); אבל טקס הענקה של זהב בתקופה הממלכה החדשה, כפי שהוא מומחש בקברי עמארנה, הוא הקרוב ביותר לתיאור המענק ליוסף.

14   שלושה פרטים בסיפור הרפורמה של יוסף תואמים להפליא את תמונת הכללה של מצרים בתקופת הממלכה החדשה, כפי שעולה מהמחקרים החדשים:
א. העיקרון של איסוף תוצרת המדינה למחסנים או לאסמים מרכזיים וחלוקתה בקרב האוכלוסייה;
ב. האסמים היו ידועים כמוסד רשמי של השלטון המצרי, והחל מימי השושלת ה־י״ח קיימת משרה מיוחדת, המכונה ׳אשר על האסמים של מצרים העליונה והתחתונה׳; מקום מושבו של נושא המשרה היה אולי עמארנה בתקופת אח״נ־אתון; ג. הכהנים היו מעמד בעל זכויות יתר במצרים הקדומה ומדי פעם זכו לפטור מתשלום מס, או להטבות אחרות. ראה: ינסן (לעיל, הערה 6), עמ׳ 184; כדרי (לעיל, הערה 6), עמ׳ 21; ורגוט (לעיל, הערה 4), עמ׳ 190 ואילך; M. Silver, *Economic Structures of the Ancient Near East*, London-Sydney 1985, pp. 19-20; J.A. Wilson, *The Culture of Ancient Egypt*, Chicago-London 1971, pp. 271-272

15   חרמחב, ׳אשר על הבית׳ בימי תות־ענח־אמון, היה אף ׳פה עליון׳ של כל הארץ. כן שימשו בתפקיד

לסיכום, יוסף ממלא שני תפקידים ריאליים בחצר פרעה. הוא משמש כ'אשר על הבית' וכ'פה' או 'פה עליון של המלך'.

ניתוח תפקידו של יוסף ומעשיו מצביע על תקופת הממלכה החדשה כמסגרת להתרחשות העלילה. הפרטים, השזורים בפרשת עלייתו לגדולה ובמעשיו, מצביעים על ימי השושלת ה-ייח, תקופת עמארנה (1400–1360 לפסה"נ בקירוב), שכן:

(א) 'פה המלך' או 'פה עליון' הם תארים קבועים לחצרני השושלת ה-ייח. 'פה עליון' כרוך בתפקידו של 'אשר על הבית', שסמכותו מגיעה לשיאה בתקופה זו. גם התואר 'אב האל' היה נפוץ בעת ההיא.[16]

(ב) בעלות מלכותית על כל אדמות מצרים מלבד אדמות המקדש, מתאימה לימי אח"ן-אתון, אשר החרים את רכוש הכוהנים המקומיים וסגר את מקדשיהם, מלבד רכושם של כוהני אתון.[17]

(ג) יוסף נושא לאשה את בת כוהן און (הליופוליס; בר' מא 45). אף פרט זה הולם את ימי שלטונו של פרעה אח"ן-אתון שהתחנך בהליופוליס, ובימים הראשונים של שלטונו ראה עצמו כ'נביאו' של האל המקומי.

(ד) ההנחה שיוסף ישב תחילה בהליופוליס ואחר כך אולי כ'אשר על הבית' במוף,[18] עולה בקנה אחד עם הפסוקים המלמדים על קרבת משכנו למושב אביו ואחיו בארץ גושן (בסביבות ואדי תומילאת בדלתה המזרחית; בר' מה 10).

(ה) בתקופת הממלכה החדשה, ובייחוד בימיו של פרעה אח"ן-אתון יכול היה שמי ממוצא נחות להגיע לתפקיד נכבד בחצר המלך המצרי. אח"ן-אתון מיהר לסלק את הפקידות הישנה, הכרוכה באמונת אמון, ולהשתית את ממשלו על פקידות חדשה, הנאמנה למשטר החדש. חלק ניכר מפקידים אלו היו נוכרים וביניהם שמיים.[19]

כפול זה נושאי המשרה 'אשר על הבית' בימי חאת-שפסות ואמנ-חותפ השני; ראה: כדרי (לעיל, הערה 6), עמ' 52.

16   ראה, כדרי, (לעיל, הערה 6), עמ' 72, וכן: LÄ, II, p. 825

17   ראה: C. Aldred, CAH, Vol.II, Part II, pp. 52-53

18   בימי אמנ-חותפ השלישי הועבר מושבו של 'אשר על הבית'. בימי בנו, אמנ-חותפ הרביעי, שומעים על שני 'אשר על הבית': האחד, אפי, שמושבו היה בממפיס, והשני, רעי, שקברו נתגלה בתבי; ראה: W. Helck, Zur Verwaltung des Mittleren und Neuen Reichs, Leiden-Köln 1958, pp. 370-371. 'אשר על הבית' היה אחראי לאסמי המלך בלבד, שלא כמו 'אשר על האסמים' (m r šn.wt) של מצרים העליונה והתחתונה', שהיה ממונה על אסמי מצרים. אי לכך, יש חוקרים הסבורים כי יוסף כיהן כ'אשר על האסמים של מצרים העליונה והתחתונה'; ראה: W.A. Ward, 'The Egyptian Office of Joseph', JSS 5 (1960), pp.144-150; idem, 'Egyptian Titles in Genesis 39-50', Bibliotheca Sacra 114 (1957), pp. 47-48; J.A.M. Janssen, 'Fonctionnaires sémites au service de l'Egypte', Chronique d'Egypte 51 (1951), p. 61. חיזוק מה לדעה זו היא העובדה שבתקופת השושלות ה-ייח וה-ייט היה 'אשר על האסמים...' אחראי על סחר החוץ בתבואה עם סוריה ואסיה הקטנה. שמא יש להבין על רקע זה את המשא ומתן של יוסף עם אחיו? אשר לדעה כי יוסף כיהן כווזיר (t3tj) במצרים, המקובלת על חוקרים אחרים (כגון: ורגוט [לעיל, הערה 4], עמ' 108–114 [עם הסתייגות], ראולי [שם], עמ' 119–120, ודירוור [לעיל, הערה 3], עמ' 773), זו מעוררת קשיים: א. בתקופת הממלכה החדשה, החל מימי תחותמס השלישי (1500–850 לפסה"נ), היו שני וזירים במצרים. האחד ישב בדרום, בתבי, והשני בממפיס או בהליופוליס (בימי רעמסס השני). יוסף, לעומת זאת, מתואר כמושל יחיד בארץ מצרים (בר' מא 43; מה 8). ב. תפקידו המרכזי של הווזיר, ניהול המערכת המשפטית, אין לו זכר בסיפור יוסף (גם אם אין ללמוד 'מן שתיקה').

19   הדמות הקרובה ביותר ליוסף מקרב פקידים אלו הוא סורי בשם טוטו/דודו, הידוע מקברו באל עמארנה וממכתבי אל עמארנה 158, 164, 167, 169. טוטו, כיוסף, היה ה'פה של המלך' ו'נביאו הראשי במקדש אתון', ובקברו מתואר טקס מינויו ונסיעה במרכבה כשהמון משתחווה לפניו; ראה: EA, VI, pp. 12-14, pls. XIX-XX. לפקידים שמיים בחצר מלך מצרים בתקופת הממלכה החדשה ראה גם:

(ו) המוטיב של הענקת זהב כחלק מטקס מינוי או כאות חסד מופיע דרך קבע בקברי השושלת
ה־יח.

(ז) השימוש במרכבה במצרים איננו קודם לימי השושלת ה־יח.[20]

תוצאות: התהוות סיפור יוסף ותולדותיו

שלב א

מבקשים אנו להניח, כי הסיפור הקדום על האב יוסף מושתת היה על אוטוביוגראפיה של פקיד
מצרי ממוצא שמי (או מוצא זר אחר), שעלה לגדולה בחצר פרעה אח'־נ־אתון או בחצרו של
אחד ממלכי השושלת ה־יח. אוטוביוגראפיה זו היתה קרובה בצורתה ובתוכנה
לאוטוביוגראפיות של פקידים גבוהים בחצר פרעה (השווה סיפור סא־נהת)[21] ולוותה באיורים
דומים לאלו שנתגלו בקברי עמארנה.

המחבר המקראי, כעמיתו החוקר המודרני, שבוי היה בקסמי תקופה זו, שהיא תקופה מיוחדת
ויוצאת דופן בקורות מצרים הקדומה, והיא שהיתה לנגד עיניו בחברו את סיפור יוסף.
אילו נחשף קברו של הפקיד, בן דמות יוסף באל עמארנה, היינו עשויים, למצוא על קירותיו
כתובת מעין זו:

שנה x, תחת כבודו של מלך מצרים העליונה והתחתונה, החי באמת, אדון שתי הארצות
נפר־ח'־פר־רע, וע'־נ־רע בן רע, החי באמת, אדון הכתרים אח'־נ־אתון גדול בימיו. אשת המלך
הגדולה, אהובתו, גברת מצרים, נפר־נפרו־רע נפרת־אתי חיה, בריאה לעולם ועד.

שנה x, החודש x של (ציון עונת השנה), יום x, אשר על בית (m r pr wr) אדון מצרים,
מושל הארץ העליונה והתחתונה, אבי האל (it nṯr) אשר הוא אוהבו, פה עליון (r ḥry) של
מצרים העליונה והתחתונה, יוסף, הוא אומר: 'הקשיבו כל האנשים גדול וקטן לדברי, כי
אספר לכם את כל החסדים אשר המלך עשה עמדי:

הייתי אדם ממוצא זר ונחות הן מצד אבי והן מצד אמי, אבל הנסיך בסססני. בארץ פא־כנען
נולדתי ונמכרתי לעבד לאיש מצרי פא־די־פא־רע שמו, הטבח (wdpw) הראשי של המלך.
הוא נתנני על ביתו והשכלתי בכל מעשי.

קרה המקרה ובהיותי לבדי בבית, אשתו לבה היה לדעתי... אך אני מאנתי ואלך לדרכי. בבוא
בעלה הפכה זאת. אדוני, פא־די־פא־רע נתנני בבית הסוהר. אבל כבודו, המלך, הרבה חסדו
עמדי. הוא מבית הסוהר הוציאני ולאשר על ביתו מינני. רביד זהב, טבעת וגם בגד נתן לי.
הוא הסב את שמי לצד־פא־נתר־אוף־ענח' ואף את בת כוהן און (Iwn) נתן לי לאשה. הוא

20   יוסן (לעיל, הערה 18), עמ' 50–62; W. Helck, *Die Beziehungen Ägypten zu
Vorderasien in 3 und 2 Jahrtausent v. Chr.*, Wiesbaden 1971, pp. 353, 359-360,
367-369; *LÄ*, I, p.1151; וכן כדרי (לעיל, הערה 6), עמ' 71–72.
ראה לעיל, הערה 11.

21   למסקנה דומה מגיע המפריס (לעיל, הערה 2), עמ' 155–157, 171, שמחקרו, המתמקד בהיבט
הספרותי של סיפור יוסף, הגיע לידינו לאחר גיבוש מאמר זה. לשיטתו, סיפור יוסף מקביל לסיפורים
מצריים, שהתפתחו מז'אנר של ה'ביוגראפיה של קבורה' השכיח במצרים, כגון, סיפור סא־נהת או
סיפור המלח שספינתו טבעה. אולם המפריס, העורך השוואה בין סיפור יוסף לסיפור סא־נהת, מסיק
כי היתה השפעה עקיפה כללית של תרבות המזרח הקדום ומנהגיו על סיפור יוסף ולא דווקא
השפעה מצרית. אף קינג מגיע למסקנה כי סיפור יוסף וסיפור סא־נהת שייכים לז'אנר ספרותי זהה
(מסוג ה־oicotype), שרווח במזרח הקדום; ראה: J.R. King, 'The Joseph Story and
Divine Politics: A Comparative Study of a Biographic Formula from the Ancient
Near East', *JBL* 106/4 (1987), pp. 577-594

גרם שאחי יהיו רבים. אספקה ומנות הובאו לי בפקודת כבודו מידי יום ביומו. לי, אשר
הייתי אדם המתחנן לפת לחם.

וכך היה הדבר: חלום חלם המלך ואני ידעתיו. שבע שנות רעב תבאנה על הארץ. אז אני
קצרתי את כל השדות של חבלי מצרים עד גבולות הצפון והדרום ונתתים באסמים, ובבוא
העת סיפקתי את צורכי העם. לא היה אדם שרעב שם. כך עשיתי עד שחזר היאור לגאותו,
עשיר בחיטה ובשעורה.

ובבוא היום, כאשר ירדה הזקנה והחולשה השיגתני, עיני כבדו, ידי רפו ורגלי תשו מלכת,
השבעתי את אחי; השבעתים כי עם מותי ישאוני מזה ויקברוני בארץ בה נולדתי, במקום
בו ישכן לבבי הוא פא־כנען׳.

סיפור יוסף הקדום מבוסס היה, אם כן, לפי הנחתנו, על אוטוביוגראפיה של פקיד מצרי
מתקופת עמארנה. הגבול התחתון ביותר לסיפור זה הוא השושלת ה־כא (1100 לפסה״נ בקירוב),
שבה הביטוי אברך, ib r.k, דהיינו, ׳שים לב׳ במצרית,[22] מוחלף ב־t3 z, כלומר ׳לארץ׳,[23] והבירה
המצרית עוברת לצוען (Sḥ.t Dˁn במצרית), שאינה נזכרת בסיפורנו.[24]

שלב ב

הסיפור הקדום נערך ועובד על ידי סופר עברי, בן תקופת המלוכה, שהשתייך לאסכולה
הצפונית. סופר זה ביקש לתת לגיטימאציה למלך מבית יוסף, קרוב לוודאי, ירבעם, על רקע
מלכותו של מלך מבית דוד. הנימוקים לכך הם אלו:

(א) בסיפור יוסף, שלא כמו ביתר האיזכורים של מצרים במקרא, היחס למצרים הוא חיובי.
מצרים איננה בית עבדים אלא מקום מקלט ומחיה בעתות משבר. תמונה זו של מצרים חוזרת
רק בראשית ימי המלוכה, בתקופת שלמה, המקיים קשרים הדוקים עם מצרים ואף נושא את
בת פרעה לאשה.

(ב) כפי שהראה פון ראד, דמות יוסף תואמת להפליא את האידיאולוגיה של החכמה, שנבעה
מחצר המלוכה הירושלמית בימי שלמה.[25]

(ג) ירבעם, בדומה ליוסף, מוצא מפלט במצרים (מל״א יא 40; יב 2).

(ד) בסיפור יוסף עומד יהודה בראש האחים והמצב תואם את ראשית תקופת המלוכה, כאשר
מלכי בית דוד תפשו את כס השלטון. לאורך הסיפור קיים עימות בין יהודה ליוסף, המשקף את
העימות בין רחבעם, המולך על יהודה ובנימין, ובין ירבעם המולך על שבטי הצפון.[26]

22 פירוש זה מובא על ידי שפיגלברג (W. Spiegelberg, *Aegyptologische Randglossen zum*
Alten Testament, Strassburg 1904, pp.14-18). אולם קיימות אפשרויות אחרות לניתוח
האטימולוגי של ׳אברך׳ לא לאור המצרית, אלא לאור השמית; ראה: ורגוט (לעיל, הערה 4),
עמ׳ 135–141; גרינץ (לעיל, הערה 4), עמ׳ 116–117; ובמיוחד כרואטו, המסביר את המונח
לאור האכדית abrikku, דהיינו, מנהל אדמיניסטראטיבי (J. S. Croatto, *VT* 16 [1966],
pp. 113-115)
23 לעניין זה ראה: קיטשן (לעיל, הערה 4), עמ׳ 162.
24 חיזוק להשערתנו שגרעין סיפור יוסף הוא קורות חייו של פקיד גבוה בחצר מלך מצרים, ניתן למצוא
גם באזכור יוסף בתה׳ קה 17–22. יוסף מתואר כאן כפרנק, כעבד שעלה לגדולה במצרים; ייתכן
והקטע בתהילים מבוסס על שלב קדום יותר בתהליך יצירת הסיפור מזה המופיע בספר בראשית;
השווה: E. Hilgert, 'The Dual Image of Joseph in Hebrew and Early Jewish
Literature', *BR* 30 (1985), p. 17 n. 5
25 השווה גם המפריס (לעיל, הערה 2), עמ׳ 147, 150, 178–181; G. von Rad, 'Josephsgeschichte und ältere Chokma', VTSup 1(1953) pp. 120-127
26 השווה, מ׳ אברבך, ׳יוסף ואחיו בראי תולדות שבטי ישראל׳, בית מקרא לב (תשמ״ז), עמ׳ 114–120;
J. Ebach, *LÄ*, I, pp. 270-273 וכן אייספלדט (לעיל, הערה 4). דעה דומה לגבי תולדותיו של

סיפור יוסף הוא, אם כן, יצירה ספרותית המושתתת על גרעין היסטורי: אוטוביוגראפיה של
עבד שמי (או נוכרי אחר), שעלה לגדולה בחצר פרעה, קרוב לוודאי בתקופת עמארנה. הסיפור
הקדום זכה מאוחר יותר ללבוש מגמתי שנועד להסביר את עלייתו של מלך מבית יוסף. הגבול
התחתון ליצירת לבוש זה הוא המאה השמינית לפסה"נ. שכן, בנבואה המקראית, השם יוסף
מציין את מלכות הצפון ולא את הפרט יוסף ובא תמיד בהקשר של מצוקה ופורענות, גם אם
מדובר בתקווה לעתיד (עמ' ה 15; ו 6; יח' לז 15–22; זכ' י 6).[27]

סיפור יוסף מביא המפריס (לעיל, הערה 2), ההולך בעקבות: G.W. Coats 'The Joseph Story
and Ancient Wisdom — A Reappraisal', *CBQ* 35 (1973), pp. 285-297. המפריס מבחין
בשני שלבים בהתהוות היצירה:

א. גרעין – סיפור אודות חצרן־חכם, שהתחבר בסוף תקופת הברונזה המאוחרת בעיר־מדינה
כנענית.

ב. נובלה, המבוססת על הרחבת סיפור הגרעין, אשר נוצרה בחצר המלך הירושלמית בראשית תקופת
הממלכה המאוחדת.

אולם לשיטתו של המפריס אין בסיפור יוסף ביקורת ברורה כלפי יהודה, ולכן אין לחפש כאן גוונים
פוליטיים; ראה שם, עמ' 171–172, 185, 190–191, 199. נימוקים נוספים לכך שסיפור יוסף נעוץ
במסגרת הכרונולוגית של תקופת הממלכה המאוחדת מביאים קוטס, שם, עמ' 291, 295;
C. Westermann, *Genesis*, trans. D. E. Greens, Michigan, 1987, p. 336

27　השווה הילגרט (לעיל, הערה 24), עמ' 5–21.